The AutoCAD® Book

Drawing, Modeling, and Applications Using AutoCAD® 2002

JAMES M. KIRKPATRICK
Eastfield College

Upper Saddle River, New Jersey
Columbus, Ohio

Library of Congress Cataloging-in-Publication Data

Kirkpatrick, James, M.
The AutoCAD book : drawing, modeling, and applications using AutoCAD 2002 / James M. Kirkpatrick.
p. cm.
ISBN 0-13-094073-9
1. Computer graphics. 2. AutoCAD. I. Title.

T385 .K4893 2002
620′.0042′02855369--dc21

2001051028

Editor in Chief: Stephen Helba
Executive Editor: Debbie Yarnell
Media Development Editor: Michelle Churma
Production Editor: Louise N. Sette
Production Supervision: Lisa Garboski
Design Coordinator: Diane Ernsberger
Cover Designer: Jason Moore
Cover art: Jason Moore
Production Manager: Brian Fox
Marketing Manager: Jimmy Stephens

This book was set in Times Roman by STELLARViSIONs. It was printed and bound by Courier Kendallville, Inc. The cover was printed by Phoenix Color Corp.

Pearson Education Ltd., *London*
Pearson Education Australia Pty. Limited, *Sydney*
Pearson Education Singapore Pte. Ltd.
Pearson Education North Asia Ltd., *Hong Kong*
Pearson Education Canada, Ltd., *Toronto*
Pearson Educación de Mexico, S. A. de C.V.
Pearson Education—Japan, *Tokyo*
Pearson Education Malaysia Pte. Ltd.
Pearson Education, *Upper Saddle River, New Jersey*

10 9 8 7 6 5 4 3 2 1
ISBN: 0-13-094073-9

Contents

Preface

The popularity of AutoCAD has generated numerous books and manuals—most of which are similar to the reference manual that accompanies the AutoCAD software. However, AutoCAD is difficult to learn using just a reference manual or a book structured like one. *The AutoCAD® Book: Drawing, Modeling, and Applications Using AutoCAD® 2002* was written in response to the need for a book with an easy-to-follow format designed for people with various educational backgrounds and at differing levels of computer experience. It was developed by people who teach AutoCAD in the classroom setting and who use AutoCAD to produce drawings for manufacturing and construction.

Using the "hands-on" approach to the AutoCAD computer package is the fastest and most effective method of learning to use this powerful and exciting drawing tool. Therefore, this text teaches students to use AutoCAD by *drawing* with it.

All the material in this textbook has been carefully class-tested. People who have used the book have learned quickly to become productive with AutoCAD, and they are pleased with the clarity of the presentation and the fact that it assumes no familiarity with computers. Many have even been inspired to create menus and customize AutoCAD for their specific situations.

FEATURES

This new edition covers AutoCAD 2002. Some of the features of this edition are

- □ Complete coverage of the features of AutoCAD 2002.
- □ Update of "Tips," "Cautions," and "Notes" in the page margins. Each of these features is designed to help the new AutoCAD user past the stumbling blocks.
- □ Illustrations of pop-down menus, dialog boxes, and toolbars for AutoCAD 2002.
- □ 3-D tutorial exercises, including an introduction to advanced modeling.
- □ Introduction to AutoCAD's DesignCenter.
- □ Application chapters for architectural, civil, electronic and electromechanical drawing, and technical illustrating.
- □ New plotting techniques.
- □ Examination of new "etransmit" and "publish to Web" features.

TEXT ORGANIZATION

The AutoCAD® Book: Drawing, Modeling, and Applications Using AutoCAD® 2002 is divided into four parts: Part I—Preparing to Draw, Part II—Basic AutoCAD, Part III—Advanced AutoCAD, and Part IV—Applications.

Part I (Chapters 1–4)

Chapter 1 outlines the types of drawings to be covered in the book; Chapter 2 describes the AutoCAD program for Windows and its uses and the equipment necessary to use AutoCAD to its fullest extent; Chapter 3 is devoted to solving common problems associated with AutoCAD; and Chapter 4 moves the reader directly into the settings needed to make drawings that are accurate and easy to produce.

Part II (Chapters 5–17)

These drawing chapters show readers step by step how to produce several different types of drawings, including orthographic, sectional, isometric, 3-D, and plan views. Dimensioning, tolerancing, geometric constructions, attributes, block diagrams, and printing are also covered in these chapters. Chapter 5 describes how to use raster images in AutoCAD drawings. Chapter 17 describes how to customize AutoCAD menus and toolbars, and introduces AutoLISP.

Part III (Chapters 18–22)

These chapters cover advanced 3-D commands, 3D Orbit, SHADE, and an introduction to advanced modeling. This part also covers how to use paper space/model space for documenting and plotting drawings.

Part IV (Chapters 23–27)

Chapters 23 through 27 provide many exercises in the application of AutoCAD. Areas covered include the following:

Architectural
Civil
Electronic
Electromechanical
Technical Illustration

CHAPTER ORGANIZATION

Each chapter in *The AutoCAD® Book: Drawing, Modeling, and Applications Using AutoCAD® 2002* features

- □ Objectives that list commands used in the chapter.
- □ Clear, concise definitions for new terms when they are first introduced.
- □ Examples of drawings relating to the chapter topic.
- □ Step-by-step listings of all commands used in examples and an illustration of each command or series of commands.
- □ Assignments of varying difficulty that are similar to the examples.
- □ Review Questions that measure readers' knowledge of the chapter material.

ACKNOWLEDGMENTS

The author would like to acknowledge the valuable assistance of the following reviewers of the text: Leo J. LaFrance, New Mexico State University; Cynthia Lang, Penn State Abington–Ogontz; Dr. Michael E. Hutchins, Eastfield College.

The author would also like to thank the following people, who contributed drawings, text, answers, and ideas: Kristi Adams, John Brooks, Allen Dodson, Ron Hixson, Dennis Hoppe, Billy Montgomery, Bill Painter, Bill Painter, Jr., John Porcheddu, Lila Seida, Bill Sorrells, Hector Sylva, Carol Ward, and Don Zeiler.

WARNING AND DISCLAIMER

This book is designed to provide tutorial information about the AutoCAD computer program. Every effort has been made to make this book complete and as accurate as possible. But no warranty or fitness is implied.

The information is provided on an "as-is" basis. The author and Pearson Education, Inc. shall have neither liability nor responsibility to any person or entity with respect to any loss or damage in connection with or arising from the information contained in this book.

PART 1 PREPARING TO DRAW

1 Introduction

OBJECTIVES

After completing this chapter, you will be able to

- □ Describe the purpose of the textbook.
- □ Identify the types of drawings to be drawn in this textbook.
- □ Describe how the textbook is organized.

PURPOSE

This textbook is intended to present information so that you can learn AutoCAD by actually drawing with it. A minimum number of pages are devoted to subjects that do not involve hands-on use of AutoCAD commands. A command is an operator response that tells the computer to do something. Step-by-step listings show you how to make each type of drawing described in the following paragraphs.

References to specific versions of AutoCAD have been avoided in this text. Users of the earlier versions will find that some commands are not available to them. When this is the case, other commands can easily be substituted, although they may be slower than those in later versions. The uneasiness felt by some who have worked with earlier versions is unnecessary. People who have learned earlier versions well will have no trouble with later versions.

TYPES OF DRAWINGS

The following are the types of drawings, dimensions, and constructions that will be produced by the student who completes this book:

- □ Geometric constructions
- □ Block diagrams
- □ Orthographic drawings (including floor plans)
- □ Dimensioned drawings
- □ Toleranced drawings
- □ Sectional drawings
- □ Three-dimensional drawings
- □ Shaded renderings
- □ Solid models

- □ Architectural applications
- □ Civil applications
- □ Electronic applications
- □ Electromechanical applications
- □ Technical illustrating applications

These drawings are described briefly in the following paragraphs. Later chapters describe them in greater detail.

Geometric Constructions

Although geometric constructions are not a type of drawing, they are the first subject in this list. These constructions are the building blocks of all types of drawings. Terms such as *parallel, perpendicular, horizontal, vertical,* and *tangent* are defined, and the concepts are used to create these constructions. The term *geometric* may sound as if higher-level math will be required; this is not the case in computer drafting. If you can add, subtract, multiply, and divide on a calculator, you can do all the drawing problems in this book.

Figure 1–1 shows several of the geometric constructions covered in Chapter 9. These constructions are often difficult to draw manually in pencil or ink, but with the computer they are easy. If the correct commands are used to draw them, the constructions can be extremely accurate and beautifully drawn.

Block Diagrams

Figure 1–2 shows examples of block diagrams drawn on a computer. These diagrams are used to show as simply as possible how a company or other group is organized and how equipment or groups function. Some of these diagrams have specific symbols and uses not shown in this figure, but they are all similar in construction. Most of them have blocks, lines connecting the blocks, and arrows showing the directional flow.

Orthographic Drawings

Two-dimensional drawings are called *orthographic drawings* in the drafting business. These drawings are the universal language of technical drawing. Only two dimensions

FIGURE 1–1
Geometric Constructions

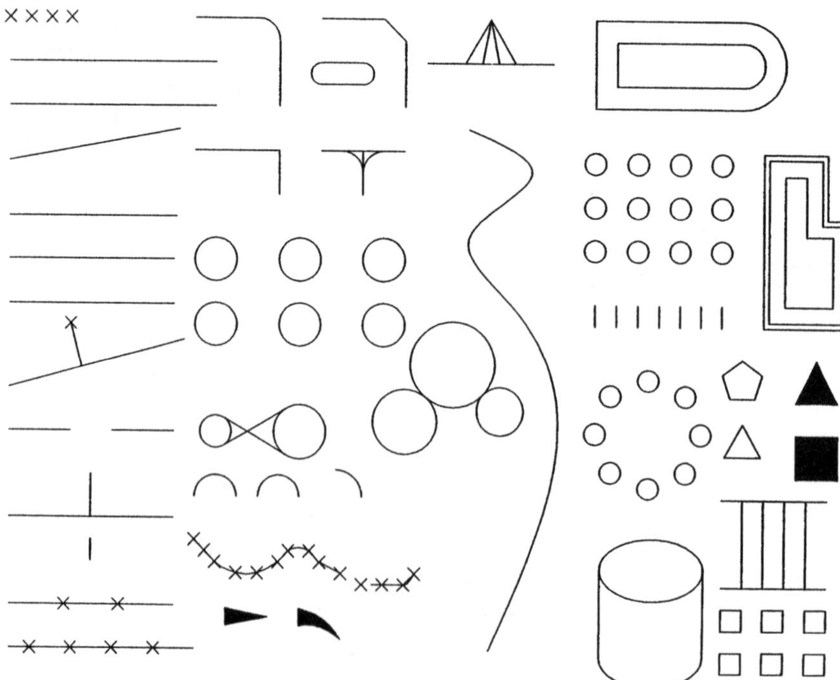

FIGURE 1–2
Block Diagrams

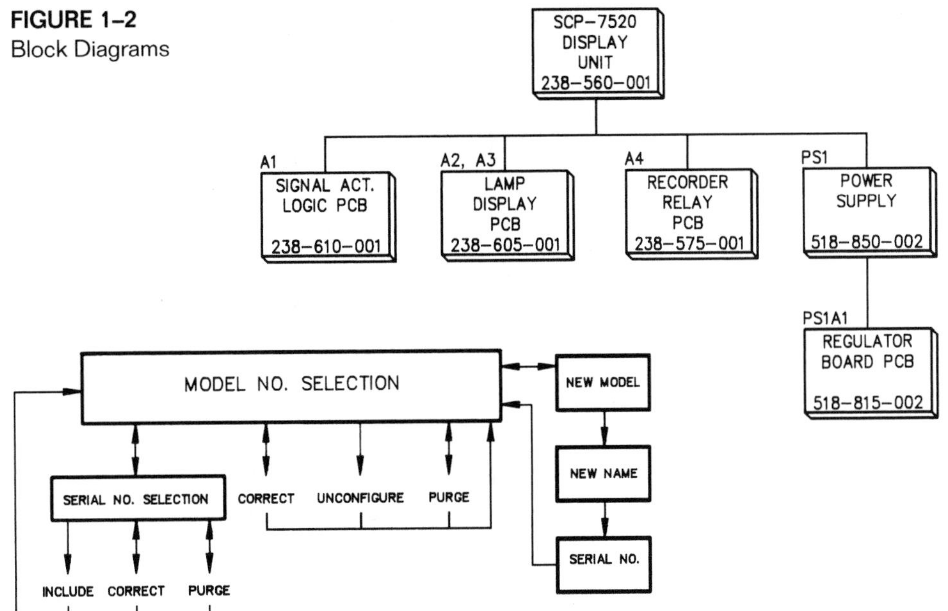

are seen in any one view. Those dimensions may be height and width, height and depth, or width and depth. Figure 1–3 shows some examples of orthographic drawings. The top drawing shows three views of a single object. The middle drawing is a two-view drawing of a design for a classic guitar. The bottom drawing is a floor plan showing a single view of a structure. Further details are presented in a later chapter.

Dimensioned Drawings

A dimensioned drawing is a type of orthographic drawing that gives the size and location of features. AutoCAD is very useful in dimensioning because it can become almost automatic when drawings are made full size. Figure 1–4 shows two drawings that have been drawn to scale and dimensioned using AutoCAD.

Toleranced Drawings

All drawings used to build parts of structures have tolerances (limits) that are placed on all dimensions. These tolerances may be very specific, as shown in Figure 1–5. For example, an understood tolerance of ±¼″ on a 3″ dimension means that a part, when inspected, must measure between 3¼″ and 2¾″ to pass. A more accurate tolerance for the same 3″ dimension could be ±.005″. The upper limit in this case would be 3.005″. The lower limit would be 2.995″. AutoCAD allows parts to be drawn with extreme accuracy using certain commands. It also allows parts that do not require accuracy to be drawn faster but with less accuracy.

Sectional Drawings

Sectional drawings are used in many different industries to clarify internal or hidden external construction. AutoCAD allows the spacing of shading lines to be very accurate and eliminates the tedious task of drawing those lines or using stick-on or rub-on shading lines. Figure 1–6 shows two sectional drawings made using AutoCAD. This type of drawing can often be done with more consistent lines and with much less effort using AutoCAD than manually. Shading lines are often drawn with a thinner pen by using LAYER or LINEWEIGHT commands, which are presented in Chapter 4. Layers are used to separate line types or other features that allow the drawing to be used more efficiently.

FIGURE 1–3
Orthographic Drawings

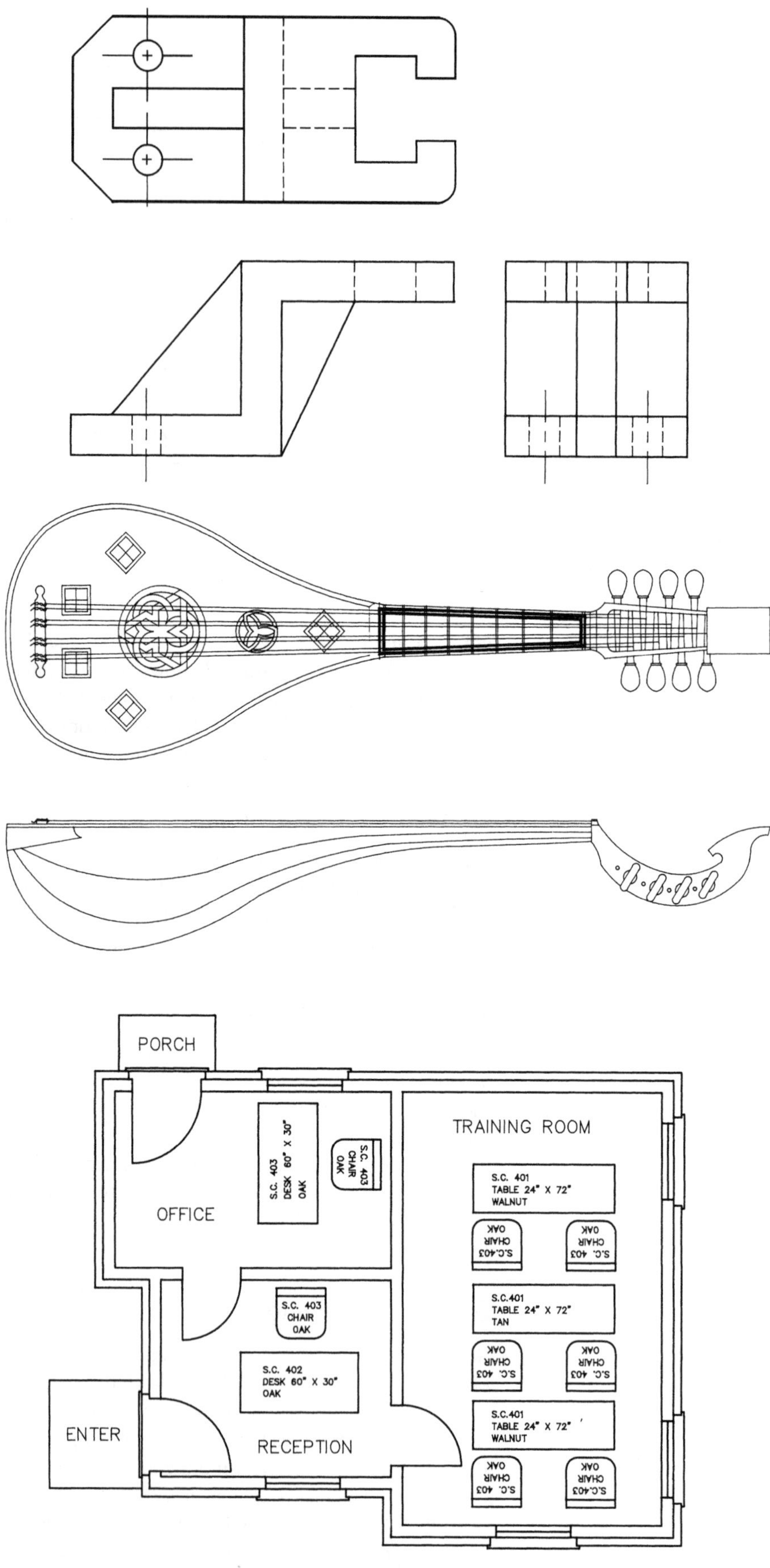

FIGURE 1–4
Dimensioned Drawings

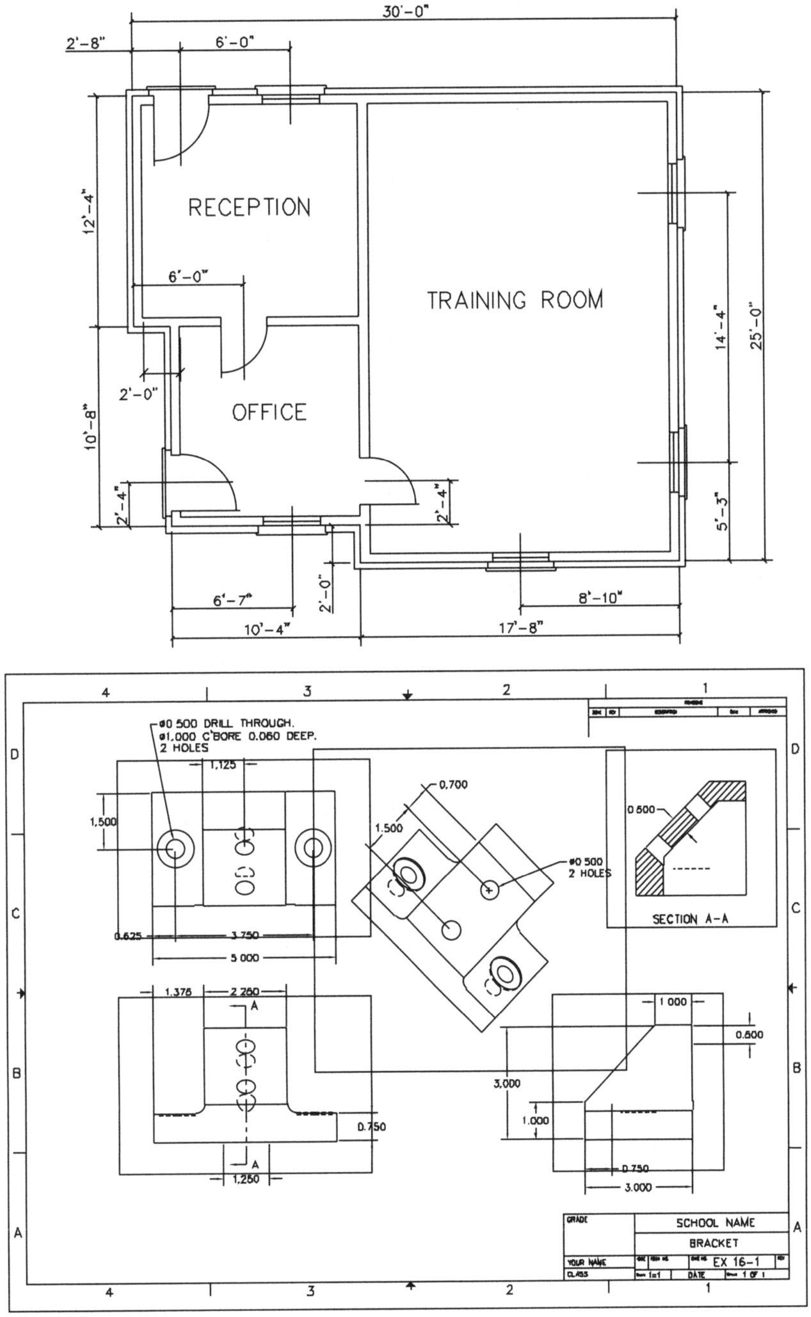

FIGURE 1–5
Toleranced Drawings

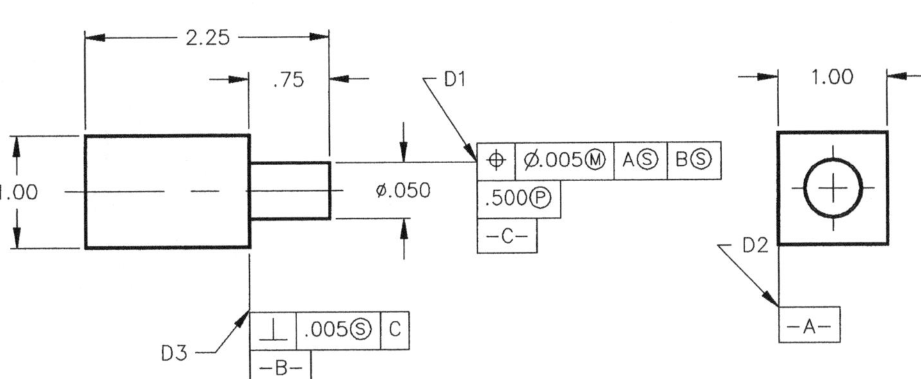

FIGURE 1–6
Sectional Drawings

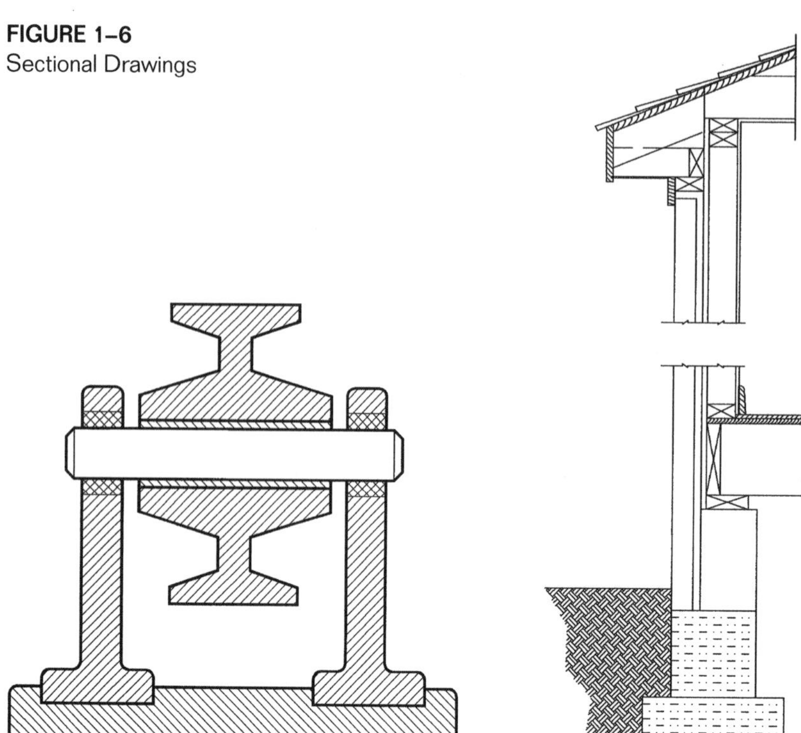

Three-Dimensional Drawings

The isometric drawing and 3-D modeling features of AutoCAD may be used to show pictorial views of objects. Figure 1–7 shows examples of three-dimensional and isometric objects drawn using AutoCAD. The 3-D feature of AutoCAD allows objects to be created in three dimensions so that they can be rotated to any desired position; limitless illustrations of an object can then be obtained from a single three-dimensional object.

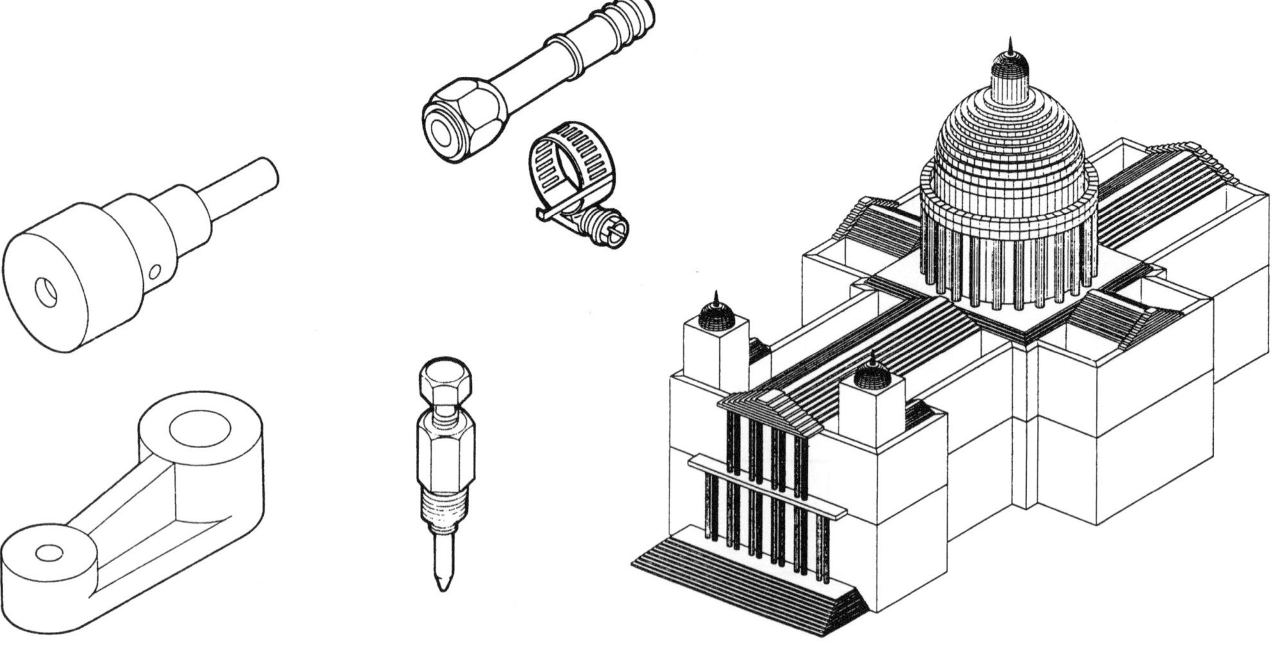

FIGURE 1–7
Three-Dimensional AutoCAD Drawings

Shaded Renderings

Figure 1–8 shows a black-and-white rendering done with the SHADE command. Shaded renderings can also be done in color. The RENDER and 3D Orbit commands are used to produce more realistic renderings. 3D Studio Max and 3D Studio VIZ (additional programs) can be used to render AutoCAD models and animate them.

Solid Models

Solid modeling allows solid shapes to be created that can be used to analyze form, fit, and functional aspects of a design. Figure 1–9 shows objects that were created using solids commands.

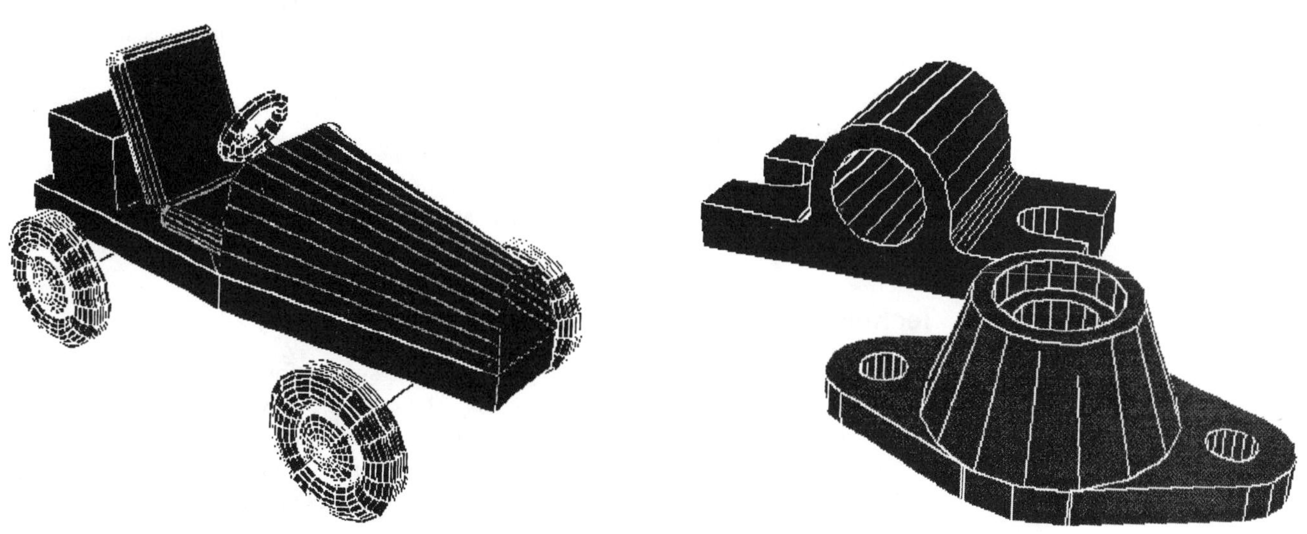

FIGURE 1–8
Shaded Models Using the SHADE Command

FIGURE 1–9
Solid Models

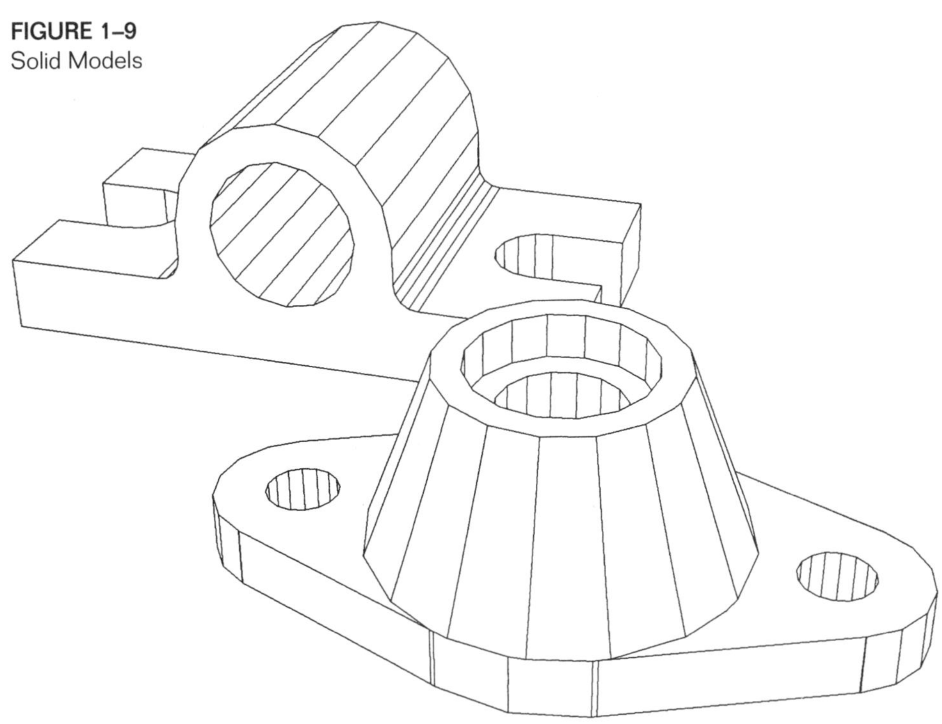

Architectural Applications

The drawing shown in Figure 1–10 is an example of the exercises that are included in Chapter 19. These are advanced AutoCAD applications for people interested in architecture.

Civil Applications

Figure 1–11 shows the advanced exercises presented in Chapter 20. This figure shows the topographical drawings of sites and the cross-sectional illustrations of such areas.

Electronic Applications

Figure 1–12 shows the drawings used to produce printed circuit boards. Although there are software packages that allow much of this work to be done automatically, AutoCAD is often used to do part or all of these drawing types. Chapter 21 provides several exercises for electronic applications.

Electromechanical Applications

Figure 1–13 shows an example of a design layout from which assembly and detail drawings are made that are used in electromechanical design. These advanced problems are included in Chapter 22.

Technical Illustrating Applications

Figure 1–14 shows examples of the types of drawings made for manuals that are used to build, assemble, install, and repair equipment. These are the drawings described in Chapter 23. Many of you have used illustrations such as these to assemble a bicycle, fix a car, or hook up a VCR. Many high-tech aircraft, electronics, and automobile companies employ large numbers of people to do these drawings. These people are called *technical illustrators.*

FIGURE 1–10
Architectural Rendering
Courtesy RTKL Associates, Inc., Bank Lobby Designer Jim Sailor, CADD Graphics Hector Silva

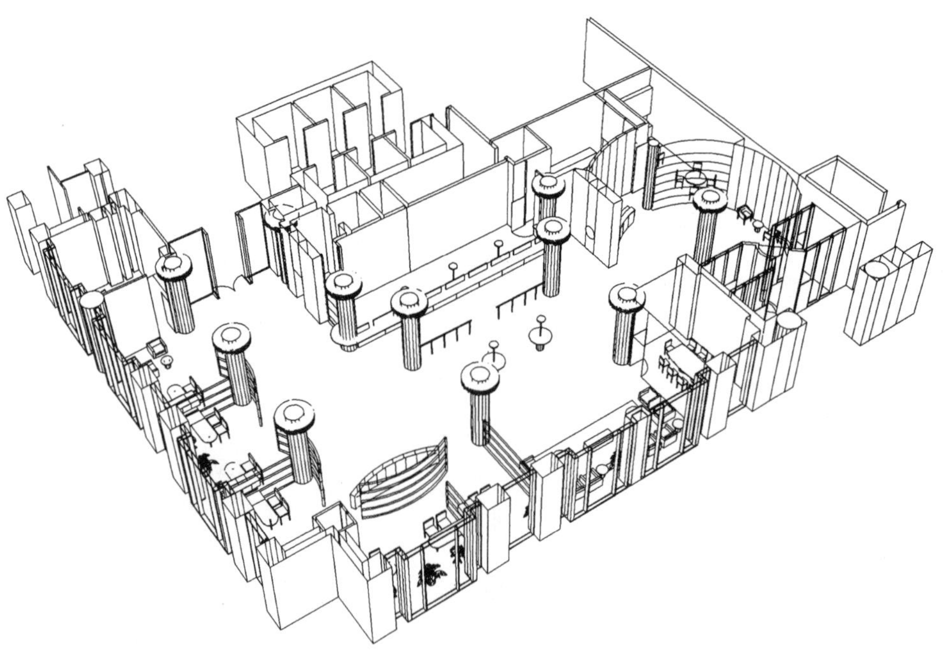

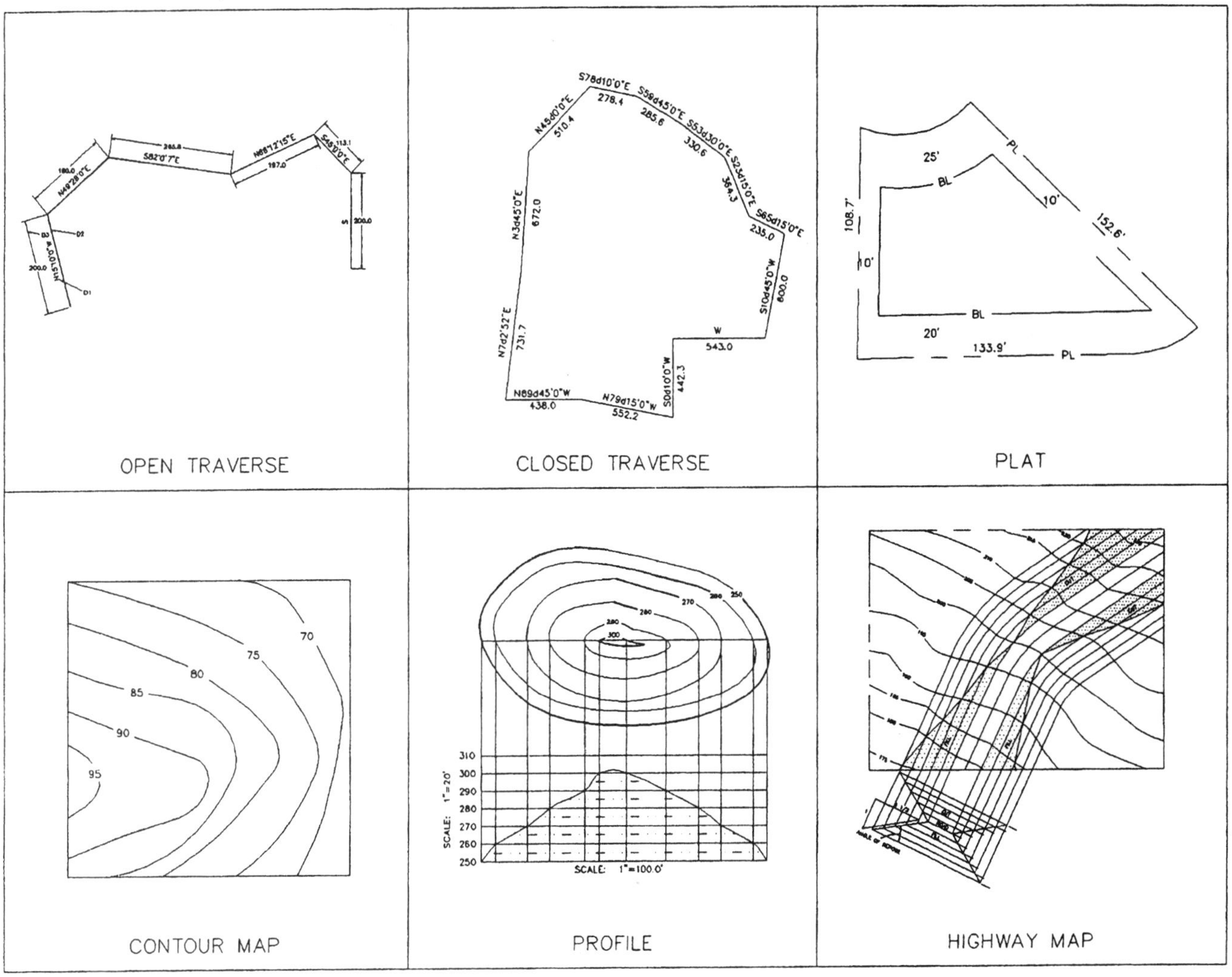

OPEN TRAVERSE | CLOSED TRAVERSE | PLAT

CONTOUR MAP | PROFILE | HIGHWAY MAP

FIGURE 1–11
Civil Applications

FIGURE 1–12
Electronic Applications

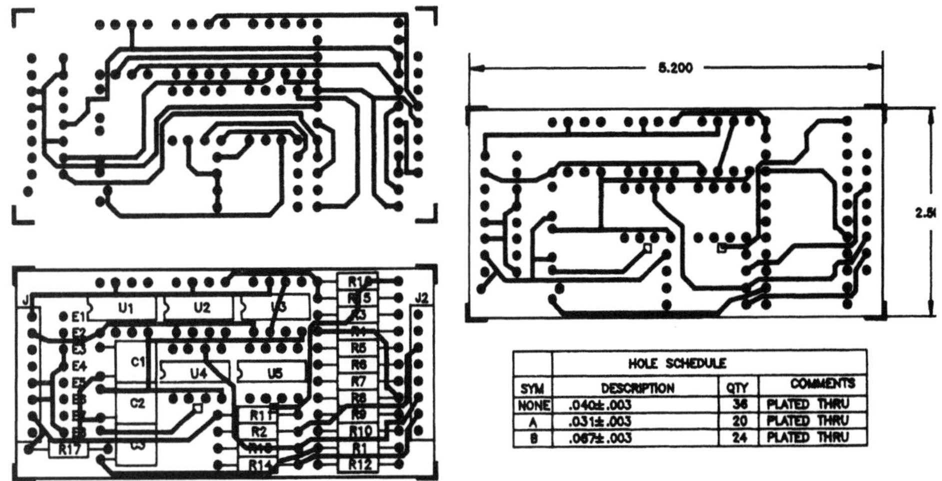

HOLE SCHEDULE

SYM	DESCRIPTION	QTY	COMMENTS
NONE	.040±.003	36	PLATED THRU
A	.031±.003	20	PLATED THRU
B	.067±.003	24	PLATED THRU

FIGURE 1–13
Electromechanical Applications

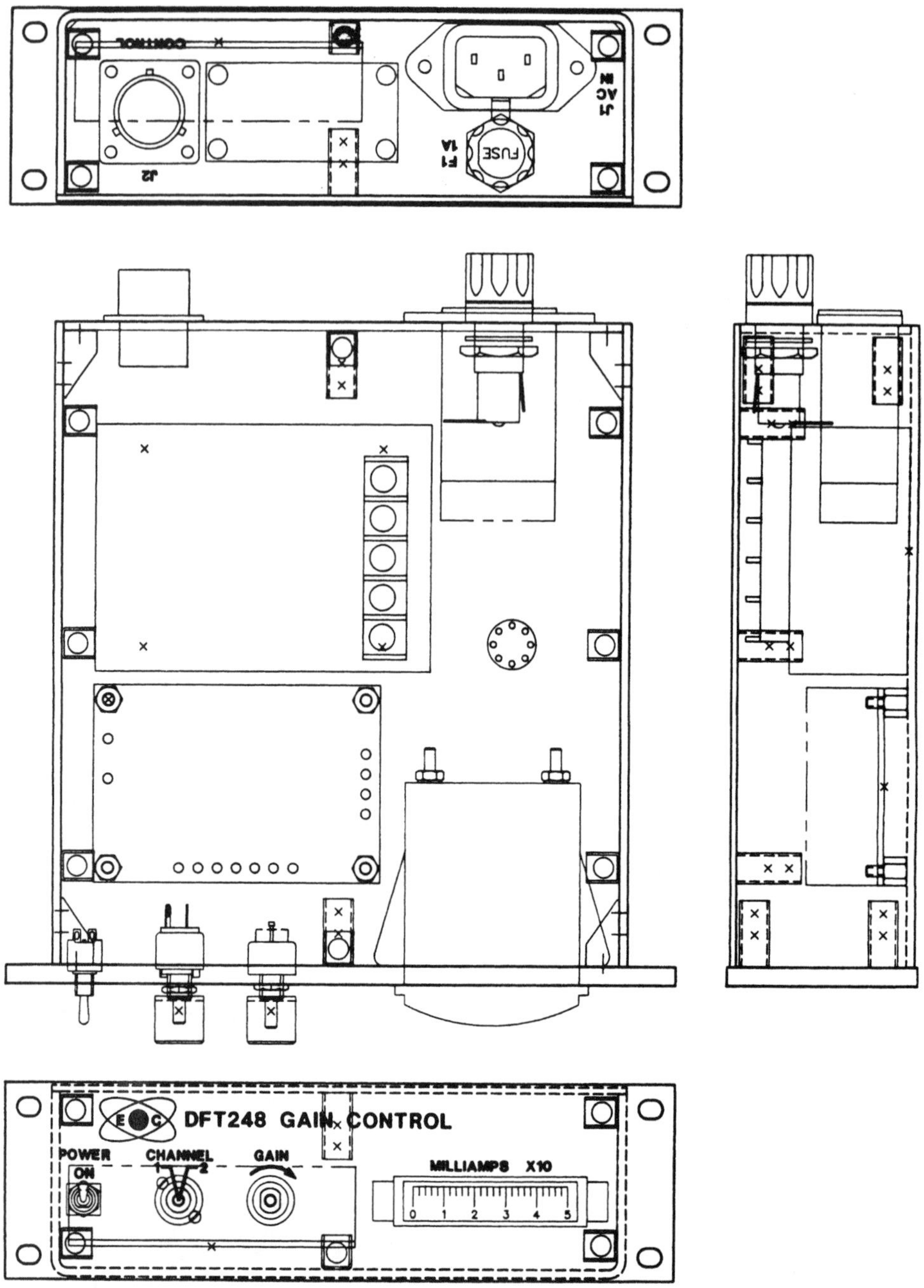

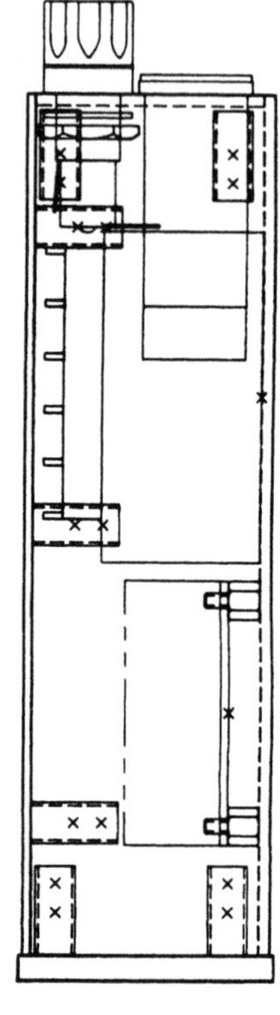

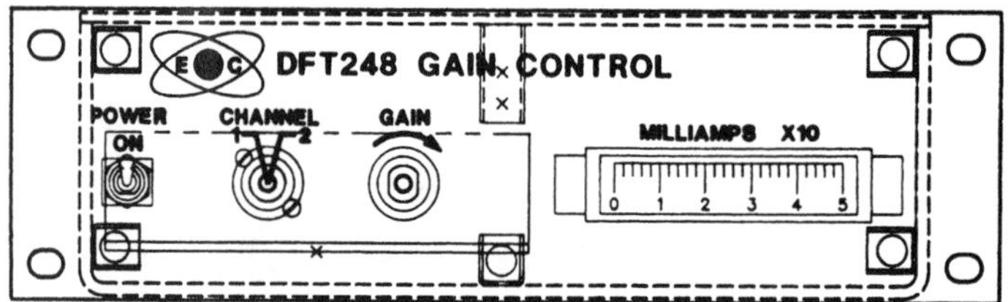

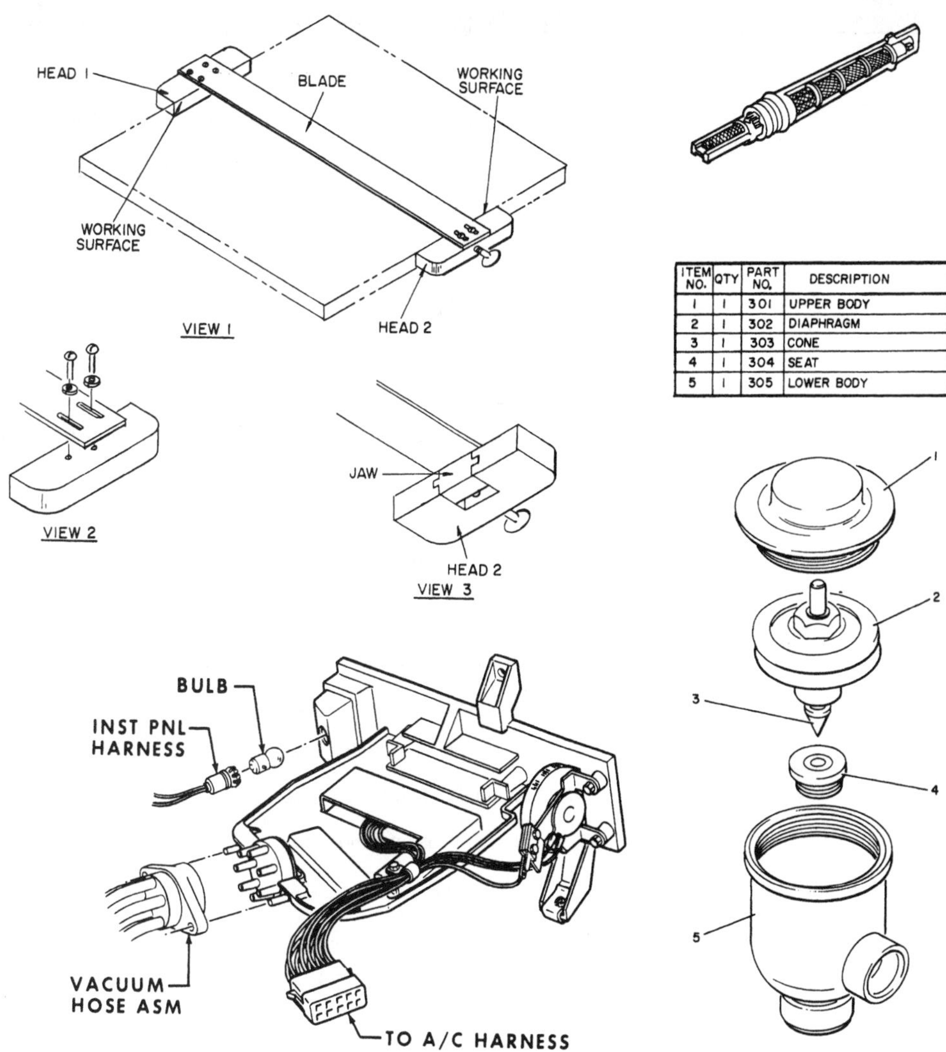

ITEM NO.	QTY	PART NO.	DESCRIPTION
1	1	301	UPPER BODY
2	1	302	DIAPHRAGM
3	1	303	CONE
4	1	304	SEAT
5	1	305	LOWER BODY

FIGURE 1–14
Technical Illustrating Applications

ADDITIONAL TOPICS

The following additional topics are described in this book:

The personal computer and the AutoCAD 2000 program
How to set up your first drawing
Using raster images (images composed of dots) in AutoCAD drawings
Common problems encountered when using AutoCAD and the solutions to those problems
Adding text to your drawings
Printing and plotting your drawings
Customizing AutoCAD menus and toolbars, creating macros, and an introduction to AutoLISP
Publishing to the Internet

AutoCAD is by far the most commonly used CAD program. The time you spend learning to use AutoCAD will give you skills that you can use and develop for the rest of your career. This book has a rich variety of exercises that we hope are fun as well as educational.

REVIEW QUESTIONS

Complete.

1. List eight types of drawings that are covered in Parts II and III of this book.

___

___

___

2. List five types of drawings that are covered in Part IV of this book.

___

___

3. List two topics other than drawing or modeling that are covered by this book.

___

___

4. Define the following:

Customized menu ___

Command ___

Tolerance ___

Dimensioned drawings ___

Sectional drawings ___

Three-dimensional modeling ___

Raster image ___

2 The AutoCAD 2002 Program

OBJECTIVES

After completing this chapter, you will be able to

- □ Describe parts of the AutoCAD hardware system.
- □ Start the Windows or Windows NT operating system.
- □ Start AutoCAD for Windows.
- □ Describe the AutoCAD for Windows screen and begin using parts of the screen.
- □ Activate, hide, dock, float, reshape, and resize toolbars.

PARTS OF THE AUTOCAD HARDWARE SYSTEM

The following are parts of a typical personal computer system on which AutoCAD software can be used:

Computer
Floppy disk drive
Hard disk drive
Compact disk drive
Display monitor
Keyboard
Mouse
Printer
Plotter

Computer

The computer should be of sufficient capacity to run AutoCAD easily. It should also have a graphics card (a printed circuit board that allows a high-quality display of graphic data) and other features that will allow the display (the screen) to be easily read and quickly generated.

Floppy Disk Drive

At least one floppy disk drive is needed to move large blocks of information into and out of the computer. Floppy disks are inserted into a floppy disk drive. AutoCAD drawings can be stored on floppy disks. Floppy disk drives are identified by a one-letter name followed by a colon (for example, A:). The 3½″ high-density disk drive uses a 3½″ floppy diskette. This diskette stores approximately 1.44 megabytes (MB) to 2 MB of information (1,440,000 to 2,000,000 bytes).

Compact Disk Drive

Compact disk drives are available in a variety of speeds and some are read/write, meaning that you can retrieve and save information on compact disks. The faster they are, the higher the price. A relatively slow compact disk drive is sufficient to load AutoCAD software, but a faster speed drive is nice to have. Because much of the new software is available on compact disks and as a result is more convenient and faster to load, a compact disk drive is a necessity. Some drawing files are now large enough that they cannot fit on a floppy disk and must be saved on compact or Zip disks. Compact disks store approximately 650 MB (650,000,000 bytes) of information.

Hard Disk Drive

A hard disk drive, also called a *hard drive* or *hard disk,* is usually permanently installed inside the computer. It can store much more information than the removable floppy disks and is used to store the AutoCAD program. AutoCAD drawings may also be stored on the hard disk drive. The hard disk drive is commonly called drive C (C:). A hard drive with adequate storage capacity for your situation is necessary. Two- to 60-gigabyte (GB) hard drives are commonly used.

Display Monitor

A display monitor is similar to a television screen. A color display monitor is a necessity. The physical size of the screen is not as important as the resolution. The resolution of the display is stated in *pixels,* which is the number of dots arranged in rows and columns to make the visual display on the screen. The finer the resolution, the better. AutoCAD requires a display screen of reasonably high resolution.

Keyboard

The keyboard has the following three parts:

Alphanumeric Keys

Located in the center of the keyboard, these are used to type the lettering and numbers that will appear on your drawings and occasionally to type commands. The number keys can also be used as a calculator with an AutoCAD command.

Function Keys

Keys labeled F1–F12, often located to the left or above the alphanumeric keys of many keyboards, are used to perform special functions such as turning a grid on or off. These keys are used and their functions are explained in later chapters.

Numeric Keys

Often located to the right of the alphanumeric keys, these keys can be used to type numbers that will appear on your drawings and can also be used as a calculator in combination with an AutoCAD command. The directional arrows, which can be toggled on or off, may be used to move the location of the pointer.

Mouse

A mouse is used to select commands from the AutoCAD menus or toolbars. The mouse allows the eyes of the operator to remain on the screen at all times. The mouse is also used to enter points of a drawing, such as where a line starts or where a circle is located. It is moved across a tabletop or pad, and its action is described on the display screen by the movement of crosshairs. The crosshairs are positioned to highlight a command or to locate a point. The pick button (usually the far-left button) on the mouse is clicked to select a command or enter a point on the drawing. The extra buttons on a mouse can be assigned to perform different tasks. Most commonly the right button is assigned return (↵) or right-click menus.

Printer

Laser printers are available that produce hard copies of excellent quality in black and white or color. Many of the newer color printers are relatively inexpensive and produce high-quality hard copies. The low-cost color printers are slow, however, so take the speed factor into account if you buy one.

Plotter

A plotter is essential for making high-quality, usable drawings (hard copies) larger than 8½ × 11. Electrostatic plotters that use an electrical charge and toner to produce an image are available, as are relatively low cost ink-jet plotters. Plotters and printers are now very similar in construction and operation.

STARTING MICROSOFT WINDOWS AND STARTING AUTOCAD 2002

Exercise 2–1: Activate Windows or Windows NT, AutoCAD, and Examine the AutoCAD Screen

Step 1. To begin Exercise 2–1, turn on the computer and observe the Windows desktop (Figure 2–1):

When Windows is started, the Windows Desktop appears on the screen. Figure 2–1 shows a typical display of the Desktop.

The Desktop has a small number of icons on it (an *icon* is a picture). Only one of these is needed to get started. That one is labeled **Start.**

Step 2. Locate the AutoCAD 2002 program and activate it (Figures 2–1 and 2–2).

Prompt	Response
The Windows Desktop is displayed:	*Click:* **the Start icon** (shown highlighted in Figure 2–2)
The Start menu is displayed:	**Move the cursor so that the word Programs is highlighted.**
The Programs list is displayed:	**Move the cursor so that the word AutoCAD 2002 is highlighted.**
The AutoCAD 2002 menu line is displayed:	*Click:* **the AutoCAD 2002 command line as shown**

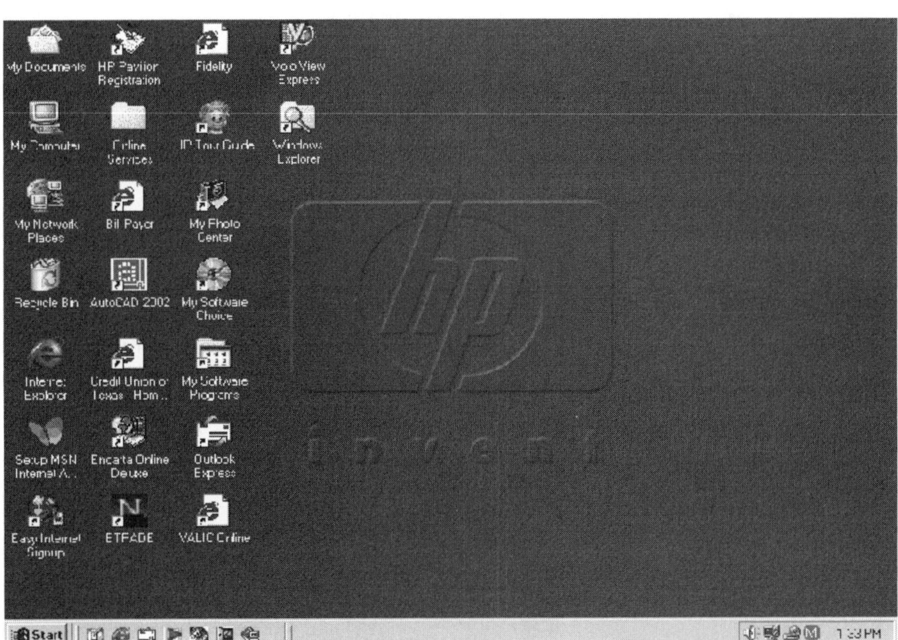

FIGURE 2–1
Windows Desktop

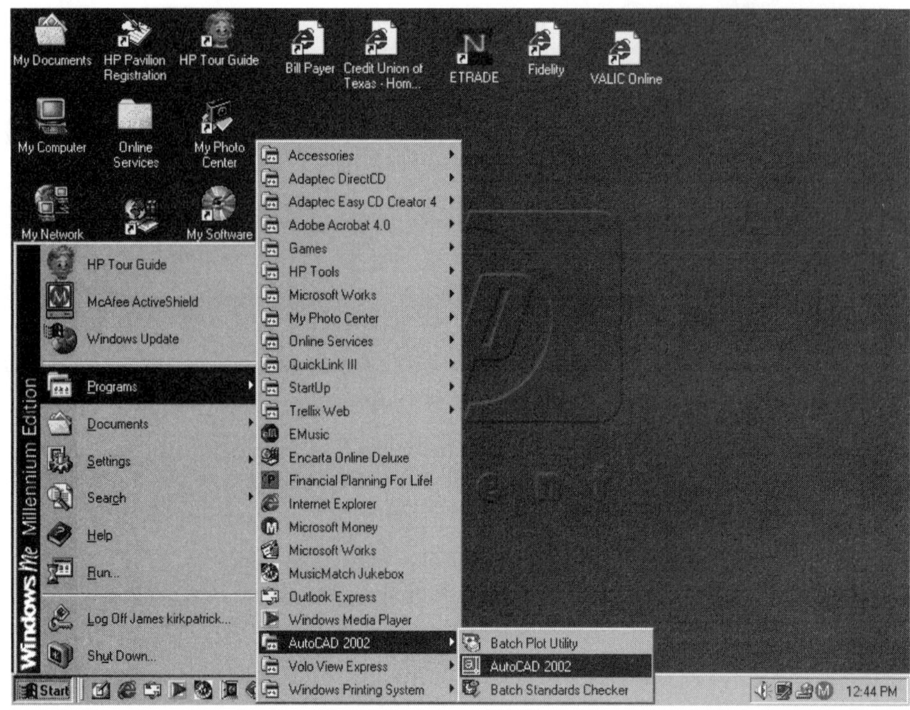

FIGURE 2–2
Starting AutoCAD 2002

Notice the AutoCAD 2002 icon at the center of the screen in Figure 2–1. This is a shortcut that Windows will create for you if you want it to allow you to activate AutoCAD more quickly.

When AutoCAD 2002 is started, the AutoCAD 2002 Today window (Figure 2–3) appears. Uses of this window are included in Chapter 4. Close this window by clicking the X in the upper right corner. When the Today window is closed, the AutoCAD 2002 graphics screen appears. It provides the display area for drawing and the commands used to create, modify, view, and plot drawings. You can begin by naming the new drawing, or you may immediately begin drawing without naming the drawing. When you are ready to end the drawing session, you must save the drawing using Save or SaveAs..., at which time you must name the drawing. AutoCAD communicates with you on various parts of the screen. You may have a slightly different appearing screen, depending on the preferences selected. A brief introduction to each part of the screen (Figure 2–4) follows.

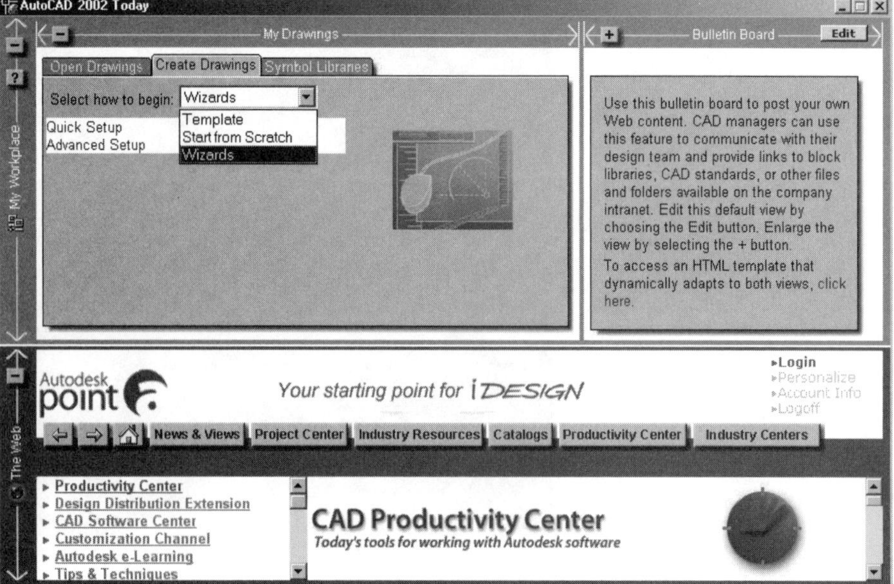

FIGURE 2–3
The AutoCAD 2002 Today Window

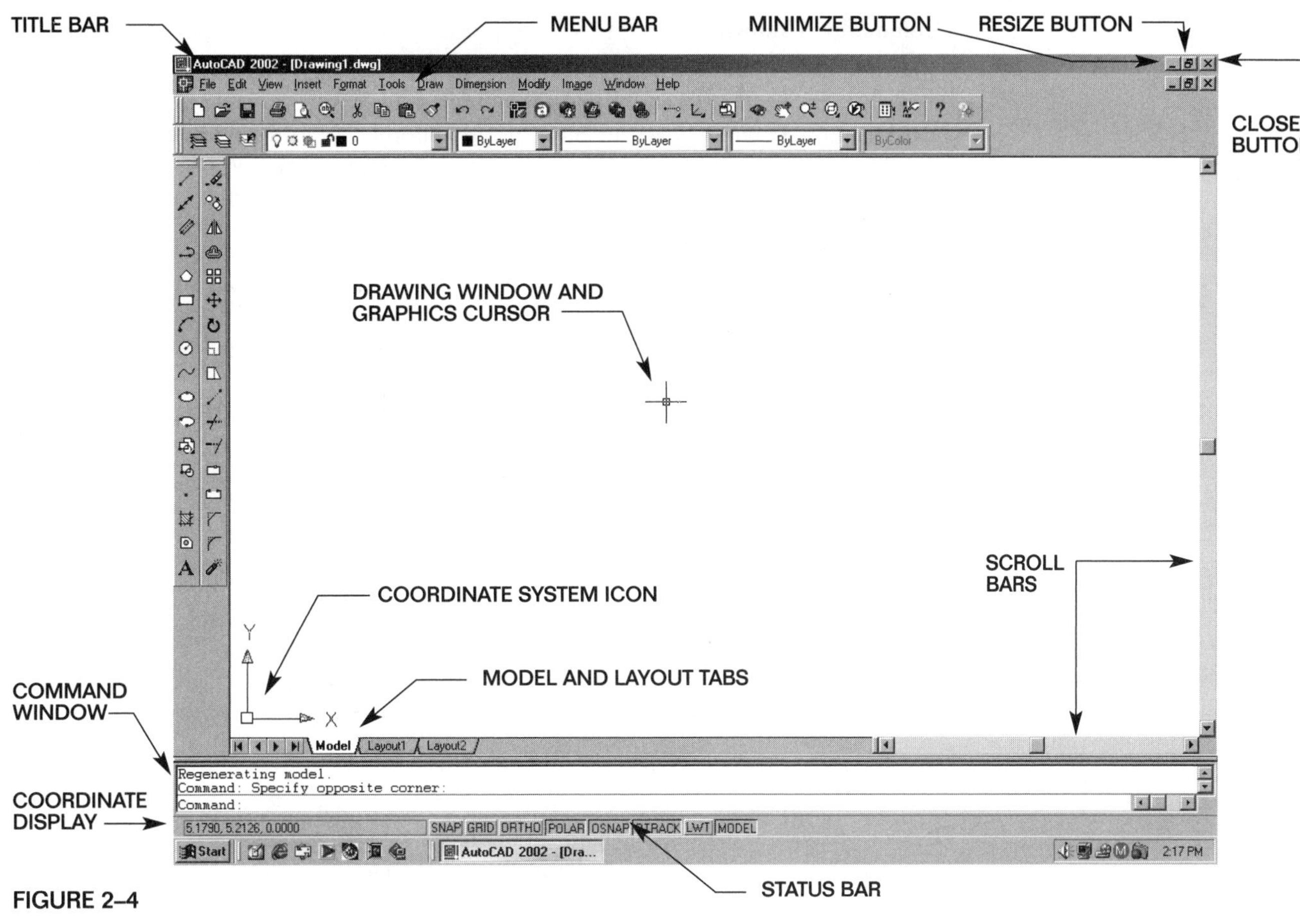

FIGURE 2–4
The AutoCAD Screen

THE AUTOCAD FOR WINDOWS SCREEN

Title Bar

The title bar contains the name of the program, AutoCAD 2002, and the name of the current drawing, in this case, [Drawing 1], because you have not yet named the drawing. The buttons on the label are listed next.

AutoCAD Program and Drawing Buttons

This button on the program window minimizes the AutoCAD program. The program remains active so you can return to it if you choose. To return to it pick the AutoCAD 2002 button on the taskbar at the bottom of the screen. A drawing can also be minimized by picking this button on the drawing window.

This button resizes the program or drawing window.

This button maximizes the size of the program or drawing window.

This button closes the AutoCAD program. It is grayed out on the drawing window, indicating the drawing cannot be closed from this button.

Drawing Window and Graphics Cursor

The drawing window is where your drawing is displayed. The graphics cursor (or crosshairs) follows the movement of a mouse or puck when points of a drawing are entered or a command is selected. To change the size of the crosshairs, click Options… on the Tools menu, then click the Display tab, then move the slider in the lower left corner to the right to increase size or left to decrease.

Command Window

The command window shown at the bottom of the screen (which may be moved and resized if you want) is where AutoCAD communicates with you once a command is activated. AutoCAD prompts you to enter specific information to further define a command and then responds with action on the screen or additional prompts. Always watch the command window to make sure you and AutoCAD are communicating.

Coordinate System Icon

The coordinate system icon in the lower left corner of the drawing window shows the orientation of the X, Y, and Z axes of the current coordinate system. When AutoCAD is started you are in the world coordinate system (WCS), as indicated by the W in the coordinate system icon.

Coordinate Display

Using an X- and Y-axis coordinate system, the coordinate display numbers in the extreme lower left corner tell you where the cursor or crosshairs on the screen are located in relation to point 0,0 (the lower left corner).

Status Bar

The status bar at the bottom of the screen keeps you informed about your drawing by displaying the status of modes that affect your drawing: SNAP, GRID, ORTHO, POLAR, OSNAP, OTRACK, LWT, and MODEL. These modes can be turned on and off by double-clicking on the mode name with the pick button of your mouse. The time is also displayed.

Scroll Bars

The scroll bars on the bottom and right side of the screen area allow you to move the drawing display at the same magnification, up and down, left and right. The scroll bars can be turned on and off using the Display tab in the Options… dialog box under Tools in the menu bar. The menu bar is described next.

Model and Layout Tabs

The model and layout tabs allow you to select different means of plotting your drawings.

Menu Bar

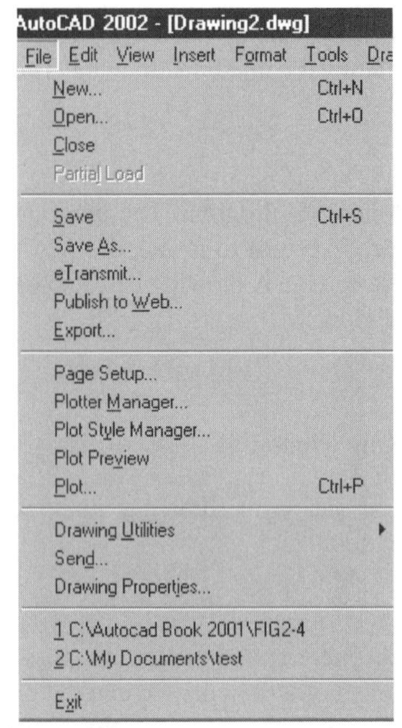

FIGURE 2–5
File Menu

Step 3. Practice using the menu bar.

You can open a menu item on the menu bar by holding the pointer on the menu name and clicking it; click the menu item again to close the menu, or use the Esc key to cancel any command activated. A pull-down menu will appear for each item on the menu bar when the item is clicked (Figures 2–5 through 2–13). Pull-down menus provide access to many of the same commands that are included on the toolbars. The commands followed by an ellipsis (…) display a dialog box when clicked. Use the Esc key or click the Cancel button in the dialog box to cancel it. Those pull-down menu items with an arrow to the right have a cascading menu.

When you hold your finger steady on the pick button of your mouse and highlight each menu bar item, pull-down menu command, or cascading menu command, a text string at the bottom of the display screen (in the coordinate display and status bar area) gives a brief description of the commands. Many of the menu bar commands are used in the following chapters; however, the following brief description of the general content of the menu bar provides an introduction:

File (Figure 2–5) This menu bar item contains the commands needed to start a new drawing, open an existing one, save drawings, print a drawing, import and export data, manage files, and exit from AutoCAD. It also shows the most recently active drawings, which may be opened by clicking on them.

Edit (Figure 2–6) This item contains the Undo command (allows you to undo or reverse the most recent command) and the Redo command (will redo one undo). It also contains the

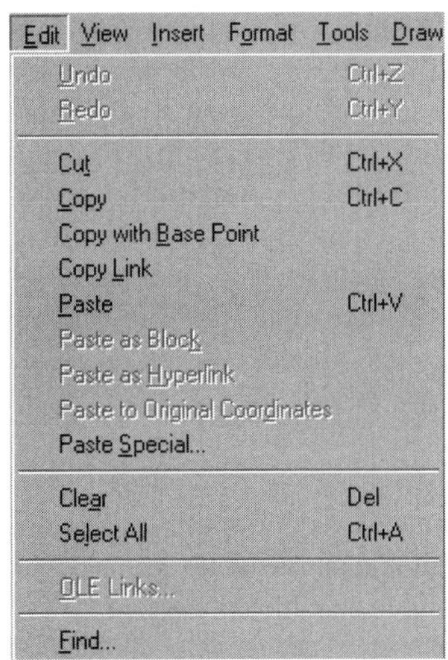

FIGURE 2–6
Edit Menu

commands related to the Windows Clipboard: Cut, Copy, Copy Link, Paste, and Paste Special… Drawings or text from other applications (such as Word or Paintbrush) can be cut or copied onto the Windows Clipboard and then pasted from the Clipboard into an AutoCAD drawing. The reverse is also possible; AutoCAD drawings can be pasted into other applications. The OLE Links… command is a Windows feature that allows you to link or unlink an AutoCAD drawing and another application's object (document or drawing). When a drawing is copied and placed in a document in another program such as Paintbrush or Word and then linked, editing it updates the information in both the original drawing and the new document.

View (Figure 2–7) This menu contains commands that control the display of your drawing. The Redraw and Regen commands redraw the display screen to remove blips, and redraw any part of the drawing that is missing. The Zoom commands control the magnification of the drawing display, and Pan allows you to move the drawing up and down, left and right. There are some 3-D commands on the pull-down menu and also commands for model space (where your drawing is created) and paper space (where a presentation is created). The Named Views… command provides a dialog box that allows you to name drawing views, save them, and restore them as needed. The Hide, Shade, and Render commands are used to render solid models, and the Toolbars… command allows you to display or hide toolbars.

Insert (Figure 2–8) This menu contains the commands that allow you to insert previously drawn objects into an AutoCAD drawing. These objects may be other AutoCAD drawings or pictures from other drawing programs.

Format (Figure 2–9) This menu bar item contains commands that help you set up your drawing environment and prepare to draw with AutoCAD. The Layer… command creates layers on which different parts of a drawing can be placed. Every drawing entity (such as an arc, line, or circle) will have a Color… and Linetype…. You will learn in later chapters to create a Text Style… and a Dimension Style… so you can add text and dimensions to your drawing. Point Style… allows you to set the style and size for points that are drawn. Multiline Style… allows you to draw up to 16 lines at a time. The Units… command establishes the drawing units. For example, an inch is a drawing unit. Thickness allows you to give an object height. The Drawing Limits command sets the page size you draw on. The Rename… command allows you to rename layers, text styles, dimension styles, and more.

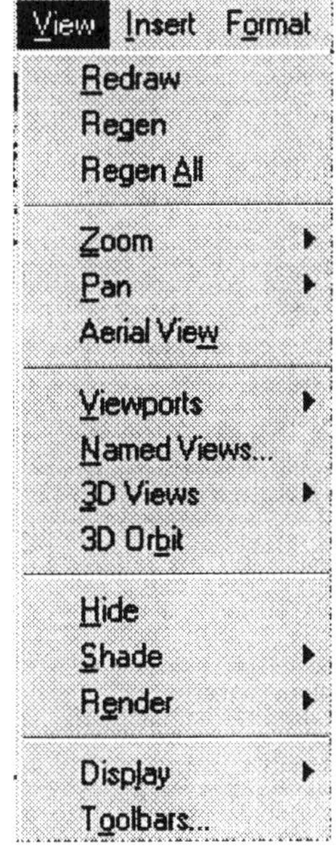

FIGURE 2–7
View Menu

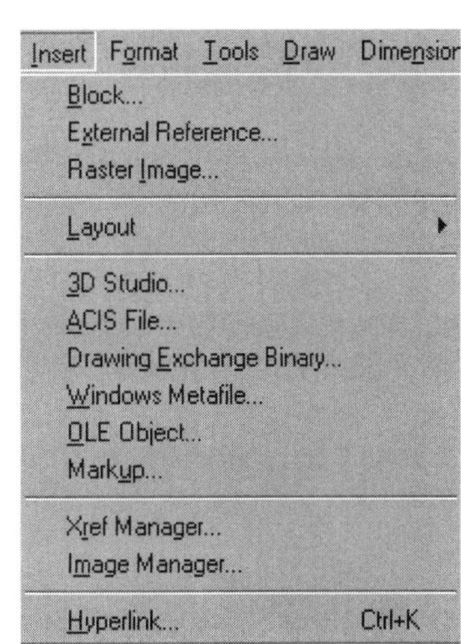

FIGURE 2–8
Insert Menu

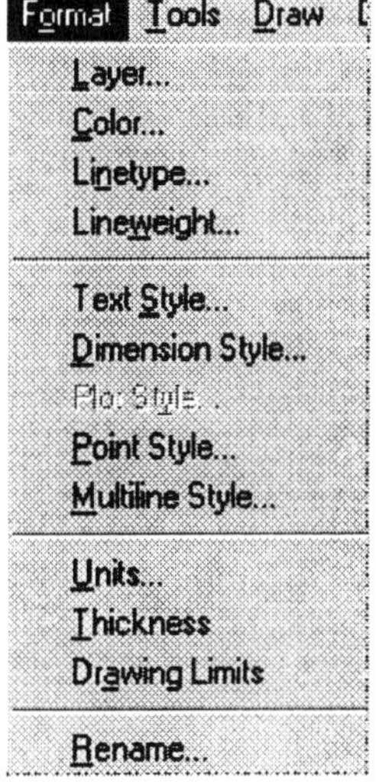

FIGURE 2–9
Format Menu

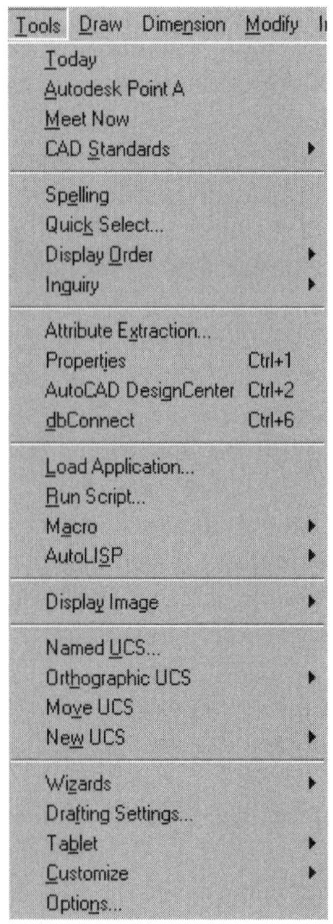

FIGURE 2–10
Tools Menu

Tools (Figure 2–10) This menu has a spell checker. A Display Order command allows you to place images on top of each other, and it also allows you to obtain information about the size and location of entities and about the amount of time spent on the drawing, when it was done, and to place a date and time stamp on your drawing. The AutoCAD Design Center is also part of the Tools menu. Tools also has commands for running scripts (described in a later chapter), loading AutoLISP programs and applications, and adding external data. UCS commands, wizards, and a dialog box for making drawing settings are located here. The Tools menu also has a command for customizing menus and toolbars, and activating the Options… dialog box. This dialog box gives you several options for arranging and coloring your screen display.

Draw (Figure 2–11) The Draw menu has all the commands used to draw objects in AutoCAD.

Dimension (Figure 2–12) This menu contains the commands used to place dimensions on drawings. All these commands are described in detail in a later chapter.

Modify (Figure 2–13) The Modify commands are used to change the position, shape, or number of objects after they have been drawn. Commands to change text are also on this menu.

Image (Figure 2-14) This menu refers to the CAD Overlay program, which is an additional program that allows you to convert scanned images into AutoCAD drawings. If you have not purchased this program, you will probably want to remove this menu.

Window (Figure 2-15) This menu is used to arrange multiple drawings when you are working on more than one drawing at the same time.

Help (Figure 2–16) This menu bar item has commands that teach you how to use the Help command. The AutoCAD Help Topics command provides information about how to use AutoCAD commands. It is a very helpful tool for any AutoCAD user. The six introductory items on this menu, Active Assistance, Developer Help, Support Assistance, Product Support on Point A, What's New, Learning Assistance, and Autodesk User Group International are very worthwhile. Take the time to run those now to familiarize yourself with the basics of this program. Other commands in this menu item provide technical information about AutoCAD.

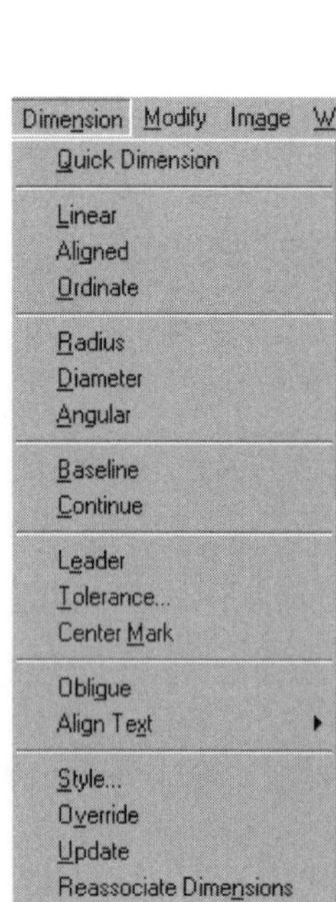

FIGURE 2–11
Draw Menu

FIGURE 2–12
Dimension Menu

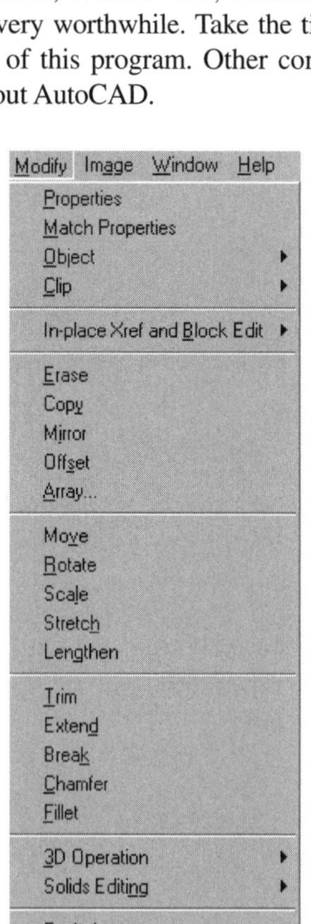

FIGURE 2–13
Modify Menu

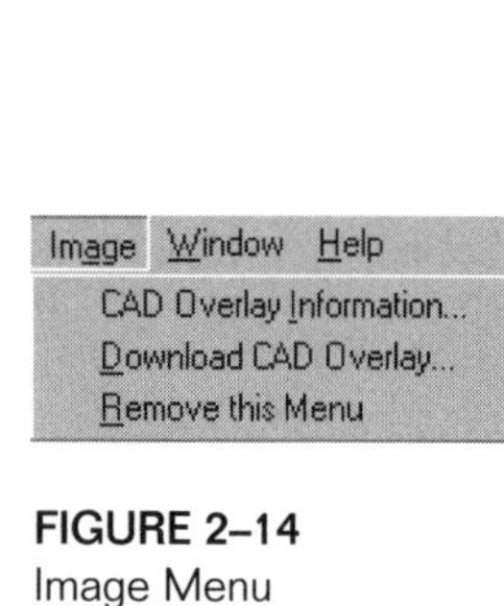

FIGURE 2–14
Image Menu

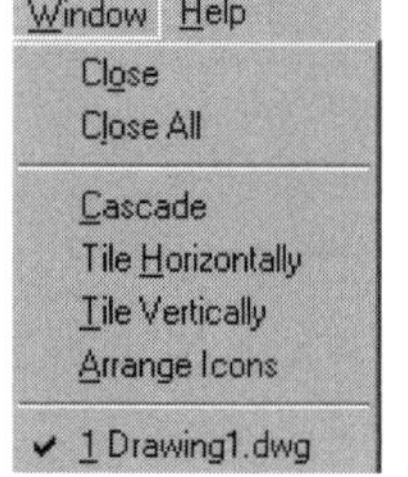

FIGURE 2–15
Window Menu

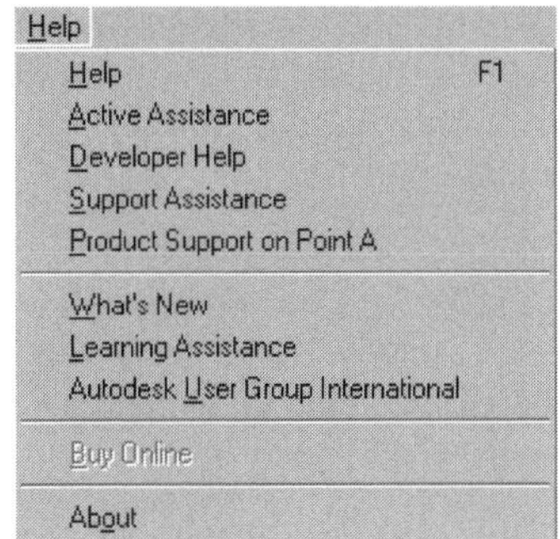

FIGURE 2–16
Help Menu

Toolbars

The AutoCAD screen shown in Figure 2–4 has four toolbars displayed: a docked Standard Toolbar and a docked Object Properties toolbar at the top of the screen, and the Draw and Modify toolbars docked at the left side of the screen. You can turn the visibility of toolbars off and on, move, resize, reshape, or customize them. The toolbars represent categories of AutoCAD commands, settings, and modes.

The Standard Toolbar (Figure 2–17) is visible by default. The Standard Toolbar contains tools that represent frequently used commands.

Step 4. Activate the Standard Toolbar's tooltips (Figure 2–17).

As you hold the mouse pointer steady (do not click) on each tool of the Standard Toolbar, tooltips will display the name of the command, as shown in Figure 2–17. A text string at the bottom of the display screen (in the coordinate display and status bar area) gives a brief description of the command.

Step 5. Activate the Standard Toolbar's flyouts (Figure 2–18).

Tools with a small black triangle have flyouts. Hold the pointer on the tool, press and hold the pick button, and the flyout will appear, as shown in Figure 2–18. When you position the pointer on a tool in the flyout and release the pick button, the command is acti-

FIGURE 2–17
Standard Toolbar with Tooltips Displayed

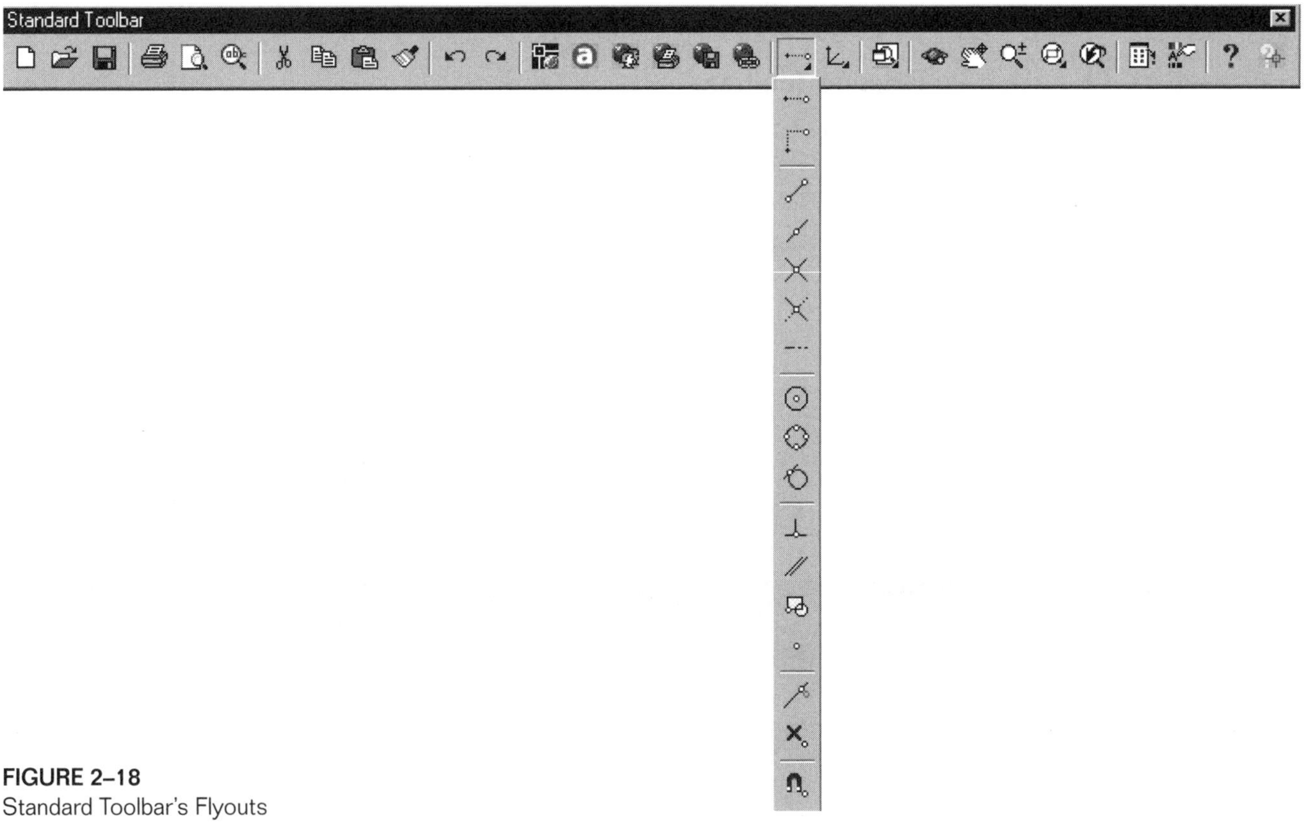

FIGURE 2–18
Standard Toolbar's Flyouts

vated; a dialog box will appear or a command sequence will begin. The most recently activated tool icon will replace the top icon that was previously visible in the standard toolbar; the location of the icon changes to reflect the most recently used command. Use the Esc key to cancel any command.

Step 6. Locate the names of the toolbars.

Prompt	Response
Command:	*Click:* **Toolbars...** (on the View menu)
The Toolbars dialog box appears.	

Many of the toolbars are used in the following chapters. Two of these toolbars are usually ON by default. They are the Standard Toolbar and the Object Properties toolbar.

Object Properties (Figure 2–19) Every drawing entity (line, arc, circle, and so on) is drawn on a layer and can inherit the properties of that layer. This toolbar contains the dialog box used to create layers and assign properties such as color and linetype. It also contains the commands for setting color and linetype, defining multiline styles, modifying drawing entities, and listing information about an entity. This toolbar is on by default.

Standard Toolbar As described earlier in this chapter, the Standard Toolbar is visible by default. The Standard Toolbar contains tools that represent frequently used commands.

The other toolbars in the Toolbars dialog box will be described as they are used.

Step 7. Activate and close the Dimension toolbar.

Note: You can also open and close toolbars by holding your mouse over any tool and right clicking. A list of the toolbars appears. Click on any toolbar name in the list to open or close it.

To activate a toolbar, pick the check box to the left of the toolbar name, so that a check mark appears in it. After studying a toolbar, you can close it by clicking the X in the upper right corner of the toolbar. You can also close a toolbar by picking the check in the Toolbars dialog box next to the toolbar name. Try this by opening and closing the Dimension toolbar.

Floating Toolbars

A *floating toolbar* floats or lies on any part of the AutoCAD for Windows screen. A floating toolbar can be moved to another part of the screen and can be reshaped and resized. Any of the top level toolbars can be displayed and will float on the screen as follows:

Step 8. Display the Draw toolbar.

Prompt	Response
Command:	*Click:* **Toolbars...** (on the View menu)
	Click: **Draw** (Figure 2–20) (from the Toolbars dialog box to put a check in the Draw box)
	Click: **OK**

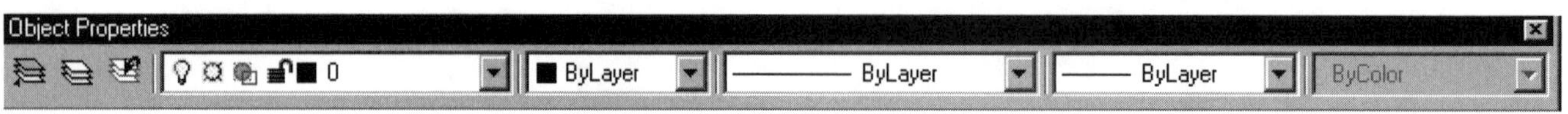

FIGURE 2–19
Object Properties Toolbar

FIGURE 2–20
Displaying the Draw Toolbar

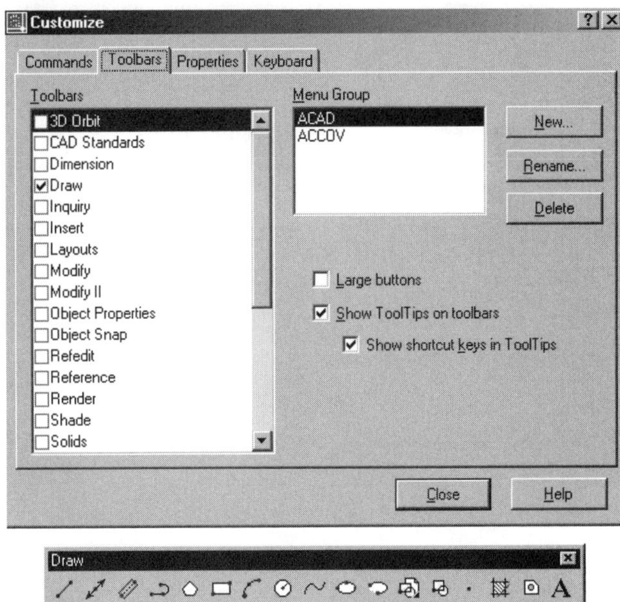

The Draw toolbar appears on the screen.

Step 9. Display the Modify toolbar.

Use the same steps to display the Modify toolbar as you used to display the Draw toolbar.

To hide any toolbar you do not want visible, click on the X in the upper right corner of the toolbar. Close the Toolbars dialog box, by clicking the X in the upper right corner, or *Click*: Close.

Step 10. Reshape and move the Draw and Modify toolbars as follows (Figure 2–21).

Change the shape of the toolbars to match those shown in Figure 2–21, by changing the width and height. Slowly move the pointer over the borders of each toolbar until you get the double-arrow pointer that allows you to resize it.

Move the Draw and Modify toolbars to the approximate position shown in Figure 2–22 by picking the title bar of each toolbar and dragging it to the new location.

FIGURE 2–21
Reshaping and Moving Toolbars

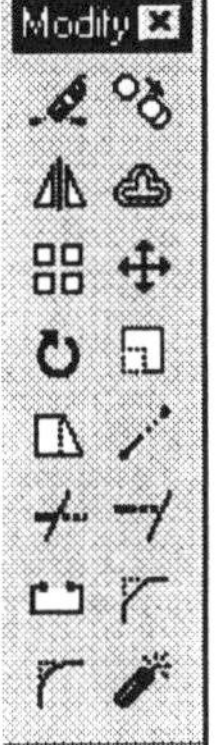

FIGURE 2–22
Moving Toolbars

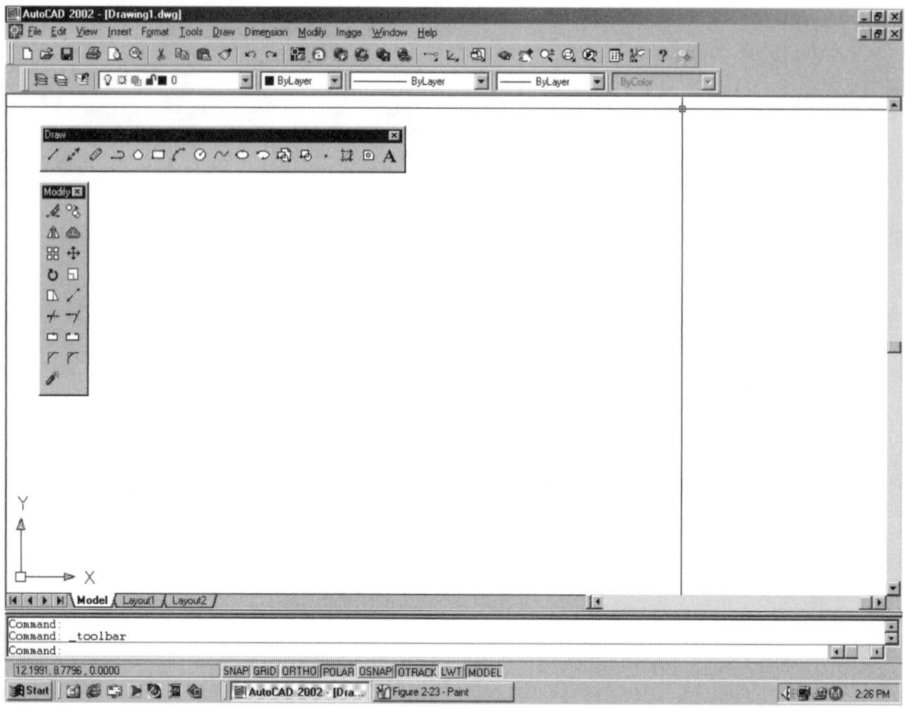

Step 11. Change the size of the toolbars (Figure 2–23) then close all toolbars at once.

Prompt	Response
Command:	*Click:* **Toolbars...** (from View on the menu bar)
The Toolbars dialog box appears (Figure 2–23):	*Click:* **Large Buttons** (the check box, to put a check in the box, turning it on)
A check appears in the Large Buttons check box:	*Click:* **Close** (to exit)
All the toolbars are larger:	**Use the same steps to change the toolbars back to the smaller size.**

FIGURE 2–23
Changing the Size of Tools on the Toolbars

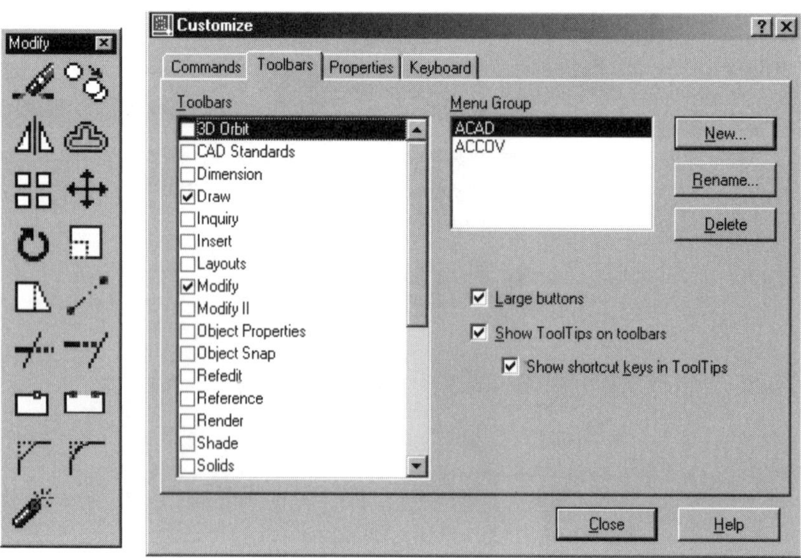

Prompt	Response
Command:	*Type:* **-TOOLBAR** ↵ (Be sure to include the minus sign.)
Toolbar name (or ALL):	*Type:* **ALL** ↵
Show/Hide:	*Type:* **H** ↵

Docked Toolbars

Step 12. Display the Draw toolbar.

Prompt	Response
Command:	*Click:* **Toolbars ...** (from View on the menu bar)
The Toolbars dialog box appears:	*Click:* **Draw**

The Draw toolbar appears on the screen.

Step 13. Dock the Draw toolbar.

A toolbar can be *docked*, which means it can be attached to any edge of the drawing window. Once docked, the toolbar does not lie on any part of the drawing area; it also cannot be reshaped. One way to dock a toolbar is to pick on the name of the toolbar and drag it to an edge. When you see an outline of the toolbar along an edge (showing you how the toolbar will look in the docking area), release the pick button on the mouse to dock the toolbar.

To undock the toolbar, pick in any part of the gray area (grab region) around the tools, and drag the toolbar away from the edge.

Pick on the name of the Draw toolbar and drag it to the left edge of the drawing area and dock it.

Toolbar Command

Step 14. Use the Toolbar command to dock the Modify toolbar on the right side of the drawing area.

Prompt	Response
Command:	*Type:* **-TOOLBAR** ↵ (Be sure to include the minus sign.)
Enter toolbar name or [ALL]:	*Type:* **MODIFY** ↵
Enter an option [Show/Hide/Left/Right/Top/Bottom/Float]:<Show>:	*Type:* **R** ↵
Enter new position (horizontal, vertical) <0, 0>:	↵
The Modify toolbar is docked on the right side of the drawing area (Figure 2–24).	

The other options of the Toolbar command, when activated, allow you to dock a toolbar on the left, top, or bottom of the drawing area, float a docked toolbar, show a not visible toolbar, or hide a visible toolbar. You can use the ALL option to make all the toolbars visible or to hide all the toolbars.

Customizing Toolbars

You can customize toolbars using the Customize dialog box under Tools in the menu bar. Using this dialog box, you can add, delete, move, or copy existing tools, or create a new toolbar using existing or new tools.

FIGURE 2–24
Modify Toolbar Docked on the Right Side of the Screen

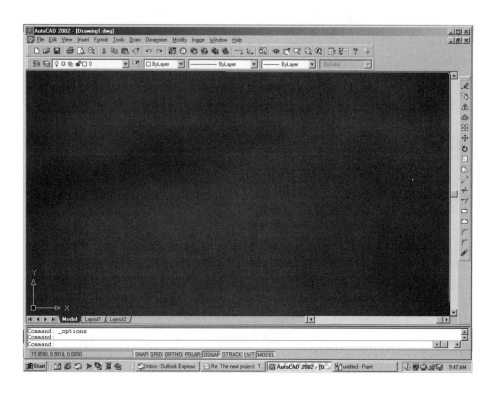

USING AUTOCAD 2002 WITH OTHER PROGRAMS

All commands related to the Windows Clipboard such as Cut, Copy, and Paste are available in AutoCAD 2002. Drawings or text from other applications (such as Word or Paint) can be cut or copied onto the Windows Clipboard and then pasted from the Clipboard into an AutoCAD drawing. The reverse is also possible: AutoCAD drawings can be pasted into other applications.

Using the Mouse and Right-Click Customization

You may be using a two-button mouse, a three-button mouse, or an IntelliMouse (with a small wheel between the buttons). With all three, the left button is the pick button used to select commands and specify points on the screen.

The Right Click Customization dialog box settings control what happens when the right mouse button (shown as ↵ in this book) is clicked. To access the Right Click Customization dialog box, select **Options...** under **Tools** in the menu bar. Select the **User Preferences** tab of the Options dialog box. Click the **Right Click Customization...** button in the Windows Standard Behavior area, and the Right Click Customization dialog box appears. By default, the Default Mode, Edit Mode and Command Mode right click menus are on:

1. *Default Mode:* In the default mode no objects on the screen are selected.
   Repeat Last Command radio button: When selected, clicking the right mouse button will repeat the last command.
   Shortcut Menu radio button: When selected, a shortcut menu appears when the right mouse button is clicked.
2. *Edit Mode:* In the edit mode no command is active, and the user selects one or more objects on the screen.

Repeat Last Command radio button: When selected, clicking the right mouse button will repeat the last command.
Shortcut Menu radio button: When selected, and the right mouse button is clicked, a shortcut menu with editing commands will appear. The menu may contain edit options specific to the object selected.

3. *Command Mode:* In the command mode a command is in progress.
ENTER: When selected, clicking the right mouse button is the same as pressing the enter key. The shortcut menus are disabled.
Shortcut Menu; always enabled: When selected, the shortcut menus are enabled.
Shortcut Menu; enabled when command options are present: When selected, the shortcut menus showing command options will appear when the right mouse button is clicked. When no command options are available, right clicking will be the same as pressing the enter key.

In the Response columns of this book ↵ indicates to click the right mouse button. Notes in parentheses are used to clarify how ↵ is used. For example, ↵ (to return the Line command prompt).

Selection Modes Settings

To access the Selection Modes settings, select **Options...** under **Tools** in the menu bar. Select the **Selection** tab of the Options dialog box. The left side of this tab shows Selection Modes and how to change the Pickbox Size. A check mark in the box indicates the mode is on:

Noun/verb selection: When on, you can select an object *before or after* invoking an edit or inquiry command.
Use Shift to add to selection: When on, you can add or remove an object from a selection set, by holding down the shift key and selecting the object. To discontinue this, click two points to draw a selection window in a blank area of the drawing.
Press and drag: When on, to draw a selection window, you have to click a point and drag the mouse to the second point. When not on, you can click two separate points to draw a selection window.
Implied windowing: When on, if you click a point outside an object, a selection window will be drawn. Drawing a window from right to left makes a crossing window and from left to right makes a window.
Object grouping: When GROUP is typed and entered at the Command: prompt, the Object Grouping dialog box appears. The dialog box allows you to create and name a group of objects. When a check mark is in this box, if you select one item in the object group, the entire object group is selected.
Associative Hatch: When using the HATCH command, if this box is checked, boundary objects are also selected when you use an associative hatch. Hatching is described later in this book.
Pickbox Size: Controls the size of the pickbox.

REVIEW QUESTIONS

Circle the best answer.

1. Which of the following is used to store the AutoCAD program?
   a. Plotter
   b. Printer
   c. Keyboard
   d. Hard drive
   e. Display monitor

2. What do you do to display the list of programs containing AutoCAD in Windows?
   a. *Type:* OPEN ↵
   b. Double-click on the icon
   c. *Click:* the Start icon and then *Click:* Programs
   d. Hold the pointer on the icon and press enter
   e. *Type:* Enter ↵
3. Clicking the X in the upper right corner of the AutoCAD program taskbar
   a. Closes the AutoCAD program
   b. Closes the Program Manager and displays the Exit Windows dialog box
   c. Enters the AutoCAD program
   d. Opens the AutoCAD screen
   e. Resizes the AutoCAD screen
4. To maximize the AutoCAD screen
   a. Click the underscore in the upper right of the screen
   b. Click the rectangle in the upper right of the screen
   c. Click the X in the upper right of the screen
   d. Click the icon to the left of File on the menu bar
   e. The AutoCAD screen cannot be maximized.
5. Which menu on the AutoCAD menu bar contains the command needed to start a new drawing?
   a. File
   b. Edit
   c. Tools
   d. Format
   e. Options
6. Which menu on the AutoCAD menu bar contains the commands related to Windows Clipboard?
   a. File
   b. Edit
   c. Tools
   d. Format
   e. Options
7. Which menu on the AutoCAD menu bar allows you to make and set layers, select drawing units, and set drawing limits?
   a. File
   b. Edit
   c. Tools
   d. Format
   e. Options
8. Which menu on the AutoCAD menu bar takes you to the Toolbars… command?
   a. File
   b. Edit
   c. Tools
   d. Format
   e. View
9. Which toolbar is usually on by default?
   a. Modify
   b. External Reference
   c. Standard Toolbar
   d. Draw
   e. Select Objects
10. Clicking GRID in the status bar when it is out does which of the following?
    a. Turns the grid OFF
    b. Displays the grid and turns snap ON
    c. Displays the grid and turns snap OFF
    d. Displays the grid
    e. Has no effect on the display screen

Complete.

11. List the eight modes displayed on the status bar.

_____ _____ _____ _____ _____ _____ _____ _____

12. If you have not named a new drawing, what name does AutoCAD assign to it?

____

13. Describe the purpose of the command window.

____

____

____

14. How many toolbars are listed in the Toolbars dialog box?

____

15. Describe how to open or activate a toolbar.

____

____

16. Describe how to close or hide a toolbar.

____

____

17. Describe how to undock a toolbar.

____

____

18. Describe how to resize a toolbar.

____

____

19. Describe the function of the scroll bars on the bottom and right side of the AutoCAD for Windows screen.

____

____

20. Describe how to activate a toolbar's tooltips and flyouts.

Tooltips: ______________________________

Flyouts: ______________________________

3 Common Problems and Solutions

OBJECTIVES

After completing this chapter, you will be able to

- Correctly answer questions regarding common problems in using AutoCAD and the solutions to those problems.

Problems occur occasionally during the use of AutoCAD. More of these problems occur when beginners use the system than when experienced AutoCAD users are at the keyboard. Most of the problems are easily remedied and are a result of not being familiar with the details necessary to ensure smooth functioning. Some of the problems, however, can result in a serious loss of time. This chapter presents the problems that commonly occur and one or more solutions for each of the problems. Cautions are presented for preventing the loss of time when problems do occur. We will begin with the cautions for preventing serious losses.

CAUTIONS

Never Work for a Long Time before Saving a Drawing

It is suggested that you use the Save command (if you have Autosave off) every hour so that no more than an hour's work will be lost in case one of the following occurs:

- Someone turns off a circuit breaker momentarily to check a circuit.
- Someone accidentally pulls the power cord to your computer out of the wall.
- Someone accidentally hits the ON/OFF switch on a power strip.
- A power failure during a storm momentarily turns off your computer.

You can set Autosave (saves automatically) to any value between 0 and 600. 0 turns Autosave OFF. Automatic save is on the Open and Save tab of the Options dialog box. Options is on the Tool menu.

Always Save a Drawing File on More Than One Disk

If your computer has adequate space on the hard drive (usually the C drive), save the drawing on both the C drive and a floppy disk or a CD. If there is not adequate space on the C drive, save the drawing on two other disks and keep them separate in case one of the following happens:

- Someone leaves the disk in a hot car and the disk warps.
- Someone mangles the disk or the metal clip on the floppy disk.
- One of the disks is lost.
- Someone exposes the disk to a magnetic field.

Note: The two precautions listed here are simple to observe and will prevent a loss of time and money. If they are not observed, serious losses can and will occur.

COMMON PROBLEMS AND SOLUTIONS

The common problems and their solutions have been divided into four groups:

- Hardware problems
- Command problems that occur before the drawing is displayed

□ Problems that occur during drawing
□ Plotting problems

The first group to be presented is hardware problems.

Common Hardware Problems

Hardware Problem 1: Mouse, tablet, printer, or plotter does not respond.

Causes

□ Device is plugged into the wrong port (a port is a connector on the back of the computer).
□ System is improperly configured for the device used.
□ Cables are not firmly plugged in or a cable is defective.
□ Device is defective.

Solution 1

Change ports for the device connector.

Solution 2

Reconfigure AutoCAD.

Solution 3

Plug in loose cables.

Solution 4

Replace defective device.

Hardware Problem 2: Visual display does not appear.

Causes

□ Power or computer cable is not plugged in.
□ Monitor power switch is off.
□ Brightness control is not turned up.
□ Defective visual display.

Solution 1

Plug in power or computer cables.

Solution 2

Turn on power switch.

Solution 3

Turn up brightness.

Solution 4

Replace or repair visual display.

Common Problems Involving Commands Before the Drawing Is Displayed

Command Problem 1: Prompt shows: "Drawing file not found."

Causes

□ Drawing name is incorrect.
□ Drawing is in a different directory.
□ Drawing is on another disk.

Method A—(For drawings that are located on the hard drive only. If you use this method to call up a drawing from the floppy disk, you run the risk of crashing when your floppy disk gets full.)

Prompt	**Response**
Command:	*Type:* **OPEN** ↵ or *Click:* **Open...**

Prompt	Response
The Select File dialog box appears:	*Double click:* **on the drive (and folder, also called directory) where you think the file is until you locate the file**
	Double click: **on the filename you want**

Method B

1. Activate a software program such as Windows Explorer and log onto the drive you wish to explore. These programs are an easy way to discover which folders (directories) and files have been created on any disk.
2. Once you have found the location and the correct name of the drawing you may activate the drawing. Be sure to locate the correct drive and folder.

Command Problem 2: AutoCAD will not call up a drawing from a floppy disk and displays a message that the disk is full.

Solution 1

Delete unnecessary files from the floppy disk (such as .bak files) and try again (see Command Problem 5).

Solution 2

Use Windows Explorer to copy the drawing to the hard disk and call it up from there.

Command Problem 3: Drawing file was lost and cannot be found.

Note: If you leave off the extension .dwg from the destination file, AutoCAD will not find the drawing. Rename the file from Draw1 to Draw1.dwg.

Cause

File was accidentally erased or deleted.

Solution 1

Recover the lost file from the Recycle Bin. Double-click on the Recycle Bin, locate the file, and restore it.

Solution 2

If the file is not in the Recycle Bin, use Windows Explorer to locate backup files. If the backup file for the last drawing exists, rename the backup file to make it the drawing file, as follows. To avoid confusion let's say the backup file is on a floppy disk in the A: drive.

1. Activate Windows Explorer by clicking Start, Programs, and Windows Explorer, as shown in Figure 3–1.
2. Select the A: drive (or the folder containing the backup file).

   Notice that the symbol or icon to the left of the filename describes the type of file. Figure 3–2 shows one file with the name Draw1. The icon shows that this is the backup file. If the drawing file is lost, the backup file is the only file with the name Draw1.
3. *Click*: **Folder Options...** on the View menu as shown in Figure 3–3. (Earlier versions of Windows will be slightly different from this picture, but the labels will be approximately the same. Windows ME has Folder Options… under the Tools menu.)
4. Remove the check in the check box before "Hide file extensions for known file types" by clicking on it (Figure 3–4).
5. *Click*: **OK**
6. The file extension is now shown after the filename (Figure 3–5).
7. *Click*: **Draw1.bak**
8. *Click:* **Rename** on the File menu (Figure 3–5)
9. *Click*: to the right of Draw1.bak and backspace over bak

   Type: **dwg** ↵ as shown in Figure 3–6
10. Close Windows Explorer by clicking the X in the extreme upper right corner.

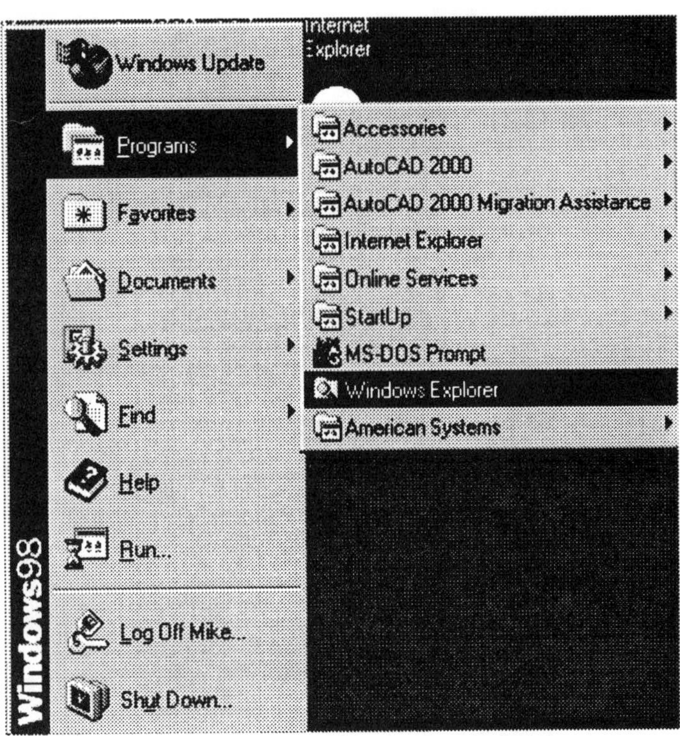

FIGURE 3–1
Activate Windows Explorer

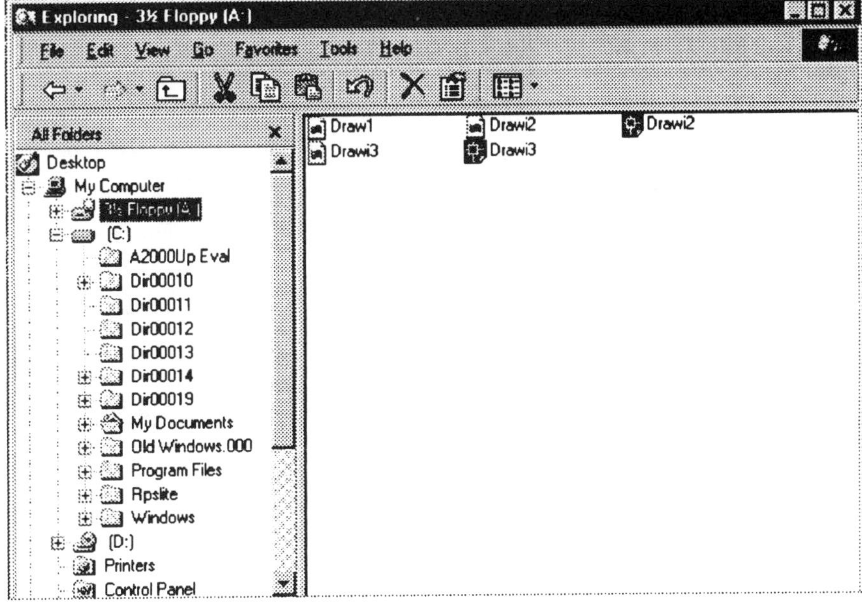

FIGURE 3–2
Locate the DRAW1 Backup File

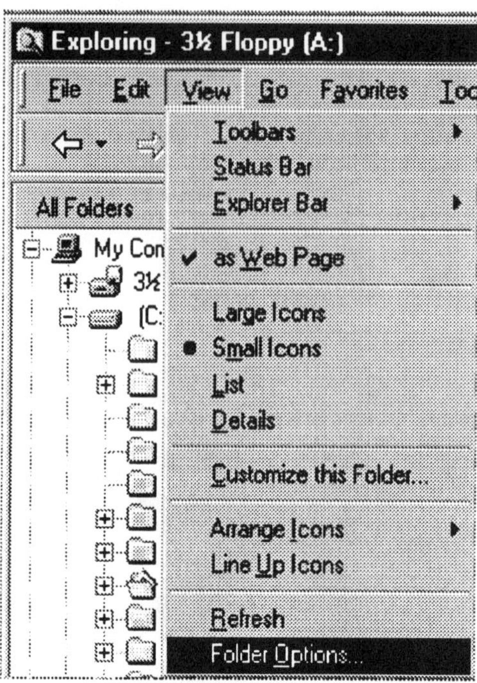

FIGURE 3–3
Click: Folder Options

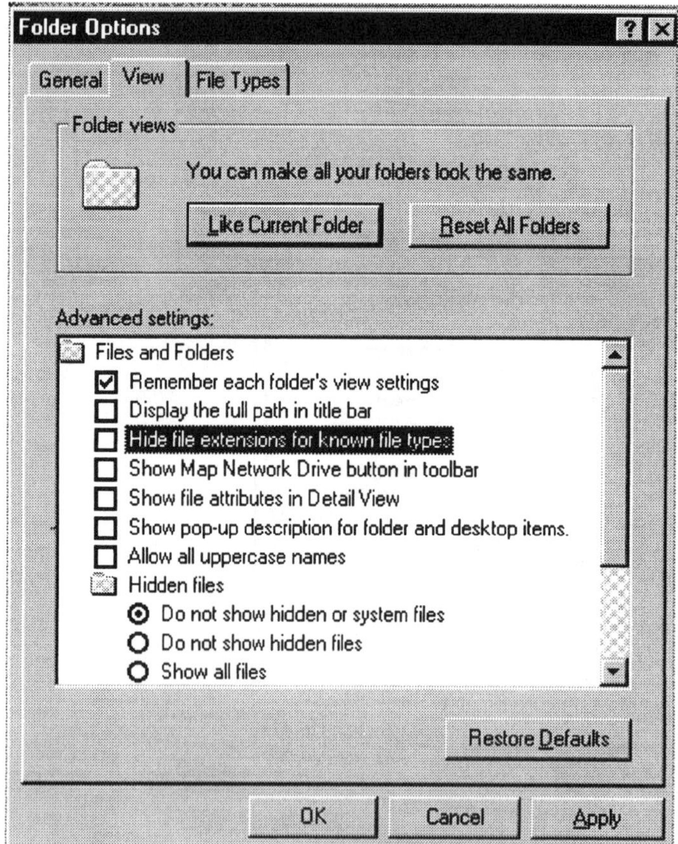

FIGURE 3–4
Remove Check in the Hide file extensions for known file types Check Box

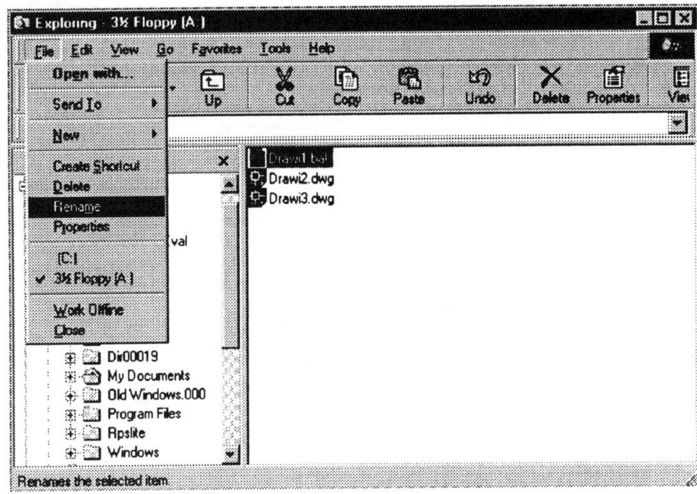

FIGURE 3–5
Click: Rename

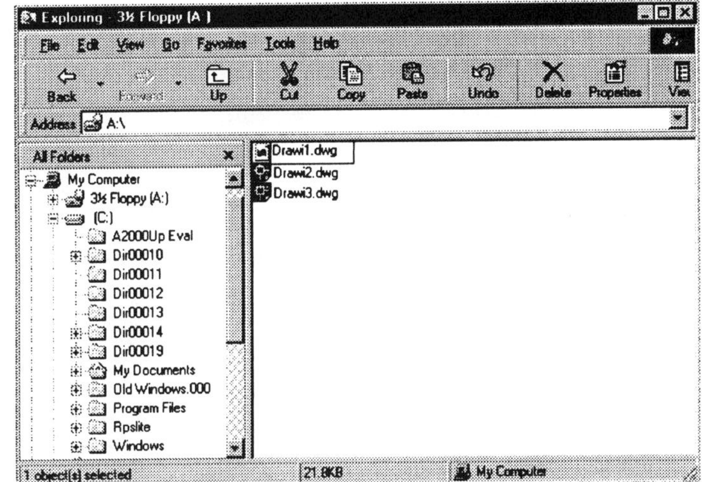

FIGURE 3–6
Draw1.bak is Renamed Draw1.dwg

A new Draw1.dwg file now exists, which was the previous version of the lost drawing file. The new drawing file may now be activated in the same manner as any other drawing file.

Command Problem 4: System response time has become very slow.

Causes

- □ Hard disk is becoming full of unnecessary files and useless bytes that accumulate during computer use.
- □ Drawing files may be unnecessarily large.

Solution 1

Delete all backup (.bak) drawing files from the hard drive. To do this:

1. Activate Windows Explorer and *Click:* **Find,** on the Tools menu, then **Files** or **Folders…** as shown in Figure 3–7.
2. In the Named: text box *Type:* ***.bak** and *Click:* **Find Now.** (Be sure that the drive you want to clean is shown in the Look in: text box and that the Include subfolders button is checked as shown in Figure 3–8.)
3. All the backup files (.bak) will appear in the area at the bottom of the dialog box as shown in Figure 3–9. *Click:* **Select All** from the Edit menu on the menu bar so that all the .bak files are highlighted.

FIGURE 3–7
Click: Find, then Files or Folder… from the Windows Explorer Tools Menu

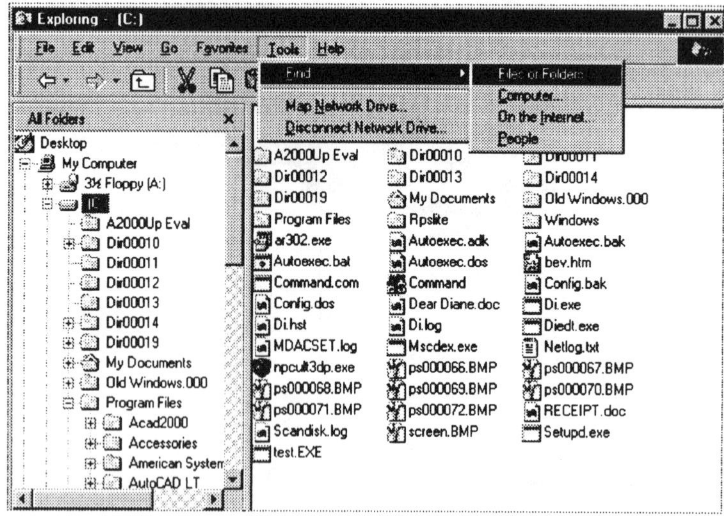

FIGURE 3–8
Type: *.bak in the Named: Text Box

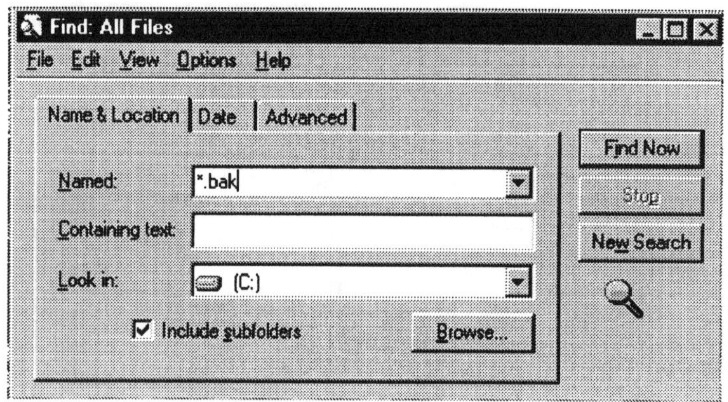

FIGURE 3–9
Select all Backup Files

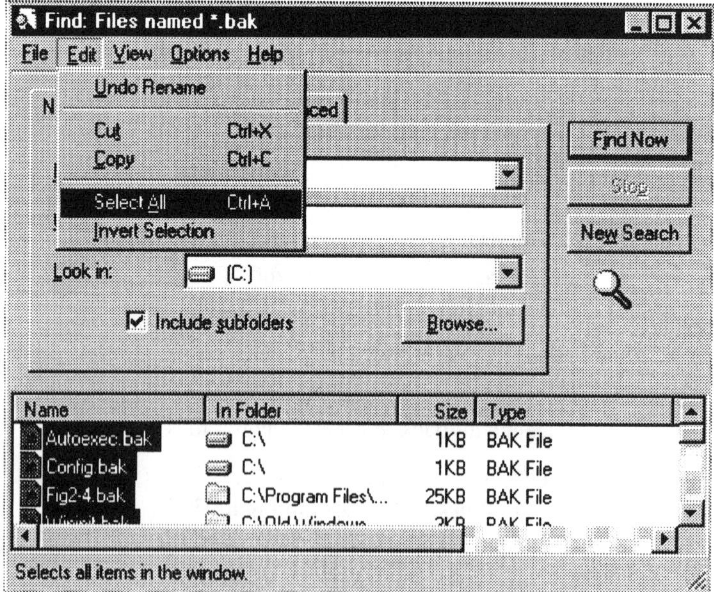

4. *Click:* **Delete** from the File menu on the menu bar or *Press*: **the Delete key** and *Click:* **Yes** when you get the Confirm File Delete message.

Solution 2

Run disk checking to check for errors on your hard disk. To run disk checking:

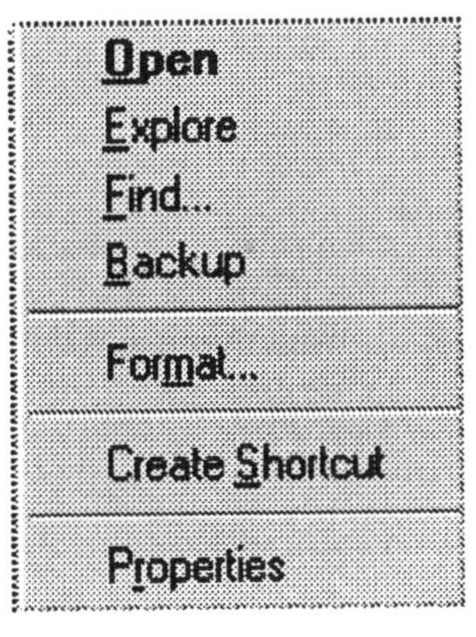

FIGURE 3–10
Select Drive with the Right Mouse Button so This Menu Appears

1. *Double click:* **My Computer,** then *Click:* the drive you want to check *with the right mouse button* so it is highlighted and the menu shown in Figure 3–10 appears. *Click:* **Properties** on the menu.
2. *Click:* **the Tools tab** on the Properties dialog box, then *Click:* **Check Now…** as shown in Figure 3–11 so that the Check Disk dialog box appears.
3. *Click:* **Thorough and Automatically fix errors**, then *Click:* **Start.**
4. When the Scan Disk Results message appears, *Click:* **Close**.
5. Close the Scan Disk dialog box by clicking the X in the upper right corner. Close the Properties dialog box in a similar manner.

Solution 3

Purge all drawing files using the Purge command (Wblock will often do a better job of purging than Purge does). To use the Purge command, call up each drawing file and do the following:

Prompt	Response
Command:	*Type:* **PURGE** ↵
Purge unused Blocks/Layers/L Types/ Shapes Styles/All:	*Type:* **ALL** ↵

Reply yes to all Purge prompts unless you plan to use that feature on the drawing again. (If you purge a feature you want to use again, you will have to recreate it.)

FIGURE 3–11
Click: Tools Tab on the Properties Dialog Box

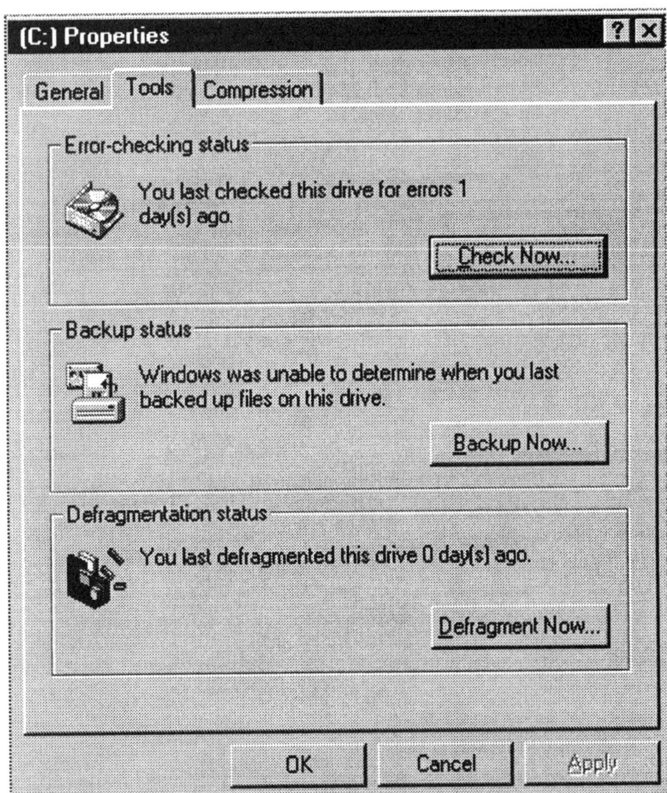

Solution 4

Use the Wblock command in AutoCAD to reduce the size of each drawing file. (Drawing files that are Wblocked are often a fraction of the size of the original file.)

To do this, call up each drawing and be sure that anything you want to save on the drawing is displayed on the screen, activate the Wblock command, respond with the same drawing name as you originally used, *Type:* **ALL** ↵ in response to the SELECT OBJECTS prompt, and then open the next drawing. Do *not* use the Save or SaveAs... commands or you will save a blank screen and overwrite your drawing with a blank screen.

Problems Occurring During Drawing

Drawing Problem 1: Commands such as Trim, Break, Erase, Change, and Extend do not work as they should.

Cause

Display is not large enough to allow the commands to work correctly.

Solution

Zoom a window to make the lines larger and try the commands again.

Drawing Problem 2: Operator makes a mistake in editing (erasing, changing, etc.) or drawing.

Solution 1

Type: U ↵ on the keyboard to UNDO the mistake.

Solution 2

If the mistake cannot be UNDONE and it occurred before a great deal of work was done, select New. . . or close the drawing without saving and select Open. . . and call the drawing up again.

Drawing Problem 3: Operator uses Undo by mistake.

Solution

Type REDO ↵ or select Redo from the menu. (The UNDO command sequence will be redone.)

Drawing Problem 4: Osnap modifiers such as Intersection, Perpendicular, Endpoint, and Midpoint do not work when used with Modify, Construct, and Draw commands.

Causes

- Lines are not quite as long as they appear to be.
- Lines or other entity selected is a block or polyline.

Solution 1

Zoom a very small window around the corner or other suspicious area and correct the problem.

Solution 2

Explode the block or polyline and try the command again.

Drawing Problem 5: Operator makes a mistake in typing or in digitizing before the command is activated.

Solution

Use backspace (if appropriate) to correct a typing error or press the Esc (Escape) key to cancel the command.

Drawing Problem 6: 2D solid command will not fill (for two-dimensional drawings).

Causes

- FILL setting is OFF.
- Solid shape was digitized in the wrong sequence.
- VPOINT is incorrectly set.

Solution 1

Set FILL to ON.

Prompt	Response
Command:	*Type:* **FILL** ↵
ON/OFF <Off>:	*Type:* **ON** ↵

Solution 2

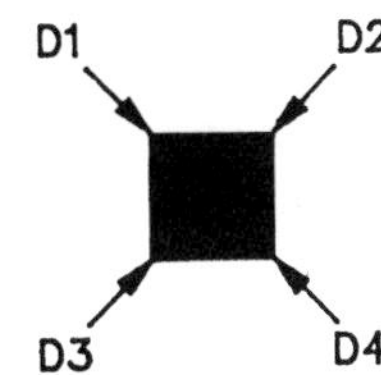

Digitize rectangles or squares in this sequence.

Prompt	Response
Command:	*Click:* **2D Solid**
First point:	**D1** (Press the pick button on the desired point.)
Second point:	**D2**
Third point:	**D3**
Fourth point:	**D4**
Third point:	↵

Digitize triangles in this sequence:

Prompt	Response
Command:	*Click:* **2D Solid**
First point:	**D1**
Second point:	**D2**
Third point:	**D3**
Fourth point:	↵

Solution 3

Reset VPOINT to 0,0,1 (this is the viewpoint for 2-D commands). To do this:

Prompt	Response
Command:	*Type:* **VPOINT** ↵ (or select from a menu.)
Rotate <Viewpoint> <X,X,X>:	*Type:* **0,0,1** ↵ (or select TOP)

Drawing Problem 7: Hidden lines display solid (they will also plot solid), dimensioning arrowheads and text size are too small, dimensioning text is the incorrect value.

Causes

- □ LTSCALE and DIMSCALE have incorrect values for the drawing scale being used.
- □ Text height using the STYLE setting is not set to 0.

Solution

Reset the LTSCALE and DIMSCALE values. To do this use the following procedure:

Prompt	Response
Command:	*Type:* **LTSCALE** ↵
New scale factor <1>:	(Enter new scale factor—examples are shown next.)

Scale or Units Used in Drawing	Response to "New Scale Factor"
Drawing in millimeters	25.4
¼″ = 1″	4
½″ = 1″	2
1″ = 1″	1
¼″ = 1′	48

½″ = 1′	24
1″ = 1′	12
1″ = 10′	120
1″ = 100′	1200
1″ = 1000′	12000

You may need to vary the scale up or down depending on the size of the drawing. Repeat for DIMSCALE.

Set text height to 0 using the STYLE setting.

Drawing Problem 8: Zoom-All places the drawing in one corner of the drawing with a great deal of open space on two sides.

Causes

- □ Drawing Limits incorrectly set.
- □ Small line, point, or text in the open space.
- □ A layer is off or frozen.

Solution 1

Set Drawing Limits correctly and then Zoom-All.

Solution 2

Erase using a crossing window in the open spaces to eliminate the object and then Zoom-All.

Solution 3

Turn ON all layers: *Type:* **LA** ↵, then ON, and then * (for ALL). THAW all layers: *Type:* **LA** ↵, then THAW, then * (for ALL), and then Zoom-All. (You may also turn on all layers using the Layer Properties Manager dialog box.)

Drawing Problem 9: System locks in Osnap when typed from the keyboard.

Solution

Press the Esc key and select Osnap from the menu (or from the mouse if the middle mouse key is so programmed).

Drawing Problem 10: Pan or Zoom command displays only part of the drawing area selected.

Cause

Drawing Limits incorrectly set.

Solution

Set Drawing Limits correctly or turn Drawing Limits OFF.

Drawing Problem 11: Command prompt will not accept a decimal response (Example: .010).

Cause

In some cases AutoCAD expects a zero before the decimal point.

Solution

Place a zero before the decimal point (Example: 0.010).

Drawing Problem 12: Change (point or line), Copy, Move, and other commands do not work as expected.

Causes

- □ ORTHO is ON (when it is not needed).
- □ Change point on the line is more than half the length of the line.
- □ Running Osnap mode is ON (when it is not needed).

Solution 1

Turn ORTHO OFF and try again.

Solution 2

Change the line in more than one step or use another command such as Trim or Break.

Solution 3

Set Osnap mode to NONE. *Type:* **OS** ↵, and then *Click:* **Clear All**, and try again.

Drawing Problem 13: LINETYPE or COLOR does not change when the proper layer is selected

Cause

LINETYPE or COLOR was inadvertently set for all layers.

Solution

Type LINETYPE ↵ or COLOR ↵ from the keyboard (*not* from inside the LAYER command) and set them to BYLAYER. BYLAYER means that the colors and linetypes are determined by the layer on which the entity is drawn.

Drawing Problem 14: Dimensions are displayed as a block.

Cause

Dimensioning variable for associative dimensioning (DIMASO) is ON.

Solution

Note: In most cases DIMASO should be ON.

Set DIMASO to OFF.

Prompt	Response
Command:	*Type:* **DIMASO** ↵
New value for DIMASO <On>:	*Type:* **OFF** ↵

Drawing Problem 15: You are stuck in the Text window.

Cause

You inadvertently selected the Text window.

Solution

Click: the minimize or close buttons in the upper right corner or Press: F2 to return to the Graphics screen.

REVIEW QUESTIONS

Circle the best answer.

1. A drawing should be Saved
   a. Only at the end of the drawing
   b. Every hour
   c. Only at the end of every working day
   d. Never
2. Which of the following values for Autosave turns it OFF?
   a. 0
   b. 10
   c. 400
   d. 500
   e. 600
3. Which of the following can damage a floppy disk?
   a. Bending the metal clip
   b. A magnetic field
   c. Excessive heat
   d. All the above

4. If the computer will not display a drawing that you know is on a disk in one of the floppy drives,
   a. A cable is loose.
   b. The drawing limits are incorrectly set.
   c. The drawing name was typed incorrectly.
   d. The drawing file is lost.
   e. None of the above
5. Which of the following is a solution to the problem in Question 4?
   a. Connect cables firmly.
   b. Reset drawing limits.
   c. Retype the drawing name correctly.
   d. Rename the drawing backup file.
   e. None of these is the correct solution.
6. If the mouse does not respond, which of the following is a possible cause?
   a. The mouse is defective.
   b. The AutoCAD program is not properly configured.
   c. The mouse cable is plugged into the wrong port.
   d. The mouse cable is not firmly plugged in.
   e. All are possible causes.
7. If the prompt shows "Drawing file not found," which of the following is a possible cause?
   a. The drawing file is too big.
   b. The disk is full.
   c. The drawing name is incorrect.
   d. The drawing file is too small.
   e. All are possible causes.
8. Which of the following is a possible solution to the problem in Question 9?
   a. List drawing files and look for the correct name.
   b. Call it up again using the same name.
   c. Clean out backup files and call it up again.
   d. Purge the drawing file to reduce its size.
   e. None of these are possible solutions.
9. Which of the following is the correct extension for a backup file?
   a. .bac
   b. .bak
   c. .back
   d. .dwgb
   e. .dbk
10. Which of the following is a possible solution to recreating a drawing file that was accidentally erased?
    a. Call the drawing file up as a block.
    b. Copy the lost file to the C drive and call it up from there.
    c. Format the floppy disk.
    d. Rename the backup file.
    e. An erased drawing file cannot be recreated.
11. Which of the following is most probably the correct solution when the Change command does not work as it should?
    a. Exit the drawing and call it up again.
    b. Change the current layer.
    c. Call a technician.
    d. Type CHANGE instead of selecting it from the menu.
    e. Zoom a window to enlarge the area.
12. Which of the following is most probably the correct solution for restoring an erased part of a drawing?
    a. Save the drawing and call it up again.
    b. Exit the drawing and call it up again.
    c. END the drawing and call it up again.
    d. Purge the drawing and call it up again.
    e. Do an INQUIRY on the drawing.

13. Which of the following should be changed when hidden lines are displayed as solid?
    a. Pdsize
    b. Pdmode
    c. Ltscale
    d. Limits
    e. Dimvar
14. Which function key switches you from the Text screen to the Graphics screen?
    a. F1
    b. F2
    c. F7
    d. F8
    e. F9

Complete.

15. List a procedure that should *never* be done while using a computer for drawing.

    ____

16. List a procedure that should always be done while using a computer for drawing.

    ____

17. Describe three ways to fix a mouse that fails to respond.

    a. ______________________________
    b. ______________________________
    c. ______________________________
18. List three possible causes for the prompt "Drawing file not found."

    a. ______________________________
    b. ______________________________
    c. ______________________________
19. List two solutions for restoring several circles that were accidentally erased.

    a. ______________________________
    b. ______________________________
20. List two possible causes for Osnap not working as it should.

    a. ______________________________
    b. ______________________________
21. List three possible causes for Solid not filling correctly.

    a. ______________________________
    b. ______________________________
    c. ______________________________

4 Preparing to Draw with AutoCAD

OBJECTIVES

After completing this chapter, you will be able to

- Make settings for an AutoCAD drawing to include Units, Limits, Grid, and Snap without a wizard.
- Create layers and assign color and linetype to each layer.
- Use function keys F2 (flip screen), F7 (grid), and F9 (snap) to control the display screen, grid, and snap as required.
- Use the commands Save, SaveAs…, and Exit to save work and exit AutoCAD.
- Save a drawing as a template.

FOLLOWING THE EXERCISES IN THIS BOOK

Before you start the exercises in this book, read the following information about how to complete them.

Drives

This book will assume that the hard drive of the computer is called drive C. It will also assume that there is a floppy disk drive called A.

Prompt and Response Columns

Throughout the exercises in this book, **Prompt** and **Response** columns provide step-by-step instructions for starting and completing a command. The Prompt column text repeats the AutoCAD prompt that appears in the Command prompt area of the display screen. The text in the Response column shows your response to the AutoCAD prompt and appears as follows:

1. All responses are shown in **bold type.**
2. ↵ is used to indicate the enter response. Either a button on the pointing device or a key on the keyboard may be used. Some keyboards may have this key marked ↵, Enter, or Return. If you use the right mouse button for enter, a pop-up menu appears that gives you comand options. When this is the required response, it is labeled Right click.
3. A response that is to be typed and entered from the keyboard is preceded by the word *Type:* and is followed by ↵ to indicate the enter response (for example, *Type:* **WALLS** ↵.
4. If the response is to pick a command or command option from a menu or toolbar on the display screen, that command is shown in the response column in bold type (for example, *Click*: **Units…**).
5. Function keys are the keys marked F1 through F10 on the keyboard (F11 and F12 are available on some keyboards). If the response is to use a function key, the key name will be preceded by the word *Press:* (for example, *Press:* **F7**).

6. When you are required to use the pick button on your digitizer (the left button on your mouse) to select an object or to specify a location, the word *Click:* is used followed by a description (for example: *Click:* **D1**).
7. Helpful notes, such as (F2 is the flip screen function key), are provided in parentheses.

Margin Illustrations

Illustrations of the AutoCAD menu bar and toolbars with items highlighted are shown in the page margins. The highlighted items illustrate the sequence menu items you must pick to arrive at specific commands. Helpful notes, tips, and warnings are also included in the margins.

INTRODUCTION

When a project that is to be manually drafted is started, decisions are made about the number of drawings required, the appropriate sheet size, scale, and so on. Similar decisions are made when preparing to draw with AutoCAD. This chapter describes the settings that must be made before drawing can begin.

The following is a hands-on, step-by-step procedure to make the setup for your first drawing exercises in Chapters 5 and 6. Each step is followed by an explanation of the command used.

MAKING THE SETUP FOR THE FIRST DRAWING EXERCISE

Exercise 4–1: Start a New Drawing without Using a Wizard

(Starting a new drawing using a wizard is covered in a later chapter.)

Clear the Screen

Step 1. Turn on the computer and start AutoCAD 2002.

Prompt	Response
The AutoCAD 2002 Today window appears:	*Click:* **Create Drawings tab**
	Click: **Start from Scratch** (from the Select how to begin: list))
	Click: **English (feet and inches)**

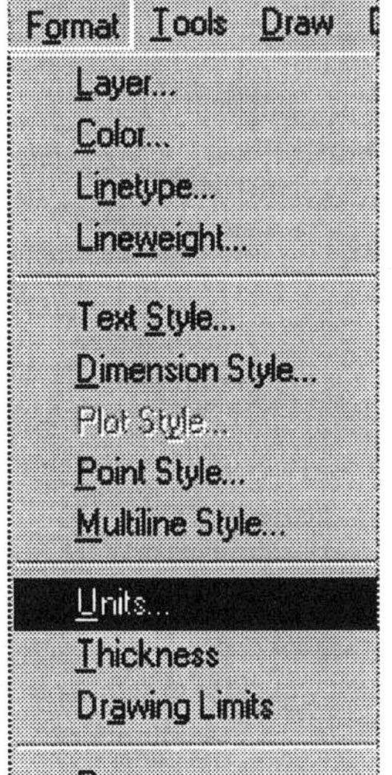

Now that you have started a new drawing, select the units that will be used in making this drawing.

Make Settings

Step 2. Select units.

Prompt	Response
Command:	*Click:* **Units . . .**
The Drawing Units dialog box appears:	*Click:* **the down arrow on the Precision: button and highlight 0.000**

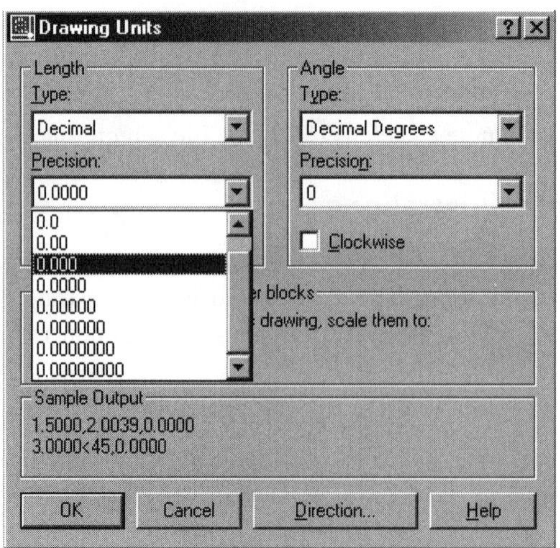

Note: The Precision: button has no bearing on how accurately AutoCAD draws. It controls the display of dimensions and other values displayed on the screen such as coordinates and defaults. No matter what the Precision: setting, AutoCAD draws with extreme accuracy.

Prompt	Response
	so that there are three places to the right of the decimal
	Click: **OK (to accept the default Decimal Units; if Decimal is not shown,** *Click:* **the down arrow, then** *Click:* **decimal from the list**

Units

Any of the units may be used. The decimal selection can be used for any units (commonly inches or millimeters). The architectural selection (4) allows feet and inches to be used. The Precision: button allows you to set the number of digits to the right of the decimal point. The remaining settings are for measuring angles. There is no reason to change these settings. By picking OK, AutoCAD's default values, which measure angles using decimal degrees in the counterclockwise direction, are accepted.

Step 3. Set the drawing limits.

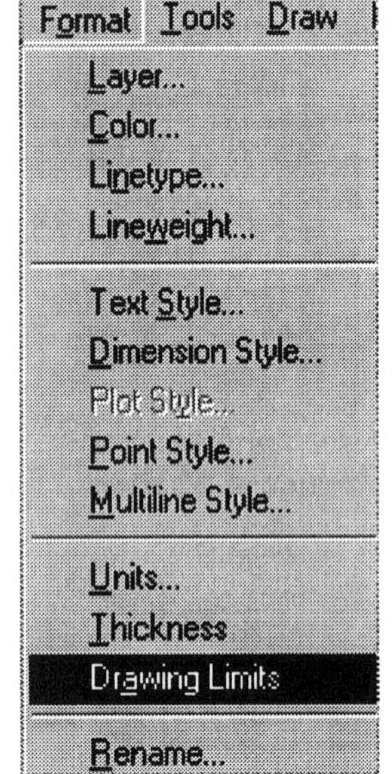

Prompt	Response
Command:	**Drawing Limits** (or *Type:* **LIMITS** ↵)
Specify lower left corner or [ON/OFF] <0.000, 0.000>:	↵ (If you press the right mouse button for ↵, the limits options menu appears. *Click*: **Enter**.)
Specify upper right corner <12.000, 9.000>:	Type: **8.5,11** ↵

Limits

Think of drawing limits as the sheet size or sheet boundaries. Here 8.5,11 was set as the drawing limits. In AutoCAD that value is entered as 8.5,11 using a comma with no spaces to separate the X and Y axes. AutoCAD defaults to inches (or any other basic unit of measure), so the inch symbol is not required. The X axis is first (8.5) and measures drawing limits from left to right. The Y axis is second (11) and measures drawing limits from bottom to top. You will be drawing in a vertical 8.5″ × 11″ area similar to a standard sheet of typing paper.

The lower left corner of the drawing boundaries is 0,0. The upper right corner is 8.5,11 (Figure 4–1). These are the limits for Chapter 5, Exercise 1. To turn the 8.5″ × 11″ area horizontally, enter the limits as 11,8.5.

FIGURE 4–1
Drawing Limits with X and Y Axes Shown

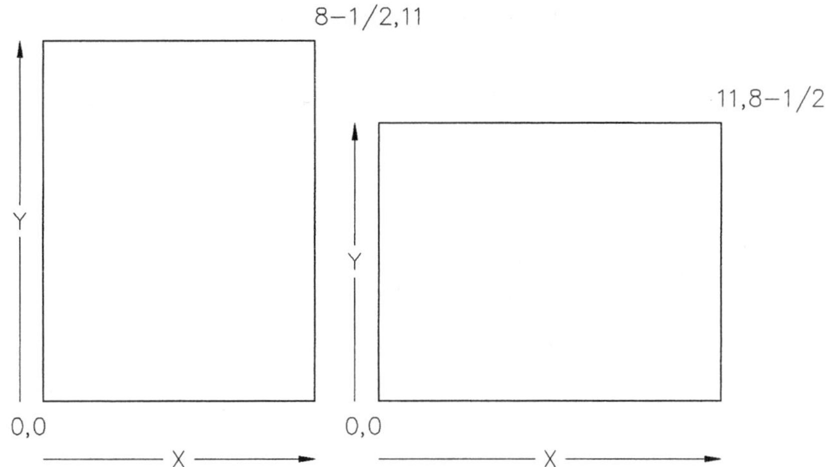

You can also respond to the Limits prompt "specify lower left corner or [ON/OFF]" by selecting ON or OFF on the menu. The ON mode, when activated, helps you avoid drawing outside the drawing limits by responding in the prompt line with "**Outside limits" if a point is selected outside the limits. Some drawing elements, such as a circle, may be started inside the limits and completed outside the limits without the appearance of this prompt. The OFF mode, when activated, allows you to draw outside the drawing limits.

If the drawing limits need to be changed, you may do so at any time by entering new limits to the "specify upper right corner>:" prompt. Changing the drawing limits will automatically change the grid pattern to the new limits.

Step 4. Set the grid and snap spacing.

Prompt	Response
Command:	*Type:* **GRID** ↵
Specify grid spacing (X) or [ON/OFF/ Snap/Aspect] <0.000>:	*Type:* **.5** ↵
Command:	*Type:* **SN** ↵
Specify snap spacing or [ON/OFF/Aspect/ Rotate/Style/Type] <0.500>	*Type:* **.125** ↵

Grid

You have just set .5 as the grid spacing. The grid is the visible pattern of dots on the display screen. It is never plotted.

Function key F7 turns the grid on or off. The grid can also be turned on and off by picking GRID at the bottom of the screen.

Snap

You have set .125 as the snap spacing. Snap is an invisible pattern of dots on the display screen. As you move the digitizer across the screen, the crosshairs will snap, or lock, to an invisible snap grid when SNAP is on. With a setting of .125, each snap point is spaced .125 horizontally and vertically.

Function key F9 turns the snap on or off. The snap can also be turned on or off by picking SNAP at the bottom of the screen. Rotate, Style and Type options are used in later chapters. The snap can be set to snap several times in between the grid points.

Some drawings or parts of drawings should never be drawn with snap off. Snap is a very important tool for quickly locating or aligning elements of your drawing. You may need to turn snap off and on while drawing, but remember that a drawing entity drawn on snap is easily moved, copied, or otherwise edited.

Drafting Settings Dialog Box and Components of All Dialog Boxes

You can also set snap and grid by using the Drafting Settings dialog box.

To locate this dialog box, move the pointer across the top of the display screen and highlight Tools on the menu bar that appears. When you *Click*: **Tools,** a pull-down menu appears under the Tools title. Move your pointer to highlight **Drafting Settings...** and *Click:* it (Figure 4–2). The Drafting Settings dialog box (Figure 4–3) now appears on your screen.

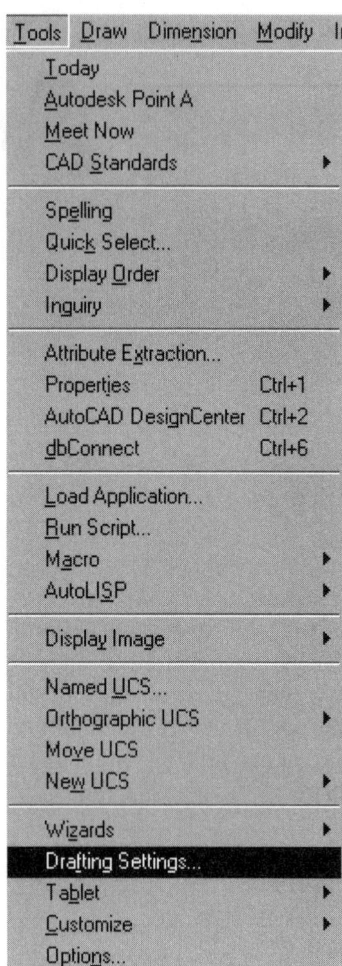

FIGURE 4–2
Click: Drafting Settings to Activate the Drafting Settings Dialog Box

All dialog boxes have some basic components. The following is a description of the Snap and Grid components that appear in the Drafting Settings dialog box (Figure 4–3) as well as in other dialog boxes you will use:

1. *Cursor:* Changes to an arrow.
2. *OK button:* Click this button to complete the command, leave the dialog box, and return to the drawing. If any changes have been made, they will remain as changes. Pressing ↵ has the same effect.
3. *Cancel button:* Click this button to cancel the command, leave the dialog box, and return to the drawing. If any changes have been made, they will be canceled and the original settings will return. Pressing the Esc key has the same effect.
4. *Input buttons:* An input button has two parts, its name and the area where changes can be made by typing new input. Click the second part of the input button Snap X Spacing, under Snap On, and experiment with the text cursor that is attached to the point of the arrow. As you move the digitizer and pick a new spot, the text cursor moves also. The following editing keys can be used to edit the text in input buttons:

   Backspace key: Deletes characters to the left of the text cursor one at a time as it is pressed.
   Delete key: Deletes characters to the right of the text cursor one at a time as it is pressed.
   Left arrow: Moves the text cursor to the left without changing the existing text.
   Right arrow: Moves the text cursor to the right without changing the existing text.
   Character keys: After existing settings are deleted, new settings can be typed.
   Highlighted text: When text is highlighted it can be replaced by simply typing the new text without backspacing or deleting. Text may be highlighted by double-clicking it.
   Snap X spacing input button: Enter the X spacing in this input button, and the Y spacing is automatically set to the same spacing.

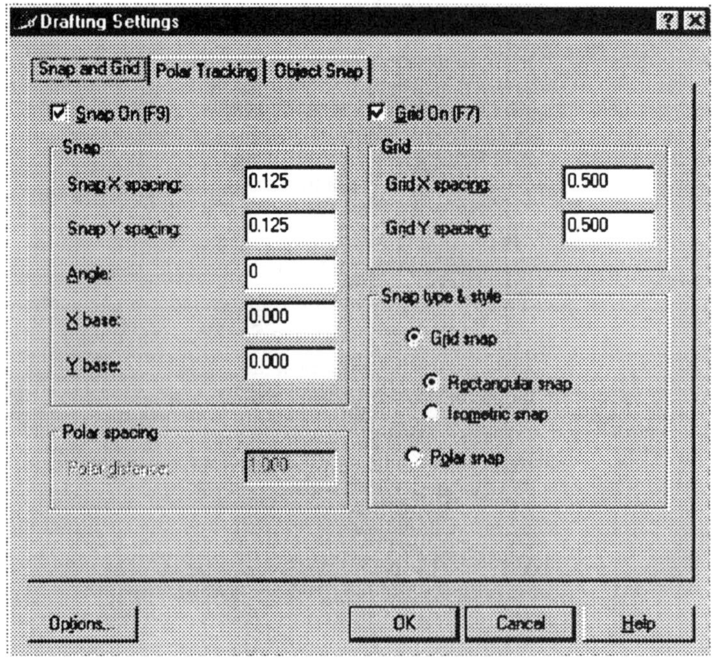

FIGURE 4–3
Drafting Settings Dialog Box

Grid X spacing input button: Enter the X spacing in this input button, and the Y spacing is automatically set to the same spacing.

Angle, X base, and Y base input buttons: These buttons relate to the Rotate option and are discussed in later chapters.

5. *Radio button*: A round button within a circle. A dark circle indicates that selection is picked.
6. *Check buttons:* A check button has two parts, its mode name and the area that can be clicked to toggle the check mark and mode on and off. A check mark in the box indicates the mode is ON.
7. *Tabs*: Tabs allow many more settings in the same dialog box. The tabs in this dialog box are Snap and Grid.

While in this dialog box, experiment with the different editing keys to become familiar with their functions. The dialog box is a handy tool to use in setting the snap and grid spacing, but if you are a fair typist, typing these commands from the keyboard is faster. After experimenting, be sure to return the grid spacing to .5 and the snap to .125 to have the correct settings for Exercise 5–1.You should have buttons picked as shown in Figure 4–3. Other items in this box will be discussed later.

Create Layers

Layers

The layer concept in AutoCAD is like using transparent overlays with a manually drafted project. Different parts of the project can be placed on separate layers. The building shell may be on one layer, the interior walls on another, the electrical on a third layer, the furniture on a fourth layer, and so on. There is no limit to the number of layers you may use in a drawing. Each is perfectly aligned with all the others. Each layer may be viewed on the display screen separately, one layer may be viewed in combination with one or more of the other layers, or all layers may be viewed together. Each layer may also be plotted separately or in combination with other layers, or all layers may be plotted at the same time. The layer name may be from 1 to 255 characters in length. You may also have "no plot" layers that are visible but do not plot.

Step 5. Create layers using the Layer Properties Manager dialog box.

Prompt	Response
Command:	**Move the pointer across the top of the display screen on the menu bar and highlight Format on the menu bar that appears.**
A pull-down menu appears under the Format title:	**Move your pointer to highlight Layer... and** *Click:* **Layer... (Figure 4–4).**
The Layer Properties Manager dialog box appears:	*Click:* **New three times**
Layer1, Layer2, and Layer3 appear in the Name list (Figure 4–5):	*Click:* **Layer1** (as shown in Figure 4–5)

Note: With the Object Properties toolbar displayed, *Click:* the following icon to activate the Layer and Linetype Properties dialog box:

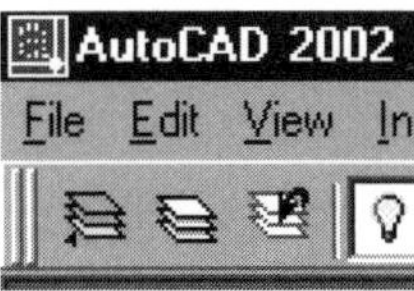

Step 6. Assign colors to layers.

Prompt	Response
	Click: **the word White under the Color button**
The Select Color dialog box, Figure 4–6, appears:	*Click:* **the color red**
	Click: **OK**

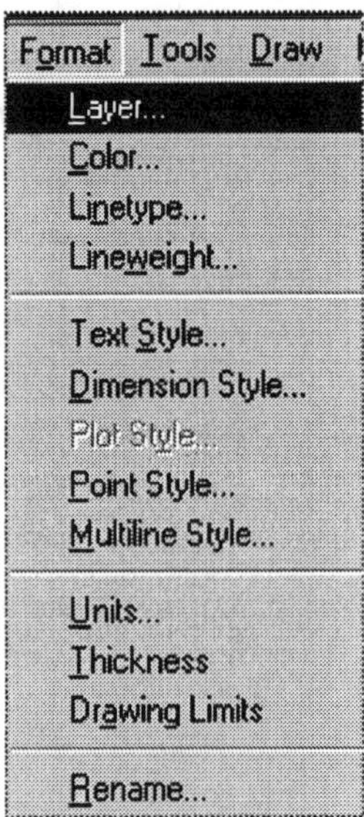

FIGURE 4–4
Click: Layer… to Activate the Layer Properties Manager Dialog Box

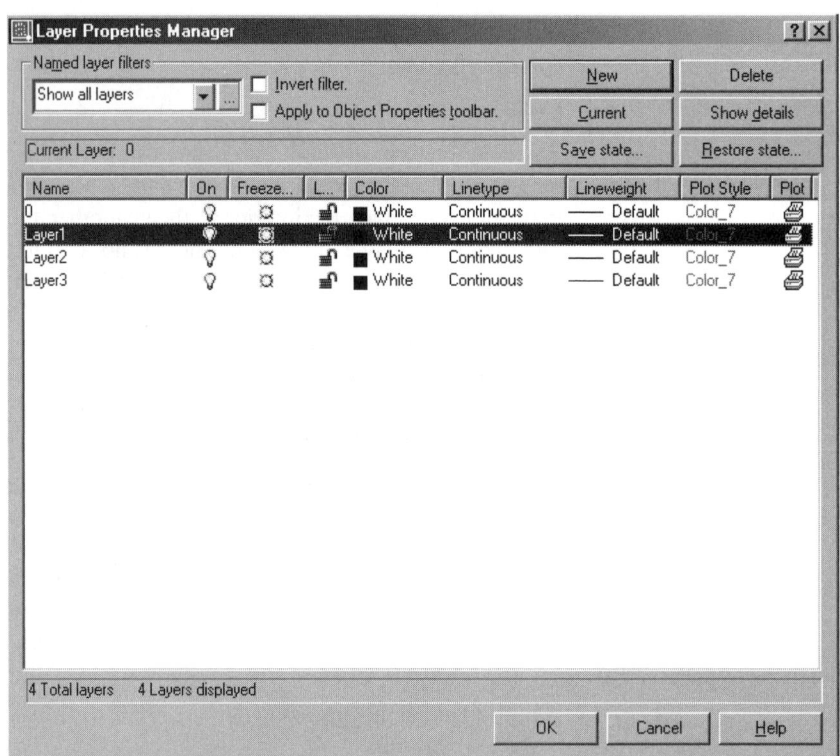

FIGURE 4–5
Layer Properties Manager Dialog Box with Layer1 Highlighted

Prompt	**Response**
The Layer Properties Manager dialog box appears:	*Click:* **Layer2 to select it**
	Click: **the word White under the Color button**
The Select Color dialog box appears:	*Click:* **the color Magenta**
	Click: **OK**
The Layer Properties Manager dialog box appears:	*Click:* **Layer3 to select it**

FIGURE 4–6
Select Color Dialog Box

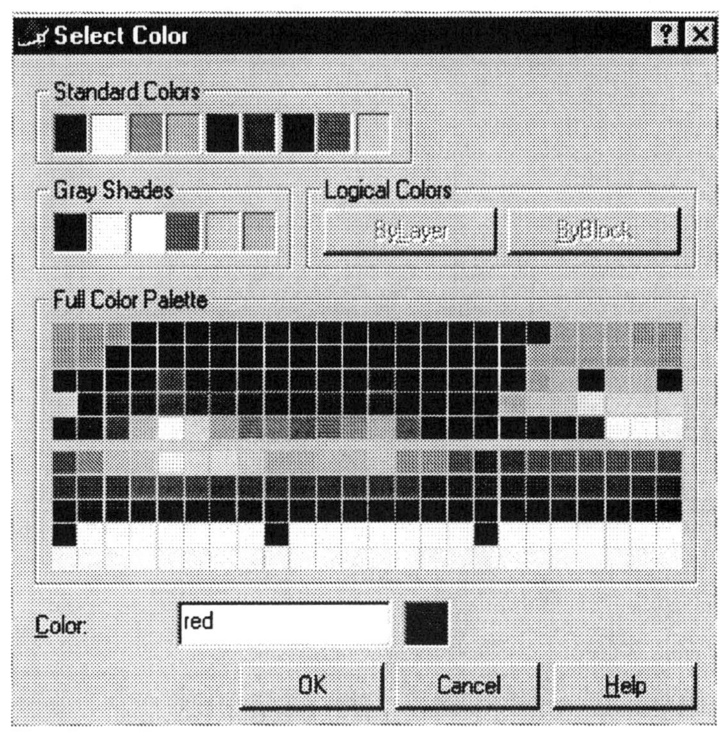

Prompt	Response
	Click: **the word White under the Color button**
The Select Color dialog box appears:	*Click:* **the color green**
	Click: **OK**

Step 7. Assign linetypes to layers.

Prompt	Response
The Layer Properties Manager dialog box appears:	*Click:* **the word Continuous on the line for Layer3**
The Select Linetype dialog box, Figure 4–7, appears:	*Click:* **Load . . .** (to load linetypes so they can be selected)

FIGURE 4–7
Select Linetype Dialog Box

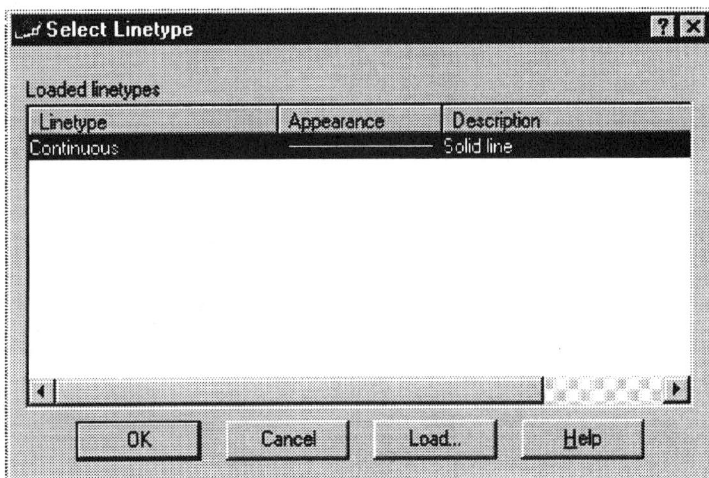

Prompt	Response
The Load or Reload Linetypes dialog box, Figure 4–8, appears:	*Click:* **the right mouse button and Select All** (You may select only the one you want to use, or select several by holding down the ctrl or shift keys.) *Click:* **OK**

The AutoCAD library of standard linetypes provides you with three different sizes of each standard linetype other than continuous. For example, the hidden line has the standard size called Hidden, a linetype half the standard size called Hidden2 [.5x], and a linetype twice the standard size called Hidden2 [2x].

Prompt	Response
The Select Linetype dialog box, Figure 4–9, appears:	*Click:* **the down arrow on the dialog box scroll bar and hold the pick button down until the HIDDEN linetype appears**

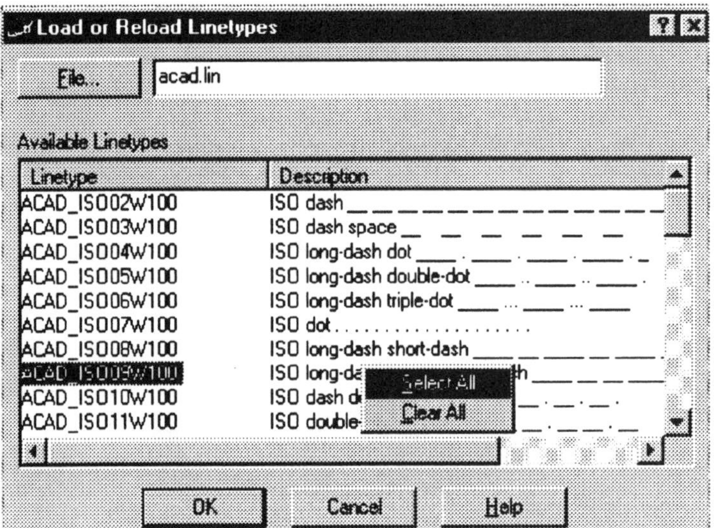

FIGURE 4–8
Load or Reload Linetypes Dialog Box

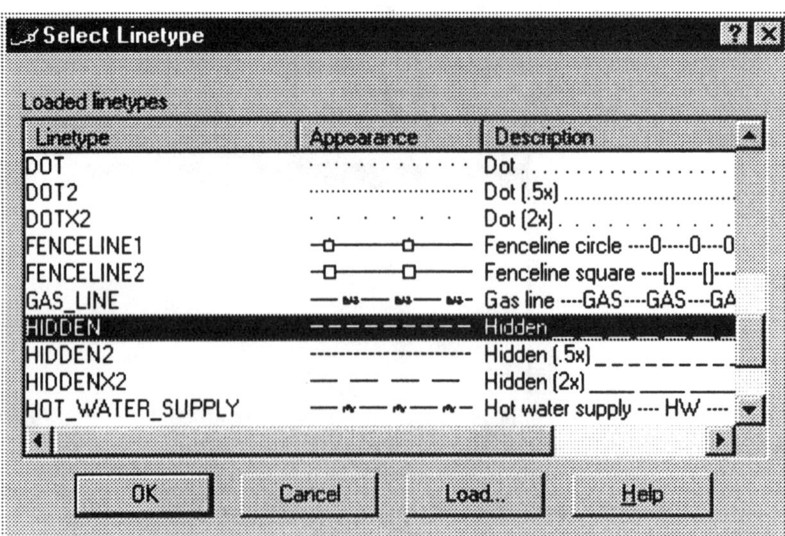

FIGURE 4–9
Select the HIDDEN Linetype

Prompt	Response
	Click: **on any point on the hidden line so the word HIDDEN is highlighted, as shown in Figure 4–9**
	Click: **OK**
The Layer Properties Manager dialog box with layer names, colors, and linetypes assigned appears as shown in Figure 4–10:	*Click:* **Layer2 to select it**
	Click: **the Current button to set Layer2 as the current layer**
	Click: **OK** (Anything drawn from this point until another layer is set current will be the color magenta on Layer2.)
Command:	*Click:* **Toolbars...** (from the View menu)
The Customize dialog box appears:	**Scroll down until Object Properties appears and** *Click*: **its check box so a check mark appears in it, as shown in Figure 4–11.**
	Click: **Close**
The Object Properties Toolbar appears docked at the top of the screen with Layer2 current:	*Click:* **the down arrow, as shown in Figure 4–12**

The small icons to the left of the layer name show the status of layers. From left to right the icons are:

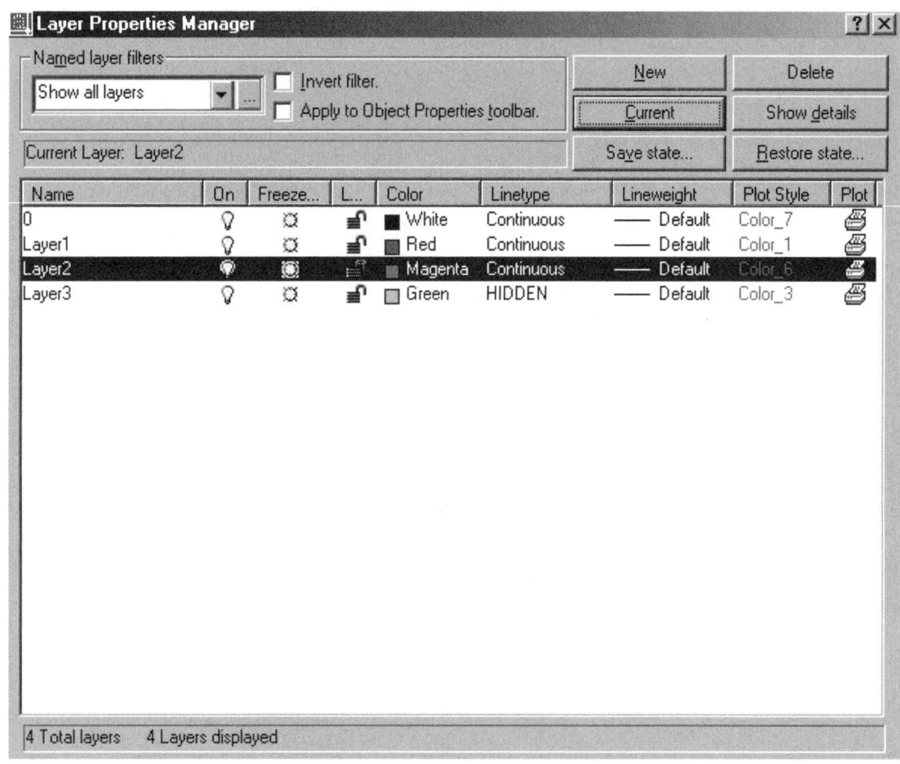

FIGURE 4–10
Layers with Colors and Linetypes Assigned and Layer2 Current

FIGURE 4–11
Select the Object Properties Toolbar

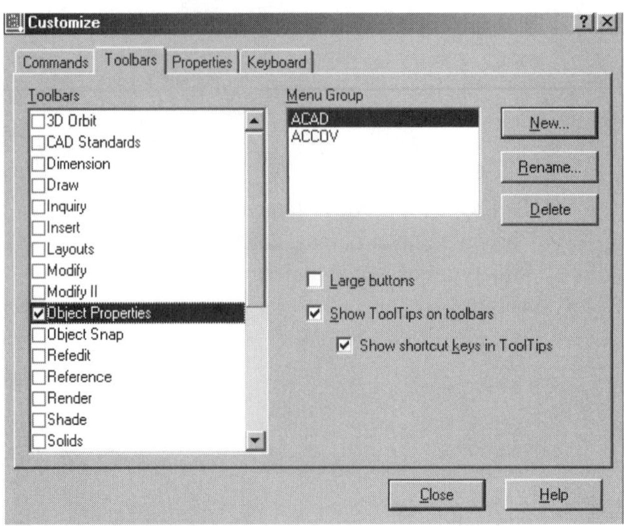

FIGURE 4–12
Show Layer Status on the Object Properties Toolbar

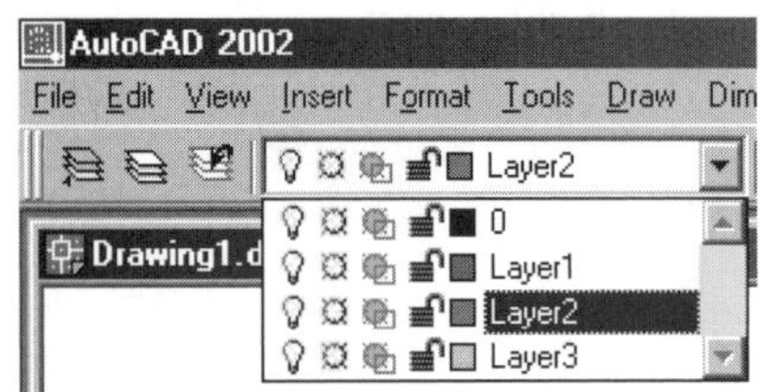

On or Off These are all on.
Frozen or Thawed These are all thawed (notice that you cannot freeze the current layer).
Frozen or Thawed in selected viewports This one is not available now because you have only one viewport, and paper space is not active. These topics will be covered later.
Locked or Unlocked These are all unlocked.
Plottable or Nonplottable These will all plot.

To change the state of any layer pick the icon to select the alternate state. For example, Figure 4–13 shows that Layer1 was turned off by picking the light bulb to turn it off. Experiment with changing the state of layers then opening the Layer Properties Manager dialog box to see the changed state reflected in it. Return all layers to their original state before you exit. Click on any open spot on the screen to close the layer list. The layer that is highlighted when you click an open spot becomes the current layer.

Experiment with all parts of the Layer Properties Manager dialog box. If you create some layers that you do not need, delete them by highlighting them and picking Delete. Be sure the layers, colors, and linetypes shown in Figure 4–10 are set for Exercise 4–1.

FIGURE 4–13
Turn Off Layer1

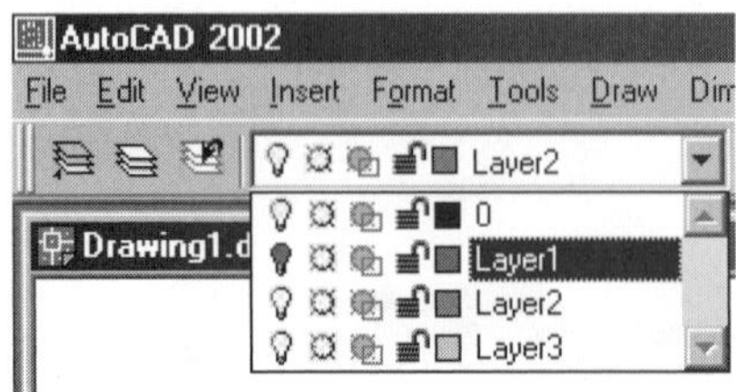

SAVING THE DRAWING AND EXITING AUTOCAD

Save the Drawing

Step 8. Save the settings and layers for Exercise 4–1 on the hard drive. The drawing name will be EX4–1 (your initials) and you will save it as a prototype drawing because you will use these same settings for drawings in Chapters 5 and 6.

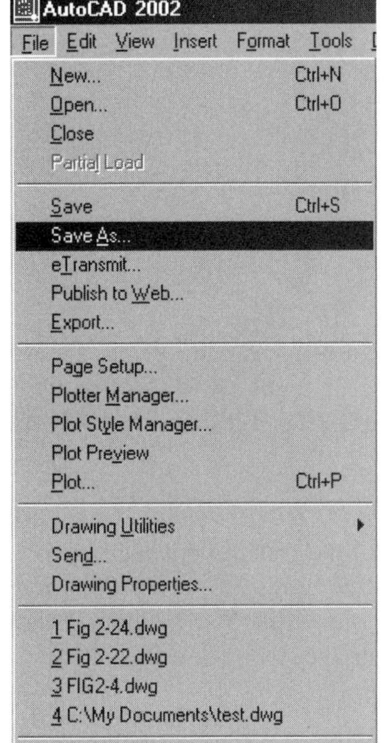

Prompt	Response
Command:	**SaveAs...** (Notice that the text to the right of the command shows that you can press the Ctrl and S keys at the same time to activate the Save command.)
The Save Drawing As dialog box appears with the File Name: Drawing highlighted:	*Type:* **EX4-1(your initials)** (Because the File Name: Drawing was highlighted, you were able to type in that place. If you had used any other part of the dialog box first, you would have had to pick to the left of Drawing, hold down the pick button, and drag the cursor across the name to highlight it and then begin typing.) The drawing name may be from 1 to 255 characters in length.
The Save Drawing As dialog box appears as shown in Figure 4–14. Notice that the drawing is being saved on the C: drive in the Acad2002 directory (or folder in Windows terms):	*Click:* **Save**

Be sure to make note of the drive and folder where the drawing is being saved so you can retrieve it easily when you need it.

Step 9. Save the same drawing to a floppy disk in the A: drive. (Substitute B: for A: if your computer is so labeled.)

Insert a formatted diskette into the A: drive.

Prompt	Response
Command:	↵ (to repeat the previous command)

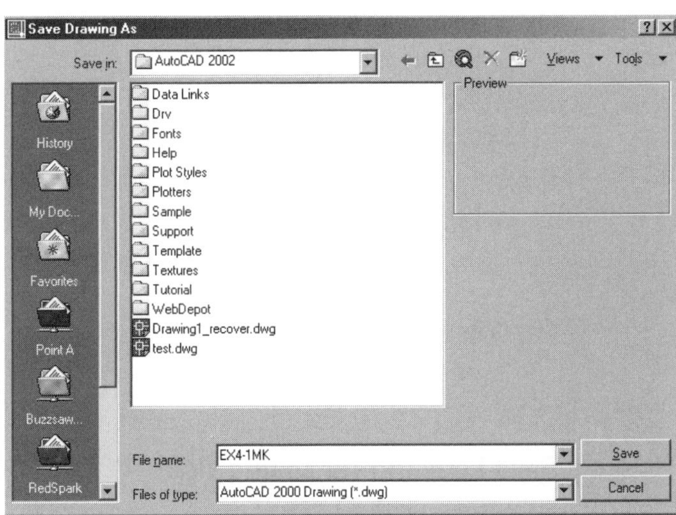

FIGURE 4–14
Save EX4–1 (your initials) in the Acad 2000 Folder on the C: Drive

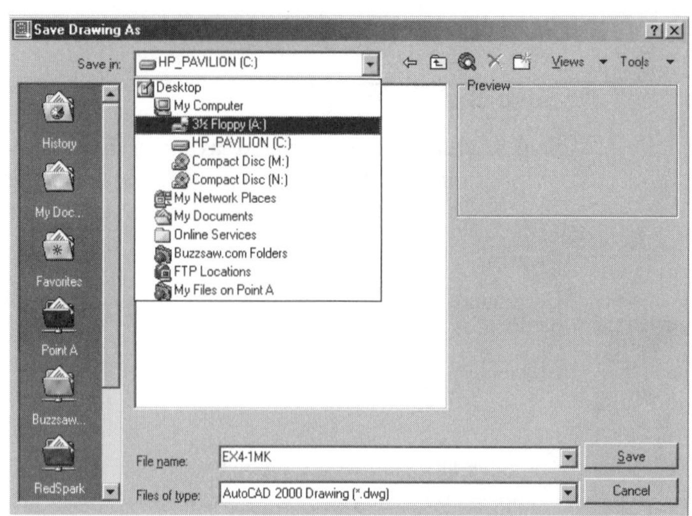

FIGURE 4–15
Save EX4–1 (your initials) on the Disk in the 3½″ Floppy [A:] Drive

Prompt	Response
The Save Drawing As dialog box appears as shown in Figure 4–14:	*Click:* **the down arrow in the Save in: button, highlight the 3½ Floppy [A:] and** *Click:* **it**
The Save Drawing As dialog box appears as shown in Figure 4–15:	*Click:* **Save**

The light should brighten on the A: drive, indicating that the drawing is being saved.

Because the drawing was named when you saved it on the hard drive, you did not have to type the name again to save it with that name on the floppy disk. You could have chosen to give the drawing another name when you saved it on the floppy disk in which case you would have had to type the new name in the File Name: input button.

Step 10. Change the GRID: to .25 and save the drawing as a template (AutoCAD saves the template file in the template folder). (You will use this drawing setup in later exercises.)

Prompt	Response
Command:	*Type:* **GRID** ↵
Grid spacing (X) or ON/OFF/Snap/ Aspect <0.500>:	*Type:* **.25** ↵
Command:	**Save As...**
The Save Drawing As dialog box appears:	*Click:* **the down arrow in the Files of type: button and move the cursor to highlight the words AutoCAD DrawingTemplate File [*.dwt]**
	Click: **Drawing Template and** *Type:* **EX5-1(your initials) in the File name: button so the dialog box appears as shown in Figure 4–16**
	Click: **Save**
The Template Description dialog box appears:	*Type:* **Setup for 8.5,11 sheet** (as shown in Figure 4–17)
	Click: **OK**

Save Drawing As Dialog Box

The parts and functions of the Save Drawing As dialog box are as follows:

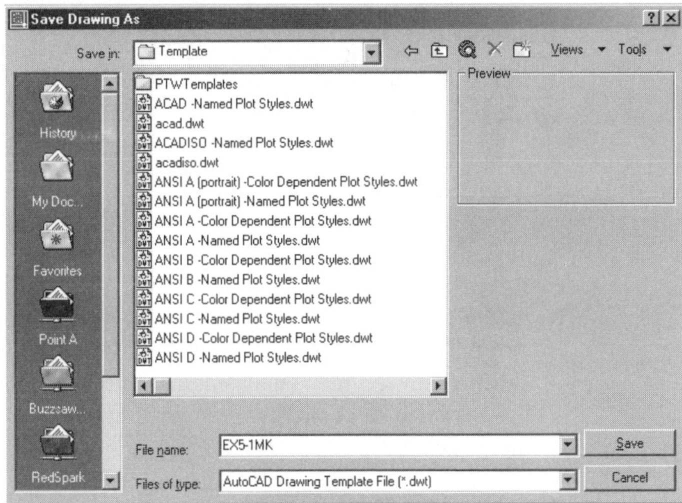

FIGURE 4–16
Save EX5–1(your initials) as a Template

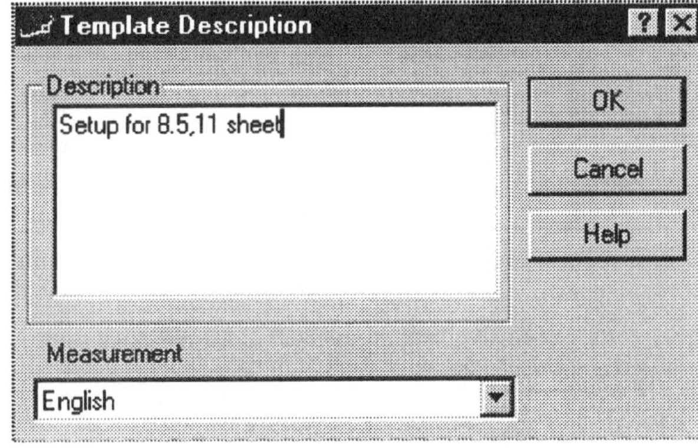

FIGURE 4–17
Template Description Dialog Box

File Name: Input Button

The drawing file name that will be saved appears here.

Save as type: Button

Note: The drawing EX4–1(your initials) could have been saved as a template (EX4–1(your initials) .dwt) with the extension .dwt instead of .dwg.

Picking the down arrow reveals a list of file types under which the drawing may be saved. The first three have the extension .dwg, and the fourth is the Drawing Template File, which has the extension .dwt. Some of these file types can be used interchangeably, but others require that a specific file type be used. In this book you will use only the Acad 2000 file type for drawings.

Save in:

The drive and folder where the file will be saved is listed in this area.

Save Button

When clicked, this button executes the SaveAs command.

Cancel Button

When clicked, this button cancels the command or closes any open button on the dialog box. The Esc key has the same effect.

Some additional features of the SaveAs command are as follows:

1. A drawing file can be saved and you may continue to work because with the SaveAs command the drawing editor is not exited.
2. If the default drive is used (the drive on which you are working), and the drawing has been opened from that drive, .dwg and .bak files are created.
3. If a different drive is specified (a floppy disk in the floppy drive), only a .dwg file is created.
4. To change the name of the drawing, you may save it under a new name by typing a new name in the File Name: button.

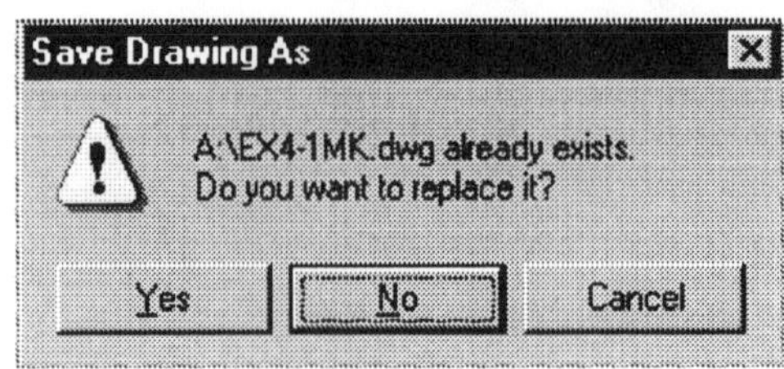

FIGURE 4–18
Save Drawing As Warning

5. If the drawing was previously saved or if a drawing file already exists with the drawing file name you typed, AutoCAD gives you the message "This file already exists. Do you want to replace it?" as shown in Figure 4–18.

   When a drawing file is updated, the old .dwg file is replaced with the new drawing, so the answer is to click Yes. If an error has been made and you do not want to replace the file, click No.

Step 11. Exit AutoCAD.

Prompt	**Response**
Command:	**Exit** (You may also *Type:* **QUIT** ↵ to exit.)

Exit

If you have not made any changes to the drawing since you last saved it, the Exit command takes you out of the AutoCAD program. If you have made changes to the drawing and have not saved these changes, AutoCAD will give you the message "Save changes to C:\Acad2002\EX4-1MK?" (or whatever the drawing name is). This is a safety feature because the Exit command, by itself, *does not update or save a drawing.* You have three options: Yes, save the changes; No, do not save changes; or Cancel the Exit command.

EXERCISE

EXERCISE 4–1. Complete Exercise 4–1 using steps 1 through 11 described in this chapter.

REVIEW QUESTIONS

Circle the best answer.

1. Which of the following is *not* in the list of units on the Unit Control dialog box?
   a. Scientific
   b. Metric
   c. Decimal
   d. Fractional
   e. Architectural
2. The Precision: button in the Units Control dialog box does which of the following?
   a. Determines how accurately AutoCAD draws
   b. Has a default value of four places to the right of the decimal point, which may not be changed
   c. Sets decimal places for fractional units
   d. Sets the places to the right of the decimal point for decimal units
   e. Sets decimal places for architectural units
3. The limits of a drawing are similar to the page size.
   a. True
   b. False
4. The default lower left corner of the drawing limits is 8.5,11.
   a. True
   b. False
5. The function key F7 described in this chapter does which of the following?
   a. Provides a check list of the layers created
   b. Turns snap ON or OFF

c. Flips the screen from the text display to the graphics display
d. Turns grid ON or OFF
e. Turns ortho ON or OFF

6. Units:, Limits:, Grid:, and Snap: can all be found under the Format menu.
   a. True
   b. False
7. Which of the following function keys is used to turn snap ON or OFF?
   a. F1
   b. F2
   c. F7
   d. F8
   e. F9
8. How many layers may be set current at the same time?
   a. 1
   b. 2
   c. 3
   d. 16
   e. An unlimited number
9. When a layer is OFF, it will regenerate but is not visible.
   a. True
   b. False
10. AutoCAD provides how many sizes of each standard linetype (except continuous)?
    a. 1
    b. 2
    c. 3
    d. 4
    e. As many as you want

Complete.

11. Describe the effect of using the Esc key while in a command.

    ____

12. What is an invisible grid to which the crosshairs will lock called?

    ____

13. What is the maximum number of characters that may be used in a layer name?

    ____

14. How many layers may be used in a drawing?

    ____

15. What is the maximum number of characters that may be used in a drawing name?

    ____

16. Explain what .dwg and .dwt files are.

    .dwg: ______________________________

    .dwt: ______________________________

17. Before a linetype other than continuous may be selected or changed in the Layer Properties Manager dialog box, what must be done?

    ____

18. List the toolbar on which the layer status is displayed.

    ____

19. What does the QUIT command do when used by itself?

    ____

20. Describe how Save differs from SaveAs when the drawing has been named.

    ____

    ____

PART II

BASIC AUTOCAD

5 Using Raster Images in AutoCAD Drawings

OBJECTIVES

When you have completed this chapter, you will be able to:

- □ Define the terms *vector* and *raster images.*
- □ List file types for raster images.
- □ Insert raster images into AutoCAD drawings.
- □ Select raster images for editing.
- □ Use grips to stretch, move, scale, copy, rotate, and mirror raster images.
- □ Clip raster images.
- □ Change the order of images lying on top of each other.
- □ Adjust the brightness and contrast of raster images.
- □ Turn image boundaries ON and OFF.
- □ Delete and Detach raster images.

INTRODUCTION

AutoCAD 2002 allows raster images to be easily imported into and exported from AutoCAD drawings. A raster image is one made up of dots similar to the photographs you find printed in newspapers and magazines. A vector image is one made up of lines and solids. Most AutoCAD drawings are made up entirely of vector images.

Being able to use raster images easily in AutoCAD drawings means that you can now bring many different types of images into your drawing. For example, you can use files from CorelDraw, Paintbrush, Powerpoint and many other popular graphics programs. You can also take photographs with a digital camera and import them into your drawing. AutoCAD uses 14 image file types that you will find listed in the Select Image File dialog box.

Many of the same commands you use with vector images can be used with raster images. How these commands are used, however, varies a little. The following exercise will give you some experience in using raster images.

Exercise 5–1 Inserting and Modifying Raster Images

The drawing template EX5-1(your initials), created in Chapter 4, will be used for this exercise. You will use that template to create a new drawing and then insert some raster images that are in the AutoCAD 2002 program. After the images are inserted some stan-

FIGURE 5–1
Exercise 5–1: Inserting and Modifying Raster Images (This material has been reprinted with permission from and under the copyright of Autodesk, Inc.)

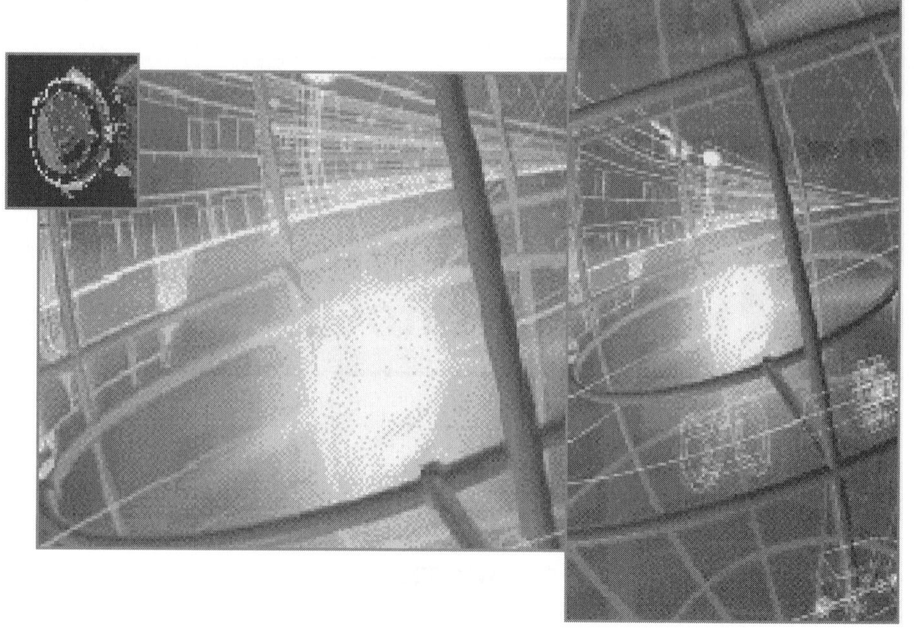

dard commands will be used to modify the images. Your final drawing will look similar to Figure 5–1.

To prepare to draw Exercise 5–1, turn on the computer and start AutoCAD. The AutoCAD 2002 Today window is displayed.

1. *Click:* **the Create Drawings tab**
2. *Click:* **Template** in the Select how to begin: list
3. **Scroll down to E (1)** and *Click:*
4. *Click:* **EX5-1(your initials).dwt** (Figure 5–2)
5. **Use SaveAs... to save the drawing on the hard drive with the name EX5-1(your initials).**
6. Use Zoom-All to view the limits of the drawing.
7. Turn GRID and SNAP ON.
8. Set Layer1 current.

FIGURE 5–2
Select the EX5-1(your initials) Template

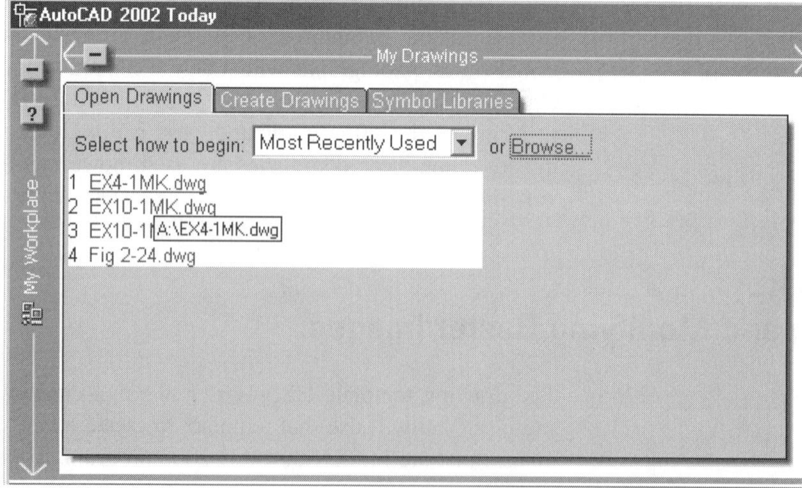

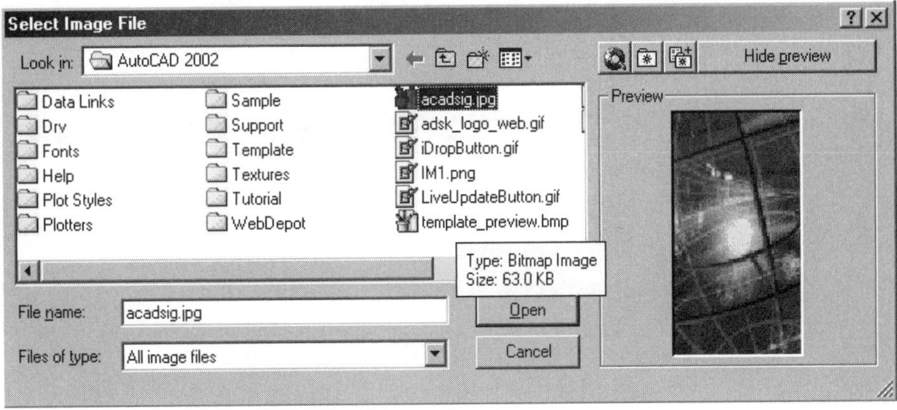

FIGURE 5–3
Double Click the acadsig.jpg File in the Acad2002 Folder

Inserting Raster Images into AutoCAD Drawings

Find the sample raster files that are in AutoCAD 2000 and insert the one named acadsig (Figure 5–3):

Prompt	Response
Command:	*Click:* **Raster Image...** (on the Insert menu)
The Select Image File dialog box appears:	*Double Click:* **acadsig.jpg** (in the Acad2002 folder)
The Image dialog box appears:	*Click:* **OK**
Specify insertion point <0,0>:	↵ (This locates the lower left corner of the picture at 0,0.)
Base image size: Width: 1.000000, Height: 1.837500, Inches Specify scale factor <1>:	*Type:* **5**↵ (This enlarges the picture to five times its original size.)

The acadsig image is inserted into the drawing.

Modifying Raster Images

Before you can do anything to an image you have to select it. Raster images have to be selected by using a window or by clicking any point on the image frame. After selecting the object, you may then move, stretch, scale, copy, mirror, or rotate it using grips or one of the standard commands.

You may also use any of the commands on the Reference toolbar to Clip, Adjust, and otherwise edit the image. Start by clipping this image to a more manageable size.

On Your Own (Figure 5–4)

1. Activate the Reference toolbar by *Clicking:* Toolbar....
2. Check the boxes to the left of Object Properties and Reference, and Close the Customize dialog box (Figure 5–4).

Clip an area from the enlarged acadsig image (Figure 5–5):

Prompt	Response
Command:	**Image Clip**

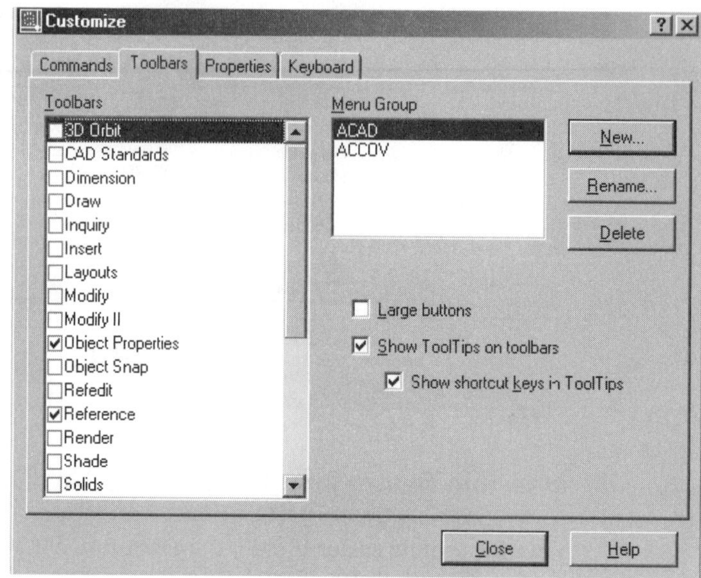

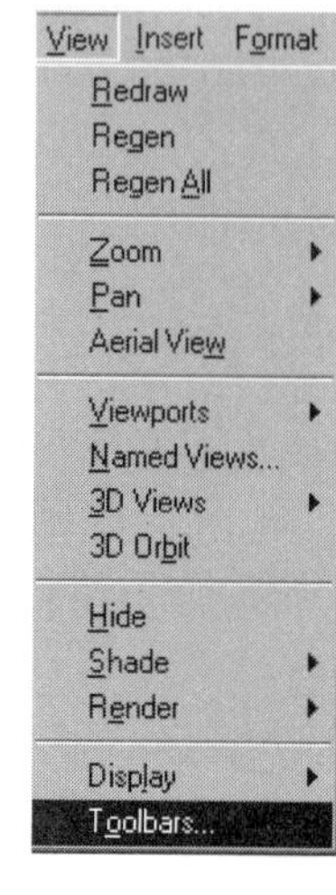

FIGURE 5–4
Activate the Reference Toolbar

FIGURE 5–5
The Clipped acadsig Image

Prompt	Response
Select image to clip:	*Click:* **any point on the frame (the outside edge) of the acadsig image**
Enter image clipping option [ON/OFF/Delete/New boundary] <New>:	↵
Enter clipping type [Polygonal/Rectangular] <Rectangular>:	↵
Specify first corner point: <Osnap off>	*Type:* **0,6.75↵**
Specify opposite corner point:	*Type:* **5.25,3.25↵**

Move the acadsig image toward the center of the drawing limits:

Prompt	Response
Command:	*Click:* **any point on the image frame**
Small blue squares (called Grips) appear on each corner of the image:	*Click:* **the square (grip) on the lower left corner of the image (to make it hot—it becomes a solid color)**
** STRETCH **	
Specify stretch point or [Base point/Copy/Undo/eXit]:	*Press:* **the space bar**
** MOVE **	

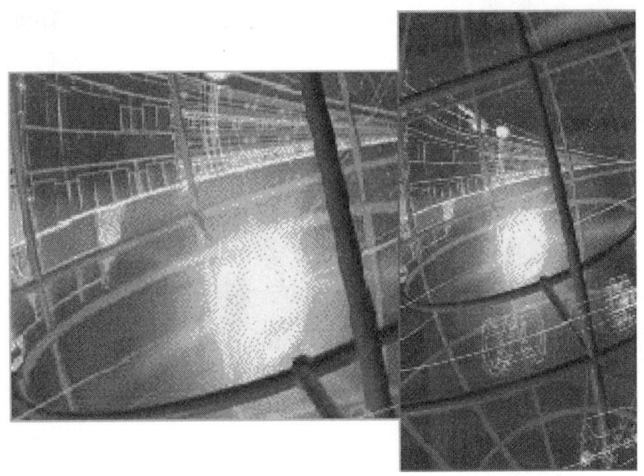

FIGURE 5–6
Insert acadsig Again

Prompt	Response
Specify move point or [Base point/Copy/Undo/eXit]:	*Type:* **1.25,3.5↵**

Insert the acadsig image again on the right side of the page (Figure 5–6):

Prompt	Response
Command**:**	**Raster Image...**
The Select Image File dialog box appears with acadsig already selected:	*Click:* **Open**
The Image dialog box appears:	*Click:* **OK**
Specify insertion point <0,0>:	*Type:* **5.25,3↵**
Base image size: Width: 1.000000, Height: 1.837500, Inches Specify scale factor <1>:	*Type:* **2.5↵**

Insert another image (a picture of a watch) on the left side of the page:

Prompt	Response
Command:	**Raster Image...**
The Select Image File dialog box appears with acadsig already selected:	*Double Click:* **the Sample folder (Figure 5–7)** *Click:* **Watch**

FIGURE 5–7
Select Image File Dialog Box

Prompt	Response
	Click: **Open**
The Image dialog box appears:	*Click:* **OK**
Specify insertion point <0,0>: <Osnap off>	*Type:* **1,6↵**
Base image size: Width: 1.000000, Height: 1.124464, Inches Specify scale factor <1>:	*Type:* **4↵**

The watch picture is too big, so you will have to scale it down.

Select the watch raster image.

Prompt	Response
Command:	*Click:* **any point on the frame of the watch image**
Small blue boxes (grips) appear at each corner of the image:	**Center the pickbox on the lower left grip.**
	Click: **the lower left grip**

The lower left grip changes to a solid color.

Scale the watch image to 1/4 its size:

Prompt	Response
STRETCH	
Specify stretch point or [Base point/Copy/ Undo/eXit]:	*Press:* ↵ **until the prompt reads as shown in the following Prompt column.**
SCALE	
Specify scale factor or [Base point/Copy/ Undo/Reference/eXit]:	*Type:* **.25↵**

The watch image is reduced to a smaller size (Figure 5–8).

Notice that Figure 5–9 shows the clipped image behind the original image. Your drawing may show the clipped image in front. In any case, complete the next step so you will know how to arrange images in overlapping order.

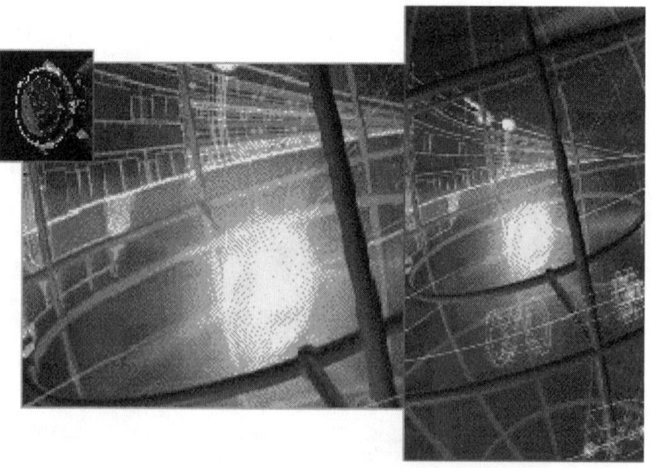

FIGURE 5–8
Watch Image Inserted and Reduced

FIGURE 5–9
Move the Clipped Image to the Front

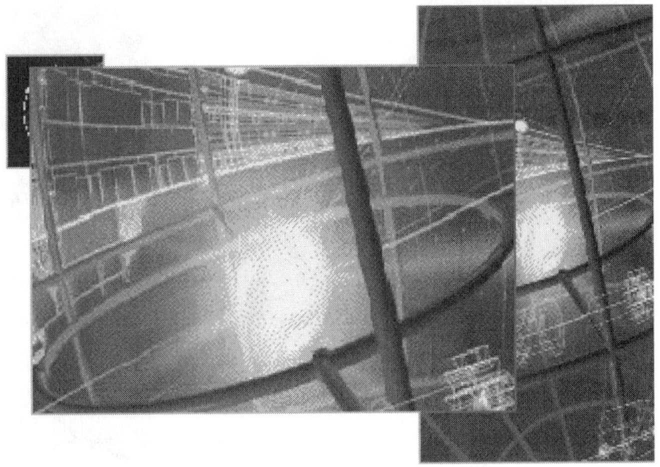

Use Display Order to move the clipped image in front of the full acadsig image (Figure 5–9):

Prompt	Response
Command:	*Click:* **Display Order**
	Click: **Bring to Front**
Select objects:	*Click:* **any point on the boundary of the clipped image**
Select objects:	↵

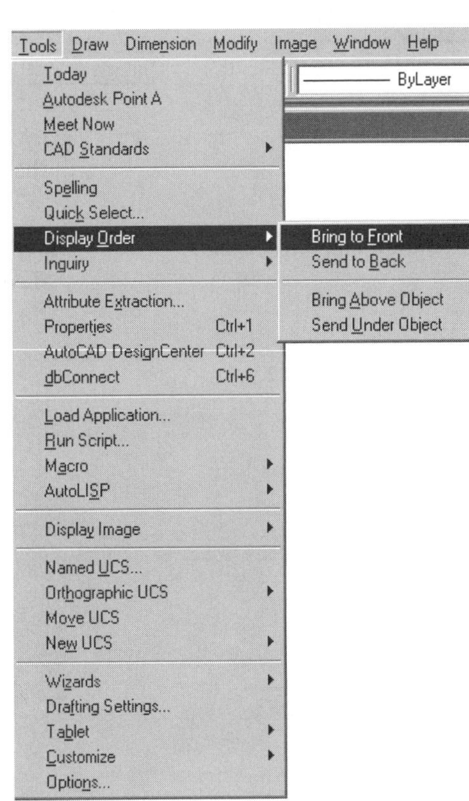

FIGURE 5–10
Exercise 5–1 Final Image

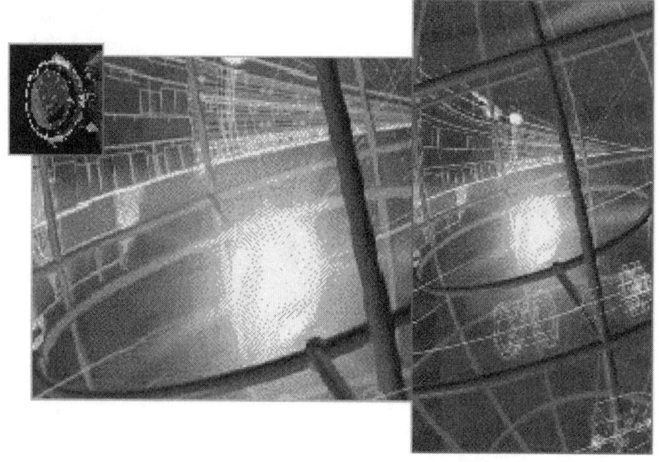

Practice a little with these commands on the Display Order menu. After you are through, your final images should look similar to Figure 5–10.

Adjusting the Brightness and Contrast of a Raster Image

Adjust the brightness and contrast of the full acadsig image (Figure 5–11):

Prompt	**Response**
Command:	*Click:* **Image Adjust**

Select image(s):	*Click:* **any point on the boundary of the full acadsig image ↵**
Select image(s):	
The Image Adjust dialog box appears:	**Move the slider for brightness to 40 and the contrast to 78 as shown in Figure 5–11.**
	Click: **OK**

FIGURE 5–11
Image Adjust Dialog Box

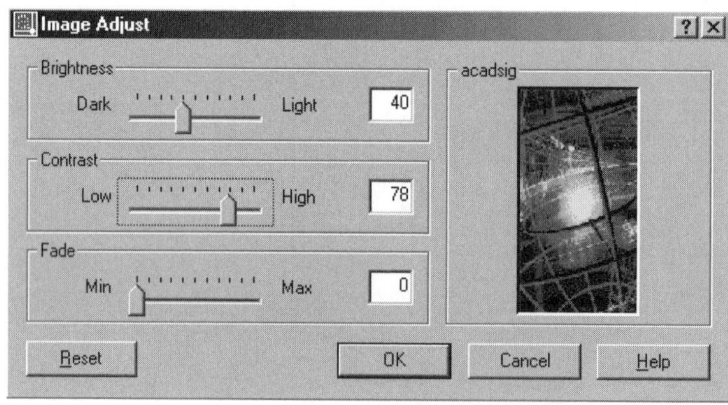

Turning Raster Image Frames On and Off

Turn image frames off:

Prompt	Response
Command:	*Click:* **Image Frame**

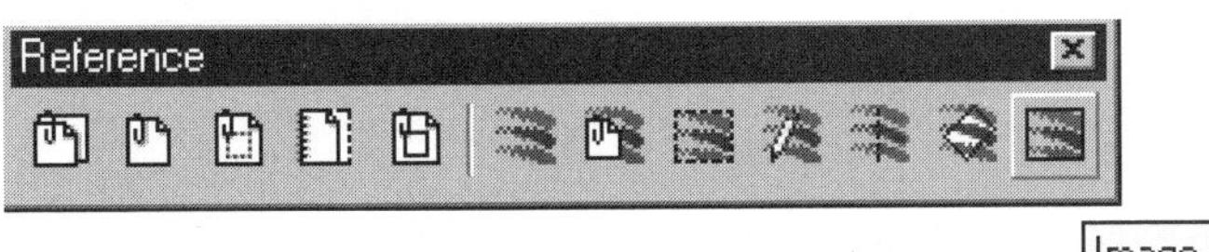

Enter image frame setting [ON/OFF]<ON>: *Type:* **OFF** ↵

You cannot select an image with the frame turned off. If you need to select an image later, you will have to turn the image frame on again using the Image Frame command.

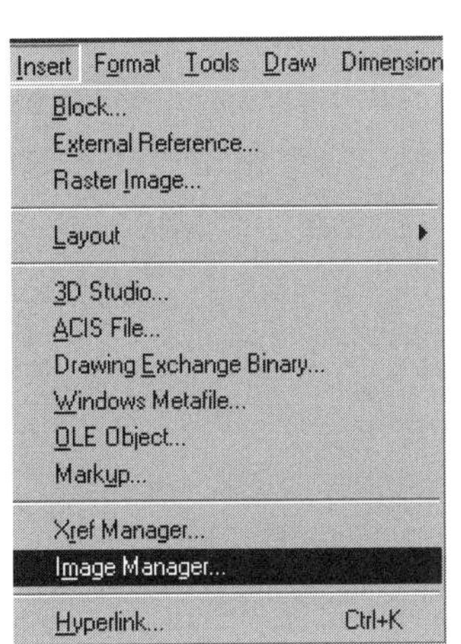

Deleting and Detaching Images

When you want to delete one or more images, select them and press the Delete key on your keyboard. You should not delete any of the images you presently have unless you have made a mistake and have more images than are shown in Figure 5–10.

Deleting the images does not detach the image from your drawing. To detach the image, activate the Image Manager (Figure 5–12), select the image file name and *Double Click:* **Detach**. When the image is detached, it is removed from the drawing database and all those images are erased from the drawing.

Save Your Drawing and Exit AutoCAD

When you have completed Exercise 5–1, save your drawing in at least two places. You can plot Exercise 5–1 after completing Chapter 8.

FIGURE 5–12
Image Manager Dialog Box

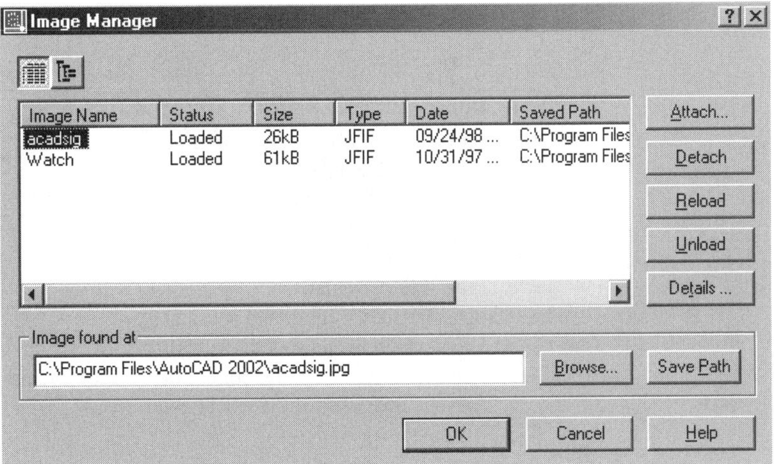

REVIEW QUESTIONS

Circle the best answer.

1. A raster image is made up of dots.
   a. True
   b. False
2. How many raster file types does AutoCAD use?
   a. 1
   b. 4
   c. 14
   d. 25
   e. An unlimited number
3. Which of the following folders contains the Watch raster image used in this chapter?
   a. Sample
   b. Acad2002
   c. Support
   d. Template
   e. Fonts
4. To select a raster image
   a. Click any point inside the frame.
   b. Click any point outside the frame.
   c. Use a dialog box to select it.
   d. Click any point on the frame.
   e. Type the name of the image.
5. When a raster image is selected
   a. It changes color.
   b. Small blue squares called grips appear on each corner.
   c. Vertical white lines appear on the image.
   d. Horizontal white lines appear on the image.
   e. A round dot appears in the center of the image.
6. When a Scale factor of .25 is used with the grips Scale mode
   a. The selected image is reduced to 1/4 its original size.
   b. The selected image is reduced to 1/2 its original size.
   c. The selected image is reduced to 1/25 its original size.
   d. The selected image is enlarged to 4 times its original size.
   e. The selected image is enlarged to 25 times its original size.
7. To activate the move grip mode, select the image, pick a grip, and press ↵
   a. Once
   b. Twice
   c. Three times
   d. Four times
   e. Do not press <enter> at all.
8. An image can be made larger or smaller with grips.
   a. True
   b. False
9. When you select Image Clip you have a choice of two types of boundaries to specify. They are
   a. Circular/<Rectangular>
   b. Rectangular/<Elliptical>
   c. Polygonal/<Rectangular>
   d. Circular/<Polygonal>
   e. Elliptical/<Circular>
10. The Display Order command is used to
    a. Show which image was inserted first
    b. Move an image from the bottom of a stack of images to the top
    c. Arrange images in alphabetical order
    d. Arrange images in rows
    e. Arrange images in columns

Complete.

11. List the command that is used to insert a raster image.

____

12. List the command that is used to clip a raster image.

____

13. List the command that is used to turn off the frame around raster images.

____

14. Write the name of the small blue squares that appear at the corners of a raster image when it is selected.

____

15. Describe how to detach a raster image from your drawing.

____

6 Adding Text to the Drawing

OBJECTIVES

When you have completed this chapter, you will be able to:

- □ Define the terms *style* and *font* and describe the function of each.
- □ Use different fonts on the same drawing.
- □ Place text on several different parts of the drawing with a single command.
- □ Use the modifiers Center, Align, Fit, Middle, Right, Top, and Style.
- □ Use the Text Style... setting to create condensed, expanded, rotated, backward, inclined, and upside-down text.
- □ Use the Text Style... setting to change any style on the drawing to a different font.
- □ Use standard codes to draw special characters such as the degree symbol, the diameter symbol, the plus and minus symbol, and underscored and overscored text.
- □ Use Mtext (multiline text) to create paragraph text.
  Spell check your drawing.

Exercise 6–1 Placing Text on Drawings

To make complete drawings with AutoCAD, you need to know how text is added to the drawings. The following AutoCAD commands, used to place lettering on drawings, are examined in Exercise 6–1.

Text Style... Used to control the appearance of text.
Single Line Text (Dtext) Used to draw text that is not in paragraph form.
Multiline Text (Mtext) Used to draw text that is in paragraph form.

When you have completed Exercise 6–1, your drawing will look similar to the drawing in Figure 6–1. To begin Exercise 6–1, turn on the computer and start AutoCAD. The Startup dialog box is displayed.

On Your Own

1. Use the same template as you used for EX5-1(your initials).
2. **Use SaveAs... to save the drawing on the hard drive with the name EX6-1(your initials).**
3. Set Layer1 current.
4. Use Zoom-All to view the limits of the drawing.

Making Settings for Text Style...

It is very important to understand the difference between the terms *Style Name* and *Font Name* with regard to text:

FIGURE 6–1
Exercise 6–1: Placing Text on Drawings

YOUR NAME CLASS NUMBER

THIS WAS TYPED WITH THE HEADING STYLE, AND THE IMPACT FONT, 1/4" HIGH, CENTERED

THIS WAS TYPED WITH THE HANDLTR SYTLE, AND THE CITY BLUEPRINT FONT, 3/16" HIGH, CENTERED

STANDARD STYLE, FIT OPTION

OVERSCORE WITH THE OVERSCORE STYLE

OVERSCORE WITH THE STANDARD STYLE

UNDERSCORE WITH THE STANDARD STYLE

STANDARD CODES WITH THE STANDARD STYLE

±1/16" 45° Ø1/2"

ARIAL FONT
WITH THE UPSIDEDOWN STYLE
UPSIDE DOWN AND BACKWARD

VERTICAL STYLE

THIS IS PARAGRAPH OR MULTILINE TEXT TYPED WITH THE SANS SERIF FONT, .125" HIGH IN AN AREA THAT MEASURES 3" X 1".

THIS IS ***PARAGRAPH OR MULTILINE TEXT*** TYPED WITH SANS SERIF FONT, .125" HIGH IN AN AREA THAT MEASURES 3" X 1".

Style Name: This is a general category that can be assigned any name you choose. The style name is used to separate fonts. You may use the same name for the style as is used for the font, or you may use a different name, single number, or letter for the style name.

Font Name: This is the name of a particular alphabet that you select to assign to a style name. A font has to be in the AutoCAD program before it can be selected and assigned to a style name.

You may have only one font per style, but you can have many styles with the same font. For example,

Style Name	Font Name
SIMPLEX	SIMPLEX
CLIENT NAME	ITALIC
NOTES	SIMPLEX
ITALIC	ITALIC
BANNER	MONOTEXT
COMPANY NAME	ROMAND
ROMAND	ROMAND

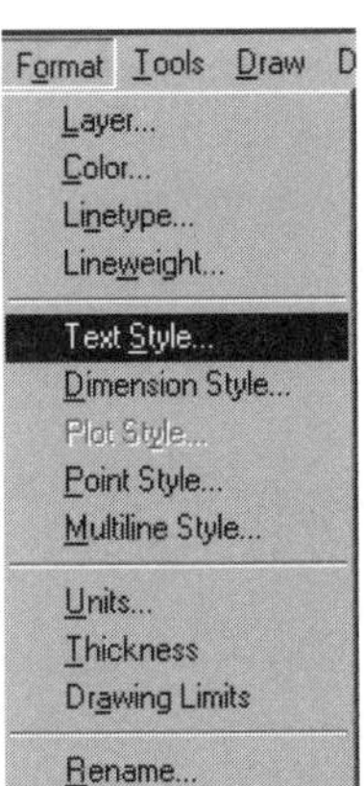

In the following procedure, the Text Style... setting is used.

Make the setting for the Standard style (Figure 6–2):

Prompt	Response
Command:	**Text Style...** (or *Type*: **ST**↵)

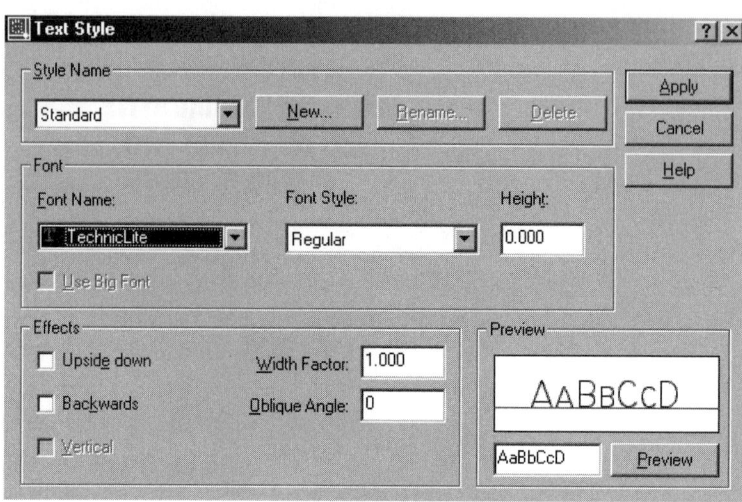

FIGURE 6–2
Select the TechnicLite Font for the Standard Style

Prompt	Response
The Text Style dialog box appears:	*Click:* **TechnicLite** (in the Font Name: list)
	Click: **Apply**

Any text typed while the Standard style is active will now contain the TechnicLite font. Notice the preview area in the lower right corner that shows you what the font looks like. Notice also that the vertical setting is grayed out, indicating that this font cannot be drawn running up and down.

The other settings should be left as they are. If you leave the text height set at 0, you will be able to draw different heights of the same style and you will be able to change the height of text if you need to. Leave the text height set to 0 in all cases. The Width Factor allows you to stretch letters so they are wider by making the width factor greater than 1, narrower by making the width factor less than 1. The Oblique Angle slants the letters to the right if the angle is positive and to the left if the angle is negative.

Make the settings for a new style that will be used on the drawing (Figures 6–3 and 6–4):

Prompt	Response
The Text Style dialog box:	*Click:* **New...**
The New Text Style dialog box appears with a Style Name that AutoCAD assigns style1:	*Type:* **HEADING** (to name the style, Figure 6–3)
	Click: **OK**
The Text Style dialog box appears:	*Click:* **romand.shx** (in the Font Name: list, Figure 6–4)
	Click: **Apply**

You now have two styles that have been defined on your drawing, Standard and HEADING.

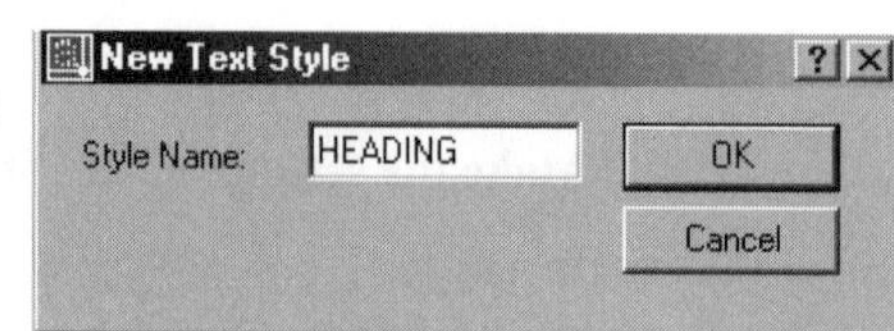

FIGURE 6–3
Name the Style, HEADING

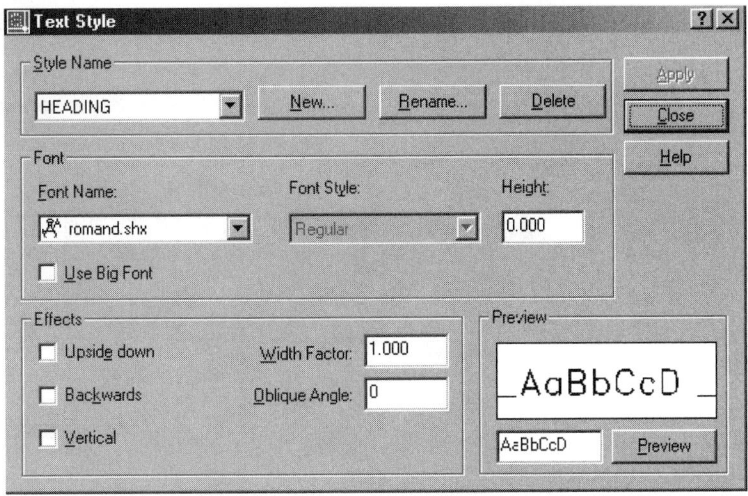

FIGURE 6–4
Select the romand.shx Font for the HEADING Style

On Your Own (Figures 6–5 and 6–6)

1. Make the settings for the following new styles:

Style Name	Font Name:	Other Settings
HANDLTR	CityBlueprint	None
OVERSCORE	Arial	None

Style Name	Font Name:	Other Settings
UPSIDEDOWN	Arial	Place checks in the Effects box labeled Upside down and the box labeled Backwards.
VERTICAL	romand.shx	Place a check in the Effects box labeled Vertical, Figure 6–5.

2. Click the down arrow in the Style Name list to determine if your list matches the one shown in Figure 6–6.
3. Click the HEADING style name to make it current.
4. Close the dialog box.

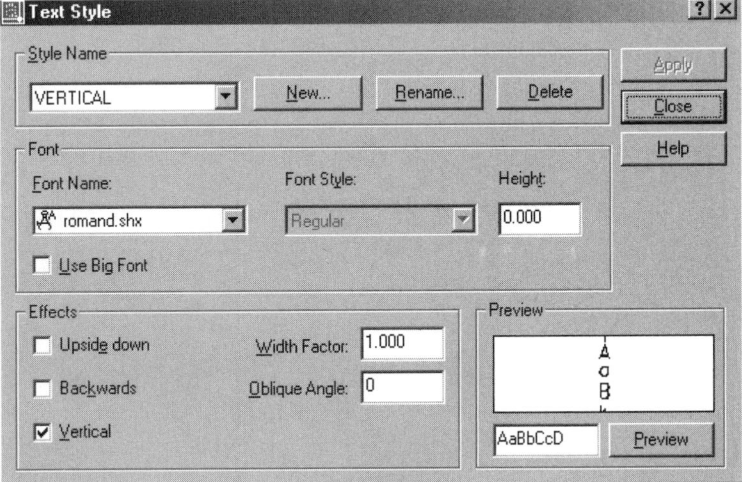

FIGURE 6–5
Make Settings for the VERTICAL Style

FIGURE 6–6
Check the Style Name List

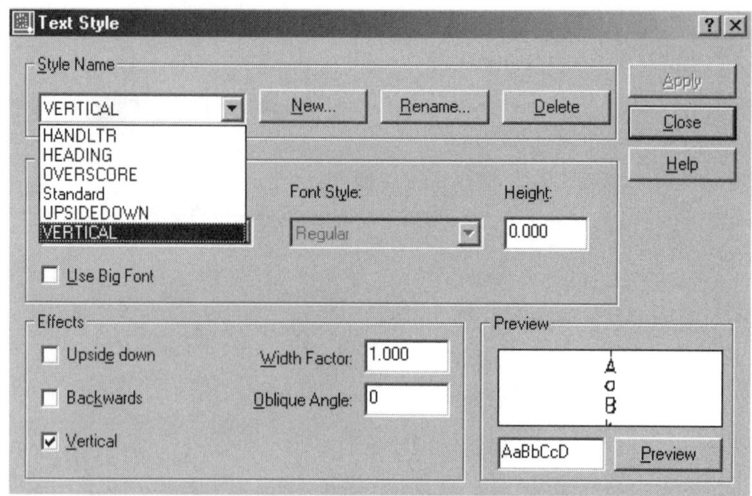

Using the Single Line Text Command to Draw Text

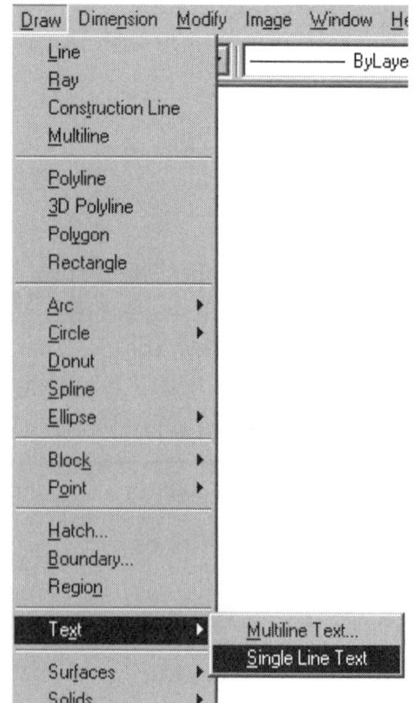

The Single Line Text command (also known as Dtext) is used to draw text that is not in paragraph form. Although the name of the command might lead you to believe that only a single line can be drawn, such is not the case. To draw one line under another just *Press:* ↵, and the next line will be ready to be drawn with the same settings as the first line. To demonstrate this, draw several of the lines of text on your current drawing.

If you are not happy with the location of the text, use the Move command to relocate it.

Draw the first two examples at the top of the page using single line text (Figure 6–7):

Prompt	Response
Command:	**Single Line Text** (or *Type*: **DT**↵)
Specify start point of text or [Justify/Style]:	*Type:* **C**↵
Specify center point of text:	*Type:* **4.25,10**↵ (You are locating the center of the line of text using absolute coordinates, 4-1/4″ to the right and 10″ up.)
Specify height <0.200>:	*Type:* **.25**↵
Specify rotation angle of text <0>:	↵
Enter text:	*Type:* **THIS WAS TYPED**↵
Enter text:	*Type:* **WITH THE HEADING STYLE,** ↵
Enter text:	*Type:* **AND THE ROMAND FONT,**↵
Enter text:	*Type:* **1/4″ HIGH**↵
Enter text:	↵

FIGURE 6–7
First Two Examples of Single Line Text

THIS WAS TYPED
WITH THE HEADING STYLE,
AND THE ROMAND FONT,
1/4" HIGH

THIS WAS TYPED
WITH THE HANDLTR SYTLE,
AND THE CITY BLUEPRINT FONT,
3/16" HIGH, CENTERED

Prompt	Response
Command:	↵ (Repeat DTEXT)
Specify start point of text or [Justify/Style]:	*Type:* **S↵** (to change styles)
Enter style name or [?] <HEADING>:	*Type:* **HANDLTR↵**
Specify start point of text or [Justify/Style]:	*Type:* **C↵**
Specify center point of text:	*Type:* **4.25,8↵**
Specify height <0.250>:	*Type:* **.188↵**
Specify rotation angle of text <0>:	↵
Enter text:	*Type:* **THIS WAS TYPED↵**
Enter text:	*Type:* **WITH THE HANDLTR STYLE,** ↵
Enter text:	*Type:* **AND THE CITY BLUEPRINT FONT,↵**
Enter text:	*Type:* **3/16″ HIGH, CENTERED↵**
Enter text:	↵

Your drawing looks like Figure 6–7.

Draw the next block of text using the Fit option of single line text with the Standard style (Figure 6–8):

Prompt	Response
Command:	**Single Line Text** (or *Type*: DT↵)
Specify start point of text or [Justify/Style]:	*Type:* **S↵**
Enter style name or [?] <HANDLTR>:	*Type:* **STANDARD↵**
Specify start point of text or [Justify/Style]:	*Type:* **F↵**
Specify first endpoint of text baseline:	*Type:* **1.5,6↵**
Specify second endpoint of text baseline:	*Type:* **7,6↵**
Specify height <0.188>:	*Type:* **.5↵**
Enter text:	*Type:* **STANDARD STYLE, FIT OPTION↵**
Enter text:	↵

When you activate the Single Line Text command, the prompt is "Specify start point of text or [Justify/Style]:". The Style option allows you to select a different style (that has already been defined) for the text you are about to draw. If you TYPE: **J**↵, the prompt then becomes "Enter an option [Align/Fit/Center/Middle/Right/TL/TC/TR/ML/MC/MR/BL/BC/BR]:".

FIGURE 6–8
Using the Fit Option of Single Line Text

THIS WAS TYPED
WITH THE HEADING STYLE,
AND THE ROMAND FONT,
1/4" HIGH

THIS WAS TYPED
WITH THE HANDLTR SYTLE,
AND THE CITY BLUEPRINT FONT,
3/16" HIGH, CENTERED

STANDARD STYLE, FIT OPTION

Align

Align draws the text between two points that you click. It does not condense or expand the font but instead adjusts the letter height so that the text fits between the two points.

Fit

Fit draws the text between two clicked points like the align option, but instead of changing the letter height, Fit condenses or expands the font to fit between the points.

Center

Center draws the text so that the bottom of the line of lettering is centered on the clicked point. Centering is not displayed until the second return is pressed. You may also choose the top or the middle of the line of lettering by typing TC or MC at the justify prompt.

Middle

Middle draws the text so that the middle of the line of lettering is centered around a clicked point. This is very useful when a single line of text must be centered in an area such as a box. Middle is not displayed until the second return is pressed. The top or bottom of the line may also be selected by typing MC or MB at the justify prompt.

Right

Right draws the text so that each line of text is right justified (ends at the same right margin). Right justification is not displayed until the second return is pressed. The top or center of the line may also be selected by typing TR or MR at the justify prompt.

TL/TC/TR/ML/MC/MR/BL/BC/BR

These are alignment options, Top Left, Top Center, Top Right, Middle Left, Middle Center, Middle Right, Bottom Left, Bottom Center, Bottom Right. They are used with horizontal text.

Draw a line of text using the VERTICAL style (Figure 6–9)

FIGURE 6–9
Using the Vertical Option of Single Line Text

THIS WAS TYPED
WITH THE HEADING STYLE,
AND THE ROMAND FONT,
1/4" HIGH

THIS WAS TYPED
WITH THE HANDLTR SYTLE,
AND THE CITY BLUEPRINT FONT,
3/16" HIGH, CENTERED

STANDARD STYLE, FIT OPTION

VERTICAL STYLE

(Remember that you checked Vertical in the Text Style dialog box for this text style.)

Prompt	Response
Command:	↵ (Repeat DTEXT)
Specify start point of text or [Justify/Style]:	*Type:* **S**↵
Enter style name or [?] <Standard>:	*Type:* **VERTICAL**↵
Specify start point of text or [Justify/Style]:	*Type:* **1,6**↵
Specify height <0.500>:	*Type:* **.25**↵
Specify rotation angle of text <270>:	↵
Enter text:	*Type:* **VERTICAL STYLE**↵
Enter text:	↵

45%%D
45°

FIGURE 6–10
Degree Symbol Code

%%C.500
∅.500

FIGURE 6–11
Diameter Symbol Code

%%P.005
±.005

FIGURE 6–12
Plus–Minus Symbol Code

Using Standard Codes to Draw Special Characters

Figures 6–10 through 6–14 show the use of codes to obtain several commonly used symbols, such as the degree symbol, the diameter symbol, the plus-minus symbol, and underscored and overscored text. The top line of Figure 6–10 shows the code that must be inserted to obtain the degree symbol following the number 45. The top line is displayed until the Enter key is pressed to obtain the degree symbol shown on the bottom line. Two percent symbols followed by the letter D produce the degree symbol.

Figure 6–11 illustrates that two percent symbols followed by the letter C produce the diameter symbol. Any text following the symbol must be typed immediately following the code.

Figure 6–12 shows the code for the plus-minus symbol.

Figure 6–13 shows the code for underscore: two percent symbols followed by the letter U. Notice that the first line contains only one code. The second line contains two codes: one to start the underline and one to stop it.

Figure 6–14 shows the code for overscored text. The same code sequence for starting and stopping the overscore applies.

Draw five lines containing special codes for the overscore, underscore, plus–minus, degree, and diameter symbols (Figure 6–15):

Prompt	Response
Command:	↵ (Repeat DTEXT)
Specify start point of text or [Justify/Style]:	*Type:* **S**↵
Enter style name or [?]<VERTICAL>:	*Type:* **OVERSCORE**↵
Specify start point of text or [Justify/Style]:	*Type:* **1.5,5**↵
Specify height <0.250>:	*Type:* **.188**↵
Specify rotation angle of text <0>:	↵
Enter text:	*Type:* **%%OOVERSCORE WITH THE OVERSCORE STYLE**↵
Enter text:	↵

%%UUNDERSCORE
UNDERSCORE

%%UUNDERSCORE%%U LETTERS
UNDERSCORE LETTERS

FIGURE 6–13
Underscore Code

%%OOVERSCORE
OVERSCORE

%%OOVERSCORE%%O LETTERS
OVERSCORE LETTERS

FIGURE 6–14
Overscore Code

FIGURE 6–15
Using Single Line Text to Draw Symbols with Standard Codes

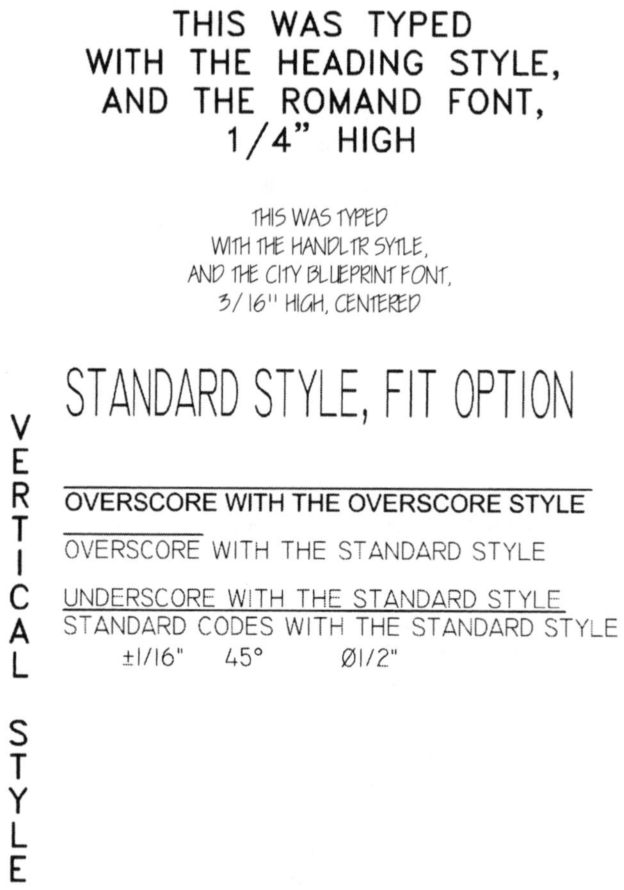

THIS WAS TYPED
WITH THE HEADING STYLE,
AND THE ROMAND FONT,
1/4" HIGH

THIS WAS TYPED
WITH THE HANDLTR SYTLE,
AND THE CITY BLUEPRINT FONT,
3/16" HIGH, CENTERED

STANDARD STYLE, FIT OPTION

VERTICAL STYLE

OVERSCORE WITH THE OVERSCORE STYLE

OVERSCORE WITH THE STANDARD STYLE

UNDERSCORE WITH THE STANDARD STYLE

STANDARD CODES WITH THE STANDARD STYLE

±1/16"   45°   Ø1/2"

Prompt	Response
Command:	↵ (Repeat DTEXT)
Specify start point of text or [Justify/Style]:	*Type:* **S↵**
Enter style name of [?]<OVERSCORE>:	*Type:* **STANDARD↵**
Specify start point of text or [Justify/Style]:	*Type:* **1.5,4.5↵**
Specify height <0.188>:	*Type:* **.188 ↵**
Specify rotation angle of text <0>:	↵
Enter text:	*Type:* **%%OOVERSCORE%%O WITH THE STANDARD STYLE ↵**
Enter text:	*Type:* **%%UUNDERSCORE WITH THE STANDARD STYLE ↵**
Enter text:	*Type:* **STANDARD CODES WITH THE STANDARD STYLE ↵**
Enter text:	*Click:* **a point in the approximate location shown in Figure 6–15**
Enter text:	*Type:* **%%P1/16″↵**
Enter text:	*Click::* **a point in the approximate location shown in Figure 6–15**
Enter text:	*Type:* **45%%D↵**
Enter text:	*Click:* **a point in the approximate location shown in Figure 6–15**
Enter text:	*Type:* **%%C1/2″↵**
Enter text:	↵

FIGURE 6–16
Draw a Phrase Upside Down and Backward with the UPSIDE-DOWN Style

THIS WAS TYPED
WITH THE HEADING STYLE,
AND THE ROMAND FONT,
1/4" HIGH

THIS WAS TYPED
WITH THE HANDLTR STYLE,
AND THE CITY BLUEPRINT FONT,
3/16" HIGH, CENTERED

STANDARD STYLE, FIT OPTION

VERTICAL STYLE

OVERSCORE WITH THE OVERSCORE STYLE

OVERSCORE WITH THE STANDARD STYLE

UNDERSCORE WITH THE STANDARD STYLE

STANDARD CODES WITH THE STANDARD STYLE

±1/16" 45° Ø1/2"

ARIAL FONT
WITH THE UPSIDEDOWN STYLE
UPSIDE DOWN AND BACKWARD

On Your Own

1. Make the Style Name UPSIDEDOWN current.
2. Use Single Line Text to draw the following phrase (.188 height) upside down and backward with its start point at 7,2.5 (Figure 6–16):

   UPSIDEDOWN AND BACKWARD↵
   WITH THE UPSIDEDOWN STYLE, ↵
   ARIAL FONT ↵ ↵.

3. Change the current style to Standard.

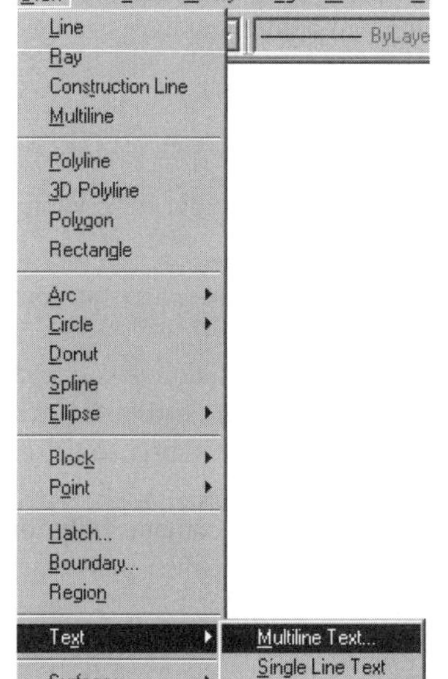

Using the Multiline Text Command to Draw Text Paragraphs

The Multiline Text command (also known as Mtext) is used to draw text in paragraph form. The command activates the Multiline Text Editor, which has many of the same features that other Windows Text Editors have. You can select a defined style, change the text height, boldface and italicize some fonts, select a justification style, specify the width of the line, rotate a paragraph, search for a word and replace it with another, undo, import text, and select symbols for use on your drawing. In this exercise you will create a paragraph using the sans serif font.

Use Multiline Text to draw a paragraph (Figure 6–17), then copy it 3.25″ to the right:

Prompt	Response
Command:	**Multiline Text** (or *Type:* **MT↵**)
Specify first corner:	*Type:* **1.5,2↵**

FIGURE 6–17
The Multiline Text Editor

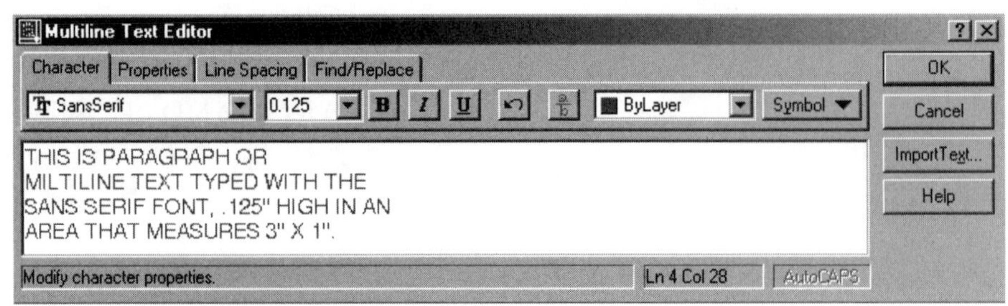

Prompt	**Response**
Specify opposite corner or [Height/Justify/ Line spacing/Rotation/Style/Width]:	*Type:* **@3,-1** (Be sure to include the minus so the vertical side of the text box is down. This makes the paragraph box 3″ × 1″ tall)
The Multiline Text Editor appears:	**Change the text height to .125 and the font to SansSerif,** then *Type*: **the paragraph shown in Figure 6–17.** (Be sure to misspell MULTILINE so it can be corrected later.)
	After the paragraph is typed correctly, *Click:* **OK**
Command:	*Type:* **CP** ↵
Select objects:	*Click:* **any point on the paragraph**
Select objects:	↵
Specify base point or displacement, or [Multiple]:	*Click:* **any point**
Specify second point of displacement or <use first point as displacement>:	*Type:* **@3.25,0**↵ (This copies the paragraph 3-1/4″ directly to the right, Figure 6–18.)

If you have trouble getting the Multiline Text to change text height, cancel the command and *Type*: **DT** to activate Single Line Text and change the default text height to .125. The Multiline Text height will then be set at .125, and you can proceed with typing the paragraph. Be sure you do not cancel the Single Line Text command before you have changed the default text height.

Changing Text Properties

There will be occasions when you will need to change the text font, height, or content. AutoCAD has several commands that can be used to do these tasks:

Text Style... Use this command to change the font of text that already exists on your drawing.

CHANGE Use this command to change the endpoint of a line, the radius of a circle, and for Single Line Text. When used for Single Line Text, you can change the text properties, the insertion point, the text style, the text height, the text rotation angle, or the text content.

DDEDIT(Edit Text) Use this command if you want to change the text contents only for Single Line Text. This command gives you the Multiline Text Editor when you select multiline text and allows you to change all its properties.

DDMODIFY(Properties) Use this command to change any of the text's characteristics: properties, origin, style, height, rotation angle, the text content, or any of several other properties.

FIGURE 6–18
Use Multiline Text to Type a Paragraph, Then Copy It

THIS WAS TYPED
WITH THE HEADING STYLE,
AND THE ROMAND FONT,
1/4" HIGH

THIS WAS TYPED
WITH THE HANDLTR SYTLE,
AND THE CITY BLUEPRINT FONT,
3/16" HIGH, CENTERED

VERTICAL STYLE

STANDARD STYLE, FIT OPTION

OVERSCORE WITH THE OVERSCORE STYLE

OVERSCORE WITH THE STANDARD STYLE

UNDERSCORE WITH THE STANDARD STYLE

STANDARD CODES WITH THE STANDARD STYLE
±1/16" 45° Ø1/2"

UPSIDE DOWN AND BACKWARD
WITH THE UPSIDEDOWN STYLE
ARIAL FONT

THIS IS PARAGRAPH OR MILTILINE TEXT TYPED WITH THE SANS SERIF FONT, .125" HIGH IN AN AREA THAT MEASURES 3" X 1".

THIS IS PARAGRAPH OR MILTILINE TEXT TYPED WITH THE SANS SERIF FONT, .125" HIGH IN AN AREA THAT MEASURES 3" X 1".

Use the Text Style... command to change the font of text typed with the HEADING name from Romand to Impact (Figure 6–19):

Prompt	Response
Command:	**Text Style...** (or *Type*: **ST↵**)
	Click: **HEADING** (in the Style Name list)
The Text Style dialog box appears:	*Click:* **Impact** (from the Font Name list, Figure 6–19)
	Click: **Apply**
	Click: **Close**

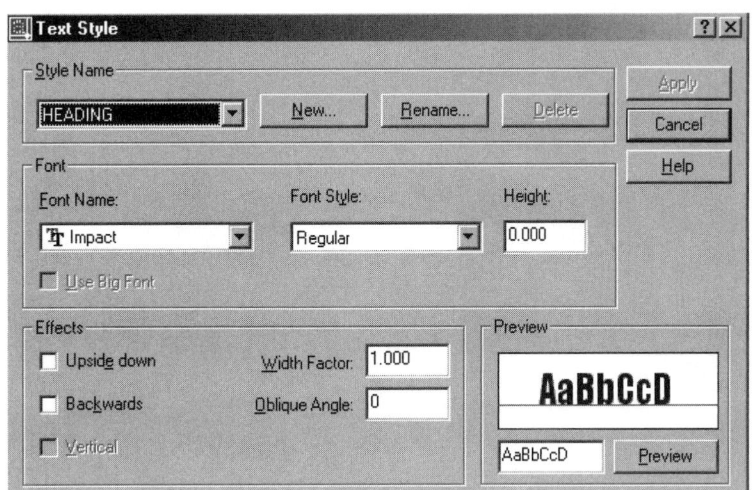

FIGURE 6–19
Select the Impact Font for the HEADING Style

Notice that everything you typed with the HEADING style name is now changed to the Impact font.

Use the CHANGE command to change the height of the phrase "VERTICAL STYLE" to 1/2″ and the contents to "VERTICAL NAME."

Prompt	Response
Command:	*Type:* **CHANGE↵**
Select objects:	*Click:* **any point on the words VERTICAL STYLE**
Select objects:	↵
Specify change point or [Properties]:	↵
Specify new text insertion point <no change>:	↵
Enter new text style <VERTICAL>:	↵
Specify new height <0.250>:	*Type:* **.5↵**
Specify new rotation angle <270>:	↵
Enter new text <VERTICAL STYLE>:	*Type:* **VERTICAL NAME ↵ "AND THE ROMAND FONT" ↵**
Oops! This is too big, and the phrase VERTICAL STYLE is better.	Change this back to the way it was by *Click*: **UNDO** (on the Standard Toolbar), or *Type*: **U ↵.**

Use the DDEDIT (Edit Text) command to change "AND THE ROMAND FONT" to "AND THE IMPACT FONT" and 1/4″ HIGH to 1/4″ HIGH, CENTERED:

Prompt	Response
Command:	**Modify-Text...** or *Type:* **DDEDIT↵**
Select an annotation object or [Undo]:	*Click:* **AND THE ROMAND FONT**
The Edit Text dialog box appears:	*Click:* **to the right of ROMAND, backspace over ROMAND** and *Type:* **IMPACT**
	Click: **OK**

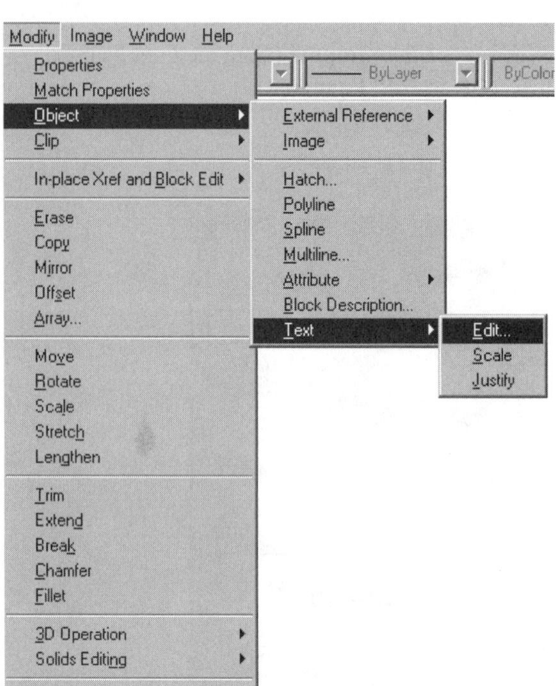

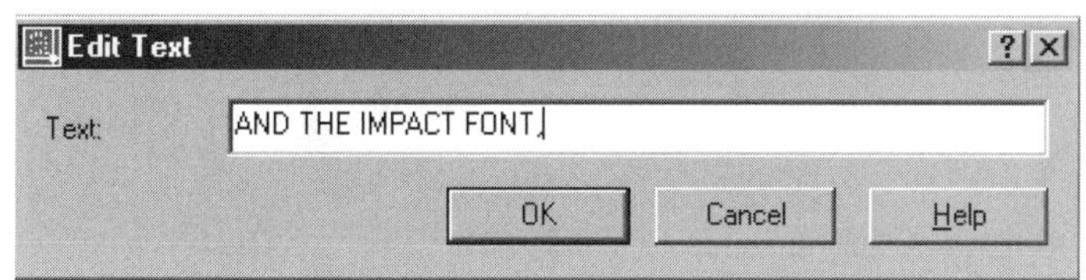

FIGURE 6–20
Changing Text Using the Edit Text Dialog Box

On Your Own

Use the Edit Text command to change the line of text that reads "1/4″ HIGH" to "1/4″ HIGH, CENTERED" (Figure 6–20).

Continue using the Edit Text command to change the words PARAGRAPH OR MULTILINE TEXT in the copied paragraph to the italic font:

Prompt	Response
Select an annotation object or [Undo]:	*Click:* **any point on the copied paragraph**
The Multiline Text Editor (Figure 6–21) appears:	*Click:* **the left mouse button to the left of the word PARAGRAPH, hold it down, and drag to the end to the word TEXT so that PARAGRAPH OR MULTILINE TEXT is highlighted,** then *Click*: **italic** in the font list
	Click: **OK**
Select an annotation object or [UNDO]:	*Press:* **ESC or ↵**

Use the DDMODIFY (Properties) command to change the vertical line of text from Layer1 to Layer2 (Figure 6–22):

Prompt	Response
Command:	*Click:* **the vertical line of text (VERTICAL STYLE)**
Command:	**Properties** (or *Type*: **DDMODIFY↵**)
The Properties dialog box appears:	*Click:* **Layer**
	Click: **the Down Arrow** (Figure 6–22)
	Click: **Layer2**
	Click: **the X in the upper right corner to close**
	Press: **Esc twice**

VERTICAL STYLE is now changed to Layer2.

Modify Image Window Help
Properties
Match Properties
Object
Clip
In-place Xref and Block Edit
Erase
Copy
Mirror
Offset
Array...
Move
Rotate
Scale
Stretch
Lengthen
Trim
Extend
Break
Chamfer
Fillet
3D Operation
Solids Editing
Explode

FIGURE 6–21
Changing Multiline Text to the Italic Font

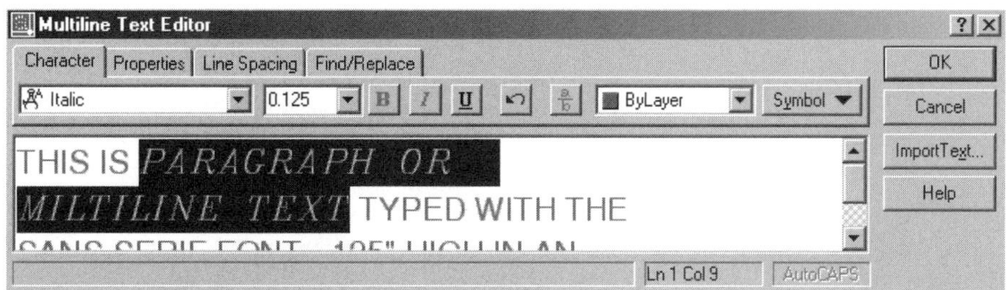

FIGURE 6–22
Change Text to Layer2

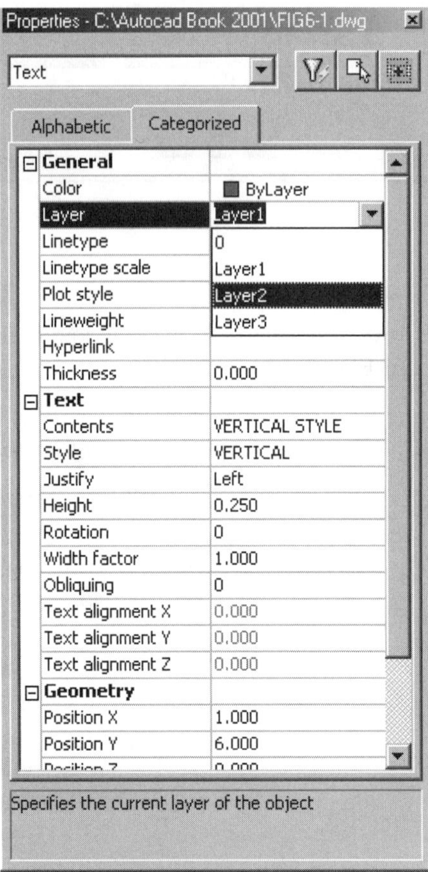

On Your Own

1. Use the Undo command to undo the layer change (*Type*: **U↵** or *Click*: **Undo** from the Standard Toolbar).
2. Use Single Line Text, Standard style, .125″ high to place your name and class number in the upper left and upper right corners, respectively. Start point for your name is 1,10.5. Use right-justified text for class number (at the Dtext prompt "Specify start point of text or [Justify/Style]:" *Type*: **R↵**. Right endpoint of text baseline is 7.5, 10.5.

Checking the Spelling

AutoCAD has a spell checker that allows you to accurately check the spelling on your drawing. If the word is correctly spelled but is not in the current dictionary, you can select Ignore All to ignore all instances of that word on the drawing. You can also add the word to the current dictionary. You can change the spelling of a single use of a word or all instances of the word on the drawing by picking Change All. AutoCAD also allows you to change dictionaries.

On Your Own

Purposely misspell the word TYPED. Use Edit Text... (or Properties) to change THIS WAS TYPED to THIS WAS TPYED.

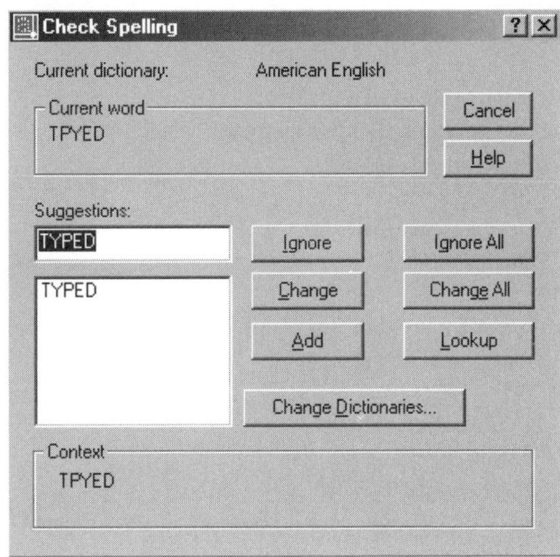

FIGURE 6–23
Change TPYED to TYPED Using Spell Check

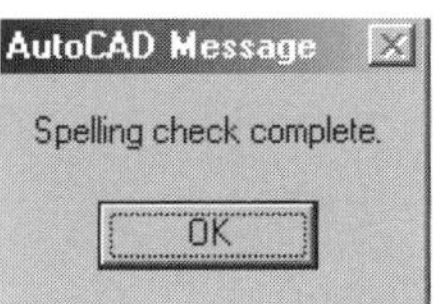

FIGURE 6–24
Click: **OK** to Complete the Spell Check

Tools Draw Dimension Modify
Today
Autodesk Point A
Meet Now
CAD Standards
Spelling
Quick Select...
Display Order
Inquiry
Attribute Extraction...
Properties Ctrl+1
AutoCAD DesignCenter Ctrl+2
dbConnect Ctrl+6
Load Application...
Run Script...
Macro
AutoLISP
Display Image
Named UCS...
Orthographic UCS
Move UCS
New UCS
Wizards
Drafting Settings...
Tablet
Customize
Options...

Use the Spelling command to check the spelling on your drawing (Figures 6–23 and 6–24):

Prompt	Response
Command:	**Spelling** (or *Type:* **SP↵**)
Select objects:	*Type:* **ALL↵** to select all the text on your drawing
Select objects:	↵
The Check Spelling dialog box appears (Figure 6–23):	*Click:* **Ignore All** for all font and command names until you reach the word TPYED
	Click: the word **TYPED** if it is not already highlighted in the Suggestions: box
	Click: **Change**
The AutoCAD Message appears:	*Click:* **OK** (Figure 6–24)

On Your Own: Change MILTILINE to MULTILINE in two places.

Save Your Drawing and Exit AutoCAD

When you have completed Exercise 6–1, save your drawing in at least two places. Exercise 6–1 will be printed in Chapter 8.

REVIEW QUESTIONS

Circle the best answer.

1. The command used in this chapter to place line text on drawings is
   a. Single Line Text (Dtext)
   b. TXT
   c. Multiline Text (Mtext)
   d. DDedit
   e. MS-DOS Text Editor
2. The command used in this chapter to place paragraph text on drawings is
   a. Single Line Text (Dtext)
   b. TXT
   c. Multiline Text (Mtext)
   d. DDedit
   e. MS-DOS Text Editor
3. Which of the following could be used as a Style name?
   a. SIMPLEX
   b. TITLE
   c. NAMES
   d. A
   e. All the above could be used as a Style name.
4. Which of the following is a font name?
   a. SIMPLEX
   b. TITLE
   c. NAMES
   d. A
   e. All the above are font names.
5. You can change from one text style to another from within the Single Line Text command.
   a. True
   b. False
6. When you set the text style, which of the following text height settings will allow you to draw different heights of the same text style?
   a. .25
   b. 0.000
   c. 1
   d. 1000
   e. -
7. Which of the following Single Line Text options draws text between two clicked points and adjusts the text height so that it fits between the two points?
   a. Fit
   b. Align
   c. Justify
   d. Middle
   e. Style
8. Which of the following Single Line Text options draws text between two clicked points and condenses or expands the text to fit between the two points but does not change the text height?
   a. Fit
   b. Align
   c. Justify
   d. Middle
   e. Style
9. The justification letters MR stand for
   a. Middle, Right-justified
   b. Margin, Right-justified
   c. Midpoint, Left-justified
   d. Bottom, Right-justified
   e. Margin Release

10. Which of the following modifiers should be selected if you want the bottom of the line of text to end 1/2″ above and 1/2″ to the left of the lower right corner of the drawing limits?
    a. TL
    b. BR
    c. BL
    d. TR
    e. MR

Complete.

11. List three commands that can be used to edit text.

    ____________ ____________ ____________

12. List the command that allows you to change only the text contents.

    ____

13. List the command that allows you to change text height, contents, properties, justification, style, and origin.

    ____

14. List the command used to create a paragraph of text.

    ____

15. List the command that will spell check any line or paragraph of text you select.

    ____

16. Describe the difference between text style name and font name.

    ____

    ____

17. List the setting for Style height that must be used for AutoCAD to prompt you for height when Dtext is used.

    ____

18. Write the description for the abbreviations TL, ML, BR.

    ____

    ____

19. Describe how to quickly change all the text on a drawing done in the Standard style, TXT font, to the SIMPLEX font.

    ____

    ____

20. List the standard codes for the following.

    a. Degree symbol: ______________________

    b. Plus–minus symbol: ______________________

    c. Diameter symbol: ______________________

    d. Underscore: ______________________

    e. Overscore: ______________________

7 Block Diagrams

OBJECTIVES

After completing this chapter, you will be able to

- Use the following commands and settings to construct block diagrams using AutoCAD:

Edit Text	Move
Copy	New
Single Line Text	Rotate
Erase	SaveAs
Exit	Scale
Grid	Snap
Layer	2DSolid
Limits	Style
Line	Zoom
Lineweight	

- Edit an existing drawing.
- Correctly answer review questions describing the function of each of the preceding commands.

DRAWING DIAGRAMS

Block diagrams are widely used in business and industry. They are used to describe organizational structure, work flow, the way parts function, and for many other purposes. Figure 7–1 is a block diagram drawn using the sequence of steps to be presented in this chapter. You will be asked to draw this diagram and a similar diagram to complete this chapter. The method used to make this diagram is not necessarily the best or the only way to do it. However, it does introduce you to some useful commands, which will be more fully developed in later chapters.

Exercise 7–1: Drawing a Block Diagram

Step 1. Load AutoCAD and begin a new drawing.

Prompt	Response
The AutoCAD 2002 Today window appears:	*Click:* **the Create Drawings tab,** then *Click:* **Wizards**
	Click: **Advanced Setup**
Units screen with Decimal Selected appears:	*Click:* **the down arrow to the right of Precision: and change Precision: to 0.000**

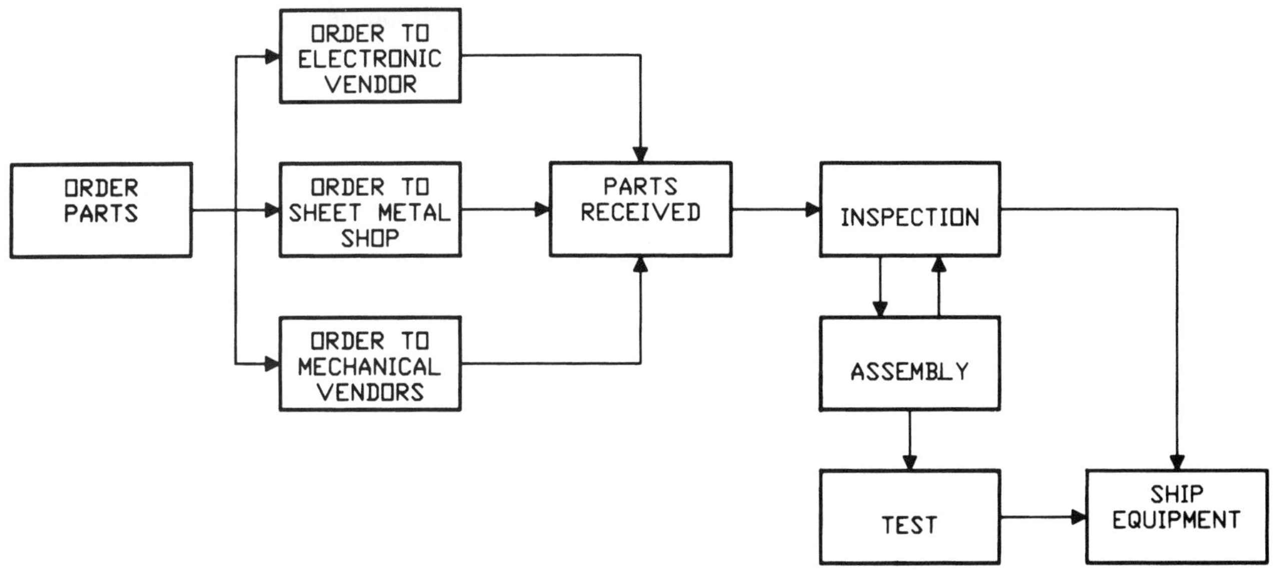

FIGURE 7–1
Block Diagram

Prompt	Response
	Click: **Next>**

Step 2. Set drawing limits.

The Advanced Setup dialog box is on the screen with Decimal Degrees for Angles	*Click:* **Next>**
Angle Measure with East checked appears:	*Click*: **Next>**
Angle Direction with Counter-Clockwise checked appears:	*Click*: **Next>**
Area with 12.000 × 9.000 appears:	*Highlight:* **12.000** in the Width: box (by double clicking it) and *Type:* **11**
	Highlight: **9.000** in the Length: box and *Type:* **8.5**.
	Click: **Finish**

This sets the drawing limits, which is the paper size on which you will draw.

Step 3. Select a GRID and a SNAP setting.

SNAP is the spacing on the display to which the crosshairs of the pointing device snap when the SNAP function is ON.

Prompt	Response
Command:	*Type:* **SN** ↵
Specify snap spacing or [ON/OFF/Aspect/Rotate/Style/Type] <0.500>:	*Type*: **.125** ↵

You have set the cursor (crosshairs or a box) to snap at every .125″.

Prompt	Response
Command:	*Type:* **GRID** ↵ (GRID is the pattern of dots displayed on your screen.)
Specify grid spacing (X) or [ON/OFF/Snap/Aspect] <0.500>:	*Type:* **.25** ↵

You now have a grid of .25″. If GRID is not visible, press the GRID function key, F7. Also turn SNAP ON by pressing F9. Turn ORTHO ON by pressing F8. This allows you to draw only horizontal or vertical lines and keeps them straight. SNAP, GRID, and ORTHO may also be turned on and off by clicking them at the bottom of your screen.

Note: Zoom-All may be picked from the pull-down View menu.

Prompt	Response
Command:	*Type:* **Z** ↵
[All/Center/Dynamic/Extents/Previous/Scale/Window] <real time>:	*Type:* **A** ↵

Step 4. Make layers on which to draw.

Note: Be sure to turn on the Object Properties toolbar.

Layers are similar to transparent overlays. You will need separate layers for the following:

- □ Boxes
- □ Connecting lines and arrows
- □ Lettering

Note: You must use the Zoom-All command periodically to see what your whole drawing looks like.

To do this, follow this sequence:

Prompt	Response
Command:	*Click:* **Layers** (from the Object Properties toolbar. Turn on the Object Properties toolbar if necessary.) (or *Type:* **LA** ↵)
The Layer Properties Manager dialog box appears:	*Click:* **New**
The name Layer1 appears highlighted:	*Type:* **THICK, THIN, LETTER**
	Click: **the word White for the LETTER layer**
The Select Color dialog box appears:	*Click:* **Green (Standard Colors)**
	Click: **OK**
The Layer Properties Manager dialog box appears (Figure 7–2):	*Click:* **on the word THIN and make that layer's color cyan**
	Click: **on the word THICK**
	Click: the word **Default** under the Lineweight column
The Lineweight dialog box appears:	*Click*: **0.40 mm** (so your boxes will be thicker than the text and connecting lines)
	Click: **OK**
The Layer Properties Manager dialog box appears:	With Layer THICK highlighted,
	Click: **Current** (at the top of the dialog box)

Note: Press F8 and F9 to turn ORTHO and SNAP ON so you can draw with ease and accuracy.

FIGURE 7–2
Assign Colors and Lineweights to the Layers

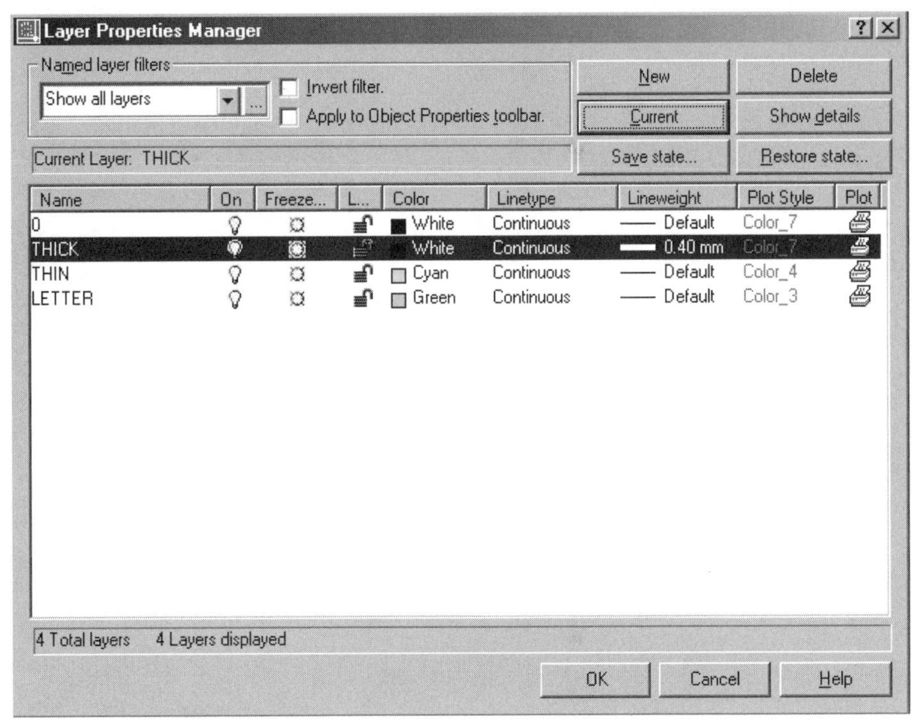

Click: **OK** (at the bottom of the dialog box)

Click: **LWT** (at the bottom of your screen) so lineweights will show on your drawing

You have now completed the setup.

Step 5. Draw the boxes and put lettering in them.

Note: Turn on the Draw toolbar if it is not on already and dock it on the left side of the screen.

Prompt	Response
Command:	*Click:* **Line** on the Draw menu or toolbar (or *Type:* **L** ↵)
Specify first point:	*Type:* **.75, 5.5** ↵ to locate **D1** (a point in the location shown in Figure 7–3; do not type the letter and number D1.)

Locate this point with the cursor (the crosshairs and pickbox controlled by the mouse) and click on that spot using the left button on the mouse.

Prompt	Response
To point:	Move the mouse 5 grids to the right and *Click:* **D2**
To point:	Move the mouse 3 grids down and *Click:* **D3**
To point:	Move the mouse 5 grids to the left and *Click:* **D4**
To point:	*Click: Type:* **C** and press ↵ to close the box

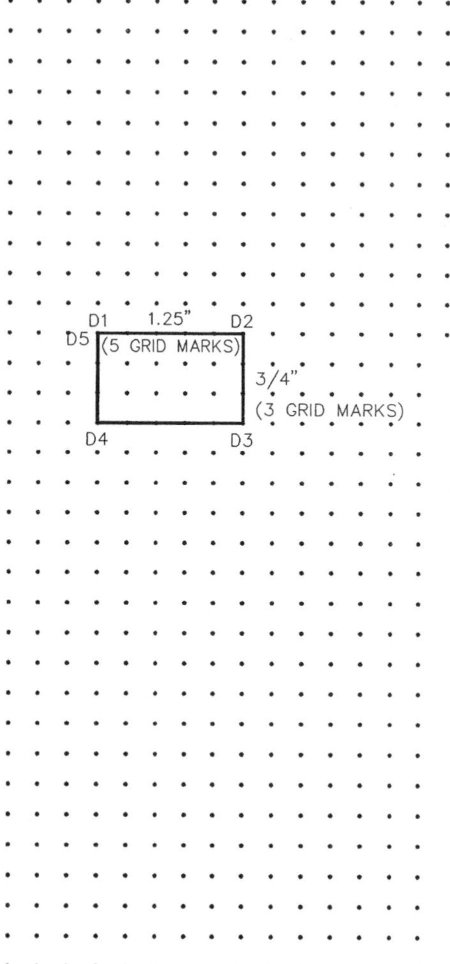

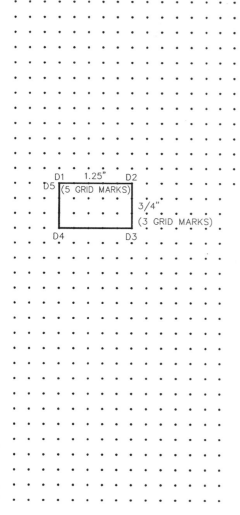

FIGURE 7–3
Click on the First Block

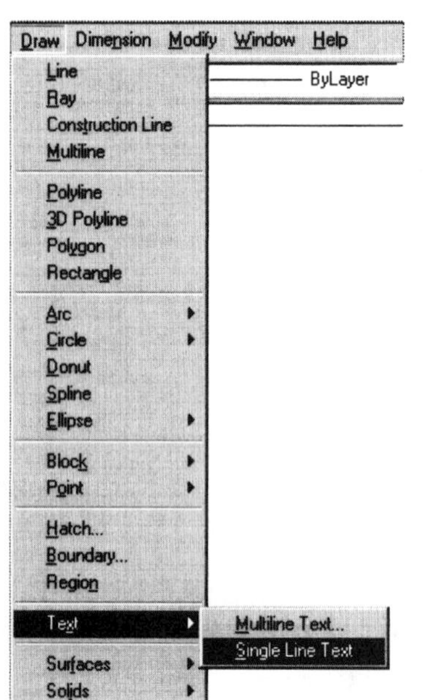

Now, depress the return button on the mouse to end the sequence, or press ↵ on the keyboard. You should have a white box.

Prompt	Response
Command:	*Click:* **Layer LETTER from the Object Properties toolbar, as shown in Figure 7–4, to make it current**
	Click: **Single Line Text** or *Type:* **DT** ↵
Specify start point of text or [Justify/Style]:	*Type:* **C** ↵
Specify center point of text:	*Click:* **D1** (Click center of box ¼″ from top, as in Figure 7–5.)
Specify height <0.2000>:	*Type:* **.1** ↵
Specify rotation angle of text <0>:	↵ (or 0 if the number shown in the brackets is not 0)
Enter text:	*Type:* **ORDER** ↵ (Be sure Caps Lock is ON.)
Text:	*Type:* **PARTS** ↵
Text:	*Type:* **XXX** ↵ (then press ↵ again)

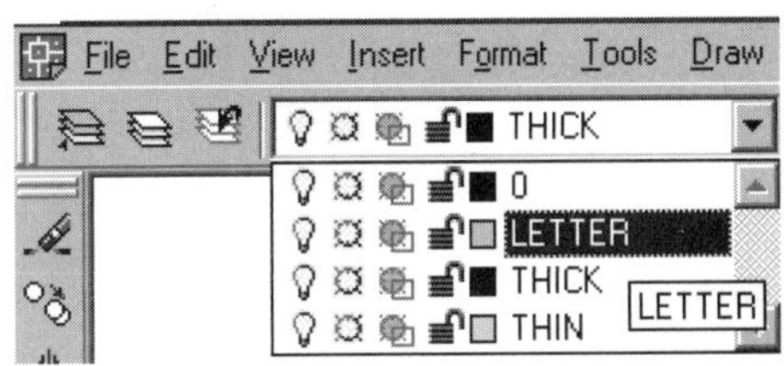

FIGURE 7–4
Layer List from the Object Properties Toolbar

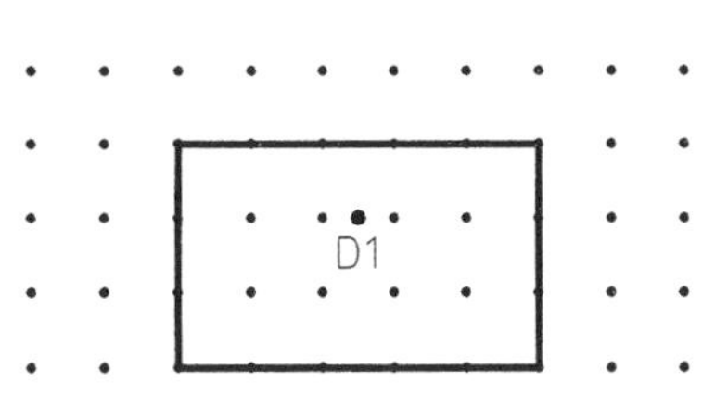

FIGURE 7–5
Locate Text

ORDER
PARTS
XXX

FIGURE 7–6
Lettering for the First Block

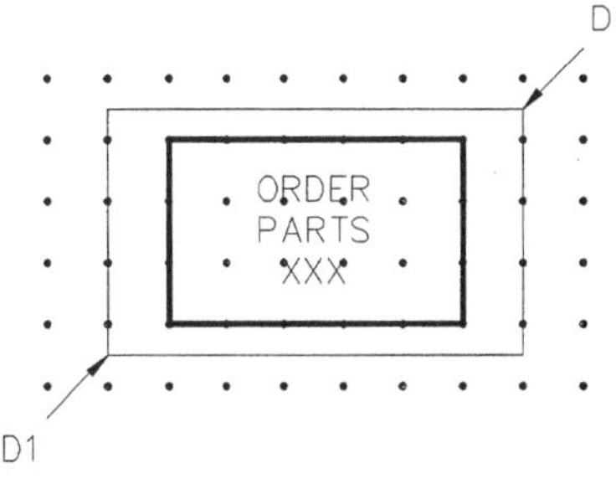

FIGURE 7–7
Window the Block to Copy

You now have three lines of text that should look like Figure 7–6. The XXX will be used later.

Note: Turn ON the Modify toolbar and dock it on the right side of the screen if it is not ON already.

Prompt	Response
Command:	*Type:* **CP** ↵ (or *Select:* **Copy** from the Modify menu or toolbar)
Select objects:	*Click:* **D1** (as in Figure 7–7)
Specify opposite corner:	*Click:* **D2** (as in Figure 7–7)
Select objects:	↵ (or return button on the mouse)
Specify base point or displacement or [Multiple]:	*Type:* **M** ↵
Specify base point:	*Click:* **D1** (Figure 7–8)
Second point of displacement or <use first point as displacement>:	*Click:* **D2** (Notice that there are three grid marks between boxes.)
Second point of displacement or <use first point as displacement>:	*Click:* **D3**

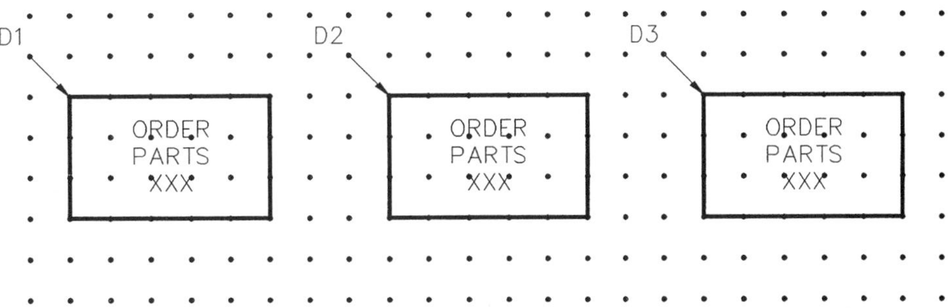

FIGURE 7–8
Multiple Copy

Prompt	Response
Second point of displacement:	*Click:* **D4, D5, D6, D7, D8, D9 (not shown).** (Place all boxes as shown in Figure 7–9.)

Note: Be sure Ortho (F8) is OFF when you copy boxes that are not lined up vertically or horizontally with the box you are copying.

Place boxes where you want them (¾″ apart horizontally and ½″ apart vertically). If you make a mistake and wish to move a box, select Move, window the box you want to move, and click the corner of the box in its original location and where you want to move it to. Press ↵.

Step 6. Change lettering in the five boxes on the left side of the drawing using the CHANGE or DDEDIT (Edit Text, from Chapter 6) commands.

Prompt	Response
Command:	*Type:* **CHANGE**
Select objects:	*Click:* **the lines ORDER,PARTS,XXX** (in the second box (Figure 7–9, D1, D2, D3))↵

You may click anywhere on the word. You may have to place SNAP in the OFF position to do this easily. Be sure to put SNAP ON again before you draw or move any lines, arrows or boxes.

Prompt	Response
Specify change point or [Properties]:	↵
Specify new text insertion point <no change>:	↵ (Do not change the insertion point.)
Enter new text style <Standard>:	↵ (Standard is the style desired.)
Specify new height <0.100>:	↵ (This is the correct height.)
Specify new rotation angle <0>:	↵ (0 is the correct angle.)
Enter new text <ORDER>:	*Type:* **ORDER TO** ↵
Specify new text insertion point <no change>:	↵ (This is so you can change the second line, PARTS, to ELECTRONIC.)

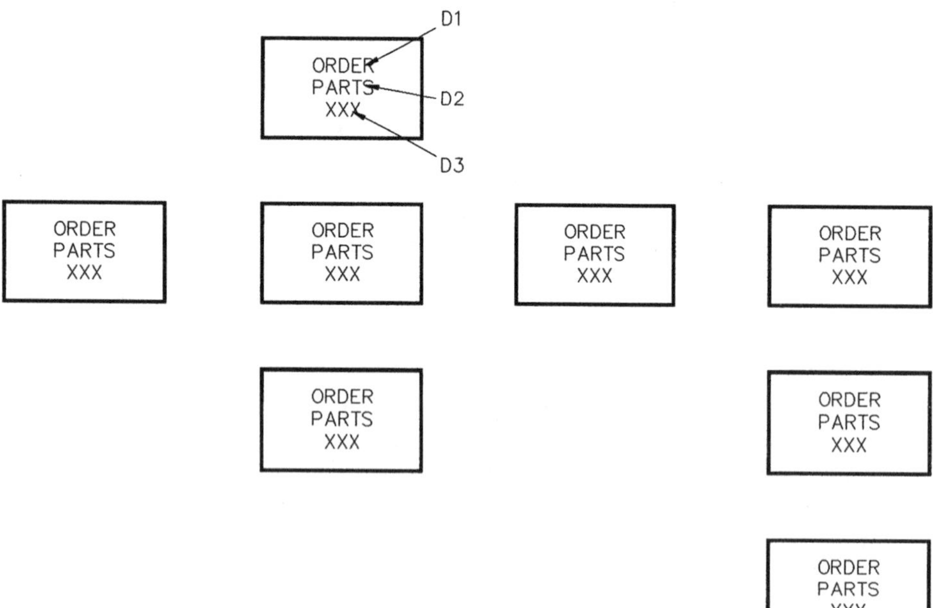

FIGURE 7–9
Change Lettering

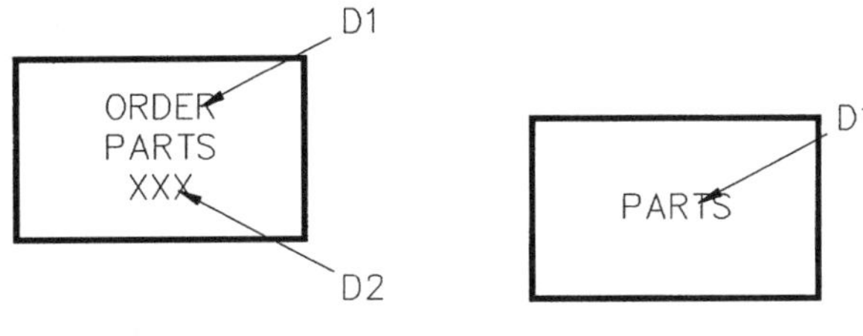

FIGURE 7–10 FIGURE 7–11

Prompts will be the same until you get to: new text <PARTS>. Just press ↵ quickly five times to get to the prompt <PARTS>; then type ELECTRONIC. Continue the same procedure for all lines of lettering in the first five boxes as shown in Figure 7–12. Use Erase as described in Step 7 to get rid of any line of lettering that is not needed. After the lettering has been completed, proceed to the next step.

Step 7. Change lettering in the other four boxes using the Erase and Properties. . . commands.

Prompt	Response
Command:	*Type:* **E** ↵
Select objects:	*Click:* **the words ORDER and XXX** (Figure 7–10)
Select objects:	↵
Command:	*Click*: **any letter or the word PARTS** (Figure 7–11)
Command:	*Select:* **Properties. . .** (from the Modify menu)
The Properties Text dialog box appears:	*Highlight*: **PARTS** (in the Contents line) *Type:* **INSPECTION**
	Click: **the X in the upper right corner to close**

The Properties dialog box allows you to change:

All the text selected
Any part of the text selected by moving your cursor to the point where the change will occur and using the Backspace or Delete keys to delete what you do not want and typing what you do want
The Color. . . of the text
The Layer. . . on which the text was created
The Linetype. . . of the text
The Origin of the justification point of the text
All the other features of the text STYLE setting such as Height and Rotation

Change the lettering in the remaining three boxes in a similar manner or use ddedit (*Click:* **Modify** on the menu bar, **Object Text Edit. . .**, or *Type:* **ED** ↵) to edit text only.

Step 8. Draw the lines connecting the boxes.

Prompt	Response
Command:	**Set Layer THIN current.**
Command:	*Select:* **Line or** *Type:* **L** ↵
Specify first point:	*Click:* **D1** (from Figure 7–12. Be sure SNAP and ORTHO (keys F8 and F9) are ON.)

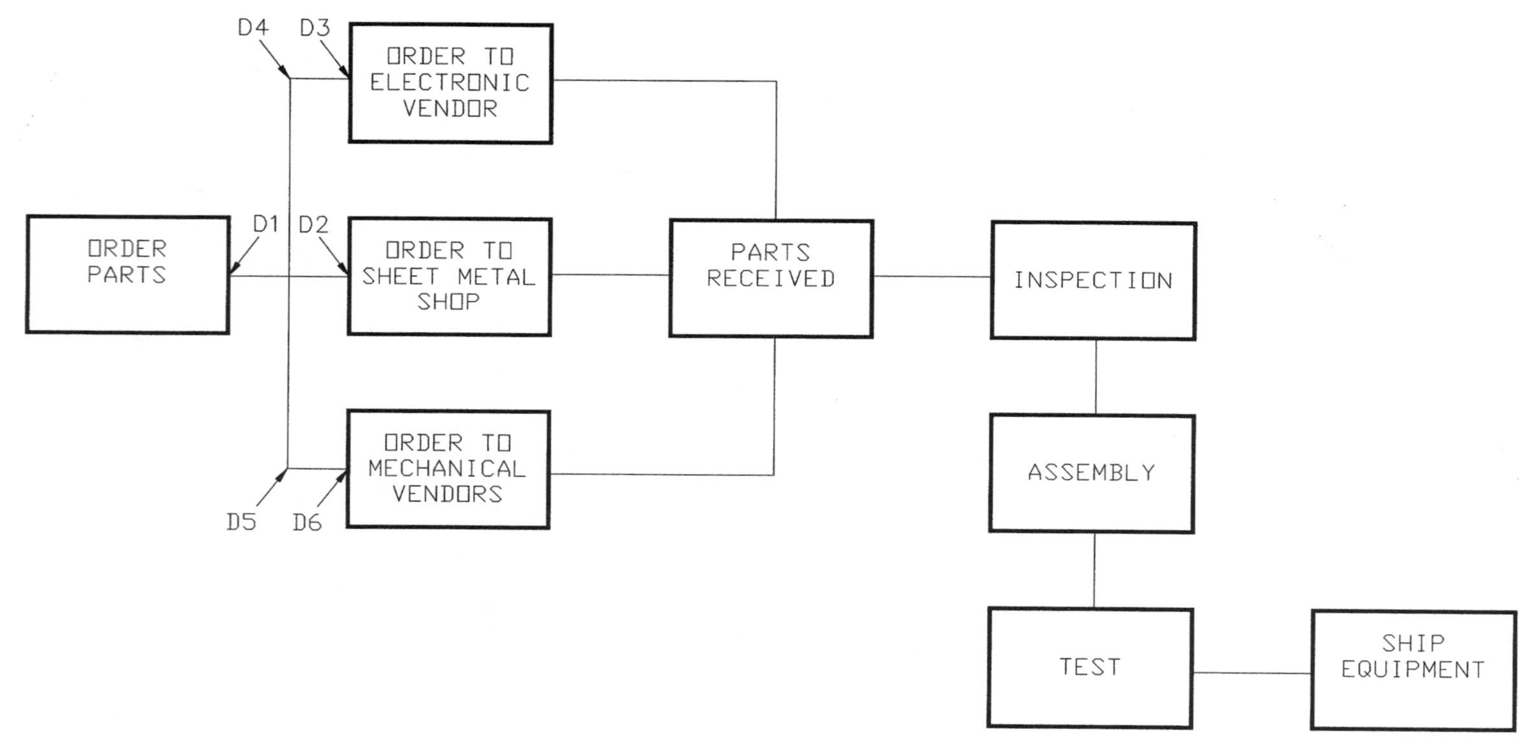

FIGURE 7–12
Drawing Connecting Lines

Prompt	Response
Specify next point or [Undo]:	*Click:* **D2**
Specify next point or [Undo]:	↵ (or the return button on the mouse)

The command is now completed.

Prompt	Response
Command:	*Press*: the Return button on the mouse. The right-click menu is activated.
Specify first point:	*Click*: **Repeat LINE** *Click:* **D3, D4, D5, D6** *Right Click*:
The Right Click menu appears:	*Click*: Enter
Command:	*Right Click*: *Click*: **Repeat LINE**
Specify first point:	**Now draw the rest of the lines; be sure to press ↵ after you have completed each line.**

Step 9. Now, draw the arrows.

Note: If you make a line in the wrong place, select Undo on the Standard Toolbar (or type U ↵ on the keyboard) and the incorrect line will disappear. If you continue to select Undo, all lines back to the start of the command will disappear. If you accidentally undo too much, type REDO ↵ from the keyboard or select it from the Standard Toolbar to replace an undone line.

Note: Be sure SNAP (F9) is ON.

Draw one in an open area beneath the drawing and copy it several times.

A good arrowhead for this size drawing is ⅛″. Change the grid to ⅛″ (.125″); draw the arrowhead ¼″ and shrink it to fit. Follow this sequence:

Prompt	Response
Command:	*Type:* **GRID** ↵
Specify grid spacing (X) or [ON/OFF/SNAP/Aspect]<0.250>:	*Type:* **.125** ↵
Command:	*Select:* **Zoom-Window** (from the View Menu) (or *Type:* **Z** ↵)

View commands are provided at both the menu bar and the Standard Toolbar.

Prompt	Response
Specify corner of window, enter a scale factor, or [All/Center/Dynamic/Extents/Previous /Scale/Window/ <real time>:	*Click:* **D1** (Figure 7–13)
Specify opposite corner:	*Click:* **D2**

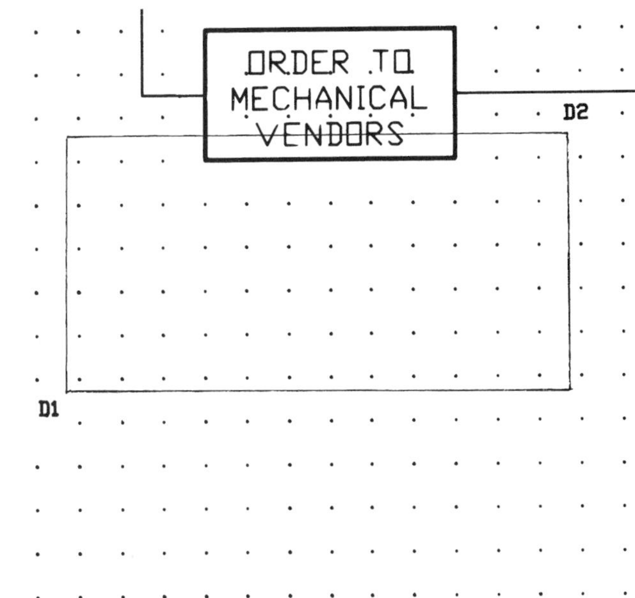

FIGURE 7–13
Click on a Window for the Arrowheads

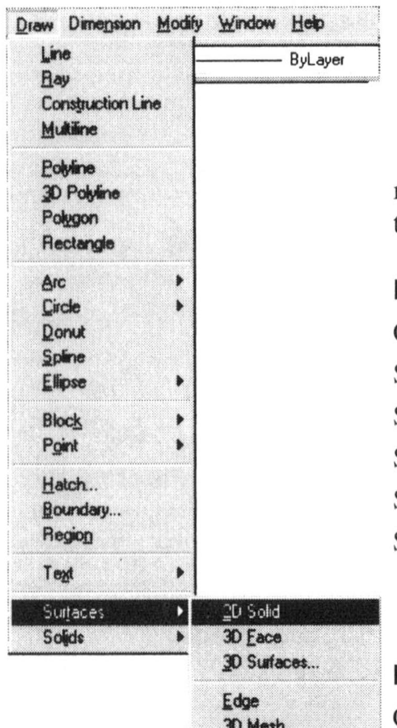

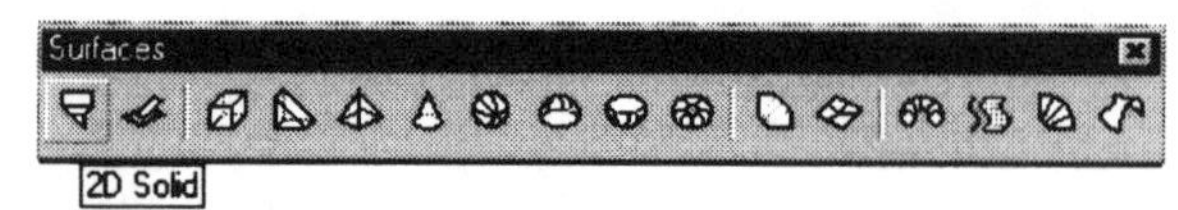

You should now have a large ⅛″ grid on your screen. Experiment with the Pan command at this point. Pan allows you to move the display area from one point to another at the same scale. You may also use the scroll bars to PAN.

Prompt	Response
Command:	*Select:* **2D Solid** or *Type*: **SO** ↵
Specify first point:	*Click:* **D1** (Figure 7–14)
Specify second point:	*Click:* **D2**
Specify third point:	*Click:* **D3**
Specify fourth point or <exit>:	↵ (Do not go to fourth point.)
Specify third point:	↵

You should have a solid ¼″ arrowhead. Now, reduce it to ⅛″:

Prompt	Response
Command:	*Select:* **Scale** from the Modify menu or toolbar (or *Type:* **SC** ↵)
Select objects:	*Click:* **on any point on the outside edge of the arrow**
Select objects:	↵
Specify base point:	*Click:* **D1** (the tip of the arrowhead as shown in Figure 7–15)
Specify scale factor or [Reference]:	*Type:* **.5** ↵ (meaning 50% of the original size)

You should now have a ⅛″ arrowhead. Three versions of it will be needed: pointing up, down, and to the right. Use Rotate on the Modify menu to do that. First, copy the arrow twice.

Prompt	Response
Command:	*Select:* **Copy** from the Modify menu or toolbar (or *Type:* **CP** ↵)
Select objects:	**Click the arrowhead D1** (Figure 7–16).

You may need to take SNAP-F9-OFF to click it. Put SNAP back ON after selecting the object.

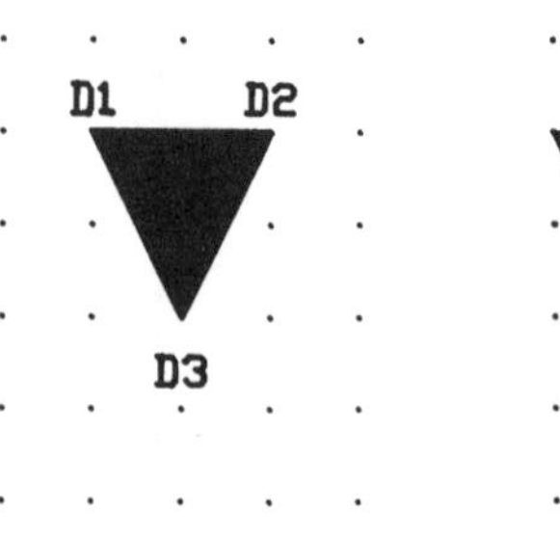

FIGURE 7–14
Make Arrowheads

FIGURE 7–15
Reduce the Arrowhead to ⅛″

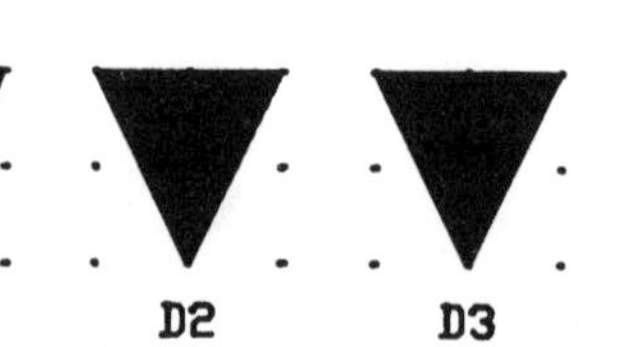

FIGURE 7–16
Copy the Arrowheads and Rotate the Copies

Prompt	Response
Select objects:	↵
Specify base point or displacement, or [Multiple]:	*Type:* **M** ↵
Specify base point:	*Click:* **D1** (tip of the arrowhead, Figure 7–16)
Specify second point of displacement or <use first as displacement>:	*Click:* **D2, D3** (Figure 7–16) ↵
Command:	*Select:* **Rotate** from the Modify menu or toolbar (or *Type:* **RO** ↵)
Select objects:	*Click:* **D2** (Click second arrowhead, Figure 7–16.)
Select objects:	↵
Specify base point:	*Click:* **D2** (Click tip of the second arrowhead.)
Specify rotation angle or [Reference]:	*Type:* **180** ↵
Command:	↵ (You may activate the command you used previously by pressing ↵, then *Click*: **Repeat ROTATE.**)
Select objects:	*Click:* **D3**
Select objects:	↵
Specify base point:	Click: **D3**
Specify rotation angle or [Reference]:	*Type:* **90** ↵

Return to the complete drawing by using the Zoom-All command. You should now have three arrowheads that may be copied onto the connecting lines, as shown in Figure 7–17. Use the Copy command and the Multiple subcommand when appropriate for speed. Be sure SNAP is ON when you select and place arrowheads.

FIGURE 7–17
Complete Block Diagram

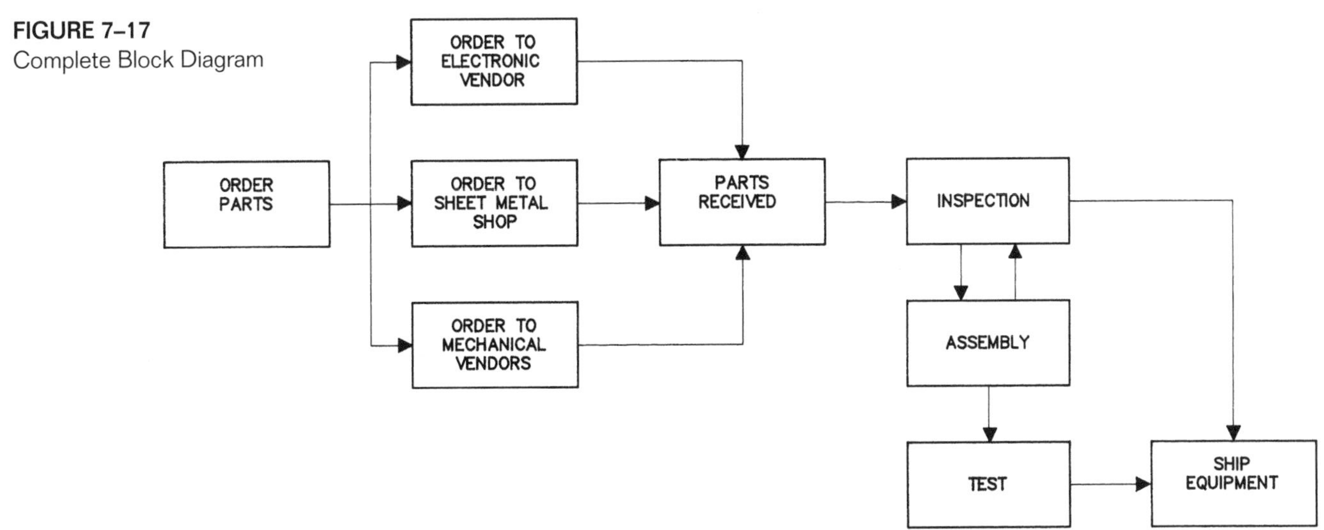

Note: Later-Release Users—The commands Erase, Move, and Copy, and other commands have the immediate-selection feature. They also have a feature allowing a selection window to be created when no entity is digitized. Moving to the right creates a selection window. Moving to the left creates a crossing window. A selection window requires that any drawing entity be contained entirely within the window. A crossing window selects any entity contained entirely within or crossed by the window.

Step 10. Clean up the drawing.

After you place the arrowheads, clean up the drawing using Erase, Erase-WINDOW from the Modify menu, and Redraw from the View menu. (You can also use Redraw by typing R ↵ from the keyboard or pressing F7 twice.)

Step 11. Change the appearance of the lettering on your drawing and draw your name with another style of lettering.

The lettering you presently have on your block diagram is in the TXT font. The *font* of a lettering *style* determines the appearance of the lettering on the drawing. The style is simply a *name* that keeps the fonts separate from each other. Let's look at a description of letter style and font.

STYLE

The *style* is the name given to all the lettering drawn on the drawing while that style is current. The default style has the name Standard. The lettering on your drawing has been typed in that style. If you want to type with a different style, you must give AutoCAD a name for the new style. That name can be anything (Example: A,B,C or 1,2,3 or MY-NAME, BOX-NAME). You give AutoCAD the name when you use the Style setting as described in the following examples.

FONT

Note: The txt font was never meant to be used on formal drawings. It looks similar to a stencil and must **always** be changed. This font regenerates faster than other fonts but should be changed before plotting.

The *font* of a lettering style determines its appearance. All fonts that exist in your AutoCAD program have specific names. They may be found in the Select Font File dialog box. Now let's put *style* and *font* together by changing your TXT font to the SIMPLEX font and creating a new style with a different font.

Change the TXT Font to the SIMPLEX Font

So that you may see clearly what happens when a font is changed, Zoom a window around one of your boxes to get a large display of the lettering inside and then follow this procedure:

Prompt	Response
Command:	*Type:* **ST** ↵
The Text Style dialog box appears:	*Click:* **Simplex** (in the Font Name: list box)
	Click: **Apply**
	Click: **Close**

Create a New Style with a Different Font and Draw Your Name With It

Prompt	Response
Command:	*Type:* **ST** ↵
	Click: **New. . .**
The New Text Style dialog box appears with a name that AutoCAD assigns, style1:	*Type:* **MY-NAME to name the style**
	Click: **OK**
The Text Style dialog box appears:	*Select:* **Complex in the Font Name: list**
	Click: **Apply**
	Click: **Close**

You now have two styles that have been defined on your drawing, Standard and MY-NAME.

Prompt	Response
Command:	*Type:* **DT** ↵
_dtext Justify/Style/<Start point>:	*Type:* **R** ↵

End point: (Click on a point .5″ up and .5″ to the left of the lower right corner of the limits of your drawing. Accept the defaults until Text: appears and *Type:* **YOUR NAME** ↵↵.)

Step 12. Save your drawing and Exit from the AutoCAD Program.

Save your drawing onto both the hard disk and your own floppy disk. Having copies in two different places is an absolute necessity as insurance in case one of them is damaged. To save a drawing, follow this procedure.

Place a formatted floppy disk in the A: drive.

Prompt	Response
Command:	*Select:* **SaveAs. . .**
_save as The Save Drawing As dialog box appears:	*Type:* **A: EX7-1(your initials)** ↵ (Choose a name of 255 characters or less, then click the OK button.)

This saves the drawing on the floppy disk, which is in the A drive.

Prompt	Response
Command:	*Select:* **Exit** (or *Type:* **QUIT** ↵)

Using Exit or QUIT after your SaveAs will discard all changes since the last Save. SAVE may also be used to save a drawing on the drive from which it was activated. Using SAVE does not prompt you with the drawing name, which is sometimes useful.

Be sure to Exit AutoCAD before turning your computer OFF to avoid creating "lost clusters"—scattered bits of information on the hard disk. These lost clusters can take up a great deal of space over a period of time.

EXERCISES

EXERCISE 7–1. If you have not already done so, draw the block diagram shown as Figure 7–17. Do it exactly as described in this chapter. Figure 7–17 shows the final drawing.

EXERCISE 7–2. Make a block diagram from the sketch shown in Figure 7–18. Put it on a horizontal A-size sheet (8 ½″ × 11″). Use the same colors, sizes, lines, and lettering as you used on your first block diagram.

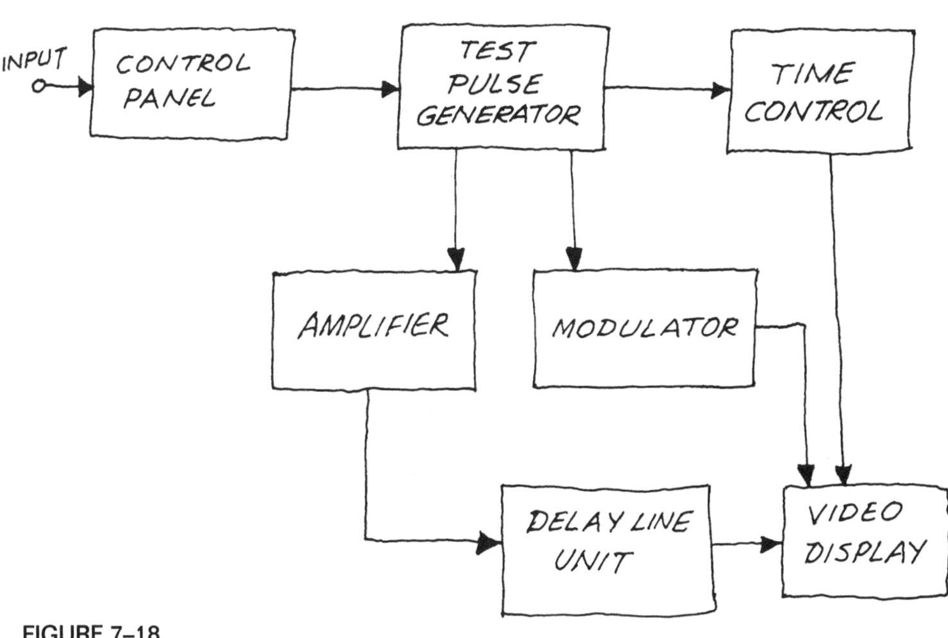

FIGURE 7–18
Exercise 7–2

Name this drawing EX7-2(your initials) (Example: EX7-2MK).

Suggestion: Copy EX7-1MK from your floppy disk to a folder on the hard drive using Windows Explorer and rename the copy EX7-2MK.

OR

Open drawing EX7-1(your initials) and save it as EX7-2(your initials), then Open EX7-2.

The original EX7-1MK remains on the A: drive in its original form. Draw the ⅛″-diameter input circle using Circle-Center, Diameter from the Draw menu on the menu bar and follow the prompts. Use the SIMPLEX font.

EXERCISE 7–3. Make an AutoCAD drawing of the block diagram in the illustration in Figure 7–19. Spaces and sizes of blocks should be approximately the same as shown. Lettering should be .08″ high using the SIMPLEX font. Place your name in the lower right corner. Drawing Limits should be 8.5″ × 11″.

The Drawing Limits command is used to control the size of your drawing. This command is found on the Format menu. To set limits for this drawing do the following:

Prompt	**Response**
Command:	*Select:* **Drawing Limits**
Lower left corner <0,0>:	↵
Upper right corner <12,9>: (or another default value)	*Type:* **8.5,11** ↵ (This gives you a vertical page.)

Use Circle-Center, Diameter from the Draw menu for input circles. (⅛″ (.125) diameter for the small circle, ⅜″ (.375) for the larger circle.) Use Donut (*Type:* **DO** ↵) for the dots (the solid circles). Use a 0 inside diameter and a ⅛″ (.125) outside diameter.

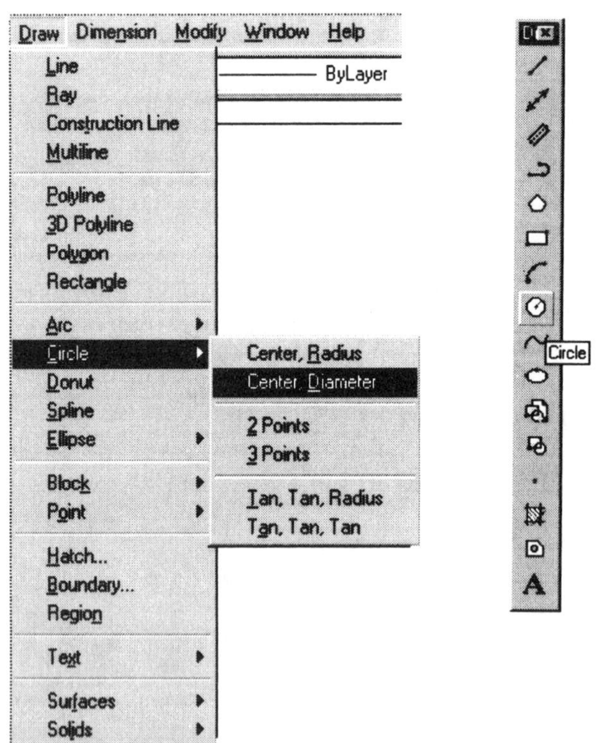

FIGURE 7–19
Exercise 7–3

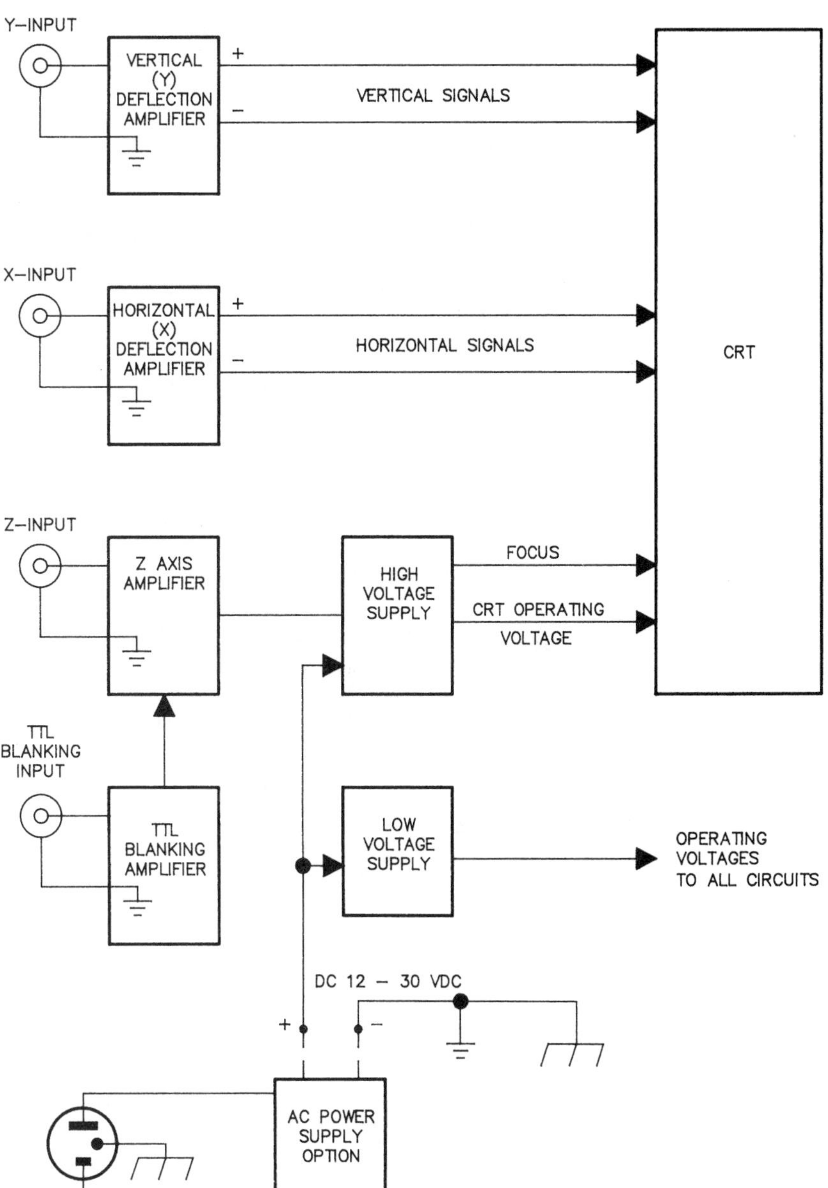

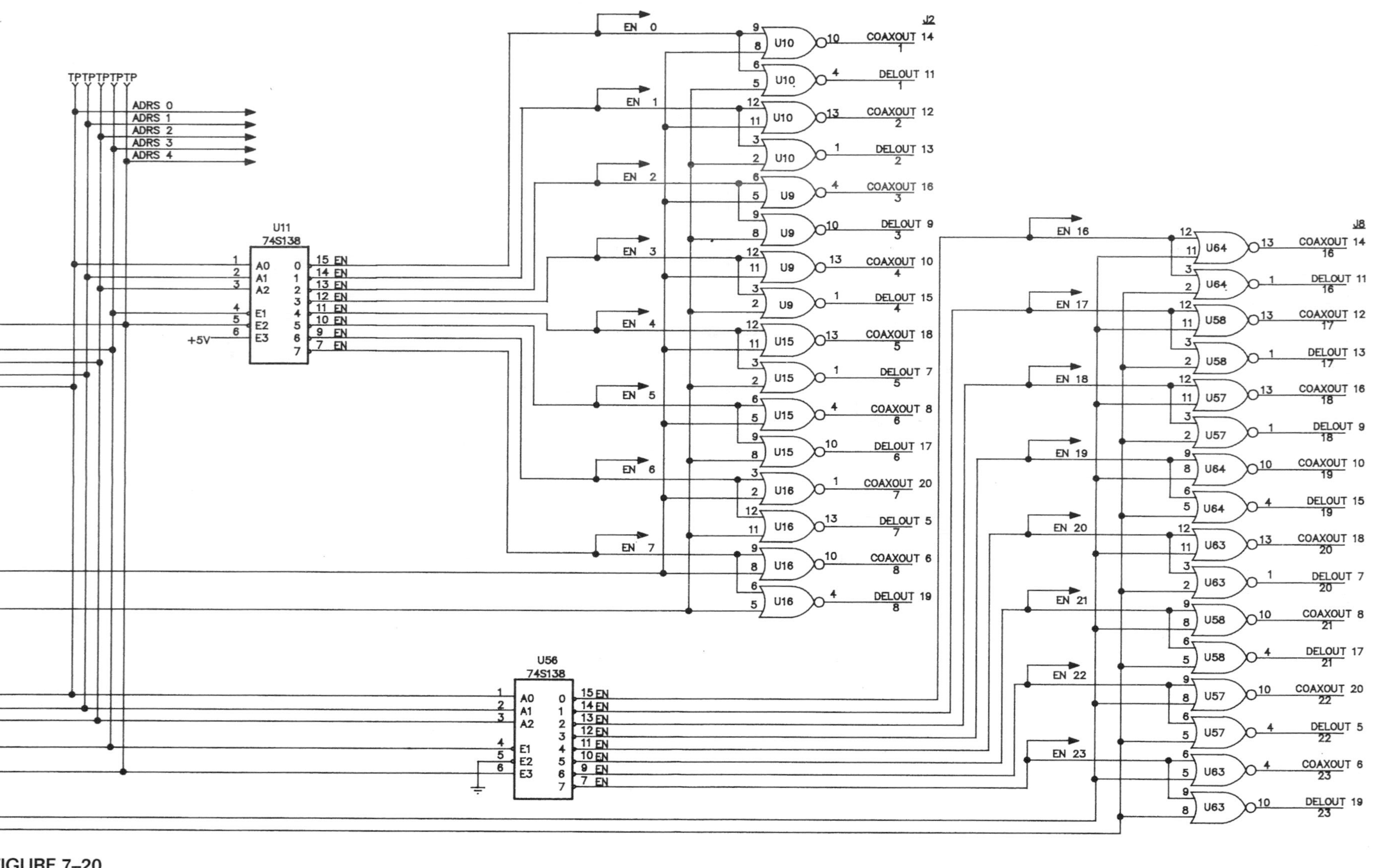

FIGURE 7–20
Exercise 7–4

EXERCISE 7–4. Make an AutoCAD drawing of the block diagram shown in Figure 7–20. Spaces, arcs, circles, and blocks should be approximately the size shown. Lettering should be approximately .05″ high using SIMPLEX font. Limits should be 17″ × 11″. Place your name in the lower right corner.

REVIEW QUESTIONS

(It is suggested that you complete this test at the computer with Figure 7–17 displayed.)

Circle the best answer.

1. What determines the paper size?
   a. Grid
   b. Paper
   c. Drawing Limits
   d. Settings
   e. Utility
2. If you want a SNAP setting of ½″, what is the correct response to the prompt Specify snap spacing or [ON/OFF/aspect/rotate/style/type] <0.125>:
   a. .5
   b. 1–2
   c. 2
   d. One-half
   e. .05 in.
3. If you have a grid setting of ¼″ (.25) and you wish to change it to ⅛″, you simply *Type*: **GRID** ↵, then *Type*: **.125** ↵.
   a. True
   b. False
4. Two layers can have the same color.
   a. True
   b. False
5. The function key F2 does which of the following when you are using AutoCAD?
   a. Sets SNAP ON or OFF
   b. Flips the screen from the text display to the graphics display
   c. Sets the GRID ON or OFF
   d. Sets ORTHO ON or OFF
   e. Sets coordinates ON or OFF
6. The function key F7 does which of the following?
   a. Sets SNAP ON or OFF
   b. Flips the screen from the text display to the graphics display
   c. Sets the GRID ON or OFF
   d. Sets ORTHO ON or OFF
   e. Sets coordinates ON or OFF
7. The function key F9 does which of the following?
   a. Sets SNAP ON or OFF
   b. Flips the screen from the text display to the graphics display
   c. Sets the GRID ON or OFF
   d. Sets ORTHO ON or OFF
   e. Sets coordinates ON or OFF
8. The function key F8 does which of the following?
   a. Sets SNAP ON or OFF
   b. Flips the screen from the text display to the graphics display
   c. Sets the GRID ON or OFF
   d. Sets ORTHO ON or OFF
   e. Sets coordinates ON or OFF
9. If the Enter key is pressed immediately after a centered line of Single Line Text has been entered on the drawing, another centered line of text may be entered after the prompt "Text."
   a. True
   b. False

10. When the Copy command is used with a selection window (not a crossing window),
    a. Everything the window touches is copied.
    b. Everything entirely within the window is copied.
    c. Only the symbols or blocks within the window are copied.
    d. Everything within the screen is copied.
    e. Everything within the window except text is copied.
11. A response of 90 to the Rotate prompt "Specify rotation angle or [Reference]" will move the arrow in Figure 7–21 to which of the following positions?

FIGURE 7–21
Question 11

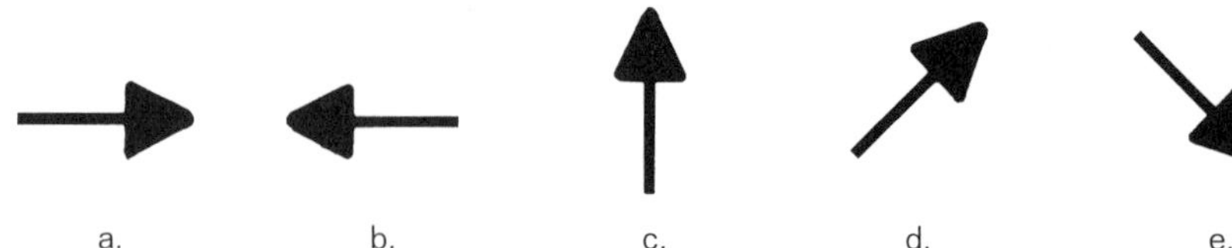

12. The Copy-Multiple command will allow how many copies to be made?
    a. One
    b. Up to five
    c. Up to 10
    d. Up to 20
    e. Unlimited
13. The Scale command can be used to do which of the following?
    a. To enlarge only
    b. To reduce only
    c. To enlarge and reduce
    d. To set the drawing units
    e. None of these
14. When a 2 is entered after the Scale prompt "Specify scale factor or [reference]:," what happens?
    a. The selected object is reduced to ½.
    b. The selected object is enlarged 2 times.
    c. Another object may be selected.
    d. A second scale is described for the entire drawing.
    e. Two images of the selected object appear.
15. Using SaveAs instead of Save has which of the following advantages?
    a. Makes a backup file
    b. Discards all changes since the last Save
    c. Allows the drawing to be saved in two places
    d. Allows an erased object to be regained
    e. Saves space on the disk

Complete.

16. Describe how Drawing Limits may be used to set a vertical and a horizontal 11″ × 8 ½″ drawing area.

    vertical ______________________________

    horizontal ______________________________

17. How is the GRID turned ON and OFF without using a function key?

    ____

18. List three choices for the text position that the Dtext command allows.

    a. ______________________________

    b. ______________________________

    c. ______________________________

19. Which command can be used to enlarge a part to 2 times its original size?

    ____

    ____

20. How many layers may be set current at the same time?

8 Plotting

OBJECTIVES

After completing this chapter, you will be able to

- □ Plot drawings to scale or to fit on standard sheets.
- □ Plot drawings for use on the Internet.

This chapter describes the parts of the Plot dialog box that are used to plot on either a printer or a plotter.

- □ Plot multiple drawings from the same screen.
- □ Save plot settings as a plot style to be used later.

PLOTTING AND PRINTING

Exercise 8–1: Making a Plot of Drawing EX7-1(your initials)

The following is a hands-on, step-by-step procedure to make a plot of drawing EX7-1(your initials). To begin, turn on the computer and start the AutoCAD program.

On Your Own

Step 1. Open drawing EX7-1(your initials) on the hard drive so it is displayed on the screen. Remember, if your drawing has been saved on a floppy disk in the A: drive, open it from the floppy disk and save it on the hard drive.

In the Open Drawings tab of the AutoCAD 2002 Today window, you can use four different methods for locating and opening a file: Most Recently Used, History by Date, History by Filename, and History by Location. Each method shows a file history list of the most recently used drawings. After selecting a method for locating a file, hold your mouse over the drawing names in the history list to view the complete drive and folder where the drawing is located and to see a thumbnail preview.

Step 2. Click the Plot command from the Standard Toolbar, or pick Plot... under File on the menu bar, *Type:* **PLOT ↵ , or hold down the control key and** *Press:* **P. The Plot dialog box (Figure 8–1) appears with the Plot Device tab selected.** (If the Plot Device tab is not selected, select it.)

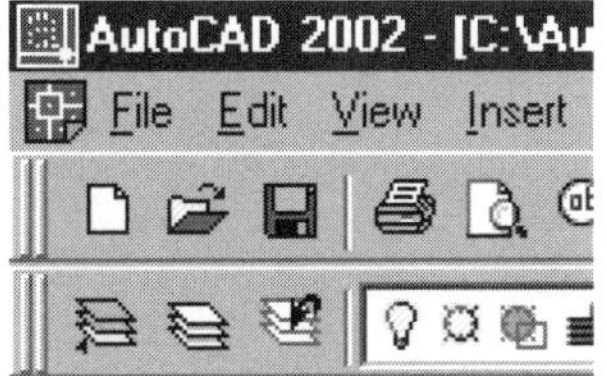

Plotter Configuration

The Name: line in the Plotter configuration area shows the current plot device. When the down arrow is picked, a list appears that shows all the plot devices configured to your computer. The device in the list box that is highlighted is the current plot device. You can select the printing or plotting device that you want to use. Each time you select a different device, the settings change to the default for that device.

FIGURE 8–1
Plot Dialog Box with Plot Device Tab Selected

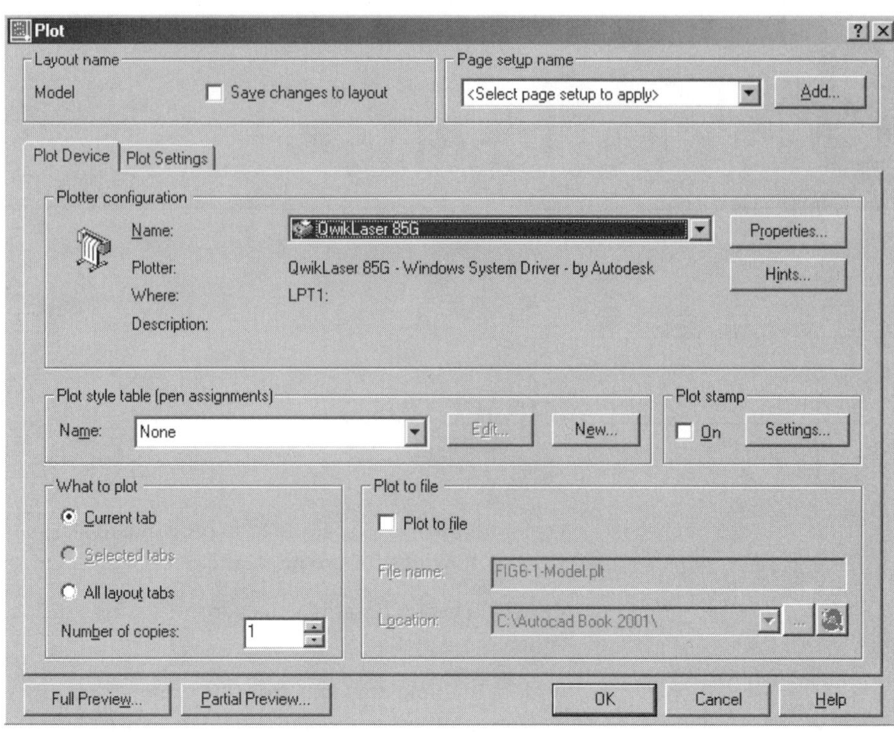

FIGURE 8–2
Printer Properties Dialog Box

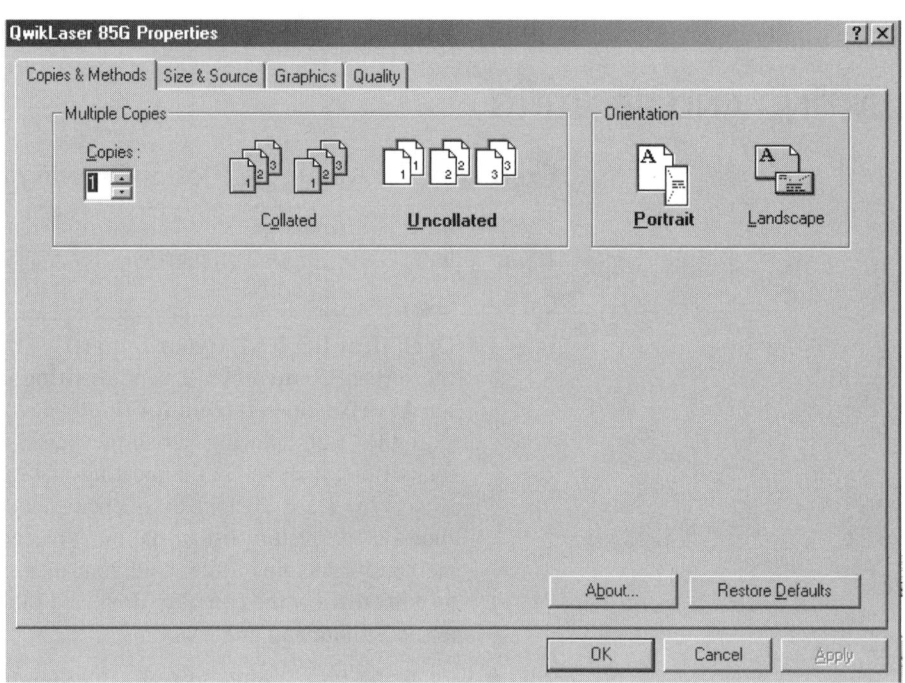

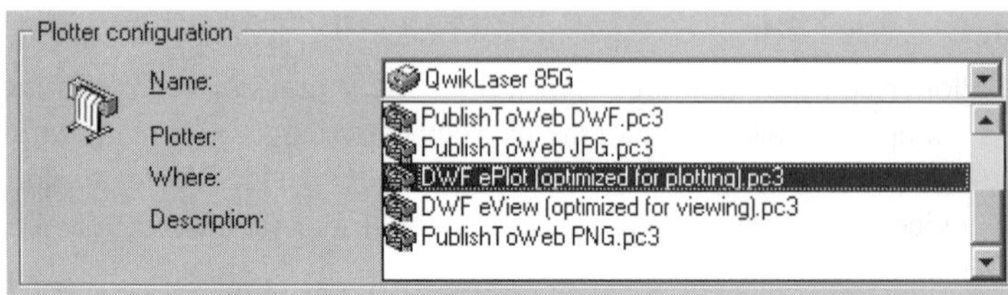

Step 3. *Click:* **the Properties…** button. The Plot Configuration Editor appears with the Device and Document Settings tab selected.
Click: **Custom Properties…** The Printer Properties Dialog Box (Figure 8–2) for that printer appears: *Click:* **The best quality for that printer,** then *Click:* **OK,** two or three times to return to the Plot dialog box. All Printer Properties dialog boxes are different, so you may have to examine other tabs to select the best quality for your plot.

Plot Style Table (pen assignments)

The plot style table allows you to select from a wide range of pen widths, screens (so areas can be grayed out but still appear on the drawing), line endings, and other features. Figure 8–3 shows the acad.ctb table being selected. After this table is selected, Edit… is clicked to display the Plot Style Table Editor (Figure 8–4). In this chapter only the basics of plotting are presented, so none of this will apply, but when you need a special type of plot, remember how to get to these dialog boxes. They give you a great number of options for determining how your final plot will appear.

Step 4. Click None in the Plot style table (pen assignments) list so it appears as shown in Figure 8–1.

What to Plot

In this area you can tell AutoCAD to plot only the current tab (the drawing you have just called up) or additional tabs. You will plot other tabs in a later chapter. For example, you will have a floor plan that shows dimensions on one tab, furniture on another, and another that shows only the floor plan without dimensions or furniture. In this chapter you will plot only the current tab and only one copy.

Plot to File

The Plot to file area, when Plot to file is checked, allows you to plot your drawings to a file on any drive and in any folder you select. A plot file is used to plot drawings on certain plot stations that do not accept a drawing file. They may also be used to insert drawings into other software programs that do not accept drawing files. Plot files are given the extension .plt. If you plotted this drawing to a file, the complete filename would be EX7-1.plt. Most likely you will not be plotting drawings to a file.

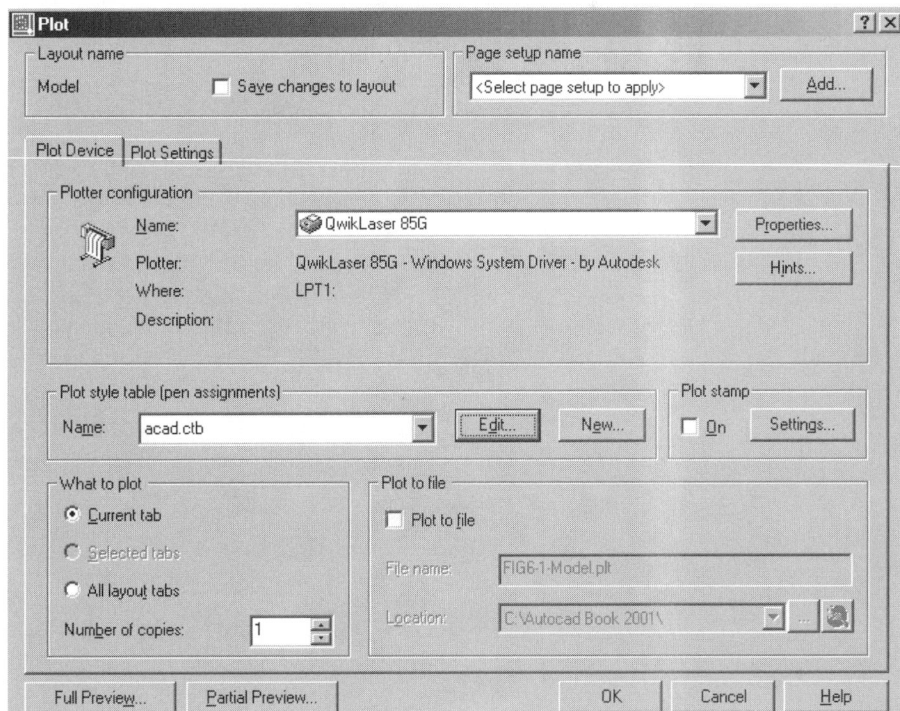

FIGURE 8–3
Selecting the acad.ctb Plot Style Table

FIGURE 8–4
Plot Style Table Editor

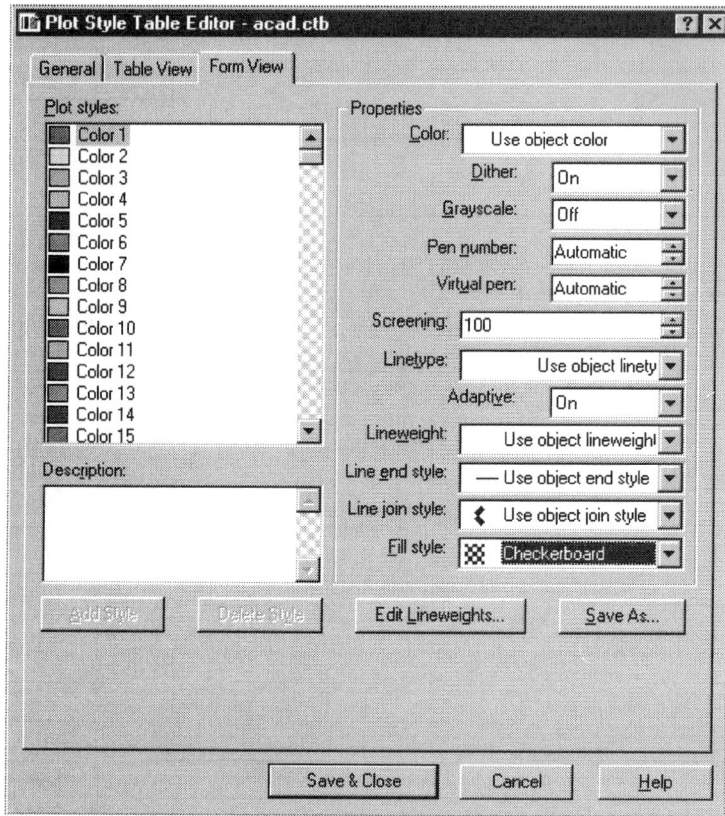

FIGURE 8–5
Plot Dialog Box with Plot Settings Tab Selected

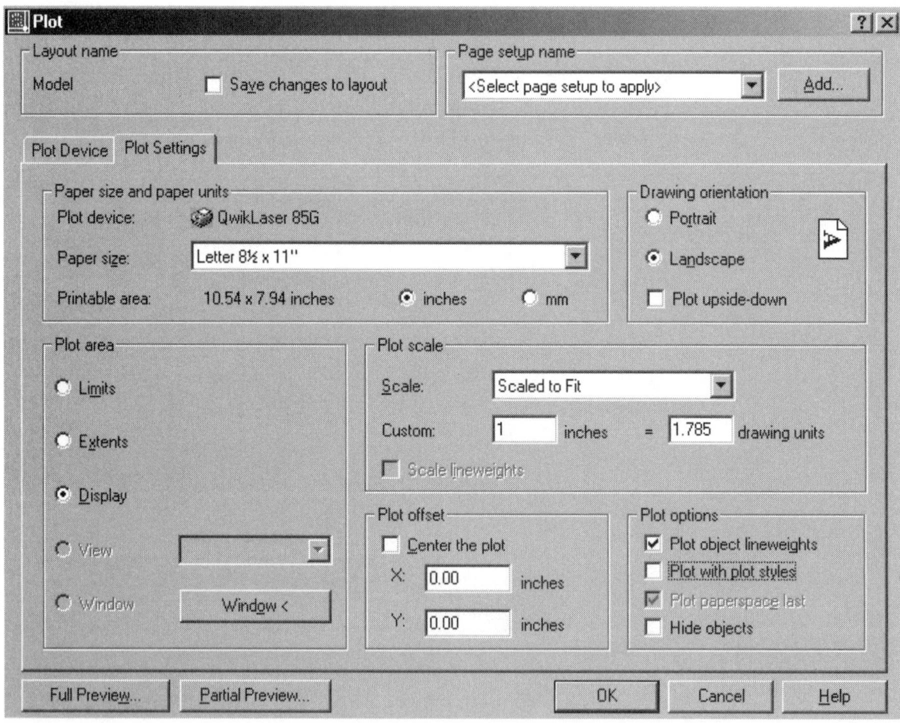

Step 5. Click the Plot Settings tab so it appears as shown in Figure 8–5.

Paper Size and Paper Units

In this area you are shown the paper sizes in inches or millimeters that the selected printer or plotter will plot. A click on the down arrow will show additional sizes that are available to you on this device. **Leave this at letter (8.50 x 11.00 Inches) for this plot.**

Drawing Orientation

The drawing orientation allows you to specify either a vertical page (Portrait), or a horizontal page (Landscape). Another button allows you to plot either portrait or landscape pages upside down. The upside down option is sometimes helpful to get a plot to fit a particular page arrangement. **Landscape should be selected, as shown in Figure 8–5.**

Plot Area

A dialog box *radio button* is a button that is part of a group that is mutually exclusive—only one button in the group can be picked. The five radio buttons in the Plot area—Display, Extents, Limits, View, and Window—specify the part of the drawing that is to be printed, and only one can be selected at a time. When the button is selected, a black dot appears inside the button.

Step 6. Pick the Limits radio button to select Limits as the part of the drawing that is to be printed.

Limits This option plots the part of the drawing that lies within the drawing limits. The limits for drawing EX7-1(your initials) are 11,8½.

Display This option plots the part of a drawing that is displayed on the screen at the time the plot is made.

Extents This option plots the drawing extents. The drawing extents are whatever graphics are actually drawn, including any graphics that lie outside the limits of the drawing area.

View This selection plots any view that has been saved and named as a result of using the View command. It is grayed out because no view was saved and selected for drawing EX7-1(your initials). If you have saved a view, click the View… button (below the Window check button) to use the View Name dialog box to select the named view.

Window This selection allows you to pick two corners of a window and plot only the part of the drawing that is within the window. When the Window< button is clicked, the dialog boxes are cleared so you can view your drawing and use your mouse to click the two corners of a window. AutoCAD will then return to the Plot box.

Plot Scale

You can specify a plot drawing scale by selecting it from the scale list. If the scale you want is not there, select Custom, then insert the plotted units on the left and drawing units on the right. Some basic calculations can help you determine the correct scale so that the drawing fits within the specified paper size. To be able to measure a plotted drawing accurately using a scale, you must enter a specific plotting scale, such as the following:

Plotted Inches	=	Drawing Units	
1	=	1	(Full size)
.5	=	1′	(½″ = 1′)
.25	=	1′	(¼″ = 1′)
.125	=	1′	(⅛″ = 1′)
.5	=	1	(Half size)
.75	=	1	(¾ size)
1	=	4	(¼ size)
2	=	1	(Twice size)

You can enter fractions in Architectural units.

You may respond by selecting Scaled to Fit instead of entering a specific scale. When you select this option, AutoCAD scales the drawing as large as possible to fit the specified paper size.

FIGURE 8–6
Select Plot Scale of 1:1

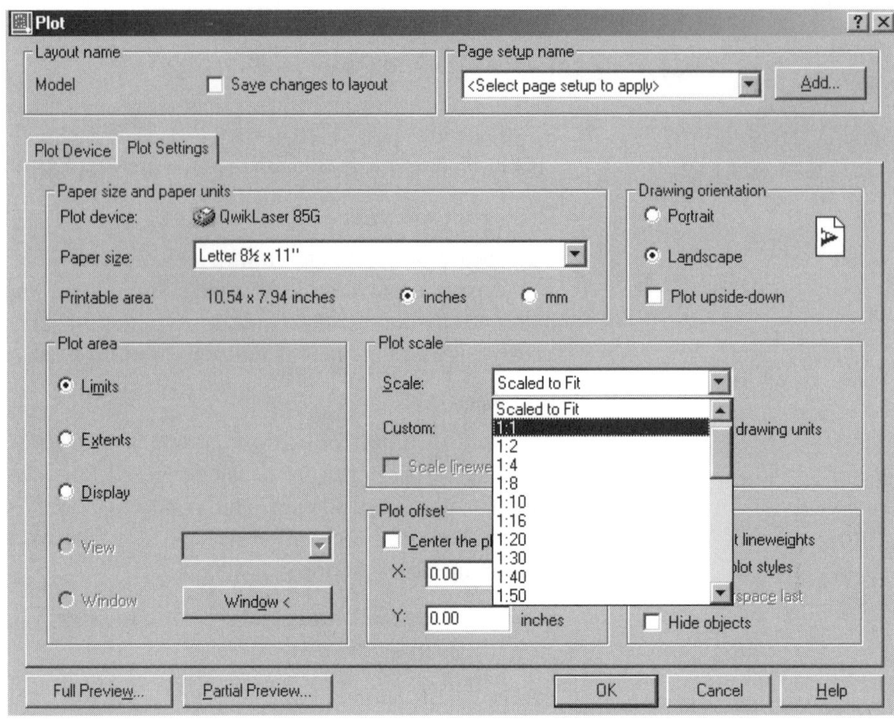

Step 7. Select 1 (Plotted Inches) = 1 (Drawing Units) for plotting your drawing EX7-1(your initials), Figure 8–6.

Plot Offset

You have three options to move your plotted area on the paper.

Center the plot A check mark in Center the plot tells AutoCAD to center the selected area (Limits, Extents, Display, View, or Window) on the printable area of your paper.

X: A positive number in this box moves the plot to the right; a negative number moves the plot to the left.

Y: A positive number in this box moves the plot up; a negative number moves the plot down.

You will not need any of the plot offset options for this drawing.

Plot Options

Plot object lineweights A check mark in this box tells AutoCAD to plot the drawing using the lineweights you have assigned to any objects in the drawing. Since you drew the boxes in your drawing with a .4mm lineweight, you should place a check in this box.

Step 8. Click: Plot object lineweights so a check appears in this box as shown in Figure 8–5.

Plot with plot styles

This option allows you to use the plot style tables to assign lineweights and patterns to objects on your drawing. You will not use this option for this drawing.

Plot paperspace last

This option applies to the layouts you will find at the bottom of your screen. You will use this option in a later chapter.

Hide Objects

The Hide objects button refers to 3-D objects only. When you use the Hide command, AutoCAD hides any surface on the screen that is behind another surface in 3-D space. If you want to do the same on your plot, you must click the Hide objects check button to

FIGURE 8–7
Partial Plot Preview

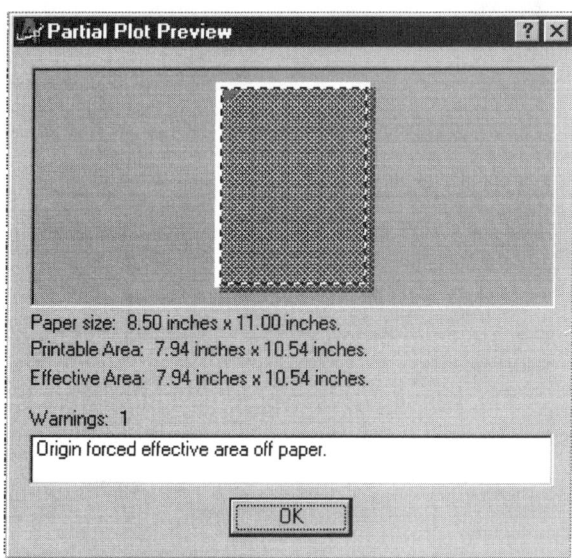

select it (a check mark will appear in the box). (If you are printing viewports in paper space, this button has no effect. The Hideplot property must be used to hide viewports in paper space.) Since you are working in 2-D, do not check this box.

Partial Preview

When you click the Partial Preview… button the Partial Plot Preview dialog box (Figure 8–7) appears. This allows you to preview the plot and, if any warnings appear, change the plotting settings. A partial preview shows only an outline of the effective plotting area of the drawing.

The effective plotting area, measured from the plot origin, is the actual size of the graphics to be plotted on the paper. If the maximum size for the printer is exceeded, AutoCAD gives you a warning, as shown in Figure 8–7. If this warning appears and seems to be a problem, or if the effective plotting area appears too small, cancel the plot and recheck the drawing limits, or extents, and any layers that are off or frozen, and see how they relate to the plot settings. Review the plot settings that include the plot offset, paper size, drawing orientation, and plot scale, and change them accordingly to get a successful plot.

Full Preview

The Full Preview button shows you exactly how the final plot will appear on the sheet.

Step 9. **Click the Full Preview radio button and preview your plot for EX7-1(your initials). It should look similar to Figure 8–8. If there is something wrong with the plot, press the spacebar and make the necessary adjustments. If the preview looks OK, press the spacebar to end the preview.**

Step 10. **If you want to keep the settings you have just made for later plots, check "Save changes to layout."**

Note: To cancel a plot after it has started, Press: Esc.

Step 11. *Click*: **OK in the Plot dialog box. The plot proceeds from this point. If you have not created a plot file, remove the completed plot from the printer or plotter and Exit AutoCAD if you are finished with this session. If you have created a .plt file, take your floppy disk to the plot station, or send your plot via a network.**

Speeding Up Plotting

If you have several drawings you want to plot, open them all. Click on the one you want to plot first, make your settings, then click on the second one and make any changes to the plot settings (if any) and plot it. Continue in this manner until all have been plotted.

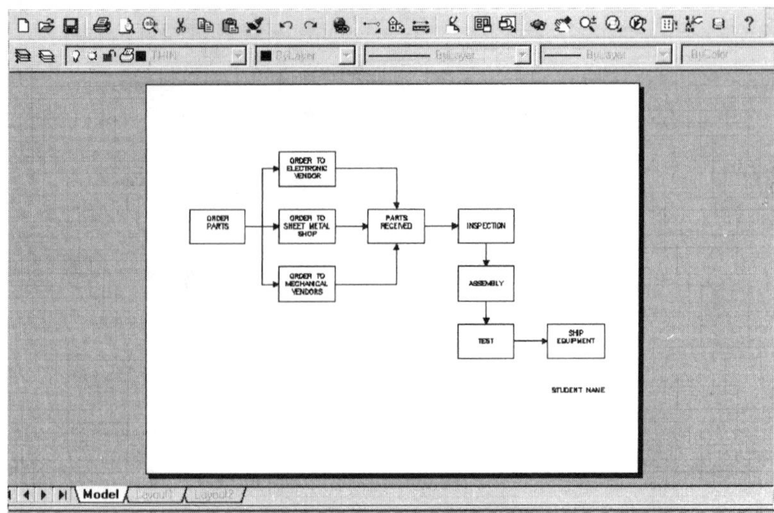

FIGURE 8–8
Full Plot Preview

Plot Styles

Plot style tables allow you to plot objects with a different appearance than you have drawn them. For example, you may want to plot a floor plan with furniture grayed out in one layout of your drawing and not in another layout. You will create and use plot style tables in a later chapter.

Using the Multiple Drawing Interface

Use the Window menu to work on and display multiple drawings in a single AutoCAD session. You can open up as many drawings as you like and cascade or tile them vertically or horizontally. When you have several drawings minimized or open, you can use Arrange Icons to clean up the display of the minimized drawing icons in the AutoCAD window. You can also select a drawing to make it the active one from the list of open drawings at the bottom of this menu.

This is especially helpful if you have several drawings you want to correct and then print at the same time.

Try this by opening three or four drawings and then use the Window menu as follows:

Window Help
Close
Close All
Cascade
Tile Horizontally
Tile Vertically
Arrange Icons
1 C:\Program Files\AutoCAD 2002\EX5-1MK.dwg
✓ 2 C:\Autocad Book 2001\FIG6-1.dwg

Prompt	Response
Command:	*Click:* **Cascade** (from the Window menu)
	Click: **Tile Vertically**
	Click: **Tile Horizontally**
	Click: **one of the drawings to make it active and print it**

To turn off the Multiple Document mode.

1. From the Tools menu, *Click*: **Options**.
2. On the System tab under General Options, *Click*: **Single Drawing Compatibility mode**. *Click*: **OK**.

or *Type*: **SDI** ↵, then *Type*: **1 or 0**

When SDI=0, Multiple Document mode is ON you can work on multiple documents. When SDI=1, you can work on only one drawing at a time.

Plotting for the Internet

Drawings used on the World Wide Web must have a different format than the standard .dwg file. AutoCAD 2002 allows you to create .dwf (drawing web format) files from the Plot dialog box. To create a .dwf plot file do the following:

1. Start the Plot command.
2. Select a dwf plotter for the plot device. AutoCAD 2002 has given you two of them by default, the DWF Classic.pc3 (similar to Release 14 .dwf files) and DWF ePlot.pc3, which shows the paper boundary.
3. When you select a dwf plotter, the Plot to file box is automatically checked as well as the filename and location. If you want to give the file a different name or location, you can do so by editing them in their text boxes.
4. To change the resolution, background color, layer information, or other properties, *Click:* **Properties...**, *Click:* **Custom Properties** in the plotter tree information, then *Click:* **Custom Properties...**when it appears on the tab.
5. *Click*: **OK**

The file is then created in the location you have specified.

Dwf files can be viewed on the Internet with a browser and the Autodesk WHIP! Plug-in.

Publish to Web

AutoCAD 2002 provides you with customizable templates that allow you to publish to the Internet. Those procedures are discussed in a later chapter.

REVIEW QUESTIONS

Circle the best answer.

1. Print quality may be selected from within the Plot dialog box.
   a. True
   b. False
2. Which of the following pull-down menus contains the Plot... command?
   a. File
   b. Edit
   c. Format
   d. Tools
   e. Window
3. Which of the following will produce a plot of the screen area only?
   a. Display
   b. Extents
   c. Limits
   d. View
   e. Window
4. Which of the following will produce a plot of the entire drawing, even if part of it is outside the limits?
   a. Display
   b. Extents
   c. Limits
   d. View
   e. Window
5. A plot file has which of the following extensions?
   a. .bak
   b. .dwg
   c. .plt
   d. .cfk
   e. .dwf
6. A plot that shows only half of what should have been plotted could probably be corrected by doing which of the following?
   a. Moving the origin .5
   b. Selecting View instead of Extents
   c. Selecting Landscape instead of Portrait
   d. Writing the plot to a file
   e. Selecting a smaller page size

7. The question "remove hidden lines?" on the plot routine refers to which of the following?
   a. 3-D objects
   b. Isometric drawings
   c. Hidden linetypes
   d. 2-D objects
   e. Slide files
8. A drawing that is to be plotted so that it fits on a particular size sheet without regard to the scale requires which scale response?
   a. 1:1
   b. Full
   c. 1:2
   d. Scaled to Fit
   e. MAX
9. A drawing that is to be plotted at a scale of ¼″ = 1′ should use which scale response?
   a. Full
   b. Scaled to Fit
   c. ⅛″ = 1′
   d. 1′0″ = 1′0″
   e. ¼″ = 1′
10. To move the Plot offset 1″ to the left, which is the correct setting? (Original setting was X Origin 0.00, Y Origin 0.00.)
   a. X 1.00 Y –1.00
   b. X –0.00 Y –1.00
   c. X 0.00 Y 0.–1
   d. X –1.00 Y 0.00
   e. X –0.10 Y 0.00

Complete.

11. Describe the uses of Plot Style tables.

____

12. List the extension for a drawing to be used on the Internet.

____

13. Describe the easiest way to center a plot on the page.

____

14. Describe how to move the plot up ½″.

____

15. Which area must be selected to make sure you plot the entire drawing even if part of it is outside the Drawing Limits?

____

9 Geometric Constructions

OBJECTIVES

After completing this chapter, you will be able to

- □ Draw and edit points, lines, circles, arcs, ellipses, solids, and polygons and use them in common geometric constructions.
- □ Answer review questions regarding the following commands and settings:

Aperture	Divide	New	Save As
Arc	Extend	Offset	Stretch
Array	Fillet	Pickbox	Trim
Chamfer	Lengthen	Polygon	Undo
Change	Line	Polyline	
Circle	Mledit	Redo	
Copy	Mline	Rotate	

Before beginning to make production drawings that can be used to build or assemble products, we need a chapter containing many of the drawing constructions. Familiarity with geometric constructions shown in this chapter will allow later drawings to be done much faster. At least one method is shown for each of the constructions presented. You will discover other methods; you may even find faster methods.

TYPES OF CONSTRUCTIONS

The following geometric constructions of this chapter are shown in Figure 9–1.

- □ Lines and points
- □ Parallel lines
- □ Perpendicular lines
- □ Breaking lines
- □ Dividing lines into equal parts
- □ Fillets
- □ Chamfers
- □ Circles
- □ Tangents
- □ Arcs
- □ Curves through points
- □ Similar shapes
- □ Arrays of circles and lines
- □ Extending lines
- □ Trimming lines
- □ Changing line length
- □ Stretching lines

CONSTRUCTION METHODS

Exercise 9–1: Geometric Constructions

(*Note:* All locations that are given for these constructions are for your convenience. If your locations vary a little, that is OK.)

Setting Up

Step 1. Load AutoCAD and begin a new drawing.

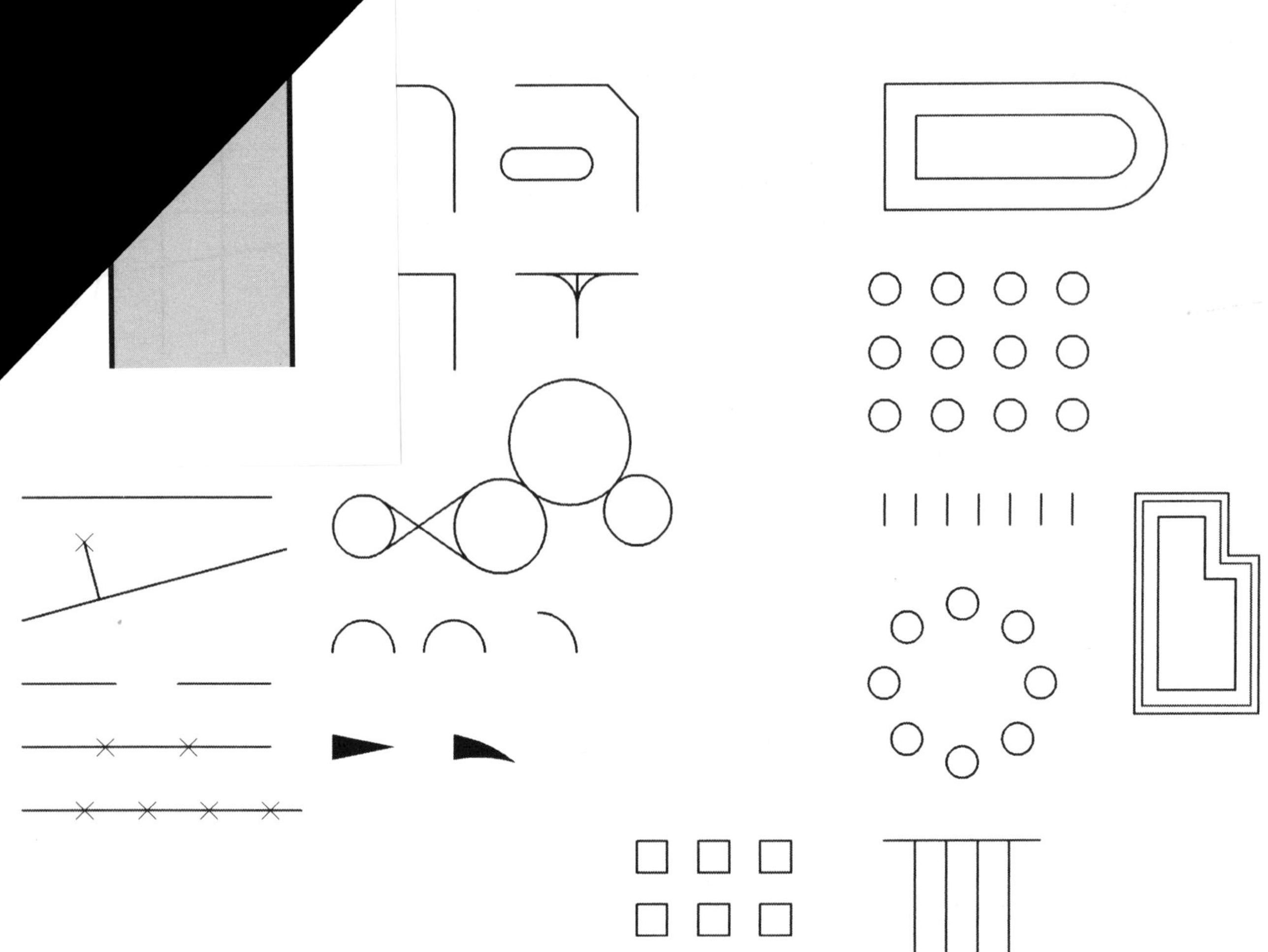

FIGURE 9–1
Geometric Constructions

Prompt	Response
AutoCAD 2002 Today window appears:	*Click:* **the Create Drawings tab** then *Click:* **Start from Scratch**
	Click: **English (feet and inches)**

Step 2. Make settings.

Prompt	Response
Command:	*Click:* **Drawing Limits** (from the Format menu) (or *Type:* **Limits** ↵)
Reset Model space limits: Specify lower left corner or [ON/OFF] <0.0000,0.0000>	↵
Specify upper right corner <Default>	*Type:* **11,8.5** ↵
Command:	*Click:* **Units…** (on the Format menu) (or *Type:* **Units** ↵)
The Drawing Units dialog box appears:	*Click:* **Decimal Units, Precision: 3 zeros after the decimal point. Accept defaults for all other Units settings.**
Command:	*Click:* **OK** *Type:* **GRID** ↵
Specify grid spacing (X) or [ON/OFF/Snap/Aspect] <0.500>	*Type:* **.25** ↵

Tip: The SNAP and GRID settings may also be made from Drafting Settings. . . on the Tools menu

Note: Do not be afraid to try any command. You can always return to where you were before the command was issued by using UNDO (type U on the keyboard). You can also REDO an UNDO by typing REDO or selecting it from the menu. Also, if you get into the middle of a command sequence and you do not want to finish it, press Esc to cancel. Undo and Redo can also be picked from the Standard Toolbar.

Prompt	**Response**
Command:	*Type:* **SN** ↵
Specify snap spacing or [ON/OFF/Aspect/Rotate/Style/Type]<0.500>:	*Type:* **.125** ↵ (to get a ⅛″ cursor movement when SNAP is ON)

You should now have an 11″ × 8.5″ drawing area with lower left corner coordinates at 0,0 and upper right corner coordinates at 11.000,8.500 (horizontal direction is first (X) and vertical direction is second (Y). You should have a ¼″ (.25) GRID and the SNAP should be on every dot on the GRID and midway between each GRID. To check this, press function key F6 (the coordinates key) to turn coordinates ON, F7 to display the GRID, and F9 to turn on SNAP. The coordinates will appear in the lower left screen. Move the cursor to the lower left corner of your page (0,0) then to the upper right corner (11.000,8.500). Now, create a magenta layer called LINE.

Prompt	**Response**
Command:	*Type:* **LA** ↵ (or *Click:* **Layer...** from the Format pull-down menu (See Chapter 4 for more on how to create layers from the pull-down menus.))
The Layer Properties Manager dialog box appears:	*Click:* **New**
	Type: **LINE** ↵
	Click: **the word White**
The Select Color dialog box appears:	*Click:* **Magenta**
	Click: **OK**
	Click: **Current**
	Click: **OK**

The LINE layer should be current on the Object Properties toolbar, and you should now have at the bottom of the screen the following buttons pushed in:

SNAP GRID ORTHO MODEL

(POLAR, OSNAP, OTRACK, and LWT will not be pushed in.)

(If this is not what you find, you may need to use the function keys to turn ON SNAP, GRID, coordinates, and ORTHO or click the word.)

F6: COORDINATES
F7: GRID FUNCTION
F8: ORTHO FUNCTION
F9: SNAP FUNCTION

Before you begin drawing, let's examine a feature of AutoCAD that you will find very helpful and in some cases absolutely essential.

Using Object Snap

Osnap

It is very important to become familiar with and use Object Snap modes while drawing. If an existing drawing entity is not drawn on a snap point, it is nearly impossible to snap a line or other drawing entity exactly to it. You may try, and think that the two points are connected, but a close examination will reveal they are not. Object Snap modes can be used to snap exactly to specific points of existing objects in a drawing. Object Snap modes need to be used constantly for complete accuracy while drawing.

Osnap commands can be activated in three different ways: by clicking Osnap icons from the Standard Toolbar, by holding down the Ctrl key and right clicking your mouse, or by typing the first three letters of the desired osnap mode from the keyboard.

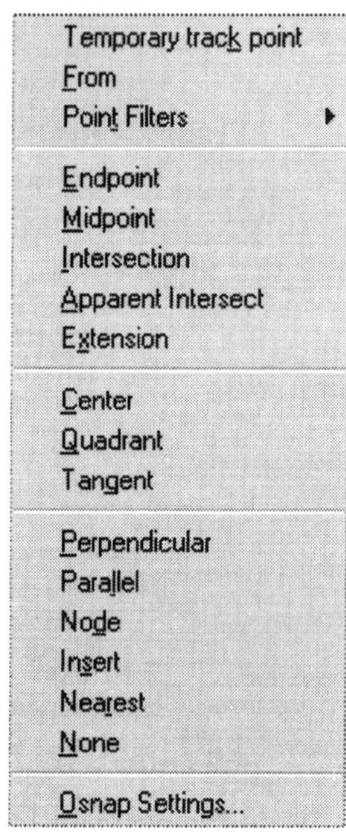

Running Osnap Modes

You may select individual modes while in another command by clicking them directly from the Osnap Settings menu or toolbar or typing them when AutoCAD prompts for a point. You may also set a "running" Osnap mode to be constantly in effect while drawing, until it is disabled. A running Osnap mode may include one or more modes. When "Osnap" is typed and entered at the Command: prompt, or "Osnap <mode>" is picked from the menu, or the function key F3 is pressed, the Osnap Settings dialog box is activated. Checks can then be placed in the desired object snap boxes. The running mode can be disabled by clicking Clear All or by clicking the existing check next to the Osnap Mode on the Running Osnap tab. You can also override the running mode for a single point by selecting another mode not included in the running mode. The running mode set by the Osnap command returns after the single override. Running Osnap can be deactivated by double clicking OSNAP at the bottom of the screen or pressing the F3 key.

When Osnap is activated, a *target symbol* is added to the screen crosshairs. This small symbol snaps to the desired point. The size and color of the symbol is controlled by the Marker setting.

Marker size

The Marker size setting can be used to change the size of the Osnap target symbol that is added to the crosshairs when Osnap is activated.

The Pickbox command that is on the Object Selection Settings dialog box can be used to change the size of the *object selection target*—the small box that replaces the screen crosshairs when the Modify commands are used.

Complete the following exercise to change the size of each.

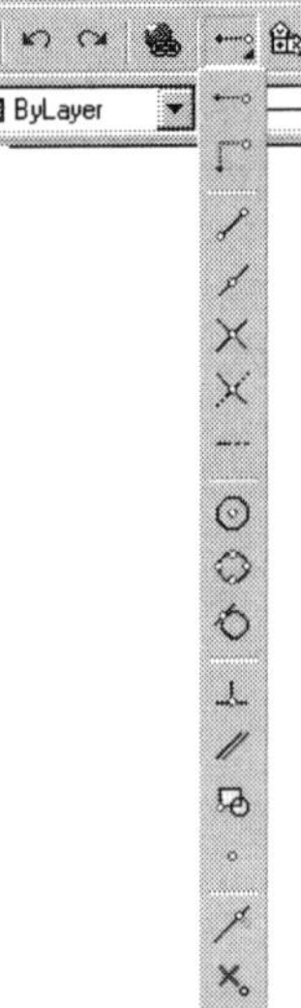

Use Marker size to change the size of the Osnap target symbol:

Prompt	Response
Command:	*Click:* **Drafting Settings...** (from the Tools menu on the menu bar.)

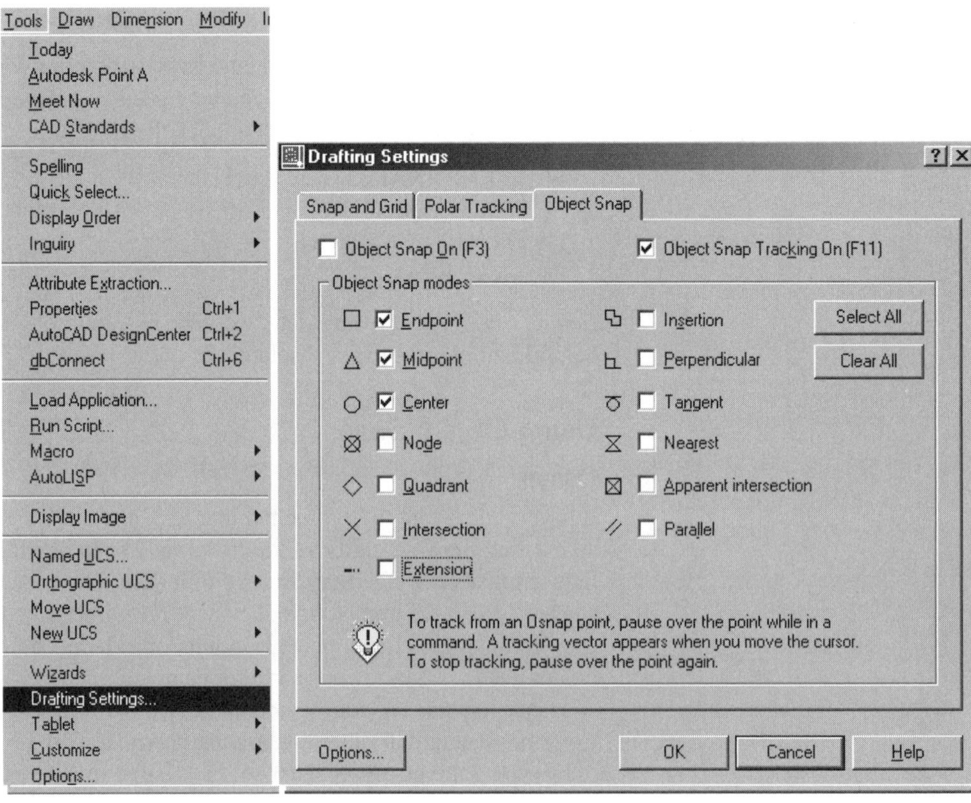

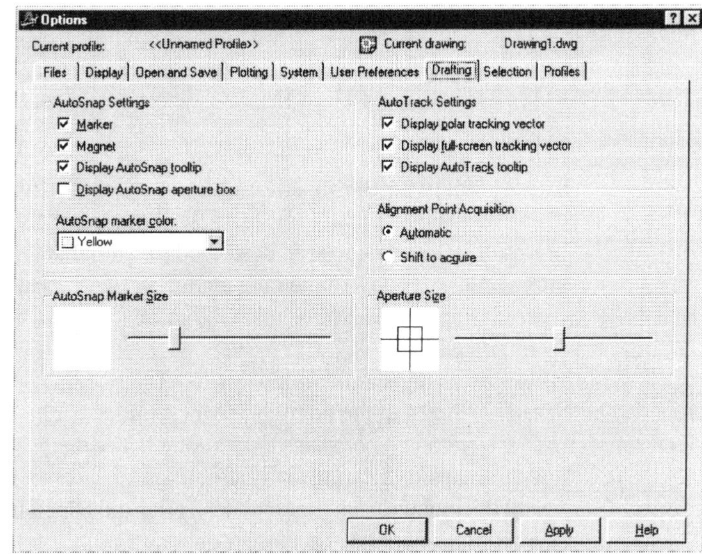

Prompt	Response
The Drafting Settings dialog box appears:	*Click:* **the Object Snap Tab** *Click:* **Options...**
The Options dialog box appears with the Drafting tab selected:	**Move the slider to the right to increase the size of the Marker or Aperture, or move the slider left to decrease the size of the Marker or Aperture.** When the size is what you want, *Click:* **OK.** You may also change the color of either on the same tab if you choose.

Select the selection tab from the Options dialog box to change the size of the pick box (the selection box) and grips.

Osnap Modes That Snap to Individual Drawing Features

Apparent Intersection Snaps to the apparent intersection of two entities even if one is below the other (helpful in 3-D drawing).

Center Snaps to the center of an Arc or Circle. (You must point to a visible part of the circumference to designate the Arc or Circle. If this mode is combined with others, you may have trouble with another object snap point being closer than the center).

Endpoint Snaps to the closest endpoint of a Line or Arc.

Extension Snaps to the extension point of an object. You set the path by moving the cursor over the endpoint of an object, then dragging the cursor along that line to the point you want to select.

From The From object snap differs from the other osnap modes in that it establishes a temporary reference point from which a point may be specified. For example, if you need to start a line 2″ in the X direction and 4″ in the Y direction from the endpoint of a line, the following sequence of steps would do that:

THE FOLLOWING IS AN EXAMPLE ONLY, NOT PART OF THE EXERCISE:

Prompt	Response
Command:	*Click:* **Line**
From point:	*Click:* **From** (from the Osnap menu) (or *Type:* **FROM** ↵)
Base point:	*Click:* **Endpoint**

Prompt	Response
of	*Click:* **the end of the line**
<Offset>	*Type:* @**2,4** ↵
To point:	

Insert Snaps to the insertion point of Text, Attribute, Attribute Definition, or Block entity. (You have already learned about Text; the other entities, Attribute, Attribute Definition, and Block are described in later chapters.)

Intersection Snaps to the intersection of two Lines, a Line with an Arc or Circle, or two Circles and/or Arcs. For this Object Snap mode, both objects must cross the target on the screen.

Midpoint Snaps to the midpoint of a Line or Arc.

Nearest Snaps to the point on a Line, Arc, or Circle that is visually closest to the position of the crosshairs, or snaps to the Point entity that is visually closest to the crosshairs.

Node Snaps to a Point entity. Points may be placed on locations in a Block definition and thus function as "snap nodes" after the Block has been inserted.

Quadrant Snaps to the closest quadrant point of an Arc, Circle, or Ellipse. These are the 0°, 90°, 180°, and 270° points on an Arc, Circle, or Ellipse (only the visible quadrants of an Arc may be selected).

Help: If you make a mistake, you can erase it by using the *Erase* command. Just *Click:* Erase then select objects by digitizing them. Press ↵ when you are finished. Erase can also be used with a window or a crossing window. *Window* selects everything entirely enclosed by the window. *Crossing window* selects everything within or crossed by the window. To use these, select Erase and then type W ↵ for *window* or C ↵ for *crossing*. Then click two points to form a box that selects objects to be erased. The selection window may also be activated by digitizing any point that does not contain an entity (such as a line or arc) and dragging to the right. The crossing window may be activated in a similar manner and dragged to the left. Windows can also be used with other commands, such as Copy and Move.

Osnap Modes That Snap to Features with Respect to the Last Point Entered

Perpendicular Snaps to the point on a Line, Circle, or Arc that forms a 90° angle from that object to the last point.

Parallel Allows you to draw lines parallel to other straight lines. Start the line by picking the start point, *Type*: **PAR** ↵ or select parallel, then hold the cursor over the existing line.

Tangent Snaps to the point on a Circle or Arc that, when connected to the last point, forms a line tangent to that object.

For the Line command, you can use the Tangent and Perpendicular Object Snap modes when specifying the first point of the line. In this case, the last point is not used in the calculation. Rather, this special case allows you to construct a line tangent to, or perpendicular to, an existing object. However, the rubber-band line normally drawn to help you select the next point will not be drawn.

TRacking

The Tracking osnap mode allows you to specify several points using individual osnap modes such as Endpoint, Center, or Midpoint without drawing anything until you reach the exact point where you want to be. An example is the center of a rectangle. You can activate tracking, click on the midpoint of one side of the rectangle, and then click on the midpoint of an adjacent side. Your cursor will then be in the exact center of the rectangle. You will use tracking in later exercises.

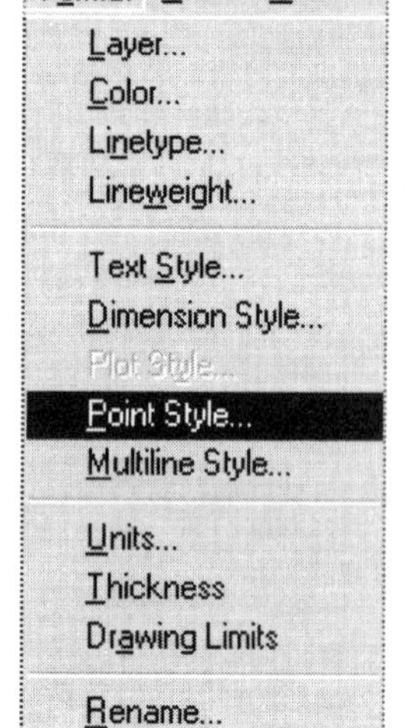

Lines and Points

Draw points, lines, circles, arcs, fillets, chamfers, and other geometric constructions.

With the coordinates, GRID, ORTHO, and SNAP ON, it is very easy to draw points or lines in increments of ¼″, or whatever your SNAP setting is. To do this, select Point and follow the given sequence. Before using Point, set Pdmode and Pdsize:

Prompt	Response
Command:	*Click:* **Point Style...**
The Point Style dialog box appears:	*Click:* **X** (■ Set size in Absolute units Point Size: 0.1)
	Click: **OK**

Pdmode and Pdsize are set and you may now proceed with the Point command.

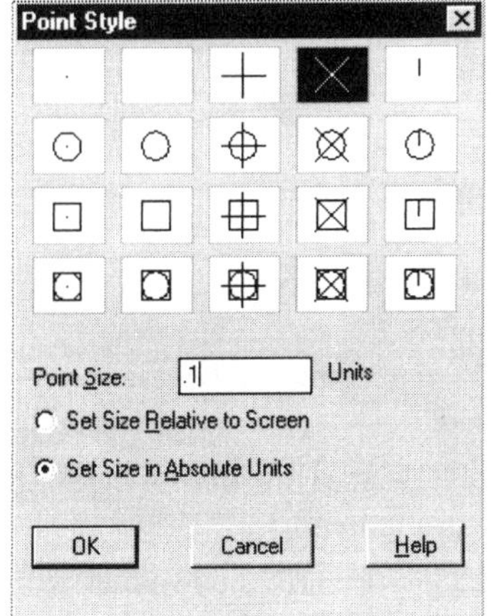

FIGURE 9–2
Points

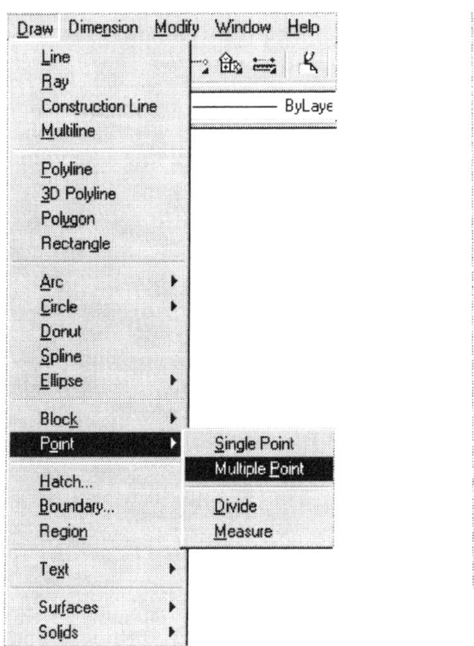

Remember: To remove digitized blips on the screen (those marks you make when you pick points), use *Redraw* from the *View* menu (or *Type:* R↵) or press the F7 (GRID) key twice to refresh the screen.

Note: Polar tracking can be used to draw lines at angles in increments of 15°.

Step 3. Draw points on a grid (Figure 9–2) (start the first point at ½″ from the left boundary and ½″ from the top—coordinates should read .500,8.000).

Prompt	Response
Command:	*Click:* **Multiple Point**
Specify a point:	*Click:* **four points; place points ¼″ apart.**
Specify a point:	*Press:* **Esc**

Step 4. Draw a horizontal line 2″ in length .500″ below the first point you drew (Figure 9–3) using polar tracking.

Prompt	Response
Command:	*Click*: **POLAR** on the status bar or *Press*: F10 to turn on Polar tracking.
Command:	*Click:* **Line** (or *Type:* **L** ↵)
Specify first point:	*Click:* **D1** (Figure 9–3; Remember, click D1 means to position your mouse so that the crosshairs are correctly positioned and click the left mouse button. Do not type D1. Start this line ½″ below the first point you drew.)
Specify next point or [Undo]:	**D2** (Move eight ¼″ grid spaces to the right, Figure 9–3.)(Polar tracking will read Polar: 2.000<0°)
Specify next point or [Undo]:	↵ (to complete the command)

FIGURE 9–3
Line 2″ Long

D1 2.00 D2

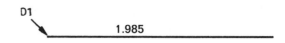

FIGURE 9–4
Horizontal Line 1.985″ Long

Step 5. Draw a horizontal line 1.9850 long (Figure 9–4).

Prompt	Response
Command:	*Click:* **Line** (or *Press:* ↵ , then *Click*: **Repeat LINE** to repeat the last command.)
Specify first point:	**D1** (Figure 9–4; start this line ½″ below the line of Figure 9–3.)
Specify next point or [Undo]:	*Type:* **@1.985<0** ↵ (Hold down the Shift key to type @ and < (on the commonly used keyboards they are above the 2 and the ,).)
Specify next point or [Undo]:	↵ then *Click*: **Enter** (To complete the command.)

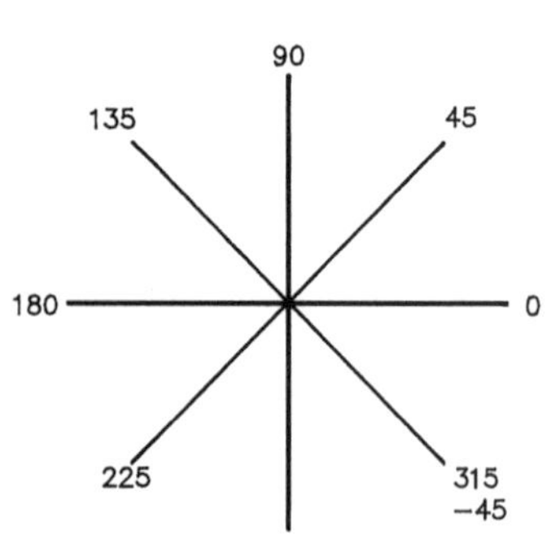

FIGURE 9–5
AutoCAD Directions

You have told AutoCAD to draw a line 1.985″ long in the 0 direction. Figure 9–5 shows the direction for all lines.

Step 6. Draw a line 2.100″ long at a 10° angle to the upper right (Figure 9–6).

Prompt	Response
Command:	*Click:* **Line**
Specify first point:	**D1** (Figure 9–6 (Start this line ⅝″ (.625) below the left end of the line in Figure 9–4.))
Specify next point or [Undo]:	*Type:* **@2.1<10** ↵
Specify next point or [Undo]:	↵ then *Click*: **Enter**

FIGURE 9–6
Line 2.100″ Long, 10° Angle

Step 7. Draw a line from one location to another location (Figure 9–7).

Note: You can turn off the right-click menus by clicking Options . . . on the Tools menu. Click the User Preferences tab, then click to remove the check mark before "shortcut menus in drawing area." Leave them on for now until you know which you prefer.

- If you use the right mouse button for ↵, you get shortcut menus.
- If you press the ↵ key on the keyboard, you do not get shortcut menus.

Start the line ½″ from the left side of the page and 5¾″ from the bottom of the page. End it 2.532″ from the left side and 5¾″ from the bottom.

Prompt	Response
Command:	*Click:* **Line**
Specify first point:	*Type:* **.5,5.75** ↵
Specify next point or [Undo]:	*Type:* **2.532,5.75** ↵
Specify next point or [Undo]:	↵

Parallel Lines Using Direct Distance Entry and Offset

Step 8. Draw 2″ lines parallel to each other, .517″ apart (Figure 9–8).

Prompt	Response
Command:	*Click:* **Line**
Specify first point:	**D1** (Start this line ½″ below the left end of the line you drew in Figure 9–7.)

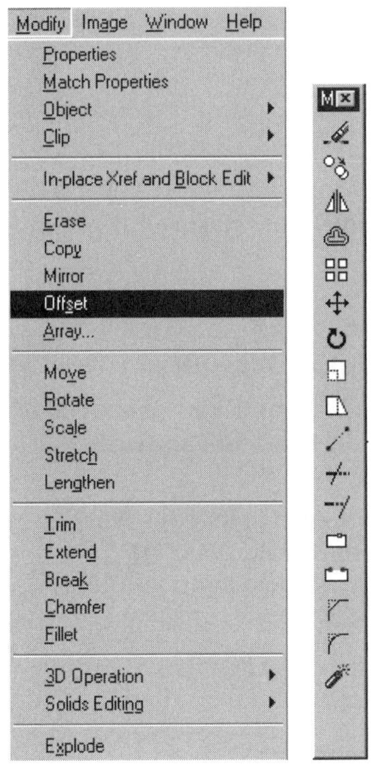

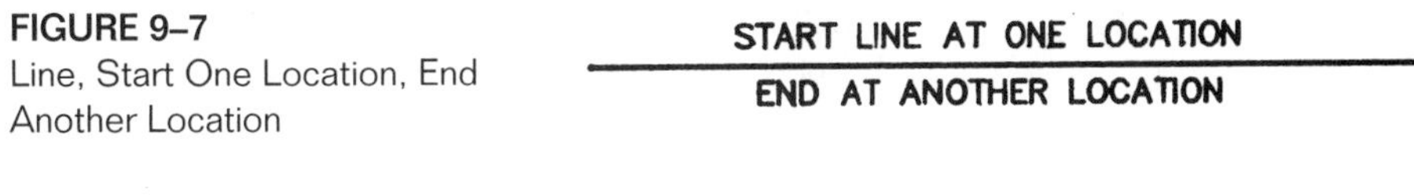

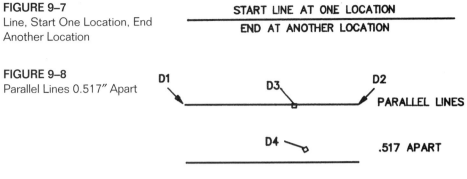

FIGURE 9–7
Line, Start One Location, End Another Location

FIGURE 9–8
Parallel Lines 0.517″ Apart

D1
D3
D2
PARALLEL LINES
D4
.517 APART

Prompt	Response
To point:	Move the cursor to the right and *Type:* **2** ↵ (SNAP and ORTHO must be ON.)
To point:	↵
Command:	*Click:* **Offset** (or *Type:* **O** ↵)
Specify offset distance or [Through] <Through>:	*Type:* **.517** ↵ (the distance that the lines are apart)
Select object to offset or <exit>:	*Click:* **D3** (Select the line anywhere on it.)
Specify point on side to offset:	*Click:* **D4** (anywhere on the side you want the other line to appear)
Select object to offset or <exit>:	↵

Note: Direct distance entry is a quick, accurate, and easy way to draw horizontal and vertical lines. With ORTHO ON move your mouse in the direction you want to draw, *Type:* the distance, and *Press:* ↵.

Help: If you draw something in the wrong location, use the *Move* command to move the object to the correct location. *Click:* Move, then select the object by clicking on it or by using a window. The base point is the point on the object that is to be moved, such as the endpoint of a line. The second point of displacement is the point to which you want to move the base point.

Perpendicular Lines

Step 9. Draw a line perpendicular to another line through a point (Figure 9–9).

Before you start, draw a line 2.200″ long at a 15° angle to the upper right and 1″ below the lines you drew in Figure 9–8. Draw a point approximately ½″ above this line near the center. After you have drawn this line and point, proceed as follows.

FIGURE 9–9
Line, Perpendicular through a Point

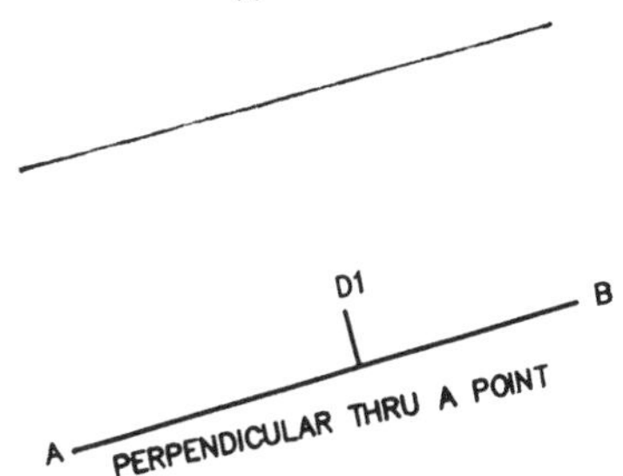

Prompt	Response
Command:	*Click:* **Line**
Specify first point:	*Click:* **Node** (from the Osnap menu) or *Type:* **NOD** ↵
of:	*Click:* **D1** (Figure 9–9) (click:the point)
Specify next point or [Undo]:	*Click:* **Perpendicular** (from the Osnap menu) (or *Type:* **PER** ↵)
to	**Click any point on the line AB**
Specify next point or [Undo]:	↵

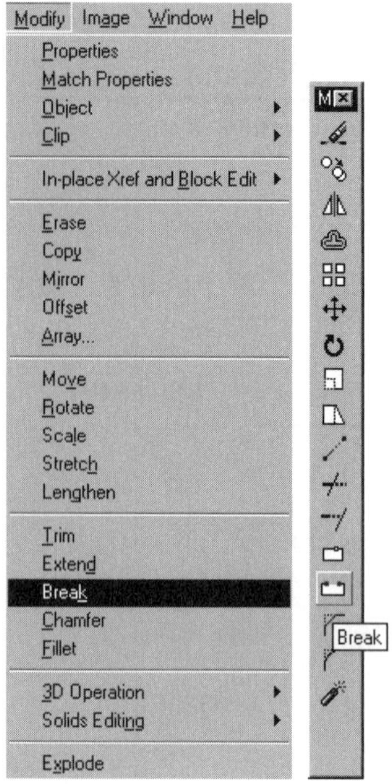

FIGURE 9–10
Simple Line Break

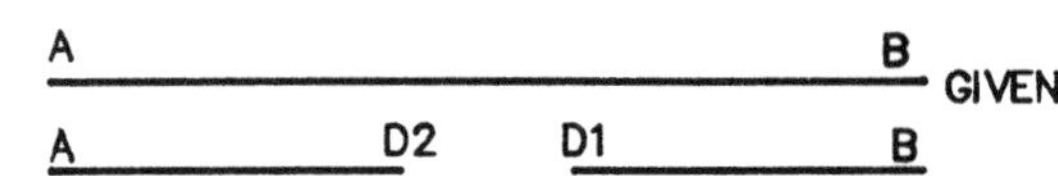

Breaking Lines

Step 10. Break a line AB with no interference from other lines (Figure 9–10).

Before you start, draw a 2″ horizontal line ½″ below the line you drew in Figure 9–9.

Prompt	Response
Command:	*Click:* **Break** (or *Type:* **BR** ↵)
Select object:	**Select the line by clicking at one end of where the break will be made. D1** ↵
Specify second break point or [First point]:	*Click:* **the second point—the other end of the break.** *Click:* **D2** ↵

Dividing Lines into Equal Parts

Step 11. Divide a given line into three equal parts (Figure 9–11).

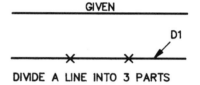

FIGURE 9–11
Divide a Line into Equal Parts

GIVEN
D1
DIVIDE A LINE INTO 3 PARTS

Note: The line has not been broken into three parts; a node, or point, has been placed at the proper interval so further construction can be done at those points.

Tip: Use *Zoom-Window* to enlarge the display of the part of the drawing on which you are working. The prompts "first corner" and "other corner" allow you to pick two points in a diagonal direction to describe the area you wish to enlarge. Use *Zoom-All* to display the entire drawing. Other display commands are described later. You will find Zoom-Window helpful for many of the exercises in this chapter.

Before you start, draw a 2″ horizontal line ½″ below the line you drew in Figure 9–10.

Prompt	Response
Command:	*Click:* **Divide** (or *Type:* **DIV** ↵)
Select object to divide:	*Click:* **anywhere on the line.** *Click:* **D1**
Enter the number of segments or [Block]:	*Type:* **3** ↵

Step 12. Divide a line into certain-size parts (Figure 9–12).

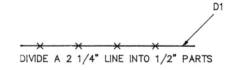

FIGURE 9–12
Divide a Line into Certain-Size Parts

D1
DIVIDE A 2 1/4" LINE INTO 1/2" PARTS

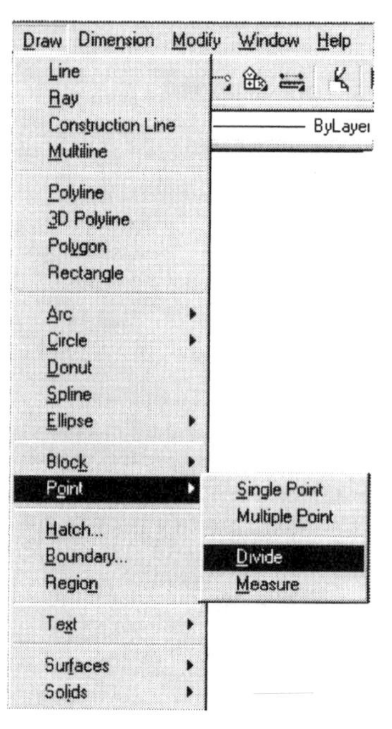

Before you start, draw a 2¼″ horizontal line ½″ below the horizontal line you drew in Figure 9–11.

Prompt	Response
Command:	*Click:* **Measure** (or *Type:* **ME** ↵)
Select object to measure:	**D1** (Figure 9–12)
Specify length of segment or [Block]:	*Type:* **.5** ↵

Note: The divisions start from the end of the line closest to the clicked point. The ¼″ left over appears on the left because the ½″ parts were measured beginning from the right end of the line.

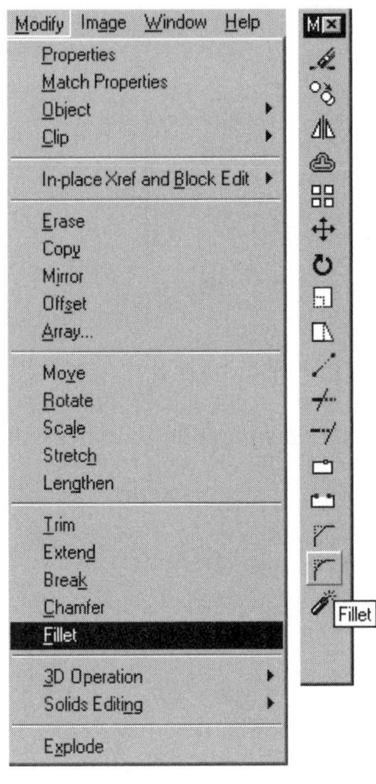

Fillets

Step 13. Make a fillet (a radius of a specific size) at the junction of two lines (Figure 9–13).

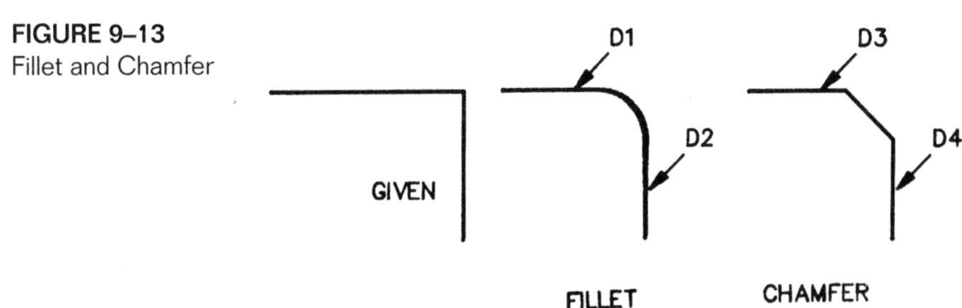

FIGURE 9–13
Fillet and Chamfer

Before you start, draw a 1″ horizontal line ½″ from coordinates 3,8 to 4,8. Draw a 1″ vertical line perpendicular to the right end of the horizontal line.

Prompt	Response
Command:	*Click:* **Fillet** (or *Type:* **F** ↵)
Select first object or [Polyline/Radius/Trim]:	*Type:* **R** ↵
Specify fillet radius <0.500>:	*Type:* **.25**
Select first object or [Polyline/Radius/Trim]:	**D1** (Figure 9–13)
Select second object:	**D2**

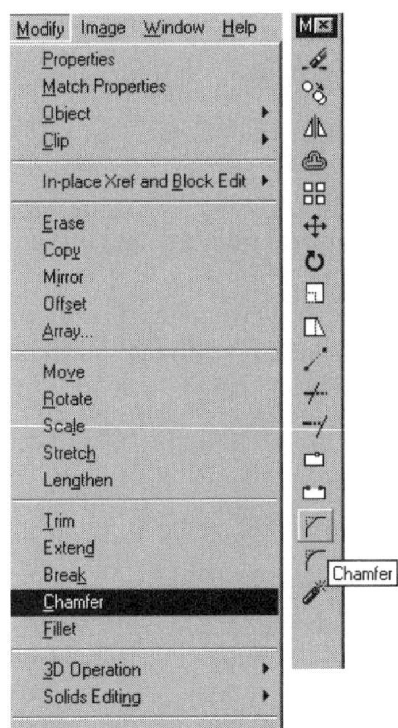

Chamfers

Step 14. Make a chamfer (an angle of a specific size) at the junction of two lines (Figure 9–13).

Before you start, draw 1″ horizontal and vertical lines as you did for Figure 9–13, FILLET. Locate these lines ½″ to the right of the fillet.

Prompt	Response
Command:	*Click:* **Chamfer** (or *Type:* **CHA** ↵)
Select first line or [Polyline/Distance/ Angle/Trim/Method]:	*Type:* **D** ↵
Specify first chamfer distance: <0.500>	*Type:* **.25** ↵
Specify second chamfer distance <0.250>:	↵ (to make a 45° chamfer)
Select first line or [Polyline/Distance/ Angle/Trim/Method]:	**D3**
Select second line:	**D4**

Suggestion: Try another chamfer, giving different measurements for each leg of the chamfer.

Zero-Radius Fillet or Chamfer

Step 15. Make a zero-radius fillet or chamfer (Figure 9–14).

You will often find it necessary to join lines that do not intersect. A zero-radius fillet or zero-distance chamfer does this easily. *Before you start,* draw a ¾″ horizontal line ½″

FIGURE 9–14
Zero-Radius Fillet

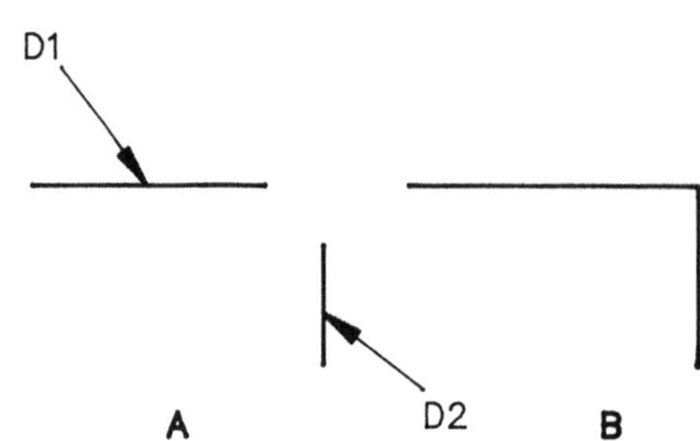

Tip: A zero-radius *fillet* or *chamfer* may also be used to connect lines that are not perpendicular. They may even be used to connect some curves with other curves or straight lines. This is a good command with which to experiment.

below the fillet of Figure 9–13. Draw a ½″ vertical line ¼″ to the right and ¼″ below the right end of the ¾″ horizontal line (Figure 9–14A). Your final drawing after the fillet will appear as in Figure 9–14B.

Prompt	Response
Command:	*Click:* **Fillet** (or *Type:* **F** ↵)
Select first object or [Polyline/Radius/Trim]:	*Type:* **R** ↵
Specify fillet radius <0.250>:	*Type:* **0** ↵
Select first object or [Polyline/Radius/Trim]:	**D1** (Figure 9–14)
Select second object:	**D2** (Figure 9–14)

Step 16. Use the No Trim option of the Fillet and Chamfer commands (Figure 9–15).

FIGURE 9–15
Using the NO TRIM Option of Fillet:

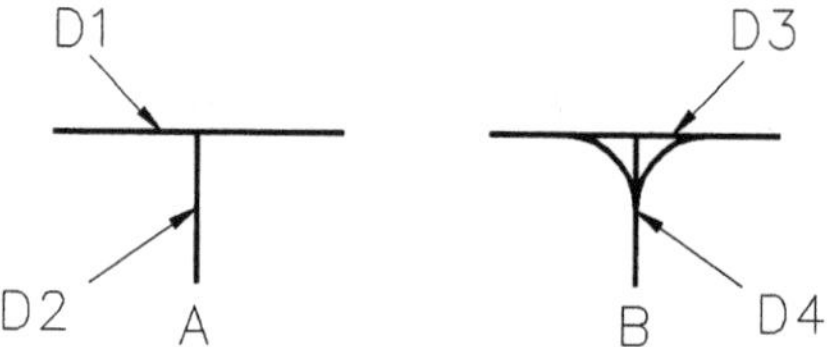

The No Trim option is often helpful when two fillets or chamfers from a single line are needed.

Before you start, draw a 1″ horizontal line ½″ to the right of the zero-radius fillet and a ½″ vertical line downward from the midpoint of the 1″ horizontal line (Figure 9–15A). Your final drawing after the fillet will appear as in Figure 9–15B.

Prompt	Response
Command:	*Click:* **Fillet**
Select first object or [Polyline/Radius/Trim]:	*Type:* **T** ↵
Enter Trim mode option [Trim/No trim] <Trim>:	*Type:* **N** ↵
Select first object or [Polyline/Radius/Trim]:	*Type:* **R** ↵
Specify fillet radius <0.000>:	*Type:* **.25** ↵
Select first object or [Polyline/Radius/Trim]:	**D1** (Figure 9–15A)
Select second object:	**D2** (Figure 9–15A)
Command:	↵
Select first object or [Polyline/Radius/Trim]:	**D3** (Figure 9–15B)
Select second object:	**D4** (Figure 9–15B)

Step 17. Use the Fillet command to make a fillet between two parallel lines, Figure 9–16.

FIGURE 9–16
Fillet to Two Parallel Lines

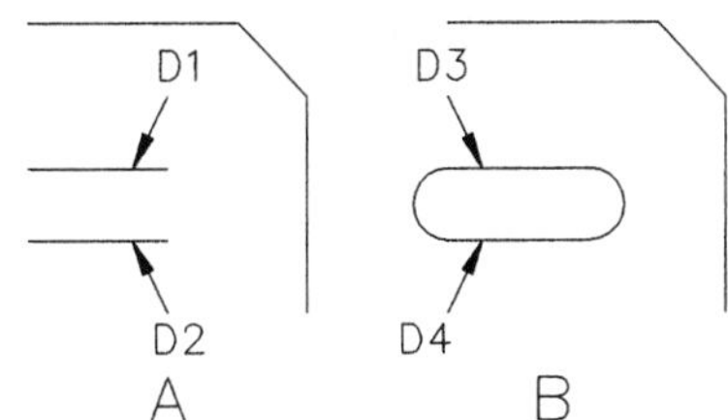

Before you start, draw two ½″ horizontal lines ¼″ apart inside the chamfered lines as shown in Figure 9–16.

Prompt	**Response**
Command:	*Click:* **Fillet**
Select first object or [Polyline/Radius/Trim]:	*Type:* **R** ↵
Specify fillet radius <default>:	*Type:* **.125** ↵
Select first object or [Polyline/Radius/Trim]:	**D1** (Figure 9–16A)
Select second object:	**D2** (Figure 9–16A)
Command:	↵
Select first object or [Polyline/Radius/Trim]:	**D3** (Figure 9–16B)
Select second object:	**D4** (Figure 9–16B)

Circles

Step 18. Draw a circle of a specific size at a specific location.

Prompt	**Response**
Command:	*Click:* **Circle-Center, Radius** (or *Type*: **C**↵)
Specify center point for circle or [3P/2P/Ttr (tan tan radius):	**D1** (with SNAP ON, 1¼″ below the left end of the zero-radius fillet and ¼″ to the right)

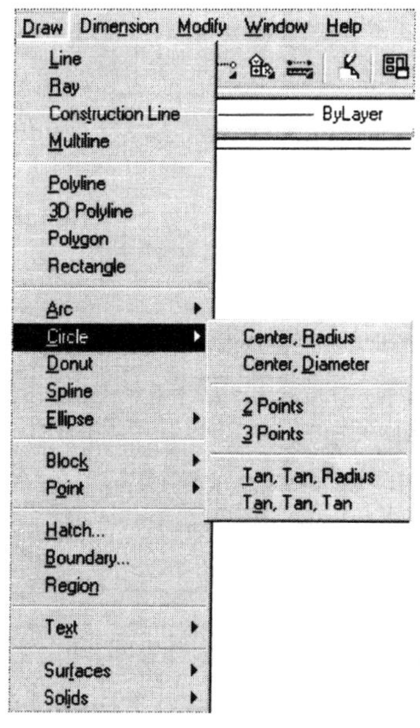

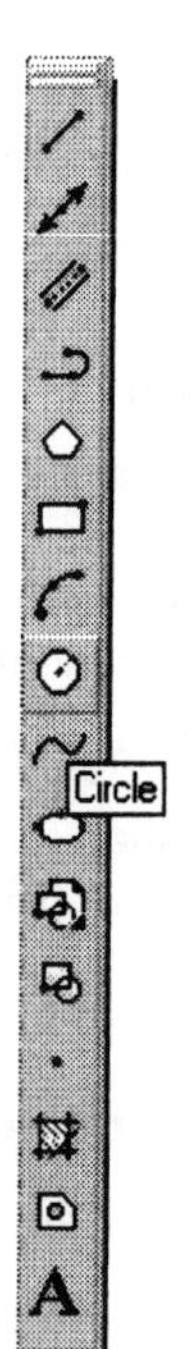

Prompt	Response
Specify radius of circle or [Diameter]:	*Type:* **.25** ↵ (.25 is the radius for this circle.) *or* *Type:* **D** ↵ (to tell AutoCAD you want to specify a diameter.)
Diameter:	*Type:* **.5** ↵

Step 19. Draw a circle by locating the two endpoints of its diameter.

Prompt	Response
Command:	*Click:* **Circle** (or *Type:* **C** ↵)
Specify center point for circle or [3P/2P/Ttr (tan tan radius)]:	*Type:* **2P** ↵
Specify first endpoint of circle's diameter:	**D3** (½″ to the right of your first circle)
Specify second endpoint of circle's diameter:	**D4** (move 3 grid spaces to the right and *Click:*)

Step 20. Draw a circle by picking three points on its circumference.

Prompt	Response
Command:	*Click:* **Circle 3 Points** (or *Type*: **C** ↵, then **3P** ↵)
Specify first point on circle:	**D5** (approximately ½″ to the right of the last circle)
Second point:	**D6** (2 grid spaces to the right)
Third point:	**D7** (1 grid space up)

You just learned three different methods of drawing circles. Experiment with different-size circles and the different methods until you become comfortable with them.

The next option on the circle command is Ttr. This stands for tangent, tangent, and radius. Tangent means to touch at a single point. To see how Ttr is used, draw the following.

Step 21. Draw a circle with a ½″ radius tangent to two other circles.

Prompt	Response
Command:	*Click:* **Circle-Tan, Tan, Radius** (or *Type:* **C** ↵)
_Circle 3P/2P/TTR/<Center point>:	*Type:* **TTR** ↵
Enter Tangent spec:	**D1** (Figure 9–17)(the second circle you drew)
Enter second Tangent spec:	**D2** (the third circle you drew)
Radius <default>:	*Type:* **.5** ↵

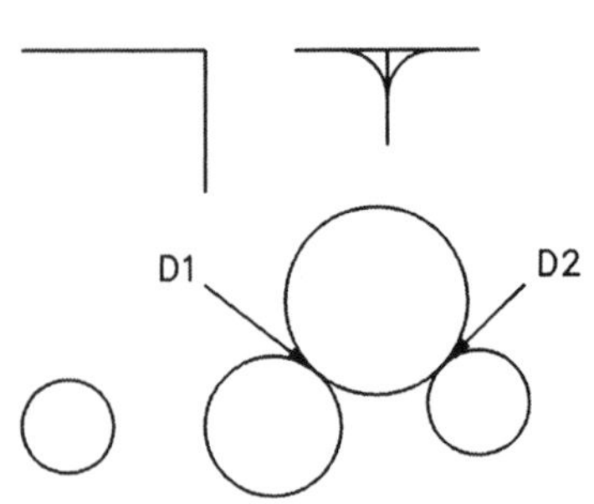

FIGURE 9–17
Drawing a Circle Using Ttr (tan tan radius)

Experiment with different-sized circles. The location of the tangent circle will change with different radius sizes.

Tangent, Tangent, Tangent Option

The last option for constructing circles is the Tan,Tan,Tan which is the tangent, tangent, tangent option. This method may be used to draw a circle tangent to three other entities.

Tangents

Step 22. Draw a line tangent to a circle (Figure 9–18).

(Use the first two circles you drew.)

FIGURE 9–18
Drawing Lines Tangent to Circles

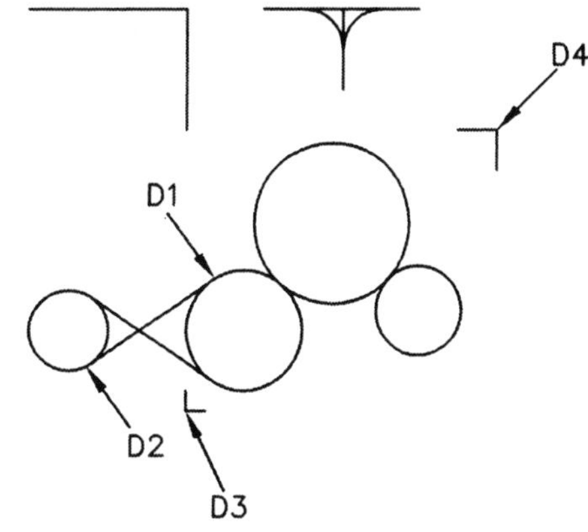

Tip: Use *Quadrant* from the OSNAP menu to draw lines or arcs to specific parts of a circle.

Note: The half of the circle that is clicked is the half where the tangent occurs. The other line tangents were drawn in the same manner.

Prompt	Response
Command:	*Click:* **Line**
From point:	*Click:* **Tangent** (from the Osnap menu) (or *Type:* **TAN** ↵)
Tangent to:	**D1**
To point:	*Click:* **Osnap-Tangent** (or *Type:* **TAN** ↵)
Tangent to:	**D2**
To Point:	↵

On your own: Draw another line tangent to these two circles, as shown in Figure 9–18.

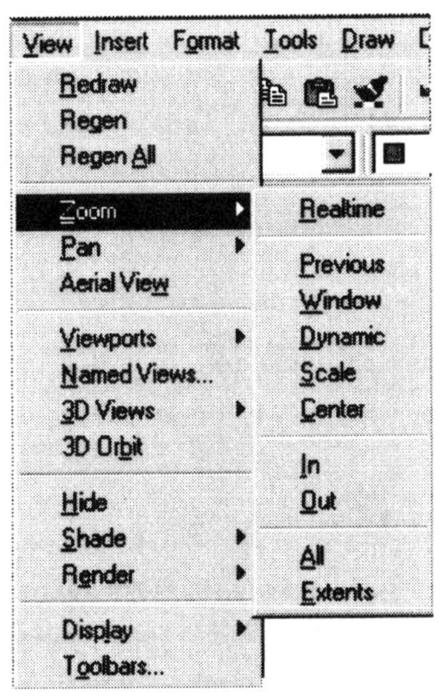

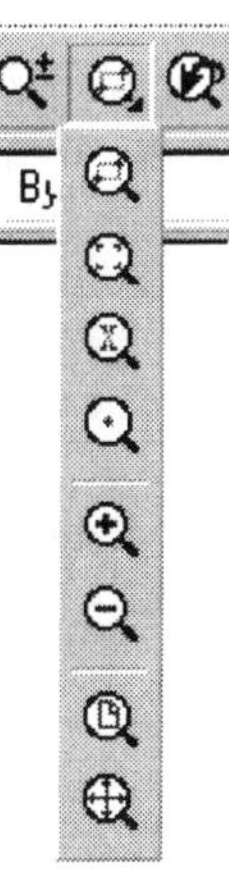

Zoom

The different Zoom commands (All, Center, Dynamic, Extents, Previous, Scale, Window, and Realtime) control how you view the drawing area on the display screen. While drawing the lines and circles for this chapter, you have been able to view the entire 8½″ × 11″ drawing limits on the screen. The Zoom-All command was used earlier to assure that view.

The following exercise uses the Zoom-Window command to look more closely at the tangent circles on the drawing. The Zoom-Window command allows you to click two opposite corners of a rectangular window on the screen.

Step 23. Use Zoom-Window.

Prompt	Response
Command:	*Click:* **Zoom window** (or *Type:* **Z** ↵)
Specify corner of window, enter a scale factor (nX or nXP) or [All/Center/Dynamic/Extents/Previous/Scale/Window]<real time>:	**D3** (lower left corner of the window, Figure 9–18)
Specify opposite corner:	**D4** (upper right corner of the window)
Command:	*Type:* **REGEN** ↵

The area that was windowed is now displayed to fill the screen. The two corners of the window may also be entered by typing and entering coordinate points.

When the magnification of the circles was enlarged with the Zoom-Window command to save regeneration time, AutoCAD did not regenerate the drawing. Only the part of the drawing that was windowed and magnified was redrawn. That is why the circles may not look like they are touching each other. Small line segments called vectors make up a circle. When the entire page is displayed, fewer line segments are used to make up the smaller circles. Zooming in and not regenerating made the small number of vectors become obvious. By typing and entering "regen," you issued a regeneration of the drawing. AutoCAD regenerated the circles with the optimal number of line segments (making the circle smoother) for the larger magnification.

Now that you have a windowed area of the drawing, how do you view the entire drawing again? Use Zoom-All in the following exercise to view the entire drawing area.

Step 24. Use Zoom-All.

Prompt	Response
Command:	*Click:* **Zoom-All** (or *Type*: **Z** ↵, then **A** ↵)

To view the tangent circles again without using Zoom-Window, use Zoom-Previous in the next exercise.

Step 25. Use Zoom-Previous.

Prompt	Response
Command:	*Click*: **Zoom-Previous** (or *Type*: **Z** ↵, then **P** ↵)

Zoom-Previous is a very convenient feature. AutoCAD remembers 10 previous views. This is especially helpful and timesaving if you are working on a complicated drawing.

Another Zoom command that saves regeneration time is Zoom-Dynamic. To understand Zoom-Dynamic, first Zoom-Window the tangent circles in your drawing again or do a Zoom-Previous to bring a windowed area of the tangent circles to the display screen. Then complete the following exercise.

Step 26. Use Zoom-Dynamic.

Prompt	Response
Command:	*Click*: **Zoom-Dynamic** (or *Type*: **Z** ↵, then **D** ↵)

There are now three areas that you see on the screen:

1. The green box is the area previously windowed.
2. The blue box shows the drawing limits or the drawing extents, whichever is larger.
3. The white (or, on some displays, black) box is the same size as the window that you just made when you windowed the circles. This window can be moved. It follows the movement of your pointer. Experiment by moving it around the screen.

The size of the window can also be changed. Change the size of the window by pushing the click button on the pointer. The X inside changes to an arrow when you push the click button. When the arrow is in the window, the movement of the pointer changes the size of the window. Experiment with changing the size of the window. Push the click button on the pointer to return the X to the center of the window. With the X in the center of the window, the size remains constant and you may move the window to the area of the drawing that you want to window or zoom in on next.

When you have decided on the area of the drawing to view next and have the size of white box (or window) needed, with an X in the center, place the white box on the area to be enlarged. Pressing the enter button on the pointer causes the area inside the white box to appear enlarged on the screen.

When you have completed the Zoom-Dynamic exercise, use the Zoom-Extents command to view the drawing, as follows.

Step 27. Use Zoom-Extents.

Prompt	Response
Command:	*Click:* **Zoom-Extents** (or *Type*: **Z** ↵, then **E** ↵)

Extents Regenerating drawing.

The Zoom-Extents command allows you to view the extents of a drawing. To understand Zoom-Extents, you need to understand the difference between drawing limits and drawing extents. The limits of a drawing are the size of the page set with the Limits command. The extents of a drawing are what are actually drawn on the page. If only half the page is full, the extents are half the page. The Zoom-All command will display the entire drawing limits or extents, whichever is larger. The extents are larger than the limits when a drawing entity is drawn outside the set limits.

The remaining Zoom commands are Scale, Center, and Realtime. A brief explanation of each follows.

Zoom-Scale

The Scale feature allows you to increase or decrease the magnification of the objects on the screen when you are viewing the entire page or a windowed view. If, while viewing the entire page or limits of the drawing, you type and enter 2 at the command prompt, the new displayed view will have a magnification twice as large as the full view. If you type and enter .25, the view will be decreased to ¼ of the full view.

While in a windowed view, with an object already zoomed in on, enter 2 followed by an X (2X) to increase the magnification of the windowed view by 2. A number followed by an X increases or decreases the object *currently* displayed. If, while in the windowed area, you enter the number 2 without the X, the full view or entire drawing area (not the windowed area) will be magnified by 2 and displayed.

The "XP" in the Scale part of the Zoom command prompt refers to paper space, which is discussed in a later chapter.

Zoom-Center

When Center is clicked in response to the Zoom prompt, AutoCAD asks you for a center point of a window. After you have clicked the center point of the window on the drawing, the prompt asks for "magnification or height <current height>:." The current height (11″ on your current drawing) is shown in default brackets. If 2 is typed and entered, a view of 2″ of the current drawing is enlarged to fill the screen. A height larger than the current height (such as 15) decreases the magnification by changing the height of the displayed view to 15″ instead of 11″.

If 2X is entered to the prompt "Magnification or Height <current height>:," the current drawing display is magnified by 2.

Zoom-Realtime

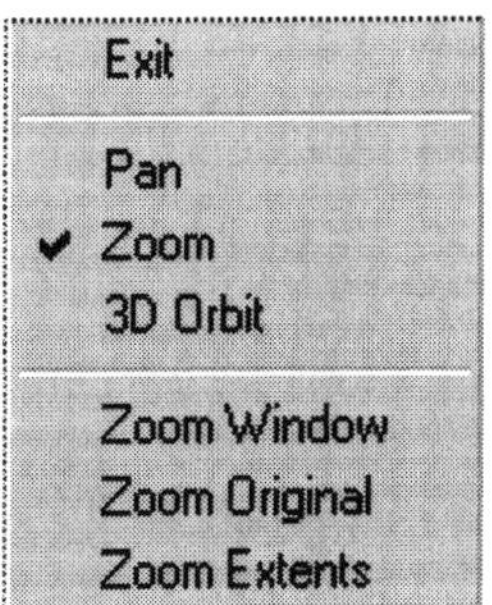

The Realtime Zoom command is located on the Standard Toolbar and on the View menu on the menu bar under Zoom. You may also type RTZOOM ↵ from the keyboard to activate this command. To zoom in or out, hold down the pick button on your mouse and move the mouse up or down to change the magnification of your drawing. Press the right mouse button to get a shortened zoom and pan menu as shown in the margin. Press Esc to exit from the command.

Zoom-In

Zoom-In magnifies the objects in the drawing.

Zoom-Out

Zoom-Out makes the objects in the drawing appear to be smaller.

Pan

The Pan command lets you stay in a windowed view and see parts of the drawing that are off the screen and not originally visible in the view. It allows you to move the drawing in any direction while still looking at the windowed view. Pan does not change the magnification of the view. To use Pan, first window a portion of the drawing and then complete the following exercise:

Prompt	Response
Command:	*Click:* **Pan**
'_pan specify base point or displacement:	*Click:* **the middle of the windowed view.**
Specify second point:	*Click:* **a point 2 grid marks to the right of the first point**

Pan-Realtime

Step 28. Use real-time pan.

The Realtime Pan command is located on the Standard Toolbar and on the View menu on the menu bar under Pan. You may also type RTPAN ↵ to activate this command. To move the view of your drawing at the same magnification, hold down the pick button on your mouse and move the mouse in any direction to change the view of your drawing. Press the right mouse button while in Realtime Pan to get a shortened Zoom and Pan menu. Press Esc to exit from the command.

Pan Scroll Bars

The scroll bars on the right and bottom of your screen may also be used to pan from one area on the drawing to another.

Transparent Commands

All the Zoom and Pan commands can be used while you are in a command that is not asking for a text entry. For example, you can do a Zoom-All from a windowed view while you are in the middle of the Line or Move command. Using Zoom or Pan in this manner is called a *transparent command.*

Redraw

Clicking Redraw (or typing R ↵) from the View command menu will cause AutoCAD to redraw and clean up your drawing. Any marker blips on the screen will disappear and drawing entities affected by editing of other objects will be redrawn. Pushing function key F7 twice will turn the grid OFF and ON and will also redraw the screen.

Viewres:

Typing VIEWRES from the keyboard causes AutoCAD to prompt: "Do you want fast zooms? <Y>." If you respond *yes,* AutoCAD will perform redraws when possible. If the response is *no,* AutoCAD will always regenerate the drawing when the view is changed. Press: ↵ to accept yes.

The next prompt from Viewres is: "Enter circle zoom percent (1–20000) <100>:." If you enter a number less than 100, the circles and arcs may not look as smooth, but the drawing will regenerate more quickly. If you enter a number higher than 100, the circles and arcs will appear very smooth as you zoom in, but regeneration time will be increased. Viewres affects only the display screen; it does not affect how the circles, arcs, and linetypes plot. (A Viewres value of 500 is a good working setting.) *Type:* **500** ↵ and Zoom-All.

Now we continue with the drawing constructions.

Arcs

Step 29. Draw arcs of a specific size or angle (Figure 9–19).

Note: These are two different methods for the same arc.

Draw these arcs approximately ½″ below the tangents.

FIGURE 9–19
Methods of Drawing Arcs

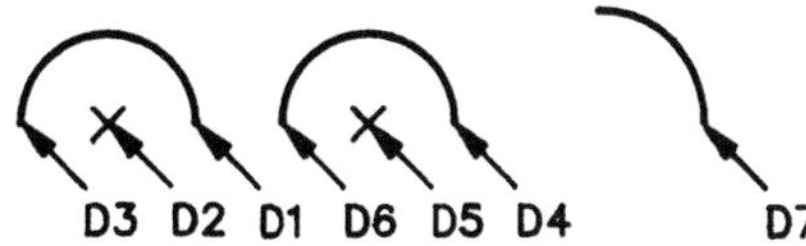

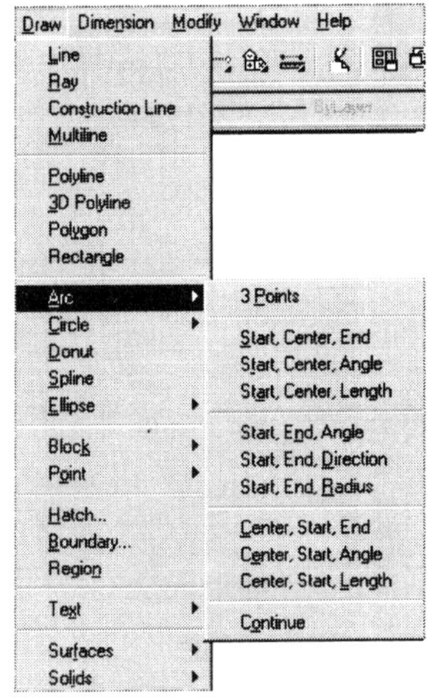

Method using three-point selection on the Arc menu:

Prompt	Response
Command:	*Click:* **Arc-3 points** (or *Type:* **A** ↵)
Specify start point of arc or [Center]:	**D1** (since default is the start point)
Specify second point of arc or [Center/End]:	*Type:* **C**↵
Specify center point of arc:	**D2** (¼″ to the left of D1)
Specify end point of arc or [Angle/chord Length]:	**D3** (¼″ to the left of D2)

Method using Start, Center, End on the Arc menu:

Prompt	Response
Command:	*Click:* **Arc-Start, Center, End**
Specify start point of arc or [Center]:	**D4**
Specify center point of arc:	**D5**
Specify end point of arc or [Angle/chord Length]:	**D6**

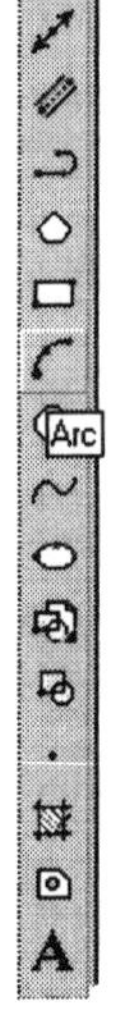

Now that you have drawn two arcs of the same size and shape, consider the choices you have in making an arc. First, look at the definitions given for the elements of an arc, Figure 9–20.

Start The beginning point of the arc (does not always have to be the first point digitized).
Center The center of the arc radius.
End The ending point of the arc.
Length The length of the chord—a straight line connecting the ends of the arc.
Direction Starting direction—used only in the Start, End, Direction sequence; all other sequences draw the arc in a counterclockwise direction (unless you specify clockwise when you set up the drawing using the Units setting).
Radius The radius of the arc.
Angle The included angle of the ends of the arc.

FIGURE 9–20
Elements of an Arc

END (E)
LENGTH OF CHORD (L)
RADIUS (R)
STARTING DIRECTION (D)
INCLUDED ANGLE (A)
CENTER (C)
START (S)

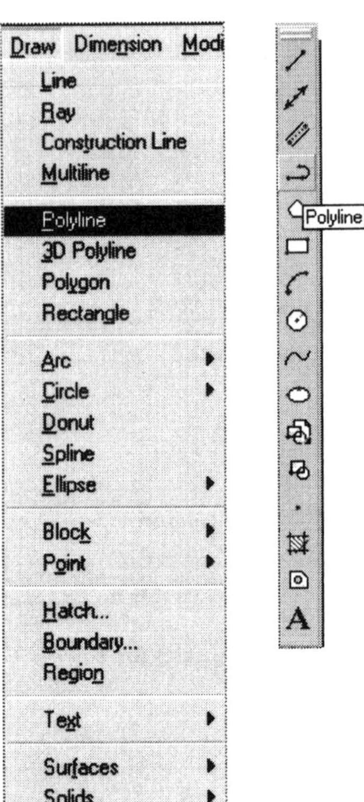

Tip: Use the same beginning and ending widths of Polyline to draw thick lines.

There are several methods of drawing arcs for specific situations or preferences. We will cover one other method in this chapter and others later where drawing problems will require the use of them.

Draw an arc of a specific radius to include a specific angle (Figure 9–19).

Radius = .315, included angle = 90°.

Prompt	**Response**
Command:	*Click:* **Arc-Start, Center, Angle**
Specify start point of arc or [CEnter]:	**D7**
Specify center point of arc :	*Type:* **@.315<180** ↵
Specify included angle:	*Type:* **90** ↵

Step 30. Draw polylines with different beginning and ending widths.

Prompt	**Response**
Command:	*Click:* **Polyline** (or *Type:* **PL** ↵)
Specify start point:	**D1** (Figure 9–21)
Specify next point or [Arc/Close/Halfwidth/Length/Undo/Width]:	*Type:* **W** ↵
Specify starting width <0.000>:	*Type:* **.2** ↵
Specify ending width <0.200>:	*Type:* **0** ↵
Specify next point or [Arc/Close/Halfwidth/Length/Undo/Width]:	**D2** (Click 2 grids to the right.) ↵
Specify next point or [Arc/Close/Halfwidth/Length/Undo/Width]:	↵
Command:	↵ (then *Select*: **(Repeat PLINE)**)
Specify start point:	**D3** (Figure 9–21)

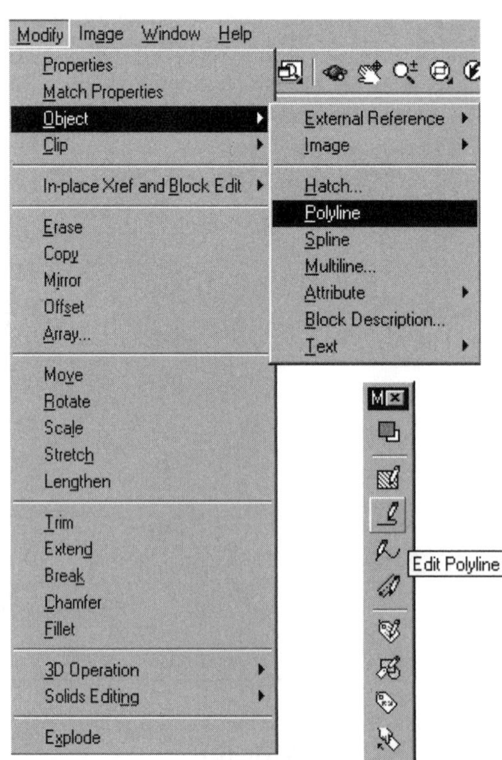

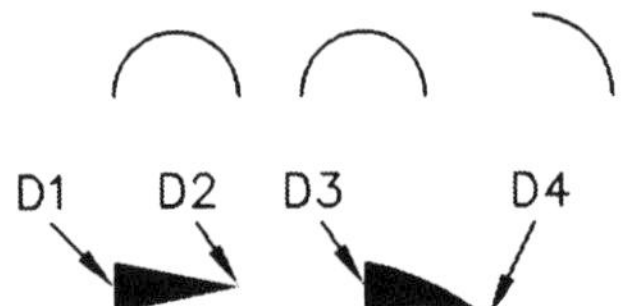

FIGURE 9–21
Polylines with Different Beginning and Ending Widths

Prompt	Response
Specify next point or [Arc/Close/Halfwidth/Length/Undo/Width]:	*Type:* **W** ↵
Specify starting width <0.000>:	*Type:* **.2** ↵
Specify ending width <0.200>:	*Type:* **0** ↵
Specify next point or [Arc/Close/Halfwidth/Length/Undo/Width]:	*Type:* **A** ↵
Specify endpoint of arc or [Angle/CEnter/CLose/Direction/Halfwidth/Line/Radius/Second pt/Undo/Width]:	**D4** (Select a curve to approximate the one shown.)
Specify endpoint of arc:	↵

Similar Shapes

Step 31. Draw a shape inside a similar shape (Figure 9–22).

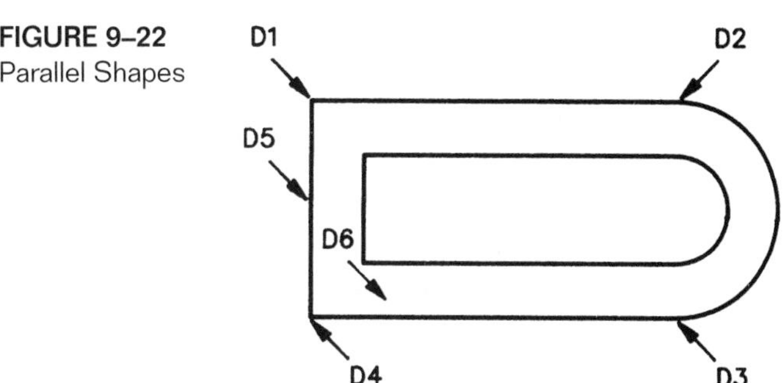

FIGURE 9–22
Parallel Shapes

All points of the inner shape are the same distance from the outer shape; the inner shape is .25″ smaller than the outer shape. Start this figure at coordinates 7.500,8.000 with SNAP ON.

Prompt	Response
Command:	*Click:* **Polyline** (or *Type:* **PL** ↵)
Specify start point:	*Type:* **7.5,8** ↵
Specify next point or [Arc/Close/Halfwidth/Length/Undo/Width]:	**D2** (or *Type:* **@2.25<0** ↵)
Specify next point or [Arc/Close/Halfwidth/Length/Undo/Width]:	*Type:* **A** ↵
Specify endpoint of arc or [Angle/CEnter/CLose/Direction/Halfwidth/Line/Radius/Second pt/Undo/Width]:	**D3** (or *Type:* **@1<270** ↵)
Specify endpoint of arc or [Angle/CEnter/CLose/Direction/Halfwidth/Line/Radius/Second pt/Undo/Width]:	*Type:* **L** ↵ (to return to the Line mode)
Specify next point or [Arc/Close/Halfwidth/Length/Undo/Width]:	**D4** or *Type*: **@2.25<180**↵
Specify next point or [Arc/Close/Halfwidth/Length/Undo/Width]:	*Type:* **C** ↵ (to close)
Command:	*Click:* **Offset** (from the Modify menu or Toolbar or *Type:* **O** ↵)
Specify offset distance or Through <Through>:	*Type:* **.25** ↵
Select object to offset or <exit>:	**D5** (anywhere on the polyline)
Specify point on side to offset:	**D6** (anywhere inside the shape)
Select object to offset or <exit>:	↵

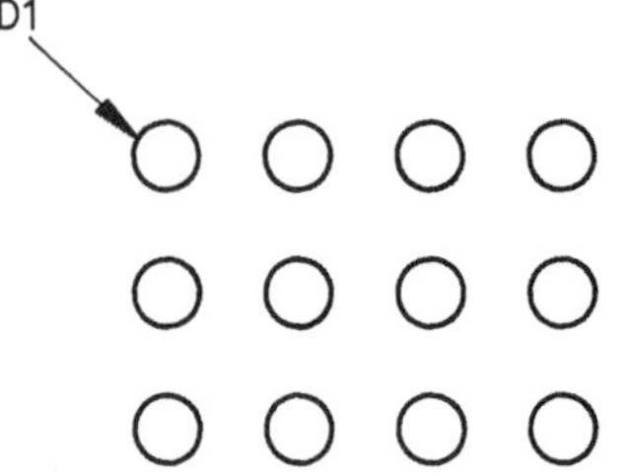

FIGURE 9–23
Rectangular Array

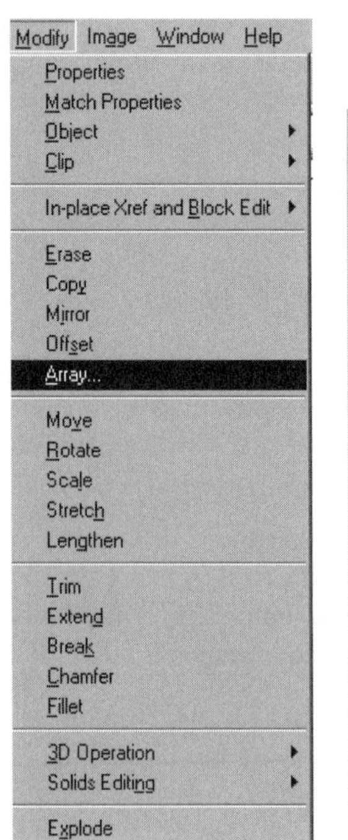

Arrays of Circles and Lines

Step 32. Draw an array of circles (Figure 9–23).

Draw three rows of four .25-diameter circles each; all circles are ½″ (.5) from center to center:

Prompt	Response
Command:	*Click:* **Circle-Center, Diameter**
Specify center point for circle or [Angle/CEnter/CLose/Direction/ Halfwidth/Line/Radius/Second pt/ Undo/Width]:	*Click:* **the center of the circle (⅝″ below the lower left corner of the shape of Figure 9–23.)**
Specify diameter of circle <1.000>:	*Type:* **.25** ↵
Command:	*Click:*
	Type: **−AR** ↵ (Be sure to include the minus sign so the dialog box does not appear this time.)
Select objects:	**D1** (any point on the circle)
Select objects:	↵
Enter the type of array [Rectangular/Polar]<R>:	*Type:* **R** ↵
Enter the number of rows (- - - - - -) <1>:	*Type:* **3** ↵
Enter the number of columns (III)<1>:	*Type:* **4** ↵
Enter the distance between rows or specify unit cell(- - - -):	*Type:* **−.5** ↵ (Rows form downward—a response of .5 forms rows upward.)
Specify the distance between columns (III):	*Type:* **.5** ↵ (Columns form to the right—a response of −.5 forms columns to the left.)

Step 33. Draw a row of seven ¼″ (.25) lines spaced ¼″ (.25) apart (Figure 9–24).

FIGURE 9–24
Rectangular Array

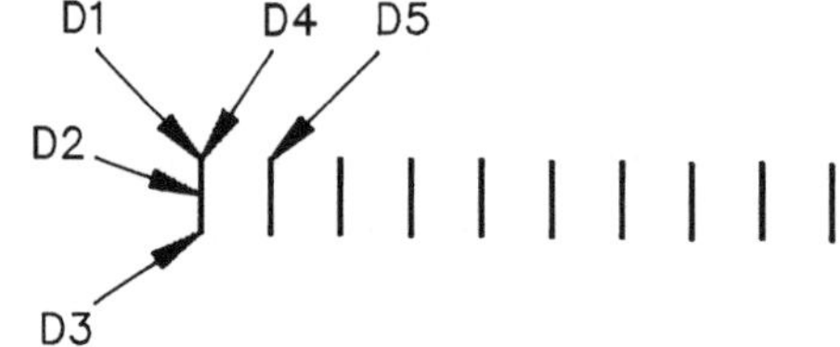

Prompt	Response
Command:	*Click:* **Line** (or *Type:* **L** ↵)
Specify first point:	**D1** (½″ below the left bottom circle of the array of Figure 9–23)
Specify next point or [Undo]:	**D3** (¼″ below D1)
Command:	*Click:* **Array** (or *Type:* **AR** ↵)
The Array dialog box appears:	*Click:* **Select Objects**
Select objects:	**D2** ↵
Select objects:	↵
The Array dialog box appears:	*Click:* **Rectangular Array**
	Type: **1** (in the Rows: box)
	Type: **7** (in the Columns: box)

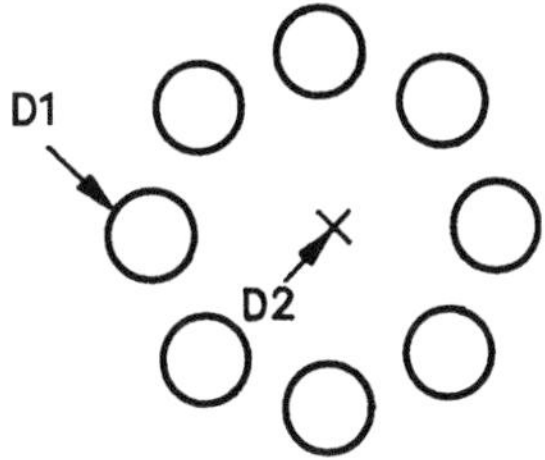

FIGURE 9–25
Polar Array

Prompt	Response
	Click: **the column offset: Arrow** (on the right)
Specify the distance between columns:	**D4** (Click two points to specify the spacing between columns or rows.)
Specify second point	**D5** (¼″ to the right of D4—SNAP must be ON)
The Array dialog box appears:	*Click:* **OK**

Step 34. Draw a circular (polar) pattern of eight ¼″- (.25-) diameter circles on a 1″-diameter bolt circle (circular center line) (Figure 9–25).

Prompt	Response
Command:	*Click:* **Circle-Center, Diameter**
Specify center point for circle or [3P/2P/Ttr (tan tan radius)]:	*Click:* **the center for the circle (1¼″ below the left line of the array of Figure 9–24.)**
Specify diameter of circle <0.250>:	↵
Command:	*Type:* **−AR** ↵ (Use the minus sign so the dialog box does not appear this time.)
Select objects:	*Click:* **D1**
Select objects:	↵
Enter the type of array [Rectangular/Polar]<R>:	*Type:* **P** ↵
Specify center point of array:	**D2** (D2 is .5″ to the right of the digitized circle from its right edge.)
Enter the number of items in the array:	*Type:* **8** ↵
Specify the angle to fill (+ = ccw, − = cw) <360>:	↵ (ccw means counterclockwise, cw is clockwise, 360 is the number of degrees in a circle—you may specify fewer than 360.)
Rotate arrayed objects [Yes/No]<Y>:	↵ (In this case yes or no will give the same pattern; rotation of the objects keeps them perpendicular to a radius drawn from the center of a circle.)

On Your Own

Undo the polar array and redo it using the Array dialog box (*Type:* **AR** ↵ or *Select:* Array from the menu or toolbar.)

Extending Lines

Step 35. Extend lines (Figure 9–26).

FIGURE 9–26
Extending Lines

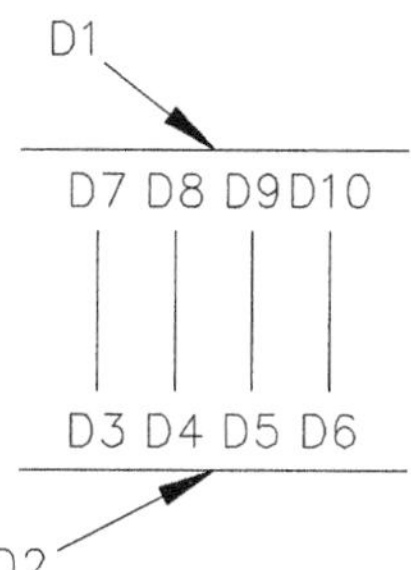

Draw four ½″ vertical lines ¼″ apart. Draw 1¼″ horizontal lines ¼″ below and above the vertical lines. Extend the vertical lines to the horizontal lines by using the Extend command. *Before you begin,* draw the lines shown in Figure 9–26, ½″ below the polar array. Extend the vertical lines to the horizontal line.

Prompt	**Response**
Command:	*Click:* **Extend** from the Modify menu or toolbar (or *Type:* **EX** ↵)
Select boundary edges… Select objects:	**D1, D2,** then *Press:* ↵ (Figure 9–26)
Select objects to extend or shift-select to trim or [Project/Edge/Undo]:	**D3, D4, D5, D6, D7, D8, D9, D10** ↵ (Click the lower ends of the vertical lines; then click the upper ends of the vertical lines.)

Trimming Lines

Step 36. Trim lines (arcs, circles, etc.).

Before you begin, draw six vertical ¾″ lines ¼″ apart 1″ to the left of Figure 9–26. Draw four horizontal 1¼″ lines ¼″ apart to form Figure 9–27A. Trim lines using crossing window to select.

Note: You may select a crossing window without typing by clicking any open point on the drawing and dragging the cursor to the left.

Prompt	**Response**
Command:	*Click:* **Trim** from the Modify menu or toolbar (or *Type:* **TR** ↵)
Select cutting edges:… Select objects:	*Click*: **D1** (Figure 9–27)
Specify opposite corner:	**D2**
Select objects:	↵ (You are finished with selecting cutting edges.)
Select object to trim or shift-select to extend or [Project/Edge/Undo]:	**D3 through D16** ↵ (Figure 9–27B; Click all lines between squares, as shown in Figure 9–1.)

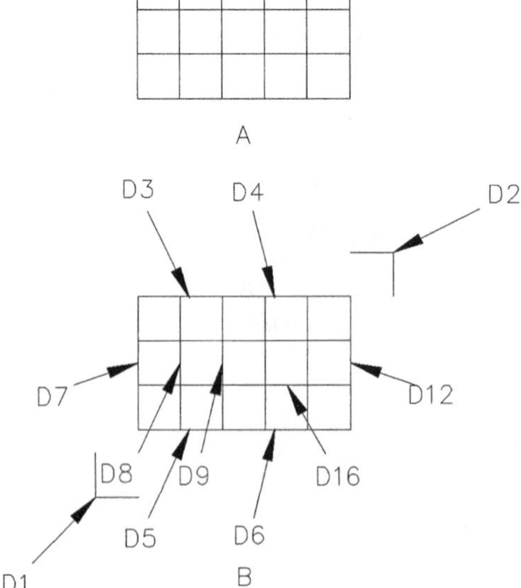

FIGURE 9–27
Trimming Lines

Changing Line Length

Step 37. Change the length of the line in Figure 9–3 from 2.000 to 2.500 using the Change command.

Prompt	Response
Command:	*Type:* **CHANGE** ↵
Select objects:	**Select the first line you drew in this exercise by clicking it.**
Select objects:	↵
Specify change point or [Properties]:	**Click a point ½″ to the right of the endpoint of the line you selected or** *Type:* **@.5<0** ↵.

Step 38. Change the length of the line in Figure 9–4 from 1.985 to 2.500 using the Lengthen command.

Prompt	Response
Command:	*Click:* **Lengthen** from the Modify menu or toolbar (or *Type:* **LEN** ↵)
Select an object or [DElta/Percent/Total/DYnamic]:	*Type:* **T** ↵
Specify total length or [Angle](1.000):	*Type:* **2.5** ↵
Select an object to change or [Undo]:	*Click:* **the second line you drew in this exercise**
Select an object to change or [Undo]:	↵

The Lengthen command allows you either to select the entity first and then specify the new length or to specify the new length and then pick one or more entities. You also have the following four options to use in specifying the new length:

DElta This option allows you to specify the amount by which you wish to lengthen an entity. For example, a DElta setting of .25 will lengthen a 2″ line to 2.25.

Percent This option allows you to specify the percentage of the original length you wish to change to. For example, a Percent setting of 150 will lengthen a 2″ line to 3″.

Total This option allows you to specify the new total length. For example, a Total setting of 2.5 will change a 2″ line to 2.5″.

DYnamic This option allows you to lengthen the entity by clicking the new length with your digitizer.

Stretching Entities

Note: *Stretch* can be used to stretch or shrink entities in one direction.

Step 39. Use the Stretch command to shorten the shape of Figure 9–22.

Prompt	Response
Command:	*Click:* **Stretch** from the Modify menu or toolbar (or *Type:* **S** ↵; be sure SNAP and ORTHO are ON.)
Select objects:	**D2** (Figure 9–28)(Picking right and dragging left gives you a crossing window.)
Specify opposite corner	**D1**
Select objects:	↵
Speify base point or displacement:	**D3**
Specify second point of displacement:	**D4** (½″ to the left)

Step 40. Draw multiple lines and clean up corners as you draw.

FIGURE 9–28
Using Stretch

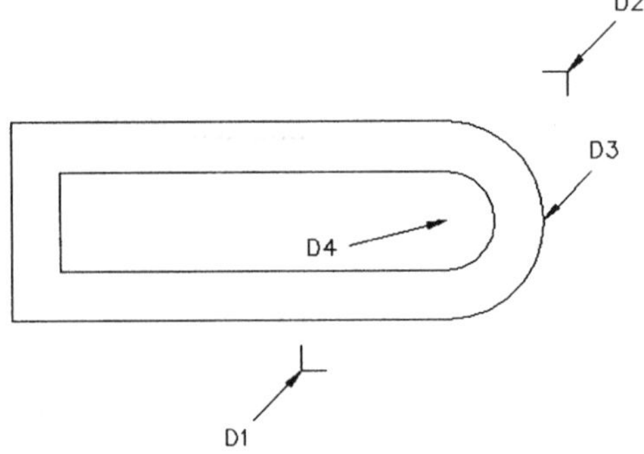

Prompt	Response
Command:	*Click:* **Multiline Style...** (or *Type:* **MLSTYLE ↵**)
The Multiline Styles dialog box appears:	*Click:* **the Name: button. Delete the word STANDARD and** *Type:* **THREE ↵** (as shown in Figure 9–29) *Click:* **the Description: button and** *Type:* **WALLS** *Click:* **Add** to make the style current *Click:* **the Element Properties... button.**
The Element Properties dialog box appears:	*Click:* **to the right of all numbers in the offset button** (or *Click:* and drag across them to highlight, or double click them) *Type:* **.75** *Click:* **the Add button** **Highlight all numbers in the Offset button.** *Type:* **.5** *Click:* **the Add button**

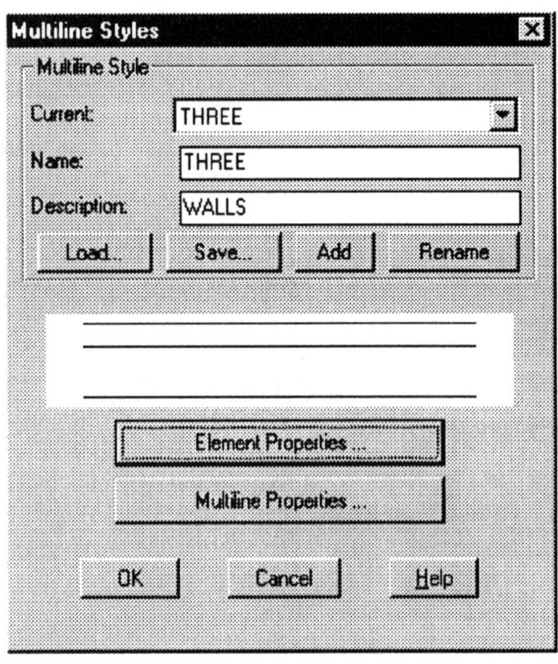

FIGURE 9–29
Multiline Styles Dialog Box

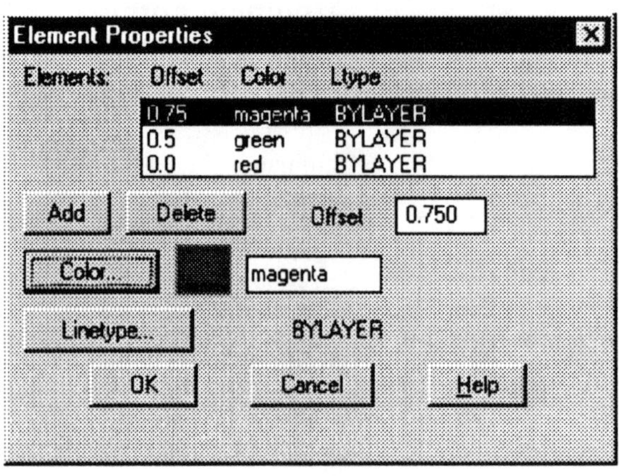

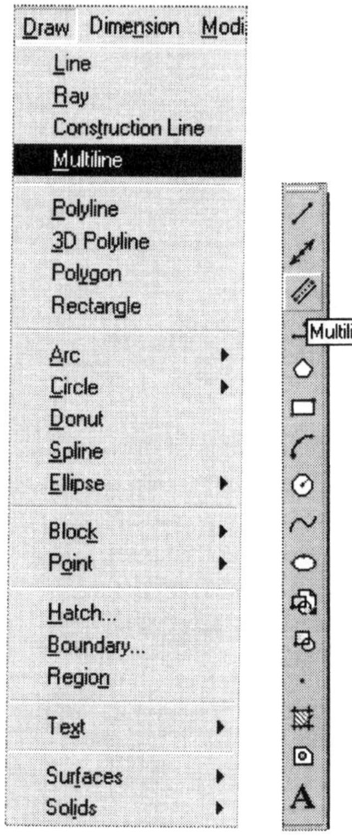

You should now have three lines with offsets of .75, .5, and 0 (Figure 9–29).

Prompt	Response
Offset 0.0 is highlighted:	*Click:* **Color... as shown in Figure 9–29.**
The Select Color dialog box appears:	*Click:* **Red** *Click:* **OK** *Highlight:* **the 0.5 Offset** *Click:* **Color...**
The Select Color dialog box appears:	*Click:* **Green** *Click:* **OK** *Highlight:* **the 0.75 Offset** *Click:* **Color...**
The Select Color dialog box appears:	*Click:* **Magenta** *Click:* **OK**
The Element Properties dialog box appears:	**Highlight any other offset lines and delete them.** *Click:* **OK**
The Multiline Styles dialog box appears:	*Click:* **Save**
The Save Multiline Style dialog box appears:	*Click:* **Save**
The Multiline Styles dialog box appears:	*Click:* **Load...**
The Load Multiline Styles dialog box appears:	*Click:* **THREE** *Click:* **OK**
The Multiline Styles dialog box appears:	*Click:* **OK**

Notice that the 0,0 red line is the origin from which all other lines are drawn. The distance from the red line to the green line when drawn at a scale of 1.000 will be 0.500. The distance from the green line to the magenta line will be 0.250 (0.750 − 0.500) or 0.750 from the green line to the red line (the origin).

Now, draw some lines at a scale of ¼ (.250).

Prompt	Response
Command:	*Click:* **Multiline** (or *Type:* **ML** ↵)
Specify start point or [Justification/Scale/STyle]:	*Type:* **S** ↵
Enter mline scale <1.000>:	*Type:* **.25** ↵
Specify start point or [Justification/Scale/STyle]:	*Type:* **9.5,4.75** ↵
Specify next point or [Undo]:	*Type:* **@.75<0**
Specify next point or [Undo]:	*Type:* **@.5<270**
Specify next point or [Undo]:	*Type:* **@.25<0**
Specify next point or [Undo]:	*Type:* **@1.25<270**
Specify next point or [Undo]:	*Type:* **@1<180**
Specify next point or [Undo]:	*Type:* **C** ↵

If you make a mistake in specifying a point, type U and press ↵ to select the Undo option from the Multiline prompt.

There are two other options on the Multiline command:

Justification This option allows you to specify whether you want the lines above or below the points specified.

STyle This option allows you to select a different style from the list of styles in the Multiline Styles dialog box.

The Multiline command allows you to draw from 1 to 16 lines at the same time and allows you to specify spacing, color, and linetype for each line.

In addition, you may also turn fill on in the Multiline Style dialog box under Multiline Properties.

You have completed Exercise 9–1.

Step 4. Print your drawing to fit on an 11″, 8.5″ sheet.

Step 5. Save your drawing in two places and Exit AutoCAD.

Prompt	**Response**
Command:	*Click:* **SaveAs...** (Save your drawing on a floppy disk and on the hard drive—you will have to initiate the SaveAs command twice, specifying the floppy drive once and the hard drive the second time. Name the drawing EX9–1(your initials), then Exit.

The preceding paragraphs cover many of the constructions you will encounter in this book and in industry. Other constructions are presented in later chapters, but understanding how to use these will provide a basis for your later work.

EXERCISES

EXERCISE 9–1. Draw Figure 9–1 using the instructions contained in this chapter.

EXERCISE 9–2. Set up an 8½″ × 11″ sheet and draw a ½″ border inside of it. Place your name ¼″ up and ¼″ over from the lower right corner in .1″-high letters. Set SNAP, ORTHO, and GRID at a setting you think is convenient. Arrange the following in order on your sheet inside the border, leaving approximately ½″ between each problem.

a. Draw a line 2.0″ long.
b. Draw a line 3.125″ long at a 30° angle upward to the right.
c. Draw two lines 3.5″ long, parallel to each other, .375″ apart.
d. Draw a 2″ line with a .5″ line perpendicular to it, .625″ from the left end.
e. Draw a line 3″ long and divide it into 7 equal parts; an X must appear where each division occurs.
f. Draw a 3″ line and divide it into .625″ segments; an X must appear where each segment ends.
g. Draw two lines 1″ long to form a 90° angle. Make a .25 chamfer at the corner.
h. Draw two 1″ lines to form a 90° angle. Make a .250 fillet at the corner.
i. Draw a polar array of eight .25″-diameter circles on a 2″-diameter circular center line.
j. Draw three 1″-diameter semicircles using three different Arc commands. Label each arc with the command used, for example: Start, Center.
k. Draw an arc with a radius of .45″ and include an angle of 60°.
l. Draw a 1½″ square using the Polyline command. Draw a 1¼″ and a 1″ square using the Offset command; all squares must be concentric.

EXERCISE 9–3. Make an AutoCAD drawing of the fan shown in Figure 9–30. Measure the picture and duplicate it on a vertical 8½″ × 11″ sheet. Place your name in the lower right corner.

EXERCISE 9–4. Make an AutoCAD drawing of the floor plan shown in Figure 9–31. Make the drawing full size and plot to fit on a horizontal 8½″ × 11″ sheet. Select architectural units and set drawing limits at 40′, 30′ for the upper right corner. Place your name in the lower right corner. Do not put any dimensions or center lines on your drawing. Make windows and doors 3′-0″ wide and walls 6″ thick.

EXERCISE 9–5. Draw Figure 9–32, following the instructions given for Exercise 9–4.

FIGURE 9–30
Exercise 9–3

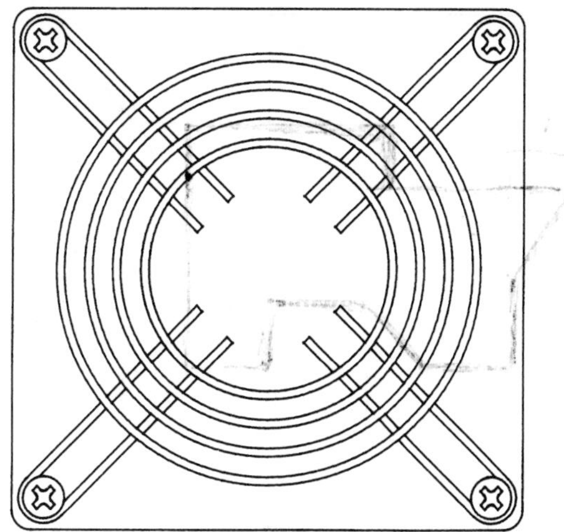

FIGURE 9–31
Exercise 9–4

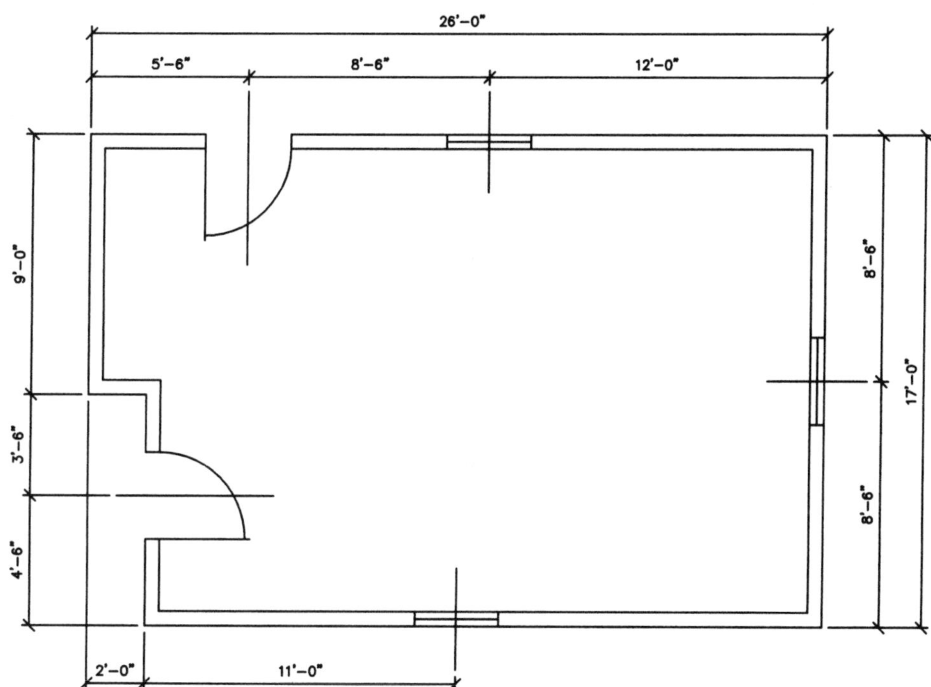

FIGURE 9–32
Exercise 9–5

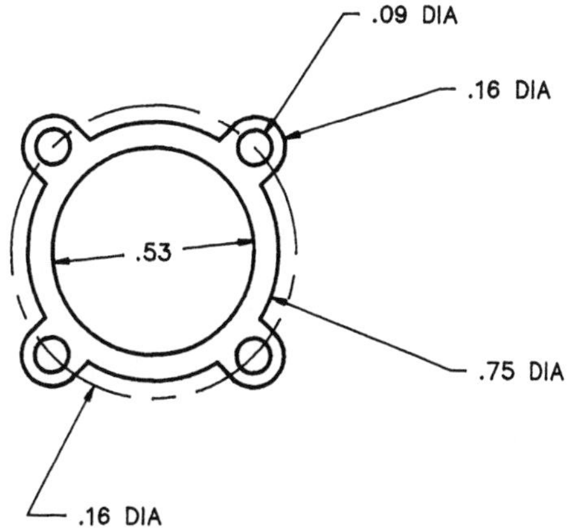

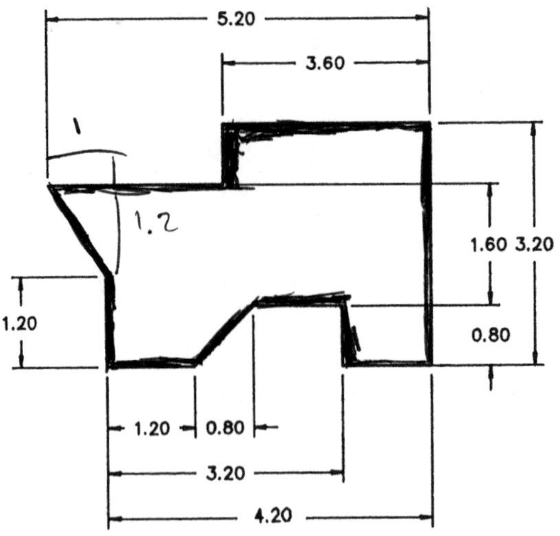

FIGURE 9–33
Exercise 9–6

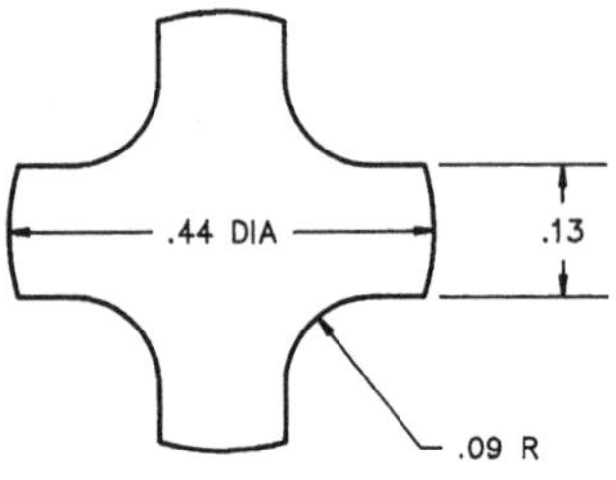

FIGURE 9–34
Exercise 9–7

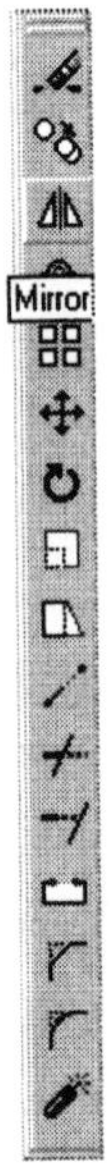

EXERCISE 9–6. Draw Figure 9–33. Make the drawing the same dimensions as shown and place it on a horizontal 11″ × 8½″ sheet. Do not put any dimensions on your drawing. Place your name in the lower right corner.

EXERCISE 9–7. Draw Figure 9–34, following the instructions given in Exercise 9–7.

EXERCISE 9–8. Make an AutoCAD drawing of the door shown in Figure 9–35. Measure the drawing and reproduce it twice its size as accurately as possible. Place it on a horizontal 8.5″ × 11″ sheet. Place your name in the lower right corner. Use the Mirror command (*Type:* **MI**↵) to produce a mirror image of any features. Leave ORTHO ON when you select mirror lines for ease in locating the second point of the mirror line. You will find Mirror to be very effective for this problem. Be sure to watch the prompts during this command and follow them carefully.

EXERCISE 9–9. Draw Figure 9–36, following the instructions given in Exercise 9–8. Place it on a horizontal 8.5″ × 11″ sheet.

EXERCISE 9–10. Draw the conference room full size as shown in Figure 9–37. Plot at ¼″=1′ on a landscape 11″ × 8½″ sheet. Place your name in the lower right corner. Select architectural units and reset drawing limits to 30′, 20′. Do not place dimensions or text as shown in the figure.

FIGURE 9–35
Exercise 9–8

FIGURE 9–36
Exercise 9–9

FIGURE 9–37
Exercise 9–10

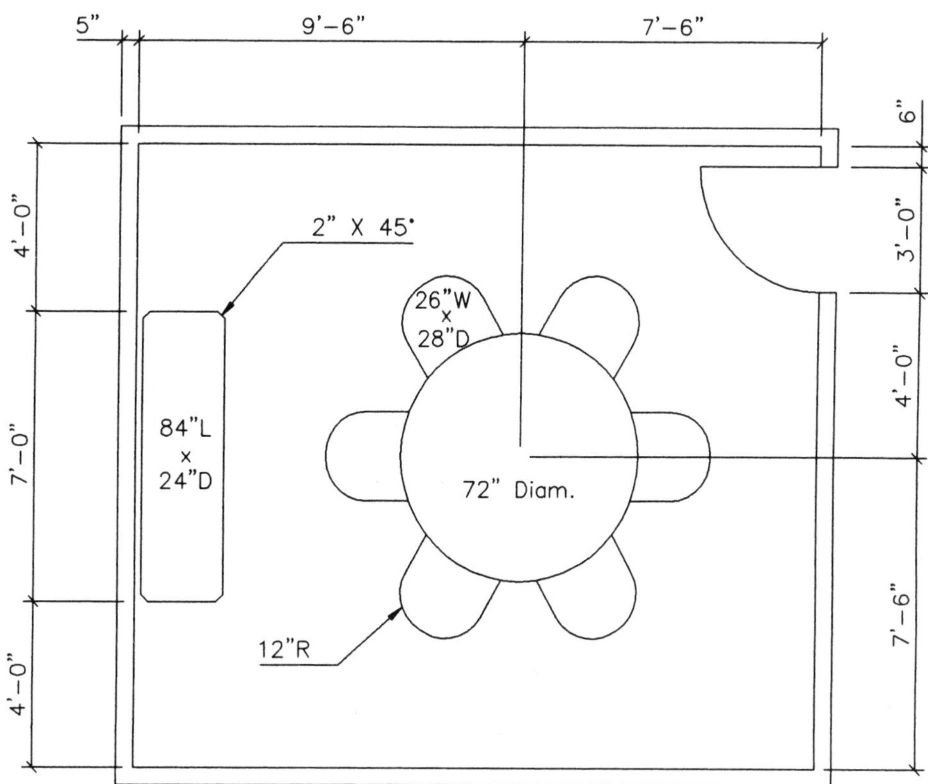

FIGURE 9–38
Exercise 9–11

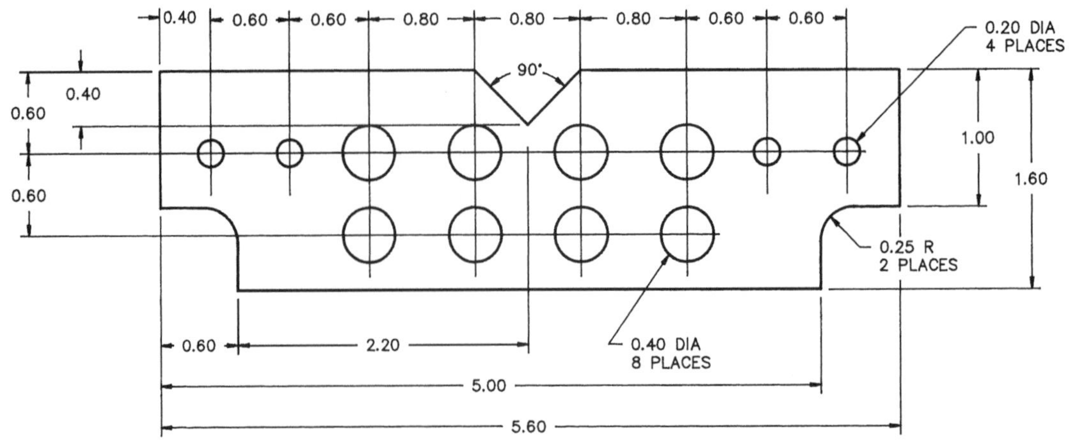

EXERCISE 9–11. Make an AutoCAD drawing of the part shown in Figure 9–38. Make the drawing the same dimensions as shown and place it on a horizontal 11″ × 8½″ sheet. Do not put any dimensions on your drawing. Place your name in the lower right corner.

REVIEW QUESTIONS

Circle the best answer.

1. What is the maximum number of characters that may be used for a drawing name?
   a. 8
   b. 32
   c. 64
   d. 255
   e. Any number
2. If the Grid spacing is .25″ and the Snap must touch every line of the GRID, at what should the Snap be set?
   a. .06
   b. .125
   c. .1
   d. .2
   e. .3
3. What is the command used to trim lines between cutting edges?
   a. Edit
   b. Trim
   c. Erase
   d. Copy
   e. Extend
4. From the Line prompt "Specify next point or [Undo]" which is the correct response to draw a horizontal line 4.501″ long to the right of the starting point?
   a. 4.501<180↵
   b. 4.501 ↵
   c. <180°<4.501↵
   d. @4.501<0 ↵
   e. <0° 4.501 ↵
5. To draw a line 5.000″ long that proceeds downward at a 45° angle to the right, which is the correct response to the prompt "Specify next point or [Undo]"?
   a. @5 <135
   b. @5.00 <45
   c. @5.00 <−45
   d. 5.000,135
   e. 5.000 <45°

6. To draw a line parallel to another line, which of the following commands should be used?
   a. Line parallel
   b. Parallel
   c. Offset
   d. Offset parallel
   e. LP
7. To draw a line perpendicular to another line from a point, which of the following options should be used?
   a. SQUARE
   b. RT ANGLE
   c. Perpendicular (from the OSNAP menu)
   d. 90° ANGLE
   e. @90°
8. If you have just drawn a line at the wrong angle and you want to return to the starting point of the line, enter
   a. Redo
   b. R
   c. U
   d. Esc
   e. Erase
9. What is the variable setting used to make a point appear as an X?
   a. Node
   b. Point Set
   c. Pdsize
   d. Pdmode
   e. Node set
10. To divide a given line into five equal parts, which of the following commands should be used?
    a. Measure
    b. Divide
    c. Break
    d. Change
    e. Polyline
11. To divide a given line into ½″ increments, which of the following commands should be used?
    a. Measure
    b. Divide
    c. Break
    d. Change
    e. Polyline
12. To make a 45° angle at the corner of two intersecting lines, which of the following commands should be used?
    a. Measure
    b. Fillet
    c. Break
    d. Change
    e. Chamfer
13. To make a ¼″ radius at the intersection of two lines, which of the following commands should be used?
    a. Measure
    b. Fillet
    c. Break
    d. Change
    e. Chamfer
14. A response of .5 to the prompt "diameter/<radius>" will produce a circle of
    a. .5000 radius
    b. .5000 diameter
    c. .5 chord
    d. .5000 circumference
    e. .5000 chord

15. The maximum number of lines that can be drawn with the Multiline command is
    a. 2
    b. 8
    c. 12
    d. 16
    e. Unlimited
16. A pattern of 16 holes on a circular centerline may be drawn fastest using
    a. RECTANGULAR ARRAY
    b. MULTIPLE COPY
    c. COPY CIRCULAR
    d. REPEAT
    e. POLAR ARRAY
17. The command _______ was used to draw the arc shown.

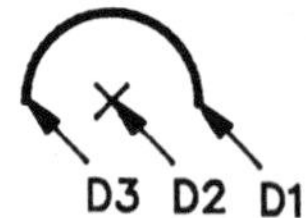

    a. ARC Center, Start, Length
    b. ARC End, Start, Center
    c. ARC Center, Start, End
    d. ARC Start, Center, End
    e. ARC Start, Center, Angle
18. A polyline is used when a series of lines must all be treated as a single entity, as in Offset.
    a. True
    b. False
19. Which of the following commands is used to extend lines to a boundary line?
    a. Move
    b. Copy
    c. Trim
    d. Edit
    e. Extend
20. Which of the following commands is used to shrink or stretch an object in one direction?
    a. Extend
    b. Trim
    c. Stretch
    d. Move
    e. Edit

10 Using 2-D Commands to Draw Orthographic Views

OBJECTIVES

After completing this chapter, you will be able to

- □ Make two-dimensional drawings to scale from two-dimensional and three-dimensional sketches using the following commands:

  Arc
  Drawing
  Limits
  Chamfer
  Line
  Circle
  Osnap
  Pan
  Fillet
  Redraw
  Point Filters
  Undo
  ID

- □ Correctly answer review questions regarding the preceding commands.

TWO-DIMENSIONAL DRAWINGS

Two-dimensional drawings are those showing only two of the three dimensions of an object in any one view. Figure 10–1 illustrates the three most commonly used two-dimensional views. The top view shows width and depth. The front view shows width and height. The right side view shows height and depth.

AutoCAD has excellent capabilities for drawing in two dimensions. The drawings can be extremely accurate and can be dimensioned in a manner ensuring correct results. Dimensioning accurately is covered in a later chapter. In this chapter the mechanics of drawing in two dimensions and the procedures needed to move quickly from one view to another are covered. Orthographic projection (two-dimensional drawing) is a major part of any good basic drafting textbook. This is a good time to review if you have questions regarding view placement or line identification. Let us begin two-dimensional drawing with a reasonably simple flat object (Figure 10–2).

Exercise 10–1: Drawing a Single Two-Dimensional View

Set Up the Drawing

Step 1. To begin Exercise 10–1, turn on the computer and start AutoCAD.

Step 2. Use a Start from Scratch to begin Exercise 10–1.

FIGURE 10–1
Standard Orthographic Views

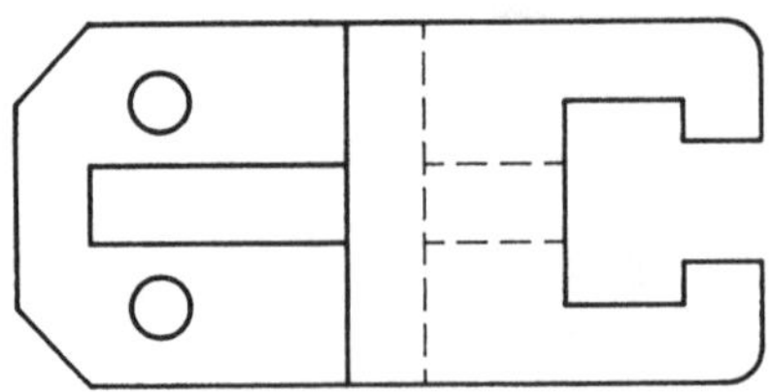

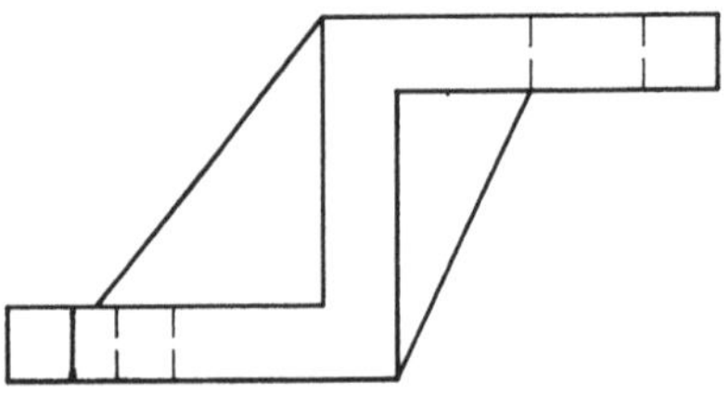

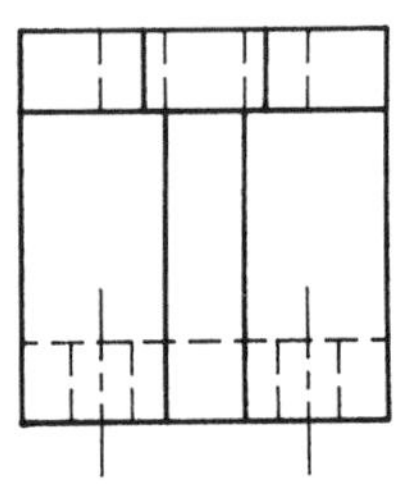

Prompt	**Response**
The AutoCAD 2002 Today window appears:	*Click:* **the Create Drawings tab**
In the Select how to begin: box	*Click:* **Start from Scratch** and make the following settings.

Step 3. Check to make sure that the following settings have been made, then save the drawing as a template under a new name. This will give you a template for a horizontal 11″ × 8.5″ page that you can use for many exercises.

Drawing Units: Decimal—2 digits to the right of the decimal point

Drawing Limits: Lower left corner: 0,0
Upper right corner: 8.5,11

Change the upper right corner limits to 11,8.5.

GRID: .25

SNAP: .125

TEXT STYLE: STANDARD FONT: SIMPLEX HEIGHT: 0

LAYERS: NAME	COLOR	LINETYPE	LINEWEIGHT
G	GREEN	HIDDEN	0.35MM
R	RED	CONTINUOUS	0.25MM
M	MAGENTA	CONTINUOUS	0.50MM

Set layer M current.

Now save the drawing as a template.

Prompt	**Response**
Command:	*Click:* **SaveAs…**
The Save Drawing As dialog box appears:	*Click:* **AutoCAD Drawing Template File (*.dwt)** in the Save as type: list box
	Type: **HOR-A** in the File name: text box
	Click: **OK**

FIGURE 10–2
Dimensions for Exercise 10–1

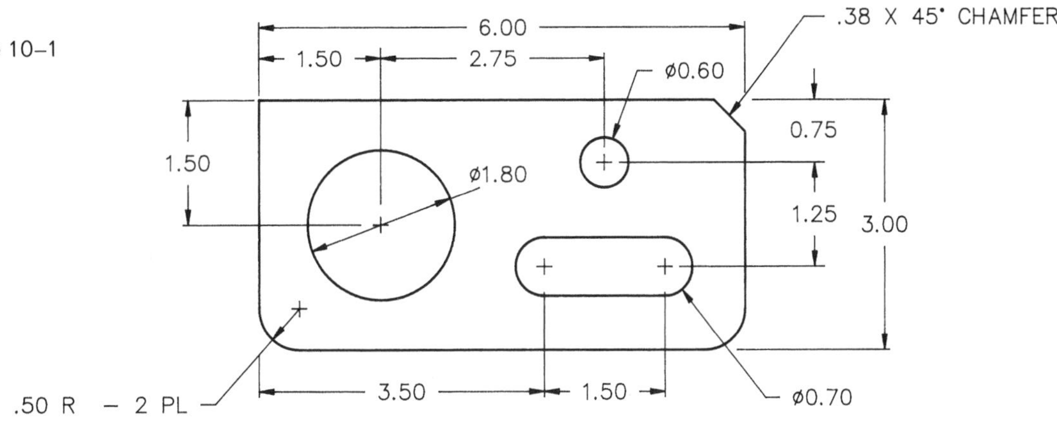

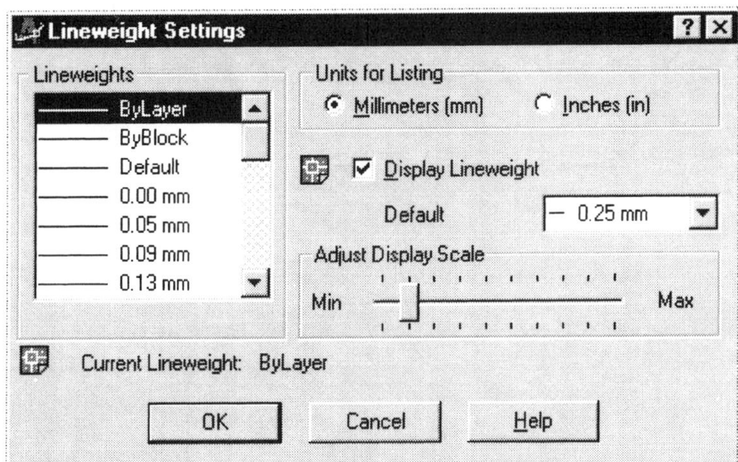

Prompt	Response
The Template Description dialog box appears:	*Type*: **HORIZONTAL A SIZE** in the Description box *Click*: **OK**

The settings for a horizontal A-size page (11″ × 8.5″) are now saved as a template with the name HOR-A.

Step 4. Use Zoom-All to view the entire drawing area.

Prompt	Response
Command:	*Click*: **Zoom-All** (or *Type:* **Z** ↵, then **A** ↵)

You are now ready to draw on layer M. Your status line at the bottom of your display should have SNAP, GRID, ORTHO, MODEL, and LWT ON. If ORTHO and SNAP are not ON, activate them from function keys F8 and F9, or double click on the label at the bottom of the screen.

Step 5. Draw the outline of Figure 10–3 using the dimensions from Figure 10–2.

Lineweight Settings Dialog Box

Before you start, take a look at the Lineweight Settings dialog box shown above. Moving the slider to the left displays the lineweight thinner; moving it to the right display the lineweight thicker. Athough the lineweight on your drawing may display very thick, it will plot in the size stated in the Layer Manager dialog box. Lineweights display in their correct width in paper space, which we will cover in a later chapter. To display the Lineweight Settings dialog box, *Right click*: **LWT** on the status bar, then *Click*: **Settings**.

FIGURE 10–3
Exercise 10–1

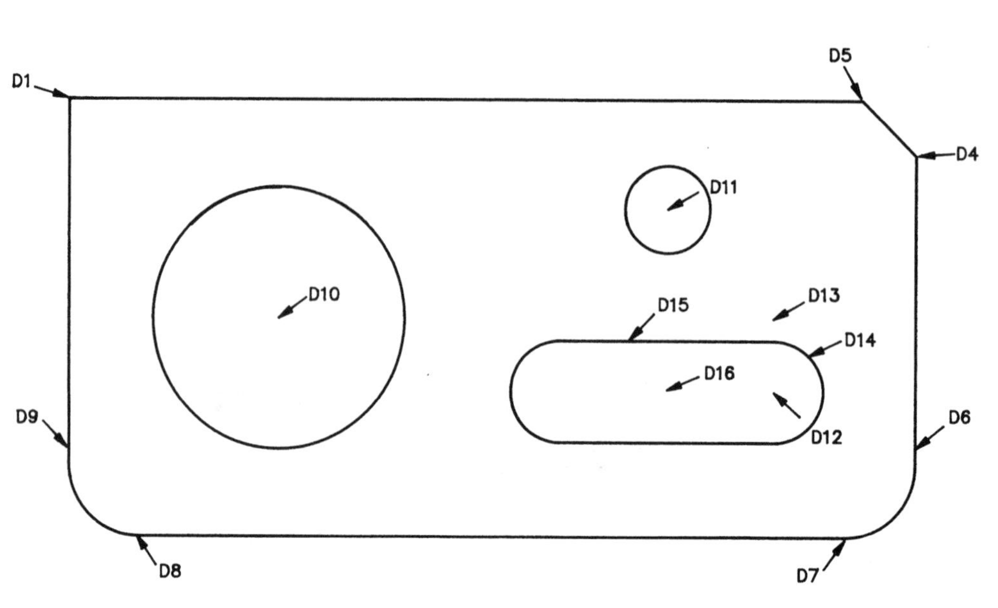

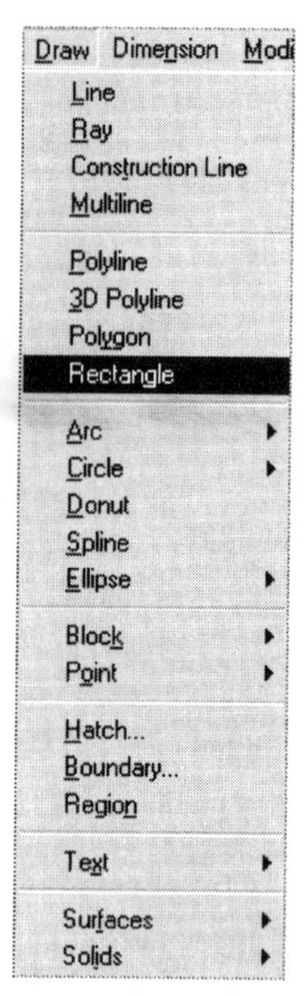

Prompt	Response
Command:	**Rectangle** (or *Type:* **REC** ↵)
Specify first corner point or [Chamfer/ Elevation/Fillet/Thickness/Width]:	*Type:* **2.5,3** ↵
Specify other corner point:	*Type:* **@6,3** ↵

Step 6. Add the chamfer to Figure 10–3.

Prompt	Response
Command:	**Chamfer** (or *Type:* **CHA** ↵)
Select first line or [Polyline/Distance/ Angle/Trim/Method]:	*Type:* **D** ↵
Specify first chamfer distance <0.00>:	*Type:* **.38** ↵
Specify second chamfer distance <0.38>:	↵
Select first line or [Polyline/Distance/ Angle/Trim/Method]:	*Click:* **D4** (Figure 10–3)
Select second line:	*Click:* **D5**

Step 7. Add fillets to Figure 10–3.

Prompt	Response
Command:	**Fillet** (or *Type:* **F** ↵)
Select first object or [Polyline/Radius/Trim]:	*Type:* **R** ↵
Specify fillet radius <0.000>:	*Type:* **.5** ↵

Prompt	Response
Select first object or [Polyline/Radius/Trim]:	*Click:* **D6** (Figure 10–3)
Select second object:	*Click:* **D7**
Command:	↵
Select first object or [Polyline/Radius/Trim]:	*Click:* **D8** (Figure 10–3)
Select second object:	*Click:* **D9**

Step 8. Add the circles to Figure 10–3.

ID

ID identifies a location from which relative coordinates may be given for a single command.

Prompt	Response
Command:	*Type:* **ID** ↵
Specify point:	**D1** (Figure 10–3)
Command:	*Type:* **C** ↵
Specify center point for circle or [3P/2P/Ttr (tan tan radius)]:	*Type:* **@1.5,−1.5** ↵
Specify radius of circle or [Diameter]:	*Type:* **.9** ↵
Command:	*Type:* **ID** ↵
Specify point:	**D1** (Figure 10–3)
Command:	*Type:* **C** ↵
Specify center point for circle or [3P/2P/Ttr (tan tan radius)]:	*Type:* **@4.25,−.75** ↵
Specify radius of circle or [Diameter]:	*Type:* **.3** ↵

Step 9. Draw the slot.

Prompt	Response
Command:	**Arc Center Start End**
Specify center point of arc:	**D12** (1″ to the left and 1″ up from the lower right corner—before it was filleted)
Specify start point of arc:	*Type:* **@.35<270** ↵
Specify endpoint of arc or [Angle/chord Length]:	**D13** (*Click:* **on any point directly above the center**)
Command:	*Type:* **L** ↵
Specify first point:	**Osnap-Endpoint**
of	**D14**
Specify next point or [Undo]:	*Type:* **@1.5<180** ↵
Specify next point or [Undo]:	↵
Command:	**Offset** (or *Type:* **O** ↵)
Specify offset distance or [Through] <Through>:	*Type:* **.7** ↵ (This sets the distance to the end of the arc.)
Select object to offset or <exit>:	**(Turn off SNAP.) D15** (Figure 10–3)

Prompt	Response
Specify point on side to offset:	**D16** (Notice how the offset line connects exactly on the end of the arc.)
Select object to offset or <exit>:	↵

Use the Fillet command to draw the other end of the slot.

Prompt	Response
Command:	**Fillet** (or *Type:* **F** ↵)
Select first object or [Polyline/Radius/Trim]:	*Type:* **R** ↵
Specify fillet radius <0.000>:	*Type:* **.35** ↵
Select first object or [Polyline/Radius/Trim]:	**D15**
Select second object:	*Click:* **on the other line of the slot**
Command:	*Type:* **R** ↵ (The REDRAW command will remove the digitized points from the screen.)

Step 10. On your own:

1. Type your name in the Simplex font in the lower right corner.
2. Save your drawing in at least two places. Name it EX10-1(your initials).
3. Plot the drawing full size on an A-size (11″ × 8½″) sheet.
4. Exit AutoCAD.

You have made and plotted a drawing with commonly used commands. Now, analyze the commands you have used and look at the following means of drawing that you must master to become an AutoCAD expert:

Absolute coordinates
Relative coordinates
Polar coordinates
ID—identify a point
Filters
Polar Tracking
Osnap Tracking

Absolute Coordinates

Absolute coordinates are given with respect to the origin 0,0. Although every point has X, Y, and Z coordinates, only X and Y are used in two-dimensional drawings. The coordinates are

X = horizontal (the first number)
Y = vertical (the second number)
Z = depth or thickness (the third number)

The Z coordinate is given a 0 or the current elevation if it is not specified. You will use Z coordinates in later chapters on three-dimensional objects.

Let's look at an example of how absolute coordinates can be used in drawing to explain this concept further. The front view of Figure 10–4 was drawn using absolute coordinates.

Exercise 10–2: Drawing Three Two-Dimensional Views of a Part

Set Up the Drawing

Step 1. To begin Exercise 10–2, turn on the computer and start AutoCAD.

Step 2. Use a template to begin Exercise 10–2.

Prompt	Response
The AutoCAD 2002 Today window appears:	*Click:* **the Create Drawings tab,** then *Click:* the template (under the letter H)
In the Select how to begin: box	*Click:* **Template, labeled HOR-A**

Step 3. Check to make sure that the following settings have been made.

Drawing Units: Decimal—3 digits to the right of the decimal point
Drawing Limits: Lower left corner: 0,0
Upper right corner: 11,8.5
GRID: .25
SNAP: .125
TEXT STYLE: STANDARD FONT: SIMPLEX HEIGHT: 0

LAYERS: NAME	COLOR	LINETYPE	LINEWEIGHT
G	GREEN	HIDDEN	0.35MM
R	RED	CONTINUOUS	0.25MM
M	MAGENTA	CONTINUOUS	0.50MM

Set layer M current.

Step 4. Use Zoom-All to view the entire drawing area.

Prompt	Response
Command:	**Zoom-All** (or *Type:* **Z** ↵, then **A** ↵)

You are now ready to draw on layer M. Your status line at the bottom of your display should have SNAP, GRID, ORTHO, MODEL, and LWT ON. If ORTHO and SNAP are not ON, activate them from function keys F8 and F9, or double click on the label at the bottom of the screen.

Step 5. Draw the outline of the front view of Figure 10–4 using absolute coordinates.

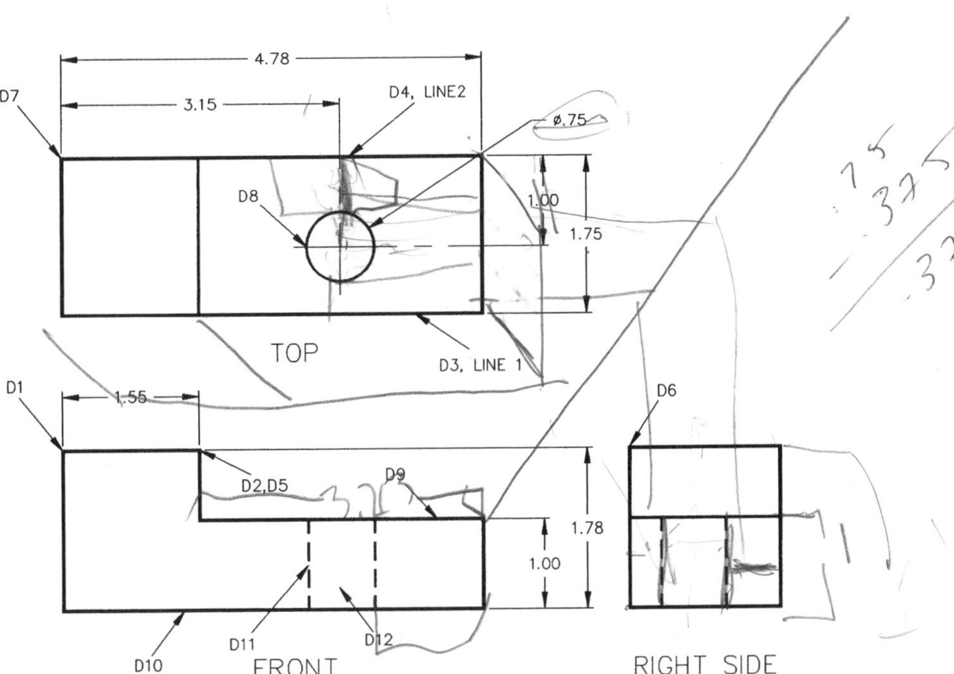

FIGURE 10–4
Dimensions for Exercise 10–2

Prompt	Response
Command:	*Type:* **L** ↵
Specify first point:	*Type:* **1,2** ↵ (1 unit in the X direction, 2 units in the Y direction)
Specify next point or [Undo]:	*Type:* **5.78,2** ↵
Specify next point or [Undo]:	*Type:* **5.78,3** ↵
Specify next point or [Undo/Close]:	*Type:* **2.55,3** ↵
Specify next point or [Undo/Close]:	*Type:* **2.55,3.78** ↵
Specify next point or [Undo/Close]:	*Type:* **1,3.78** ↵
Specify next point or [Undo/Close]:	*Type:* **C** ↵

Now, draw the top view using relative coordinates.

Relative Coordinates

Relative coordinates (relative to the point just entered) are taken from the previous point entered. The symbol @ must precede relative coordinates.

Suppose you are going to draw the outline of the top view using relative coordinates, but you do not want to do the arithmetic necessary to use absolute coordinates to locate the lower left corner of the top view. All you know is that you want the views to be 1″ apart. Osnap From allows you to do that.

OSNAP FROM

Osnap From identifies a location from which relative coordinates may be given. Therefore, every point in the outline of the top view can be drawn using relative coordinates as follows.

Step 6. Draw the outline of the top view using relative coordinates, Figure 10-4.

Prompt	Response
Command:	**Line** (or *Type:* **L** ↵)
Specify first point:	**Osnap-From** (or *Type*: **FRO** ↵)
Base point:	*Click:* **D1** (the upper left corner of the front view using Osnap-Endpoint)
Offset:	*Type:* **@0,1** ↵ (0 units in the X direction and 1 unit in the Y direction from the Base point)
Specify next point or [Undo]:	*Type:* **@4.78,0** ↵
Specify next point or [Undo]:	*Type:* **@0,1.75** ↵
Specify next point or [Undo/Close]:	*Type:* **@−4.78,0** ↵
Specify next point or [Undo/Close]:	*Type:* **C** ↵

Now draw the vertical inside line of the top view using point filters to locate the first point.

Point Filters

Point filters relate to the X, Y, and Z coordinates of a point. Point filters allow you to avoid unnecessary construction lines and to save considerable time when they are used effectively. An XZ filter, for example, says to AutoCAD, "I am pointing to the XZ location for the point now; then I will point to the Y location. Use that information to locate my point." You may filter one or two of the X, Y, and Z coordinates in any command that requires the location of a point.

Let's use a point filter to draw the vertical inside line of the top view of Figure 10–4.

Step 7. Use a point filter to draw the vertical inside line of the top view.

Prompt	Response
Command:	*Type:* **L** ↵
Specify first point:	*Type:* **.X** ↵ (or *Click:* **the .X icon on the Standard Toolbar)**
of	**D2** (Use Osnap-Endpoint and click. You are pointing to the X coordinate of the point you want.)
(need YZ)	**D3** (Use Osnap-Nearest or Endpoint and *Click:* **any point on line 1 of the top view**. You are pointing to the Y coordinate of the point. The Z coordinate in 2-D is 0 or the current elevation.)
Specify next point or [Undo]:	**D4** (Use Osnap-Perpendicular and *Click:* **on any point on line 2 of the top view.)**
Specify next point or [Undo]:	↵

Now use a Y filter to locate the top left corner of the right side view.

Step 8. Locate the top left corner of the right side view using a Y point filter.

Prompt	Response
Command:	*Type:* **L** ↵
Specify first point:	*Type:* **.Y** ↵
of:	**D5** (Use Osnap-Endpoint to pick the Y coordinate of the point.)
Need XZ:	**D6** (*Click:* **on a point approximately 1.5″ from the extreme right end of the front view. Put SNAP ON.)**
Specify next point or [Undo]:	

You will now draw the outline of the right side view using polar coordinates.

Let's look briefly at the parts of a polar coordinate.

Polar Coordinates

A polar coordinate involves distance and direction. The @ symbol indicates that a distance will follow. The response @1.75 tells AutoCAD to move 1.75 units. The < symbol indicates that an angle will follow. The response <0 tells AutoCAD to move horizontally to the right. Figure 10–5 shows the values for polar angles. Now draw the outside lines of the right side view.

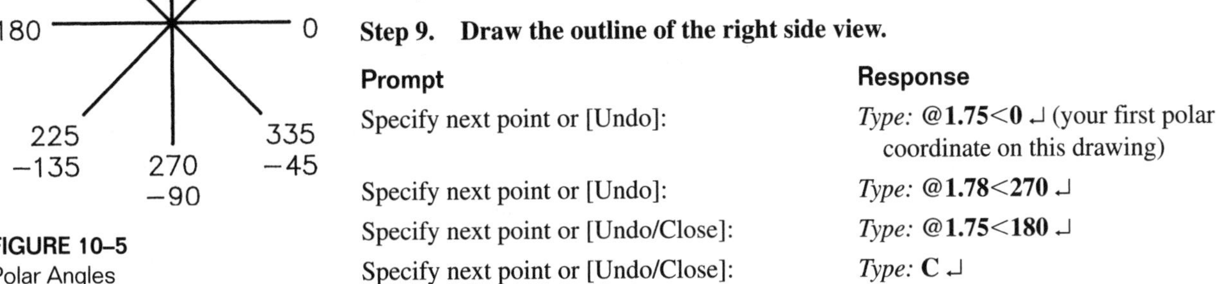

FIGURE 10–5
Polar Angles

Step 9. Draw the outline of the right side view.

Prompt	Response
Specify next point or [Undo]:	*Type:* **@1.75<0** ↵ (your first polar coordinate on this drawing)
Specify next point or [Undo]:	*Type:* **@1.78<270** ↵
Specify next point or [Undo/Close]:	*Type:* **@1.75<180** ↵
Specify next point or [Undo/Close]:	*Type:* **C** ↵

Step 10. Now use relative coordinates to locate and draw the circle in the top view.

Prompt	Response
Command:	*Type:* **ID** ↵
Specify point:	**D7** (Use Osnap-Endpoint.)
Command:	**Circle-Center, Diameter**
Specify center point for circle or [3P/2P/Ttr (tan tan radius):	*Type:* **@3.15,−1** ↵
Specify diameter of circle:	*Type:* **.75** ↵

Now use point filters to draw the hidden lines in the front view. Set layer G current and use the following procedure.

Step 11. Draw the hidden lines in the front view using point filters.

Prompt	Response
Command:	**Set Layer G current.**
Command:	*Type:* **L** ↵
Specify first point:	*Type:* **.X** ↵
of:	**D8** (Use Osnap-Quadrant.)
Need YZ:	**D9** (Use Osnap-Nearest (any point on this line).)
Specify next point or [Undo]:	**D10** (Use Osnap-Perpendicular.)
Specify next point or [Undo]:	↵
Command:	**Offset** (or *Type:* **O** ↵)
Specify offset distance or through <Through>:	*Type:* **.75** ↵
Select object to offset or <exit>:	**D11**
Specify point on side to offset:	**D12**
Select object to offset or <exit>:	↵

Step 12. On your own:

1. Set layer M current.
2. Turn SNAP ON and draw the horizontal line in the right side view.

Step 13. Duplicate the two hidden lines in the front view to the right side view.

Prompt	Response
Command:	*Type:* **CP** ↵
Select objects:	*Click:* **the two hidden lines in the front view**
Select objects:	↵
Specify base point or displacement or [multiple]:	**With SNAP OFF, use Osnap-ENDpoint to select the endpoint of one of the hidden lines.**
Specify second point of displacement or <Use first point as displacement>:	**Press F9 to turn SNAP back ON. Use the grid points to locate the correct point to pick the copied location.**

Step 14. On your own:

1. Save your drawing in at least two places. Name it EX10-2(your initials).
2. Plot the drawing full size (1 Plotted inch = 1 Drawing unit) on an 11″ × 8.5″ sheet.

3. Exit AutoCAD.

The next exercise involves a more complex part drawn in millimeters and uses a different format. The Prompt–Response format used in the earlier exercises introduces you to commands and gives you a reference that you may need later. If you have any difficulty using the following steps, refer to earlier exercises in this chapter and to the exercises in Chapter 9.

Exercise 10–3: Drawing Three Two-Dimensional Views of a More Complex Part (Figure 10–6)

Set Up the Drawing

Step 1. To begin Exercise 10–3, turn on the computer and start AutoCAD.

Step 2. Use the HOR-A template to begin Exercise 10–3.

Step 3. Change settings to the following:

UNITS: Decimal—2 digits to the right of the decimal point

LIMITS: Lower left corner: 0,0
Upper right corner: 420,297 (This sets up a metric drawing on a 17″×11″ sheet.)

GRID: 10

SNAP: 5

TEXT STYLE: STANDARD   FONT: SIMPLEX   HEIGHT: 0

LAYERS: NAME	COLOR	LINETYPE	LINEWEIGHT
G	GREEN	HIDDEN	0.35 MM
R	RED	CONTINUOUS	0.25MM
M	MAGENTA	CONTINUOUS	0.50MM

Set layer M current.

Set linetype scale to 15 (*Type*: **LTSCALE**↵, then *Type*: **15** ↵).

Step 4. Use Zoom-All to view the entire drawing area.

Step 5. Save this drawing as a template file using the name Metric-B.

Step 6. Draw part of the front view, Figure 10–7. Use absolute coordinates to locate the lower left corner of the front view at 80,50. Use the Line command with relative or polar coordinates to draw the remainder of Figure 10–7. Use dimensions from Figure 10–6.

Direct Distance Entry

Direct distance entry allows you to specify a point (to draw, move, copy, etc.) by moving your mouse to indicate the direction and typing the distance, then pressing ↵ . This is the fastest way to draw many objects. It is most useful with ORTHO ON so that it is easy to indicate the direction.

Calculator

You will have to do some adding and subtracting to find the right coordinates. You can use the calculator from Windows in the Accessories folder. Figure 10–8 shows the path to the calculator. You can move the calculator if you choose and minimize it for use whenever you need it. The view option on the calculator allows you to display either a scientific or a standard calculator.

Step 7. Use the Rectangle command to draw the outline of the top view as shown in

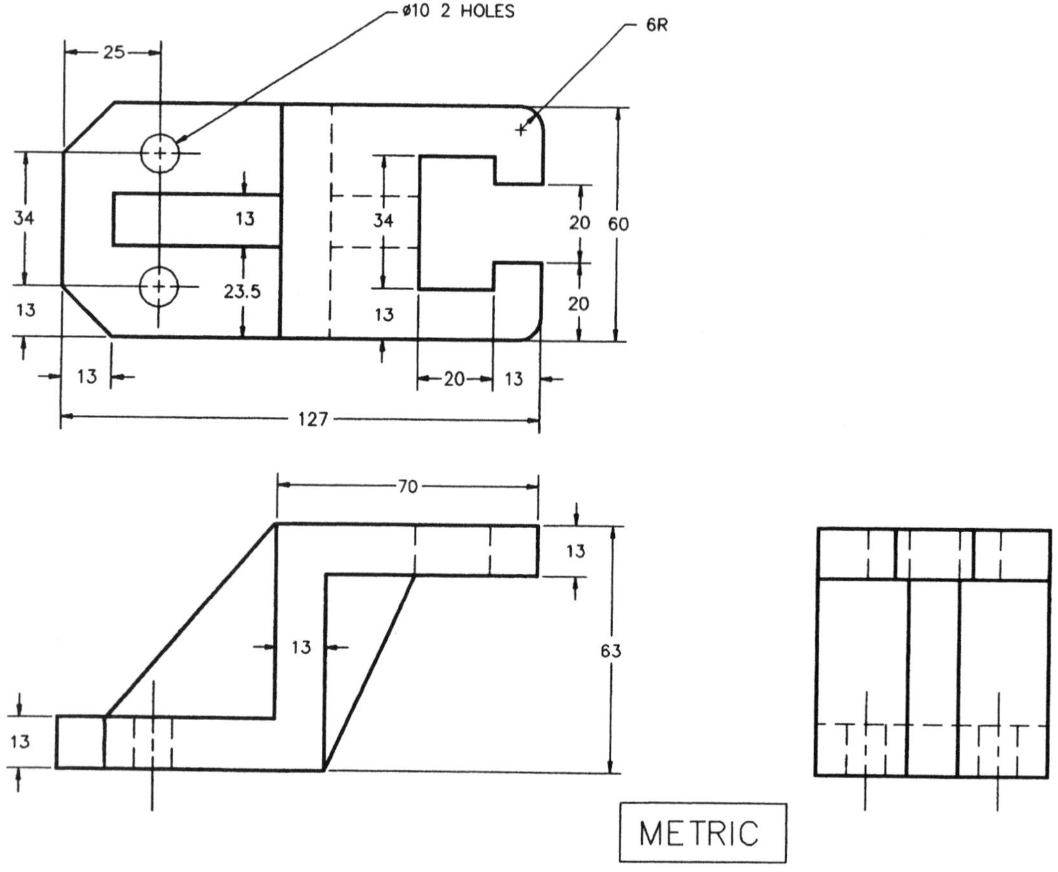

FIGURE 10–6
Dimensions for Exercise 10–3

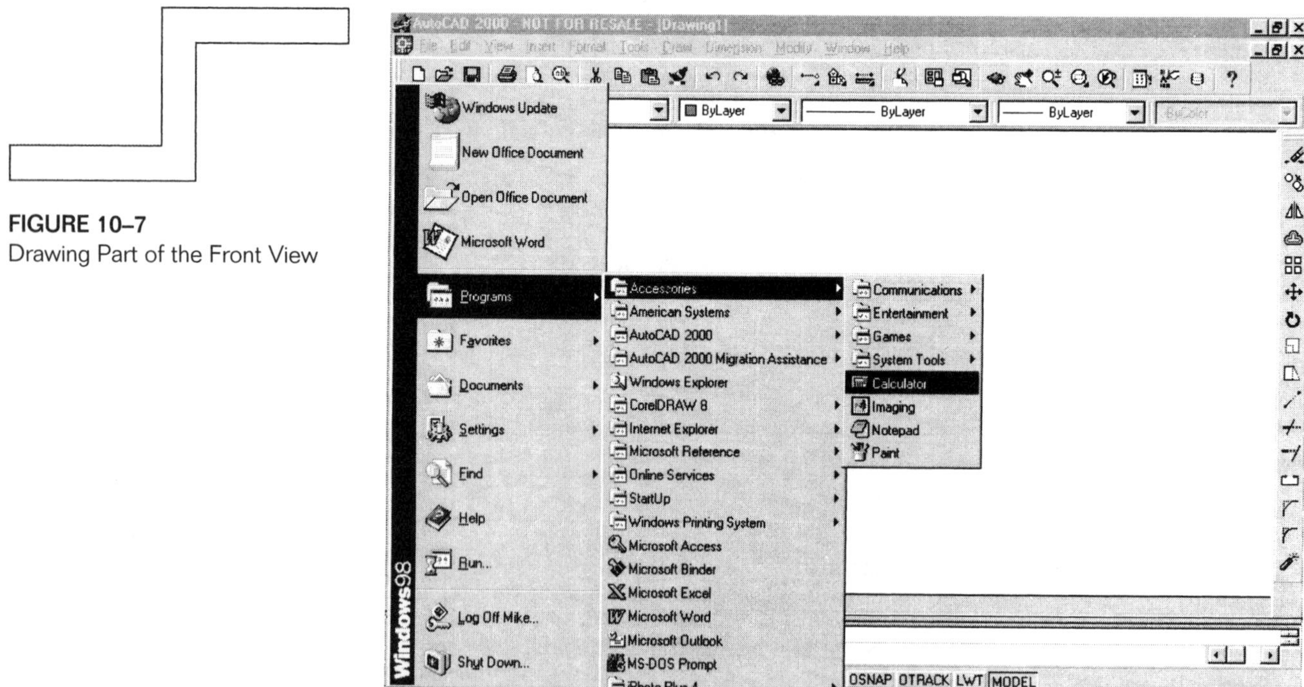

FIGURE 10–7
Drawing Part of the Front View

FIGURE 10–8
Path to the Windows Calculator

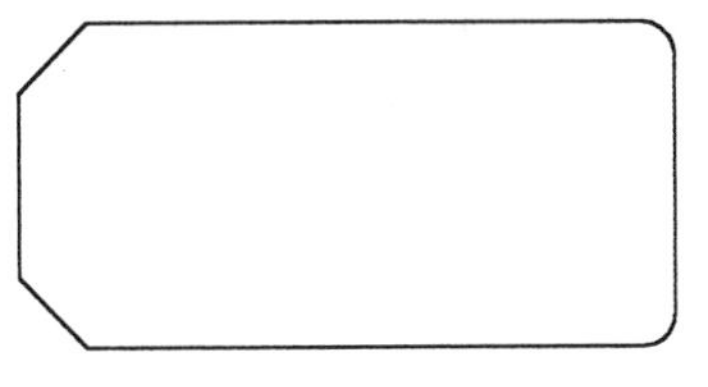

Figure 10–9. Locate the lower left corner of the rectangle at coordinates 80,180. Use the Chamfer and Fillet commands to create chamfers and fillets.

Step 8. Use point filters with the Line command to draw the continuous vertical line in the top view (Figure 10–10).

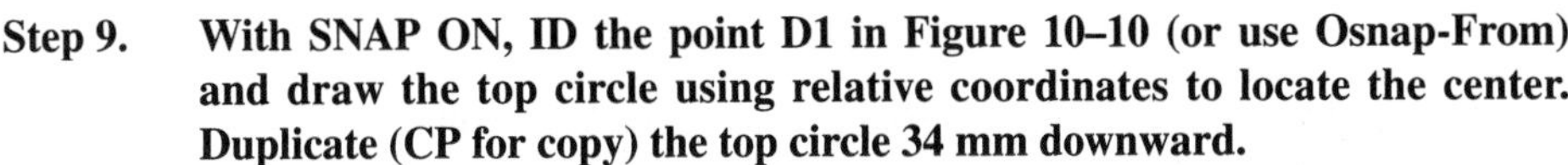

Step 9. With SNAP ON, ID the point D1 in Figure 10–10 (or use Osnap-From) and draw the top circle using relative coordinates to locate the center. Duplicate (CP for copy) the top circle 34 mm downward.

Step 10. Draw the top view of the wedge shape using the line command and the From Osnap mode (Figure 10–11). When AutoCAD asks "Specify first point:", activate Osnap-From. At the "Base point:" prompt activate Osnap-Endpoint and click the lower end of the inside vertical line. At the <Offset>: prompt *Type:* **@23.5<90.** This locates the right end of line 1, which is 44 units long. Use relative or polar coordinates to draw the first two lines, then use Osnap-Perpendicular to complete the third line.

Step 11. Use the Line command with Osnap-From and point filters to locate the first point, D1, and relative or polar coordinates to draw the cutout in the right end of the part. Use the Trim command to delete the line across the right end of the cutout.

Step 12. Use the Line command with Osnap-Endpoint for the first point and point filters for the second point to draw the wedge shapes in the front view.

Another way to do this is to use the Construction Line command to draw vertical construction lines through points in the top view as shown in Figure 10–12. Erase the construction lines when you have drawn the wedge shapes.

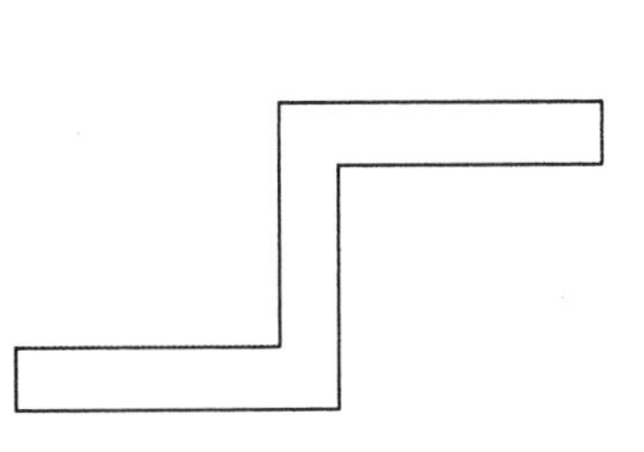

FIGURE 10–9
Drawing the Outline of the Top View

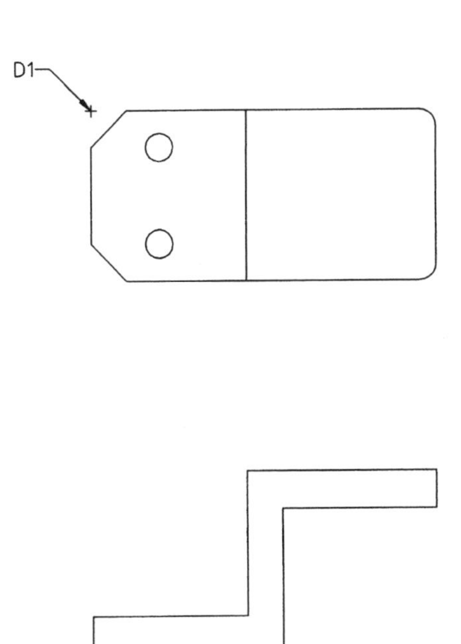

FIGURE 10–10
Drawing the Continuous Vertical Line and the Two Circles

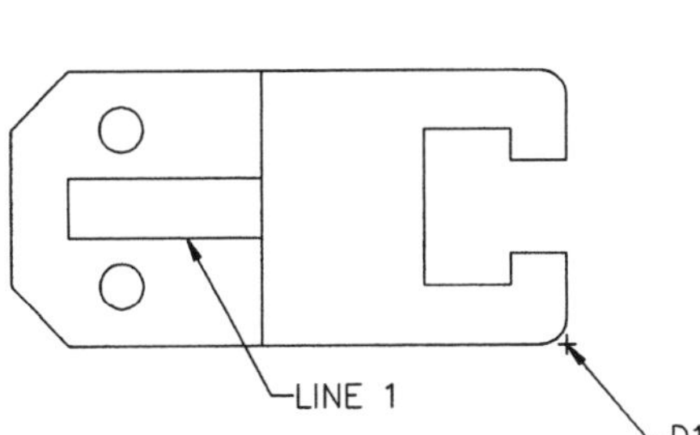

FIGURE 10–11
Drawing the Top View of the Wedge Shape and the Cutout

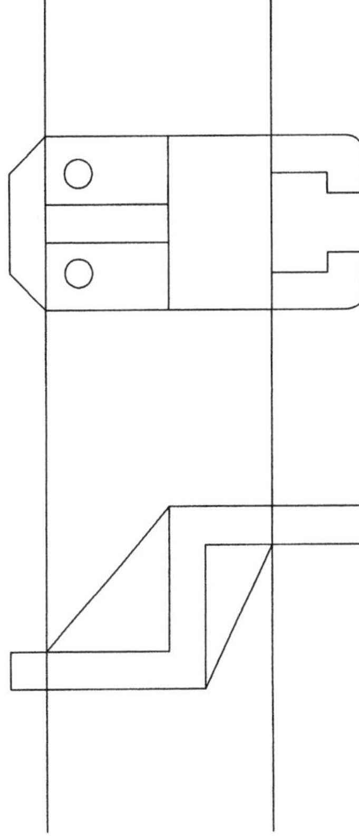

FIGURE 10–12
Drawing the Wedge Shapes in the Front View

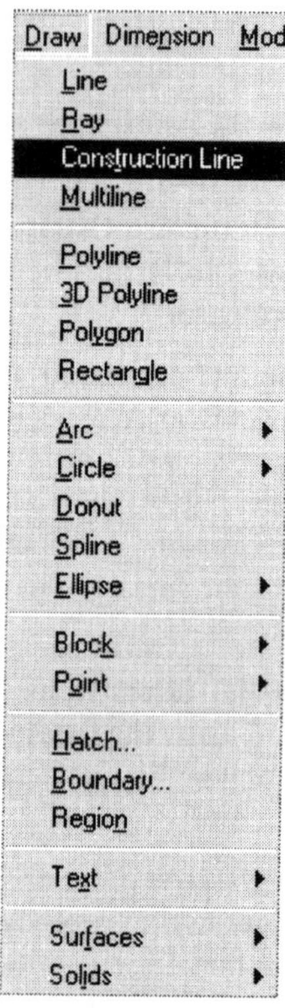

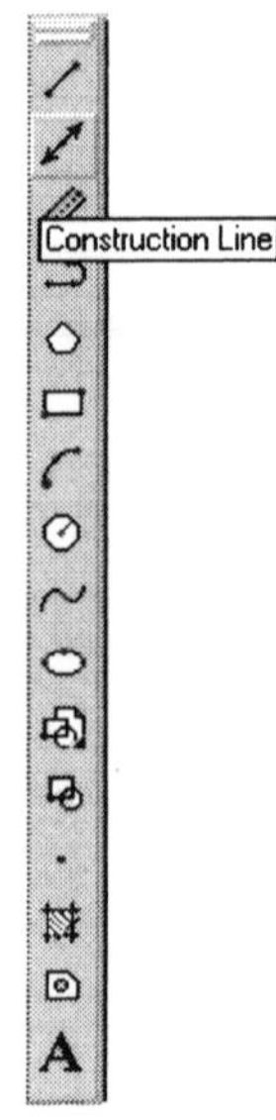

Step 13. Make layer G (with the HIDDEN linetype) current. Use the Line command and point filters to draw the hidden lines in the top view. Draw the vertical line first and the short horizontal lines second (Figure 10–13). If the HIDDEN linetype does not appear, set Linetype Scale (*Type:* LTSCALE ↵) to a value between 15 and 25.4. Start with 15. It is necessary to change the scale of linetypes because of the metric measurements.

Step 14. Use the Line command to draw the hidden line in the front view from the endpoint of the wedge shape perpendicular to the top line. Use the Offset or Duplicate command to copy this line 20 units to the right.

Use the Line command with an X point filter through the left and right quadrants of one of the circles (Figure 10–14) (Y coordinate is Osnap-Nearest on the top or bottom edge) to draw the two hidden lines for the circles in the front view.

Step 15. Set layer R current and use the Angle option of the Construction Line command to draw a 45° construction line through the upper right corner of the front view as shown in Figure 10–15. Draw a horizontal construction line through an endpoint of the bottom line of the top view and the bottom line of the front view. Finally, draw a vertical construction line through the intersection of the two construction lines just drawn.

Step 16. Set layer M current and use the Rectangle command to draw a rectangle measuring 60 mm wide by 63 mm high with its lower left corner at the intersection of the vertical construction line and the horizontal construction line in the front view. Erase the vertical and horizontal construction lines because they are no longer needed, but leave the 45° construction line.

Step 17. Use the Explode command to explode the rectangle into lines (after you explode the rectangle it will appear to be the same but instead of being a single polyline it will now be four separate lines). Use the Offset command to offset the top and bottom horizontal lines 13 units as shown in Figure 10–16. Use Properties... from the Modify menu on the menu bar to change the bottom offset line to the G layer (G layer is assigned the HIDDEN linetype).

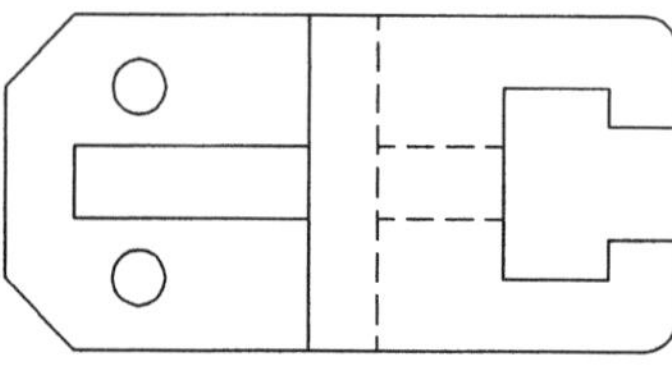

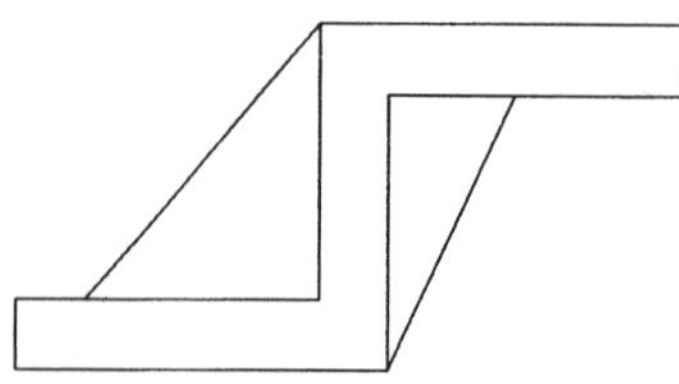

FIGURE 10–13
Drawing Hidden Lines in the Top View

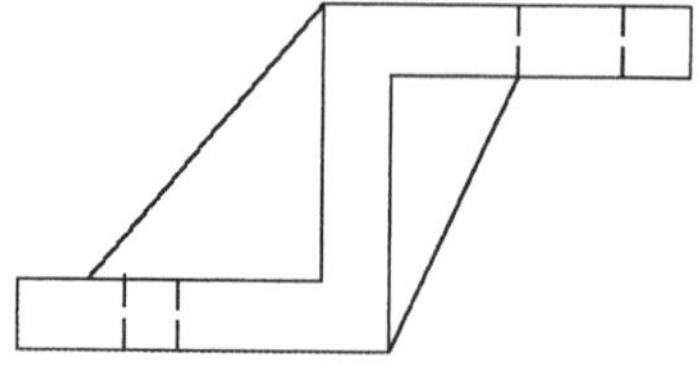

FIGURE 10–14
Drawing Hidden Lines in the Front View

FIGURE 10–15
Using Construction Lines to Draw the Rectangle for the Right Side View

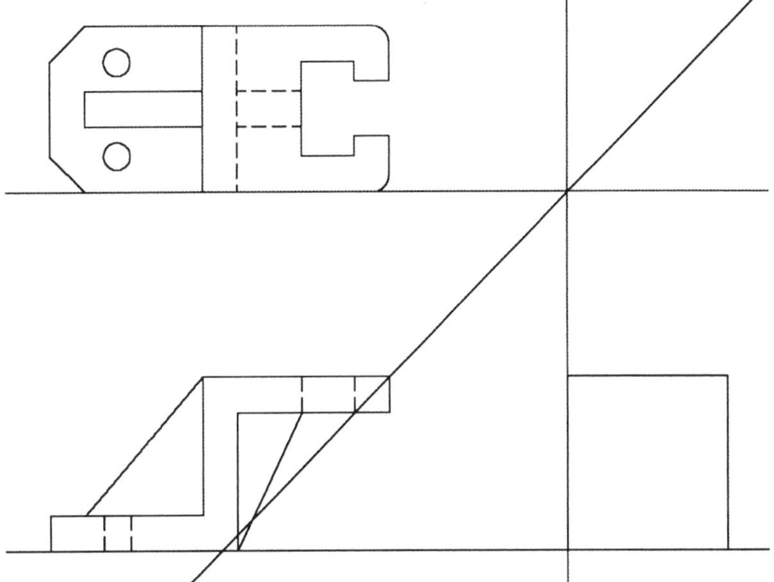

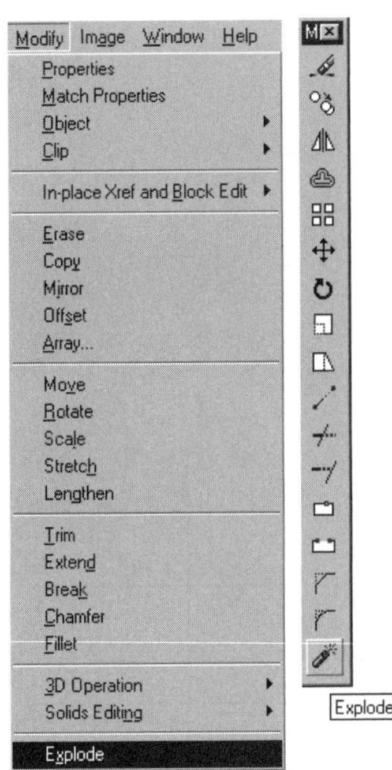

Step 18. **Draw construction lines through the endpoint of the cutout and the endpoint of the bottom horizontal line of the wedge shapes in the top view, Figure 10–17. Use the line command and point filters at the intersections of the construction lines and the 45° angle to draw the two inside vertical lines in the right side view.**

Step 19. **Offset the shorter vertical line 20 mm to the right and the longer vertical 13 mm to the right, Figure 10–18. Erase the two horizontal construction lines.**

Step 20. **Set layer G current and draw horizontal construction lines through the outermost lines of the cutout as shown in Figure 10–19. Draw vertical construction lines through the intersections of the horizontal construction lines with the 45° line. Use the Trim command to trim the two vertical construction lines as shown in Figure 10–20. Draw the two inside short vertical lines using Osnap-Endpoint and Osnap-Perpendicular. Erase the two horizontal construction lines.**

Step 21. **Draw horizontal construction lines through the top and bottom quadrants of the two circles as shown in Figure 10–21. Draw vertical construction lines through the intersections of the horizontal construction lines with the 45° line. Use the Trim command to trim the vertical lines as shown in Figure 10–22. Erase the remaining construction lines.**

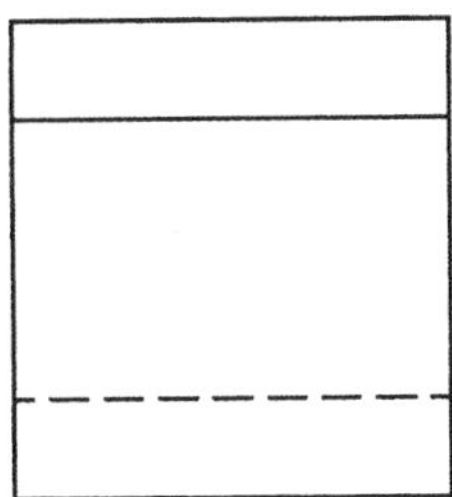

FIGURE 10–16
Offsetting the Horizontal Lines

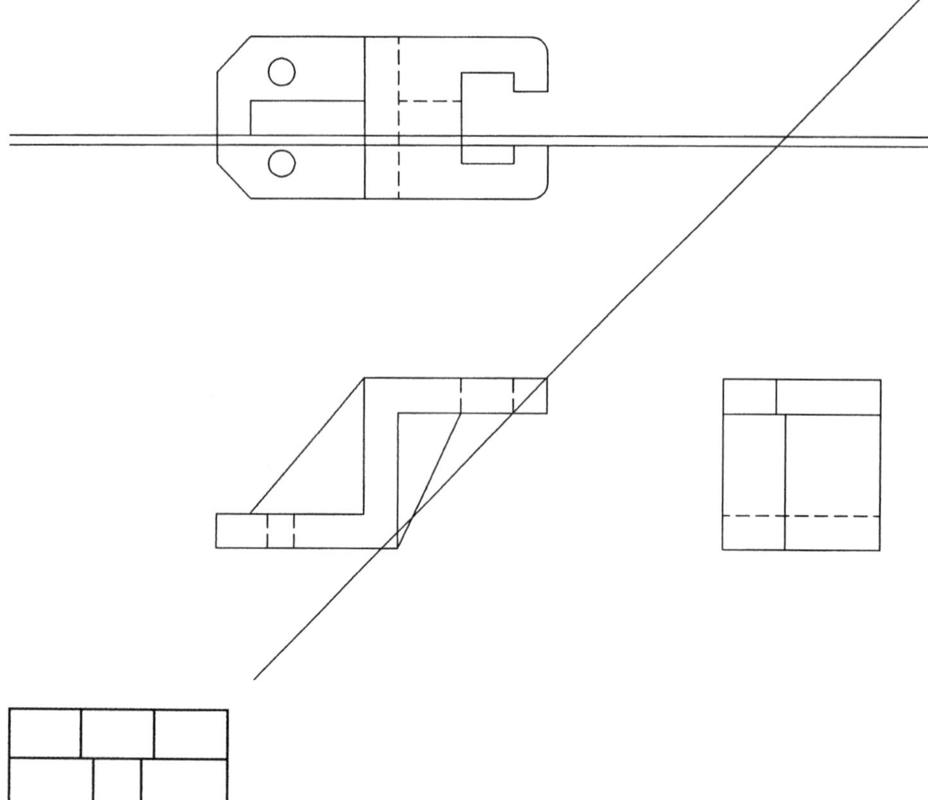

FIGURE 10–17
Projecting Lines through the 45° Angle and Using the Intersections to Draw Two Vertical Inside Lines

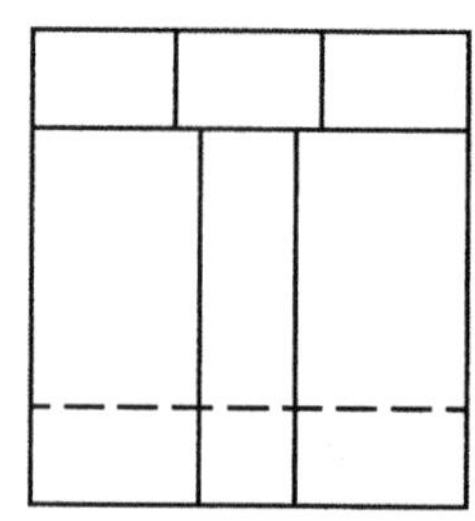

FIGURE 10–18
Offsetting the Vertical Lines

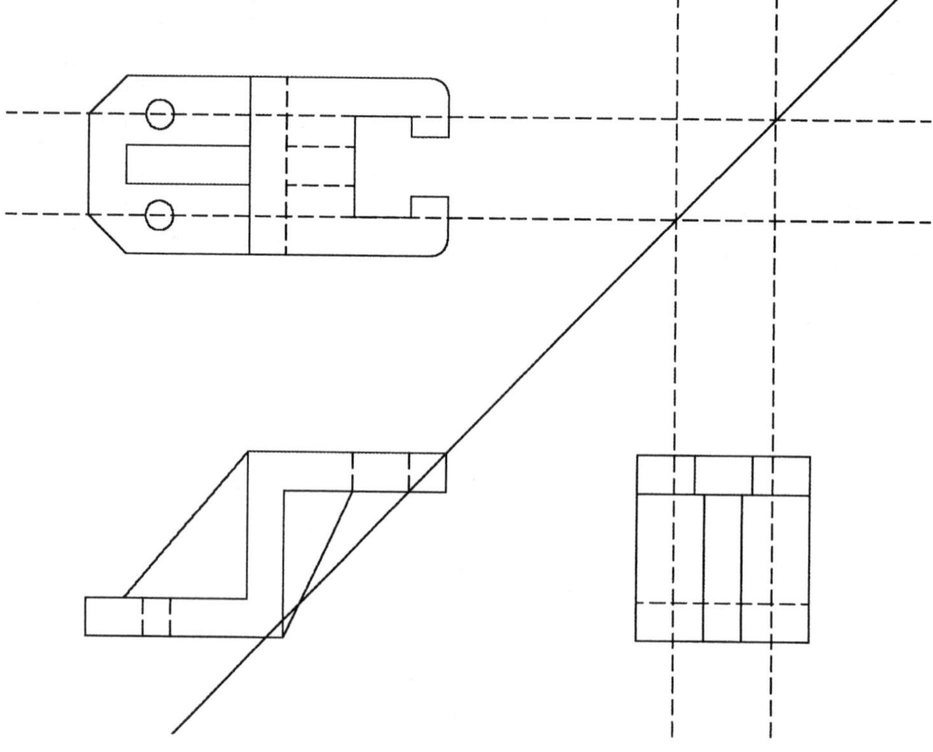

FIGURE 10–19
Drawing Hidden Construction Lines

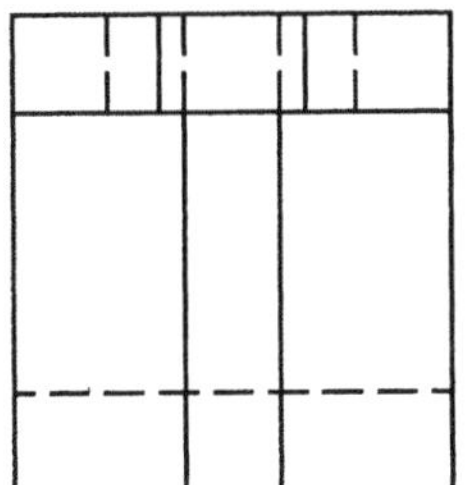

FIGURE 10–20
Trimming the Vertical Construction Lines and Drawing Two Short Hidden Lines

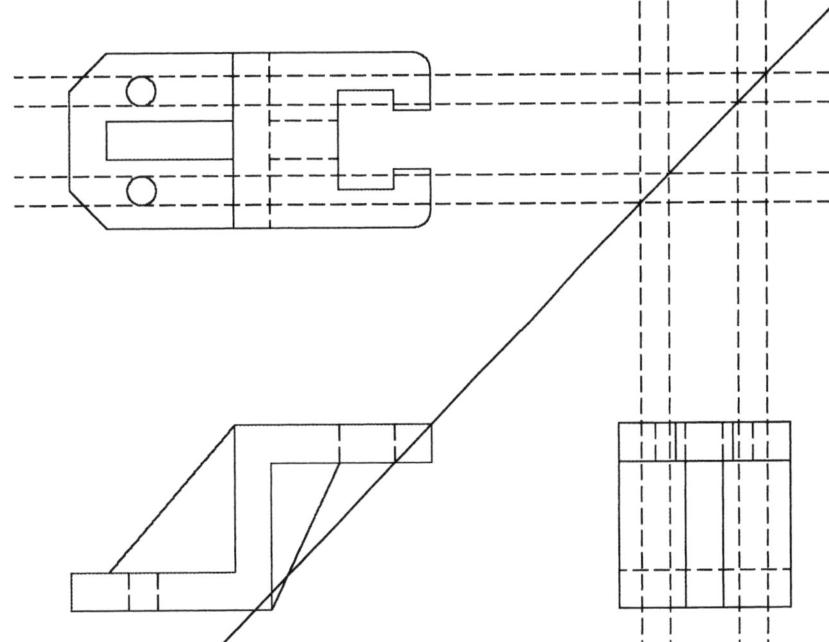

FIGURE 10–21
Drawing Horizontal and Vertical Construction Lines

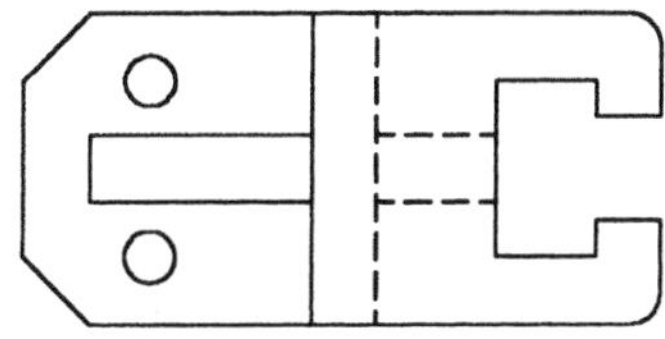

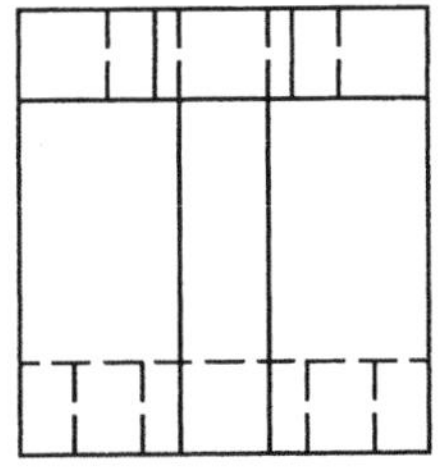

FIGURE 10–22
Vertical Construction Lines Trimmed

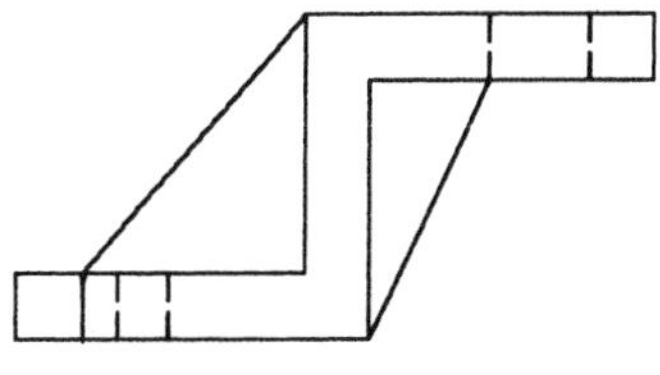

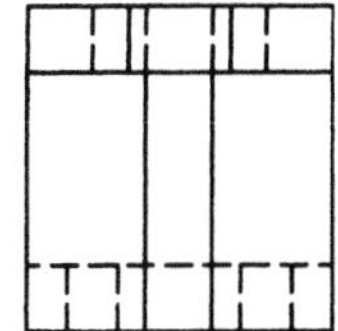

FIGURE 10–23
Exercise 10–3 Complete

The drawing is now complete, as shown in Figure 10–23. Center lines and dimensions will be added to this drawing in a later chapter.

Step 22. On your own:

1. Save your drawing in at least two places. Name it EX10-3(your initials).
2. Plot the drawing full size (1 Plotted MM = 1 Drawing Unit) on a 17″ × 11″ sheet or half size (1 Plotted MM = 2 Drawing Units) on an 11″ × 8.5″ sheet. Be sure to select mm in the Plot dialog box.
3. Exit AutoCAD.

EXERCISES

EXERCISE 10–1. Complete Exercise 10–1 using steps 1 through 10 described in this chapter.

EXERCISE 10–2. Complete Exercise 10–2 using steps 1 through 14 described in this chapter.

EXERCISE 10–3. Complete Exercise 10–3 using steps 1 through 22 described in this chapter.

EXERCISE 10–4. Draw the front, top, and right side orthographic views of the object shown in Figure 10–24 using the following specifications:

Full scale
17″ × 11″ sheet of paper
Name in the lower right corner
No dimensions

EXERCISE 10–5. Draw the front, top, and right side orthographic views of the object shown in Figure 10–25 using the following specifications:

Full scale
17″ × 11″ sheet of paper
Name in the lower right corner
No dimensions

EXERCISE 10–6. Draw the front, top, and right side orthographic views of the object shown in Figure 10–26 using the following specifications:

Full scale
17″ × 11″ sheet of paper
Name in the lower right corner
No dimensions

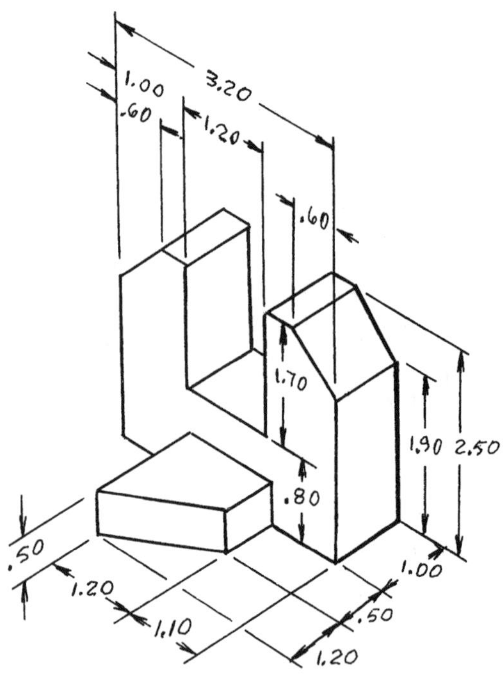

FIGURE 10–24
Exercise 10–4

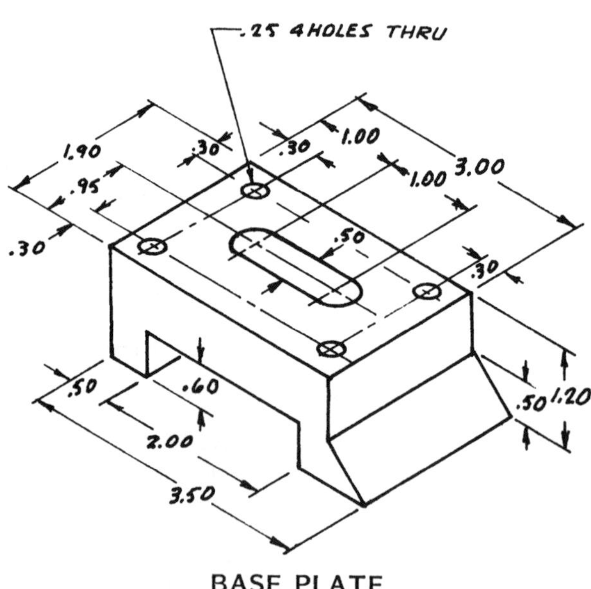

FIGURE 10–25
Exercise 10–5

FIGURE 10–26
Exercise 10–6

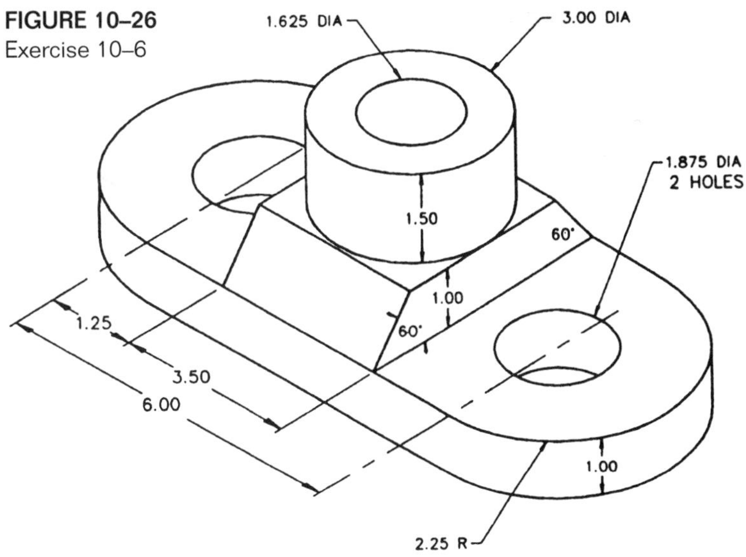

FIGURE 10–27
Exercise 10–7

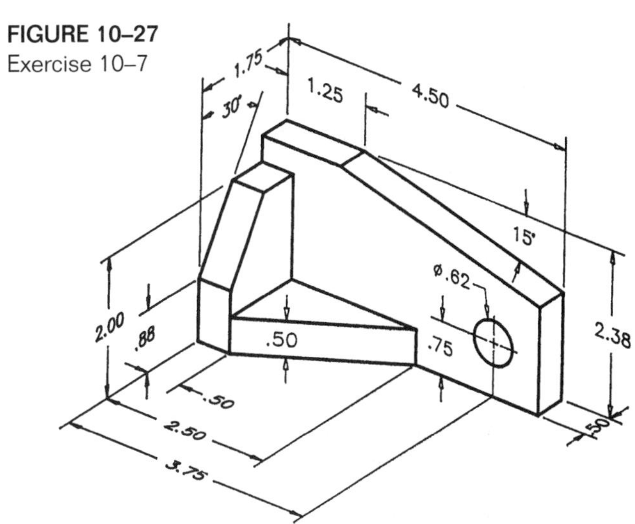

EXERCISE 10–7. Draw the front, top, and right side orthographic views of the object shown in Figure 10–27 using the following specifications:

Full scale
17″ × 11″ sheet of paper
Name in the lower right corner
No dimensions

EXERCISE 10–8. Draw the front, top, and right side orthographic views of the object shown in Figure 10–28 using the following specifications:

Full scale
17″ × 11″ sheet of paper
Name in the lower right corner
No dimensions

FIGURE 10–28
Exercise 10–8

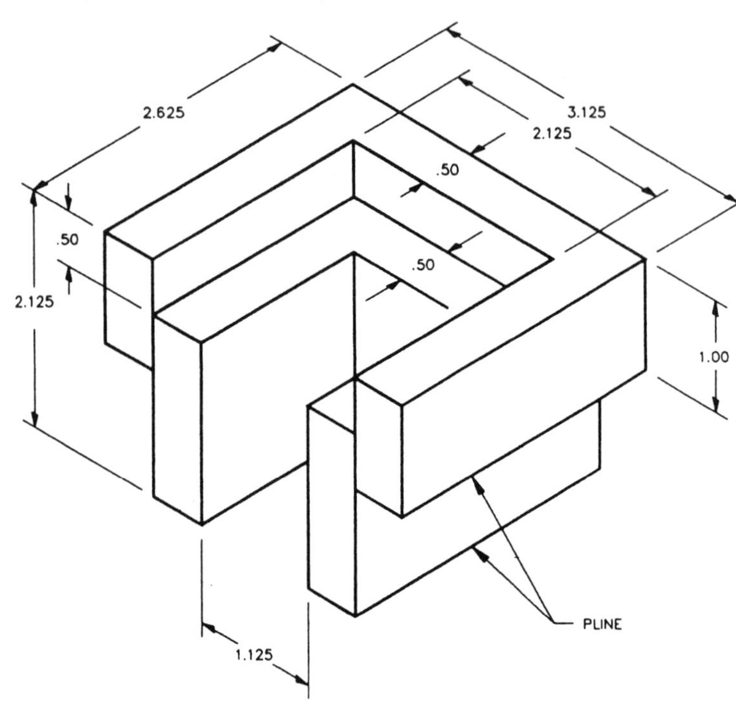

REVIEW QUESTIONS

Circle the best answer.

1. The top view of an object shows
   a. Height and depth
   b. Width and length
   c. Width and depth
   d. Length and height
   e. Width and height
2. Another name for two-dimensional drawing is
   a. Isometric projection
   b. Perspective projection
   c. Oblique projection
   d. Auxiliary projection
   e. Orthographic projection
3. All template files (by default) are stored in the same directory.
   a. True
   b. False
4. When you activate the Rectangle command and AutoCAD prompts you with "Specify first corner point", to locate the lower left corner of a rectangle 2½″ to the right and 3″ up from coordinates 0,0, you must type which of the following?
   a. 2.5,3 ↵
   b. 3,2.5 ↵
   c. @2.5,3 ↵
   d. @3,2.5 ↵
   e. @3<25 ↵
5. To make a rectangle 6″ wide by 3″ high when you are prompted with "Specify other corner point", you must type
   a. 6,3 ↵
   b. 3,6 ↵
   c. @6,3 ↵
   d. @3,6 ↵
   e. @6<30 ↵
6. To set the chamfer distance to ½″ from the Chamfer prompt "Select first line or [Polyline/Distance/Angle/Trim/ Method]:", you must first type
   a. P ↵
   b. D ↵

c. .5 ↵
d. R ↵
e. A ↵
7. The ID command allows you to identify a point to AutoCAD that can be used several times in the same drawing.
a. True
b. False
8. To locate any point such as the center of a circle 2″ to the right and 1″ down from a point defined with the ID command, you must type
a. 2,1 ↵
b. 1,2 ↵
c. @2,−1 ↵
d. @1,2 ↵
e. @2<1 ↵
9. The Fillet command may *not* be used to do which of the following?
a. Make a semicircle between two parallel lines
b. Make a square corner
c. Make a radius between two perpendicular lines
d. Make a radius without trimming the straight lines
e. Make a complete circle
10. Absolute coordinates are specified with respect to
a. The last point entered
b. The current viewport
c. 0,0 (the origin)
d. Any point identified with the ID command
e. All points entered

Complete.

11. Fill in the blanks using the Line command and absolute coordinates to draw a rectangle that is 3″ long and 2″ high.
From point: 4,3 (lower left corner)
To point: ___________
To point: ___________
To point: ___________
To point: ___________
12. Fill in the blanks using the Line command and relative coordinates to draw a rectangle that is 3″ long and 2″ high.
From point: 4,3 (lower left corner)
To point: ___________
To point: ___________
To point: ___________
To point: ___________
13. Fill in the blanks using the Line command and polar coordinates to draw a rectangle that is 3″ long and 2″ high.
From point: 4,3 (lower left corner)
To point: ___________
To point: ___________
To point: ___________
To point: ___________
14. Fill in the blanks to describe how to use point filters to start a line from a point that has its X component at the center of a circle and its Y component at the endpoint of a line.
From point: *Type:* ___________________________
of ___________________________
Need YZ ___________________________
15. List the metric equivalent of a 17″ × 11″ sheet.

____

11 Drawings, Formats, Blocks, and Attributes

OBJECTIVES

After completing this chapter, you will be able to

- □ Draw a small office floor plan full scale.
- □ Draw desks, tables, and chairs full scale as blocks.
- □ Assign attributes to all furniture.
- □ Insert furniture into the small office floor plan.
- □ Describe how to make a list of furniture part numbers from the floor plan (extract data).
- □ Describe how to plot the floor plan on a standard-size sheet.
- □ Draw a standard-size format, assign attributes, and insert a drawing into it.
- □ Correctly answer questions regarding the following commands:

Attdef	Multiline
Attedit	Multiline Style
Attext	Node
Block	Offset
DDatDef	Pedit
Explode	PERpendicular
Extend	Pline
Insert	Plot
Limits	Scale
MIDpoint	Wblock

APPLICATION OF AUTOCAD TO FLOOR PLANS

Advantages

AutoCAD has a distinct advantage over manual drafting in drawing floor plans. The plan can be drawn full size and plotted at a size that will fit on a standard-size sheet of paper instead of being drawn at a reduced scale. In this chapter you will draw a floor plan and create a library of symbols you will use to insert windows, doors, and furniture and to label rooms correctly. The libraries you create will suffice for the drawings in this chapter, but professional use requires so many different symbols that it is often economical to buy disks containing architectural symbols for use with AutoCAD. You will find many of these symbols in the DesignCenter which is part of the AutoCAD 2002 program.

Another major advantage of many CAD programs is the ability of the program to make accurate lists of parts from the drawing. Space planning in commercial buildings is often extremely complex and tedious. After all the furniture, bookcases, shelves, partitions, lighting, and electrical outlets are drawn in place, they must be carefully counted and accurately listed. Errors in this type of work can be very costly. AutoCAD allows these lists to be made from the drawing with ease. Each part of the plan (chair, bookcase, end plate, etc.) is given a part number, a description, and any other needed information such as color and price.

These part numbers and descriptions are called *attributes.* When the item is placed into the floor plan, its attributes accompany it. After the floor plan is completed, the attributes may be used to make a complete and accurate list of all the items placed on the floor plan. AutoCAD will write the information to a file, but the file must be totaled and rearranged with the use of another software program.

In this chapter you will make a floor plan of a small office, draw furniture as blocks, assign attributes to each block, insert the furniture into the floor plan, and examine the processes necessary to make an automatic listing of all the furniture. Begin by drawing the office.

Exercise 11–1: Drawing a Floor Plan of a Small Office

None of the templates you presently have will help with this drawing, so use a wizard to begin Exercise 11–1. Your final drawing will look similar to the drawing in Figure 11–1.

Step 1. To begin Exercise 11–1, turn on the computer and start AutoCAD.

Step 2. Use a wizard to begin Exercise 11–1.

Prompt	Response
The AutoCAD 2002 Today window appears:	*Click:* **the Create drawings tab**
	Click: **Wizards** (Figure 1–2)
	Click: **Quick Setup**
The Quick Setup dialog box appears:	
The Units tab appears:	*Click:* **Architectural**
	Click: **Next>**
The Area tab appears:	*Type:* **45′ in the Width box** (be sure to include the foot symbol)
	Type: **40′ in the Length box**
	Click: **Finish**

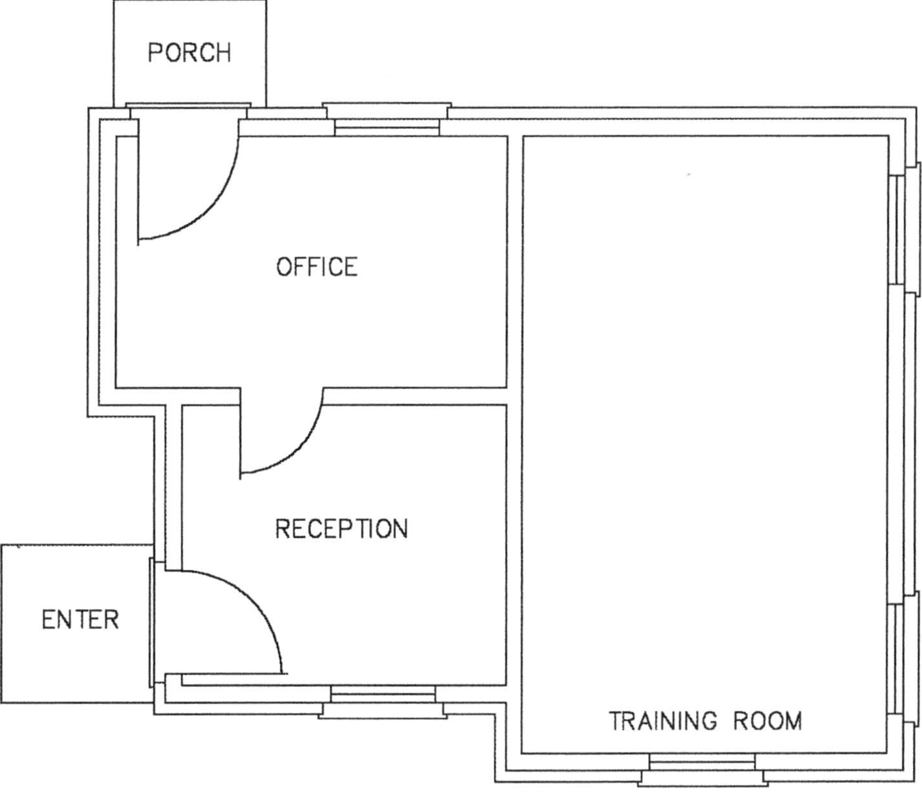

FIGURE 11–1
Completed Exercise 11–1

FIGURE 11–2
AutoCAD 2002 Today with Create Drawings-Wizards Selected

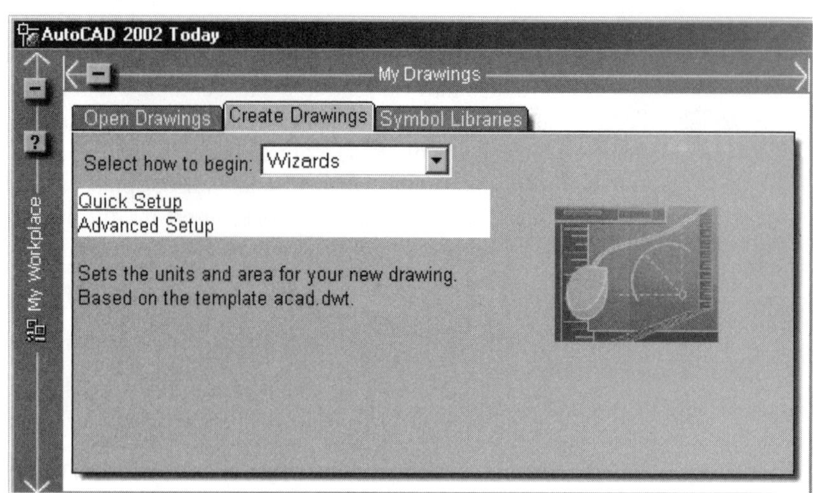

Step 3. Make the following settings:

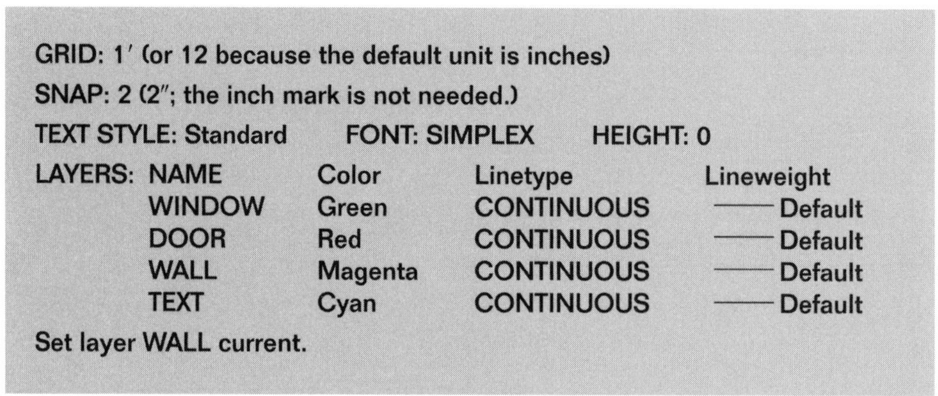

GRID: 1′ (or 12 because the default unit is inches)
SNAP: 2 (2″; the inch mark is not needed.)
TEXT STYLE: Standard FONT: SIMPLEX HEIGHT: 0

LAYERS:	NAME	Color	Linetype	Lineweight
	WINDOW	Green	CONTINUOUS	—— Default
	DOOR	Red	CONTINUOUS	—— Default
	WALL	Magenta	CONTINUOUS	—— Default
	TEXT	Cyan	CONTINUOUS	—— Default

Set layer WALL current.

Step 4. Use Zoom-All to view the entire drawing area.

Prompt	Response
Command:	**Zoom-All** (or *Type:* **Z** ↵, then **A** ↵)

Draw the Outside Walls of the Office (Figure 11–3)

You will not be required to place dimensions on this drawing now.

Step 5. Check the screen. The Layer list box on the Object Properties toolbar should read WALL. If it doesn't, review the procedures for setting and making layers. The status bar at the bottom of the screen should show the coordinates as you move your mouse around the screen, and SNAP, GRID, ORTHO, and MODEL should be ON. If any one of them is not on, click it to turn it on or use the appropriate function key to turn it on; F6—coordinates, F7—GRID, F8—ORTHO, F9—SNAP.

The wall sections can now be drawn.

Step 6. Set a Multiline Style for the outside walls.

Now set the Multiline Style so that you have the correct distance between the lines that show the walls of the office space.

Prompt	Response
Command:	*Click:* **Multiline Style...**

FIGURE 11–3
Dimensions for Office

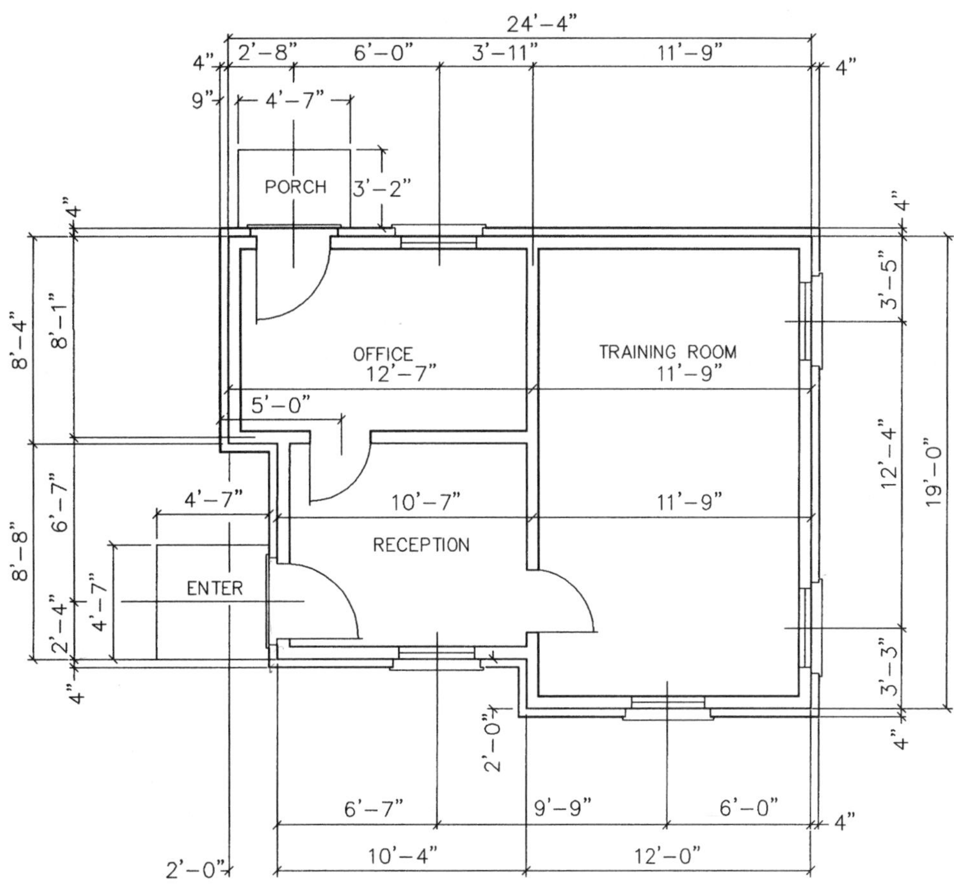

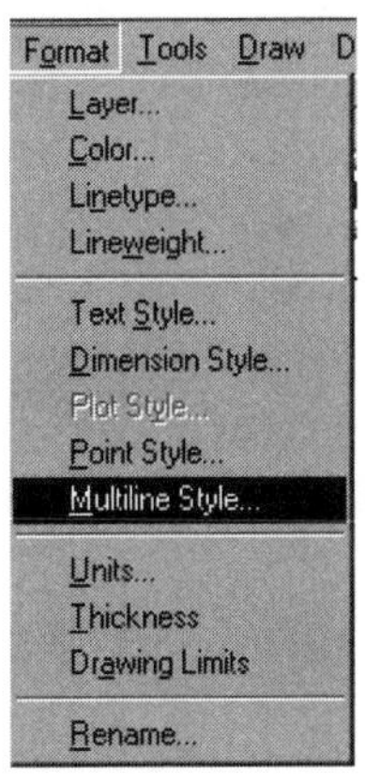

Prompt	**Response**
The Multiline Styles dialog box appears:	*Click:* **the Name: text box and backspace over the existing name, or highlight the name, then** *Type:* **WALLS**
	Click: **the Add button**
	Click: **the Save… button**
The Save multiline style dialog box appears:	*Click:* **the Save button**
The Multiline Styles dialog box appears:	*Click:* the **Load… button**
The Load Multiline Styles dialog box appears:	*Click:* **WALLS**, then *Click:* **OK**
The Multiline Styles dialog box appears:	*Click:* **the Element Properties button**
The Element Properties dialog box appears:	*Click:* **the Offset text box and backspace over all numbers, or highlight the number, then** *Type:* **4.**
	Click: **the Add button**
	Click: **the Offset button and backspace over all numbers then** *Type:* **−6**
	Click: **the Add button**
	Click: **the Color… button and select a color for each line or leave the color as is so that the lines assume the color of the current layer**

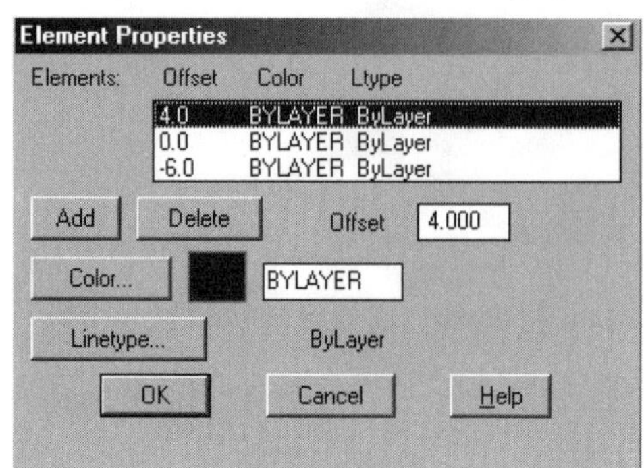

FIGURE 11–4
Element Properties Dialog Box

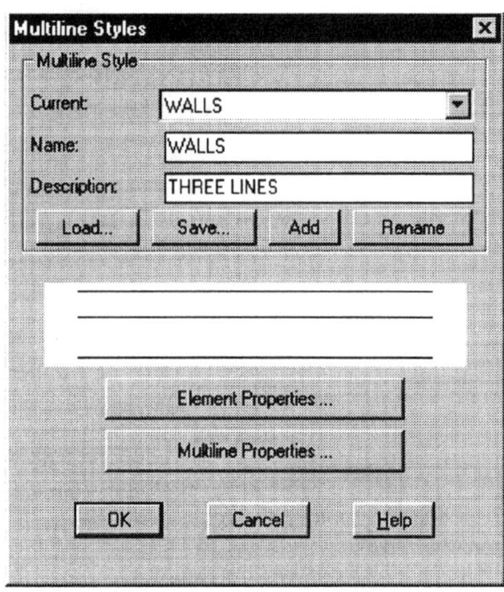

FIGURE 11–5
Multiline Styles Dialog Box

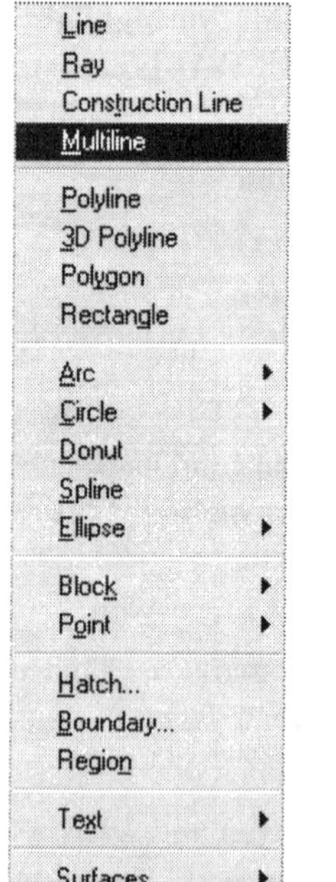

The Element Properties dialog box should appear as shown in Figure 11–4. If you have other offset elements, click them so that they are highlighted and *Click:* the **Delete** button to get rid of them. When the Element Properties dialog box is correct, *Click:* **OK.** Type a description such as "three lines" in the Description: box when the Multiline Styles dialog box appears, then *Click:* **OK** (Figure 11–5).

Step 7. Use the Multiline command to draw the outside walls.

Prompt	Response
Command:	**Multiline** (or *Type:* **ML** ↵)
Specify start point or [Justification/Scale/STyle]:	*Type:* **7′,32′** ↵
Specify next point:	**Move the mouse to the right with ORTHO ON and** *Type:* **24′4** ↵
Specify next point or [Undo]:	**Move the mouse down and** *Type:* **19′** ↵
Specify next point or [Close/Undo]:	**Move the mouse to the left and** *Type:* **12′** ↵
Specify next point or [Close/Undo]:	**Move the mouse up and** *Type:* **2′** ↵
Specify next point or [Close/Undo]:	**Move the mouse to the left and** *Type:* **10′4** ↵

Prompt	Response
Specify next point or [Close/Undo]:	**Move the mouse up and** *Type:* **8′8** ↵
Specify next point or [Close/Undo]:	**Move the mouse to the left and** *Type:* **2′** ↵
Specify next point or [Close/Undo]:	*Type:* **C** ↵

Step 8. Use the Explode, Extend, and Trim commands to draw the inside walls.

Prompt	Response
Command:	**Explode** (from the Modify menu or toolbar, or *Type:* **X** ↵)
Select objects:	*Type:* **ALL** ↵
Select objects:	↵
Command:	**Extend** (from the Modify menu or toolbar, or *Type:* **EX** ↵)
Select boundary edges ... Select objects:	**D1** (Figure 11-6) (You may need to zoom in closer to make it easier to click on these lines.)
Select objects:	↵
Select object to extend or Shift-select to trim or [Project/Edge/Undo]:	**D2 and D3** and *Press:* ↵
Command:	*Right click* and *click*: **Repeat EXTEND**
Select boundary edges ... Select objects:	**D4** (Figure 11–6) (You may need to zoom in closer to make it easier to click on these lines.)
Select objects:	↵
Select object to extend or Shift-select to trim or [Project/Edge/Undo]:	**D5 and D7;** *Press:* ↵

Note: The Extend command allows you to trim objects while in the Extend command by holding down the Shift key and selecting the object to be trimmed. The Trim command allows you to extend objects while in the Trim command by holding down the Shift key and selecting the object to extend.

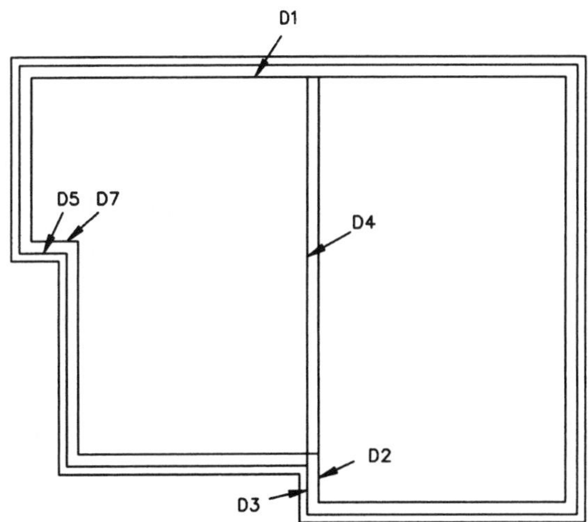

FIGURE 11–6
Extend Lines to Form Inside Walls

FIGURE 11–7
Trim Inside Walls

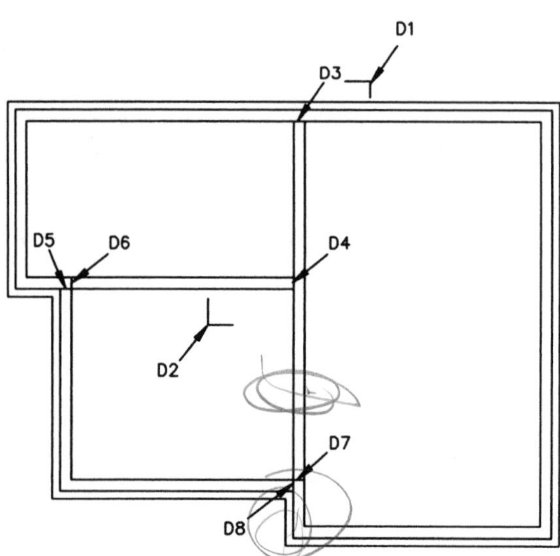

The Trim command is used to edit the interior walls. First Zoom closer to the sections to be trimmed, as shown in Figure 11–7.

Prompt	**Response**
	Click: **Zoom-Window** (or *Type:* **Z** ↵)
Specify corner of window, enter a scale factor (nX or nXP), or [All/Center/Dynamic/Extents/ Previous/Scale/Window]<real time>:	**D1** (Figure 11–7)
Specify opposite corner:	**D2**
Command:	**Trim** (or *Type:* **TR** ↵)
Select cutting edges ... Select objects:	*Type:* **All** ↵
Select objects:	↵
Select object to trim or Shift-select to extend or [Project/Edge/Undo]:	**D3 and D4**
Use the scroll bars to pan to the left: (or type: **`P**↵)	**D5 and D6**
Use the scroll bars to pan to the right and down:	**D7 and D8** ↵, then *Click*: **Enter**

The walls are now drawn. The next steps are to draw the windows and doors, save them as blocks, and insert them into the walls.

Draw, Block, and Insert Windows and Doors

Block (*Type:* **B** ↵) The Block command creates a figure or symbol that can be inserted at any point you specify into the current drawing. It can be scaled, rotated, mirrored, or exploded as it is inserted. The Block command does not write the drawing to a disk and can, therefore, normally be used only on the drawing on which the block was created. (Blocks can be copied from one drawing to another in the DesignCenter.)

Step 9. On your own:
Use the Line, Arc, and Mirror commands with the dimensions shown in Figure 11–8 to draw the doors and the window in an open area of your drawing. Make the door line extend 3″ beyond the end of the arc.

Step 10. Make a block of the window.

FIGURE 11–8
Dimensions for Windows and Doors

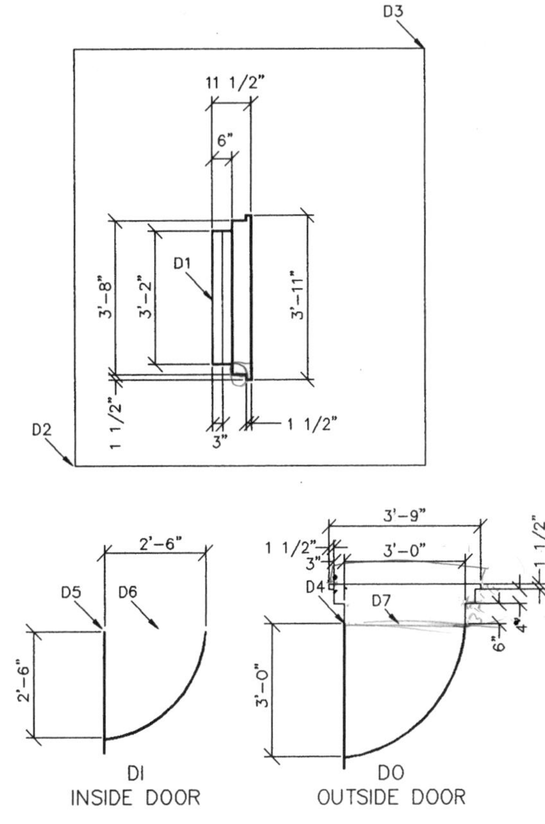

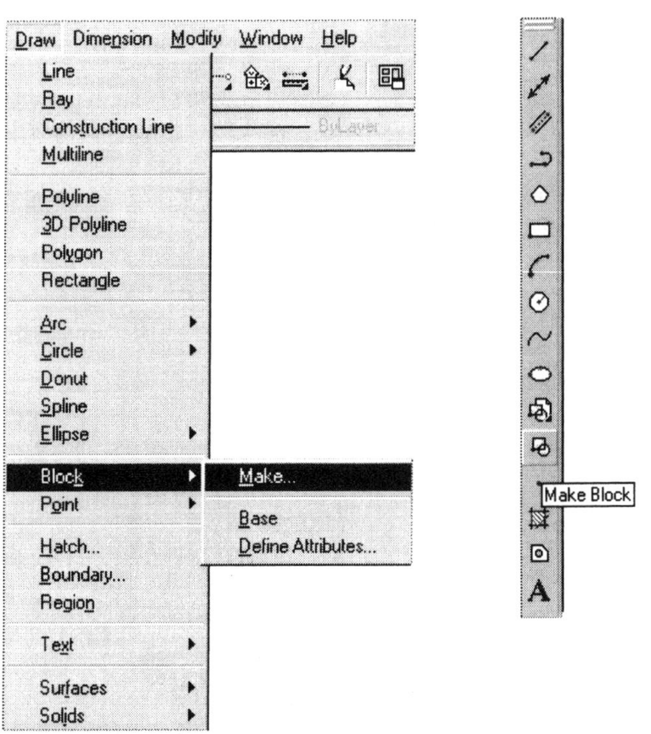

Prompt	Response
Command:	*Type:* **B** ↵ (or *Select:* **Block-Make…** to obtain the Block Definition dialog box)
The Block Definition dialog box appears:	*Type*: **W** (in the Name: text box to name the block) *Click*: **Pick point:** (in the Base point area so that you can return to the drawing to pick the base point (the midpoint of a certain line on the window))
Specify insertion base point:	**Osnap-Midpoint**
of	**D1** (Figure 11–8)
The Block Definition dialog box appears:	*Click*: **Select objects** (in the Objects area)
Select objects:	**D2** (Figure 11–8)
Specify opposite corner:	**D3**
Select objects	↵
The Block Definition dialog box appears:	Type: **3′-8″ Window** (in the Description text box as shown in Figure 11–9) *Click*: the **Delete radio button** (in the Objects area so that a dot appears in it as shown). The objects you select for the block will then be deleted from the drawing but can be inserted later. *Click*: the **Create icon from block geometry** radio button (in the Preview icon area so that a dot appears in it as shown). You will then be able to preview blocks as you insert them. *Click*: **OK**

The drawing should vanish. You now have a block named "W" that you may call up anytime this drawing is active. If you want to use this same block on later drawings, place a copy of it on your floppy disk (or the hard disk if you are using your own computer)

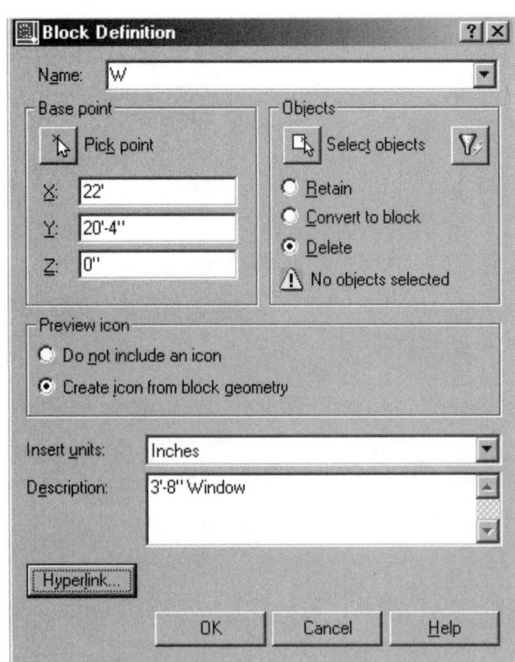

FIGURE 11–9
Block Definition Dialog Box

using the Wblock command so it may be inserted on any drawing you choose. This is called *writing it out to disk.*

Wblock (*Type:* **WBLOCK** ↵) The Wblock command creates a drawing file that is just like any other drawing file stored on either the hard disk or your floppy disk. AutoCAD asks you for the Wblock name, then the block name. The Wblock name is the name of the new drawing file that will be created. The block name allows you to do one of the following:

If you type the name of an existing block, AutoCAD saves that block as the drawing file using the insertion point specified for that block.

If you type an equal (=) sign, the block and the Wblock have the same name.

If you type an asterisk (*), AutoCAD saves the entire drawing to the new drawing file.

If you press ↵ to the block name prompt, AutoCAD prompts you to select objects to save as the drawing (Wblock).

Step 11. Make a Wblock of the block named W.

Prompt	**Response**
Command:	*Type:* **W** ↵
The Write Block dialog box (Figure 11–10) appears:	*Click*: the **Block: radio button** (in the Source area so you can use a defined block as the WBLOCK)
	Click: **the down arrow in the Source area and** *Click*: **W (the defined block)**
	Type: **WINDOW** in the File name: text box (in the destination area)
	Click: **the three dots (the ellipsis)** to the right of the Location: text box
The Browse for Folder dialog box (Figure 11–11) appears:	*Click*: **3½ Floppy [A:]** *Click:* **OK**
The Write Block dialog box appears:	When your dialog box looks like Figure 11–10, *Click:* **OK**

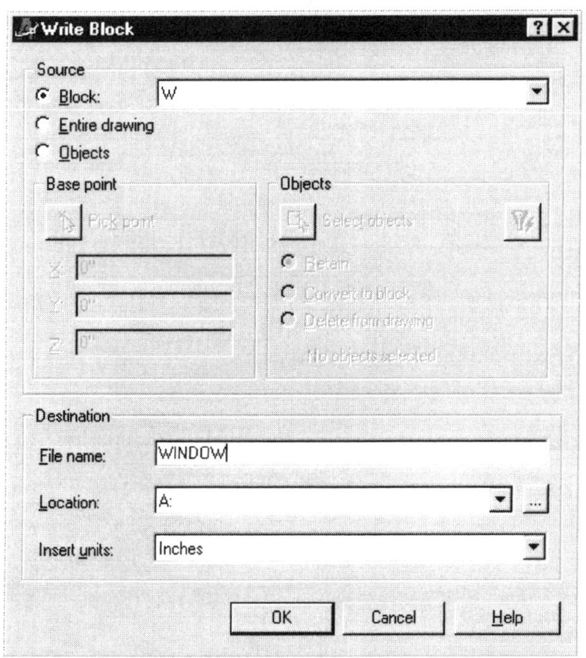

FIGURE 11–10
Write Box Dialog Box

FIGURE 11–11
Browse for Folder Dialog Box

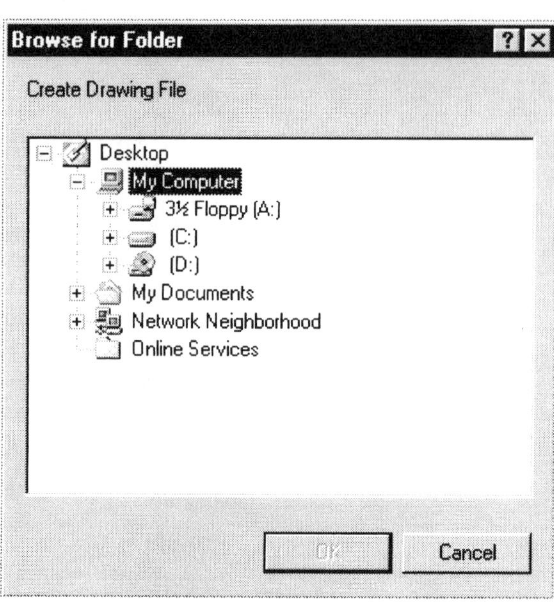

A drawing named WINDOW now exists on your floppy disk in the A: drive. If you leave the A: off the response, a drawing will be created on the hard drive of your computer. As you will see later in this chapter, any drawing may be inserted into any other drawing.

Step 12. Make a Wblock of the inside door. Use Osnap-From to identify a point that may be used to specify the insertion point of the Wblock.

Prompt	**Response**
Command:	*Type:* **W** ↵
The Write Block dialog box appears:	*Click:* **the Objects radio button** (in the Source area) *Type*: **DI** (for inside door) in the File name: text box (in the destination area) *Click*: **the three dots (the ellipsis)** to the right of the Location: text box
The Browse for Folder dialog box (Figure 11–11) appears:	*Click:* **3½ Floppy [A:]** *Click:* **OK**
The Write Block dialog box appears:	When your dialog box looks like Figure 11–12, *Click:* **Pick Point** (in the Base point area)
Specify insertion base point:	**Osnap-From** (or *Type*: **FRO** ↵)
Base point:	**Osnap-Endpoint** (or *Type:* **END** ↵)
of	**D5** (Figure 11–8)
Offset:	*Type*: **@1′3<0** ↵ (This defines the insertion point, D6.)
The Write Block dialog box appears:	*Click:* **Select objects** (in the Objects area)
Select objects:	**Use a window to select the lines forming the inside door.**
Select objects:	↵
The Write Block dialog box appears:	*Click:* **OK**

FIGURE 11–12
Write Block Dialog Box for Inside Door

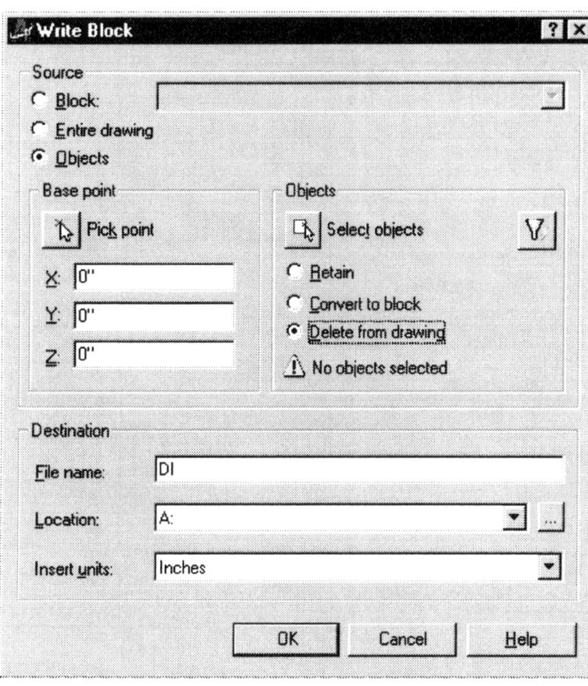

Step 13. On your own:

Make a Wblock of the outside door. Use Osnap-From to identify a point, D4, that may be used to specify the insertion point, D7, of the Wblock. Name the outside door DO.

You should now have three Wblocks on your floppy disk: DI, DO, and WINDOW. Remember where their insertion points are and proceed to the next step.

Step 14. Insert the first window (Figure 11–13).

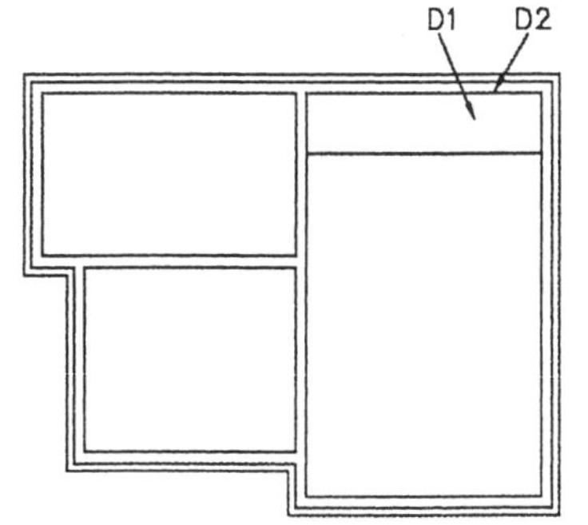

FIGURE 11–13
Locating the Insertion Point for the Window Using Offset

Insert (*Type:* **I** ↵) The Insert command allows you to bring any drawing into any other drawing or to insert a block created on the active drawing. The Insert dialog box allows you to scale, rotate, mirror, or explode the drawing as it is inserted at any point you pick. You may also specify the scale, rotation, and insertion point by picking the points on the screen and typing numbers when the Specify On-screen button is checked. When you use the scale option, you may enlarge or reduce a block using numbers larger than 1 to enlarge or smaller than 1 to reduce. A response of 2 will make the block twice the size; .5 will make the block half the size. (PScale/PX/PY/PZ/PRotate allow you to preview any of these options.)

Use the dimensions from Figure 11–2 to locate the centers of windows and doors. Two different methods can be used to identify the insertion points. The first method uses the Offset command to draw a construction line perpendicular to the location of the insertion point. This line will be erased later.

Prompt	Response
Command:	**Offset** (or *Type*: **O**↵)
Specify offset distance or [Through]<Through>:	*Type:* **2′11** ↵ (Subtract the 6″ wall from the 3′5″ dimension shown in Figure 11–3. You can use one of the two outside lines to offset, but you will have to Explode them first.)

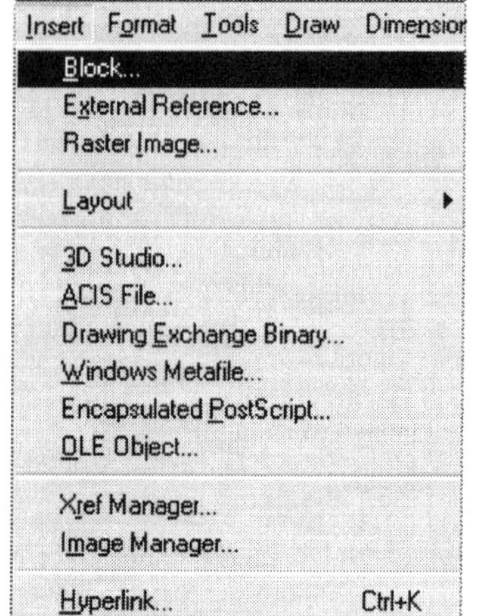

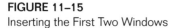

Prompt	**Response**
Select object to offset or <exit>:	**D2** (Figure 11–13)
Side to offset?	*Click:* **D1**
Command:	**Insert-Block...** (or *Type:* **I** 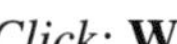)
The Insert dialog box (Figure 11–14) with a list of all blocks defined in the present drawing appears when the down arrow is picked. (Notice that only the block W has been defined on this drawing. DI and DO are drawings on a floppy disk. AutoCAD will define them as blocks when they are inserted into this drawing.)	*Click:* **W** *Click:* **the Specify On-screen button if it does not already have a check in it** *Click:* **OK**
Specify insertion point or [Scale/X/Y/Z/Rotate/PScale/PX/PY/PZ/Protate]:	**Osnap-Intersection**
of	**D1** (Figure 11–15)

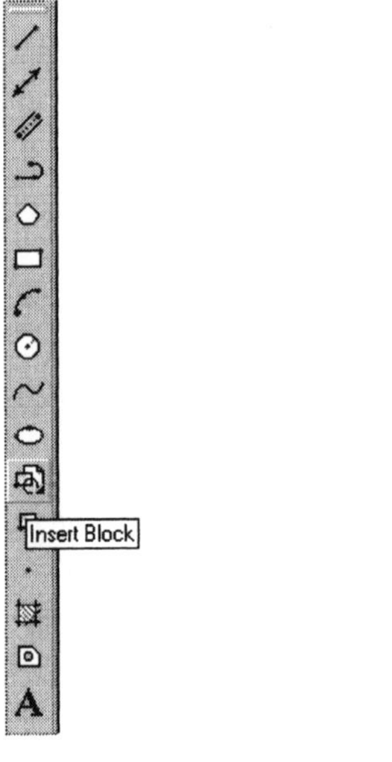

Step 15. Insert the second window.

Another means of placing the block is to identify the location of corners of the house and place the wblock using tracking.

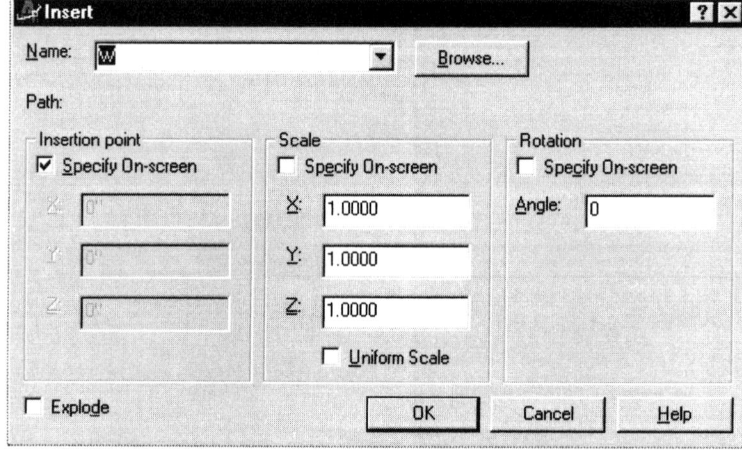

FIGURE 11–14
Insert Dialog Box

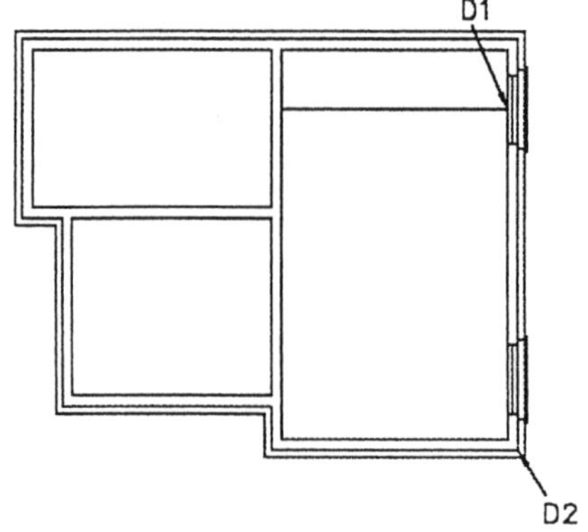

FIGURE 11–15
Inserting the First Two Windows

Prompt	Response
Command:	**Insert-Block** (or *Type:* **I** ↵)
The Insert dialog box appears:	*Click:* **W**
	Click: **OK**
Specify insertion point or [Scale/X/Y/Z/ Rotate/PScale/PX/PY/PZ/PRotate]:	*Type:* **TRACK** ↵
First tracking point:	**Osnap-Endpoint** (or *Type:* **END** ↵)
of:	**D2** (Figure 11–15)
Next point (Press Enter to end tracking):	*Type:* **@–6,3'3** ↵ (–6 is the wall thickness, and 3'3" is the distance shown in Figure 11–3)
Next point (Press Enter to end tracking):	↵

Step 16. Insert the remaining windows and doors.
Use a procedure similar to the ones described to insert the other windows and the doors. When you insert the doors you will have to pick Browse... in the Insert dialog box, then pick the A: drive to locate those wblocks.

Step 17. Clean up the drawing.
After all doors and windows are in place, use the Break or Trim commands to remove unwanted lines. Explode blocks and polylines before using Trim or Break if needed. Draw the ends of the partitions next to the doors using the Line command. Use the Zoom command if necessary to make the drawing larger on the screen.

Step 18. Add the ENTER slab and the PORCH using the Line command. You will find Osnap-From to be useful. Try it.

Step 19. Add labels to the rooms, the porch, and the entry using the Single Line Text command with 6″ high letters (Figure 11–16).

Step 20. On your own:

1. Save your drawing on at least two different disks. Name it EX11-1(your initials).
2. Plot the drawing at ¼″ = 1′ (¼ Plotted inch = 1′ Drawing unit) on an 11″ × 8.5″ sheet.
3. Exit AutoCAD.

In the next exercise you will add furniture containing attributes to your floor plan. An *attribute* is a label that contains text. These labels are placed on drawings of parts. They contain important information, such as the part number and description of the part. These part numbers and descriptions may later be extracted from the drawing to form a list of all of the parts (in this case the furniture) used in the drawing. This becomes an important function of the system. The command used to extract data is Attribute Extract and must be used with a spreadsheet to obtain a parts list.

The command that allows you to assign attributes is Attribute Definition.

Exercise 11–2: Adding Furniture with Attributes

Your final drawing will look similar to Figure 11–17.

Step 1. To begin Exercise 11–2, turn on the computer and start AutoCAD.

Step 2. Open drawing EX11-1(your initials).

Step 3. Use the SaveAs... command to save the drawing as EX11-2(your initials).
Doing this now renames the current drawing to EX11-2(your initials) and eliminates the possibility of overwriting EX11-1(your initials) with the new drawing.

Step 4. Add a new layer named FURNITURE, color white, and set it current.

FIGURE 11–16
Exercise 11–1 Complete

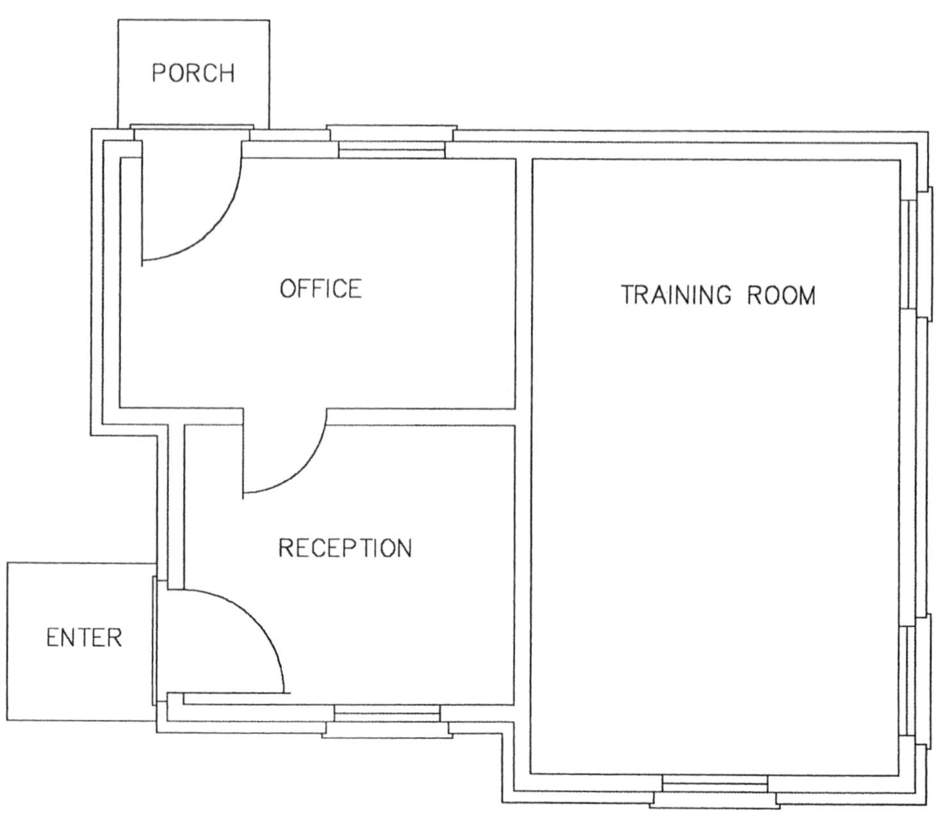

FIGURE 11–17
Floor Plan with Furniture Containing Attributes

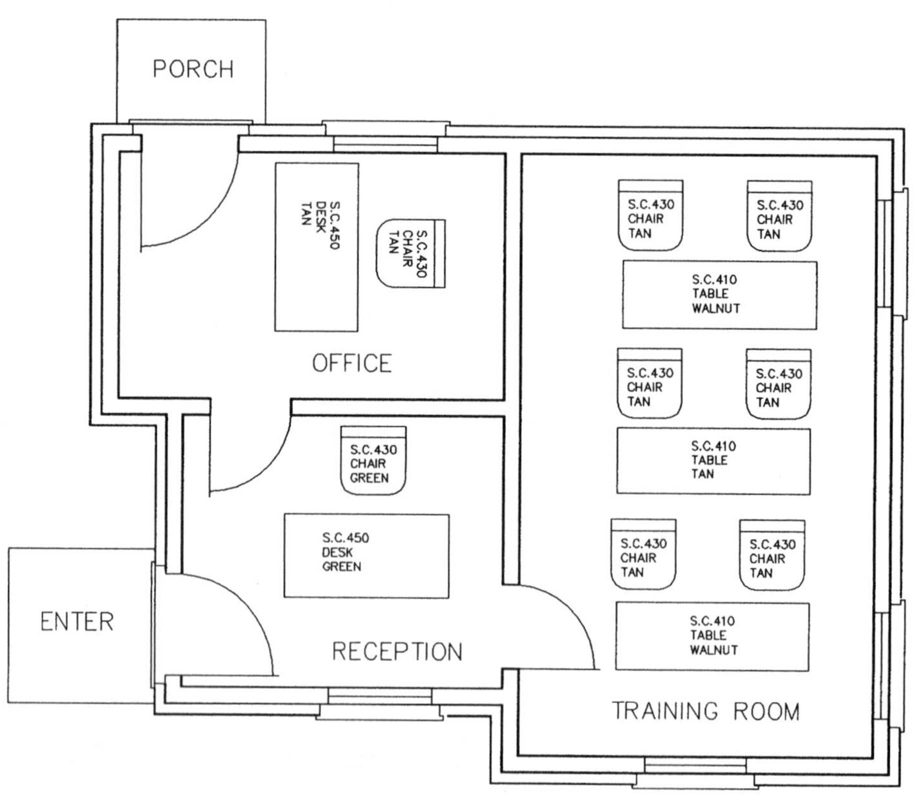

FIGURE 11–18
Furniture Dimensions

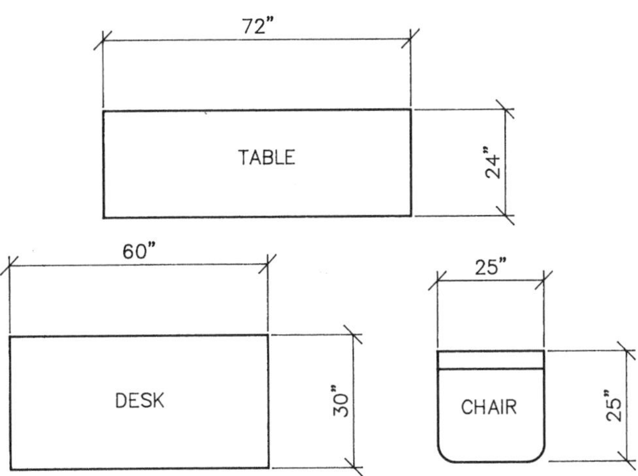

Draw the furniture using the dimensions shown in Figure 11–18. You may draw these objects in any open area. Use the Line or Rectangle commands for drawing the rectangles and the Fillet command for rounding the corners on the chair (use a 4″ fillet) and make the chair back 4″ thick.

Before you assign the first attribute to the table examine the Attribute Definition command and the parts of the Attribute Definition dialog box, Figure 11–19.

Attribute Definition *(Type:* ATTDEF ↵.*)*

The parts of the Attribute Definition dialog box are as follows:

Mode

Invisible The attribute will not appear on the drawing when the block is inserted. You want these to be invisible. (The "price" might be something that should be invisible.)

Constant The attribute is the same for every insertion of the block and cannot be changed.

Verify The value of the attribute is verified during insertion so that you may correct any mistake or change your mind about the value you have inserted.

Preset The attribute is variable but is not requested when the block is inserted. This is similar to a constant attribute in that the default value appears on the drawing. It is different from the constant attribute in that it can be changed later with the ATTEDIT command. It is used to limit the number of prompts to which you must respond.

FIGURE 11–19
Attribute Definition for the First Attribute

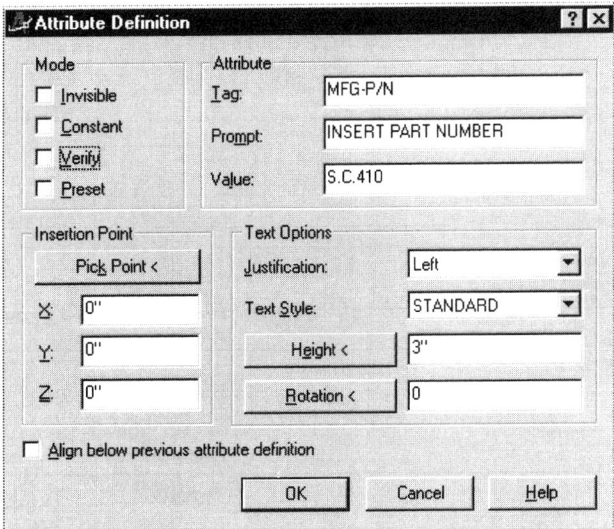

If none of these modes is selected, the attribute is a variable one.

Attribute

Tag: This is the label's identifying text, which may be used later to extract the Value from the drawing. Spaces may not be used in the Tag: text.

Prompt: This is the prompt that will appear on the command line when you insert the block. Make the prompt whatever is necessary to make sure the correct information is inserted. Spaces may be used in the Prompt: text.

Value: This is the label that will be inserted if one is not typed in response to the prompt. Spaces may be used in the Value: text.

Text Options

Justification: This establishes the point around which the attribute tag (when the attribute is defined) and the attribute value (when the block is inserted) are drawn.

Text Style: Allows you to select any of the styles you have defined on the drawing.

Height < Allows you to specify the height of the attribute text for the tag and the value.

Rotation < Allows you to specify the rotation angle of the attribute text for the tag and the value.

Insertion Point

Pick Point < Allows you to pick a point on the drawing for the attribute to be inserted. In most cases you will use Pick Point to define the insertion point.

X: Allows you to specify the X component of the point at which the attribute will be inserted.

Y: Allows you to specify the Y component of the point at which the attribute will be inserted.

Z: Allows you to specify the Z component of the point at which the attribute will be inserted.

Align Below Previous Attribute

Checking this box after the first attribute has been defined aligns the next attribute below the first one.

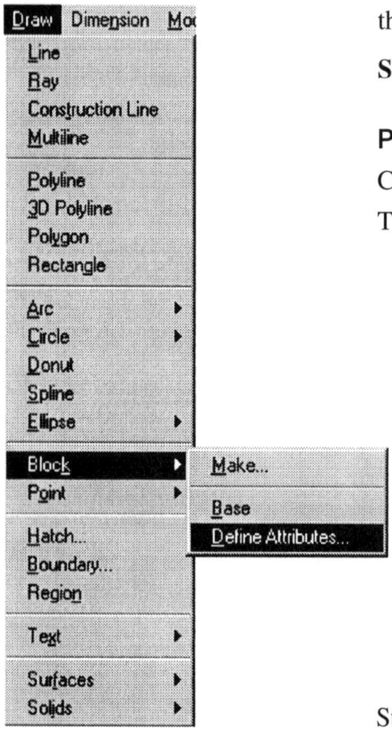

Step 5. Assign the first attribute to the table (Figure 11–19).

Prompt	Response
Command:	**Define Attribute** (or *Type:* **ATTDEF↵**)
The Attribute Definition dialog box appears:	In the Tag: box *Type:* **MFG-P/N** (Spaces are *not* allowed in the tag.)
	In the Prompt: box *Type:* **INSERT PART NUMBER.** (Spaces *are* allowed in the prompt.)
	In the Value: box *Type:* **S.C.410** (Spaces *are* allowed in the value. S.C.410 was chosen as the default value because all the tables carry this part number.)
	In the Height < box *Type:* **3** (the height of the attribute text) (Replace any value in the Height < box with 3.)
	Click: **the Pick Point < button**
Start point:	**D1** (Figure 11–20)

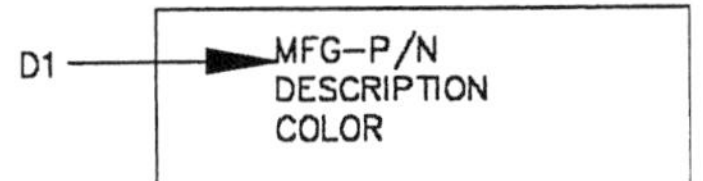

FIGURE 11–20
Assigning Attributes to the Table

Prompt	**Response**
The Attribute Definition dialog box reappears:	*Click:* **OK**

The attribute just assigned is a variable one.

Step 6. On your own:
Assign the second attribute to the table (Figure 11–21). Make the Attribute Definition dialog box look like Figure 11–21. Make sure that the Constant and the Align below previous attribute boxes are checked, and *Click:* **OK** instead of Pick Point < this time. This attribute will not change, so it can be a constant one.

Step 7. On your own:
Assign the third attribute to the table (Figure 11–22). Make the Attribute Definition dialog box look like Figure 11–22. Make sure that the Verify and the Align below previous attribute boxes are checked, and *Click:* **OK** instead of Pick Point < this time. This attribute will be variable, and AutoCAD will prompt you to verify any value you assign when the block is inserted with this attribute.

Step 8. Make a block of the table (Figure 11–23).

Prompt	**Response**
Command:	*Type:* **B** ↵ (or *Select*: **Make Block**)
The Block Definition dialog box appears:	*Type:* **TABLE** (in the Name: text box to name the block) *Click:* **Pick point:** (in the Base point area so you can return to the drawing to pick the base point (the midpoint of a certain line on the window)
Specify insertion base point:	**D1** (Figure 11–23)
The Block Definition dialog box appears:	*Click*: **Select objects** (in the Objects area)
Select objects:	**D2** (Figure 11–23)
Specify opposite corner:	**D3**
Select objects:	↵
The Block Definition dialog box appears:	*Click*: **the Delete radio button** (in the Objects area so a dot appears in it as shown). The objects you select for the block will then be deleted from the

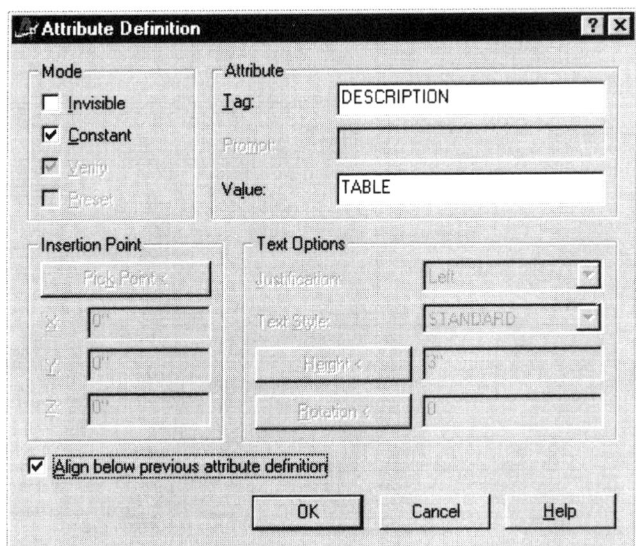

FIGURE 11–21
Attribute Definition for the Second Attribute

FIGURE 11–22
Attribute Definition for the Third Attribute

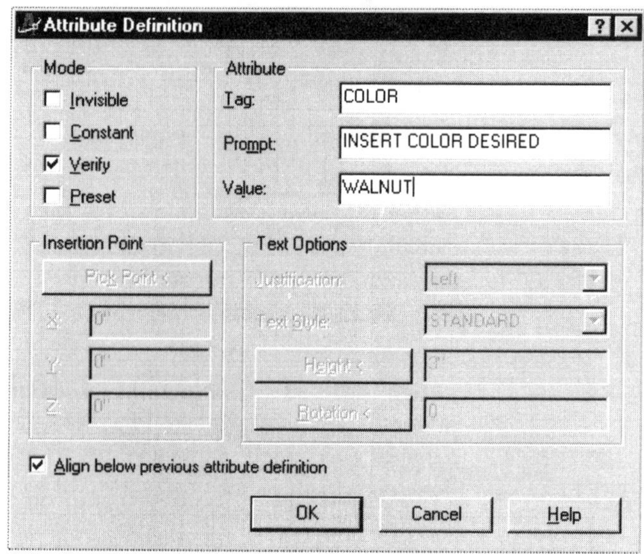

FIGURE 11–23
Making a Block of the Table

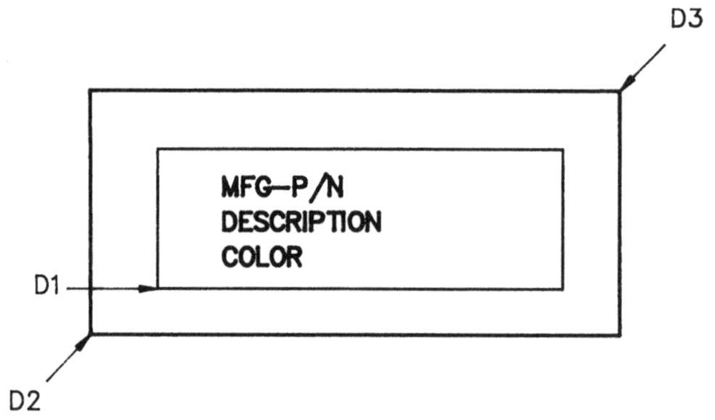

Prompt	Response
	drawing but can be inserted later.
	Click: **the Create icon from block geometry** radio button (in the Preview icon area so a dot appears in it as shown). You will then be able to preview blocks as you insert them.
	Click: **OK**

The table disappears.

Step 9. Insert the table and answer the prompts you assigned (Figure 11–24).

S.C.410
TABLE
WALNUT

FIGURE 11–24
Inserting the Table with Attributes

Prompt	Response
Command:	**Insert-Block...** (or *Type:* **I** ↵)
The Insert dialog box appears:	*Click:* **the down arrow**
	Click: **TABLE**
	Click: **the Specify On-screen button if it does not already have a check in it**
	Click: **OK**
Specify insertion point or [Scale/X/Y/Z/Rotate/PScale/PX/PY/PZ/PRotate]:	*Click:* **on any point where you want to place the table** (similar to the locations shown in Figure 11–25)

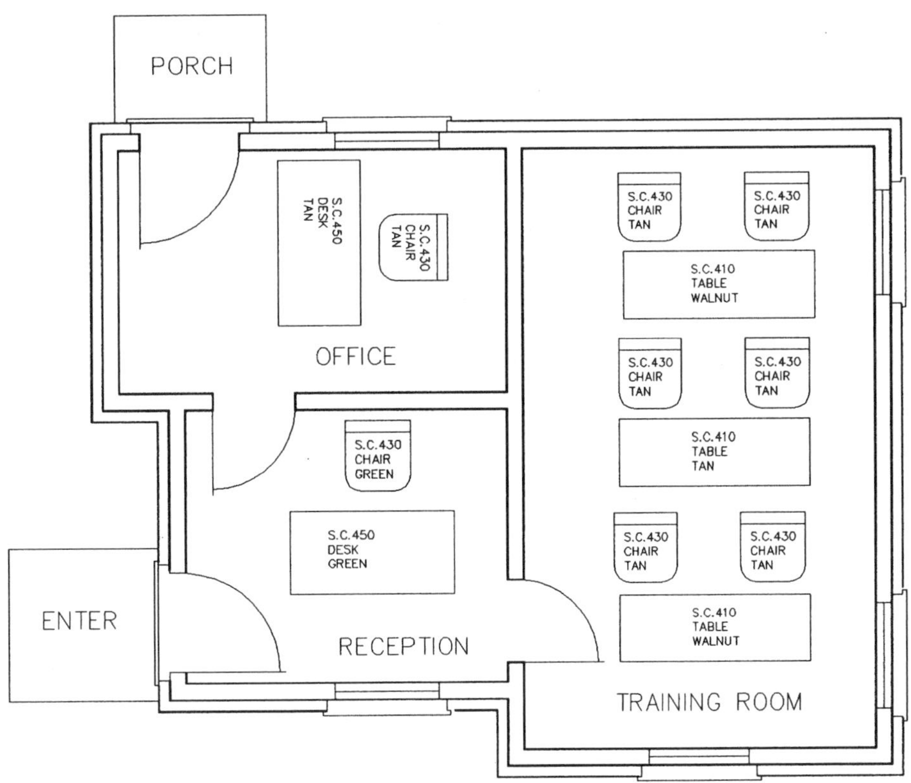

FIGURE 11–25
Approximate Locations of Furniture

Prompt	**Response**
INSERT COLOR DESIRED <WALNUT>:	↵ (to accept the default color WALNUT)
INSERT PART NUMBER <S.C.410>:	↵ (to accept the default part number S.C.410)
INSERT COLOR DESIRED <WALNUT>:	↵ (to verify that WALNUT is correct)

The table inserted should appear as shown in Figure 11–24.

Step 10. On your own:

1. Assign attributes to the chair and desk in the same manner as you did for the table. The part number will be a variable attribute. The description will be a constant attribute. The color will be a verify variable attribute.
2. Use the Block command to make blocks of the chair and desk.
3. Insert the tables, chairs, and desks in the approximate locations shown in Figure 11–25, and move room labels to appear as shown.
4. Save your drawing on at least two different disks. Name it EX11-2(your initials).
5. Plot the drawing at ¼″ = 1′ (¼ Plotted inch = 1′ Drawing unit) on an 11″ × 8.5″ sheet.
6. Exit AutoCAD.

Note: If you make a mistake and insert a block with an incorrect attribute, use the command Edit Attribute (*Type:* **ATTEDIT ↵**) to fix it.

DRAWING FORMATS

Most manufacturing and construction drawings must be placed in a standard format. This format consists of the border, title blocks, revision block, and standard notes. The drawing is drawn full scale for convenience in measuring and then reduced to fit within a standard-size format in paper space.

The format may be called up as a block with attributes and inserted around the drawing. The following are standard-size sheets:

A: 11″ × 8 ½″ or 12″ × 9″
B: 17″ × 11″ or 18″ × 12″
C: 22″ × 17″ or 24″ × 18″
D: 34″ × 22″ or 36″ × 24″

The larger sheets in each size are architectural sheet sizes.

AutoCAD has several templates that are standard title blocks that can be modified by labeling areas with text and assigning attributes to items that will change such as the drawing name, number, date, and scale. In Exercises 11–3 and 11–4 you will modify a B-size format and insert it around a reduced drawing, then plot it with different layers ON.

Exercise 11–3: Drawing a B-Size Format with Attributes

Modify the template named ansi b.dwt and save it as a drawing file.

Your final drawing will look similar to Figure 11–26.

Step 1. To begin Exercise 11–3, turn on the computer and start AutoCAD.

Step 2. Use a template to begin Exercise 11–3.

Prompt	Response
The AutoCAD 2002 Today window appears:	*Click:* **the Create Drawings tab**
	Click: **Template** in the **Select how to begin:** box
	Click: **the template labeled ANSI b-Color Dependent Plot Styles.dwt (under the letter A)**

The ANSI B Title Block drawing appears in paper space as shown in Figure 11–27. Paper space is where you can plot and use formats more easily than in model space. Model space is where the drawing or model is created. Model space and paper space are discussed in detail in a later chapter.

Step 3. Make the following settings.

UNITS: Decimal—3 digits to the right of the decimal point
LIMITS: Lower left corner: accept default
Upper right corner: accept default
GRID: .5
SNAP: .125

TEXT STYLE: Standard	FONT: simplex.shx	HEIGHT: 0
TEXT STYLE: ITALIC	FONT: italicc.shx	HEIGHT: 0
TEXT STYLE: BOLD	FONT: Technic Bold	HEIGHT: 0
TEXT STYLE: Roman	FONT: romans.shx	

LAYERS:	NAME	Color	Linetype	Lineweight
	BORDER	Green	CONTINUOUS	Default
	FTEXT	Red	CONTINUOUS	Default
	ATEXT	Magenta	CONTINUOUS	Default

Set layer FTEXT current.

Step 4. Use Zoom-All to view the entire drawing area.

Prompt	Response
Command:	**Zoom-All** (or *Type:* **Z** ↵, then **A** ↵)

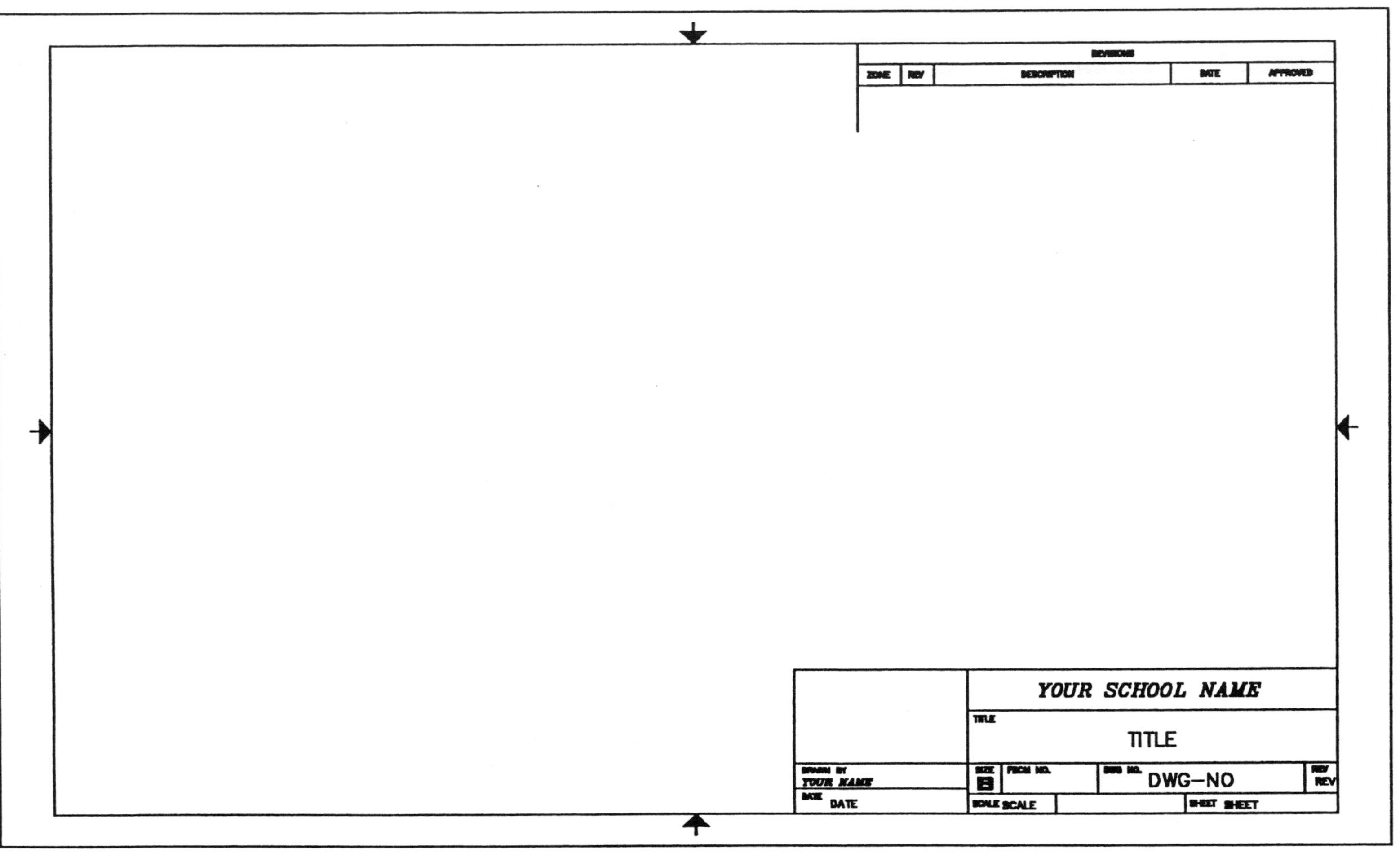

FIGURE 11–26
B-Size Format Complete

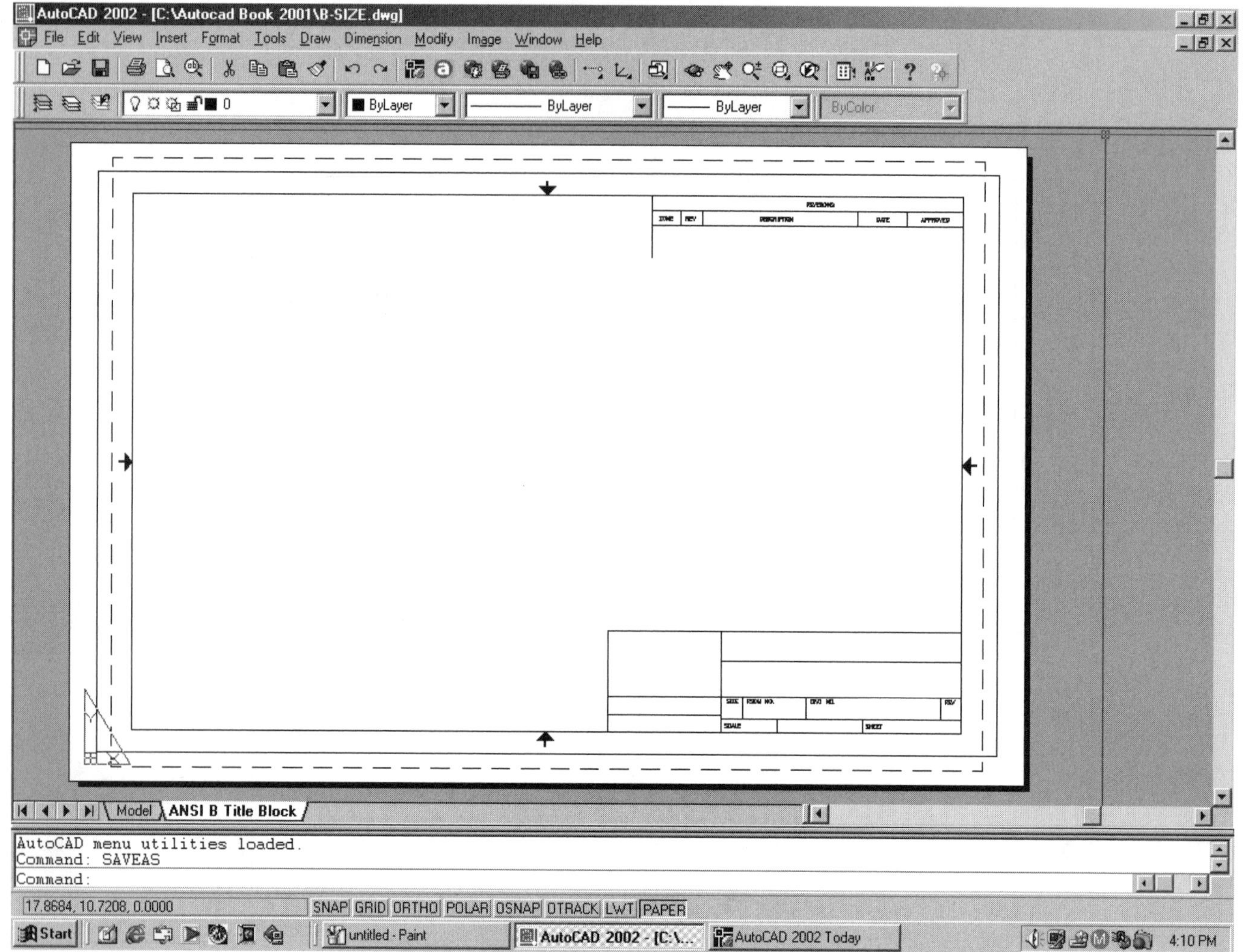

FIGURE 11–27
ANSI B Format in Paper Space.

Step 5. **With layer FTEXT current and text style Standard current, use the Dtext command to add format text in spaces for TITLE, DRAWN BY, and DATE as shown in Figure 11–28. The format text consists of all the smallest lettering that labels each space, height: .06.** Make sure all boxes are labeled as shown. If you have to explode the ansi b template to erase an item, do so using the Explode command.

Step 6. **With layer FTEXT current and style ITALIC current, use DTEXT to draw the following:**

Your name—height: .08
School name—height: .15

Step 7. **With layer FTEXT current and style BOLD current, use DTEXT to draw a B in the SIZE box—height: .15.**

Step 8. **With layer ATEXT current and style Standard current, assign VARIABLE ATTRIBUTES to the following: Use the label of the box as the tag and make up your own prompts. Remember you cannot have spaces in the tag, so you will have to put a hyphen in DWG-NO.**

SCALE (default 1/1)—height: .08—justified flush left
DATE (default *Type:* NONE)—height: .08—justified flush left
TITLE (default *Type:* NONE)—height: .15—centered

FIGURE 11–28
The Title Block with Attributes Defined

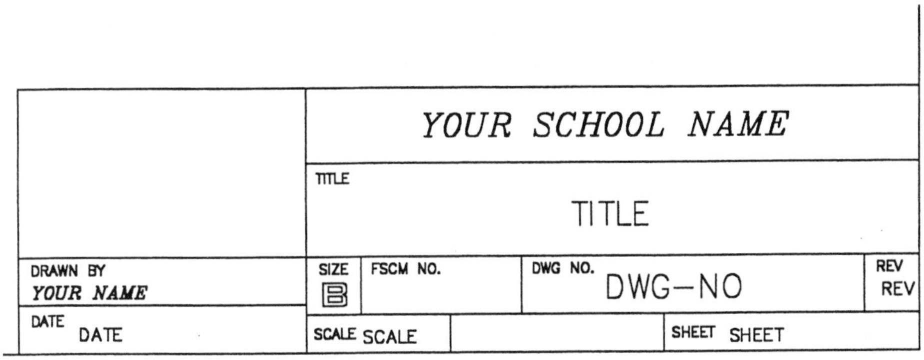

YOUR SCHOOL NAME
TITLE
TITLE
DRAWN BY
YOUR NAME
SIZE
B
FSCM NO.
DWG NO.
DWG–NO
REV
REV
DATE
DATE
SCALE SCALE
SHEET SHEET

DWG NO. (default *Type:* NONE)—height: .15—justified flush left
REV (default *Type:* a dash)—height: .08—centered
SHEET (default 1/1)—height: .08—justified flush left

Step 9. On your own:

1. Explode the template and erase the lettering that is outside the border on the left and bottom of the drawing if your template has some items there that you will not use.
2. Block the drawing using the name FORMAT. (Because the Insert command does not recognize anything that is in paper space you must insert this drawing into model space on the same drawing.) When you select objects *Type:* **ALL** ↵ to be sure you get the complete drawing. Use 0,0 as the insertion point.
3. *Click:* **the Model tab** (to the left of the ANSI B Title Block tab).
4. Insert the FORMAT block in model space using 0,0 as the insertion point. Accept defaults for all attributes.
5. Explode this block so the attributes will apply when you insert it around other drawings.
6. Save your drawing on at least two different disks using the name B-SIZE.
7. Plot the drawing half size (1 Plotted inch = 2 Drawing units) on an 11″ × 8.5″ sheet.
8. Exit AutoCAD.

In the next exercise you will insert this format around the floor plan that you drew in Exercise 11–1.

Exercise 11–4: Inserting the Format around the Floor Plan

Open the drawing of your floor plan and insert your B-size format as Layout1, then reduce your drawing on the layouts to ¼″ = 1′, using Zoom 1/48 XP. This zoom factor sets up a relationship between model space (where you made the drawing) and paper space (where you will annotate and plot the drawing).

Your final drawing will look similar to Figure 11–29.

Step 1. To begin Exercise 11–4, turn on the computer and start AutoCAD.

Step 2. Open drawing EX11-2(your initials).

Step 3. Rename Layout1 as Floor Plan.

Prompt	Response
	Click: **Layout1 at the bottom of your screen**
The Page Setup — Layout1 dialog box appears:	*Double-click*: **Layout1 in the Layout name box** *Type:* **Floor Plan** (in the Layout name box) *Click:* **OK**

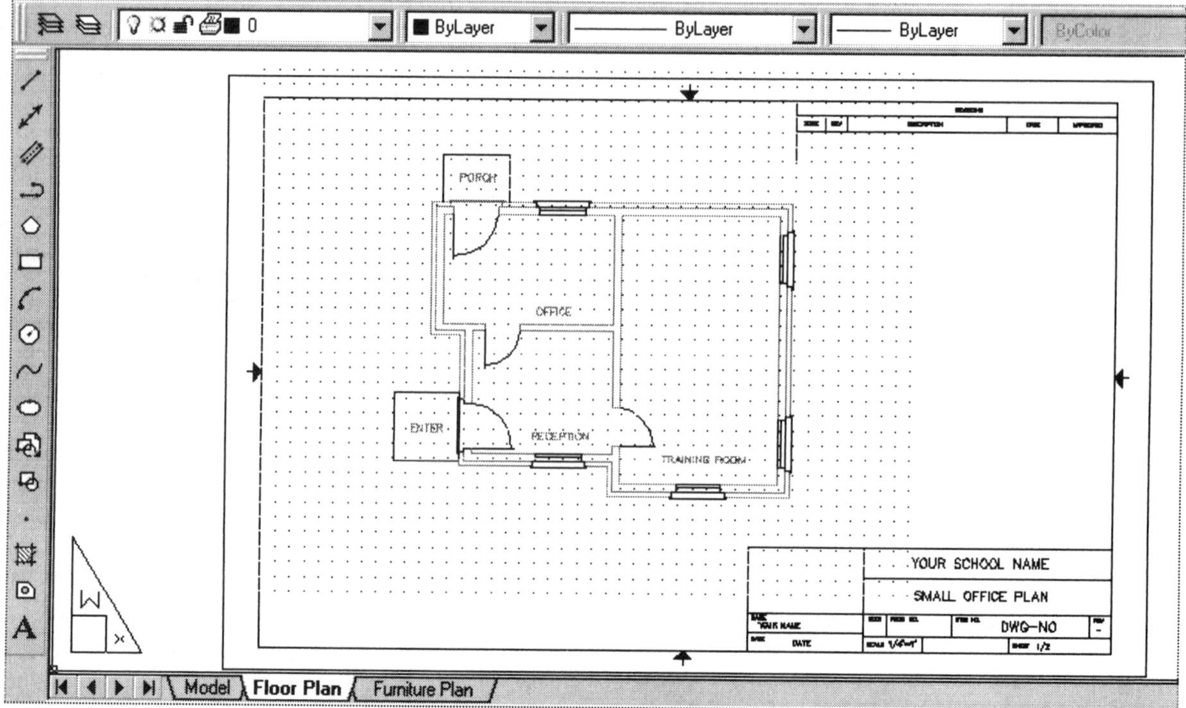

FIGURE 11–29
Exercise 11–4 Complete

Step 4. Insert the drawing B-SIZE into Layout1.

Prompt	Response
Command:	*Type*: **I** ↵
The Insert dialog box appears:	*Click*: **Browse…** and *Click*: **B-SIZE** (on the floppy disk containing the B-Size drawing in the A: drive) *Click:* **OK**
Specify insertion point or [Scale/X/Y/Z/ Rotate/PScale/PX/PY/PZ/PRotate]:	*Type:* **0,0** ↵

Answer the prompts you assigned for the variable attributes for your format with the following:

SCALE: Type: ¼″ = 1′
DATE: Type: **(the current date)**
TITLE: Type: **SMALL OFFICE PLAN**
DWG NO. Type: **EX11-4P**
REV: **(accept the default — a dash)**
SHEET: Type: **1 / 2**

Step 5. Set the scale for the layout page, and move the viewport so that the drawing is centered in the format.

Prompt	Response
Command:	*Click:* **The Outside edge of the viewport surrounding the floor plan so that grips appear at all four corners** *Click:* **Properties** on the Modify menu

Prompt	Response
The Properties dialog box appears	*Click:* **Standard Scale**
A down arrow appears:	*Click:* **The down arrow** and *Select:* **the scale:** ¼″ = **1**′ (It is near the bottom of the list.)
	Close: **the Properties box.**

If you need to, use the Move command to move the drawing so it is centered in the format. *Type:* **M** ↵ and click the boundary around the viewport to select the viewport, *Press:* ↵, then click a base point, then click another point for the second point of displacement.

Step 6. Copy the Floor Plan layout page and delete Layout2.

Prompt	Response
Command:	**Hold your mouse over the words Floor Plan at the bottom of the screen and right click.**
The Layout right-click menu appears:	*Click:* **Move or Copy**
The Move or Copy dialog box (Figure 11–30) appears:	*Click:* **the check box to the left of Create a copy as shown**
	Click: **(move to end)**
	Click: **OK**
	Hold the mouse over Layout2 and right click.
The Layout right-click menu appears:	*Click:* **Delete**
An AutoCAD warning appears:	*Click:* **OK**

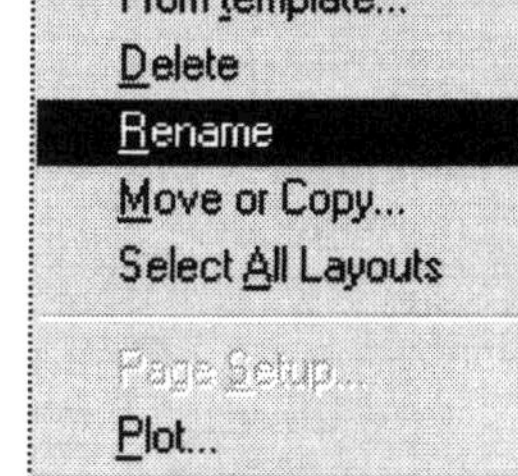

Step 7. Rename layout Floor Plan (2).

Prompt	Response
Command:	**Hold the mouse over Floor Plan (2) and right click.**
The Layout right-click menu appears:	*Click:* **Rename**

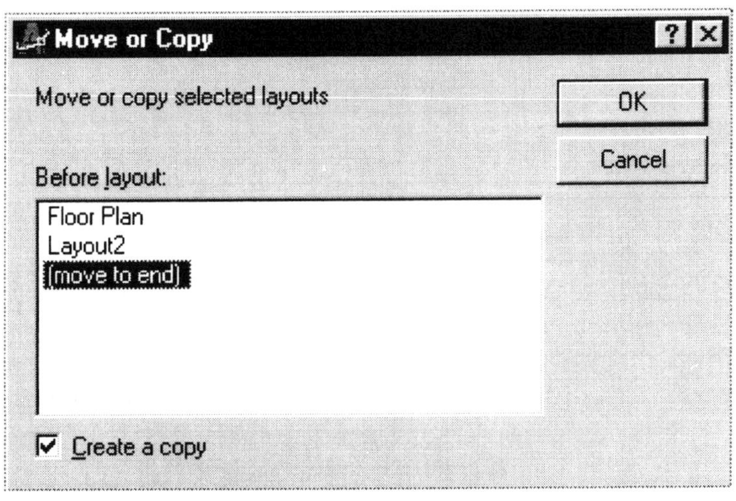

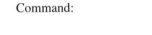

FIGURE 11–30
Move or Copy (Layout) Dialog Box

FIGURE 11–31
Rename Layout (Floor Plan 2) as Furniture Plan

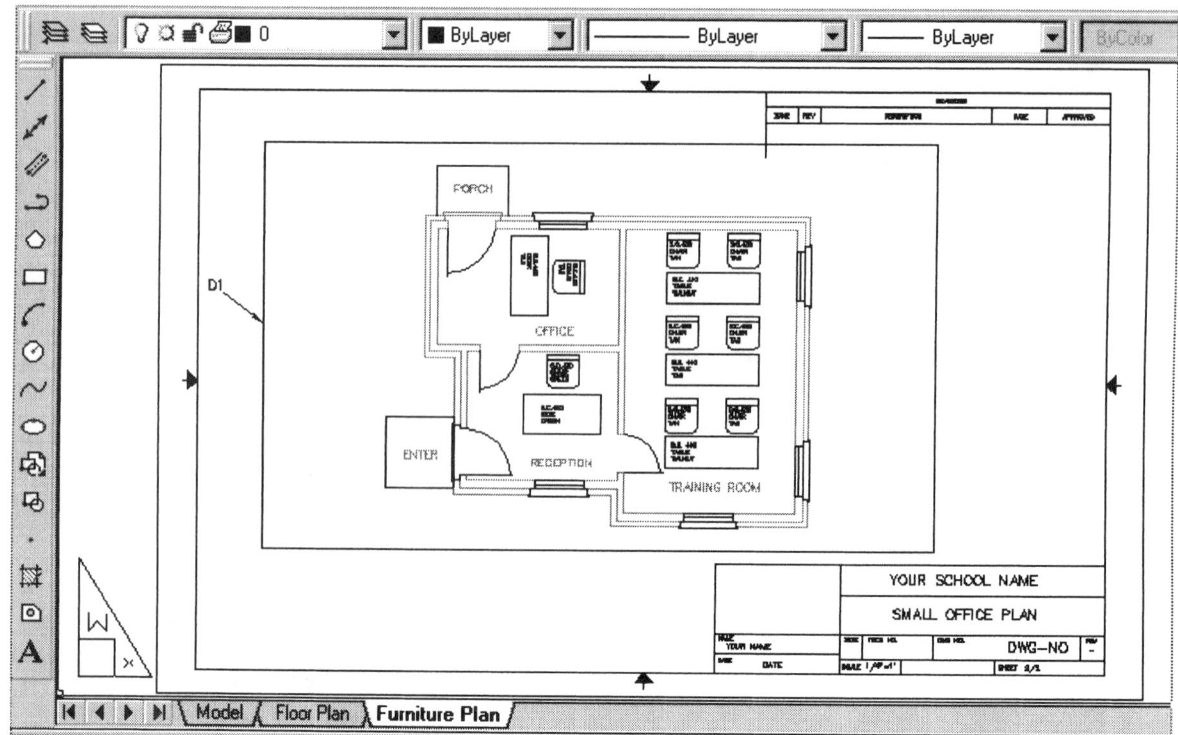

FIGURE 11–32
Change the Boundary of the Viewport to the Viewport Layer

Prompt	Response
The Rename Layout dialog box (Figure 11–31) appears:	*Type:* **Furniture Plan** *Click:* **OK**

Step 8. Move the viewport boundary to the Viewport layer and turn it off, as shown in Figure 11–32.

Prompt	Response
Command:	*Click:* **D1** (Figure 11–32) to select the viewport boundary *Click:* **the Layer List on the Object Properties toolbar (Figure 11–33)** *Click:* **the Viewport Layer** *Click:* **the lightbulb to turn off the layer if it is not off already**

FIGURE 11–33
Change the Viewport Boundary to the Viewport Layer and Turn It OFF

Step 9. On your own:

1. Save your drawing in at least two places. Name it EX11-4 (your initials).
2. *Click:* **Floor Plan** at the bottom of your screen to make that layout active. Turn OFF the FURNITURE layer and print this layout full size on a 17″ × 11″ sheet if you have a printer that accepts that size sheet. If your printer prints only 11″ × 8½″ sheets, print to fit.
3. *Click:* **Furniture Plan** at the bottom of your screen to make that layout active. Use ATTEDIT (Edit Attribute) to change the sheet attribute from 1 / 2 to 2 / 2. (This is sheet 2 of a two-sheet drawing). Turn ON the FURNITURE layer and print this layout full size on a 17″ × 11″ sheet if you have a printer that accepts that size sheet. If your printer prints only 11″ × 8½″ sheets, print to fit.
4. Exit AutoCAD.

EXTRACTING ATTRIBUTES

The Attribute Extraction wizard in AutoCAD2002 can be used to produce a parts list or bill of materials directly from a drawing that contains blocks with attributes. The drawing you have done in this chapter is an excellent example of this type of drawing. With the Attribute Extract wizard you can extract existing attributes and save them to an external file in one of two formats. This file can then be used in another software program to produce the exact form you want. Exercise 11–5 is used to extract the attributes from the drawing done for Exercise 11–2, save it to a txt format, and print it as an external file.

Exercise 11–5: Extracting Attributes from Drawing EX11-2(your initials)

Step 1. To begin Exercise 11–5, turn on the computer and start AutoCAD.

Step 2. Open drawing EX11-2(your initials).

Step 3. Extract attributes from this drawing using the Enhanced Attribute Extraction command.

Prompt	Response
Command:	**Attribute Extraction...** (or *Type:* **EATTEXT**)
The Attribute Extraction Wizard with Select Drawing tab selected appears (Figure 11–34):	**With the Current Drawing radio button selected** *Click:* **Next.**
The Settings tab is selected:	*Click:* **Next>**
The Use Template tab is selected:	**With the No Template radio button selected** *Click:* **Next>.**
The Select Attributes tab is selected:	There should be checks to the left of **DESK, CHAIR, and TABLE** in the Block Name list. If not, *Click:* **Check All** under the Blocks area.
	With **DESK highlighted** in the Block Name list, under the Attributes for block <DESK> *Click:* **Uncheck All** (so that no attributes are selected).

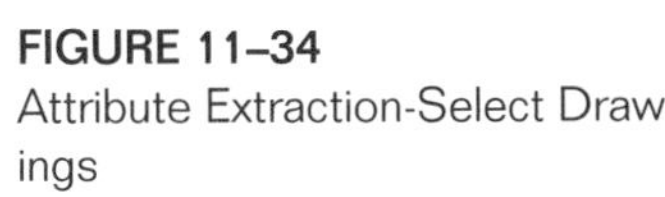

FIGURE 11–34
Attribute Extraction-Select Drawings

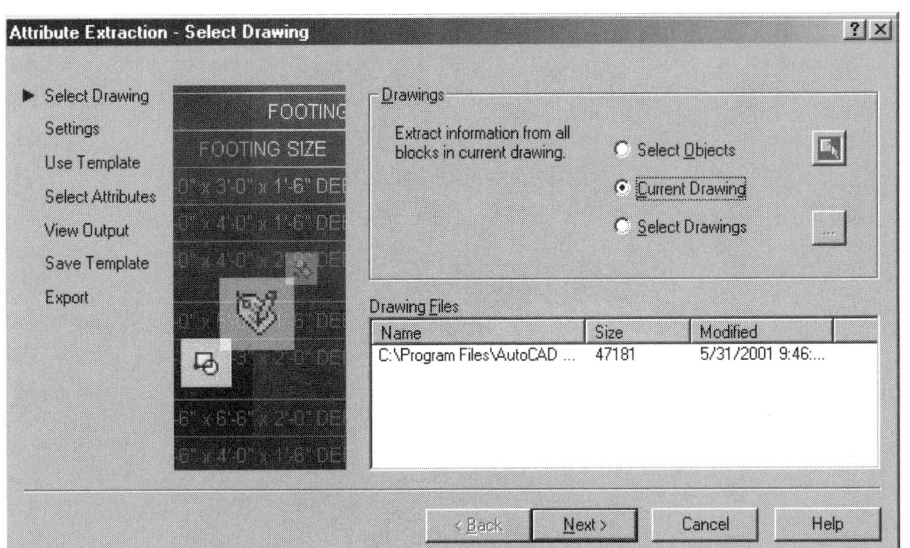

FIGURE 11–35
Attribute Extraction-Select Attributes

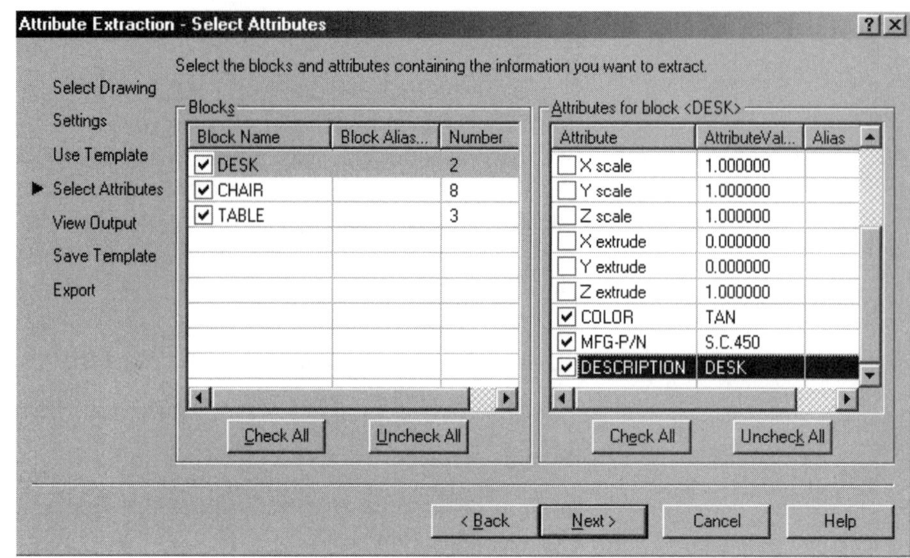

Check: **COLOR, MFG-P/N, and DESCRIPTION,** as shown in Figure 11–35

With **CHAIR highlighted** in the Block Name list, under the Attributes for block <CHAIR> *Click:* **Uncheck All** (so that no attributes are selected).

Check: **COLOR, MFG-P/N, and DESCRIPTION,** as shown in Figure 11–35

With **TABLE highlighted** in the Block Name list, under the Attributes for block <TABLE> *Click:* **Uncheck All** (so that no attributes are selected).

Check: **COLOR, MFG-P/N, and DESCRIPTION,** as shown in Figure 11–35

Click: **Next>**

The View Output tab is selected:

Click: **Alternate View** once or twice so the screen appears as shown in Figure 11–36.

Click: **Next>**

The Save Template tab is selected:

Click: **Next>**

The Export tab is selected:

In the File Name text box, *Type:* **A:EX11-5(YOUR INITIALS)** (Figure 11–37).

In the File Type text box, *Select:* **Tab Delimited File (*.txt)**

Click: **Finish**

Step 4. Open Notepad in Windows (Figure 11–38)

Click: **Start**
Click: **Accessories**
Click: **Notepad**

FIGURE 11–36
Attribute Extraction-View Output

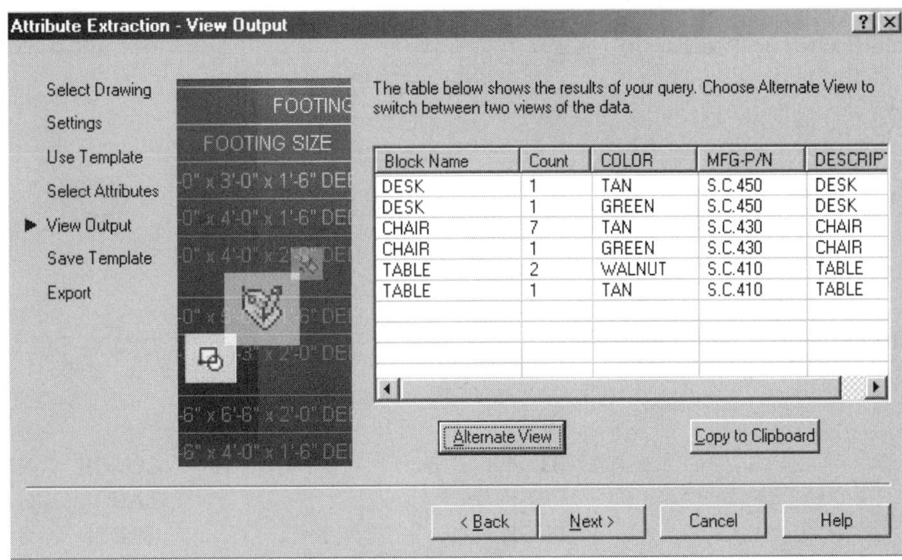

FIGURE 11–37
Attribute Extraction-Export

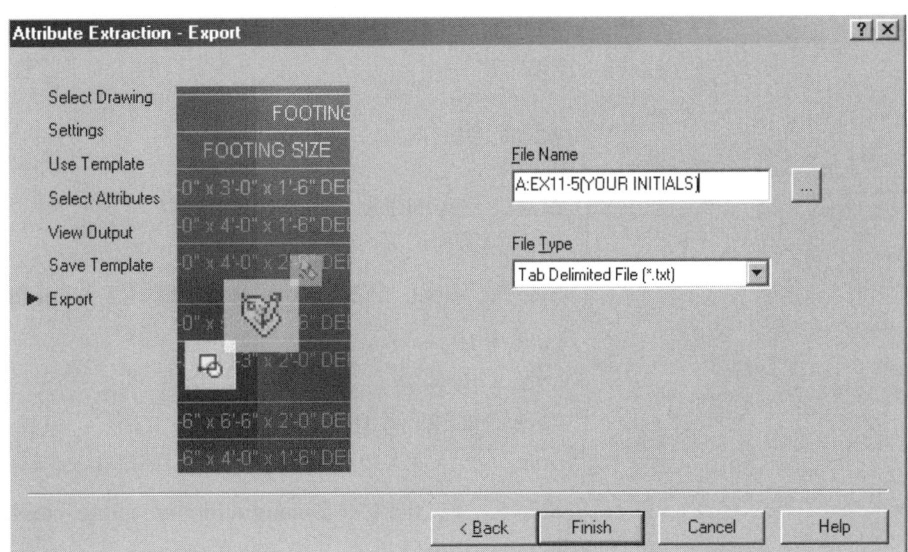

FIGURE 11–38
Open Notepad in Windows

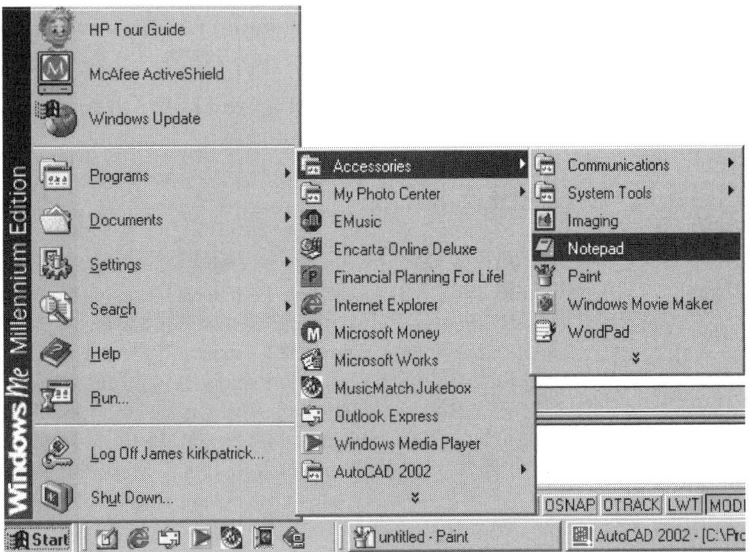

FIGURE 11–39
Fix the Text File in Notepad

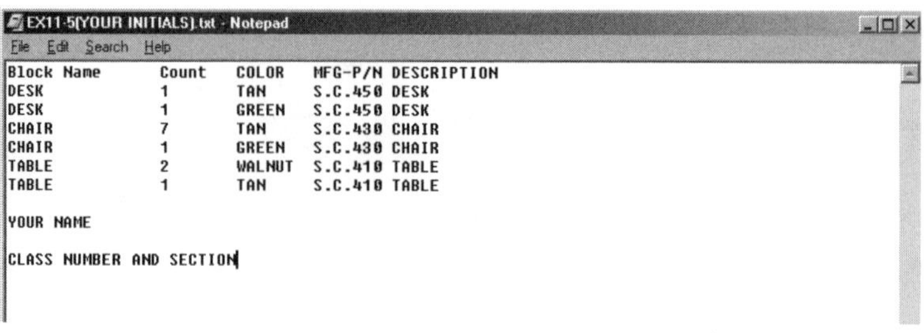

```
Block Name      Count   COLOR   MFG-P/N DESCRIPTION
DESK            1       TAN     S.C.450 DESK
DESK            1       GREEN   S.C.450 DESK
CHAIR           7       TAN     S.C.430 CHAIR
CHAIR           1       GREEN   S.C.430 CHAIR
TABLE           2       WALNUT  S.C.410 TABLE
TABLE           1       TAN     S.C.410 TABLE

YOUR NAME

CLASS NUMBER AND SECTION
```

FIGURE 11–40
Print Exercise 11–5

```
EX11-5(YOUR INITIALS) .txt

Block Name       Count   COLOR   MFG-P/N DESCRIPTION
DESK             1       TAN     S.C.450 DESK
DESK             1       GREEN   S.C.450 DESK
CHAIR            7       TAN     S.C.430 CHAIR
CHAIR            1       GREEN   S.C.430 CHAIR
TABLE            2       WALNUT  S.C.410 TABLE
TABLE            1       TAN     S.C.410 TABLE

YOUR NAME

CLASS NUMBER AND SECTION
```

Step 5. Open EX5-11(YOUR INITIALS) from the floppy disk in the A: drive

Click: **File**

Click: **Open**

Click: **3 ½ Floppy Drive [A:]**

Double-click: **EX11-5(YOUR INTIALS).txt**

Step 6. Fix the text file and add your name, class and section (Figure 11–39).

Click: **To the left of the number 1 (between DESK and 1) and press the Tab key.**

The number 1 should then be aligned under the Count column.

Repeat step 6 for the remaining numbers and add your name, class, and section number as shown in Figure 11–39.

Step 7. Print this file (Figure 11–40), to complete the exercise.

EXERCISES

EXERCISE 11–1. Complete Exercise 11–1 using steps 1 through 26.

EXERCISE 11–2. Complete Exercise 11–2 using steps 1 through 10.

EXERCISE 11–3. Complete Exercise 11–3 using steps 1 through 4.

EXERCISE 11–4. Complete Exercise 11–4 using steps 1 through 9.

EXERCISE 11–5. Complete Exercise 11–5 using steps 1 through 7.

EXERCISE 11–6. Draw an A-size format using the dimensions shown in Figure 11–41. Assign attributes as you did for Exercise 11–4 using the same settings and letter sizes. Reset limits to 11,8.5. Make this Drawing Number EX11-5. Keep this format on file to use in later chapters. Name it A-SIZE. Start with the ansi.a template.

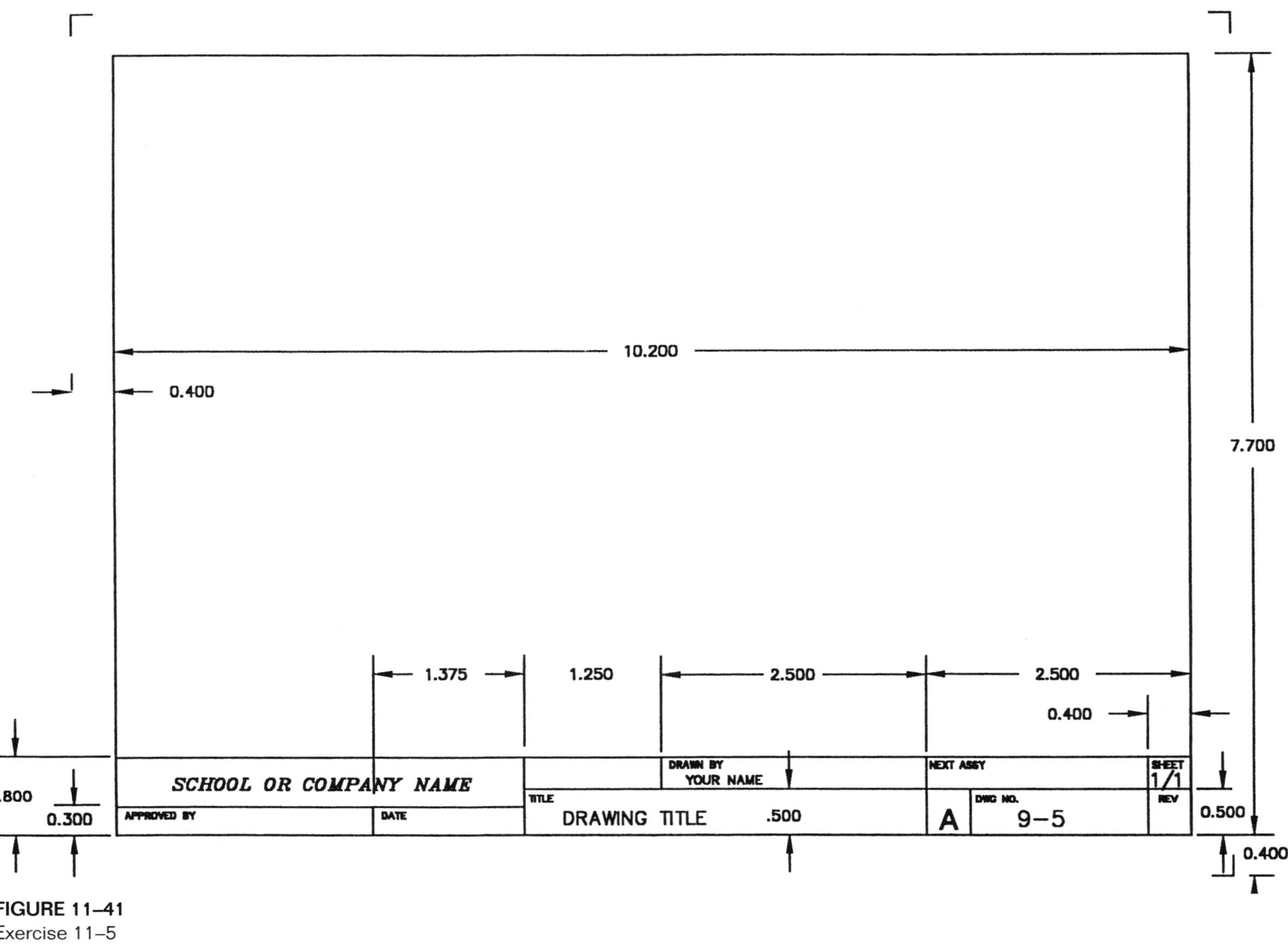

FIGURE 11–41
Exercise 11–5

EXERCISE 11–7. Draw a C-size format using the template ansi c.dwt and modify it so it appears as shown in Figure 11–42. Assign attributes as you did for Exercise 11–4 using the same settings and letter sizes. Reset limits to 22,17. Keep this format on file to use in later chapters. Name it C-SIZE.

EXERCISE 11–8. Draw the floor plan shown in Figure 11–43 full scale. Approximate any dimensions not shown. Use a polyline with a 10″ width for the outside walls; 6″ width for inside walls. Set limits to 140′, 90′ for the upper right corner. Insert your C-size format from Exercise 11–6 into Layout1. Set the scale at ⅛″ = 1″ using Properties in paper space. Plot on a C-size sheet at a scale factor of 1 = 1.

EXERCISE 11–9. Draw the floor plan shown in Figure 11–44 full scale. Approximate any dimensions not shown or measure with an architect's scale and draw to size. Use the wall technique used for Exercise 11–7. Limits should be 120′,100′ for the upper right corner. Use the settings from Exercise 11–1. Insert your B-size format from Exercise 11–4 into Layout1. Set the scale at ⅛″ = 1″ using Properties in paper space. Plot on a B-size sheet at a scale factor of 1 = 1.

REVIEW QUESTIONS

Circle the best answer.

1. AutoCAD contains most of the symbols needed for complete space planning.
   a. True
   b. False
2. What was the GRID setting for Figures 11–1 through 11–12?
   a. 1″ b. 1′ c. ¼″ d. ½″ e 6″
3. What was the SNAP setting for the floor plan in this chapter?
   a. ¼″ b. 3″ c. 2″ d. ⅛″ e. 1″
4. How many layers are needed if furniture outlines are on one layer, text is on another, walls are on another, and doors and windows occupy the same layer?
   a. 1 b. 2 c. 3 d. 4 e. 5
5. Which of the following commands will most easily produce three lines showing a wall?
   a. Copy
   b. Pline
   c. Line
   d. Offset
   e. Multiline
6. Which command must be used *before* the Multiline command can be used to draw a specified number of lines?
   a. Style
   b. Format
   c. Pline
   d. Multiline Style
   e. Offset
7. On which menu is the Attribute Extraction… command located?
   a. Insert
   b. Format
   c. Draw
   d. Image
   e. Tools
8. Which of the following commands creates a block that may be used on the current drawing only?
   a. Block
   b. Wblock
   c. Attdef
   d. Attext
   e. Attblock

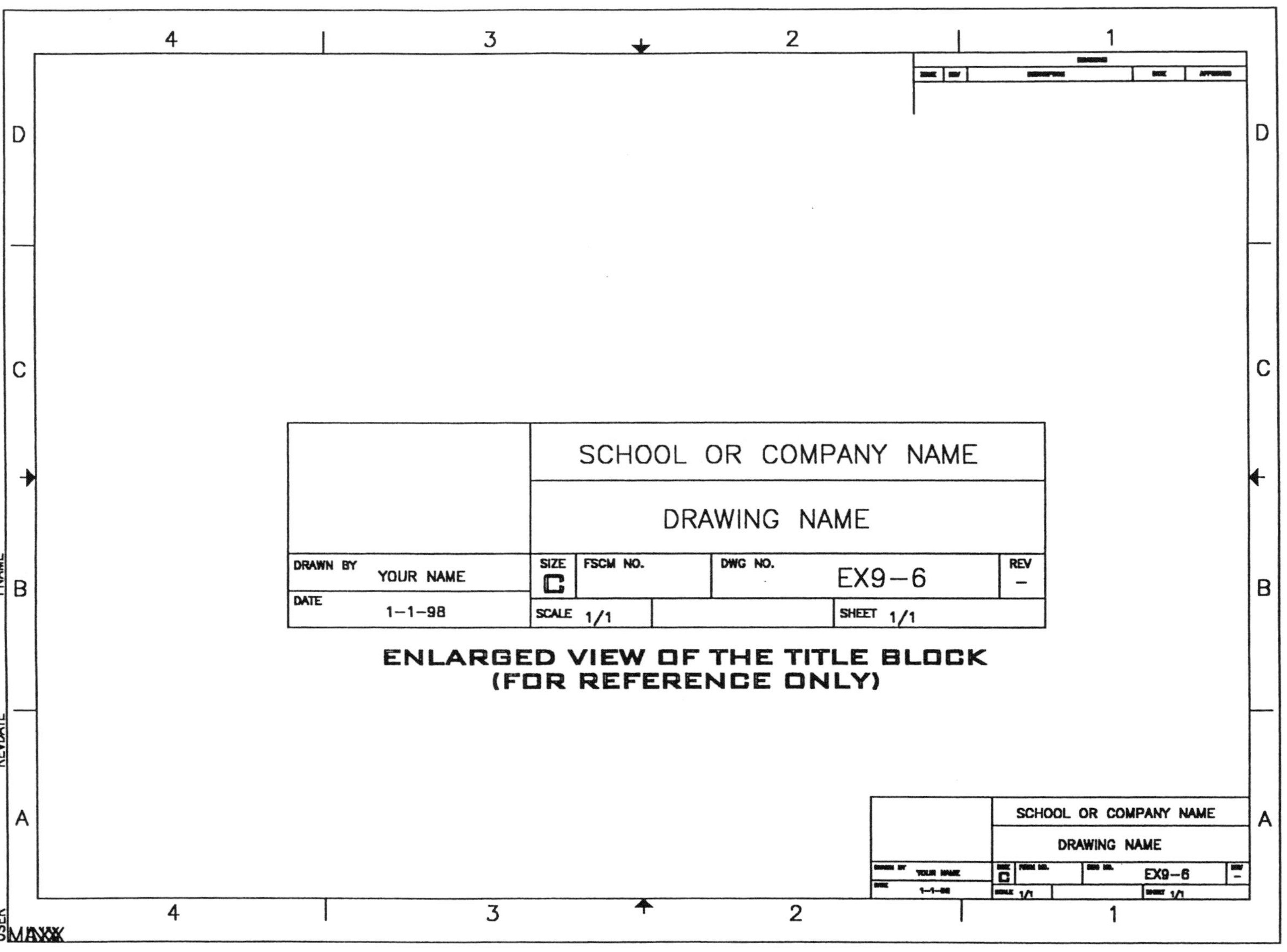

FIGURE 11–42
Exercise 11–6

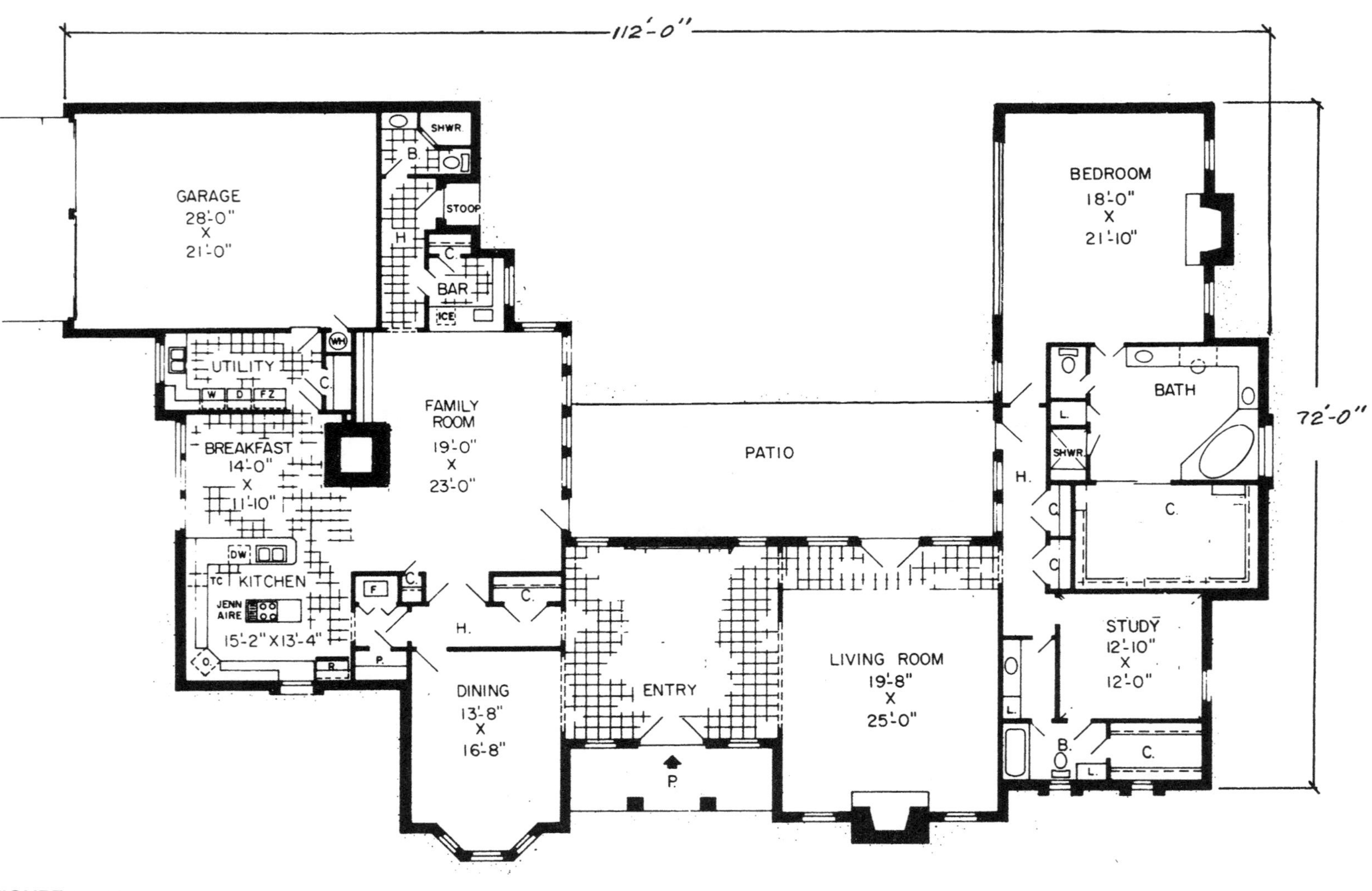

FIGURE 11–43
Exercise 11–7

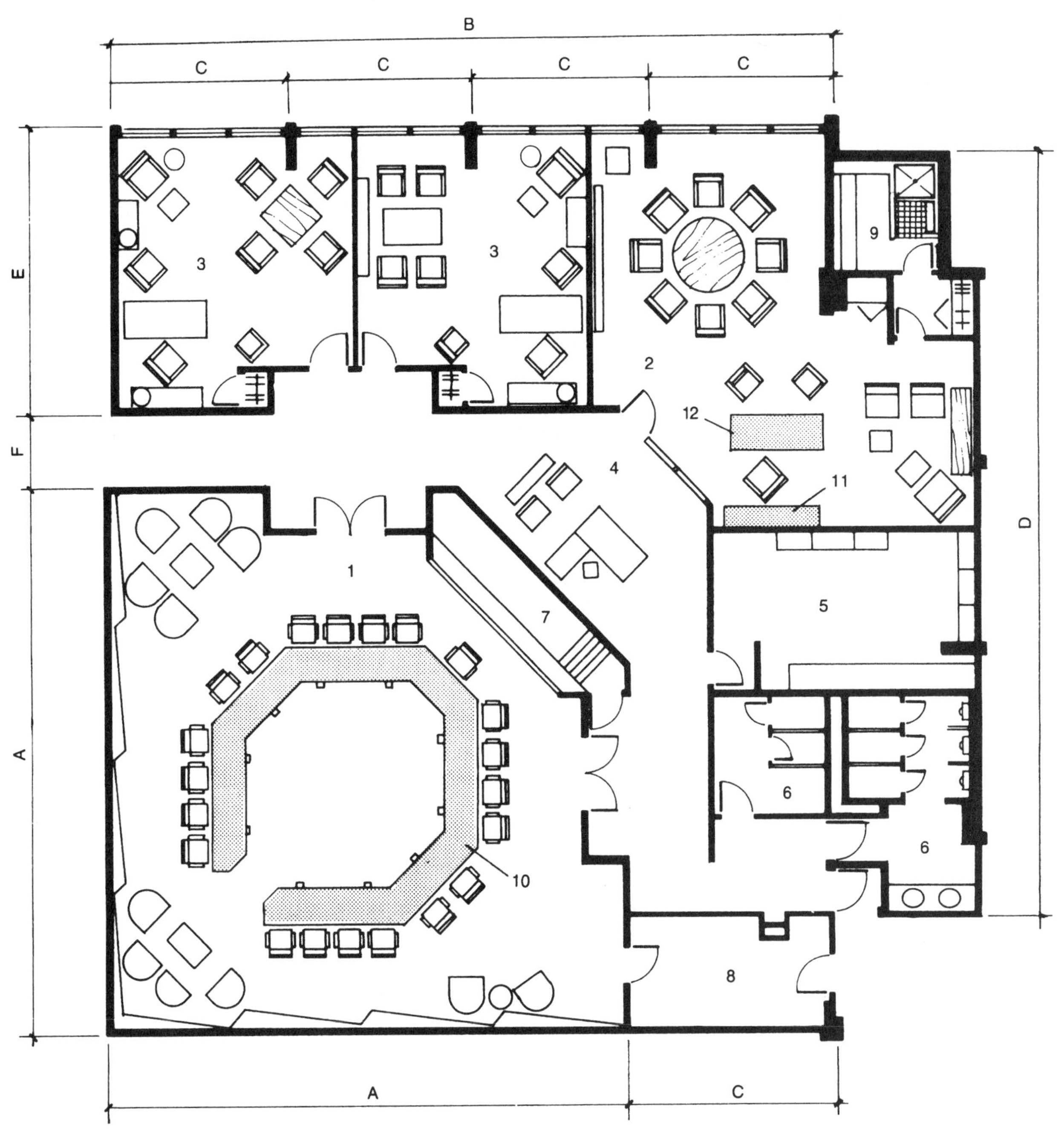

Dimensions:

		ft/in.	m
A	=	46 6	14.17
B	=	62	18.90
C	=	15 6	4.72
D	=	69±	21.03
E	=	24±	7.32
F	=	6±	1.83

FIGURE 11–44
Exercise 11–8

9. Which of the following commands creates a block that may be used on any drawing?
   a. Block
   b. Wblock
   c. Attdef
   d. Attext
   e. Attblock
10. Which of the following toolbars contains the Insert Block command?
    a. Draw
    b. Modify
    c. Standard
    d. Object Properties
    e. Attribute
11. Which of the following menus contains the Define Attribute command?
    a. Draw
    b. Modify
    c. Edit
    d. Insert
    e. Format
12. Which of the following commands is used to assign attributes to a drawing?
    a. Define Attribute
    b. Edit Attribute
    c. Edit Attribute Globally
    d. Block
    e. Wblock
13. Which of the following commands may be used to identify a location from which a block may be inserted with the @2′6″<0 response?
    a. Tracking
    b. Zero
    c. Osnap-Intersection
    d. Osnap-Nearest
    e. Distance
14. In which of the following may spaces not be used?
    a. Attribute Value
    b. Attribute Prompt
    c. Attribute Tag
    d. Default attribute value
    e. None of these may contain spaces.
15. To insert a format around an existing drawing on the screen, which of the following commands is used?
    a. Insert Block...
    b. Block
    c. Format
    d. Draw
    e. Change

12 External References (XREFs)

OBJECTIVES

After completing this chapter, you will be able to

- Attach one or more drawings to another without the use of blocks.
- Correctly answer review questions regarding the following commands:

  External Reference
    Bind
    Detach
    Path
    Reload
    Attach
  XrefCtl
  External Reference Clip
  External Reference Clip Frame

INTRODUCTION

Combining drawings in AutoCAD has two distinct benefits: It can result in a considerable savings in time, and it can result in more accurate and current drawing revision.

AutoCAD provides two methods for combining drawings.

Method 1 Inserting one or more drawings into another.
The Insert command allows you to copy one drawing into another. The copy and the active drawing are permanently combined as one. The original of the copied drawing and the combined drawing have no relationship to each other.

Method 2 Attaching one or more drawings to one or more other drawings.
The XREF command allows you temporarily to combine two or more drawings into a single drawing. The data of each drawing are stored in their own separate files so that changes made to the external references are reflected in the combined drawing file.

TERMS

So that some confusion can be avoided, let's begin this explanation by defining the terms that will be used to refer to drawings.

Current drawing The drawing to which the xref is attached.
External reference The drawing that is attached to the current drawing.

ADVANTAGES OF USING EXTERNAL REFERENCES

There are two distinct advantages to using external references:

1. The current drawing always contains the most recent version of the external reference.

2. There are no conflicts in layer names and other similar features (called named objects) such as linetypes, text styles, and block definitions. AutoCAD automatically places the drawing name of the External Reference followed by a / in front of the inserted layer name or other object name. (Example: The current drawing and the external reference (named CHAIR) have a layer named SYMBOL. The current drawing layer retains the name SYMBOL, and the external reference layer in the current drawing becomes CHAIR/SYMBOL.)

USES OF EXTERNAL REFERENCES

There are many ways external references may be used. The following are three examples of their use.

Example 1. Mechanical assembly drawings. Drawings of detail parts are created and attached as external references to any assembly drawing that contains the parts. Each time a detail part drawing is changed, all assembly drawings containing that detail part are updated automatically.

Example 2. Schematic diagrams. Complex symbols are created as external references and attached to a current drawing that is the complete schematic diagram. Any change in the complex symbol drawing is reflected in all schematic diagrams to which the symbol is attached.

Example 3. Space planning. A common space such as a typical executive's office is created as an external reference and attached to several drawings, each representing one floor of a multistory building. When changes are made to the manager's office (as a result of furniture substitution, for example) the change is reflected on each floor to which the executive's office is attached.

Now let's look at the options that the External Reference (XREF) command contains.

EXTERNAL REFERENCE OPTIONS

When the Xref Manager command is activated, the following options in the Xref Manager dialog box are displayed.

The dialog box displays a list of all external references contained in the current drawing and the drawing files to which each one is attached.

Bind Creates a block of the external reference in the current drawing and erases any reference to it as an external reference for that block.

Detach Lets you remove unneeded external references from your drawing.

Browse... and Save Path Allows you to change the path (the drive and folder containing the external reference) and save it.

Reload Allows you to update the current drawing with an external reference that has been changed since you began the current drawing. You do not have to exit from the current drawing to update it with an external reference that you or someone else changed while in the current drawing.

Attach Allows you to attach any drawing to the current drawing as an external reference.

Now let's make a drawing and attach it to another drawing as an external reference.

Exercise 12–1: Attach an External Reference to the Floor Plan in Exercise 11–4

Your final drawing will look similar to Figure 12–1.

Make a drawing of a typical office work station (Figure 12–2). (This will be the external reference.)

FIGURE 12–1
Completed Exercise 12–1

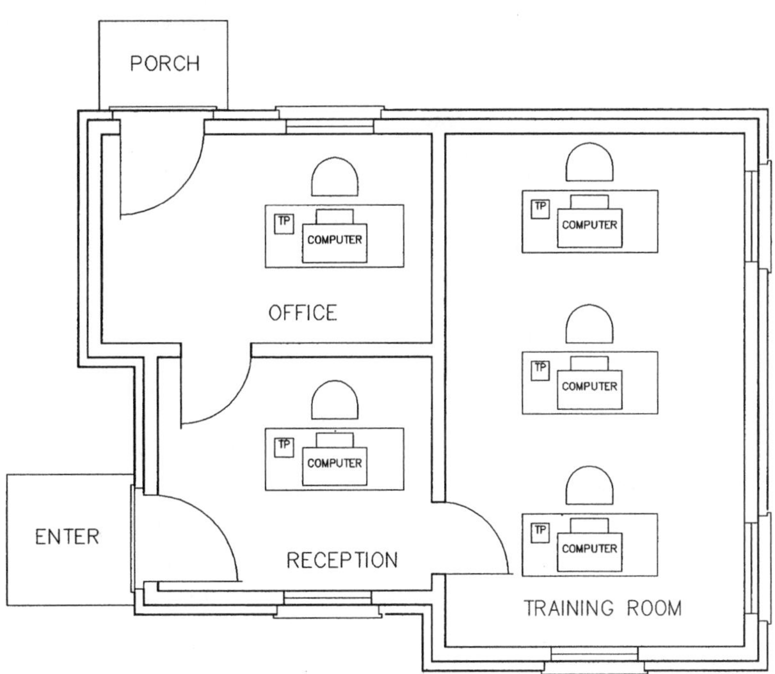

FIGURE 12–2
Dimensions for the Typical Work Station

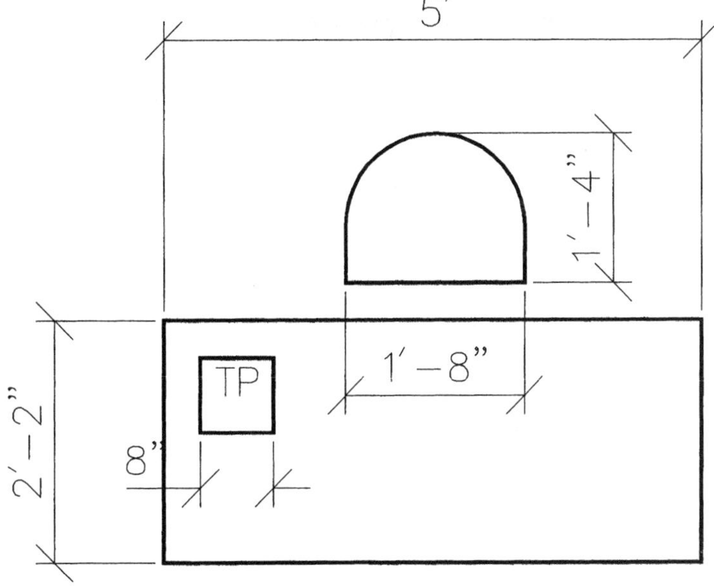

Step 1. To begin Exercise 12–1, turn on the computer and start AutoCAD.

Step 2. On your own:

1. Open drawing EX11-1(your initials) so that you may use the layers and settings from Exercise 11–1. Both the status bar and MODEL tab should read MODEL. (You must be in model space.)
2. In an open area draw Figure 12–2. Make the text 3″ high. Approximate any dimensions not shown.
3. Wblock WS-(your initials) to a floppy disk in the A: drive. Use the upper quadrant of the chair as the insertion point.
4. Exit EX11-1(your initials) and do not save changes.

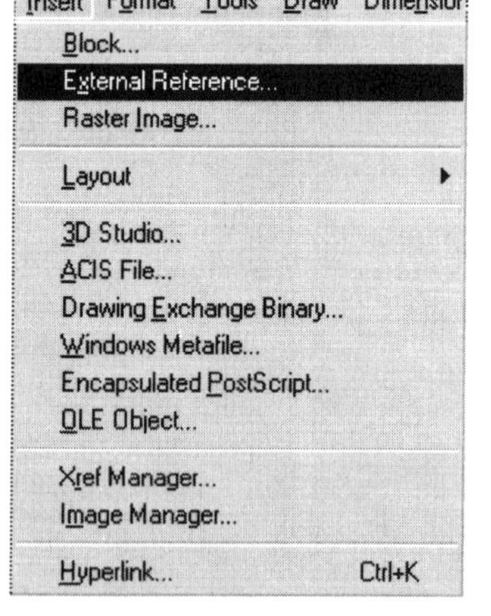

Open the drawing you did of the floor plan in Chapter 11 and attach the work station drawing to it using External Reference-Attach.

Step 3. Open drawing EX11-1(your initials). If you have not drawn Exercise 11–1, draw the floor plan as described in Chapter 9. Erase all furniture from the floor plan so that you have a drawing similar to Figure 12–3. *Click:* **MODEL** at the bottom of your screen so you will be in model space to add to your drawing.

Step 4. Attach the work station drawing to the Current Drawing in the following manner.

Prompt	Response
Command:	*Click:* **External Reference... from the menu bar, or External Reference Attach from the Reference toolbar**

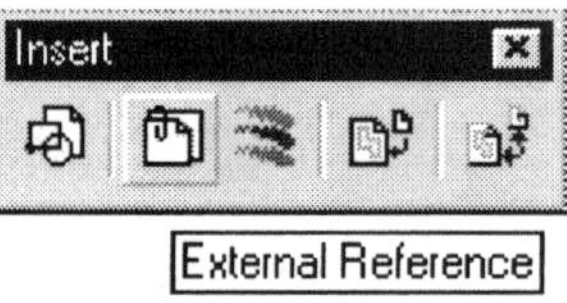

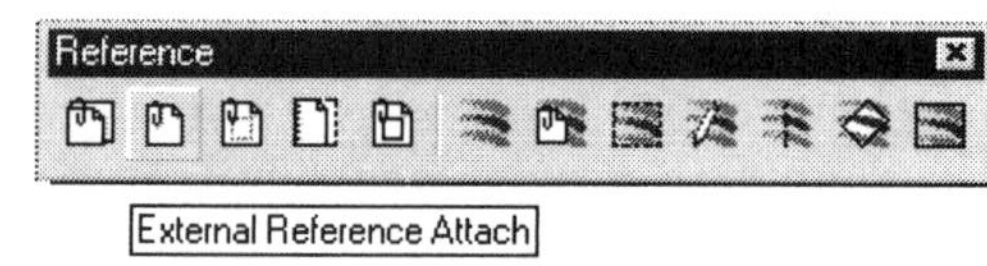

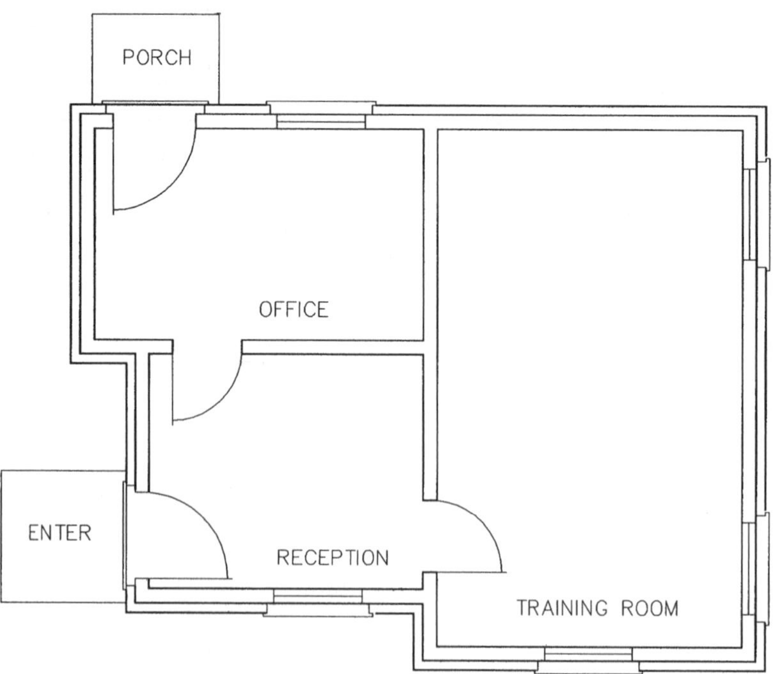

FIGURE 12–3
Floor Plan from Exercise 11–1

Note: The External Reference icon on the Insert toolbar leads you to the External Reference dialog box, then to the Select Reference File dialog box. The External Reference Attach icon on the Reference toolbar leads you directly to the Select Reference File dialog box.

Prompt	Response
The Select Reference File dialog box (Figure 12–4) appears:	*Click:* **3½ Floppy [A:]**
	Click: **WS-(your initials)**
	Click: **Open**
The External Reference dialog box (Figure 12–5) appears:	*Click:* **OK**
Insertion point:	**D1** (Figure 12–6)

That's all there is to attaching a drawing as an external reference to another drawing.

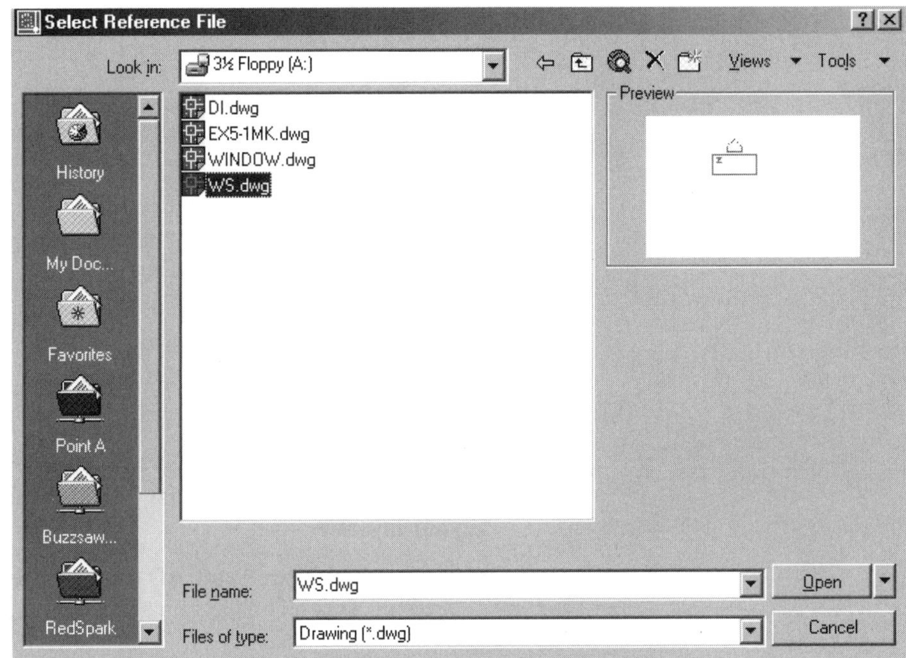

FIGURE 12–4
Select Reference File Dialog Box

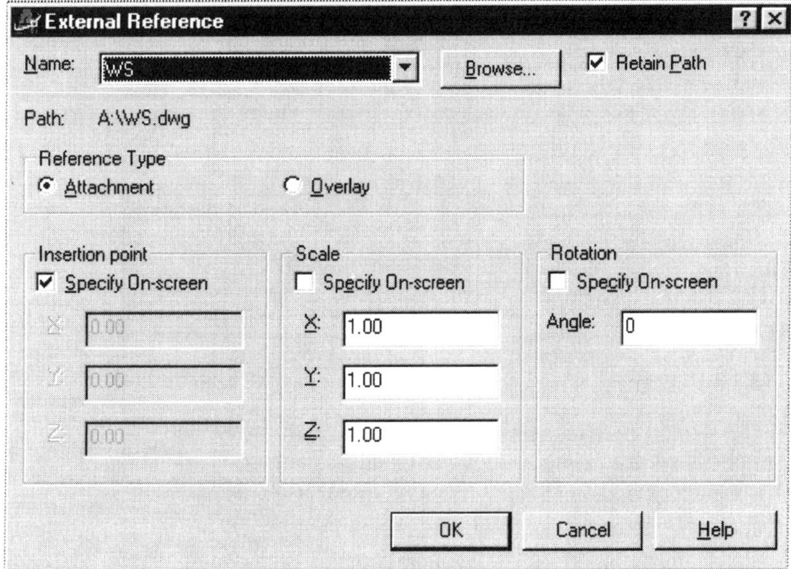

FIGURE 12–5
External Reference Dialog Box

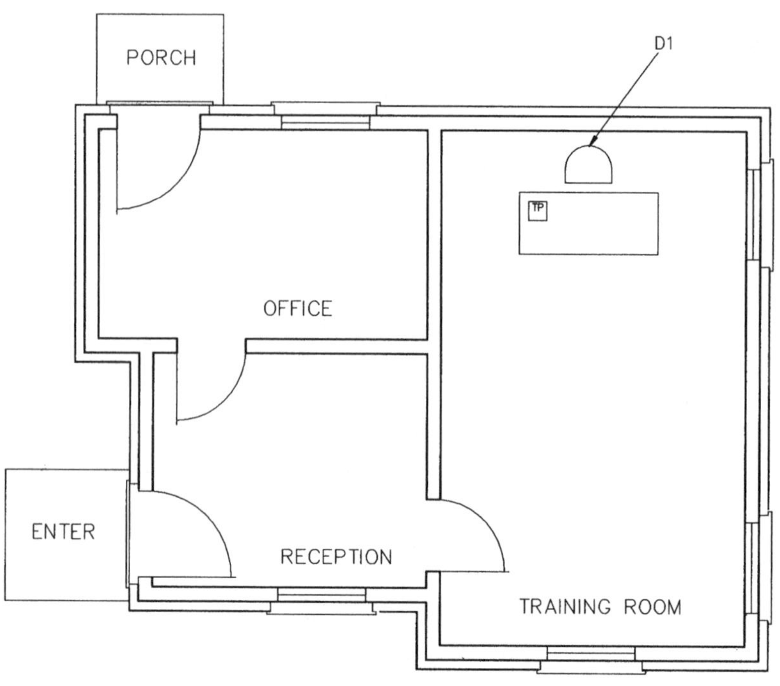

FIGURE 12–6
Attaching the External Reference

Step 5. On your own:
Copy the external reference to four other locations in the floor plan, as shown in Figure 12–7.

Step 6. Use the SaveAs... command to save your drawing as EX12-1(your initials) on the same floppy disk that contains the external reference drawing WS-(your initials).

If you are working with other AutoCAD operators, be sure that everyone is able to locate the external reference based on the path and filename stored with the drawings.

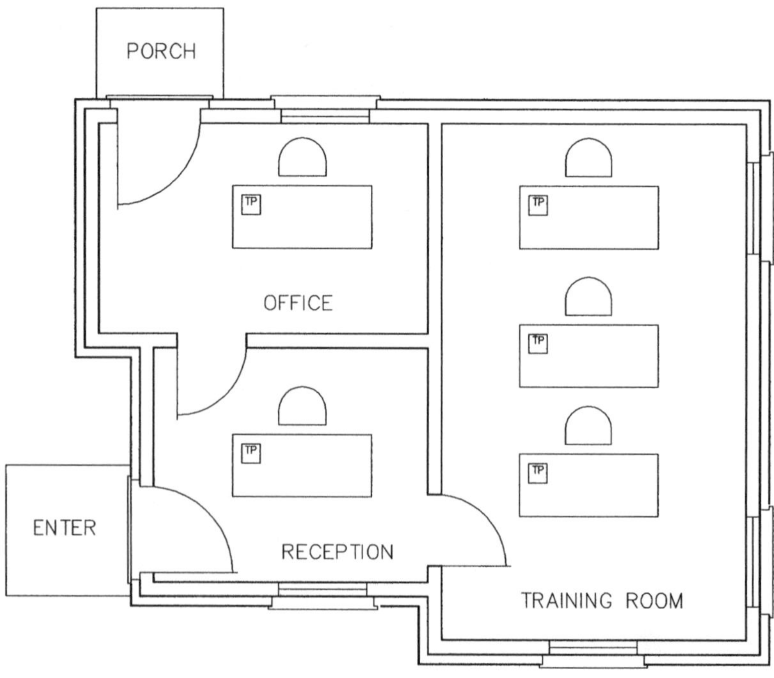

FIGURE 12–7
Copying the Work Station as an External Reference to Four Other Locations

FIGURE 12–8
New Executive Work Station

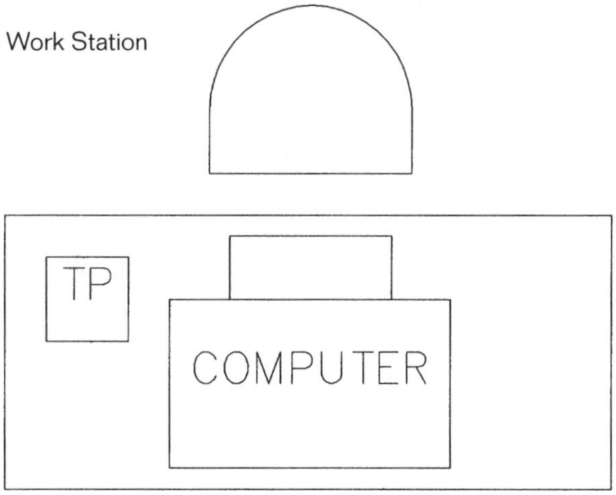

Note: You do not have to close the drawing EX12-1 to open WS-(your initials) and change it. If you change WS-(your initials) and save it, you will have to close WS-(your initials), then reload it as an xref from the Xref Manager.

Edit the existing drawing WS-(your initials) and open drawing EX12-1(your initials) to display the new external references as described in steps 7 and 8.

You have been informed that all executive workstations should now have a computer, as shown in Figure 12–8.

Step 7. On your own:
Open drawing WS-(your initials) and draw a computer approximately the size shown and label it. Save the new workstation drawing in the same place from which it came.

Step 8. Open drawing EX12-1(your initials). It should appear as shown in Figure 12–9.

Step 9. On your own:

1. Save your drawing in at least two places.
2. Plot the drawing at a scale of ¼″ = 1′ (¼ Plotted inch = 1′ Drawing unit) on an 11″ × 8½″ sheet.
3. Exit AutoCAD.

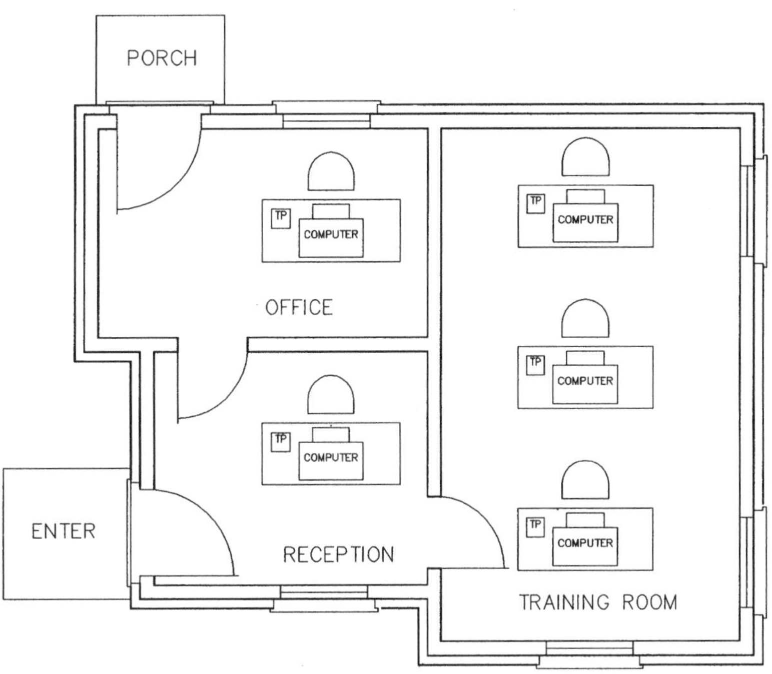

FIGURE 12–9
Exercise 12–1 Complete

FEATURES OF EXTERNAL REFERENCES

- □ An external reference cannot be exploded.
- □ An external reference can be changed into a block with the bind option of the external reference command and then exploded. The advantage of using the external reference is then lost. The bind option would be used if you wanted to send a client a disk containing only the current drawing without including external references on the same disk, for example.
- □ External references can be nested. That means that a current drawing containing external references can itself be used as an external reference on another current drawing. There is no limit to the number of drawings you can nest like this.
- □ External references can be clipped (parts of the xref can be cut out using the external reference Clip command). The external reference Clip Frame command puts a border around the clipped area.

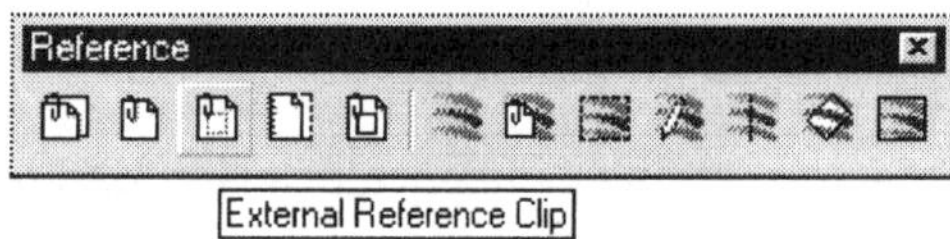

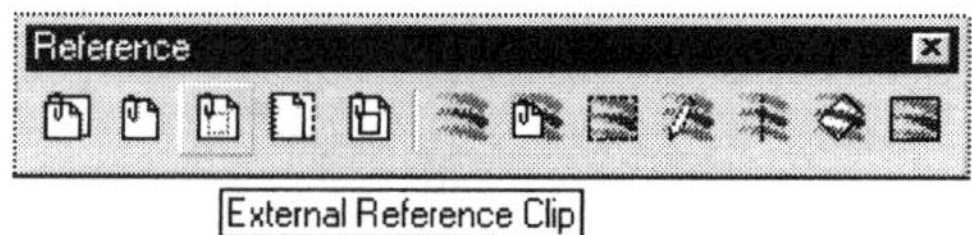

THE LOG FILE

AutoCAD maintains a log of the activities associated with each drawing containing external references. The log file is an ASCII file that can be printed or examined with a text editor. The log is maintained only if the variable XREFCTL is set to 1 (ON). The default is 0 (OFF), so you will have to set XREFCTL to 1 if you want a log file. To do that *Type:* **XREFCTL** ↵ at the Command: prompt, and *Type:* **1** ↵ to change the setting.

XREF MANAGER

The Xref Manager displays the external references in the drawing in a tree view or a list view. You can use the F3 and F4 keys to switch between list view and tree view.

List View

The list view shows a list of the attached external references. You can sort the list of references by name, status, type, file date, file size, or the saved path and file name.

Reference Name

Lists the names of the external references.

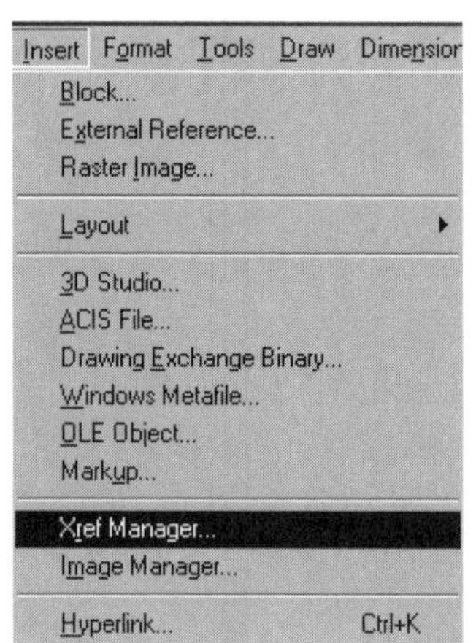

Status

Shows whether the external reference is loaded, unloaded, unreferenced, not found, unresolved, or orphaned

- □ *Loaded:* Currently attached to the drawing.
- □ *Unloaded:* Marked to be unloaded from the drawing once the Xref Manager is closed.
- □ *Unreferenced:* Attached to the drawing but erased.
- □ *Not Found:* No longer exists in the search paths.
- □ *Unresolved:* Cannot be read by AutoCAD.
- □ *Orphaned:* Attached to another external reference that is unreferenced, unresolved, or not found.

Size

Shows the file size of the loaded external reference.

FIGURE 12–10
Xref Manager Displaying Xrefs in Tree View

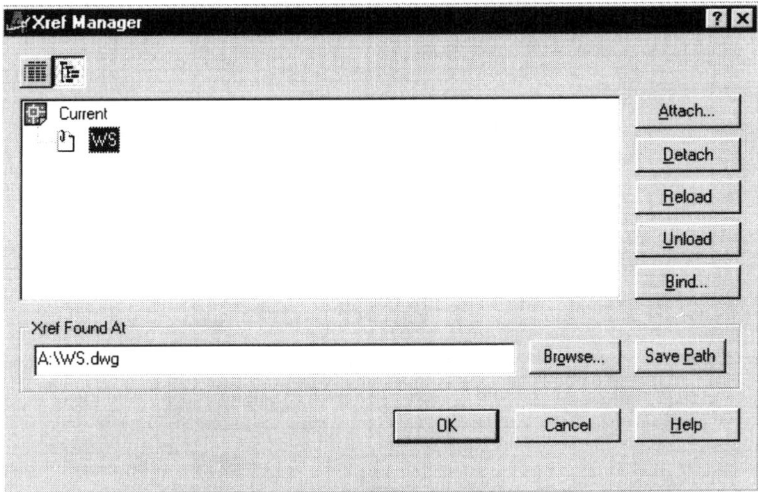

Type

Tells whether the external reference is an attachment or an overlay. An overlay is not shown on the current drawing if it is nested. This is helpful when one user needs the overlay to be displayed and another user does not.

Date

Shows the last date the loaded drawing was modified.

Saved Path

Shows the saved path of the associated external references (this is not necessarily where the xref is found).

Tree View

Tree view displays external references in a chart form (Figure 12–10). Tree view shows the level of nesting relationship of the attached external references, whether they are attached or overlaid, and whether they are loaded or unloaded.

EXERCISES

EXERCISE 12–1. Complete Exercise 12–1 using steps 1 through 9.

EXERCISE 12–2. Bind drawing WS-(your initials) to drawing EX12-1(your initials) using the Bind option of the External Reference command.

REVIEW QUESTIONS

Circle the best answer.

1. Which of the following External Reference options creates a block of the external reference and erases any reference to it as an external reference?
   a. Bind
   b. Detach
   c. Attach
   d. Reload
   e. Clip

2. Which of the following lets you remove unneeded external references from your drawing?
   a. Bind
   b. Detach
   c. Attach
   d. Reload
   e. Clip
3. Which of the following allows you to attach any drawing to the current drawing?
   a. Bind
   b. Detach
   c. Attach
   d. Reload
   e. Clip
4. Which of the following lets you change the current drawing with an external reference that has been changed since you began the current drawing?
   a. Bind
   b. Detach
   c. Attach
   d. Reload
   e. Clip
5. An external reference cannot be exploded.
   a. True
   b. False

Complete.

6. Explain what is meant by the term *nested external reference.*

   ____

   ____

7. Describe the function of the XREFCTL setting.

   ____

8. Describe the function of the Path option of the External Reference command.

   ____

9. Describe how the Attach option of the External Reference command differs from the Bind option.

   ____

   ____

10. Describe why an external reference is sometimes used instead of a block.

   ____

   ____

13 Dimensioning and Tolerancing

OBJECTIVES

After completing this chapter, you will be able to

- □ Use the Dimensioning menu to dimension full-scale drawings of
  Architectural floor plans.
  Mechanical parts using decimal parts of an inch.
  Mechanical parts using metric measurements.
- □ Provide positive and negative tolerances for specific dimensions.
- □ Use the geometric tolerance feature to dimension mechanical parts.
- □ Correctly answer questions regarding dimensioning variables and commands.

DIMENSIONING

Up to this point, you have made several different types of drawings. You have made block diagrams, architectural floor plans, drawings of furniture containing attributes, and two-dimensional drawings of mechanical parts.

For manufacturing and construction drawings to be used to manufacture a part or to construct a building, dimensions must be added. Adding dimensions to a drawing manually is a very time consuming process. With AutoCAD, adding dimensions is much easier. In addition, the AutoCAD dimensioning process verifies the accuracy of the drawing. The associative dimensioning feature of AutoCAD also allows a part size to be changed or corrected, automatically changing the dimension with it.

In this chapter you will dimension some of the drawings you have already made and you will make some simple drawings to demonstrate other dimensioning features. Remember that you have made these drawings full size, so the dimensioning procedure is relatively simple; however, the following settings must be checked or set before you begin dimensioning:

Units The correct system of units must be selected, and the places to the right of the decimal must be correctly set if decimals are used. DIMUNIT, a dimensioning variable, sets the dimensioning system of units.

Text Style The lettering style desired must be defined and the height for that style must be set at 0. DIMTXSTY sets the dimensioning text style.

Layer The correct layer for dimensions must be current.

DIMVARS The dimensioning variables that control the length, height, and spacing of the many elements of dimensions must be set correctly. These dimensioning variables are described next.

Warning: If you set the letter style height to 0, AutoCAD will prompt you each time you use DTEXT for the height so that you may have two or more heights of the same style. This setting of 0 also has no effect on the height of the text used for dimensions (DIMTXT). *If you set the letter style height to something other than 0, only one height can be drawn for that style.* The change command cannot be used to change letter height. The letter height for dimensioning text (DIMTXT) is overridden by the style height. *Leave the style height at 0.*

Dimensioning Variables

Although the following list is long, you will set only a few variables for any drawing. Once these are set you may make a template (or a prototype drawing) containing all the settings (Layers, Units, Limits, etc.) for a particular type of drawing. Notice that the variable names begin to make sense when you know what they are. For example: DIM-

FIGURE 13–1
DIMALT

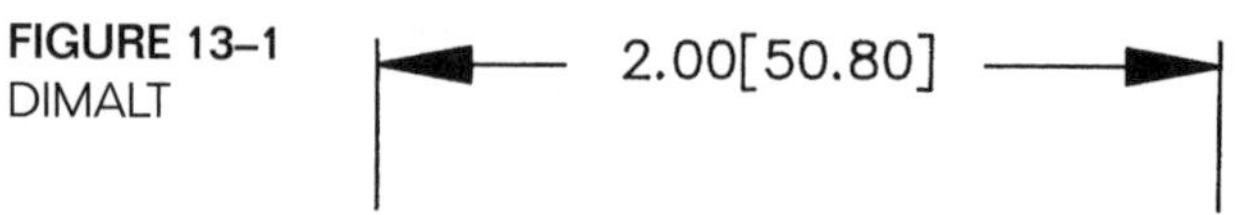

SCALE is dimensioning scale, DIMTXT is dimensioning text, and DIMSTYLE is dimensioning style.

DIMADEC Angular decimal places.

DIMALT Alternate units selected (Figure 13–1). If a drawing must show two sets of dimensions, such as inches and millimeters, this variable is turned on.

DIMALTD Alternate unit decimal places. This variable sets the number of places to the right of the decimal for the second set of dimensions. (Example: For DIMALTD = 2, the dimension will read 12.70.)

DIMALTF Alternate unit scale factor. This is the number by which the primary dimension is multiplied to get the alternate dimension. (Example: For DIMALTF = 25.40, if the primary dimension is 2″, the alternate dimension is 50.80.)

DIMALTRND Alternate units rounding value. This rounds off the alternate dimension.

DIMALTTD Alternate dimension tolerance decimal places. DIMALTTD sets the number of decimal places for the tolerance values of an alternate units dimension.

DIMALTTZ Alternate tolerance zero suppression. DIMALTTZ suppresses zeros in alternate tolerance values to the right of the decimal point.

DIMALTU Alternate units. This variable sets units for alternate dimensions.

DIMALTZ Alternate units zero suppression. DIMALTZ suppresses zeros in alternate dimension values to the right of the decimal point as follows:

- **0** Zeros are not suppressed (are shown; Example: 2.00)
- **1** Zeros are suppressed (are not shown; Example: 2)

DIMAPOST Suffix for alternate text. This is the marking placed after the alternate dimension. (Example: For DIMAPOST = mm, the alternate dimension reads 50.80 mm.)

Note: There are advantages and disadvantages to setting DIMASO on.
Disadvantages:
1. If you want to erase an extension line or any other part of the dimension, you must use the Explode command to break the dimension into separate entities and then use the Properties… command to change the color of the dimension elements to BYLAYER and change the exploded lines back to the layer from which they were exploded.
2. If you reduce the drawing using the SCALE command, the dimensions change with it.

Advantages:
1. If you decide to change a dimensioning variable after part of the drawing has already been dimensioned, you can change the existing dimensions to the new dimensioning variables with the UPDATE command.
2. If you decide to change the text of the dimension, you can do it with the DDEDIT (Modify Text…) command or the location of text with grips.
3. If you change the length of a dimensioned feature, the dimension changes with it. For example if you STRETCH a 3″ line to 4″, the dimension changes from 3″ to 4″.

DIMASO Create associative dimensions. When DIMASO is on, the complete dimension (dimension lines, arrowheads, extension lines, and text) comes in as a block.

DIMASZ Arrow size. DIMASZ sets the length of the arrowhead (Figure 13–2).

DIMATFIT Arrow and text fit. This variable determines where text and arrows are placed when there is not enough space between extension lines.

- **0** Places both text and arrows outside extension lines
- **1** Places arrows first, then text
- **2** Places text first, then arrows
- **3** Moves text or arrows, whichever fits best

DIMAUNIT Angular unit format. This variable sets the angle format for angular dimensions.

DIMAZIN Angular zero supression. DIMAZIN displays or suppresses leading and trailing zeros.

DIMBLK Arrow block name. If you want to use something other than the standard arrowhead or tick (Figure 13–2), change this to the desired block name and then create a block with that name. Example: DIMBLK = DOT. If you have a block with the name DOT that is a circle, that circle will appear instead of an arrowhead. When you want to return to the arrowhead, change DIMBLK to . (a period). Consult the *AutoCAD User's Guide* for details on how to construct a DIMBLK.

FIGURE 13–2
Arrowhead and Tick

ARROWHEAD

TICK

3'–0"

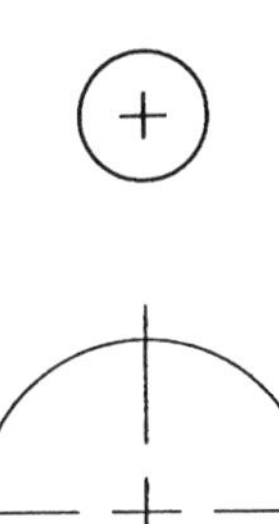

center lines

FIGURE 13–3
DIMCEN

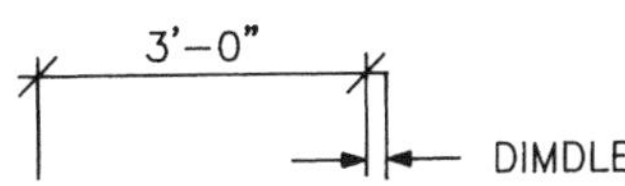

FIGURE 13–4
DIMDLE

DIMBLK 1; DIMBLK 2 First and second arrow block names. If you want to use one block (a circle) at one end of the dimension line and something else (a square) at the other end, give DIMBLK 1 and DIMBLK 2 different names and draw blocks with these names. Turn DIMSAH on to activate these two variables.

DIMCEN Center mark size (Figure 13–3). DIMCEN sets the size of the center mark that appears at the center of circles and radii. A negative value for the center mark draws center lines that extend outside the circle by that amount.

DIMCLRD Dimension line color. If you want the dimension line, extension lines, leaders, and the dimension text to be different colors, AutoCAD gives you that option with DIMCLRD, DIMCLRE, and DIMCLRT. The default of BYBLOCK (color is assigned by the layer on which it is inserted) is acceptable for most situations.

DIMCLRE Extension line and leader color.

DIMCLRT Dimension color.

DIMDEC Decimal places. This variable sets the number of decimal places to the right of the decimal point for the dimension value.

DIMDLE Dimension line extension (Figure 13–4). DIMDLE allows you to extend the dimension line past the extension line. This feature is useful for some architectural styles.

DIMDLI Dimension line increment for continuation (Figure 13–5). DIMDLI allows you to set the space between dimension lines when BASELINE or CONTINUE dimensioning is used.

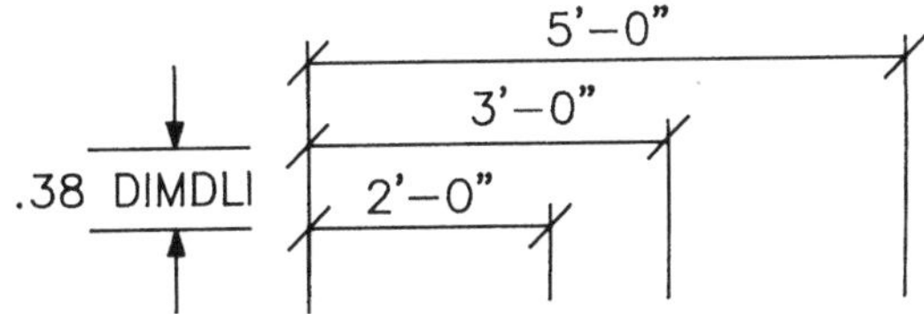

FIGURE 13–5
DIMDLI

DIMDSEP Decimal separator. DIMDSEP specifies a character to be used to separate decimals. The default is a decimal point.

DIMEXE Extension above dimension line (Figure 13–6). DIMEXE allows you to set the length of the extension line past the arrowhead.

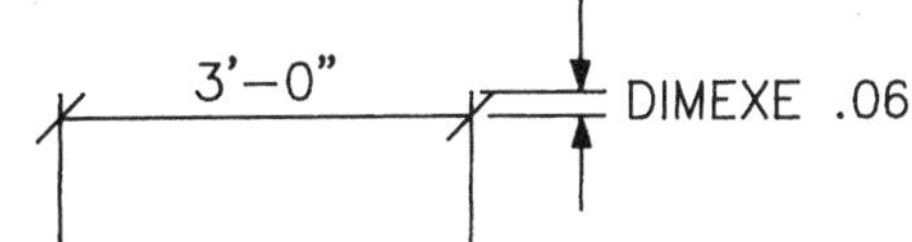

FIGURE 13–6
DIMEXE

DIMEXO Extension line origin offset (Figure 13–7). DIMEXO allows you to set the space between the object and the extension line.

FIGURE 13–7
DIMEXO

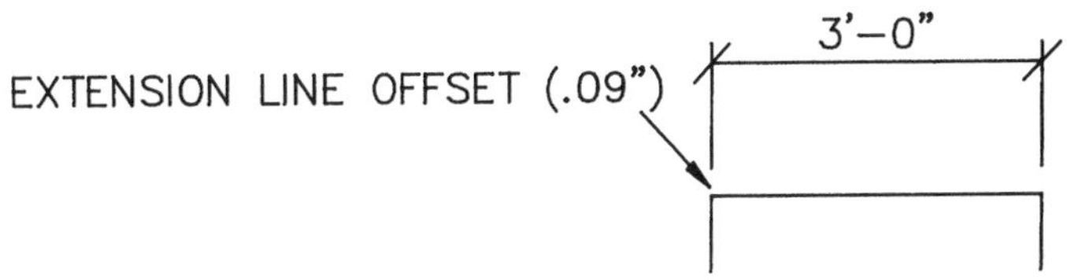

EXTENSION LINE OFFSET (.09")

3'–0"

DIMFRAC Fraction format. This variable allows you to set the way you want fractions to appear.

- **0** Horizontal
- **1** Diagonal
- **2** Not stacked (1/2)

DIMGAP Gap from dimension line to text (Figure 13–8). DIMGAP sets this space.

DIMJUST Justification of text on dimension line. Controls the horizontal position of the text in the dimension as follows:

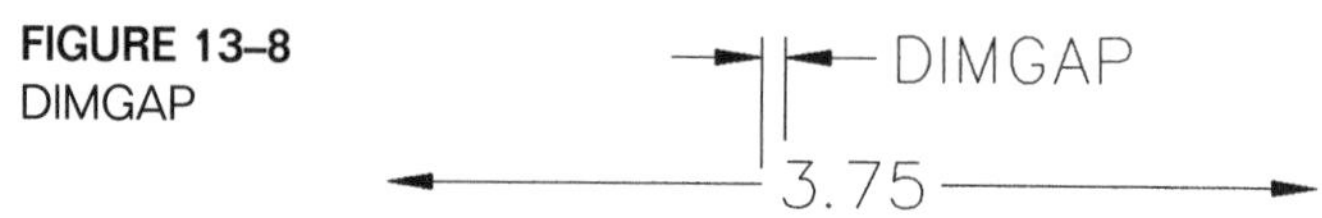

FIGURE 13–8
DIMGAP

0 Positions the text above the dimension line and centers it between the extension lines.

1 Positions the text above the dimension line and next to the first extension line.

2 Positions the text above the dimension line and next to the second extension line.

3 Positions the text above the dimension line and rotates it so that it is centered above the first extension line.

4 Positions the text above the dimension line and rotates it so that it is centered above the second extension line.

DIMLDRBLK Leader block name. Allows you to specify the appearance of the arrow on the end of a leader.

DIMLFAC Linear unit scale factor (Figure 13–9). DIMLFAC is the factor by which the measured distance is multiplied to obtain the dimension shown on the drawing. This is used to dimension drawings that have been drawn to a scale other than full size. If a drawing has been drawn one-fourth size, the DIMLFAC is set to 4 to obtain the full-size dimension.

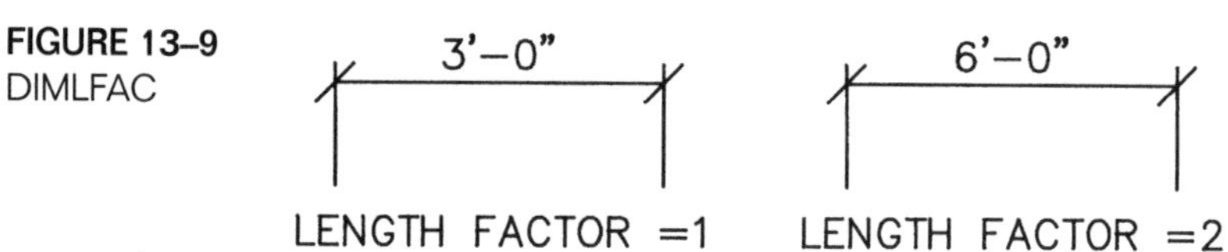

FIGURE 13–9
DIMLFAC

DIMLIM Generates dimension limits (Figure 13–10). This setting is turned on if a limit dimension is necessary. A limit dimension shows the upper and lower limits of tolerance for a dimension. For example, if the dimension is 2.50 with a tolerance of +.02 (set with DIMTP) and −.01 (set with DIMTM), the limits are 2.52 and 2.49, as shown.

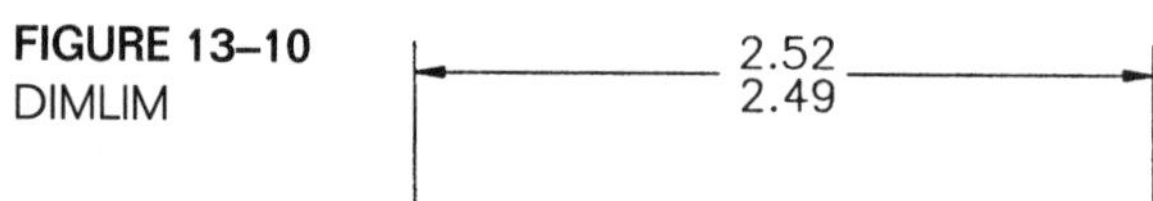

FIGURE 13–10
DIMLIM

DIMLUNIT Linear unit format. Allows you to set units for all dimensioning types except angular.

DIMLWD Dimension line and leader lineweight. DIMLWD sets the lineweight for dimensions and leaders.

DIMLWE Extension line lineweight. DIMLWE sets the lineweight for extension lines.

DIMPOST Default suffix for dimension text. This variable allows units such as feet, inches, or millimeters to be added after the dimension. (Example: When DIMPOST = ″, the dimension is displayed as 12.00″. When DIMPOST = mm, the dimension reads 12.00 mm.)

DIMRND Rounding value. This variable is used for rounding dimensions. (Example: When DIMRND = .005, all dimensions are rounded to the nearest .005 unit. When DIMRND = 1.0, the dimension is rounded to the nearest full unit, so 2.40 becomes 2.)

FIGURE 13–11
DIMSAH

DIMSAH Separate arrow blocks (Figure 13–11). When this variable is on, DIMBLK1 and DIMBLK2 define the shape that is used on each end of the dimension line. It is used for shapes other than the arrowhead or tick at each end of the dimension line.

DIMSCALE Overall scale factor. This variable allows you to set all the other variables at the size you want them to be plotted and then set DIMSCALE to the same value as the plotting ratio. For example, a drawing of a house drawn full scale (40′ × 30′) is plotted at a scale of ¼″ = 1′ to fit comfortably on a 17″ × 11″ sheet. DIMSCALE must be set to 48 (the same ratio as ¼″ = 1′, or 4 × 12) for dimensions to show in their correct proportions. You may also set DIMSCALE = 0 so that AutoCAD may set a DIMSCALE for you. This DIMSCALE is the ratio between model space and paper space limits. You must first set paper space limits and create a paper space viewport before DIMSCALE = 0 will work. (Tilemode must also be 0.)

DIMSD1 Suppress the first dimension line. When DIMSD1 is on, the dimension line nearest the first extension line origin is not drawn.

DIMSD2 Suppress the second dimension line. When DIMSD2 is on, the dimension line nearest the second extension line origin is not drawn.

Note: Use DIMSE1 and DIMSE2 to avoid overlapping two extension lines. Although overlapping is not noticeable in many cases, it increases the size of the drawing file, which is usually undesirable.

DIMSE1 Suppress the first extension line (Figure 13–12). When DIMSE1 is on, the first extension line of any dimension is not drawn.

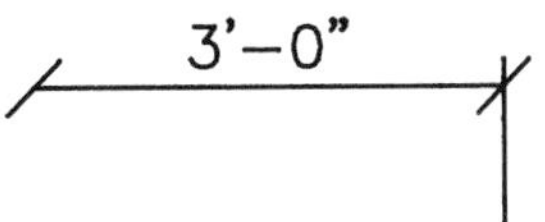

FIGURE 13–12
DIMSE1

DIMSE2 Suppress the second extension line (Figure 13–13). When DIMSE2 is on, the second extension line of any dimension is not drawn.

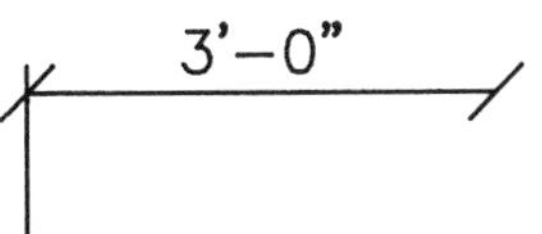

FIGURE 13–13
DIMSE2

DIMSOXD Suppress outside extension dimension (Figure 13–14). Dimension lines outside the extension lines are not drawn when DIMSOXD is on.

0.50

FIGURE 13–14
DIMSOXD

DIMSTYLE Current dimension style. This variable allows you to have several sets of different dimensioning variables saved under style names that can be recalled quickly with the Restore option.

DIMTAD Controls vertical position of text in relation to the dimension line (Figure 13–15).

0 Centers the dimension text between the extension lines.

1 Places the dimension text above the dimension line except when the dimension line is not horizontal and text inside the extension lines is forced horizontal (DIMTIH = 1). The distance from the dimension line to the baseline of the lowest line of text is the current DIMGAP value.

2 Places the dimension text on the side of the dimension line farthest away from the defining points.

3 Places the dimension text to conform to a Japanese Industrial Standards (JIS) representation.

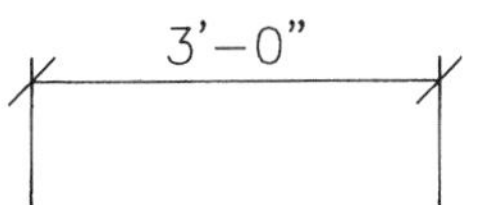

FIGURE 13–15
DIMTAD

DIMTDEC Tolerance decimal places. Sets the number of decimal places in the tolerance value for a dimension.

DIMTFAC Tolerance text scaling factor (Figure 13–16). Multiplying DIMTEXT, the dimension text height, times DIMTFAC equals the height of the tolerance text. In the case of Figure 13–16, DIMTFAC = .5.

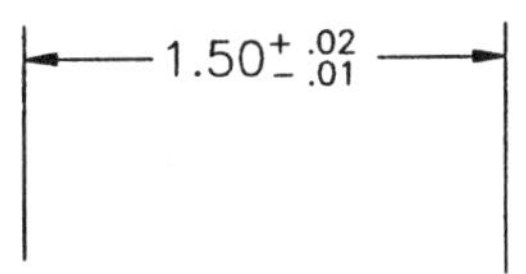

FIGURE 13–16
DIMTFAC

DIMTIH Text inside dimensions is horizontal (Figure 13–17). All dimensions inside extension lines are drawn horizontally when DIMTIH is on.

DIMTIX Place text inside extension. This variable forces the text inside the extension lines whether it fits or not.

DIMTM Minus tolerance (Example: 1.500 − .005).

DIMTMOVE Text movement. This variable sets text movement rules if there is not enough space for the dimension.

0 Moves the dimension line with the text
1 Adds a leader when the text is moved
2 Moves text without a leader

DIMTOFL Force line inside extension line (Figure 13–18). A line is drawn inside the extension lines.

DIMTOH Text outside extensions is horizontal (Figure 13–19). Text outside the extension lines is horizontal; inside it is aligned with the dimension line unless DIMTIH is also on.

FIGURE 13–17
DIMTIH

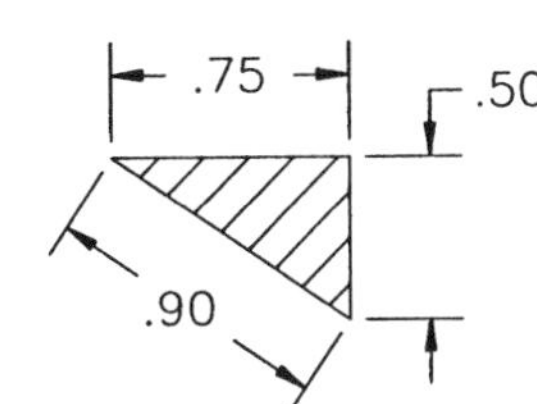

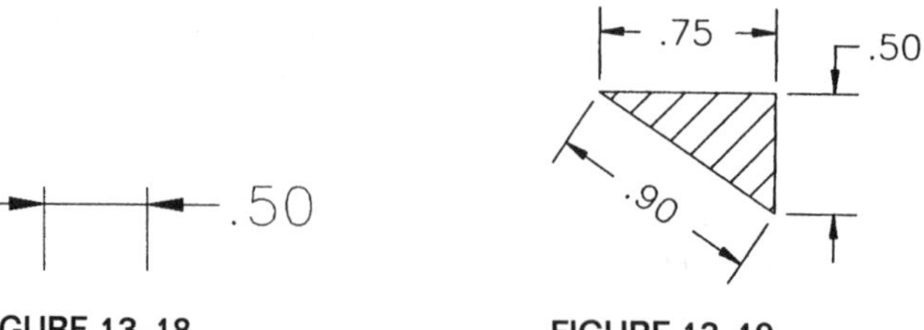

FIGURE 13–18
DIMTOFL

FIGURE 13–19
DIMTOH

DIMTOL Generates dimension tolerances (Figure 13–20). When DIMTOL is on and DIMTP and DIMTM are the same (Example: .02), the dimension is displayed as 3.37 ± .02. If they are different (Example: DIMTP = .02, DIMTM = .01), the dimension is displayed as 3.37 + .02 − .01.

FIGURE 13–20
DIMTOL On

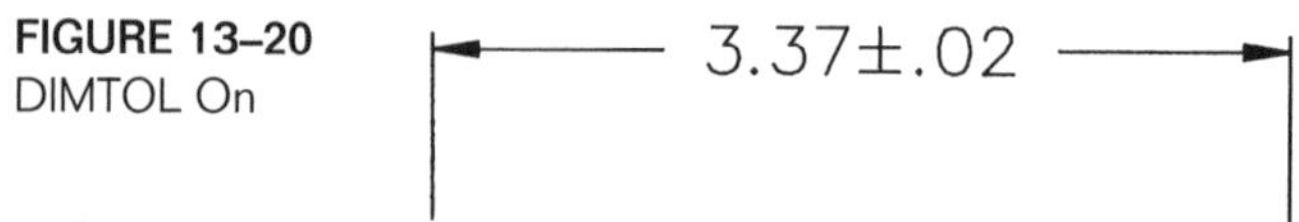

DIMTOLJ Tolerance vertical justification. Controls the vertical placement of tolerance values relative to the dimension text as follows:

- **0** Top
- **1** Middle
- **2** Bottom

DIMTP Plus tolerance (Example: 1.500 + .005).
DIMTSZ Tick size (Figure 13–21).

FIGURE 13–21
DIMTSZ

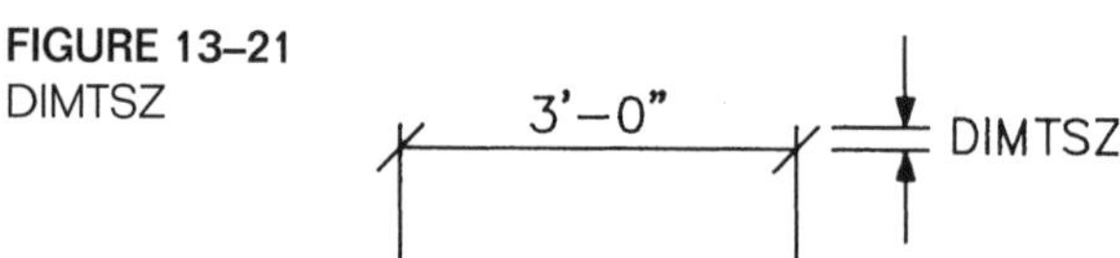

DIMTVP Text vertical position. This is the factor by which the DIMTXT height is multiplied to obtain the location of text above or below the dimension line.
DIMTXSTY Text style. Specifies the text style of the dimension. The style chosen must be defined in the current drawing. See Chapter 6 for setting styles with the STYLE command.
DIMTXT Text height. This variable sets the height of the text if the current text height under the STYLE setting is 0. DIMTXT is multiplied by DIMSCALE.
DIMTZIN Tolerance zero suppression. Suppresses zeros in tolerance values to the right of the value as follows:

- **0** Zeros are not suppressed (are shown; Example: .0500)
- **1** Zeros are suppressed (not shown; Example: .05)

DIMUPT User-positioned text. When this variable is on, it allows you to click the point where you wish the dimension line and the text to appear. If you want the text to appear nearer one end of the dimension line, select a single point that will place the dimension line where you want it and will place the text on the same point. The setting is:

- **0** Off
- **1** On

DIMZIN Zero suppression. This factor allows several different variations of feet and inches display, as follows.

DIMZIN Value	Meaning	Examples
0	Suppress zero feet and inches	¼″, 3″, 2′, 1′-0 ½″
1	Include zero feet and inches	0′-0 ¼″, 0′-3″, 2′-0″, 1′-0 ½″

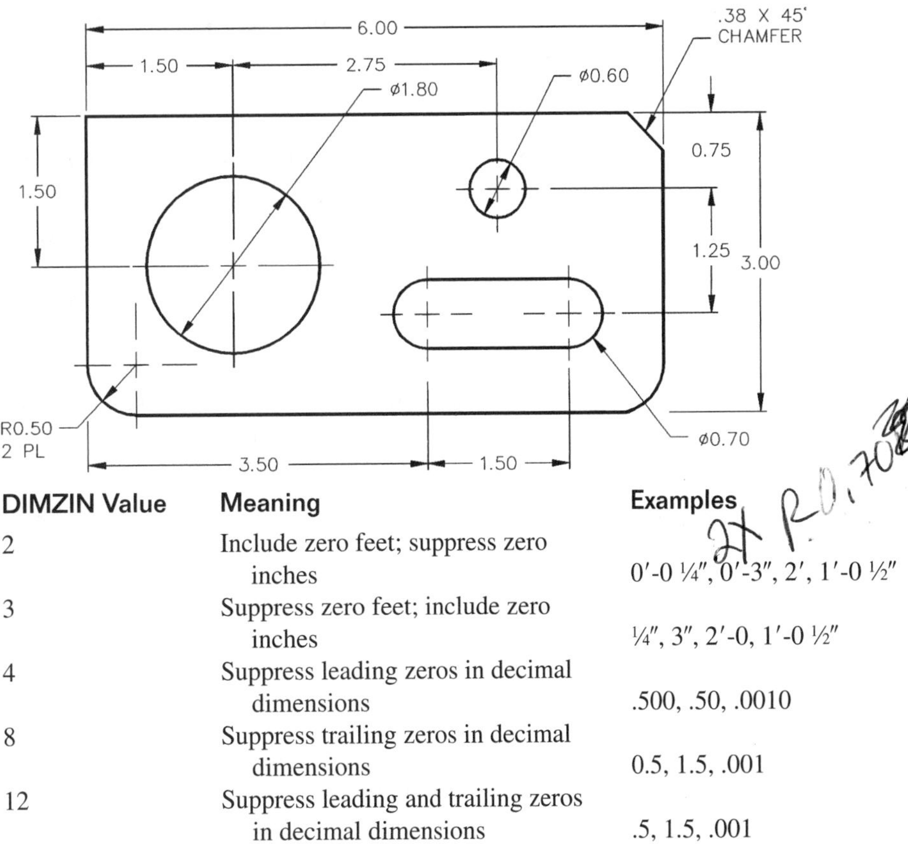

FIGURE 13–22
Drawing to Be Dimensioned

DIMZIN Value	Meaning	Examples
2	Include zero feet; suppress zero inches	0′-0 ¼″, 0′-3″, 2′, 1′-0 ½″
3	Suppress zero feet; include zero inches	¼″, 3″, 2′-0, 1′-0 ½″
4	Suppress leading zeros in decimal dimensions	.500, .50, .0010
8	Suppress trailing zeros in decimal dimensions	0.5, 1.5, .001
12	Suppress leading and trailing zeros in decimal dimensions	.5, 1.5, .001

Now that you have been introduced to dimensioning variables, let's dimension some drawings to see how this works. Begin with a mechanical part (Figure 13–22). Use the drawing you did in Exercise 1, Chapter 10.

Exercise 13–1: Dimensioning a Mechanical Part

Set Up the Drawing

Step 1. To begin Exercise 13–1, turn on the computer and start AutoCAD.

Step 2. On your own:

1. Open drawing EX10-1(your initials).
2. Use the SaveAs… command to save the drawing as EX13-1(your initials).

Step 3. Check to make sure that the following settings have been made:

Units: Decimal—2 digits to the right of the decimal point. (Also *Type:* DIMDEC ↵, then *Type:* 2 ↵ for the new value.

LIMITS: Lower left corner: 0,0
Upper right corner: 11,8.5

GRID: .25

SNAP: .0625

TEXT STYLE: Standard FONT: simplex.shx HEIGHT: 0

LAYERS: NAME	Color	Linetype	Lineweight
R	Red	CONTINUOUS	0.25 mm
M	Magenta	CONTINUOUS	0.50 mm
G	Green	HIDDEN	0.35 mm

Set layer R current.

Step 4. Use Zoom-All to view the entire drawing area:

Prompt	Response
Command:	**Zoom-All** (or *Type:* **Z** ↵, then **A** ↵)

Step 5. Check the current status of dimensioning variables and make necessary changes.

Note: You can save a dimension style after you have set all other dimensioning variables. *Select:* **Dimension Style...**; then *Type:* **SE1–2** ↵ in the Namebox (or any other name you choose) and *Click:* **Save** to save all your settings under this style name. You may have another dimension style (Example: SE1) that has DIMSE1 on, DIMTIX off, and DIMTOFL on that will allow you to suppress the first extension line and dimension the larger circle in a different manner. You may quickly move from one set of dimensioning variables to another set by clicking another defined style current in the Dimension Styles dialog box.

Prompt	Response
Command:	*Type:* **DIM** ↵
Dim:	*Type:* **STATUS** ↵

A listing of all dimensioning variables appears. Compare the listing on your screen with the list shown in Figure 13–23. Make the following changes so that your list matches Figure 13–23. When you compare the two lists make any other changes needed.

Change three dimensioning variables from the keyboard.

Prompt	Response
Command:	*Type:* **DIMASZ** ↵ (or any other variable)
Enter new value for DIMASZ <0.18>:	*Type:* **.125** ↵ (Because Units are set to two places to the right of the decimal, .125 will be rounded to .13. The actual value will be .125.)
Command:	*Type:* **DIMCEN** ↵
Enter new value for DIMCEN<0.09>:	*Type:* **−.0625** ↵ (The negative sign gives you a center mark that extends outside the circle or arc.)
Command:	*Type:* **DIMEXE** ↵
Enter new value for DIMEXE <0.18>:	*Type:* **.0625** ↵

Change three dimensioning variables from the Dimension Style Manager dialog box.

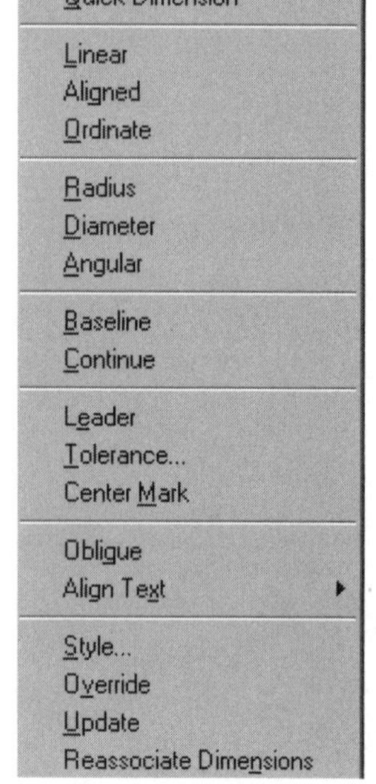

Prompt	Response
Command:	**Dimension Style...** (or *Type:* **DDIM** ↵)
The Dimension Style Manager dialog box shown in Figure 13–24 appears:	*Click:* **Modify...**
The Modify Dimension Style: Standard dialog box with the Lines and Arrows tab current appears (Figure 13–25):	When your dialog box looks like Figure 13–25, *Click:* **the Text tab** (Notice that Center Marks for Circles shows Line for the Type:, and the size is 0.0625. The negative value you typed for DIMCEN determines the Type:) If you click the down arrow for Type:, you get three choices, Line, Mark, and None. Click each one of them and observe how it affects the example, then go back to Line and *Click:* **the Text tab**.
The Text tab (Figure 13–26) appears:	*Double-click:* **0.180 in the Text height: box and** *Type:* **.125** as shown. When your dialog box looks like Figure 13–26, *Click:* **the Fit tab**.

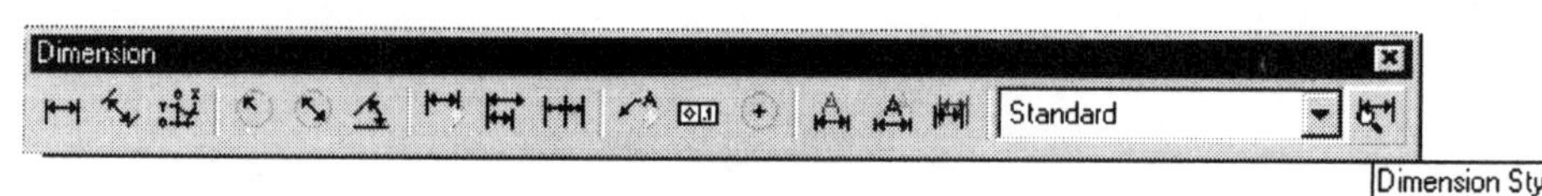

FIGURE 13–23
Dimensioning Variables for Exercise 13–1

DIMADEC	0	Angular decimal places
DIMALT	Off	Alternate units selected
DIMALTD	2	Alternate unit decimal places
DIMALTF	25.40	Alternate unit scale factor
DIMALTRND	0.00	Alternate units rounding value
DIMALTTD	2	Alternate tolerance decimal places
DIMALTTZ	0	Alternate tolerance zero suppression
DIMALTU	2	Alternate units
DIMALTZ	0	Alternate unit zero suppression
DIMAPOST		Prefix and suffix for alternate text
DIMASZ	0.13	Arrow size
DIMATFIT	3	Arrow and text fit
DIMAUNIT	0	Angular unit format
DIMAZIN	0	Angular zero supression
DIMBLK	ClosedFilled	Arrow block name
DIMBLK1	ClosedFilled	First arrow block name
DIMBLK2	ClosedFilled	Second arrow block name
DIMCEN	−0.06	Center mark size
DIMCLRD	BYBLOCK	Dimension line and leader color
DIMCLRE	BYBLOCK	Extension line color
DIMCLRT	BYBLOCK	Dimension text color
DIMDEC	2	Decimal places
DIMDLE	0.00	Dimension line extension
DIMDLI	0.38	Dimension line spacing
DIMDSEP	.	Decimal separator
DIMEXE	0.06	Extension above dimension line
DIMEXO	0.06	Extension line origin offset
DIMFRAC	0	Fraction format
DIMGAP	0.09	Gap from dimension line to text
DIMJUST	0	Justification of text on dimension line
DIMLDRBLK	ClosedFilled	Leader block name
DIMLFAC	1.00	Linear unit scale factor
DIMLIM	Off	Generate dimension limits
DIMLUNIT	2	Linear unit format
DIMLWD	−2	Dimension line and leader lineweight
DIMLWE	−2	Extension line lineweight
DIMPOST		Prefix and suffix for dimension text
DIMRND	0.00	Rounding value
DIMSAH	Off	Separate arrow blocks
DIMSCALE	1.00	Overall scale factor
DIMSD1	Off	Suppress the first dimension line
DIMSD2	Off	Suppress the second dimension line
DIMSE1	Off	Suppress the first extension line
DIMSE2	Off	Suppress the second extension line
DIMSOXD	Off	Suppress outside dimension lines
DIMTAD	0	Place text above the dimension line
DIMTDEC	4	Tolerance decimal places
DIMTFAC	1.00	Tolerance text height scaling factor
DIMTIH	On	Text inside extensions is horizontal
DIMTIX	Off	Place text inside extensions
DIMTM	0.00	Minus tolerance
DIMTMOVE	0	Text movement
DIMTOFL	Off	Force line inside extension lines
DIMTOH	On	Text outside horizontal
DIMTOL	Off	Tolerance dimensioning
DIMTOLJ	1	Tolerance vertical justification
DIMTP	0.00	Plus tolerance
DIMTSZ	0.00	Tick size
DIMTVP	0.00	Text vertical position
DIMTXSTY	Standard	Text style
DIMTXT	0.13	Text height
DIMTZIN	0	Tolerance zero suppression
DIMUPT	Off	User positioned text
DIMZIN	0	Zero suppression

Prompt	Response
The Fit tab (Figure 13–27) appears:	Make your dialog box look like Figure 13–27 if it does not already, and *Click:* **the Primary Units tab**.
The Primary Units tab (Figure 13–28) appears:	*Click:* **the down arrow in the Precision box and** *Click:* **0.00 as shown.** All dimensions will have two places to the right of the decimal point. When your Primary Units tab looks like Figure 13–28, *Click:* **the Alternate Units tab.**
The Alternate Units tab (Figure 13–29) appears:	You should not have to change anything here, but check to see if your tab matches Figure 13–29, and *Click:* **the Tolerances tab.**

FIGURE 13–24
Dimension Style Manager

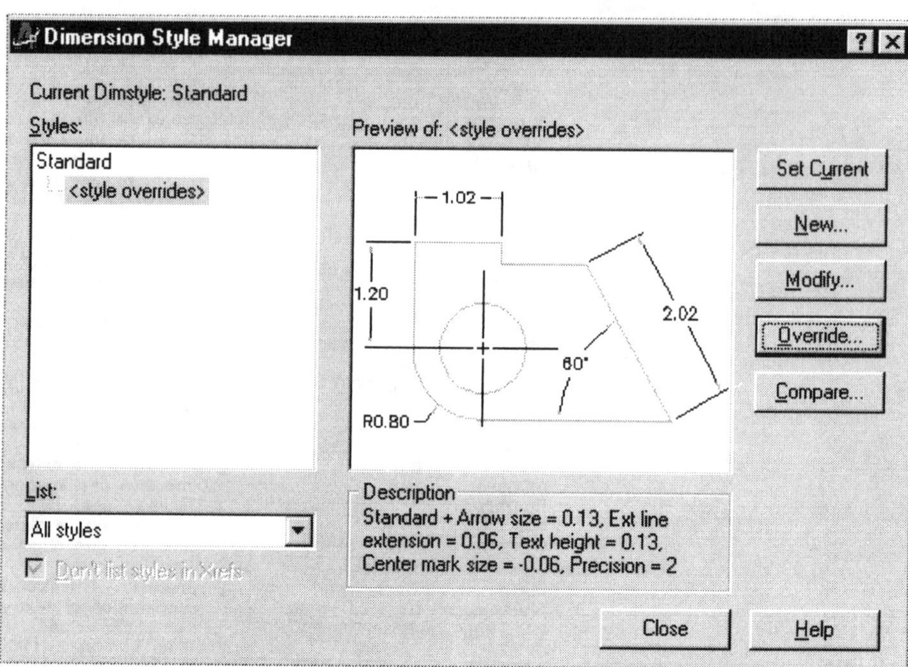

FIGURE 13–25
Lines and Arrows Tab

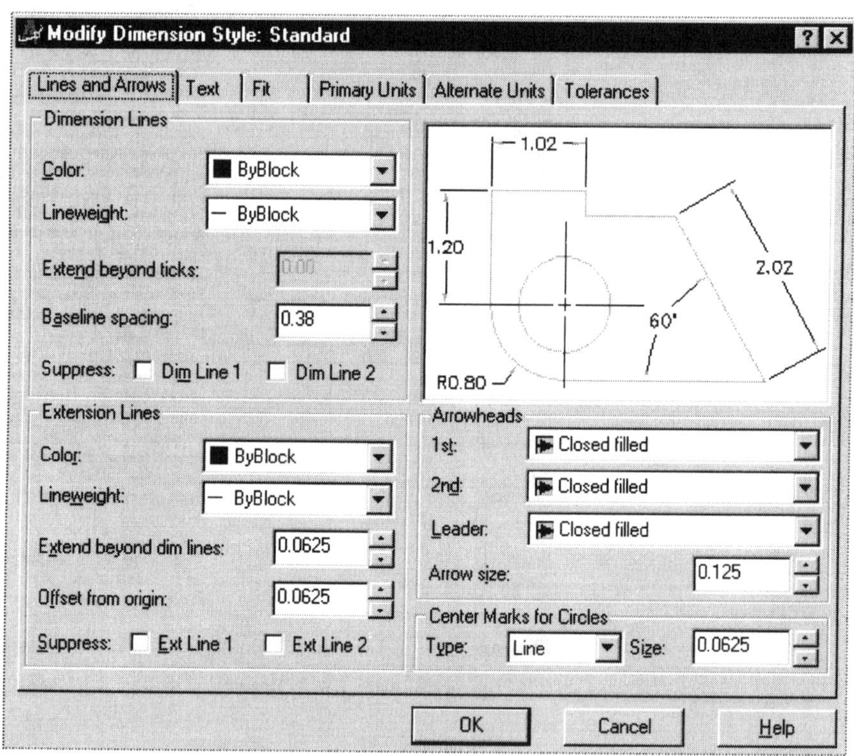

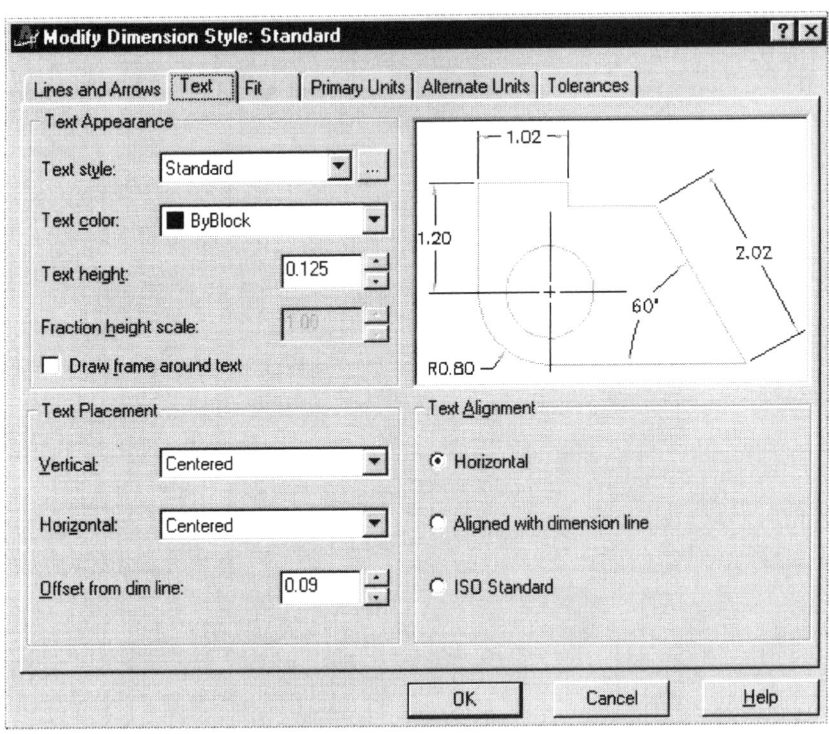

FIGURE 13–26
Text Tab

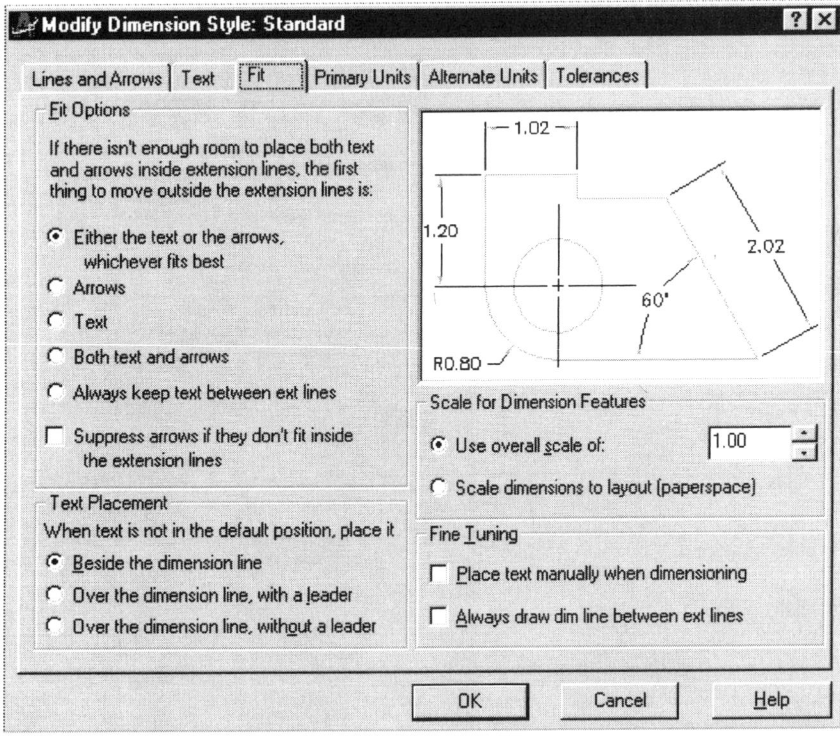

FIGURE 13–27
Fit Tab

FIGURE 13–28
Primary Units Tab

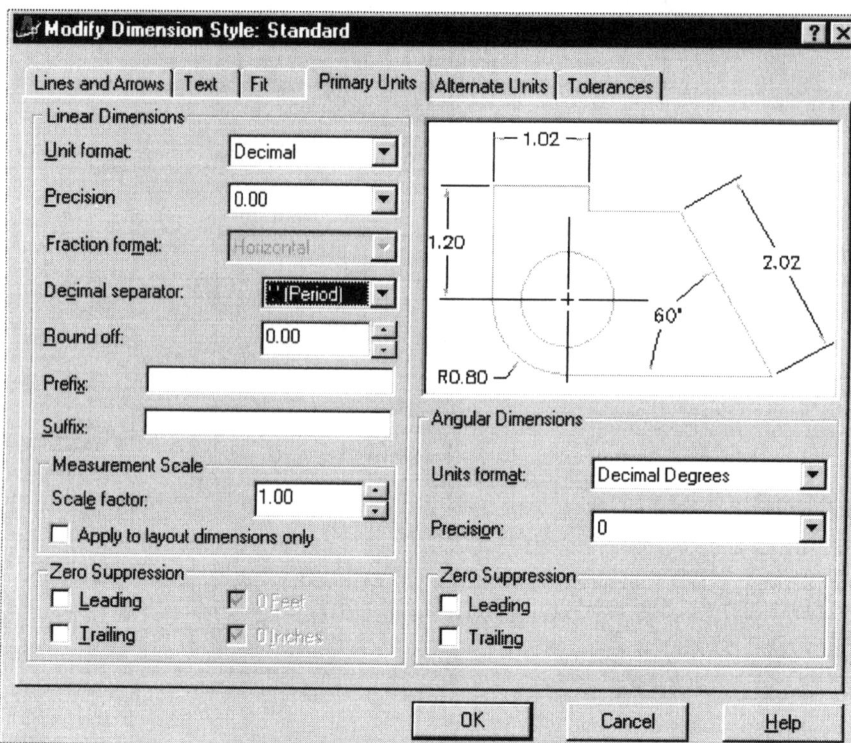

FIGURE 13–29
Alternate Units Tab

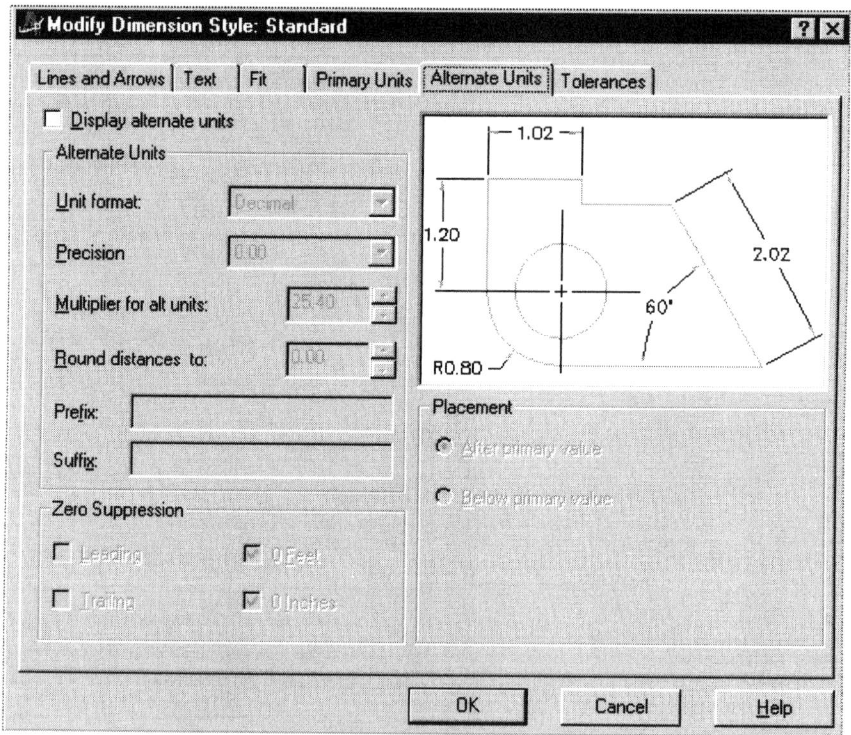

Prompt	Response
The Tolerances tab (Figure 13–30) appears:	You should not have to change anything here either, but check to see if your tab matches Figure 13–30, and *Click:* **OK**.
The Dimension Style Manager dialog box appears:	

FIGURE 13–30
Tolerances Tab

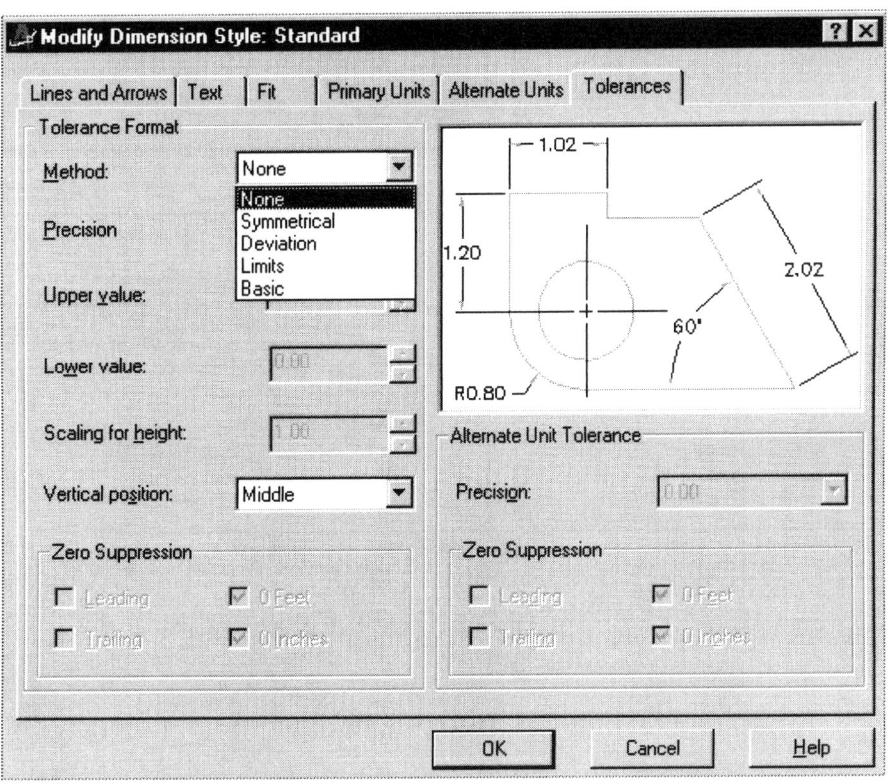

The five buttons on the right of the Dimension Style Manager dialog box allow you to do the following:

Set Current If you have more than one dimension style defined in this drawing, this button allows you to select the one you wish to be current. Because you will not define a new dimension style in this drawing only one style, Standard, will be available.

New... This button allows you to name a new style and set dimensioning variables for it.

Modify... This button allows you to modify the current style (in this case, Standard) so that new variable settings become effective for any dimensions drawn after you have modified this style. To make existing dimensions take on the new variable settings, the Update command on the dimensioning menu is used.

Override... This button allows you to set variables that take effect when override to the current style is selected. You may have a set of variables that are fine most of the time but need to be different for a specific situation. Override allows you to do that easily.

Compare... This button allows you to compare two dimensioning styles or to compare the existing style with the override settings.

Prompt	Response
The Dimension Style Manager dialog box is open:	*Click:* **Close**

You are now ready to dimension your drawing from Chapter 10.

Dimension the Drawing

Step 6. Place center marks at the centers of all circles and radii (Figure 13–31).

Activate the Dimension toolbar or use commands from the Dimension menu on the menu bar.

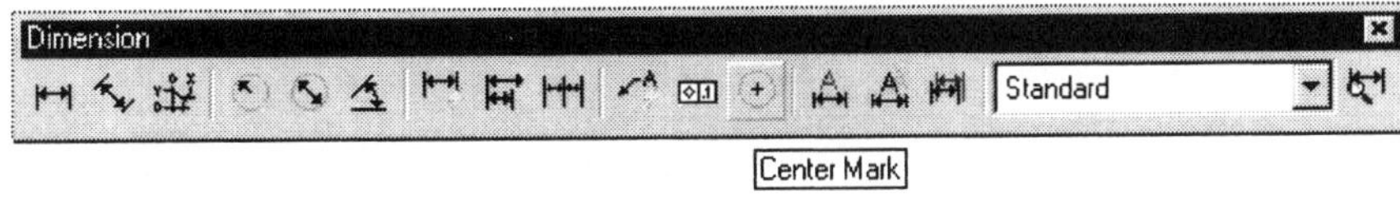

FIGURE 13–31
Dimension Steps

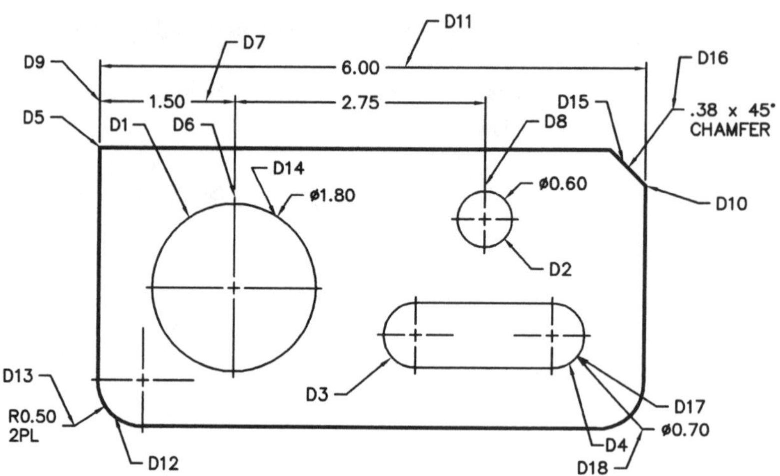

Prompt	Response
Command:	**Center Mark**
Select arc or circle:	**D1** (Figure 13–31)
Command:	↵
Select arc or circle:	**D2**
Command:	↵
Select arc or circle:	**D3**
Command:	↵
Select arc or circle:	**D4**

Step 7. Make all horizontal dimensions (Figure 13–31).

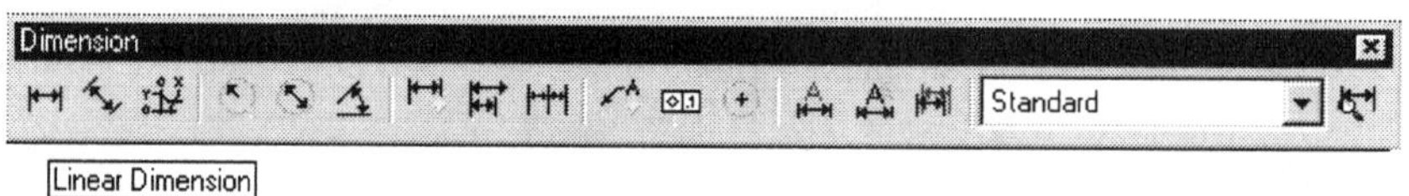

Prompt	Response
Command:	**Linear Dimension**
Specify first extension line origin or <select object>:	**Osnap-Endpoint**
of	**D5**
Specify second extension line origin:	**Osnap-Endpoint**
of	**D6**
Specify dimension line location or [Mtext/Text/Angle/Horizontal/Vertical/Rotated]:	**D7** (½″ from the top line of the object)
Dimension text = 1.50:	
Command:	**Continue Dimension**
Specify a second extension line origin or [Undo/Select] <Select>:	**Osnap-Endpoint**
of	**D8**
Dimension text <2.75>:	

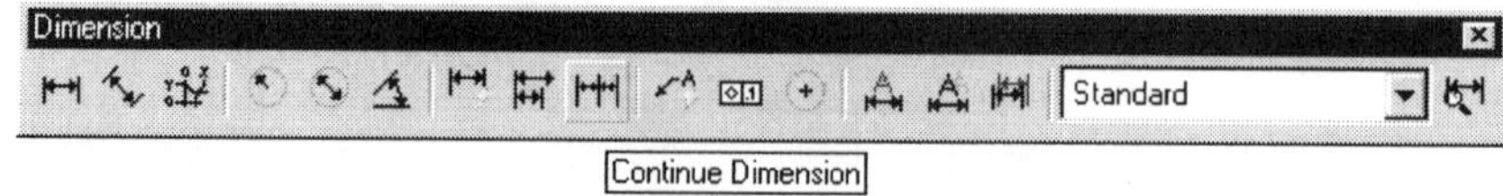

Prompt	Response
Specify a second extension line origin or [Undo/Select] <Select>:	*Press:* **Esc**
Command:	**Linear Dimension**
Specify first extension line origin or <select object>:	**Osnap-Intersection**
of	**D9**
Second extension line origin:	**Osnap-Endpoint**
of	**D10**
Specify dimension line location or [Mtext/Text/Angle/Horizontal/Vertical/Rotated]:	**D11** (⅜″ from the first dimension line)
Dimension text = 6.00:	
Command:	

Draw the remainder of the horizontal dimensions shown at the bottom of Figure 13–22 in a similar manner. **Make sure you place those dimensions ½″ from the drawing.**

Step 8. On your own:
Make all vertical dimensions shown in Figure 13–22 using the Linear Dimension and Continue Dimension commands. Notice that the direction in which you move your digitizer determines whether the dimension is vertical or horizontal. **The dimensions closest to the drawing are ½″ from it. All other dimensions are ⅜″ from the first set of dimensions.**

Step 9. Dimension radii (Figure 13–31).

Note: You may need to highlight the two lines of text and *Click:* 0.125 in the text height box if the text height is still .200.

Prompt	Response
Command:	**Radius Dimension**
Select arc or circle:	**D12** (Figure 13–31)
Specify dimension line location or [Mtext/Text/Angle]:	*Type:* **M** ↵
The Multiline Text Editor program appears:	(Set text height to .125 if it is not already.) **Highlight the brackets, then** *Type:* **R0.50** ↵**, and on the second line** *Type:* **2 PL** (meaning 2 places).
	Click: **the Properties tab**
	Click: **Bottom Left in the Justification: list box**
	Click: **OK**
Specify dimension line location or [Mtext/Text/Angle]:	**D13**

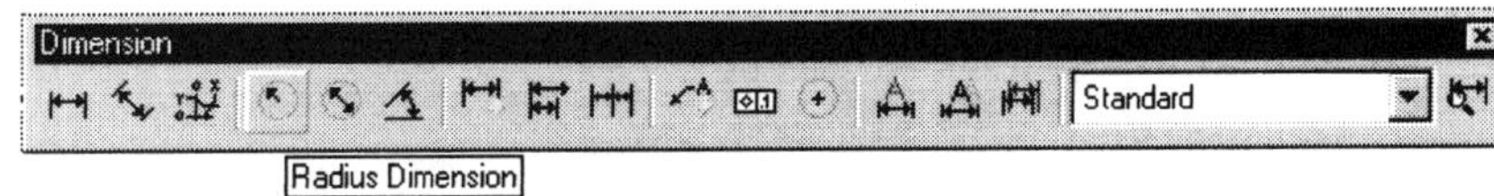

Step 10. Dimension diameters (Figure 13–31). (If your diameter dimensions do not look the same as Figure 13–31, you can change them in step 13.)

Prompt	Response
Command:	**Diameter Dimension**

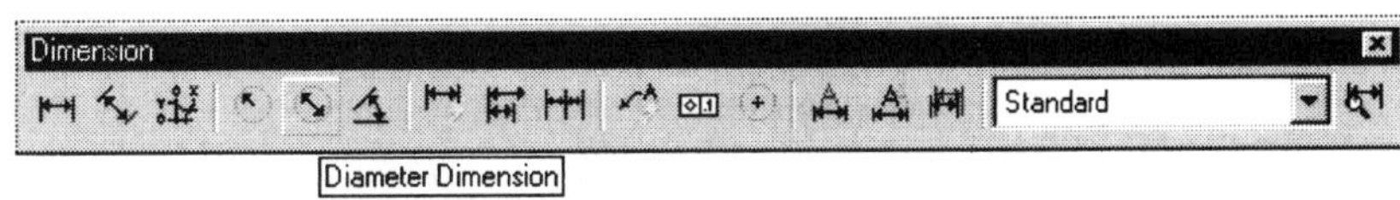

Prompt	Response
Select arc or circle:	**D1** (Figure 13–31)
Dimension text = 1.80: Specify dimension line location or [Mtext/Text/Angle]:	**D14**
Command:	↵
Select arc or circle:	**D2** (Figure 13–31)
Dimension text = 0.60: Specify dimension line location or (Mtext/Text/Angle]:	↵

Step 11. Dimension the chamfer (Figure 13–31).

Prompt	Response
Command:	**Leader**
Specify first leader point or [Settings] <Settings>:	**Osnap-Midpoint**
of	**D15** (Figure 13–31)
Specify next point:	**D16**
Specify next point:	↵
Specify text width <0.00>	↵
Enter first line of annotation text <Mtext>:	*Type:* **.38 × 45%%D** ↵
%%D is the code for the degree symbol.	
Enter next line of annotation text:	*Type:* **CHAMFER** ↵
Enter next line of annotation text:	↵

Step 12. Dimension the slot diameter (Figure 13–31).

Prompt	Response
Command:	↵ (to repeat the leader command)
Specify first leader point or [Settings] <Settings>:	**Osnap-Nearest**
to	**D17** (Figure 13–31)
Specify next point:	**D18**
Specify next point:	↵
Specify text width <0.00>:	↵
Enter first line of annotation text <Mtext>:	*Type:* **%%C0.70** ↵
Enter next line of annotation text:	↵
%%C is the code for the diameter symbol.	

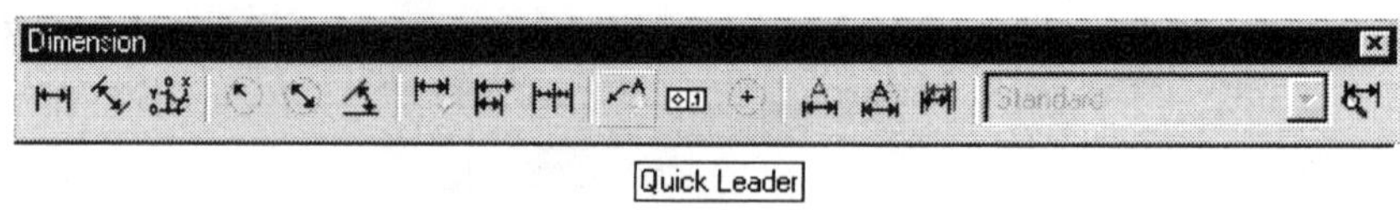

Clean Up the Dimensions

Step 13. Modify diameters (Figure 13–32).
Now fix the diameters so they look like Figure 13–22.

Prompt	Response
Command:	*Click:* **Dimension Style**
The Dimension Style manager appears:	*Click:* **Modify**
The Lines and Arrows tab appears:	*Click:* **the Fit tab**

FIGURE 13–32
Modify Diameter Dimensions

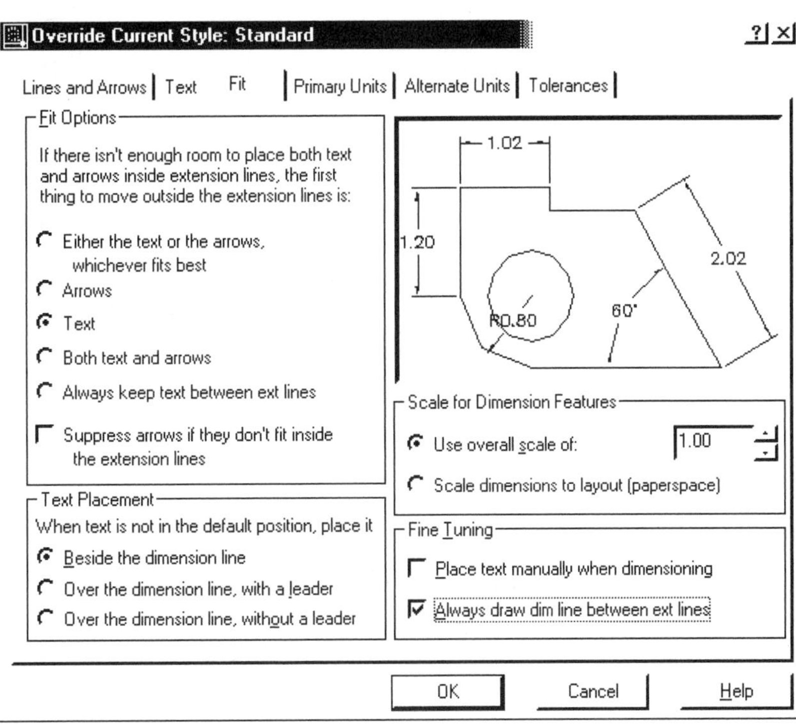

Prompt	Response
The Fit Tab appears:	*Click:* **Text** and **Always draw dim line between ext lines,** as shown in Figure 13–32.
	Click: **OK**
The Dimension Style manager appears:	*Click:* **Close**
Command:	**Dimension Text Edit** (or *Type:* **DIMTEDIT** ↵)
Select Dimension:	*Click:* **any point on the 1.80 diameter dimension**
Specify new location for dimension text or [Left/Right/Center/Home/Angle]:	**D1** (Figure 13–33)

FIGURE 13–33
Use DIMTEDIT to Relocate Dimension Text

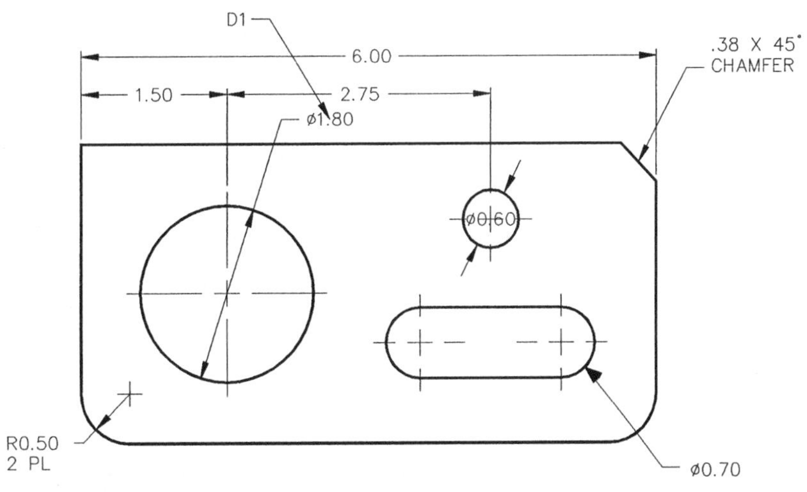

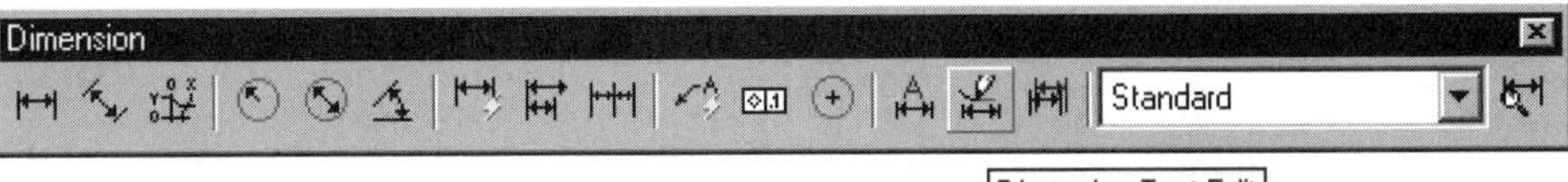

Prompt	Response
Command:	**Dimension Update** (or *Type:* **DIM** ↵ then **UP** ↵)
Select objects:	*Click:* **any point on the 1.80 diameter dimension**

On your own: Fix the 0.60 diameter dimension so it appears as shown in Figure 13–22. Use Grips to move it. From the command prompt, click the 0.60 dimension, click the text grip to make it hot, and move the text to the new location.

Be sure your final drawing looks like Figure 13-22.

Step 14. On your own:

1. Save your drawing in at least two places.
2. Plot the drawing full size (1 Plotted inch = 1 Drawing unit) on an 11″ × 8.5″ sheet.
3. Exit AutoCAD.

Next, dimension the floor plan you drew in Chapter 11.

Exercise 13–2: Dimensioning a Full-Size Floor Plan

Set Up the Drawing

Step 1. To begin Exercise 13–2, turn on the computer and start AutoCAD.

Step 2. On your own:

1. Open drawing EX11-1(your initials).
2. Use the SaveAs… command to save the drawing as EX13-2(your initials).

Step 3. Check to make sure that the following settings have been made:

Units: Architectural
LIMITS: Lower left corner: 0,0
Upper right corner: 45′,40′
GRID: 1′ (or 12 because the default unit is inches)
SNAP: 2
TEXT STYLE: Standard FONT: simplex.shx HEIGHT: 0

LAYERS: NAME	Color	Linetype	Lineweight
WINDOW	Green	CONTINUOUS	Default
DOOR	Red	CONTINUOUS	Default
WALL	Magenta	CONTINUOUS	Default
TEXT	Cyan	CONTINUOUS	Default
FURNITURE	White	CONTINUOUS	Default

Add the following layer:

DIM	Green	CONTINUOUS	Default

Turn off the FURNITURE layer.
Set layer DIM current.

Step 4. Use Zoom-All to view the entire drawing area:

Prompt	Response
Command:	**Zoom-All** (or *Type:* **Z** ↵, then **A** ↵

Step 5. Check the current status of dimensioning variables and make necessary changes.

Prompt	Response
Command:	*Type:* **DIM** ↵
Dim:	*Type:* **STATUS** ↵

FIGURE 13–34
Dimensioning Variables for the Full-Size Floor Plan

DIMADEC	0	Angular decimal places
DIMALT	Off	Alternate units selected
DIMALTD	2	Alternate unit decimal places
DIMALTF	25.4000	Alternate unit scale factor
DIMALTRND	0"	Alternate units rounding value
DIMALTTD	2	Alternate tolerance decimal places
DIMALTTZ	0	Alternate tolerance zero suppression
DIMALTU	2	Alternate units
DIMALTZ	0	Alternate unit zero suppression
DIMAPOST		Prefix and suffix for alternate text
DIMASZ	0"	Arrow size
DIMATFIT	3	Arrow and text fit
DIMAUNIT	0	Angular unit format
DIMAZIN	0	Angular zero supression
DIMBLK	ClosedFilled	Arrow block name
DIMBLK1	ClosedFilled	First arrow block name
DIMBLK2	ClosedFilled	Second arrow block name
DIMCEN	1/16"	Center mark size
DIMCLRD	BYBLOCK	Dimension line and leader color
DIMCLRE	BYBLOCK	Extension line color
DIMCLRT	BYBLOCK	Dimension text color
DIMDEC	4	Decimal places
DIMDLE	0"	Dimension line extension
DIMDLI	3/8"	Dimension line spacing
DIMDSEP		Decimal separator
DIMEXE	1/16"	Extension above dimension line
DIMEXO	1/16"	Extension line origin offset
DIMFRAC	0	Fraction format
DIMGAP	1/16"	Gap from dimension line to text
DIMJUST	0	Justification of text on dimension line
DIMLDRBLK	ClosedFilled	Leader block name
DIMLFAC	1.0000	Linear unit scale factor
DIMLIM	Off	Generate dimension limits
DIMLUNIT	4	Linear unit format
DIMLWD	-2	Dimension line and leader lineweight
DIMLWE	-2	Extension line lineweight
DIMPOST		Prefix and suffix for dimension text
DIMRND	0"	Rounding value
DIMSAH	Off	Separate arrow blocks
DIMSCALE	48.0000	Overall scale factor
DIMSD1	Off	Suppress the first dimension line
DIMSD2	Off	Suppress the second dimension line
DIMSE1	Off	Suppress the first extension line
DIMSE2	Off	Suppress the second extension line
DIMSOXD	Off	Suppress outside dimension lines
DIMTAD	2	Place text above the dimension line
DIMTDEC	4	Tolerance decimal places
DIMTFAC	1.0000	Tolerance text height scaling factor
DIMTIH	Off	Text inside extensions is horizontal
DIMTIX	Off	Place text inside extensions
DIMTM	0"	Minus tolerance
DIMTMOVE	0	Text movement
DIMTOFL	On	Force line inside extension lines
DIMTOH	On	Text outside horizontal
DIMTOL	Off	Tolerance dimensioning
DIMTOLJ	1	Tolerance vertical justification
DIMTP	0"	Plus tolerance
DIMTSZ	1/16"	Tick size
DIMTVP	0.0000	Text vertical position
DIMTXSTY	Standard	Text style
DIMTXT	1/8"	Text height
DIMTZIN	0	Tolerance zero suppression
DIMUPT	Off	User positioned text
DIMZIN	1	Zero suppression

A listing of all dimensioning variables appears. Compare the listing on your screen with the list shown in Figure 13–34. Make any necessary changes so that your list matches Figure 13–34.

Be sure you do not overlook the following:

DIMASZ = 0	DIMASO = ON (or 1)	DIMZIN = 1
DIMSCALE = 48	DIMTIH = OFF (or 0)	DIMLUNIT = 4
DIMTAD = ON (or 2)	DIMTOH = OFF (or 0)	DIMTOFL = ON
DIMTXT = ⅛	DIMTSZ = 1⁄16	DIMEXE = 1⁄16

Dimension the Drawing

Dimension to the center of all doors, windows, and inside partitions. Dimension to the outside of the outside walls.

Step 6. On your own:

Zoom a window to include just the north side of the office (Figure 13–35).

FIGURE 13–35
Dimension the North Side

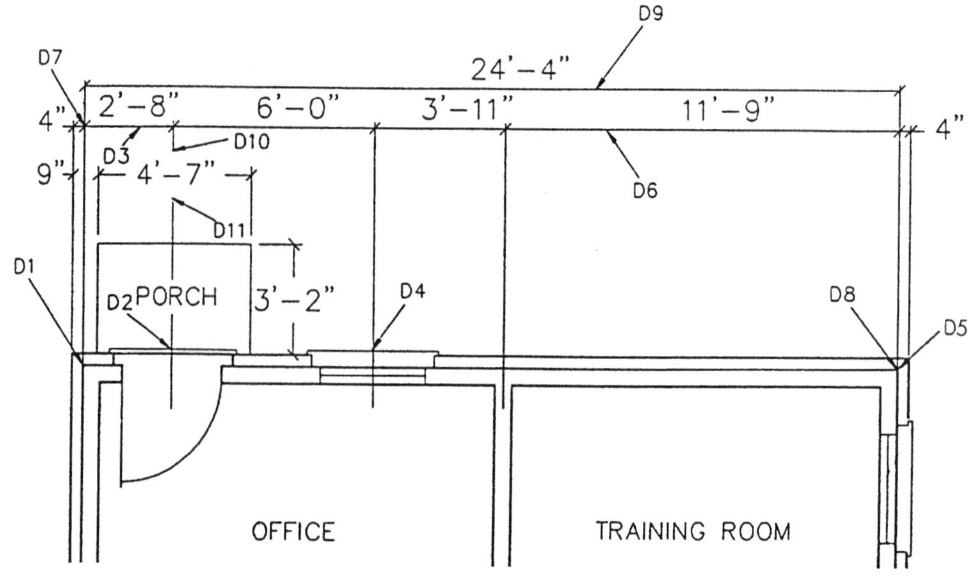

Step 7. Make all dimensions on the north side (the top) of the floor plan.

Prompt	Response
Command:	**Linear**
Specify first extension line origin or <select object>:	**Osnap-Endpoint**
of	**D1**
Specify second extension line origin:	**Osnap-Midpoint**
of	**D2**
Specify dimension line location or [Mtext/Text/Angle/Horizontal/Vertical/Rotated]:	**D3** (Use an appropriate distance from the drawing of the office, usually ½″ on the plotted drawing—in this case the porch interfered with that, and the available space allowed the dimension to be placed farther from the outline of the office itself.)
Dimension text = 2′-8″:	

Before clicking D3, you may change the dimension text if needed by typing T ↵ and then the correct dimension.

Prompt	Response
Command:	**Continue Dimension**
Specify a second extension line origin or [Undo/Select]<Select>:	**Osnap-Midpoint**
of	**D4**
Dimension text = 6′-0″:	
Specify a second extension line origin or [Undo/Select]<Select>:	↵
Select continued dimension:	↵

Now, dimension to the center of the partition from the outside wall. Since the drawing was made full scale and the partition was to have been 11′-9″ from the right corner of the building, follow this procedure:

Prompt	Response
Command:	**Linear Dimension**
Specify first extension line origin or <select object>:	**Osnap-Endpoint**
of	**D5**
Specify second extension line origin:	*Type:* **@11′9<180** ↵

Prompt	Response
Specify dimension line location or [Mtext/ Text/Angle/Horizontal/Vertical/Rotated]:	**D6**
Dimension text = 11′-9″:	
Command:	**Continue Dimension**
Specify a second extension line origin or [Undo/Select] <Select>:	**Osnap-Intersection**
of	*Click:* **the intersection of the 6′-0″ dimension and the 3′-11″ dimension**
Dimension text = 3′-11″:	
Specify a second extension line origin or [Undo/Select] <Select>:	↵
Select continued dimension:	↵

Now, place the overall dimension as the outside dimension.

Prompt	Response
Command:	**Linear Dimension**
Specify first extension line origin or <select object>:	**Osnap-Endpoint**
of	**D7**
Specify second extension line origin:	**Osnap-Endpoint**
of	**D8**
Specify dimension line location or [Mtext/ Text/Angle/Horizontal/Vertical/Rotated]:	**D9**
Dimension text = 24′-4″:	

On your own: Add other dimensions as shown in Figure 13–35. Set dimensioning variables DIMSE1 and DIMSE2 on if needed to avoid overlapping dimension lines. Set DIMTXT to 3/32 and update all existing dimensions before proceeding. To update dimensions, *Type:* **DIM ↵, then** *Type:* **UP ↵, then** *Type:* **ALL ↵** *Press:* **↵.**

Step 8. Explode any dimensions that interfere with lettering or dimension lines and break extension lines of the exploded dimensions so that they no longer cross lettering or dimension lines.

Prompt	Response
Command:	**Explode** (or *Type:* **X** ↵)
Select objects:	*Click:* **D10** (Figure 13–35)
Select objects:	↵
Command:	**Break** (or *Type:* **BR** ↵)
Select object:	**D10** (Figure 13–35)
Enter second point (or F for first point):	**D11**

Step 9. On your own:

Use the Properties… command to change the exploded lines back to the DIM layer and their color to BYLAYER.

Step 10. On your own:

Complete dimensions for the floor plan (Figure 13–36). Use methods similar to the ones used to dimension the north side of this floor plan.

Step 11. On your own:

1. Save your drawing in at least two places.
2. Plot the drawing at a scale of ¼″ = 1′ (¼ Plotted inch = 12 Drawing units) on an 11″ × 8.5″ sheet or insert into Layout1 (zoom factor 1/48 XP) and plot full scale.
3. Exit AutoCAD.

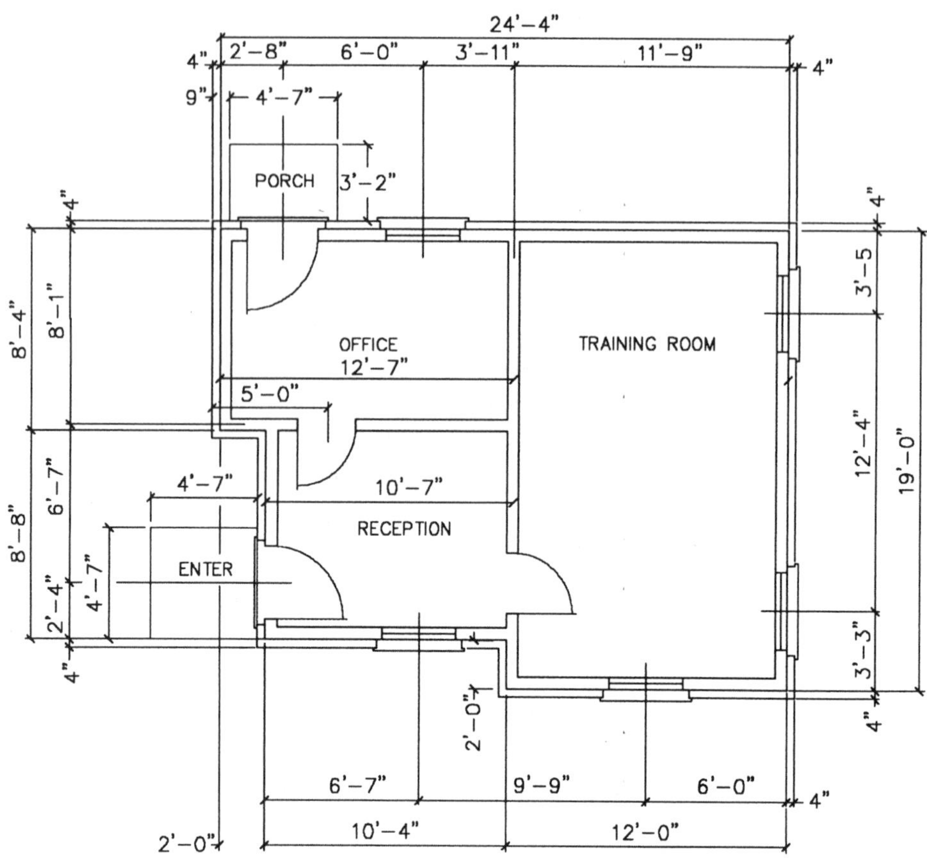

FIGURE 13–36
Exercise 13–2 Completely Dimensioned

GEOMETRIC DIMENSIONING AND TOLERANCING

Now that you have dimensioned a mechanical part and a floor plan, let's look at a specific type of dimensioning of mechanical parts. This type, called *geometric dimensioning and tolerancing,* allows parts to be manufactured with required accuracy and economy so that mating parts fit with the least cost. The following paragraphs will acquaint you with what this type of dimensioning looks like, what the standard symbols mean, and how you can use AutoCAD to easily construct the required frames containing those symbols. This is just an introduction to this topic. There are several good books devoted to the subject of geometric dimensioning and tolerancing.

What Geometric Dimensioning and Tolerancing Looks Like

Let's say, for example, that one surface on a part needs to be perpendicular to another surface within two parallel lines (called a tolerance zone) that are .005″ apart. One of these surfaces must be identified as a theoretically exact flat plane so that a note on the other surface can refer to it. Figure 13–37 shows one surface identified as surface A (called a *datum*). A datum is a plane used as a reference. The other surface is described as being perpendicular (the *symbol*) within a tolerance zone of .005 to datum A. Other examples of this type of dimensioning are shown in Figure 13–38.

What the Standard Symbols Mean

Figure 13–39 lists the standard symbols, describes the general terms applied to those symbols, and identifies the types of tolerances:

Location A location tolerance, for example, is often applied to the centers of holes.

Orientation An orientation tolerance, such as parallelism or perpendicularity, is often applied to two planes.

FIGURE 13–37
The Top Plane Is Perpendicular to the Right Side within .005

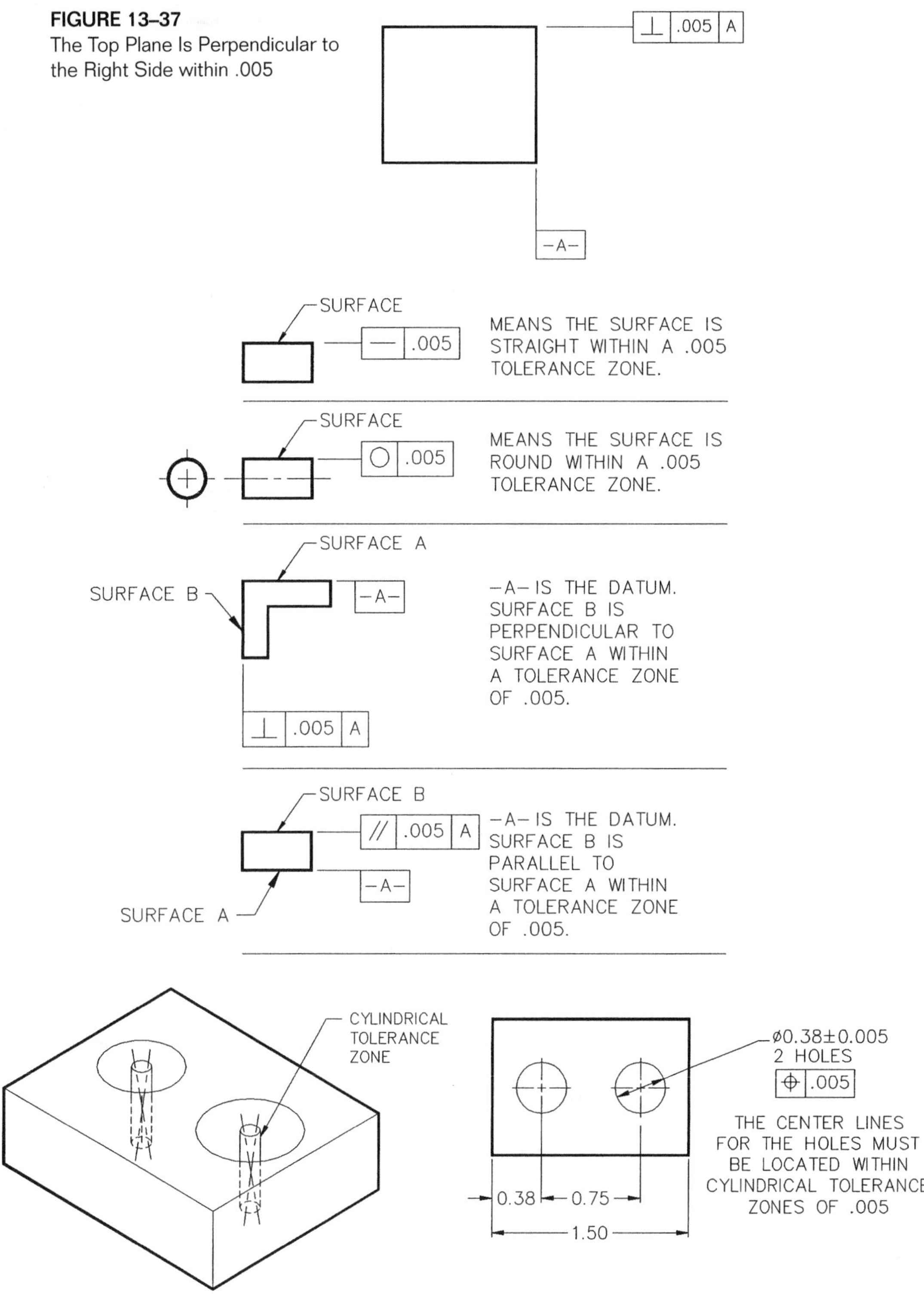

.005 A
-A-
SURFACE
.005
MEANS THE SURFACE IS STRAIGHT WITHIN A .005 TOLERANCE ZONE.
SURFACE
.005
MEANS THE SURFACE IS ROUND WITHIN A .005 TOLERANCE ZONE.
SURFACE A
SURFACE B
-A-
.005 A
-A- IS THE DATUM. SURFACE B IS PERPENDICULAR TO SURFACE A WITHIN A TOLERANCE ZONE OF .005.
SURFACE B
.005 A
-A-
SURFACE A
-A- IS THE DATUM. SURFACE B IS PARALLEL TO SURFACE A WITHIN A TOLERANCE ZONE OF .005.
CYLINDRICAL TOLERANCE ZONE
⌀0.38±0.005
2 HOLES
.005
THE CENTER LINES FOR THE HOLES MUST BE LOCATED WITHIN CYLINDRICAL TOLERANCE ZONES OF .005
0.38
0.75
1.50

FIGURE 13–38
Examples of Geometric Dimensioning and Tolerancing

FIGURE 13–39
Standard Geometric Tolerance Symbols

Symbol	Characteristic	Type
⌖	Position	Location
◎	Concentricity or coaxiality	Location
⌯	Symmetry	Location
//	Parallelism	Orientation
⊥	Perpendicularity	Orientation
∠	Angularity	Orientation
⌭	Cylindricity	Form
▱	Flatness	Form
○	Circularity or roundness	Form
—	Straightness	Form
⌓	Profile of a surface	Profile
⌒	Profile of a line	Profile
↗	Circular runout	Runout
⌰	Total runout	Runout

Form A form tolerance, such as roundness or straightness, is often applied to a shaft so that it will fit into a cylindrical opening.

Profile Profile describes the tolerance zone within which the shape of a surface must lie.

Runout Runout describes the movement of the dial of a precise measuring instrument as a shaft to be inspected is rotated in it.

All dimensions have tolerances whether they are stated directly on the drawing or contained in a general note. A dimension of .500 with a standard tolerance of ± 0.010 could measure (when inspected) .510 or .490 or any measurement between those two numbers and pass the inspection. When these tolerances are applied to cylinders such as shafts and holes the following terms are often necessary:

Maximum Material Condition This is the condition in which the most material is present within the tolerance limits, such as the largest shaft and the smallest hole.

Least Material Condition This is the opposite of maximum material condition—the smallest shaft and the largest hole.

Regardless of Feature Size This term means that no matter how large or small the feature is within its tolerance limits, the tolerance shown for the particular geometry holds. Figure 13–40 shows the material condition symbols.

Ⓜ MAXIMUM MATERIAL CONDITION

Ⓛ LEAST MATERIAL CONDITION

Ⓢ REGARDLESS OF FEATURE SIZE

FIGURE 13–40
Material Condition Symbols

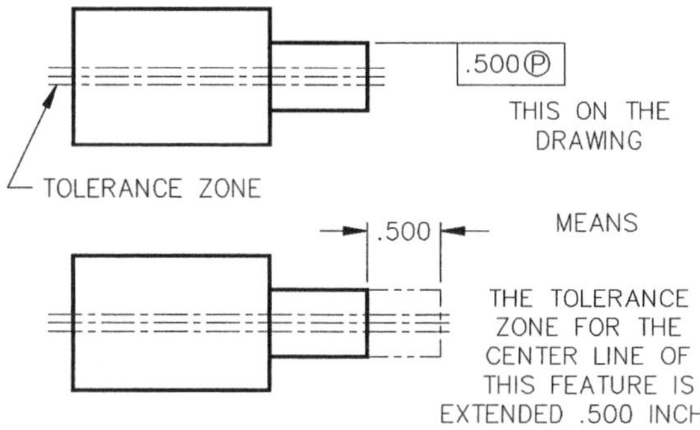

FIGURE 13–41
Projected Tolerance Zone

Projected Tolerance Zone The standard positional tolerance means that the center line of a hole, for example, must lie within a cylindrical tolerance zone that extends through the thickness of the part. In some situations where there are mating parts the cylindrical tolerance zone is extended to accommodate the mating part so that screws, studs, or other fasteners fit when the parts are assembled. Figure 13–41 describes the projected tolerance zone.

Exercise 13–3: Using the Tolerance Option of AutoCAD Dimensioning to Create the Control Frames Used in Geometric Dimensioning and Tolerancing

Step 1. To begin Exercise 13–3, turn on the computer and start AutoCAD.

Step 2. Open drawing EX13-1(your initials), erase all of it, and save it as EX13-3(your initials). You will still have drawing EX13-1 and you will have used the settings from that drawing for your new EX13-3 drawing.

Step 3. Check or make the following settings:

Units: Decimal—2 digits to the right of the decimal point
LIMITS: Lower left corner: 0,0
Upper right corner: 11,8.5
GRID: .25
SNAP: .125
TEXT STYLE: Standard FONT: simplex.shx HEIGHT: 0

LAYERS: NAME	Color	Linetype
R	Red	CONTINUOUS
M	Magenta	CONTINUOUS
G	Green	CENTER

Check dimensioning variables so they are as shown in Figure 13–23.

Step 4. Use Zoom-All to view the entire drawing area.

Prompt	Response
Command:	**Zoom-All** (or *Type:* **Z** ↵, then **A** ↵)

Step 5. On your own:

1. Draw and dimension the shape shown in Figure 13–42. Use layers as follows:

Center line on layer G
Object lines on layer M
Dimension lines on layer R

FIGURE 13–42
Dimensions for Exercise 13–3

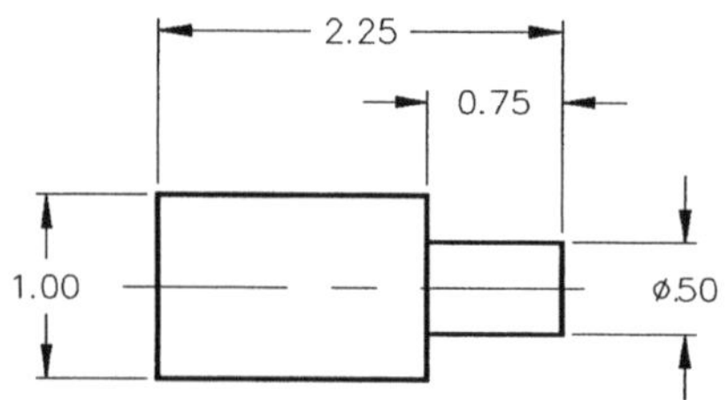

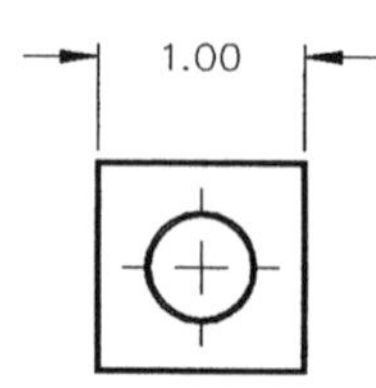

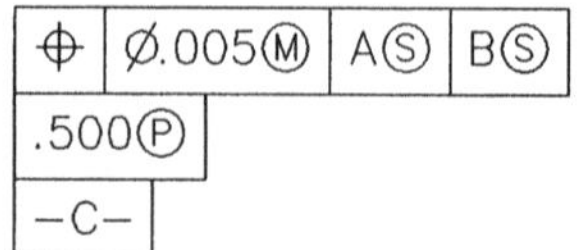

FIGURE 13–43
Feature Control Frame

2. Set Ltscale (Linetype Scale (*Type:* **LTSCALE** ↵)) to 1 so the center line will have two long dashes and a short dash.
3. Set layer R current to complete Step 6.

Step 6. Complete the feature control frame shown in Figure 13–43.

Let's start with one feature control frame, Figure 13–43, that uses all the values in the Geometric Tolerance dialog box, Figure 13–44.

FIGURE 13–44
Geometric Tolerance Dialog Box

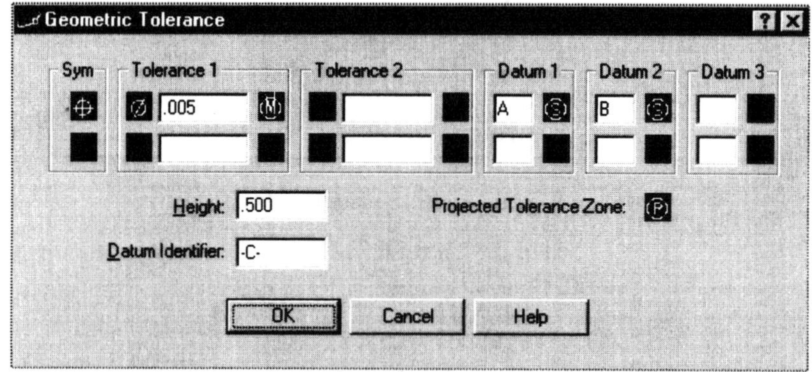

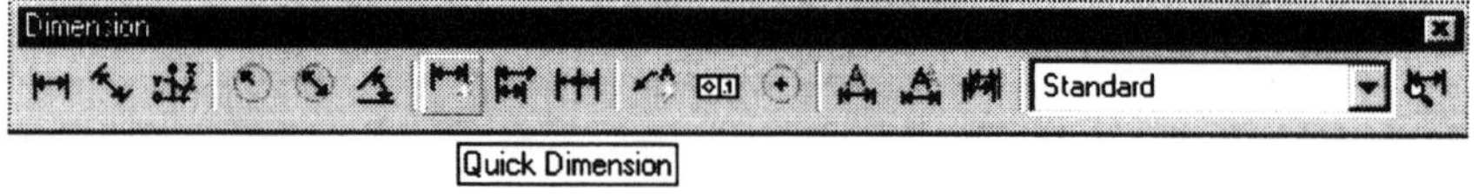

Symbol

FIGURE 13–45
Symbol Dialog Box

Material Condition

FIGURE 13–46
Material Condition Dialog Box with Maximum Material Condition Picked

Prompt	Response
Command:	**Tolerance**
The Geometric Tolerance dialog box appears:	*Click:* **The black square under the word Sym**
The Symbol dialog box, Figure 13–45, appears:	*Click:* **the Position symbol as shown**
The Geometric Tolerance dialog box appears:	*Click:* **the Dia button (the left uppermost square) in the Tolerance 1 area so that the diameter symbol appears as shown**
	Click: **the Value button (the rectangle in the center)**
	Type: **.005**
	Click: **the MC button (the square on the right)**
The Material Condition dialog box, Figure 13–46, appears:	*Click:* **the Maximum Material Condition symbol as shown**
The Geometric Tolerance dialog box appears:	*Click:* **the Datum button (the open rectangle) in the Datum 1 area**

Prompt	Response
	Type: **A**
	Click: **the MC button (the black square) in the Datum 1 area**
The Material Condition dialog box, Figure 13–47, appears:	*Click:* **the Regardless of Feature Size symbol as shown**
The Geometric Tolerance dialog box appears:	*Click:* **the Datum button in the Datum 2 area**
	Type: **B**
	Click: **the MC button in the Datum 2 area**
The Material Condition dialog box, Figure 13–47, appears:	*Click:* **the Regardless of Feature Size symbol as shown**
The Geometric Tolerance dialog box, Figure 13–44, appears.	*Click:* **the Height below the Tolerance 1 area**
	Type: **.500**
	Click: **the Projected Tolerance Zone button so that the Projected Tolerance Zone symbol appears**
	Click: **the Datum Identifier button**
	Type: **-C-**
	Click: **OK**
Enter tolerance location:	**D1** (Figure 13–48)

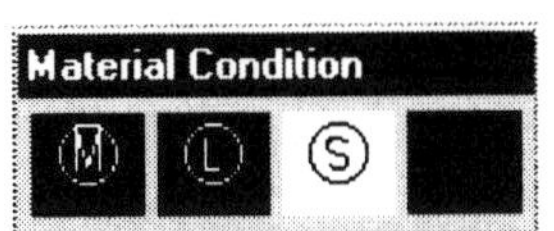

FIGURE 13–47
Material Condition Dialog Box with Regardless of Feature Size Picked

FIGURE 13–48
Applying Feature Control Frames

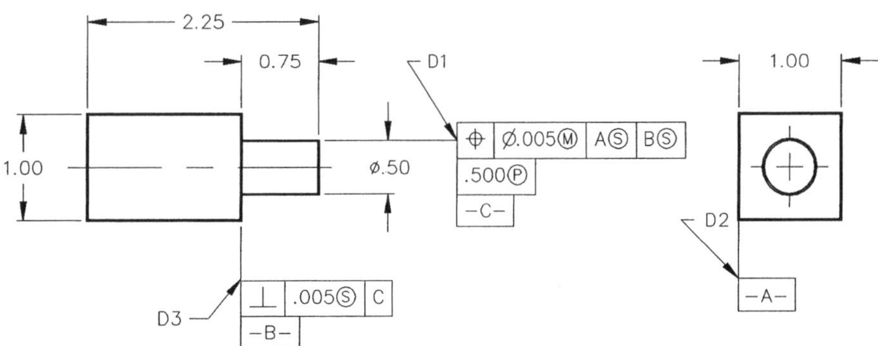

Step 7. On your own:

1. Add the -A- datum identifier by completing the Geometric Tolerance dialog box as shown in Figure 13–49 and clicking D2, Figure 13–48.
2. Add the perpendicularity tolerance by completing the Geometric Tolerance dialog box as shown in Figure 13–50 and clicking D3, Figure 13–48.
3. Add or extend any necessary lines so that the drawing appears as shown in Figure 13–48. (Do not add D1, D2, and D3 and their leaders.)

If you make a mistake after you have completed the Geometric Tolerance dialog box, use Text… from the Modify (DDEDIT) menu on the menu bar to correct it.

Exercise 13–3 is now complete.

Step 8. On your own:

1. Save your drawing in at least two places.

FIGURE 13–49
Adding Datum-A-

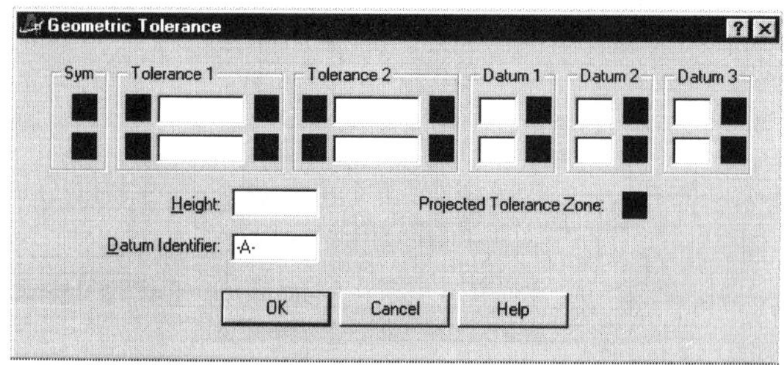

FIGURE 13–50
Adding Perpendicularity Tolerance

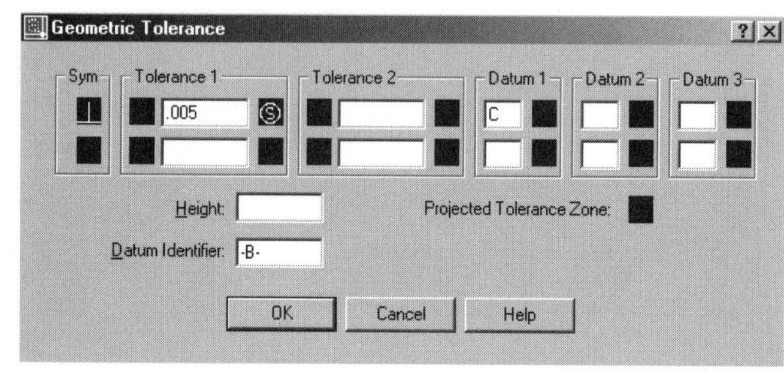

2. Plot the drawing full size (1 Plotted inch = 1 Drawing unit) on an 11″ × 8.5″ sheet.
3. Exit AutoCAD.

To dimension a drawing in millimeters using one-place decimals:

Dimensioning a metric drawing is similar to dimensioning a drawing drawn in inches, but there are a few differences. The differences are shown next. Set dimensioning variables in the same manner as you chose for dimensioning in inches (Figure 13–23), except:

Note: LTSCALE for metric drawings may have to be more or less than 25.4, depending on the size of the drawing.

DIMSCALE = 25.4
LTSCALE = 25.4 (LTSCALE may need to be set to 1 if metric linetypes are the default.)

Use the Units Control dialog box to set Units to Decimal. Precision to a single 0.

Additional Dimensioning Features

Feature 1. Respond with ↵ to the Linear Dimension prompt. This will eliminate some prompts. You will discover where it can be used most effectively, for example: overall dimensions of parts (Figure 13–51).

D2
35.6
D1

FIGURE 13–51
Selected Line for Dimension

Prompt	Response
Command:	**Linear Dimension**
Specify first extension line origin or <select object>:	↵
Select object to dimension:	**D1** (the line, arc, or circle to be dimensioned)
Specify dimension line location or [Mtext/Text/Angle/Horizontal/Vertical/Rotated]:	**D2**
Dimension text <35.6>:	

Feature 2. Notice that the sequence of extension lines selection determines where the small dimension is placed. See examples in Figure 13–52.

Feature 3. For baseline dimensioning (Figure 13–53):

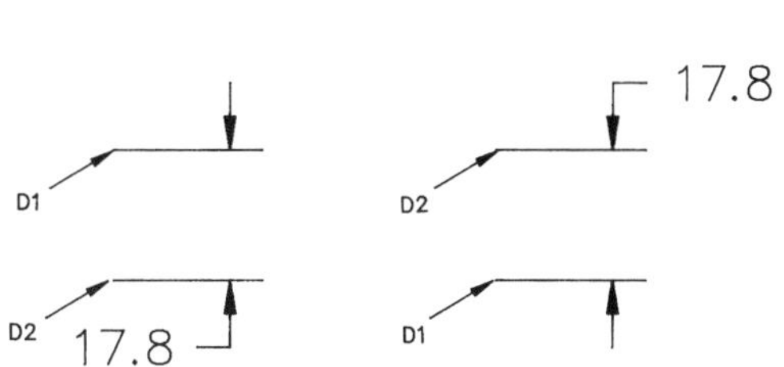

FIGURE 13–52
Dimension Placement

FIGURE 13–53
Baseline Dimensioning

Prompt	**Response**
Command:	**Linear Dimension**
Specify first extension line origin or <select object>:	**D1**
Specify second extension line origin:	**D2**
Specify dimension line location or [Mtext/Text/Angle/Horizontal/Vertical/Rotated]:	**D3**
Dimension text = 40.6:	
Command:	**Baseline Dimension**

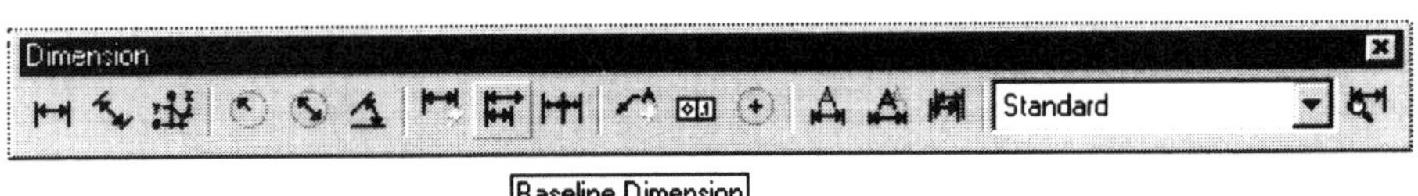

Specify a second extension line origin or [Undo/Select]<Select>:	**D4**
Specify a second extension line origin or [Undo/Select]<Select>:	**D5**
Specify a second extension line origin or [Undo/Select]<Select>:	*Press:* **Esc**

Feature 4. Associative dimensioning—use the Stretch command to shrink or enlarge any drawing already dimensioned.
Observe that the dimension text changes with the size of the drawing (DIMASO must be on). When DIMAZO is on, the dimension, dimension lines, arrowheads, and extension lines are inserted as a block.

Feature 5. Adding tolerances to specific dimensions—to add tolerances to a specific dimension (Figure 13–54), make settings as shown in Figure 13–54 and then dimension. If you wish to add tolerances to an existing dimension (Example: 3.37), use the Edit Text... command, select the dimension, then type 3.37%%P.02 in the Edit MText dialog box and delete the <>. %%P is a code for ±.

Feature 6. The command DIMEDIT or GRIPS is used to control the placement and orientation of the text within an associative dimension.

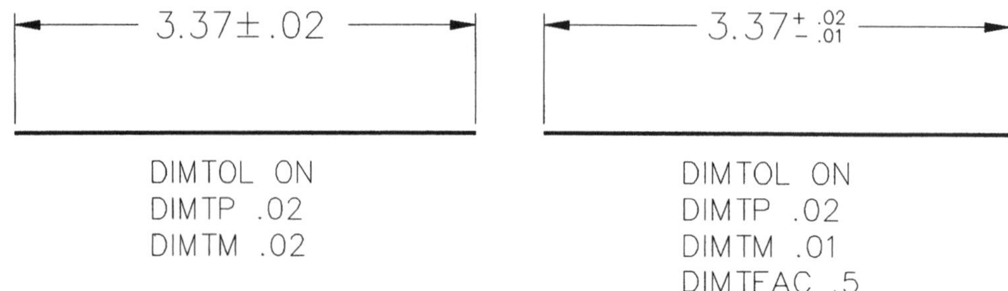

FIGURE 13–54
Tolerances

Feature 7. Use NEWTEXT (*Type:* **NEWTEXT↵**) from the Dim: prompt or Modify Text… (*Type:* **DDEDIT↵**) to correct dimension text in an associative dimension.

Feature 8. The Ordinate Dimension command is used to create dimensions from a 0,0 datum similar to Figure 13–55. The current UCS is used to define where 0,0 is located. To place 0,0 at the upper left corner of this drawing, do the following:

Note: UCS (user coordinate system) will be explained in depth in later chapters on 3-D.

Remember: Return the origin to its original location before plotting. (Select UCS and then World, which is the default.)

Prompt	Response
Command:	*Type:* **UCS** ↵
Enter an option [New/Move/orthoGraphic/Prev/Restore/Save/Del/Apply/?/World] <World>:	*Type:* **O** ↵ (for origin)
Origin point<0,0,0>:	*Click:* **the upper left corner of the part.** This is now the origin 0,0 of the current UCS. (The UCSICON, the arrow in the lower left corner of the display, will not move to the new origin unless directed to do so.) Now Ordinate Dimensioning can be used by clicking the beginning and ending point for the extension line.

Dimension
Standard
Quick Dimension

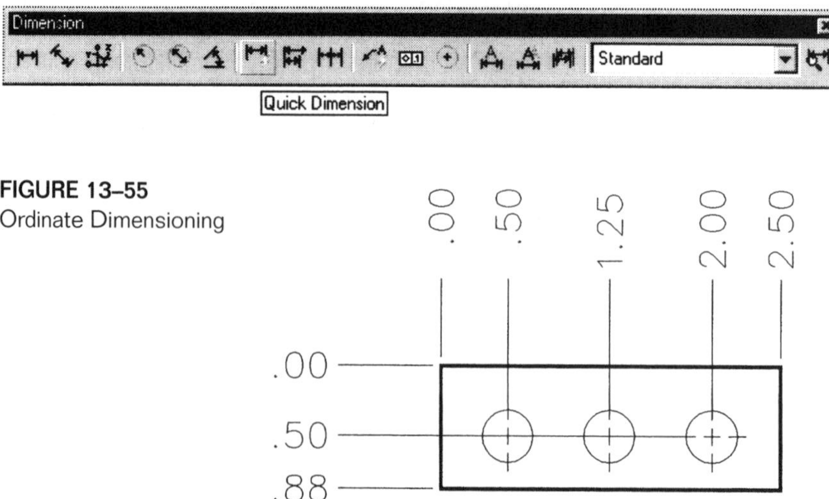

FIGURE 13–55
Ordinate Dimensioning

Feature 9. **Quick Dimension** is used to make a series of dimensions at the same time. Start Quick Dimension, then select the items on the object you want to dimension and specify how you want to dimension them. AutoCAD dimensions them all at the same time:

Prompt	Response
Command:	**Quick Dimension** (from the Dimension menu or *Type:* **QDIM** ↵)
Select geometry to dimension:	*Click:* (the objects you want to dimension)
Specify dimension line position, or [Continuous/Staggered/Baseline/Ordinate/Radius/Diameter/datumPoint/Edit] <Baseline>:	*Type:* (the capital letter of the method you want to use)

AutoCAD then dimensions the objects for you. Exercises 13–4, 13–5, and 13–7 are excellent examples of where Quick Dimension can be used effectively.

DIMASSOC System Variable

This new AutoCAD 2002 setting is not one of the dimensioning variables but does affect how dimensions behave in relation to the object being dimensioned. It has three states:

0 Creates exploded dimensions. Each part of the dimension (arrowheads, lines, text) is a separate object.

1 Creates dimensions that are single objects but are not associated with the object being dimensioned. When the dimension is created, definition points are formed (at the ends of extension lines, for example). If these points are moved, as with the Stretch command, the dimension changes, but it is not directly associated with the object being dimensioned.

2 Creates associative dimension objects. The dimensions are single objects, and one or more of the definition points on the dimension are linked to association points on the object. When the association point on the object moves, the dimension location, orientation, and text value of the dimension change. For example: Check DIMASSOC to make sure the setting is 2. (*Type:* **DIMASSOC** ↵. If the value is not 2, *Type:* 2 ↵) Draw a 2″ circle and dimension it using the diameter dimensioning command. With no command active, *Click:* any point on the circle so that grips appear at the quadrants of the circle. *Click:* any grip to make it hot, and move the grip. The dimension changes as the size of the circle changes.

EXERCISES

EXERCISE 13–1. Dimension the mechanical part shown as Figure 13–22. Use the basic drawing from Chapter 10. *Click:* Layout1, then insert an A-size format around the drawing. Plot the drawing or save it on a floppy disk according to your instructor's plan.

EXERCISE 13–2. Dimension the floor plan (Figure 13–36) using the procedures described in this chapter. Use the floor plan from Chapter 11 for the basic drawing. *Click:* **Layout1**, *Click:* the outside edge of the viewport, and insert a C-size format around the drawing and select a scale of ¼″ = 1′ in the Properties dialog box. Plot the drawing on an 11″ × 8½″ sheet.

EXERCISE 13–3. Complete Exercise 13–1 (Figure 13–48) as described in the section on geometric dimensioning and tolerancing. Plot the drawing or save it on a floppy disk for later use according to your instructor's plan.

EXERCISE 13–4. Draw and dimension the part shown in Figure 13–56 using metric dimensions and Quick Dimension. Make the drawing full scale. Set the dimensioning variables using the procedures described for Figure 13–23. Set DIMSCALE 5 25.4. Insert an A-size format around this drawing in Layout1. Make center

FIGURE 13–56
Exercise 13–4

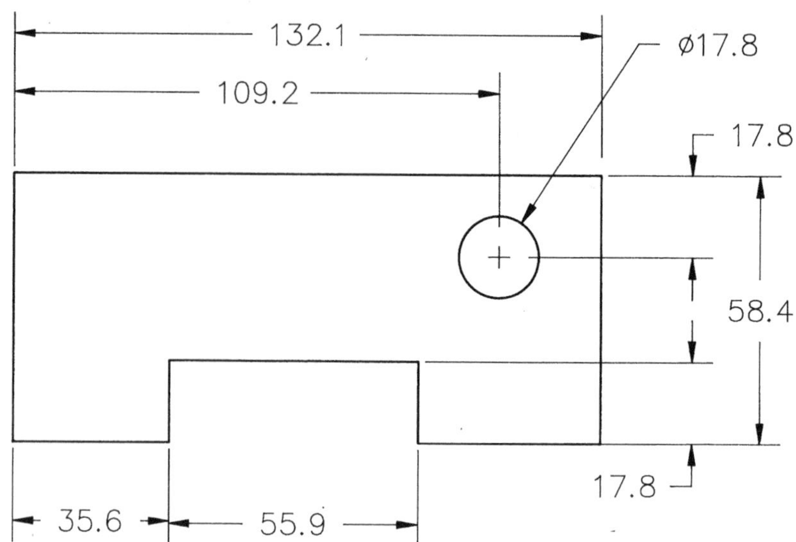

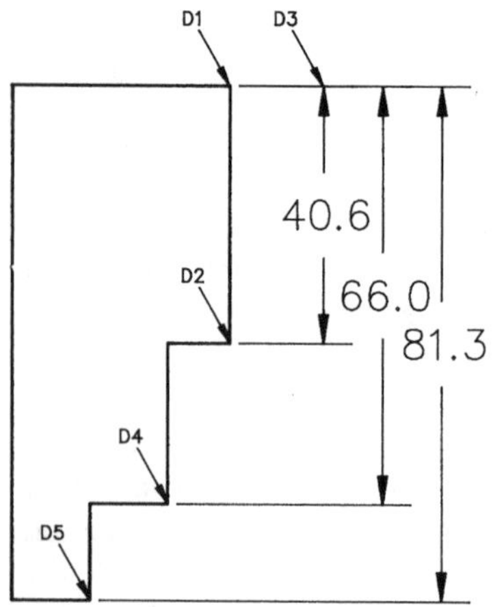

FIGURE 13–57
Exercise 13–5

mark first so you can select it for Quick Dimension. Plot or save according to your instructor's plan.

EXERCISE 13–5. Draw and dimension the part shown in Figure 13–57 using 1-place decimal dimensions in millimeters. Use settings from Exercise 13–4. Use Quick Dimension with the Baseline option. Estimate horizontal dimensions. Set DIMSCALE = 25.4. Insert an A-size format around this drawing in Layout1. Plot or save according to your instructor's plan. When Quick Dimension prompts you to select objects, use a window to select the entire drawing, drag to the right, then *Type:* **B** ↵ to select the Baseline option.

EXERCISES 13–6A and 13–6B. Dimension the drawings done for Chapter 10, Exercises 10–2 and 10–3. Use settings from Exercise 13–1. Change drawing limits to 17,11 for Exercise 10–2, DIMSCALE to 25.4 for Exercise 10–3. Plot these drawings on a 17″ × 11″ sheet. Insert a B-size format around each drawing before plotting.

EXERCISE 13–7. Draw full size, set indicated variables, and use Quick Dimension to dimension the drawings shown in Figure 13–58. Use settings from Exercise 13–1. Draw center marks before you start Quick Dimension. Then use a crossing window to select just the vertical lines, including center marks; *Type:* **O** ↵ to specify the ordinate option. Repeat for just the horizontal lines.

DIMDEC = 2
DIMUNITS = 2
DIMTXT = .25
DIMAS2 = .2
EXTENSION LINE OFFSET = .06
EXTENSION LINE EXTENSION = .06

Use 2-place decimals for all dimensions.
Insert an A-size format around this drawing in Layout1.

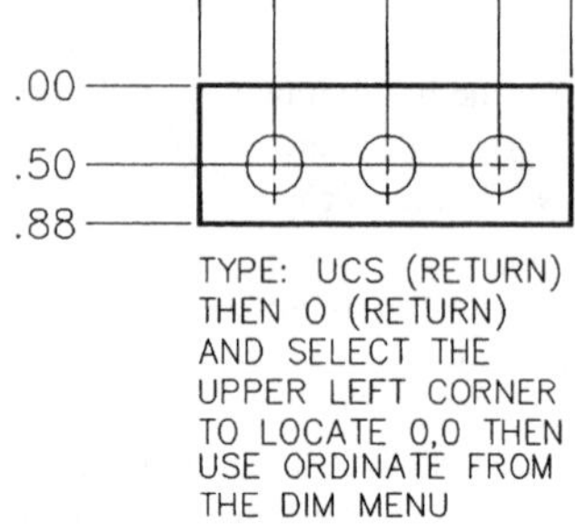

.00
.50
.88
TYPE: UCS (RETURN)
THEN O (RETURN)
AND SELECT THE
UPPER LEFT CORNER
TO LOCATE 0,0 THEN
USE ORDINATE FROM
THE DIM MENU

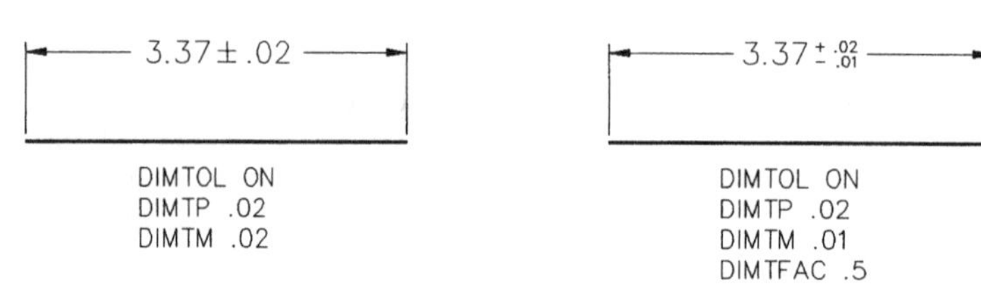

FIGURE 13–58
Exercise 13–7

Hint: Dimensioning diameters, radii, and special features before making horizontal and vertical linear dimensions is often helpful. Planning the complete dimensioning procedure for a drawing before dimensioning often saves time.

EXERCISE 13–8. Draw full size and dimension the part shown in Figure 13–59. Set limits of 44,34 (twice the C-size of 22,17). Use the following dimensioning variables:

DIMDEC = 2
DIMUNITS = 2
DIMTXT = .12
DIMASZ = .12
DIMEXE = .06
DIMEXO = .06
DIMSCALE = 2

Use 3-place decimals for hole sizes.
Use 2-place decimals for all other dimensions.
Insert a C-size format around this drawing in Layout1.

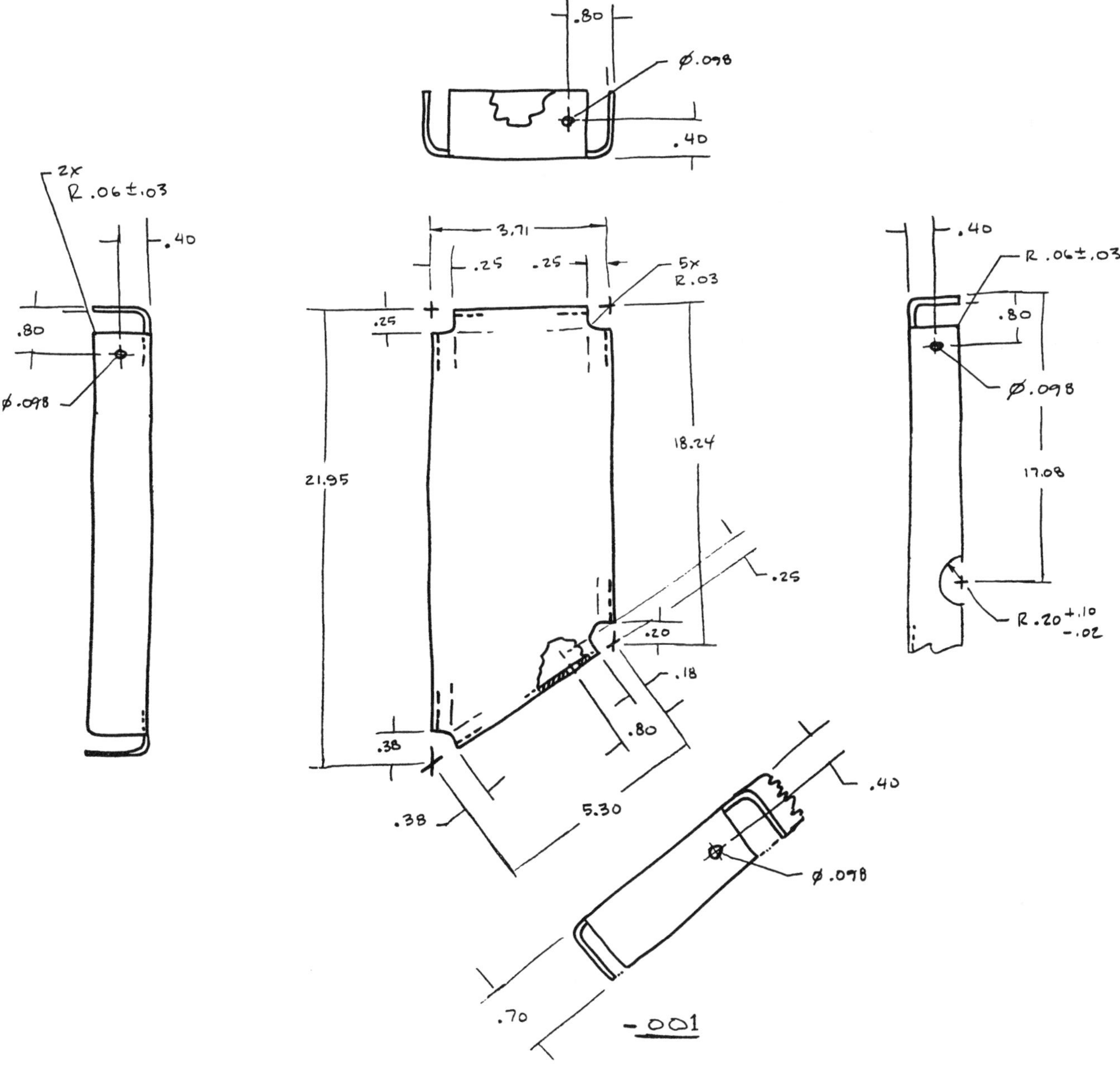

FIGURE 13–59
Exercise 13–8

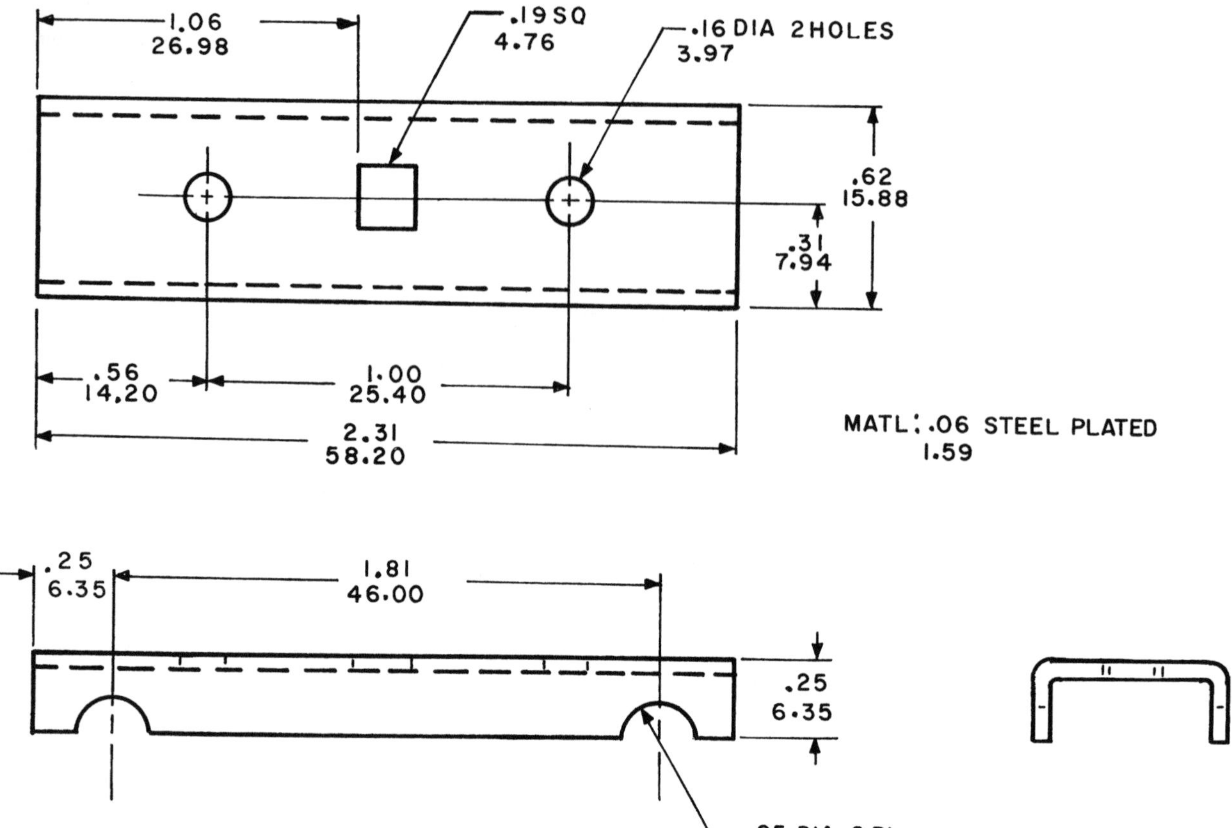

FIGURE 13–60
Exercises 13–9A and 9B

EXERCISES 13–9A and 13–9B. Draw full size and dimension the part shown in Figure 13–60. Make the drawing twice its size and place it on an A-size horizontal sheet. Name the drawing 13-9A and copy it under the name 13-9B. Use the following dimensioning variables:

DIMDEC = 2
DIMUNITS = 2
DIMTXT = .10
DIMASZ = .12
DIMEXE = .06
DIMEXO = .06
DIMSCALE = 2
DIMLFAC = .5

a. Use 2-place decimal inch dimensions for Drawing 13-9A.
b. Use 2-place decimal millimeter dimensions for Drawing 13-9B. Use DIMSCALE = 25.4 and DIMLFAC = 12.7 for Drawing 13-9B.

Insert an A-size format around these drawings in Layout1.

EXERCISES 13–10A and 13–10B. Draw full size and dimension the part shown in Figure 13–61. Make the drawing full size and place it on an A-size horizontal sheet. Name the drawing 13-10A and copy it under the name 13-10B. Use the following dimensioning variables:

DIMDEC = 2
DIMUNITS = 2
DIMTXT = .10

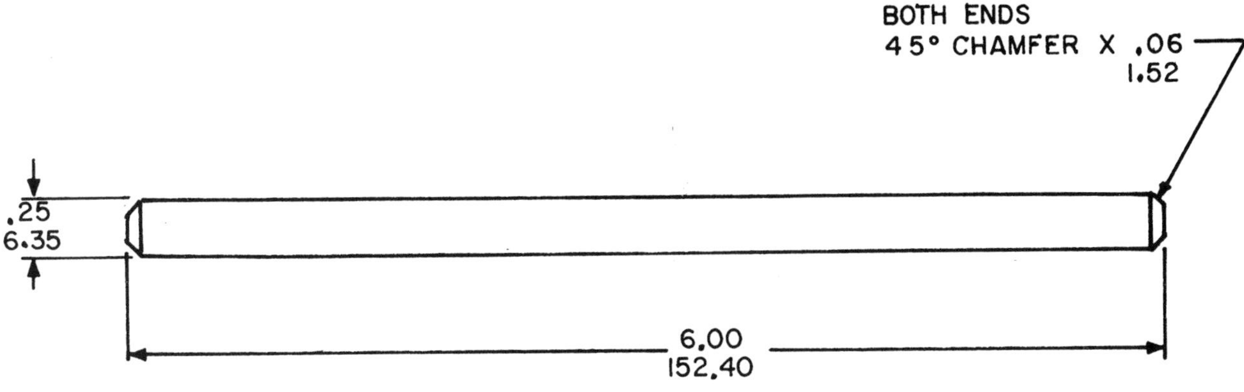
BOTH ENDS
45° CHAMFER X .06
1.52
.25
6.35
6.00
152.40

FIGURE 13–61
Exercises 13–10A and 10B

DIMASZ = .12
DIMEXE = .06
DIMEXO = .06
DIMSCALE = 1
DIMLFAC = 1

a. Use 2-place decimal inch dimensions for Drawing 13-10A. (Inch dimensions are above the metric dimensions.)
b. Use 2-place decimal millimeter dimensions for Drawing 13-10B. Use DIMSCALE = 25.4 and DIMLFAC = 25.4 for Drawing 13-10B.

Insert an A-size format around these drawings.

EXERCISE 13–11. Draw and dimension the part shown in Figure 13–62. Use the Tolerance option on the Dimensioning toolbar to add a feature control frame as stated in Figure 13–62. Insert an A-size format around the drawing in Layout1.

EXERCISE 13–12. Draw and dimension the part shown in Figure 13–63. Use the Tolerance option on the Dimensioning toolbar to add a feature control frame as stated in Figure 13–63. Insert an A-size format around the drawing in Layout1.

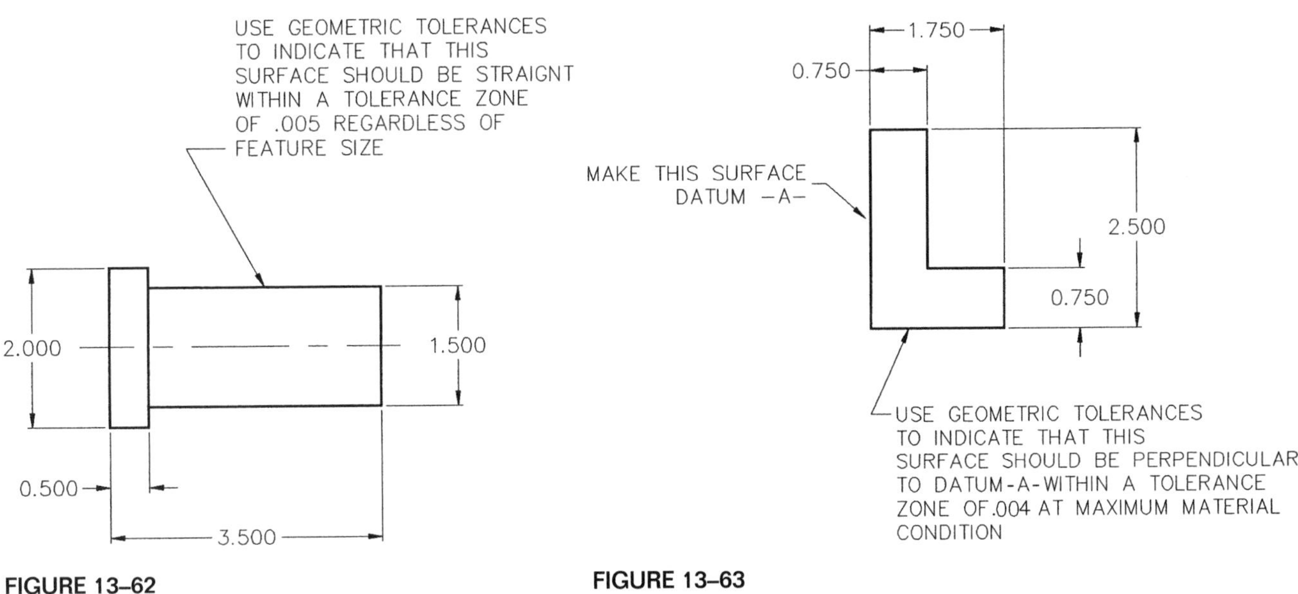
USE GEOMETRIC TOLERANCES
TO INDICATE THAT THIS
SURFACE SHOULD BE STRAIGNT
WITHIN A TOLERANCE ZONE
OF .005 REGARDLESS OF
FEATURE SIZE
2.000
1.500
0.500
3.500
1.750
0.750
MAKE THIS SURFACE
DATUM -A-
2.500
0.750
USE GEOMETRIC TOLERANCES
TO INDICATE THAT THIS
SURFACE SHOULD BE PERPENDICULAR
TO DATUM-A-WITHIN A TOLERANCE
ZONE OF.004 AT MAXIMUM MATERIAL
CONDITION

FIGURE 13–62
Exercise 13–11

FIGURE 13–63
Exercise 13–12

EXERCISE 13–13. Draw and dimension the part shown in Figure 13–64. Use the Tolerance option on the Dimensioning toolbar to add a feature control frame as stated in Figure 13–64. Insert an A-size format around the drawing in Layout1.

EXERCISE 13–14. Draw and dimension the top view only of the part shown in Figure 13–65. Use 3-place decimals on all dimensions. Use the Tolerance option on the Dimensioning toolbar to add feature control frames as stated below.
Make the horizontal center lines of the holes datums -A- and -B-.
Make the bottom edge datum -C-.
Locate holes with a positional tolerance of .005 at maximum material condition with reference to datums -A- and -B-. Holes should have a projected tol-

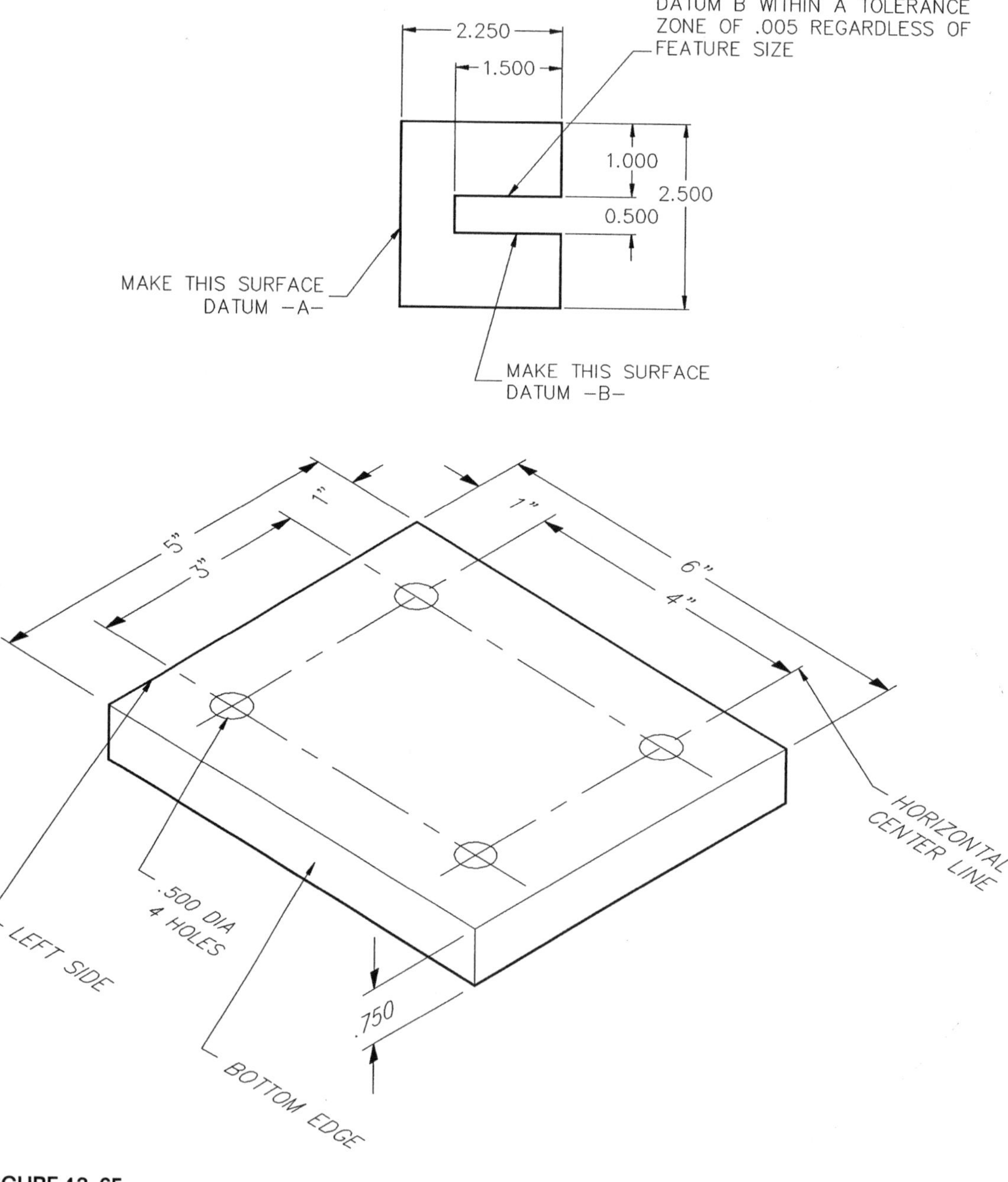

USE GEOMETRIC TOLERANCES TO INDICATE THAT THIS SURFACE IS PERPENDICULAR TO DATUM A WITHIN A TOLERANCE ZONE OF .002 AT MAXIMUM MATERIAL CONDITION AND PARALLEL TO DATUM B WITHIN A TOLERANCE ZONE OF .005 REGARDLESS OF FEATURE SIZE
2.250
1.500
1.000
2.500
0.500
MAKE THIS SURFACE DATUM –A–
MAKE THIS SURFACE DATUM –B–
5"
3"
1"
1"
6"
4"
HORIZONTAL CENTER LINE
.500 DIA 4 HOLES
LEFT SIDE
.750
BOTTOM EDGE

FIGURE 13–64
Exercise 13–13

FIGURE 13–65
Exercise 13–14

erance zone height of .375. Show the projected tolerance zone symbol.
Make the left side of the part perpendicular to the bottom edge within a tolerance zone of .005 regardless of feature size.
Insert an A-size format around the drawing in Layout1.

REVIEW QUESTIONS

Circle the best answer.

1. Which of the following sets the text style of the dimension?
   a. DIMTXT
   b. DIMTXSTY
   c. DIMUNIT
   d. DIMDEC
   e. DIMUPT
2. DIMASZ determines
   a. The height of the alternate text
   b. The height of the arrowhead
   c. The length of the arrowhead
   d. The direction of the azimuths
   e. The length of the bearing
3. DIMEXO sets
   a. The distance from the X and Y coordinates
   b. The execute file for dimensions
   c. The distance from the object to the beginning of the extension line
   d. The distance from the end of the extension line to the dimension line
   e. The distance from the beginning of the extension line to the end of the extension line
4. DIMDLI sets
   a. The dimension length in inches
   b. The length of the arrowhead
   c. The distance from the beginning of the dimension line to the extension line
   d. The length of dimension lines
   e. The spacing between dimension lines
5. With DIMSCALE set at 48 and DIMTXT set at 1⁄8″, text for dimensions will measure
   a. 1⁄16″
   b. 1⁄8″
   c. 1⁄4″
   d. 3″
   e. 6″
6. Which of the following places the text above the extension line?
   a. DIMSE1
   b. DIMSE2
   c. DIMTAD
   d. DIMLIM
   e. DIMTOL
7. Which of the following (when ON) produces a dimension with no extension line at the beginning of the dimension?
   a. DIMSE1
   b. DIMSE2
   c. DIMTAD
   d. DIMLIM
   e. DIMTOL
8. Which of the following must be set to ON for tolerances to be added to dimensioning text?
   a. DIMSE1
   b. DIMSE2
   c. DIMTAD
   d. DIMLIM
   e. DIMTOL

9. Which of the following must be set ON for metric dimensions to be displayed with inch dimensions?
   a. DIMLIM
   b. DIMTOL
   c. DIMALT
   d. DIMALTF
   e. DIMALTD
10. Which of the following sets the number of decimal places to the right of the decimal point in the alternate dimension?
    a. DIMDEC
    b. DIMTOL
    c. DIMALT
    d. DIMALTF
    e. DIMALTD
11. Which of the following sets the number of decimal places to the right of the decimal point for the standard dimension?
    a. DIMDEC
    b. DIMTOL
    c. DIMALT
    d. DIMALTF
    e. DIMALTD
12. To pick the exact location of the upper right corner of the floor plan, which of the following Osnap modifiers should be used?
    a. Perpendicular
    b. Intersection
    c. Center
    d. Midpoint
    e. Nearest
13. When DIMSCALE = 0, AutoCAD computes a DIMSCALE that is the ratio
    a. Between model space and paper space limits
    b. Between DIMLFAC and DIMALTF
    c. Between the plotting scale and the drawing size
    d. Between DIMTXT and STYLE height
    e. Between drawing size and plotting units
14. Which of the following dimension commands produces feature control frames for geometric tolerances?
    a. Tolerance
    b. Linear
    c. Ordinate
    d. Baseline
    e. Continue
15. If DIMSCALE is set at 1.0000, what must the setting be for an arrowhead to be ⅛″ long?
    a. DIMASZ = .125
    b. DIMASZ = 1.00
    c. DIMTSZ = .125
    d. DIMTSZ = 1.00
    e. DIMASZ = 0
16. Which of the following variables must be activated if some symbol other than the tick or the arrowhead is to be used for the ends of a dimension line?
    a. DIMSHO
    b. DIMPOST
    c. DIMBLK
    d. DIMALT
    e. DIMALT2
17. If all dimensions are to originate from the same edge, which of the following dimensioning commands should be used?
    a. Continue
    b. Datum
    c. Origin
    d. Originate
    e. Baseline

18. If you wish to begin all extension lines 1/16″ from the object lines, which of the following is the correct setting?
    a. DIMZIN = 0
    b. DIMEXE = 1
    c. DIMEXO = .0625
    d. DIMLIM = .0625
    e. DIMLIM = 1
19. If the DIMASSOC system variable is set to 2 and a circle has been dimensioned with this setting ON,
    a. When the size of the circle is changed, the dimension text and the elements of the dimension (such as arrowheads) change.
    b. The dimension is exploded.
    c. The dimension remains the same when the size of the circle is changed.
    d. AutoCAD prompts you to change the setting.
    e. The text changes, but the other elements of the dimension stay where they were.
20. Which of the following is used to make several dimensions at the same time?
    a. Ordinate
    b. Baseline
    c. Quick Dimension
    d. Continue
    e. Linear

14 Sectional Drawings and Hatching

OBJECTIVES

After completing this chapter, you will be able to

- Use the Hatch command in conjunction with other draw and modify commands to produce sectional views of detail (single) parts.
- Use the Hatch command in conjunction with other draw and modify commands to produce assembly and wall sections.
- Correctly answer questions regarding the use of the commands used to produce sectional views; these commands are:

  Array
  Break
  Copy
  Erase
  Explode
  Extend
  Hatch
  Hatchedit
  Offset
  Scale
  Snap (Rotate)
  Stretch
  Trim

USE OF SECTIONAL DRAWINGS

Sectional drawings are used to show the internal construction of parts (Figure 14–1) or external features that cannot easily be understood with external views (Figure 14–2). Sectional drawings are used not only to show someone how to make a part but also to show someone how several parts function or how to assemble parts (Figure 14–3). The construction of sectional views is reviewed for your information in the following paragraphs. If you need further information regarding sectional views, consult any good technical drawing textbook.

Constructing a Sectional View

Sectional views are easy to construct if you follow a simple series of steps. These steps are shown in Figure 14–4. The object shown in Figure 14–4 is a rather complex shape. Its features could be misunderstood if only external views were used. To clear up any misunderstanding, a sectional view is chosen. To draw the sectional view, use the following steps.

Step 1. Decide which view would best show the hidden feature. In your mind, cut off the part that is hiding the feature.

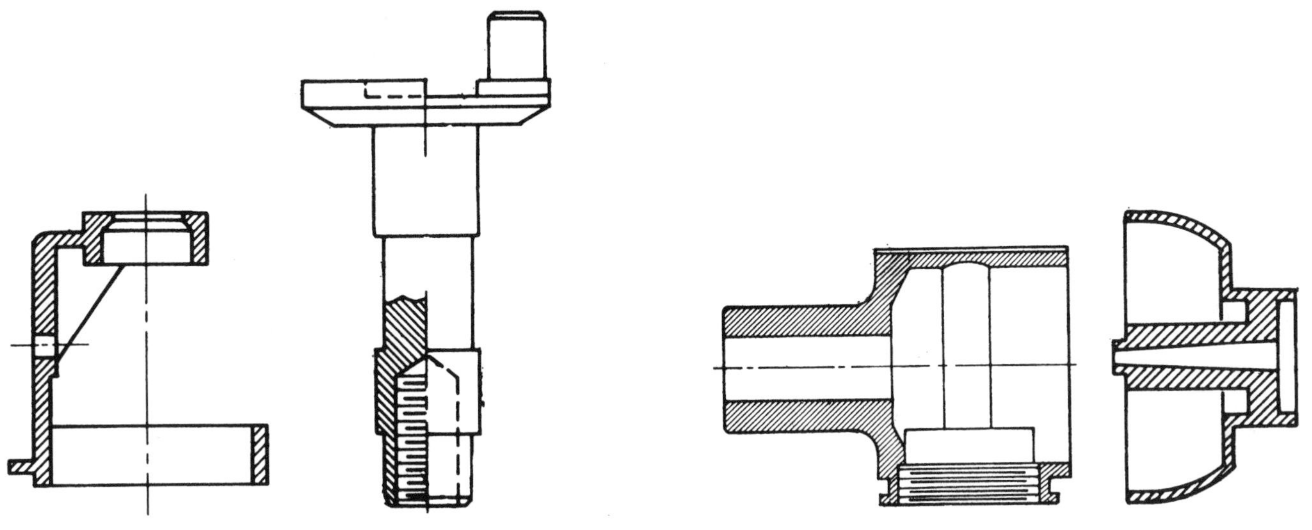

FIGURE 14–1
Internal Construction

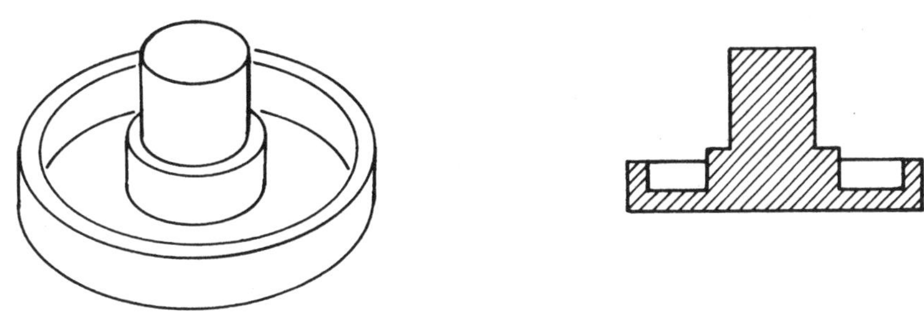

FIGURE 14–2
External Features Shown in Section

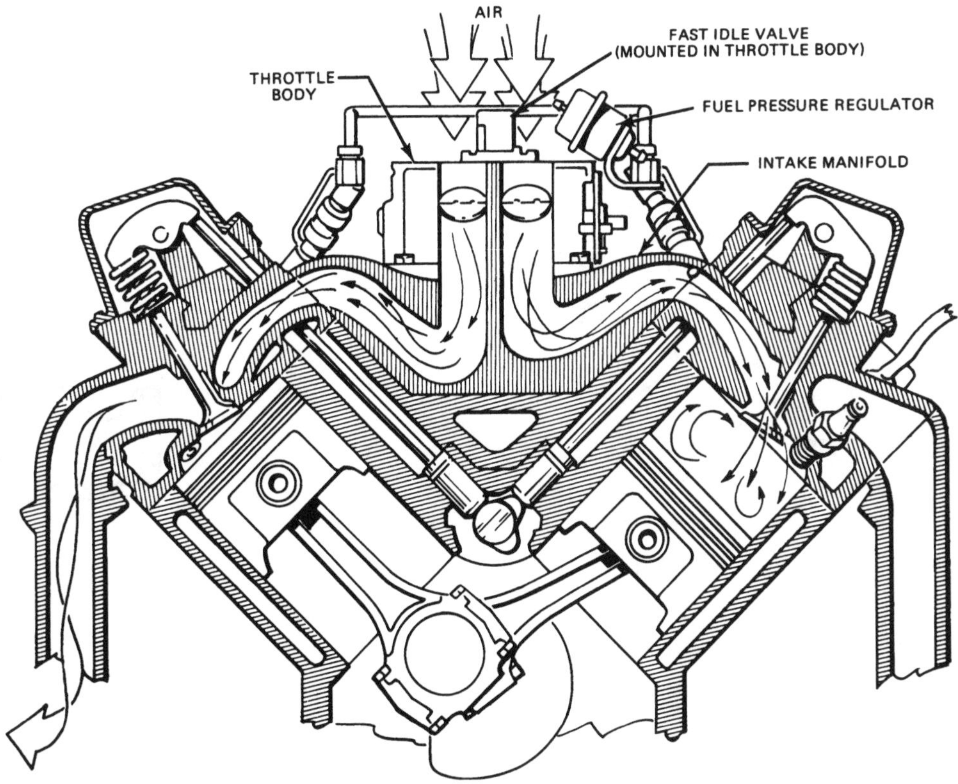

FIGURE 14–3
Sectioned Assembly Drawing

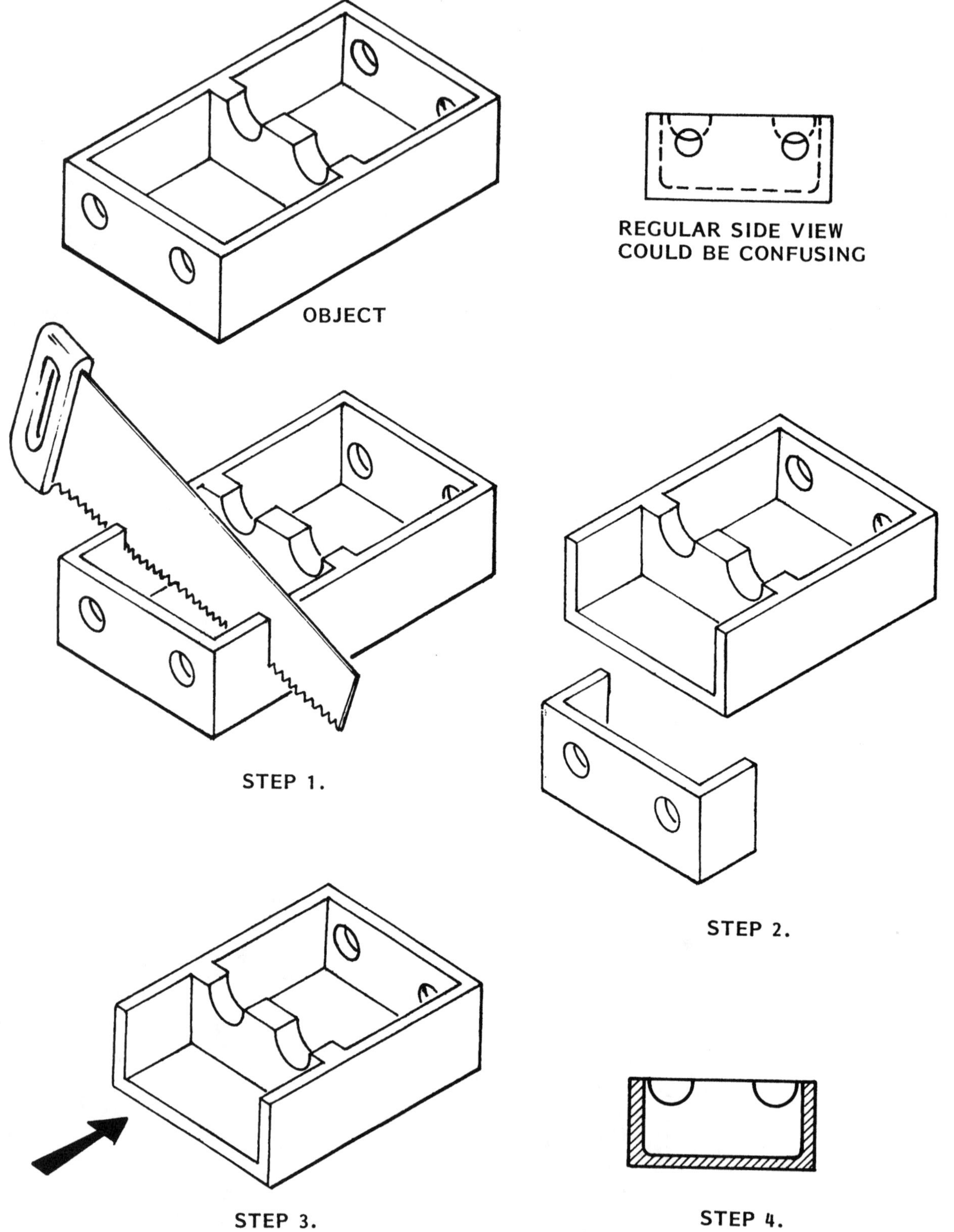

FIGURE 14–4
Constructing a Sectional Drawing

Step 2. Throw away the part you cut off and do not think of it again.

Step 3. Look into the part that is left.

Step 4. Draw the shape of what you see. Place the sectional view in the standard view arrangement—for example, right side, left side, top, bottom.

Occasionally, sections are placed away from the other views to show details. Put section or crosshatch lines on the part that was cut. You can think of putting saw marks on the part of the object that the saw actually touched. Section lines are often drawn at a 45° angle and are spaced approximately 1/10″ apart. They may be spaced wider apart on very large drawings.

HATCH PATTERNS

Section lining in AutoCAD can take many forms. You will find these patterns listed in the Boundary Hatch dialog box along with a view of any pattern you select.

In this chapter you will use these patterns:
U: the standard equally spaced, solid lines
A curved line symbolizing wood
MUDST: a standard for symbolizing concrete
EARTH: a standard for symbolizing the earth
Other patterns of your choice under hatch patterns

Showing Hatch Patterns in the Boundary Hatch Dialog Box

Figure 14–5 describes how to show the pattern for any of the predefined hatch patterns in AutoCAD:

Step 1. *Click:* **Hatch. . . from the Draw menu or the Draw toolbar** (or *Type:* **H** ↵). **The Boundary Hatch dialog box appears.**

Step 2. *Click:* **the down arrow on the Pattern: button to find the pattern you want to view.**

Click: **the pattern, and the new pattern appears in the Swatch: area.**

Step 3. *Click:* **Swatch: (or the ellipsis—the three dots to the right of the Pattern: box) and the Hatch Pattern Palette appears.**

Click: **one of the tabs to view the next page of patterns.**

Click: **the picture of the pattern you want to make it current.**

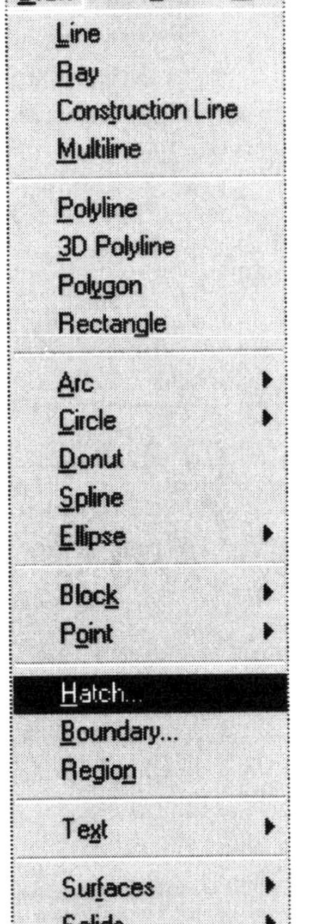

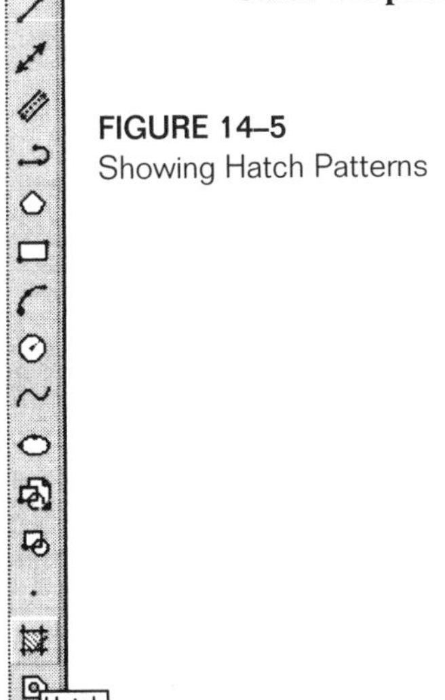

FIGURE 14–5
Showing Hatch Patterns

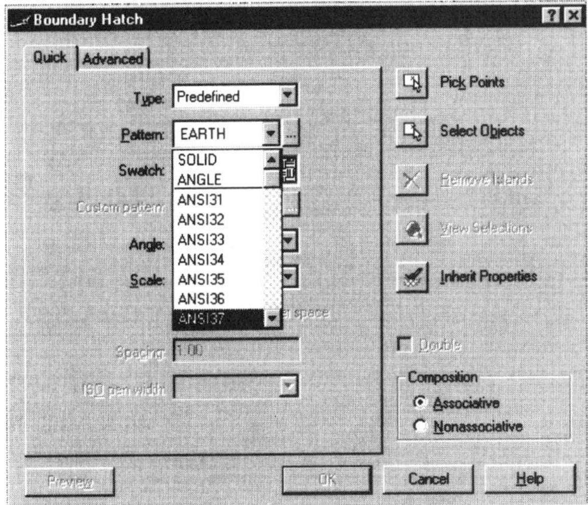

Other Buttons and Features of the Boundary Hatch Dialog Box

ISO pen width: If you select one of the 14 ISO (International Organization of Standardization) patterns on the ISO tab, you can select a pen width for the pattern when you plot. Each of these pattern names begins with ISO.

Custom tab: This tab shows a custom pattern name when you have defined one.

Scale: This allows you to enlarge or shrink the hatch pattern to fit the drawing. It is not available if you have selected User Defined in the Pattern Type box.

Angle: Allows you to specify an angle for the hatch pattern relative to the X axis of the current UCS. For now only the world UCS is used. Other UCSs will be used in the chapters on 3-D.

Spacing: Allows you to specify the space between lines on a user-defined hatch pattern.

Double When you pick this button so that a check appears in it, the area is hatched with a second set of lines at 90° to the first hatch pattern. The pattern must be user defined.

Pick Points Allows you to pick points inside a boundary to specify the area to be hatched.

Select Objects Allows you to select the outside edges of the boundary to specify the area to be hatched.

Remove Islands Allows you to remove from the boundary set objects defined as islands by the Pick Points option. You cannot remove the outer boundary.

View Selections Displays the currently defined boundary set. This option is not available when no selection or boundary has been made.

Advanced Tab Displays the Advanced Options shown at the end of the description of the Boundary Hatch dialog box.

Preview Allows you to preview the hatch pattern before you apply it to the drawing.

Inherit Properties Allows you to pick an existing hatch pattern to specify the properties of that pattern. The pattern picked must be associative (attached to and defined by its boundary).

Associative When a check appears in this button, the hatch pattern stretches when the area that has been hatched is stretched.

Nonassociative When you pick this button so that a check appears in it, the hatch pattern is applied as individual line segments instead of a single entity. If you think you may have an overlapping hatch pattern, you should bring in the pattern exploded (nonassociative) and then use the Trim command to correct the overlap.

OK Allows you to apply the hatch pattern to the drawing.

Advanced Tab

When you pick the Advanced tab, the Advanced Options appear:

Island detectionstyle: Hatch Style: options, Figure 14–6

> **Normal** When style is set to Normal (and a selection set is composed of areas inside other areas), alternating areas are hatched as shown in the Advanced tab on the left.
>
> **Outer** When style is set to Outer (and a selection set is composed of areas inside other areas), only the outer area is hatched as shown in the Advanced tab in the center.
>
> **Ignore** When style is set to Ignore (and a selection set is composed of areas inside other areas), all areas are hatched as shown in the Advanced tab on the right.

Retain Boundaries Specifies whether the boundary objects will remain in your drawing after hatching is completed.

Object type: Controls the type of the new boundary object. When the boundary is created, AutoCAD uses a region or polyline. For now this box should read Polyline.

New Allows you to create a new hatch boundary

Island detection method Flood allows you to use islands; Ray casting does not.

FIGURE 14–6
Advanced Options for Hatching

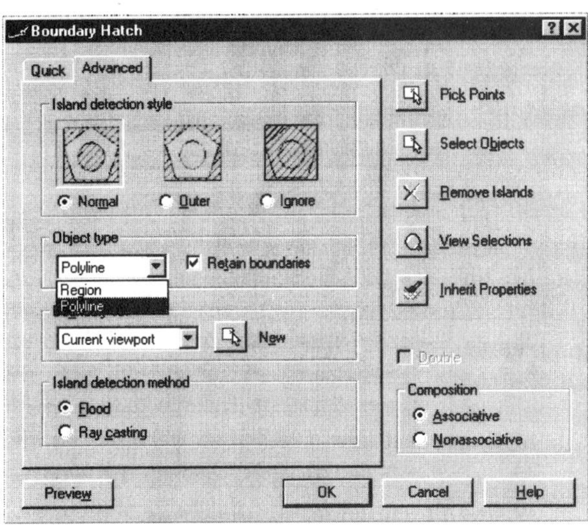

Using Hatch to Make Sectional Drawings

Warning: Those of you who are still working on your floppy disk are even more likely to lose some of your work with Hatch. Hatching often creates a huge drawing file. Be aware of how large that file is and be sure it will fit comfortably on your floppy disk when you save it.

In Exercise 14–1 the Hatch command is used so that you will have the experience of selecting objects to create a boundary for the hatch pattern. Picking points inside an area often creates a boundary more easily but you need to know both methods. Exercises 14–2 and 14–3 use Hatch with the pick points option to create the boundary.

Exercise 14–1: Placing Hatch Patterns on a Single Part

The given drawing (Figure 14–7) contains a front view and a side view. The side view should be shown as a sectional view. (It will be to your advantage to place hatching on a layer different from the one containing the other lines of the drawing.) Your final drawing will look similar to the drawing in Figure 14–7.

Set Up the Drawing

Step 1. To begin Exercise 14–1, turn on the computer and start AutoCAD.

Step 2. Use a template to begin Exercise 14–1.

FIGURE 14–7
Placing Hatch Patterns on a Simple Part

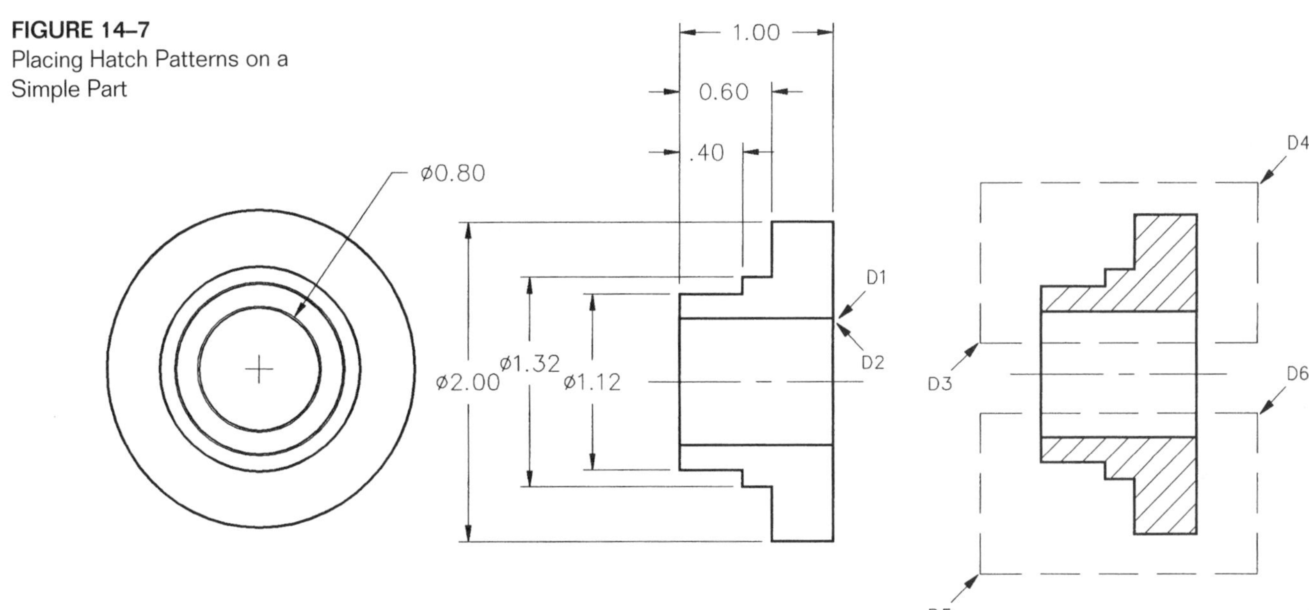

Prompt	Response
The AutoCAD 2002 Today window appears:	*Click:* **Template (from the Create Drawings tab)**
The Template alphabet list appears:	*Click:* **E**, then *Click:* **the template labeled ex10-1(your initials).dwt (If you cannot find the template,** *Click:* **Start from Scratch** and **English and make the settings in step 3.)**

Step 3. Check to make sure that the following settings have been made:

Units: Decimal—2 digits to the right of the decimal point

LIMITS: Lower left corner: 0,0
Upper right corner: 11,8.5

GRID: .25

SNAP: .125

TEXT STYLE: Standard FONT: simplex.shx HEIGHT: 0

LAYERS: NAME	Color	Linetype	Lineweight
Layer 1	Red	CONTINUOUS	0.25 mm
Layer 2	Magenta	CONTINUOUS	0.50 mm
Layer 3	Green	HIDDEN	0.35 mm

Set Layer2 current.

Step 4. Use Zoom-All to view the entire drawing area.

Draw the Figure without Hatching and Prepare It for Hatching

Step 5. On your own:
Use the Line and Mirror commands to draw only the right side view of Figure 14–7 using the dimensions shown. Do not dimension the drawing.

Step 6. Set Layer 1 current.

Step 7. Prepare the areas to be hatched.
If the views to be hatched have already been drawn, it is often necessary to break some of the lines so the area to be hatched does not contain lines that extend outside the area. To do this, use the Break command in this manner:

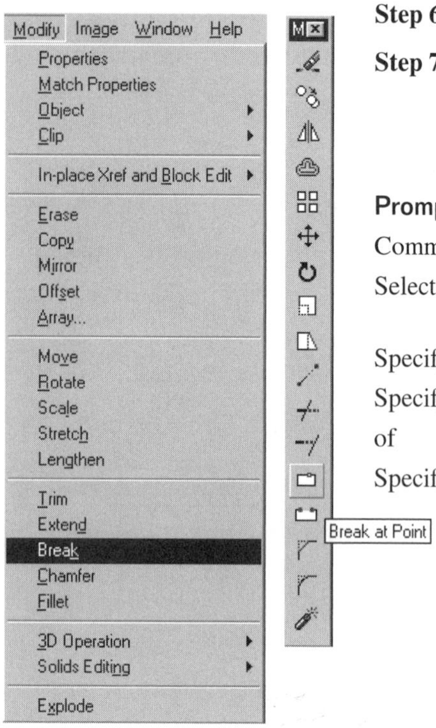

Modify Image Window Help
Properties
Match Properties
Object
Clip
In-place Xref and Block Edit
Erase
Copy
Mirror
Offset
Array...
Move
Rotate
Scale
Stretch
Lengthen
Trim
Extend
Break
Chamfer
Fillet
3D Operation
Solids Editing
Explode

Break at Point

Prompt	Response
Command:	Break (or *Type:* **BR** ↵)
Select object:	*Click:* **D1** (Select the vertical line.) (Figure 14–7)
Specify second break point or [First point]:	*Type:* **F** ↵
Specify first break point:	**Osnap-Intersection**
of	**D2**
Specify second break point	*Type:* @ ↵

Note: If you use Break at Point from the toolbar, only one pick is necessary. Try both methods so you know how both perform.

Be sure to perform the break on both vertical lines at the top and bottom areas to be hatched. After both areas to be hatched have been properly prepared, proceed as follows:

Hatch the Drawing

Step 8. Hatch the areas.

Prompt	Response
Command:	*Click:* **Hatch** (or *Type:* **H↵**)
The Boundary Hatch dialog box appears:	*Click:* **User defined** in the Type: list↵
	Type: **45** in the Angle: box
	Type: **.08** in the Spacing box
	Click: **Select Objects**
Select objects:	**D3**
Specify opposite corner:	**D4**
8 found. Select objects.	**D5**
Specify opposite corner:	**D6**
Select objects:	↵
The Boundary Hatch dialog box appears as shown in Figure 14–8:	*Click:* **OK**

Both top and bottom halves of the right-side view should now be hatched to complete the figure.

Step 9. On your own:

1. **Setup Layout1 so you can plot the drawing full scale:**

   Click: **Layout1** at the bottom of your screen, *Click:* **OK** in the Page Setup dialog box, *Click:* any point on the outside edge of the paper space viewport and *Select:* the **Properties** command on the Modify menu. *Click:* **1:1** on the Standard scale list.

   Insert your 8.5″ × 11″ horizontal format around the drawing full scale. Complete the title block as described at the end of this chapter.
2. **Save your drawing in at least two places.**
3. **Plot the drawing full size** (1 Plotted inch = 1 Drawing unit) on an 8.5″ × 11″ sheet.
4. **Exit AutoCAD.**

Now, use Boundary Hatch to place some of the same hatch patterns on an assembly section drawing (Figure 14–9).

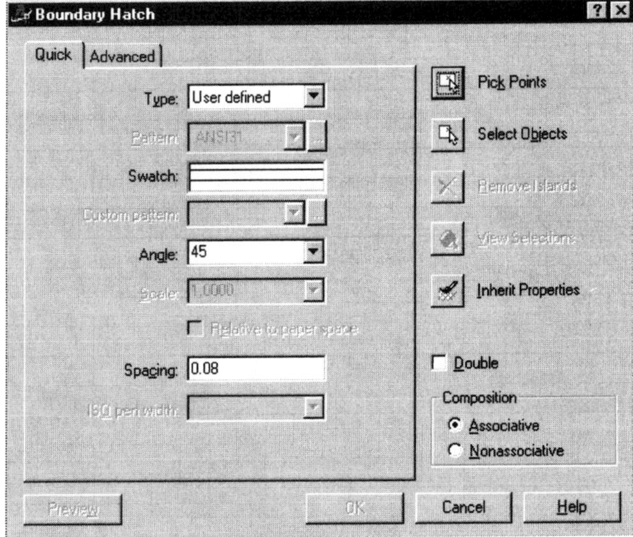

FIGURE 14–8
Boundary Hatch Dialog Box with 45° Angle

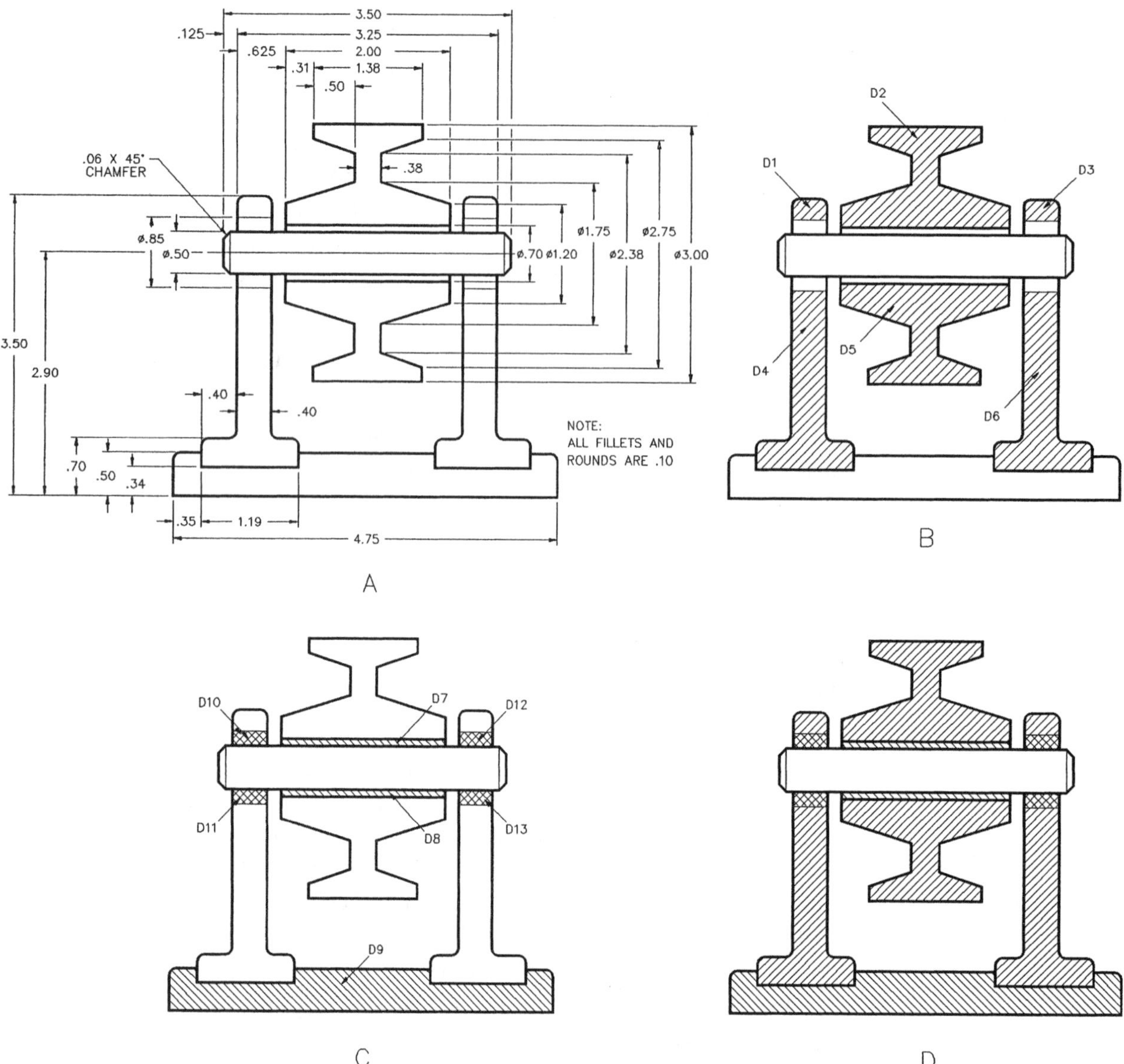

FIGURE 14–9
Placing Hatch Patterns on an Assembly Section Drawing

Exercise 14–2: Placing Hatch Patterns on an Assembly Section Drawing

Set Up the Drawing

Step 1. To begin Exercise 14–2, turn on the computer and start AutoCAD.

Step 2. Use a template to begin Exercise 14–2.

Prompt	Response
The AutoCAD 2002 Today window appears:	*Click:* **Template (from the Create Drawings tab)**
The Template alphabet list:	*Click:* **E**, then *Click:* **the template labeled ex10-1(your initials).dwt** (or *Click:* **Start from Scratch,** then **English** and make the settings in step 3.)
	Click: **OK**

Step 3. Check to make sure that the following settings have been made:

Units: Decimal—2 digits to the right of the decimal point

LIMITS: Lower left corner: 0,0
Upper right corner: 11,8.5

GRID: .25

SNAP: .125

TEXT STYLE: Standard FONT:simplex.shx HEIGHT: 0

LAYERS: NAME	Color	Linetype	Lineweight
Layer3	Green	HIDDEN	0.35 mm
Layer1	Red	CONTINUOUS	0.25 mm
Layer2	Magenta	CONTINUOUS	0.50 mm

Set Layer2 current.

Step 4. Use Zoom-All to view the entire drawing area.

Draw the Figure without Hatching

Step 5. On your own:

1. Use the Line, Fillet, Chamfer, Offset, and Mirror commands to draw the assembly using the dimensions shown in Figure 14–9A.
2. Set layer R current.

Hatch the Drawing

Step 6. Hatch the areas shown in Figure 14–9B.

Prompt	Response
Command:	*Select:* **Hatch. . .** (or *Type:* **H** ↵)
	Click: **the Quick tab**
The Boundary Hatch dialog box, Figure 14–8, appears:	*Click:* **the down arrow in the Type: button**
	Click: **User-defined so that it appears in the button as shown**
	Click: **the Angle: button and use the down arrow to select 45 as shown**
	Click: **the Spacing: button, highlight or backspace over anything in this box, and** *Type:* **.08**

All other buttons in the Boundary Hatch dialog box should appear as shown in Figure 14–8.

Prompt	Response
	Click: **Pick Points**
Select internal point:	**D1,D2,D3,D4,D5,D6** (Figure 14–9B)
Select internal point:	↵
The Boundary Hatch dialog box appears:	*Click:* **Preview**
<Hit enter or right click to return to the dialog>	***Right-click***
The Boundary Hatch dialog box appears:	*Click:* **OK** (if the preview shows the hatching to be correct; if it is not correct, find out what is wrong and correct it)

Prompt	Response
Command:	↵ **Repeat BHATCH**
The Boundary Hatch dialog box, Figure 14–10, appears:	*Click:* **the left side of the 4 in 45 and** *Type:* − (so that the angle reads −**45**); then Press: ↵
The Angle: button changes to 315 (the same as −45).	

All other buttons in the Boundary Hatch dialog box should appear as shown in Figure 14–10.

Prompt	Response
	Click: **Pick Points** <
Select internal point:	**D7,D8,** and **D9** (Figure 14–9C)
Select internal point:	↵
The Boundary Hatch dialog box appears:	*Click:* **Preview** (You can skip Preview if you are sure the hatching will be OK.)
<Hit enter or right click to return to the dialog>	***Right-click***
The Boundary Hatch dialog box appears:	*Click:* **OK** (if the preview shows the hatching to be correct; if it is not correct, find out what is wrong and correct it)
Command:	↵ **Repeat BHATCH**
The Boundary Hatch dialog box, Figure 14–11, appears:	*Click:* **the Double check box so a check appears in it as shown in Figure 14–11**

All other buttons in the Boundary Hatch dialog box should appear as shown in Figure 14–11.

Prompt	Response
	Click: **Pick Points**
Select internal point:	**D10,D11,D12,** and **D13** (Figure 14–9C)
Select internal point:	↵

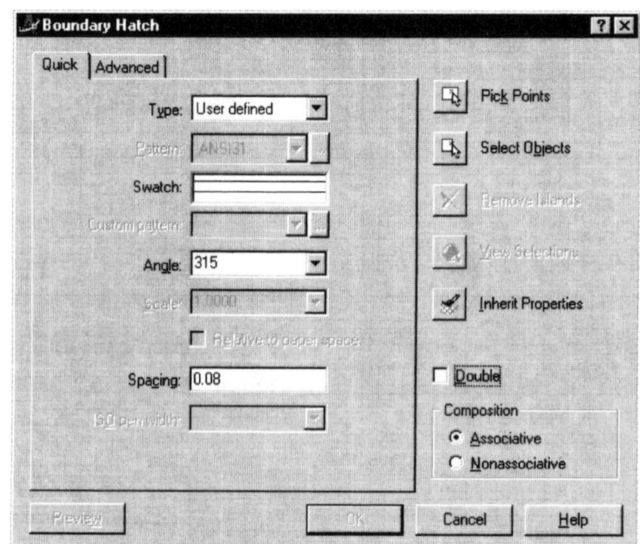

FIGURE 14–10
Boundary Hatch Dialog Box with 315° Angle

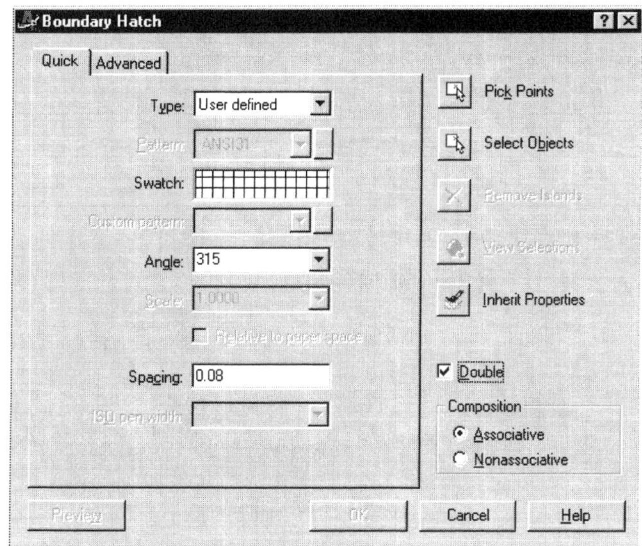

FIGURE 14–11
Boundary Hatch Dialog Box with User-Defined Pattern Double Hatch Selected

Prompt	Response
The Boundary Hatch dialog box appears:	*Click:* **Preview** (You can skip Preview if you are sure the hatching will be OK.)
<Hit enter or right click to return to the dialog>	***Right-click***
The Boundary Hatch dialog box appears:	*Click:* **OK** (if the preview shows the hatching to be correct; if it is not correct, find out what is wrong and correct it)

The complete drawing should now appear with hatching as shown in Figure 14–9D.

Step 7. On your own:

1. **Setup Layout1 so you can plot the drawing full scale:**

   Click: **Layout1** at the bottom of your screen, *Click:* **OK** in the Page Setup dialog box, *Click:* any point on the outside edge of the paper space viewport and *Select:* the **Properties** command on the Modify menu. *Click:* **1:1** on the Standard Scale list (to set the scale of 1=1 for Layout1).

   Insert your 8.5″ × 11″ horizontal format around the drawing full scale. Complete the title block as described at the end of this chapter.
2. Save your drawing in at least two places.
3. Plot the drawing full size (1 Plotted inch = 1 Drawing unit) on an 8.5″ × 11″ sheet.
4. Exit AutoCAD.

Now, make an architectural wall section as shown in Figure 14–12.

Exercise 14–3: Placing Hatch Patterns on an Architectural Wall Section, Figure 14–12

Set Up the Drawing

Step 1. To begin Exercise 14–3, turn on the computer and start AutoCAD.

Step 2. *Click:* **the Create Drawings tab, then Start from Scratch, then English (feet and inches) to begin Exercise 14–3.**

Step 3. Make the following settings:

Units: Architectural

LIMITS: Lower left corner: 0,0

Upper right corner: 17′,11′ (Be sure to include the foot symbols)

GRID: 6

SNAP: 1

TEXT STYLE: Standard FONT: simplex.shx HEIGHT: 0

LAYERS:	NAME	Color	Linetype	Lineweight
	WALL	Magenta	CONTINUOUS	Default
	WOOD	Red	CONTINUOUS	Default
	EARTH	Green	CONTINUOUS	Default
	TEXT	Cyan	CONTINUOUS	Default

Set layer WALL current.

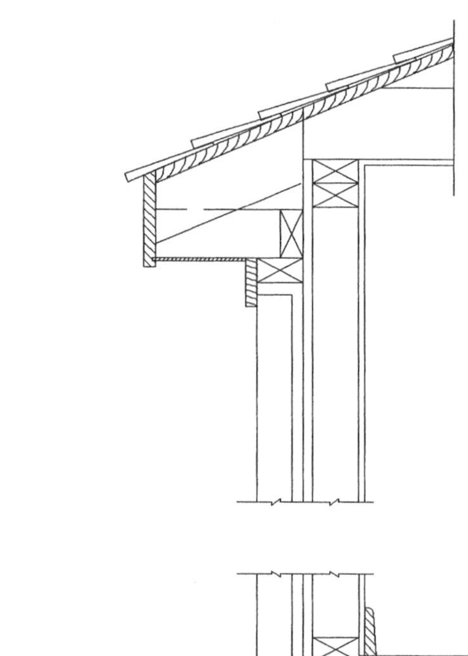

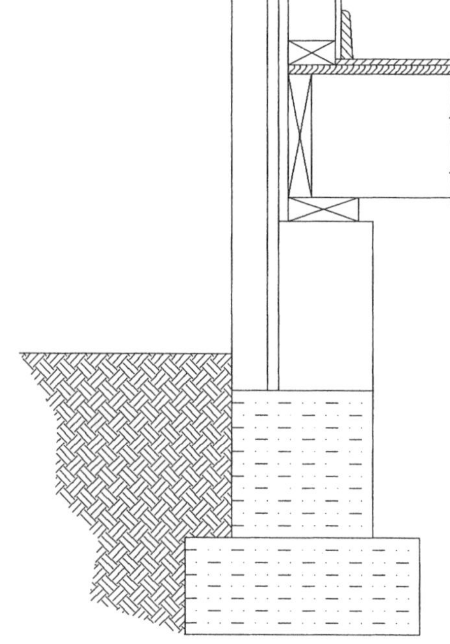

FIGURE 14–12
Wall Section

Step 4. Use Zoom-All to view the entire drawing area.

Draw the Wall without Hatching

Step 5. On your own:

Draw the wall without hatching.

Draw all the wall section components using the dimensions shown in Figure 14–13. Drawing some of the components separately, as shown in Figure 14–14, and copying or moving them into place will be helpful. You will have to approximate the length of some of the components. As long as the drawing looks the same as Figure 14–12 it will be fine for this exercise. After the drawing has been completed, begin hatching as described in step 6.

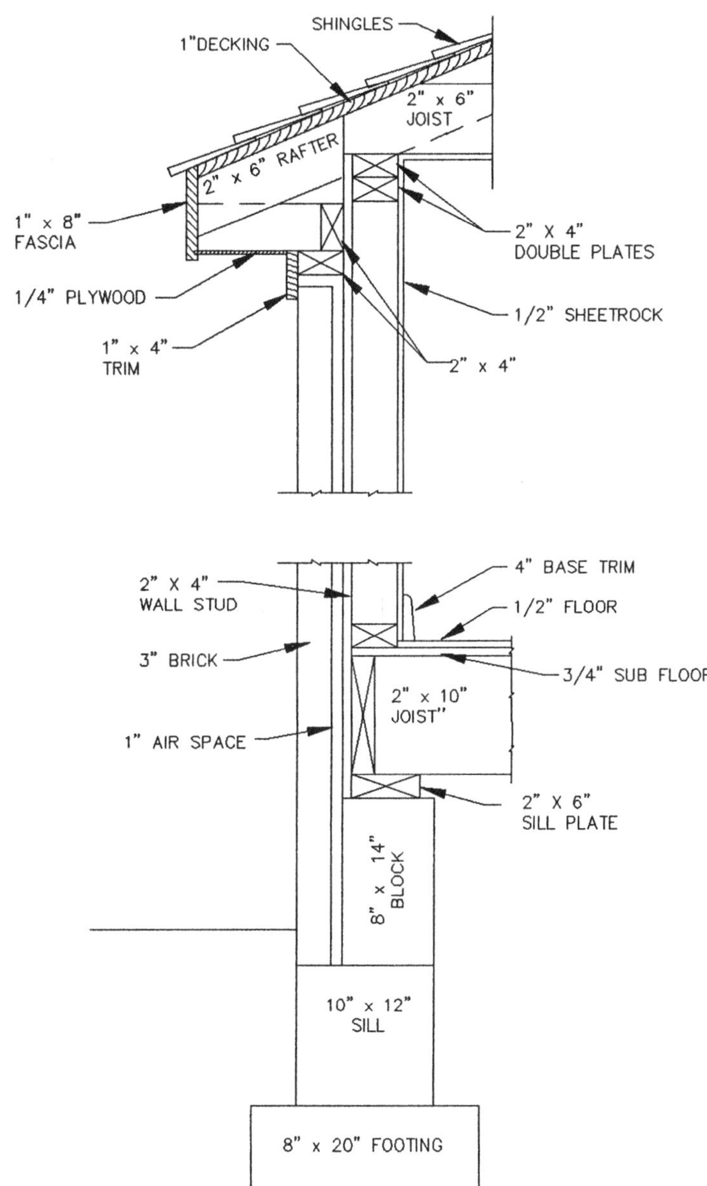

FIGURE 14–13
Dimensions for the Wall Section

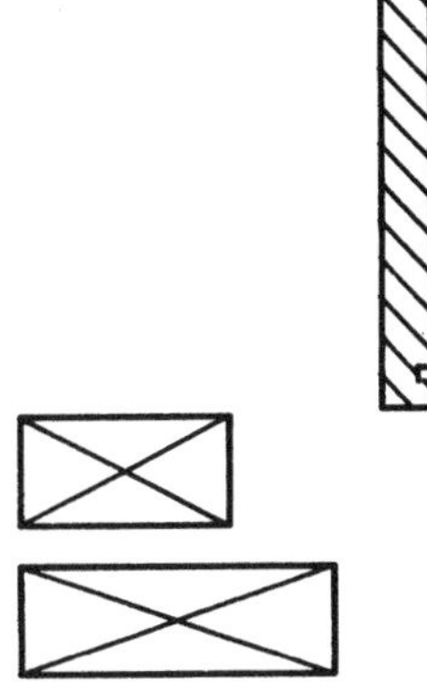

FIGURE 14–14
Draw Some Components Separately

Tip: You can also right-click on OSNAP on the status bar and *Click:* **Settings** to get the Drafting Settings dialog box.

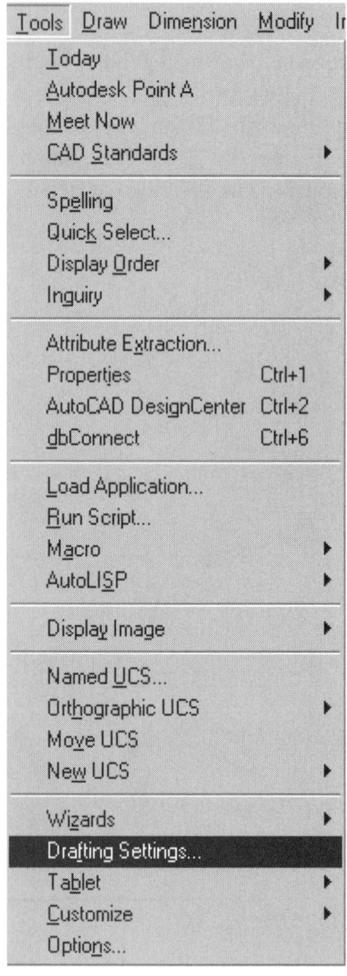

FIGURE 14–15
Running Osnap Settings Endpoint and Intersection

Hatch the Wall Section with Standard Patterns

Step 6. Hatch footing, sill, and the ground.

Before you begin hatching, set running osnap modes so that snapping to endpoints and intersections will be automatic:

Prompt	Response
Command:	*Click:* **Drafting Settings. . .**
The Drafting Settings dialog box, Figure 14–15, appears:	*Click:* **Endpoint and Intersection buttons so that a check appears in those buttons as shown**

Now proceed with the hatching of the wall section, Figure 14–16.

Prompt	Response
Command:	*Type:* **HATCH** ↵
Enter a pattern name or [?/Solid/User defined]<ANSI 31>:	*Type:* **EARTH** ↵
Specify a scale for the pattern <1.0000>:	*Type:* **10** ↵
Specify an angle for the pattern <0>:	*Type:* **135** ↵
Select objects:	↵
Retain polyline boundary? [Yes/No]<N>	↵
Specify start point:	**D1** (Figure 14–16A)
Specify next point or [Arc/Close/Length/Undo]:	**D2, D3, D4, D5, D6, D7, D8, D9**
Specify next point or [Arc/Close/Length/Undo]:	*Type:* **C** ↵
Specify start point for new boundary or <apply hatch>:	↵
Command:	*Click:* **Hatch. . .** (or *Type:* **H** ↵)

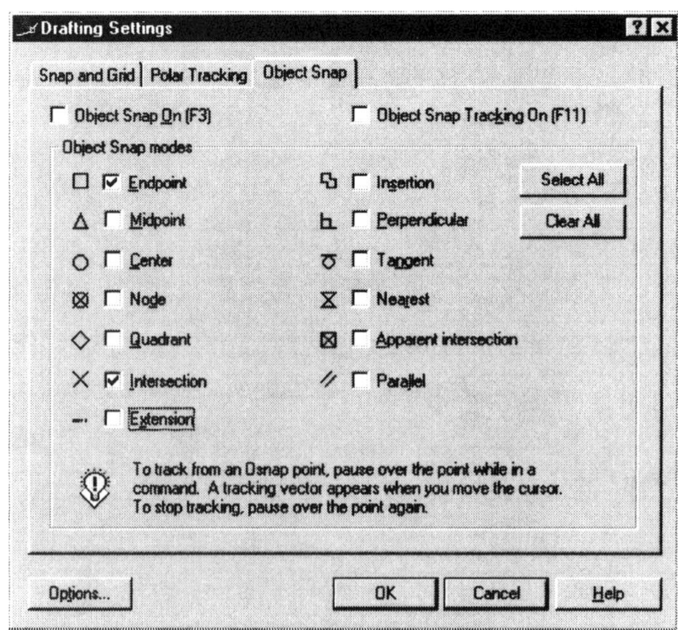

FIGURE 14–16
EARTH and MUDST Hatching

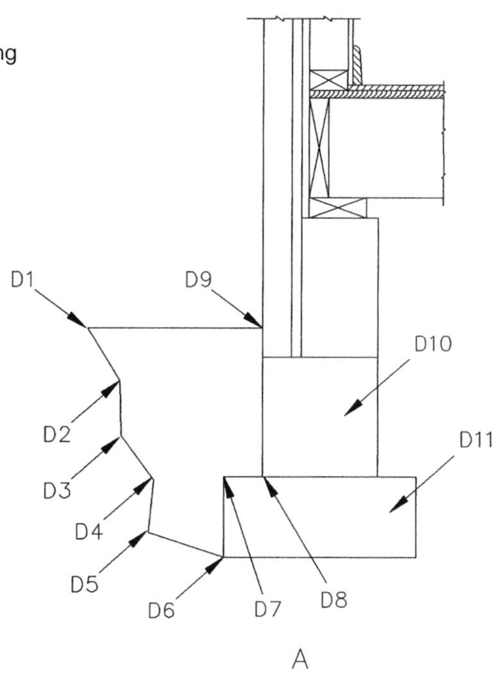

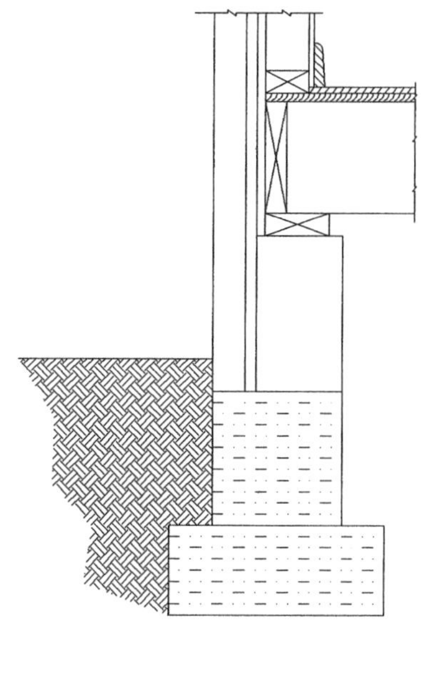

Prompt	Response
The Boundary Hatch dialog box, Figure 14–17, appears:	*Click:* **the Pattern: down arrow and select the MUDST pattern**
	Double-click: **the Scale button and** *Type:* **5**

All other buttons in the Boundary Hatch dialog box should appear as shown in Figure 14–17.

Prompt	Response
	Click: **Pick Points**

FIGURE 14–17
Boundary Hatch Dialog Box with MUDST Pattern Selected

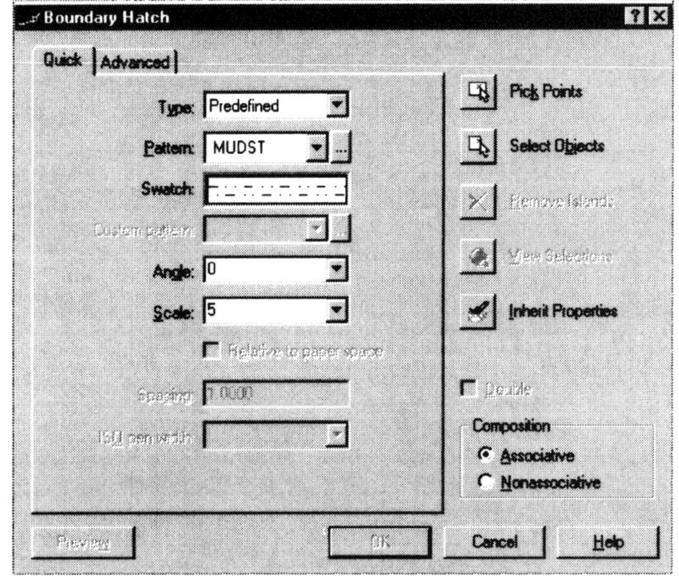

Prompt	Response
Select internal point:	**D10** and **D11,** Figure 14–16A
Select internal point:	↵
The Boundary Hatch dialog box appears:	*Click:* **Apply (if you are reasonably sure the hatching will be correct; if not,** *Click:* **Preview and proceed as before)**

The hatching should appear as shown in Figure 14–16B.

Step 7. Hatch areas using the 45° U pattern.

The fascia, 1″ × 4″ trim, floor, and subfloor may all be hatched using the standard 45° or 135° User-defined patterns, Spacing: .5 as shown in Figures 14–16B and 14–18. Use the same sequence of steps as you used to complete parts of Figure 14–7.

Hatch Using a Rotated Array

Step 8. Draw the wood grain pattern.

Occasionally it may become necessary to create a different pattern from the standard ones available. To create a wood grain such as the one shown in Figure 14–18, the Spline command is used. Begin by enlarging an area for creating the pattern:

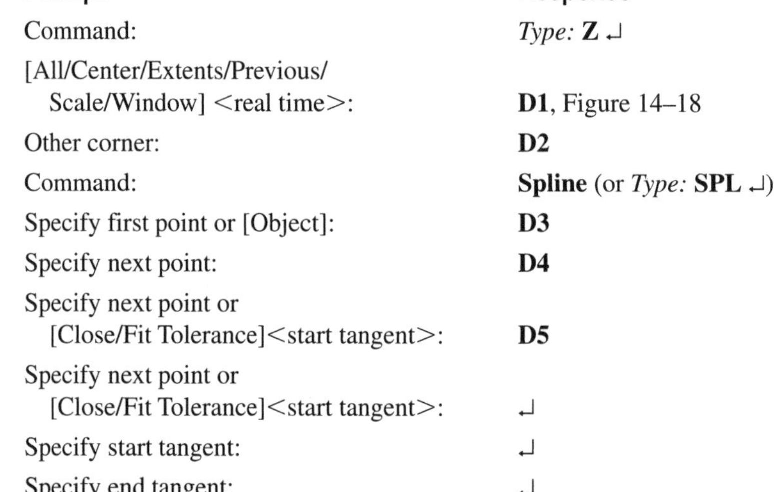

Prompt	Response
Command:	*Type:* **Z** ↵
[All/Center/Extents/Previous/ Scale/Window] <real time>:	**D1**, Figure 14–18
Other corner:	**D2**
Command:	**Spline** (or *Type:* **SPL** ↵)
Specify first point or [Object]:	**D3**
Specify next point:	**D4**
Specify next point or [Close/Fit Tolerance]<start tangent>:	**D5**
Specify next point or [Close/Fit Tolerance]<start tangent>:	↵
Specify start tangent:	↵
Specify end tangent:	↵

Step 9. Array the Spline at an angle to form the wood pattern.

Prompt	Response
Command:	**Array** (or *Type:* **AR** ↵)
The Array dialog box appears:	*Click:* **Select Objects**
Select objects:	**D4** (again)
Select objects:	↵
The Array dialog box appears:	*Click:* **Rectangular Array**
	Type: **1** in the Rows: box
	Type: **30** in the Columns: box

This may be too many or too few, so choose the number of lines you think you need to fill the area. If you choose more than enough, you can erase those you don't need.

Prompt	Response
	Click: **the Column offset: arrow** (on the right)

FIGURE 14–18
Creating a Wood Pattern

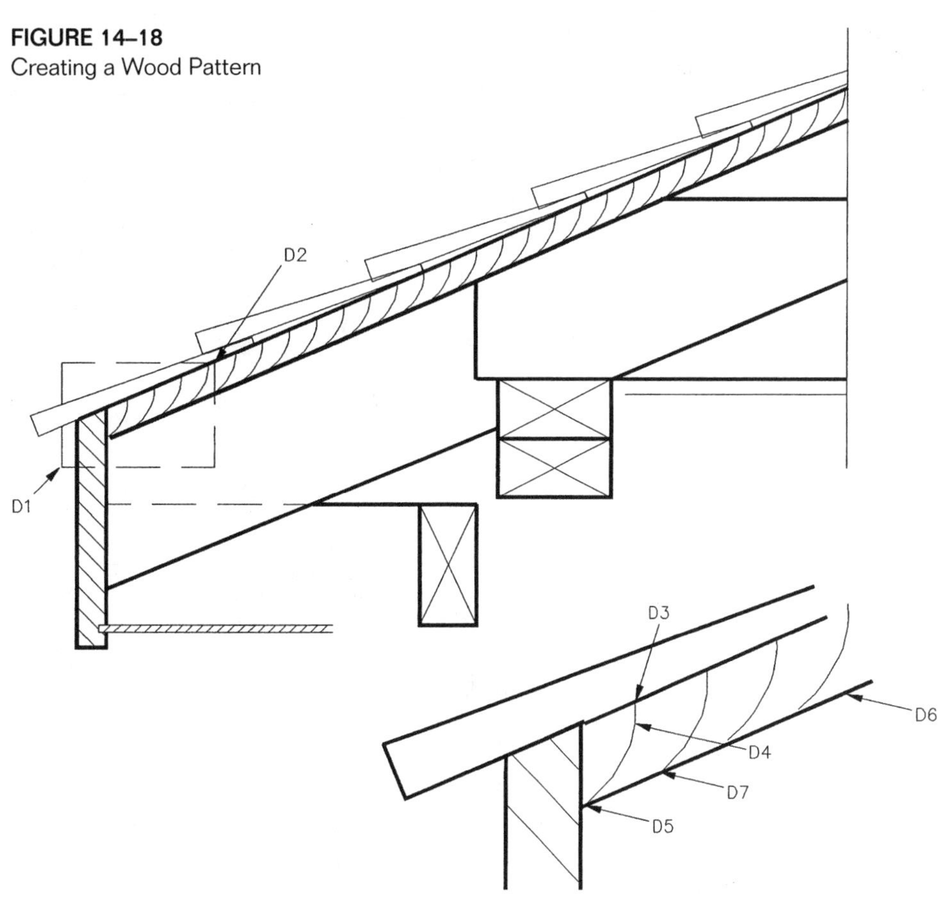

Prompt	Response
Specify the distance between columns (111):	**D5** (again)
Specify second point:	**D7** (Click a point the approximate distance shown.)
The Array dialog box appears:	*Click:* **the Angle of array: arrow** (on the right)
Specify angle of array:	**D5** (again)
Specify second point:	**Osnap-Nearest**
to	**D6** (any point on this line)
The Array dialog box appears:	*Click:* **OK**

Step 10. On your own:

1. **Draw the shingles and array them in a similar manner.** You will have to draw the first one; Copy it and Rotate the copy so that the second shingle rests on top of the first, then use the Array command.
2. **Setup Layout1 so you can plot the drawing full scale:** *Click:* **Layout1** at the bottom of your screen, *Click:* **OK** in the Page Setup dialog box. *Click:* any point on the outside edge of the paper space viewport and *Select:* the **Properties** command on the Modify menu. *Click:* **1″= 1′** on the Standard Scale list to set the scale of 1″=1′ for Layout1.

   Insert your 17″ × 11″ format around the drawing. Complete the title block as described at the end of this chapter.
3. **Save your drawing in at least two places.**
4. **Plot the drawing full scale on a 17″ × 11″ sheet.**
5. **Exit AutoCAD.**

FIGURE 14–19
BRICK and AR-SHAKE Hatch Patterns

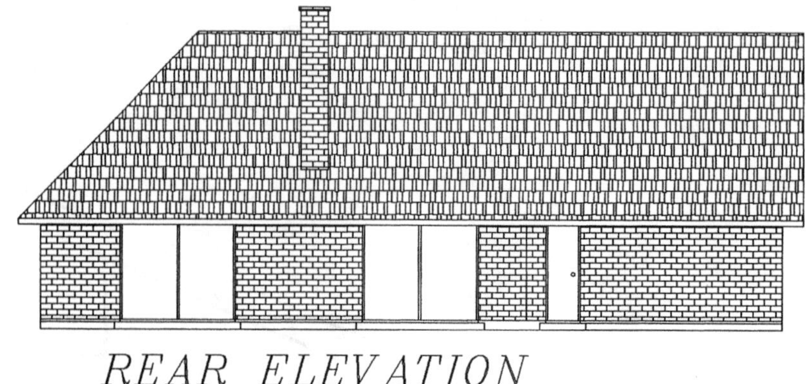

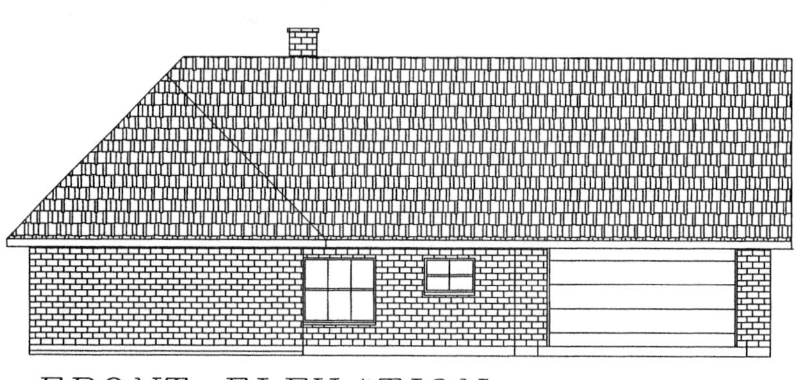

You should now have a wall section complete with hatching. These exercises will give you the information and skills you need to render any type of sectional view. You may use the same skills to place hatch patterns on other types of drawings.

Other Uses for Hatching

The following examples show other uses for hatching using the standard hatch patterns. Figure 14–19 was hatched using BRICK (scale 24) as the pattern for the brick veneer of the elevations, and AR=SHAKE (scale 30) was used to represent shingles.

Figure 14–20 shows shading performed using the DOTS pattern .5, .75, and 1.00. Figure 14–21 shows a geological drawing using LINE, EARTH, and AR-CONC as patterns.

FIGURE 14–20
DOTS Hatch Pattern

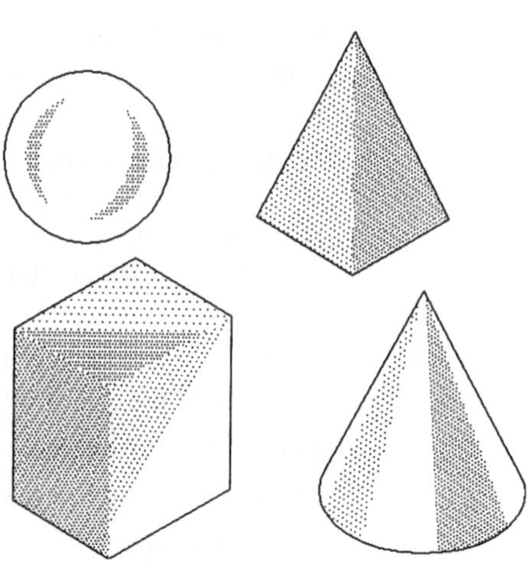

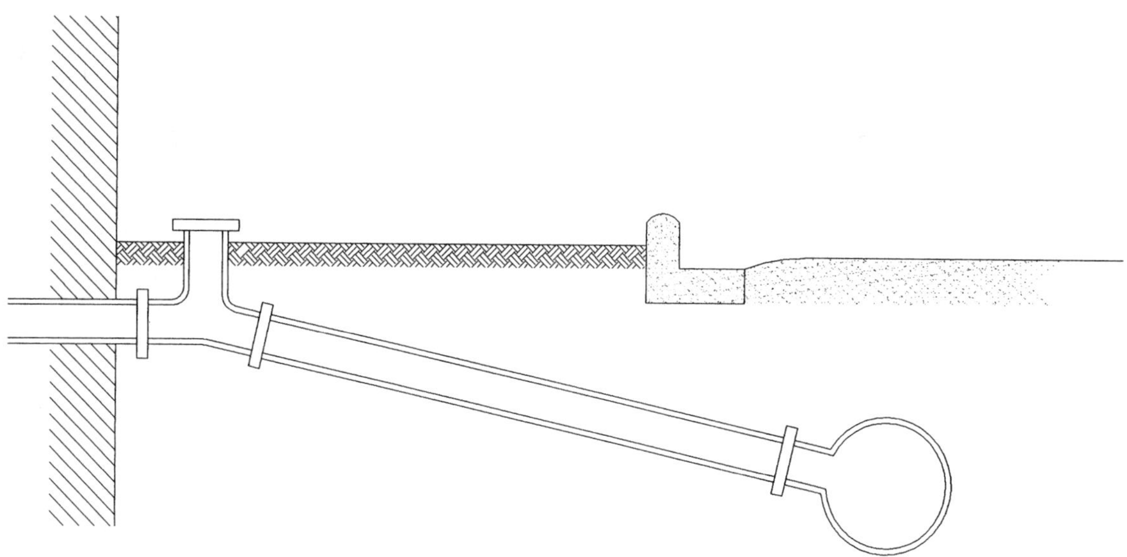

FIGURE 14–21
LINE, EARTH, and AR-CONC Hatch Patterns

You will find many other applications for the Hatch command. You may even decide to create your own Hatch pattern, as explained in detail in the *AutoCAD User's Guide.*

EXERCISES

EXERCISE 14–1. Complete Exercise 14–1 using steps 1 through 9 described in this chapter. Insert your 8½″ × 11″ horizontal format around the drawing full scale. Complete the title block:

Drawing Title: Pipe Flange
Assignment Number: 14–1
Date: Current date
Scale: 1 = 1

Center the drawing in the drawing field. Plot the drawing on an 11″ × 8.5″ sheet.

EXERCISE 14–2. Complete Exercise 14–2 using steps 1 through 7 described in this chapter. Insert your 8½″ × 11″ horizontal format around the drawing full scale. Complete the title block:

Drawing Title: Shaft Support Assembly
Assignment Number: 14–2
Date: Current date
Scale: 1 = 1

Center the drawing in the drawing field. Plot the drawing on an 11″ × 8.5″ sheet.

EXERCISE 14–3. Complete Exercise 14–3 using steps 1 through 12 described in this chapter. Insert your 17″ × 11″ format around the drawing full scale. Complete the title block:

Drawing Title: Wall Section
Assignment Number: 14–3
Date: Current date
Scale: 1 = 1

Center the drawing in the drawing field. Plot the drawing on a horizontal 17″ × 11″ sheet.

EXERCISE 14–4. Open drawing EX14-2 (your initials) and use the SaveAs command to save it as EX14-4 (your initials). Erase everything but the title block, then draw the

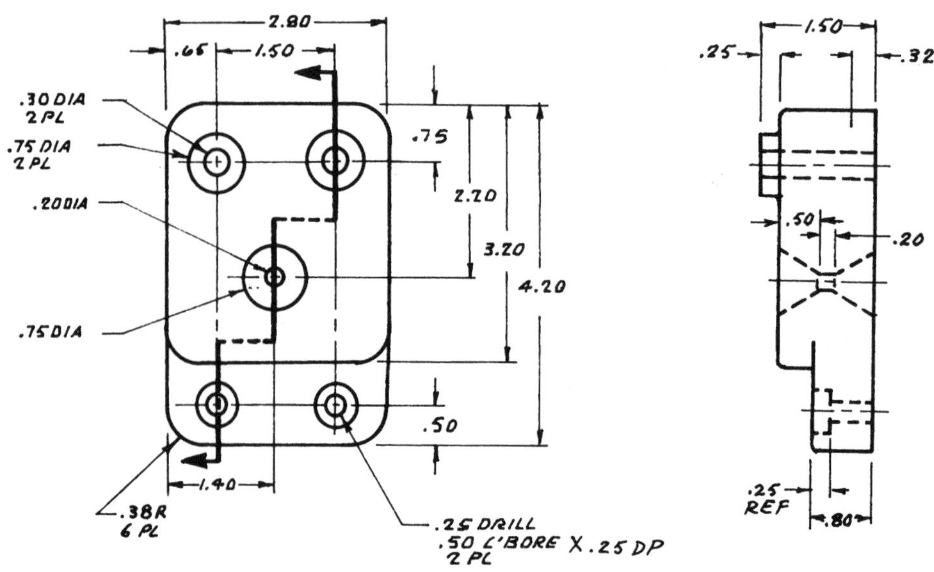

FIGURE 14–22
Exercise 14–4

figure (Figure 14–22) for this exercise full size in the 11″ × 8.5″ format. Draw a front view and a right side view. Make the right side a sectional view. Use ATTEDIT to change:

Drawing Title: Cover
Assignment Number: 14–4
Date: Current date
Scale: 1 = 1

Plot the drawing on a horizontal 11″ × 8.5″ sheet.

EXERCISE 14–5. Open drawing EX14-2 (your initials) and use the SaveAs command to save it as EX14-5 (your initials). Erase everything but the title block, then measure Figure 14–23 for this exercise and draw it twice size on the horizontal 11″ × 8.5″ format. Use hatching as shown. Use ATTEDIT to change. Use a solid fill hatch pattern on the black rectangle.

Drawing Title: Vacuum Switch
Assignment Number: 14–5
Date: Current date
Scale: 2X

Plot the drawing on a horizontal 11″ × 8.5″ sheet.

EXERCISE 14–6. Use settings from Exercise 14–2. Double the dimensions given and make sectional drawings (Figures 14–24, 14–25, and 14–26) of the following figures. Draw all views and insert your A-size horizontal format around each of the drawings. Do not show dimensions. (Upper numbers are in inches; lower numbers are in millimeters.)

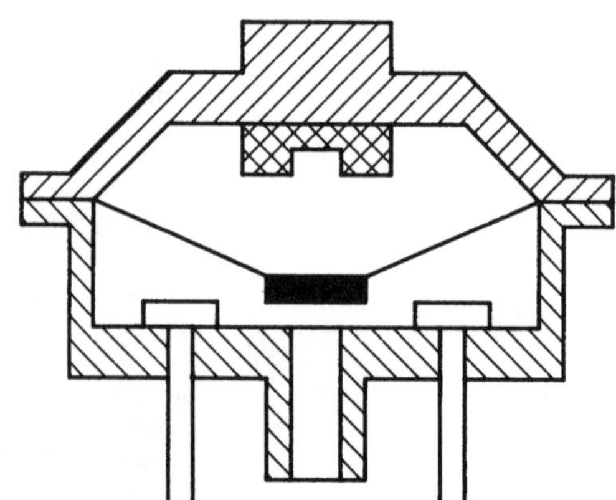

FIGURE 14–23
Exercise 14–5

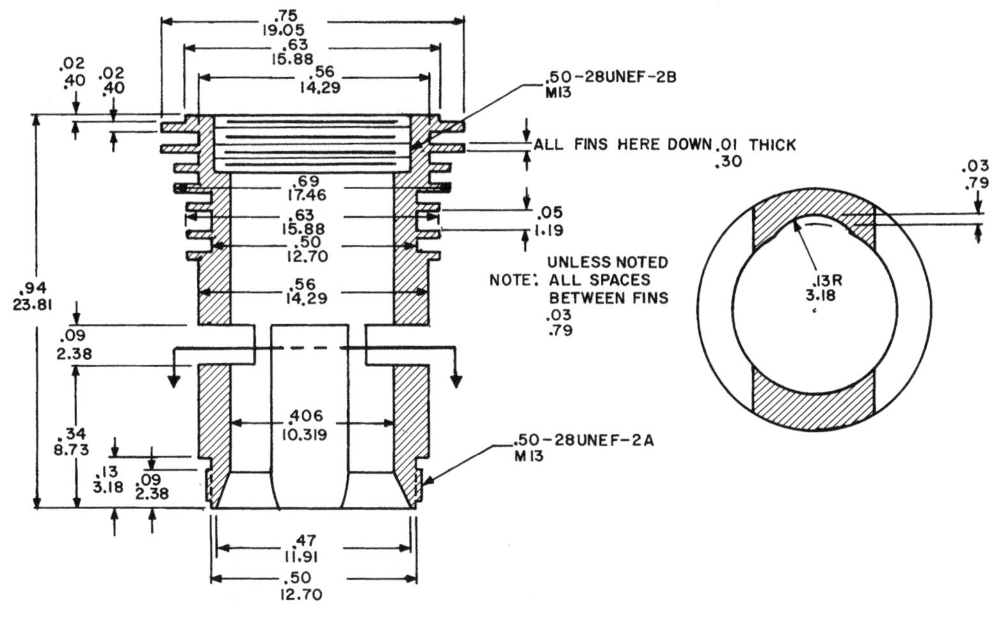

FIGURE 14–24
Exercise 14–6A

FIGURE 14–25
Exercise 12–6B

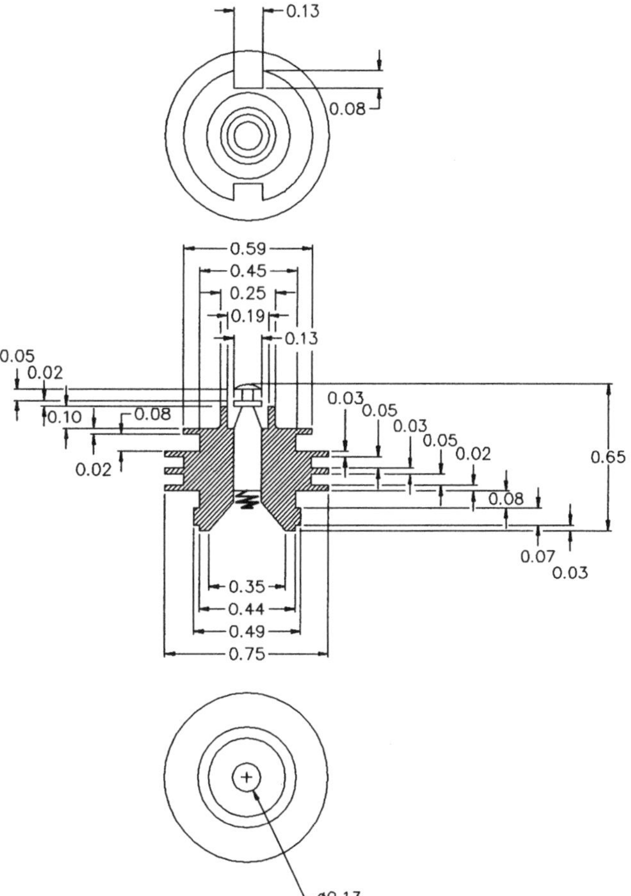

FIGURE 14–26
Exercise 14–6C

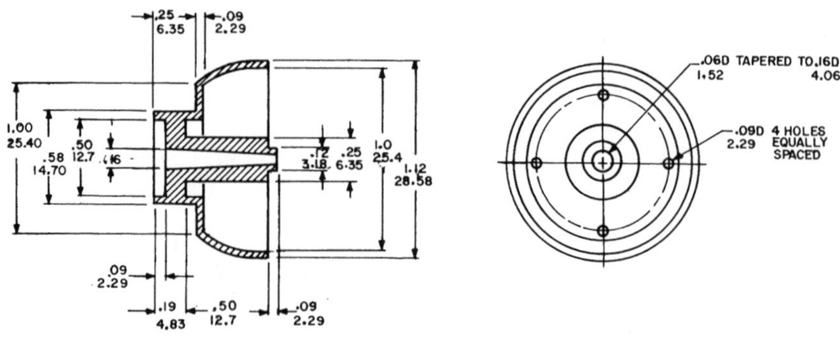

Assignment Numbers	Drawing Title	Scale
14–6A	Cylinder	2X
14–6B	Head	2X
14–6C	Fuel tank	2X

Use the current date. Plot each drawing on an 8.5″ × 11″ sheet.

EXERCISE 14–7. Make a sectional drawing of the crank shown in Figure 14–27. Use settings from Exercise 14–2. Draw all given views and insert a horizontal A-size format around the drawing. Make the drawing four times the dimensions shown. Do not show dimensions. (Upper numbers are in inches; lower numbers are in millimeters.)

Drawing Title: Crank
Assignment Number: 14–7
Scale: 4X

Plot on an 11″ × 8.5″ sheet.

EXERCISE 14–8. Make a drawing of the assembly section shown in Figure 14–28. Measure the drawing and make your drawing twice the size. Show a parts list on the drawing, and draw leaders and index numbers as shown. Your lettering should be simplex, .08″ high. Place it on a horizontal A-size format.

Drawing Title: Routing Holder
Assignment Number: 14–8
Date: Current date
Scale: 1 5 1

Plot on an 11″ × 8.5″ sheet.

EXERCISE 14–9. Make a drawing of the diagram shown in Figure 14–29. Use hatch patterns that are similar to the shaded areas. Make the drawing and lettering twice the size shown. Place the drawing on a B-size format.

Drawing Title: Subcool
Assignment Number: 14–9
Date: Current date
Scale: None

Plot on a 17″ × 11″ sheet.

FIGURE 14–27
Exercise 14–7

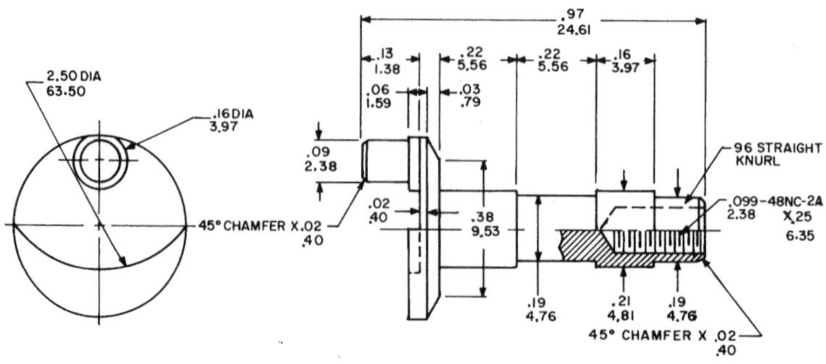

FIGURE 14–28
Exercise 14–8

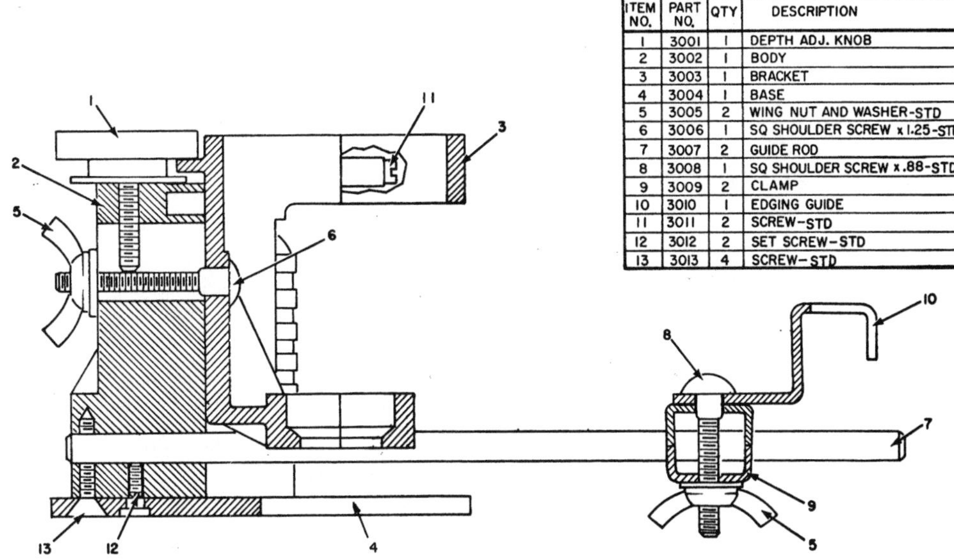

ITEM NO.	PART NO.	QTY	DESCRIPTION
1	3001	1	DEPTH ADJ. KNOB
2	3002	1	BODY
3	3003	1	BRACKET
4	3004	1	BASE
5	3005	2	WING NUT AND WASHER-STD
6	3006	1	SQ SHOULDER SCREW x 1.25-STD
7	3007	2	GUIDE ROD
8	3008	1	SQ SHOULDER SCREW x .88-STD
9	3009	2	CLAMP
10	3010	1	EDGING GUIDE
11	3011	2	SCREW-STD
12	3012	2	SET SCREW-STD
13	3013	4	SCREW-STD

FIGURE 14–29
Exercise 14–9

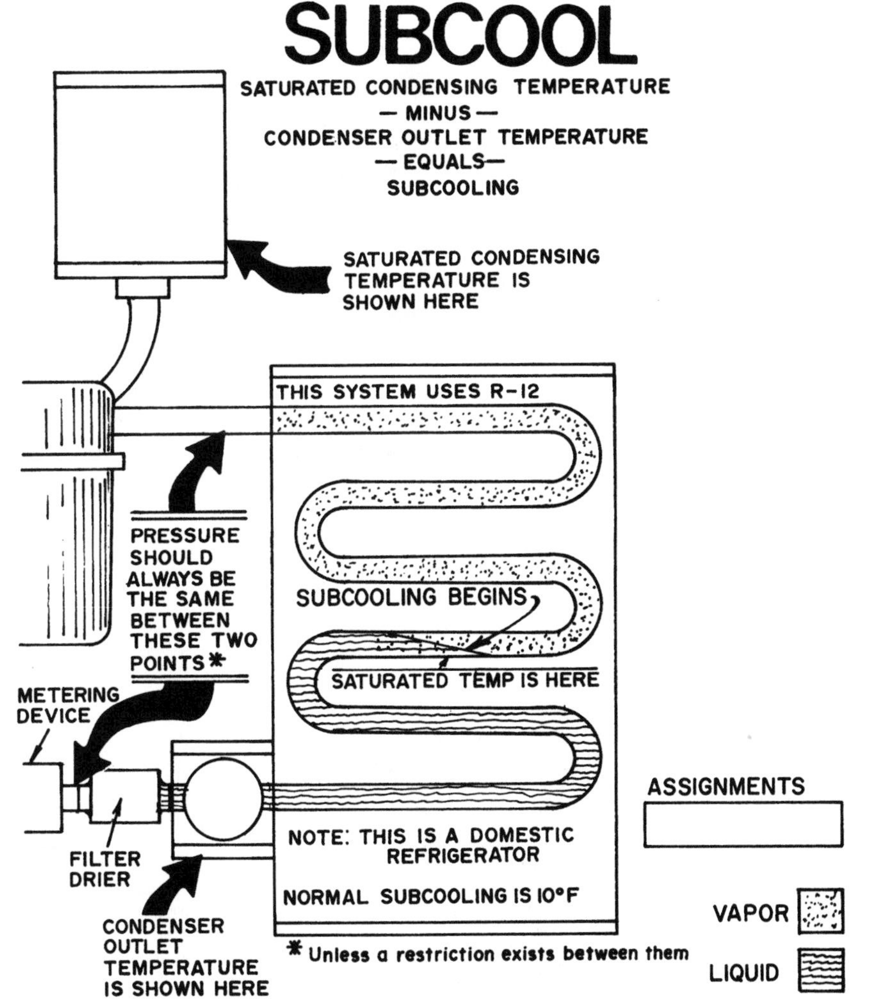

EXERCISE 14–10. Make a drawing similar to Figure 14–30. Approximate any dimensions not shown. Use BRICK and AR=SHAKE patterns at a scale that gives the same appearance as shown. Insert a B-size format around this drawing in Layout1. Use Properties to set a scale for the paper space viewport of ⅛″ = 1′. Complete the title block:

Drawing Title: Elevations
Assignment Number: 14–10
Date: Current date
Scale: ⅛″ = 1′

Center the drawing in the drawing field. Plot on a 17″ × 11″ sheet at a scale of 1=1.

EXERCISE 14–11. Make a drawing of Figure 14–31. (Show only step 4 twice the size.) Use DOTS pattern at a scale that gives the same appearance as shown. Insert an A-size format around the drawing. Complete the title block:

Drawing Title: Illustration
Assignment Number: 14–11
Date: Current date
Scale: Full

Plot on an 11″ × 8.5″ sheet.

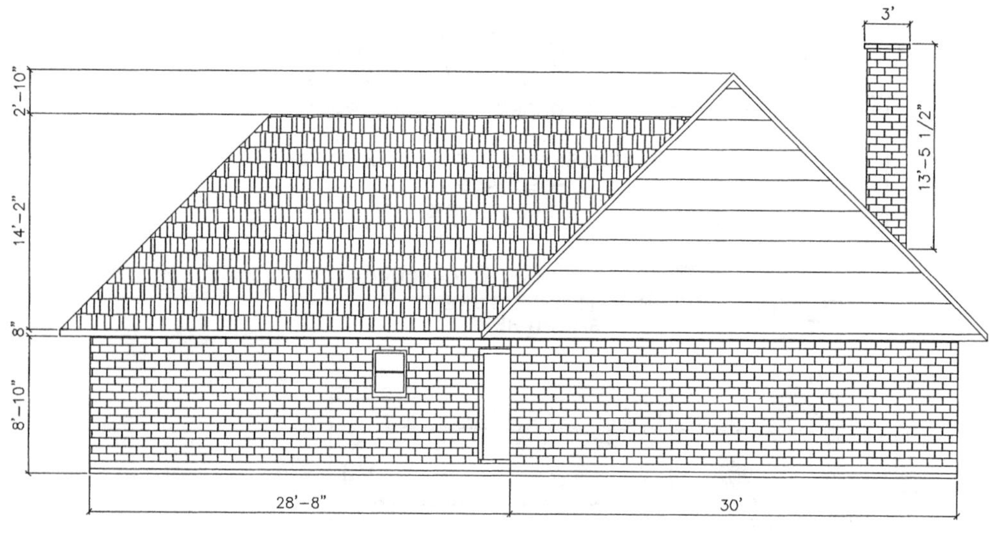

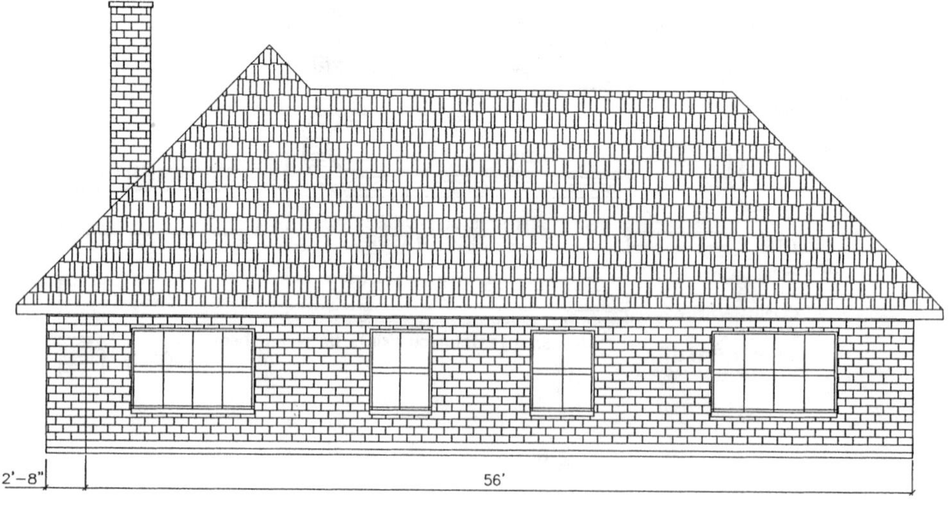

FIGURE 14–30
Exercise 14–10

STEP 1

STEP 2

STEP 3

STEP 4

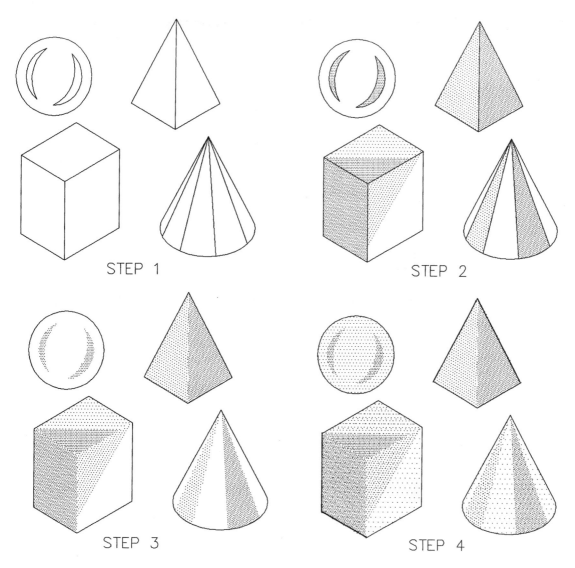

FIGURE 14–31
Exercise 14–11

REVIEW QUESTIONS

Circle the best answer.

1. Which of the following patterns produces continuous, evenly spaced lines?
   a. ANSI31
   b. MUDST
   c. PAT LINE
   d. U-Line
   e. EARTH

2. Which of the following angles produces the User-defined pattern shown?
   a. 45
   b. 90
   c. 0
   d. 135
   e. 105

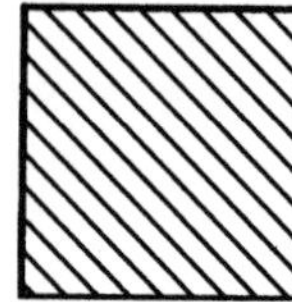

3. Which of the following angles produces the User-defined pattern shown?
   a. 45
   b. 90
   c. 0
   d. 135
   e. 105
4. Which of the following commands can be used to correct an overlapping hatching pattern after it has been exploded?
   a. Array
   b. Change
   c. Move
   d. Trim
   e. Mirror

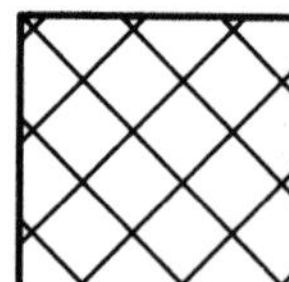

5. Which of the following describes the pattern shown?
   a. X Pat
   b. 45, 145
   c. Double Hatch
   d. Double Section
   e. Line-Two
6. Which of the following entries in the Spacing: button will produce hatch lines ¼″ apart (User-defined pattern)?
   a. 1-4
   b. .25
   c. 2.5
   d. 1,4
   e. 25
7. After a hatching command that spaces lines .10″ apart has been performed, what is the default response in the Spacing: button (original default was .08)?
   a. 0
   b. .10
   c. .08
   d. .125
   e. It is impossible to tell.
8. Which of the following entries in the Spacing: button will produce lines approximately 1⁄12″ apart when the drawing is plotted at a scale of 1″ = 1′ (U pattern)?
   a. 1-12
   b. 1/12
   c. 1
   d. .085
   e. .12
9. Which of the following commands is used to make a smooth curve?
   a. Decurve
   b. Edit vertex
   c. Spline
   d. Curve
   e. Join
10. The Array dialog box allows you to create an array of objects at an angle.
    a. True
    b. False

15 Isometric Drawing

OBJECTIVES

After completing this chapter, you will be able to

- □ Make isometric drawings to scale from two-dimensional drawings.
- □ Correctly answer questions regarding the following commands and features:

Array	Ellipse	Osnap	Toggle
Block	Explode	Polygon	
Break	Isoplane	Snap Style	

ISOMETRIC DRAWING SETTINGS

Note: Isometric drawings are not 3-D objects. This drawing form is a 2-D drawing used to give the appearance of a 3-D object. 3-D objects created in AutoCAD can be viewed from any angle so that a variety of pictures can be made from a single object.

Isometric drawings can be done quickly and easily using AutoCAD software. Once the GRID and SNAP settings are properly made, the drawing itself proceeds with little difficulty. The three isometric axes are 30° right, 30° left, and vertical. All measurements are made full scale on all three axes.

We will begin with four simple shapes (Figure 15–1):

FIGURE 15–1
Isometric Shapes

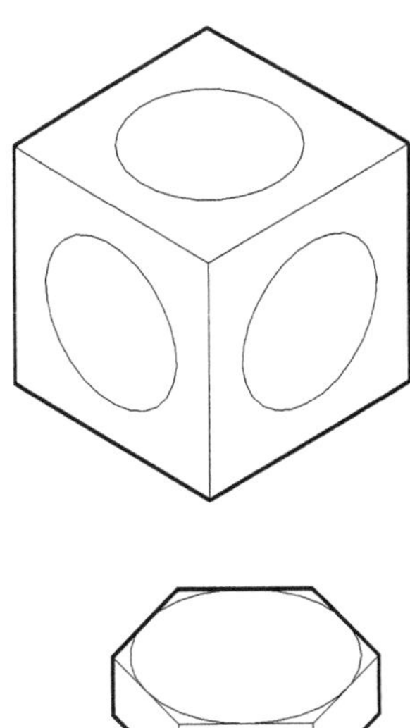

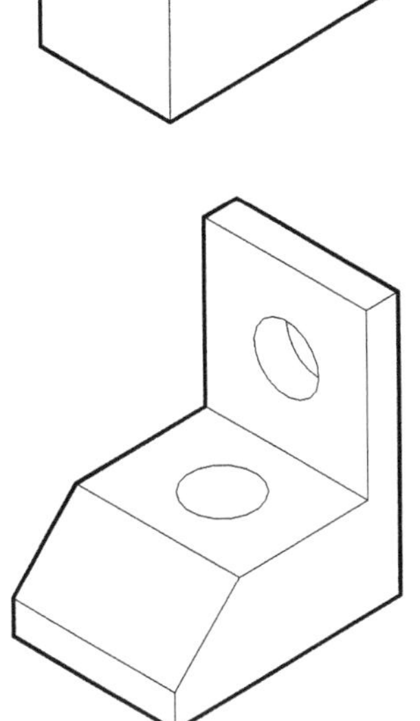

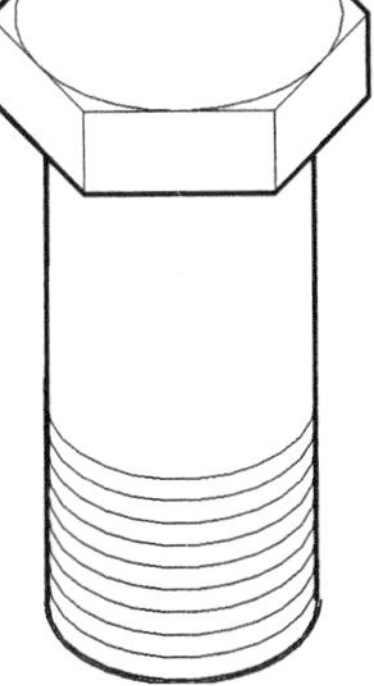

An isometric box
An isometric cube with an ellipse on each of the three isoplanes
An isometric view of a part from a 2-D drawing
An isometric hexagonal head bolt

Exercise 15–1: Drawing Isometric Shapes

Step 1. Turn on your computer and start the AutoCAD program.

Prompt	Response
The AutoCAD Today window appears:	*Click:* **Use a Template**
The Select a Template file list box appears:	*Click:* **the template labeled EX5-1(your initials).dwt**

Step 2. Check to make sure the following settings have been made:

Units: Decimal—2 digits to the right of the decimal point
LIMITS: Lower left corner: 0,0
Upper right corner: 11,8.5
TEXT STYLE: Standard FONT: simplex.shx HEIGHT: 0

LAYERS: NAME	Color	Linetype	Lineweight
Layer1	Red	CONTINUOUS	0.25 mm
Layer2	Magenta	CONTINUOUS	0.50 mm
Layer3	Green	CONTINUOUS (Change from HIDDEN)	0.35 mm

Set Layer2 as the current layer.

Set GRID and SNAP for isometric, as follows:

Prompt	Response
Command:	*Type:* **SN** ↵
Specify snap spacing or [ON/OFF/ Aspect/Rotate/Style/Type]<0.50>:	*Type:* **S** ↵
Enter snap grid style [Standard/Isometric]<S>:	*Type:* **I** ↵
Specify vertical spacing<0.50>:	*Type:* **.125** ↵
Command:	*Type:* **GRID** ↵
Specify grid spacing (X) or [ON/OFF/ Snap]<0.1250>:	*Type:* **.25** ↵

The isometric grid should appear. You may now get control of the plane (or surface) that you will be working. To do this press the Ctrl and the E keys on your keyboard simultaneously or *Press:* **F5** so that you "toggle" among the left, right, and top isometric planes. Now you are ready to draw the shape shown in Figure 15–1. With the cursor for the isometric plane in the position shown in Figure 15–2, follow this sequence:

To draw an isometric rectangle measuring 1″ × 2″ × 1″ (Figure 15–2):

Step 1. Draw the right plane.

Prompt	Response
Command:	*Click:* **Line** (or *Type:* **L** ↵)
Specify first point:	*Type:* **2.17,5.38** ↵ (or *Click:* **D1** in this approximate location: Watch your coordinate display.)

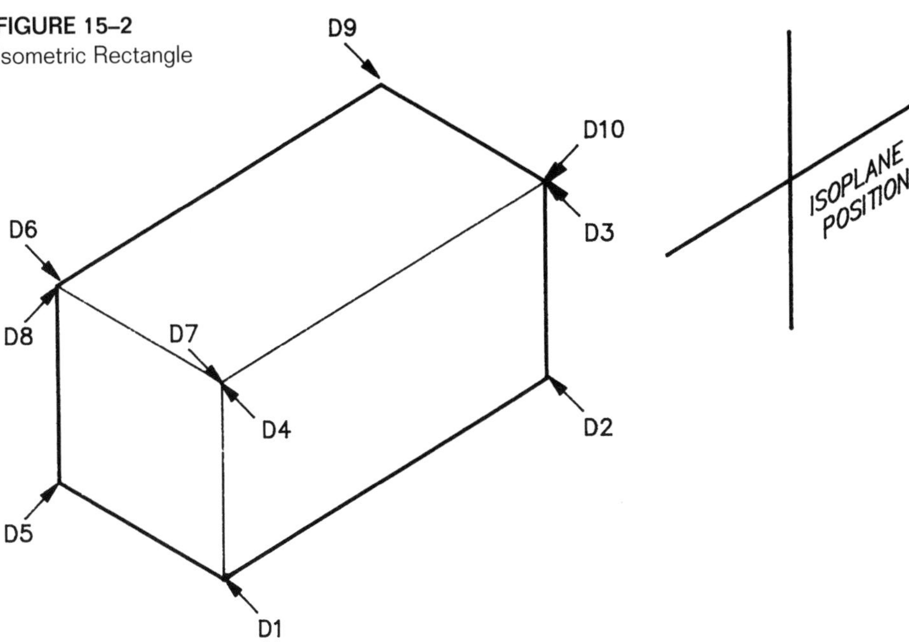

FIGURE 15–2
Isometric Rectangle

Time Saving Tip: Instead of using polar coordinates for drawing lines, use Direct Distance Entry. Just turn on ORTHO, move your mouse in the direction you want the line to go, *Type:* the distance, and *Press:* ↵. Direct Distance Entry can also be used for specifying points in any command such as Copy or Move.

Prompt	Response
Specify next point or [Undo]:	**D2** (Move eight .25 spaces upward to the right or *Type:* **@2<30.**)↵
Specify next point or [Undo]:	**D3** (Move four .25 spaces upward or *Type:* **@1<90.**)↵
Specify next point or [Undo/Close]:	**D4** (Move eight .25 spaces downward to the left or *Type:* **@2<210.**)↵
Specify next point or [Undo/Close]:	*Type:* **C** ↵

You have drawn the right plane. You may leave the isometric plane the same to finish the rectangle, or you may toggle to the left plane.

Step 2. Draw the left plane.

Prompt	Response
Command:	*Click:* **Line** (or *Type:* **L** ↵)
Specify first point:	↵ (Notice that the beginning point for this line is the endpoint of the last line you drew.)
Specify next point or [Undo]:	**D5** (or *Type:* **@1<150**) ↵
Specify next point or [Undo]:	**D6** (or *Type:* **@1<90**) ↵
Specify next point or [Undo/Close]:	**D7** ↵ (or *Type:* **@1<330**) ↵ ↵

Step 3. Draw the top plane.

Prompt	Response
Command:	↵
Specify first point:	**D8**
Specify next point or [Undo]:	**D9** (or *Type:* **@2<30**) ↵
Specify next point or [Undo]:	**D10** ↵ (or *Type:* **@1<330**) ↵ ↵

You have now drawn your first isometric rectangle on AutoCAD. To provide some variety in line weights, you may wish to change the inside lines to another layer, for example: Layer1, which is .25 mm wide (half what Layer2 is). Select the inside lines, then the G layer on the layer list to change the inside lines to the G layer.

The next problem is to draw a 1½″ isometric cube with a 1″ ellipse on each surface. This will introduce you to the standard isometric planes with which you must be very familiar to be successful with isometric drawing.

To draw a 1½″ isometric cube with a 1″ ellipse on each surface (Figure 15–3):

Step 1. Draw the right plane (A).

Toggle to the right Isoplane by pressing th F5 key.

Prompt	Response
Command:	*Click:* **Line** (or *Type:* **L** ↵)
Specify first point:	*Type:* **7.36,5** ↵
Specify next point or [Undo]:	**D2** (or *Type:* **@1.5<30**) ↵
Specify next point or [Undo]:	**D3** (or *Type:* **@1.5<90**) ↵
Specify next point or [Undo/Close]:	**D4** (or *Type:* **@1.5<210**) ↵
Specify next point or [Undo/Close]:	*Type:* **C** ↵

Step 2. Draw the top plane (B) and the left plane (C).

Now do something a little different.

Prompt	Response
Command:	*Click:* **Mirror** (or *Type:* **MI** ↵)

FIGURE 15–3
Drawing the Isometric Cube

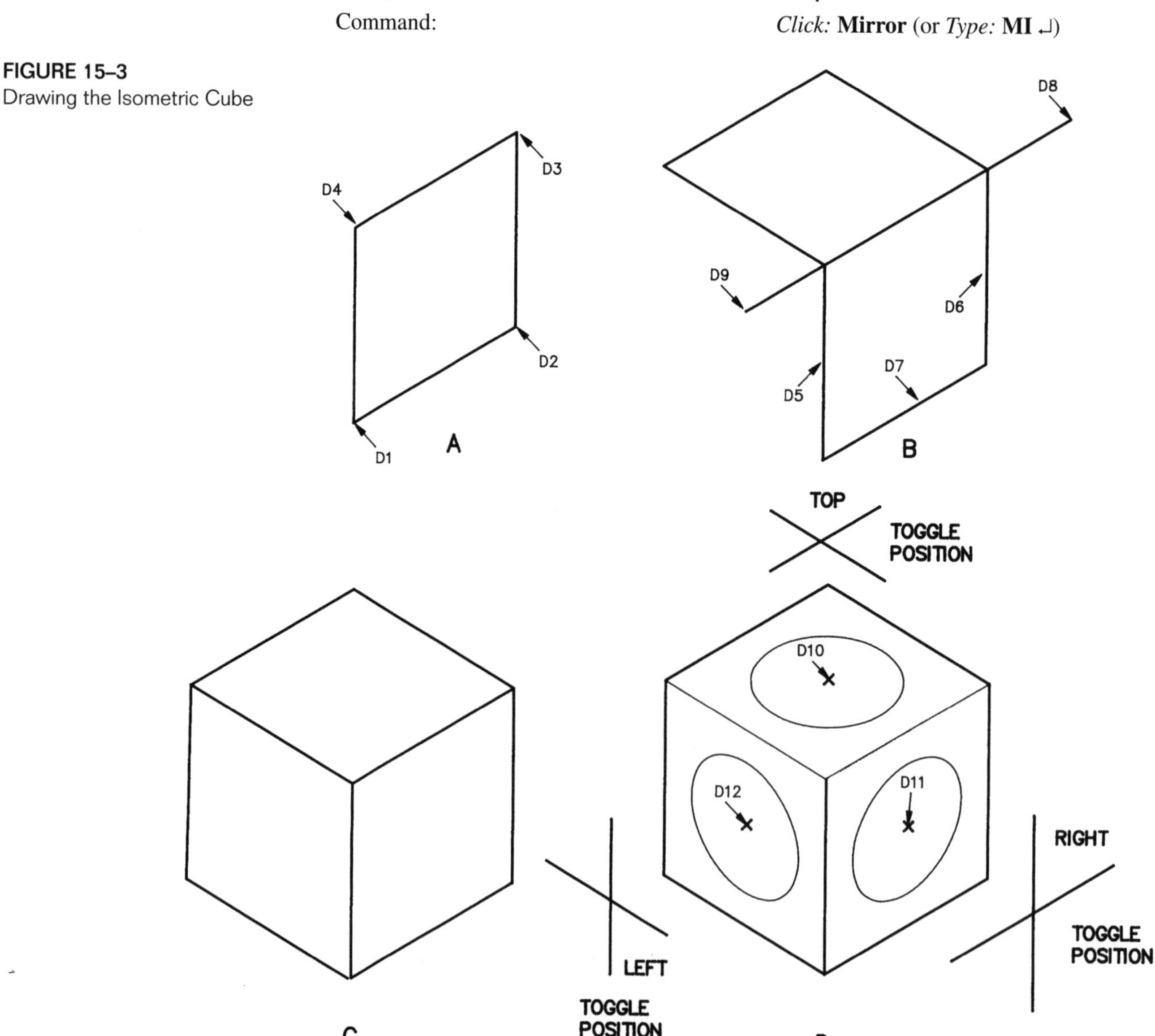

Prompt	Response
Select objects:	**D5, D6, D7** ↵
Specify first point of mirror line:	**D8**
Specify second point of mirror line:	**D9**
Delete source objects: [Yes/No]<N>	↵

You should have the figure shown at B in Figure 15–3. To draw the other face, you may use either Copy or the Line command.

Once you have the figure shown as C in Figure 15–3, you are ready to draw ellipses in these cube surfaces. To do this, use Ctrl-E or F5 to toggle to the top surface as shown at D. Follow these steps:

Step 3. Draw ellipses.

Prompt	Response
Command:	*Click:* **Ellipse** (or *Type:* **EL** ↵)
Specify axis endpoint of ellipse or [Arc/Center/Isocircle]:	*Type:* **I** ↵
Specify center of isocircle:	**D10**
Specify radius of isocircle or [Diameter]:	*Type:* **.5** ↵ (The default is radius.)
Command:	

Now toggle using Ctrl-E or F5 to the right isometric plane.

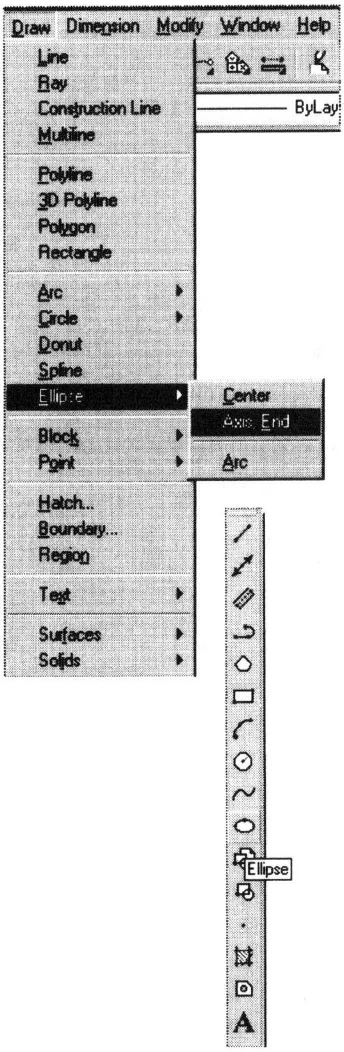

Prompt	Response
	Click: **Ellipse**
Specify axis endpoint of ellipse or [Arc/Center/Isocircle]:	*Type:* **I** ↵
Specify center of isocircle:	**D11**
Specify radius of isocircle or [Diameter]:	*Type:* **.5** ↵
Command:	

Now toggle to the left isometric plane.

Prompt	Response
	Click: **Ellipse**
Specify axis endpoint of ellipse or [Arc/Center/Isocircle]:	*Type:* **I** ↵
Specify center of isocircle:	**D12**
Specify radius of isocircle or [Diameter]:	*Type:* **.5** ↵

Take a few minutes to study the position of the ellipses on the isometric planes. These positions are the same for all normal (perpendicular) surfaces and must not be rotated in any direction. Remember where Figure 15–3 is in case you need to return to it to refresh your memory.

Now turn to Figure 15–4 and observe how to draw a slightly more complex part.

To draw an isometric view of a part from a two-dimensional drawing:

Be sure SNAP (F9) is ON, ORTHO is OFF, and the toggle and cursor are in the correct isometric plane (Figure 15–4).

Step 1. Draw the front surface (A).

Prompt	Response
Command:	*Click:* **Line** (or *Type:* **L** ↵)
Specify first point:	*Type:* **2.17,1.38** ↵

FIGURE 15–4
Drawing a Complex Isometric Shape

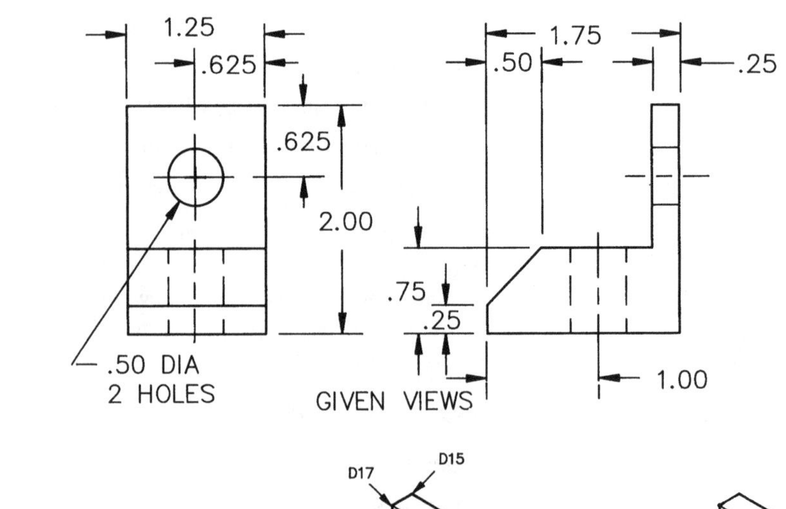

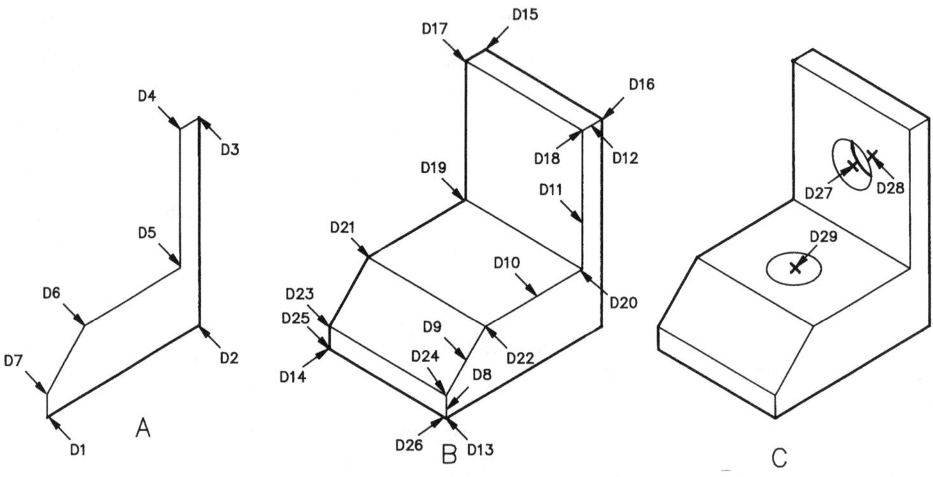

Prompt	Response
Specify next point or [Undo]:	**D2** (Count seven ¼″ spaces (1.75 or 1¾″) on the 30° isometric axis upward to the right or *Type:* **@1.75<30.**) ↵
Specify next point or [Undo]:	**D3** (Count eight ¼″ spaces (2.00″) on the vertical axis or *Type:***@2<90.**) ↵
Specify next point or [Undo/Close]:	**D4** (Count one ¼″ space downward on the 30° isometric axis to the left or *Type:* **@.25<210** (210 is 180 + 30).) ↵
Specify next point or [Undo/Close]:	**D5** (Count five ¼″ spaces downward on the vertical axis or *Type:* **@1.25<−90** (or 270).) ↵
Specify next point or [Undo/Close]:	**D6** (count four ¼″ spaces downward on the 30° isometric axis to the left or *Type:* **@1<210.**) ↵

Now you have a problem because this angle cannot be identified easily on an isometric drawing; therefore, the other end of the angle, which is .25 upward on the vertical axis from D1, must be located. Find that point and D7. The angle can be identified by using the List command, but you do not need that information now.

Prompt	Response
Specify next point or [Undo]:	**D7**
Specify next point or [Undo]:	*Type:* **C** ↵

Since you have already put some time into drawing the front surface, copy appears to be a good approach to drawing the identical back plane.

Step 2. Draw the back surface (Figure 15–4B).

Prompt	Response
Command:	*Click:* **Copy** (or *Type:* **CP** ↵)
Select objects:	**D8, D9, D10, D11, D12** (or window the area)
Select objects:	↵
Specify base point or displacement, or [Multiple]:	**D13**
Specify second point of displacement or <use first point as displacement>:	**D14** (Count five ¼″ spaces on the 30° isometric axis upward to the left, or *Type:* **@1.25<150** ↵)

Step 3. Connect the front and back surfaces.

With the SNAP ON (ORTHO OFF), lines will be cleanly drawn to the correct points, so no cleanup is necessary.

Prompt	Response
Command:	*Click:* **Line** (or *Type:* **L** ↵)
Specify first point:	**D15**
Specify next point or [Undo]:	**D16** ↵
Command:	↵

Repeat the preceding for lines D17–18, D19–20, D21–22, D23–24, and D25–26, or copy the line in four places using Copy-Multiple.

Step 4. Draw the holes (Figure 15–4C).

To complete this figure you must draw three ellipses, apply any finishing touches such as varying line weights, and clean up any excess lines. To draw the ellipses:

Prompt	Response
Command:	*Click:* **Ellipse** (or *Type:* **EL** ↵)
Specify axis endpoint of ellipse or [Arc/Center/Isocircle]:	*Type:* **I** ↵

Be sure to toggle to the left isoplane.

Prompt	Response
Specify center of isocircle:	**D27**
Specify radius of isocircle or [Diameter]:	*Type:* **.25** ↵ (the radius of the .5-diameter circles)
Command:	↵
Specify axis endpoint of ellipse or [Arc/Center/Isocircle]:	*Type:* **I** ↵
Specify center of isocircle:	**D28**

Move one GRID space back on the 30° axis to the right.

Prompt	Response
Specify radius of isocircle or [Diameter]:	*Type:* **.25** ↵
Command:	↵
Specify axis endpoint of ellipse or [Arc/Center/Isocircle]:	*Type:* **I** ↵

Be sure to toggle to the top isoplane.

Prompt	Response
Specify center of isocircle:	**D29**
Specify radius of isocircle or [Diameter]:	*Type:* **.25** ↵
Command:	

Now use Trim to get rid of the back part of the ellipse formed from the D28 click. Select Trim, crossing, window the entire area, press Enter, and select the unwanted portion.

Change the interior lines to Layer1 so they will be thinner than the outside lines, as the last step in Figure 15–4 shows. Use a different method to accomplish this task this time:

Click: those lines you want to move to Layer1 so they are selected, then *Click:* **Layer1** from the layer list on the Object Properties toolbar.

To draw an isometric hexagonal head bolt (Figure 15–5):

Some of the commonly used parts in many manufacturing firms are bolts, screws, and other threaded fasteners (Figure 15–5).

This part, once drawn, can be scaled up or down, modified, and rotated to fit into many different illustrations.

To allow this bolt to be drawn as simply as possible, make the threads of the bolt 1″ in diameter and the hexagonal head 1½″ (1.50) in diameter. Start with the hexagonal head.

Step 1. Draw the isometric hexagonal head in the top isoplane.

FIGURE 15–5
Drawing an Isometric Hexagonal Head Bolt

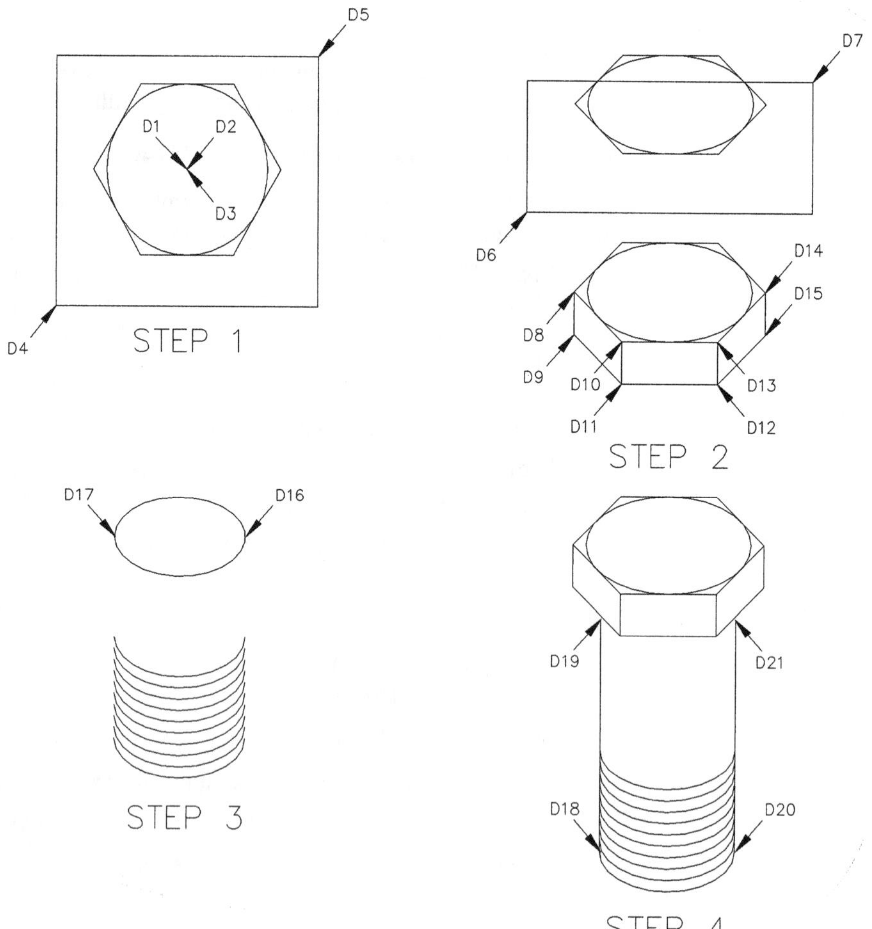

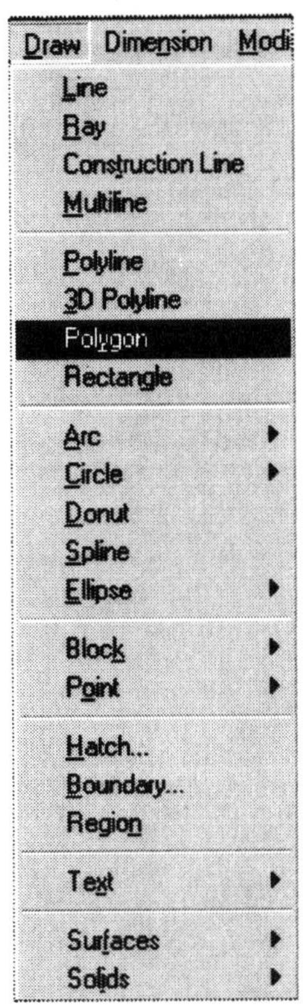

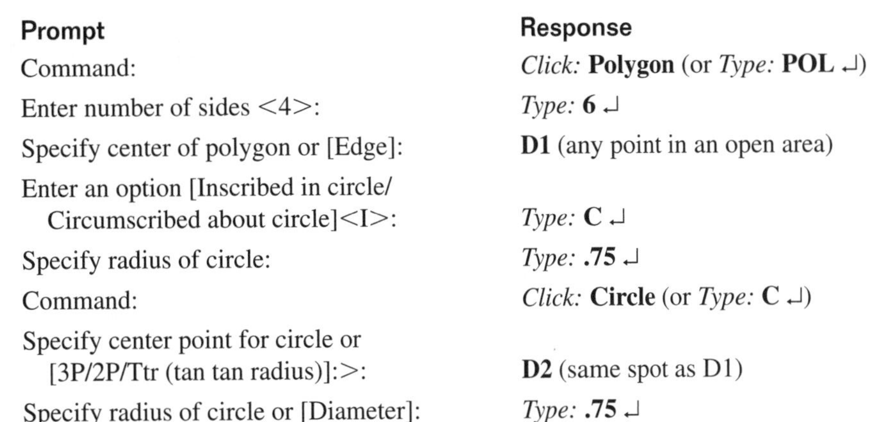

Prompt	Response
Command:	*Click:* **Polygon** (or *Type:* **POL** ↵)
Enter number of sides <4>:	*Type:* **6** ↵
Specify center of polygon or [Edge]:	**D1** (any point in an open area)
Enter an option [Inscribed in circle/ Circumscribed about circle]<I>:	*Type:* **C** ↵
Specify radius of circle:	*Type:* **.75** ↵
Command:	*Click:* **Circle** (or *Type:* **C** ↵)
Specify center point for circle or [3P/2P/Ttr (tan tan radius)]:>:	**D2** (same spot as D1)
Specify radius of circle or [Diameter]:	*Type:* **.75** ↵

Step 2. Change the hexagonal head to isometric.

Now you have a hexagon circumscribed about a 1½″-diameter circle. You must now block it and bring it back into the drawing as an isometric hexagonal shape. Follow these steps:

Prompt	Response
Command:	*Click:* **Block** (or *Type:* **B** ↵)
The Block Definition dialog box appears:	*Type:* **IH** in the Name: text box
	Click: **Pick Point**

The block name may be up to 255 characters long and can use spaces and any special characters not used by Microsoft.

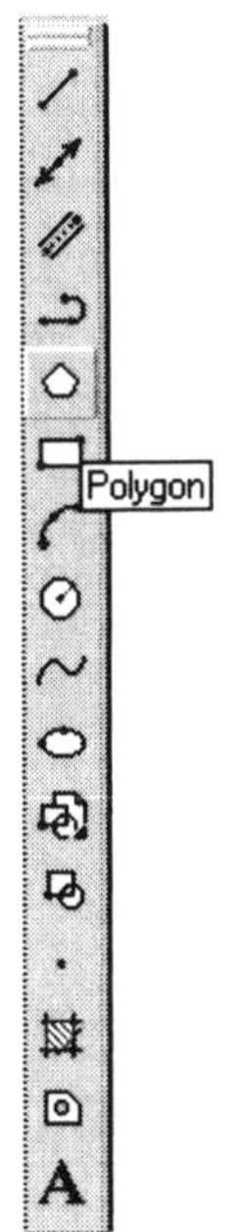

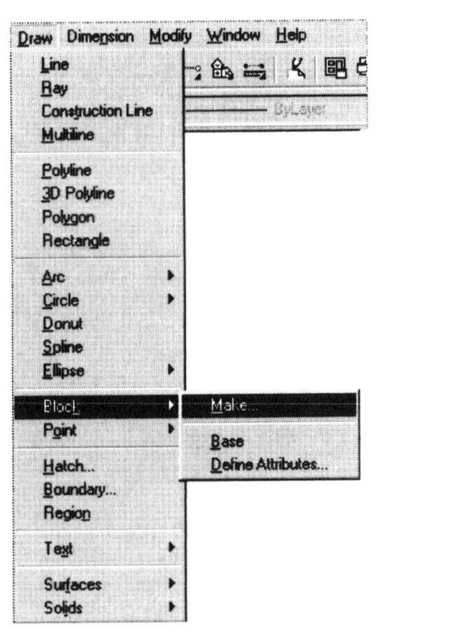

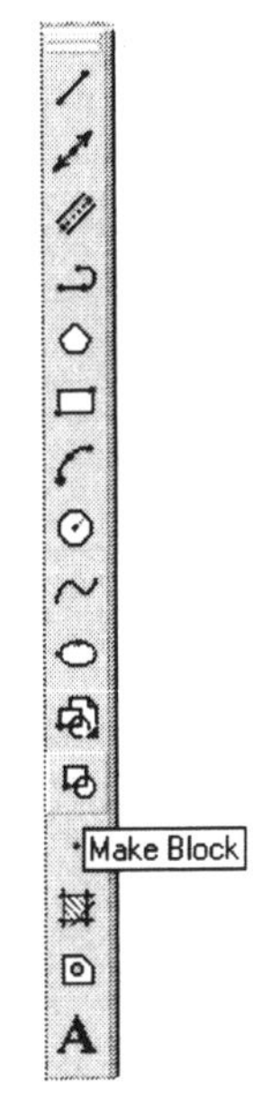

Prompt	Response
Specify insertion base point:	**D3** (same spot as D1 and D2)
The Block Definition dialog box reappears:	*Click:* **Select objects**
Select objects:	**D4**
Other corner:	**D5**
3 found-Select objects:	↵
The Block Definition dialog box appears:	*Click:* **OK**

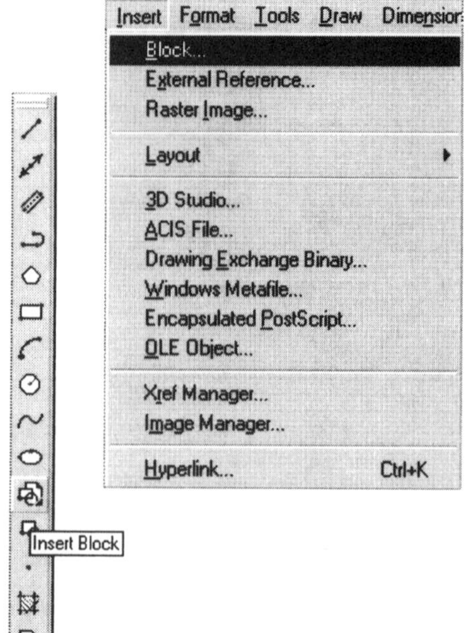

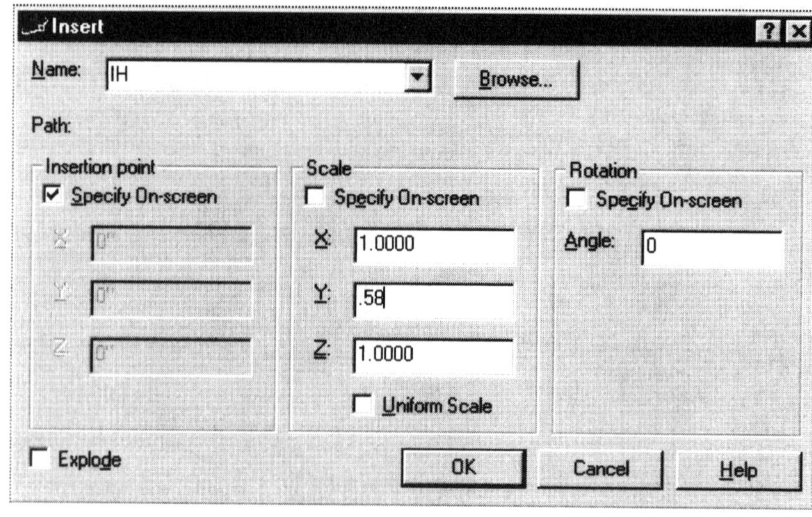

FIGURE 15–6
Insert Block 1H with Y-Scale Set at .58

Prompt	Response
Command:	**Insert Block** (or *Type:* **I** ↵)
The Insert dialog box (Figure 15–6) appears:	*Click:* **IH** (in the Name: box)
	(Make sure a check appears in the Specify On-screen box for Insertion point and .58 appears in the Y: scale box as shown

The value .58 is a very close approximation of the isometric Y-axis scale factor.

Prompt	Response
	Click: **OK**
Specify insertion point or [Scale/X/Y/Z/Rotate/PScale/PX/PY/PZ/PRotate]:	*Type:* **7.58,4.38** ↵

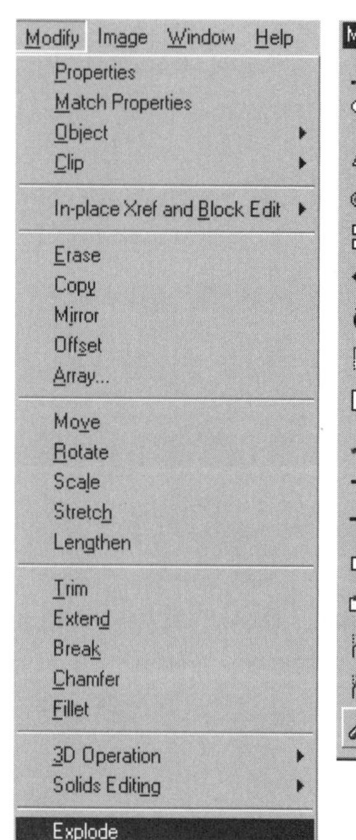

Now, Copy the bottom half of the hexagonal head. Before you do this you must Explode the block.

Prompt	Response
Command:	**Explode** (or *Type:* **X** ↵)
Select objects:	*Click:* **any point on the hexagonal head**
Select objects:	↵
Command:	**Copy** (or *Type:* **CP** ↵)
Select objects:	**D6**
Specify opposite corner:	**D7**
Select objects:	↵
Base point or displacement, or [Multiple]	*Click:* **any point.**
Specify second point of displacement or <use first point as displacement>:	*Type:* **@.375<−90** ↵

Now, connect the top and bottom planes. To make sure you have accurately connected lines, use Osnap in this manner:

Prompt	Response
Command:	*Click:* **Object Snap Settings...** (or *Type:* **OS** ↵)
The Object Snap tab appears:	*Click:* **Endpoint**
	Click: **OK**

Now you will be able to use Osnap-Endpoint without having to select endpoint each time. (You may also use other Osnap modes, such as Center, while you are in the Endpoint mode by selecting them. After you use another mode Osnap returns to the Endpoint mode.)

Tip: You may select more than one running Osnap mode at a time so that Endpoint, Midpoint, and Intersection, for example, are all in effect at the same time. The mode that becomes active is the one that is appropriate for the digitized point. You should experiment with this technique.

Prompt	Response
Command:	*Click:* **Line** (or *Type:* **L** ↵)
Specify first point:	**D8**
Specify next point or [Undo]:	**D9** ↵
Command:	↵
Specify first point:	**D10**
Specify next point or [Undo]:	**D11** ↵
Command:	↵
Specify first point:	**D12**
Specify next point or [Undo]:	**D13** ↵
Command:	↵
Specify first point:	**D14**
Specify next point or [Undo]:	**D15** ↵
Command:	*Type:* **OS** ↵
The Object Snap tab appears:	*Click:* **Clear all** (takes you out of the Endpoint Osnap mode)
	Click: **OK**

The hexagonal head of the bolt is now complete. The next step is to draw the threads and connect them to the head to complete the drawing.

Step 3. Draw the threads.

Prompt	Response
Command:	*Click:* **Ellipse** (or *Type:* **EL** ↵)
Specify axis endpoint of ellipse or [Arc/Center/Isocircle]:	*Type:* **I** ↵
Specify center of isocircle:	*Type:* **7.58,2.63** ↵
Specify radius of isocircle or [Diameter]:	*Type:* **.5** ↵ (the radius for a 1″-diameter circle)

The ellipse must now be broken in half to form the threads.

Prompt	Response
Command:	*Click:* **Break** (or *Type:* **BR** ↵)
Select object:	**D16**
Specify second break point or [First point]:	**D17**

You should now have the bottom half of an isometric ellipse. Array it to form the screw threads.

Prompt	Response
Command:	*Click:* **Array** (or *Type:* **AR** ↵)
The Array dialog box appears:	*Click:* **Select Objects**
Select objects:	*Click:* **any point on the half ellipse**
Select objects:	↵
The Array dialog box appears:	*Click:* **Rectangular Array**
	Type: **10** in the Rows: box (could be more or less depending on how long the screw is)
	Type: **1** in the Columns: box
	Type: **−.1** in the Row offset: box (.1″ is a good space for this size thread.)
	Click: **OK**

Caution: Be sure to make the distance negative (−.1) so that the array will be downward.

Important: Toggle to left or right isoplane before drawing the vertical lines.

Step 4. You must now connect the threads to the head to complete the bolt drawing.

Prompt	Response
Command:	*Click:* **Line**
Specify first point:	*Click:* **Osnap-Endpoint D18**

Be sure ORTHO is ON so you will get a straight line.

Prompt	Response
Specify next point or [Undo]:	**D19**↵
Command:	*Click:* **Line**
Specify first point:	*Click:* **Osnap-Endpoint D20**
Specify next point or [Undo]:	**D21** ↵

The bolt is now complete. Save the drawing in two places and Exit AutoCAD.

DIMENSIONING IN ISOMETRIC

Placing dimensions on isometric drawings is a problem that can be fully resolved by buying a third-party software package for isometric dimensioning. Isometric dimensioning may also be done by drawing isometric extension lines and creating arrowheads with the Solid command as BLOCKs that have an "isometric slant" for the base of the arrowhead. The dimension text may be placed in the horizontal position or parallel with the extension lines as shown in Figure 13–65. Chapters 10, 13, and 16 have several good examples of isometric dimensioning in the exercise illustrations. You can use the Mirror command effectively to create arrowheads in a different isoplane by using Ctrl-E or F5 to move from one isoplane to another while you are in the middle of the Mirror command.

EXERCISES

EXERCISE 15–1. Reproduce Figure 15–1 on a horizontal 8½″ × 11″ format and plot the drawing according to your teacher's instructions. Use the following attribute values when you insert your horizontal A-size format:

Drawing Title: Isometric Shapes
Assignment 15–1
Scale: 1/1
Date: Current date

EXERCISE 15–2. Draw the figure shown in Figure 15–7 approximately twice the size shown using the isometric method. Center the drawing in a horizontal 8½″ × 11″ for-

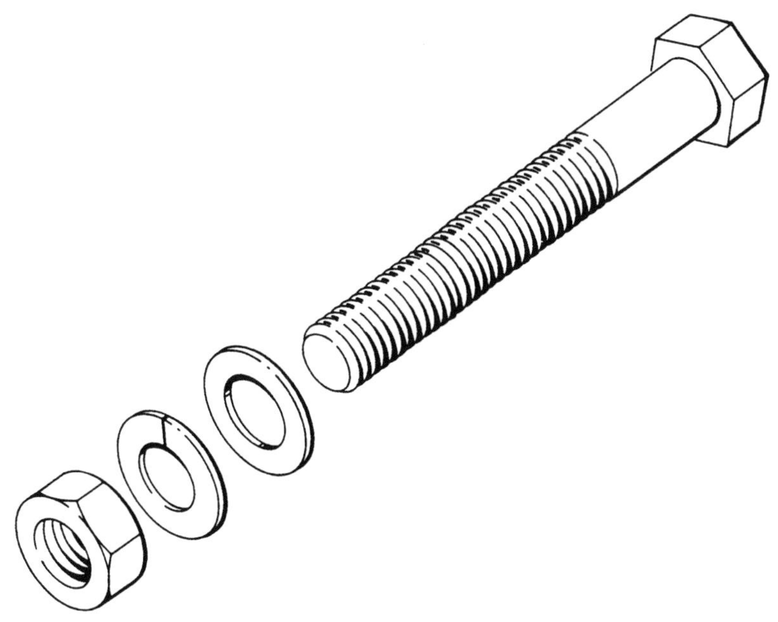

FIGURE 15–7
Exercise 15–2

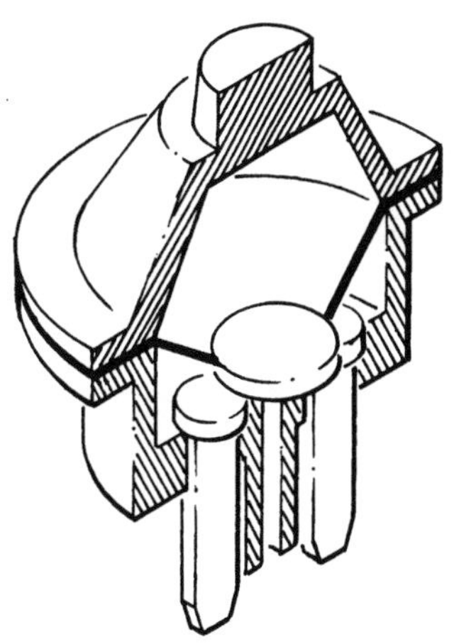

FIGURE 15–8
Exercise 15–3

mat. The shaded threads and other shading techniques are described in Chapter 27. Do not shade this drawing unless your instructor instructs you to do so. Plot as directed by your instructor. Use the following attribute values:

Drawing Title: Isometric Bolt
Assignment 15–2
Scale: None
Date: Current date

EXERCISE 15–3. Draw the figure shown in Figure 15–8 approximately the size shown using the isometric method. Center the drawing in a vertical 8½″ × 11″ format. The shading techniques are described in Chapter 27. Do not shade this drawing unless your instructor instructs you to do so. Plot as directed by your instructor. Use the following attribute values:

Drawing Title: Isometric Cutaway
Assignment 15–3
Scale: None
Date: Current date

EXERCISE 15–4. Make an isometric view from the orthographic views shown in Figure 15–9. Center your drawing on an 8½″ × 11″ horizontal format and plot it as your instructor directs. Use the following attribute values:

Drawing Title: Base
Assignment 15–4
Scale: None
Date: Current date

EXERCISE 15–5. Make isometric drawings from the 2-D drawings shown in Figure 15–10. Let the grid represent ¼″. Divide a horizontal A-size format into four equal spaces and place one drawing in each space. You will have two sheets when you finish. Complete the title block using the following attribute values:

Drawing Title: Isometric Sketches
Assignment 15–5
Scale: None
Date: Current Date

FIGURE 15–9
Exercise 15–4

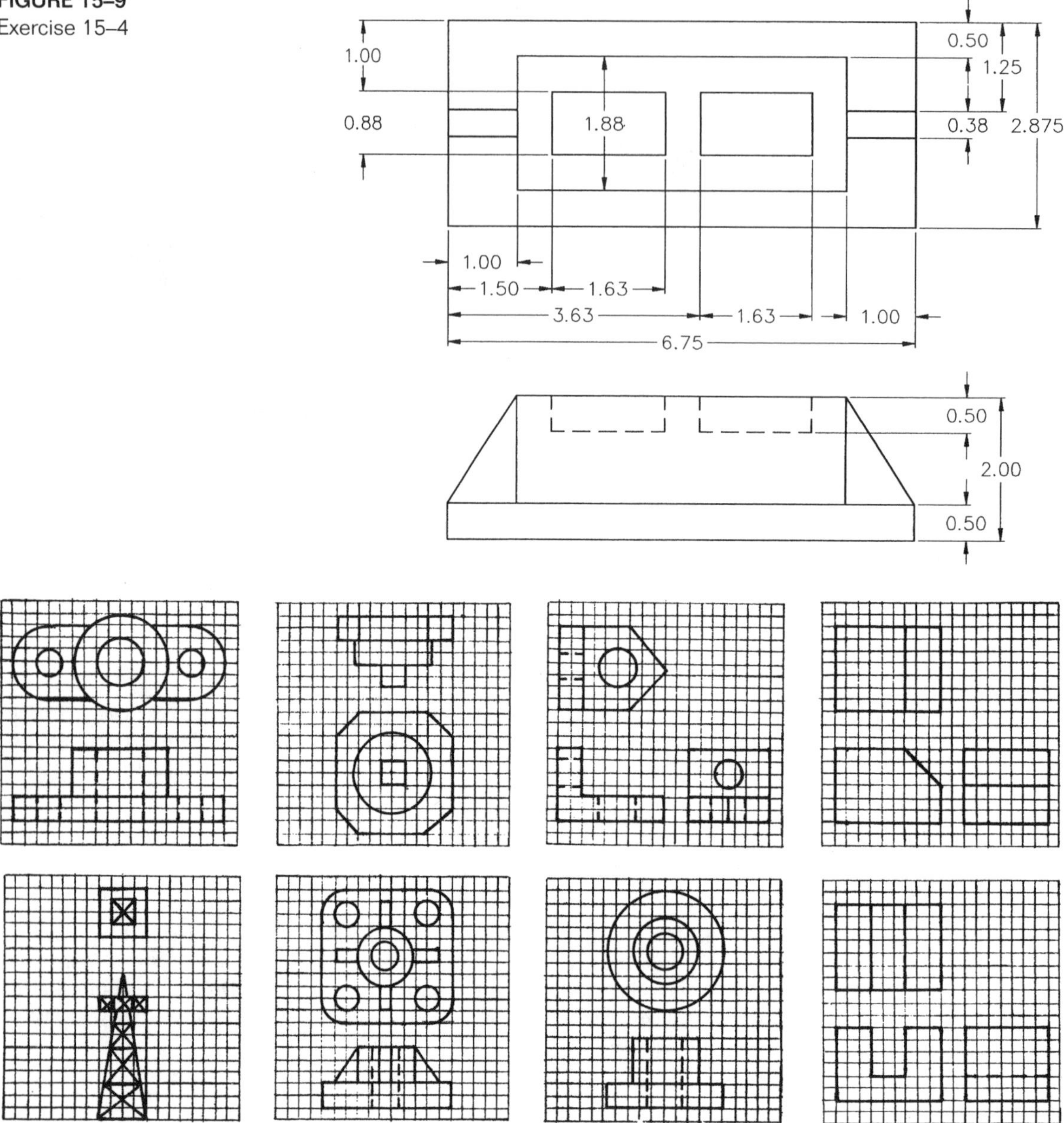

FIGURE 15–10
Exercise 15–5

EXERCISE 15–6. Make AutoCAD isometric drawings of Figures 15–11 through 15–17. Measure the drawings and make your drawings approximately the same size. Center each one in an 8½″ × 11″ format. Make the lettering on Exercise 15–6 SIMPLEX, .08″ high. Use the following attribute values:

Title:	Assignment	Scale	Date
a. Frame	15–6a	None	Current date
b. Gear	15–6b	None	Current date
c. Fitting	15–6c	None	Current date
d. Condenser	15–6d	None	Current date
e. TV	15–6e	None	Current date
f. Clock Radio	15–6f	None	Current date
g. Drill Holder	15–6g	None	Current date

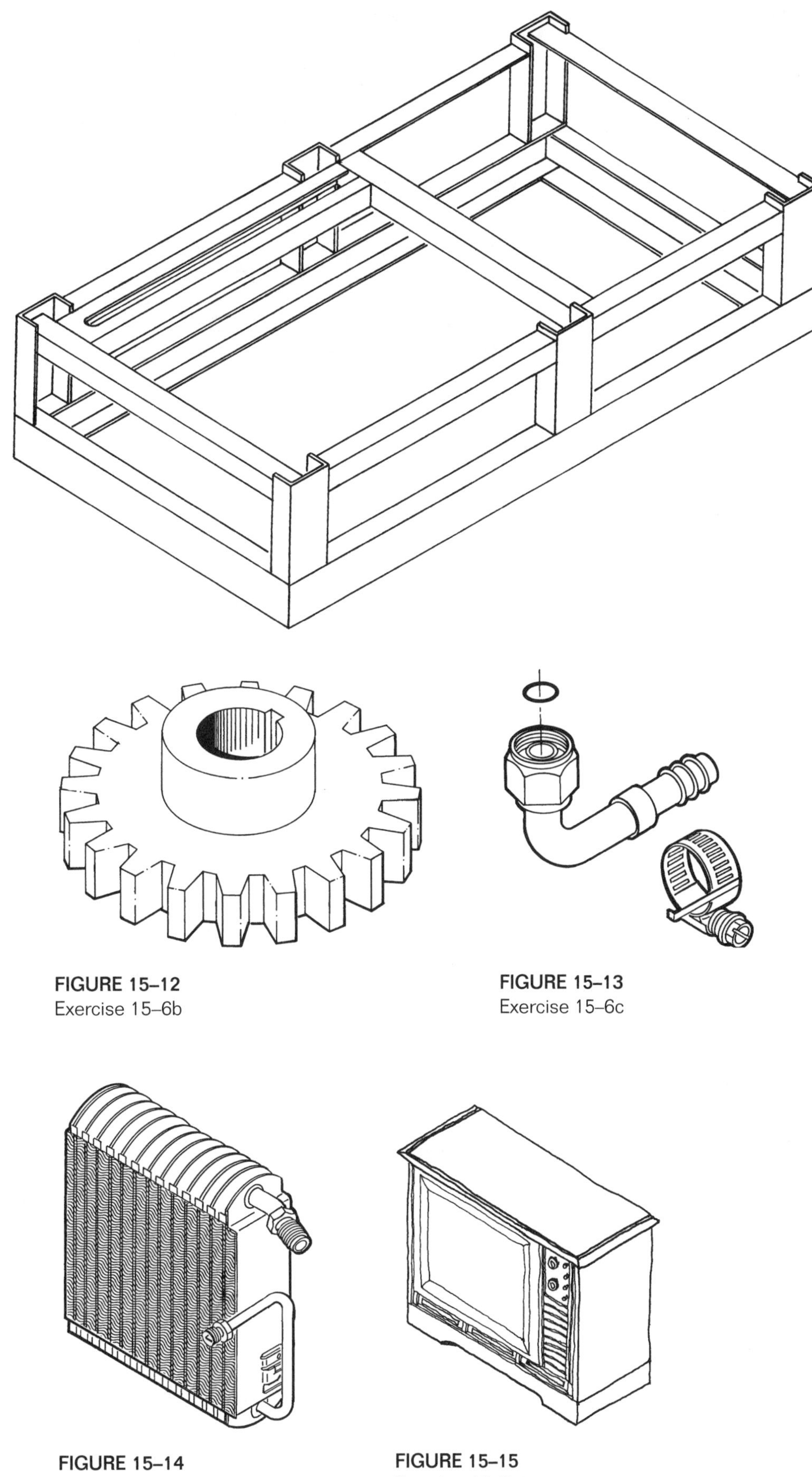

FIGURE 15–11
Exercise 15–6a

FIGURE 15–12
Exercise 15–6b

FIGURE 15–13
Exercise 15–6c

FIGURE 15–14
Exercise 15–6d

FIGURE 15–15
Exercise 15–6e

FIGURE 15–16
Exercise 15–6f

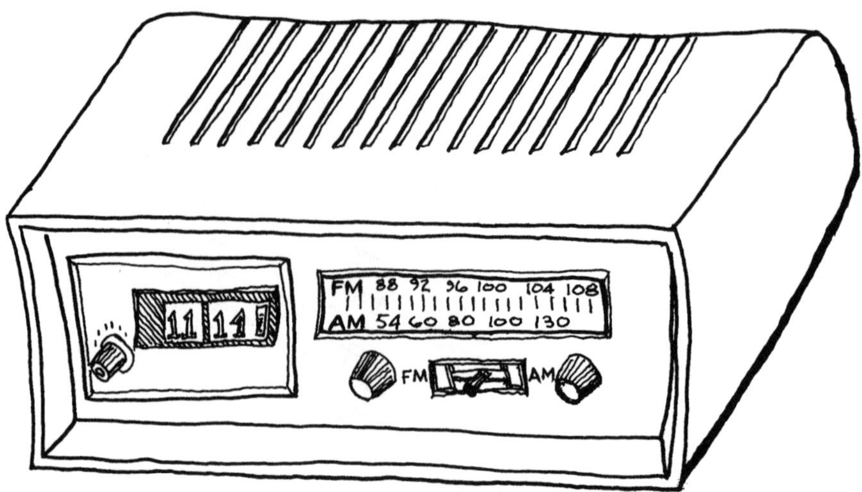

FIGURE 15–17
Exercise 15–6g

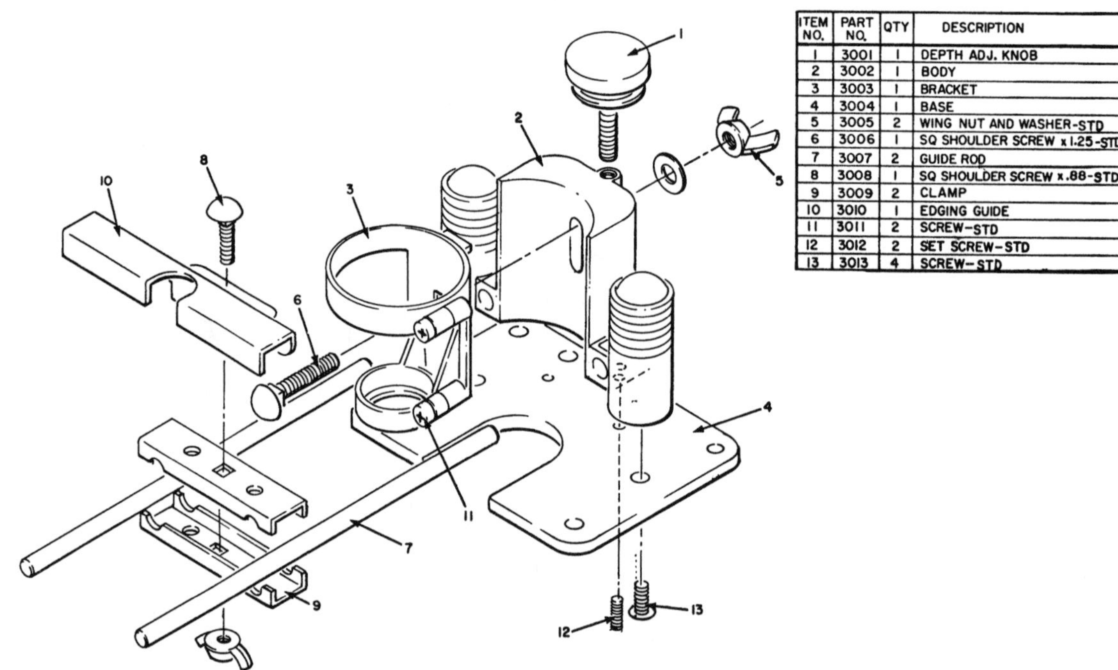

ITEM NO.	PART NO.	QTY	DESCRIPTION
1	3001	1	DEPTH ADJ. KNOB
2	3002	1	BODY
3	3003	1	BRACKET
4	3004	1	BASE
5	3005	2	WING NUT AND WASHER-STD
6	3006	1	SQ SHOULDER SCREW x 1.25-STD
7	3007	2	GUIDE ROD
8	3008	1	SQ SHOULDER SCREW x .88-STD
9	3009	2	CLAMP
10	3010	1	EDGING GUIDE
11	3011	2	SCREW-STD
12	3012	2	SET SCREW-STD
13	3013	4	SCREW-STD

REVIEW QUESTIONS

It is suggested that you complete this test at the computer after reproducing Figure 15–1. Circle the best answer.

1. The isometric grid is obtained from which of the following commands?
   a. ELEV
   b. LINE
   c. SNAP
   d. 3-D
2. Which of the following is used to toggle from one isoplane to another?
   a. F3
   b. F5
   c. Ctrl-T
   d. Ctrl-P

3. What happens when the C key is pressed as a response to the prompt: "Specify next point or [Undo/Close]:"?
   a. The rectangle is copied.
   b. The rectangle is changed to layer C.
   c. The rectangle is opened.
   d. The rectangle is closed.
4. In response to the prompt "Line: Specify first point:" which of the following starts a line from the endpoint of the last line drawn?
   a. ↵
   b. F6
   c. Ctrl-E
   d. REPEAT
5. An ellipse that appears in the following position would have been drawn in the
   a. Left isoplane
   b. Right isoplane
   c. Top isoplane
   d. None of the above

6. An ellipse that appears in the following position would have been drawn in the
   a. Left isoplane
   b. Right isoplane
   c. Top isoplane
   d. None of the above

7. An ellipse that appears in the following position would have been drawn in the
   a. Left isoplane
   b. Right isoplane
   c. Top isoplane
   d. None of the above

8. Which of the following is the same as $-30°$?
   a. 60°
   b. 150°
   c. 210°
   d. 330°
9. Which of the following commands has a feature labeled "multiple"?
   a. Copy
   b. Change
   c. Line
   d. Array
10. Which of the following commands is used to change lines from one layer to another?
    a. Color
    b. Layer
    c. Properties. . .
    d. Break
11. Which of the following is a reason for changing lines to another layer?
    a. So that line weights may be varied during plotting
    b. So that the drawing will be more accurate
    c. So that circles may be drawn
    d. So that ellipses may be drawn
12. Which of the following isoplanes will not allow vertical lines to be drawn with a mouse when ORTHO is ON?
    a. Left
    b. Right
    c. Top
    d. All will allow vertical lines to be drawn.

13. A hexagon may be drawn most easily with which of the following commands?
    a. Polygon
    b. Line
    c. Pline
    d. Shape
14. Inserting a polygon so that it appears correct in an isometric top plane requires a scale of ________ in the Y axis.
    a. .30
    b. .90
    c. .58
    d. .355
15. A hexagon inserted as a block so that it appears correct in an isometric top plane may not be exploded.
    a. True
    b. False

16 Basic 3-D and the AutoCAD DesignCenter

OBJECTIVES

After completing this chapter, you will be able to

- Describe the differences between working in 2-D and 3-D.
- Use Elevation, Thickness, UCS, and Viewports to create 3-D objects in space.
- Use Viewpoint to display different views of the same object.
- Describe the difference between model space and paper space.
- Describe the uses of model space viewports.
- Correctly answer questions regarding the following commands and settings:

Properties...	Mview
2D Solid	UCS
Elevation	Plan
Thickness	3D Viewpoint
Hide	Pspace
Mspace	Viewports
Tilemode	AutoCAD DesignCenter

THINKING IN 3-D

Up to this point, you have been working in 2-D AutoCAD. Beginning with this chapter you will be working in three dimensions. No longer will you be making 2-D drawings of objects; now you will be creating these objects. Although you will use many of the same commands, such as Line, Solid, Circle, Duplicate, and Move, your concept of what you are doing now must change. You are building models, not drawing pictures. In this chapter you will begin your model building with the basic 3-D concepts of:

Thickness
Elevation

You will be able to use the following commands to view these objects from several different angles:

3D Viewpoint
Viewports

Finally, you will be able to use the following to build your models and then arrange them as 2-D pictures so that they are documented to the best advantage:

UCS
Model space
Paper space

Let's begin with a model containing several solid shapes of varying heights (Figure 16–1). Because of the orientation of these views, these heights are called Thickness. Until now you have worked in only the X and Y directions. You are now going to add a Z dimension to give thickness and vertical shape to your objects. Creating this model will demonstrate the uses of Elevation and Thickness.

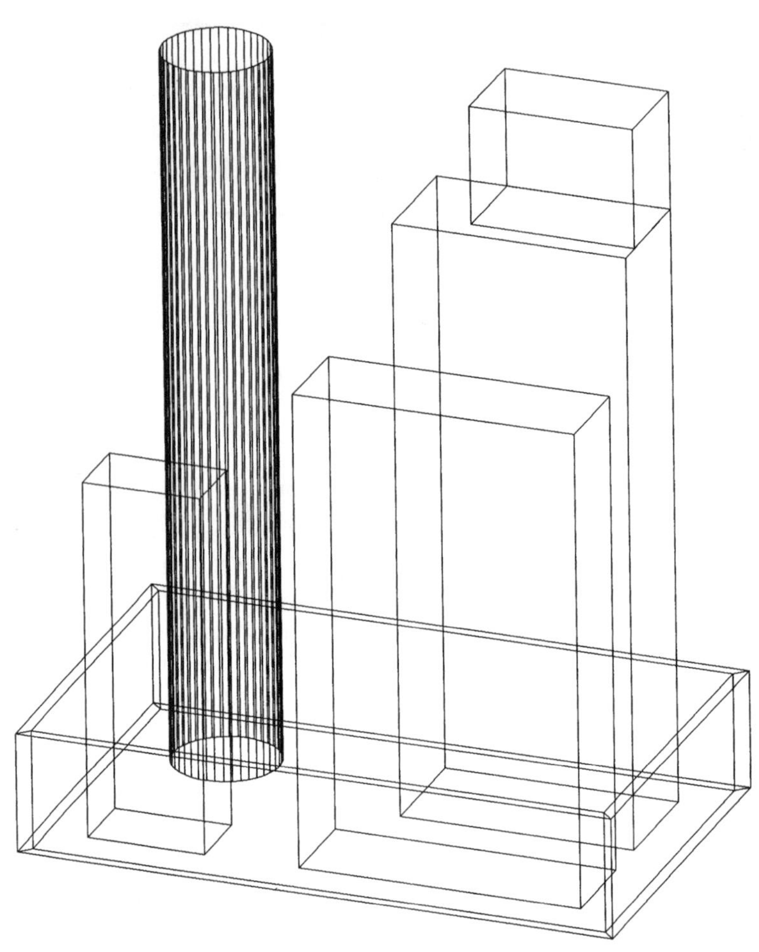

FIGURE 16–1
3-D Model—Shapes with Varying Thicknesses

THE AUTOCAD DESIGNCENTER

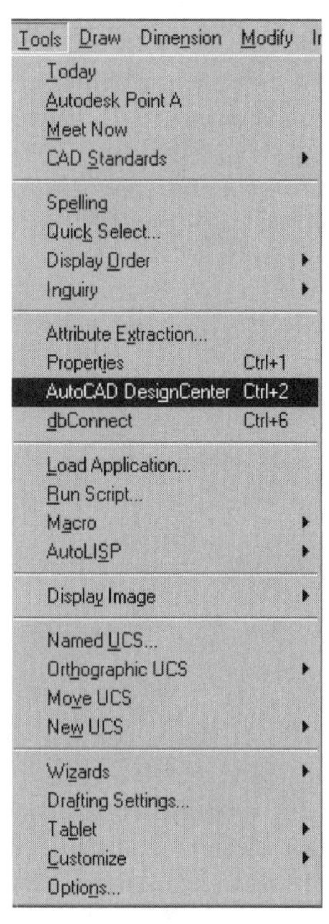

Before you begin working in 3-D, let's take a look at the AutoCAD DesignCenter. This feature allows you to do several things that can save you a great deal of time:

Use several existing blocks arranged in categories provided with AutoCAD R2000.
Use blocks, layers, layouts, linetypes, text and dimension styles, and external references from any existing drawing using drag and drop.
Examine drawings and blocks as either drawing names or pictures.
Search for drawings and other files.

To see how the DesignCenter operates, open it, examine it, and use it to begin your first drawing in 3-D:

Exercise 16–1

Step 1. To begin Exercise 16–1, turn on the computer and start AutoCAD.

Step 2. Activate the AutoCAD DesignCenter and examine it.

Prompt	Response
The AutoCAD 2002 Today window is displayed:	*Click:* **the Create Drawings tab**
	Click: **Start from Scratch**
	Click: **English (feet and inches)**
	Click: **OK**
Command:	**AutoCAD DesignCenter** (or *Type:* **ADC ↵**)

FIGURE 16–2
AutoCAD DesignCenter

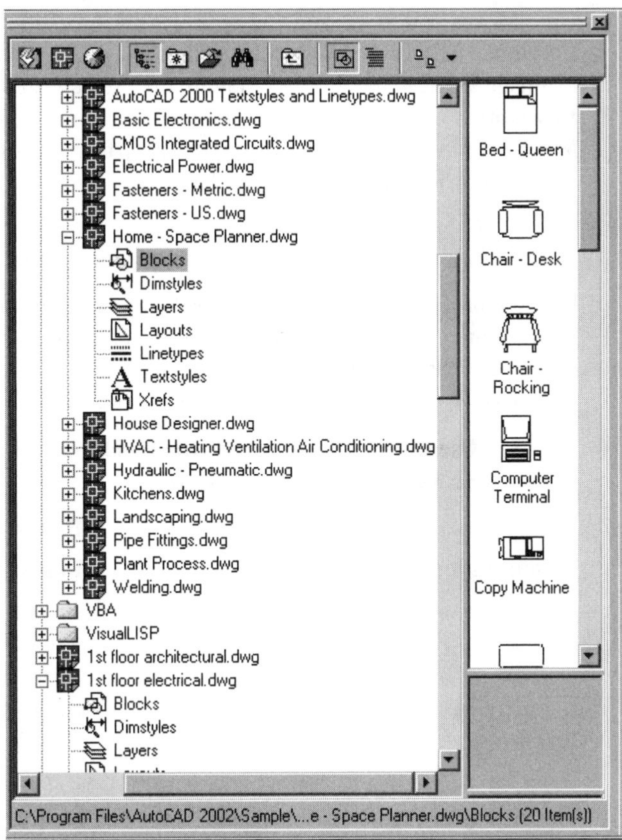

Note: The width of the DesignCenter areas can be changed by placing your mouse over the right edge of the area boundary until it changes to a double arrow. Hold down the pick button and drag to the left or right.

The DesignCenter can also be opened from the Symbol Libraries tab of the Today window.

Prompt	**Response**
The DesignCenter appears:	*Double-click:* **The DesignCenter folder**
The folders of predefined blocks and other items, Figure 16–2, appears:	*Double-click:* **Home-Space Planner.dwg**
The defined folders under Home-Space Planner appear:	*Double-click:* **Blocks**
All the predefined blocks for this folder appear:	

You can now click on any of these drawings, hold down the mouse button, drag the drawing into the current drawing and drop it. Don't do that for this exercise. Now, let's examine the other buttons in the DesignCenter, then use one of your previous drawings to set up Exercise 16–2.

DesignCenter Buttons (Figure 16–3)

Tree View Toggle The first button on the left displays and hides the tree view. The tree view shows the structure of the files and folders in the form of a chart.

Favorites The next button, Favorites, shows what is in the Favorites folder.

Load This button allows you to load drawings and other items that you want to use in your current drawing.

Find Find allows you to search for and locate data that you need.

FIGURE 16–3
DesignCenter Buttons

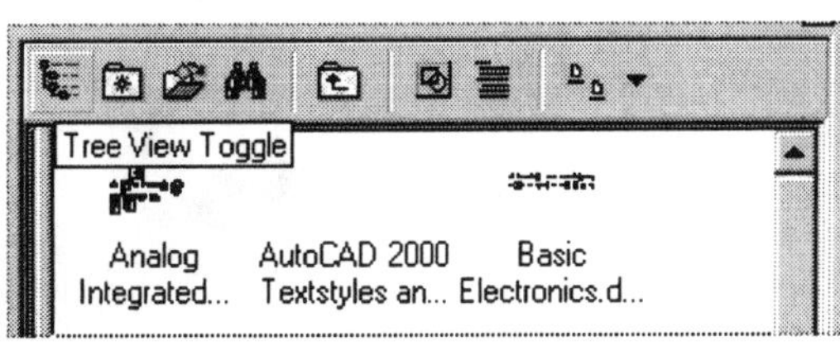

Up Moves you to the drawing or folder one level above the active one.

Preview Allows you to look at a preview of any selected item. If there is no preview image saved with the selected item, the Preview area is empty.

Description Shows a text description of any selected item.

Views Provides you with different display formats for the selected items. You can select a view from the View list, or choose the View button again to cycle through display formats.

The down arrow at the far right gives you the following:

Large Icon Shows the names of loaded items with large icons.

Small Icon Shows the names of loaded items with small icons.

List View Shows a list of loaded items.

Detail View Gives you additional information about the loaded items.

Step 3. Use layers 1, 2, 3, 4 and title block: layout, Floor Plan, and text styles from EX12–1 to begin Exercise 16–1.

Prompt	Response
Command:	**Place the floppy disk containing EX12-1 (your initials) in the A: drive**
	Click: **Load** (the third button to the right of the Tree View toggle)
	Click: **3½ Floppy [A:]** and *Double click:* **EX12-1 as shown in Figure 16–4.**
The display in Figure 16–5 appears:	*Double-click:* **Layers**
The display in Figure 16–6 appears:	*Click:* **Layer ATEXT 1, hold down the pick button, drag it into the current drawing (to the right of the Design-Center), and release the pick button.**
	Repeat the previous step for layers BORDER, DOOR, TEXT, WALL, WINDOW, and title block
	Click: **UP**

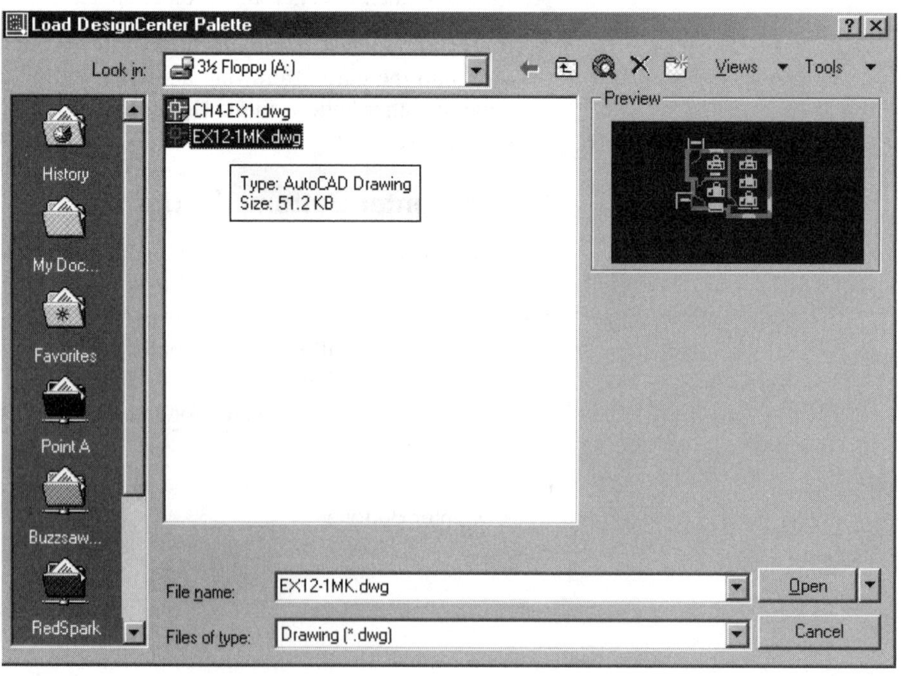

FIGURE 16–4
Load EX12-1(your initials)

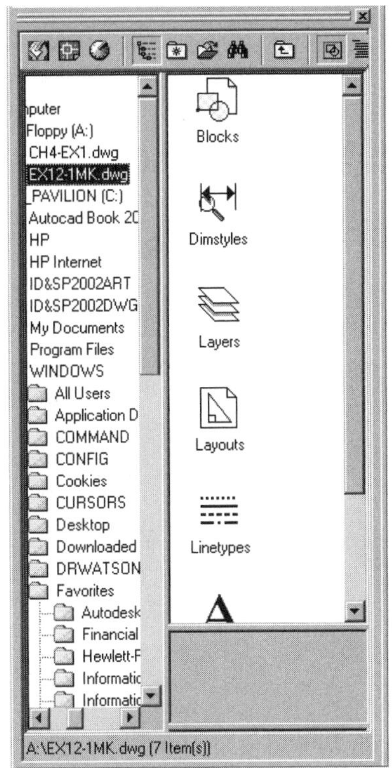

FIGURE 16–5
Items Contained in EX12-1

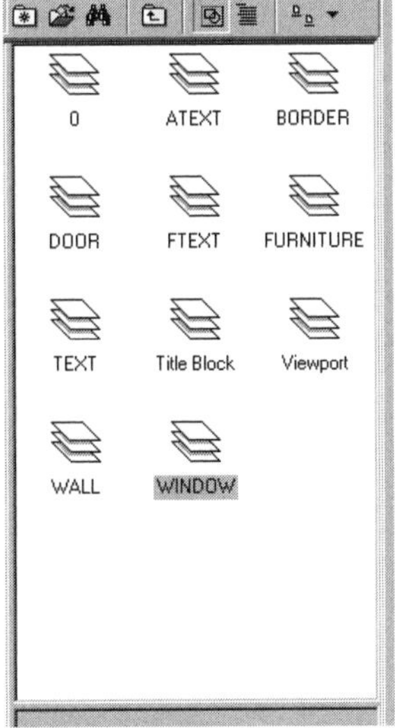

FIGURE 16–6
Layers Contained in EX12-1

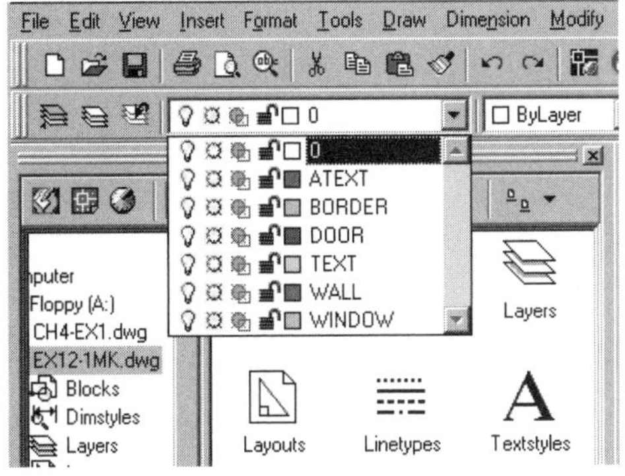

FIGURE 16–7
Check Layer List

Prompt	Response
Now check to see if your layers are OK:	*Click:* **the Layer List** as shown in Figure 16–7
	Click: **any point in an open area of the screen**
	Double-click: **Layouts**
The Layouts display appears:	**Drag and drop the Floor Plan Layout into the current drawing.**
	Hold your mouse over Layout2 in the current drawing and right click.
The right-click menu (Figure 16–8) appears:	*Click:* **Delete**
An AutoCAD warning appears:	*Click:* **OK**
	Delete Layout1 in the same manner.

FIGURE 16–8
Layout Right Click Menu

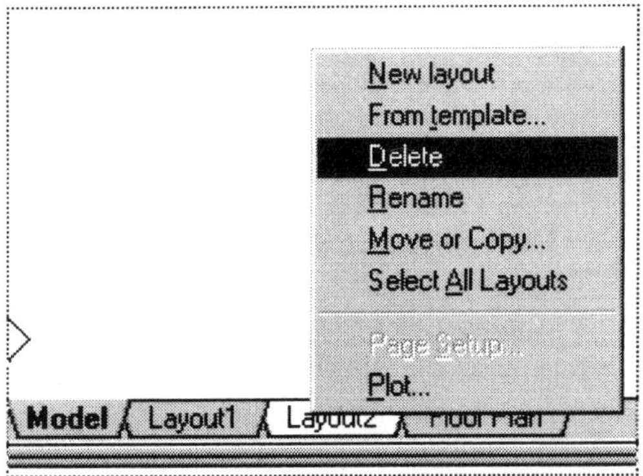

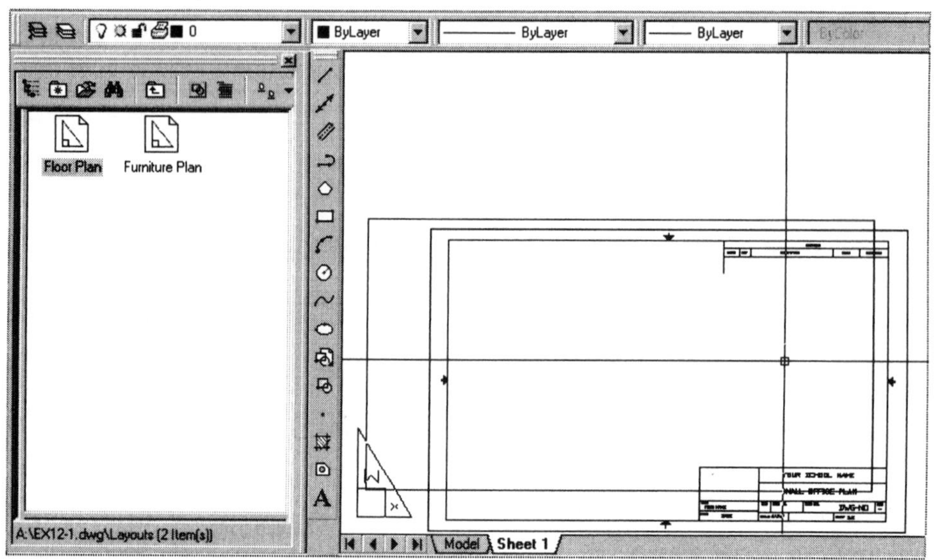

FIGURE 16–9
Layouts Deleted and Renamed

Prompt	Response
	Hold your mouse over the Floor Plan Layout in the current drawing and right click.
The right click menu appears:	*Click:* **Rename**
The Rename Layout dialog box appears:	*Type:* **Sheet 1** (to rename Floor Plan, Sheet 1, Figure 16–9)
	Click: **OK**

On Your Own:

1. Drag and drop Textstyles: Standard and Roman into the current drawing.
2. Close the DesignCenter by clicking the **X** in its upper right corner.
3. Exit AutoCAD and do not save this exercise.

CREATING 3-D MODELS

Exercise 16–2: Creating a 3-D Model Using Elevation and Thickness

In Chapter 10, the settings and layers were made for template HOR-A. You will now use that template file to begin Exercise 16–1. Your final drawing will look similar to the drawing in Figure 16–1.

Step 1. Load AutoCAD and begin a new drawing.

Prompt	Response
The AutoCAD 2002 Today window appears:	*Click:* **the Create Drawings tab**
	Click: **Template**
	Click: **the letter H, then** *Click:* **HOR-A**

Step 2. Check to make sure the following settings have been made. (If you cannot locate the template HOR-A, start from scratch and make the following settings.) You will have to change the grid and snap settings.

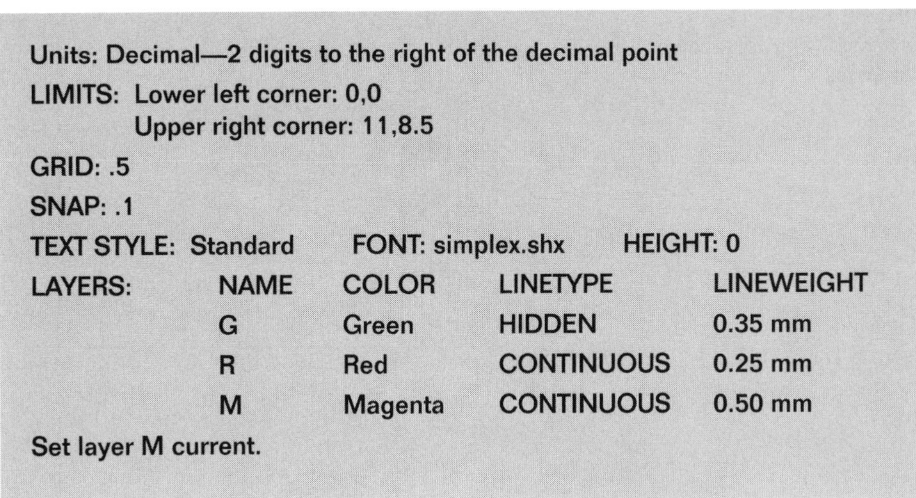

Units: Decimal—2 digits to the right of the decimal point

LIMITS: Lower left corner: 0,0
Upper right corner: 11,8.5

GRID: .5

SNAP: .1

TEXT STYLE: Standard FONT: simplex.shx HEIGHT: 0

LAYERS:	NAME	COLOR	LINETYPE	LINEWEIGHT
	G	Green	HIDDEN	0.35 mm
	R	Red	CONTINUOUS	0.25 mm
	M	Magenta	CONTINUOUS	0.50 mm

Set layer M current.

Step 3. Use Zoom-All to view the entire drawing area.

Step 4. Set elevation and thickness.

Prompt	Response
Command:	*Type:* **ELEV** ↵
Specify new default elevation <0.00>:	↵
Specify new default thickness <0.00>:	*Type:* **1** ↵

Now everything you draw will be at elevation 0 (the ground level for this drawing) with a thickness of 1″.

Use the dimensions in Figures 16–10 and 16–11 with the proper elevation and thickness to draw the shapes described in steps 7 through 12.

Step 5. Draw the outside wall.

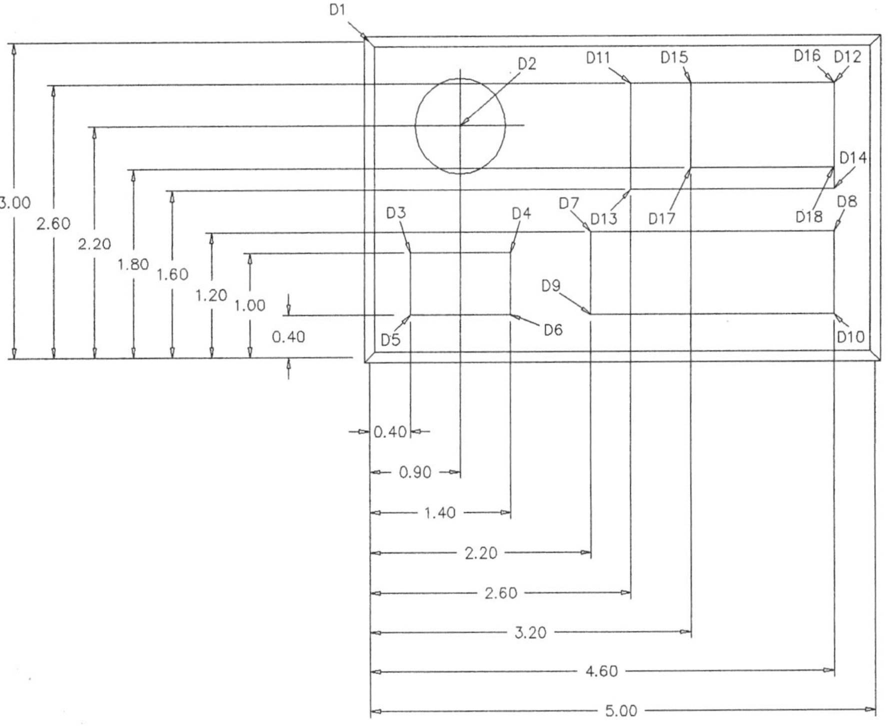

FIGURE 16–10
Dimensions from the Top View

FIGURE 16–11
Dimensions for Elevation and Thickness

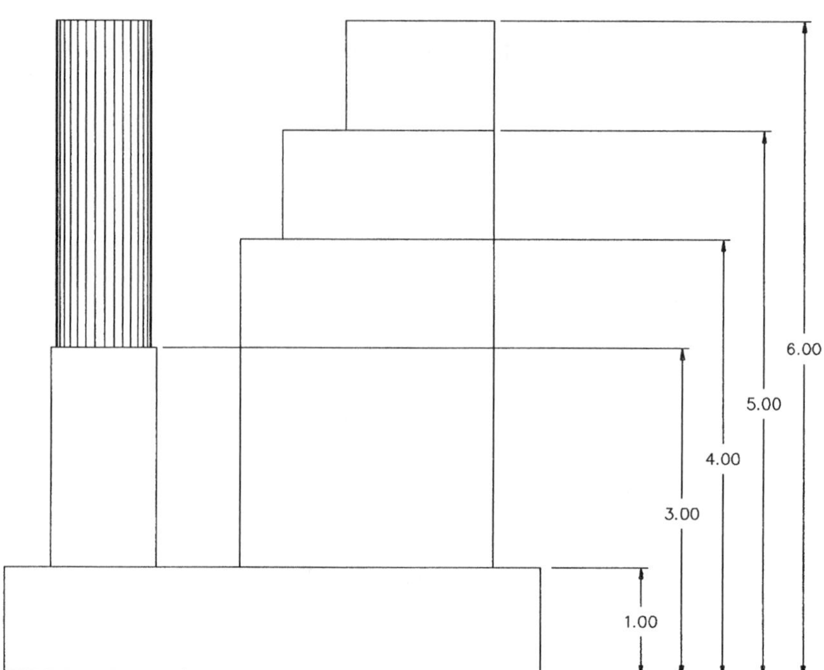

Prompt	Response
Command:	**Polyline** (or *Type:* **PL** ↵)
Specify start point:	**D1** (Figure 16–10) (Click on a point to locate the upper left corner of the wall. Plan your drawing so it is approximately centered within the drawing limits.)
Specify next point or [Arc/Close/Halfwidth/Length/Undo/Width]:	*Type:* **W** ↵
Specify starting width <0.00>:	*Type:* **.1** ↵
Specify ending width <0.10>:	↵
Specify next point or [Arc/Close/Halfwidth/Length/Undo/Width]:	With ORTHO ON, **move the cursor to the right and** *Type:* **5** ↵
Specify next point or [Arc/Close/Halfwidth/Length/Undo/Width]:	With ORTHO ON, **move the cursor down and** *Type:* **3** ↵
Specify next point or [Arc/Close/Halfwidth/Length/Undo/Width]:	**Move the cursor to the left and** *Type:* **5** ↵
Specify next point or [Arc/Close/Halfwidth/Length/Undo/Width]:	*Type:* **C** ↵

The wall is done.

Step 6. Draw the circle that has an elevation of 0, a thickness of 6″, and a diameter of 1″. Set thickness and UCS origin before you begin to draw.

Prompt	Response
Command:	*Type:* **TH** ↵
Enter new value for THICKNESS:	*Type:* **6** ↵

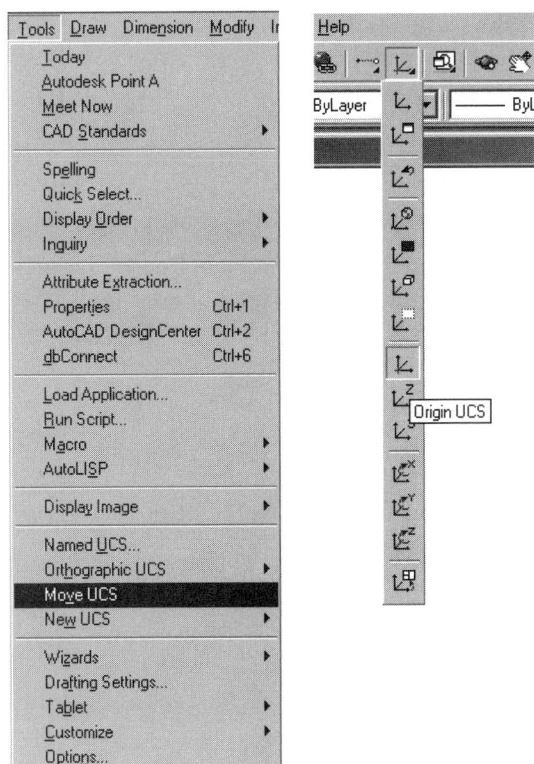

Note: Don't be concerned because you don't see thickness at this point. Remember, you are looking directly down on the plan (or top) view of this model. You will see the thickness when you change your view of the object.

Now everything you draw will have an elevation of 0 and a thickness of 6. Set the UCS origin to the lower left corner of the polyline to simplify your drawing.

Prompt	**Response**
Command:	*Type:* **UCS** ↵
Enter an option [New/Move/orthoGraphic/ Prev/Restore/Save/Del/Apply/?/World] <World>:	*Type:* **O** ↵
Specify new origin point <0,0,0>:	**Osnap-Endpoint**
of	*Click:* **the lower left corner of the wall you drew with the Polyline command**
Command:	**Circle Center, Diameter**
Specify center point for circle or [3P/2P/Ttr/ (tan tan radius)]:	*Type:* **.9,2.2** ↵

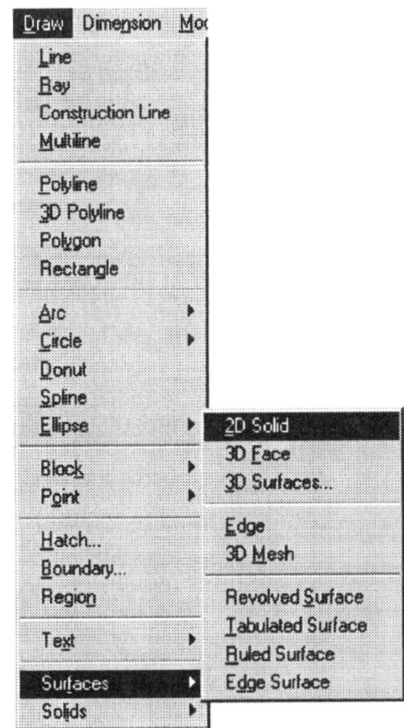

Notice that you are using absolute coordinates with respect to the new UCS origin.

Specify diameter of circle:	*Type:* **1** ↵

That finishes the circle.

Step 7. Draw the solid in front of the circle.

Prompt	**Response**
Command:	**2D Solid** (or *Type:* **SO** ↵)

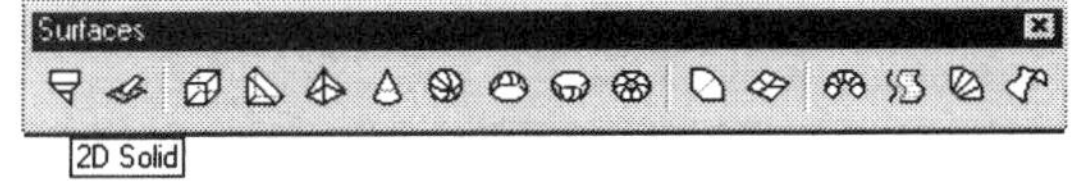

Prompt	Response
Specify first point:	**D3** (Figure 16–2) (or *Type:* **.4,1** ↵)
Specify second point:	**D4** (or *Type:* **1.4,1** ↵)
Specify third point:	**D5** (or *Type:* **.4,.4** ↵)
Specify fourth point or <exit>:	**D6** (or *Type:* **1.4,.4** ↵)
Specify third point:	↵

Note: You may turn on the coordinates display (F6) and identify locations to be picked by watching this display, or you may use absolute coordinates to draw from the newly defined UCS origin.

You have now drawn the solid in front of the circle, but you drew it with a thickness of 6 instead of 3, as Figure 16–11 shows. Let's change that after the view shows three dimensions. Now draw another three solids:

Step 8. Draw the second solid.

Prompt	Response
Command:	*Type:* **TH** ↵
Enter new value for THICKNESS <6.00>:	*Type:* **4** ↵

Now everything you draw will have an elevation of 0 and a thickness of 4.

Prompt	Response
Command:	**2D Solid** (or *Type:* **SO** ↵)
Specify first point:	**D7** (Figure 16–10) (or *Type:* **2.2, 1.2** ↵)
Specify second point:	**D8** (or *Type:* **4.6,1.2** ↵)
Specify third point:	**D9** (or *Type:* **2.2,.4** ↵)
Specify fourth point or <exit>:	**D10** (or *Type:* **4.6,.4** ↵)
Specify third point:	↵

Step 9. Draw the third solid.

Prompt	Response
Command:	*Type:* **TH** ↵
Enter new value for THICKNESS <4.00>:	*Type:* **5** ↵

Now everything you draw will have an elevation of 0 and a thickness of 5.

Prompt	Response
Command:	**2D Solid** (or *Type:* **SO** ↵)
Specify first point:	**D11** (Figure 16–10) (or *Type:* **2.6, 2.6** ↵)
Specify second point:	**D12** (or *Type:* **4.6,2.6** ↵)
Specify third point:	**D13** (or *Type:* **2.6,1.6** ↵)
Specify fourth point or <exit>:	**D14** (or *Type:* **4.6,1.6** ↵)
Specify third point:	↵

Step 10. Draw the fourth solid.

Prompt	Response
Command:	*Type:* **ELEV** ↵
Specify new default elevation <0.00>:	*Type:* **5** ↵
Specify new default thickness <1.00>:	*Type:* **1** ↵

The smallest solid is sitting on top of the 5″ solid, so its elevation, or base, is 5″. Set layer R as the current layer (so you can see it on top of the solid beneath it).

Prompt	Response
Command:	**2D Solid** (or *Type:* **SO** ↵)
Specify first point:	**D15** (Figure 16–10) (or *Type:* **3.2, 2.6** ↵)
Specify second point:	**D16** (or *Type:* **4.6,2.6** ↵)
Specify third point:	**D17** (or *Type:* **3.2,1.8** ↵)
Specify fourth point or <exit>:	**D18** (or *Type:* **4.6,1.8** ↵)
Specify third point:	↵

Now let's take a look at what you have built; AutoCAD gives you several ways of doing that.

Viewports

Step 11. Divide the screen into four viewports.

Before changing the viewpoint, divide the screen into four viewing areas so that you can clearly see just what is happening. Use the Vports command to do this.

Prompt	Response
Command:	**Viewports-4 Viewports** (or *Type:* **VPORTS** ↵, then *Select:* **Four: Equal and** *Click:* **OK**)

The display area is now divided into four viewports. The active viewport is outlined with a solid line and displays the lines of the cursor when the cursor is moved into the active viewport. Inactive viewports display an arrow when the cursor is moved into those areas. To make a different viewport active, position the arrow in the desired viewport and press the click button on your digitizer to select a different viewport as the current one. The other selections on the viewports command are as follows.

New Viewports... Allows you to name a set of viewports in model space from a dialog box and save it for future use. Named Viewports... recalls the saved viewports. Any number of sets may be named, saved, and recalled.

Named Viewports Restores a saved set of viewports. AutoCAD gives you a dialog box with the list of named viewports. You can recall or delete by selecting the viewport set from the list.

Join Joins two viewports into one larger one. The resulting view is the dominant viewport. AutoCAD asks you the following:

Note: The display screen may be divided into as many viewports as your monitor will support. Each active viewport may be divided into two, three, or four areas.

Prompt	Response
Command:	**Viewports-Join**
Select dominant viewport <current viewport>:	↵ (to accept the current active viewport, or click the one you want)
Select viewport to join:	*Click:* **the other viewport**

(Note: This is an example only. Do not do this as part of the exercise.)

Single (or 1 Viewport on the menu bar) Returns the display to a single viewport. The resulting view is the current active viewport before single was selected.

2, 3, 4 (or 2 Viewports, 3 Viewports, 4 Viewports on the menu bar) Divides the current viewport into two, three, or four viewports with the same view, snap, and grid settings. Selections 2 and 3 allow you to select a vertical or horizontal arrangement. Selection 3 also allows for two smaller viewports to the left or right of one larger viewport.

Polygonal Viewport Allows you to draw an irregular shape and use it as a viewport.

Object Allows you to draw an object such as a circle or an ellipse and use it as a viewport.

Viewpoint

In this chapter, the Viewpoint command is used to allow you to look at the model from any point you choose. There are four means of selecting the viewing point (the location of the eye that is looking at your model):

Select the Viewpoint using the Viewpoint Presets dialog box.
Type the X, Y, and Z coordinates of the viewpoint from the keyboard.
Pick the Viewpoint from the View menu on the menu bar.
Pick a point on the Viewpoint Tripod.

Many people prefer the first three methods because the resulting viewpoint is always the same. Using the AutoCAD Tripod is not quite as predictable.

To select viewpoint from the Viewpoint Presets dialog box:

Prompt	Response
Command:	*Click:* **3d Views-Viewpoint Presets**

The Viewpoint Presets dialog box, Figure 16–12, appears. The first two buttons in this box allow you to select whether you want the viewpoint to be taken with respect to the World UCS or to the UCS that is current in the drawing:

Absolute to WCS When this button is selected, the resulting viewpoint is relative to the World UCS.

Relative to UCS When this button is selected, the resulting viewpoint is relative to the UCS that is current in the drawing at the time.

The two charts in this box allow you to specify the precise viewpoint you want:

The chart on the left, consisting of a square with a circle in it, may be thought of as a viewpoint looking down on the top of an object:

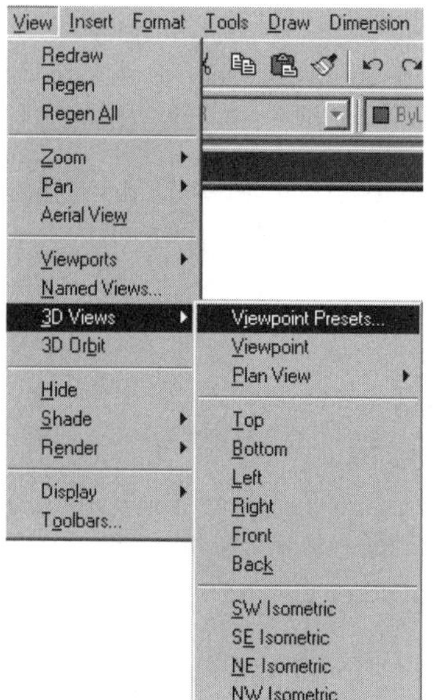

270 Places your view directly in front of the object.
315 Places your view to the right and in front of the object.
0 Places your view on the right side of the object.
45 Places your view to the right and behind the object.
90 Places your view behind the object.

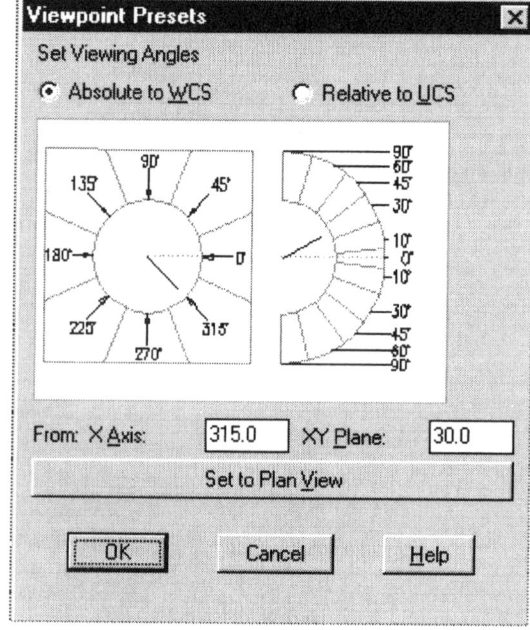

FIGURE 16–12
Select a Viewpoint for the Upper Right Viewport

135 Places your view to the left and behind the object.
180 Places your view on the left side of the object.
225 Places your view to the left and in front of the object.

The chart on the right, consisting of two semicircles, allows you to specify whether the viewpoint is to be above or below the object:

0 Places your view directly perpendicular to the chosen angle. For example, a view of 270 on the left chart and 0 on the right chart places the viewpoint directly in front of the object.
10 to 60 Places your view above the object.
90 Places your view perpendicular to the top view of the chosen angle.
−10 to −60 Places your view below the object.
−90 Places your view perpendicular to the bottom view of the chosen angle.

The buttons From: X Axis: and XY Plane: allow you to type the values of the two charts instead of selecting them. The two buttons also display these values when they are selected from the charts.

Set to Plan View When this button is clicked, the plan view (270, 90) of the object in the World or Current UCS is selected.

Step 12. Use the Viewpoint Presets dialog box to change the upper right viewport to a view above, and to the right in front.

Click the upper right viewport to make it the active viewport.

Prompt	Response
Command:	*Click:* **3D-Viewpoint Presets**
The Viewpoint Presets dialog box appears:	*Click:* **315°** in the left chart (Figure 16–12)
	Click: **30°** in the right chart
	Click: **OK**

To select Viewpoint by typing coordinates:

Figure 16–13 shows the results of four typed viewpoints. The first (0,0,1) is the plan view (the view you are looking at now). The second (−1,−1,1) means that you have moved the viewing point 1 unit to the left, 1 unit in front, and 1 unit above the object with respect to the plan view. The third (1,−1,1) says you have moved the viewpoint 1 unit to the right, 1 unit in front, and 1 unit above the model. The fourth (1,−1,−1) indicates that the viewpoint is 1 unit to the right, 1 unit in front, and 1 unit below the model. AutoCAD adjusts the magnification of the view so that all objects are displayed. Because the Viewpoint command specifies only a view direction, viewpoint 2,−2,2 is the same as 1,−1,1.

To select Viewpoint from the View menu on the menu bar:

The top two selections on the 3D Views menu provide access to the two other means of selecting the viewpoint. The other items are described next:

Plan View Allows you to select the plan view of the current UCS, the World UCS, or a saved and named UCS
Top Gives you the top view of the model.
Bottom Gives you the bottom view of the model.
Left Gives you the left side view of the model.
Right Gives you the right side view of the model.
Front Gives you the front view of the model.
Back Gives you the back view of the model.
SW Isometric Gives you an isometric view from the front, to the left, above.
SE Isometric Gives you an isometric view from the front, to the right, above.
NW Isometric Gives you an isometric view from the back, to the left, above.
NE Isometric Gives you an isometric view from the back, to the right, above.

Note: The front view is a 90° clockwise rotation of the plan view of the object looking straight into it. Left side, right side, and rear views are also 90° rotations.

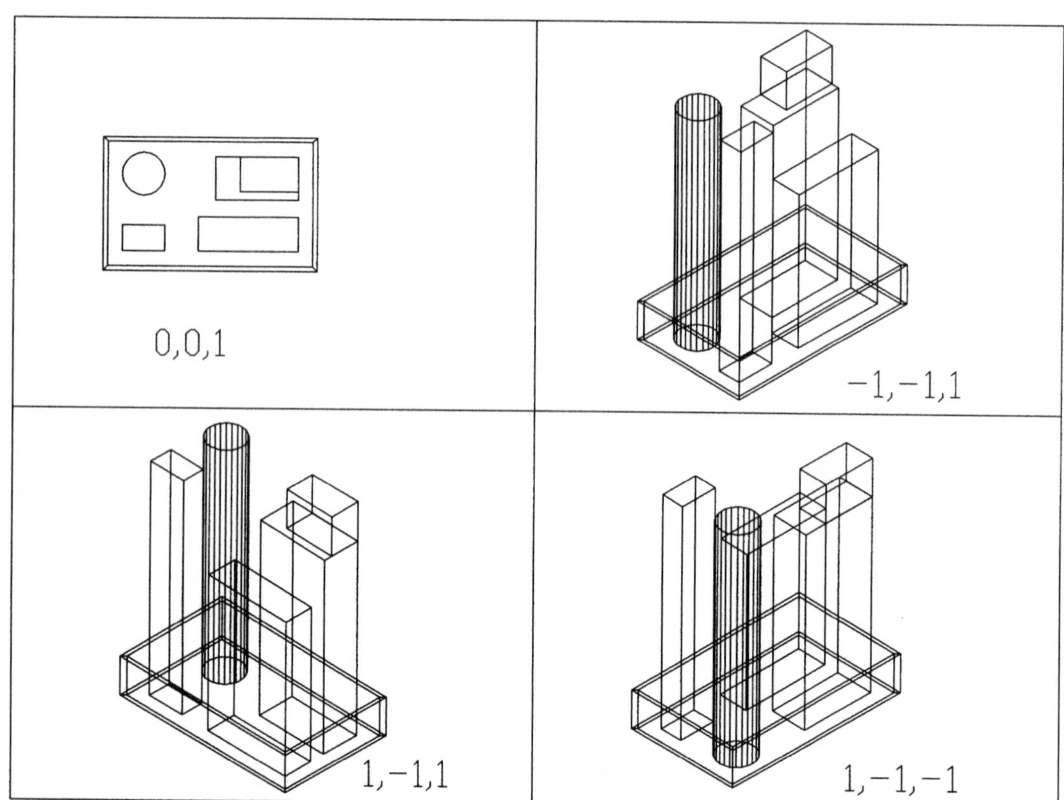

FIGURE 16–13
3D Viewpoints

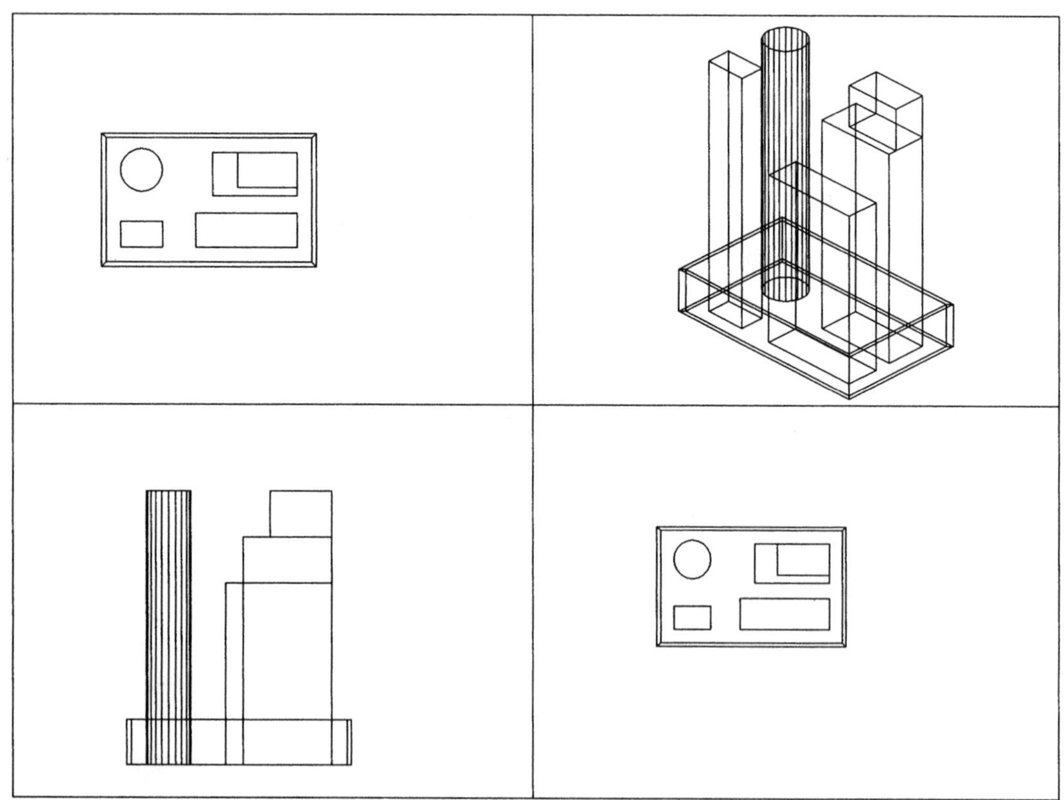

FIGURE 16–14
Changing Viewpoints

Step 13. Use 3D Views on the menu bar to change the lower left viewport of Figure 16–14 to a front view.

Use the click button on your mouse to make the lower left viewport active.

Prompt	Response
Command:	**3D Views-Front**

Step 14. Zoom out to obtain a better view of the front view of the model.

Prompt	Response
Command:	*Type:* **Z** ↵
Specify corner of a window, enter a scale factor, or [All/Center/Dynamic/Extents/Previous/Window]<real time>:	*Type:* **.75X** ↵

Step 15. Use the Pan command to center the front view of the model in the lower left viewport.

Prompt	Response
Command:	*Type:* **P** ↵
Press ESC or ENTER to exit, or right click to display the shortcut menu:	*Click:* **a point near the center of the model itself, hold down the pick button and move the display to a point in the approximate center of the viewport so the view is centered as shown in Figure 16–14**

To select VPOINT using the AutoCAD Tripod:

The AutoCAD Tripod is another convenient way to select a viewpoint. Although the tripod provides a visual insight into what the resulting display will be, you cannot click the same spot on the tripod every time. The resulting display does not give you exactly the same orientation each time, as the previously described methods do.

The AutoCAD Tripod is shown in Figure 16–15. As you move the cursor inside the tripod, the tripod with its X, Y, and Z axes moves to give you an idea of what the resulting display will be. When the tripod appears to have the desired orientation, click that spot inside the tripod to produce the desired viewpoint.

Study Figure 16–15 a few moments to obtain an understanding of what each area on the tripod signifies. The inner circle is above the object. The outer circle is below it. Any point below the horizontal line is in front of the object. Any point above the horizontal

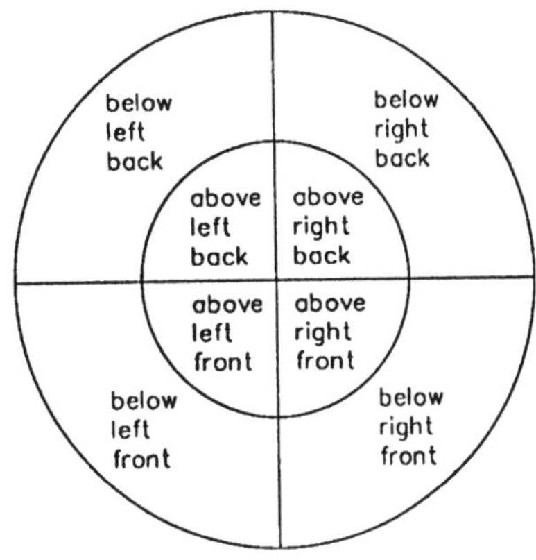

FIGURE 16–15
AutoCAD LT Tripod

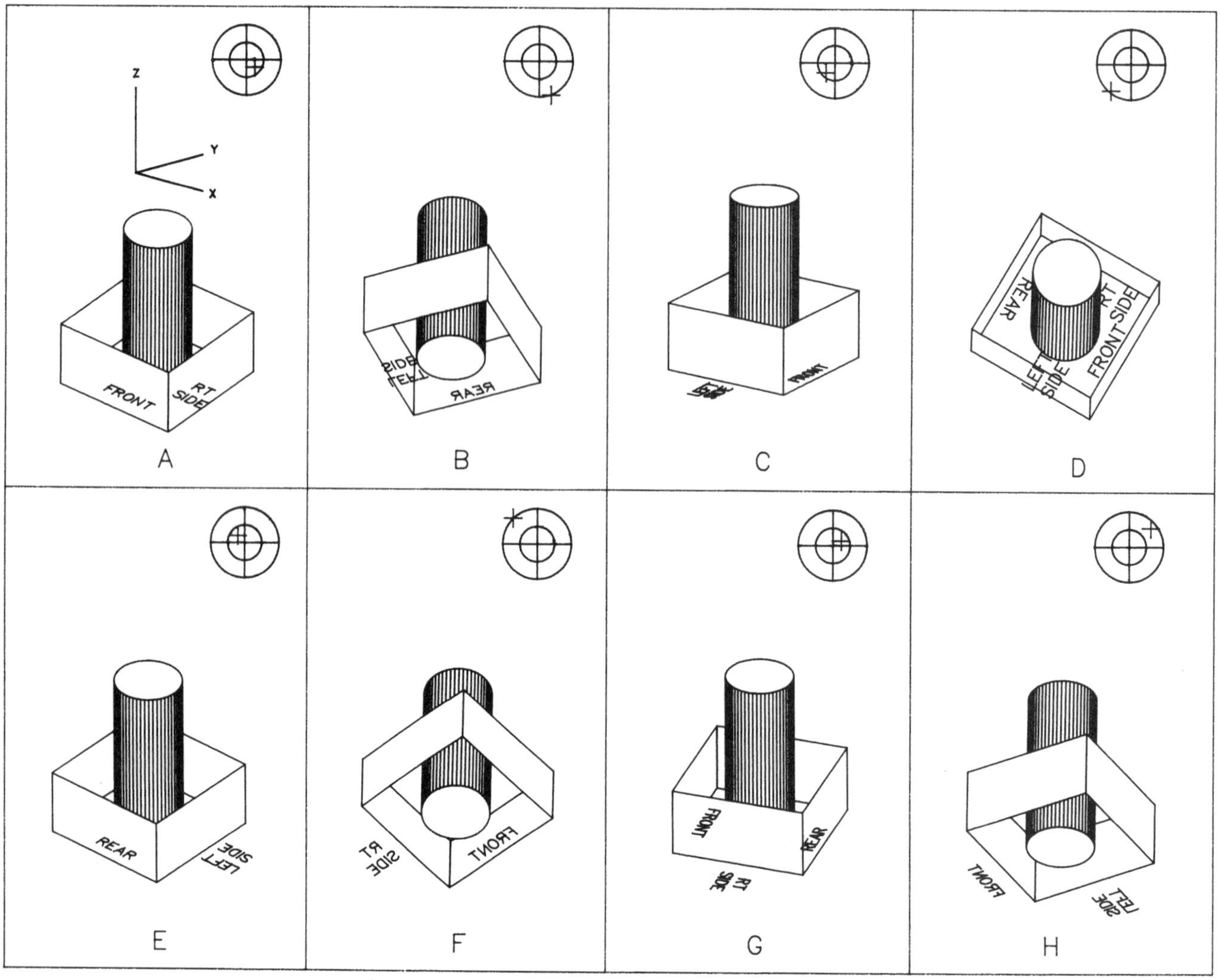

FIGURE 16–16
Tripod Viewpoints

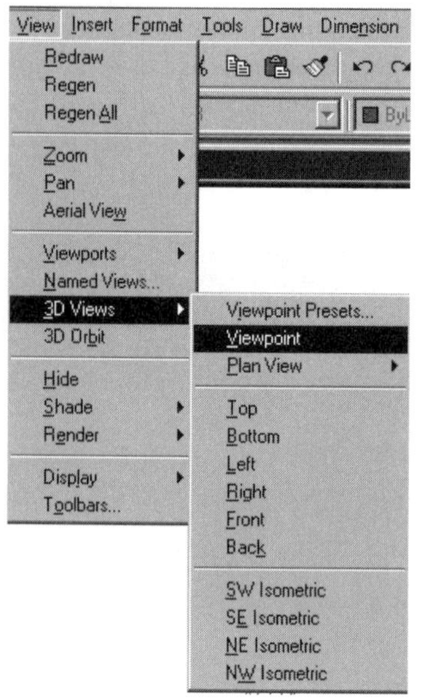

line is behind it. Any point to the right of the vertical line is looking at the viewer's right side of the object; left of the vertical line is the viewer's left side. Clicking a point on the inner circle right of the vertical line and below the horizontal line produces a viewpoint above, in front of, and to the right of the object. Figure 16–16 shows examples of eight different picks on the Tripod.

Step 16. Use the AutoCAD Tripod to change the lower right viewport of Figure 16–17 to a view below, in back, and to the right.

Use the click button on your mouse to make the lower right viewport active.

Prompt	Response
Command:	**3D Views-Viewpoint** (or *Type:* **VPOINT** ↵ and ↵ again)
The AutoCAD Tripod appears:	*Click:* **the location on the tripod shown as Figure 16–16H to create the display shown in Figure 16–17.**

Step 17. On your own:

Use Zoom and Pan (or the scroll bars) to create the display shown in Figure 16–17 if it is not that already.

FIGURE 16–17
Final Display

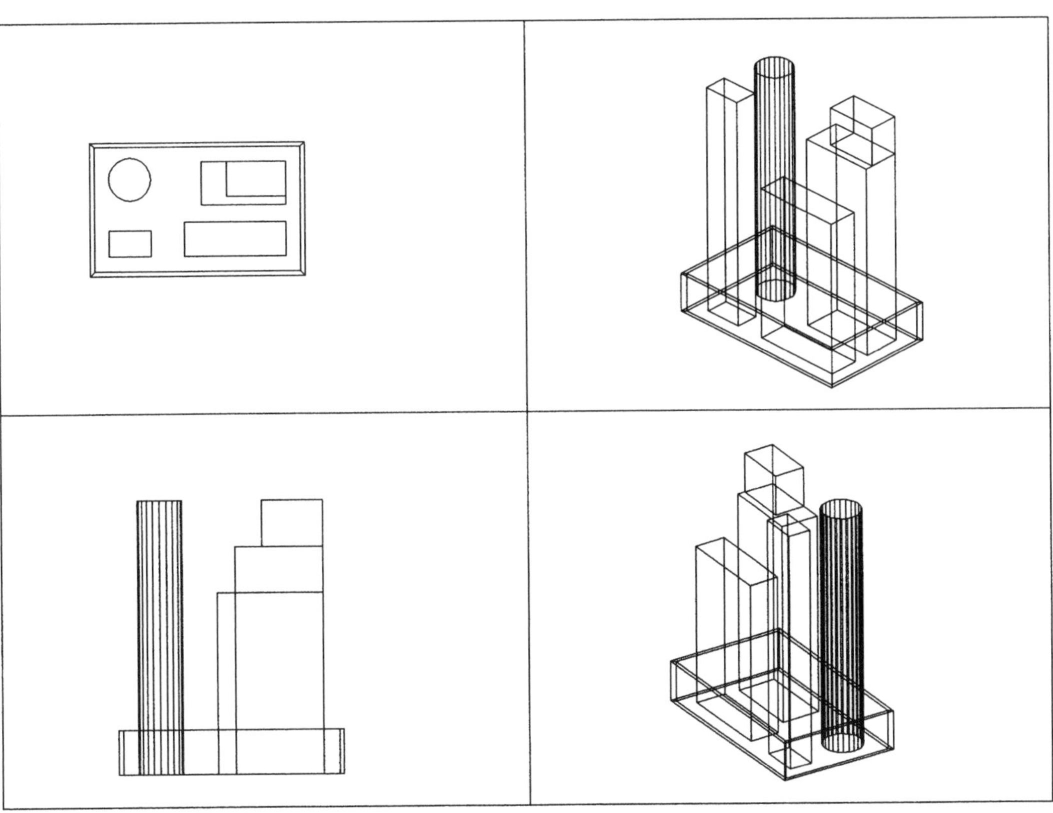

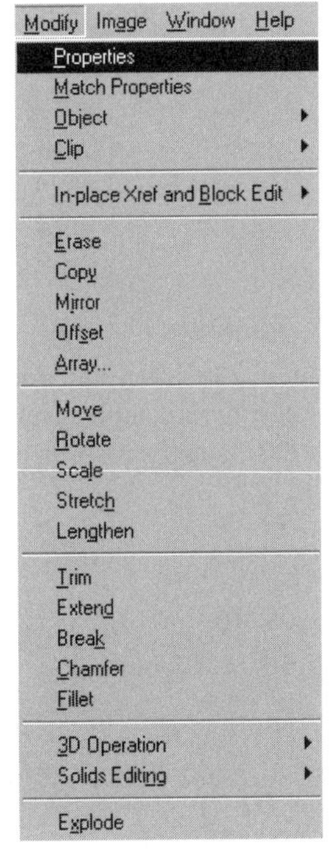

Warning: When you are working in 3-D, there are times when you absolutely *must* use Osnap to move or insert objects. An object that appears to be placed on the endpoint of a line, for example, may be in front of, behind, below, or above where it appears to be unless Osnap is used to designate the endpoint of the line.

Correcting Your Drawing

Before proceeding, use the Properties... command to change the thickness of the solid that is presently 6″ to 3″, as shown in Figure 16–11.

Step 18. Use Properties... to change the height (thickness) of the solid in front of the cylinder from 6″ to 3″.

Prompt	Response
Command:	*Click:* **the SOLID in front of the cylinder**
Command:	**Properties...**
The Properties dialog box (Figure 16–18) appears:	*Click:* **Thickness,** then **change the thickness from 6.000 to 3.000, as shown in Figure 16–18.**
	Click: **the X in the upper right corner to close**

The height (thickness) of the object changes. To change the elevation, use the Move command and use relative coordinates to move the object in the Z direction. (Example: @0,0,−2 moves the object 2″ downward.)

Step 19. Hide surfaces that are behind other surfaces.

Now that you have acceptable viewpoints, select the upper right viewport to set it current and remove all lines that are covered by surfaces that are in front of them. AutoCAD uses the Hide command to do that.

Pick the upper right viewport to make it active.

Prompt	Response
Command:	**Hide** (or *Type:* **HI** ↵)

FIGURE 16–18
Use the Properties Dialog Box to Change Thickness

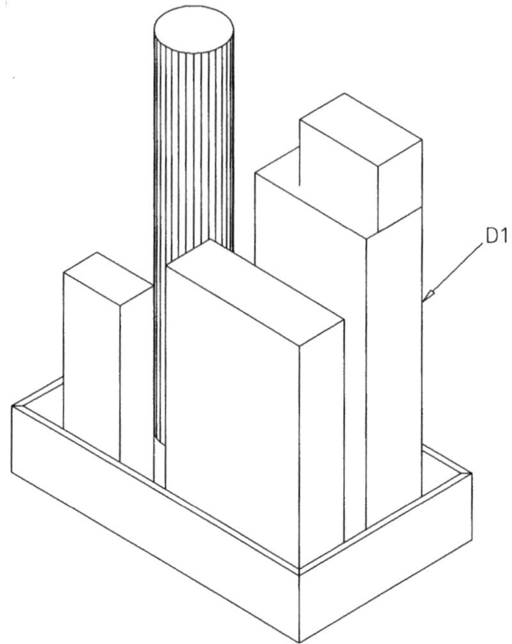

FIGURE 16–19
Hide Results

Note: Your display may not show a line missing. If it doesn't, you were lucky. You will have similar problems on other 3-D models, so read this information carefully.

View Insert Format
Redraw
Regen
Regen All
Zoom
Pan
Aerial View
Viewports
Named Views...
3D Views
3D Orbit
Hide
Shade
Render
Display
Toolbars...

The resulting display is shown in Figure 16–19.

Step 20. Correct Hide problems.

Notice that the bottom line of the top solid does not show (you may be lucky and not have this problem). When surfaces touch, the Hide command displays unpredictable results. To correct the display, either move the top box up a little or make the supporting box a little shorter (less thick).

Prompt	Response
Command:	*Click:* **D1** (Figure 16–19)
The Properties dialog box appears:	**Change the thickness from 5.000 to 4.98**
	Click: **OK**
Command:	**Hide** (or *Type:* **HI** ↵)

Figure 16–20 is displayed.

Other problems that are encountered may be solved in a similar manner. Cylinders inside other cylinders, such as a shaft in a support, may produce lines that do not hide correctly. Increase the clearance between the hole and the shaft by making the hole bigger or the shaft smaller to correct the problem. On full-scale models of machine parts, a clearance of .02 seems to work well. You may need to experiment with this on larger models.

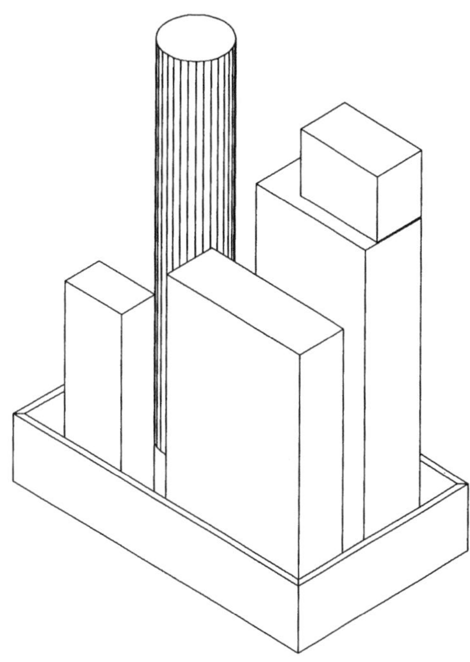

FIGURE 16–20 Hide Results after Changing Thickness

UCS and 3D Viewpoint

Warning: 3D Viewpoint is only a point from which the view is taken. Nothing is moved, nor are multiple objects displayed. This is all the same model, so if you do anything to move or alter the model itself in one view, you are doing it to all views. Keep in mind the distinction between *viewing* and *creating* the model.

The 3D Viewpoint command describes viewpoints for the current UCS (user coordinate system). A user coordinate system may be thought of as the grid on which you are drawing or creating your model. If, for example, you want to draw a series of blocks to represent windows on one of the vertical faces of the model, you will have to rotate the grid to that vertical face. The plan viewpoint will then be perpendicular to that UCS, and all viewpoints selected after that will relate to that UCS.

The next step involves restoring a viewport configuration in paper space. There has been no mention of paper space until now. A full discussion of model space and paper space appears in the next chapter. The following is an introduction to plotting multiple viewports, which can be done only in paper space. The commands associated with this procedure will be described in detail in Chapter 20.

Step 21. Save the current viewport configuration and restore it in paper space (Sheet 1).

Prompt	Response
Command:	**New Viewports...**
The Viewports dialog box appears:	*Type:* **VP1** (in the New name: box)
Command:	*Click:* **OK**
	Click: **Layout1** (the tab next to Model at the bottom of your screen.)

Clicking Layout1 sets Tilemode to 0 and places you into paper space.

Status Bar

The status bar at the bottom of your display shows you when you are in model space or paper space, with Tilemode OFF.

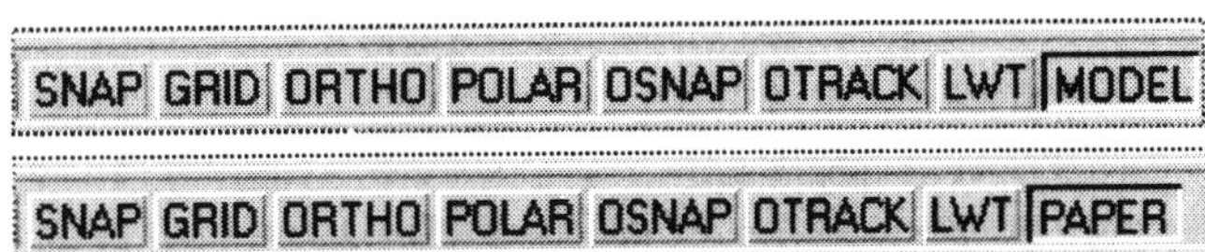

Tilemode

The Tilemode setting may be ON (1) or OFF (0). When you *Click:* the Model tab (next to Layout1), you turn Tilemode ON. When you *Click:* any of the layout tabs (Layout1, in this case), you turn Tilemode OFF.

1 When Tilemode is ON, you are in model space, where the model is created.

0 When Tilemode is OFF, you may be in either model space, where you can alter the model, or in paper space, where you cannot change the model but you can plot multiple viewports and otherwise document the model. With Tilemode OFF you can switch from model space to paper space by typing PS or go from paper space to model space by typing MS. You may also switch by clicking MODEL or PAPER. More details on this topic are contained in Chapter 17.

You have another large viewport now that you don't need. Erase it by clicking on its outside edge, then *Press:* the Delete key or *Type:* **E↵↵.**

Note: If your viewport views are too big, *Click:* PAPER on the status bar to move to model space and use a zoom factor of .4XP in each viewport.

Prompt	Response
Command:	**Named Viewports...**
The Viewports dialog box appears:	*Click:* **VP1**
	Click: **OK**
Specify first corner or [Fit]<Fit>:	*Type:* **2.5,2.5** ↵
	Click: **OK**
Specify opposite corner:	*Type:* **11.5,8.5** ↵

MVIEW

The MVIEW command may be used to turn an individual paper space viewport on or off (visible or not); remove hidden lines in individual viewports when the drawing is plotted in paper space; fit a viewport configuration within the available display area; create two, three, or four viewports with a single operation; restore a saved VPORT configuration; or set paper space limits by locating the lower left corner with the first point and the upper right corner with the second point. When a new viewport is created, you also have the choice of fitting the new viewports within the display area or digitizing a window for the new viewport.

Step 22. Insert your drawing B-size (the B-size format) at 0,0 insertion point. Answer prompts as shown in Figure 16–21.

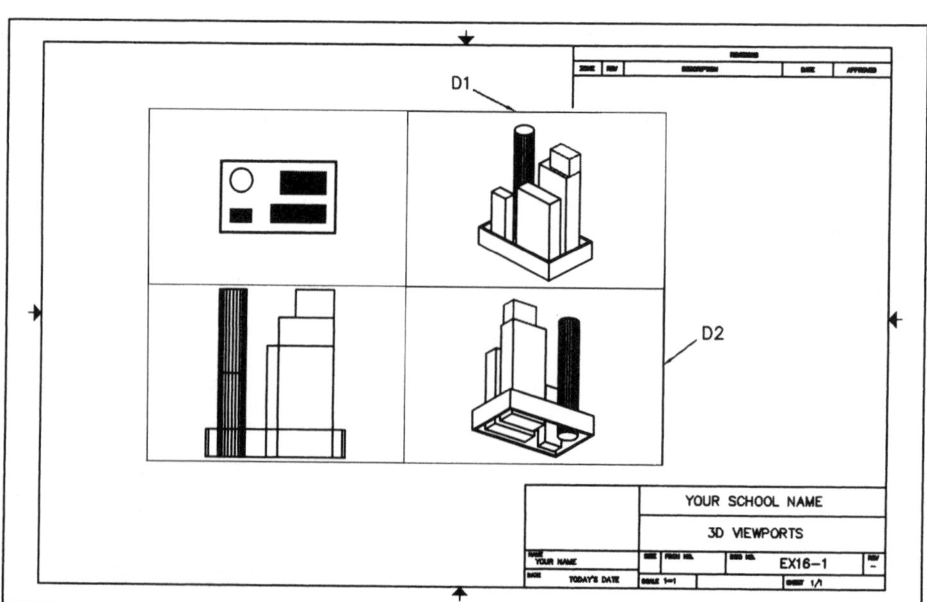

FIGURE 16–21
Final Appearance for Plotting

Step 23. Use the Hideplot option of MVIEW to remove hidden lines in the two right viewports on the plotted drawing.

Prompt	**Response**
Command:	*Type:* **MV** ↵, then *Type:* **H** ↵ for Hideplot
Hidden line removal for plotting [ON/OFF]:	*Type:* **ON** ↵
Select objects:	**D1, D2** (Figure 16–21) (You may click any point on the outside edge of any viewport in which you want hidden lines removed.)

The display will not show hidden lines removed, but the plot preview will, and the drawing will plot with hidden lines removed.

Note: All construction for 2-D and 3-D models should be done in model space, as was done in all previous chapters. Paper space allows you to plot all your viewports at once and permits annotating within and across viewports. Paper space also allows viewports to overlap, creating a varied and flexible drawing space. These viewports may be erased, moved, or otherwise edited. Model space does not allow viewports to overlap, and only one model space viewport may be plotted at a time.

Step 24. On your own:

1. Make a new layer, name it VIEWPORT, and turn it OFF.
2. Use Properties to change the outside boundary of all viewports to the viewports layer, or *Click:* all four boundaries and *Click:* the VIEWPORT layer on the layer list on the Object Properties toolbar.
3. Save your drawing in at least two places.
4. Plot the drawing 1/2 size (1 Plotted inch = 2 Drawing units) centered on an 11″ × 8.5″ sheet.
5. Exit AutoCAD.

Other Objects for Basic 3-D

Shapes that you want to appear as solids must be drawn as solids, polylines, circles, donuts, or other objects. Figure 16–22 shows several solids. If you are drawing polylines, solids, or donuts, be sure to change elevation and thickness before you draw these shapes.

FIGURE 16–22
3-D Shapes

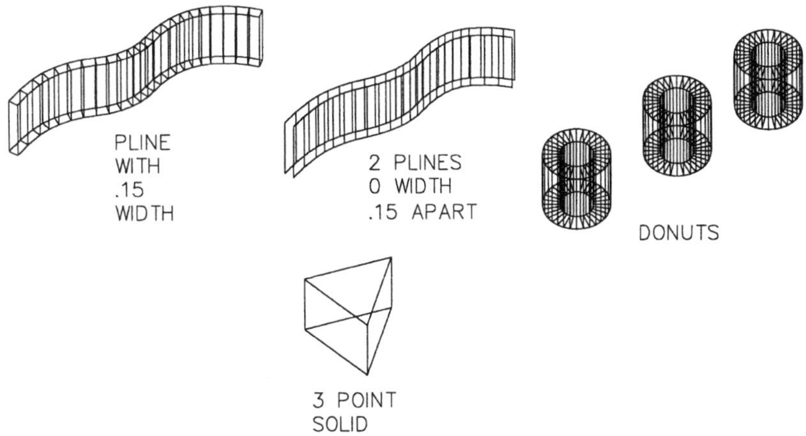

EXERCISES

EXERCISE 16–1. Complete Exercise 16–1 using steps 1 through 24 described in this chapter.

EXERCISE 16–2. Create a 3-D model from Figure 16–23.

Use settings from Exercise 16–1.
Draw this as two cylinders (use Circle or Donut) with a 0 width polyline (height 1″) around them.
Use two viewports.
Pick one viewpoint above and to the right (SE Isometric) and one beneath and to the left (1, −1, −1).
Place your name in the lower right corner in Layout1 using the simplex font.

FIGURE 16–23
Exercise 16–2

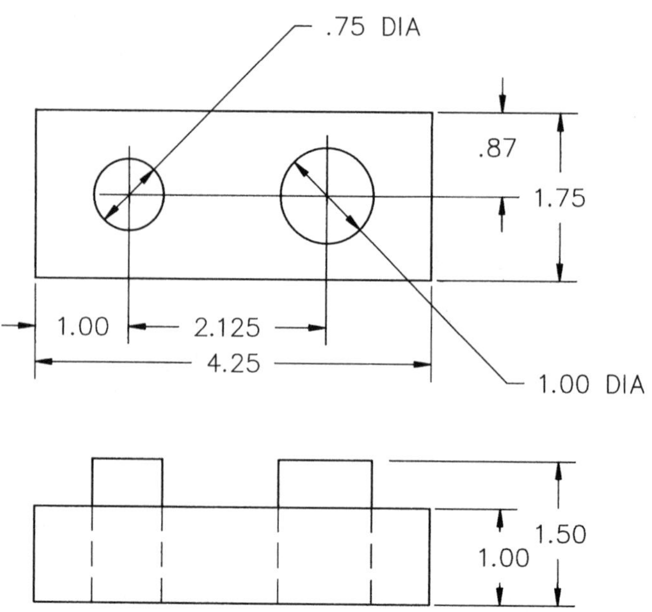

Use the Hideplot option of the Mview command for both viewports.

Plot the drawing to include both viewports to fit on a horizontal 11″ × 8.5″ sheet.

EXERCISE 16–3. Create a 3-D model of the chair shown in Figure 16–24.

Use settings from Exercise 16–1. Reset Limits to 30,40 (upper right corner), Grid to 2, Snap to 1, Units to Architectural.

FIGURE 16–24
Exercise 16–3

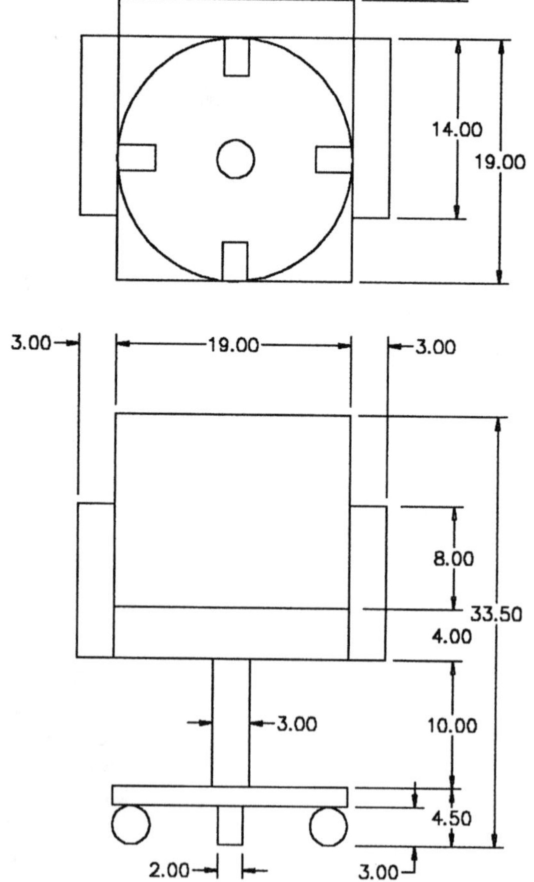

Split the screen into two vertical viewports, one with the top viewpoint, the other with the front viewpoint—so you can see where the parts of the model are.
Use the 2D Solid command or Polyline with width to draw the seat, arms, and back of the chair. Use donut or circle for the base, support, and casters. You will have to rotate your UCS 90° about the X axis to draw the casters, or draw one caster in the World UCS and use Rotate 3D to rotate it into position, then use Polar Array to copy the other three.
Use a single viewport when you have completed the model.
Pick a viewpoint of 1,−1,1.
Be sure the UCS is set to World.
Make sure a check appears in the Hide Lines check box in the Plot Configuration dialog box.
Plot the drawing to fit on a horizontal 8½″ × 11″ sheet.
Write your name on the finished plot (the hard copy).

EXERCISE 16–4. Create the table shown in Figure 16–25.

Use settings from Exercise 16–3. Reset Limits to 80,80 (upper right corner).
Make sure the bottom of the base rests on elevation 0.00. Draw the table with three circles with different elevations and thickness.
Pick a viewpoint of 1,−1,1.
Be sure the UCS is set to World.
Plot the drawing to fit on a horizontal 8½″ × 11″ sheet (remove hidden lines).
Write your name on the hard copy.

EXERCISE 16–5. Create the walls for a small office, as shown in Figure 16–26. The walls should have a thickness of 8′. With the UCS set to World, insert the table and four chairs from Exercises 16–3 and 16–4.

FIGURE 16–25
Exercise 16–4

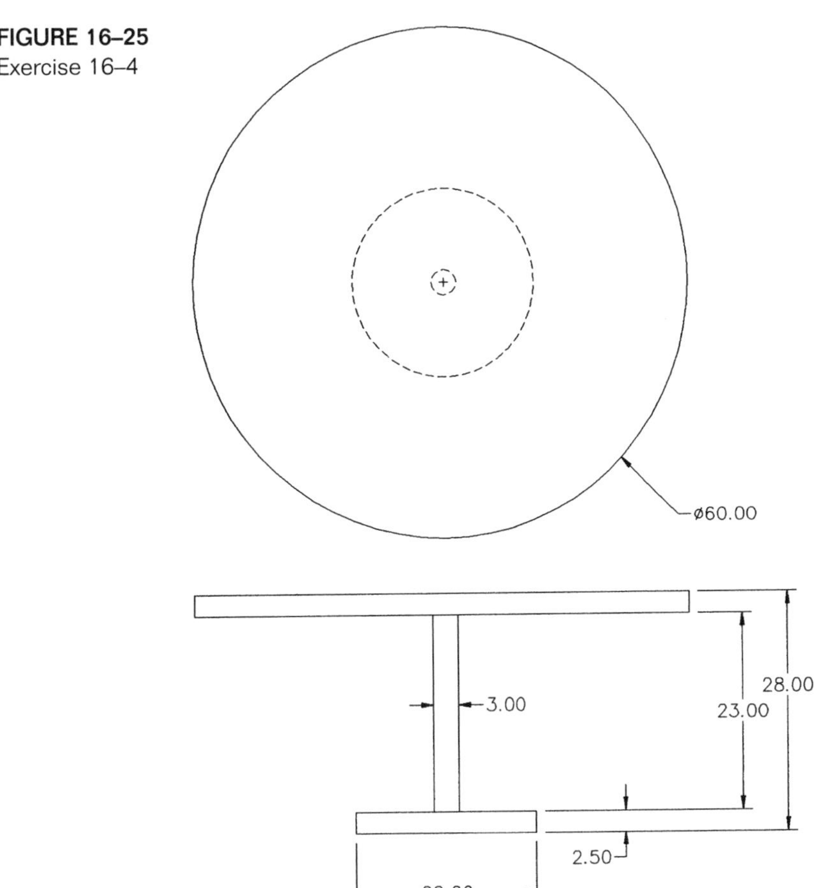

FIGURE 16–26
Exercise 16–5

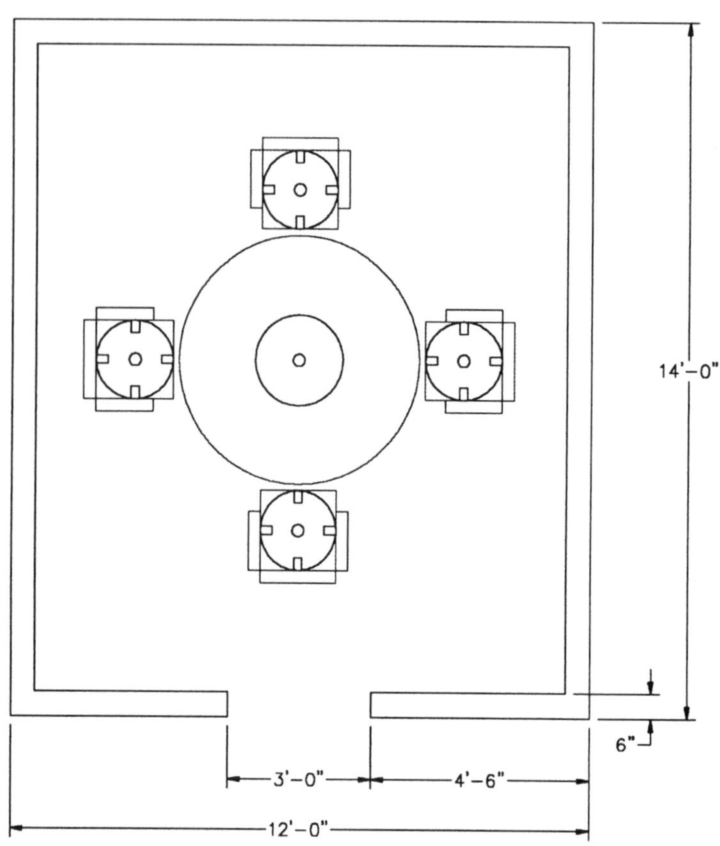

Use settings from Exercise 16–3. Reset Limits to 20′,30′ (upper right corner). Be sure to include the foot (′) mark.
Reset GRID to 12, SNAP to 3.
Pick a viewpoint on the 3D Viewpoint Tripod that is above and to the left of the completed room.
Use the Viewports (VPORTS) command and create three viewports, two on the left and one on the right.
Make the top viewport on the left the top view.
Make the bottom viewport on the left the front view.
Leave the right viewport as a 3-D view.
Use Zoom and Pan to position the objects in the viewports so that they are centered with adequate space around them.
Save this viewport configuration in model space and restore it on Layout1 with the first point at .5,.5 and the second point at 10.5,8.
Place your name in the lower right corner in paper space.
Use the Hideplot option of the MVIEW command to remove hidden lines in the right viewport.
Plot the drawing to fit on a horizontal 8½″ × 11″ sheet.

EXERCISE 16–6. Create 3-D objects of Figures 16–27 through 16–30. Place each one on a separate horizontal 8½″ × 11″ sheet. Use a polyline with width and thickness for all solid rectangles.

Exercise 16–6C is three cylinders that can be drawn with either the Circle or Donut commands.
Use settings from Exercise 16–1.
Pick a pleasing 3-D viewpoint for each object.
Use Set UCS-View and use Dtext to place your name in the lower right corner.
Plot each one at a ratio of 1 = 1 on a horizontal 8½″ × 11″ sheet. Remove hidden lines when you plot.

FIGURE 16–27
Exercise 16–6A

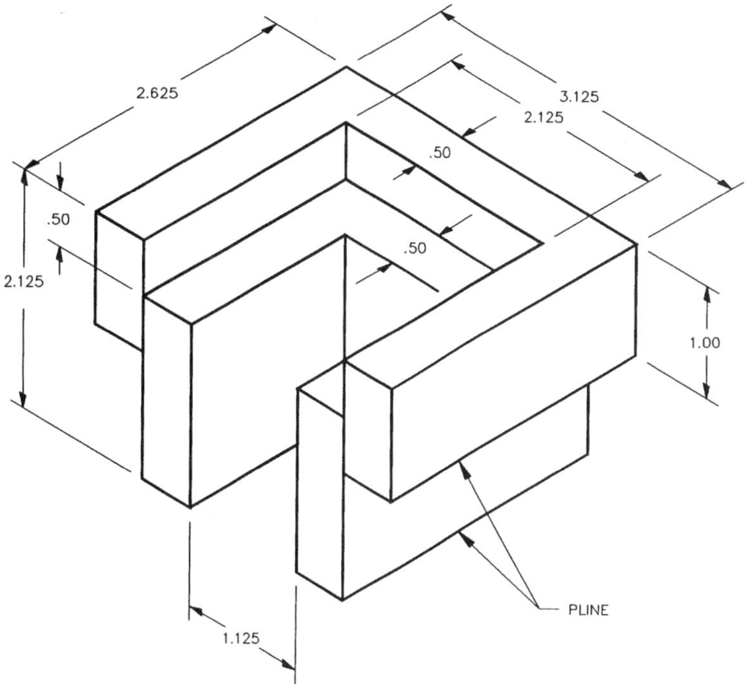

FIGURE 16–28
Exercise 16–6B

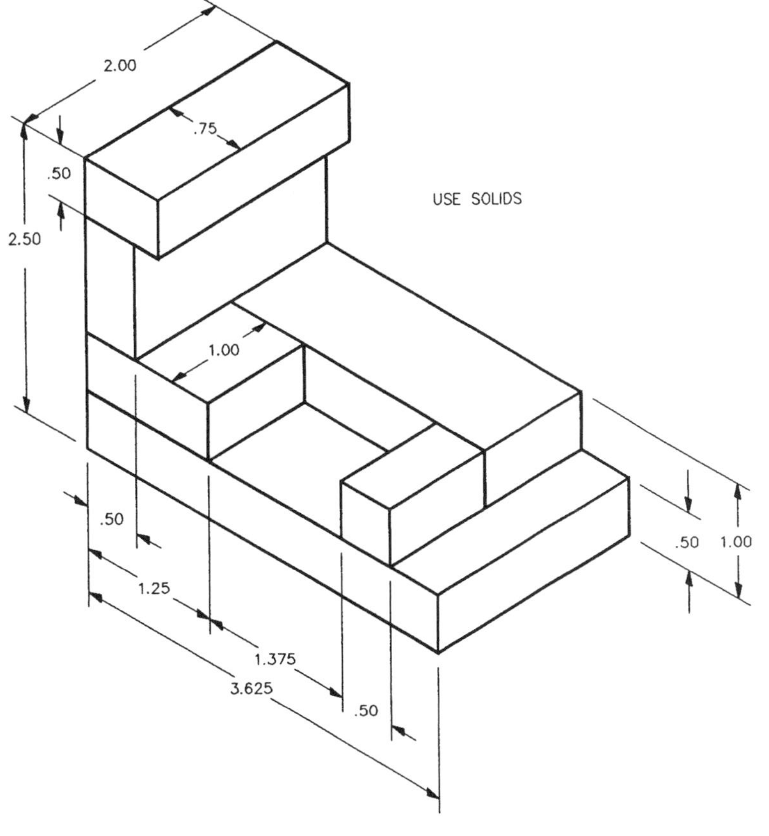

FIGURE 16–29
Exercise 16–6C

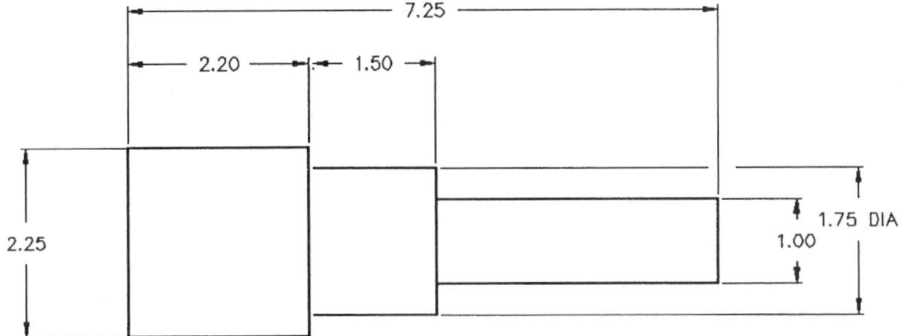

FIGURE 16–30
Exercise 16–6D

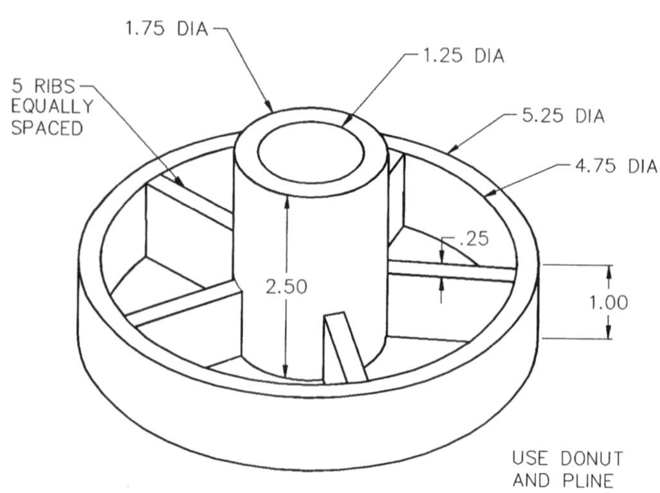

REVIEW QUESTIONS

Circle the best answer.

1. Drawing in three dimensions requires the same concepts of space as drawing in two dimensions.
   a. True
   b. False
2. Thickness values may be set with the use of which of the following settings?
   a. Layer
   b. Tilemode
   c. Viewport
   d. Elev
   e. Mview
3. Which command is used to remove lines hidden by surfaces that are in front of them?
   a. UCS
   b. 3D Viewpoint-Save
   c. Hide
   d. Tripod
   e. Floating Viewports
4. The AutoCAD DesignCenter allows you to use blocks from another drawing.
   a. True
   b. False
5. Which of the following UCS options is used to change 0,0,0 from the lower left corner of the screen to a corner of the drawing?
   a. View
   b. Restore
   c. Origin (or Move)
   d. Rotate
   e. x,y,z
6. Which of the following viewpoints from the Viewpoint Presets dialog box displays a view above and to the right of the model?
   a. 315,30
   b. 225,30
   c. 45,−30
   d. 315,−30
   e. 135,30
7. Which of the following viewpoints displays a view above and to the left of the model?
   a. 315,30
   b. 225,30
   c. 45,−30
   d. 315,−30
   e. 135,30

8. Models are constructed in
   a. Model space
   b. Paper space
9. When the tab Layout1 is active you can be in model space only.
   a. True
   b. False
10. To create a shape that is 3″ from the floor and 5″ tall, which is the correct setting?
    a. Elevation 3, thickness 5
    b. Elevation 0, thickness 8
    c. Elevation 5, thickness 3
    d. Elevation 8, thickness −3
    e. Elevation 0, thickness 3,5

Complete.

11. Write the command described in this chapter that allows you to view an object in three dimensions.

    ____

12. Write the command that splits the display into two, three, or four areas.

    ____

13. Write the command that allows you to set thickness only.

    ____

14. Write the command that allows you to set elevation and thickness.

    ____

15. Write the command that allows you to change the thickness of an existing entity.

    ____

16. Describe the uses of model space and paper space.
    Model space:

    ____

    ____

    Paper space:

    ____

    ____

17. Describe the view obtained when you pick NE Isometric from 3D Viewpoint from the View menu on the menu bar.

    ____

18. Describe the view obtained when you pick SW Isometric from 3D Viewpoint from the View menu on the menu bar.

    ____

19. Describe how to activate the 3D Viewpoint Tripod from the View menu on the menu bar.

    ____

20. List five categories of objects that the AutoCAD DesignCenter allows you to use on a new drawing from an existing drawing (for example: Layers).

    ____

17 Customizing Toolbars and Menus

OBJECTIVES

After completing this chapter, you will be able to

- □ Make new toolbars.
- □ Add tools to a toolbar.
- □ Delete tools from a toolbar.
- □ Move tools from one toolbar to another toolbar.
- □ Copy tools from one toolbar to another toolbar.
- □ Delete toolbars.
- □ Position toolbars.
- □ Display toolbars.
- □ Hide toolbars.
- □ Create and edit tools.
- □ Make a new menu bar.
- □ Make a new .mnu (menu) file.
- □ Copy the acad.mnu file under another name.
- □ Add macros to a menu.
- □ Delete commands from a menu.
- □ Move commands from one position to another.
- □ Copy commands from one menu to another.
- □ Delete menus.
- □ Position menus on the menu bar.
- □ Load menus.
- □ Unload menus.

CUSTOMIZING TOOLBARS

AutoCAD allows you to create custom toolbars that allow you to be more productive by arranging tools so they can be found easily and quickly. In this chapter you will make new toolbars, delete old ones, and create and edit your own tools. Also in this chapter you will learn to customize items on the menu bar to complete this introduction to customizing. Let's begin by making a new toolbar.

MAKING A NEW TOOLBAR

When you make a new toolbar it has no tools. You have to drag tools onto the new toolbar from the Customize Toolbars dialog box. In Exercise 17–1 you will start a new toolbar and load it with tools you use frequently.

Exercise 17–1: Create a New Toolbar and Load It with Tools

Your final toolbar will look similar to the one shown in Figure 17–1.

FIGURE 17–1
Your New Toolbar

Step 1. To begin Exercise 17–1, turn on the computer and start AutoCAD. *Click:* **Start from Scratch,** then **English (feet and inches)**

Step 2. Make a new toolbar.

Prompt	Response
Command:	**Toolbars...** (from the View menu) (or *Click:* **any tool with the RETURN button of your pointing device,** then *Click:* **Customize...**)
The Customize dialog box appears:	*Click:* **the Toolbars tab,** then *Click:* **New:**
The New Toolbar dialog box (Figure 17–2) appears:	*Type:* **(your initials)TOOLS** in the Toolbar Name: text box
	Click: **OK**

Your new toolbar (Figure 17–3) is displayed. (If the toolbar is not visible, it is hidden behind other toolbars. Either move the other toolbars or turn them OFF.)

Step 3. On your own:

Move your new toolbar to the left side of the screen (Figure 17–4) so it will be to the left of the Customize dialog box. Position your cursor over the toolbar title area, hold down the click button on your pointing device, and release the click button when the toolbar is where you want it to be.

Adding Tools to Toolbars

Step 4. Add tools to your new toolbar from the Customize dialog box.

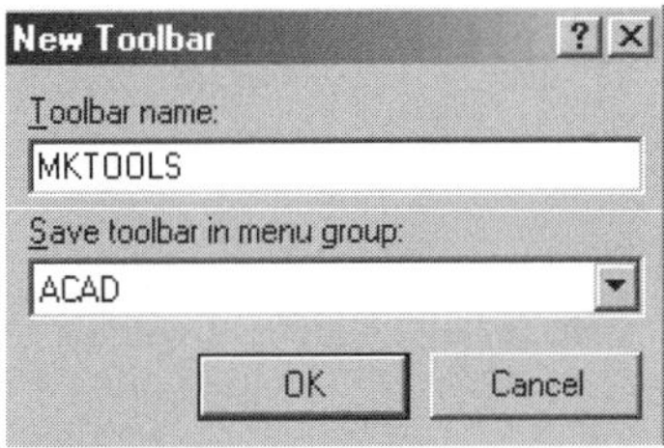

FIGURE 17–2
New Toolbar Dialog Box with Your New Name

FIGURE 17–3
Your New Toolbar

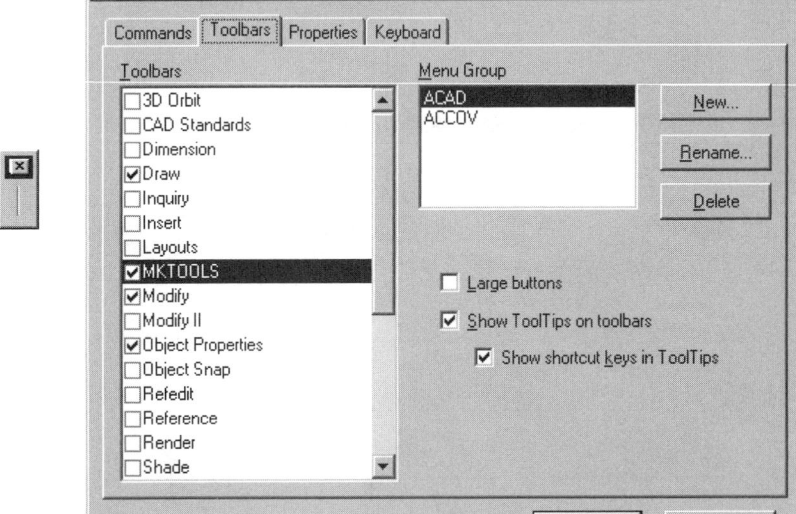

FIGURE 17–4
Move the New Toolbar to the Left Side of the Screen

Prompt	Response
With the Customize dialog box displayed:	*Click:* **the Commands tab**
The Commands tab (Figure 17–5) appears:	*Click:* **Draw** from the list of categories
The tools on the Draw toolbar appear on the right side of the dialog box:	**Copy the Line tool from the Draw category to your toolbar by moving the cursor so it is over the Line tool, then press the click button and hold it down while you drag the Line tool and release it inside your new toolbar.**
Your new toolbar now contains the Line tool:	**Copy the Polyline, Donut, and Single Line Text icons to your toolbar as shown in Figure 17–6.** (You will have to click the scroll bar to find the icons.)
	Click: **the Modify category** (Figure 17–7)
	Copy the Move, Copy Object, Mirror, Offset, Chamfer, and Fillet tools to your toolbar as shown in Figure 17–7
	Click: **the Dimension category** (Figure 17–8)
	Copy the Linear Dimension and Radius Dimension tools to your toolbar as shown in Figure 17–8.
	Click: **Close**

Note: If the shape of your toolbar is different from the one in Figure 17–6, that's OK. It can be changed later.

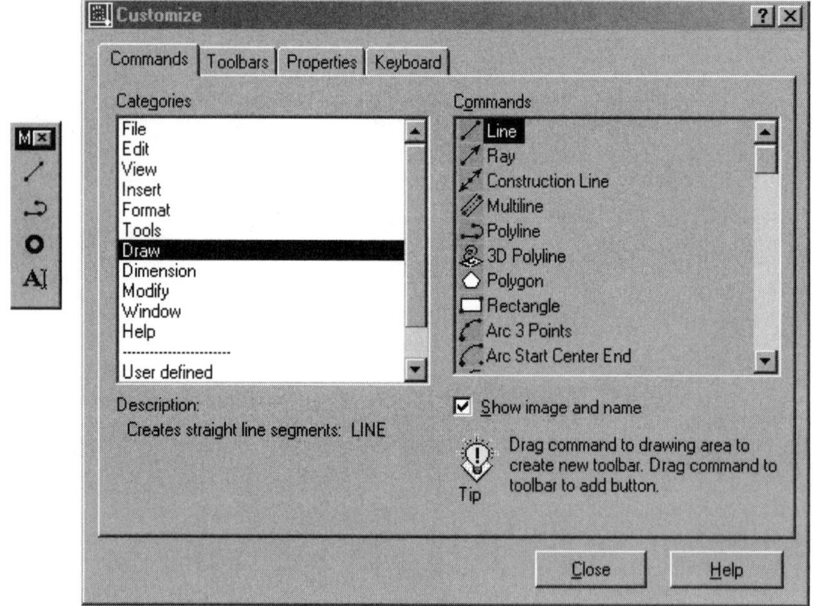

FIGURE 17–5
Customize Dialog Box with Draw Category

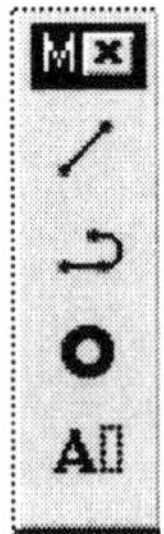

FIGURE 17–6
New Toolbar with Line, Polyline, Donut, and Dtext Tools

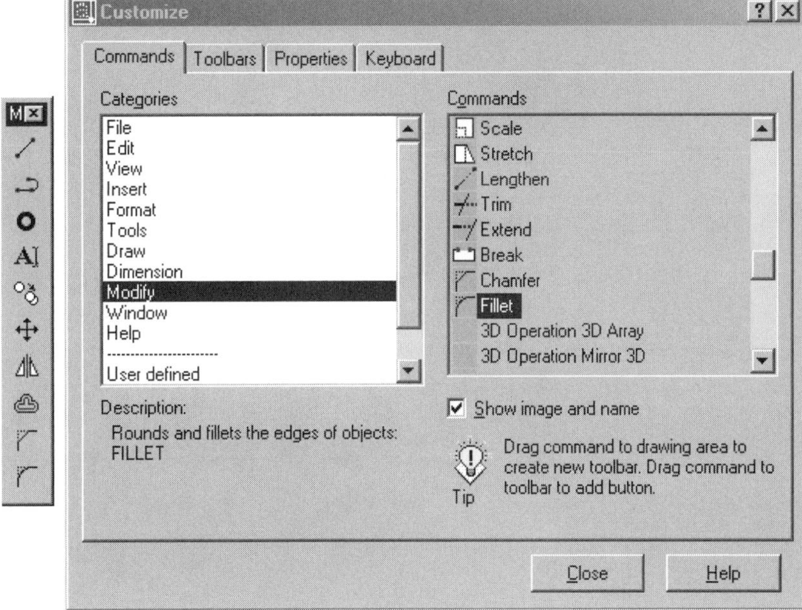

FIGURE 17–7
Select Tools from the Modify Category

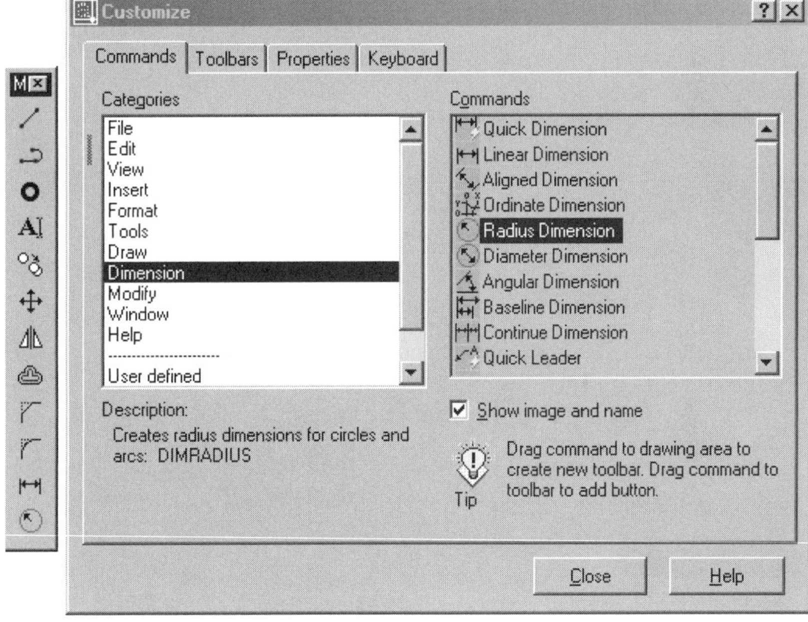

FIGURE 17–8
Select Tools from the Dimension Category

Deleting Tools from Toolbars

Step 5. Delete the dimensioning tools from your new toolbar.

Prompt	Response
Command:	**Toolbars...** (from the View menu)
The Customize dialog box (Figure 17–9) appears:	*Click:* **the Linear Dimension tool on your toolbar by moving the cursor over the Linear Dimension tool and holding down the click button. Continue holding down the click**

FIGURE 17–9
Customize Dialog Box

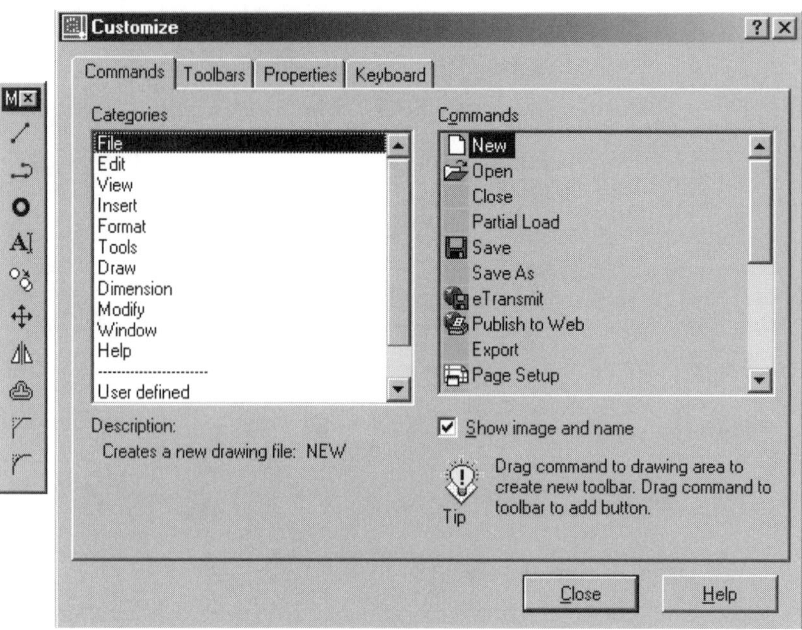

Prompt	Response
	button and drop the tool into the Customize dialog box or onto any open area.
	Delete the Radius Dimension tool in a similar manner.
	Click: **Close**

If you accidentally delete a standard tool from a toolbar, you can replace it from the Customize dialog box. If you delete a tool you have customized, you cannot retrieve it.

Displaying Toolbars

You can display all toolbars (and eliminate your drawing area) or only the ones you use often. To display all toolbars:

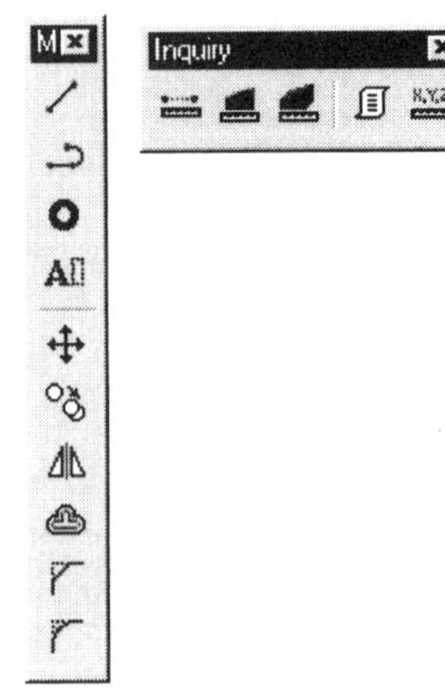

FIGURE 17–10
Toolbars

Prompt	Response
Command:	*Type:* **-TOOLBAR** ↵
Enter toolbar name or [ALL]:	*Type:* **ALL** ↵
Enter an option [Show/Hide]:	*Type:* **S** ↵

Now, hide all toolbars. Follow the same procedure but substitute H ↵ for S ↵.

You can also display only the ones you need presently.

Step 6. Display your new toolbar and the Inquiry toolbar.

Prompt	Response
Command:	**Toolbars...** (from the View menu)
The Customize dialog box appears:	**Check the Inquiry and (your initials)-TOOLS toolbars so they appear on the screen as shown in Figure 17–10.**
	Click: **Close**

FIGURE 17–11
Copying and Moving Tools

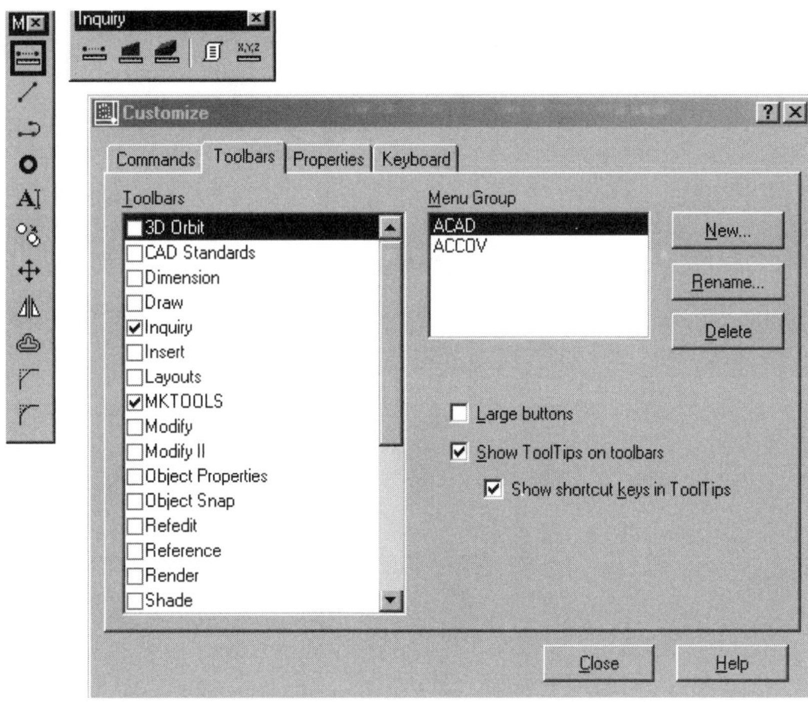

Moving Tools from One Toolbar to Another

Step 7. Move the Distance icon from the Inquiry toolbar to your new toolbar.

Prompt	Response
Command:	**Toolbars…**
The Customize dialog box appears:	**Hold down the click button over the Distance icon on the Inquiry toolbar and drop it onto your new toolbar (Figure 17–11).**

When the Customize dialog box is displayed, you can move or copy a tool from one toolbar to another.

Copying Tools from One Toolbar to Another

Step 8. Copy the Distance icon from your new toolbar back to the Inquiry toolbar.

Prompt	Response
With the Customize dialog box still displayed:	**Press and hold the Ctrl key while you hold down the click button over the Distance icon on your new menu and drop it onto the Inquiry toolbar (Figure 17–11).**

Step 9. On your own:

1. Copy (not move) the List icon from the Inquiry toolbar to your new toolbar.
2. Close the Customize dialog box.

Making New Toolbars and Letting AutoCAD Name Them

You can also make new toolbars by choosing the Commands tab in the Customize dialog box and dragging an icon off the dialog box and dropping it anywhere but onto another toolbar.

FIGURE 17–12
Creating Two New Toolbars, Toolbar1 and Toolbar2

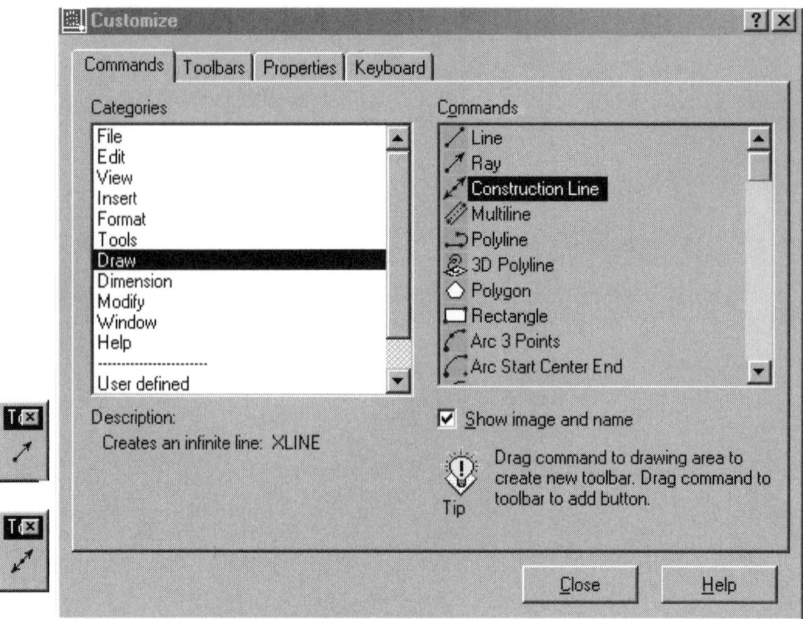

Step 10. Make two new toolbars and let AutoCAD name them for you.

Prompt	Response
Command:	**Toolbars…**
The Customize dialog box appears:	*Click:* **the Commands tab**
	Hold down the click button over any of the icons on the Draw category (any toolbar category will do) and drop it onto an open area off the Customize dialog box (Figure 17–12).
	Repeat the preceding procedure so you have the two toolbars as shown in Figure 17–12.

You could now proceed to load tools onto these toolbars as described previously.

Response
Click: **Close.**

Deleting Toolbars

You may delete toolbars from the Toolbars dialog box. AutoCAD will ask you if you really want to delete the toolbar because you cannot undo this action. If you delete one of the major toolbars such as the Draw toolbar, you can recreate it by making a new toolbar, naming it the Draw toolbar and dragging tools onto it from the Draw category after clicking Customize on the Toolbars dialog box. You can also reload the acad.mnu file from Options on the Tools menu on the menu bar. Reload the acad.mnu by clicking **Menu and Miscellaneous file names Help**, then Browse…, then *Double-click:* **Menu File**, then *Double-click:* **C:\PROGRAM FILES\AutoCAD2002\support\acad**, then *Click:* the acad.mnu file, then *Click:* **OK**. When the warning appears, *Click:* **Yes**. You will replace any customizing you have done.

Step 11. Delete the two new toolbars that AutoCAD named for you.

Prompt	Response
With the Customize dialog box displayed:	**Use the scroll bars in the Toolbars: list box to locate Toolbar1, and use the click button to highlight it.**

Prompt	Response
	Click: **Delete**
The AutoCAD warning appears —Delete toolbar ACAD.Toolbar1?	*Click:* **Yes**
	Delete Toolbar2 in a similar manner.

CHANGING A TOOLBAR

You can change the shape, name, and appearance of a floating toolbar, move it, dock it, float a docked toolbar, reposition tools on a toolbar, and add space between tools.

Let's start with a relatively uncluttered screen.

Step 12. Hide all toolbars.

Prompt	Response
Command:	*Type:* **-TOOLBAR** ↵
Enter toolbar name or [ALL]:	*Type:* **ALL** ↵
Enter an option [Show/Hide]:	*Type:* **H** ↵

Step 13. Display your new Toolbar.

Prompt	Response
Command:	**Toolbars...**
The Customize dialog box appears:	**Check the (your initials)TOOLS check box**
	Click: **Close**
The floating (your initials)TOOLS toolbar appears:	

Changing the Shape of a Floating Toolbar

A floating toolbar can be reshaped from vertical to horizontal or somewhere in between. The horizontal toolbar can also be reshaped to vertical. Docked toolbars cannot be reshaped.

Step 14. Change the shape of the floating (your initials)TOOLS toolbar.

If your toolbar is vertical:

Note: You can also *Click:* the top border, hold down the *Click:* button, and move your mouse down.

Prompt	Response
Command:	*Click:* **the bottom border so that the cursor changes to a double arrow and hold down the click button while you move your mouse up.** (You will have to move it over halfway before a change occurs.)

If your toolbar is horizontal:

Prompt	Response
	Click: **a side border so that the cursor changes to a double arrow and hold down the click button while you move your mouse to the left or right**

Renaming a Toolbar

There will be a time when you will need to change the name of a toolbar. This is how to do it.

FIGURE 17–13
Selecting the (your initials)TOOLS Toolbar and Renaming It

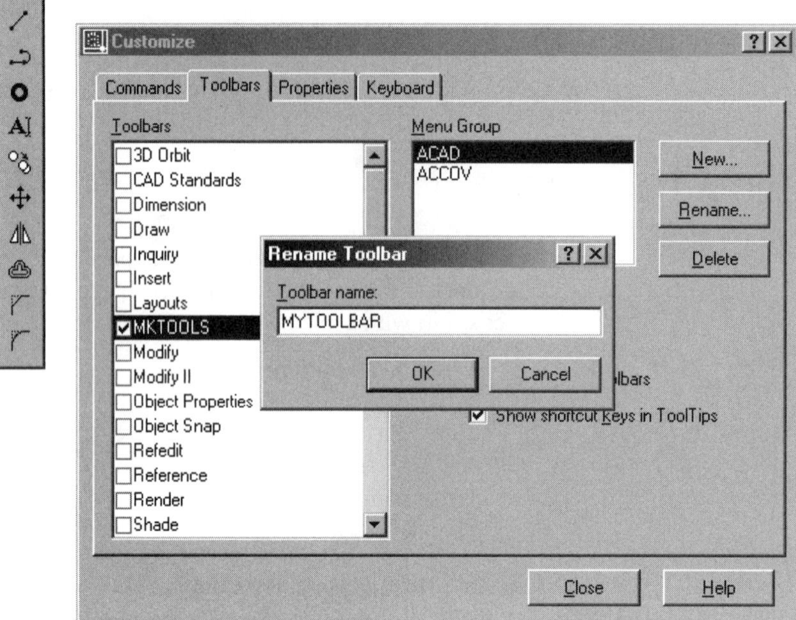

Step 15. Rename the (your initials)TOOLS toolbar.

Prompt	Response
Command:	**Toolbars...**
The Customize dialog box appears:	**Locate (your initials)TOOLS in the Toolbars list box and highlight it as shown in Figure 17–13.**
	Click: **Rename...**
The Rename Toolbar dialog box appears with the word (your initials) TOOLS highlighted:	*Type:* **MY TOOLBAR**
	Click: **OK**
The Customize dialog box appears:	*Click:* **Close**

The (your initials)TOOLS toolbar is now renamed MY TOOLBAR.

Step 16. On your own:
Rename the MY TOOLBAR to the (your initials)TOOLS toolbar.

Changing the Appearance of the Toolbar

The Toolbars dialog box allows you to change the size of the tools on the toolbar, whether toolbars are displayed in color or black and white, and whether tooltips (the text that appears when you hold the cursor over the tool) are displayed.

Step 17. Change the appearance to large buttons.

Prompt	Response
Command:	**Toolbars...**
The Customize dialog box appears:	**Check Large Buttons as shown in Figure 17–14.**
	Click: **Close**

The (your initials)TOOLS toolbar now has large tools.

FIGURE 17–14
Check Large Buttons

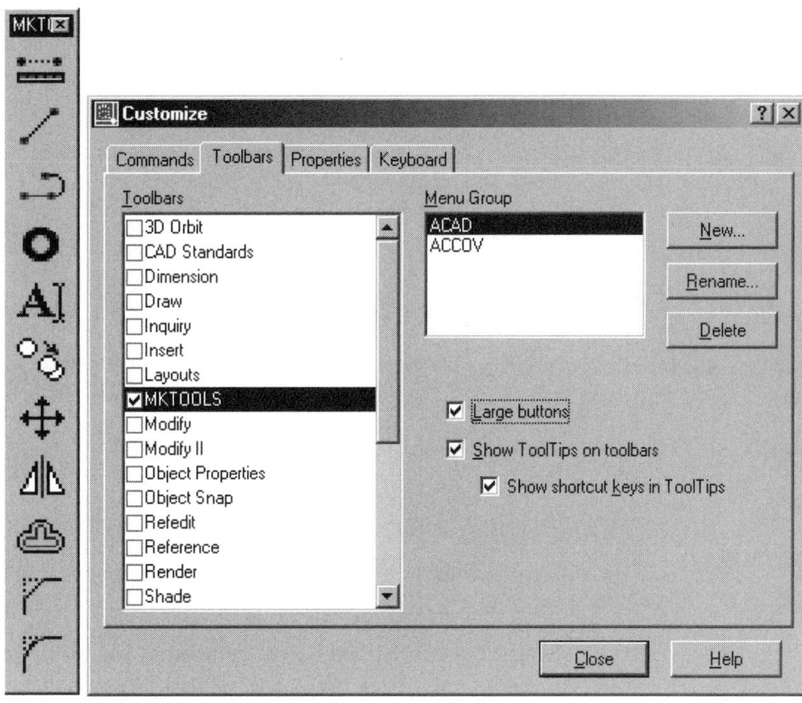

Moving Toolbars

You can move toolbars by picking the area between the outside border of the toolbar and the area surrounding the tools, holding down the click button, and moving the toolbar where you want it.

Step 18. Move the (your initials) TOOLS toolbar.

Prompt	Response
Command:	*Click:* **the area between the outside border of the (your initials)TOOLS toolbar and the area surrounding the tools (or the area at the top of the toolbar), hold down the click button, and move the toolbar to another area**

Docking a Toolbar

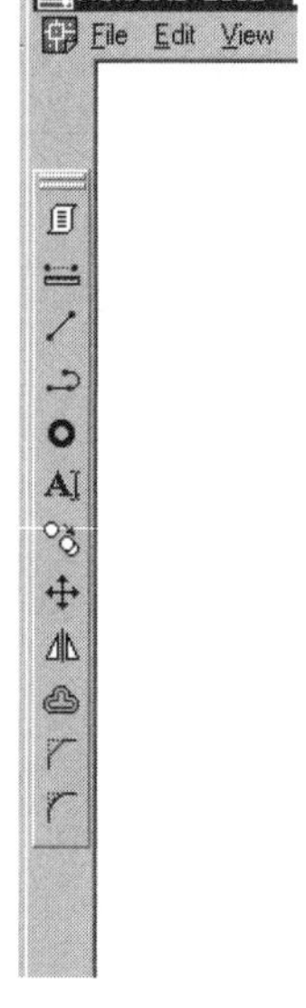

FIGURE 17–15
A Docked Toolbar

It is sometimes helpful to get the toolbars out of the drawing area. They can be placed on the outside edges of the screen in what is known as a *docked position*, as shown in Figure 17–15.

Step 19. On your own:

1. Change the icons back to small buttons.
2. Dock the (your initials)TOOLS toolbar on the left side of the screen by moving it as you did in step 18, except move it to the extreme left side so it appears as shown in Figure 17–15.

Floating a Docked Toolbar

Toolbars can be removed from their docked position by clicking the area between the tools and the toolbar border (or the title area), holding down the click button, and moving the toolbar.

Step 20. On your own:
Float the (your initials)TOOLS toolbar.

Repositioning the Tools on a Toolbar

You can change the position of tools on a toolbar from the Customize dialog box. When you click the tool and move it, you must drag the tool more than halfway across the tool that already exists in the new location.

Step 21. Reposition a tool on the (your initials)TOOLS toolbar.

Prompt	Response
Command:	**Toolbars...**
The Customize dialog box appears:	**Position your cursor over the List tool, hold down the click button, and move the List tool so it is a little more than halfway past the Distance tool.**

The (your initials)TOOLS toolbar appears as shown in Figure 17–16.

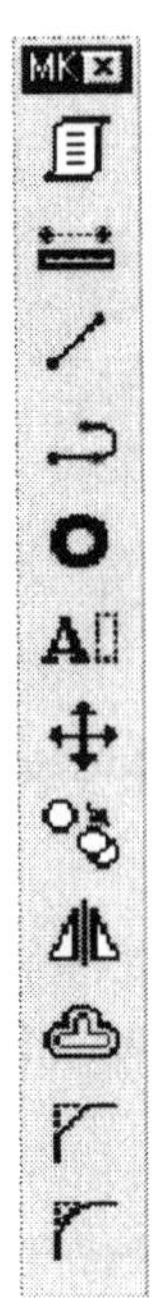

FIGURE 17–16
(your initials)TOOLS Toolbar with List Tool Position Changed

Adding Space between Tools on a Toolbar

If you prefer to have a little space between tools on the toolbar, you can change the spacing from the Customize dialog box.

Step 22. Add space between tools on the (your initials)TOOLS toolbar. (Make your toolbar a horizontal shape if it is not.)

Prompt	Response
Command:	**Toolbars...**
The Customize dialog box appears:	**Position your cursor over the List tool, hold down the click button, and move the List tool to the right or left but not more than half the distance of a side of the tool.**
	Repeat the preceding steps for all tools on the (your initials)TOOLS toolbar so it appears as shown in Figure 17–17.

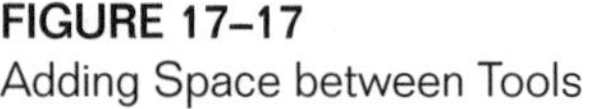
FIGURE 17–17
Adding Space between Tools

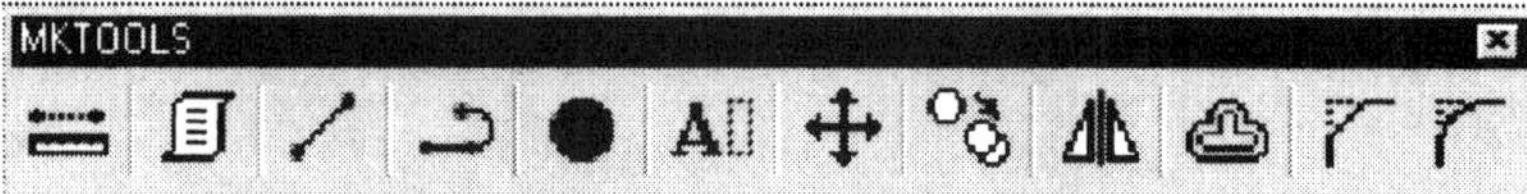

CREATING AND MODIFYING TOOLS

You can create your own tools by modifying or combining the tools that are supplied with AutoCAD. The following will provide you with the basics of customizing tools.

Basic Keystrokes Used to Modify Tool Macros

AutoCAD recognizes commands in a macro (a command line) as if they were typed from the keyboard. The following keystrokes represent pressing the return key, an operator response, canceling a command, a transparent command, and international versions:

; The semicolon is the same as pressing ↵.
\ The backslash tells AutoCAD to wait for the operator to do something.
^C^C Two Ctrl-Cs cancel a previous command and any option of that command.
' An apostrophe preceding the command allows it to be used transparently.
__ An underscore enables commands to work on international versions of AutoCAD.

The best way to understand how these work is to create a tool using some of these keystrokes.

Creating Tools

Step 23. Create a tool.

Prompt	Response
Command:	**Toolbars...**
The Customize dialog box appears:	**Place your cursor over the Donut tool on the (your initials)TOOLS toolbar and press the RETURN button on your mouse.**
Button Properties tab (Figure 17–18) appears:	**Change the information in the Name: box, the Help box, and the Macro: box as shown in Figure 17–19.** (The

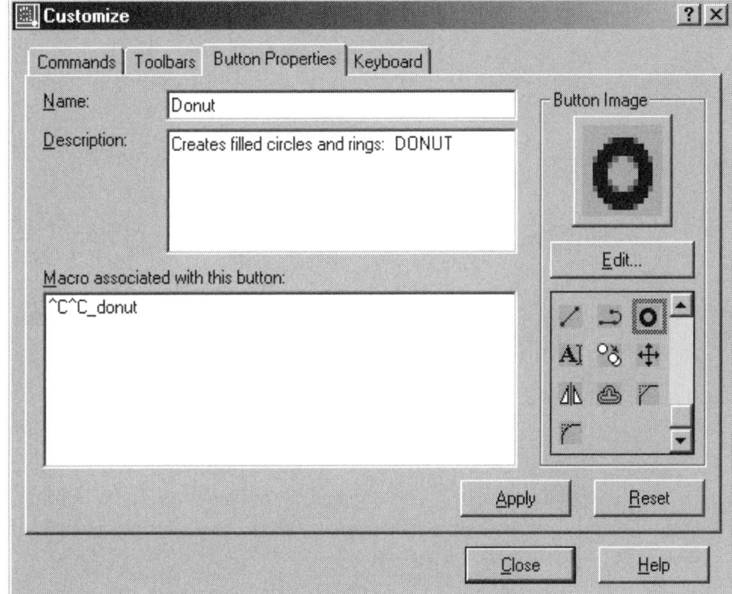

FIGURE 17–18
Button Properties Tab

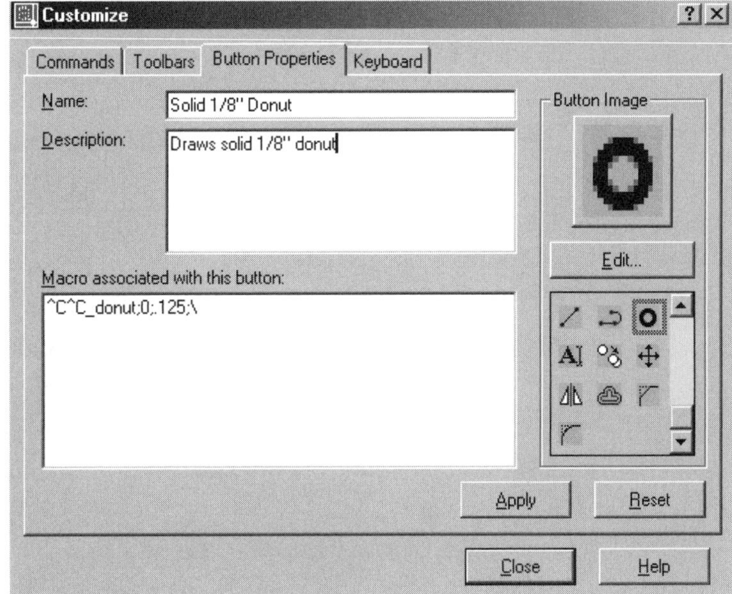

FIGURE 17–19
Button Properties Tab for Solid ⅛″ Donut

Prompt	Response
	line in the Macro: box should read: ^C^C_donut;0;.125;\)

Let's look at this line for a minute:

Macro Elements

^C^C_donut This is already here and it means that you are canceling previous commands (^C^C), making the command available to international versions (_), and activating the Donut command.

; This acts as a ↵, as if you had typed DONUT and then pressed ↵.

The Donut command then asks you for an inside diameter.

0; This tells AutoCAD you want an inside diameter of 0, as if you had typed 0 ↵.

The Donut command then asks you for an outside diameter.

.125; This tells AutoCAD you want an outside diameter of .125, as if you had typed .125 ↵.

The Donut command then asks you to pick (or type coordinates for) the center of the donut.

\ The backslash tells AutoCAD you will pick the center or type coordinates—an operator response.

Changing or Making Tool Icons

When you create a new command, AutoCAD allows you to change an existing icon or create an entirely new one with the Button Editor. When you open the Button Editor (Figure 17–20), you have an abbreviated paint program available to you. The four tools at the top of the editor from left to right are:

Pencil tool Changes one pixel at a time.
Line tool Draws lines in a selected color.
Circle tool Draws circles in a selected color. Hold down the click button on your mouse to select the center of the circle; continue to hold the click button as you drag the circle to the desired radius.
Erase tool Erases pixels as you move the cursor with the click button depressed over the area you want to erase.

The color bar to the right allows you to select from 16 colors by selecting one with the click button.

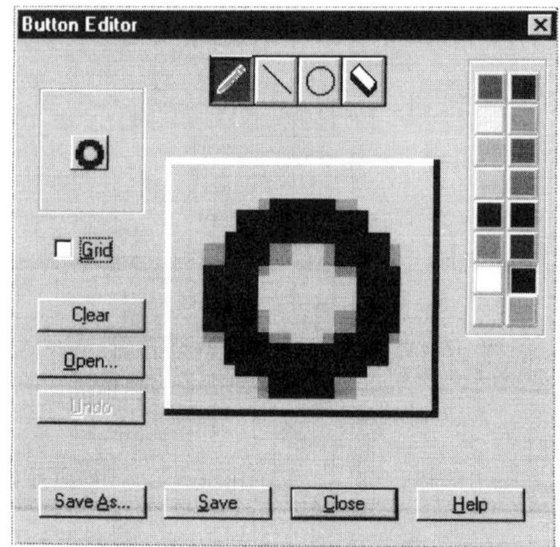

FIGURE 17–20
Button Editor

The **Grid** button gives you a grid.
The **Clear** button clears the image.
The **Open** button opens images you have saved previously.
The **Undo** button undoes the previous single action.

SaveAs..., Save, Close, and Help perform the standard functions for the tool icons.

Step 24. Change the new tool icon to a solid circle.

Prompt	Response
With the Button Properties tab displayed:	*Click:* **Edit... in the Button Image area**
The Button Editor appears:	**Click the same color in the color bar as the donut image if it is not already selected.**
	Use the Pencil tool to color all pixels of the inside of the donut as shown in Figure 17–21. (Hold down the click button with the Pencil tool selected and move it across the area.)

You could now save this icon to a file but you do not need to at this time.

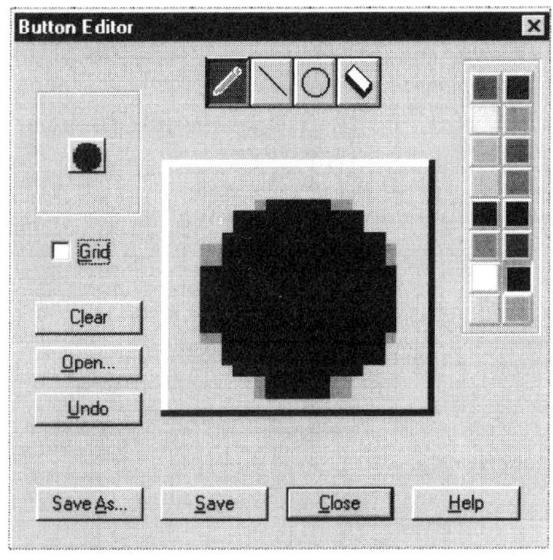

FIGURE 17–21
Color the Inside of the Donut Icon

Prompt	Response
	Click: **Close**
Would you like to save the changes made to your button?	*Click:* **Yes**
The Button Properties tab appears:	*Click:* **Apply**
	Click: **Close**

Your (your initials)TOOLS toolbar should now look like Figure 17–22. When you hold the cursor over the new tool, its tooltip now reads Solid ⅛″ Donut.

Step 25. On your own:
Add the original donut command to the (your initials)TOOLS toolbar (from the Draw category) so it appears as shown in Figure 17–23.

FIGURE 17–22
(your initials)TOOLS Toolbar with the Solid Donut Tool

FIGURE 17–23
(your initials)TOOLS Toolbar with the Donut Tool Added

Step 26. On your own:

1. Save your drawing as EX17-1(your initials) in two places.
2. Exit AutoCAD.

CUSTOMIZING MENUS

The standard arrangement of the AutoCAD package is often not the most convenient or productive for many situations. The structure of the AutoCAD menu makes it easy to customize by rearranging commands on the menus, adding new commands, rearranging the menus, and creating keyboard aliases. This chapter will give you some basic tools for menu customizing. Remember to keep accurate notes containing the exact commands that you use. Commands must contain exactly the same spelling, punctuation, and spacing every time. Let us begin by rearranging menus on the menu bar using the Customize Menus... command.

REARRANGING AND DELETING MENUS FROM THE MENU BAR

Exercise 17–2: Making a New Menu Bar Using the Customize Menus... Command

Sometimes having fewer menus on the menu bar is better than having the full menu. If you occasionally need a command that is no longer on the menu bar, you can type it or

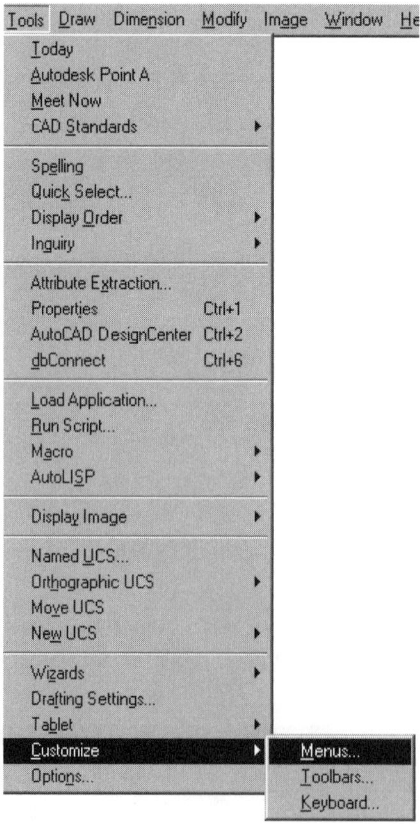

FIGURE 17–24
Shortened Menu Bar

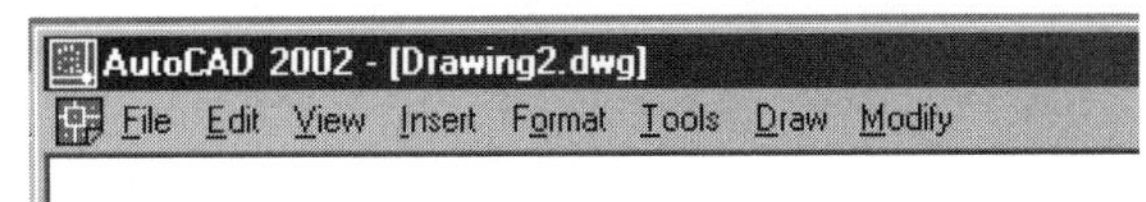

access it from a toolbar. Assume that you need a menu bar that has only the File, Edit, View, Insert, Format, Tools, Draw, and Modify menus. Your final menu will look similar to the one shown in Figure 17–24.

Step 1. To begin Exercise 17–2, turn on the computer and start AutoCAD, and cancel the Today window.

Step 2. Remove the File and Edit menus from the menu bar.

Prompt	Response
Command:	**Customize Menus...**
The Menu Customization dialog box appears:	*Click:* **Menu Bar tab**
The Menu Bar page appears:	*Click:* **File** in the Menu Bar: list as shown in Figure 17–25
	Click: << **Remove**
	Click: **Edit**
	Click: << **Remove**

Step 3. Replace the File Menu on the menu bar.

Prompt	Response
	With **View** highlighted on the Menu Bar: list, *Click:* **File** in the Menus: list as shown in Figure 17–26.
	Click: **Insert>>**

Step 4. On your own:

1. Remove the Dimension, Image, Window, and Help menus from the menu bar.

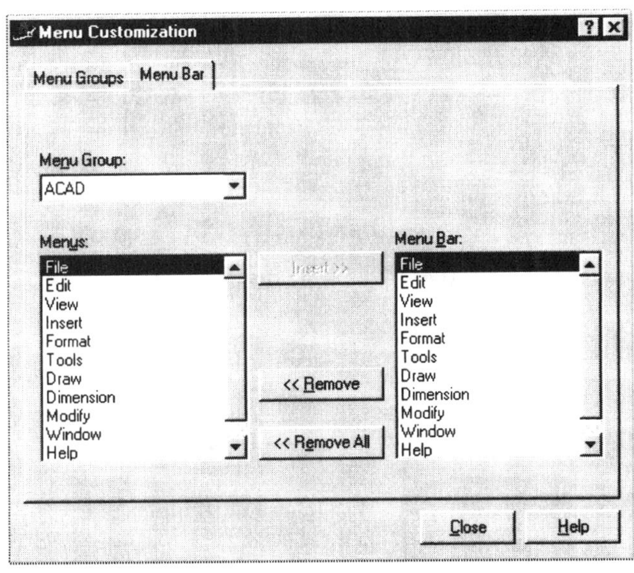

FIGURE 17–25
Click: File in the Menu Bar: List to Remove

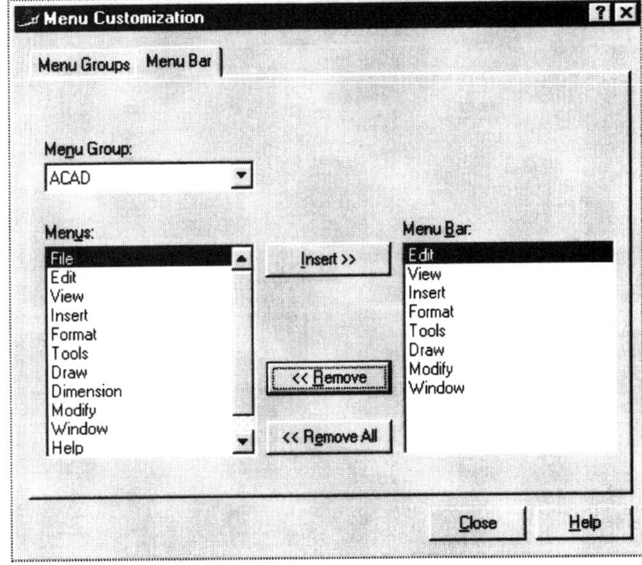

FIGURE 17–26
Click: File in the Menus: List to Insert

FIGURE 17–27
Your New Menu Bar

2. Close the Menu Customization dialog box so your menu bar appears as shown in Figure 17–27.

Exercise 17–2 is now complete.

MAKING A NEW MENU FILE

In Exercise 17–3 you will make a new menu file that contains new macros that you add to menus on the menu bar, commands that are rearranged, deleted, and copied. To do that you must begin by copying the standard AutoCAD menu file under another name.

Exercise 17–3: Making a New Menu Called Menu1 (Menu1.mnu)

Step 1. On your own:

1. Exercise 17–3 requires that the complete menu bar be present, so begin by returning all menus to their original location as shown in Figure 17–25 using Customize Menus... You will have to remove Window and insert it and the Help menu to get it in its correct location.
2. Close the Menu Customization dialog box.

Locating the File Containing the Standard AutoCAD Menu (acad.mnu)

Step 2. Find out where the acad.mnu file is located so you can copy it to a floppy disk under the name menu1.mnu.

Prompt	Response
Command:	**Options...**
The Options dialog box appears:	*Click:* **Files tab**
The Files tab appears as shown in Figure 17–28:	*Double-click:* **Menu, Help, and Miscellaneous File Names**
	Double-click: **Menu File**
	Make a note of the drive, folder, and subdirectory where the Menu File is located. In this case: C:\PROGRAM FILES\AutoCAD2002\support\acad
	Click: **OK**

Copying the acad.mnu File to a Floppy Disk in the A or B Drive

Step 3. Copy the acad.mnu and acad.mnl files to a floppy disk.

Prompt	Response
Command:	*Click:* **Start**
	Click: **Programs**
	Click: **Windows Explorer** (Figure 17–29)
The Support dialog box appears:	*Click:* **Program Files Folder**
	Click: **AutoCAD2002 Folder**
	Click: **Support folder**

FIGURE 17–28
Locating the Menu File

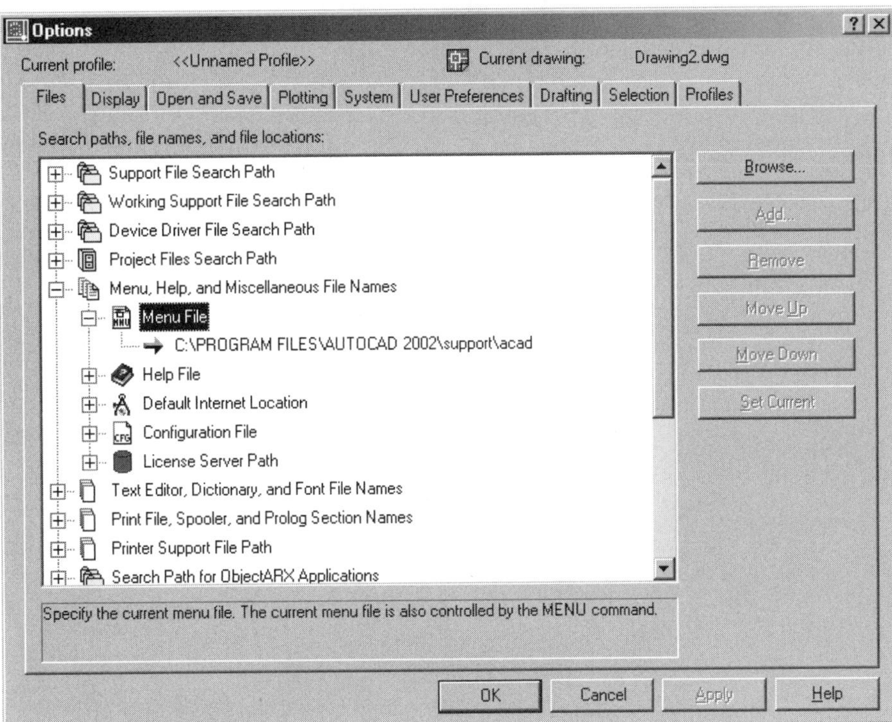

FIGURE 17–29
Start Windows Explorer

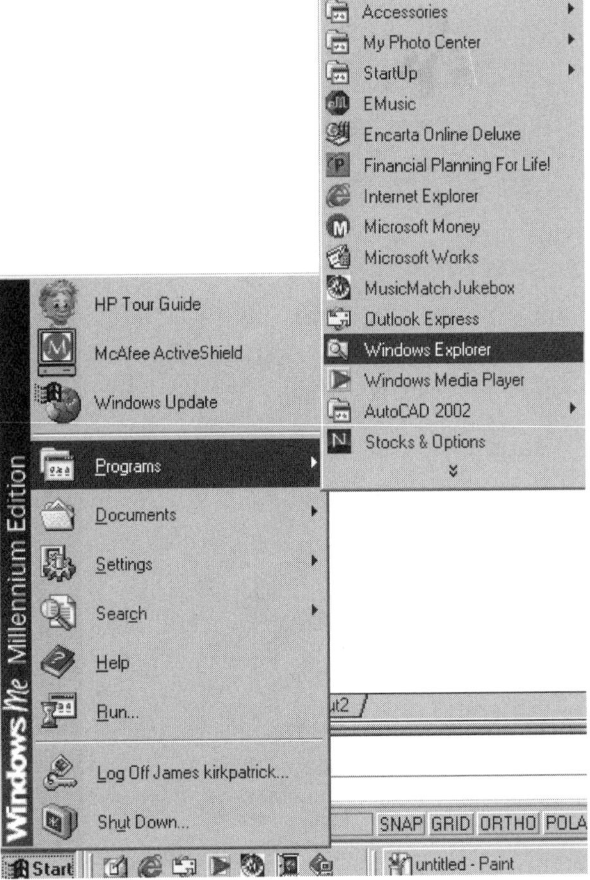

FIGURE 17–30
Click: the acad.mnu and acad.mn1 Files

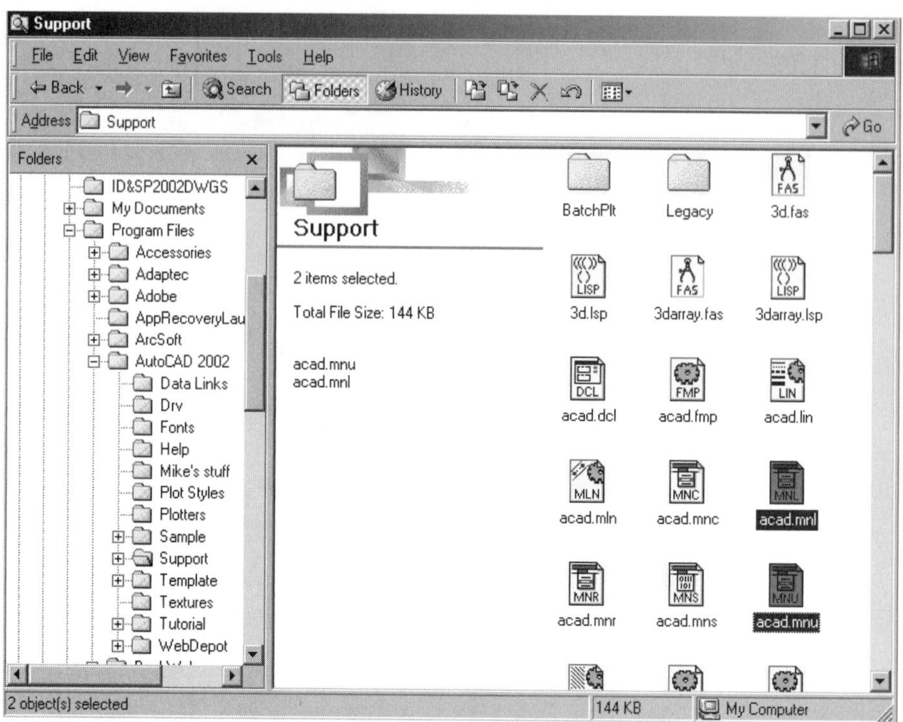

Prompt	Response
	The contents of the Support folder are displayed on the right side of the dialog box:
	Hold down the Ctrl key and *Click:* **the acad.mnu and the acad.mnl files** (Figure 17–30) then, *Click:* **File, Send To, 3½ Floppy (A)** or to whichever drive contains your floppy disk (Figure 17_31). (You can also drag and drop the file into the floppy diskette.)
The "copying from AutoCAD to A:" message appears:	

Renaming the acad.mnu File Menu1.mnu

Step 4. Rename the acad.mnu file, Menu1.mnu.

Prompt	Response
	Click: **the vertical scroll bar in the Folders box and scroll up to the floppy drive containing the copied acad.mnu file**
	Click: **the floppy drive**
The contents of the floppy drive are displayed in the right panel:	*Right-click:* **the acad.mnu file**
	Click: **Rename** (Figure 17–32)

FIGURE 17–31
Send the File to a Floppy Disk

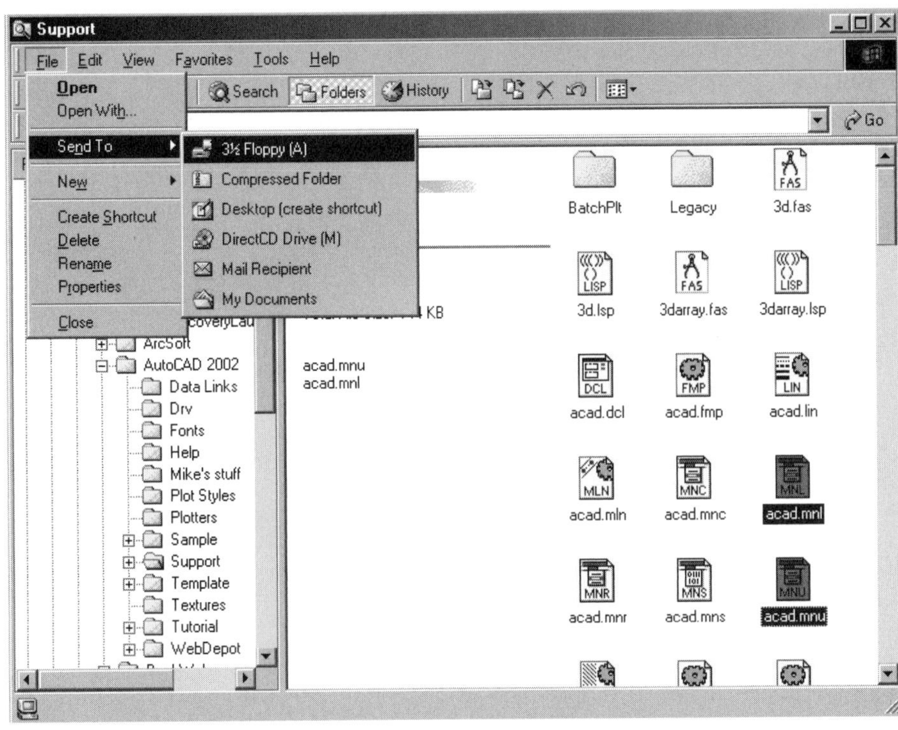

FIGURE 17–32
Rename the acad.mnu File, Menu 1.mnu

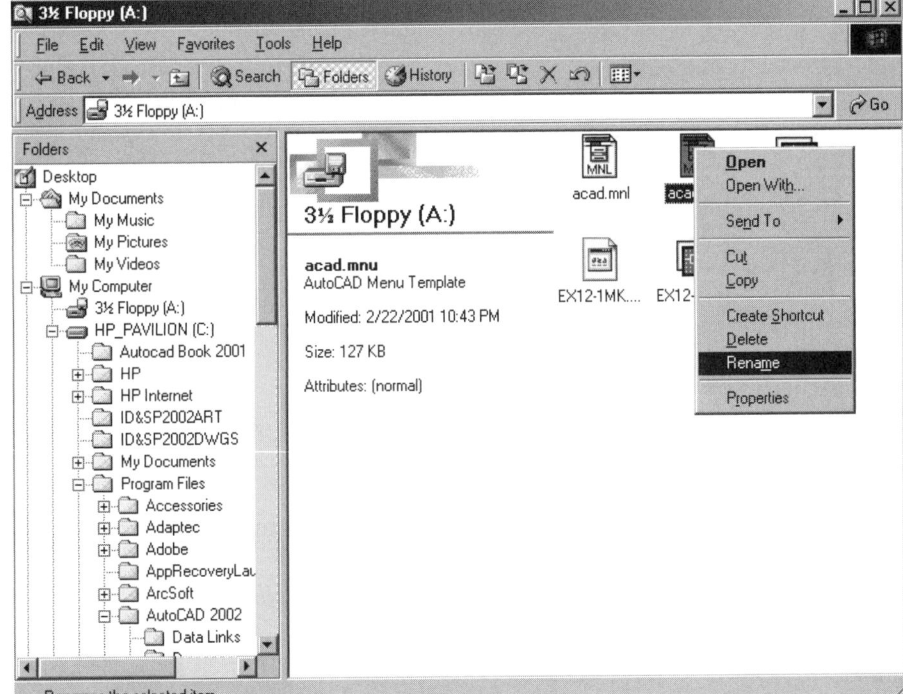

FIGURE 17–33
Type: Menu1.mnu to Rename the acad.mnu File

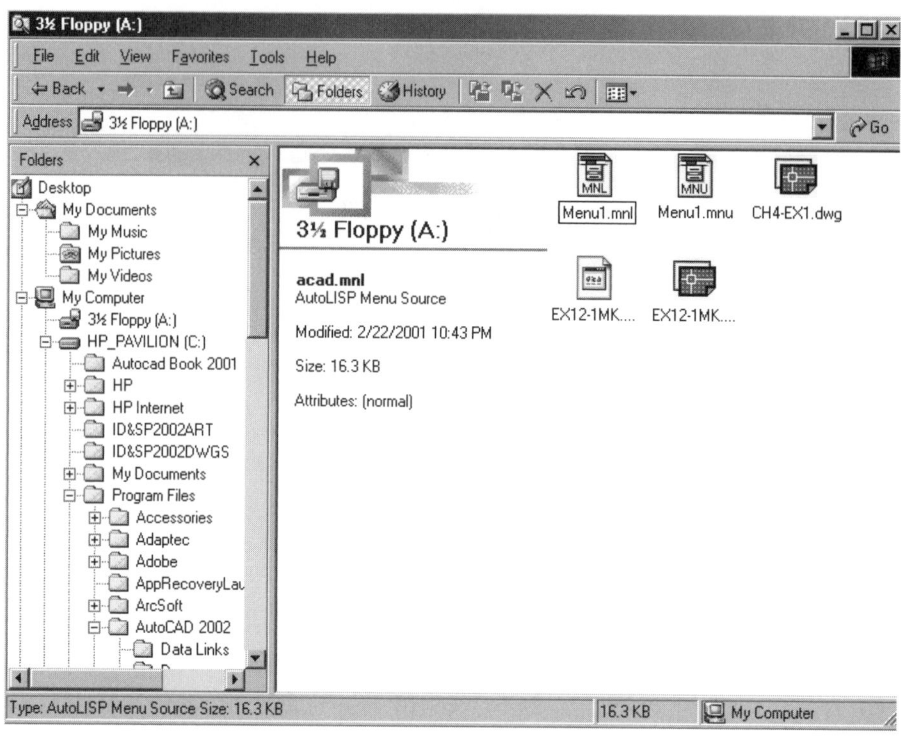

Prompt	Response
The acad.mnu file is highlighted:	*Type:* **Menu1.mnu** (Figure 17–33) (Be sure to include the .mnu extension.)

Step 5. Rename the acad.mnl file, Menu1.mnl in a similar manner.

Opening the Menu1.mnu File So You Can Modify the Menu

Step 6. Open the Menu1.mnu file on the floppy disk using a text editor such as Wordpad, Word, or Word Perfect.

Prompt	Response
	Click: **Open** (Figure 17–34) *Click:* **All documents** in the Files of type: list
The Menu1.mnu file is displayed:	**Maximize the display**

FIGURE 17–34
Open the Menu1.mnu File with Wordpad in Accesories

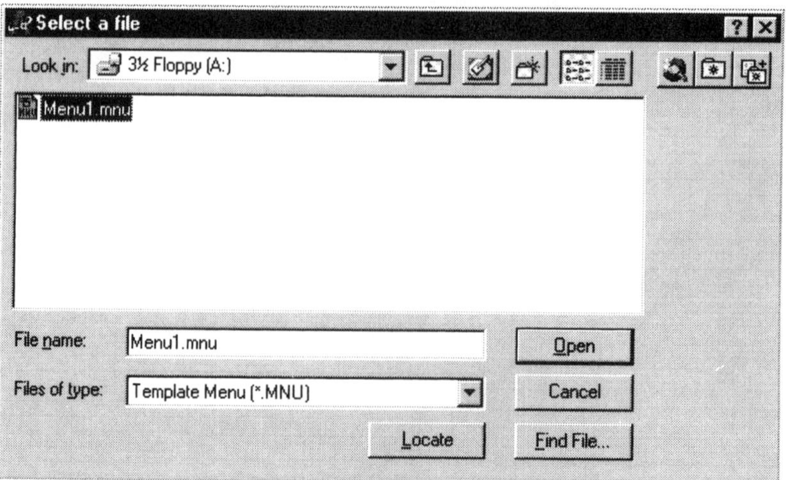

FIGURE 17–35
Change ***MENUGROUP=acad to ***MENUGROUP=Menu1

```
//      NOTE:   AutoCAD looks for an ".mnl" (Menu Lisp) file whose name is
//              the same as that of the menu file, and loads it if
//              found.  If you modify this menu and change its name, you
//              should copy acad.mnl to <yourname>.mnl, since the menu
//              relies on AutoLISP routines found there.
//

//
//      Default AutoCAD NAMESPACE declaration:
//
***MENUGROUP=Menu1
//
//   Begin AutoCAD Digitizer Button Menus
//
***BUTTONS1
// Simple + button
// if a grip is hot bring up the Grips Cursor Menu (POP 500), else send a
carriage return
// If the SHORTCUTMENU sysvar is not 0 the first item (for button 1) is NOT
USED.
$M=$(if,$(eq,$(substr,$(getvar,cmdnames),1,5),GRIP_),$P0=ACAD.GRIPS $P0=*);
$P0=SNAP $p0=*
```

Modifying the Menu

Step 7. Relabel the MENUGROUP so AutoCAD will recognize this as a menu different from the original.

	Response
	Scroll down to the label ***MENUGROUP = ACAD and change ACAD to Menu1 (Figure 17–35).

Step 8. Scroll down through the menu through the AutoCAD Button Menus (*Press:* the down arrow) so you become familiar with what the menu looks like.

Step 9. Locate the line "Begin AutoCAD Pull-down Menus."

Deleting Commands from a Menu on the Menu Bar

You will now find the menus on the menu bar labeled ***POP1 through ***POP10. Begin modifying this menu by deleting some commands on ***POP7 that are not used a great deal.

Step 10. Locate the ***POP7 pull-down menu.

Prompt	Response
	Click: **Find...**(from search or edit on the menu bar)
The Find and Replace dialog box, Figure 17-36, appears:	*Type:* *****POP7** in the Find what: text box
	Click: **Find Next**
	Close the Find and Replace dialog box by clicking the X in the upper right corner.

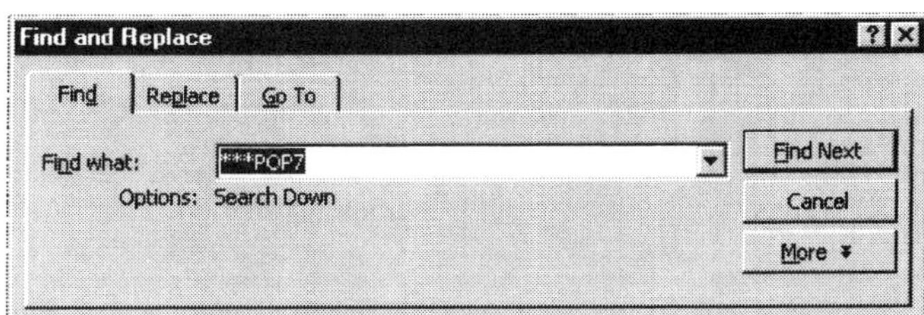

FIGURE 17–36
Find and Replace Dialog Box

Step 11. Delete the following commands from the ***POP7 menu.

Line
Ray
Xline
Circle3pt
CircleTTR
EllipseAx
Boundary
Mtext
Solid

To delete a line of text, move your cursor to one end of the line, hold down the click button on your mouse, drag the cursor across the line to highlight the text, and press the Delete key. *Press:* **Backspace** to delete the space between lines.

If you make a mistake, *Click:* **Undo** from the Edit menu.

Adding Macros to a Menu on the Menu Bar

Adding macros to a menu requires that you know what the command is going to ask, and what response is required. For example, the Insert (*Type:* **-INSERT** ↵) command when typed from the keyboard asks:

Prompt	Response
Enter block name [or ?]:	Your response is to type the block name and press ↵.
Specify insertion point or [Scale/X/Y/Z/ Rotate/PScale/PX/PY/PZ/PRotate]:	Your response is to click a point with your mouse or type X and Y coordinates and press ↵. The symbol in a macro that requires an operator response is the backslash (\).
Enter X scale factor, specify opposite corner, or [Corner/XYZ]<1>:	If you want the X scale factor to be 1, the correct response is to press ↵. The symbol in a macro that represents ↵ is the semicolon (;).
Enter Y scale factor <use x scale factor>:	If you want the Y scale factor to be the same as the X scale factor, the correct response is to press ↵. The symbol in a macro that represents ↵ is the semicolon (;).
Specify rotation angle <0>:	If you want the rotation angle to be the same as the original block orientation, the correct response is to press ↵. If you want to change the rotation angle often, leave this semicolon off the end of the macro.

In this exercise you will add four macros to the Draw pull-down menu. The first macro when picked will execute the Insert command, insert a block named BLOCK1 (which you will have to make and save on a floppy disk in the A: drive), insert it at an X scale factor of 1 and a Y scale factor of X, and it will ask you for a rotation angle. The other three macros will do the same thing for BLOCK2, BLOCK3, and BLOCK4.

Now add the macros to ***POP7 on the menu bar.

Step 12. Type the three lines at the top of the ***POP7 menu as shown in Figure 17–37.

FIGURE 17–37
Type the Three Macros at the Top of POP7

```
***POP7
**DRAW
ID_MnDraw      [&Draw]
ID BLOCK1      [BLOCK1]^C^C_-INSERT;A:BLOCK1;\;;
ID BLOCK1      [BLOCK2]^C^C_-INSERT;A:BLOCK2;\;;
ID BLOCK1      [BLOCK3]^C^C_-INSERT;A:BLOCK3;\;;
ID_Mline       [&Multiline]^C^C_mline
               [--]
ID_Pline       [&Polyline]^C^C_pline
ID_3dpoly      [&3D Polyline]^C^C_3dpoly
ID_Polygon     [Pol&ygon]^C^C_polygon
ID_Rectang     [Rectan&gle]^C^C_rectang
               [--]
ID_MnCircle    [->&Circle]
ID_CircleRad     [Center, &Radius]^C^C_circle
ID_CircleDia     [Center, &Diameter]^C^C_circle \_d
```

Give careful attention to the arrangement of the text and the exact position of each character. If you make even the slightest change, it will most likely be reflected in your menu.

Moving Commands from One Position to Another

Commands are easily moved from one position to another. Now that you have deleted several commands the arrangement of the commands on the Draw menu does not follow any particular pattern. Move the commands so that they are in alphabetical order. Begin by moving the Arc commands to the top of the menu.

Step 13. Move the Arc commands to the top of the menu.

Prompt	Response
Command:	**Position your cursor at the beginning of the Arc commands, hold down the click button, and drag the cursor so that the lines are highlighted as shown in Figure 17–38.**

FIGURE 17–38
Highlight the Arc Commands and Cut and Paste Them to the Windows Clipboard

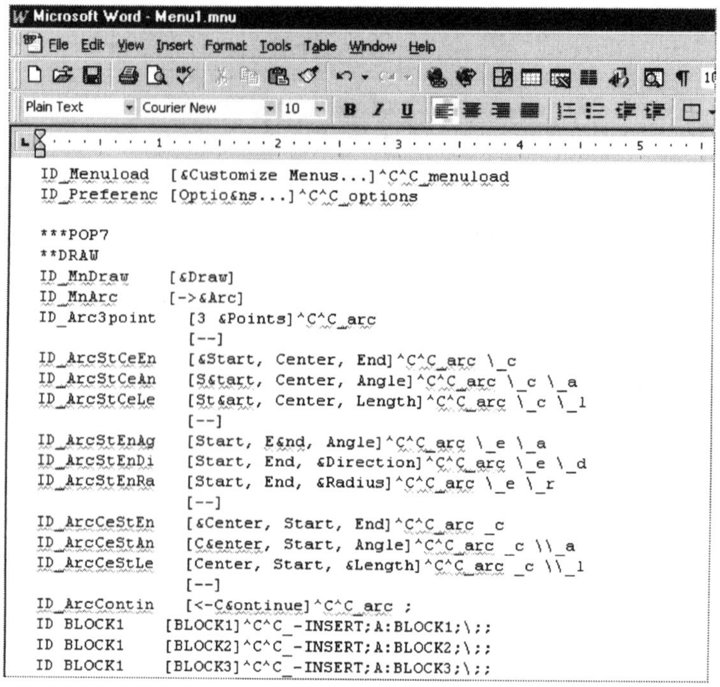

```
ID_Menuload  [&Customize Menus...]^C^C_menuload
ID_Preferenc [Optio&ns...]^C^C_options

***POP7
**DRAW
ID_MnDraw      [&Draw]
ID_MnArc       [->&Arc]
ID_Arc3point    [3 &Points]^C^C_arc
                [--]
ID_ArcStCeEn    [&Start, Center, End]^C^C_arc \_c
ID_ArcStCeAn    [S&tart, Center, Angle]^C^C_arc \_c \_a
ID_ArcStCeLe    [St&art, Center, Length]^C^C_arc \_c \_l
                [--]
ID_ArcStEnAg    [Start, E&nd, Angle]^C^C_arc \_e \_a
ID_ArcStEnDi    [Start, End, &Direction]^C^C_arc \_e \_d
ID_ArcStEnRa    [Start, End, &Radius]^C^C_arc \_e \_r
                [--]
ID_ArcCeStEn    [&Center, Start, End]^C^C_arc _c
ID_ArcCeStAn    [C&enter, Start, Angle]^C^C_arc _c \\_a
ID_ArcCeStLe    [Center, Start, &Length]^C^C_arc _c \\_l
                [--]
ID_ArcContin    [<-C&ontinue]^C^C_arc ;
ID BLOCK1     [BLOCK1]^C^C_-INSERT;A:BLOCK1;\;;
ID BLOCK1     [BLOCK2]^C^C_-INSERT;A:BLOCK2;\;;
ID BLOCK1     [BLOCK3]^C^C_-INSERT;A:BLOCK3;\;;
```

FIGURE 17–39
Arc Commands Are Moved

Prompt	Response
	Click: **Cut**
	Position your cursor to the left of ID_BLOCK1.
	Click: **Paste**

The menu appears as shown in Figure 17–39.

Copying Commands from One Menu to Another

You may decide that you would like to have other commands from other menus on the Draw menu. You can copy them from other menus using the Copy command found on the Edit menu of Notepad, then use Paste to place the copy in the correct location.

Step 14. On your own:

1. Save your Menu1.mnu file to your floppy disk using the Save as command from your text editor. Be sure to save the file as menu1.mnu..
2. Make four drawings of items you often use and wblock or save them on the floppy disk in the A: drive with the names BLOCK1, BLOCK2, BLOCK3, and BLOCK 4.

Now comes the test of your first menu. Do not be surprised if you have to make several corrections and return to your menu several times.

Step 15. *Click:* **the AutoCAD 2000 label at the bottom of your screen to activate AutoCAD.**

Loading a Menu

Menus are loaded with the MENULOAD command. You can either *Type:* **MENULOAD** ↵, or *Click:* **Customize Menus...** from Tools on the AutoCAD menu bar. When the menu is loaded, it then displays the commands in the new menu arrangement. You must also *Click:* the menu file from Options on the Tools menu on the menu bar. To provide a shortcut for loading the menu go directly to Options.

Step 15. Load Menu1.mnu from the floppy disk in the A: drive.

Prompt	Response
Command:	**Options...**
The Options dialog box with the Files tab is displayed:	*Double-click:* **Menu, etc.**
	Double-click: **Menu File**
	Highlight: **the location of the Menu File**
	Click: **Browse**
	Click: **3½ Floppy (A:) or whichever drive contains your floppy disk with the Menu1.mnu file on it**
	Click: **Menu Template (*.mnu) in the Files of type: box**
	Click: **Menu1.mnu so the name appears in the File name: box as shown in Figure 17–40.**
	Click: **Open**
The Options dialog box (Figure 17-41) appears with A:\ menu1 highlighted:	*Click:* **OK**
The AutoCAD customization warning appears:	*Click:* **Yes**
The Menu1.mnu file loads:	*Click:* **OK**
	Click: **Draw on the menu bar**

Your menu should appear as shown in Figure 17–42. Test the command.

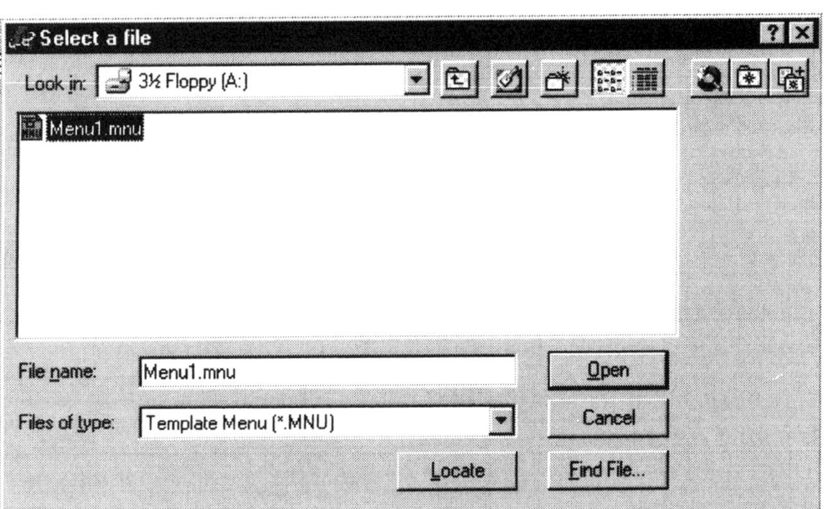

FIGURE 17–40
Select the Menu1.mnu File on the Floppy Disk

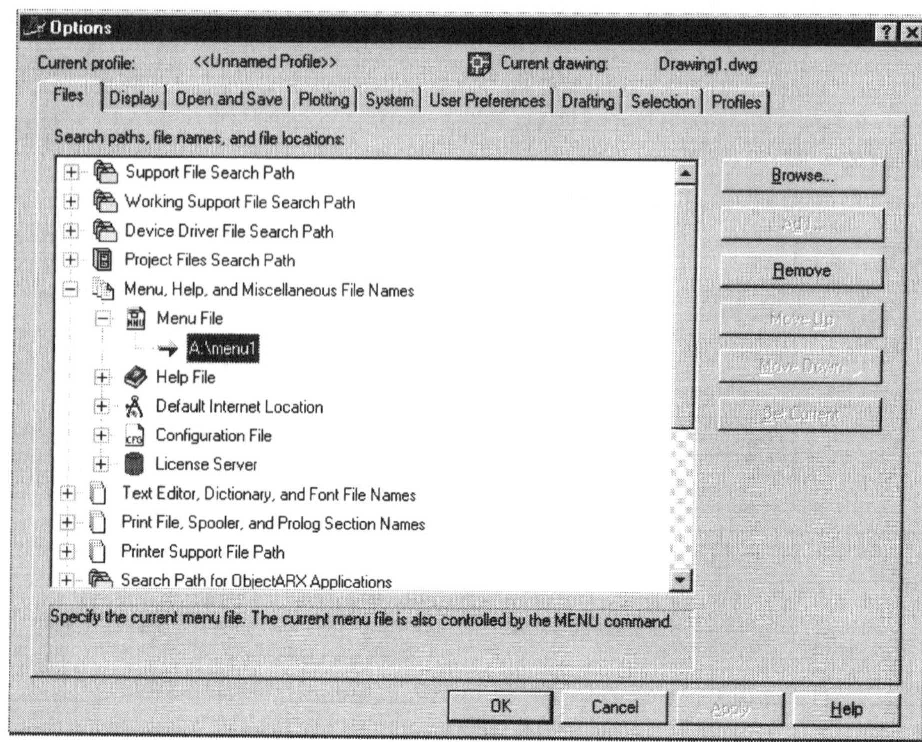

FIGURE 17–41
Options Dialog Box with A:\menu1 as the Menu File

FIGURE 17–42
POP7 on the Menu1 Menu

If you have any errors, *Click:* Menu1.mnu at the bottom of the screen to return to Notepad and the Menu1.mnu file. Make any necessary changes and return to AutoCAD.

Because you have loaded the Menu1.mnu file previously, you will get the "Error loading menu file" message when you try to load the file again. You will have to unload the Menu1.mnu file before you can load your new version of it again.

Unloading a Menu

To unload a menu, *Click:* **Customize Menus...**, then *Click:* **Unload** to unload the Menu1.mnu file, since it will be the one highlighted. Then *Click:* **Browse** and locate the Menu1.mnu file on your floppy disk again and reload it.

Step 16. On your own:

1. When your menu is correct, use SaveAs... to save it on two floppy disks.
2. Return to AutoCAD and load the acad.mnu file.
3. Exit AutoCAD.

EXERCISES

EXERCISE 17–1. Complete Exercise 17–1 using steps 1 through 26 described in this chapter. Show and demonstrate your (your initials) TOOLS toolbar to your instructor.

EXERCISE 17–2. Complete Exercise 17–2 using steps 1 through 4 described in this chapter. Show and demonstrate your abbreviated menu bar to your instructor.

EXERCISE 17–3. Complete Exercise 17–3 using steps 1 through 16 described in this chapter. Show and demonstrate your Menu1 menu to your instructor.

EXERCISE 17–4. Make a toolbar named My Blocks containing four of your most commonly used blocks.

1. Make four drawings of items you use often or call them up from an old drawing.
2. Wblock each drawing onto a floppy disk in the A drive using the names A:BLOCK1, A:BLOCK2, A:BLOCK3, and A:BLOCK4 or any other names you want.
3. Create four tools using icons that you will recognize as tools that insert your blocks. Name and describe them as you choose. Use the following as the Macro: for BLOCK1:

^C^C_insert;A:BLOCK1;
Repeat the Macro: for BLOCK2, BLOCK3, and BLOCK4.

EXERCISE 17–5. Modify Menu1 in the following manner:

Rearrange the Modify menu on the menu bar so that all commands are in alphabetical order. Leave the flyouts as they are but put the flyout labels in alphabetical order. Show and demonstrate your modified Menu1 menu to your instructor.

REVIEW QUESTIONS

Circle the best answer.

1. To create a new toolbar, *Click:* Toolbars…, then *Click:* the Toolbars tab in the Customize dialog box and *Select:*
   a. New
   b. Delete
   c. Customize
   d. Custom
   e. File
2. Which of the following is *not* a category in the Customize dialog box with the Commands tab current?
   a. Attributes
   b. Draw
   c. Custom
   d. Modify
   e. Edit
3. When you delete a standard tool from a toolbar you cannot retrieve it.
   a. True
   b. False
4. To display all toolbars, *Type:* -TOOLBAR ↵, then *Type:* ALL ↵, then Type:
   a. S ↵
   b. D ↵
   c. H ↵
   d. A ↵
   e. T ↵
5. To copy a tool from one toolbar to another, *Click:* the tool and drag it to the other toolbar while holding down which key?
   a. Shift
   b. Alt
   c. Ctrl
   d. Esc
   e. F1
6. AutoCAD will make a new toolbar and name it for you when you *Click:* the Commands tab from the Customize dialog box, *Click:* any tool from any category, and
   a. *Press:* New
   b. Drop it on an existing toolbar
   c. Drop it in an open area.
   d. *Press:* Ctrl
   e. *Press:* Esc

7. If you have made a mess of your toolbars and the menu and you want to reload the acad.mnu file, where can you find it?
   a. On the Options menu
   b. In the Customize dialog box
   c. From File System in the Options dialog box on the Tools menu
   d. *Type:* MENU ↵
   e. From Files in the Customize dialog box
8. If you wish to change the shape of a floating horizontal toolbar to vertical
   a. Drag the bottom border
   b. Drag the right border
   c. Drag the left border
   d. Drag the tool label
   e. Floating toolbars cannot be reshaped
9. If you wish to change the shape of a docked vertical toolbar to horizontal
   a. Drag the bottom border
   b. Drag the right border
   c. Drag the top border
   d. Drag the tool label
   e. Docked toolbars cannot be reshaped.
10. To change the name of a toolbar from the Toolbars tab of the Customize dialog box, *Click:*
    a. Customize...
    b. New...
    c. Custom...
    d. Rename...
    e. Toolbars...
11. The command used to rearrange menus on the menu bar is
    a. Customize Menus...
    b. Customize Toolbars...
    c. Customize Menu Bar
    d. Preferences...
    e. Properties...
12. The Menu file has the extension
    a. .bak
    b. .dwg
    c. .mnu
    d. .men
    e. .scr
13. The standard AutoCAD menu file is named
    a. aclt
    b. Menu1
    c. acad
    d. AutoCAD
    e. lt
14. The standard AutoCAD menu file in this chapter was located in which drive, folder, and subfolder?
    a. C:\acad\Program\
    b. C:\program files\autocad\
    c. C:\autocad\
    d. C:\program\acad\
    e. C:\PROGRAM FILES\AutoCAD2002\support
15. The Windows program used to copy and rename the AutoCAD menu file in this chapter is
    a. WordPad
    b. Files
    c. Windows Explorer
    d. Notepad
    e. StartUp

16. The item that was changed to allow AutoCAD to recognize the Menu1 menu file as different from the standard AutoCAD menu file is
    a. MENU1
    b. The File menu on the menu bar
    c. ***POP0
    d. ***MENUGROUP=
    e. The Button menu
17. The Dimension menu on the menu bar is labeled
    a. ***POP1
    b. ***POP4
    c. ***POP6
    d. ***POP7
    e. ***POP8
18. The first response AutoCAD asks from you when the Insert command is activated is
    a. Insertion point:
    b. X scale factor
    c. Y scale factor
    d. Block name
    e. Rotation angle:

PART III ADVANCED AUTOCAD

18 Advanced 3-D

OBJECTIVES

After completing this chapter, you will be able to:

- □ Define wire frame.
- □ Define surface modeling.
- □ List the 3-D surface commands and describe how each is used.
- □ List the settings needed for 3-D models.
- □ Create wire frames.
- □ Add surfaces to wire frames.
- □ Correctly answer questions regarding the following commands and settings:

Edgesurf	Revsurf	Tabsurf	UCS
FILTERS	Rulesurf	3DFace	UCSICON
Pedit	Surftab1	3DMesh	
PFace	Surftab2	3DPoly	

INTRODUCTION

The commands and settings used in the advanced 3-D versions of AutoCAD are simple and essential. As with other concepts in AutoCAD, none is difficult, but they do provide you with more details to remember. Let's begin by taking a look at wire frames and surface models. Figure 18–1 is a wire frame. This model is composed of boundary edges of the object. The wire frame has no surface attached to it. Figure 18–2 is a surface model. This is a wire frame that has had surfaces attached to it. The surface model is hollow inside but gives the appearance of being solid. Figure 18–3 is a surface model after hid-

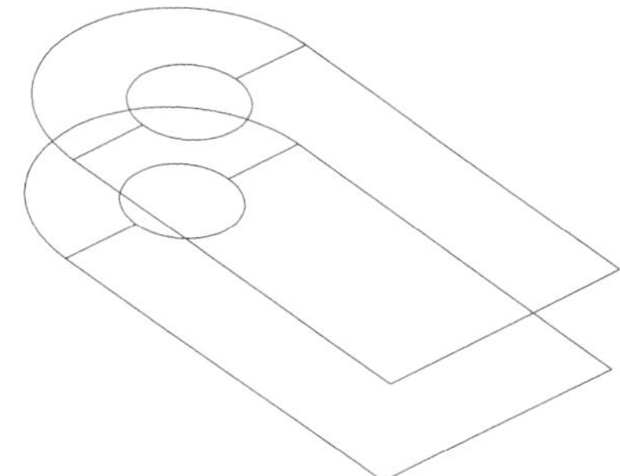

FIGURE 18–1
Wire Frame

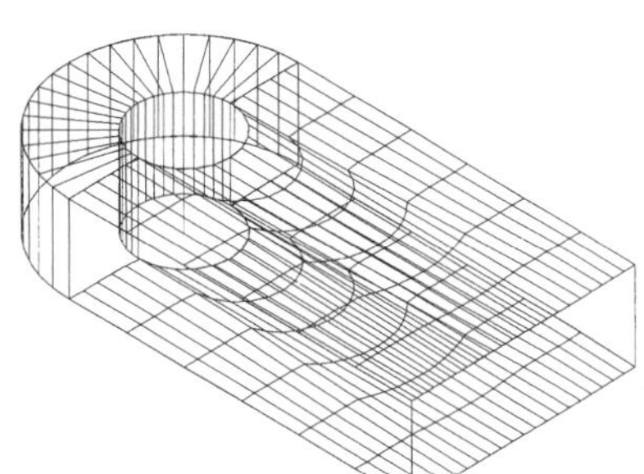

FIGURE 18–2
Surface Model

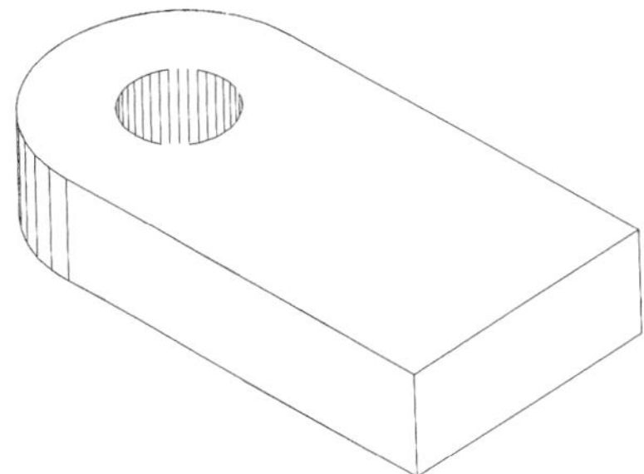

FIGURE 18–3
Surface Model with HIDE

den lines have been removed and layers containing meshes have been turned off. Solid modeling is covered in a later chapter.

COMMANDS USED TO CREATE 3-D SURFACES

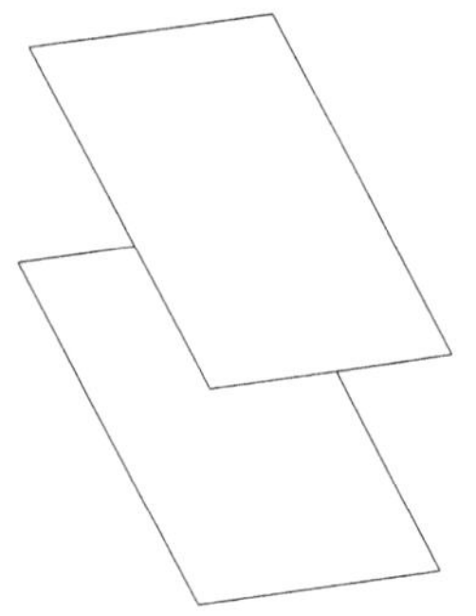

FIGURE 18–4
3DFACEs

The commands used to create wire frames are the same as those used in 2-D drawing, except that the Z dimension now plays an important part. The commands used to create 3-D surfaces are not used in 2-D drawing:

3DPOLY (3D Polyline) This command allows a polyline to be drawn and edited using X, Y, and Z coordinates with all the options available to a 2-D polyline except width and tangent. A 3D polyline can be given a lineweight.

3DFACE (Figure 18–4) This command allows a flat surface to be formed with three or more points making a three- or many-sided shape. Any surface behind this 3-D face will not be seen when the Hide command is executed.

3DMESH (Figure 18–5) This command forms a 3-D surface composed of a mesh whose length and width are defined in drawing units. The intersection of each segment of the mesh can be in a different plane.

PFACE (Figure 18–6) This command forms a 3-D mesh except that intersections can be at any distance from each other.

EDGESURF (Edge Surface) (Figure 18–7) This command forms a 3-D surface called a Coon's Patch between four adjoining edges.

REVSURF (Revolved Surface) (Figure 18–8) This command forms a 3-D surface by rotating it around a selected axis.

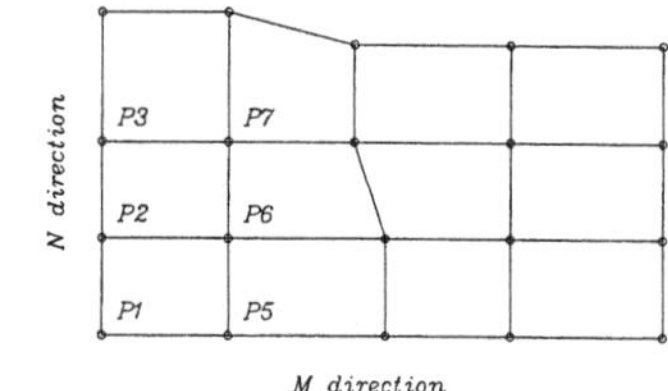

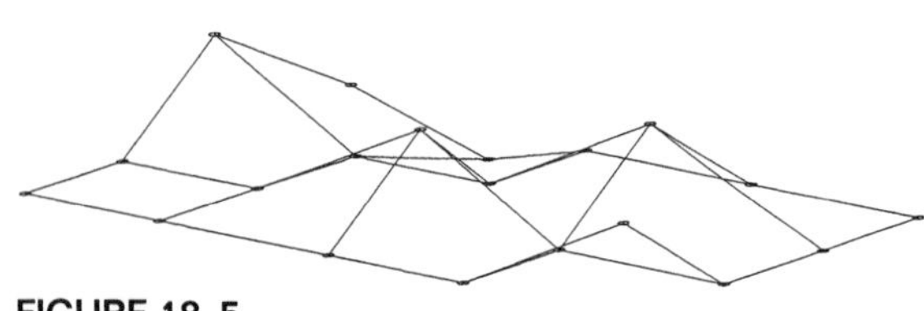

FIGURE 18–5
3DMESH

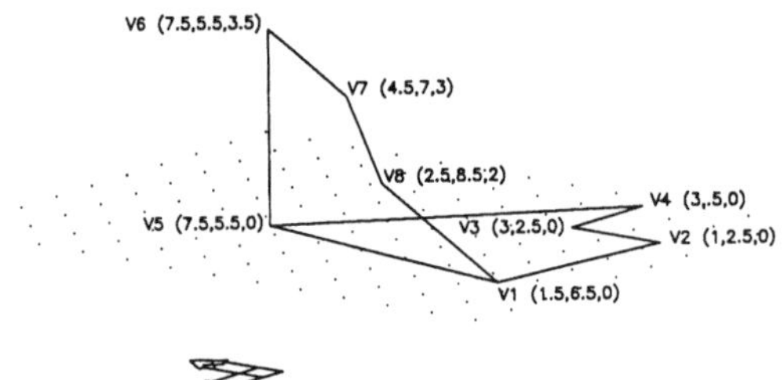

FIGURE 18–6
PFACE Mesh

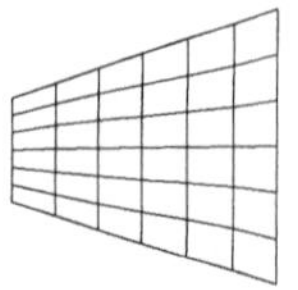

FIGURE 18–7
EDGESURF

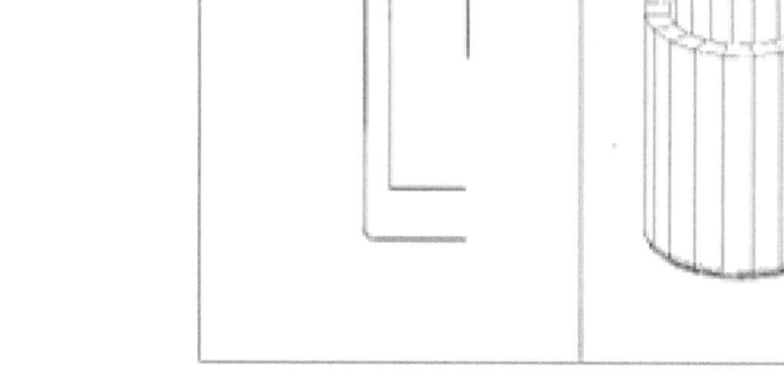

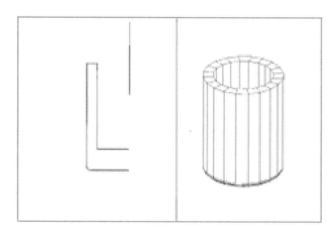

FIGURE 18–8
REVSURF

Note: 3DMESH and PFACE meshes are tedious and time-consuming because the X, Y, and Z components of each vertex must be specified. The other mesh commands—EDGESURF, RULESURF, TABSURF, and REVSURF—are preferred for most uses. The 3DMESH is most often used for topological applications.

RULESURF (Ruled Surface) (Figure 18–9) This command creates a 3-D surface between two curves or straight lines.

TABSURF (Tabulated Surface) (Figure 18–10) This command creates a 3-D surface defined by a shape and a line showing the direction of the surface formation.

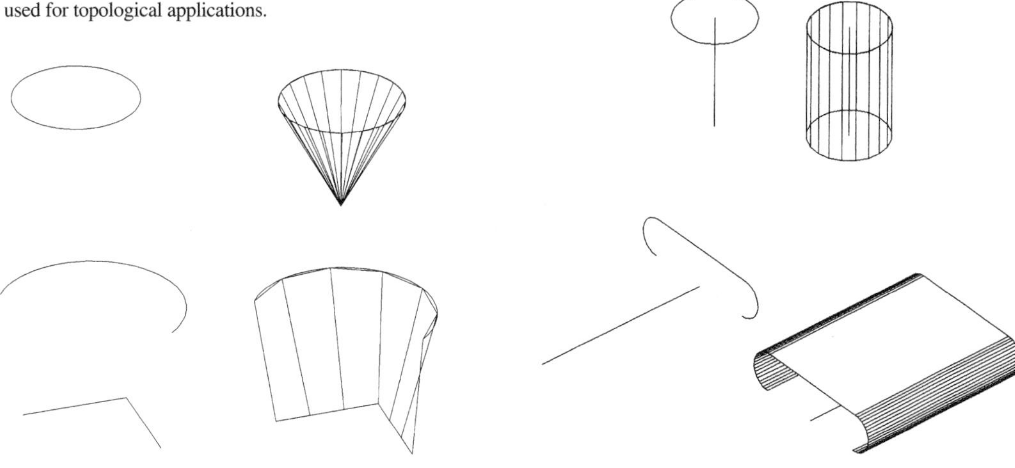

FIGURE 18–9
RULESURF

FIGURE 18–10
TABSURF

SETTINGS USED FOR 3-D SURFACES

There are several settings that affect the formation of these surfaces. Some settings that would also have a use in 2-D drawing have been included because they are particularly useful in 3-D:

MIRRTEXT When the Mirror command is used the text is not mirrored if MIRRTEXT is set to 0.

SURFTAB1 Sets the number of segments in the M direction of Rulesurf, Tabsurf, Revsurf, and Edgesurf surfaces. (Keep these numbers small, not more than 20, to avoid lengthy delays in hide, plot, and regen situations.)

SURFTAB2 Sets the number of segments in the N direction of Revsurf and Edgesurf surfaces.

UCS

Note: If you do not like the surface created with SURFTAB1 and SURFTAB2 settings at a specified value, you will have to erase the surface and redraw it with new SURFTAB1 and SURFTAB2 settings. No UPDATE is available for these meshes.

The user coordinate system is used to allow drawing on any surface. It is important to practice the UCS concept *and* understand how to use it. Usually it is better to construct a feature on what appears to be a 2-D plane. For example, features on a slanted surface should be drawn in a UCS that is parallel to and on the slanted surface. The UCS options are:

M(Move) Defines a new UCS at a different origin but uses the same directions for the X, Y, and Z axes as previously defined.

N(New) Defines a new UCS with a new origin or one of the following options:

- **ZA(ZAxis)** Defines a new UCS at a different origin and a point on the positive Z axis. In effect the new UCS becomes tilted with the new Z axis.
- **3(3point)** Allows you to define a UCS using three points, most often three points on an existing plane.
- **OB(OBject)** Allows you to define a UCS by pointing to any object except a 3-D polyline or polygon mesh. This option is very useful when an object has been created and something needs to be added to it.
- **F(Face)** Allows you to define a new UCS by clicking a face on a solid object. Face will not work on a surface model.

V(view) This modifier creates a new coordinate system whose XY plane is parallel to a screen. This is the UCS that must be used when a 3-D drawing is to be placed into an apparent 2-D format. A good way to combine the 3-D drawing and the 2-D format is to arrange the 3-D drawing as you wish it to appear, set the UCS to "view," and insert a previously drawn format around it.

X/Y/Z This allows the UCS to be rotated around any of the three normal axes. If you want to rotate the UCS about the X axis, type X at the UCS prompt.

G(OrthoGraphic) Allows you to define a new UCS using standard orthographic terms.

P(Prev) Restores the previous UCS.

R(Restore) Restores a UCS that has been saved under a name.

S(Save) Names and saves the current UCS.

D(Del) Deletes specified UCSs (those that have been named and saved).

A(Apply) Allows you to apply the current UCS to other viewports.

? Lists all UCSs that have been saved with the Save option.

W(World) Sets the UCS to the world coordinate system.

UCSICON Controls the display of the UCS arrows, their location, and whether they are visible. OFF removes the UCS arrows from the display. The UCSICON does not automatically move when a new UCS is defined. The UCSICON option, Origin, moves the UCSICON to the new UCS origin. The Properties option allows you to use a 2D or 3D icon and make several settings from a dialog box that controls the UCS icon display.

VIEWCTR Identifies the center of the view in the current viewport.

VIEWDIR Identifies the direction of the view in the current viewport.

In addition there are several LISP routines and other drawing aids that are useful in 3-D.

MODIFYING 3-D OPERATION COMMANDS

Rotate 3D Allows any part of the drawing to be rotated around the X, Y, or Z axis. This is very useful in 3-D.

EDGE Allows you to change the visibility of 3DFACE edges. If an edge is visible, you can make it invisible and vice versa.

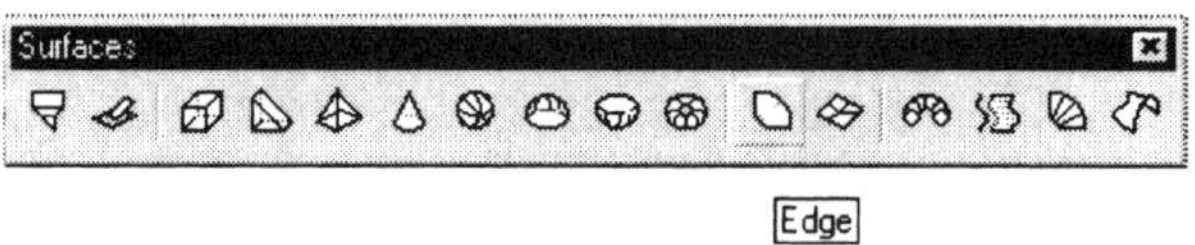

Align Allows you to move and rotate a 3-D shape at the same time and to align it with points on another object.

3D Array This command draws 3-D rectangular or polar arrays on the X, Y, and Z axes.

Mirror 3D This command creates a mirror image of an object about a plane.

Other Drawing Aids

FILTERS Using X, Y, and Z filters is often useful in 3-D drawing. Filters allow you to specify one or two of the X, Y, Z components when the other one or two are known.

You will not use all these commands and settings in this chapter, but knowing that they are available will be of use to you in later 3-D modeling.

Now for a few general guidelines before you begin creating wire frames and surface models.

FIGURE 18–11
3D and 2D USCICONS

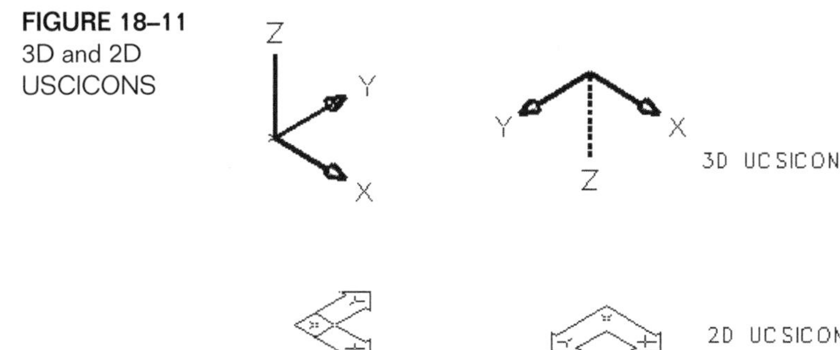

3-D GUIDELINES

- ☐ Create the wire frame first on a layer separate from 3-D surfaces.
- ☐ Create the 3-D surfaces on a visible layer and change them to a layer that has been turned off (*not* frozen) so that the wire frame may be clean for other surfaces to be created. Trying to pick a wire-frame line that has a visible surface attached to it is often difficult.
- ☐ Create surfaces in a positive Z direction whenever possible so that resulting viewpoints will not be a surprise.
- ☐ Follow the right-hand rule to determine the positive Z direction. The right-hand rule is as follows: Look at the UCSICON and hold your right hand in front of you with your palm up and your thumb pointing to the right. Point your middle finger up so that thumb, index finger, and middle finger are perpendicular to one another. Point your thumb in the X direction of the UCSICON and your index finger in the Y direction. The middle finger shows the positive Z direction (Figure 18–11).
- ☐ Use Hide occasionally if you get confused about what view is displayed.
- ☐ Positive Z is shown in the 3D UCSICON with a solid line. Negative Z is shown with a dashed line. The 2D UCSICON does not show the Z dimension as graphically as the 3D UCSICON, so if you are using the 2D UCSICON, apply the right-hand rule to determine the positive Z direction.

So now let's create a 3-D wire frame similar to Figure 18–1 and hang some surfaces on it.

Exercise 18–1: Create a Wire Frame and Add Surfaces Using RULESURF, TABSURF, and 3DFACES Commands

To create 3-D wire frame and surfaces:

Step 1. Load AutoCAD. *Click:* **Create Drawings-Wizards-Quick Setup.**

Step 2. Make the following settings:

Tip: When you *Click:* New and type the Layer name, WIRE, type commas to make the second and third layers.

Units: Decimal—3 places to the right of the decimal point

Area: Width: 11.000
Length: 8.500

GRID: .2

SNAP: .1

TEXT STYLE: Standard FONT: simplex.shx HEIGHT: 0

LAYERS: NAME	Color	Linetype	Lineweight
WIRE	Magenta	CONTINUOUS	Default
R	Red	CONTINUOUS	Default
G	Green	CONTINUOUS	Default

Set layer WIRE current. Set SNAP, GRID, and ORTHO ON.

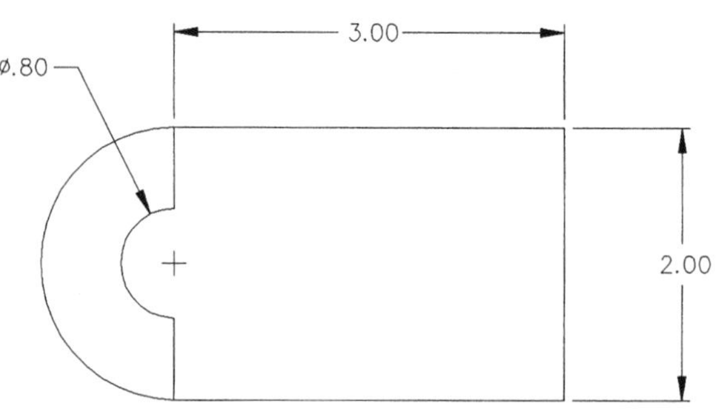

FIGURE 18–12
Dimensions

FIGURE 18–13
Create Surfaces

Step 3. Draw Figure 18–12 using the Line and Arc (or circle and trim) commands.

Step 4. Mirror the small arc to create Figure 18–13.

Step 5. Draw a line from the center of the small arc ¾″ in the positive Z direction.

Prompt	Response
Command:	*Click:* **Line**
Specify first point:	**D1** (Figure 18–13)
Specify next point or [Undo]:	*Type:* **@0,0, .75** ↵
Specify next point or [Undo]:	↵

Step 6. Make a polyline out of the right small arc and the two short vertical lines.

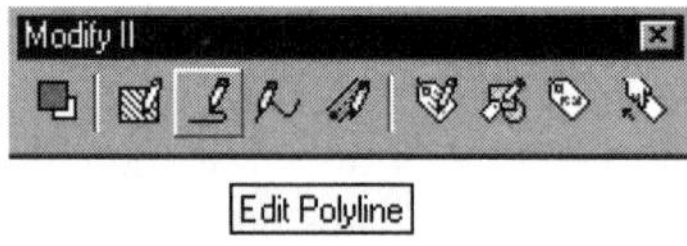

Note: These three segments must be joined into a single edge for the EDGESURF command to work. EDGESURF requires four adjoining edges.

Prompt	Response
Command:	*Click:* **Edit Polyline** (or *Type:* **PE** ↵)
Select polyline or [Multiple]:	**D2** (Figure 18–13)
Object selected is not a polyline. Do you want to turn it into one? <Y>	↵
Enter an option [Close/Join/Width/Edit vertex/Fit/Spline/Decurve/Ltype Gen/Undo]:	*Type:* **J** ↵
Select objects:	**D3, D4, D5** ↵ ↵

The bottom edges of the wire frame are now complete. Before copying this to form the top edges, let's *hang* some surfaces on it.

Step 7. Create RULESURF and EDGESURF surfaces. Set layer R current and set SURFTAB1 and SURFTAB2 to 20.

Prompt	Response
Command:	*Type:* **SURFTAB1** ↵
Enter new value for SURFTAB1 <6>:	*Type:* **20** ↵
Command:	*Type:* **SURFTAB2** ↵
Enter new value for SURFTAB2 <6>:	*Type:* **20** ↵

Set layer R current using the Layer list.

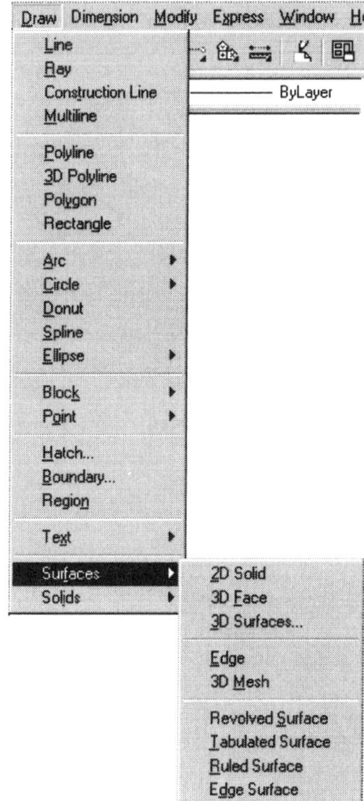

Prompt	Response
Command:	*Click:* **Ruled Surface** (or *Type:* **RULESURF** ↵)
Select first defining curve	**D6** (Figure 18–13)
Select second defining curve	**D7**

If one of the Rulesurf curves, such as a circle, is closed, the other curve must also be closed. When constructing a ruled surface between open curves, AutoCAD starts from the endpoint of each curve nearest the point where you digitized the curve; therefore, don't pick opposite ends of the defining curves unless you want a bow-tie effect.

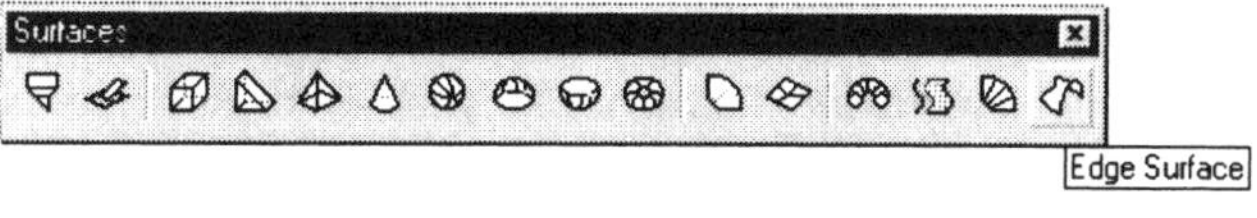

Prompt	Response
Command:	*Click:* **Edge Surface** (or *Type:* **EDGESURF** ↵)
Select object 1 for surface edge:	**D8** (Figure 18–13)
Select object 2 for surface edge:	**D9**
Select object 3 for surface edge:	**D10**
Select object 4 for surface edge:	**D4**

Tip: Instead of typing R↵ to remove an object from the selection set, hold down the Shift key and click the object.

The edges may be selected in any order. The first edge you click determines the M direction of the mesh divisions (controlled by the Surftab1 setting) and the second click determines the N direction of the mesh divisions (controlled by the Surftab2 setting). The default is 6. These settings are changed often, depending on the surface needed.

Step 8. Copy this entire figure to form the top surfaces of the object.

Prompt	Response
Command:	*Click:* **Copy** (or *Type:* **CP** ↵)
Select Objects:	**Window the entire area. Hold down the Shift key to remove the perpendicular line at the center of the small circle from this command.** ↵
Specify Base point or displacement, or [Multiple]:	**D1** (Any point is OK.) (Figure 18–13)
Specify second point of displacement or <Use first point as displacement>:	*Type:* **@0,0, .75** ↵

The surfaces and wire frame are copied .75 in the positive Z direction. Now let's see what you've done.

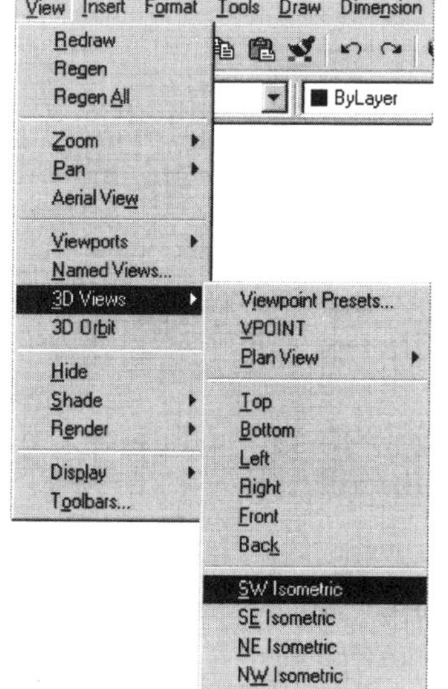

Prompt	Response
Command:	*Type:* **VPOINT** ↵
Specify a viewpoint or [Rotate]<display compass and tripod>:	*Type:* **1,−1,1** ↵

FIGURE 18–14
Create TABSURFs and 3DFACEs

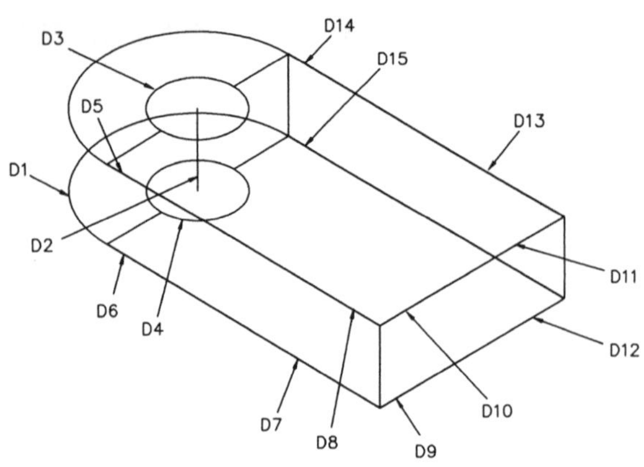

Warning: Do not skip turning off layer R before proceeding, or the other commands will not work.

Step 9. Form other surfaces (Figure 18–14).

Now, turn off layer R so that other surfaces can be formed from the same wire frame. Set layer G as the current layer.

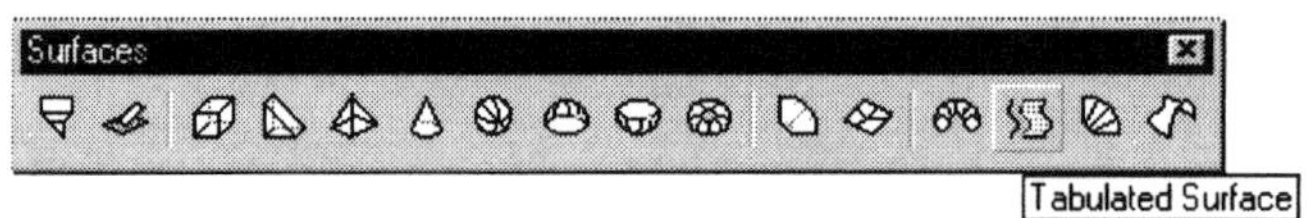

Prompt	Response
Command:	*Click:* **Tabulated Surface** (or *Type:* **TABSURF ↵**)
Select object for path curve:	**D1** (Figure 18–14)
Select object for direction vector:	**D2** (Be sure to click the bottom part of line D2.)

The surface will be drawn starting at the point on the curve closest to your pick point when you select path curve D1. The direction vector is the displacement from the endpoint closest to your pick point to the other end of the line used as the direction vector.

Prompt	Response
Command:	↵
Select object for path curve:	**D3**
Select object for direction vector:	*Click:* **the top part of line D2**

Before proceeding, **use the Explode command to explode the bottom polyline (D4)** so the TABSURF command can be used to create the other half of the hole.

Prompt	Response
Command:	*Click:* **Tabulated Surface** (or *Type:* **TABSURF ↵**)
Select object for path curve:	**D4**
Select object for direction vector:	**D2** (for the third time)

Now set a running Osnap mode of Endpoint and create all the 3DFACE surfaces.

Prompt	Response
Command:	*Click:* **OSNAP** (from the status bar, or *Type:* **OS ↵**)

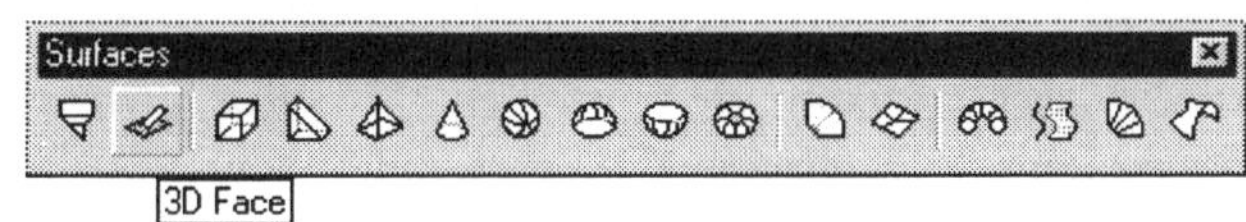

Prompt	Response
Object snap tab appears:	*Click:* **Endpoint**
	Click: **OK**
Command:	*Click:* **3DFace** (or *Type:* **3DFACE** ↵)
Specify first point or [Invisible]:	*Type:* **i** ↵ **D5**
Specify second point or [Invisible]:	**D6**
Specify third point or [Invisible]<exit>:	**D7**
Specify fourth point or [Invisible]<create three-sided face>:	**D8**
Specify third point or [Invisible]<exit>:	↵

Typing *i* before digitizing the first point of an edge makes that edge invisible. In this case, the vertical edge should be invisible so that it doesn't show when a HIDE is executed. You may continue with additional points beyond the fourth point to form more edges of the 3DFACEs and even specify differing Z coordinates. Most 3DFACEs, however, have all their points in the same plane (coplanar). They must all be in the same plane for the surface to be considered opaque by the Hide command.

Prompt	Response
Command:	↵
Specify first point or [Invisible]:	**D9**
Specify second point or [Invisible]:	**D10**
Specify third point or [Invisible]<exit>:	**D11**
Specify fourth point or [Invisible]<create three-sided face>:	**D12**
Specify third point or [Invisible]<exit>:	↵
Command:	↵
Specify first point or [Invisible]:	**D12**
Specify second point or [Invisible]:	**D13**
Specify third point or [Invisible]<exit>:	*Type:* **i** ↵ **D14**
Specify fourth point or [Invisible]<create three-sided face>:	**D15**
Specify third point or [Invisible]<exit>:	↵

The figure is now complete.

Step 10. Now perform a HIDE.

Prompt	Response
Command:	**Hide** (or *Type:* **HI** ↵)

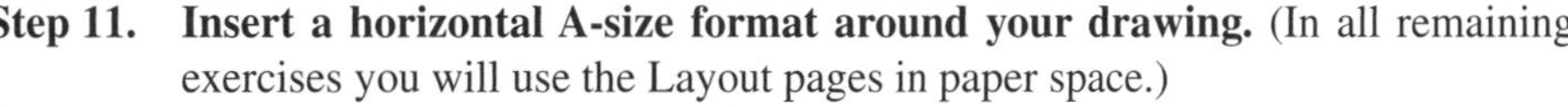

Step 11. Insert a horizontal A-size format around your drawing. (In all remaining exercises you will use the Layout pages in paper space.)

Prompt	Response
Command:	*Click:* **UCS-View** (from the Tools menu or toolbar) (or *Type:* **UCS** ↵)
Enter an option [New/Move.../Origin/Zaxis/3point/Entity/World]<World>:	*Type:* **V**↵
Command:	*Type:* **I**
The Insert dialog box appears:	*Click:* **Browse and locate the name of the A-size format you created in an earlier chapter. Be sure to locate the drive and folder (if any) that contains the drawing.** *Click:* **OK. Answer the prompts with: Assignment: 18–1; Title: GUIDE; Date: Current date.**

Step 12. Print the drawing on an 11″ × 8½″ sheet. Move the model so it is centered in the format. Be sure to have an X in the Hide Objects button (Plot options on the Plot Settings tab).

Step 13. Save the drawing in two places with the name EX18-1(your initials) and continue using AutoCAD.

You have used Rulesurf, Edgesurf, Tabsurf, and 3DFace commands.

To create a model using the REVSURF command (Figure 18–15):

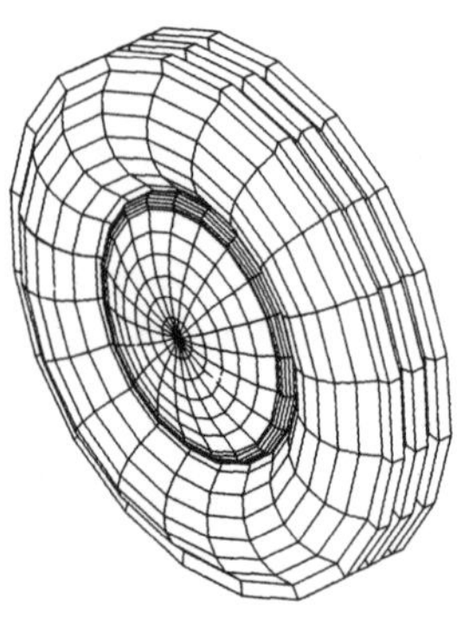

FIGURE 18–15
Completed Tire and Hubcap

Exercise 18–2: Creating a Surface Model Using Revsurf

Step 1. *Click:* **New.** *Click:* **Create Drawings-Wizards-Quick Setup.**

Step 2. Make the following settings:

Units Decimal—3 places to the right of the decimal point.
Area: Width: 8.5
Length: 11
GRID: .2
SNAP: .1
TEXT STYLE: Standard FONT: simplex.shx HEIGHT: 0

LAYERS: NAME	Color	Linetype	Lineweight
WIRE	Magenta	CONTINUOUS	Default

Set layer 0 current. Turn GRID and SNAP ON.

Because you will Wblock this drawing, you should create it on the construction layer 0. When the block is inserted into a drawing, it assumes the color of the layer on which it is inserted. Blocks constructed on layers other than 0 retain the color of the layers on which they were constructed.

Note: Be sure to join all the segments into a single polyline. The REVSURF command allows you to pick only one entity.

Step 3. Draw the tire (Figure 18–16). Using the dimensions shown (approximate any not shown), use Arc and Line commands; then Pedit (Edit Polyline) to join all segments into a single polyline.

Step 4. Draw a centerline 4″ from the inside of the tire centered along its width. (You will use this centerline as an insertion point for a later drawing.)

Step 5. Draw the hubcap as a single polyline, as shown.

FIGURE 18–16
Tire and Hubcap Dimensions

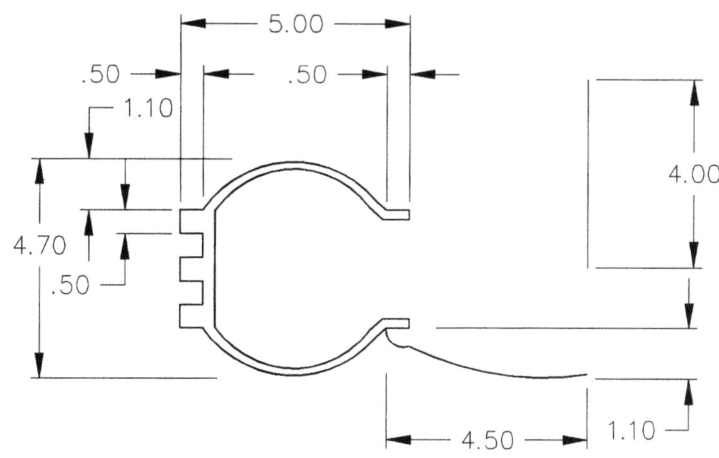

Step 6. Set SURFTAB1=20. (*Type:* **SURFTAB1** ↵)

Step 7. Create a REVSURF of the hubcap wire frame.

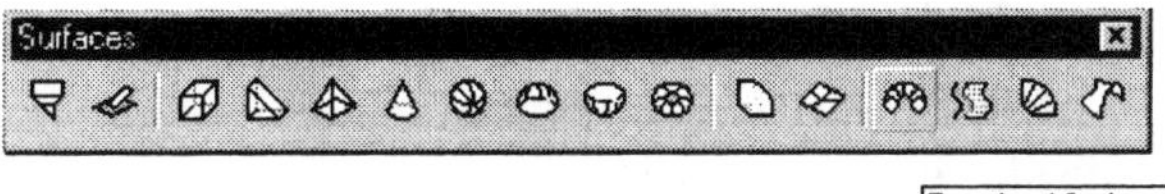

Prompt	Response
Command:	*Click:* **Revolved Surface** (or *Type:* **REVSURF** ↵)
Select object to revolve:	*Click:* **on the hubcap polyline**
Select object that defines the axis of revolution:	*Click:* **on the centerline**
Specify start angle <0):	↵
Specify included angle (+=ccw,−=cw) <360>:	↵

Step 8. Create a REVSURF of the tire wire frame.

Prompt	Response
Command:	*Click:* **Revolved Surface** (or *Type:* **REVSURF** ↵)
Select object to revolve:	*Click:* **on the tire polyline**
Select object that defines the axis of revolution:	*Click:* **on the centerline**
Start angle <0):	↵
Specify included angle (+=ccw,−=cw) <360>:	↵

Step 9. Now, take a look at what you have done.

Prompt	Response
Command:	*Type:* **VP** ↵
The Viewpoint Presets dialog box appears:	*Click:* **315° on the left chart**
	Click: **30° on the right chart**
	Click: **OK**

Step 10. Use Hide to remove hidden lines.

Step 11. **Print the drawing on an 11″ × 8½″ sheet. Write your name on the printed sheet in the lower right corner. No format is needed on this drawing. You will use it as a block on a later drawing. The drawing must remain in the world UCS so that it may be inserted properly into another drawing. Do not change the UCS.**

Step 12. **Wblock the drawing using the Endpoint of the centerline as the insertion point, and Exit. Because the centerline is covered by the hubcap, use two viewports and select a view in one that will allow the insertion point to be selected.**

Prompt	Response
Command:	*Click:* **Viewports-2 Viewports** (or *Type:* **VPORTS** ↵, then *Type:* **2** ↵)
Enter a configuration option [Horizontal/Vertical]<Vertical>:	↵
Command:	*Type:* **VPOINT** ↵
Specify a viewpoint or [Rotate] <display compass and tripod>:	*Type:* **1, 1, 1**↵

Click the right viewport to make it active. Now **Zoom a window to enlarge the display of the centerline.**

Prompt	Response
Command:	*Type:* **WBLOCK** ↵
The Write Block dialog box appears:	*Type:* **WHEEL-(your initials)** (in the File Name button, *Click:* **A: from…** in the Location button, and *Click:* **Pick Point** in the Base point area)
Specify insertion base point:	**Use Osnap-Endpoint to select the endpoint of the centerline farthest from the tire in the right viewport** (Figure 18–17).

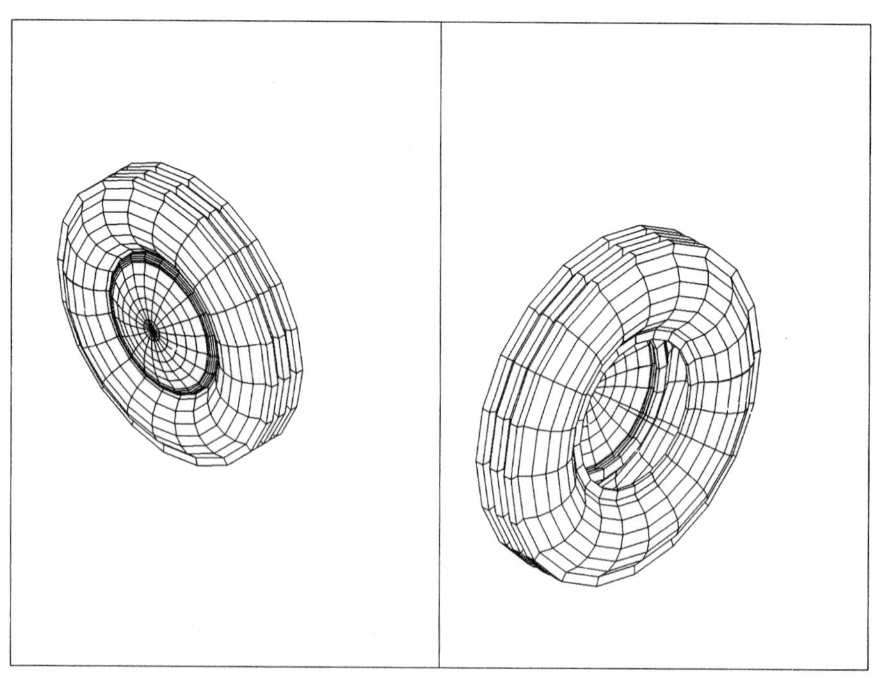

FIGURE 18–17
Front and Rear Views of the Wheel

Prompt	Response
The Write Block dialog box appears:	*Click:* **Select objects**
Select objects:	*Type:* **All** ↵
Select objects:	↵
The Write Block dialog box appears:	*Click:* **OK**

One more example will complete the commands in this chapter.

Step 13. Close AutoCAD and do not save changes to any drawing.

Exercise 18–3: Using Rotate 3D to Rotate Views of Existing Drawings

The Rotate 3D command makes it possible to rotate flat views of existing drawings to form a 3-D wire frame on which surfaces can be created if necessary. Let's examine one of a simple block shape. Because you don't presently have this drawing, you will have to draw it and pretend it existed.

Step 1. Load AutoCAD. *Click:* **Create Drawings-Wizards-Quick Setup.**

Step 2. Make the following settings:

Units: Decimal—3 places to the right of the decimal point.

Area: Width: 11.000
Length: 8.500

GRID: .2

SNAP: .1

TEXT STYLE: Standard FONT: simplex.shx HEIGHT: 0

LAYERS: NAME	Color	Linetype	Lineweight
WIRE	Yellow	CONTINUOUS	Default
R	Red	CONTINUOUS	Default
G	Green	CONTINUOUS	Default

Set layer WIRE current. Set SNAP, GRID, and ORTHO ON.

Step 3. Draw the three views of Figure 18–18 using the dimensions shown. (Do not dimension the drawing.)

Step 4. Set layer R current and create 3DFACEs on front and right side views. You will have to use three 3DFACEs on the front view. Make inside edges of the 3DFACEs invisible.

Step 5. Draw a line from the center of each circle to @0,0,−2 and then create TABSURFs to form the holes. Turn layer R off. Erase the centerlines when you are through.

Step 6. Set layer WIRE current and draw a line across the midpoints of the surfaces with the holes, trim out the line inside of the circle, and trim half of the circle. Use Pedit (Edit Polyline) to make a single polyline out of the half circle and two short lines. Set layer G current, set SURFTAB1 and SURFTAB2 = 20, form an EDGESURF, and Mirror it to form the other half of the upper surface. Do this for both surfaces with holes. Erase the polyline after the EDGESURF surfaces have been created.

Step 7. Turn all layers ON and move all the flat surfaces up 2″ so that the bottom of the model will rest on elevation 0 when the model is completed.

FIGURE 18–18
Existing Views

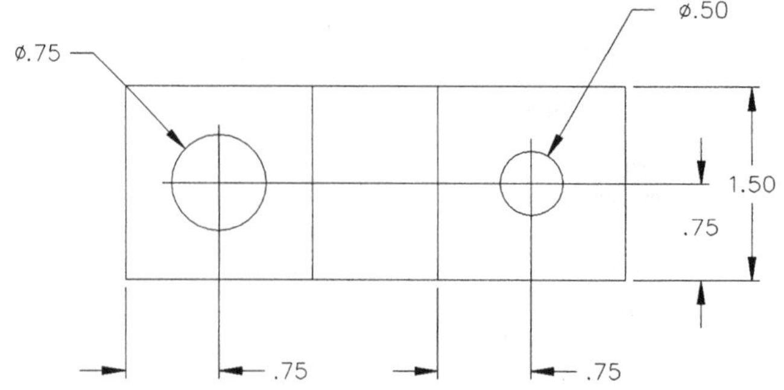

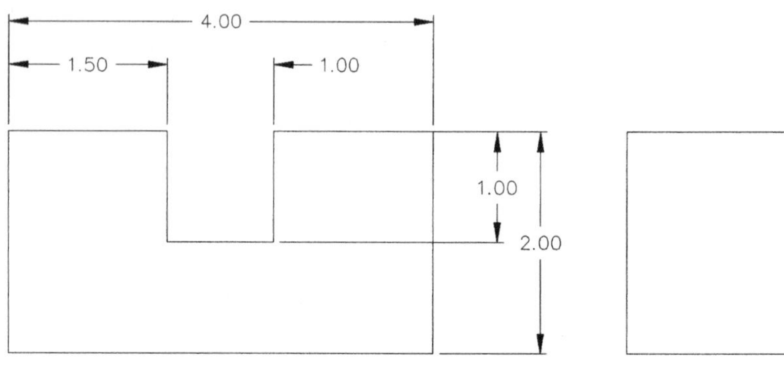

Tip: Use viewports with two or more views of the same object to make it easier to locate points and draw shapes. Many shapes can be drawn in 2-D and rotated to their desired positions.

Prompt	**Response**
Command:	*Click:* **Move** (or *Type:* **M** ↵)
Select objects:	*Click:* **on everything except the holes**
Specify base point or displacement:	*Click:* **on an intersection**
Specify second point of displacement or <use first point as displacement>:	*Type:* **@0,0,2** ↵

Step 8. Use Rotate 3D to rotate surfaces to their correct orientation and move them into position using Osnap (Figure 18–19).

Prompt	**Response**
Command:	*Type:* **VPOINT** ↵ (or *Click:* **SE Isometric** from 3D Views)
Select a viewpoint or [Rotate] <display compass and tripod>:	*Type:* **1,−1,1** ↵

Modify Window Help
Properties
Match Properties
Object
Clip
In-place Xref and Block Edit
Erase
Copy
Mirror
Offset
Array...
Move
Rotate
Scale
Stretch
Lengthen
Trim
Extend
Break
Chamfer
Fillet
3D Operation
Solids Editing
Explode
3D Array
Mirror 3D
Rotate 3D
Align

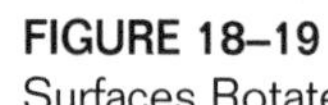

FIGURE 18–19
Surfaces Rotated

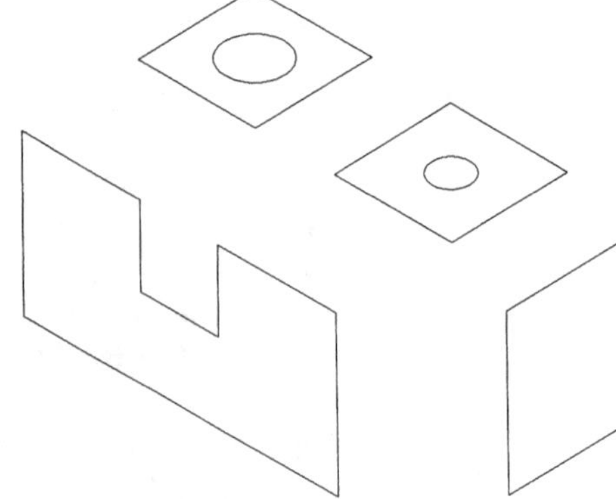

Prompt	**Response**
Command:	*Click:* **Rotate 3D** (or *Type:* **ROTATE 3D ↵**)
Select objects:	*Click:* **front- and right-side surfaces and wire frames**
Specify first point on axis or define axis by [Object/Last/Xaxis/Yaxis/Zaxis/2 points]:	*Type:* **X** ↵
Specify a point on the X axis <0,0,0>:	*Click:* **the upper left corner of the front view using Osnap-Endpoint**
Specify rotation angle or [Reference]:	*Type:* **90** ↵ (for counterclockwise rotation)
Command:	↵ **(Repeat ROTATE3D.)**
Select objects:	*Click:* **right-side surfaces and wire frame**
Specify first point on axis or define axis by [Object/Last/Xaxis/Yaxis/Zaxis/2 points]:	*Type:* **Z** ↵
Specify a point on the Z axis <0,0,0>:	*Click:* **the upper left corner of the right-side view**
Specify rotation angle or [Reference]:	*Type:* **90** ↵

Step 9. Copy the front-view wire frame and surfaces to the rear of the model using Osnap.

Step 10. Move the front- and right-side-view wire frames and surfaces to their correct locations using Osnap.

Step 11. Turn off layers R and G and, with layer R current, create 3DFACEs on the sides and bottom of the slot.

Step 12. Turn on layer R and use Hide to remove all hidden lines. (Leave layer G OFF.)

Note: If necessary, *Click:* on the paper space viewport boundary and use Properties from the Modify menu to set the scale to 1:1.

Step 13. *Click:* **Layout1 and insert your A-size horizontal format. Answer prompts with**

Assignment: 18–3
Drawing Title: FIXTURE
Date: Current date

Move the model viewport so it is centered in the format.

Step 14. Print the drawing on a horizontal 11″ × 8.5″ sheet. Be sure to remove hidden lines with MVIEW-Hideplot. (See step 25 of Exercise 16–1.)

Step 15. Save the drawing in two places and Exit AutoCAD.

EXERCISES

Hint: Use different colors to separate parts. Assign a different color to each layer and turn layers on and off as needed.

EXERCISE 18–1. Complete Exercise 18–1 as described in this chapter.
EXERCISE 18–2. Complete Exercise 18–2 as described in this chapter.
EXERCISE 18–3. Complete Exercise 18–3 as described in this chapter.
EXERCISE 18–4. Create a 3-D model of the figure shown in Figure 18–20. Use surfaces described. Your final model should look like the figure on the lower right. Insert a horizontal A-size format around the model in Layout1 and plot it on an A-size sheet. Answer the prompts with:

FIGURE 18–20
Exercise 18–4

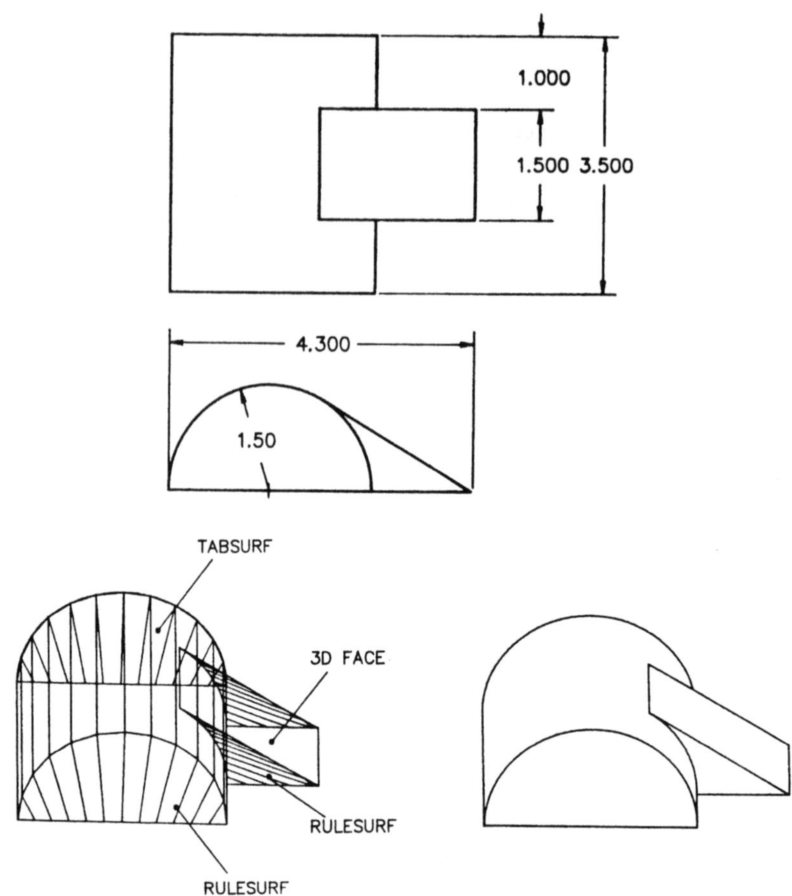

Assignment: 18–4
Drawing Title: HUT
Date: Current date

Be sure to remove hidden lines with MVIEW-Hideplot.

EXERCISE 18–5. Create a 3-D model as shown in Figure 18–21. You will find it helpful to rotate the UCS to the inclined surface to create those surfaces. Select a viewpoint that gives approximately the same appearance as shown. Insert a horizontal A-size format around the model in Layout1 and answer the prompts with:

Assignment: 18–5
Drawing Title: STOP
Date: Current date

Remove hidden lines with MVIEW-Hideplot.

EXERCISE 18–6. Create a 3-D model as shown in Figure 18–22. Select a viewpoint that gives approximately the same appearance as shown. Insert a horizontal A-size format around the model in Layout1 and answer the prompts with

Assignment: 18–6
Drawing Title: BRACKET
Date: Current date

Remove hidden lines with MVIEW-Hideplot.

EXECISE 18–7. Create a 3-D model as shown in Figure 18–23. Select a viewpoint that gives approximately the same appearance as shown. Insert a horizontal A-size format around the model in Layout1 and answer the prompts with

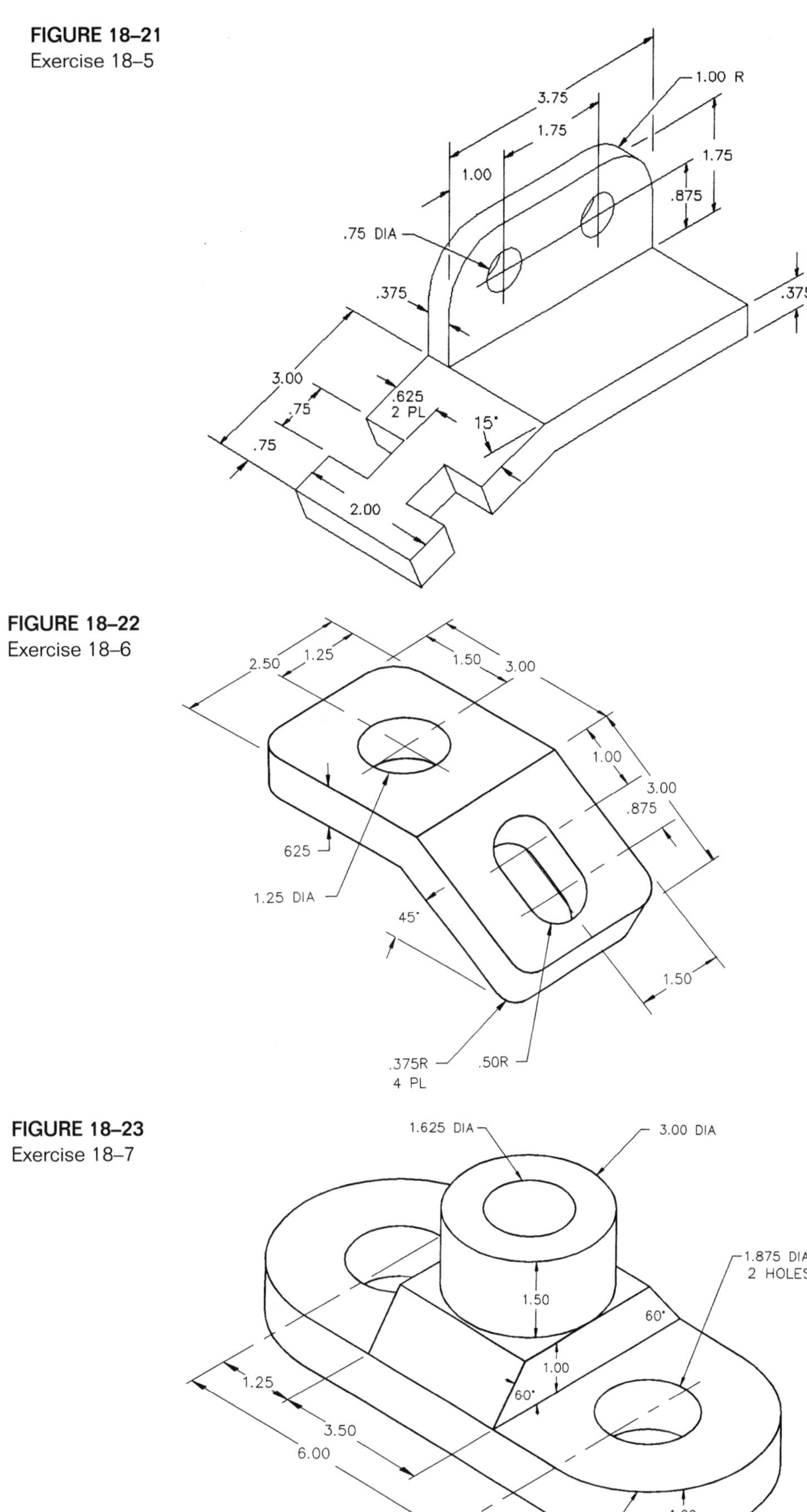

FIGURE 18–21
Exercise 18–5

FIGURE 18–22
Exercise 18–6

FIGURE 18–23
Exercise 18–7

FIGURE 18–24
Exercise 18–8

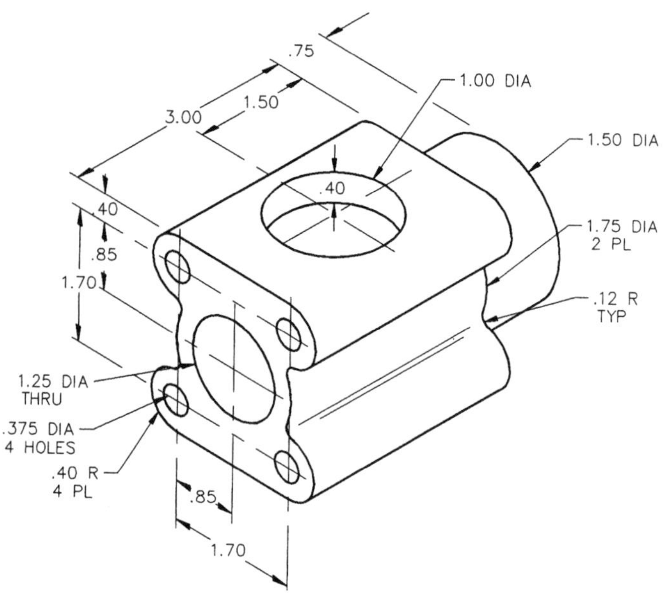

Tip: Use *Donut* for the top cylinder.

Assignment: 18–7
Drawing Title: BASE
Date: Current date

Remove hidden lines with MVIEW-Hideplot.

EXERCISE 18–8. Create a 3-D model as shown in Figure 18–24. Select a viewpoint that gives approximately the same appearance as shown. Insert a horizontal A-size format around the model in Layout1 and answer the prompts with

Assignment: 18–8
Drawing Title: HOUSING
Date: Current date

Remove hidden lines with MVIEW-Hideplot.

REVIEW QUESTIONS

Circle the best answer.

1. The command used to create a flat surface without a mesh is
   a. PFace
   b. 3DFace
   c. Edgesurf
   d. Revsurf
   e. Rulesurf
2. The command that forms a mesh between four adjoining edges is
   a. PFace
   b. 3DFace
   c. Edgesurf
   d. Revsurf
   e. Rulesurf
3. The command that forms a 3-D surface by rotating it around a selected axis is
   a. PFace
   b. 3DFace
   c. Edgesurf
   d. Revsurf
   e. Rulesurf

4. The command that forms a surface between two curves or straight lines is
   a. PFace
   b. 3DFace
   c. Edgesurf
   d. Revsurf
   e. Rulesurf
5. The command that forms a surface defined by a shape and line showing the direction of surface formation is
   a. Tabsurf
   b. 3DFace
   c. Edgesurf
   d. Revsurf
   e. Rulesurf
6. The length and width of a 3-D mesh is labeled (see Figure 18–5)
   a. M and N
   b. X and Y
   c. A and B
   d. Y and Z
   e. Varies, depending on orientation of the UCS
7. You must use MVIEW-Hideplot to remove hidden lines in paper space.
   a. True
   b. False
8. The setting that controls the number of segments in one direction of a mesh is
   a. Splinesegs
   b. Surftype
   c. UCSICON
   d. Surftab1
   e. Splframe
9. The command that allows an object to be rotated around X, Y, and Z axes is
   a. Rotate
   b. Rotate 3D
   c. Array
   d. Move
   e. Revolve
10. The 3D UCSICON shows negative Z direction
    a. With a solid line
    b. With a solid line and an arrowhead
    c. With a dashed line
    d. With a dashed line and an arrowhead
    e. It does not show negative Z.

19 Advanced 3-D: Blocks, Dview, and 3D Orbit

OBJECTIVES

After completing this chapter, you will be able to

- □ Create complex surface models.
- □ Create and use blocks with different X, Y, and Z scales.
- □ Use Dview and 3D Orbit to display models in parallel and perspective projections.

The previous chapters on 3-D have introduced many commands, settings, and LISP routines that can be effectively used to create surface models. This chapter continues to use those features in a complex assembly. In addition, this chapter provides information regarding the use of blocks to form surfaces and Dview and 3D Orbit to view them in parallel and perspective projection. 3D Orbit is also used to render the model.

Before beginning to construct the assembly shown in Figure 19–1, some blocks must be constructed that will make this assembly considerably easier.

BLOCKS IN 3-D

Many of the standard 3-D objects can be used in forming complex surface models. A *box,* for example, can be inserted with different X, Y, and Z dimensions using the 3-D object BOX. Other shapes, however, are sometimes necessary to speed up the creation of complex shapes. This can be done with blocks constructed within a 1-unit cube and inserted

FIGURE 19–1
Complete Assembly

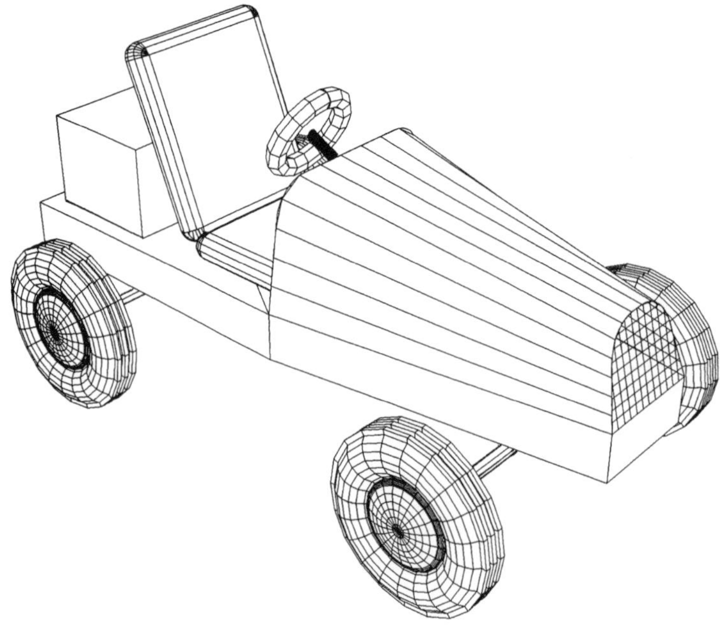

FIGURE 19–2
3-D Fillet

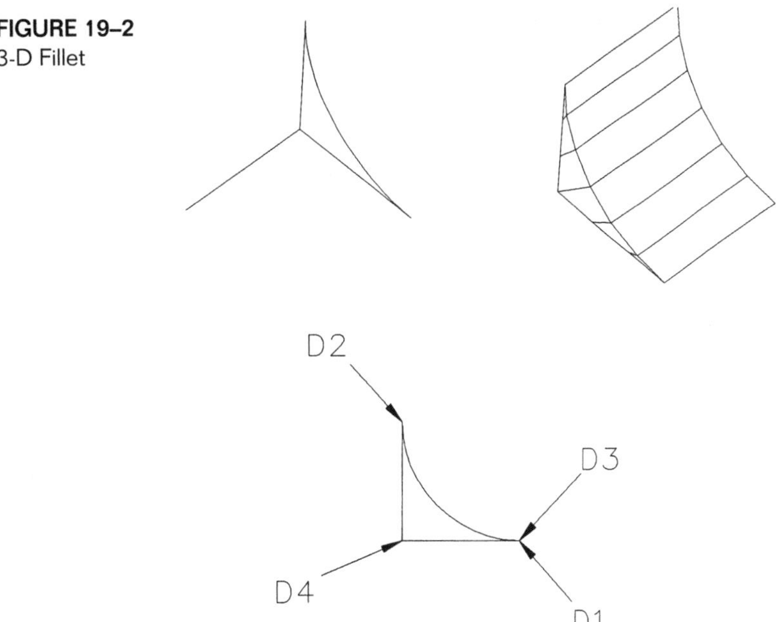

with different X, Y, and Z scales. For example, the fillet (Figure 19–2) was constructed with 1″ length, width, and depth and then Wblocked. It can be inserted with an X-scale factor of .25, a Y-scale factor of .25, and a Z-scale factor of 6 for a ¼″ fillet weld along a 6″ length of metal. The shapes you will draw in this exercise are a fillet, a half-round, and a ¼″ end cap. Let's consider these shapes now.

CONSTRUCTING 3-D BLOCKS

Exercise 19–1A: Drawing a 3-D Fillet, Half-Round, and ¼ End Cap

Step 1. Load AutoCAD. *Click:* **Create Drawings-Wizards-Quick Setup.**

Step 2. Make the following settings:

Units: Decimal—3 places to the right of the decimal point
Area: Width: 8.500
Length: 11.00
GRID: .5
SNAP: .1
TEXT STYLE: Standard FONT: simplex.shx HEIGHT: 0

LAYERS:	NAME	Color	Linetype	Lineweight
	WIRE	Yellow	CONTINUOUS	Default

Set layer WIRE current. Turn SNAP, GRID, and ORTHO ON.
Zoom-All to see the whole grid.
Set surftab1: 20

Step 3. Construct the fillet (Figure 19–2).

Prompt	Response
Command:	*Click:* **Polyline** (or *Type:* **PL** ↵)
Specify start point:	**D1** (Figure 19–2)

Prompt	Response
Specify next point or [Arc/Close/Halfwidth/ Length/Undo/Width]:	**With Ortho ON, move the cursor to the left and** *Type:* **1** ↵
Specify next point or [Arc/Close/Halfwidth/ Length/Undo/Width]:	**Move the cursor up and** *Type:* **1** ↵
Specify next point or [Arc/Close/Halfwidth/ Length/Undo/Width]:	↵
Command:	*Click:* **Arc-Start, End, Radius**
Specify start point of arc or [Center]:	**D2**
Specify end point of arc:	**D3**
Specify radius of arc:	*Type:* **1** ↵
Command:	*Click:* **Line**
Specify first point:	**D4**
Specify next point or [Undo]:	*Type:* **@0,0,1** ↵
Specify next point or [Undo]:	↵
Command:	*Type:* **VPOINT**↵ (or select SW Isometric from 3D Views)
Specify a view point or [Rotate] <display compass and tripod>:	*Type:* **1,−1,1** ↵
SET LAYER 0 CURRENT.	
Command:	*Click:* **Tabulated Surface** (or *Type:* **TABSURF** ↵)
Select object for path curve:	*Click:* **on the arc**
Select object for direction vector:	*Click:* **on the Z axis line near its lower end. Turn layer 0 OFF (even though it is current).**
Command:	*Click:* **Ruled Surface** (or *Type:* **RULESURF** ↵)
Select first defining curve:	*Click:* **on the Polyline**
Select second defining curve:	*Click:* **on the arc. Turn layer 0 ON.**
Command:	*Click:* **Copy**
Select objects:	*Click:* **on the RULESURF**
Select objects:	↵
Specify base point or displacement, or [Multiple]:	**Use Osnap to click on the endpoint of the Z-axis line closest to the RULESURF.**
Specify second point of displacement or <use first point as displacement>:	**Use Osnap to click on the other endpoint of the Z-axis line.**

On your own:

Change all entities of the fillet to the 0 layer; use Properties or the Layer list.

Prompt	Response
Command:	*Click:* **Wblock** (or *Type:* **W** ↵)
The Write Block dialog box appears:	*Type:* **FILL-(your initials)** in the File Name: button. *Click:*... to the right of the Location: button and *Click:* **3½ Floppy (A:)**

Prompt	Response
	Click: **OK**
	Click: **Pick point**
Insertion base point:	*Click:* **on the intersection of the two straight lines of one of the RULESURFs.**
The Write Block dialog box appears:	*Click:* **Select objects**
Select objects:	**Window the entire drawing to select all objects.**
Select objects:	↵
The Write Block dialog box appears:	*Click:* **OK**

Step 4. Construct the half-round on the 0 layer (Figure 19–3) in a similar manner and Wblock it using A:HR-(your initials) for the WBLOCK name. Be sure to make the diameter and length 1 unit each. Use the intersection of one of the half-rounds and the Z-axis line as the insertion point.

Step 5. Construct end cap (Figure 19–4) on the 0 layer.

Prompt	Response
Command:	*Click:* **Line**
Specify start point:	**D1** (Figure 19–4)
Specify next point or [Undo]:	**With ortho ON: Move the cursor up and** *Type:* **1** ↵
Specify next point or [Undo]:	↵
Command:	*Click:* **Arc-Start, End, Radius**
Specify start point of arc or [Center]:	**D2**
Specify end point of arc:	**D3**
Specify radius of arc:	*Type:* **.5** ↵
Command:	*Click:* **Revolved Surface** (or *Type:* **REVSURF** ↵)
Select object to revolve:	*Click:* **on the arc**
Select object that defines the axis of revolution:	*Click:* **on the line**
Specify start angle <0>:	↵
Specify included angle (+=ccw,−=cw><360>	*Type:* **90** ↵

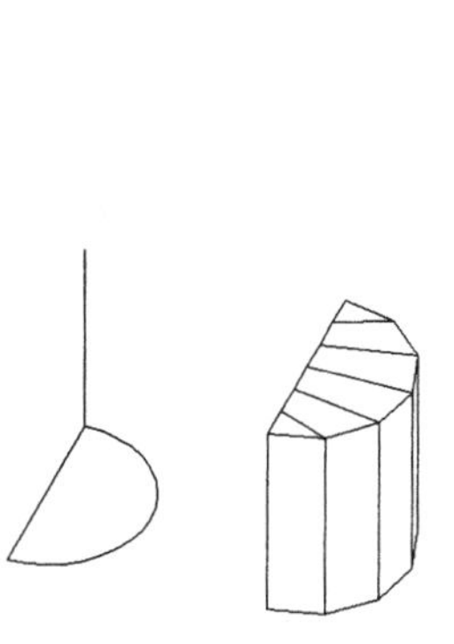

FIGURE 19–3
Half-Round

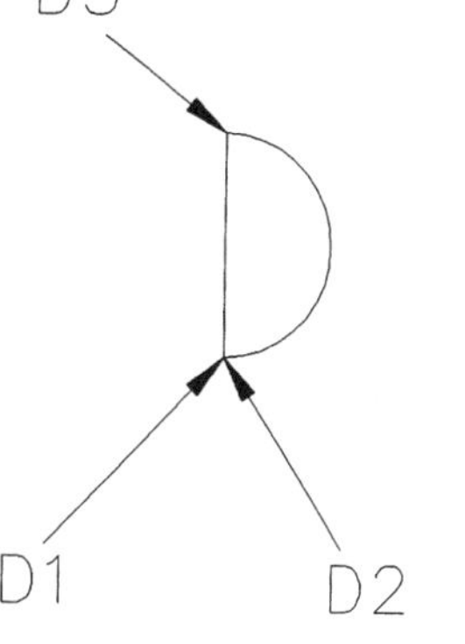

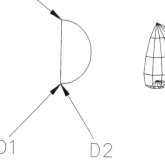

FIGURE 19–4
End Cap

WBlock the end cap to the floppy disk (A:) using the name EC and use D1 (Figure 19–4) as the insertion point.

Step 6. Exit

CREATING A COMPLEX 3-D SURFACE MODEL

Now, draw the assembly shown as Figure 19–1. There are several ways to do this. In the previous chapter you rotated parts that had all been drawn on the same plane to form a 3-D part. In this chapter, you will use that technique as well as rotating the construction plane (the UCS) so that the parts can be created in the correct plane and thus do not have to be rotated after they are constructed.

Exercise 19–1B: Drawing the assembly (Figure 19–1)

Step 1. Load AutoCAD. *Click:* **Create Drawings-Wizards-Quick Setup.**

Step 2. Make the following settings:

Units Decimal—2 places to the right of the decimal point

Area: Width: 100
Length: 50

GRID: 4

SNAP: 1

TEXT STYLE: Standard FONT: simplex.shx HEIGHT: 0

LAYERS: NAME	Color	Linetype	Lineweight
M	Magenta	Continuous	Default
R	Red	Continuous	Default
G	Green	Continuous	Default
B	Blue	Continuous	Default

Set layer M current.

Surftab1: 20

Zoom-All

Warning: Users of previous versions of AutoCAD should be aware that a different UCS can be specified in each viewport.

Begin by drawing everything that can be drawn on the default construction plane, the world coordinate system.

Step 3. Draw the axles.

Prompt	Response
Command:	Set Elevation: to 9; Thickness: to 0; (*Type:* **ELEV** ↵)
Command:	*Click:* **Line** (or *Type:* **L** ↵)
Specify first point:	**D1** (Figure 19–5)
Specify next point or [Undo]:	**With Ortho ON: move the cursor down and** *Type:* **28** ↵
Specify next point or [Undo]:	↵
Command:	*Click:* **Offset** (or *Type:* **O** ↵)
Specify offset distance or [Through] <1.000>:	*Type:* **48** ↵
Select object to offset or <exit>:	*Click:* **on the line just drawn**
Specify point on side to offset:	*Click:* **to the left**

FIGURE 19–5
Base, Axles, and Engine-Compartment Dimensions

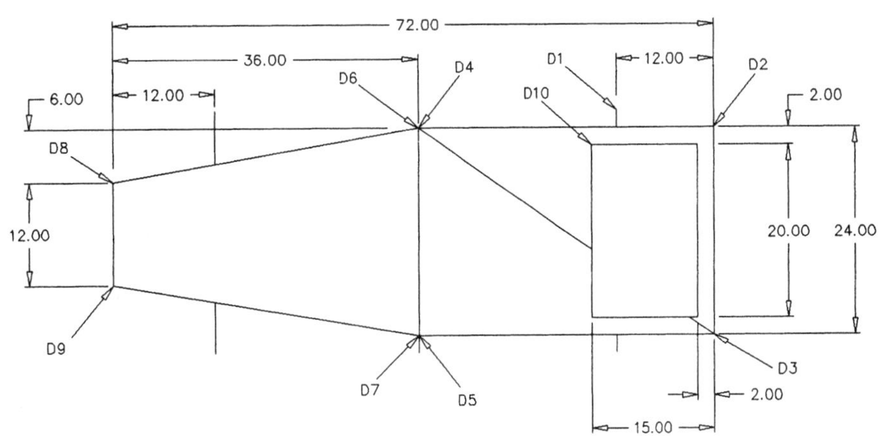

Step 4. Draw the base (Figures 19–5 and 19–6). Begin by setting the elevation and thickness for the base.

Prompt	Response
Command:	**Set Elevation: to 12; Thickness: to 5**
Command:	*Click:* **2D Solid** (*Type:* **SO** ↵)
Specify first point:	**D2** (Figure 19–5) (3 grid marks to the right and 2 snaps down from D1)
Specify second point:	*Type:* **@24<−90** ↵
Specify third point:	*Type:* **@−36,24** ↵
Specify fourth point or <exit>:	*Type:* **@24<−90** ↵
Specify third point:	*Type:* **@24<90** ↵ (to locate D6)
Specify fourth point or <exit>:	*Type:* **@24<−90** ↵ (to locate D7)
Specify third point:	*Type:* **@−36,18** ↵ (to locate D8)
Specify fourth point or <exit>:	*Type:* **@12<−90** ↵ (to locate D9)
Specify third point:	↵

Step 5. Draw the engine compartment (Figure 19–5). Set Layer R current and reset elevation and thickness (Figure 19–6).

Prompt	Response
Command:	**Set Elevation: to 17; Thickness: to 10**
Command:	*Click:* **2D Solid** (*Type:* **SO** ↵)
Specify first point:	**D10** (Figure 19–5) (4 snaps down and 4 snaps to the left of D1)

FIGURE 19–6
Elevation and Thickness Dimensions

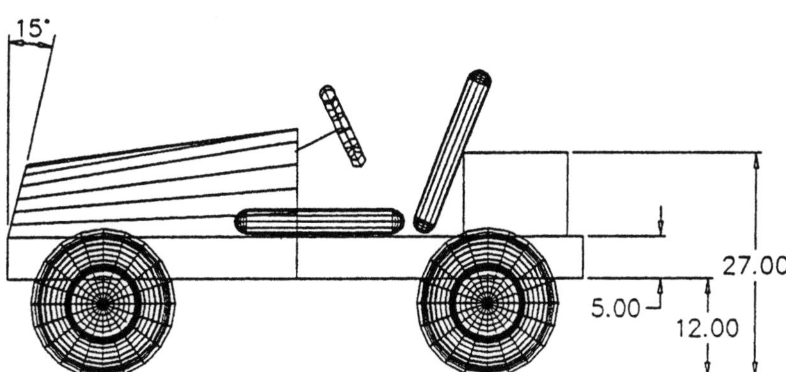

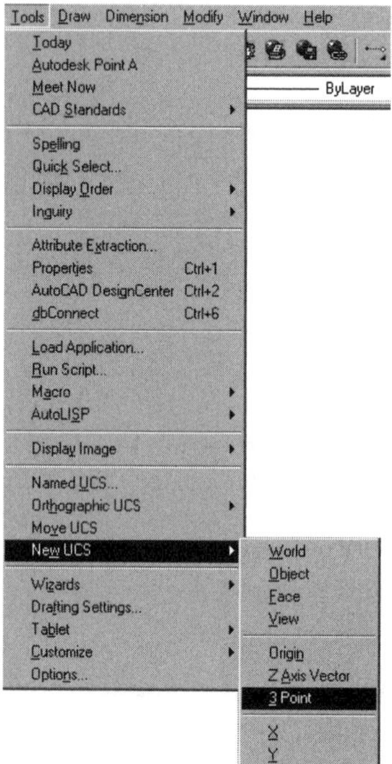

Prompt	Response
Specify second point:	*Type:* **@13,0↵**
Specify third point:	*Type:* **@−13,−20** ↵
Specify fourth point or <exit>:	*Type:* **@13,0↵**
Specify third point:	↵

Step 6. Draw the back end of the hood (Figure 19–7). You may draw this in the current UCS. Then use Move and Rotate 3D to move it into its correct location. Another way is to position the UCS at the left corner of the hood end and draw the hood in its correct location. Let's use the second way so you know how to do that. Begin by selecting a viewpoint similar to Figure 19–8.

Prompt	Response
Command:	*Click:* **New UCS-3Point** (or *Type:* **UCS↵** then, *Type:* **3↵**)
Specify new origin point <0,0,0>:	*Click:* **Osnap-Intersection**
of	**D1** (Figure 19–8)
Specify point on positive portion of X-axis <current>:	*Click:* **Osnap-Endpoint D3**
Specify point on positive-Y portion of the UCS XY plane <current>:	*Click:* **Osnap-Endpoint D2**
Command:	*Click:* **New UCS-Origin** (or *Type:* **UCS** ↵, then *Type:* **O** ↵
Specify new origin point <0,0,0>:	*Click:* **Osnap-Intersection D2** (Figures 19–8 and 19–9 (to move the origin to the lower left corner of the object to be drawn))

Tip: If your Osnap-Intersection does not work, use Endpoint or Zoom in closer.

Note: Any time you want to look directly down on the construction plane, as you will when you draw any detailed item, select *Plan* (a plan view of the correct UCS). (Or *Type:* PLAN ↵)

Now save this UCS to be used again later.

Prompt	Response
Command:	*Type:* **UCS** ↵
Enter an option [New/Move/orthoGraphic/ Previous/Restore/Save/Del/Apply/?/ World]<World>:	*Type:* **S↵**
Enter name to save current USC or [?]:	*Type:* **HOOD** ↵
Command:	

Note: The line from the endpoint of one fillet to the other gives you a line to hang the steering column on.

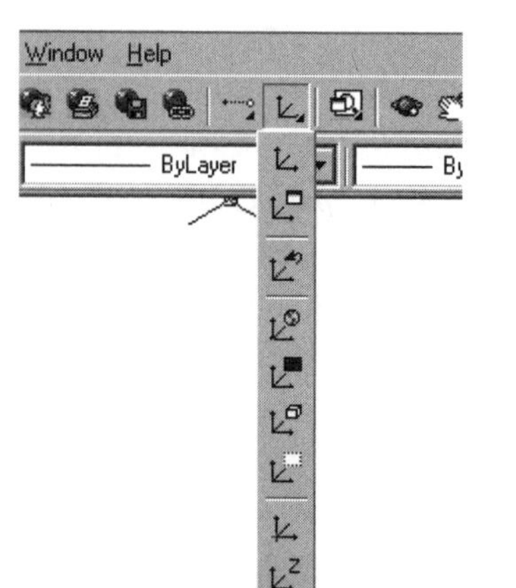

R4.00
20.00
13.00
24.00

FIGURE 19–7
Back End of Hood Dimensions

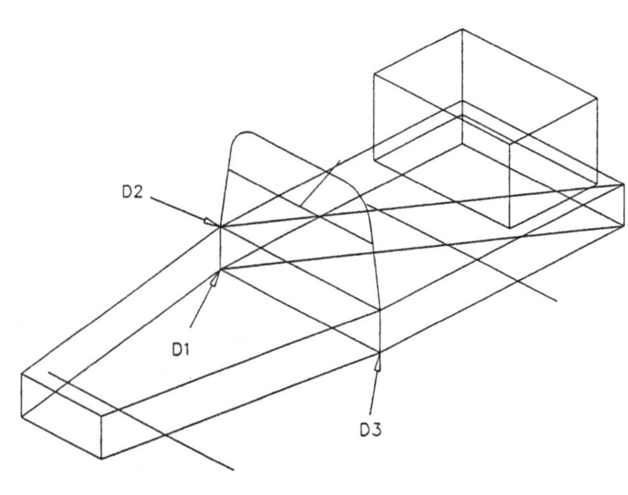

FIGURE 19–8
Setting UCS for Drawing

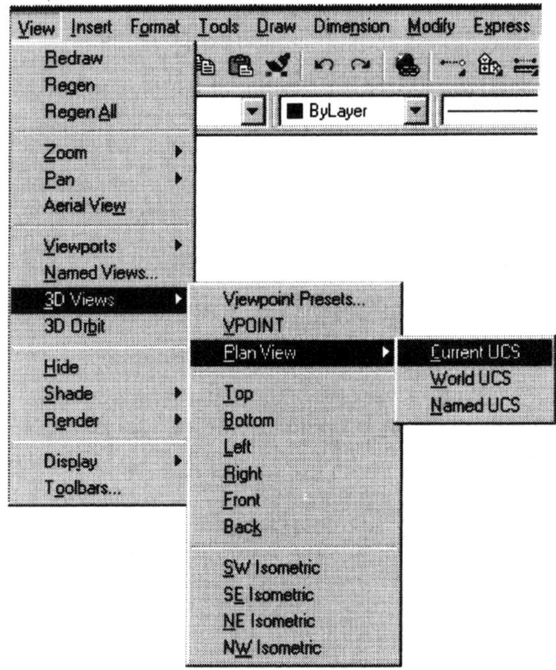

On your own:

Draw the back end of the hood using the dimensions shown in Figure 19–7. Be sure to include the line from the endpoint of one fillet to the other. (**Reset elevation and thickness to 0** before you start. Your first point is 0,0; second point is @2,13; third point is @20,0; fourth point is @2,−13. Use the fillet command for the 4″ radius.)

Prompt	**Response**
Command:	*Click:* **Edit Polyline** (or *Type:* **PE** ↵) (You must join all lines of Figure 19–7 into a single Polyline.)

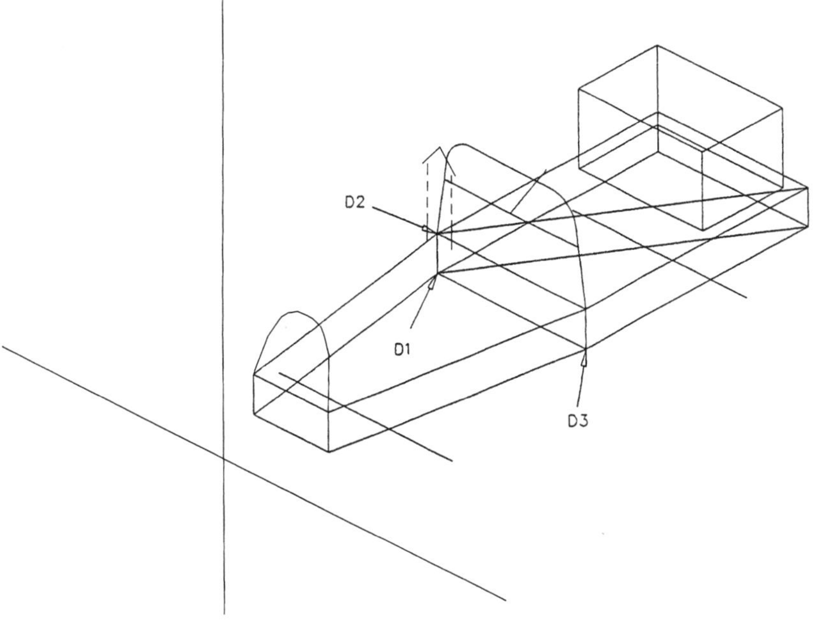

FIGURE 19–9
UCS Orientation

Select polyline:	*Click:* **on one of the lines you just drew**
Prompt	**Response**
Object selected is NOT a polyline.	
Do you want to turn it into one?<Y>:	↵
Enter an option [Close/Join/Width/ Edit vertex/Fit/Spline/Decurve/ Ltype gen/Undo]:	*Type:* **J** ↵
Select objects:	*Click:* **on all lines (except the line at the bottom of the fillets) of the back end of the hood (Window or Crossing, etc.)**
Enter an option [Close/Join . . . Undo]:	↵
Command:	*Click:* **Viewports-2 Viewports**
Enter a configuration option [Horizontal/Vertical]<Vertical>:	↵

Now use two viewports to execute one command. You will start a command in one viewport and complete it in another. Before doing that, however, the right viewport must be oriented so that the object can be viewed from another angle (Figure 19–10).

To do that:

1. Set the viewpoint in the left viewport to −1,−1,1.
2. *Click:* the right viewport to make it active.
3. *Click:* **New UCS-World**
4. *Click:* **New UCS-X-Rotate 90**
5. *Type:* **PLAN** ↵ then ↵ again to obtain a plan view of the current UCS.
6. Save this UCS as SIDE. (*Type:* **UCS** ↵, then **S** ↵, then **SIDE** ↵.)
7. *Click:* **the left viewport to make it active**
8. *Click:* **Named UCS...** (from the Tools menu)
9. *Click:* **SIDE**
10. *Click:* **Set current**
11. *Click:* **OK**

Step 7. Draw the center line of the steering column.

Click the left viewport to make it active. (Zoom in on both viewports if you need to.)

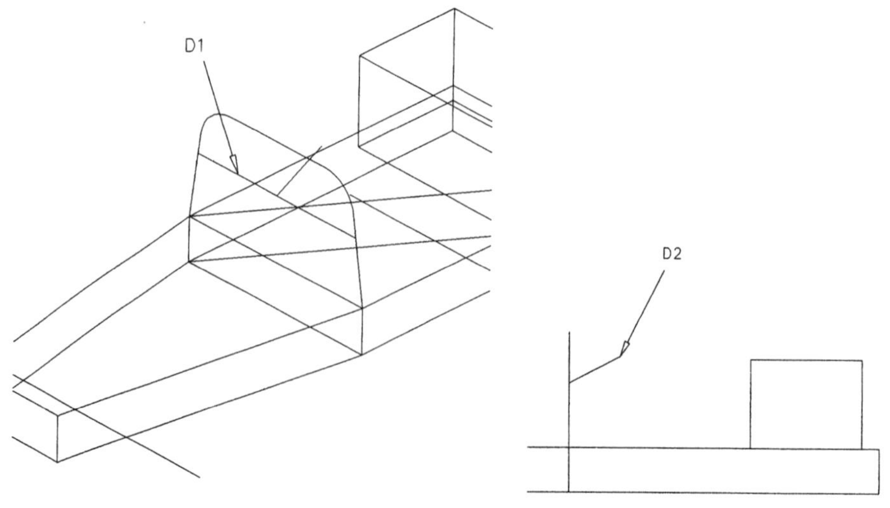

FIGURE 19–10
Two Viewports with Different Views

Prompt	Response
Command:	*Click:* **Line** (or *Type:* **L** ↵)

Prompt	Response
Select first point:	*Click:* **Osnap-Midpoint** **D1** (Figure 19–10)
Select next point or [Undo]:	*Type:* **.Z** ↵.
of:	*Click:* **Midpoint of the line D1.**
(Need XY):	*Click:* **the right viewport to make it active**; then *Click:* **D2** (Figure 19–10)
Specify next point or [Undo]:	↵

Step 8. Draw the steering wheel (Figure 19–11). In the right viewport, draw a 1½″ circle above the centerline of the steering wheel in the approximate location shown and use Revolved Surface to create the steering wheel (Figure 19–12). (Use the Z filter to locate the center of the circle.)

Step 9. Draw the front end of the hood (Figure 19–13) in the left viewport. Position the UCS where the grill is to be drawn.

Prompt	Response
Command:	*Click:* **the left viewport to make it active**
Command:	*Type:* **UCS** ↵, then *Type:* **R**
Enter name of UCS to restore or [?]:	*Type:* **HOOD** ↵
Command:	↵ **(Repeat UCS.)**
Enter an option [New/Move/orthoGraphic/…/World] <World>:	*Type:* **O**↵
Specify new origin point <0,0,0>:	*Click:* **Osnap-Intersection** (*Click:* **the upper left corner of the front of the car** (Figure 19–13).)
Command:	↵ **(Repeat UCS.)**
Enter an option [New/Move/orthoGraphic/…/World] <World>:	*Type:* **X** ↵ (to rotate UCS around the X axis)
Specify rotate angle about x axis <90>	Type: **–15** ↵ (to create the UCS (Figure 19–13))

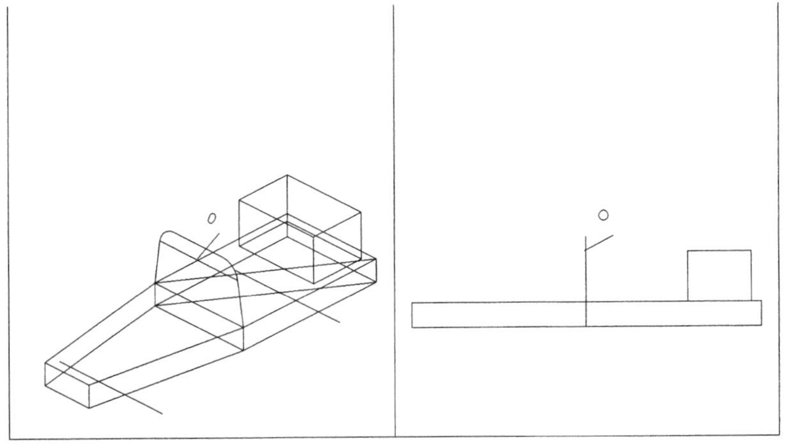

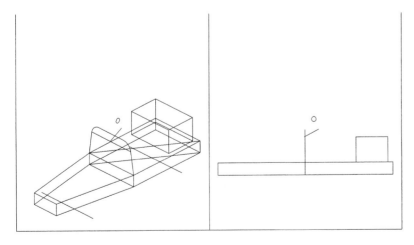

FIGURE 19–11
Drawing the Steering Wheel

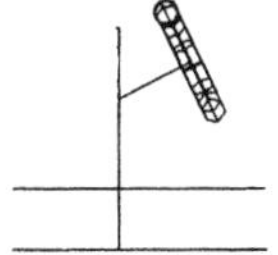

FIGURE 19–12
Drawing the Steering Wheel

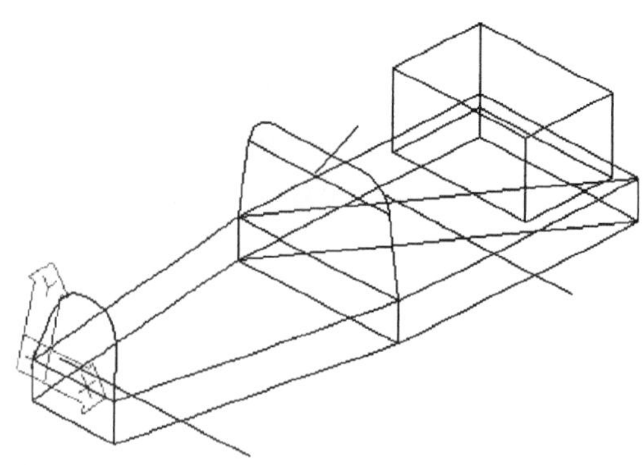

FIGURE 19–13
Positioning the UCS

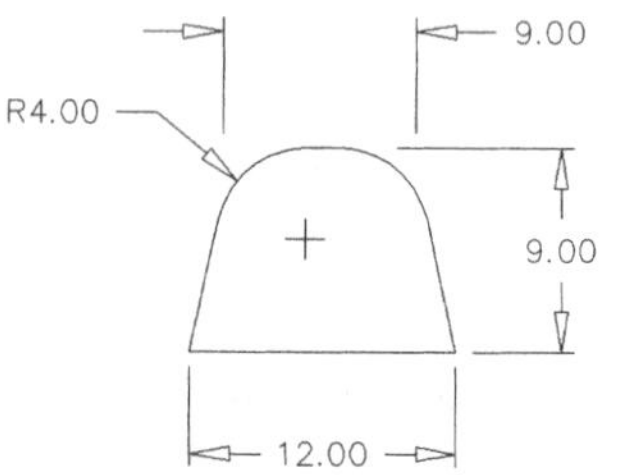

FIGURE 19–14
Front End of Hood Dimension

On your own:

Draw the front end of the hood using the dimensions shown in Figure 19–14. Use four lines and then a 4″ fillet. Use Pedit (Edit Polyline) to make a single polyline out of the front end. Do not include the bottom horizontal line in the polyline, but do draw it so you can use it later. (Your first point is 0,0—see step 6 **On your own** if you need help.)

Step 10. Draw the grille using Bhatch.
Set Elevation and Thickness to 0.

Set layer B current. Use the User-defined pattern with a 1.00 spacing, 0 angle, and double hatch area. You may need to select objects to get the double hatch.

Step 11. Create a Rulesurf to form the hood (Figure 19–15).

1. Turn layer B OFF until the hood is formed so you will not have problems selecting the front PLINE.
2. Set Layer G current.
3. Select a Viewpoint similar to Figure 19–15, the left viewport.
4. Select Ruled Surface, then click on the front and back ends of the hood to form the surface.
5. Turn layer B ON after this surface is formed.

Note: Be sure the FRONT UCS is current when you insert the box. Any other orientation will require a different sequence of dimensions for length, width, and height.

FIGURE 19–15
Form Hood with Ruled Surface

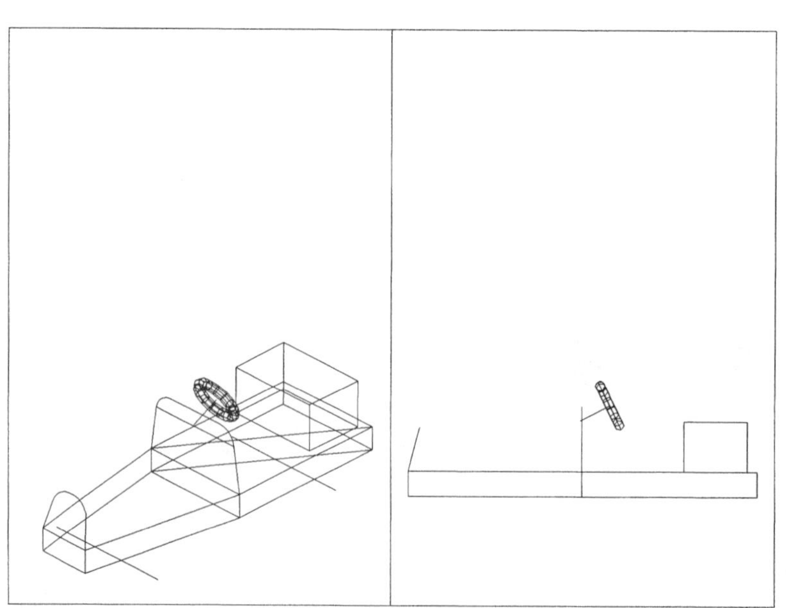

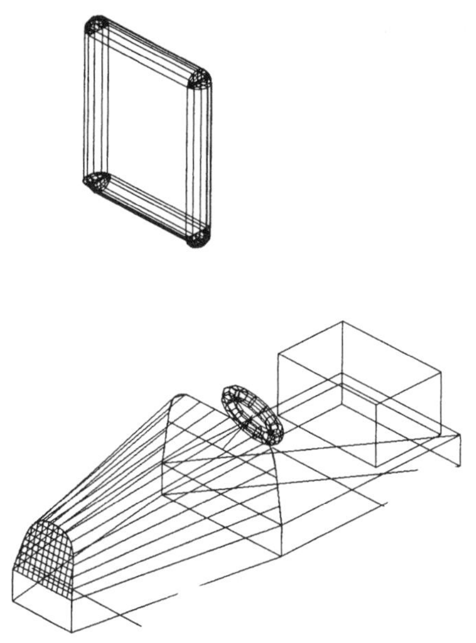

FIGURE 19–16
Create Pads for Seat and Back Cushions

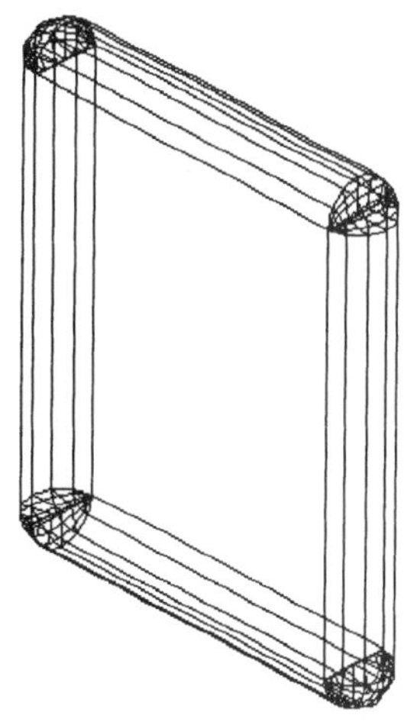

FIGURE 19–17
HOOD UCS

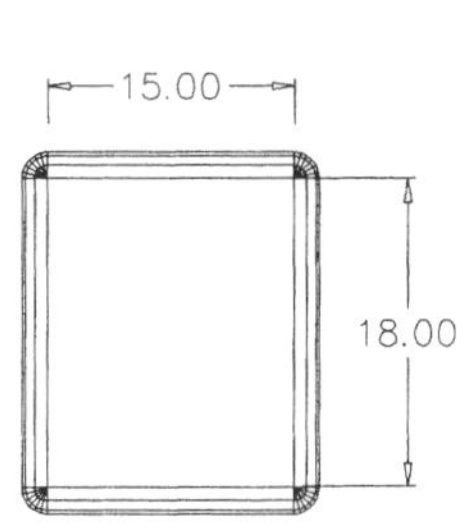

FIGURE 19–18
Dimensions for Pads

Step 12. Create pads to form seat and back cushions (Figure 19–16).

1. Restore the HOOD UCS (Figure 19–17). (*Click:* **Named UCS...** then *Click:* **HOOD**; then *Click:* **Set Current**; *Click:* **OK**.)
2. Use dimensions from Figure 19–18 to create a 3-D object, BOX. (The cushion thickness is 4″.)

Prompt	Response
Command:	*Click:* **Box3d** (from the 3D Surfaces menu)
Specify corner point of Box:	*Click:* **on a point above the model in the approximate location of Figure 19–16.)**

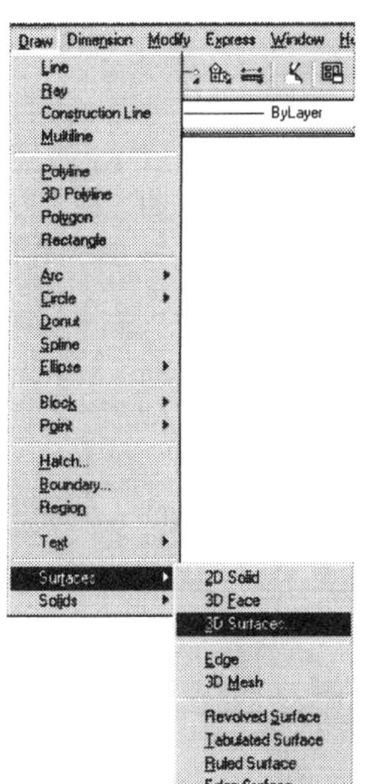

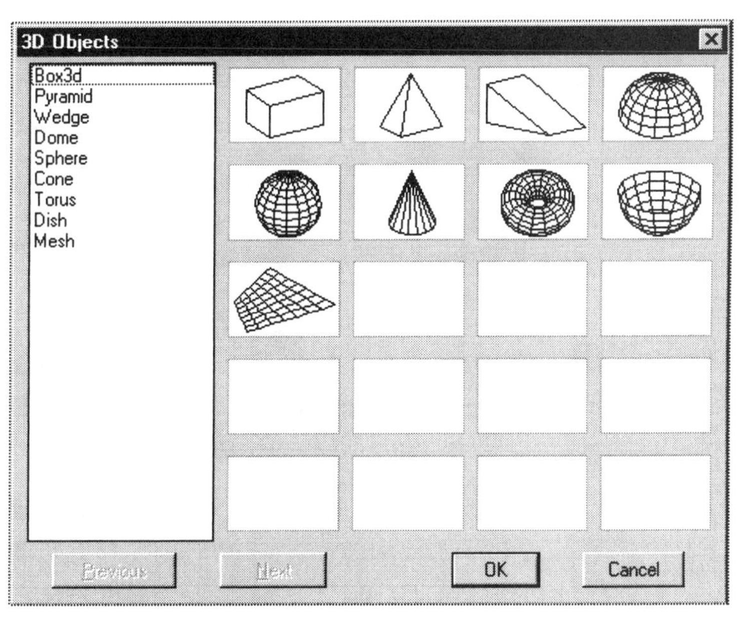

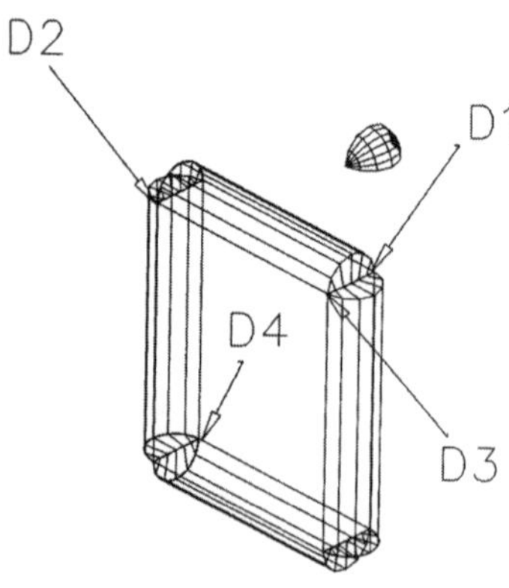

FIGURE 19–19
Insert Rounds and End Caps

Prompt	**Response**
Specify length of box:	*Type:* **18** ↵
Specify width of box or [Cube]:	*Type:* **15** ↵
Specify height of box:	*Type:* **4** ↵
Specify rotation angle about the Z axis or [Reference]:	*Type:* **0** ↵

Now, insert the rounds that you drew and saved on a floppy disk to form the edges of the pads.

Prompt	**Response**
Command:	*Click:* **New UCS-Y**
Specify rotation angle about Y axis<90>:	↵
Command:	*Click:* **Insert** (or *Type:* **I** ↵)
The Insert dialog box appears:	*Click:* **Browse and locate HR (your initials)(on your disk);** *Click:* **OK**
Specify insertion Point or [Scale/X/Y/Z/Rotate/PScale/PX/PY/PZ/PRotate]:	*Type:* **X** ↵
Specify X scale factor:	*Type:* **4** ↵
Specify insertion point:	*Type:* **Y** ↵
Specify Y scale factor:	*Type:* **4** ↵
Specify insertion point:	*Type:* **Z** ↵
Specify Z scale factor:	*Type:* **18** ↵
Specify insertion point:	*Type:* **R** ↵
Specify rotation angle:	*Type:* **180** ↵
Specify insertion point:	**D2** (Figure 19–19; use Osnap-Intersection)
Command:	↵ (If the round is not in the correct position, use Rotate 3D and Move to position it correctly.)
The Insert dialog box appears with HR-your initials in the Name: box:	*Click:* **OK**
Specify insertion point or [Scale/X/Y/Z/...PRotate]:	*Type:* **X** ↵
Specify X scale factor:	*Type:* **4** ↵
Specify insertion point :	*Type:* **Y** ↵
Specify Y scale factor:	*Type:* **4** ↵
Specify insertion point:	*Type:* **Z** ↵
Specify Z scale factor:	*Type:* **18** ↵
Specify insertion point:	*Click:* **Osnap-Endpoint D4**
Command:	*Click:* **New UCS-X**
Specify rotation angle about X axis<90>:	↵
Command:	*Click:* **Insert** (or *Type:* **I** ↵)
The Insert dialog box appears with HR-your initials in the Name: box:	*Click:* **OK**
Specify insertion point or [Scale/X/Y/Z/...PRotate]:	*Type:* **X** ↵
Specify X scale factor:	*Type:* **4** ↵
Specify insertion point:	*Type:* **Y** ↵

Note: Rotating the UCS is necessary so that the rounds are inserted in the correct orientation.

Prompt	Response
Specify Y scale factor:	*Type:* **4** ↵
Specify insertion point:	*Type:* **Z** ↵
Specify Z scale factor:	*Type:* **15** ↵
Specify insertion point:	*Type:* **R** ↵
Specify rotation angle:	*Type:* **180** ↵
Specify insertion point:	*Click:* **Osnap-Intersection D3** (Figure 19–19) (Repeat INSERT)
Command:	↵
The Insert dialog box appears:	*Click:* **OK**
Specify insertion point or [Scale/X/Y/Z/...PRotate]:	*Type:* **X** ↵
Specify X scale factor:	*Type:* **4** ↵
Specify insertion point:	*Type:* **Y** ↵
Specify Y scale factor:	*Type:* **4** ↵
Specify insertion point:	*Type:* **Z** ↵
Specify Z scale factor:	*Type:* **15** ↵
Specify insertion point:	*Click:* **Osnap-Intersection D4**

Now, **move this half-round to its correct location** by specifying the second point of displacement as **@0,0,−15**. Insert the end caps to complete the pads (Figure 19–19).

1. Return the UCS to World and Insert an end cap at a scale of 4 for X, Y, and Z axes above the cushion, as shown in Figure 19–19. If it is not in the correct orientation, experiment with the Insert rotation angle and the UCS rotation angle until the correct orientation is obtained, or use Rotate 3D to rotate the end cap to the correct position.
2. Move the first end cap to the location identified as D3. Use Osnap-Intersection for the base point and second point of displacement.
3. Copy end caps at the other corners using Osnap-Intersection and use Rotate 3D to rotate end caps to the correct positions.

Step 13. Restore the SIDE UCS in the right viewport, draw 2″-diameter circles around the axles, and use Tabulated Surface to create axle thickness (Figure 19–20).

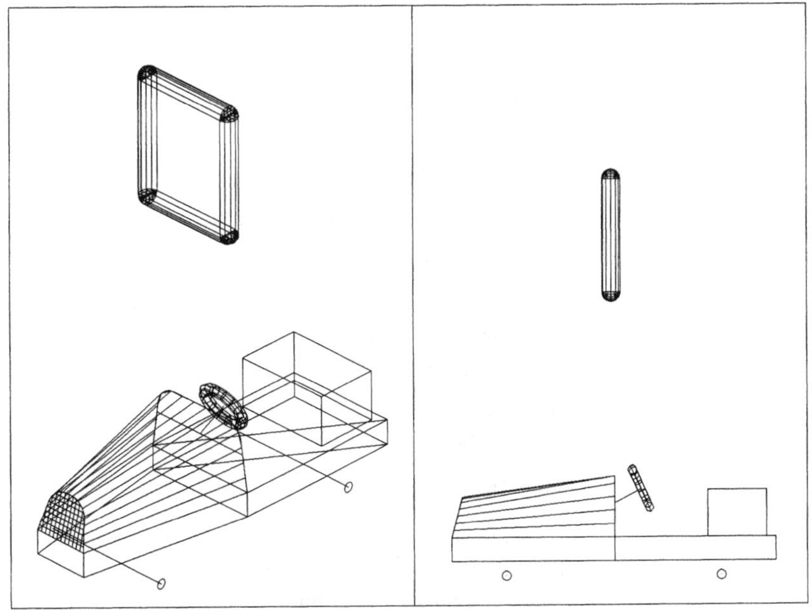

FIGURE 19–20
Viewports for Moving Cushions

FIGURE 19–21
Locate UCS

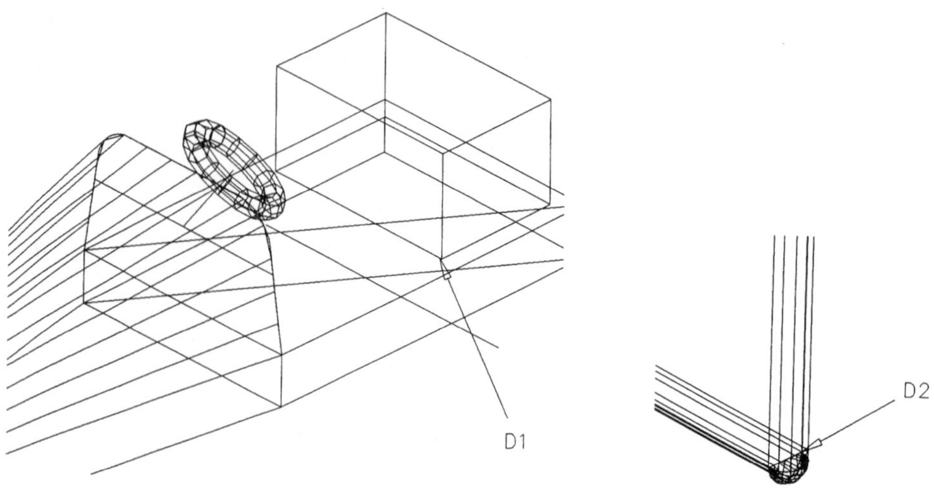

Step 14. Copy the cushion into its correct location, rotate the seat cushion, and move it to its correct location.

1. Click the right viewport to make it active and restore the SIDE UCS, then *Type:* **PLAN** ↵ to obtain the views shown in Figure 19–20. Click the left viewport and restore the SIDE UCS in this viewport also.
2. Click the left viewport, then move the origin of the UCS to the lower right corner of the engine compartment (Figure 19–21), D1.
3. Copy the complete cushion.

Prompt	Response
Command:	*Click:* **Copy** (or *Type:* **CP** ↵)
Select objects:	*Click:* **on the entire cushion**
Specify base point or displacement or [Multiple]:	*Click:* **Osnap-Endpoint D2** (Figure 19–21)
Specify second point of displacement or <use first point as displacement>:	*Type:* **0,2,−3** ↵

The cushion should appear as shown in Figure 19–22.

1. Rotate the back cushion −15° using Rotate. The point of rotation is the top left corner of the engine compartment (Figure 19–23).
2. Rotate the cushion that is in space 90° (Figure 19–23).
3. Move the cushion using Osnap-Endpoint and click on the lower right back corner of the cushion in the left viewport as the base point. Use −8,0,−1 as the second point of displacement (Figure 19–24).

Tip: Move the cushions as needed to obtain a view similar to Figure 19–24 if you have used a different construction method.

Step 15. Insert wheels onto axles (Figures 19–25 and 19–26).

1. Set UCS to World in both viewports.
2. Click the left viewport and, using Osnap-Endpoint, Insert the block you created in Chapter 18 named WHEEL onto the ends of the axles on the side presently visible (Figure 19–25). (You may need to rotate the tire 90° as you insert.)
3. Reset the VPOINT to the back side of the go-cart and Insert the Wblock WHEELS onto the axles on that side (Figure 19–26).

Note: The Dview viewpoint is always specified relative to viewpoint of the current UCS. If you are surprised at the views you get or have difficulty in controlling Dview, return to the World UCS and select the plan view before you rotate.

Step 16. Give the steering column thickness.

Select a UCS perpendicular to the steering column by using UCS-Object, then click on the steering column and rotate the UCS if necessary. Draw a 1″-diameter circle and use Tabulated Surface to complete the drawing.

FIGURE 19–22
Cushion in Position

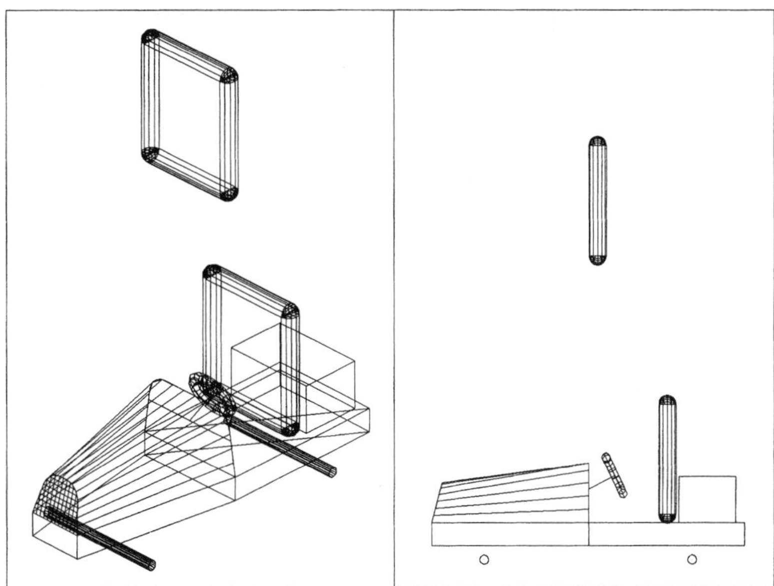

FIGURE 19–23
Rotate Cushions

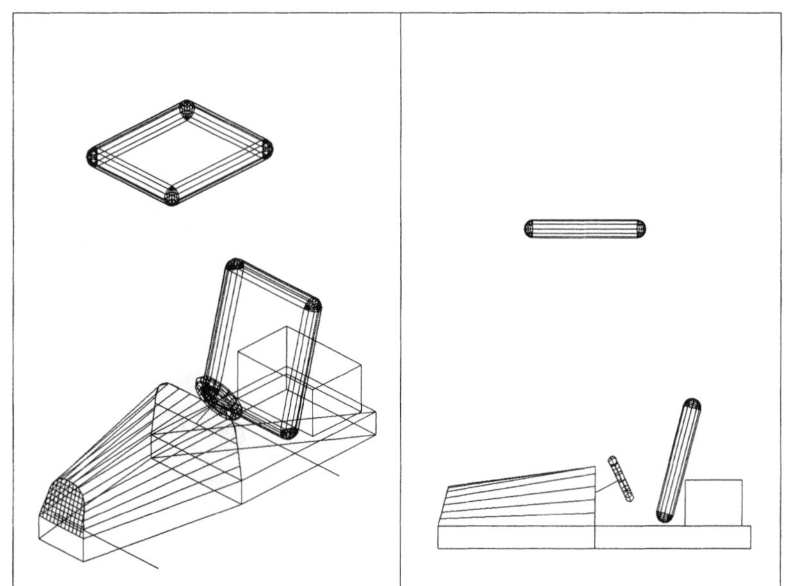

Step 17. Use 3D Dynamic View (Dview) (*Type:* DV ↵) to obtain a perspective view of the model.

You have used Dview very little to this point; therefore, a brief discussion of Dview will help. The Dview command allows you to view either parallel projections such as the views you have been seeing with Viewpoint or perspective projection, which gives you a very realistic view of a model. You may use angles typed from the keyboard or a scroll bar in two directions. The resulting view is similar to a camera rotating first in a vertical plane and second in a horizontal plane around the object as a whole or around a specified target point.

The Distance option of the Dview command places you in the perspective mode and allows you to specify a distance from the model. Dview options are as follows:

CA (Camera) Rotates the camera around the view or the target point.

TA (Target) Allows you to specify where on the model your line of sight is pointed toward.

FIGURE 19–24
Cushions in Place

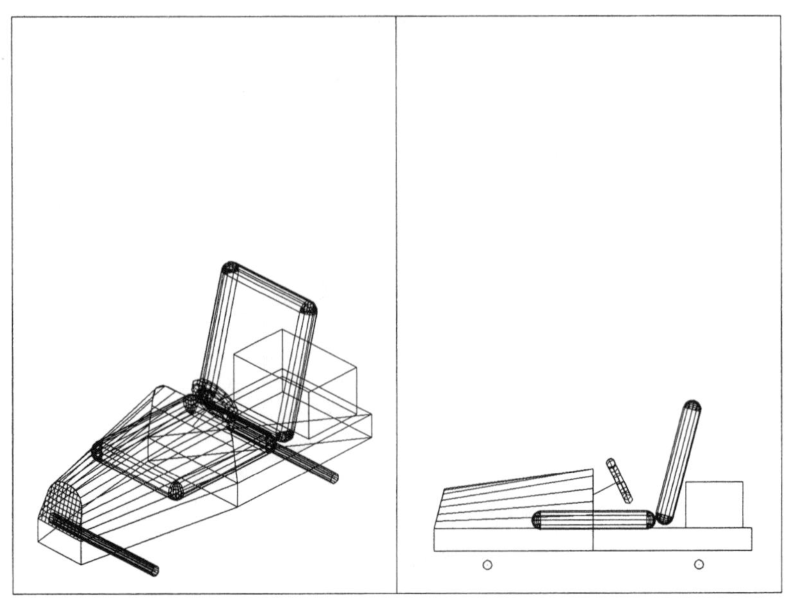

FIGURE 19–25
Insert Wheels

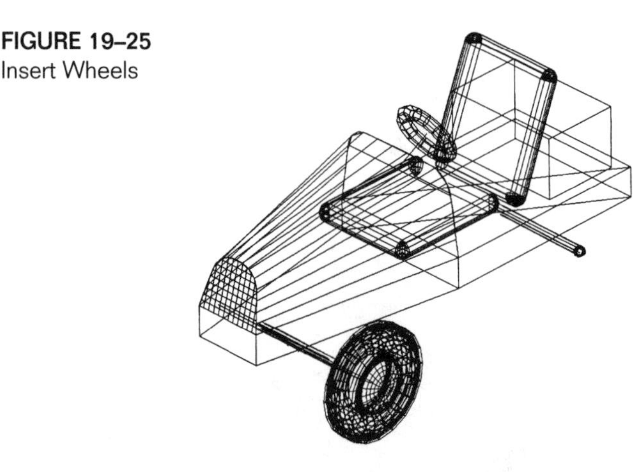

FIGURE 19–26
Insert Wheels

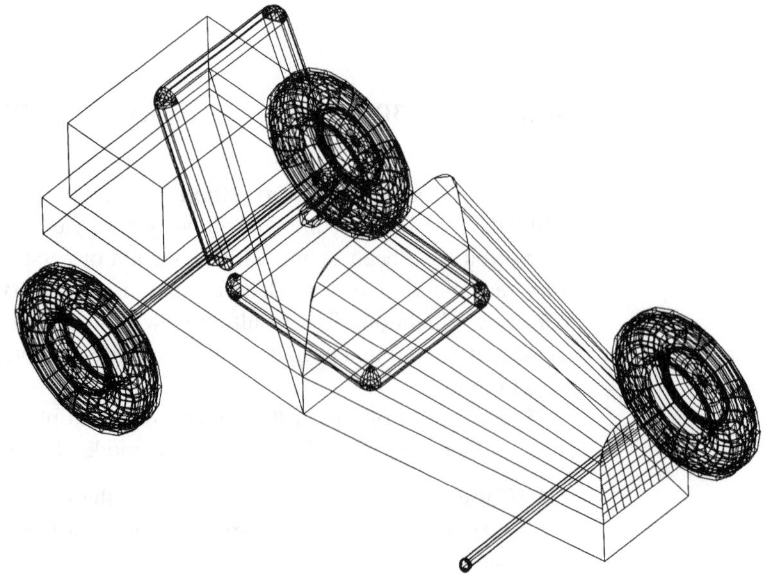

D (Distance) Turns perspective mode on and moves the camera into or away from the view or target point. The UCSICON changes to a perspective box when the display is in perspective mode.

PO (Points) Allows you to locate camera and target points using X, Y, and Z coordinates. This option is useful for identifying different camera locations inside a room, for example.

PA (Pan) Allows you to shift the view just as Pan under the display menu does.

Z (ZOOM) If perspective mode is on, this option allows you to change the camera's lens length. The default lens length is 50 mm. Decreasing the lens length widens the view and vice versa. If perspective mode is not on, this option acts as Zoom-Center and allows you to select a magnification factor.

TW (Twist) Allows you to tilt the view.

CL (Clip) The front and back clipping planes allow you to position these planes so that they obscure what is in front or behind them.

H (Hide) Removes hidden lines as any Hide command does.

O (Off) Turns perspective mode off.

U (Undo) Undoes the last Dview operation.

X (Exit) Ends the Dview command but leaves you with the view you have selected.

Now, use Dview to get the perspective view shown in Figure 19–1.

Prompt	Response
Command:	*Type:* **DV** ↵)
Select objects or <use DVIEWBLOCK>:	*Type:* **ALL** ↵ ↵
Enter option [CAmera/TArget/Distance/ POints/PAn/Zoom/TWist/CLip/Hide/ Off/Undo]:	*Type:* **CA** ↵
Specify camera location, or enter angle from XY plane or [Toggle (angle in)] <30.0000>:	**Move the cursor so that the view appears as shown and press ↵.**
Specify camera location or enter angle in XY plane from X axis or [Toggle (angle from)] <30.0000>:	**Move the cursor so that the coordinate angle reads 120° and click on that point** or *Type:* **120** ↵.

You should have a parallel projection in the orientation of Figure 19–1.

Prompt	Response
Enter option [CAmera/TArget/Distance/ POints/PAn/Zoom/TWist/CLip/Hide/ Off/Undo]:	*Type:* **D** ↵
Specify new camera–target distance <1.0000>:	*Type:* **150** ↵

This is still too close, so type D ↵ again and type a greater distance (200).

Prompt	Response
Enter option [CAmera/Target/. . . /Undo]:	*Type:* **H** ↵
Enter option [CAmera/Target/. . . /Undo]:	*Type:* **X** ↵

Step 18. Set Vports to single. *Click:* **Layout1, then** *Click:* **OK. Insert a horizontal format around your drawing at an appropriate scale. Answer the prompts with:**

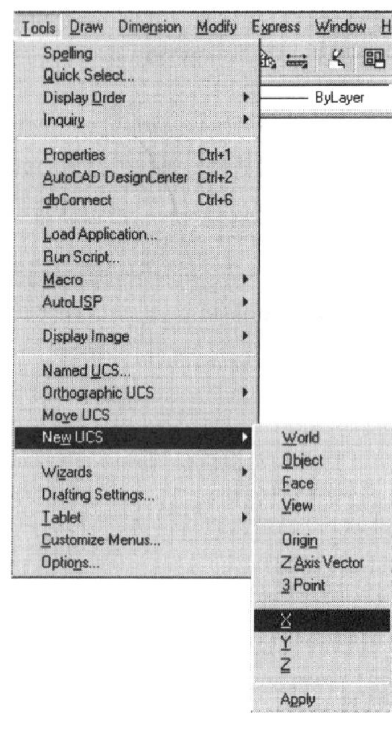

Assignment: 19–1
Drawing Title: GO-CART
Date: Current date

Step 19. Print the drawing on an 11″ × 8.5″ sheet.

Step 20. Save the drawing in two places as EX19-1(your initials).

3D Orbit

3D Orbit allows you to obtain a 3-D view in the active viewport. The 3D Orbit shows an arcball. An *arcball* is a large circle with a small circle at each of its four quadrants. When you start 3D Orbit, the target of the view remains stationary while the camera, or your point of view, orbits around the target. The center of the arcball (not the center of the model) is the target point. When you move your mouse over different parts of the arcball, the direction in which the view rotates changes.

When 3D Orbit is active, you can right click in the drawing area to activate the shortcut menu shown in the margin. This menu allows you to render the object and select parallel or perspective views while the object is being orbited. You can also access these options from the 3D Orbit toolbar.

Let's spend a few minutes with 3D Orbit and take a good look at this new AutoCAD 3-D tool.

Step 21. Use 3D Orbit to render and animate the model you have just completed.

Prompt	Response
Command:	*Click:* **the Model tab next to Layout1**
	Activate the 3D Orbit toolbar.
	3D Orbit (or *Type:* **3DO↵**)
The arcball with smaller circles at its quadrants appears:	*Click:* **One of the circles, hold down the click button, and slowly move the mouse so you get a feel for how the view changes.** Practice a moment with each of the quadrant circles.
	Click: **the down arrow at the right side of the 3D Orbit toolbar** and *Click:* **SW Isometric**
	Right click: **to obtain the shortcut menu**
	Click: **Projection on the shortcut menu,** then *Click:* **Perspective.**
	Click: **Shading Modes on the shortcut menu,** then *Click:* **Gouraud shading**
	Click: **3D Continuous Orbit on the 3D Orbit toolbar**

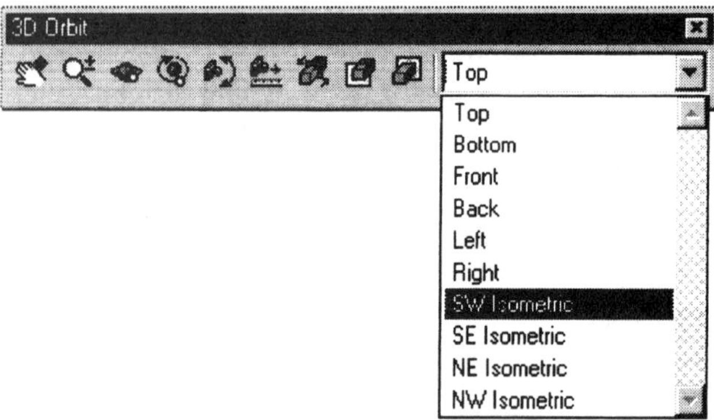

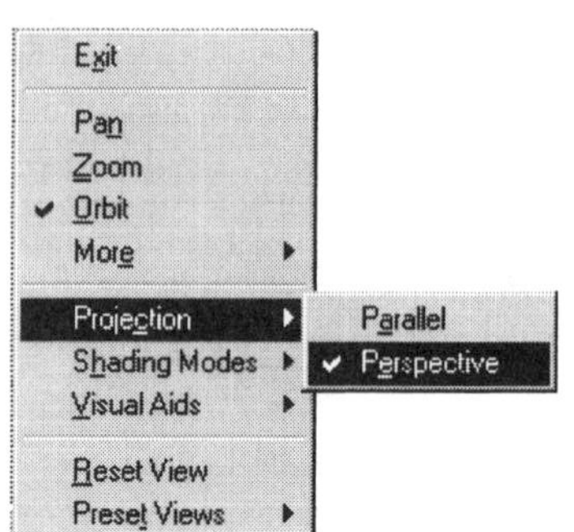

Prompt	Response
	Click: **a point at the upper left edge of the display, hold down the click button, and describe a very small circle so the model rotates continuously.** Experiment with the continuous orbit display until you feel comfortable with it.

You may need to return to 3D Orbit and click SW Isometric occasionally to return the display to a manageable view.

Prompt	Response
	Click: **3D Orbit and rotate the view with perspective projection and Gouraud shading ON to obtain a view similar to Figure 19–27.**

Click the other commands (3D Swivel, 3D Adjust Distance, and 3D Adjust Clip Planes) on the 3D Orbit toolbar to see how they operate.

Refer to Chapter 22 for a procedure on how to print a shaded model if your lab instructions indicate a printed copy is needed.

Step 22. Save your drawing in two places as EX19-1A(your initials).

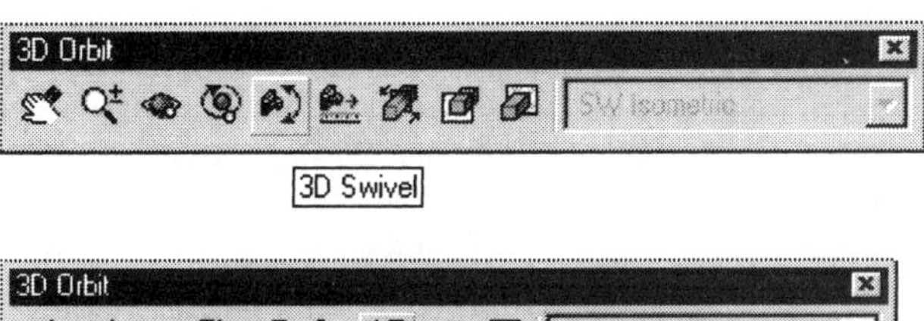

3D Orbit

SW Isometric

3D Adjust Distance

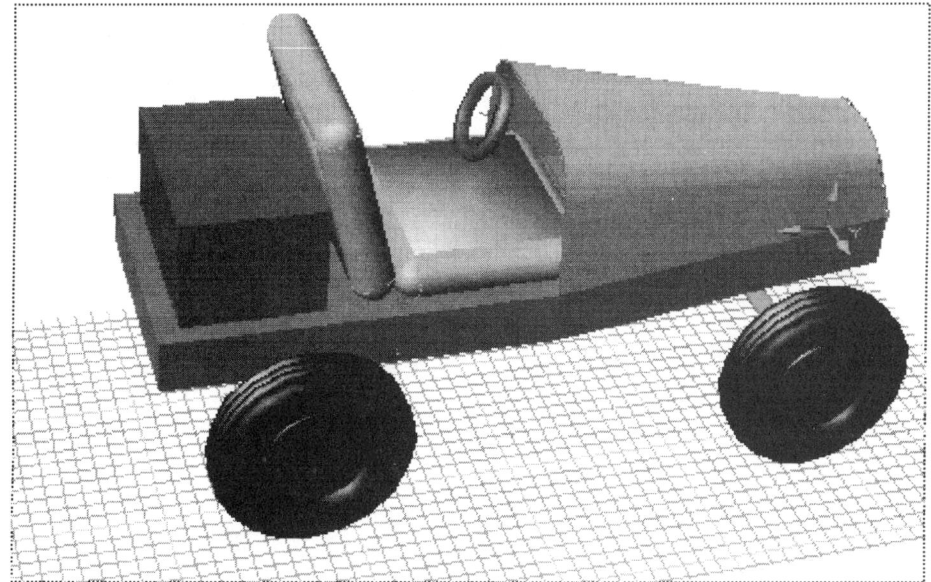

FIGURE 19–27
3D Orbit Shaded Model

EXERCISES

EXERCISE 19–1. Follow the steps outlined in this chapter to complete the model shown as Figure 19–1. Insert your 11″ × 8½″ horizontal format around it in Layout1 and plot the drawing on an 11″ × 8½″ sheet. Answer prompts as described in the chapter.

EXERCISE 19–2. Use the Revsurf command to create 3-D models of the parts shown in Figure 19–28. Notice that these are very small model-airplane engine parts. Scale them to 2 times the dimensions shown (approximate any dimensions not shown) and center all three in one 11″ × 8½″ format in Layout1. Answer prompts with:

Assignment: 19–2
Title: REVSURFs
Date: Current date

EXERCISE 19–3. Use the Rulesurf command to make 3-D models of the sheet metal parts shown in Figure 19–29. Scale all of them to fit on one 11″ × 8½″ format in Layout1. Answer prompts with:

Assignment: 19–3
Title: RULESURFs
Date: Current date

EXERCISE 19–4. Use the Tabsurf command to make 3-D models of the parts shown in Figure 19–30. Scale all to fit on on 11″ × 8½″ format with pleasing page arrangement. Answer prompts with:

Assignment: 19–4
Title: TABSURFs
Date: Current date

EXERCISE 19–5. Draw shapes of four common objects around your house or office using 3-D commands. Suggestions are a bottle, vase, glass, pitcher, or pen.

EXERCISE 19–6. Make a 3-D model of the barge shown in Figure 19–31. Let each mark on the scale equal ¼″. Select two viewports for your final drawing. Create two different perspective views, one in the left viewport and one in the right viewport. Place your name in the lower right corner. Print them both in paper space on the same 11″ × 8½″ sheet.

EXERCISE 19–7. Make a 3-D model of the model airplane shown in Figure 19–32. Use the scale shown in the upper right for your dimensions. Select two viewports for your final drawing. Create two perspective views, one in the left viewport and one in the right viewport. Place your name in the lower right corner. Print them both in Layout1 on the same 11″ × 8½″ sheet.

EXERCISE 19–8. Make a 3-D model of the towboat shown in Figure 19–33. Let each mark on the scale equal ¼″. Select two viewports for your final drawing. Create two perspective views, one in the left viewport and one in the right viewport. Place your name in the lower right corner. Print them both in Layout1 on the same 11″ × 8½″ sheet.

EXERCISE 19–9. Create a 3-D model of the vehicle shown in Figure 19–34. Let each mark on the scale equal ¼″. Select two viewports for your final drawing. Create two perspective views, one in the left viewport and one in the right viewport. Place your name in the lower right corner. Print them both in Layout1 on the same 11″ × 8½″ sheet.

FIGURE 19–28
Sheet 1 of 3
Exercise 19–2

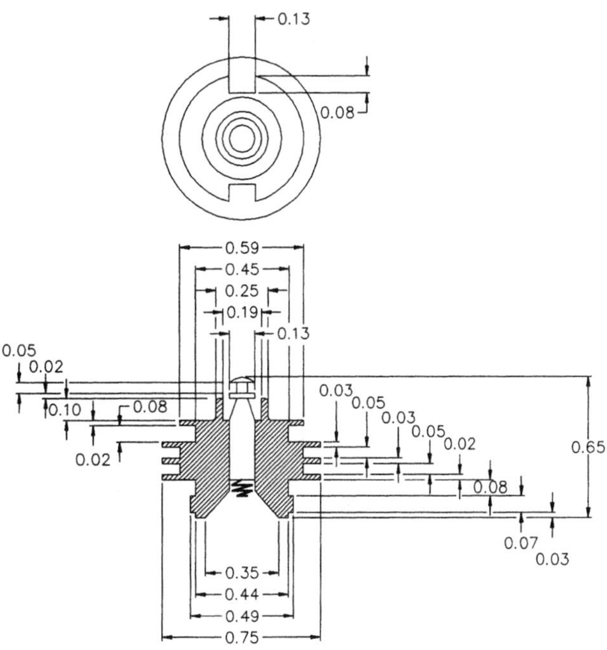

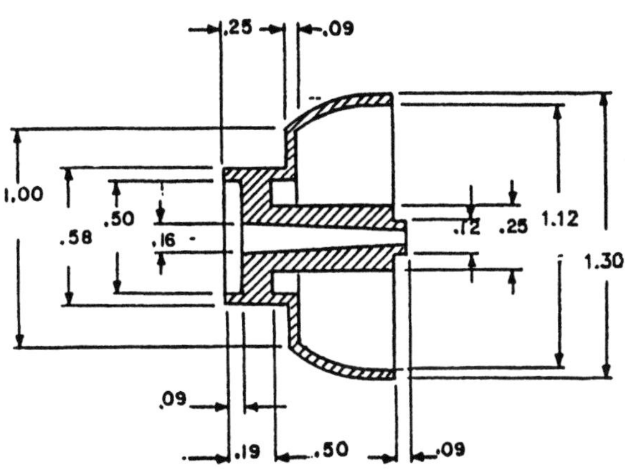

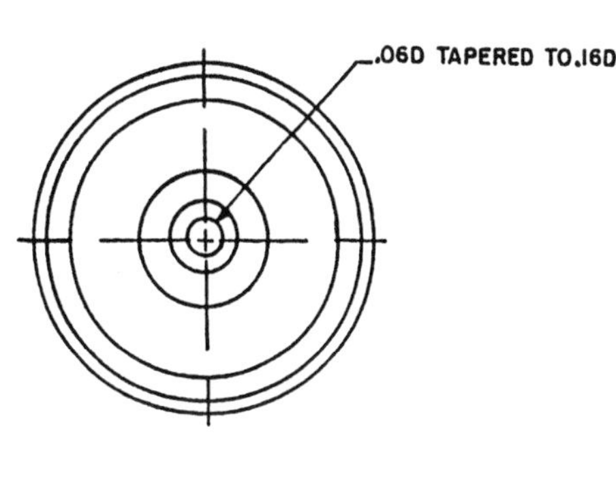

FIGURE 19–28
Sheet 2 of 3
Exercise 19–2

FIGURE 19–28
Sheet 3 of 3
Exercise 19–2

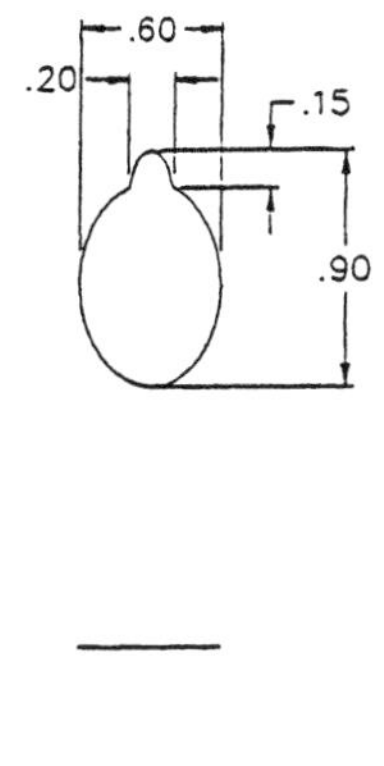

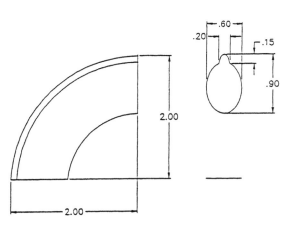

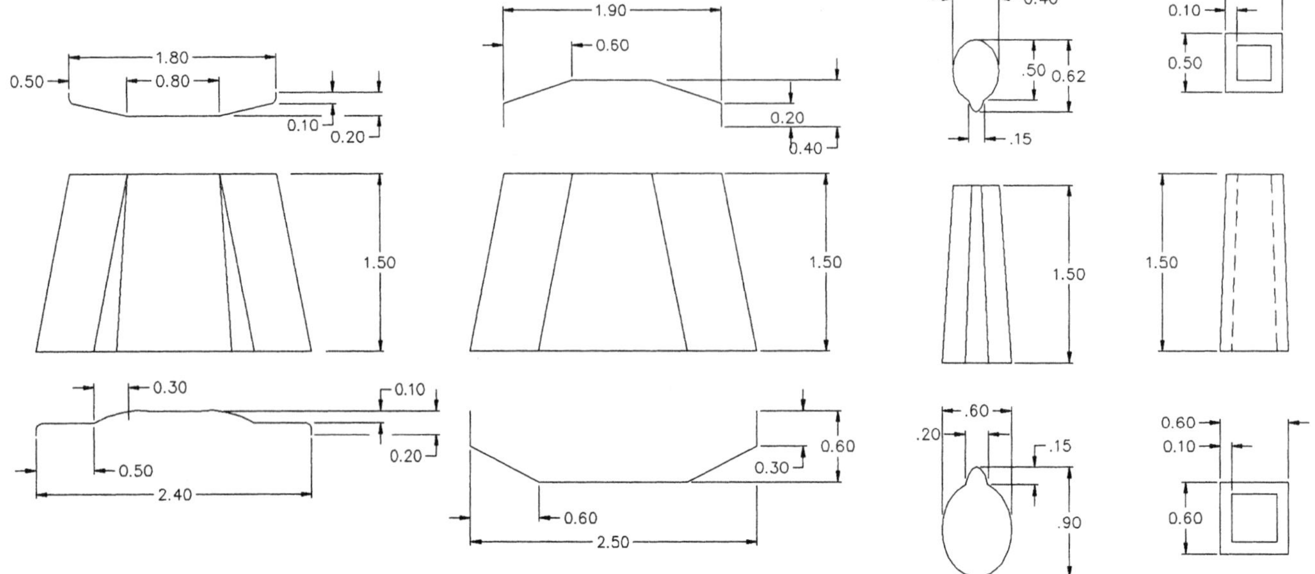

FIGURE 19–29
Exercise 19–3

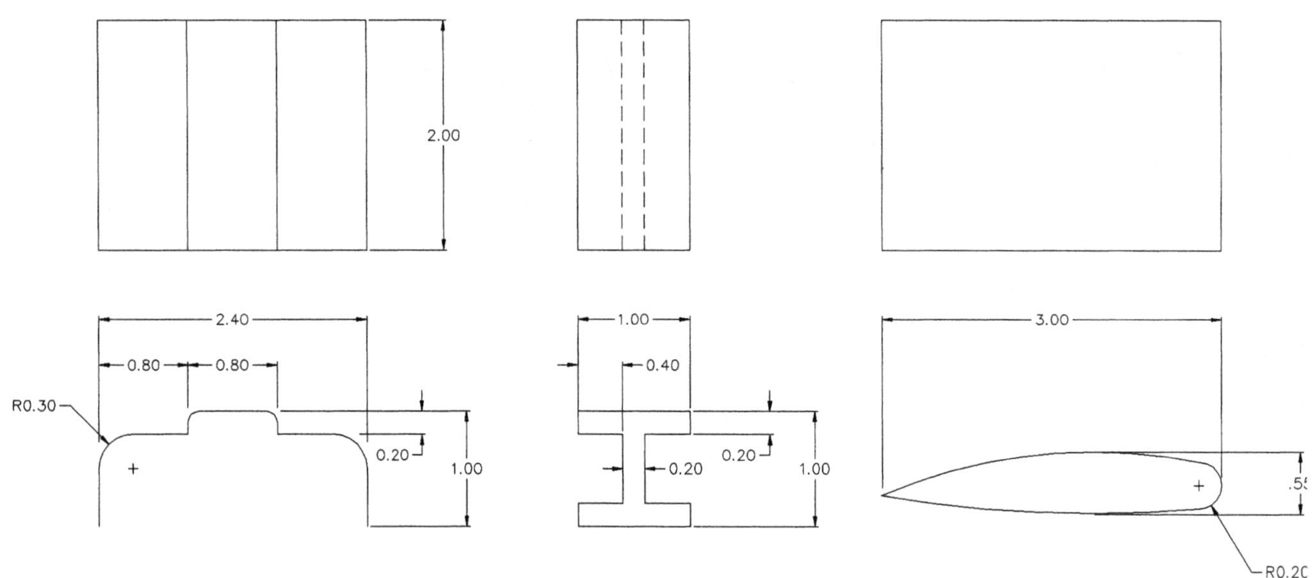

FIGURE 19–30
Exercise 19–4

FIGURE 19–31
Exercise 19–6

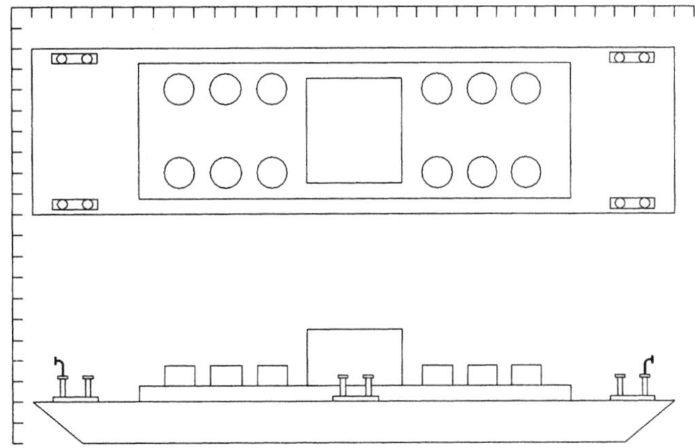

FIGURE 19–32
Exercise 19–7

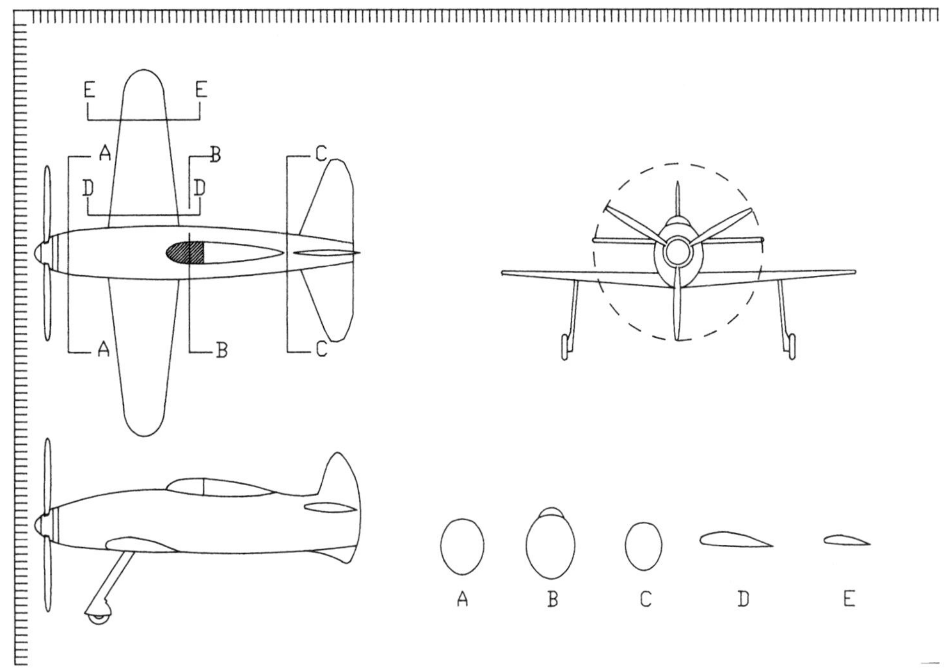

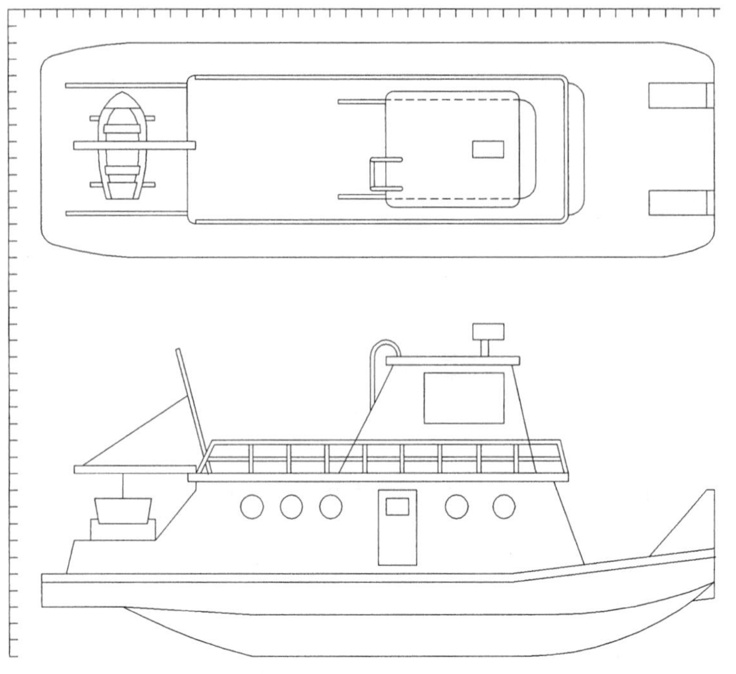

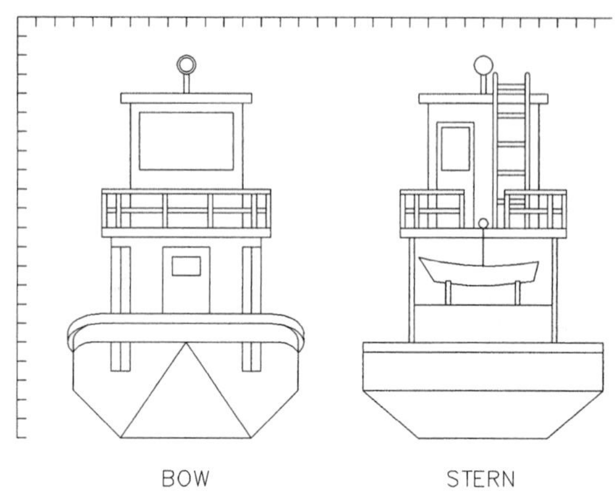

FIGURE 19–33
Exercise 19–8

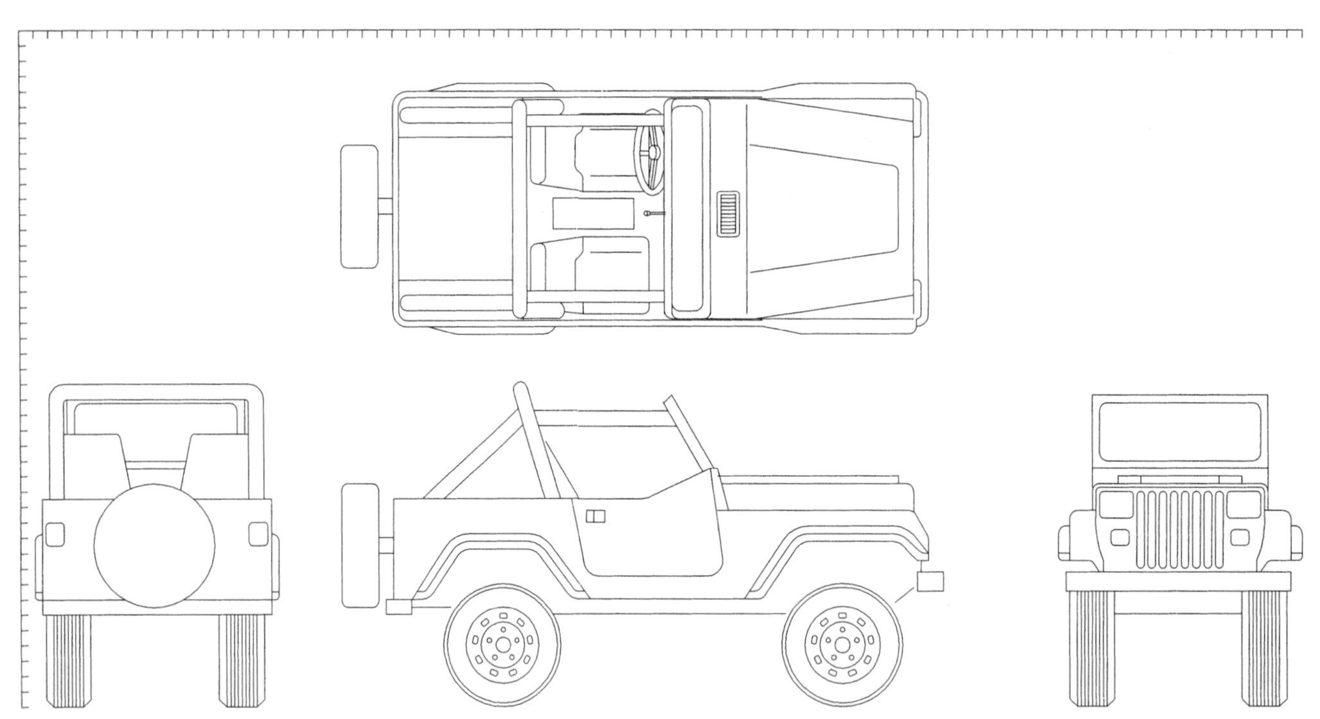

FIGURE 19–34
Exercise 19–9

REVIEW QUESTIONS

Circle the best answer.

1. Which of the following SURFACE commands was used to create the pad for the seat cushions described in this chapter?
   a. Pad
   b. Block
   c. Box
   d. Polygon
   e. Cube
2. Ruled Surface requires which of the following?
   a. Two defining lines or curves
   b. A curve and a direction vector
   c. Four adjoining edges
   d. A curve and an axis of rotation
   e. Coplanar points
3. Tabulated Surface requires which of the following?
   a. Two defining lines or curves
   b. A curve and a direction vector
   c. Four adjoining edges
   d. A curve and an axis of rotation
   e. Coplanar points
4. Revolved Surface requires which of the following?
   a. Two defining lines or curves
   b. A curve and a direction vector
   c. Four adjoining edges
   d. A curve and an axis of rotation
   e. Coplanar points
5. Edge Surface requires which of the following?
   a. Two defining lines or curves
   b. A curve and a direction vector
   c. Four adjoining edges
   d. A curve and an axis of rotation
   e. Coplanar points
6. Which of the following DVIEW options can be used to obtain a perpective view?
   a. CAmera
   b. TArget
   c. Distance
   d. POints
   e. Hide
7. Which of the following could be rotated instead of using Rotate 3D to rotate parts during INSERTion into their correct position?
   a. Axis
   b. Vpoint
   c. Dview
   d. Vport
   e. UCS
8. Which of the following UCS options is used to save a UCS for later use?
   a. Save
   b. Restore
   c. X,Y,Z
   d. Window
   e. Name

9. 3D Orbit perspective views are obtained from:
   a. Projection on the shortcut menu
   b. Visual Aids on the shortcut menu
   c. Shading modes on the shortcut menu
   d. Swivelcamera from More on the shortcut menu
   e. Adjust distance from More on the shortcut menu
10. Many commands can be started in one viewport and ended in another.
   a. True
   b. False

20 Using Model Space, Paper Space, and Layouts to Create, Document, and Present 2-D and 3-D Shapes

OBJECTIVES

After completing this chapter, you will be able to

- □ Define the terms associated with paper space and model space.
- □ Use the commands associated with paper space to annotate and plot multiple viewports.
- □ Use SHADE to render 3-D models.
- □ Make slides of your work.
- □ Make a script file to run a slide show of your work.
- □ Demonstrate your slide show on a computer.
- □ Correctly answer questions regarding the following commands:

Delay
Slide-Create… (Mslide)
Model Space
Mview
Layout
Layout Wizard
Paper Space (Pspace)
Script
Shade
Tilemode
UCSICON
Vplayer
Viewports (Vports)
Slide-View… (Vslide)

INTRODUCTION

You have used UCS and multiple viewports and have been introduced to paper space in the preceding chapters. This chapter presents the details of how to use model space and paper space; how to shade 3-D models using the SHADE command; how to put all this together into a slide presentation of your work; and how to plot multiple viewports to scale.

WHY PAPER SPACE AND MODEL SPACE?

Let's begin with the concepts of paper space and model space. Model space is the 3-D environment in which you worked in previous versions of AutoCAD. It is limited in that only one viewport can be active at a time, and only one of these viewports can be plotted. Model space is where your 3-D model or 2-D drawing (really 3-D—the Z dimension is 0) is created and modified. When you start a new drawing, you are in model space.

Paper space allows you to bring model space viewports into paper space; move, copy, stretch, erase, or scale them; put callouts and other identifying text and symbols on the drawing; and plot the whole thing at one time. For example, you can use paper space to do the following:

Display a 2-D drawing (Figure 20–1) in four viewports (Example: A floor plan with furniture) as follows:

One viewport with only the floor plan
One viewport with the floor plan with dimensions
One viewport with the floor plan with furniture and no dimensions
One viewport with floor plan, furniture, and dimensions

Insert a border and title block around the whole display. Plot all viewports with border and title block on a single sheet of paper to scale.

When you click any of the Layout tabs, your drawing is placed into paper space.

TILED AND NONTILED VIEWPORTS

Two types of viewports, tiled and nontiled, are now available to you. Tiled viewports are the 3-D viewports used in previous versions of AutoCAD.

Features of Tiled Viewports

- Tiled viewports are available in model space only.
- They fill the graphics display and lie side by side like ceramic tile.

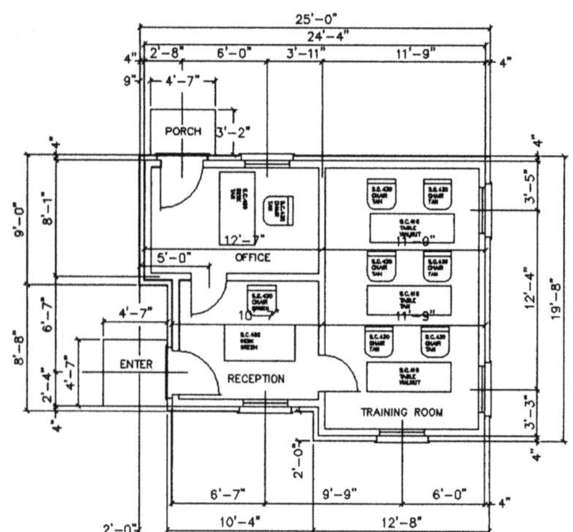

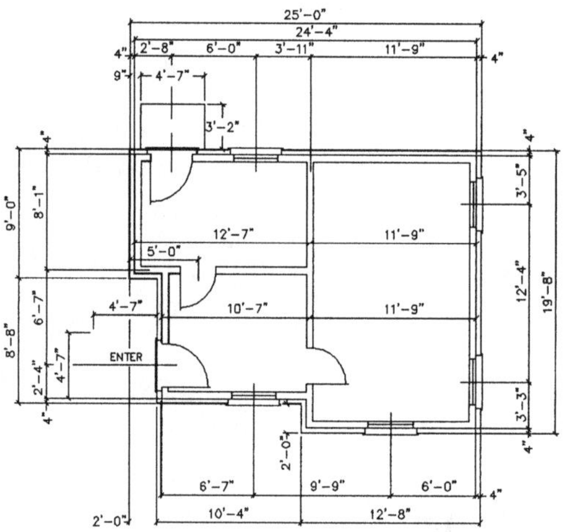

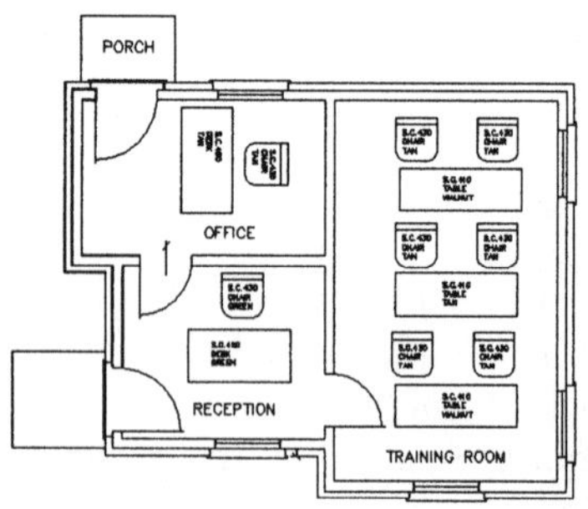

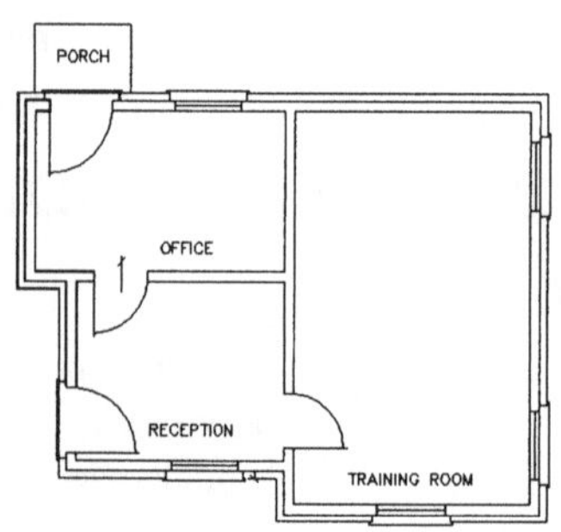

FIGURE 20–1
Uses of Paper Space for a 2-D Drawing

- They are fixed and cannot overlap.
- They can be deleted only by changing the viewport configuration.
- Only one tiled viewport can be active at a time.
- Only the active viewport can be plotted.

Nontiled viewports are used in paper space or in model space. These viewports are essentially 2-D in paper space and have a great deal of flexibility.

Features of Nontiled Viewports

- Nontiled viewports are available in either model space or paper space after they have been created in paper space.
- They may or may not fill the graphics screen.
- They can overlap.
- They can be moved, copied, scaled, stretched, or erased.
- They can have different layers turned on or off in any viewport.
- They can all be plotted at the same time.
- Anything drawn in a nontiled viewport cannot be edited in a tiled viewport.

COMMANDS USED IN PAPER SPACE

The commands, settings, and other features you will use in paper space are as follows:

Mview

Mview operates only in paper space and is used to create and control viewport display. Its options are:

ON Turns selected viewports on. Models are regenerated in these viewports.
OFF Turns off selected viewports so AutoCAD doesn't have to regenerate them until needed.
Hideplot The same as the Hide command except that individual viewports can be selected during paper space plotting.
Lock Allows you to lock a viewport so no one else can edit it.
Object Allows you to create a new viewport by selecting an existing object such as a circle.
Polygonal Allows you to draw an irregularly shaped viewport using polyline lines and arcs.
Fit Creates a single viewport to fill the current paper space display.
2,3,4 Creates two, three, or four viewports in a specified area or to fit the current display.
Restore Restores saved model space viewports in paper space.
<point> Creates a new viewport defined by digitizing two corners or by typing the X, Y coordinates of the lower left and upper right corners.

Model Space

Switches to model space with Tilemode OFF. (*Click*: **PAPER** on the status bar)

Paper Space

Switches to paper space. (*Click*: **MODEL** on the status bar)

VPlayer

Allows you to turn layers on or off in select viewports.

Tilemode

A setting that must be off for you to work in paper space (0 is off, 1 is on). You can work in model space, however, with tilemode off. The default is ON.

UCSICON

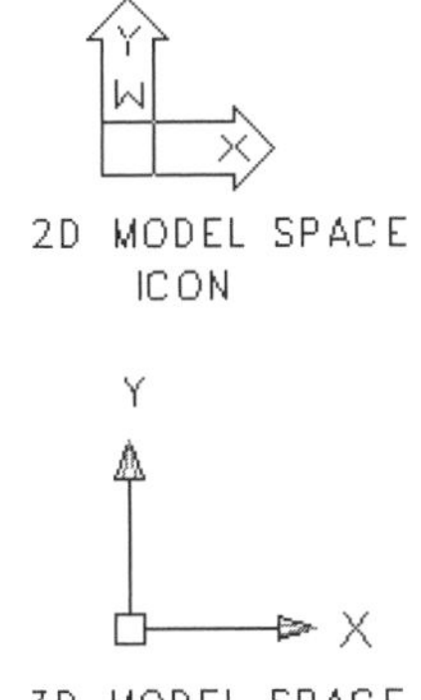

FIGURE 20–2
UCSICONS

The UCSICON, Figure 20–2, changes from the arrows to a triangle when you enter paper space. The status bar at the bottom of your screen also displays PAPER when you enter paper space. The UCSICON can be turned ON or OFF and can be placed at the UCS origin by selecting the Origin option. You can use either 2D or or 3D UCSICONS for 2-D objects. The same is true for 3-D objects.

COMMANDS THAT CANNOT BE USED IN PAPER SPACE

3D Viewpoint
Tiled Viewports (Vports)
3D Dynamic View (Dview)
Plan
3D Orbit

All other Draw, Modify, and View commands can be used in both model space and paper space.

Now, use these commands to produce a drawing containing four viewports with different layers frozen in each viewport (Figure 20–1).

CREATING A DRAWING WITH DIFFERENT LAYERS FROZEN IN EACH VIEWPORT

Exercise 20–1: Creating a Drawing with Different Layers Frozen in Each Viewport

Your final drawing will look similar to the drawing in Figure 20–1.

Set Up the Drawing

Step 1. To begin Exercise 20–1, turn on the computer and start AutoCAD.

Step 2. On your own:

1. Open drawing EX13-2(your initials).
2. Use the SaveAs... command to save the drawing as EX20-1(your initials).

Step 3. Check to make sure that the following settings have been made:

UNITS: Architectural
LIMITS: Lower left corner: 0,0
Upper right corner: 45′,40′
GRID: 12″
SNAP: 2″
TEXT STYLE: Standard FONT: simplex.shx HEIGHT: 0

LAYERS:	NAME	Color	Linetype	Lineweight
	WINDOW	Green	Continuous	Default
	DOOR	Red	Continuous	Default
	WALL	Magenta	Continuous	Default
	TEXT	Cyan	Continuous	Default
	FURNITURE	Magenta	Continuous	Default
	DIM	Green	Continuous	Default

Step 4. Use Zoom-All to view the entire drawing area.

Step 5. On your own:
Change all parts of the drawing to the following layer structure using the Properties... command if the drawing is not presently in this form:

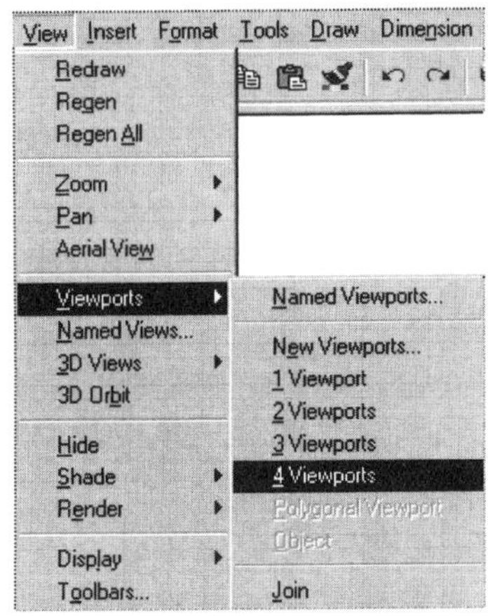

Walls and porches on the WALL layer
Doors on the DOOR layer
Windows on the WINDOW layer
ROOM, PORCH, and ENTER labels on the TEXT layer
Furniture on the FURNITURE layer
Dimensions on the DIM layer

Create Viewports in Model Space

Step 6. Use the Viewports command to change the display to four equal viewports, as shown in Figure 20–1.

Prompt	Response
Command:	**Viewports-4 Viewports** (or *Type:* **VPORTS** ↵ and then *Type:* **4** ↵)

Step 7. Use the Viewports command to save the current viewport configuration.

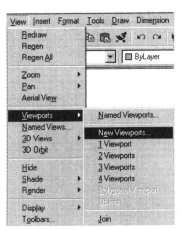

Prompt	Response
Command:	**New Viewports** (or *Type:* **-VPORTS** ↵, then *Type:* **S** ↵, and then *Type*: **VP1** ↵)
The viewports dialog box with the New Viewports tab appears:	*Type:* **VP1** in the New name: box *Click*: **OK**

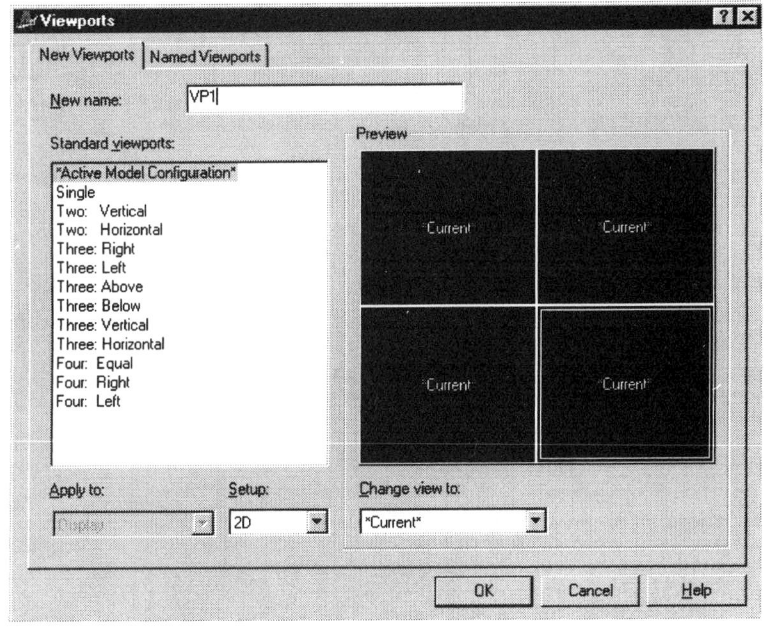

Restore Saved Model Space Viewports in Paper Space

Step 8. Switch to paper space and restore saved viewport configuration to new paper space limits of 22″ × 17″ with a 1″ margin around the space.

Prompt	Response
Command:	*Click:* **Layout Wizard**
The Layout Wizard appears with the name Layout2:	*Click:* **Next**

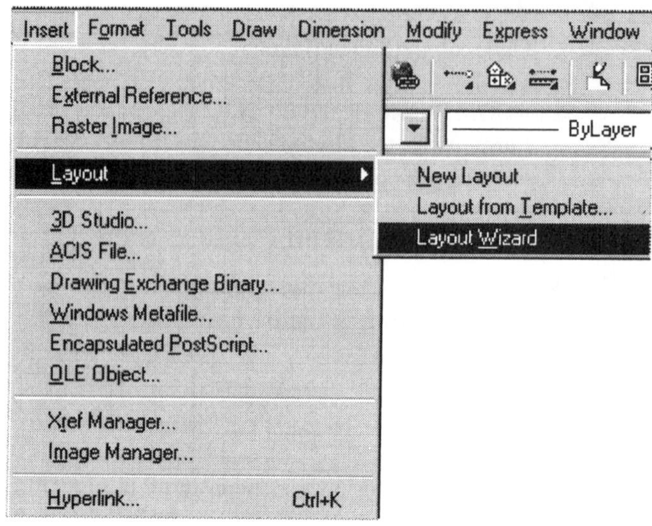

Prompt	Response
The Printer option appears:	*Click:* **DWF ePlot (optimized for plotting).pc3**
	Click: **Next**
The Paper size option appears:	**Locate ANSI C [22.00 x 17.00 Inches] in the paper size list and click on it.**
	Click: **Next**
The Orientation option appears:	*Click:* **Landscape**
	Click: **Next**
The Title block option appears:	*Click:* **None**
	Click: **Next**
The Define viewports option appears:	*Click:* **None**
	Click: **Next**
The Finish option appears:	*Click:* **Finish**
Command:	*Type:* **Z** ↵ then **A** ↵
Command:	**MV** ↵ and then *Type:* **R** ↵ (for MVIEW-Restore)
?/Name of window configuration to insert <VP1>:	*Type:* **VP1** ↵ (or just press ↵ if VP1 is the default)
Fit/<First Point>:	*Type:* **1,1** ↵
Second point:	*Type:* **21,16** ↵ (This creates the 1″ margin on a 22″ × 17″ sheet.)

The restored viewports now fill the paper space limits, which you have set at 22″ × 17″ with a 1″ border all around. At this point anything you add to the drawing must be edited in paper space. Each viewport is a separate snapshot that cannot be edited except in its entirety. You may erase, move, copy, stretch, or otherwise edit individual viewports as a complete entity. If you need to change something within the viewport, you must switch back to model space using the Model Space command (or *Type:* **MS** ↵ or *Click:* **PAPER** at the bottom of your screen).

Freeze Different Layers in Three Viewports in Model Space

Step 9. Return to model space with Tilemode set to 0.

Note: You can use the Layers Properties Manager to freeze layers in the same manner as using the VPLAYER command. The "Current" column on the extreme right side of the dialog box can be used to freeze layers in the current nontiled viewport.

Prompt	Response
Command:	*Click:* **PAPER** (on the status bar) (or *Type:* **MS** ↵)

Step 10. Use the Viewport Layer Controls (VPlayer) command to freeze the FURNITURE and TEXT layers in the upper right viewport.

Click: The upper right viewport to make it active.

Prompt	Response
Command:	*Type:* **VPLAYER** ↵
Enter an option [?/Freeze/Thaw/Reset/Newfrz/Vpvisdflt]:	*Type:* **F** ↵
Enter layer name(s) to freeze:	*Type:* **FURNITURE,TEXT** ↵
Enter an option [All/Select/Current]<Current>:	*Type:* **S** ↵
Select objects:	*Click:* **on any point on the outside edge of the upper right viewport**
Select objects:	↵
Enter an option [?/Freeze/Thaw/Reset/Newfrz/Vpvisdflt]:	↵

Step 11. Use the Viewport Layer Controls (VPlayer) command to freeze the DIM layer in the lower left viewport.

Click: The lower left viewport to make it active.

Prompt	Response
Command:	*Type:* **VPLAYER** ↵
Enter an option [?/Freeze/Thaw/Reset/Newfrz/Vpvisdflt]:	*Type:* **F** ↵
Enter layer name(s) to freeze:	*Type:* **DIM** ↵
Enter an option [All/Select/Current]<Current>:	↵

Step 12. Use the Viewport Layer Controls (VPlayer) command to freeze the DIM and FURNITURE layers in the lower right viewport.

Click: The lower right viewport to make it active.

Prompt	Response
Enter an option [?/Freeze/Thaw/Reset/Newfrz/Vpvisdflt]:	*Type:* **F** ↵
Enter layer name(s) to freeze:	*Type:* **DIM, FURNITURE** ↵
Enter an option [All/Select/Current]<Current>:	↵

Viewport Layer Controls (Vplayer)

The following options are available to you with the Viewport Layer Controls command:

All Changes the visibility of layers in all viewports.
Select Allows you to select individual viewports for visibility changes.
Current Changes visibility in the current viewport only.

?(LIST) Tells you which layers are frozen in the viewports you select.
Freeze Asks you for the layers you want to freeze.
Thaw Asks you for the layers you want to thaw.
Reset Restores the default visibility setting for a layer in a selected viewport.
Newfrz Creates new layers that are frozen in all viewports.
Vpvisdflt Changes the default visibility for layers in all viewports.

Hide the Outlines of the Individual Viewports

Step 13. On your own:

1. Make a new layer named VP and turn it off.
2. Go into paper space if you are not there already and use the Properties… command or the Layer list to change the outside edge of all viewports to the VP layer so that the lines describing the limits of the viewports are no longer visible.

In paper space you may add notations to the drawing, overlap viewports, add viewports, and completely document all viewports at once. Complete this exercise by adding your name to the lower right corner.

Complete the Drawing

Step 14. Add your name to the lower right corner.

Prompt	Response
Command:	**Single-Line Text** (or *Type:* **DT** ↵)
Specify start point of text or [Justify/Style]:	*Type:* **R** ↵
Specify right endpoint of text baseline:	*Click:* **on a point ½″ above and to the left of the lower right corner**
Specify height <.200>:	↵
Specify rotation angle of text<0>:	↵
Enter text:	*Type:* **(your name)** ↵
Enter text:	↵

Step 15. On your own:

1. Save your drawing in at least two places.
2. Plot the drawing "Extents" half size (1 Plotted inch = 2 Drawing units) on an 11″ × 8.5″ sheet.
3. Exit AutoCAD.

CREATING A FOUR-SHEET DRAWING WITH DIFFERENT LAYERS FROZEN ON EACH SHEET

Exercise 20–2: Creating a Four-Sheet Drawing with Different Layers Frozen on Each Sheet (Figure 20–3)

Your final drawing will look similar to the drawing in Figure 20–3.

Step 1. To begin Exercise 20–2, turn on the computer and start AutoCAD.

Step 2. On your own:

1. Open drawing EX13-2(your initials).
2. Use the SaveAs... command to save the drawing as EX20-2(your initials).
3. Check to make sure the settings and layer structure are the same as shown in steps 3, 4, and 5 of Exercise 20–1.

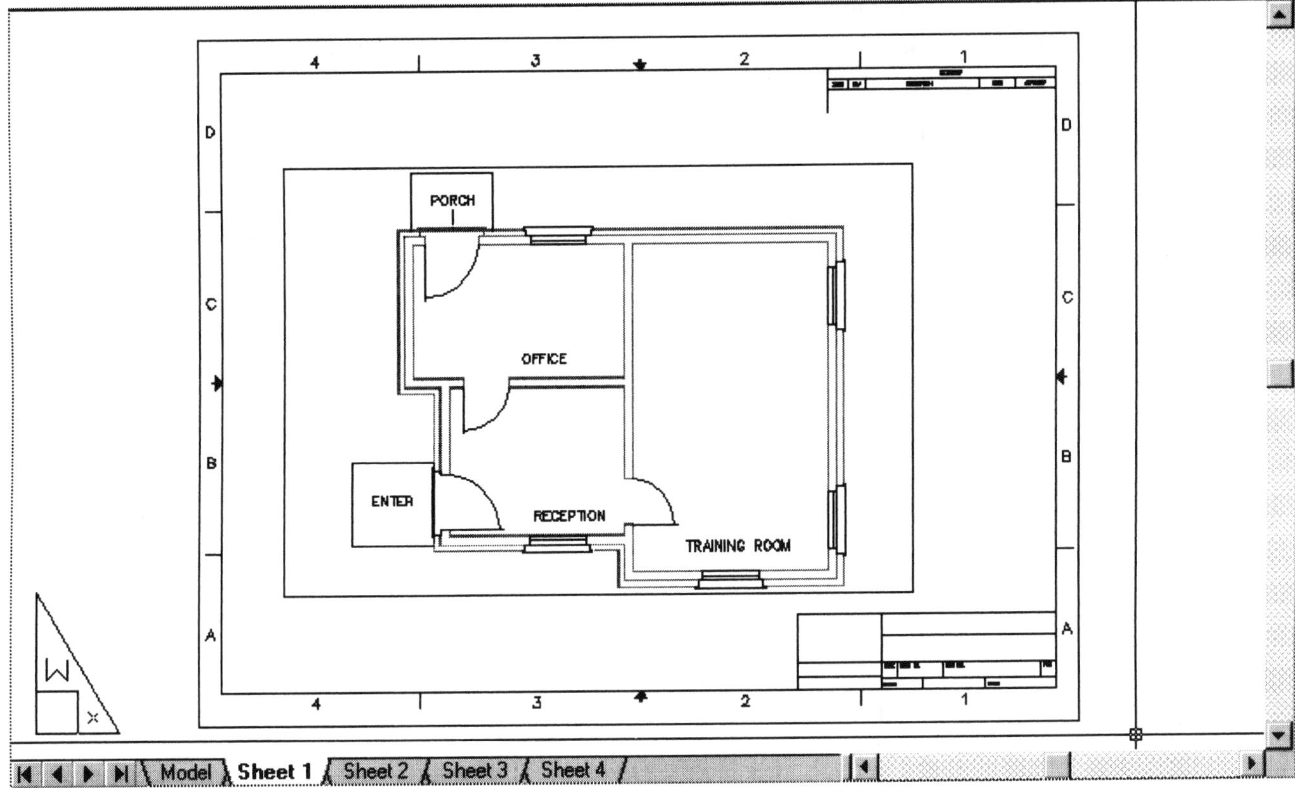

FIGURE 20–3
A Four-Sheet Drawing

Step 3. Delete any existing layouts. *Click:* **the layout name,** *Right click:* **to get the shortcut menu, then** *Click:* **Delete.**

Step 4. Add a new layout named Sheet 1.

Prompt	Response
Command:	*Click:* **Layout Wizard**
The Layout Wizard appears with the name Layout 1:	*Type:* **Sheet 1** *Click:* **Next**
The Printer option appears:	*Click:* **the appropriate printer configured for your computer.** *Click:* **Next**
The Paper size option appears:	**Locate ANSI C [22 × 17 Inches] in the paper size list and click on it.** *Click:* **Next**
The Orientation option appears:	*Click:* **Landscape** *Click:* **Next**
The Title block option appears:	*Click:* **ANSI C Title block.dwg** *Click:* **Next**
The Define viewports option appears:	*Click:* **Single** *Click:* **¼″ = 1′0″** (in the Viewport Scale list) *Click:* **Next**
The Pick Location option appears:	*Click:* **Select location <**
Specify first corner:	*Type:* **2,3** ↵
Specify other corner:	*Type:* **17,13** ↵

Note: If your printer does not print a sheet of 22″ × 17″ use the DWF ePlot (optimized for plotting).pc3 option.

Prompt	Response
The Finish option appears:	*Click:* **Finish**

Step 5. On your own:

1. Use the VPLAYER command to freeze layers DIM and FURNITURE
2. Complete the title block of the format using the following: (Refer to Figure 11–31 for the location of items.)
   Title: SMALL OFFICE PLAN
   Name: Your Name
   School: Your school name
   Date: Current date
   Drawing Number: EX20–2
   Sheet no. 1 of 4

Step 6. Add a new layout named Sheet 2.

On your own:

1. Use the Layout Wizard to make the new layout as described in step 5. Name the new layout Sheet 2.
2. Use the VPLAYER command to freeze layer DIM. (Thaw layer FURNITURE if necessary.)
3. Complete the title block of the format using the following:
   Title: SMALL OFFICE PLAN
   Name: Your Name
   School: Your school name
   Date: Current date
   Drawing Number: EX20–2
   Sheet no. 2 of 4

Step 7. Add a new layout named Sheet 3.

On your own:

1. Use the Layout Wizard to make the new layout described in step 5. Name the new layout Sheet 3.

3. Use the VPLAYER command to freeze layers FURNITURE and TEXT. (Thaw layer DIM if necessary.)
4. Complete the title block of the format using the following:
   Title: SMALL OFFICE PLAN
   Name: Your Name
   School: Your school name
   Date: Current date
   Drawing Number: EX20–2
   Sheet no. 3 of 4

Step 8. Add a new layout named Sheet 4.

On your own:

1. Use the Layout Wizard to make the new layout as described in step 5. Name the new layout Sheet 4.
2. Use the VPLAYER command to thaw all layers.
3. Complete the title block of the format using the following:
   Title: SMALL OFFICE PLAN
   Name: Your Name
   School: Your school name
   Date: Current date
   Drawing Number: EX20–2
   Sheet no. 4 of 4

Step 9. Save and print your drawing.

1. Save your drawing in at least two places
2. Plot each layout of the drawing half size (1 plotted inch = 2 drawing units) on four 11″ × 8.5″ sheets.
3. Exit AutoCAD.

CREATING A DRAWING WITH FIVE DIFFERENT VIEWS OF A 3-D OBJECT

Exercise 20–3: Creating a Drawing with Five Viewports, Each with a Different View of a 3-D Object (Figure 20–4)

Your final drawing will look similar to the drawing in Figure 20–4.

Set Up the Drawing

Step 1. To begin Exercise 20–3, turn on the computer and start AutoCAD.

Step 2. On your own:

1. Open drawing EX19-2(your initials).
2. Use the SaveAs… command to save the drawing as EX20-3(your initials).

Create Four Viewports using the Layout Wizard

Step 3. Make sure you are in a single viewport with UCS set to World.

Prompt	Response
Command:	*Click:* **Viewports-Single** (or *Type:* **-VPORTS** ↵, then *Type:* **SI** ↵)
Command:	*Click:* **New UCS-World** (Or *Type:* **UCS** ↵, then *Press:* ↵ to accept the default of World UCS

Step 4. Delete any existing layouts. *Click:* **the layout name,** *Right click:* **to get the shortcut menu, then** *Click:* **Delete.**

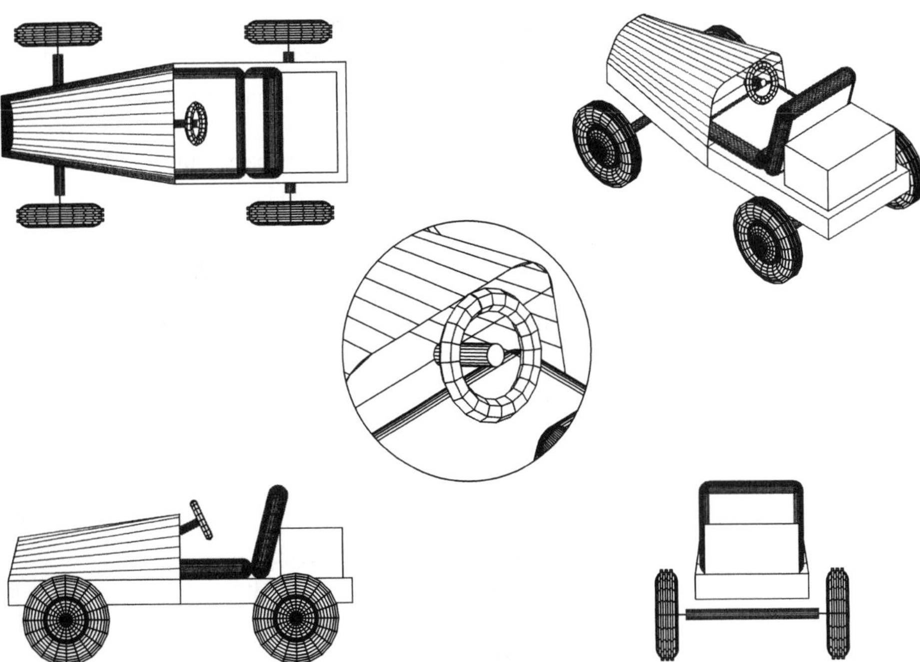

FIGURE 20–4
Completed Exercise 20–3

Step 5. Add a new layout named Layout1.

Prompt	Response
Command:	*Click:* **Layout Wizard**
The Layout Wizard appears with the name Layout1:	*Click:* **Next**
The Printer option appears:	*Click:* **DFW ePlot (optimized for plotting).pc3** *Click:* **Next**
The Paper size option appears:	**Locate ANSI C [22.00 × 17.00 Inches] in the paper size list and click on it.** *Click:* **Next**
The Orientation option appears:	*Click:* **Landscape** *Click:* **Next**
The Title block option appears:	*Click:* **None** *Click:* **Next**
The Define viewports option appears:	*Click:* **Std. 3D Engineering Views** *Click:* **Next**
The Pick Location option appears:	*Click:* **Select location** <
Specify first corner:	*Type:* **1,1** ↵
Specify other corner:	*Type:* **20,16** ↵
The Finish option appears:	*Click:* **Finish**

Step 6. Use the MVSETUP command to scale viewports so that all four views are the same scale.

Prompt	Response
Command:	*Type:* **MVSETUP** ↵
Enter an option [Align/Create/ Scale viewports/Options/Title block/Undo]:	*Type:* **S** ↵
Select the viewports to scale...	*Type:* **ALL** ↵ (or select all four viewports using a crossing window)
Select objects:	↵
Set zoom scale factors for viewports. Interactively/<Uniform>:	↵
Set the ratio of paper space units to model space units...	
Enter the number of paper space units <1.0>:	↵
Enter the number of model space units <1.0>:	*Type:* **10** ↵
Enter an option [Align/Create/ Scale viewports/Options/Title block/Undo]:	↵

Step 7. Draw a circle near the center of the new layout and use the MVIEW command to make a new viewport with a circular shape.

Prompt	Response
Command:	*Type:* **PS** ↵ (to make sure you are in paper space)
Command:	*Type:* **C** ↵
Specify center point for circle or [3P/2P/Ttr (tan tan radius)]:	*Click:* **a point near the center of the layout**
Specify radius of circle or [Diameter]:	*Type:* **2** ↵

Prompt	**Response**
Command:	*Type:* **MV** ↵
Specify corner of viewport or [ON/OFF/Fit/Hideplot/Lock/Object/ Polygonal/Restore/2/3/4]<Fit>:	*Type:* **O** ↵
Select object to clip viewport:	*Click:* **the circle you just drew**

Step 8. Zoom in on the newly created viewport, return to model space, set a viewpoint of 315 30, zoom a window to obtain the view shown in Figure 20–4, return to paper space, and zoom all.

Prompt	**Response**
Command:	*Type:* **Z** ↵
Specify corner of window, enter a scale factor (nX or nXP), or [All/Center/Dynamic/Extents/ Previous/Scale/Window]<real time>:	*Click:* **D1, Figure 20–5** (the view in your circle may not look like this figure right now—it will later.)
Specify opposite corner:	*Click:* **D2**
Command:	*Type:* **MS** ↵ (or *Click:* **PAPER** on the status bar)
Command:	*Type:* **VP** ↵
The Viewpoint Presets dialog box appears:	*Click:* **315 in the left chart** *Click:* **30 in the right chart** *Click:* **OK**
Command:	*Type:* **Z** ↵
Specify corner of window, enter a scale factor (nX or nXP), or [All/Center/Dynamic/Extents/ Previous/Scale/Window]<real time>:	*Click:* **D1, Figure 20–6**

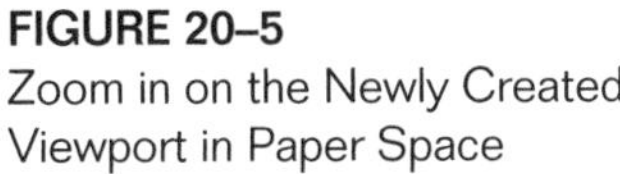

FIGURE 20–5
Zoom in on the Newly Created Viewport in Paper Space

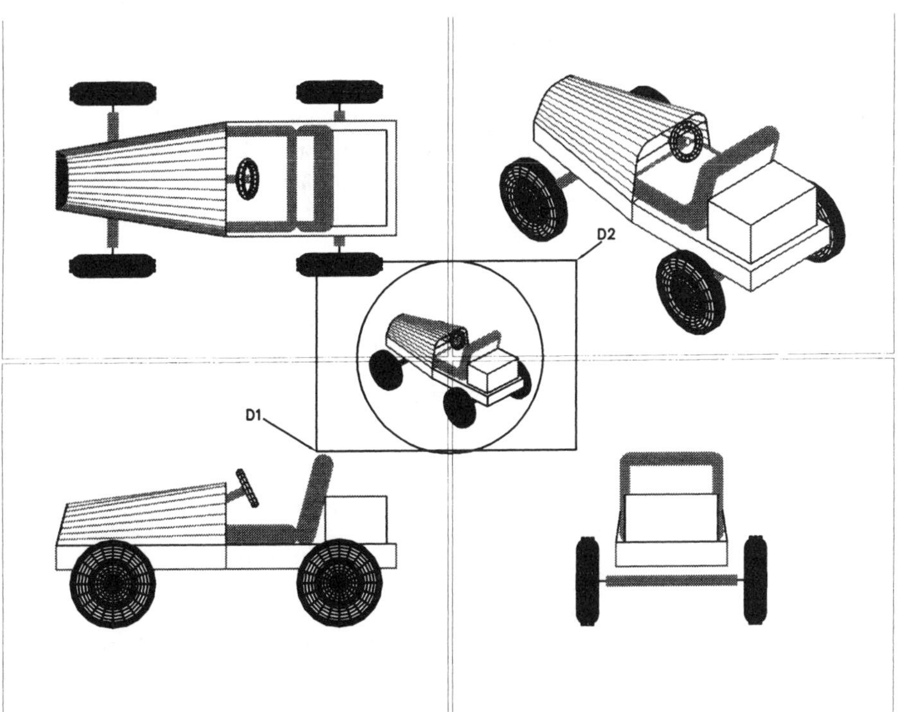

FIGURE 20–6
Zoom a Window in Model Space to Obtain an Enlarged View

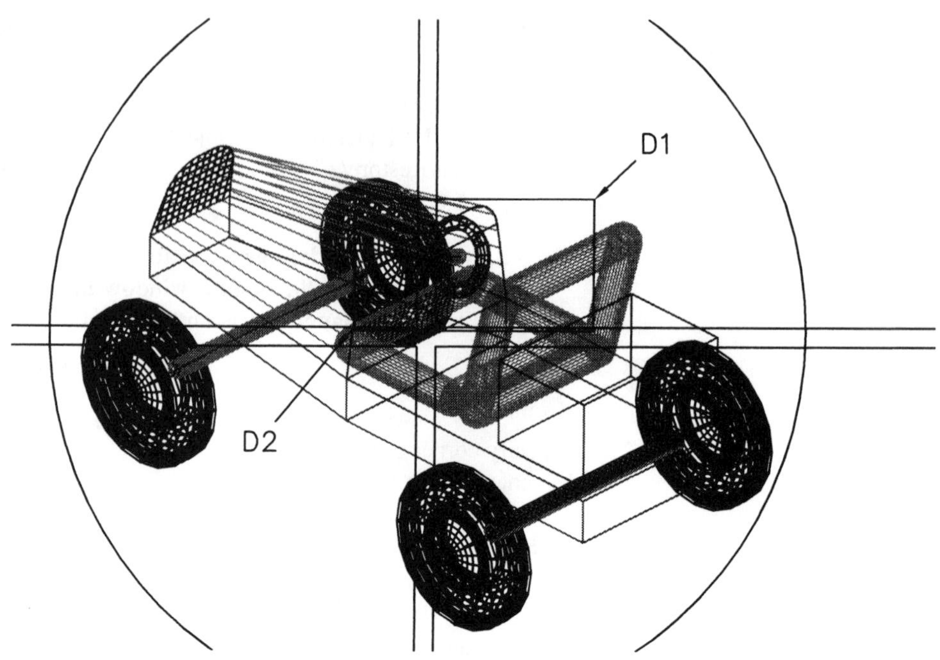

Prompt	Response
Specify opposite corner:	*Click:* **D2**
Command:	*Type:* **PS** ↵ (or *Click:* **MODEL** on the status bar)(to return to paper space)
Command:	*Type:* **Z** ↵
Specify corner of window, enter a scale factor (nX or nXP), or [All/Center/Dynamic/Extents/Previous/Scale/Window]<real time>:	*Type:* **A** ↵

Step 9. Use Mview-Hideplot to remove hidden lines for plotting.

Prompt	Response
Command:	*Type:* **MV** ↵
Specify corner of viewport or [ON/OFF/Fit/Hideplot/Lock/Object/Polygonal/Restore/2/3/4]<Fit>:	*Type:* **H** ↵
Hidden line removal for plotting [ON/OFF]:	*Type:* **ON** ↵
Select objects:	*Type:* **ALL** ↵
Select objects:	↵

Step 10. On your own:

1. Make a new layer, name it VP1, and turn it OFF.
2. Use the Properties command or the Layer list to change the four rectangular viewports to the VP1 layer.
3. Type your name in the lower right corner; simplex font, .2″ high.

Step 11. Save and print your drawing.

1. Save your drawing in at least two places.
2. Plot this layout of the drawing half size (1 plotted inch = 2 drawing units) on an 11″ × 8.5″ sheet.
3. Exit AutoCAD.

CREATING A SLIDE SHOW

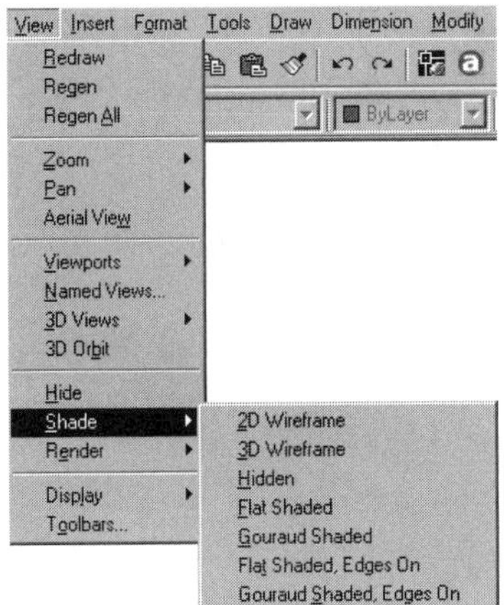

Now that you have paper space under control, you can use models and drawings in both model space and paper space to create slides to be used in a slide show. A slide is a snapshot of a drawing. It can be quickly generated for viewing but cannot be edited in any way as a slide.

Slide shows are easily produced with AutoCAD. They can be a valuable tool for selling ideas and products to supervisors or customers.

Exercise 20–4: Making a Slide Show of the Drawings You Have Created

Step 1. Select drawings to be included in the slide show.

Decide which drawings you wish to include in the slide show. Make a storyboard consisting of quick sketches of the drawings in the order in which you want them to appear. Identify each drawing by the name under which you have it stored. You may include as many drawings as you want; usually 10 with a title slide is a good number.

Use the Shade command to provide shading on any 3-D models you choose. Let's shade a 3-D model you have already drawn.

Step 2. On your own:

1. Open drawing EX16-1(your initials).
2. *Click:* the Model tab.
3. Make the viewport containing the 3-D view shown in Figure 20–7 active, and return the display to a single viewport.

You can create different effects when you use different options of the Shade command. Four of these options are shown in Figures 20–7 through 20–10.

Step 3. Shade the drawing with four Shade options.

Prompt	Response
Command:	**Shade-Flat Shaded**
The view shown as Figure 20–7 appears:	
Command:	**Shade-Flat Shaded, Edges On**
The view shown as Figure 20–8 appears:	
Command:	**Shade-Hidden**
The view shown as Figure 20–9 appears:	
Command:	**Shade-Gouraud Shaded**
The view shown as Figure 20–10 appears:	

FIGURE 20–7
Flat Shaded

FIGURE 20–8
Flat Shaded, Edges On

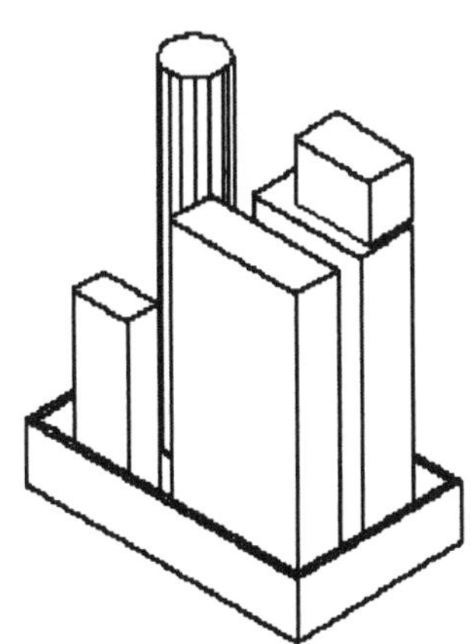

FIGURE 20–9
Hidden

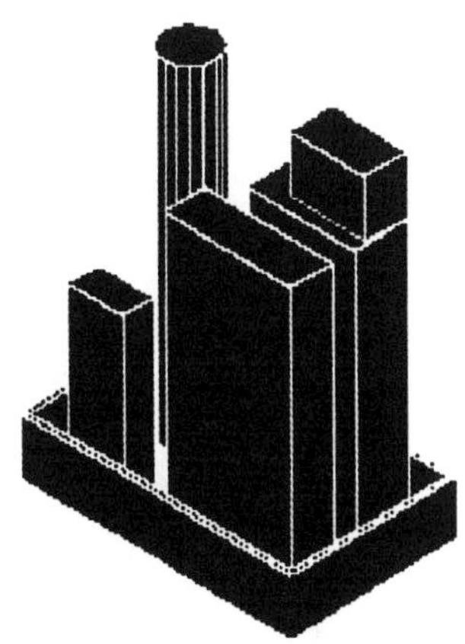

FIGURE 20–10
Gouraud Shaded

Step 4. Make a slide of your shaded drawing using Shade-Gouraud Shaded, Figure 20–10.

Prompt	Response
Command:	*Click:* **Shade-Gouraud Shaded**
Command:	*Type:* **MSLIDE** ↵
The Create Slide File dialog box (Figure 20–11) appears:	*Click:* **3½ Floppy [A:] in the Save in: box**
	Type: **SLIDE1** in the File Name: text box so that your Create Slide File dialog box looks like Figure 20–11
	Click: **OK**

Step 5. On your own:

1. Make slides of the other drawings you have chosen for your slide show.
2. Number the slides consecutively. Be sure to save the slides on the floppy disk in the A drive.

Note: If Shade does not give you an acceptable image, use the Render command and accept all the defaults.

Using AutoCAD, bring each drawing to be included in the slide show from the floppy disk to the hard drive, one at a time. Inserting drawings into a blank area may be the fastest means of accomplishing this. Insert, make the slide, and then UNDO to get rid of the block. You may want to ZOOM a window around a drawing so that it fills the screen. The view of the drawing as displayed on the screen is what your slide will look like. Make slides of each displayed drawing as you did in step 4. Use Shade or Render for 3-D drawings only.

Step 6. Make a script file for your slide show.

AutoCAD provides a script facility that allows commands to be read and executed from a script file. To make a script file for your slide show:

Prompt	Response
Command:	*Click:* **Start** in the lower left corner of your screen
	Locate: **Notepad** as shown in Figure 20–12 and start it.

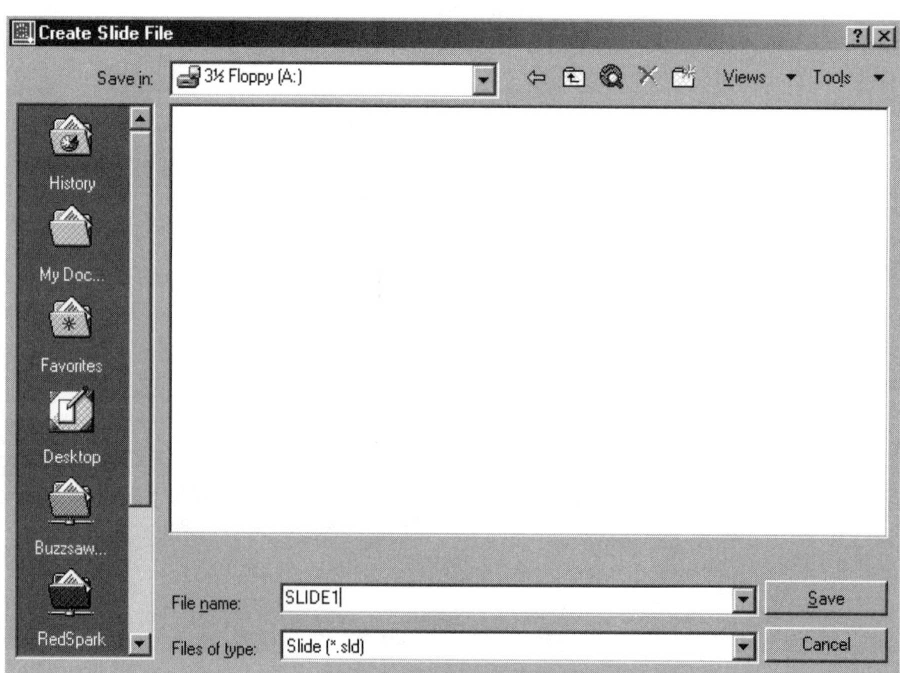

FIGURE 20–11
Create Slide File Dialog Box

FIGURE 20–12
Locate Notepad

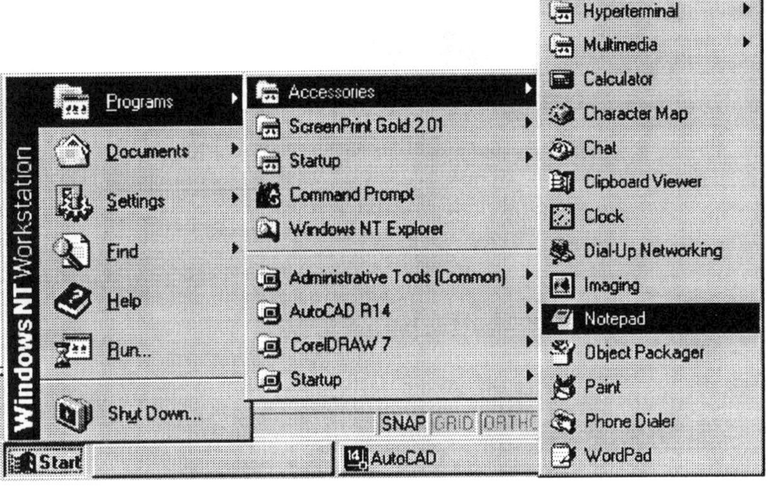

Prompt	Response
	Type: **VSLIDE A:SLIDE1** ↵
	VSLIDE *A:SLIDE2 ↵
	DELAY 2500 ↵
	VSLIDE ↵
	VSLIDE *A:SLIDE3 ↵
	DELAY 2500 ↵
	VSLIDE ↵

Be careful when typing the script file—do not press the space bar and create a space at the end of any line of text. Press the return key only once to go to the next line. Do not create any spaces between the lines of text. If you have any spaces at the end of any lines or between the lines, the script file will not run. The * in the script file means load. VSLIDE means view the slide. Delay 2500 means delay 2500 milliseconds (1000 is approximately 1 second). The maximum delay is 32767, slightly less than 33 seconds. Be sure to use the same slide name you used when you made slides of each drawing and saved them to your floppy disk.

You must have the following three lines for each slide after the first one.

VSLIDE *A:SLIDE4
DELAY 2500
VSLIDE

To save some time, use the Copy command to copy the last six lines as a block as shown in Figure 20–13, then change the slide numbers for each slide:

FIGURE 20–13
Block the Text to Be Copied

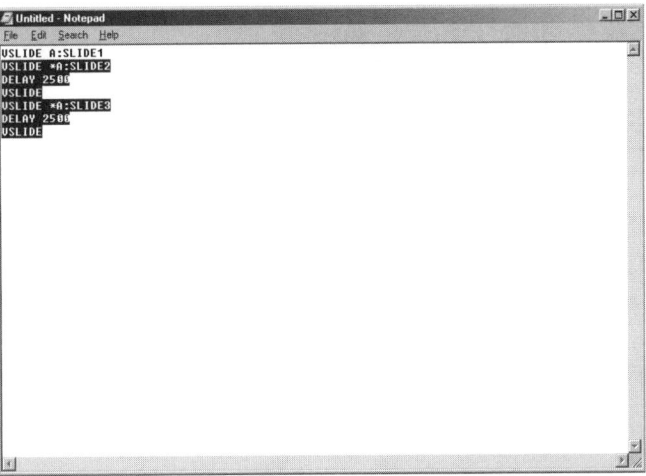

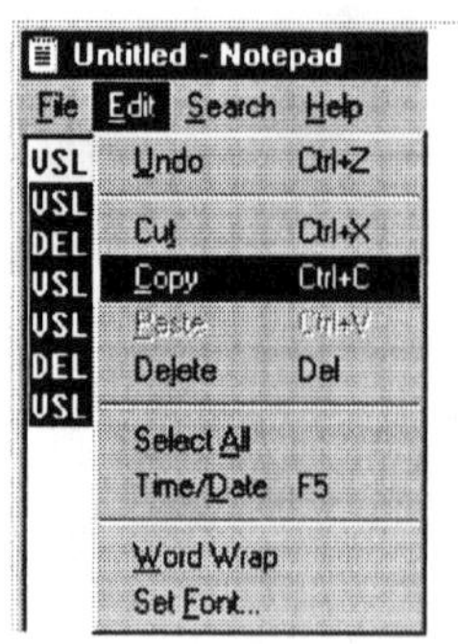

FIGURE 20–14
Copy the Text

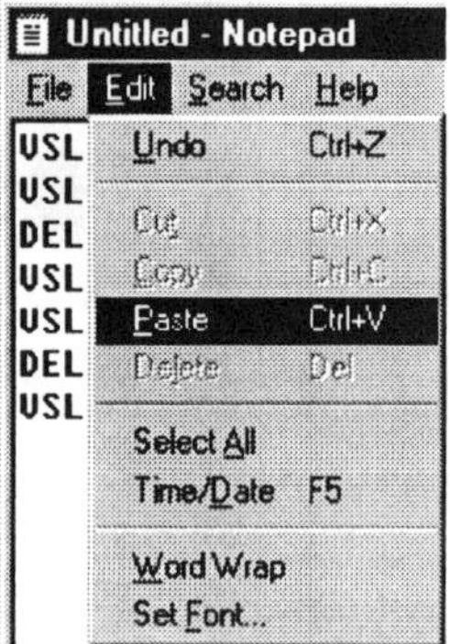

FIGURE 20–15
Paste

Prompt	Response
	Click: **to the left of VSLIDE *A:SLIDE2 Hold down the click button and move the cursor so that the last six lines are highlighted** (Figure 20–13)
	Click: **Copy** (Figure 20–14)
	Move the cursor to where you want to copy and *Click:* **Paste** (Figure 20–15).
	Change the slide numbers of the copied lines so they look like Figure 20–16.
	The last line you must add to the script file is **RSCRIPT** (*Press:* ↵ after typing this.)

This command reruns your script file until you interrupt it by pressing **Esc.** If you want it to continue, *Type:* **RESUME** ↵.

Step 7. Save your script file.

Prompt	Response
	Click: **SaveAs...** from the File menu
	Click: **the 3½ Floppy (A:) drive**

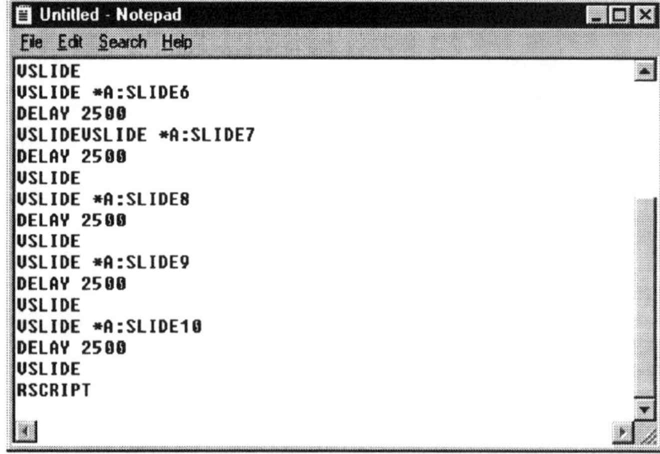

FIGURE 20–16
The Last Lines of the Script File

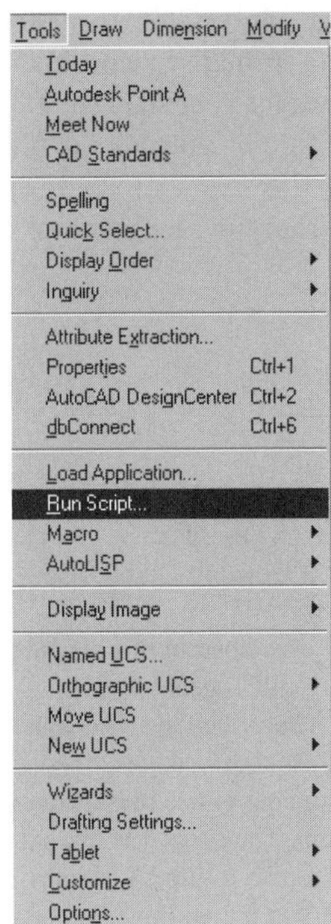

Prompt	Response
	Type: **SLDSCRIP.SCR** in the File name: box, Figure 20–17
	Click: **Save**
	Exit Notepad

At this point you should have a floppy disk containing your script file named Sldscrip.scr and 10 slides named SLIDE1.SLD through SLIDE10.SLD. Your script file should contain references to 10 slide files (Example: VSLIDE A:SLIDE1 through VSLIDE *A:SLIDE10, DELAY 2500, VSLIDE).

Step 8. Test your slide show and script file.

Prompt	Response
Command:	**Run Script...**
The Select Script File dialog box appears:	*Click:* **the A: drive**
	Click: **Sldscrip** from the File name: list so it appears as shown in Figure 20–18
	Click: **OK**

Your slide show should now run until you decide to stop it. To stop the slide show at any point, *Press:* **Esc**. To start it again, *Type:* **RESUME** ↵.

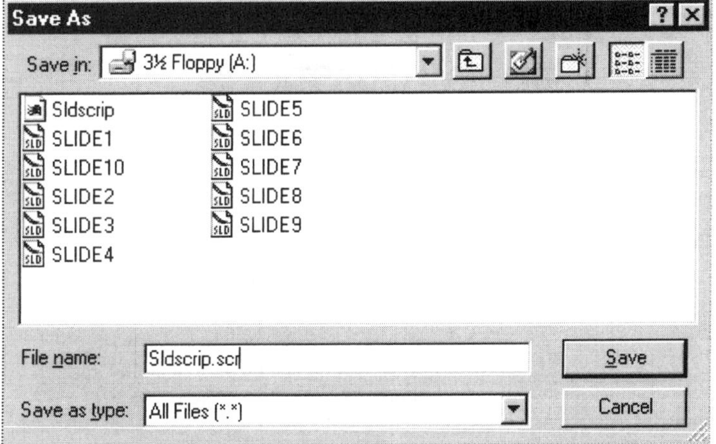

FIGURE 20–17
Save the Script File on the Floppy Disk

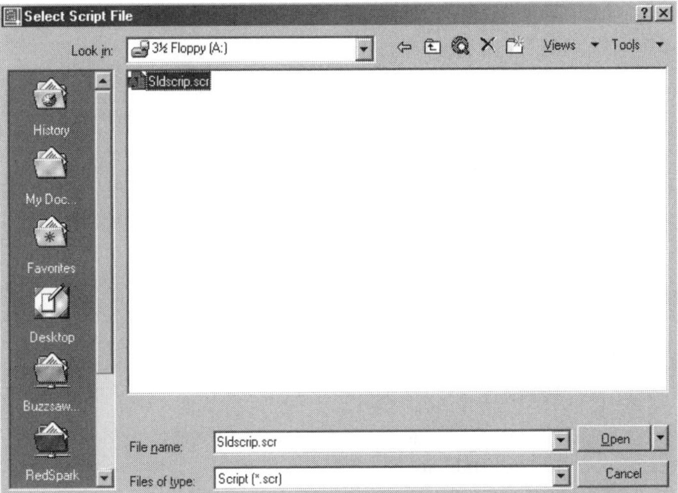

FIGURE 20–18
Select the Script File Dialog Box

To change the delay period, edit the script file and change the number 2500 to 3000 for a longer delay or to 2000 for a shorter delay. These numbers are in milliseconds. You may want to experiment with this value until you find just the right one for your slide show.

If the slide show does not run correctly, you may need to edit your script file (or rename slide files or make slide files with the correct name).

To edit the script file, start Notepad again and use Open from the File menu to open your script file and correct it.

Step 9. Exit AutoCAD.

EXERCISES

EXERCISE 20–1. Complete Exercise 20–1 using steps 1 through 15 described in this chapter. Plot the drawing at a scale of 1 Plotted Inch = 2 Drawing Units on an 11″ × 8.5″ sheet.

EXERCISE 20–2. Complete Exercise 20–2 using steps 1 through 8 described in this chapter. Plot each sheet of this drawing half size on four 8½″ × 11″ sheets.

EXERCISE 20–3. Complete Exercise 20–2 using steps 1 through 13 described in this chapter.

EXERCISE 20–4. Prepare a slide show containing a minimum of 10 slides, as described in this chapter. Shade at least three of your 3-D solids using either the Shade or the Render command before you make slides of them. The script file and all slide files should be contained on one floppy disk. Prepare a title slide as SLIDE1 containing your name and the course number, if you are taking a course. (You will have to rename SLIDE1 from the exercise; make it SLIDE0 if you like, then you will not have to rename all your slides.) Run the slide show as directed by your instructor.

REVIEW QUESTIONS

Circle the best answer.

1. A tiled viewport is used in
   a. Model space
   b. Paper space
2. Which of the following is a characteristic of tiled viewports?
   a. They can overlap.
   b. Only one viewport can be active at one time.
   c. Multiple viewports can be plotted at once.
   d. They can be copied, moved, or erased.
   e. All are characteristics of tiled viewports.
3. Which of the following commands switches the display to paper space?
   a. Mview
   b. Viewports
   c. Vplayer
   d. Vpoint
   e. Paper Space
4. Which of the following Mview options removes hidden lines in selected viewports during plotting?
   a. Hide
   b. Hideplot
   c. Viewports Off
   d. Restore
   e. Vplayer
5. Which of the following allows different layers to be turned off in selected viewports?
   a. Mview
   b. Vplayer
   c. Viewports
   d. Tilemode
   e. Hideplot

6. Which of the following commands cannot be used in paper space?
   a. Dtext
   b. Zoom
   c. Move
   d. Erase
   e. 3D Viewpoint
7. You cannot work in model space when Tilemode is ON.
   a. True
   b. False
8. Which of the following Vplayer options allows a new layer to be created that is frozen in all viewports?
   a. Vpvisdflt
   b. Freeze
   c. Newfrz
   d. New
   e. Select
9. Which of the following Vplayer options changes the default visibility for all layers?
   a. Vpvisdfltd
   b. Freeze
   c. Newfrz
   d. New
   e. Select
10. Which of the following commands is used to make a slide of a drawing?
    a. SLIDE
    b. Slide-View…
    c. MSLIDE
    d. *VSLIDE
    e. Save

21 Advanced Modeling: Solids and Regions

OBJECTIVES

After completing this chapter, you will be able to

- □ Define solid modeling.
- □ Create solid primitives.
- □ Create composite solids.
- □ Edit solid models.
- □ Create solid models from regions.
- □ Render solid models.
- □ Create a cross section of a solid model.
- □ Generate 2-D drawings from a solid model.

SOLID MODELING

Solid modeling is a major step toward three-dimensional CAD in manufacturing and construction industries. Those commands create solid models that can be analyzed as if they existed outside of the computer. They can be rendered, indexed, rotated, sectioned, and viewed from any angle. These models may also be documented as 2-D drawings.

Solid modeling differs from the 3-D wire frame with its accompanying 3-D surfaces in that the solid is just that—it's solid. The solid has been molded as a solid block. The 3-D wire frame with its surfaces attached is a hollow model that can be made to look solid. The solid model can be weighed and otherwise analyzed to determine how well it will function. Let's begin the description of Solid Modeling by looking at the Solids menus and other commands that may now be used to create and modify AutoCAD solids.

SOLIDS COMMANDS

The Solids and Solids Editing menus and toolbars are shown in Figure 21–1.

Solids Commands Used to Create Basic Shapes

Box Used to make a solid box. The base of the box is parallel to the XY plane of the current UCS.

Sphere Used to make a solid sphere. The sphere is created by specifying its center point and then specifying either its radius or its diameter. Keep in mind that the center specified is the center of the ball, not top or bottom center.

Cylinder Used to make a solid cylinder. The base of the cylinder may be circular or elliptical and is parallel to the XY plane of the current UCS. The height of the cylinder is parallel to the Z axis of the current UCS and may be positive or negative.

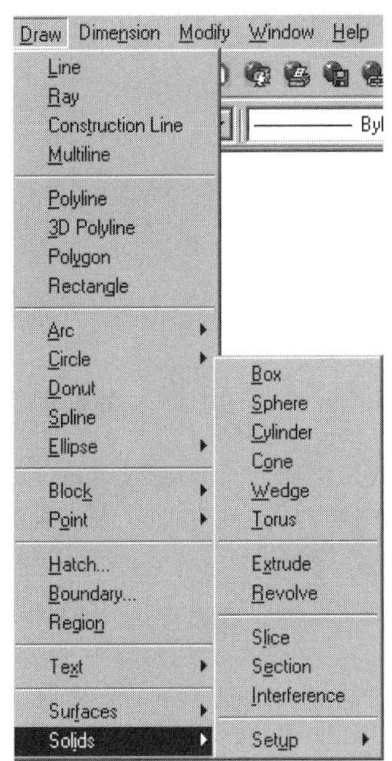

FIGURE 21–1
Solids and Solids Editing Menus and Toolbars

Cone Used to make a solid cone. The base of the cone may be circular or elliptical and is parallel to the XY plane of the current UCS. The height of the cone is parallel to the Z axis of the current UCS and may be positive or negative.

Wedge Used to make a solid wedge. The base of the wedge is parallel to the XY plane of the current UCS with the sloped face opposite the first corner. The height may be positive or negative parallel to the Z axis.

Torus Used to make a solid torus (a shape similar to an inner tube or a real donut). The XY plane of the current UCS cuts horizontally through the center of the torus if the center specifies a 0 Z value. The torus radius or diameter is the outside measurement of the inner tube. The tube diameter or radius is the dimension of tube that holds the air. You can create a football shape by specifying a negative torus radius and a positive tube radius of greater magnitude (e.g., −2 torus radius, +3 tube radius).

Extrude Used to add thickness to shapes such as closed polylines, polygons, rectangles, circles, ellipses, closed splines, donuts, and regions. The vertical thickness may be straight or tapered. In the process of having thickness added, the object is made into a solid. An object may also be extruded along a curved or straight path. 3-D objects, blocks, or polylines that have crossing or intersecting segments may not be extruded.

Revolve Used to make a solid by revolving a closed object about an axis. Draw the cross-sectional shape of the object, then draw a center line and revolve the shape about the center line. The object or shape must be a single polyline or other entity, so if the object was drawn with lines and arcs, use the Join option of Pedit: to join all lines into a single shape. You cannot revolve objects in blocks or other 3-D objects, and the object cannot intersect itself.

Solids Commands Used to Create Composite Solids

Note: The commands Union, Subtract, and Intersect are located on the Modify menu on the menu bar and on the Modify II toolbar.

Union Used to make a composite solid from two or more solids or two or more regions.

Subtract Used to remove the common area of one solid from another. (Example: subtracting cylinders from a solid to create holes.)

Intersect Used to make a composite solid from the common volume of two or more overlapping solids. Intersect removes the nonoverlapping areas and creates a composite solid from the common volume.

Interference Does the same thing as Intersect except it retains the two original objects.

EDITING SOLIDS

Solids Commands Used to Edit Solids

Slice Used to create a new solid by cutting the existing solid into two pieces and removing or retaining either or both pieces.

Section Used to create the cross-sectional area of a solid. That area may then be hatched using the Hatch or Bhatch commands with any pattern you choose. Be sure the section is parallel with the current UCS when you hatch the area.

SOLIDEDIT

The SOLIDEDIT command has several options that allow you to change features of 3-D solid objects. These options are shown as separate tools on the Solids Editing toolbar, Figure 21–1, and as separate commands on the Solids Editing menu from the Modify menu on the menu bar.

With SOLIDEDIT, you can change solid objects by extruding, moving, rotating, offsetting, tapering, copying, coloring, separating, shelling, cleaning, checking, or deleting features such as holes, surfaces and edges.

When you type: SOLIDEDIT ↵, the following prompt appears:

Enter a solids editing option [Face/Edge/Body/Undo/eXit]<eXit>:

When you type: F ↵ for face, the following options appear for changing surfaces:

Extrude Allows you to extrude an existing surface or surfaces on a solid along a path.

Move Allows you to move surfaces such as holes or objects in the solid from one point to another.

Rotate Allows you to rotate surfaces in a solid such as slots, or other shapes.

Offset Allows you to create new surfaces by offsetting existing ones.

Taper Allows you to taper surfaces on a solid along a path.

Delete Allows you to delete surfaces (such as holes and other features) from the solid.

Copy Allows you to copy existing surfaces from a solid model.

coLor Allows you to assign a color to any surface of the solid model.

All these options are similar to commands you have already used.

When you *Type:* **E for Edge, the following options appear for changing edges:**

Copy Allows you to copy existing edges from a solid model.

coLor Allows you to assign a color to any edge of the solid model.

When you *Type:* **B ↵ for body, the following options appear for changing the body of the model:**

Imprint Allows you to imprint a shape onto a solid. The object to be imprinted must intersect one or more faces on the selected solid in order for imprinting to be successful. You can imprint the following objects: arcs, circles, lines, 2-D and 3-D polylines, ellipses, splines, regions, and 3-D solids.

seParate solids Allows you to separate some solids that have been joined together to form a composite solid.

Shell Shelling creates a hollow, thin wall with a specified thickness. You can specify a constant wall thickness for all the faces. You can also exclude faces from the shell by selecting them. A 3-D solid can have only one shell.

Clean Clean removes any unused or duplicated geometry from the model.

Check Allows you to verify that the object is a valid solid.

Other Commands That Can Be Used to Edit Solids

Rotate 3D Used to rotate solids about X, Y, or Z axes.

3D Array Used to create three-dimensional arrays of solids.

Mirror 3D Used to create mirror images of solids about a plane specified by three points.

Trim Used to trim lines, polylines, and similar entities in 3-D space, but this command will not trim a solid shape.

Extend Used to extend lines, polylines, and similar entities in 3-D space, but this command will not extend a solid shape.

Fillet Used to create fillets and rounds. Specify the radius for the fillet and then digitize the edge or edges to be filleted.

Chamfer Used to create chamfers. Specify the distances for the chamfer and then digitize the edge or edges to be chamfered.

Align Used to move a solid so that a selected plane on the first solid is aligned with a selected plane on a second solid.

Explode Used to explode a solid into regions. (Example: An exploded solid box becomes six regions: four sides, a top, and a bottom.)

All the following commands may be used to edit or view solids in the same manner as you have used them previously.

Move	**Dview**
Properties. . .	**Vpoint**
Erase	**Mview**
Scale	**Zoom**
UCS	**Pan**

Settings That Control How the Solid Is Displayed

FACETRES Used to make shaded solids and those with hidden lines removed smoother. Values range from 0.01 to 10.0. The default value is 0.5. Higher values take longer to regenerate but look better. To change the FACETRES value, *Type:* **FACETRES** ↵, then type the new value. Try 2. If you have created a solid with FACETRES at 0.5, you can update the solid to the new value by using the Shade or Hide command again.

ISOLINES Sets the number of lines per surface on solids. Values range from 0 to 2047. The default value is 4. To change the ISOLINES value, *Type:* **ISOLINES** ↵, then type the new value. Try 10. If you have created a solid with ISOLINES at 4, you can update the solid to the new value by typing or selecting **REGEN** ↵.

CREATING SOLIDS USING SOLIDS COMMANDS

Exercise 21–1: Creating the First Solid Model

Refer to Figure 21–2 for dimensions.

Step 1. Load AutoCAD. *Click:* **Create Drawings-Wizards-Quick Setup.**

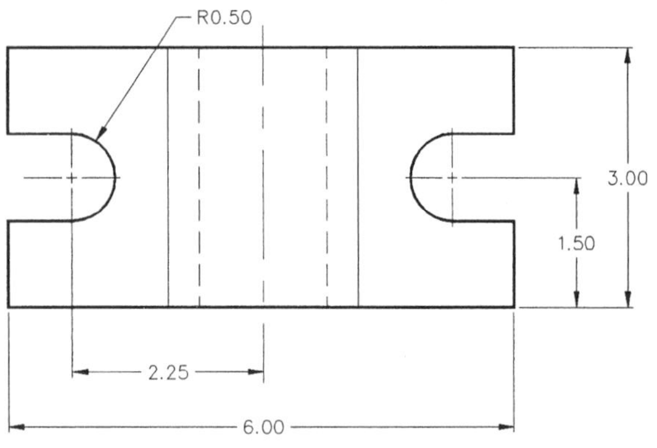

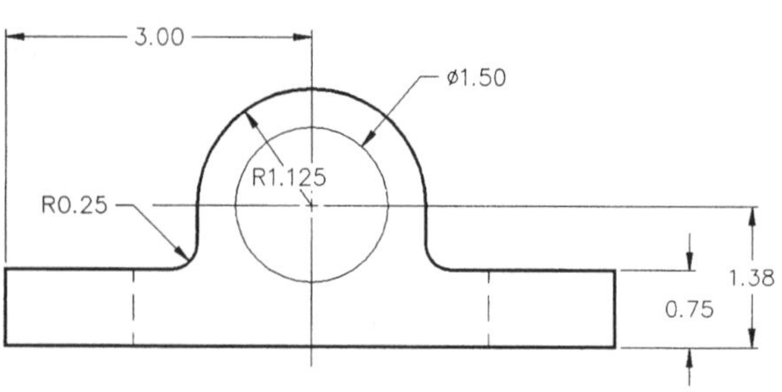

FIGURE 21–2
First Model

Step 2. Make the following settings:

Units: Decimal—2 digits to the right of the decimal point				
Area: Width: 11				
Length: 8.5				
GRID: .2				
SNAP: .1				
TEXT STYLE: Standard		**FONT: simplex.shx**	**HEIGHT: 0**	
LAYERS:	**NAME**	**Color**	**Linetype**	**Lineweight**
	M	**Magenta**	**Continuous**	**Default**
	R	**Red**	**Continuous**	**Default**
	G	**Green**	**Continuous**	**Default**
Set layer G current. Set SNAP ON.				

Help: The UCSICON arrows will not move to the new origin unless instructed to do so. To do that, *Type:* or *Select:* **UCSICON ↵**; then *Type:* **OR ↵**.

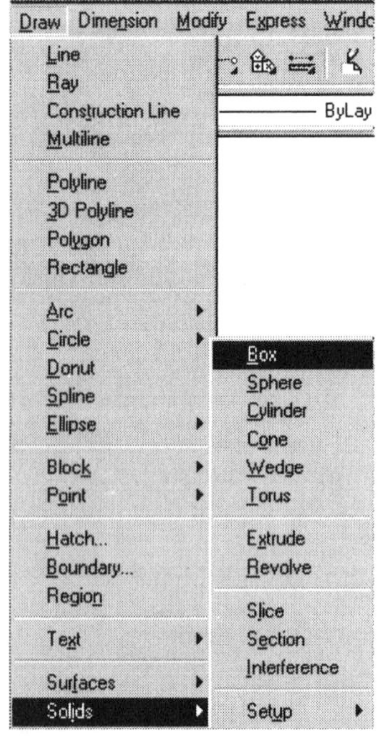

Step 3. Create the base (Figure 21–3).

Prompt	Response
Command:	**Box** (or *Type:* **BOX ↵**)
Specify corner of box or [CEnter]<0,0,0>:	*Click:* **on a point on the screen to locate the lower left corner of the box (Figure 21–3)**
Specify corner or [Cube/Length]:	*Type:* **@6,3 ↵**
Specify height:	*Type:* **.75 ↵**
Command:	**Move UCS** (or *Type:* **UCS ↵**, then **O ↵**) (Move the UCS origin to the lower left corner of the box for convenience in drawing other shapes (Figure 21–3).)
Specify new origin point or [Zdepth]<0,0,0>:	*Click:* **on the lower left corner of the box using Osnap-Endpoint**
Command:	*Type:* **VPOINT ↵**

Solids

Box

FIGURE 21–3
Move the UCS Origin

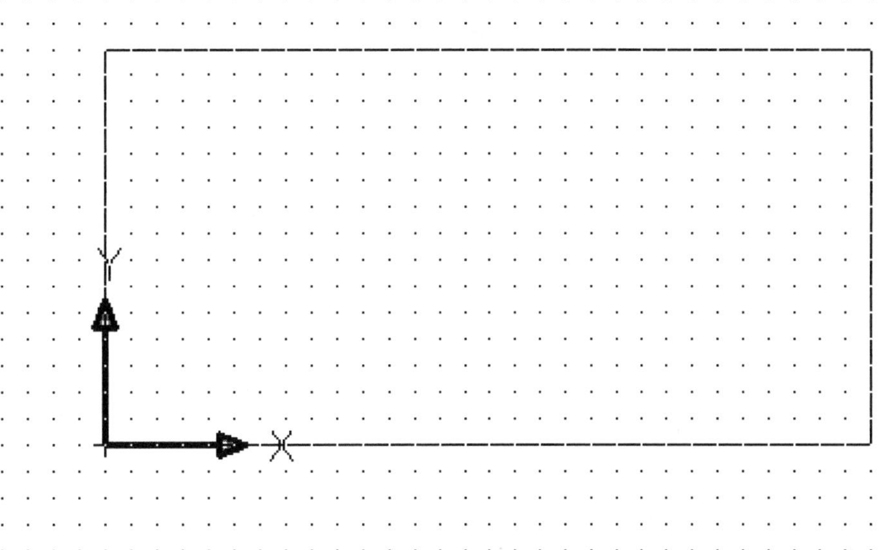

Prompt	Response
Specify a viewpoint or [Rotate]<display compass and tripod>:	*Type:* **1,−1,1** ↵ (or select your favorite viewpoint so that you can see what you are doing)
Command:	*Click:* **Polyline** (or *Type:* **PL** ↵) (Figure 21–4)
Specify start point:	*Type:* **0,1** ↵ (0 in the X direction, 1 in the Y direction (Figure 21–2))
Specify next point or [Arc/Close/Halfwidth/Length/Undo/Width]:	*Type:* **@.75,0** ↵
Specify next point or [Arc/Close/Halfwidth/Length/Undo/Width]:	*Type:* **A** ↵
Specify Endpoint of arc or [Angle/CEnter/CLose/Direction/Halfwidth/Line/Radius/Second pt/Undo/Width]:	*Type:* **@0,1** ↵

FIGURE 21–4
Construct Slots

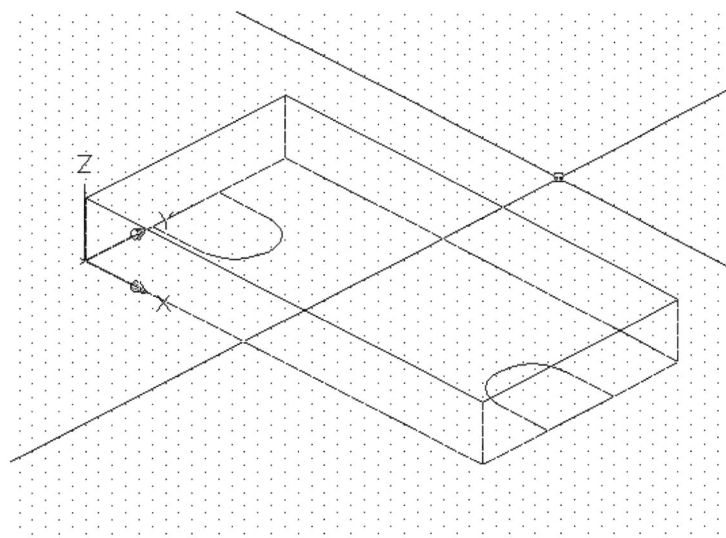

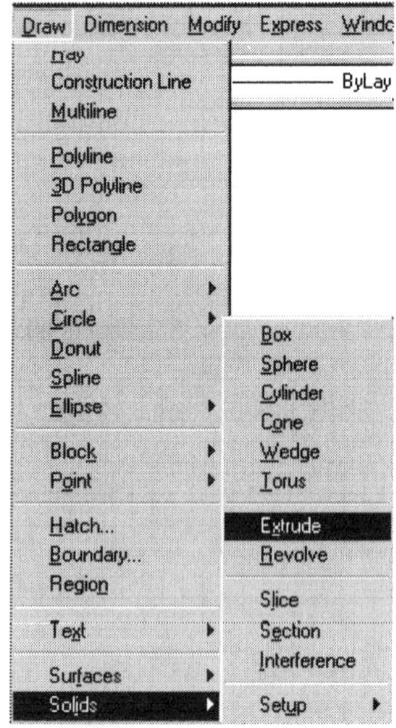

Prompt	Response
Specify Endpoint of arc or [Angle/CEnter/ CLose/Direction/Halfwidth/Line/Radius/ Second pt/Undo/Width:	*Type:* **L** ↵
Specify next point or [Arc/Close/Halfwidth Length/Undo/Width]:	*Click:* **on the left edge of the box using Osnap-Perpendicular**
Specify next point or [Arc/Close/Halfwidth Length/Undo/Width]:	*Type:* **C** ↵
Command:	*Type:* **ISOLINES** ↵
Enter new value for ISOLINES <4>:	*Type:* **10** ↵
Command:	**Extrude** (or *Type:* **EXT** ↵) (Figure 21–5)
Select objects:	*Click:* **on the Polyline you just drew.** ↵
Specify height of extrusion or [Path]:	*Type:***.75** ↵
Specify angle of taper for extrusion <0>:	↵
Command:	*Click:* **Mirror** (or *Type:* **MI** ↵)

Mirror the slot using the midpoints of the long sides of the box as the mirror line.

Step 4. Create the cylinder and the hole to be subtracted (Figure 21–6).

Prompt	Response
Command:	**UCS** (or *Type:* **UCS** ↵)

Rotate the UCS 90° about the X axis so that you may draw the cylinders, then draw the cylinders as follows:

Prompt	Response
Command:	**Cylinder** (or *Type:* **CYLINDER** ↵)

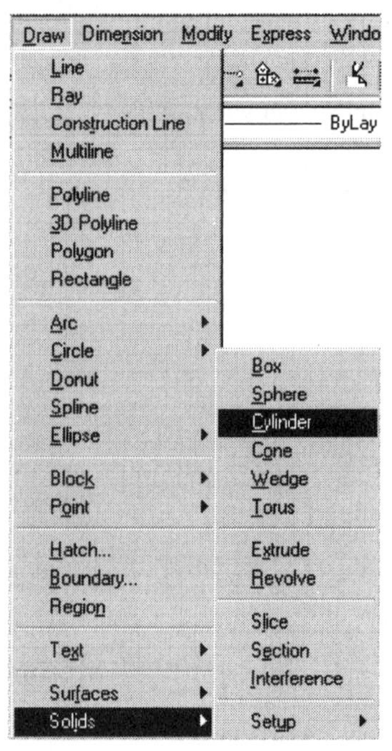

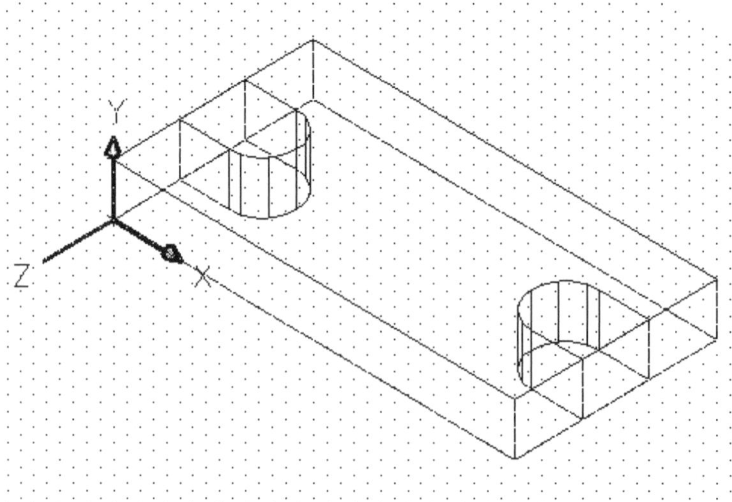

FIGURE 21–5
Extrude the polyline, Mirror It, and Rotate the UCS.

FIGURE 21–6
Construct Cylinders

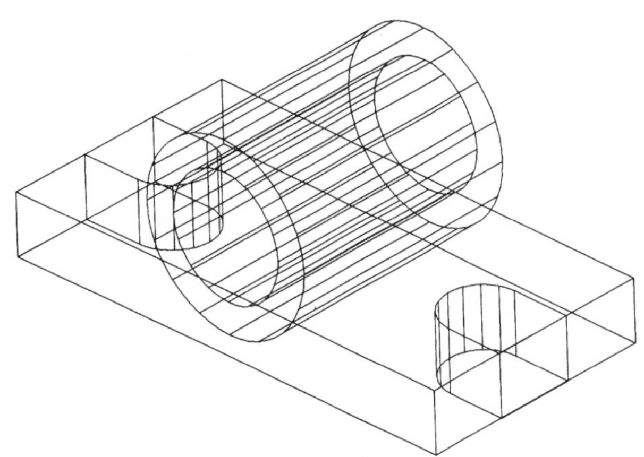

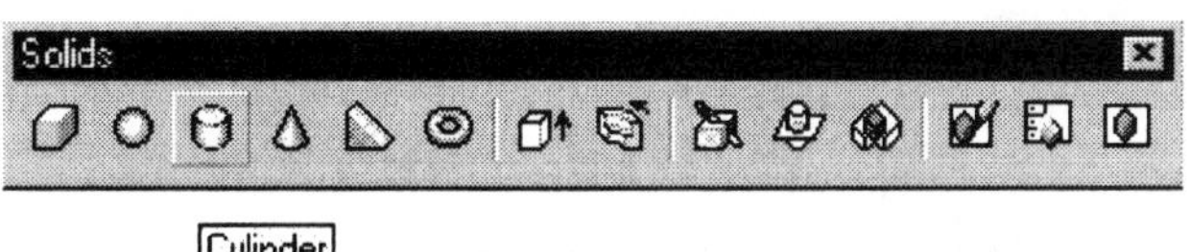

Prompt	Response
Specify center point for base of cylinder or [Elliptical]<0,0,0>:	*Type:* **3,1.38** ↵
Specify radius for base of cylinder or [Diameter]:	*Type:* **D** ↵
Specify diameter for base of cylinder:	*Type:* **1.5** ↵
Specify height of cylinder or [Center of other end]:	*Type:* **−3** ↵
Command:	↵ **(Repeat CYLINDER)**
Specify center point for base of cylinder or [Elliptical]<0,0,0>:	*Type:* **3,1.38** ↵
Specify radius for base of cylinder or [Diameter]:	*Type:* **1.125** ↵
Specify height of cylinder or [Center of other end]:	*Type:* **−3** ↵

Step 5. Combine the larger cylinder and the base into one solid (Figure 21–7).

Now let's build in a mistake so that you can learn how to correct it easily. In most cases it is better to create all solid primitives before combining them into a single solid model and

FIGURE 21–7
Incorrect Model

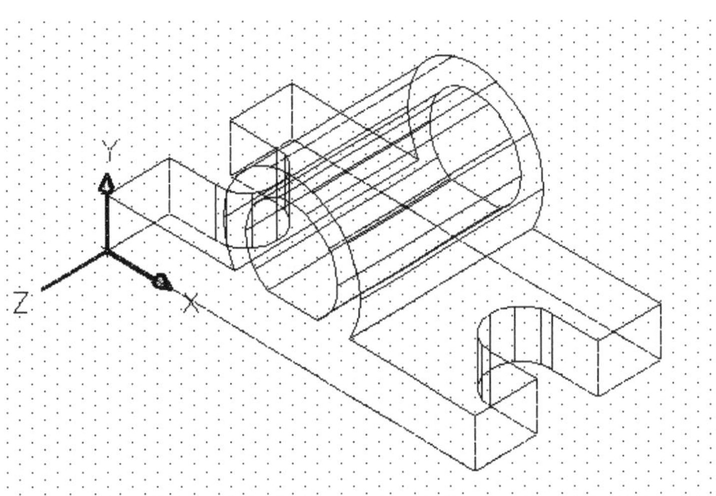

then to subtract all holes at the same time. They can be combined in stages, however, and in this case combining in stages will create a model that is incorrect. Let's do it in stages so you can see the result. Begin by subtracting holes from the base and then from the cylinder.

Prompt	Response
Command:	**Subtract** (or *Type:* **SU** ↵)
Select solids and regions to subtract from . . .	
Select objects:	*Click:* **on the box**
Select objects:	↵
Select objects and regions to subtract . . .	
Select objects:	*Click:* **on the two slots**
Select objects:	↵
Command:	↵ **(Repeat SUBTRACT)**
Select objects:	*Click:* **on the larger cylinder**
Select objects:	↵
Select objects and regions to subtract . . .	
Select objects:	*Click:* **on the smaller cylinder**
Select objects:	↵
Command:	*Click:* **Union** (or *Type:* **UNION** ↵)
Select objects:	*Click:* **on the base and the cylinder**
Select objects:	↵

The bottom of the cylindrical hole is flattened (Figure 21-7). **Instead of backing up and redoing part of the model, correct the mistake by creating the small cylinder again and subtracting it from the unified model.** You will find this technique useful when you create more complex models. The correct way to create this part is to use the Union command to make a composite solid of the base and the large cylinder before subtracting the slots and the cylindrical hole.

Step 6. Create the small cylinder again in the same location and subtract it.

Step 7. On your own:
Fill the area between cylinder and base and add fillets.

Now, a polyline must be drawn so that the area between the cylinder and the base can be filled, then fillets can be created to complete the part.

Prompt	Response
Command:	*Click:* **Polyline** (or *Type:* **PL** ↵)
Specify start point:	**D1** (Osnap-Quadrant (Figure 21–8)
Specify next point or [Arc/Close/Halfwidth/Length/Undo/Width]:	**D2** (Osnap-Perpendicular)
Specify next point or [Arc/Close/Halfwidth/Length/Undo/Width]:	**D3** (Osnap-Endpoint)
Specify next point or [Arc/Close/Halfwidth/Length/Undo/Width]:	*Type:* **C** ↵

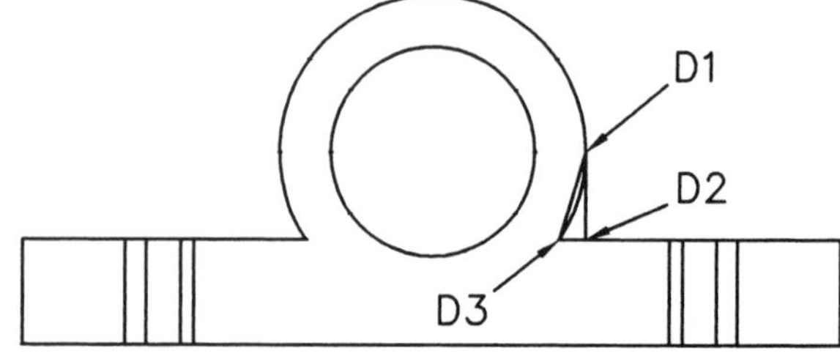

FIGURE 21–8
Fill Area Between Cylinder and Base

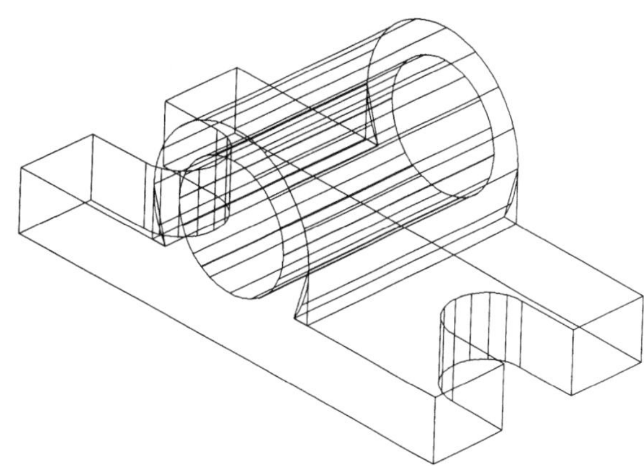

FIGURE 21–9
Extrude Polylines

Prompt	Response
Command:	**Extrude** (or *Type:* **EXT** ↵)
Select objects:	*Click:* **on the Polyline** ↵
Specify height of extrusion or [Path]:	*Type:* **−3** ↵
Specify angle of taper for extrusion:	↵

Now, Mirror the extruded polyline to the other side of the cylinder using Osnap-Midpoint to select the midpoints of the long sides of the base for the mirror line (Figure 21–9).

Before the intersections of the polylines and the base can be filleted, the polylines and the rest of the model must be unified. To do that:

Prompt	Response
Command:	*Click:* **Union** (or *Type:* **UNION** ↵)
Select objects:	*Type:* **ALL** ↵
Command:	**Fillet** (or *Type:* **F** ↵)
Select first object or [Polyline/Radius/Trim]:	**D1** (the intersection of the extruded polyline and the base of one side of the cylinder, Figure 21–10)
Enter fillet radius<0.5000>:	*Type:* **.25** ↵
Select an edge or [Chain/Radius]:	**D2**
Select an edge or [Chain/Radius]:	↵

The edges have now been filleted, as shown in Figure 21–11.

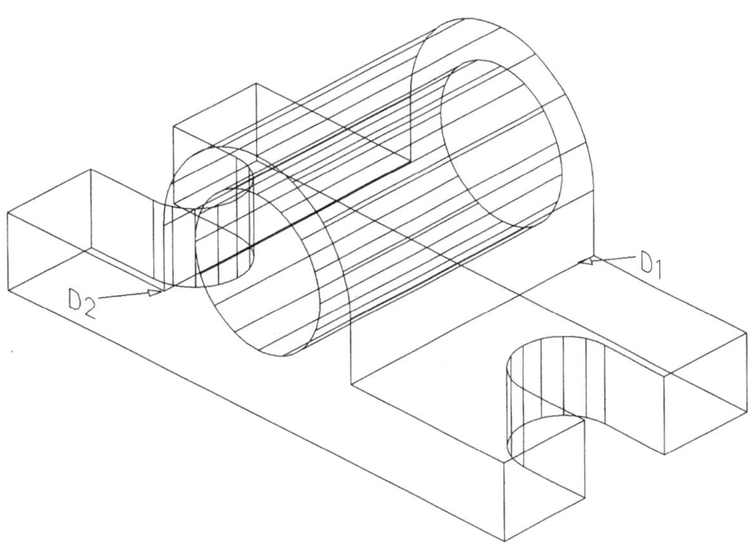

FIGURE 21–10
Add Polylines to the Model and Fillet Points

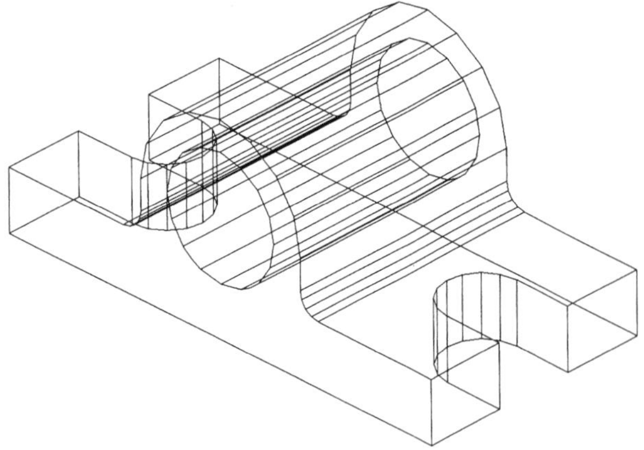

FIGURE 21–11
Fillet the Intersections

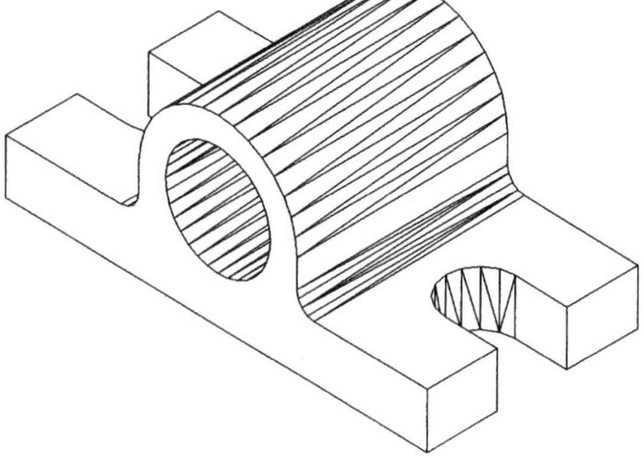

FIGURE 21–12
Hidden Lines Removed

Step 8. Remove hidden lines.

Prompt	Response
Command:	*Click:* **Hide** (or *Type:* **HI** ↵)

The model appears with hidden lines removed (Figure 21–12). The model may now be rendered with Shade, 3D Orbit, or 3D Studio Max.

Step 9. *Click:* **Layout2, put your name in the lower right corner, use MVIEW-Hideplot to hide lines, and print the drawing on an 11″ × 8½″ sheet.**

Step 10. Save the model in two places as EX21-1(your initials) and exit AutoCAD.

Now let's create another model that will give you the opportunity to use other modeling commands and extract some 2-D drawings from it.

Exercise 21–2: Creating the Second Model

Use dimensions from Figure 21–13.

FIGURE 21–13
Second Model Dimensions

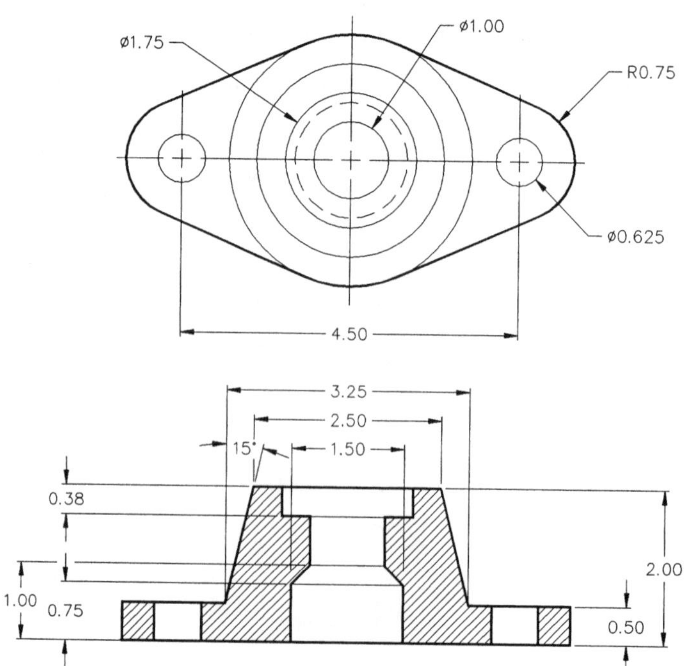

FIGURE 21–14
Create Cylinders and Draw a Construction Line

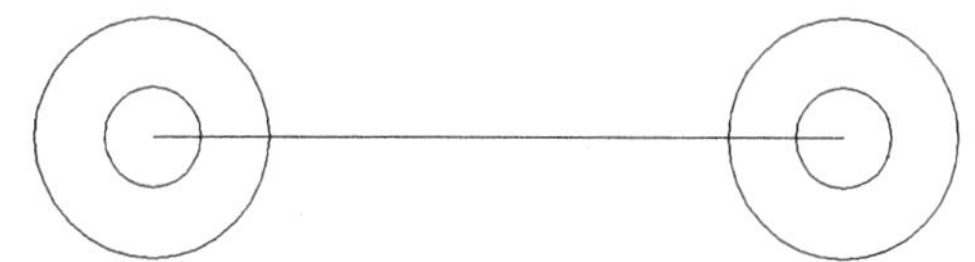

Step 1. Load AutoCAD. *Click:* **Create Drawings-Wizards-Quick Setup.**

Step 2. Make the following settings:

Units: Decimal—2 digits to the right of the decimal point

Area: Width: 11
Length: 8.5

ISOLINES: 20

FACETRES: 2

GRID: .2

SNAP: .1

TEXT STYLE: Standard FONT: simplex.shx HEIGHT: 0

LAYERS: NAME	Color	Linetype	Lineweight
R	Red	Continuous	Default
M	Magenta	Continuous	Default
G	Green	Continuous	Default

Set layer G as the current layer. Set SNAP ON.

Step 3. Draw cylinders for the two end radii (.75 radius) and the holes (.625 diameter) in them (Figure 21–14) using Cylinder with a height of .5.

Draw a construction line between the two cylinder centers to position a UCS for creating a sectional view.

Step 4. Draw the center cylinder (3.25 diameter) for the base only (Figure 21–15) using Cylinder with a height of .5.

Step 5. Draw lines to fill an area around the base circles using Osnap-Quadrant, Nearest, and Tangent (Figure 21–16). (You may use the Polyline command instead and skip the Edit Polyline-Join step.)

Note: You may find that the Mirror command creates a larger drawing file than drawing the Polyline area four times. If file size is a consideration, you may need to check this.

If Osnap-Tangent does not work, use Nearest and then use the Change command and select Tangent for the change point.) Use Edit Polyline-Join to join all three lines into a single polyline.

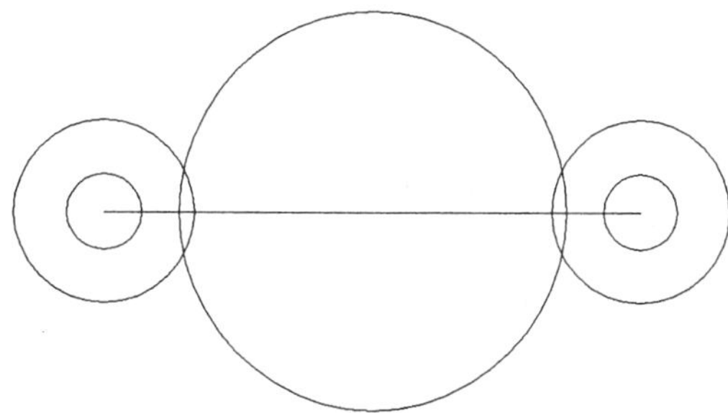

FIGURE 21–15
Create the Center Cylinder for the Base Only

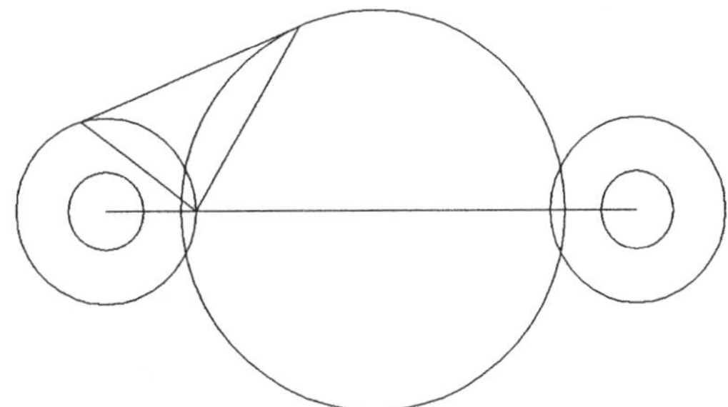

FIGURE 21–16
Fill Areas Using Line and Edit Polyline-Join to Form a Polyline

FIGURE 21–17
Mirror Polylines Twice

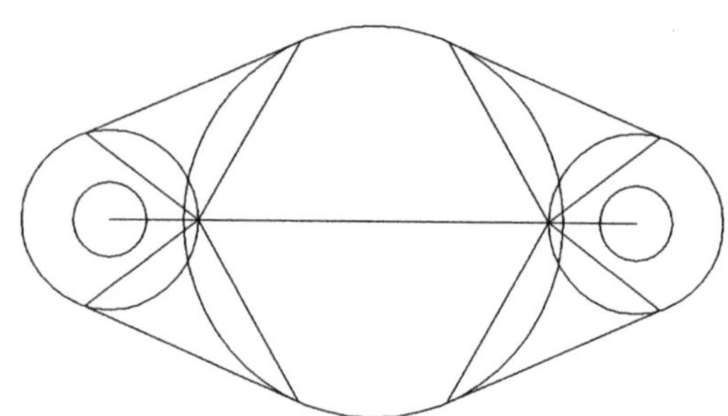

FIGURE 21–18
Draw a Circle and Extrude It

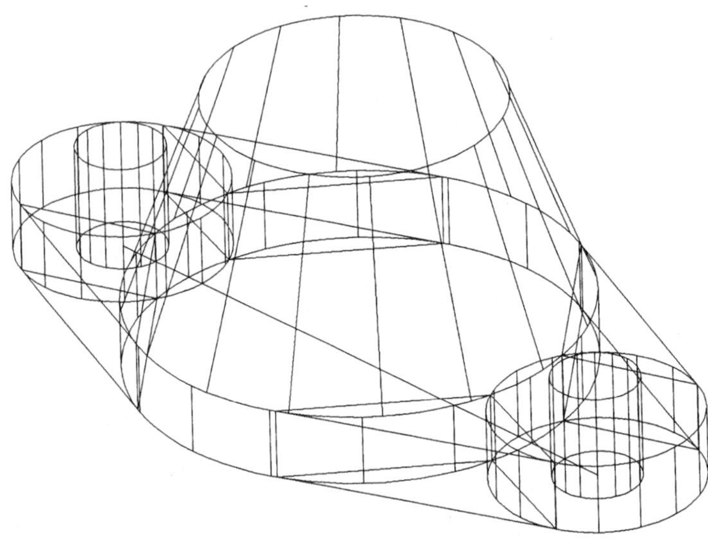

Step 6. Mirror the Polylines twice to fill in all four areas (Figure 21–17) and extrude all fill areas .5 using Extrude.

Step 7. Draw a circle on top of the center cylinder and extrude it (Figure 21–18).

Select a viewpoint similar to Figure 21–18, then follow these steps:

Prompt	Response
Command:	**Circle-Center, Diameter**
Specify center point for circle or [3P/2P Ttr (tan tan radius)]:	*Click:* **on the top edge of the big cylinder using Osnap-Center**
Specify diameter of circle:	*Type:* **3.25** ↵
Command:	**Extrude** (or *Type:* **EXT** ↵)
Select objects:	*Click:* **on the circle just drawn** ↵
Specify height of extrusion or [Path]:	*Type:* **1.5** ↵
Specify angle of taper for extrusion <0>:	*Type:* **15** ↵

Step 8. Move the UCS origin to the midpoint of the construction line and rotate it 90° around the X axis (Figure 21–19).

Step 9. Draw the shape of the center hole (Figure 21–20).

Type PLAN ↵ to obtain the flat view as shown, then draw a polyline as shown. You can use Osnap-Center to start the line on the top cylinder face and Center to end it on the bottom cylinder face even if you see these faces only as edges. Use the dimensions from Figure 21–20 and a combination of direct distance entry and *relative* coordinates to draw this shape on your own.

FIGURE 21–19
Move UCS to the Midpoint of the Construction Line and Rotate It 90°

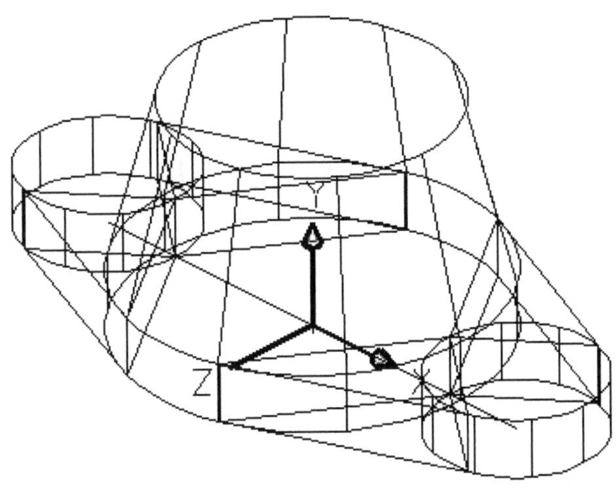

FIGURE 21–20
Draw the Shape of the Center Hole

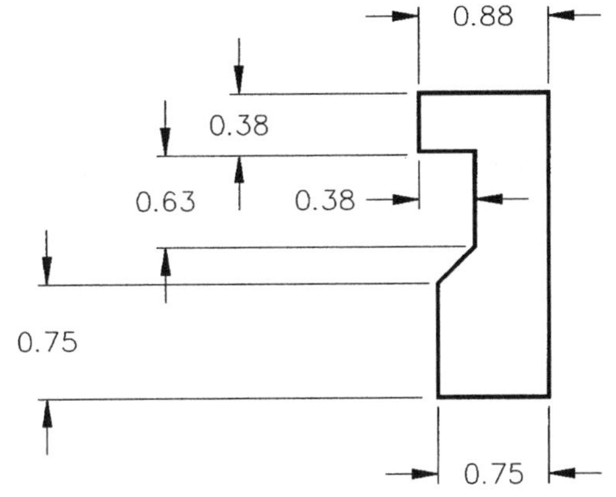

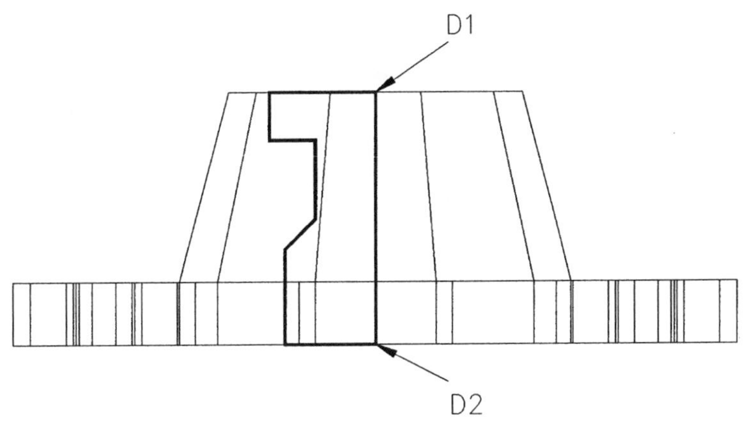

FIGURE 21–21
Create the Center Hole

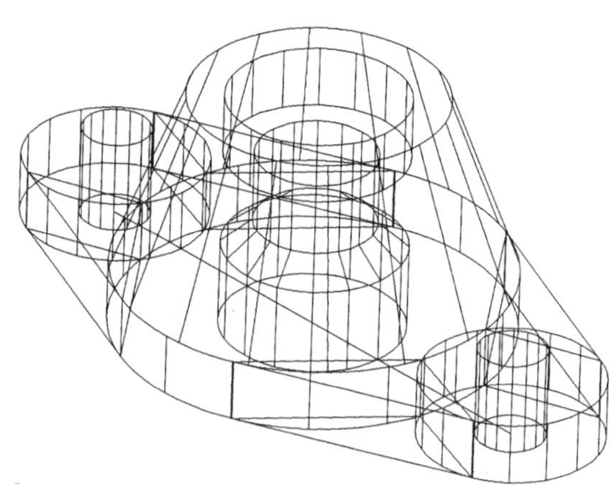

Step 10. Use Revolve to create the interior solid (Figure 21–21).

Note: Be sure to include the top and bottom horizontal lines of the shape so that the complete solid is formed during Revolve. This is a little different from the method used in surface modeling using Revsurf. Remember that you are creating a solid shape that will be subtracted from a larger one.

Select a VPOINT that gives you a view similar to Figure 21–21, then follow these steps:

Prompt	Response
Command:	*Click:* **Revolve** (or *Type:* **REV** ↵)
Select objects:	*Click:* **on the polyline just drawn**
Select objects:	↵
Specify start point for axis of revolution or define axis by [Object/X (axis)/Y (axis)]:	**D1** (the beginning of the polyline using Osnap-Endpoint (Figure 21–20))
Specify endpoint of axis:	**D2** (the end of the polyline using Osnap-Endpoint (Figure 21–20))
Specify angle of revolution <360>:	↵

Step 11. Unify the primitives into a solid and subtract the holes.

Prompt	Response
Command:	**Union** (or *Type:* **UNION** ↵)

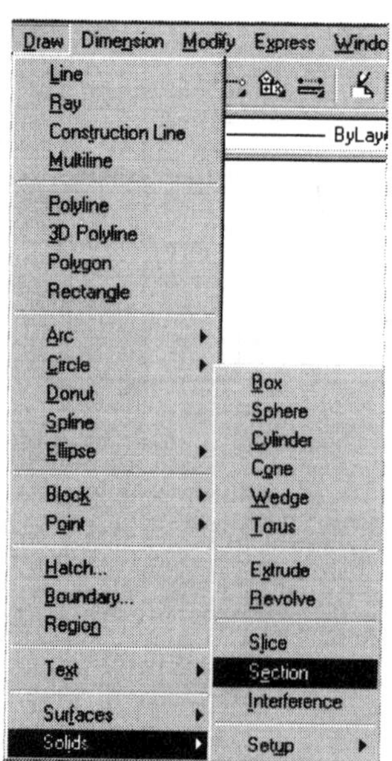

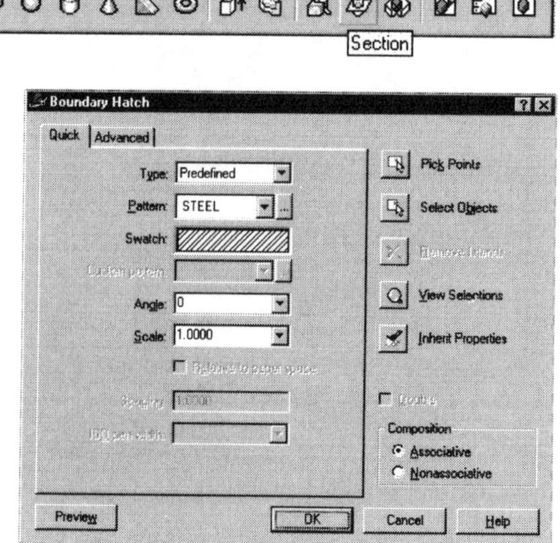

Prompt	Response
Select objects:	*Click:* **on all parts of the model except the holes** ↵
Select objects:	↵
Command:	**Subtract** (or *Type:* **SU** ↵)
Select solids and regions to subtract from . . .	
Select objects:	*Click:* **on the model** ↵
Select solids and regions to subtract:	
Select objects:	*Click:* **on the three holes** ↵

Step 12. Create a sectional view using Section (Figure 21–22).

Prompt	Response
Command:	**Section**
Select objects:	*Click:* **on the model** ↵
Specify first point on section plane by [Object/Zaxis/View/XY/YZ/ZX/3 points] <3 points>:	*Type:* **XY** ↵
Specify a point on the XY plane <0,0,0>:	↵
Command:	*Click:* **Hatch** (or *Type:* **H** ↵)
The Boundary Hatch dialog box appears:	*Click:* **STEEL** (in the Pattern: button)
	Click: **Select Objects** <
Select objects:	*Click:* **on any point on the section view just created**
Select objects:	↵
The Boundary Hatch dialog box appears:	*Click:* **OK**

Step 13. Remove the sectional view from the model (Figure 21–23).

Prompt	Response
Command:	**Move** (or *Type:* **M** ↵)
Select objects:	*Click:* **on the section and its hatch pattern**

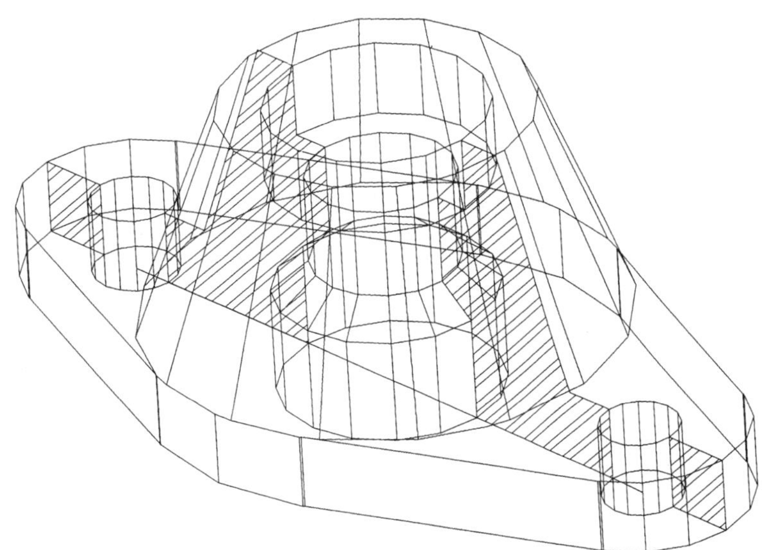

FIGURE 21–22
Create a Sectional Drawing

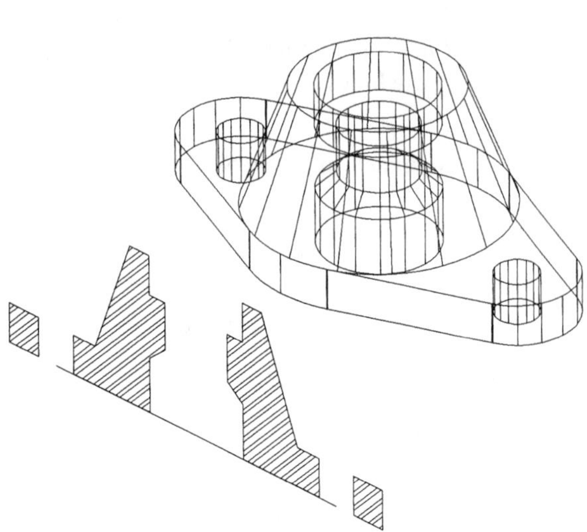

FIGURE 21–23
Remove Sectional View

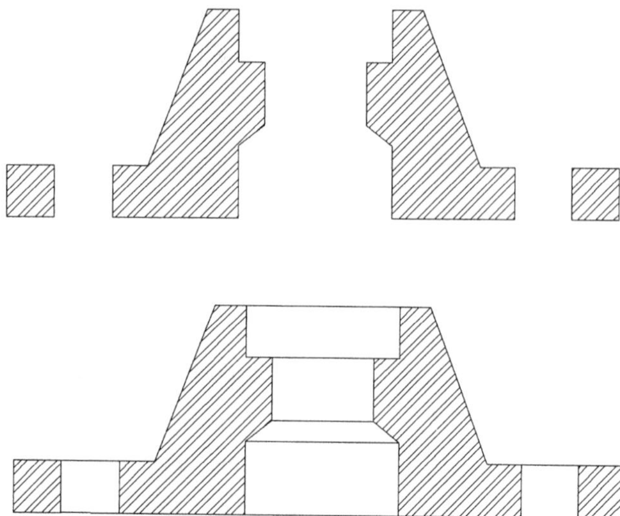

FIGURE 21–24
Draw Lines to Complete the Sectional View

Tip: After you have selected Move, digitize a window to include the entire model. Then select Remove and digitize any point on the model to remove the model from the selection set. Only the section is thereby selected.

Prompt	Response
Select objects:	↵
Specify base point or displacement:	*Click:* **on a point on the surface**
Specify second point of displacement or <use first point as displacement>:	*Click:* **on a point far enough from the model so that it can be Wblocked easily**

Step 14. Complete a 2-D sectional drawing and Wblock it (Figure 21–24).

Prompt	Response
Command:	*Click:* **Plan** (or *Type:* **PLAN** ↵)

The sectional view may now be modified to include lines, as shown. After the view is complete, Wblock the drawing with the name EX21-2SEC(your initials).

Step 15. Return the model to a 3-D viewpoint and perform a Hide on the model (Figure 21–25).

FIGURE 21–25
The Complete Model with Hidden Lines Removed

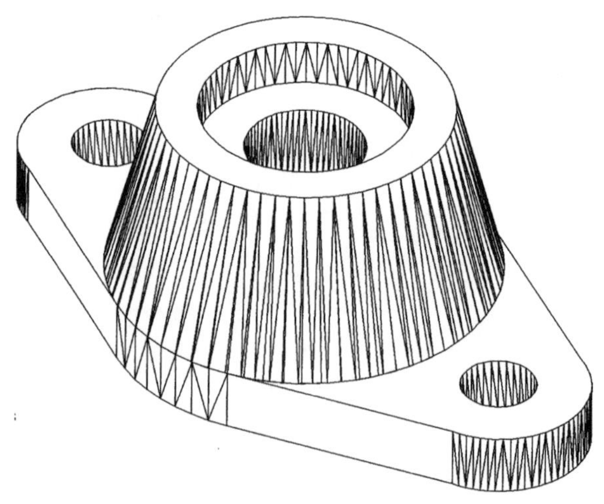

Note: To use Purge *Type:* **PURGE ↵** and then type the first letter of the unused objects you want to remove from the drawing.

Step 16. The model and the accompanying section drawing are now complete. Use Purge (ALL) to reduce the size of the model drawing, then print each drawing on an 11″ × 8½″ sheet.

Step 17. Save the model drawing in two places with the name EX21-2(your initials) and exit AutoCAD.

Exercise 21–3: Creating the Third Model

Your final model will appear as shown in Figure 21–26.

Step 1. Load AutoCAD. *Click:* **Create Drawings-Wizards-Quick Setup.**

Step 2. Make the following settings:

Units: Decimal—2 digits to the right of the decimal point

Area: Width: 50
Length: 50

ISOLINES: 20

FACETRES: 2

GRID: .5

SNAP: .1

TEXT STYLE: Standard   FONT: simplex.shx   HEIGHT: 0

LAYERS: NAME	Color	Linetype	Lineweight
R	Red	Continuous	Default
M	Magenta	Continuous	Default
G	Green	Continuous	Default

Set layer G as the current layer. Set SNAP ON.

Step 3. Split the screen into two vertical viewports, select a 3-D viewpoint in the right viewport, and Zoom-All in both viewports.

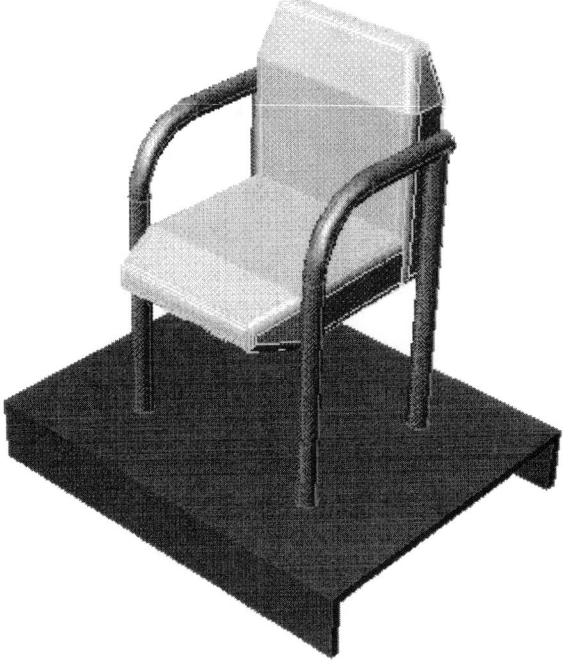

FIGURE 21–26
Exercise 21-3 Complete (on Screen)

Prompt	Response
Command: _	**Viewports-2 Viewports**
Enter a configuration option [Horizontal/Vertical]<Vertical>:	↵
Regenerating model.	
Command:	*Click:* **the right viewport**
Command:	*Type:* **VP** ↵
The Viewpoint Presets dialog box appears:	*Click:* **315 in the left chart, 30 in the right chart**
Command:	*Type:* **Z** ↵, then **A** ↵ *Click:* **the left viewport**
Command:	*Type:* **Z** ↵, then **A** ↵

Step 4. Define a UCS that is parallel to the side of the chair legs and arms.

Prompt	Response
Command: _	*Type:* **UCS** ↵
Enter an option [New/Move/ orthoGraphic/Prev/Restore/Save/ Del/Apply/?/World]<World>:	*Type:* **X** ↵
Specify rotation angle about X axis <90>:	↵
Command:	↵ **(Repeat UCS)**
Enter an option [New/Move/ orthoGraphic/Prev/Restore/Save/ Del/Apply/?/World]<World>:	*Type:* **Y** ↵
Specify rotation angle about Y axis <90>:	↵

Step 5. Draw a path for the chair arm and front leg (two lines and a fillet and join them together using Pedit), draw a circle to form the metal tube, rotate the circle, and extrude it along the path.

Prompt	Response
Command:	*Type:* **L** ↵
Specify first point:	*Type:* **8,12** ↵
Specify next point or [Undo]:	*Type:* **@0,27** ↵
Specify next point or [Undo]:	*Type:* **@16.5,0** ↵
Specify next point or [Close/Undo]:	↵
Command:	*Type:* **F** ↵
Select first object or [Polyline/Radius/Trim]:	*Type:* **R** ↵
Specify fillet radius <0.5000>:	*Type:* **5** ↵
Select first object or [Polyline/Radius/Trim]:	*Click:* **one of the lines**
Select second object:	*Click:* **the other line**
Command:	*Type:* **PE** ↵
Select polyline:	*Click:* **one of the lines** (Figure 21–27)
Object selected is not a polyline Do you want to turn it into one?<Y>	↵
Enter an option [Close/Join/ Width/Edit vertex/Fit/Spline/ Decurve/Ltype gen/Undo]:	*Type:* **J** ↵
Select objects:	*Type:* **ALL** ↵
Select objects:	↵

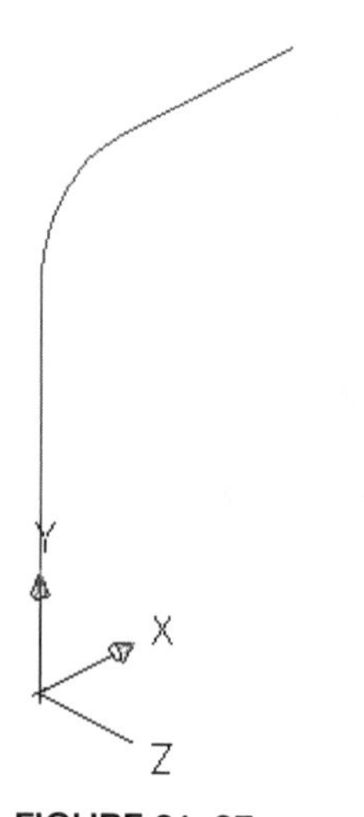

FIGURE 21–27
Draw a Path to Extrude a Circle

Prompt	Response
2 segments added to polyline	
Enter an option [Close/Join/ Width/Edit vertex/Fit/Spline/ Decurve/Ltype gen/Undo]:	↵
Command:	*Type:* **C ↵**
CIRCLE Specify center point for circle or [3P/2P/Ttr (tan tan radius)]:	*Type:* **END ↵**
of	*Click:* **the lower end of the vertical line**
Specify radius of circle or [Diameter]:	*Type:* **1 ↵**
Command:	**Rotate 3D**
Select objects:	*Click:* **the circle**
Select objects:	↵
Specify first point on axis or define axis by [Object/Last/ View/Xaxis/Yaxis/Zaxis/2points]:	*Type:* **X ↵**
Specify a point on the X axis <0,0,0>:	*Type:* **END ↵**
of	*Click:* **the lower end of the vertical line**
Specify rotation angle or [Reference]:	*Type:* **90 ↵**
Command:	*Type:* **EXT ↵**
Select objects:	*Click:* **the circle ↵**
Specify height of extrusion or [Path]:	*Type:* **P ↵**
Select extrusion path:	*Click:* **the polyline**

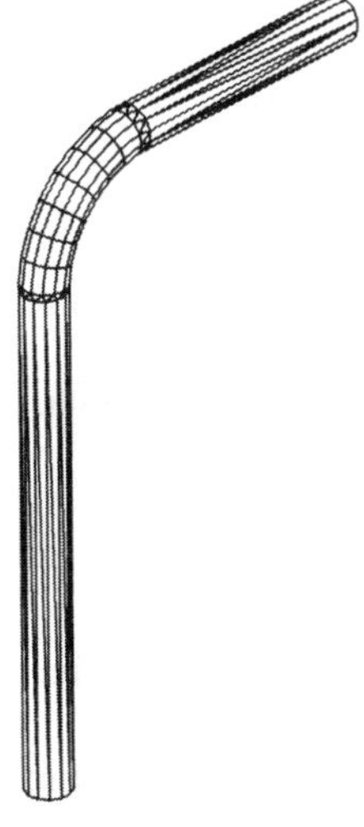

FIGURE 21–28
Chair Leg-Arm Extrusion Complete

The right viewport should appear as shown in Figure 21–28.

Step 6. Set a new UCS that is parallel to the world UCS (the cushion of the chair) that has an origin at the bottom of the chair leg.

Prompt	Response
Command: _	*Type:* **UCS ↵**
Enter an option [New/Move/ orthoGraphic/Prev/Restore/Save/ Del/Apply/?/World]<World>:	↵
Command:_	**↵ (repeat UCS)**
Enter an option [New/Move/ orthoGraphic/Prev/Restore/Save/ Del/Apply/?/World]<World>:	*Type:* **M ↵**
Specify new origin point or [Zdepth]<0,0,0>:	*Type:* **CEN ↵**
of	*Click:* **the bottom of the left chair leg** (Figure 21–29)

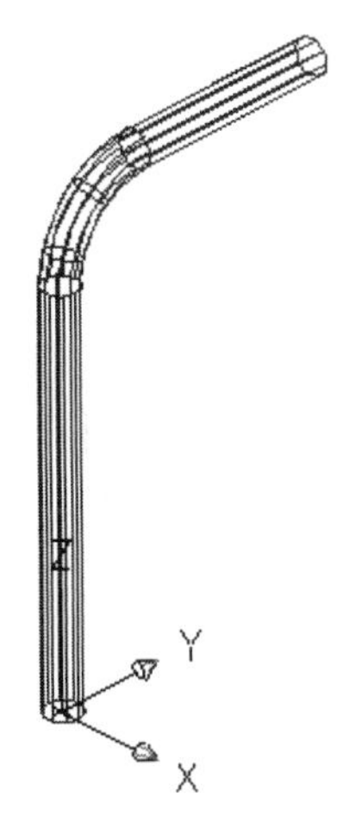

FIGURE 21–29
Move the UCS

Step 7. Set layer M current. Draw a box for the chair cushion and extrude and taper the front of it.

On your own: Set layer M current.

Prompt	Response
Command:	**Box (or *Type:* BOX ↵)**
Specify corner of box or [CEnter] <0,0,0>:	*Type:* **1,13,14 ↵**
Specify corner or [Cube/Length]:	*Type:* **@18,−13**
Specify height:	*Type:* **5 ↵**

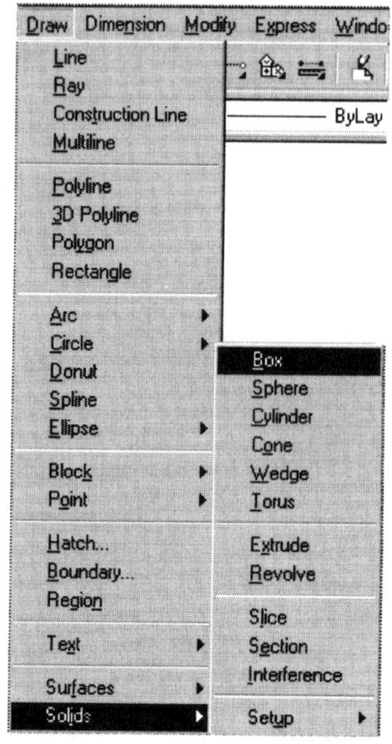

Command:	*Type:* **SOLIDEDIT ↵**
Enter a solids editing option [Face/Edge/Body/Undo/eXit] <eXit>:	*Type:* **F ↵** (for face or surface)
Enter a face editing option [Extrude/Move/Rotate/Offset/Taper/Delete/Copy/coLor/Undo/eXit] <eXit>:_	*Type:* **E ↵**
Select faces or [Undo/Remove]:	*Click:* **D1**, Figure 21–30
Select faces or [Undo/Remove/ALL]:	*Type:* **R ↵** (to remove any surfaces that you do not want to extrude. You will probably have one that needs to be removed.)
Remove faces or [Undo/Add/ALL]:	*Click:* **any extra faces so the model appears as shown in Figure 21–31**
Remove faces or [Undo/Add/ALL]:	↵
Specify height of extrusion or [Path]:	*Type:* **5 ↵**
Specify angle of taper for extrusion <0>:	*Type:* **15 ↵** ↵ ↵

The model appears as shown in Figure 21–32.

Step 8. Draw a box for the back of the chair.

Prompt	Response
Command:	**Box (or** *Type:* **BOX ↵)**
Specify corner of box or [CEnter] <0,0,0>:	*Type:* **END ↵** (or select Osnap-endpoint)
of	*Click:* **D1**, Figure 21–32
Specify corner or [Cube/Length]:	**@20,5 ↵**
Specify height:	*Type:* **16 ↵**

Step 9. Oops, the back is too long. Correct it by moving the right surface of the box 2″ to the left, then Extrude the top face of the back 5″ with a 15° taper as shown in Figure 21–33 and use the Fillet command to round all the box edges, Figure 21–34.

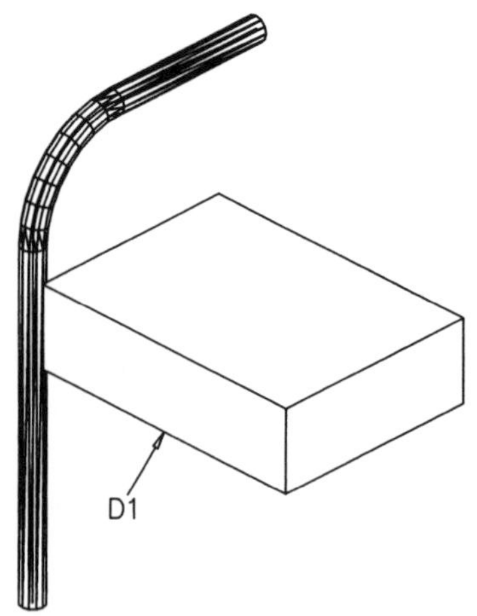

FIGURE 21–30
Click the Face to Extrude

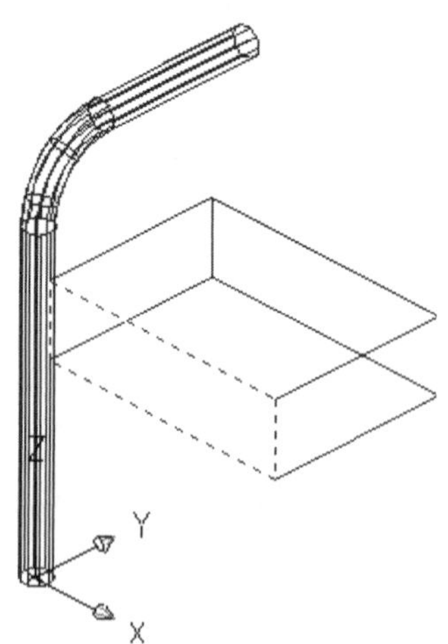

FIGURE 21–31
Select Front Face to Extrude

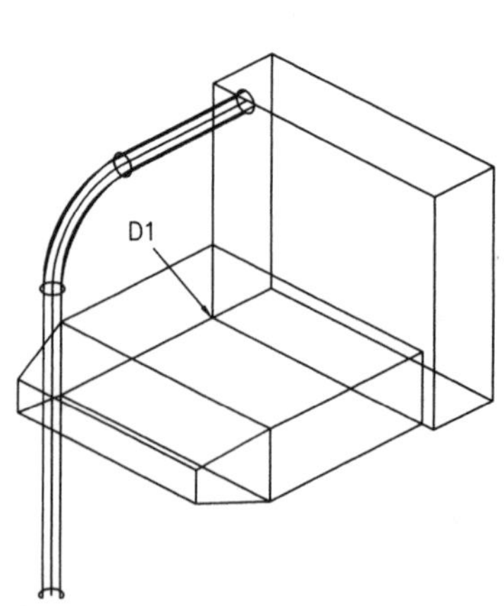

FIGURE 21–32
Draw the Box for the Back of the Chair

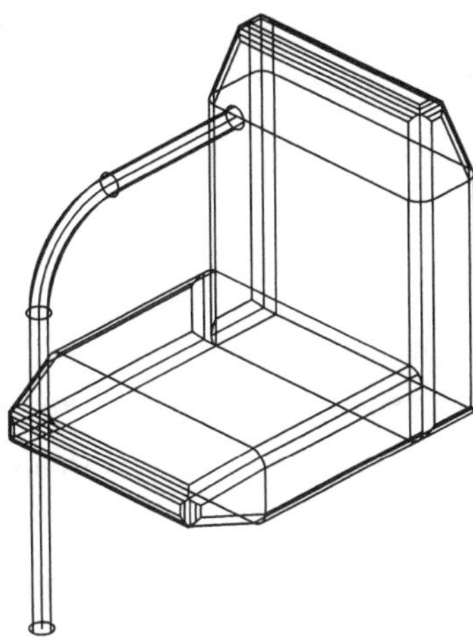

FIGURE 21–33
Correct the Back, Extrude Its Top Surface, and Fillet All Sharp Edges 1″.

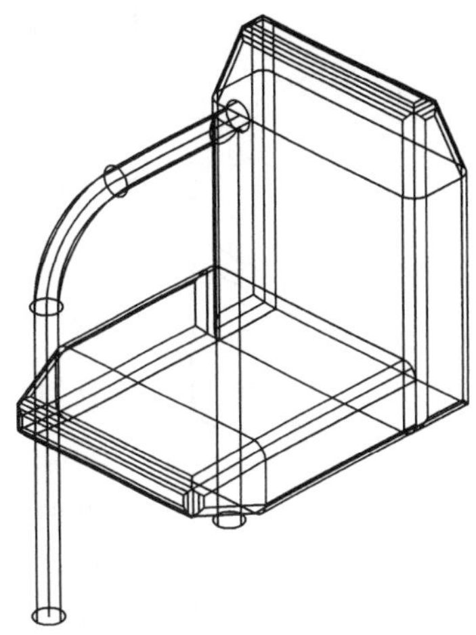

FIGURE 21–34
Draw a Circle for the Back Leg, Extrude It, and Union It With the Back Leg

On your own:

1. **Use the Move Faces option of the Solids Editing (SOLIDEDIT) command to move the right side of the back of the chair 2″ to the left.** Be sure that only the right side of the box is selected. **Select any point as a base point,** then *Type:* **@2<180** ↵ as the second point of displacement. You can skip several prompts by using either the Solids Editing toolbar or Solids Editing-Move Faces from the Modify menu on the menu bar. Typing the command as demonstrated in step 7 shows you the complete structure of the SOLIDEDIT command.
2. **Use the Extrude Faces option of the Solids Editing (SOLIDEDIT) command to extrude the top of the chair back 5″ with a 15° taper.** You can skip several prompts by using either the Solids Editing toolbar or Solids Editing-Extrude Faces from the Modify menu on the menu bar.
3. **Use the Fillet command to round all sharp edges of the chair cushion and back.** *Type:* **F** ↵ for fillet, then *Type:* **R** ↵ for radius, then *Type:* **1** ↵ to set the radius. *Press:* ↵ to repeat FILLET, then select edges when you get the prompt: "Select an edge or [Chain/Radius]:". **Pick the edges of the right side of the cushion, for example, then** *Press:* ↵. If you try to select all edges at the same time, you will get an error message.

Step 10. Set layer G current. Draw a circle for one of the back legs, extrude it, and combine front and back legs into a single object using the Union command (Figure 21–34).

Prompt	Response
Command:	*Type:* **C** ↵
Specify center point for circle or [3P/2P/Ttr (tan tan radius)]:	*Type:* **0,15.5** ↵ (This makes the center point of the circle 15.5″ in the Y direction from the UCS origin.)
Specify radius of circle or [Diameter]:	*Type:* **1** ↵
Command:	*Type:* **EXT** ↵
Select objects:	*Click:* **the circle you just drew**
Select objects:	
Specify height of extrusion or [Path]:	*Type:* **27** ↵ (The back leg is 27″ high.)

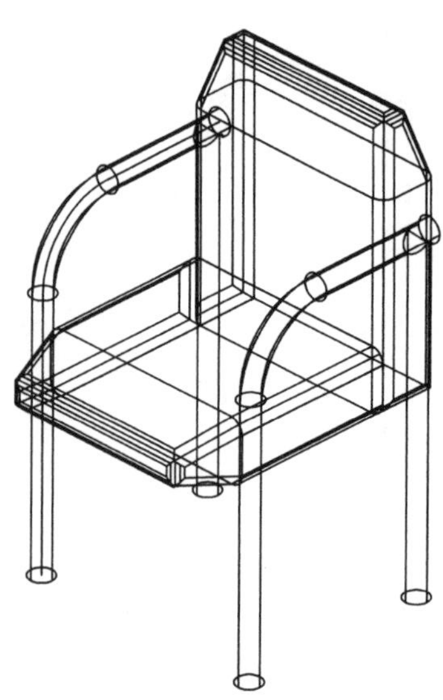

FIGURE 21–35
Copy the Leg Assembly to the Right Side of the Chair

Prompt	Response
Specify angle of taper for estrusion <0>:	↵
Command	**Union** (or *Type:* **UNION** ↵)
Select objects:	*Click:* **the chair front leg and the back leg.** (This makes the two pieces into a single piece.)
Select objects:	↵

Step 11. Copy the leg assembly to the right side of the chair (Figure 21–35).

Prompt	Response
Command:	*Type:* **CP** ↵
Select objects:	*Click:* **the chair leg assembly**
Select objects:	↵
Specify base point or displacement, or [Multiple]:	*Click:* **any point**
Specify second point of displacement, or <use first point as displacement>:	*Type:* **@20<0** ↵

Step 12. Draw a box and make a shell out of it.

Prompt	Response
Command:	*Type:* **BOX** ↵
Specify corner of box or [CEnter] <0,0,0>:	*Type:* **−10,−8,−6** ↵ (Notice that these are absolute coordinates based on the UCS located on the bottom of the front left leg.)
Specify corner or [Cube/Length]:	*Type:* **30,23.5,0** ↵ (absolute coordinates again)
Command:	**Solids Editing-Shell** (from the Modify menu or toolbar)
Select a 3D solid:	*Click:* **the box you just drew**
Remove faces or [Undo/Add/ALL]:	*Click:* **D1 and D2** (Figure 21–36)

FIGURE 21–36
Draw a Box and Make a Shell of It

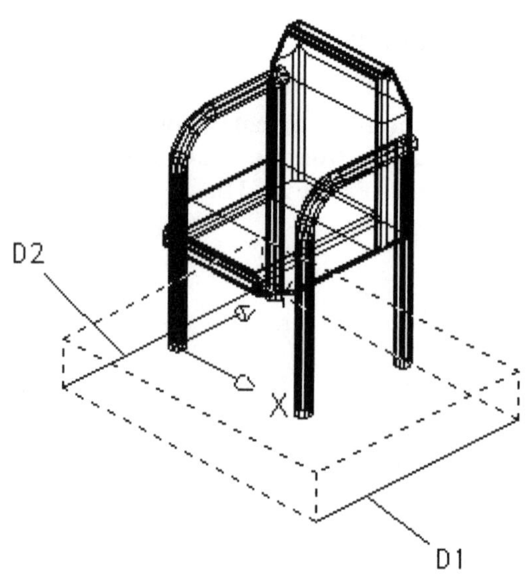

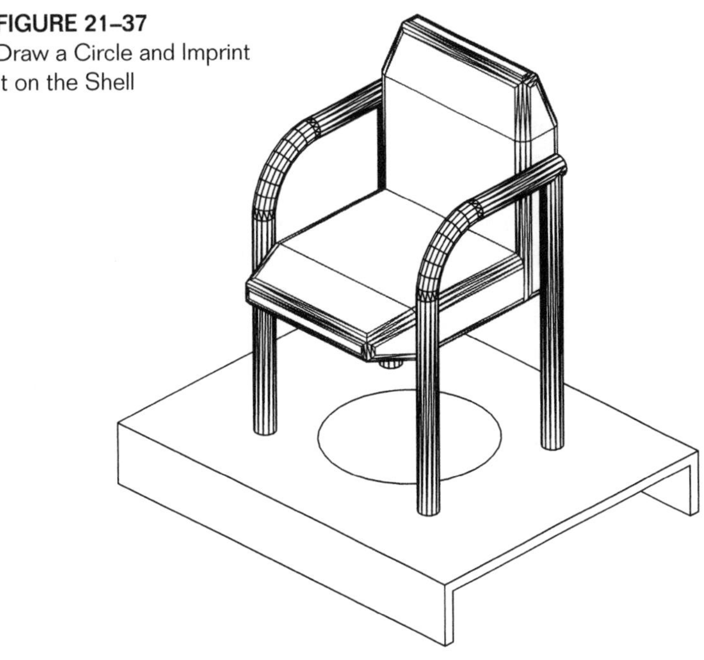

FIGURE 21–37
Draw a Circle and Imprint It on the Shell

Prompt	Response
Remove faces or [Undo/Add/ALL]:	↵
Enter the shell offset distance:	*Type:* **1** ↵
[Imprint/seParate solids/Shell/cLean/ Check/Undo/eXit] <eXit>:	↵

Step 13. Draw a circle and imprint it on the shell (Figure 21–37).

Prompt	Response
Command:	*Type:* **C** ↵
Specify center point for circle or [3P/2P/Ttr (tan tan radius)]:	*Type:* **10,7.75** ↵
Specify radius of circle or [Diameter]<0′-1″>:	*Type:* **9** ↵
Command:	**Solids Editing-Imprint**
Select a 3D solid:	*Click:* **the shell under the chair**
Select an object to imprint:	*Click:* **the circle you just drew**
Delete the source object <N>:	*Type:* **Y** ↵
Select an object to imprint:	↵
Enter a solids editing option [Imprint/seParate solids/Shell/cLean/Check/Undo/eXit]<eXit>:	↵
Enter a body editing option [Face/Edge/ Body/Undo/eXit]<eXit>:	↵

Step 14. On your own:

Use 3D Orbit to obtain a view similar to Figure 21–26. Use Perspective Projection, Gouraud shaded.

Step 15. *Click:* **Layout1, put your name in the lower right corner in the simplex font, .25 high. Use Mview-Hideplot to hide lines, and print the drawing on an 11″ × 8.5″ sheet.**

Step 16. Save your drawing in two places and exit AutoCAD.

Now let's look at another means of creating 2-D and 3-D models, Region Modeling.

REGION MODELING

The purpose of Region Modeling is to create two-dimensional areas that can easily be analyzed and that can be used in creating solid models. *Regions* are 2-D areas that can contain holes. After these areas have been constructed, you can use the Area command to calculate their areas by subtracting the inner loops from the outer loops.

You can create solids from regions and vice versa. The cross section of the solid you just made in Exercise 21-2, for example, is a 2-D region. A 2-D region can be extruded or revolved to create complex solid models. Let's begin the exercise on Region Modeling by constructing the outline of an external rachet. The shape could just as easily be the elevation of a building or any other flat plane containing one or more holes.

CREATING SOLIDS FROM REGIONS

Exercise 21–4: Creating a Solid Model from a 2-D Region

Step 1. Load AutoCAD. *Click:* **Create Drawings-Wizards-Quick Setup.**

Step 2. Make the following settings:

Units: Decimal—2 digits to the right of the decimal point
Area: Width: 11
Length: 8.5
ISOLINES: 20
FACETRES: 2
GRID: .2
SNAP: .1
TEXT STYLE: Standard FONT: simplex.shx HEIGHT: 0

LAYERS: NAME	Color	Linetype	Lineweight
R	Red	Continuous	Default
M	Magenta	Continuous	Default
G	Green	Continuous	Default

Set layer G as the current layer. Set SNAP ON.

Step 3. Draw Figure 21–38 to create a shape for Exercise 21–4.

Prompt	Response
Command:	*Click:* **Line** (or *Type:* **L** ↵)
Specify first point:	*Type:* **4.2,5.6** ↵
Specify next point or [Undo]:	*Type:* **@3<0** ↵
Specify next point or [Undo]:	↵
Command:	↵ **(Repeat LINE)**
Specify first point:	*Type:* **4.2,5.6** ↵
Specify next point or [Undo]:	*Type:* **@3<30** ↵
Specify next point or [Undo]:	↵
Command:	↵ **(Repeat LINE)**
Specify first point:	*Click:* **Osnap-From** (or *Type:* **FROM** ↵)
Base point:	**D1** (Figure 21–39) (Use Osnap-Endpoint)
<Offset>:	*Type:* **@.5<210** ↵
Specify next point or [Undo]:	*Click:* **Osnap-Endpoint** (or *Type:* **END** ↵)
of	**D2** (Figure 21–39)

FIGURE 21–38
Figure to Be Drawn for Exercise 21–4

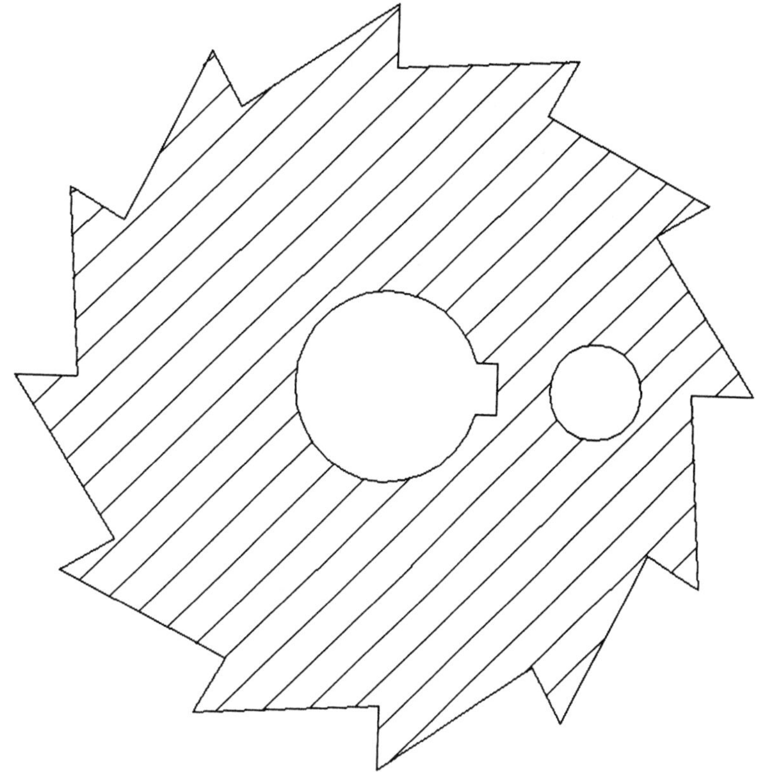

FIGURE 21–39
Construction Lines for Rachet

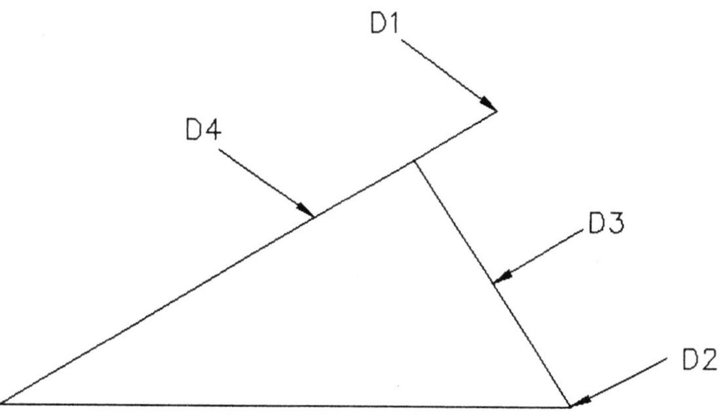

Prompt	Response
Specify next point or [Undo]:	↵
Command:	**Trim** (or *Type:* **TR** ↵)
Select cutting edge(s). . .	
Select objects:	**D3** (Figure 21–39) ↵
Select objects:	↵
Select object to trim or [Project/Edge/Undo]:	**D4** ↵
Command:	**Array** (or *Type:* **AR** ↵)
The Array dialog box appears:	*Click:* **Select objects**
Select objects:	**D1,D3** (Figure 21–39)↵
The Array dialog box appears:	*Click:* **Polar Array**
	Click: **the arrow to the far right of Center point:**

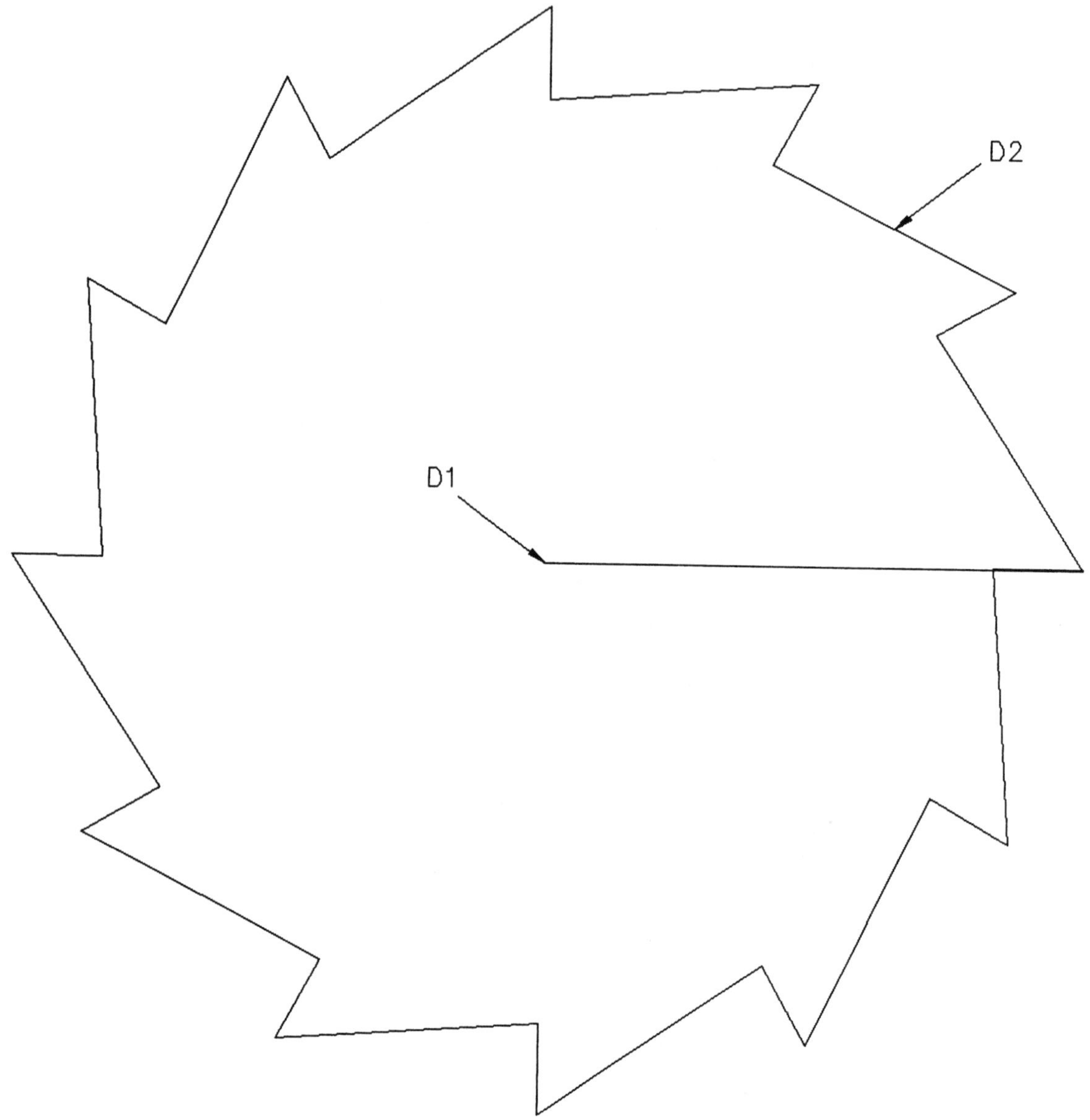

FIGURE 21–40
Array Notches and Join Them to Form One Polyline

Note: The short line was drawn on a 30° angle. Therefore, the notches on the ratchet are 30° apart; 360° in a circle divided by 30° = 12.

Prompt	**Response**
Specify center point of array:	**D1** (Figure 21–40; pick the endpoint of the line shown.)
The Array dialog box appears:	*Type:* **12 in the Total number of items: box**
	Check: **the Rotate items as copied button** if there is no check in that button
	Click: **OK**
Command:	*Type:* **E** ↵
Select objects:	**D1** (Pick any point on the horizontal line.)↵
Command:	*Click:* **Edit Polyline** (or *Type:* **PE** ↵)
Select polyline:	**D2** (Figure 21–40)

Prompt	Response
Object selected is not a polyline. Do you want to turn it into one?<Y>	↵
Enter an option [Close/Join/Width/ Edit vertex/Fit/Spline/Decurve/ Ltype gen/Undo]:	*Type:* **J** ↵
Select objects:	*Type:* **ALL**↵
Select objects:	↵
23 segments added to polyline	
Enter an option [Close/Join/Width/ Edit vertex/Fit/Spline/Decurve/ Ltype gen/Undo]:	↵
Command:	*Type:* **C** ↵
Specify center point for circle or [3P/2P/Ttr (tan tan radius)]:	*Type:* **4.2,5.6** ↵
Specify radius of circle or [Diameter]:	*Type:* **.75** ↵
Command:	*Click:* **Rectangle** (or *Type:* **REC** ↵)
Specify first corner point or [Chamfer/ Elevation/Fillet/Thickness/Width]:	*Type:* **4,6.2** ↵
Specify other corner point:	*Type:* **4.4,6.5** ↵

Draw Dimension Modi
Line
Ray
Construction Line
Multiline
Polyline
3D Polyline
Polygon
Rectangle
Arc
Circle
Donut
Spline
Ellipse
Block
Point
Hatch...
Boundary...
Region
Text
Surfaces
Solids

You can also use polar or relative coordinates or pick points with a mouse to form a rectangle. Use Zoom-Window to zoom in closer to the circle and rectangle (Figure 21–41). Notice that the Rectangle command allows you to chamfer or fillet the corners of the rectangle and give it elevation, thickness, and width. This will be very useful for block diagrams and other similar drawings.

Prompt	Response
Command:	**Trim**
Select cutting edge(s). . .	
Select objects:	**D1,D2** (Figure 21–41; this creates a crossing window that selects the circle and the rectangle as cutting edges.)
Select objects:	↵
Select object to trim or [Project/Edge/Undo]:	**D3,D4,D5,D6** ↵

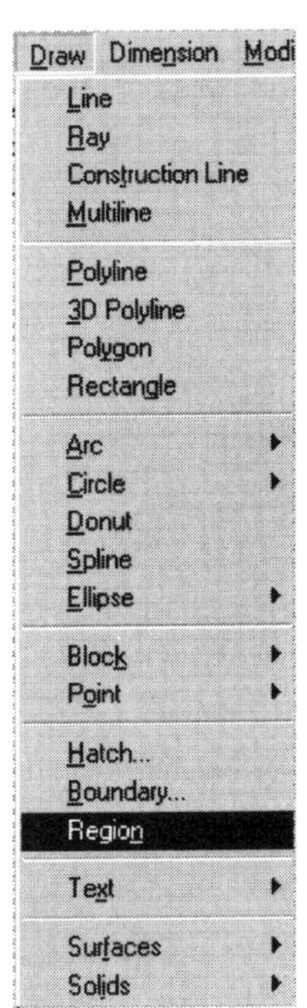

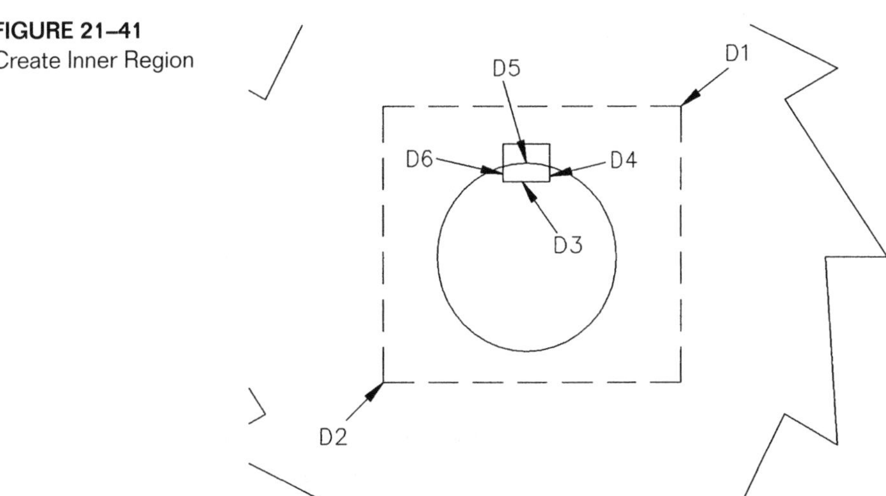

FIGURE 21–41
Create Inner Region

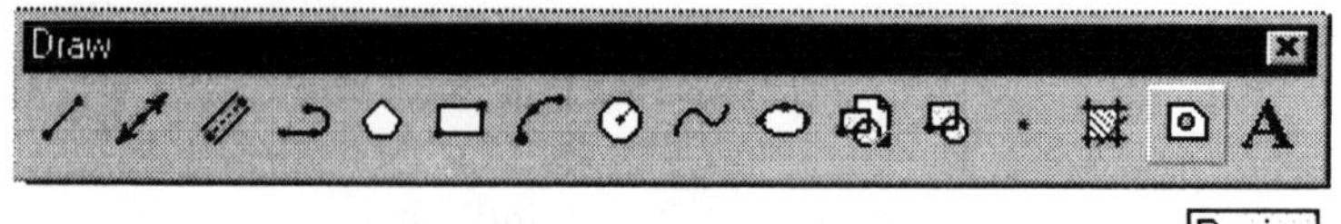

Prompt	Response
Command:	**Edit Polyline** (or *Type:* **PE** ↵)
Select polyline:	**D1**
Object selected is not a polyline. Do you want to turn it into one?<Y>	*Type:* J ↵
Enter an option [Close/Join/Width/ Edit vertex/Fit/Spline/Decurve/ Ltype gen/Undo]:	*Type:* **J**↵
Select objects: (Figure 21-42)	*Click:* D2
Specify opposite corner:	*Click:* D3
Select objects:	↵
3 segments added to polyline	
Enter an option [Close/Join/Width/ Edit vertex/Fit/Spline/ Decurve/Ltype gen/Undo]:	↵
Command:	*Click:* **Zoom-All**

Step 4. Create region primitives.

Prompt	Response
Command:	*Click:* **Region** (or *Type:* **REG** ↵)
Select objects:	*Click:* **on the outer polyline**
Select objects:	↵

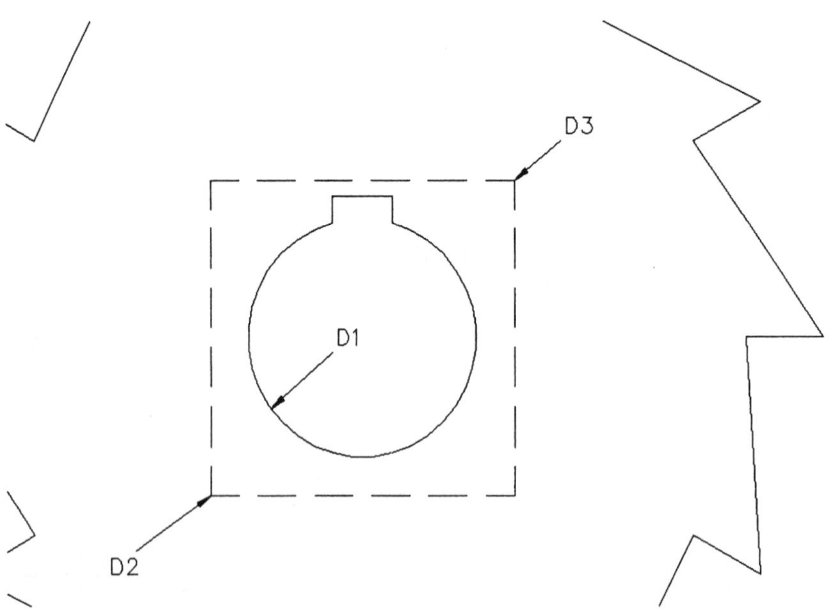

FIGURE 21–42
Join Lines into a Polyline

A region is created, and the polyline is removed from the drawing.

Prompt	**Response**
Command:	*Click:* ↵ **(Repeat Region)**
Select objects:	*Click:* **on the polyline forming the hole**
Select objects:	↵

Make a copy of the region forming the hole so that it may be subtracted from the shoulder when it is placed over the hole.

Prompt	**Response**
Command:	*Click:* **Copy** (or *Type:* **CP** ↵)
Select objects:	*Click:* **on the region forming the hole**
Select objects:	↵
Specify base point or displacement or [Multiple]:	*Click:* **any point**
Specify second point of displacement or <use first point as displacement>:	*Type:* @ ↵

The regions shown in Figure 21–43 are formed. (The hatching will not appear on your drawing). Now subtract the hole from the outer region.

Step 5. Subtract the inner region from the outer one.

Prompt	**Response**
Command:	**Subtract** (or *Type:* **SU** ↵)
Select solids and regions to select from . . .	
Select objects:	*Click:* **on any line on the outer region**
Select objects:	↵
Select objects and regions to subtract. . .	
Select objects: 1 found	*Click:* **on any point on the hole region**
Select objects:	↵

Step 6. Create another hole and subtract it.

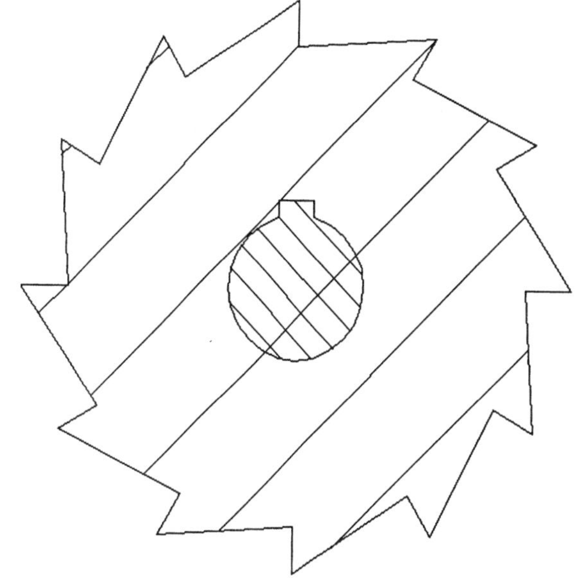

FIGURE 21–43
Create Inner and Outer Regions

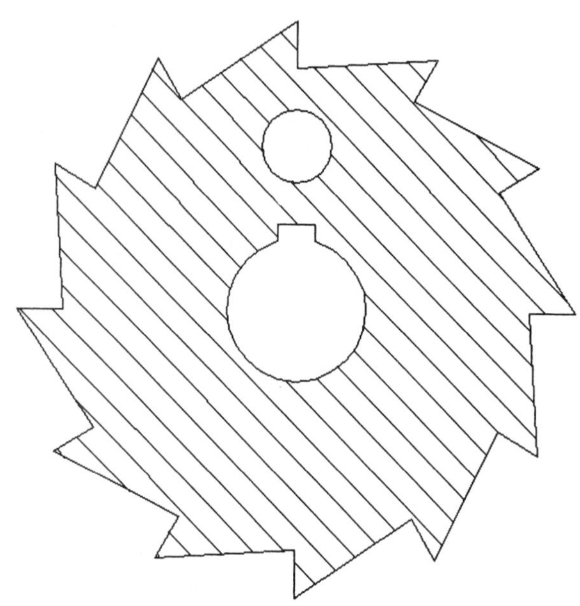

FIGURE 21–44
Subtract Holes

Prompt	Response
Command:	*Type:* **C** ↵
Specify center point for circle or [3P/2P/Ttr (tan tan radius)]:	*Type:* **4.2,7.3** ↵
Specify radius of circle or [Diameter]<0.75>:	*Type:* **.375** ↵
Command:	*Click:* **Region**
Select objects:	*Click:* **on the circle just created** (Figure 21–44).
Select objects:	↵
Command:	*Click:* **Subtract** (or *Type:* **SU** ↵)
Select solids and regions to select from. . .	
Select objects:	*Click:* **on any line on the outer region**
Select objects:	↵
Select objects and regions to subtract. . .	
Select objects:	*Click:* **on any point on the new hole region**
Select objects:	↵

Step 7. Create a shoulder for this ratchet and subtract a copy of the inner hole from it.

On your own: Set the R layer current and do the following:

Note: Shading (hatching) will not appear on your regions. It is shown for your reference only.

1. Draw a 2.4″-diameter circle in the lower right corner of the limits and make a region of it (Figure 21–45).
2. Use the Move command to move the 2.4″-circle region to the center of the ratchet (Figure 21–46).
3. Use Subtract to subtract the copy of the center hole from the 2.4″-diameter-circle region (Figure 21–47). (You will have to use a window to click the copy of the center hole.)

FIGURE 21–45
Create a Region for the Shoulder

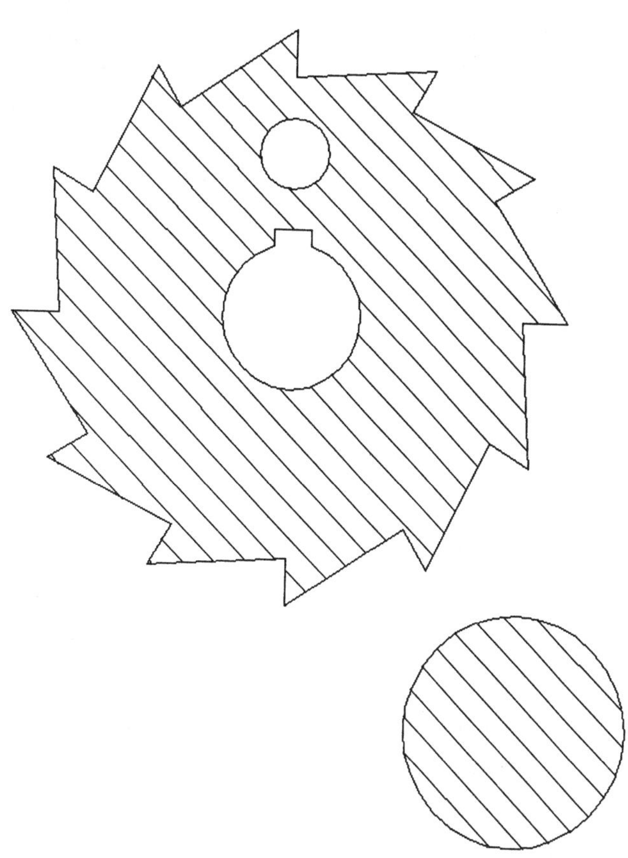

FIGURE 21–46
Move 2.4" Circle to the Center of the Ratchet

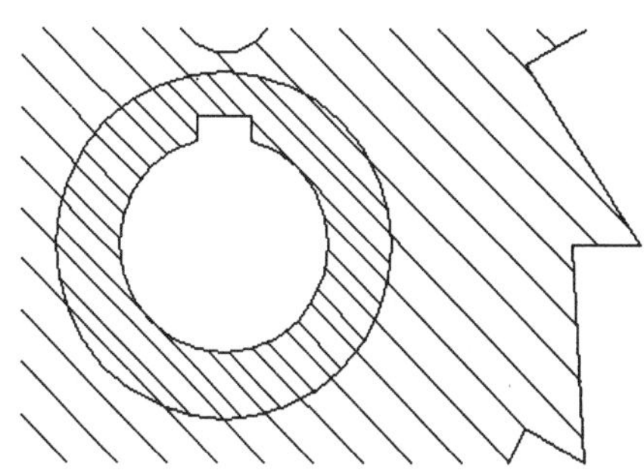

FIGURE 21–47
Place Shoulder and Subtract Hole

FIGURE 21–48
Extrude the Inner Region

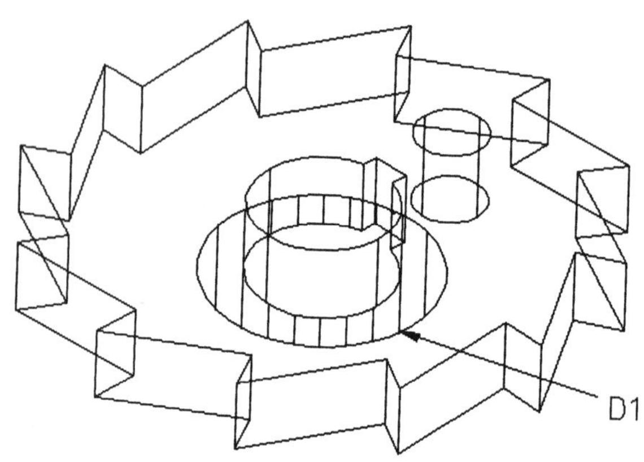

Step 8. Select a 3-D viewpoint and extrude regions to form a solid model.

Prompt	Response
Command:	*Type:* **VPOINT** ↵
Specify a viewpoint or [Rotate] <display compass and tripod>:	*Type:* **1, −1,1** ↵
Command:	**Extrude** (or *Type:* **EXT** ↵)
Select objects:	*Click:* **on the outer region**
Select objects:	↵
Specify height of extrusion or [Path]:	*Type:* **.75** ↵
Specify angle of taper for extrusion<0>:	↵
Command:	↵ **(Repeat EXTRUDE)**
Select objects:	*Click:* **on the inner region; D1** (Figure 21–48)
Select objects:	↵
Specify height of extrusion or [Path]:	*Type:* **1.25**↵
Specify angle of taper for extrusion <0>:	↵
Command:	**Union** (or *Type:* **UNION** ↵)
Select objects:	Click: **on the inner and outer extruded regions**
Select objects:	↵

The Union command makes one solid from the two extruded regions.

Prompt	Response
Command:	**Hide** ↵ (or *Type:* **HI** ↵)

Figure 21–49 is displayed, and this exercise is complete.

Step 9. Save your drawing in two places with the name EX21-4(your initials). *Click:* **Layout1, put your name in the lower right corner, use Mview-Hideplot to remove hidden lines, and print the drawing on an 11″ × 8½″ sheet.**

Step 10. Exit AutoCAD.

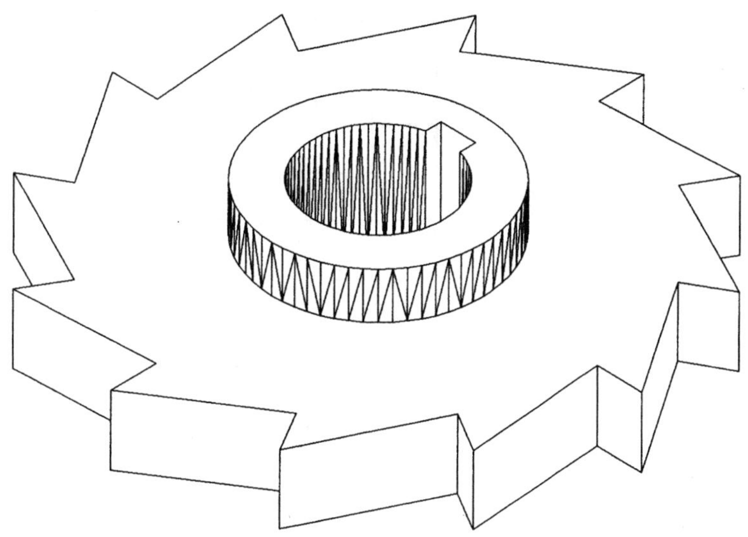

FIGURE 21–49
Completed Model

EXERCISES

EXERCISE 21–1. Complete the first model as described in this chapter using the dimensions from Figure 21–2. Print a view of the model similar to Figure 21–12 with hidden lines removed. Center the drawing on an 11″ × 8.5″ sheet.

EXERCISE 21–2. Complete the second model as described in this chapter using the dimensions from Figure 21–13. Print a view of the model similar to Figure 21–25 with hidden lines removed. Center the drawing on an 11″ × 8.5″ sheet. In addition, complete a 2-D drawing similar to Figure 21–13 with dimensions using the 2-D sectional view described in this chapter. Center this drawing in a horizontal 11″ × 8.5″ format and print it on an A-size sheet.

EXERCISE 21–3. Complete the third model using steps 1 through 16 described in this chapter.

EXERCISE 21–4. Create a solid from a region as described in this chapter. Print a view of the model similar to Figure 21–49 with hidden lines removed. Center the drawing on an 11″ × 8.5″ sheet.

EXERCISE 21–5. Make a solid model from the drawing shown in Figure 21–50. Print a pleasing perspective view using 3D Orbit. Make the view similar to Figure 21–25 and center it on an 11″ × 8.5″ sheet.

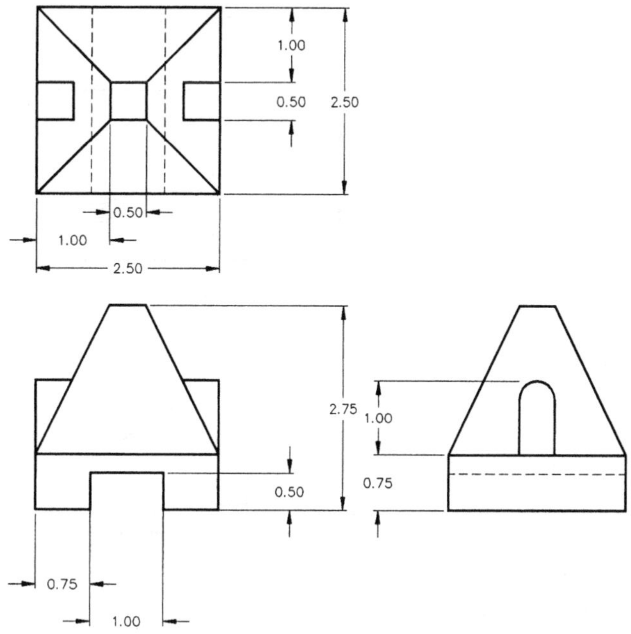

FIGURE 21–50
Exercise 21–5

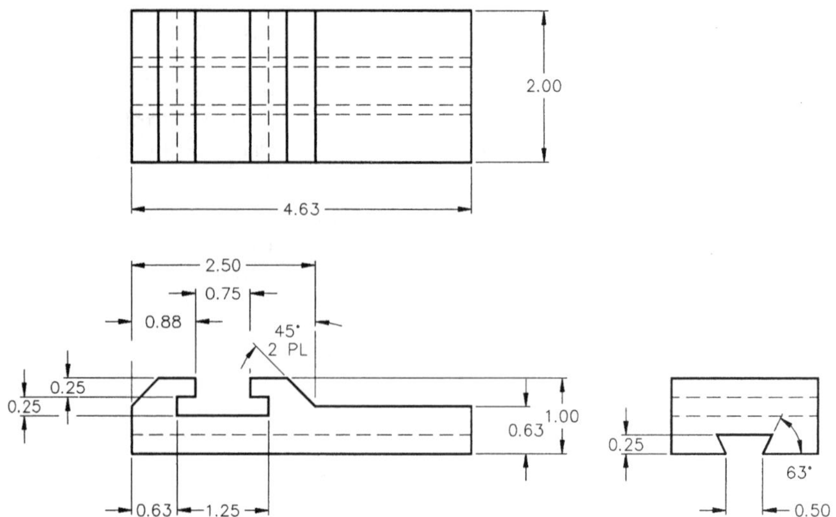

FIGURE 21–51
Exercise 21–6

EXERCISE 21–6. Make a solid model from the drawing shown in Figure 21–51. Plot a pleasing perspective view using 3D Orbit. Make the view similar to Figure 21–25 and center it on an 11″ × 8.5″ sheet.

EXERCISE 21–7. Make a solid model from the drawing shown in Figure 21–52. Print a pleasing perspective view using 3D Orbit. Make the view similar to Figure 21–25 and center it on an 11″ × 8.5″ sheet.

EXERCISE 21–8. Make a solid model from the drawing shown in Figure 21–53. Print a pleasing perspective view using 3D Orbit. Make the view similar to Figure 21–25 and center it on an 11″ × 8.5″ sheet.

EXERCISE 21–9. Make a solid model from the drawing shown in Figure 21–54. Print a pleasing perspective view using 3D Orbit. Make the view similar to Figure 21–25 and center it on an 11″ × 8.5″ sheet.

EXERCISE 21–10. Make a solid model from the drawing shown in Figure 21–55. Print a pleasing perspective view using 3D Orbit. Make the view similar to Figure 21–25 and center it on an 11″ × 8.5″ sheet.

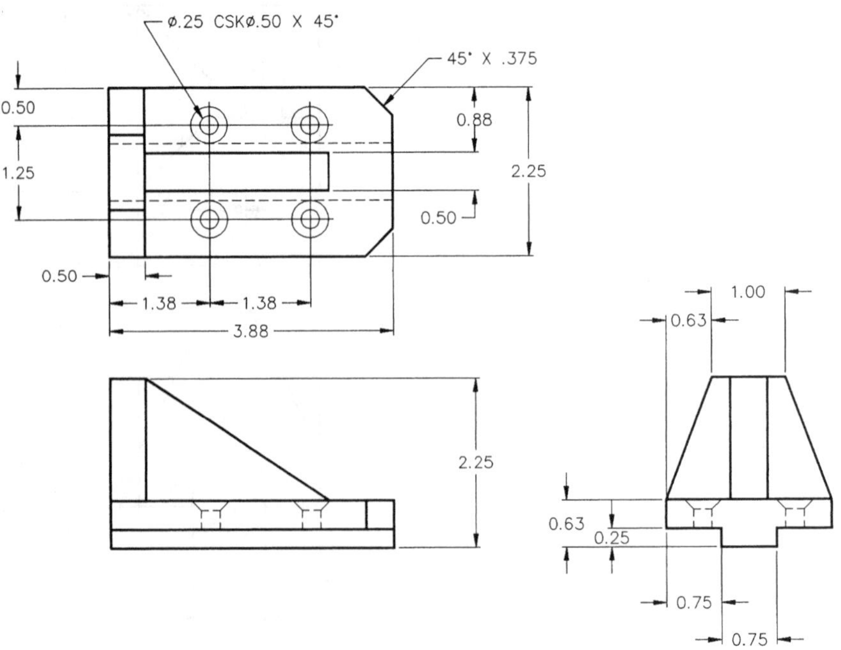

FIGURE 21–52
Exercise 21–7

FIGURE 21–53
Exercise 21–8

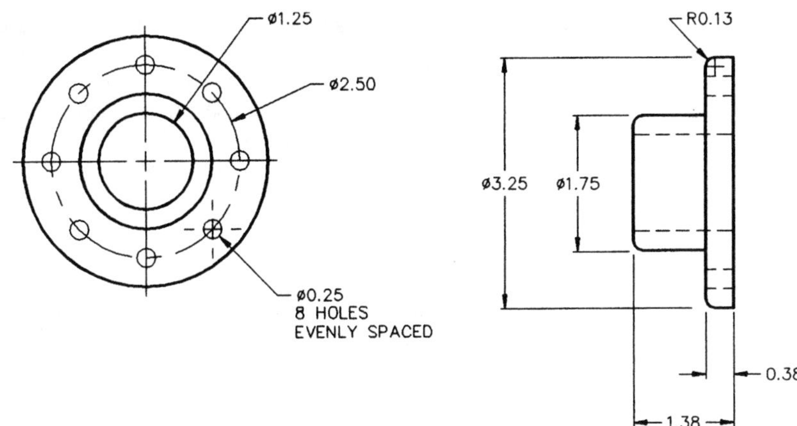

FIGURE 21–54
Exercise 21–9

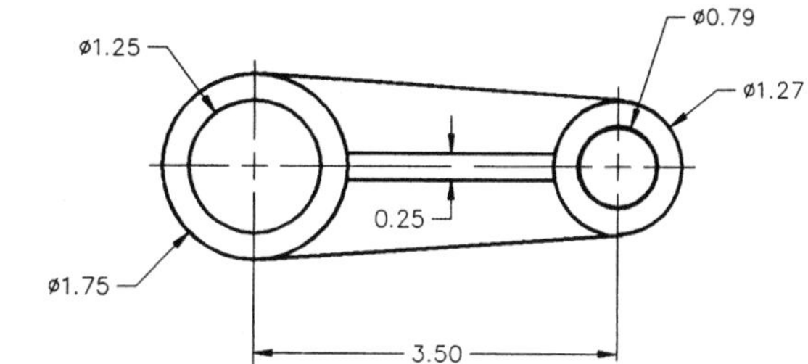

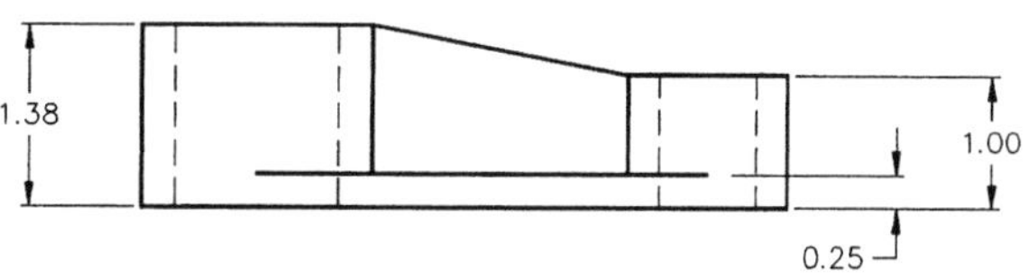

FIGURE 21–55
Exercise 21–10

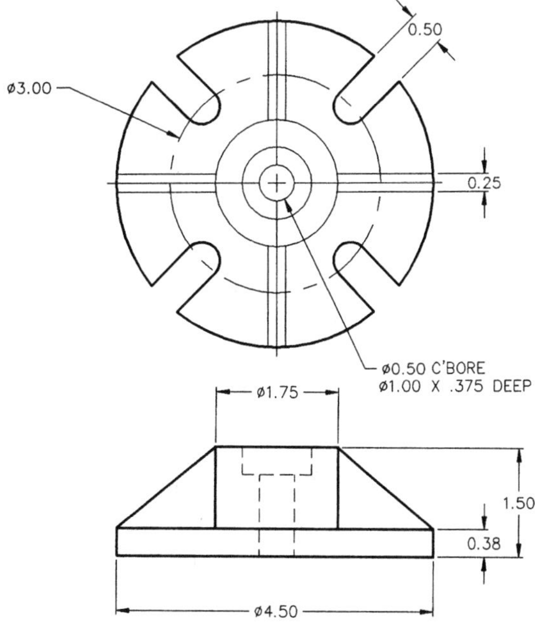

EXERCISE 21–11. Make a solid model from the drawing shown in Figure 21–56. Print a pleasing perspective view using 3D Orbit. Make the view similar to Figure 21–25 and center it on an 11″ × 8.5″ sheet.

EXERCISE 21–12. Make a solid model from the drawing shown in Figure 21–57. Print a pleasing perspective view using 3D Orbit. Make the view similar to Figure 21–25 and center it on an 11″ × 8.5″ sheet.

FIGURE 21–56
Exercise 21–11

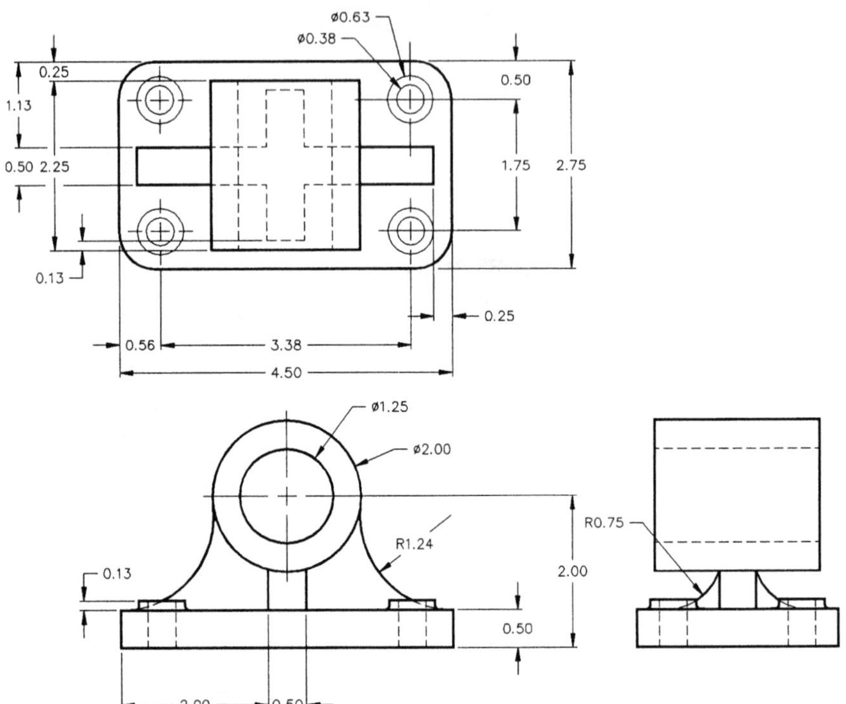

FIGURE 21–57
Exercise 21–12

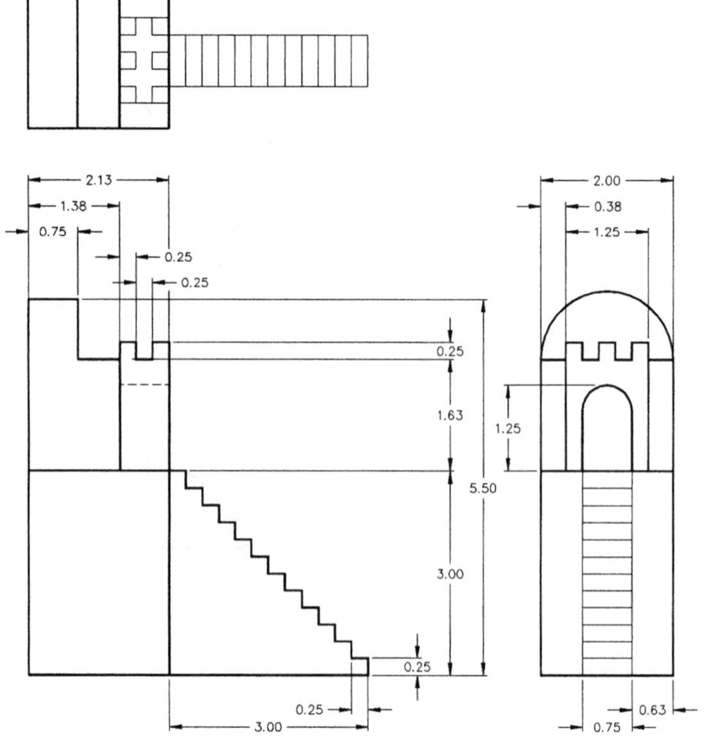

EXERCISE 21–13. Make a solid model from the drawing shown in Figure 21–58. Print a pleasing perspective view using 3D Orbit. Make the view similar to Figure 21–25 and center it on an 11″ × 8.5″ sheet.

EXERCISE 21–14. Create regions for the shape shown as Figure 21–59A. Extrude the shape so that it appears as shown in Figure 21–59B. You may find it helpful to extrude inner loops at different heights. Print the shape shown in Figure 21–59B in the center of an 8½″ × 11″ sheet.

EXERCISE 21–15. Draw the individual shapes using the dimensions shown at the top of Figure 21–60. Remember that each shape has to be a continuous polyline, so you will have to draw them first, then use PEDIT to join lines together. Stack them on top of each other as shown in the middle figure. Use Revolve to revolve the shaft (4.50 × 0.3) 360°. Revolve all other shapes 270° using the center of the shaft as the axis of revolution. Use Rotate3D if necessary to obtain the view shown on the bottom. *Click:* Layout1, place your name in the simplex font, .2 high, use Mview-Hideplot to remove hidden lines, and plot on an 11″ × 8.5″ sheet.

FIGURE 21–58
Exercise 21–13

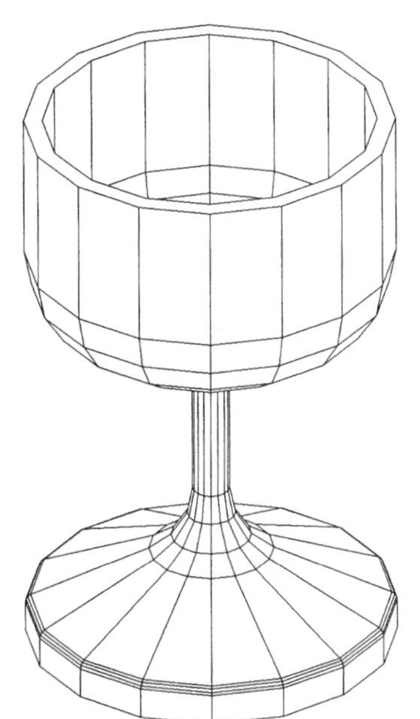

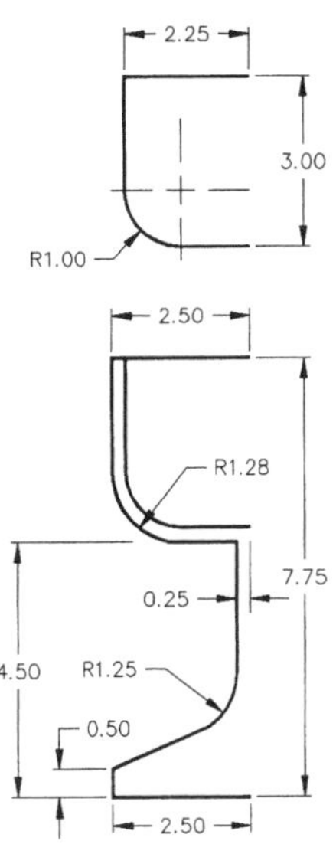

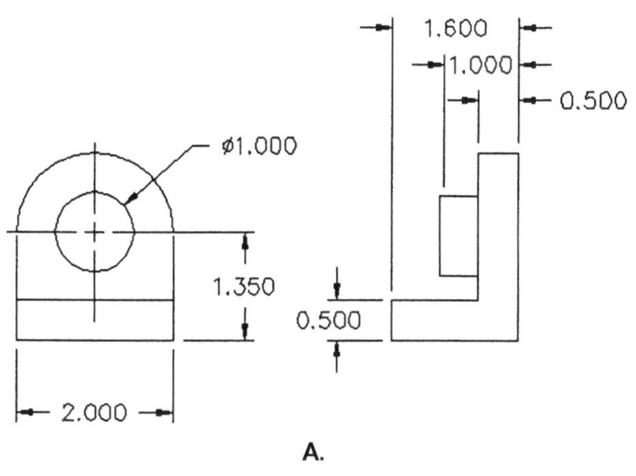

A.

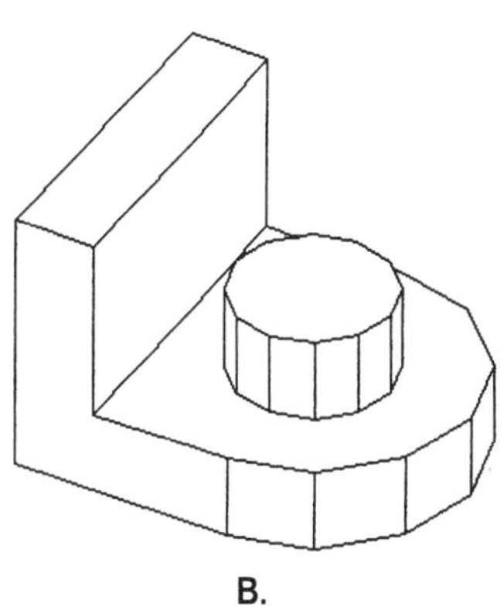

B.

FIGURE 21–59
Exercise 21–14

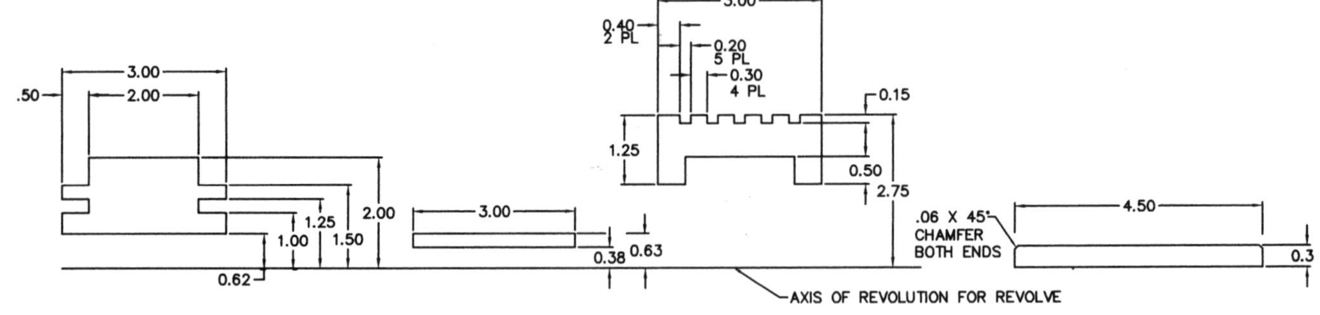

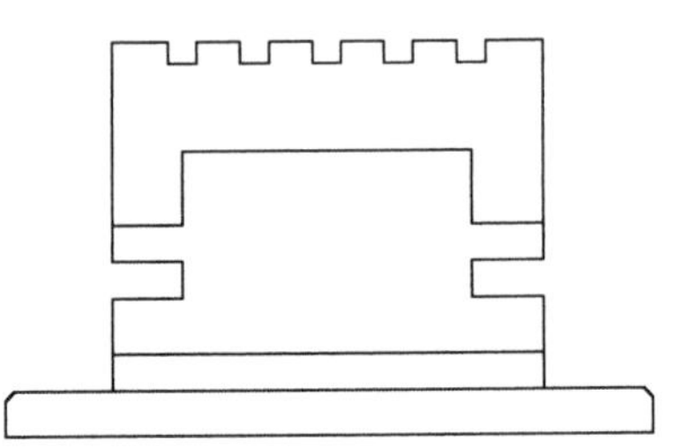

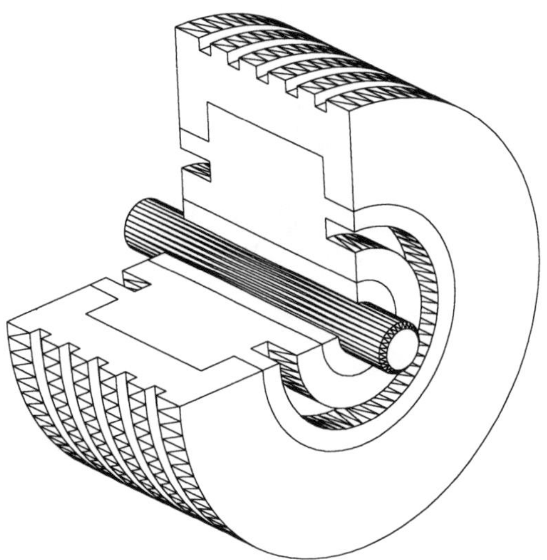

FIGURE 21–60
Exercise 21–15

REVIEW QUESTIONS

Circle the best answer.

1. Which menu on the menu bar contains the Solids menu?
   a. Draw
   b. Insert
   c. Modify
   d. View
   e. Window

2. Which Toolbar contains the Solids commands?
   a. Draw
   b. Render
   c. Solids
   d. View
   e. Window
3. Which menu on the menu bar contains the Subtract command?
   a. Draw
   b. Modify
   c. Tools
   d. Solids
   e. Window
4. Which menu on the menu bar contains the solids editing commands?
   a. Draw
   b. Modify
   c. Solids
   d. Express
   e. Window
5. Which of the following commands creates a round cylinder that can be used as a hole?
   a. Subtract
   b. Cylinder
   c. Hole
   d. Revolve
   e. Edit Polyline
6. Which of the following commands can be used to remove material from a hole?
   a. Subtract
   b. Cylinder
   c. Hole
   d. Revolve
   e. Edit Polyline
7. Which of the following commands is used to combine several solids into a single solid?
   a. Solidfy
   b. Extrude
   c. Combine
   d. Union
   e. Region
8. Which of the following commands is used to give thickness to a circle or polyline?
   a. Solidfy
   b. Extrude
   c. Combine
   d. Revolve
   e. Region
9. Which of the following commands sets the number of lines per surface on a solid?
   a. Dview
   b. Units
   c. Viewres
   d. FACETRES
   e. ISOLINES
10. Which of the following commands makes solids that have had hidden lines removed appear smoother?
    a. Dview
    b. Units
    c. Viewres
    d. FACETRES
    e. ISOLINES
11. Which of the following solids editing commands can be used to extrude a surface or surfaces to a specific height or along a path?
    a. Extrude
    b. Extrude faces
    c. Copy faces
    d. Imprint
    e. Shell

12. Which of the following solids editing commands can be used to make a box with thin walls from a solid box?
    a. Extrude faces
    b. Separate
    c. Imprint
    d. Shell
    e. Box
13. Which of the following solids editing commands can be used to make an object such as a circle or polyline a permanent part of an object?
    a. Extrude faces
    b. Separate
    c. Imprint
    d. Shell
    e. Box
14. Which of the following solids editing commands can be used to separate some solids that have been joined to form a composite solid?
    a. Extrude faces
    b. Separate
    c. Imprint
    d. Shell
    e. Box
15. Which of the following commands has the options to extrude, move, rotate, offset, taper, shell, check, or delete features such as holes, surfaces, and edges?
    a. PEDIT
    b. SOLIDEDIT
    c. MODIFY
    d. PROPERTIES
    e. UNION

22 Three-Dimensional Tutorial Exercises, Including Rendering and Publishing to the Web

OBJECTIVES

After completing this chapter, you will be able to

- □ Cut solids using Slice.
- □ Use solids commands to create counterbored and countersunk holes in a solid.
- □ Use solids editing commands to move holes and surfaces.
- □ Use Wblock to create solid blocks for use in any drawing.
- □ Use Insert to insert solids into the current drawing.
- □ Use Render to shade solid objects in color.
- □ Use Intersection to form a solid from the common volume of two intersecting solids.
- □ Use MV Setup to make four standard engineering views of a model and insert a standard format around those views.
- □ Correctly answer questions regarding the following commands:

Slice	MV Setup	Render
Interfere	Intersect	SOLIDEDIT

Let's begin by constructing a cylindrical object and then cutting it.

CUTTING A SOLID USING SLICE AND SAVING IT

Exercise 22–1: Constructing a 3-D Model and Cutting It in Half

Use dimensions from Figure 22–1.

Step 1. Load AutoCAD. *Click:* **Create Drawings-Wizards-Quick Setup.**

Step 2. Make the following settings:

Units: Decimal—2 places to the right of the decimal point

Area: Width: 11 Length: 8.5

ISOLINES: 30

FACETRES: 2

GRID: .2

SNAP: .1

TEXT STYLE: Standard FONT: simplex.shx HEIGHT: 0

LAYERS: NAME	Color	Linetype	Lineweight
R	Red	Continuous	Default
M	Magenta	Continuous	Default
G	Green	Continuous	Default

Set layer M current. Set SNAP ON.

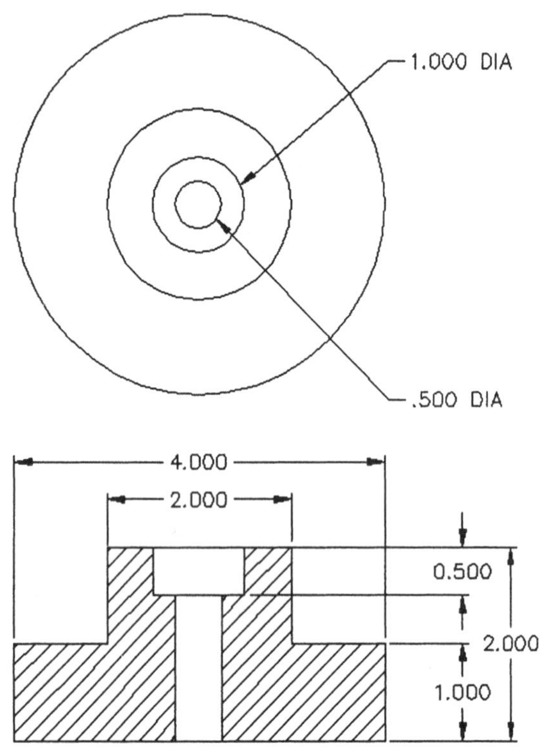

FIGURE 22–1
Dimensions for Exercise 22–1

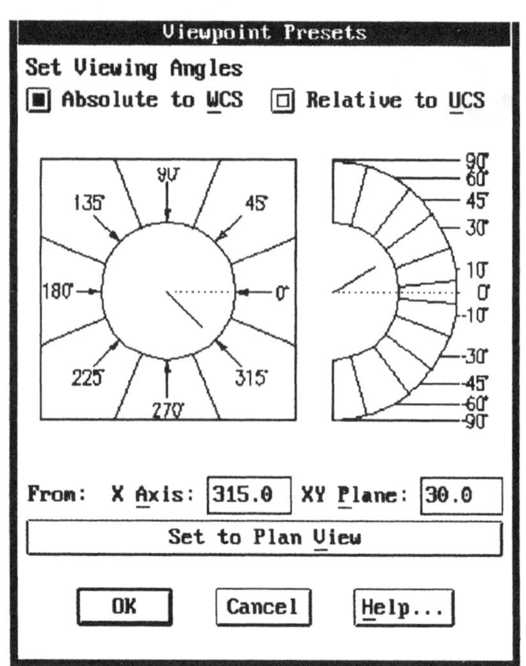

FIGURE 22–2
Viewpoint Setting

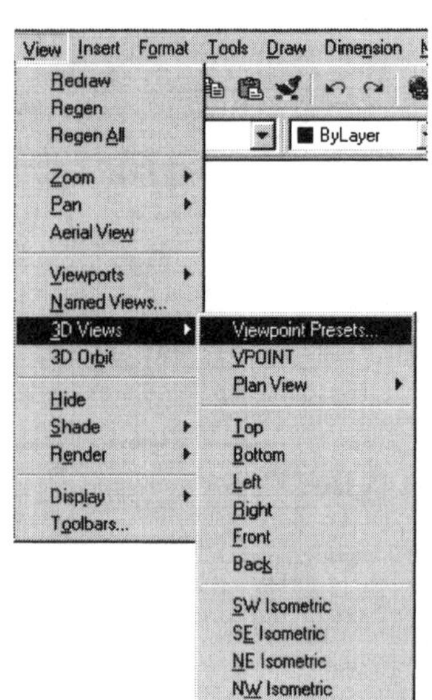

Select a 3D Viewpoint.

Prompt	Response
Command:	**3D Views-Viewpoint Presets** (Viewpoint Presets dialog box) **X Axis: 315.0** **XY Plane: 30.0** (as shown in Figure 22–2)

Step 3. Construct the model.

Prompt	Response
Command:	**Cylinder** (from the Solids menu or toolbar) (or *Type:* **CYLINDER** ↵)
Specify center point for base of cylinder or [Elliptical]<0,0,0>:	*Type:* **5,5** ↵ (To locate a convenient point near the center of the display with the Z component of the point set at 0.)
Specify radius for base of cylinder or [Diameter]:	*Type:* **2** ↵
Specify height of cylinder or [Center of other end]:	*Type:* **1** ↵
Command:	↵ **(Repeat CYLINDER)**
Specify center point for base of cylinder or [Elliptical]<0,0,0>:	*Type:* **5,5,1** ↵ (to locate the second cylinder on the same XY point with the Z component of the point set at 1—on top of the larger cylinder)
Specify radius for base of cylinder or [Diameter]:	*Type:* **1** ↵

Prompt	Response
Specify height of cylinder or [Center of other end]:	*Type:* **1** ↵
Command:	↵ **(Repeat CYLINDER)**
Specify center point for base of cylinder or [Elliptical]<0,0,0>:	*Type:* **5,5** ↵ (to draw the hole in the center of the cylinder with the Z component of the point set at 0)
Specify radius for base of cylinder or [Diameter]:	*Type:* **.25** ↵
Specify height of cylinder or [Center of other end]:	*Type:* **2.5** ↵ (Any height greater than 2″—the depth of the hole—is all right.)
Command:	↵ **(Repeat CYLINDER)**
Specify center point for base of cylinder or [Elliptical]<0,0,0>:	*Type:* **5,5,1.5** ↵ (to locate the bottom of the counterbore in the cylinder)
Specify radius for base of cylinder or [Diameter]:	*Type:* **.5** ↵
Specify height of cylinder or [Center of other end]:	*Type:* **1** ↵ (Any height greater than .5, the depth of the counterbore, is all right.)
Command:	**Union** (or *Type:* **UNION** ↵)
Select objects:	*Click:* **on the two largest cylinders**
Command:	**Subtract** (or *Type:* **SU** ↵)
Select solids and regions to subtract from. . .	
Select objects:	*Click:* **on any point on the largest cylinder**
Select objects:	↵
Select solids and regions to subtract. . .	
Select objects:	*Click:* **on the two smallest cylinders)**
Select objects:	↵

The object appears as shown in Figure 22–3.

Step 4. Cut the object in half using Slice (Figure 22–4).

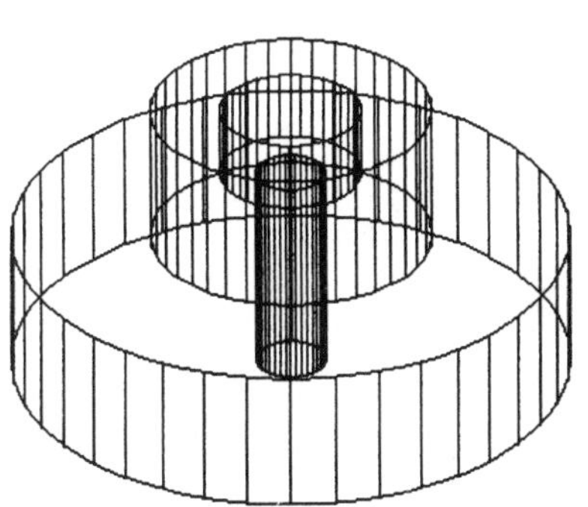

FIGURE 22–3
The Complete Cylinder

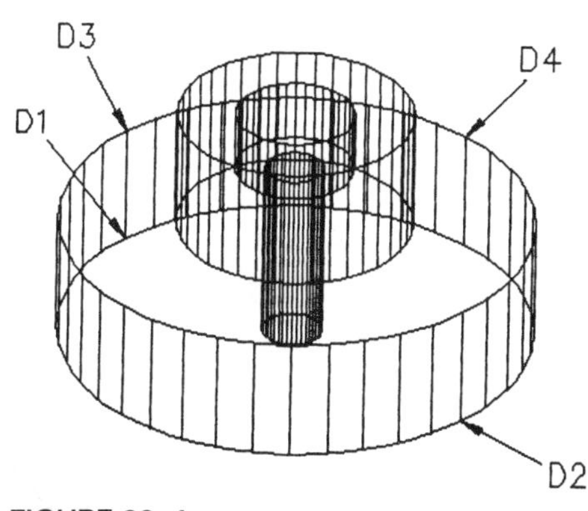

FIGURE 22–4
Selecting the Cutting Plane

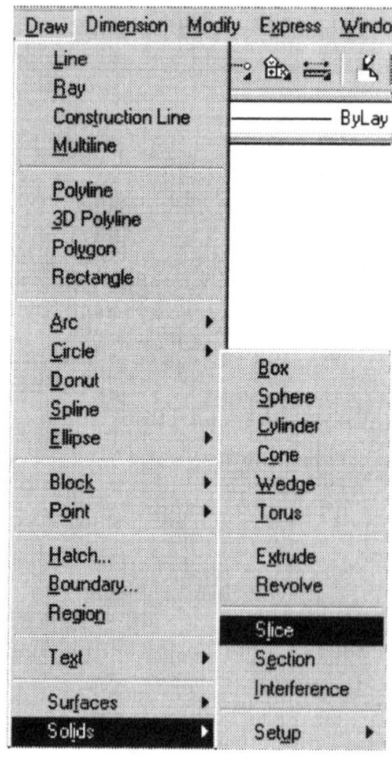

Prompt	Response
Command:	**Slice** (or *Type:* **SL** ↵)
Select objects:	*Click:* **on any point on the model**
Select objects:	↵
Specify first point on slicing plane by [Object/Zaxis/View/XY/ YZ/ZX/3points]<3points>:	↵
Specify first point on plane:	**D1** (Use Osnap-Quadrant.)
Specify second point on plane:	**D2** (Use Osnap-Quadrant.)
Specify third point on plane:	**D3** (Use Osnap-Quadrant.)
Specify a point on desired side of the plane or [keep Both sides]:	**D4** (*Click:* **on any point on the back side of the object**)

Step 5. Use Hide to be sure the model is correct (Figure 22–5).

Prompt	Response
Select objects:	↵
Command:	*Type:* **HI** ↵ (or *Click:* it)

If your model looks like the one shown in Figure 22–5, it is ready to be rendered. Let's wait to render this model until you have constructed another model and used a few more new commands so you can render them all at the same time.

Now, use the Wblock (*Type:* **W** ↵) command to save this drawing to a floppy disk (or any other disk, for that matter).

Step 6. **On your own:** Save the model to a floppy disk in the A: drive using WBlock. Name the drawing: CYLINDER. Use the insertion point, D1, shown in Figure 22–6. Check "Delete from drawing" in the Write Block dialog box so the object does not remain on the screen. The screen should be blank after you have Wblocked this model.

Now let's create another model of a plate with countersunk and counterbored holes in it.

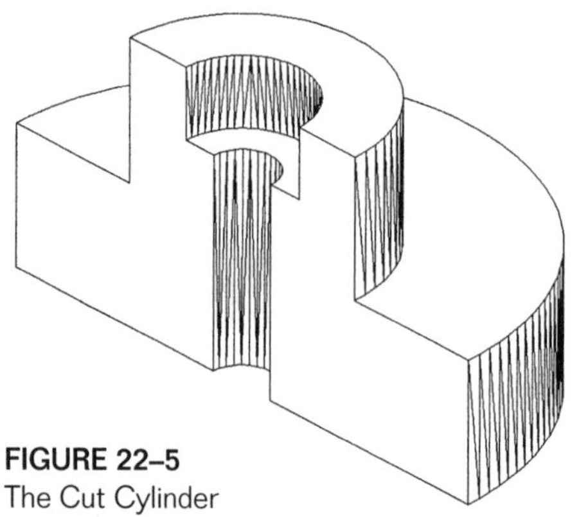

FIGURE 22–5
The Cut Cylinder

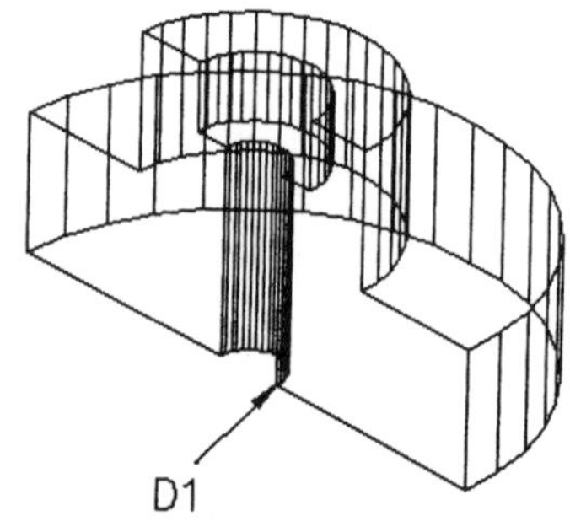

FIGURE 22–6
Pick the Insertion Point

CREATING A SOLID MODEL WITH COUNTERBORED AND COUNTERSUNK HOLES

Use dimensions from Figure 22–7.

Step 7. Create the base plate using Box.

Now return to the plan view of the World UCS so that the model can be oriented properly.

Prompt	Response
Command:	*Type:* **PLAN** ↵
Enter an option [Current UCS/ Ucs/World]<Current>:	*Type:* **W** ↵
Command:	**Zoom-All**
Command:	**Box** (or *Type:* **BOX** ↵)
Specify corner of box or [CEnter]<0,0,0>:	*Type:* **2,2** ↵ (to locate the first corner of the model so that it will be centered in the display with the Z coordinate at 0)
Specify corner or [Cube/Length]:	*Type:* **8,6** ↵
Specify height:	*Type:* **1** ↵
Command:	*Click:* **on the same viewpoint as you did for the cylindrical model so that your view appears as shown in Figure 22–8.**

Step 8. Draw holes in the plate (Figure 22–9).

Prompt	Response
Command:	*Click:* **New UCS-3Point** ↵
Specify new origin point <0,0,0>:	**D1** (Use Osnap-Endpoint.)

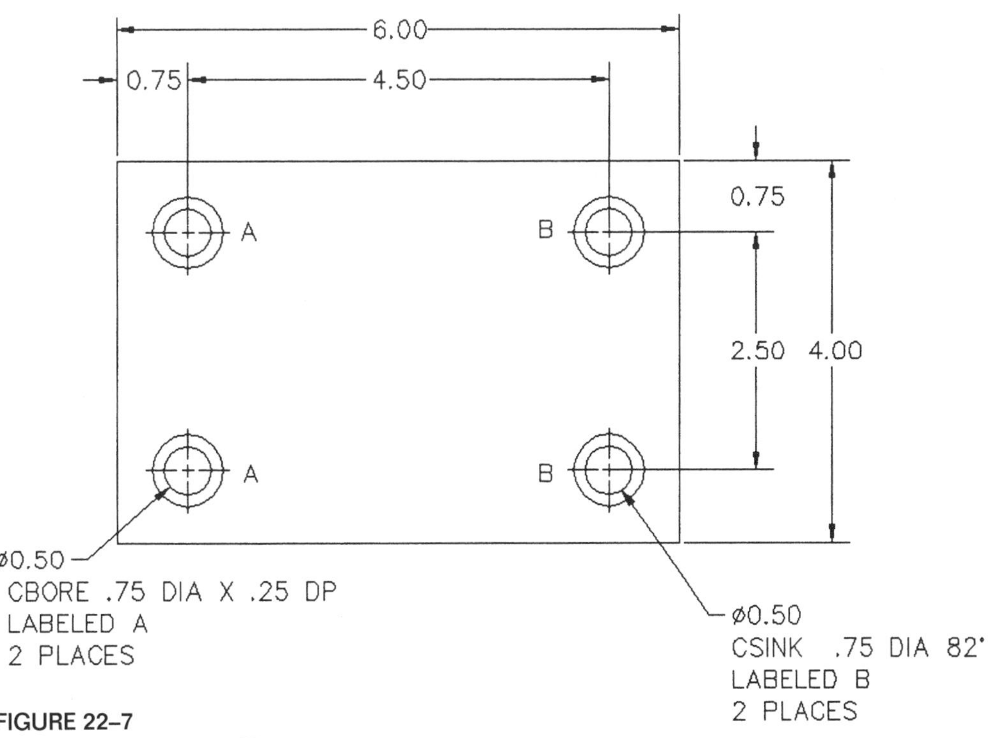

FIGURE 22–7
Dimension for the Base Plate

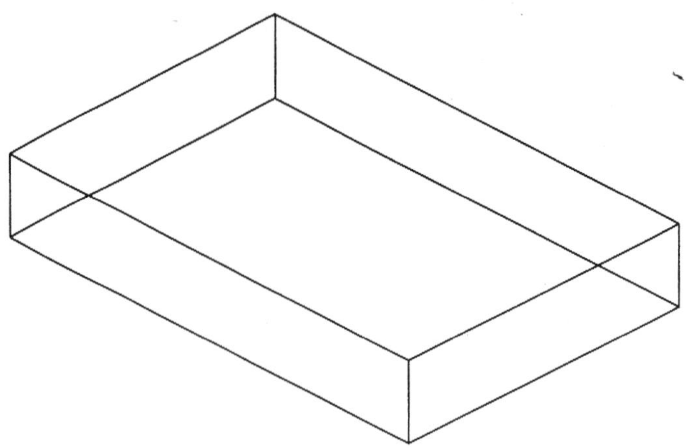

FIGURE 22–8
Base Plate without Holes

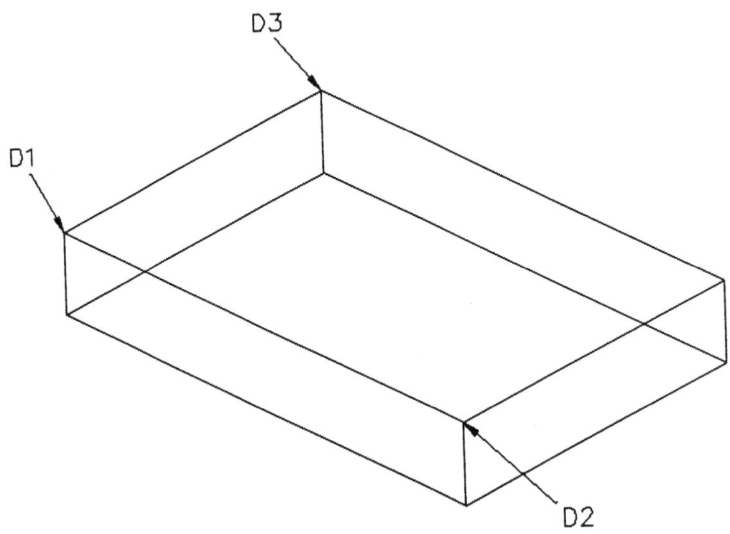

FIGURE 22–9
Locating a Construction Plane Using UCS 3 point

Prompt	**Response**
Specify point on positive portion of the X axis <default>:	**D2** (Use Osnap-Endpoint.)
Specify point on positive-Y portion of the UCS XY plane <default>:	**D3** (Use Osnap-Endpoint.)
Command:	**Cylinder** (or *Type:* **CYLINDER** ↵)
Specify center point for base of cylinder or [Elliptical]<0,0,0>:	*Type:* **.75,.75** ↵ (to locate the center of the cylinder with the Z component of the point set at the top of the plate)
Specify radius for base of cylinder or [Diameter]:	*Type:* **.25** ↵
Specify height of cylinder or [Center of other end]:	*Type:* **−1.1** ↵ (the thickness of the plate plus a little more to make sure the hole goes completely through the plate)
Command:	*Click:* **Mirror** (or *Type:* **MI** ↵)
Select objects:	*Click:* **on the cylinder**
Select objects:	↵
Specify first point of mirror line:	**D1** (Use Osnap-Midpoint (Figure 22–10).)

FIGURE 22–10
Draw Holes Using Cylinder

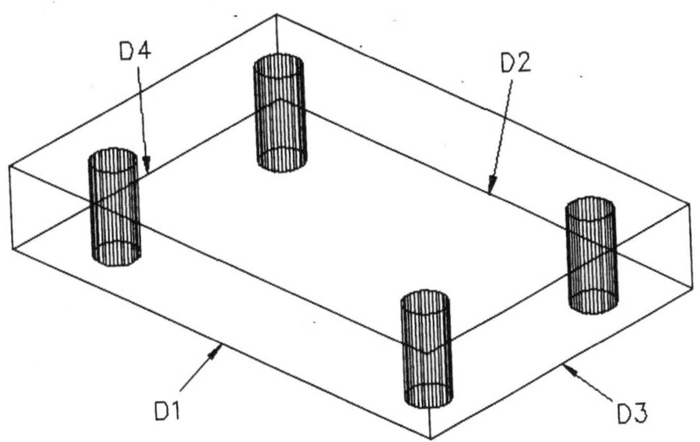

Prompt	Response
Specify second point of mirror line:	**D2** (Use Osnap-Midpoint.)
Delete source objects? [Yes/No]<N>	↵
Command:	↵ **(Repeat MIRROR)**
Select objects:	*Click:* **on the two cylinders**
Select objects:	↵
Specify first point of mirror line:	**D3** (Use Osnap-Midpoint (Figure 22–10).)
Specify second point of mirror line:	**D4** (Use Osnap-Midpoint.)
Delete source objects? [Yes/No]<N>	↵

Step 9. Create two counterbored holes and two countersunk holes using the Cylinder and Chamfer commands (Figure 22–11).

Prompt	Response
Command:	**Cylinder** (or *Type:* **CYLINDER** ↵)
Specify center point for base of cylinder or [Elliptical]<0,0,0>:	*Type:* **.75,.75** ↵ (to locate the counterbore at the top of the first hole with the Z component of the point set at 0)
Specify radius for base of cylinder or [Diameter]:	*Type:* **D** ↵
Specify diameter for base of cylinder:	*Type:* **.75** ↵
Specify height of cylinder or [Center of other end]:	*Type:* **−.25**

FIGURE 22–11
The Plate with Counterbored and Countersunk Holes

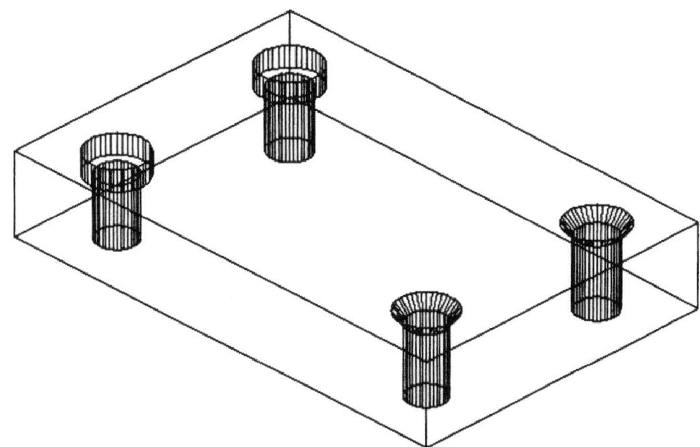

Prompt	Response
Command:	*Click:* **Copy** (or *Type:* **CP** ↵)
Select objects:	*Click:* **on the cylinder just formed**
Specify base point or displacement or [Multiple]:	**Use Osnap-Center to click on the top of the first hole on the left end of the base plate.**
Specify second point of displacement or <use first point as displacement>:	**Use Osnap-Center to click on the top of the second hole on the left end of the base plate.**
Command:	*Click:* **Subtract** (or *Type:* **SU** ↵)
Select solids and regions to subtract from. . .	
Select objects:	*Click:* **on the box**
Select objects:	↵
Select solids and regions to subtract. . .	
Select objects:	*Click:* **on all the cylinders on both ends of the base plate**
Select objects:	↵
Command:	*Click:* **Chamfer** (or *Type:* **CHA** ↵)
Select first line or [Polyline/ Distance/Angle/Trim/Method]:	*Click:* **on the top of one of the holes in the right end of the base plate**
Enter surface selection option [Next/OK (current)]<OK>:	*Type:* **N** ↵ or if the top surface is highlighted press: ↵ **(to accept OK)**

The top surface should be highlighted. If it is not, continue typing N ↵ (for next) until it is.

Prompt	Response
Specify base surface chamfer distance <0.50>:	*Type:* **.125** ↵
Specify other surface chamfer distance <0.50>:	*Type:* **.125** ↵
Select an edge or [Loop]:	*Click:* **on the top edges of the two holes in the right end of the plate**
Select an edge or [Loop]:	↵

Step 10. Use the SOLIDEDIT command to move the counterbored holes 1″ to the right and the left side of the base .5″ to the right.

Prompt	Response
Command:	**Solids Editing-Move Faces**
Select faces or [Undo/Remove]:	*Type:* **c** ↵ to activate a crossing window
Specify first corner: Specify opposite corner:	*Click:* **two corners crossing both counterbored holes.** (You will get surfaces other than the counterbored holes so you must remove those from the selection set.)
10 faces found.	
Select faces or [Undo/Remove/ALL]:	*Type:* **R** ↵
Remove faces or [Undo/Add/ALL]:	*Click:* **any highlighted surface that is not one of the counterbored holes**

Prompt	Response
Remove faces or [Undo/Add/ALL]:	↵
Specify a base point or displacement:	*Click:* **any point**
Specify a second point of displacement:	With Ortho on, **move your mouse to the right and** *Type:* **1** ↵
Enter a face editing option [Extrude/Move/Rotate/Offset/Taper/Delete/Copy/coLor/Undo/eXit]<eXit>:	*Type:* **M** ↵
Select faces or [Undo/Remove/ALL]:	*Click:* **the left side of the base so it is highlighted. Remove any**
other	**surfaces**
Select faces or [Undo/Remove/ALL]:	↵
Specify a base point or displacement:	*Click:* **any point**
Specify a second point of displacement:	With ortho on, **move your mouse to the right and** *Type:* **.5** ↵
[Extrude/Move/Rotate/Offset/Taper/Delete/Copy/coLor/Undo/eXit]<eXit>:	↵
Enter a solids editing option [Face/Edge/Body/Undo/eXit]<eXit>:	↵

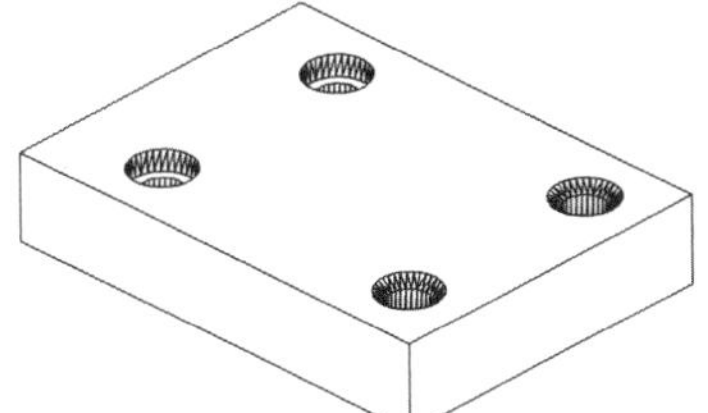

Step 11. Execute the Hide command so that the model appears as shown in Figure 22–12.

Step 12. Insert the cut cylinder into the existing drawing.

FIGURE 22–12
The Completed Plate

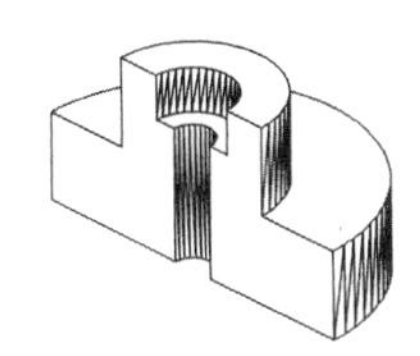

Prompt	Response
Command:	*Type:* **I** ↵
The Insert dialog box appears:	*Click:* **Browse and locate CYLINDER on the A: drive.** *Check:*in the Insertion point area **Specify On screen.** *Click:* **OK** ↵
Specify insertion point or [Scale/X/Y/Z/Rotate/PScale/PX/PY/PZ/PRotate]:	*Type:* **3,2,4** ↵ (This will place the cylinder near the center of the base plate, 3″ above the top surface of the base plate.)
Command:	**Zoom-All**
Command:	**Hide** (or *Type:* **HI** ↵)

Your drawing should now look like Figure 22–13.

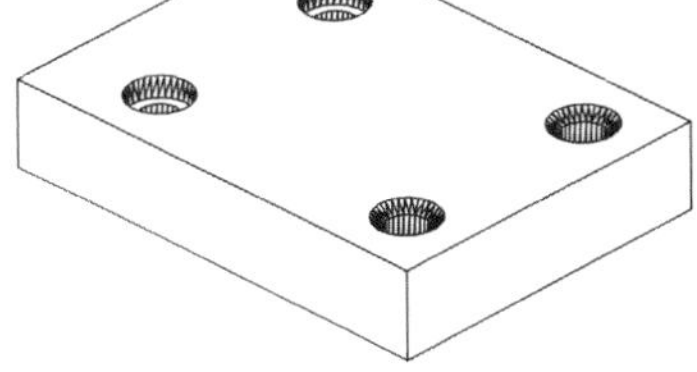

FIGURE 22–13
Exercise 22–1: Completed Model without Rendering

Step 13. *Click:* **Layout1, put your name in the lower right corner, use Mview-Hideplot to remove hidden lines and print the drawing to fit on an 8.5″ × 11″ sheet.**

Step 14. Save your drawing in two places with the name EX22-1(your initials) and Exit AutoCAD.

USING RENDER TO SHADE SOLIDS

The Render command includes many of the features of the 3D Orbit. You have the opportunity to set lights, scenes, and finishes, make film rolls, and modify other parts of this program. This chapter gives information on how to select a material, how to modify the lighting, and how to apply these to render the existing model.

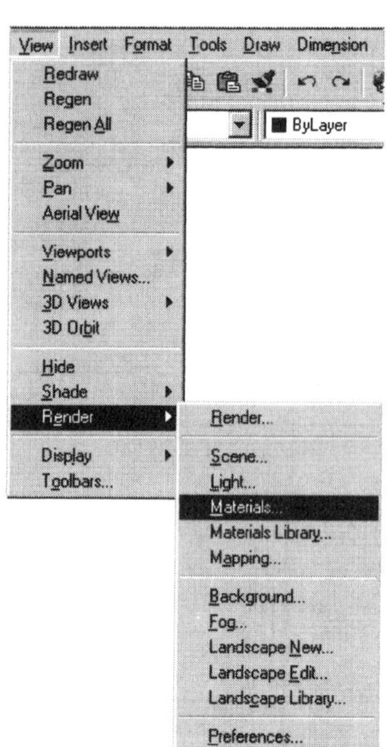

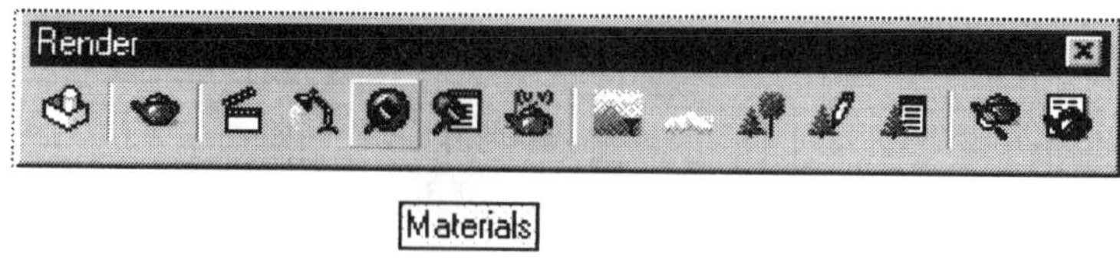

Exercise 22–2: Using Render to Render a Scene

Step 1. **Load AutoCAD.** *Click:* **Open a drawing. . .,** *Click:* **A:EX22-1 and save it to the hard drive of your computer.**

Step 2. **Create a New Material and apply it to the model.**

Prompt	Response
Command:	*Click:* **Materials. . .**
The Materials dialog box (Figure 22–14) appears:	*Click:* **New. . .**
The New Standard Material dialog box (Figure 22–15) appears:	*Type:* **BRASS** (in the Material Name: button)
	Click: **By ACI. . .** (so that the check is removed)
	With the **Color/Pattern button checked,** set **Red=0.84 Green=0.80 Blue=0.09**
	Click: **the Ambient button. Use the slider bar or arrows to set Ambient Light at .50.**
	Set Reflection at .30.
	Set Roughness at .60.
	Click: **Preview**
	Click: **OK**
The Materials dialog box appears:	*Click:* **Attach**
Select objects to attach "BRASS" to:	*Click:* **on the two objects in your display**
Select objects:	↵

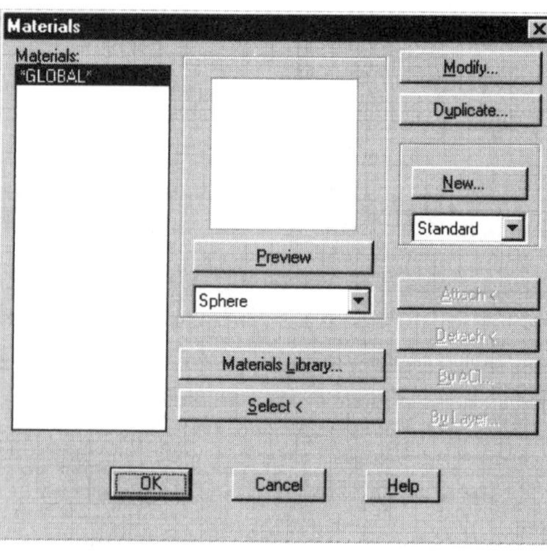

FIGURE 22–14
Materials Dialog Box

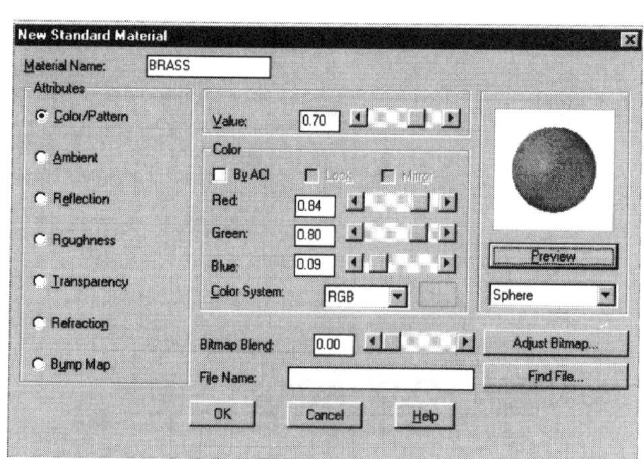

FIGURE 22–15
New Standard Materials Dialog Box

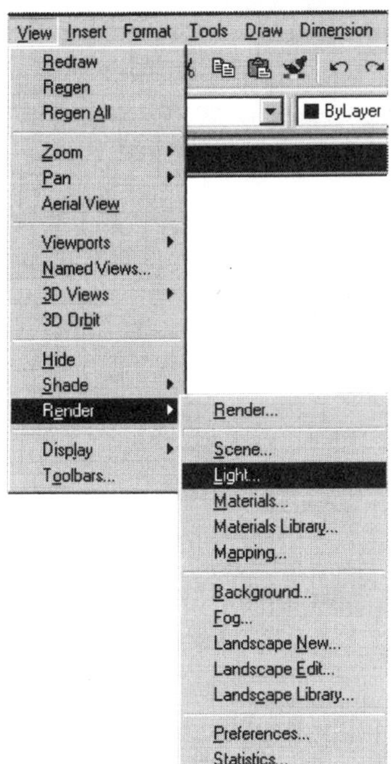

Prompt	Response
Updating drawing. . .done.	
The Materials dialog box appears:	*Click:* **OK**

Step 3. Locate new lights and make new settings for other lighting factors.

Prompt	Response
Command:	**Lights. . .**
The Lights dialog box (Figure 22–16) appears:	*Click:* **New. . .**
Point Light is indicated in the Light Type button (Figure 22–16) (A point light spreads light in all directions.)	
The New Point Light dialog box (Figure 22–17) appears:	*Type:* **L1** (in the Light Name: box)
	Click: **the Modify < box**
Enter light location <current>:	*Type:* **0,0,8** ↵
The New Point Light dialog box appears:	*Click:* **Show. . .**

FIGURE 22–16
Lights Dialog Box with Point Light Indicated

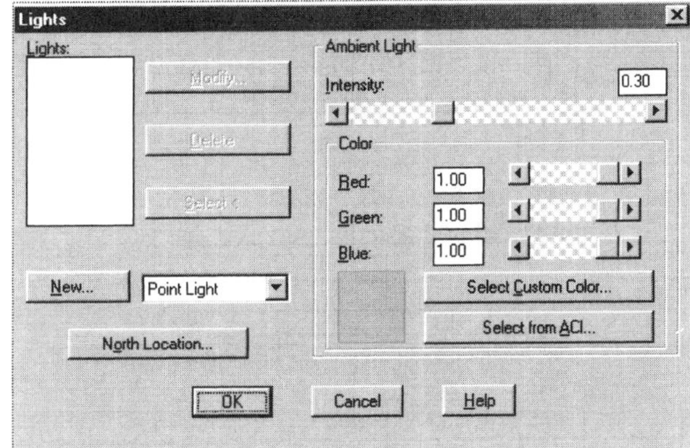

FIGURE 22–17
New Point Light Dialog Box

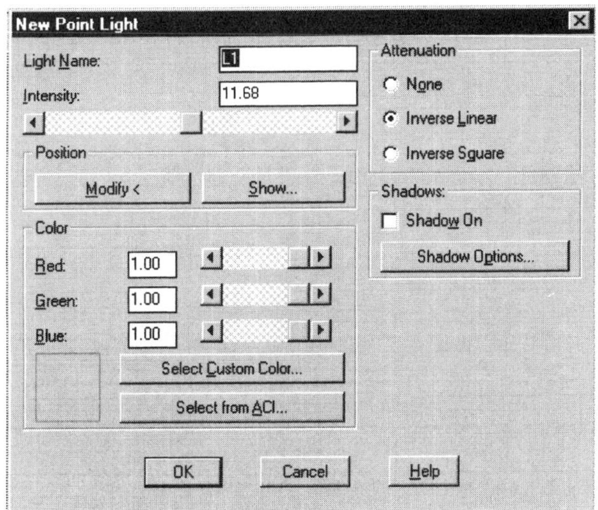

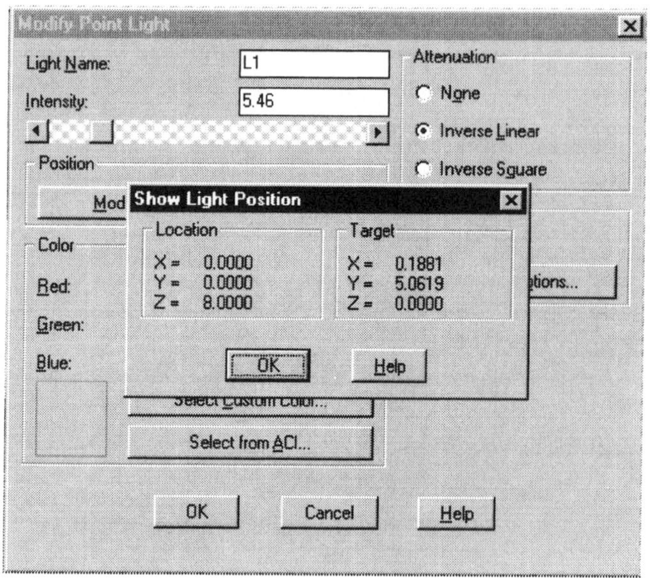

FIGURE 22–18
Show Light L1 Position Dialog Box

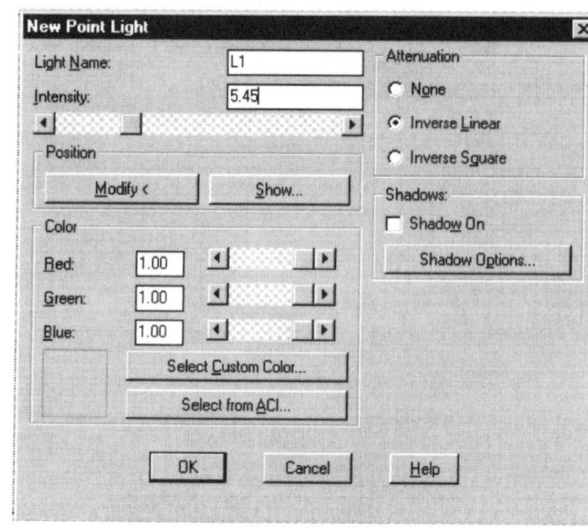

FIGURE 22–19
Set L1 Intensity

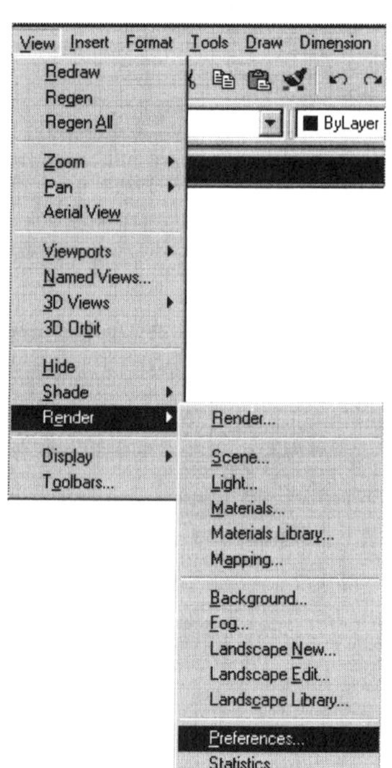

Prompt	Response
The Show Light Position dialog box (Figure 22–18) appears:	*Click:* **OK** (If your light position does not read 0,0,8 as shown, modify the Light Position to correct your mistake.)
The New Point Light dialog box (Figure 22–19) appears:	*Click:* **on the Intensity: slider bar until the light intensity reads approximately 5.46. The maximum light intensity is related to the extents of the drawing and other settings. Experiment with light settings to achieve the desired effect.**
	Click: **OK**

On your own: Locate two more point lights, L2 and L3, with Light Intensity and Position as shown in Figures 22–20 and 22–21. Then set Ambient Light to .30, as shown in Figure 22–22, and *Click:* **OK.**

Let's make one final setting before you render your drawing.

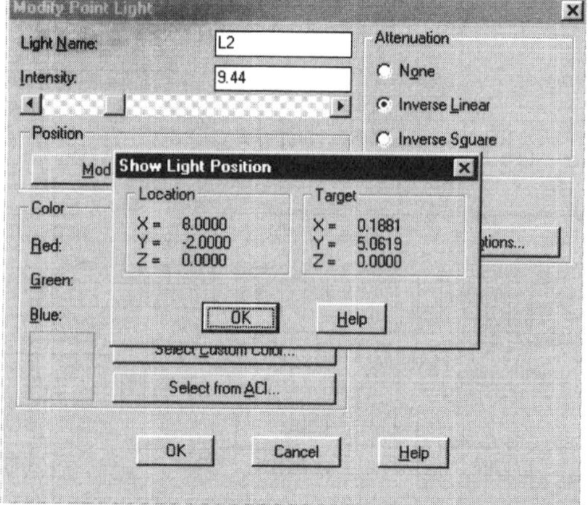

FIGURE 22–20
Light L2 Intensity and Position

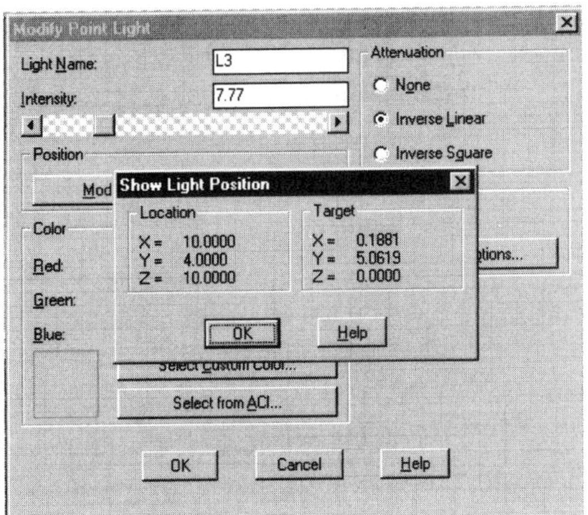

FIGURE 22–21
Light L3 Intensity and Position

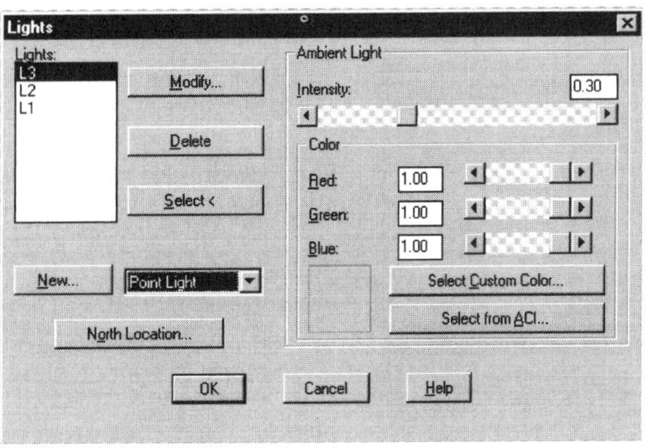

FIGURE 22–22
Final Light Settings

Step 4. Make Rendering Preferences settings.

Prompt	**Response**
Command:	*Click:* **Render-Preferences. . .**
The Rendering Preferences Dialog box (Figure 22–23) appears:	*Click:* **Photo Real in the Rendering Type: box in the Render dialog box,** *Check:* **Smooth Shade,** and **Apply Materials** (if they are not already selected; your display should appear as shown in Figure 22–23.)
	Click: **OK**

Now you are ready to render this drawing.

Step 5. Render the drawing.

FIGURE 22–23
Rendering Preferences Dialog Box

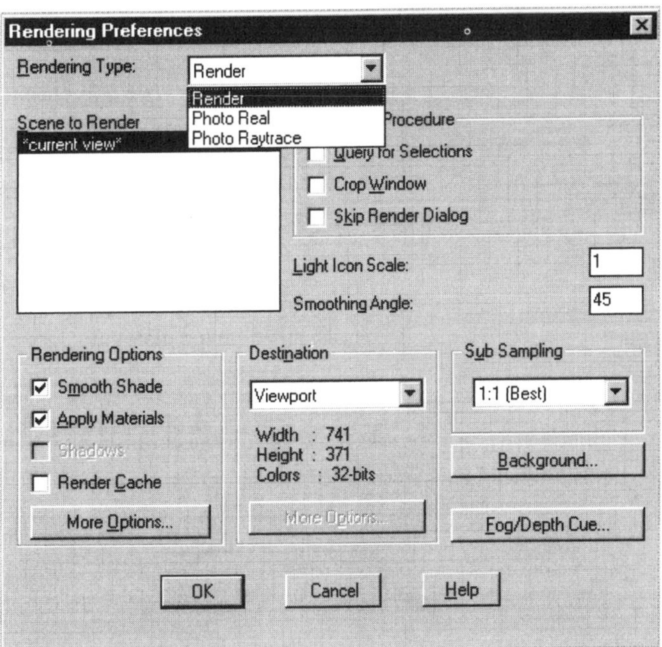

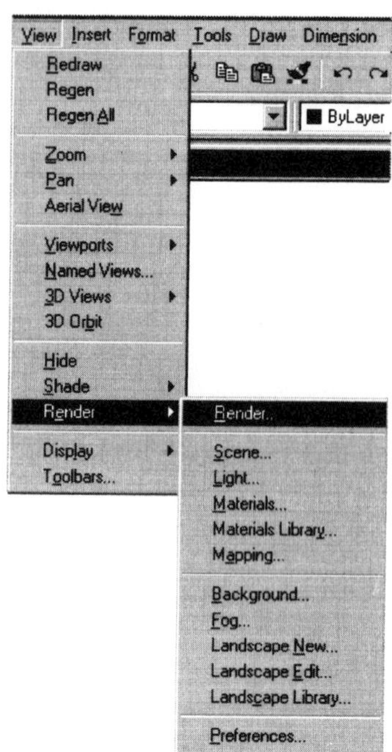

Prompt	Response
Command:	*Click:* **Render-Render. . .** then *Click:* **Background. . .**
The Background dialog box appears:	*Check:* **Gradient**
	Click: **OK**
The Render dialog box appears:	*Click:* **Render**

AutoCAD will display messages indicating that the drawing is being processed; then the display will go blank for a few moments, depending on the power of your computer. Finally, the rendered drawing will appear. You may wish to adjust your rendering by adding or deleting lights, applying new materials, or examining other settings that are available to you.

To return to your drawing display, *Type:* **REGEN** ↵.

Step 6. Save your drawing in two places with the name EX22-2(your initials).

Step 7. Print your rendered drawing on a color printer.

1. Render the drawing again using the Render command.

Prompt	Response
Command:	**Render** (or *Type:* **RENDER** ↵)
The Render dialog box appears:	*Click:* **File in the Destination Area** (You are rendering this drawing to a file.)
The Rendering File dialog box appears with the name EX22-2(your initials) in the File name: text box.	*Click:* **a folder on the hard drive (or a compact or zip drive)** and make a note of where you are saving the file
	Click: **Save**

2. Insert the rendered file in paper space.

Prompt	Response
Command:	*Click:* **Layout1** to enter paper space
The Page Setup dialog box appears:	*Click:* **OK**
	Erase the paper space viewport that appears. (If you get the message that the object is on a locked layer, unlock the layer by *Clicking:* on the locked lock in the layer list, then erase it.)
Command:	*Click:* **Insert-raster image…**
The Select Image File dialog box appears:	**Locate your rendered file and** *Click:* **on it so the name EX22-2(your initials) appears in the File name: text box.**
	Click: **Open**
The Image dialog box appears:	*Click:* **OK** (Checks should appear in the Specify on-screen boxes in both Insertion point and Scale areas.)
Specify insertion poin (0,0):	*Click:* **a point inside the lower left corner of the dashed lines**
Specify scale factor or [Unit]<1>:	**Move your mouse very slowly upward to the right to** *Click:* **the upper right corner of the image.** (The image will be much larger than the distance you moved the mouse.)

3. **Use Dtext (*Click:* Single Line Text or *Type:* DT ↵) to place your name in the lower right corner of the page using some readable font other than txt.**
4. **Print the drawing to fit on an 11″ × 8½″ sheet.**

Exercise 22–3: Using Intersection to Form a Solid Model from the Common Volume of Two Intersecting Solids

Drawing the solid model in Exercise 22–3 demonstrates some powerful tools that can be used to form complex models. In this exercise two separate solid shapes are drawn and moved so that they intersect. Interfere is used to combine the shapes to form one solid model from the common volume of the two intersecting solids. Figure 22–24 shows the two separate solid shapes and the solid model that is formed from the common volume of the two solid shapes.

Step 1. Load AutoCAD. *Click:* **Create Drawings-Wizards-Quick Setup.**

Step 2. Make the following settings:

Units: Decimal—2 digits to the right of the decimal point
Area: Width: 11
Length: 8.5
ISOLINES: 20
FACETRES: 2
GRID: .2
SNAP: .05
TEXT STYLE: Standard FONT: simplex.shx HEIGHT: 0

LAYERS: NAME	Color	Linetype	Lineweight
R	Red	Continuous	Default
M	Magenta	Continuous	Default
G	Green	Continuous	Default

Set layer M as the current layer.
Split the screen into two vertical viewports. Select a viewpoint of 315°–30° from the Viewpoint Presets dialog box in the right viewport.

FIGURE 22–24
Two Separate Solids and the Model Created with the Intersection Command

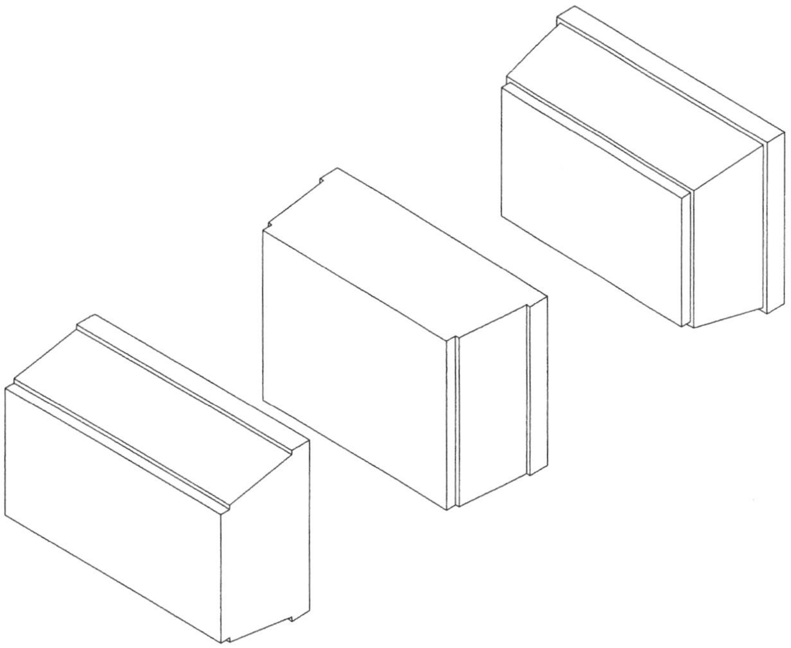

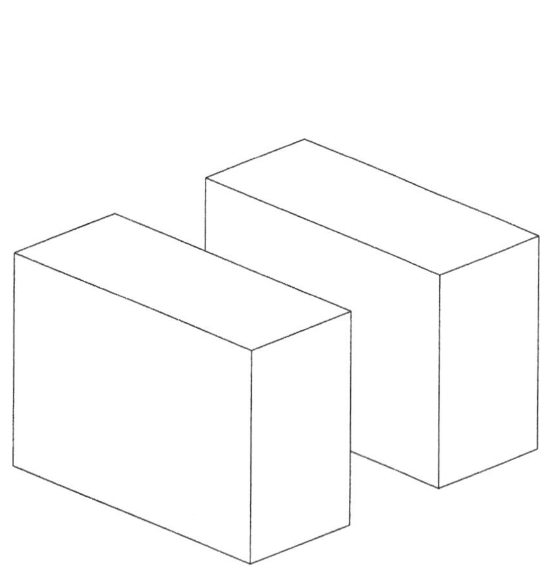

FIGURE 22–25
Draw Two Boxes the Same Size

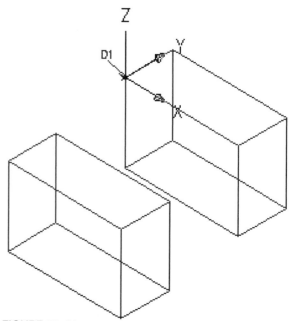

FIGURE 22–26
Move the UCS to the Top of One of the Boxes

Step 3. Draw two boxes.

On your own (Figure 22–25):

With SNAP ON, **draw two boxes measuring 6 (length) × 2.5 (width) ×** 4 **(height)** (you can draw one and copy it) as shown in Figure 22–25. These boxes will be used to help draw the two separate solids. Their location is not critical.

Step 4. Draw solid shape 1.

Draw shape 1 using the box in the back, as follows:

Use UCS to relocate the UCS to the top of the box in the back (Figure 22–26):

Prompt	Response
Command:	*Click:* **New UCS-Origin**
Specify new origin point <0,0,0>:	*Type:* **END** ↵
of	**D1**

Use Plan to change the view in the left viewport to the plan view of the new UCS:

Prompt	Response
Command:	*Click:* **3D Views-Plan view-current UCS** (or *Type:* **PLAN** ↵, then *Press:* ↵)

On your own (Figure 22–27):

1. Set layer R current.
2. With SNAP ON (OSNAP OFF), use the Polyline command to draw the right side *only* of the outline shown in Figure 22–27 on the top surface of the box in the back.
3. Complete the outline as follows:

Mirror the polyline you just drew (Figure 22–27):

Prompt	Response
Command:	*Click:* **Mirror**
Select objects:	*Click:* **on the Polyline you just drew**

FIGURE 22–27
Dimensions for the Top of the Box

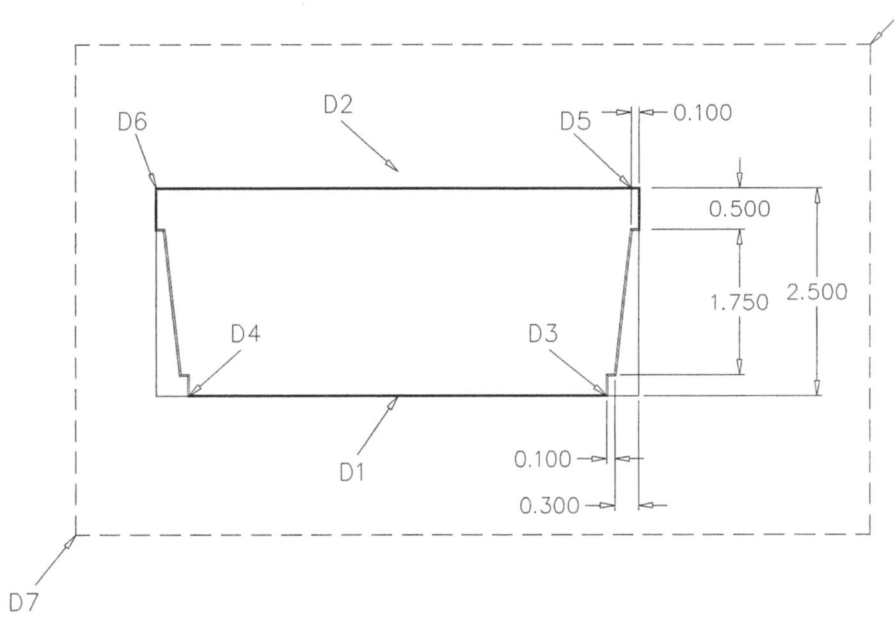

Prompt	Response
Select objects:	↵
Specify first point of mirror line:	**D1** (Use Osnap-Midpoint.)
Specify second point of mirror line:	**With ORTHO ON, click on a point above the first point, D2.**
Delete source objects? [Yes/No] <N>	↵

Use Polyline to draw lines connecting the two ends of the outline (Figure 22–27):

Prompt	Response
Command:	*Type:* **PL** ↵
Specify start point:	**D3** (Use Osnap-Endpoint.)
Specify next point or [Arc/Close/Halfwidth/Length/Undo/Width]:	**D4** (Use Osnap-Endpoint.)
Specify next point or [Arc/Close/Halfwidth/Length/Undo/Width]:	↵
Command:	↵ **(Repeat PLINE)**
Specify start point:	**D5** (Use Osnap-Endpoint.)
Specify next point or [Arc/Close/Halfwidth/Length/Undo/Width]:	**D6** (Use Osnap-Endpoint.)
Specify next point or [Arc/Close/Halfwidth/Length/Undo/Width]:	↵

Use Pedit (Edit Polyine) to combine all the polylines forming the outline into a single polyline (Figure 22–27):

Prompt	Response
Command:	**Edit Polyline** (or *Type:* **PE** ↵)
Select polyline:	*Click:* **on one of the polylines you just drew** ↵
Enter an option [Close/Join/Width/Edit vertex/Fit/Spline/Decurve/Ltype gen/Undo]:	*Type:* **J** ↵
Select objects:	**D7**

Prompt	Response
Specify opposite corner:	**D8**
Select objects:	↵
2 segments added to polyline	
Enter an option [Close/Join/Width/Edit vertex/ Fit/Spline/Decurve/Ltype gen/Undo]:	↵ (to exit the Pedit (Edit Polyline) command)

On your own:

1. Erase the solid box; it was used for construction only.
2. Return to the World UCS.

Use Extrude to complete shape 1 by extruding the polyline, −4 height, 0 degrees extrusion taper angle (Figure 22–28):

Prompt	Response
Command:	**Extrude** (or *Type:* **EXT**↵)
Select objects:	**D1**
Select objects:	↵
Specify Height of extrusion or [Path]:	*Type:* **−4** ↵
Specify angle of taper for extrusion <0>:	↵

The display of solid shape 1 should appear as shown in Figure 22–29.

Step 5. Draw solid shape 2.

Draw the second solid using the other box to help with construction, as follows:

On your own:

1. Set layer G current.
2. Freeze layer R, to more easily see what you are doing on the left box.
3. Relocate the UCS to the right side of the front box (Figure 22–30) in the right viewport.

On your own (Figures 22–31 and 22–32):

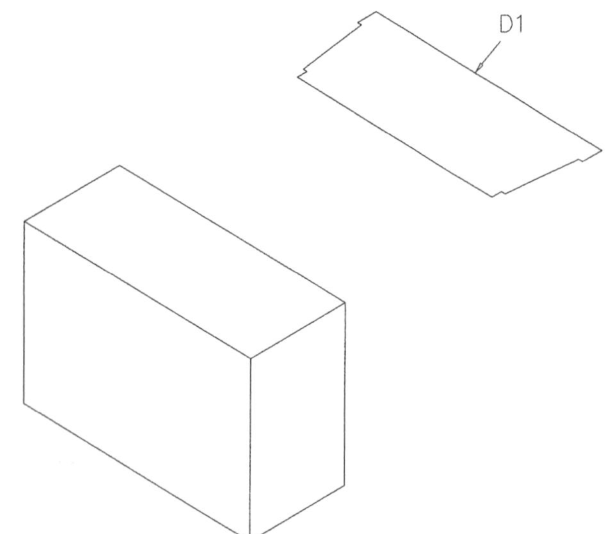

FIGURE 22–28
Click: The Polyline to Extrude It.

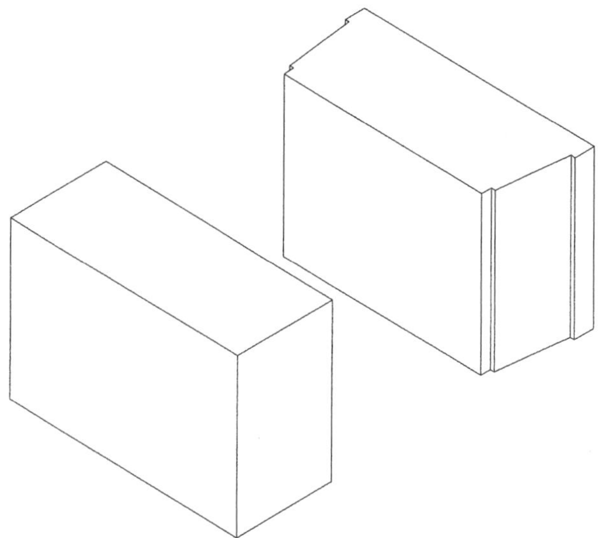

FIGURE 22–29
The Top Polyline Extruded

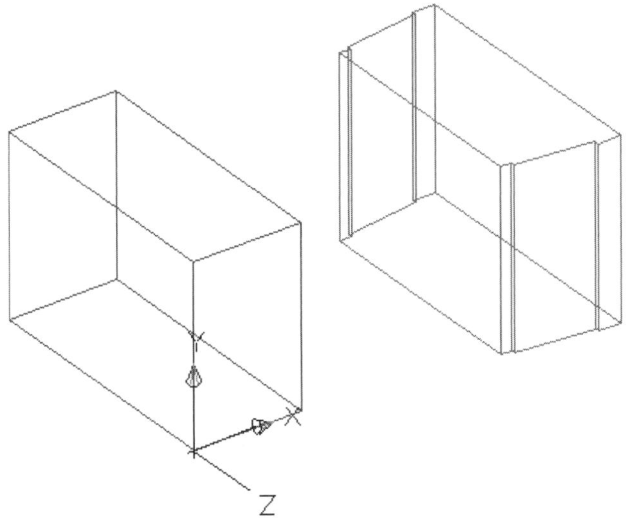

FIGURE 22–30
Move the UCS Using UCS-3 Point

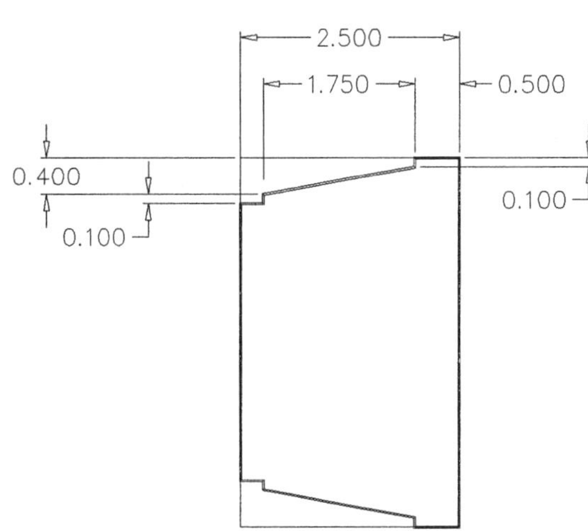

FIGURE 22–31
Dimensions for the Right Side of the Other Box

1. With SNAP ON, use the Polyline command to draw the top part *only* of the outline shown in Figure 22–31 on the side surface of the box.
2. Mirror the top part of the outline using the midpoint of the vertical edge of the box as the first point on the mirror line. Pick any other point to the right of the first point with ORTHO ON.
3. Complete drawing the outline (lines connecting the top and bottom polylines) using Polyline and Osnap-Endpoint.
4. Use the Pedit (Edit polyline) command to join all the polylines drawn into a single polyline.
5. Erase the box.
6. Use the Extrude command to extrude the polyline −6 in the negative Z direction.
7. Return to the world UCS.
8. Thaw layer R.

The display should appear as shown in Figure 22–32.

FIGURE 22–32
The Side Polyline Extruded

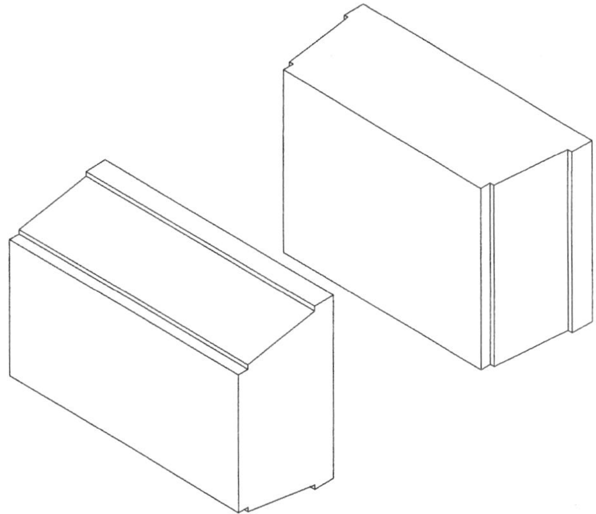

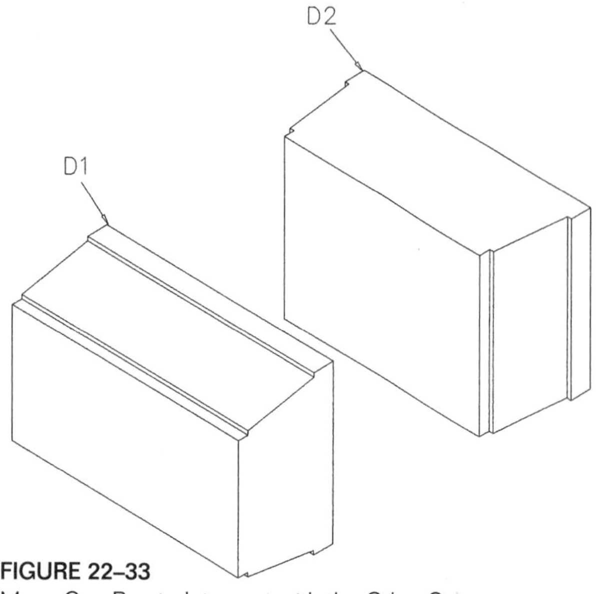

FIGURE 22–33
Move One Box to Intersect with the Other One

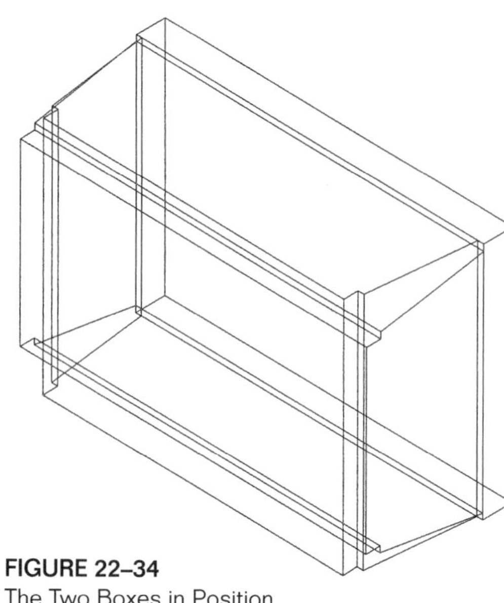

FIGURE 22–34
The Two Boxes in Position

Step 6. Move one solid to intersect with the other solid.

Use the Move command to move the solid in front to intersect with the other solid (Figure 22–33):

Prompt	Response
Command:	*Click:* **Move** (or *Type:* **M** ↵)
Select objects:	*Click:* **on the shape in front**
Select objects:	↵
Specify base point or displacement:	*Type:* **END** ↵
of	**D1**
Specify second point of displacement or <use first point as displacement>:	*Type:* **END** ↵
of	**D2**

On your own (Figure 22–34):

Zoom in on the two intersecting solids, so your display appears similar to Figure 22–34.

Step 7. Use Intersect to form a solid model from the common volume of the two intersecting solids (Figure 22–35).

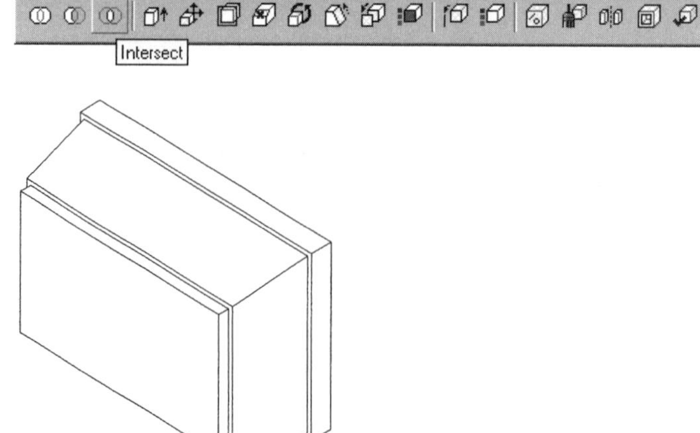

FIGURE 22–35
The Intersected Model

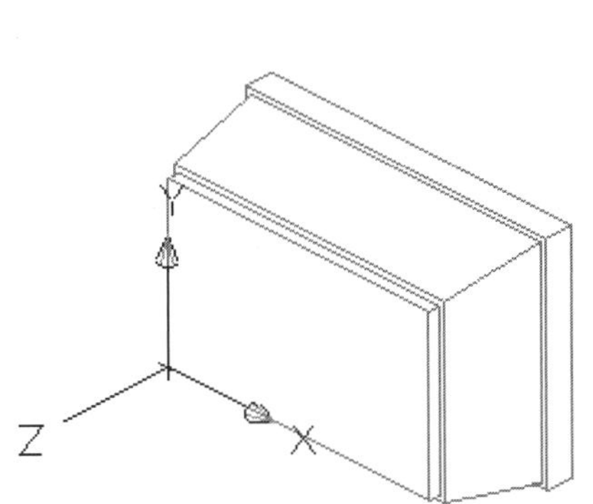

FIGURE 22–36
Move the UCS to the Front of the Model

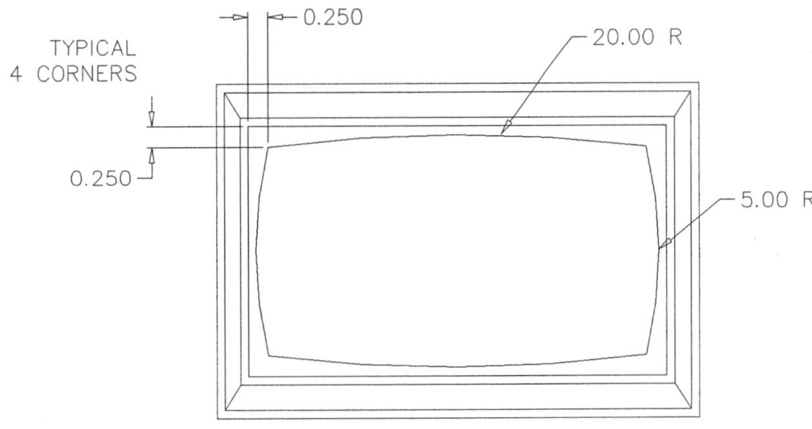

FIGURE 22–37
Dimensions for the Front Face

Prompt	**Response**
Command:	*Click:* **Intersect** (or *Type:* **IN** ↵)
Select objects:	*Click:* **on both shapes**
Select objects:	↵

The display should appear as shown in Figure 22–35.

Step 8. Complete drawing the combined solid.

On your own (Figures 22–36, 22–37, and 22–38):

Select a UCS that is common with the front surface of the solid, Figure 22–36, and select Plan so that you can easily draw the outline shown in Figure 22–37.
Use Arc-Start, End, Radius to draw the curved outline for the front face. Use the dimensions shown in Figure 22–37.
Join all four arcs to form a single polyline using Pedit.
Use Extrude to extrude the single polyline −.25 (in the negative Z direction).
Use Subtract to subtract the extruded polyline from the combined solid, Figure 22–38.

The display should appear as shown in Figure 22–38.

Step 9. Use Layout Wizard to create a 4-view drawing and scale and align the views. Make sure you are in a single viewport with UCS set to World.

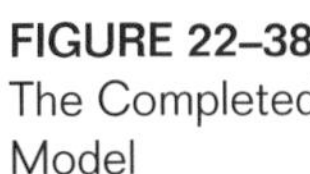

FIGURE 22–38
The Completed Model

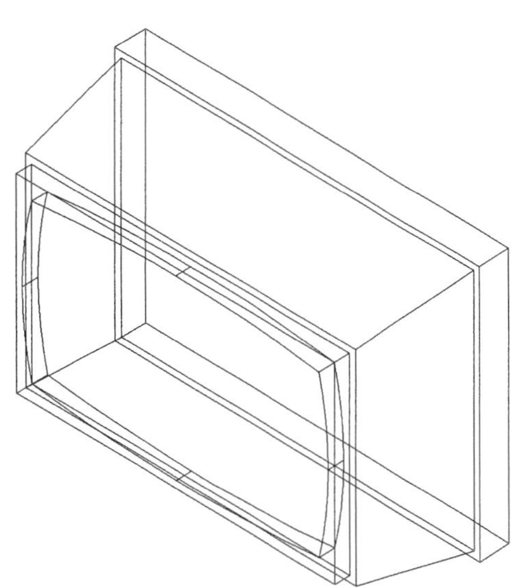

Prompt	Response
Command:	*Click:* **Viewports-Single** (or *Type:* **VPORTS** ↵, then *Type:* **SI** ↵)
Command:	*Click:* **New UCS-World** (or *Type:* **UCS** ↵, then *Press:* ↵ to accept the default, world UCS)

Delete any existing layouts. *Click:* **the layout name,** *Right click:* **to get the shortcut menu, then** *Click:* **Delete.** (You will not be able to delete the last layout—Layout1.)

Add a new layout named Layout2.

Prompt	Response
Command:	*Click:* **Wizards-Create Layout...** (from the Tools menu)

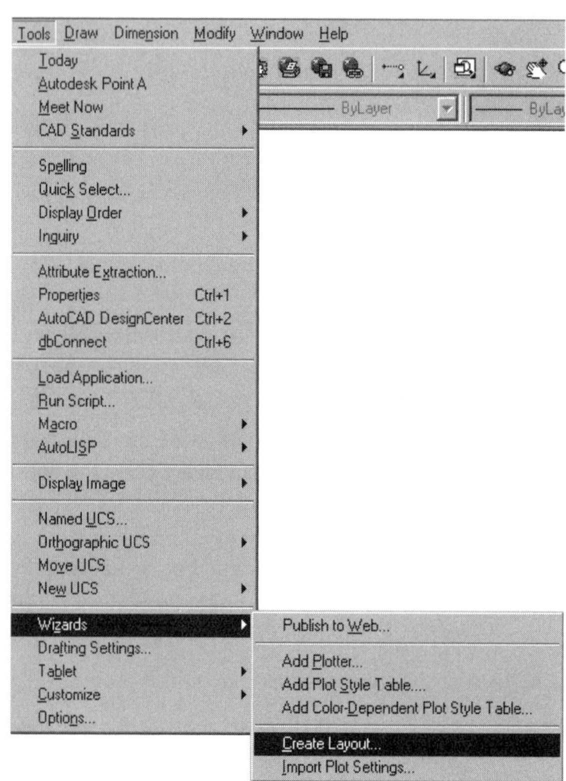

The Layout Wizard appears with the name Layout1:	*Click:* **Next**
The Printer option appears:	*Click:* **DFW ePlot(optimized for plotting).pc3** *Click:* **Next**
The Paper size option appears:	Locate **ANSI B [17.00 × 11.00 Inches] in the paper size list and click on it.** *Click:* **Next**
The Orientation option appears:	*Click:* **Landscape** *Click:* **Next**
The Title block option appears:	*Click:* **ANSI B title block.dwg** *Click:* **Next**
The Define viewports option appears:	*Click:* **Std. 3D Engineering Views** *Click:* **Next**
The Pick Location option appears:	*Click:* **Select location <**

Prompt	Response
Specify first corner:	*Type:* **.5,.5** ↵
Specify other corner:	*Type:* **10.5,8** ↵
The Finish option appears:	*Click:* **Finish** (Figure 22–39)

Use the MVSETUP command to scale viewports so all four views are the same scale (Figure 22–40).

Prompt	Response
Command:	*Type:* **MVSETUP** ↵
Enter an option [Align/Create/Scale viewports/Options/Title block/Undo]:	*Type:* **S** ↵
Select the viewports to scale. . .	*Type:* **ALL** ↵ (or select all four viewports using a crossing window)
Select objects:	↵
Set zoom scale factors for viewports. Interactively/<Uniform>:	↵
Set the ratio of paper space units to model space units. . .	
Enter the number of paper space units <1.0>:	↵
Enter the number of model space units <1.0>:	*Type:* **2** ↵
Enter an option [Align/Create/Scale viewports/Options/Title block/Undo]:	↵ **(Use the align option (*Type:* A ↵ and follow the prompts) of the MVSETUP command to align viewports if necessary)**

All four views are scaled the same, as shown in Figure 22–40.

Step 10. On your own:

1. Use the Move command to move the four viewports so they are arranged as shown in Figure 22–41.

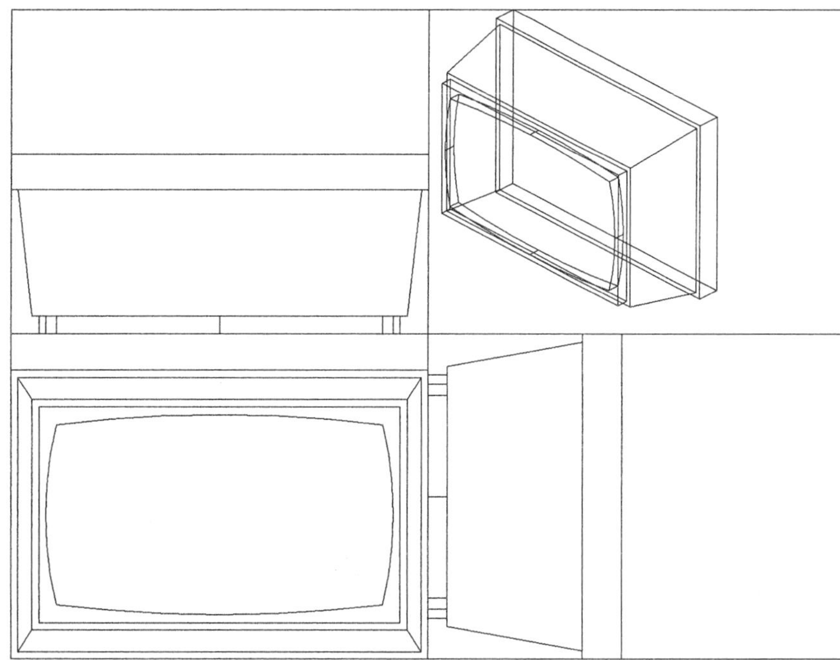

FIGURE 22–39
Views Obtained by Selecting Std. 3D Engineering Views

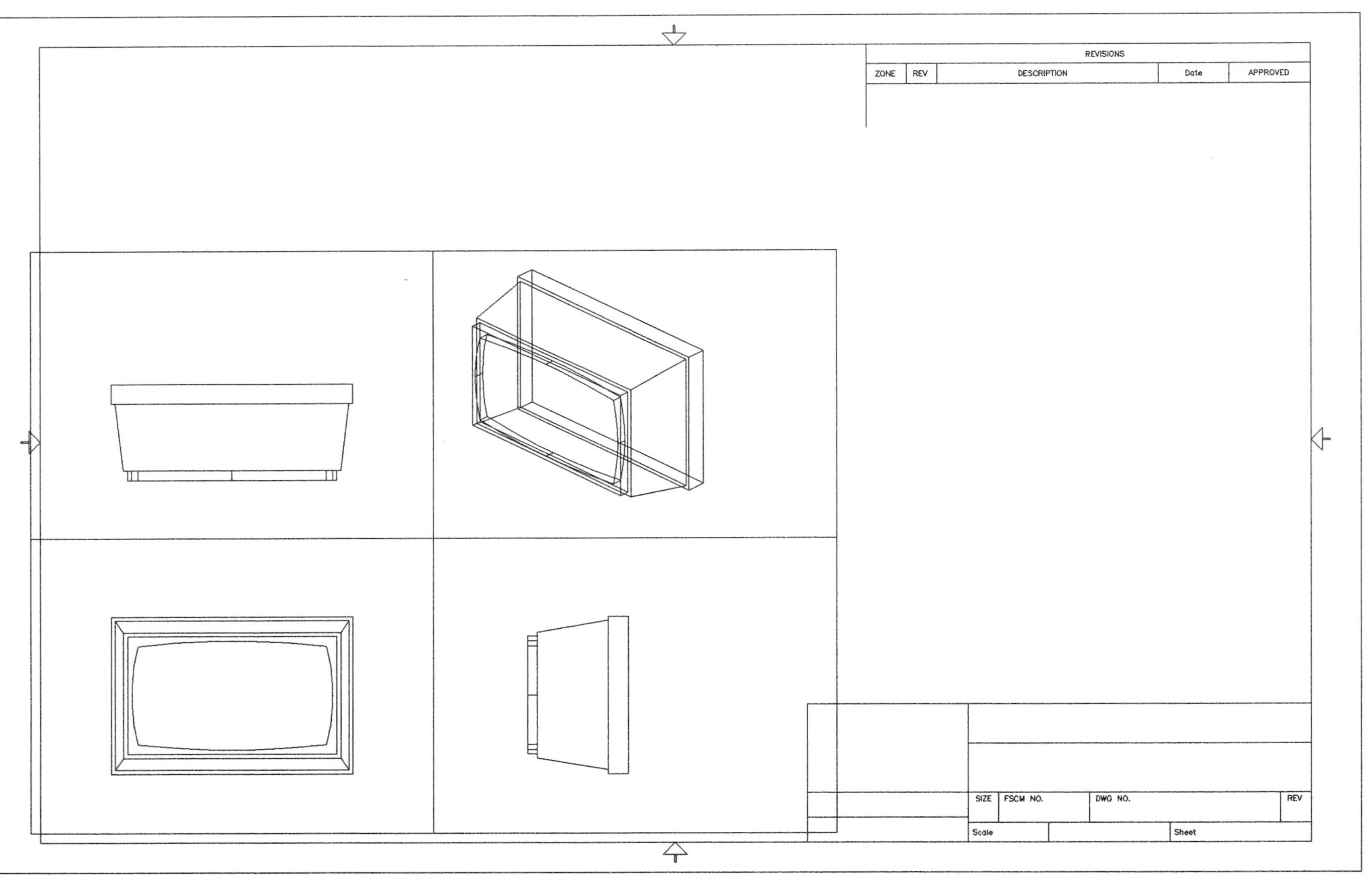

FIGURE 22–40
All viewports are the same scale

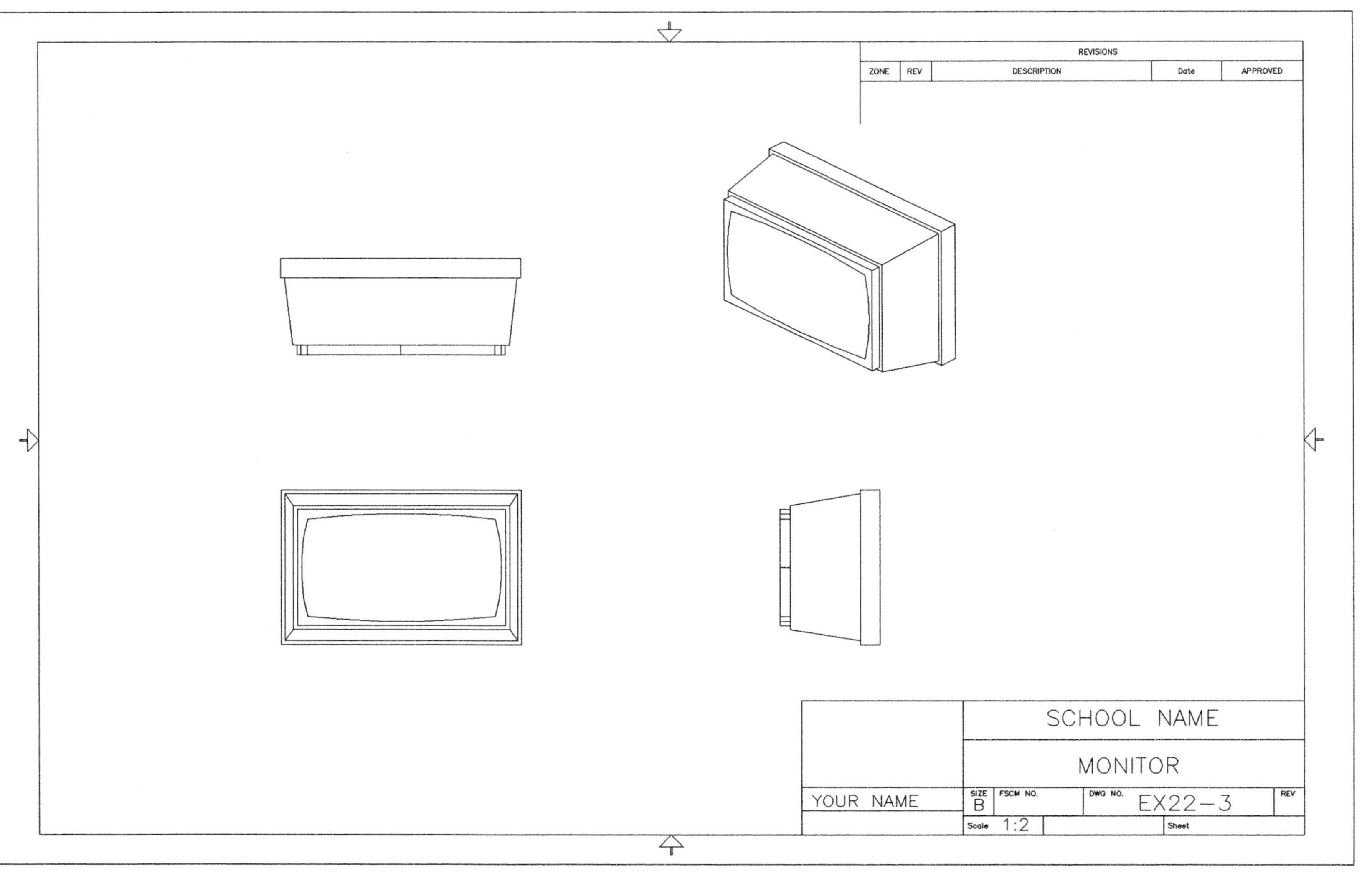

FIGURE 22–41
Exercise 22–3 Complete

2. Use the Hideplot option of Mview to remove hidden lines in the 3-D view before plotting.
3. Create a new layer named VP, turn it OFF, and use the Properties. . . command to change the outside edge of each viewport to that layer.
4. Fill out the title block with the correct information as shown in Figure 22–41.

Step 11. Print the drawing on a standard 17″ × 11″ sheet.

Step 12. Save the drawing in two places with the name EX22-3(your initials) and exit AutoCAD.

PUBLISHING TO THE WEB

The Publish to Web Wizard allows you to create a Web page for the Internet using the following options.

Image Types You can choose from three image types (file formats).
Templates You can select one of four templates for the layout of your Web page, or you can design your own template.
Themes You can choose a theme for the template. Themes allow you to change the colors and fonts in your Web page.
i-drop You can select the i-drop property for your Web page so that visitors to your page can drag drawing files into AutoCAD. The i-drop feature is ideally suited for publishing block libraries (a group of drawings) to the Internet.
Select Drawings This option allow you to select any of your drawings and choose any or all of the layouts in that drawing to display on your Web page.
Generate Images Here you can regenerate images for drawings that have changed or regenerate all the images.
Preview and Post This option allows you to see what your Web page will look like before you post it onto the Internet.

Let's use the Publish to Web Wizard to create a Web page.

Exercise 22–4: Create a Web Page

If you are still in AutoCAD, *Click:* **Wizards-Publish to Web** from the Tools menu. If not, enter AutoCAD and do the same.

Prompt	Response
Command:	*Click:* **Wizards-Publish to Web** (from the Tools menu)
The Publish to Web-Create Web Page Wizard appears:	*Click:* **the Create New Web Page button** if it is not already active.
	Click: **Next>**
The Create Web Page screen appears:	*Type:* **(YOUR NAME)'s HOME PAGE** in the upper open box (Figure 22–42).
	Type: **THIS IS A WEB PAGE FOR MY CLASS WORK** in the Provide a description to appear on your Web page box.
	Click: **Next>**
The Select Image Type screen appears:	*Click:* **Next>** (or select another of three types from the list)
The Select Template screen appears:	*Click:* **List plus summary** (or another template if you choose)

FIGURE 22–42
The Publish to Web Wizard

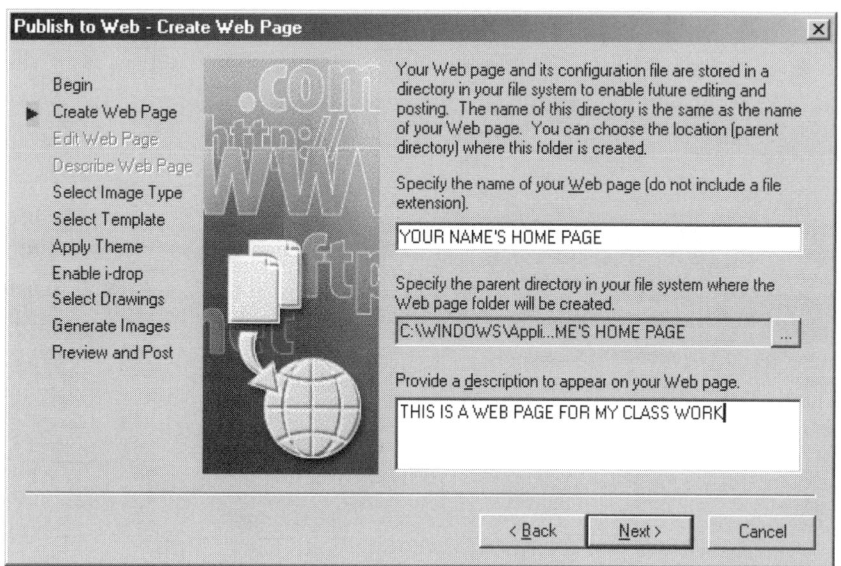

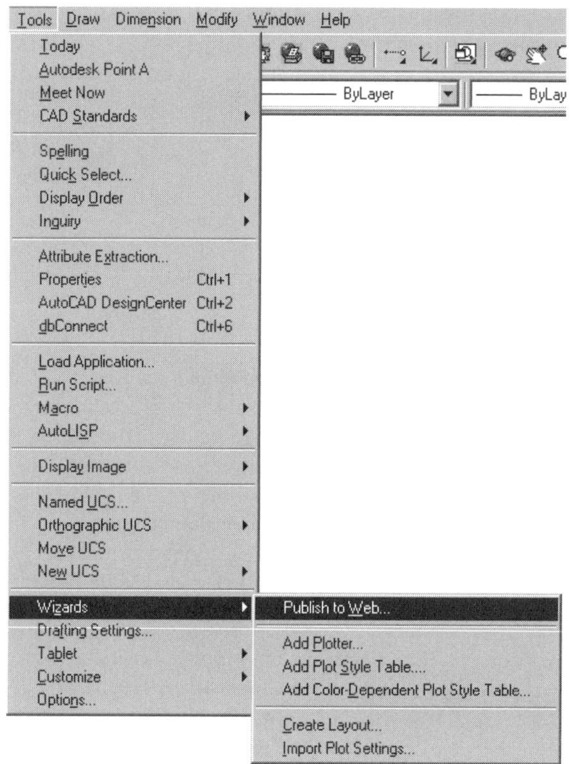

Prompt	**Response**
	Click: **Next>**
The Apply Theme screen appears:	*Click:* **Any of the 7 themes from the list** (I chose Supper Club.)
	Click: **Next>**
The Enable i-drop screen appears:	*Check:* **Enable i-drop**
	Click: **Next>**
The Select Drawings screen appears:	*Click:* **the Ellipsis (the three dots to the right of the Drawing: list) and find your drawing of EX20-2(your initials) on a disk or in a folder on**

Prompt	Response
	the hard drive. When you find it *Click:* **Open**
	Click: **the Layout list:**
	Click: **Next>**
	Click: **each one of the Layouts** and *Click:* **Add>**
	When all the Layouts are in the Image list, *Click:* **Next>**
The Generate Images screen appears:	*Click:* **Next>**
The Preview and Post screen appears:	*Click:* **Preview**
A preview of your Web page appears:	*Click:* **Post Now (or** *Click:* **<Back if you want to change something.) (You can also edit this page with this wizard.)**
The Posting Web dialog box appears:	*Click:* **Save**
The Posting successfully completed Message appears:	*Click:* **OK**
The Preview and Post screen appears:	*Click:* **send Email and send yourself an email if you have an email address so you have a link to the location of your Web page.**
The Preview and Post screen appears:	*Click:* **Finish**

EXERCISES

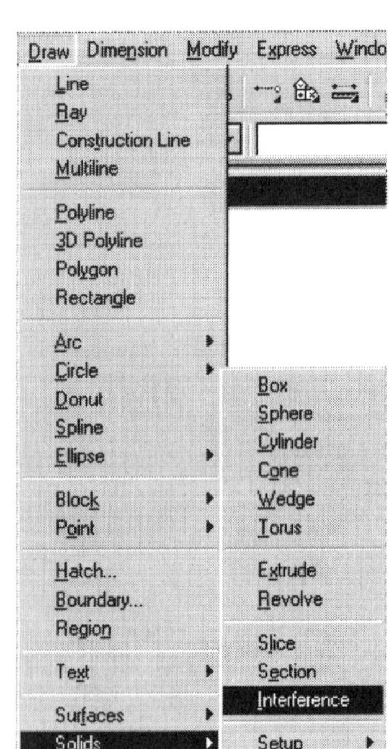

EXERCISE 22–1. Construct the cylindrical object and the base plate in Figure 22–13 using the steps described in this chapter. Print the drawing and turn it in.

EXERCISE 22–2. Use Render to render the model as described in this chapter. Show the rendered drawing to your instructor.

EXERCISE 22–3. Construct the solid model as described in this chapter. Use Layout Wizard and MV Setup to make the four views, scale and align the views, and print the drawing as stated in the instructions.

EXERCISE 22–4. Complete Exercise 22–4 as described in this chapter.

EXERCISE 22–5. Use Box to construct two solids as follows:

Box 1: First corner: Type: 2,2
Other corner: Type: 8,6
Height: Type: 1

Box 2 First corner: Type: 4,4
Other corner: Type: 10,8
Height: Type: 1

Use Interference to create a solid of the overlapping area of the two models. (The display will appear the same but a new solid is created of the overlapping area.) Move the new solid to one side, then use Dist to determine the length and width of the resulting solid:

Length: ____________

Width: ____________

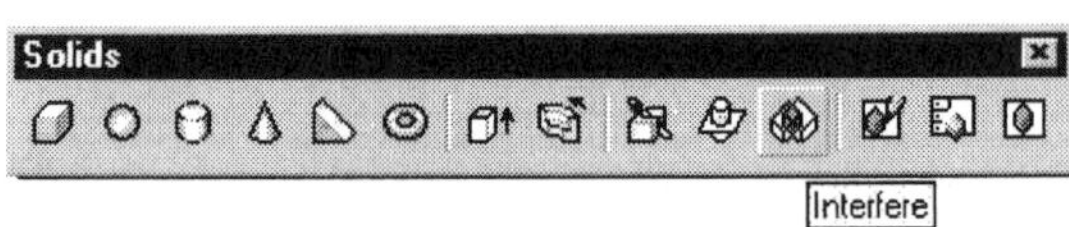

EXERCISE 22–6. Use Solids commands (Extrude) to make a solid model of the object shown in the engineering sketch shown in Figure 22–43. Pick a viewpoint that will display the model in approximately the same orientation as shown in Exercise 22–1. Render the solid in any color you choose.

EXERCISE 22–7. Use Solids commands (Draw the front view as a polyline and extrude it) to make a solid model of the object shown in the engineering sketch shown in Figure 22–44. Pick a viewpoint that will display the model in approximately the same orientation as shown in Exercise 22–1. Render the solid in any color you choose.

EXERCISE 22–8. Make a solid model of the micrometer shown in Figure 22–45. Use the dimensions shown to draw the object full size. Use three viewports as shown in Figure 22–45. Your final drawing should look like that figure without dimensions.

EXERCISE 22–9. Use Solids commands to make a solid model of the object shown in the engineering sketch shown in Figure 22–46. Use Slice to cut the pulley and bushing only. Measure this drawing and make your model the same size. All these objects are found in the 3-D model. Pick a viewpoint that will display the model in approximately the same orientation as shown in Exercise 22–1. Render the solid in any color you choose.

FIGURE 22–43
Exercise 22–6

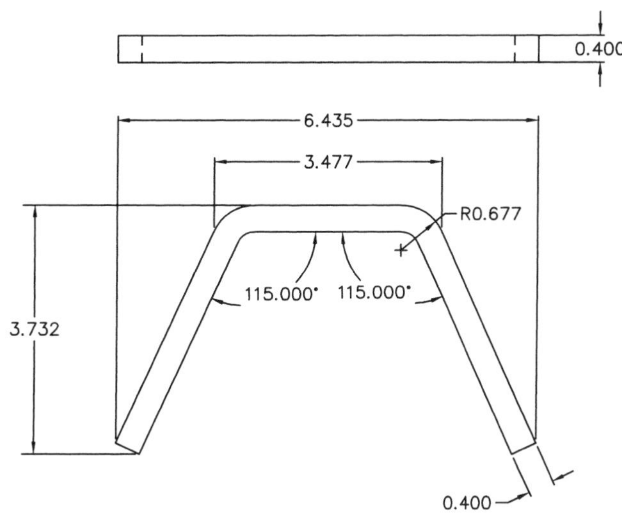

FIGURE 22–44
Exercise 22–7

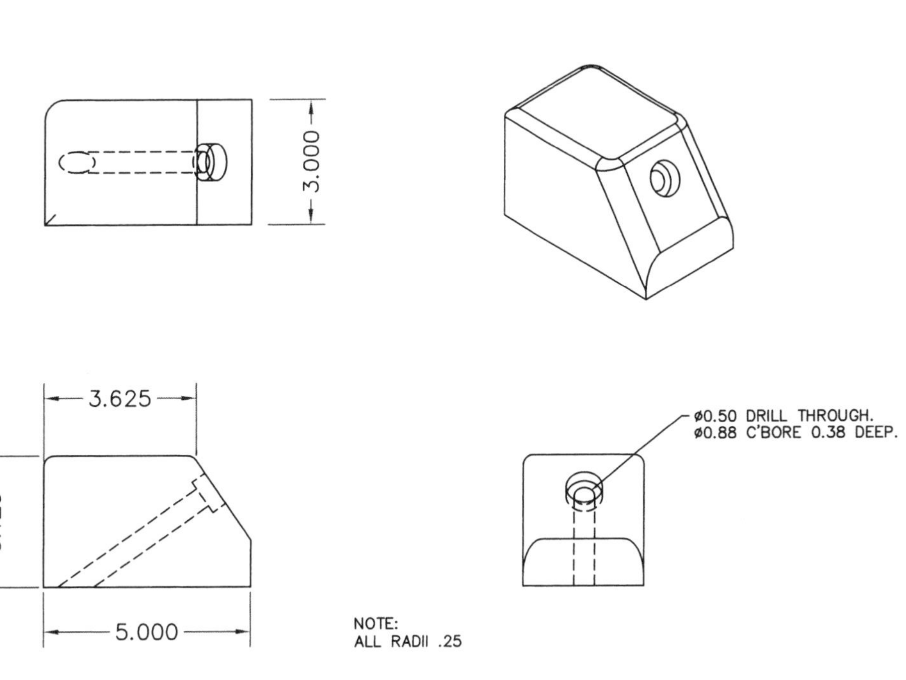

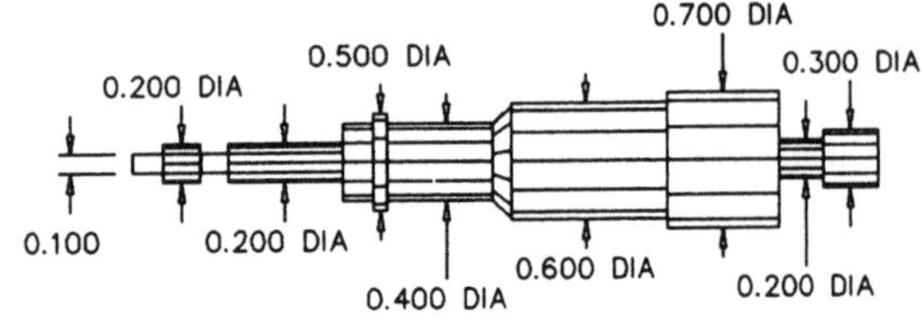

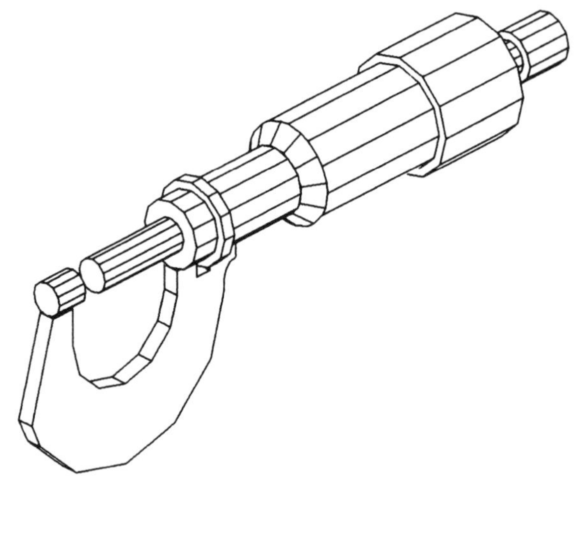

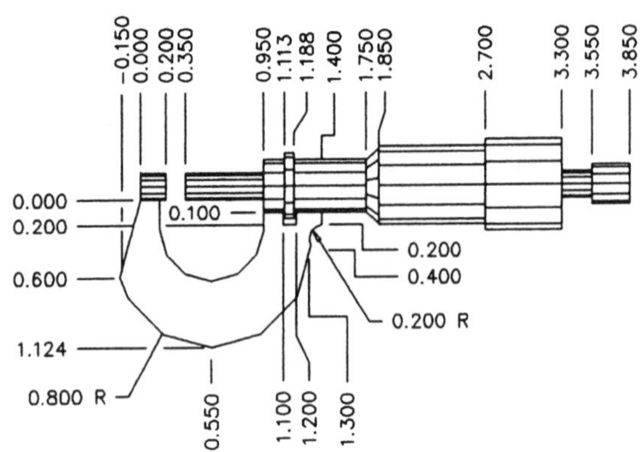

FIGURE 22–45
Exercise 22–8

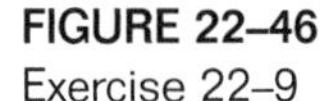

FIGURE 22–46
Exercise 22–9

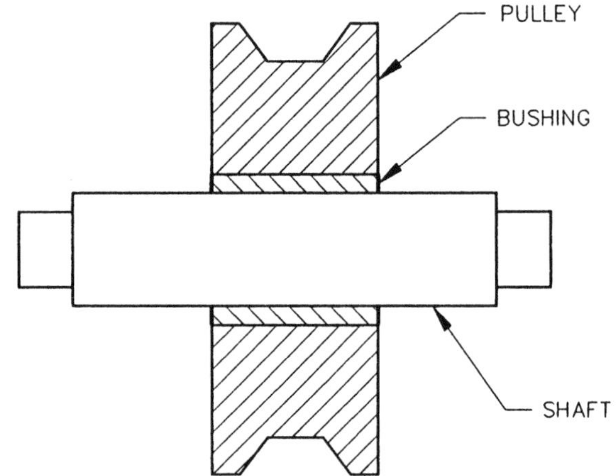

EXERCISE 22–10. Make a solid model of the lounge chair shown in Figure 22–47. Use the grid and the callouts to draw the object full size. Each grid mark is 2″. The slats are 40″ long. Your final drawing should look like the 3-D view of Figure 22–47. Assign appropriate materials from the render materials library, position three lights, and render the model using 3D Orbit in the perspective mode with Gouraud shading. Plot the drawing to fit on an 11″ × 8.5″ sheet.

EXERCISE 22–11. Make a solid model of the mounting flange shown in Figure 22–48. Use the dimensions shown to draw the object full size. Choose a viewpoint similar to that in Figure 22–13 and use 3D Orbit to obtain a perspective view and render it with Gouraud shading. Plot the drawing to fit on an 11″ × 8.5″ sheet.

FIGURE 22–47
Exercise 22–10

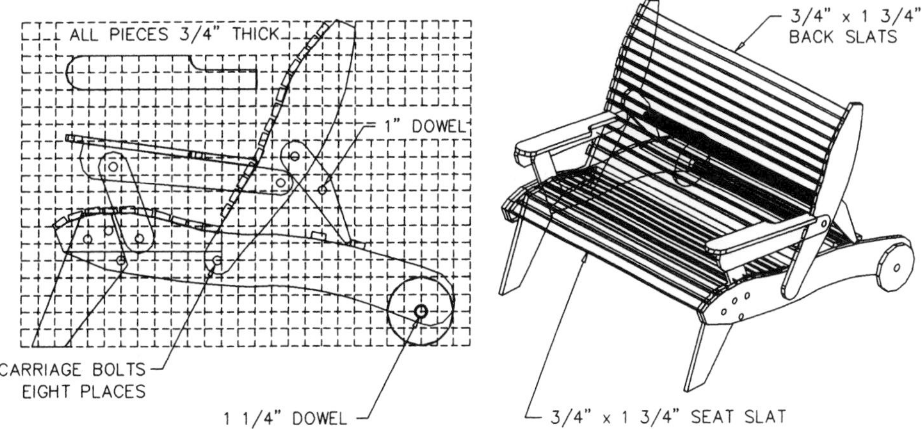

FIGURE 22–48
Exercise 22–11

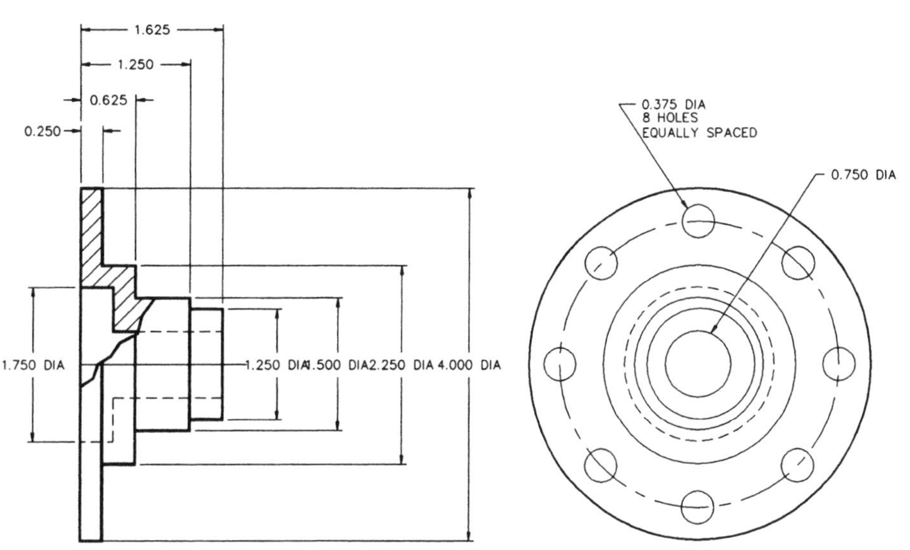

REVIEW QUESTIONS

Circle the best answer.

1. The setting that makes cylindrical objects appear more or less round is
   a. ISOLINES
   b. SURFTAB1
   c. FACETRES
   d. SNAP
   e. GRID
2. The Solids command used to create a cylinder is
   a. Circle
   b. Cylinder
   c. Cylsol
   d. Round
   e. Donut
3. The command used to combine two or more solids into one is
   a. Subtract
   b. Combine
   c. Unify
   d. Union
   e. Solidfy

4. The command used to cut a solid and retain either or both parts is
   a. Render
   b. Slice
   c. Section
   d. Solidfy
   e. Solcut
5. The command used in this chapter to make a countersunk hole is
   a. Hole
   b. Chamfer
   c. Round
   d. Fillet
   e. Countersink
6. The setting used to make shaded or hidden lines appear smoother is
   a. FACETRES
   b. ISOLINES
   c. SURFTAB1
   d. SNAP
   e. GRID
7. If the correct base surface is not selected in using the Chamfer command, which option must be selected?
   a. OK
   b. Loop
   c. Select edge
   d. Next
   e. Dist1
8. Which option on the Layout Wizard (Wizards-Create Layout) allows you to create four views of a solid model?
   a. Begin
   b. Paper Size
   c. Orientation
   d. Title Block
   e. Define Viewports-Std 3D Engineering Views
9. Which of the following would position a light 2″ in the X direction, 3″ in the Y direction, and 6″ in the Z direction using absolute coordinates?
   a. @2,3,6
   b. @3,2,6
   c. 3,2,6
   d. 2,3,6
   e. 2,3,<90
10. If you want to print a rendered model which option do you choose in the Destination area of the Render dialog box?
    a. Render Window
    b. Viewport
    c. File
    d. Plot
    e. Print Rendering

PART IV APPLICATIONS

23 Architectural Applications

OBJECTIVES

After completing this chapter, you will be able to

- □ Make the following drawings.

  Plot plan
  Floor plan
  Electrical plan
  Exterior elevation plans
  Wall section and detail plan
  Foundation plan
  Perspective

INTRODUCTION

More and more architectural drawings are being created on computers. Because contractors, designers, architects, and others involved in construction all share these drawings, the trend toward using AutoCAD to create them is likely to gain momentum in the near future. This chapter presents exercises that create AutoCAD drawings for most of the drawing types used in residential construction, including

Plot plan
Floor plan
Electrical plan
Exterior elevations
Wall section and details
Foundation plan
Perspective

The plot plan is the first exercise to be presented.

PLOT PLAN

The plot plan is often taken from a site plan such as the one shown as Figure 23–1. The lot is selected and then an accurate drawing is made of the property line, building lines, and all easements and construction. For this example lot number 11 was selected. To make the plot plan drawing follow these steps:

FIGURE 23–1
Site Plan

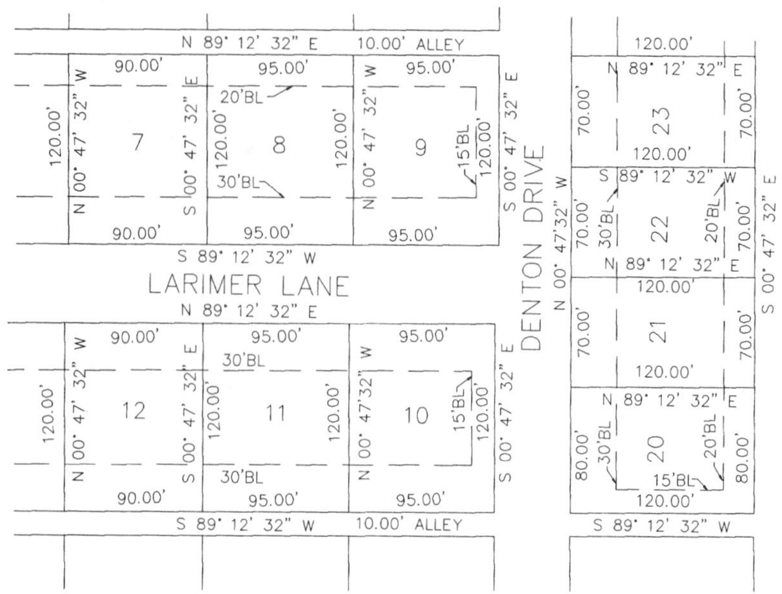

* UNLESS OTHERWISE MARKED ALLOW 10' FROM THE PROPERTY LINE TO THE BUILDING LINE.

Exercise 23–1: Drawing a Plot Plan

Step 1. Load AutoCAD. *Click:* **Create Drawings-Wizards-Quick Setup.**

Step 2. Make the following settings:

Units: Architectural: Surveyor's units. Be sure to select surveyor's units in the Angles list.

Area: Width: 125′
Length: 160′

LTSCALE = 211 (You are going to plot on a 9″ × 12″ sheet. The image will be 7″ wide. 125′, the width of the drawing limits, times 12″ is 1500″. Divide that by 7″ to obtain 211.)

GRID: 4′

SNAP: 1′

TEXT STYLE: Standard FONT: simplex.shx (Try CIBT or COBT for a different architectural font.) HEIGHT: 0

LAYERS:

NAME	Color	Linetype	Lineweight
PL	Red	Dashdot	Default
BL	Yellow	Dashed	Default
BUILDING	Green	Continuous	Default
LABELS	Blue	Continuous	Default

Set layer PL as the current layer.

Zoom-All

Step 3. Draw the property lines (Figure 23–2).

Prompt	Response
Command:	*Select:* **Line** (or *Type:* **L** ↵)
Specify first point:	*Type:* **15′, 20′** ↵ (This point will locate the drawing in the center of the limits.)

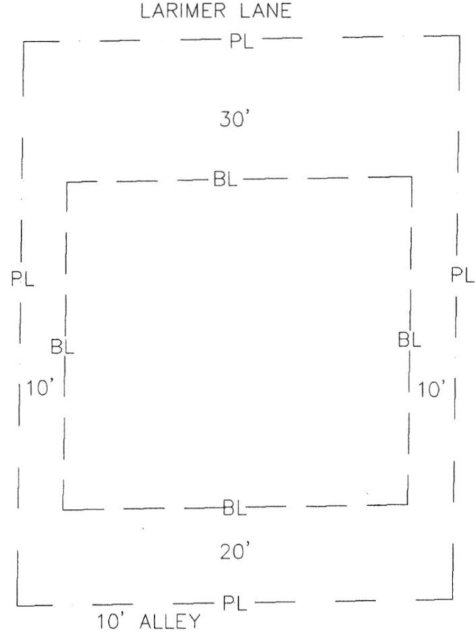

FIGURE 23–2
Plot Plan

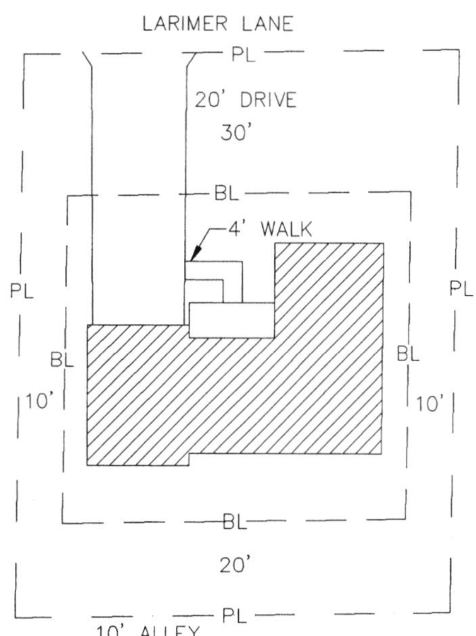

FIGURE 23–3
Plot Plan with House, Drive, and Walks

Prompt	**Response**
Specify next point:	*Type:* **@120′<N0D47′32″W**↵ (These bearings are taken from the site plan (Figure 23–1).)
Specify next point:	*Type:* **@95′<N89D12′28″ E** ↵
Specify next point:	*Type:* **@120′<S0D47′32″ E** ↵
Specify next point:	*Type:* **C** ↵

Step 4. Draw building lines (Figure 23–2).

On the north and south sides of this lot, the building lines are taken from the site plan. They are the lines labeled BL. On the east and west sides of the lot, many building codes require a 10′ distance from the building to the property line. Use Offset and Trim to make the building lines; then use Properties. . . to change them to layer BL.

Step 5. Draw the house outline inside the building lines (Figure 23–3). Locate the house shown as Figure 23–4 inside the building lines. Use only the outside dimensions of the building (Figure 23-6) and Hatch the house as shown in Figure 23–3.

Step 6. Add the driveway and walks to the plot plan (Figure 23–3).

Step 7. Add labels as indicated (Figure 23–3), using Dtext, 3′ high.

Step 8. Insert a 9″ × 12″ format around the drawing in Layout1. When you construct Layout1, use a scale of 1 = 240. (after you are in Layout1, *Type:* **MS ↵ to go to Model Space, then** *Type:* **Z ↵, then Type: 1/240xp↵). Title your drawing Plot Plan.**

Step 9. Print the drawing on a 12″ × 9″ sheet, full scale.

Step 10. Save the drawing in two places with the name EX23-1(your initials) and exit AutoCAD.

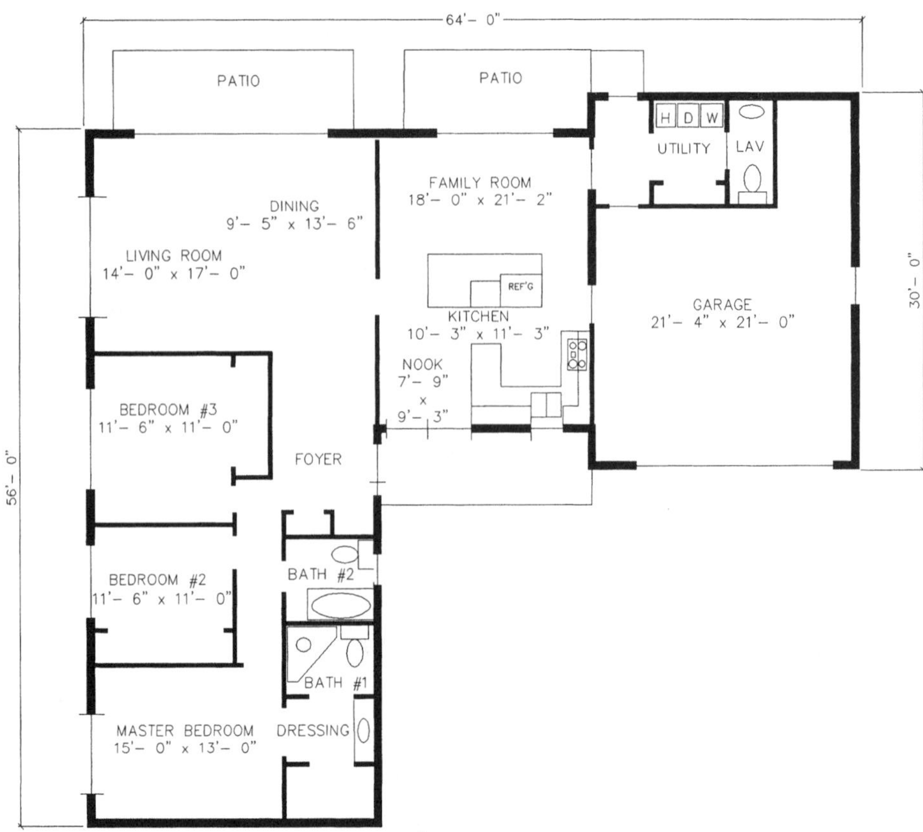

FIGURE 23–4
Preliminary Floor Plan

FLOOR PLAN

Draw Figure 23–5. Take the general room sizes from Figure 23–4 and maintain the overall building dimensions. Modify interior dimensions as necessary to make room sizes total to the overall dimensions. Use architectural graphic standards or a similar reference for bath and kitchen fixtures (Figure 23–4).

Exercise 23–2: Drawing a Floor Plan

Step 1. Load AutoCAD. *Click:* **Create Drawings-Wizards-Quick Setup.**

Step 2. Make the following settings:

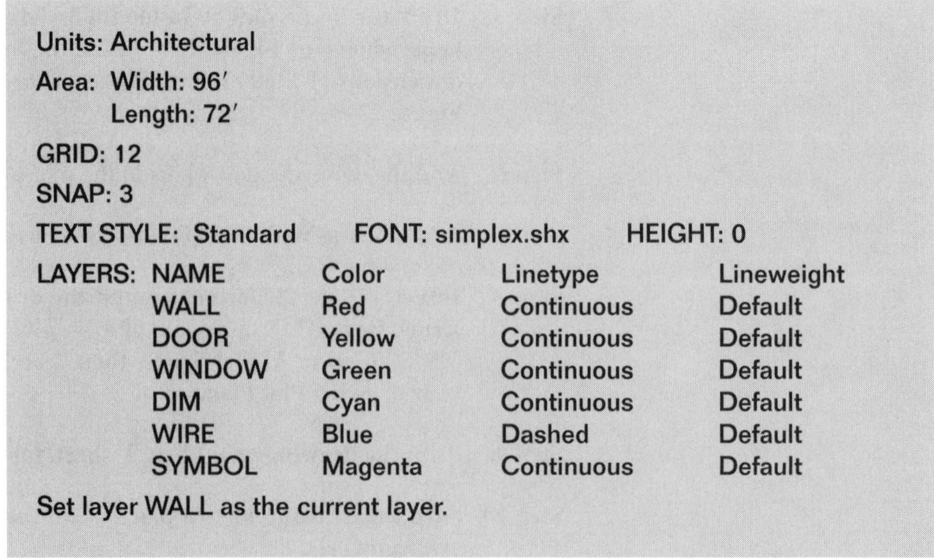

Units: Architectural
Area: Width: 96′
Length: 72′
GRID: 12
SNAP: 3
TEXT STYLE: Standard FONT: simplex.shx HEIGHT: 0

LAYERS: NAME	Color	Linetype	Lineweight
WALL	Red	Continuous	Default
DOOR	Yellow	Continuous	Default
WINDOW	Green	Continuous	Default
DIM	Cyan	Continuous	Default
WIRE	Blue	Dashed	Default
SYMBOL	Magenta	Continuous	Default

Set layer WALL as the current layer.

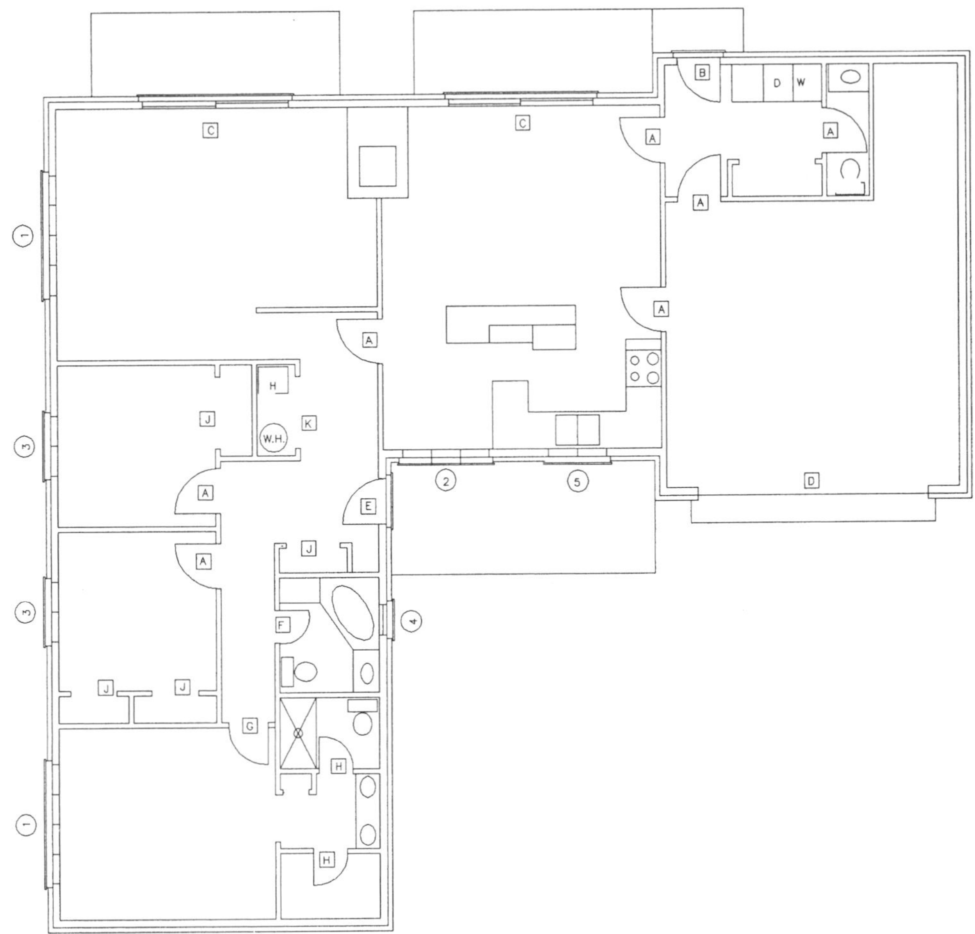

FIGURE 23–5
Floor Plan without Dimensions and Electrical Plan

Step 3. Draw walls using the Multiline command.
Set a multiline style with offsets of 0, 6″, and 10″.

Prompt	Response
Command:	*Click:* **Multiline** (or *Type:* **ML** ↵)
Specify start point or [Justification/Scale/STyle]:	*Type:* **16′,5′** ↵
Specify next point:	*Type:* **@24′ <0** ↵
Specify next point or [Undo]:	*Type:* **@31′4 <90** ↵

Continue drawing outside walls using polar coordinates or direct distance entry with ORTHO ON (Figure 23–6). Draw interior walls using Multiline. Trim intersections as needed.

Step 4. Add windows and doors.

Make blocks of windows and doors (Figure 23–7) on the 0 layer. Insert window and door blocks on window and door layers. Use dimensions from Figure 23–6 for any locations that are questionable. Your locations may be a little different from those in Figure 23–6. Trim walls from behind windows and doors if necessary.

Step 5. Add index numbers and letters.

Add circles and numbers for all windows and squares and letters for all doors (Figure 23–5). These indexes identify windows and doors on window and door schedules, which will appear in later drawings. Notice that all windows and doors that are the same size and style have the same index number or letter.

Tip: Explode windows and doors before Trimming. You may also precede the block name with an asterisk when you Insert it so that it comes in as separate entities (Example: *WINDOW) or check Explode in the Insert dialog box.

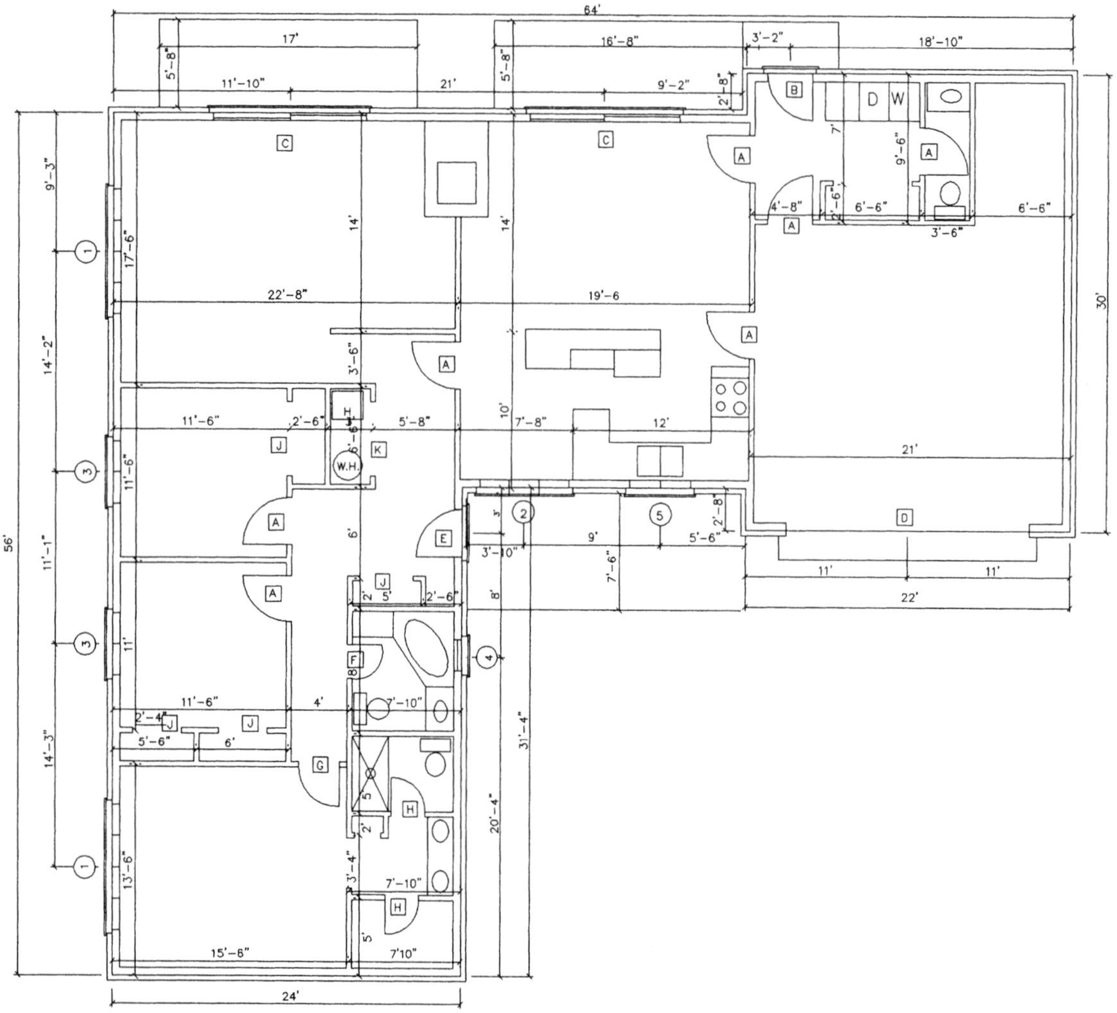

FIGURE 23–6
Floor Plan with Dimensions

FIGURE 23–7
Symbols

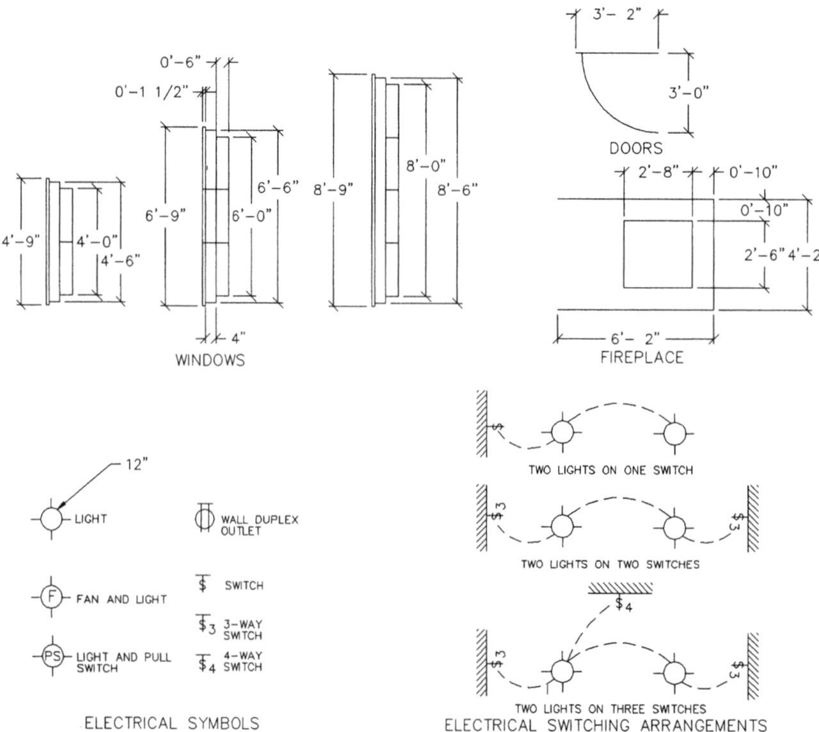

Step 6. Complete all remaining features such as patios and porches.

Step 7. Add dimensions.

Add dimensions on the DIM layer, as shown in Figure 23–6. Dimensions should be made from the outside of the framing wall to the centers of interior walls, windows and doors. Use the following DIMVARS settings:

Note: You may instead use DIMSCALE = 0. Set paper space limits to 24″ × 18″. Use MVIEW FIT to create a paper space viewport. You must do all three before DIMSCALE = 0 will work. Return to model space before dimensioning. Any dimensions you do in paper space exist only in paper space.

DIMASO: ON
DIMASZ: 0
DIMEXE: 1/16
DIMEXO: 1/16
DIMSCALE: 48
DIMTAD: ON
DIMTIH: OFF
DIMTOH: OFF
DIMTXT: 1/8
DIMTSZ: 1/16

Step 8. Use the Layout Wizard, select ARCH C (24 × 18) size, select none for Title Block, and set a Viewport Scale of 1/4″=1′. Insert a 24″ × 18″ format around the drawing and complete the format information. Title your drawing Floor Plan 1.

Step 9. Print the drawing on a 24″ × 18″ sheet.

Step 10. Save the drawing in two places with the name EX23-2(your initials) and exit AutoCAD.

ELECTRICAL PLAN

Now add the electrical plan to your floor plan.

Exercise 23–3: Adding the Electrical Plan

Step 1. Load AutoCAD, select Open a drawing. . . , and select EX23-2(your initials).

Step 2. Turn off layer DIM.

Step 3. Make blocks of all electrical symbols.

Make blocks of the electrical symbols shown in Figure 23–7 on the 0 layer and Insert them in appropriate locations on the SYMBOL layer, as shown in Figure 23–8.

For two switches to turn on the same light(s), use two three-way switches. For three switches to turn on the same light(s), use a four-way switch and two three-way switches.

Step 4. Draw electrical lines.

Set layer WIRE current and draw dashed lines connecting switches and lights using Arc, Spline, or Polyline—then use Edit Polyline-Fit Curve. Set LTSCALE = 48 for lines to appear DASHED.

When you construct Layout1 use the Layout Wizard as in Step 7 above. Use a Viewport Scale of 1/4″=1′.

Note: You may wish to set LTSCALE to a value higher or lower than 48 for your drawing.

Step 5. Print the drawing on a 24″ × 18″ sheet.

Step 6. Save the drawing in two places with the name EX23-3(your initials) and exit AutoCAD.

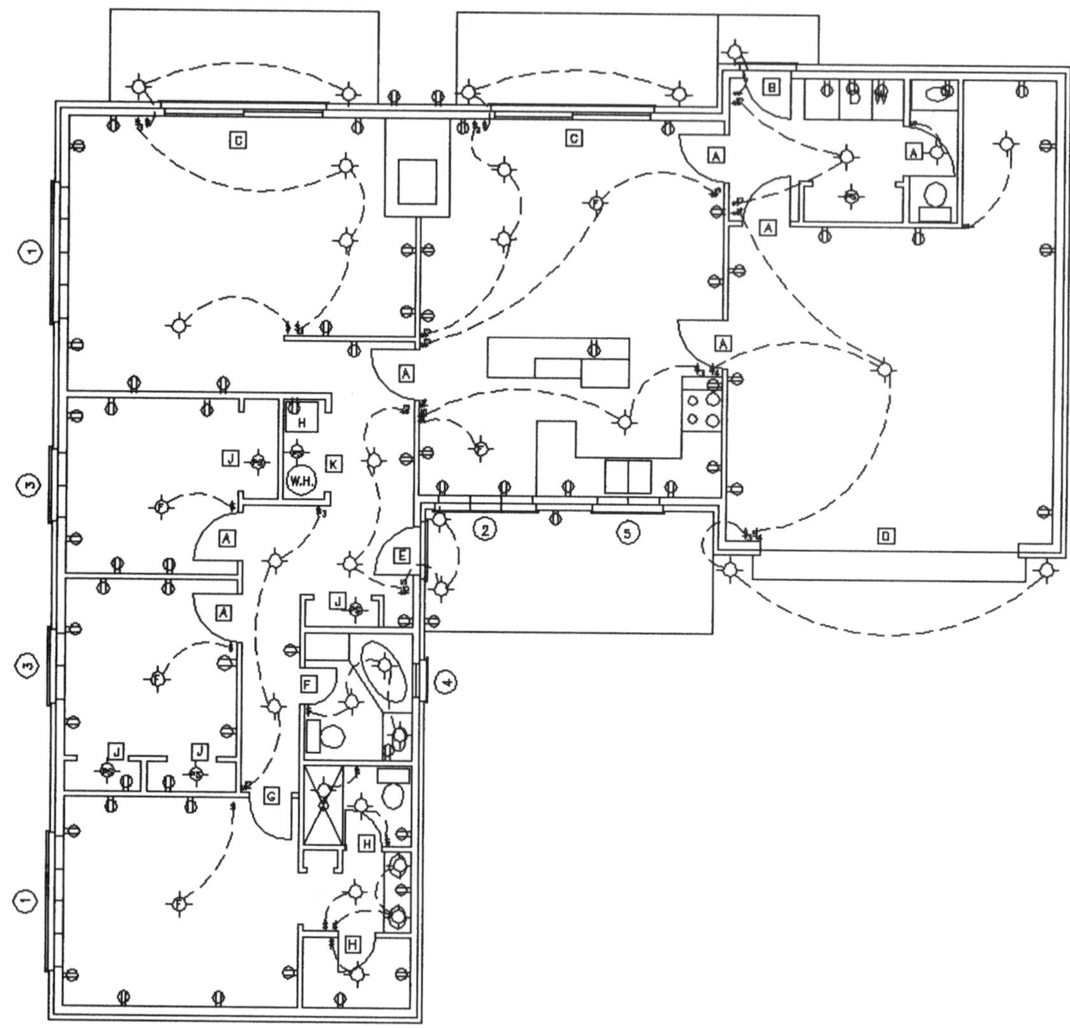

FIGURE 23–8
Electrical Plan

FRONT AND REAR ELEVATIONS

Exercise 23–4: Drawing Front and Rear Elevations

Load AutoCAD, *Click:* **Create Drawings-Wizards-Quick Setup,** and save the drawing as EX23-3(your initials). Draw front and rear elevations (Figure 23–9) and print on one 24″ × 18″ sheet. Create layers and make settings that you think are appropriate. If you would like to use different windows and doors from a standards book or catalog sheets, do so. Be sure windows and doors can be purchased from stock, and be sure their locations match the floor plan. Draw the chimney for the fireplace in the same location as shown on the floor plan. Use DOLMIT or AR-RSHKE HATCH pattern for the roof and AR-B816 or BRICK HATCH pattern for the brick.

RIGHT AND LEFT ELEVATIONS

Exercise 23–5: Drawing Right and Left Elevations

Load AutoCAD, open the drawing EX23-3(your initials), and save it as EX23-4(your initials). Erase anything you do not need. Draw right and left elevations (Figure 23–10) to match the floor plan using the directions described for front and rear elevations. Add win-

FIGURE 23–9
Front and Rear Elevations

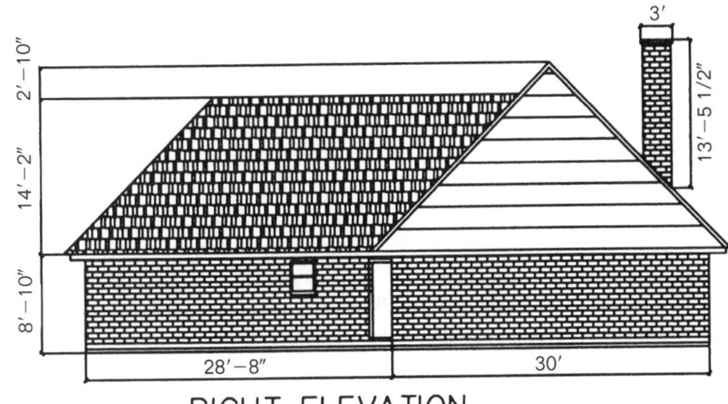

DOOR SCHEDULE

MARK	SIZE	TYPE	REMARKS
A	3′–0″ × 6′–8″ × 1 3/8″	7 INTERIOR	PINE
B	3′–0″ × 6′–8″ × 1 3/4″	1 EXTERIOR BACK	PINE
C	10′–0″ × 6′–8″	2 SLIDING	ALUM FR. TM. GL.
D	16′–0″ × 8′–0″	1 GARAGE	ALUM
E	3′–0″ × 6′–8″ × 1 3/4″	1 EXTERIOR FRONT	SOLID PINE
F	2′–2″ × 6′–8″ × 1 3/8″	1 INTERIOR	HOL. PINE
G	2′–8″ × 6′–8″ × 1 3/8″	1 INTERIOR	HOL. PINE
H	2′–4″ × 6′–8″ × 1 3/8″	2 INTERIOR	2 DR. UNIT
J	1′–7″ × 6′–8″ × 1 3/8″	8 INTERIOR	2 DR. UNIT
K	2′–5″ × 6′–8″ × 1 3/8″	2 INTERIOR	2 DR. UNIT

WINDOW SCHEDULE

MARK	SIZE	TYPE	REMARKS
1	2′–0″ × 5′–0″	D.H.	ALUM. 4 WINDOW GROUP
2	2′–0″ × 5′–0″	D.H.	ALUM. 3 WINDOW GROUP
3	2′–0″ × 5′–0″	D.H.	ALUM. 2 WINDOW GROUP
4	2′–0″ × 2′–6″	D.H.	ALUM. FROSTED
5	2′–0″ × 2′–6″	D.H.	ALUM. CLEAR

FIGURE 23–10
Left and Right Elevations

dow and door schedules as shown. Change dimensions on these schedules to match your sizes if you selected different windows or doors. Use Single Line Text, SIMPLEX font, with a height of 6″. Print on a 24″ × 18″ sheet.

WALL SECTION AND DETAILS

Exercise 23–6: Drawing Wall Sections and Details

Load AutoCAD, *Click:* **Create Drawings-Wizards-Quick Setup**, and make appropriate settings. Draw a typical wall section similar to Figure 23–11. Select a wall section from a graphic standards book for construction in your area of the country or use the one shown.

FIGURE 23–11
Wall Section

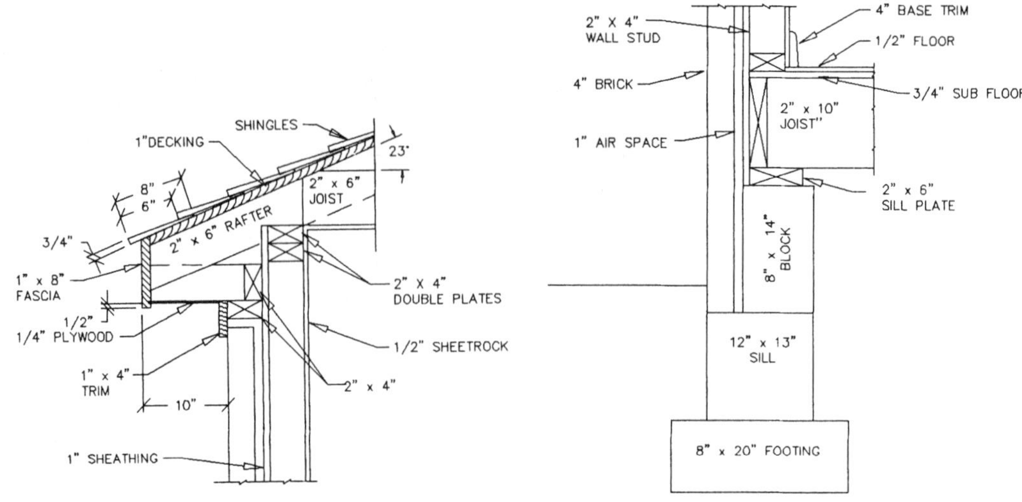

Draw interior details as shown in Figures 23–12 through 23–20. Estimate any dimensions not shown. Reduce or enlarge drawings using the Scale command if necessary so that the wall section and all interior details are contained within the same 24″ × 18″ format. Print the drawing on a 24″ × 18″ sheet. Save it as EX23-6(your initials).

FIGURE 23–12
Kitchen, Elevation 1

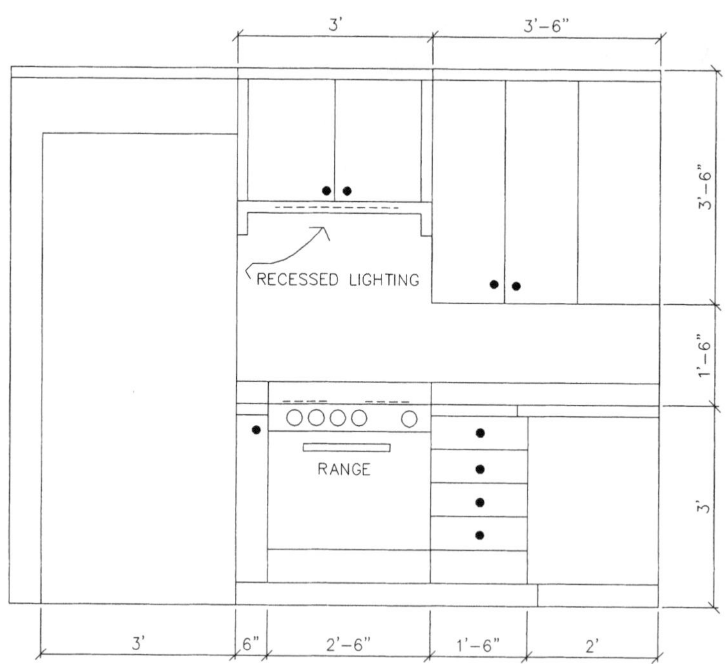

FIGURE 23–13
Kitchen, Elevation 2

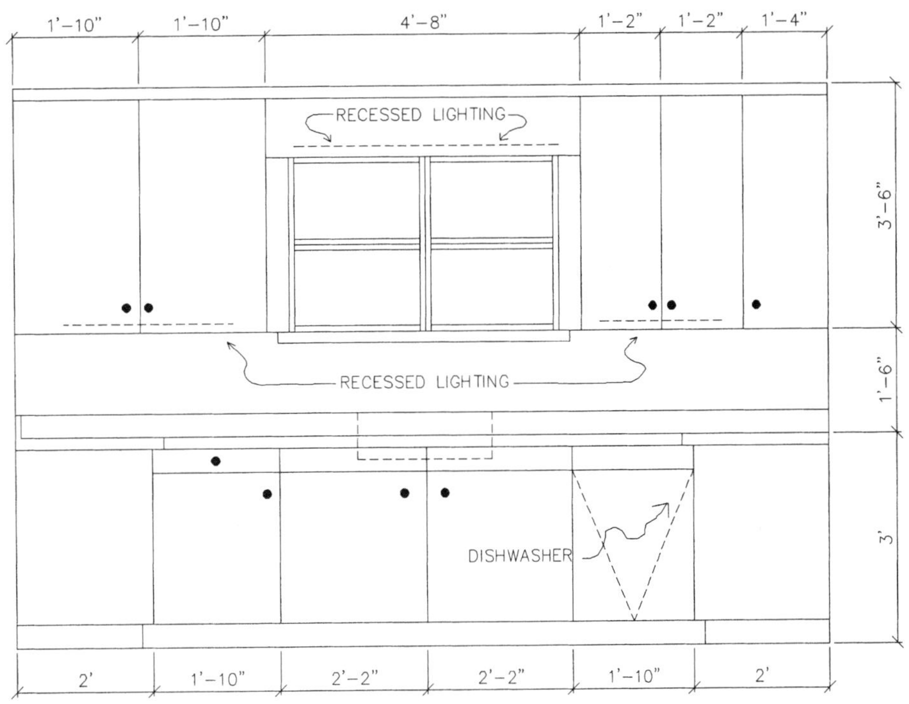

FIGURE 23–14
Kitchen, Elevation 3

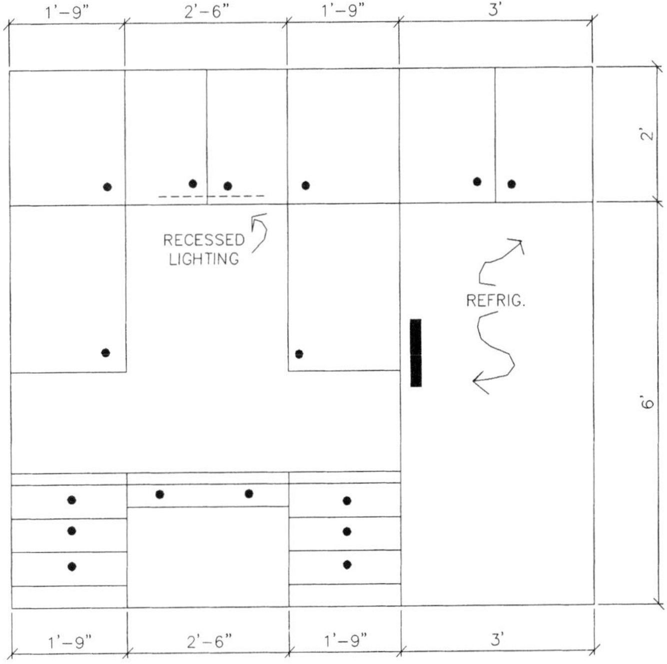

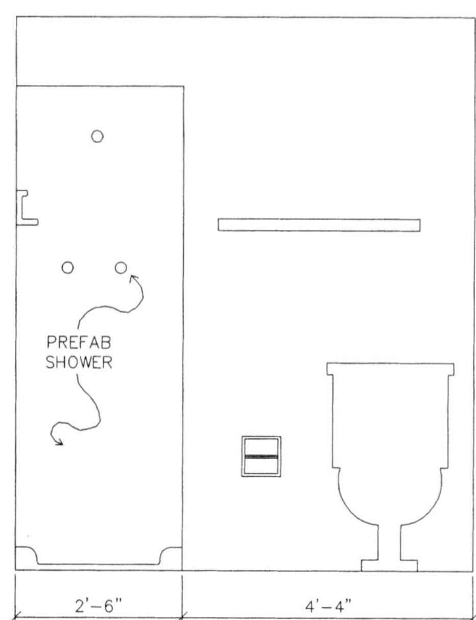

FIGURE 23–15
Master Bath, Elevation 1

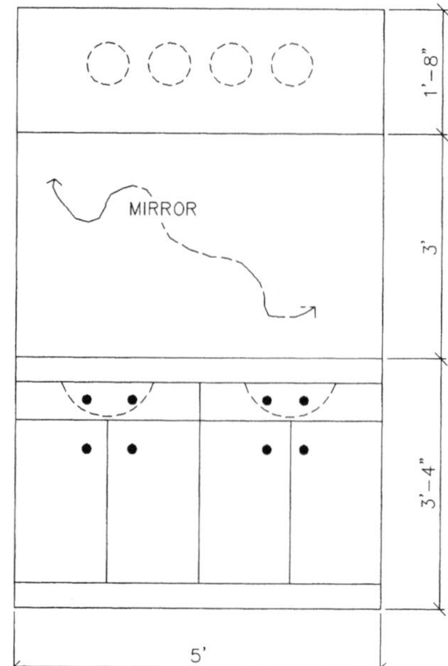

FIGURE 23–16
Master Bath, Elevation 2

FIGURE 23–17
Bath 1, Elevation 1

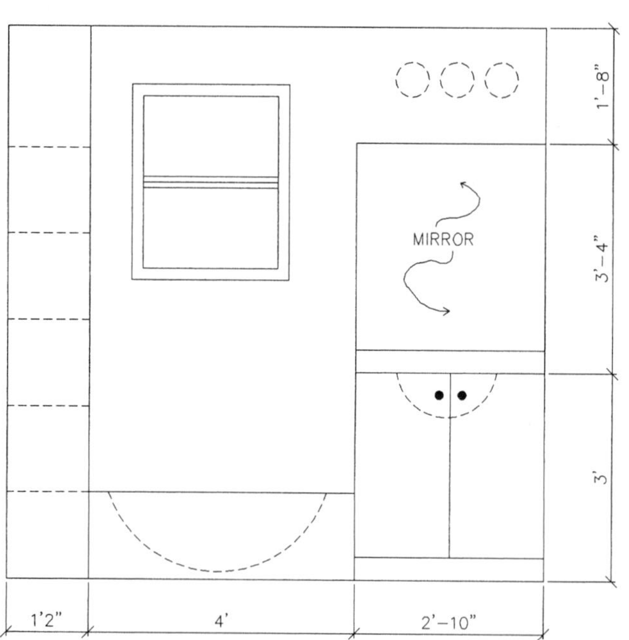

FIGURE 23–18
Bath 1, Elevation 2

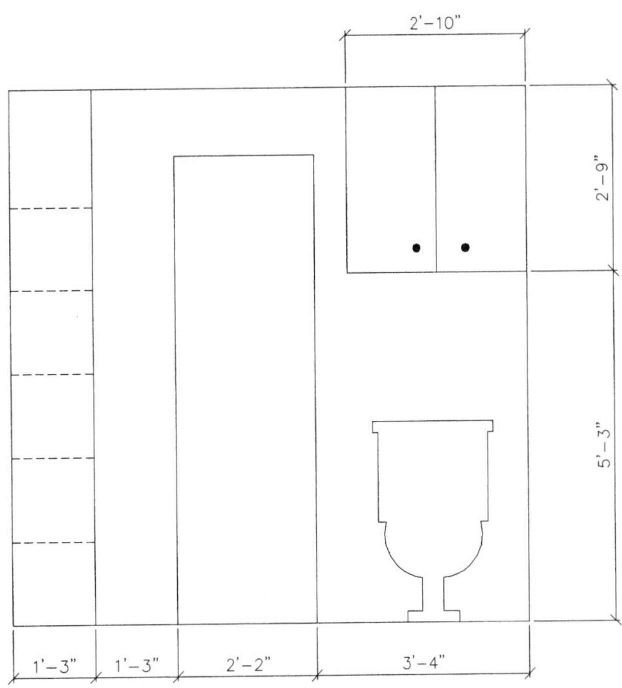

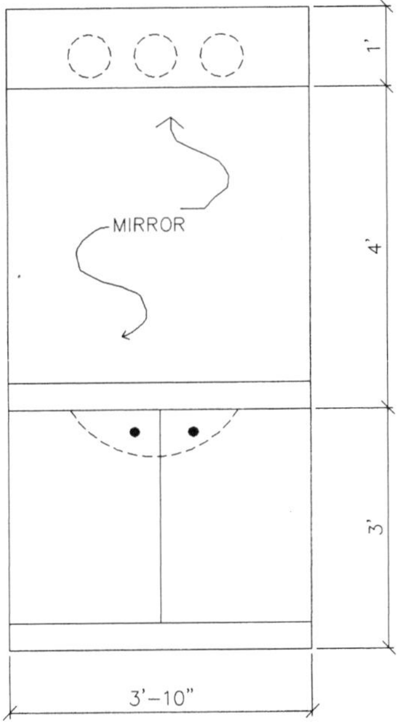

FIGURE 23–19
Bath 2, Elevation 1

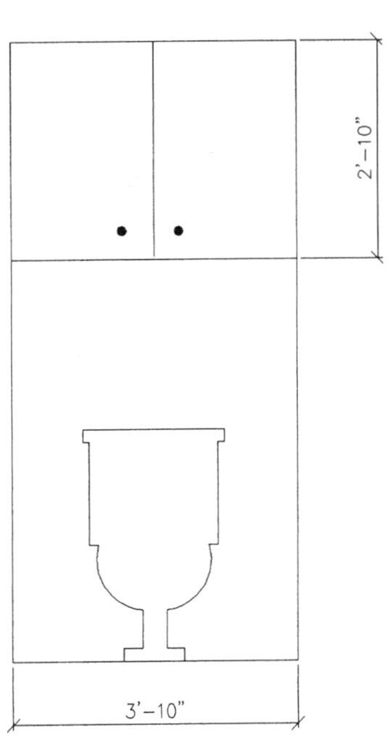

FIGURE 23–20
Bath 2, Elevation 2

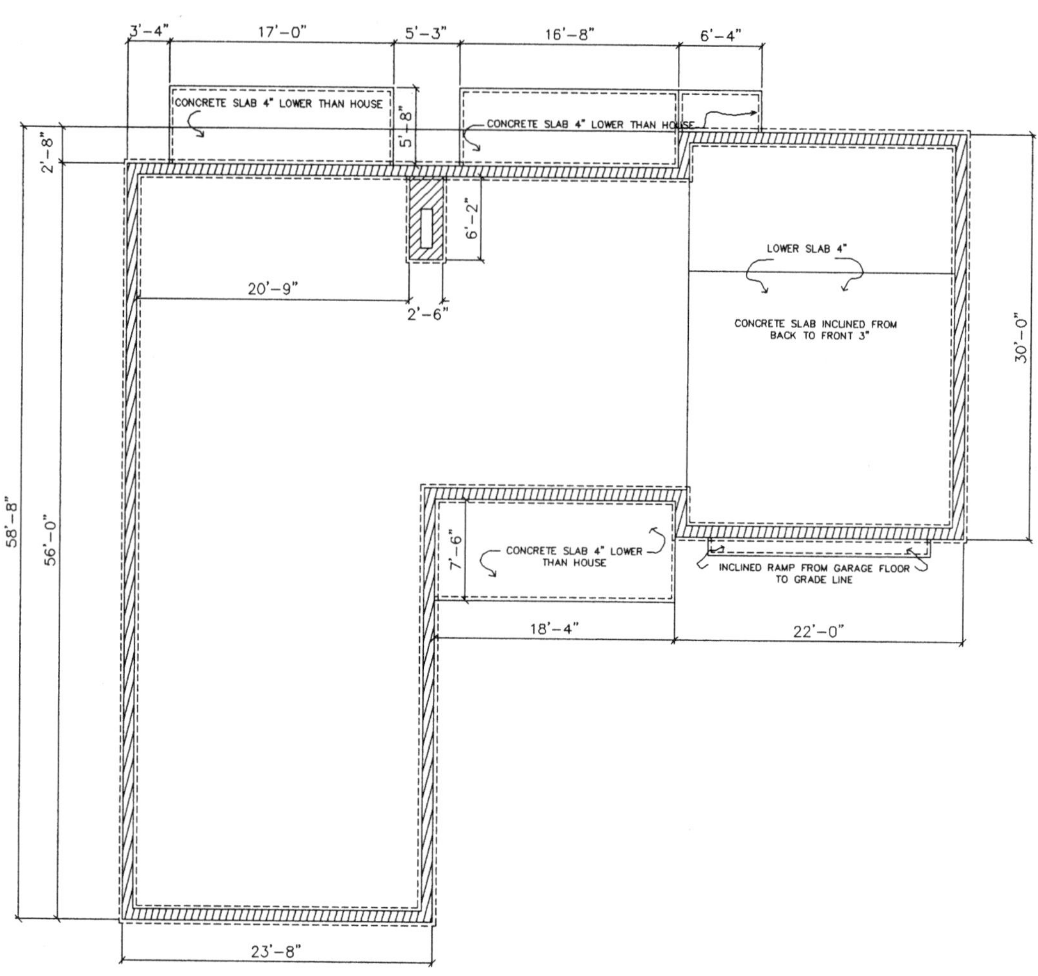

FIGURE 23–21
Foundation Plan

FOUNDATION PLAN

Tip: Use the floor plan to draw your foundation plan so that you can be sure they match. Open the floor plan drawing and save it as EX23-7(your initials). Then, Erase everything you do not need and draw the foundation plan with the confidence that it matches the floor plan.

Exercise 23–7: Drawing the Foundation Plan

Draw the foundation plan (Figure 23–21) after creating appropriate layers and making appropriate settings. The dashed line around the foundation is the footing shown on the wall section. Make sure these lines agree with the wall section. Use a foundation plan that fits construction in your section of the country. Print on a 24″ × 18″ sheet. Save it as EX23-7(your initials).

PERSPECTIVE

Exercise 23–8: Drawing a Perspective

Create a 3-D model from the floor plan and elevations just drawn. The perspective shown as Figure 23–22 was created using primarily elevation and thickness. Your perspective will require some 3Dfaces for the roof, but polylines with thickness will create the walls and sections of the windows and doors.

It is not necessary to create interior walls. Use 3D Orbit to obtain a perspective view after the model is created. Some guidelines you may find useful are the following:

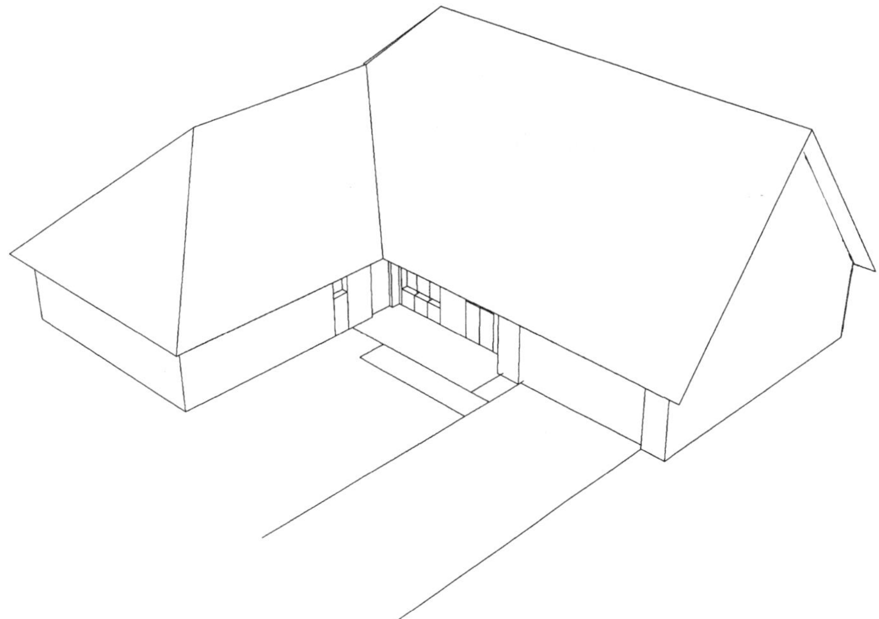

FIGURE 23–22
3-D Perspective

Note: Some residential architects create a 3-D model first and then extract elevations from the model. Use of AutoLISP to create 3-D windows, doors, walls, roofs, cornices, and other construction features makes 3-D an economical and useful tool.

- □ Create hidden layers and turn them off so that you can avoid using the "remove hidden lines" option to the Print command for complex models. To create a hidden layer, make a layer with the same name as a visible layer and precede the name with the word HIDDEN (Example: HIDDENWALLS).
- □ Create 3-D windows and door blocks with a wall section above and below the window or door so that they are located in the correct position vertically when inserted.
- □ Create all entities above the grid (elevations should not be negative if you can avoid it.
- □ Use Properties. . . to give polylines thickness or use the Extrude command.
- □ Draw roof lines before creating 3Dfaces for the roof surfaces.
- □ Avoid having broad flat planes covering other broad flat planes to avoid long delays when the Hide command is used.
- □ Choose an appropriate plot scale for Layout1 and use Mview-Hideplot.

Print the perspective to fit on a horizontal 12″ × 9″ sheet within an A-size format.

EXERCISES

EXERCISES 23–1 through 23–8. Prepare a set of plans for the house described in this chapter using the instructions for each type of drawing.

EXERCISE 23–9. Construct a 3-D model from the floor plan and elevation shown in Figure 23–23, then extract a front elevation and the floor plan as shown. You should have three final plots: a floor plan, a front elevation, and a 3-D perspective from your model. Plot each drawing on a separate 12″ × 9″ sheet.

EXERCISE 23–10. Prepare a set of plans for the house shown in Figure 23–24. Select the smallest possible lot from Figure 23–1 that will accommodate this building. Include all drawings shown for Exercises 23–1 through 23–8.

EXERCISE 23–11. Prepare a set of plans for the house shown in Figure 23–25. Notice that this house is identical to the house in Exercise 23–3 except for the front elevation. Select the smallest possible lot from Figure 23–1 that will accommodate this building. Include all drawings shown for Exercises 23–1 through 23–8. Copy drawings as necessary from Exercise 23–10.

EXERCISE 23–12. Prepare a set of plans for the house shown in Figure 23–26. Select the smallest possible lot from Figure 23–1 that will accommodate this building. Include all drawings shown for Exercises 23–1 through 23–8.

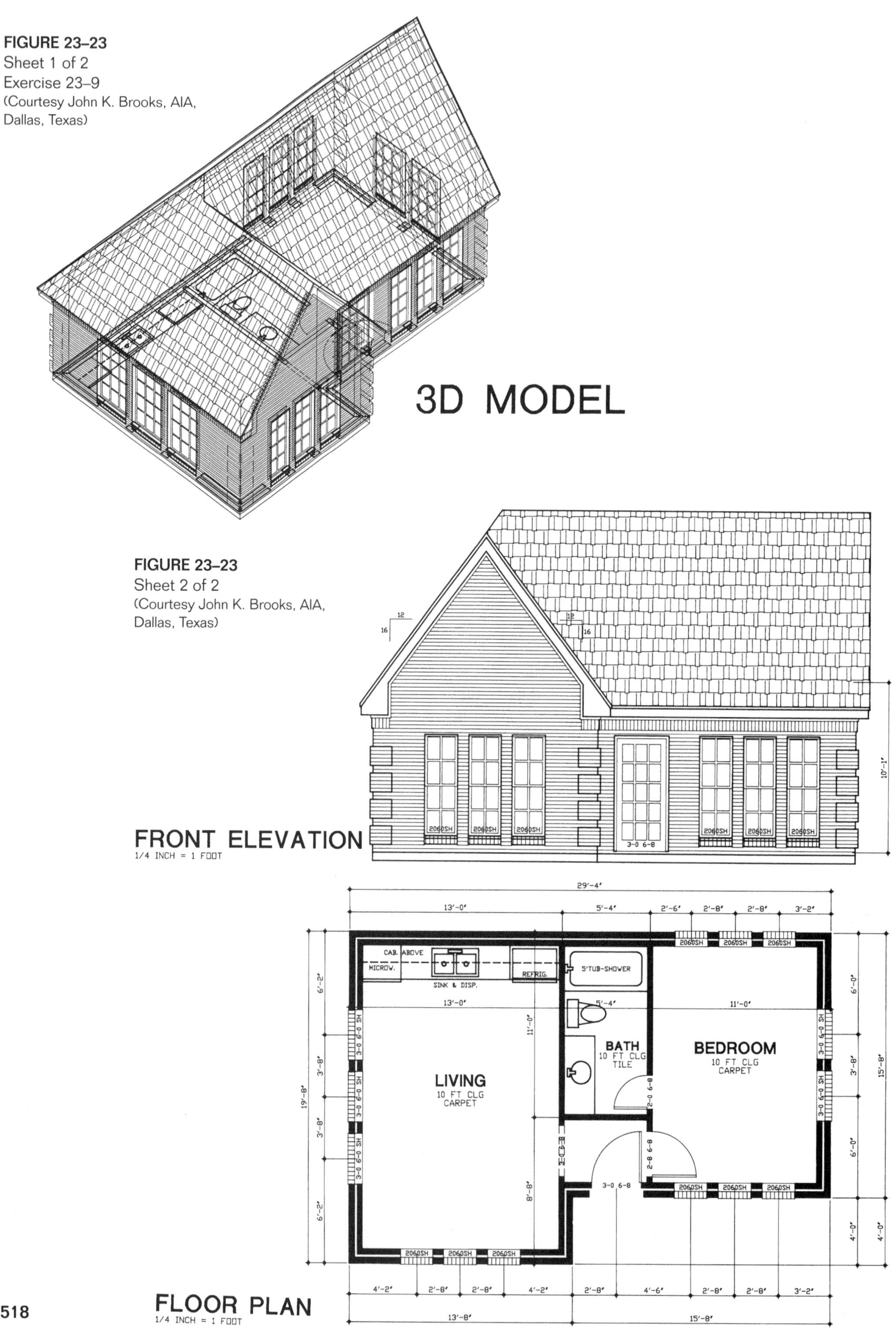

FIGURE 23–23
Sheet 1 of 2
Exercise 23–9
(Courtesy John K. Brooks, AIA, Dallas, Texas)

FIGURE 23–23
Sheet 2 of 2
(Courtesy John K. Brooks, AIA, Dallas, Texas)

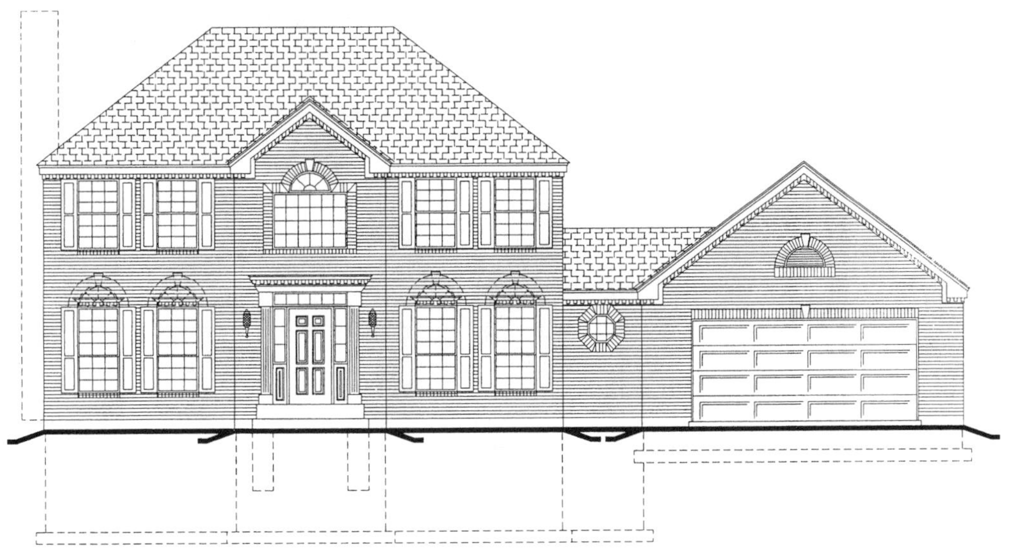

FIGURE 23–24
Sheet 1 of 2
Exercise 23–10
(Courtesy AmeriCAD, Inc., Plano, Texas)

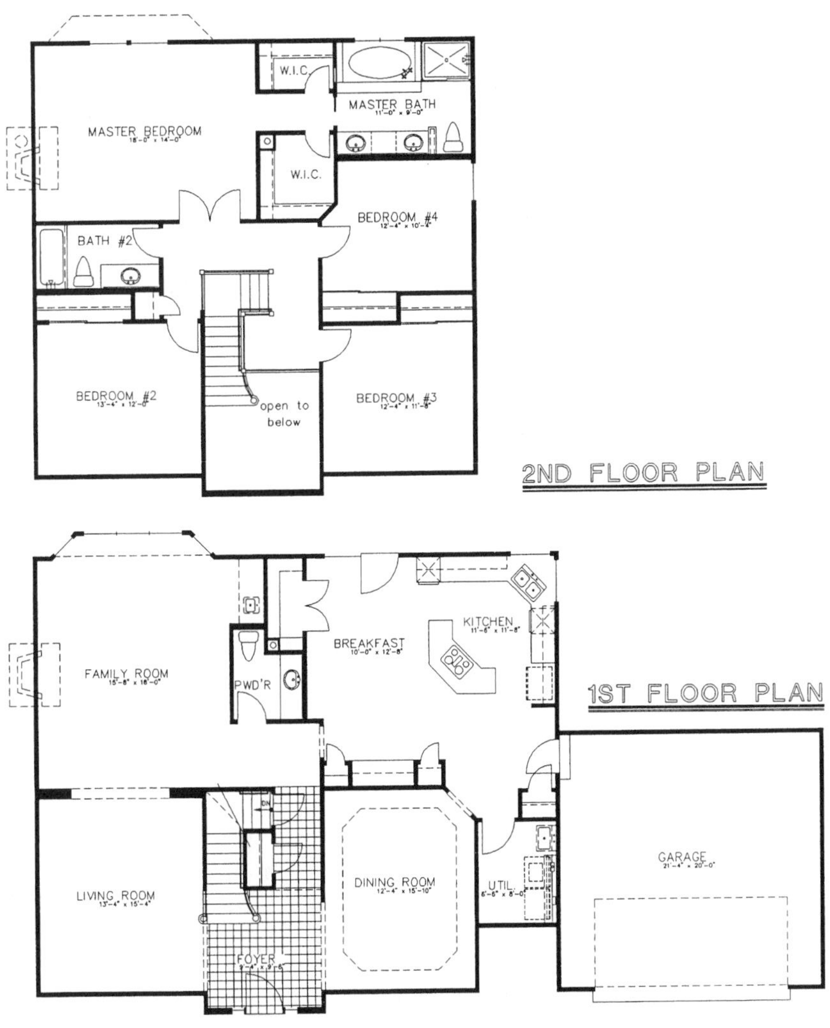

FIGURE 23–24
Sheet 2 of 2
(Courtesy AmeriCAD, Inc., Plano, Texas)

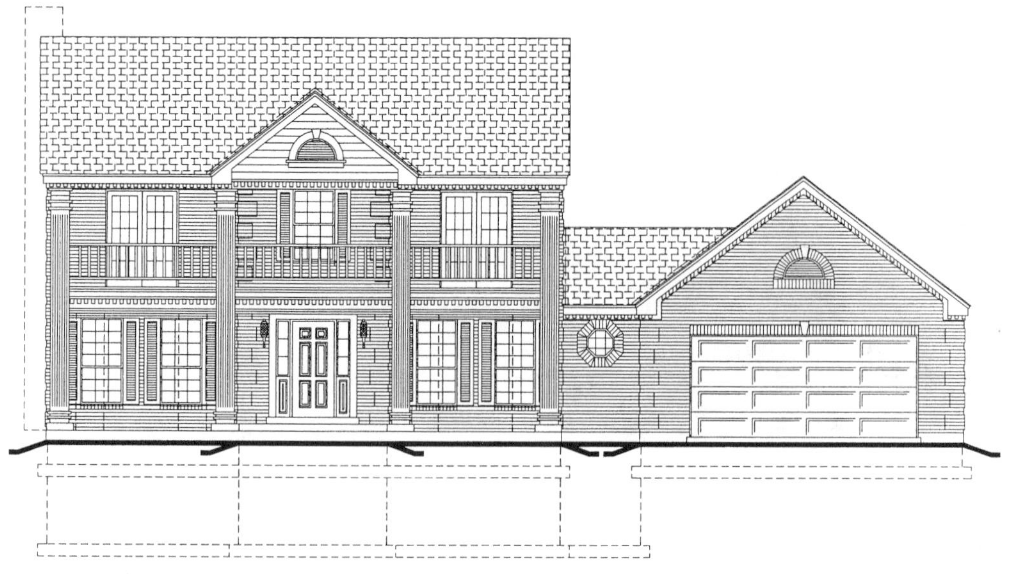

FIGURE 23–25
Sheet 1 of 2
Exercise 23–11
(Courtesy AmeriCAD, Inc., Plano, Texas)

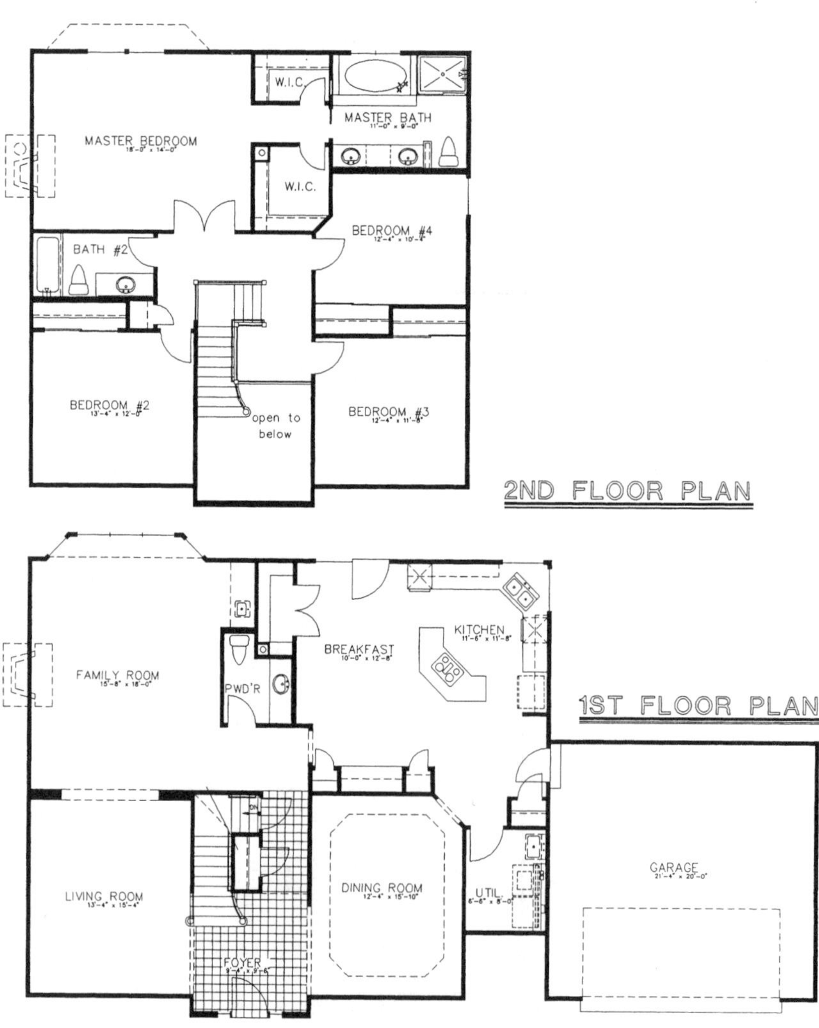

FIGURE 23–25
Sheet 2 of 2
(Courtesy AmeriCAD, Inc., Plano, Texas)

FIGURE 23–26
Sheet 1 of 2
Exercise 23–12
(Courtesy AmeriCAD, Inc., Plano, Texas)

FIGURE 23–26
Sheet 2 of 2
(Courtesy AmeriCAD, Inc., Plano, Texas)

2ND FLOOR PLAN

W.I.C.
BEDROOM #3
BATH
DRESSING
W.I.C.
BEDROOM #2

1ST FLOOR PLAN

BREAKFAST
KITCHEN
FAMILY ROOM
GARAGE
WET BAR
BATH #2
LINEN
UTIL
DINING ROOM
W.I.C.
W.I.C.
WINDOW SEAT
FOYER
SITTING/ BEDROOM #4
W.I.C.
LIVING ROOM
POR.
MASTER BEDROOM
MASTER BATH

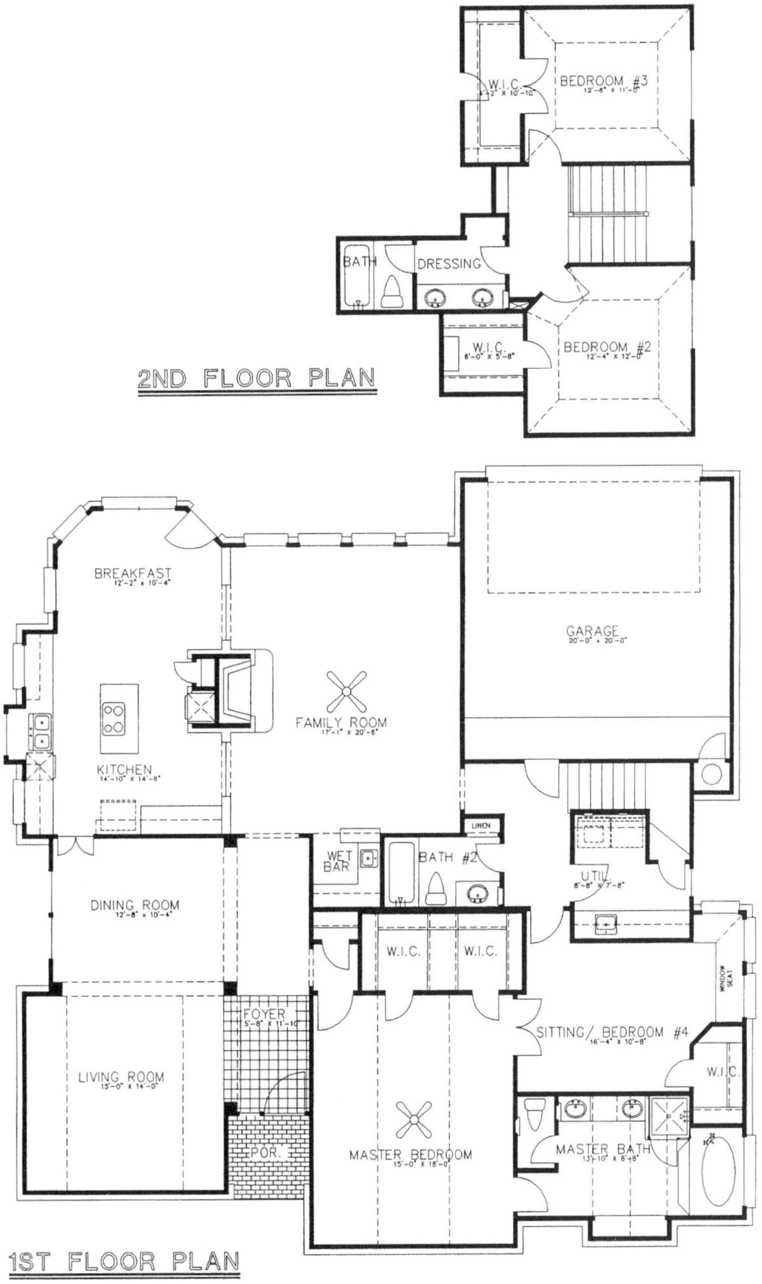

FIGURE 23–27
Sheet 1 of 2
Exercise 23–13
(Courtesy AmeriCAD, Inc., Plano, Texas)

FIGURE 23–27
Sheet 2 of 2
(Courtesy AmeriCAD, Inc., Plano, Texas)

2ND FLOOR PLAN

1ST FLOOR PLAN

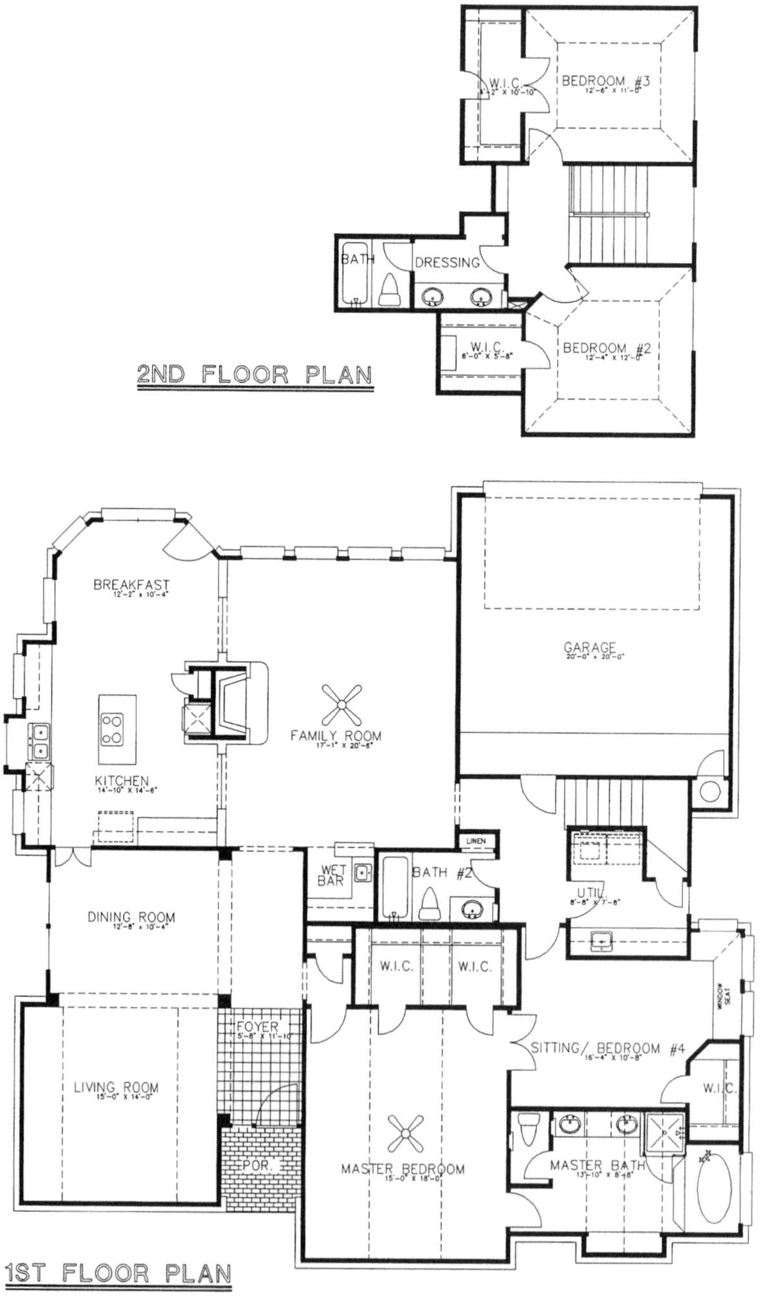

EXERCISE 23–13. Prepare a set of plans for the house shown in Figure 23–27. Select the smallest possible lot from Figure 23–1 that will accommodate this building. Include all drawings shown for Exercises 23–1 through 23–8. Copy drawings as necessary from Exercise 23–12.

EXERCISE 23–14. Design a house whose outside dimensions of living areas measure 60′ × 30′. The house should have three bedrooms, two baths, a kitchen, utility room, living/dining room, den, and a two-car garage. Prepare a set of plans to include all drawings indicated in Exercises 23–1 through 23–8.

EXERCISE 23–15. Design a residence of 2500 ft^2 living area that will fit on one of the lots in Figure 23–1. The house should have four bedrooms, three baths, a kitchen, utility room, living/dining room, den, and a two-car garage. Prepare a set of plans to include all drawings indicated in Exercises 23–1 through 23–8.

REVIEW QUESTIONS

Circle the best answer.

1. The setting for "Angle Type:" on UNITS that allows you to use bearings to draw property lines is
   a. Surveyor's units
   b. Bearings
   c. Decimal
   d. Architectural
   e. Civil engineering
2. The property line and the building line are often the same line.
   a. True
   b. False
3. The building line may be obtained from the property line most easily with the use of which of the following commands?
   a. Line
   b. Offset
   c. Move
   d. Copy
   e. Rotate
4. Which of the following commands draws a double line and cleans up the corners?
   a. Pline
   b. Line
   c. Trace
   d. Multiline
   e. There is no such command.
5. Which of the following commands is used to change a line from one layer to another?
   a. Layer
   b. Move
   c. Properties. . .
   d. Line
   e. Xplode
6. Which of the following block names will INSERT the block WINDOW with all lines as separate entities?
   a. *WINDOW
   b. WINDOW
   c. WINDOW@
   d. WINDOW*
   e. @WINDOW
7. Windows on the floor plan are identified with circles and letters.
   a. True
   b. False
8. A DIMSCALE of 48 with DIMTXT = 1⁄16 will produce a letter with a height of
   a. 4″
   b. 3″
   c. 2.5″
   d. 48″

e. 1/16″
9. A drawing measuring 48′ × 36′ at a Plot scale of 1 = 24 will produce a plot measuring
   a. 48″ × 36″
   b. 30″ × 20″
   c. 24″ × 18″
   d. 20″ × 15″
   e. 15″ × 10″
10. For DASHED lines to appear as dashed lines on the electrical plan for Exercise 23–1, LTSCALE must be set to approximately
   a. 1
   b. 12
   c. 24
   d. 48
   e. 96

Complete.

11. List the commands and their options used to draw DASHED lines on the electrical plan.

____

____

____

12. Describe the uses of three-way and four-way light switches.

____

____

13. Sketch the correct symbol for each of the following.

   Wall plug

   Light

   Light with fan

   Three-way switch

   Four-way switch

14. List four HATCH patterns that represent brick.

____

____

____

____

15. List two HATCH patterns that can be used to represent shingles.

____

____

16. Describe the uses of the window and door schedules.

____

____

17. Describe the uses of the wall section.

____

____

18. Describe what parts of the foundation plan must match the floor plan and the wall section.

____

19. How are thickness and elevation used to create a 3-D model of a window?

____

20. List two architectural fonts that are standard in the AutoCAD program.

____

24 Civil Applications

OBJECTIVES

After completing this chapter, you will be able to

□ Produce the following drawings.

Open traverse
Closed traverse
Plat
Contour map
Profile
Highway map

DRAWING TYPES

The most common types of drawings used in civil drafting are those just listed. These are easily produced using AutoCAD. Figure 24–1 is a composite of these drawing types. To make these types of drawings, some information about how to collect data is necessary. Let's begin with *surveying basics.*

Surveying Basics

All maps and associated drawings begin with a survey. A survey is a process used to measure land. The basic elements of this measuring process are distance, direction, and elevation.

Distance

Distance along a line is measured in feet and decimal parts of a foot (252.5′) or feet and inches (252′6″). Many AutoCAD drafters or engineers find it convenient to work full scale and use the plotting ratio to reduce a map to a standard plot size, or use the Layout Wizard to reduce the drawing to fit the layout and plot full scale.

Direction

Note: There are 60 seconds in an angular minute; 60 minutes in a degree. The symbol ° indicates degrees, the symbol ′ indicates minutes, and the symbol ″ indicates seconds.

The direction of a surveying line is most often shown as a bearing. Bearings are measurements of angles. They measure from 0 to 90°, taken from a north or south line, and point either east or west (e.g., N49°15′E). AutoCAD allows you to specify a bearing in these same terms using surveyor's units.

Elevation

The elevation or height of a point is measured from sea level. This measurement is often taken from any known point, and further elevation readings are measured from there. AutoCAD provides an elevation setting or Z-axis measurement to provide the elevation measurement.

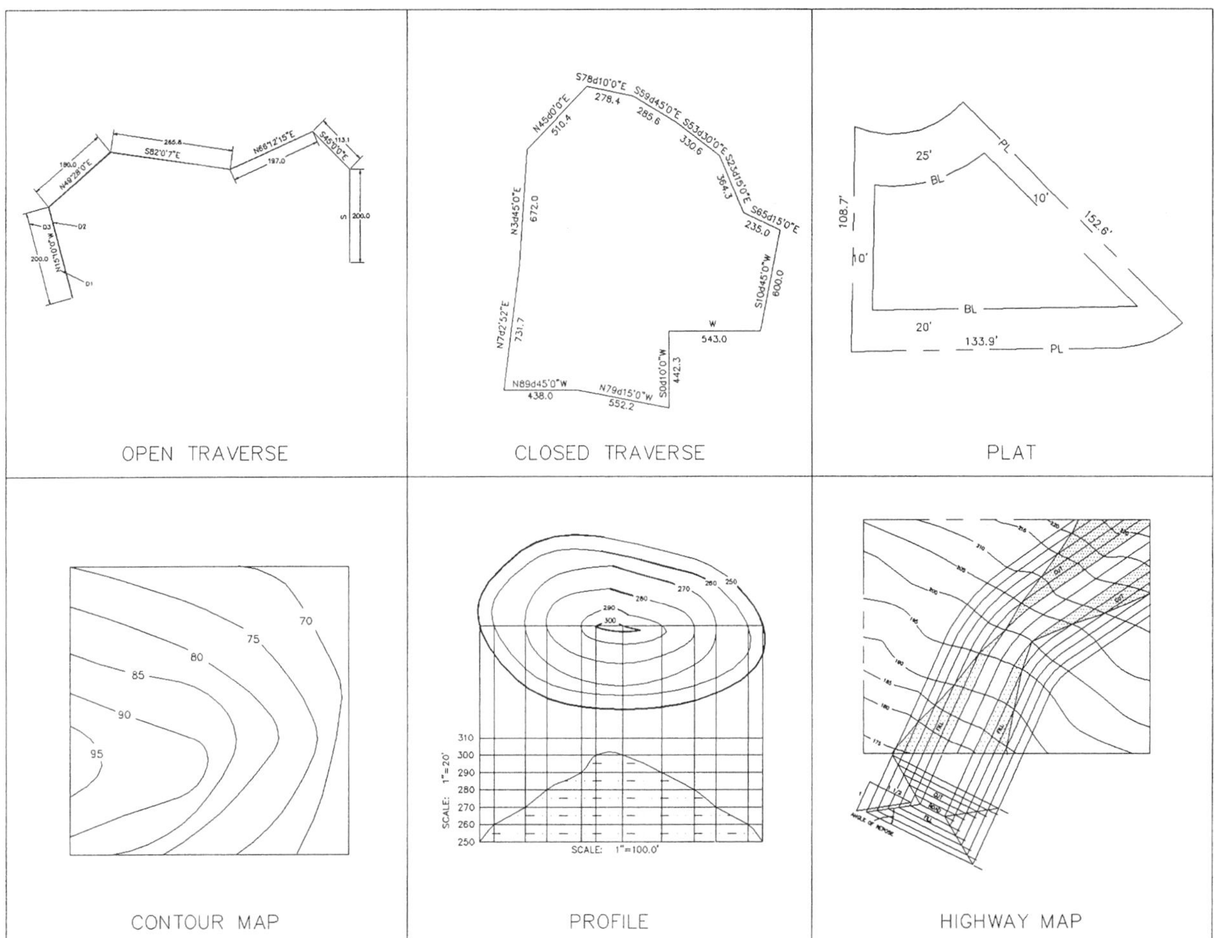

FIGURE 24–1
Drawing Types

The three elements of distance, direction, and elevation are used to collect data for the six survey types. The procedure of surveying is not included in this book. The six survey types are as follows.

Land or boundary survey The plat is one of the most commonly used boundary surveys. It is used to describe any tract when it is not necessary to show elevation (often called *relief*). Any property you own should have a plat describing its boundaries.

Topographic survey This survey is used to produce maps that show the elevations (artificial or natural) and features of the land. These are contour maps.

Geodetic survey This is a survey covering large areas, often entire countries. These areas are so large that the curvature of the earth is a factor in measurement.

Photo survey This survey consists of a series of aerial photographs that are combined to produce a complete photogrammetric map.

Route survey This survey is used to describe highways, pipelines, or power lines. It consists of straight lines and angles originating from an identified point. No elevations are shown on a route survey.

Construction survey This survey is used in the construction of buildings and highways where the elevation of points is needed. It is often used to show where earth must be removed (cut) or added (fill).

Now that you have an idea of how data are gathered, let's use AutoCAD to produce some maps from this data. Let's begin with traverses (a series of straight lines showing distance and direction) that are used to create site plans and highway maps.

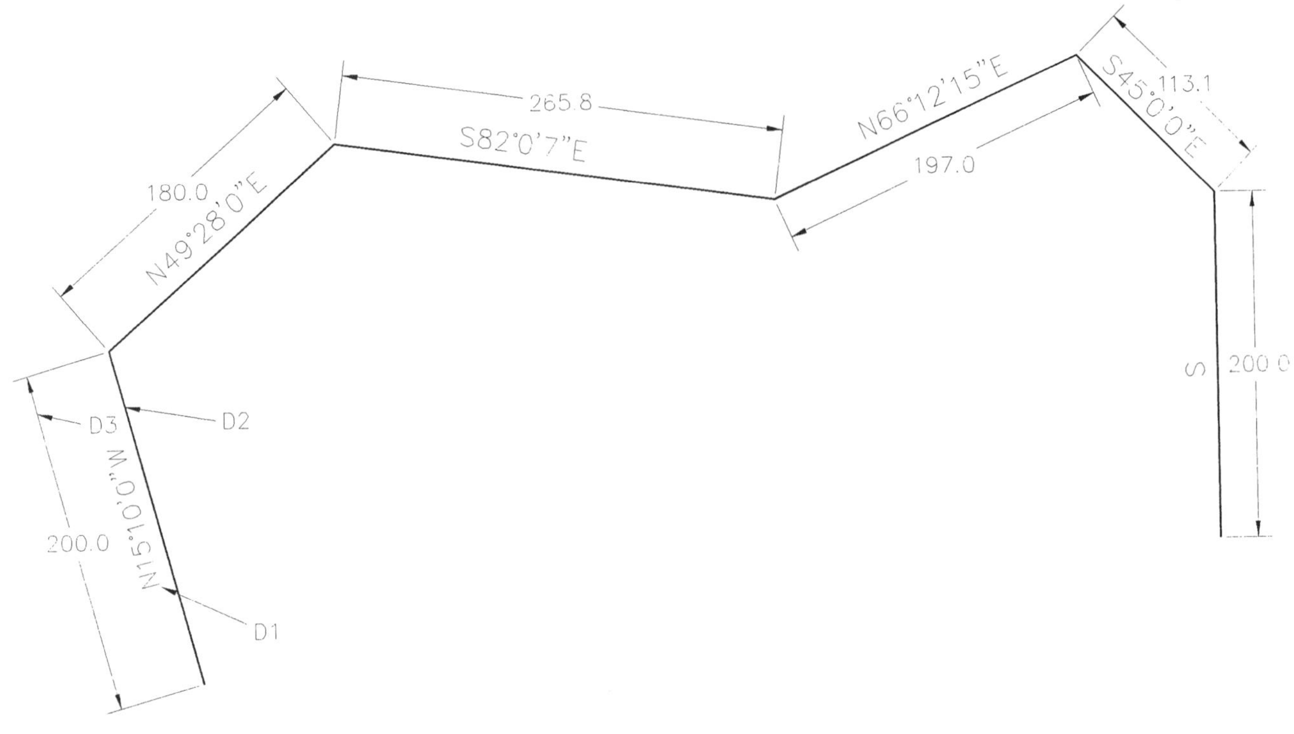

FIGURE 24–2
Open Traverse

OPEN TRAVERSE

Exercise 24–1: Drawing an Open Traverse (Figure 24–2)

Step 1. Load AutoCAD. Close the AutoCAD2002 Today window.

Prompt	Response
Command:	*Type:* **-UNITS** ↵ (or *Type:* **UNITS** ↵ and use the Drawing Units dialog box)
Enter Choice, 1 to 5 <2>:	↵ (to select decimal units)
Number of digits to right of decimal point, 0 to 8 <4>:	*Type:* **1** ↵
Enter Choice, 1 to 5 <1>:	*Type:* **5** ↵ (to select surveyor's units)

Note: Either decimal or engineering can be selected. Decimal allows any units to be entered without respect to feet or inches. Engineering sets inches as the default and allows feet and inches to be entered.

Press Return to accept the defaults for the rest of the unit prompts. Press F2 (or *Click:* the down arrow) to flip back to the graphics display if necessary.

Step 2. Make the following settings:

Note: Use Wizards-Advanced Setup or Quick Setup instead of setting units and limits individually. Area: Length and Width are the values for the upper right corner.

LIMITS: Lower left corner: 0,0
Upper right corner: 800,500

SNAP: 20

GRID: 40

LAYERS: NAME	Color	Linetype	Lineweight
BEARING	Yellow	Continuous	Default
TEXT	Green	Continuous	Default

Zoom-All

Step 3. Set BEARING as the current layer and proceed as follows:

Prompt	Response
Command:	**Polyline** (or *Type:* **PL** ↵)
Specify start point:	*Type:* **133,47** ↵
Specify next point or [Arc/Close/Halfwidth/Length/Undo/Width]:	*Type:* **@200<N15D10′W** ↵
Specify next point or [Arc/Close/Halfwidth/Length/Undo/Width]:	*Type:* **@180<N49D28′E** ↵
Specify next point or [Arc/Close/Halfwidth/Length/Undo/Width]:	*Type:* **@265.8<S82DO′7″E** ↵
Specify next point or [Arc/Close/Halfwidth/Length/Undo/Width]:	*Type:* **@197<N66D12′15″E** ↵
Specify next point or [Arc/Close/Halfwidth/Length/Undo/Width]:	*Type:* **@113.1<S45DE** ↵
Specify next point or [Arc/Close/Halfwidth/Length/Undo/Width]:	*Type:* **@200<S** ↵
Specify next point or [Arc/Close/Halfwidth/Length/Undo/Width]:	↵

The traverse of Figure 24–2 is now complete. Add identifying text and dimensions using the following procedures:

Set Text as the current layer.
Choose Text Font—simplex.
Press Return to accept all the defaults until you return to the command prompt.

Note: The rotation angle for the text is the same as the bearing angle.

Note: You may use Osnap-Endpoint and digitize both ends of each bearing to obtain the rotation angle for bearing text.

Note: %%D is the code for the degree symbol.

Step 4. Place text on all bearings using the following procedure.

Prompt	Response
Command:	**Single Line Text** (or *Type:* **DT** ↵)
Specify start point of text or [Justify/Style]:	**D1** (the starting point for the label)
Specify height <.18>:	*Type:* **10** ↵
Specify rotation angle of text <N90dE>:	*Type:* **N15D10′W** ↵ (or click on the endpoints of the line)
Text:	*Type:* **N15%%D10′10″W** ↵
Text:	↵

Use a similar procedure to place text on all other bearings.

Step 5. Place dimensions on all bearings using the following procedure:

Prompt	Response
Set: DIMSCALE=50	
Command:	*Click:* **Aligned** (from the Dimensioning menu)
First extension line origin or <select object>:	↵
Select object to dimension:	**D2** (Figure 24–2)
Specify dimension line location or [Mtext/Text/Angle]:	**D3**
Command:	↵ **(Repeat Aligned)**
First extension line origin or <select object>:	↵

Select object to dimension:	**Continue selecting lines as described previously**

Note: You can also set the scale by clicking on the paper space viewport boundary, *Click:* Properties and select a scale of 1=100.

Step 6. Complete the drawing by clicking Layout1, then *Click:* OK, and set a scale of 1 = 100 (after you are in Layout1, *Type:* MS ↵ to go to model space, then *Type:* Z ↵, then *Type:* 1/100xp ↵). Place your name in the lower right corner and print the drawing on an 8½″ × 11″ sheet. Save the drawing in two places with the name EX24-1(your initials) to ensure that it will be there when you want it again, then exit AutoCAD.

Now let's draw a closed traverse.

CLOSED TRAVERSE

Exercise 24–2: Drawing a Closed Traverse

The closed traverse of Figure 24–3 is drawn in a manner similar to the one used to draw the open traverse of Figure 24–2. The last bearing, however, may be drawn with the *C,* or *Close,* modifier to the line command. An inquiry using the command Distance (*Type:* **DIST** ↵) will provide a positive check to determine how accurately you have drawn the traverse. Many of the settings of Figure 24–2 can be used to draw Figure 24–3, so let's use them. The procedure is as follows.

Step 1. Load AutoCAD, open drawing EX24-1(your initials) and save it as EX24-2(your initials).

Help: Press Esc to exit from the Erase command.

Prompt	Response
Command:	**Zoom-All**
Command:	**Erase** (or *Type:* **E** ↵)
Select objects:	*Type:* **ALL** ↵
Select objects:	↵

FIGURE 24–3
Closed Traverse

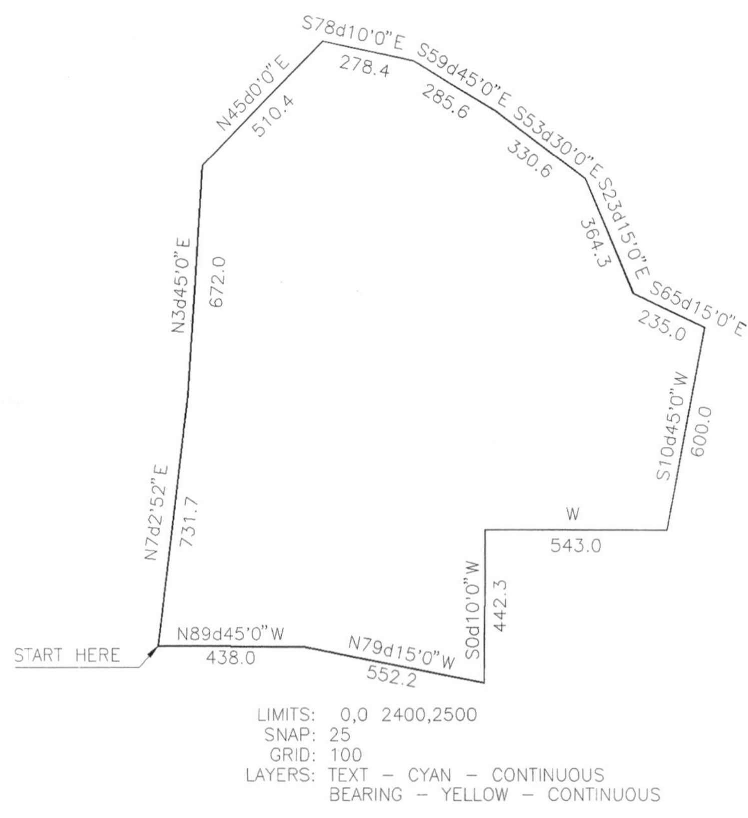

Step 2. Make the following settings:

> LIMITS: Lower left corner: 0,0
> Upper right corner: 2400,2500
>
> SNAP: 25
>
> GRID: 100
>
> Set BEARING as the current layer. (Layers and units settings already exist from Exercise 24–1.)

Step 3. Draw the traverse.

Prompt	Response
Command:	**Line** (or *Type:* **L** ↵)
Specify point or [Undo]:	*Type:* **400,400** ↵
Specify next point or [Undo]:	*Type:* **@731.7<N7D2′52″E** ↵
Specify next point or [Close/Undo]:	*Type:* **@672<N3D45′E** ↵
Specify next point or [Close/Undo]:	*Type:* **@510.4<N45DE** ↵
Specify next point or [Close/Undo]:	*Type:* **@278.4<S78D10′E** ↵

Continue drawing bearings around the traverse, as shown in Figure 24–3, until you come to the last bearing, N89D45′0″W. For this bearing:

Prompt	Response
Specify next point or [Close/Undo]:	*Type:* **C** ↵

Note: The Area command allows you to pick points to describe an enclosed area by digitizing points immediately after the first Area prompt. It also allows you to add or subtract areas from other areas. This is a good command with which to experiment a little.

Now check to see how well you drew the traverse:

Prompt	Response
Command:	**List** (or *Type:* **LIST** ↵)
Select objects:	*Click:* **on the last bearing (the one drawn with the *C* response)**
Select objects:	↵

A description of the bearing appears. It should show an angle in the X-Y plane of N89D45′0″W and a length of 438.0.

Prompt	Response
Command:	*Click:* **F2** (to return to the graphics screen)

Now set the current layer to TEXT and place text describing the bearing direction and length on the drawing as you did in Figure 24–2. Use simplex font, height: 10. Do not use arrowheads and dimension lines. Place your name in the lower right corner of the drawing.

Now use Area to find the area and perimeter of the closed traverse.

Prompt	Response
Command:	**Boundary**
The Boundary Creation dialog box appears:	*Click:* **Pick Points <**
Select internal point:	*Click:* **on any point inside the closed traverse**
Select internal point:	↵
BOUNDARY created 1 polyline Command:	**Area** (or *Type:* **AREA** ↵)
Specify first point or [Object/Add/Subtract]:	*Type:* O ↵

Note: *Click:* F2 (or the down arrow) to return to the graphics screen.

Prompt	Response
Select objects:	*Click:* **on any point on the closed traverse**
Area=2063952.5, Perimeter=5983.5	Exit

Step 4. Save the drawing in two places with the name EX24-2(your initials), then *Click:* **OK, and set a scale of 1 = 300 (after you are in Layout1,** *Type:* **MS ↵ to go to model space, then** *Type:* **Z ↵, then** *Type:* **1/300xp ↵). Place your name in the lower right corner and print the drawing full scale.**

PLAT

Exercise 24–3: Drawing a Plat

The plat of Figure 24–4 has many of the same elements as the closed traverse. It also has curve data and building line offsets that must be accurately drawn. The final figure should appear as shown in Figure 24–5, but all the data shown in Figure 24–4 are needed to draw Figure 24–5. Follow this procedure.

Step 1. Load AutoCAD. *Click:* **Create Drawings-Wizards-Quick Setup.**

Step 2. Make the following settings:

Area: Width: 200
Length: 160

SNAP: 2.

GRID: 10.0

LTSCALE: 10

Units: Decimal units—1 digit to the right of the decimal point. Surveyor's units. Accept the defaults for all other unit prompts.

LAYERS: NAME	Color	Linetype	Lineweight
BL	Magenta	Dashed X2	Default
PL	Green	Phantom 2	Default
TEXT	Cyan	Continuous	Default

Set PL as the current layer.

Zoom-All

CURVE DATA

CURVE	CHORD BEARING	CHORD LENGTH	CURVE RADIUS
C70	S68D44'47"W	33.4'	50'
C74	N77°50'57"E	55.4'	50'

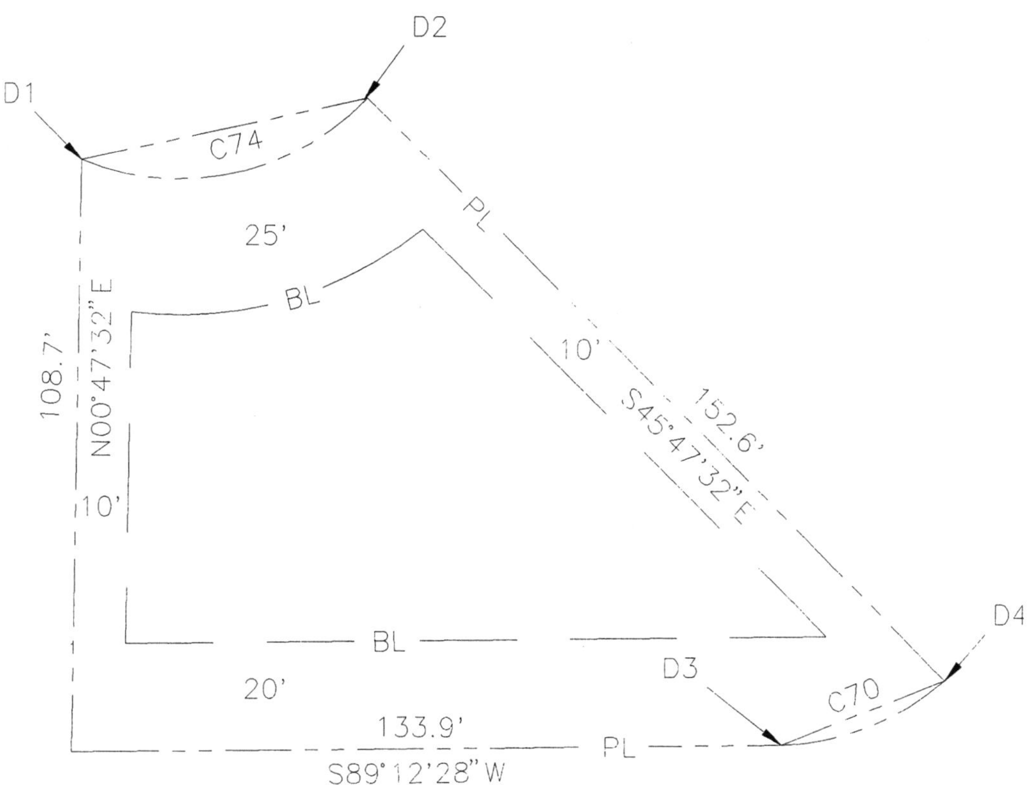

FIGURE 24–4
Information Needed to Draw the Plat, Figure 24–5

FIGURE 24–5
Plat

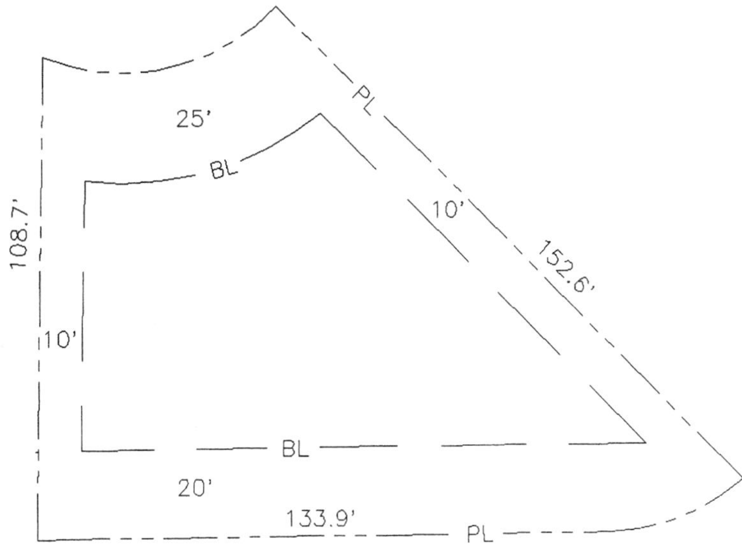

Step 3. Use the following procedure to draw Figure 24–5.

Prompt	Response
Command:	*Click:* **Line** (or *Type:* **L** ↵)
Specify first point:	*Type:* **20,10** ↵
Specify next point or [Undo]:	*Type:* **@108.7<N0D47′32″E** ↵
Specify next point or [Undo]:	*Type:* **@55.4<N77D50′57″E** ↵ (This is the bearing for curve C74.)

Notice that the bearing for the curve C74 was taken from the curve data chart shown on Figure 24–4. Curve data are an essential part of the information you need for this type of drawing.

Prompt	Response
Specify next point or [Close/Undo]:	*Type:* **@152.2<S45D47′32″E** ↵
Specify next point or [Close/Undo]:	*Type:* **@33.4<S68D44′47″W** ↵
Specify next point or [Close/Undo]:	*Type:* **C** ↵

Use the Arc command to draw the curves C70 and C74.

Prompt	Response
Command:	**Arc-Start, End, Radius**
Specify start point of arc or [CEnter]:	**D1** (Use Osnap-Endpoint.)
Specify end point of arc:	**D2** (Use Osnap-Endpoint.)
Specify radius of arc:	*Type:* **50** ↵
Command:	**Arc-Start, End, Radius**
Specify start point of arc or [CEnter]:	**D3** (Use Osnap-Endpoint.)
Specify end point of arc:	**D4** (Use Osnap-Endpoint.)
Specify radius of arc:	*Type:* **50** ↵

Step 4. Erase the two chords of C70 and C74.

Step 5. Use Offset to form the building line (BL).

Step 6. Use *zero-radius* **Fillet to clean up the corners of the building line.**

Step 7. Place the required Text in the locations shown on Figure 24–5 using Single Line Text 3.5-unit-high simplex font.

Step 8. Break lines where they cross Text, as shown in Figure 24–5.

Step 9. Place your name in the lower right corner using Single Line Text.

Step 10. *Click:* **Layout1, then** *Click:* **OK and set a plot scale of 1 = 30 (after you are in Layout1,** *Click:* **the paper space viewport boundary and use Properties to set the scale. Place your name in the lower right corner and print the drawing on an 11″ × 8½″ sheet.**

Step 11. Save the drawing in two places with the name EX24-3(your initials) and exit AutoCAD.

CONTOUR MAP

Exercise 24–4: Drawing a Contour Map

The contour map shown in Figure 24–6C was drawn from the field notes in that figure. The surveyor laid out a grid with all vertical and horizontal lines 20′ apart and then took elevation readings from an identified 0 elevation at each intersection. The grid was drawn in the same manner and the elevation of each intersection was labeled on the grid. Contours were drawn in 5′ increments by interpolating (estimating the location) for contour point on each grid line. Your final drawing should appear as shown in Figure 24–6B and C.

To draw this figure:

Step 1. Load AutoCAD. *Click:* **Create Drawings-Wizards-Quick Setup.**

Step 2. Make the following settings:

> **Units: Decimal —1 digit to the right of the decimal point.**
> **Area: Width: 320**
> **Length: 160**
> **GRID: 10**
> **SNAP: 2**

LAYERS: NAME	Color	Linetype	Lineweight
CONTOUR	Green	Continuous	Default
GRID	Cyan	Continuous	Default
TEXT	Magenta	Continuous	Default

> **Set GRID as the current layer. Set SNAP and ORTHO ON.**
> **Zoom-All**

Step 3. Draw B and C of Figure 24–6.

Prompt	**Response**
Command:	**Line** (or *Type:* **L** ↵)
Specify first point:	*Type:* **30,30** ↵

	A	B	C	D	E	F	
	75	74	72	70	69	68	0+00
	82	80	77	75	71	68	0+20
	88	86	85	80	75	68	0+40
	97	92	91	85	78	68	0+60
	95	93	90	80	75	65	0+80
	88	84	78	75	70	65	1+00

KKK

KKK

A

FIELD NOTES

STATION	ELEVATION	STATION	ELEVATION
A–0+00	75.0	D–0+00	70.0
A–0+20	82.0	D–0+20	75.0
A–0+40	88.0	D–0+40	80.0
A–0+60	97.0	D–0+60	85.0
A–0+80	95.0	D–0+80	80.0
A–1+00	88.0	D–1+00	75.0
B–0+00	74.0	E–0+00	69.0
B–0+20	80.0	E–0+20	71.0
B–0+40	86.0	E–0+40	75.0
B–0+60	93.0	E–0+60	78.0
B–0+80	95.0	E–0+80	75.0
B–1+00	84.0	E–1+00	70.0
C–0+00	72.0	F–0+00	68.0
C–0+20	77.0	F–0+20	68.0
C–0+40	85.0	F–0+40	68.0
C–0+60	91.0	F–0+60	68.0
C–0+80	90.0	F–0+80	65.0
C–1+00	78.0	F–1+00	65.0

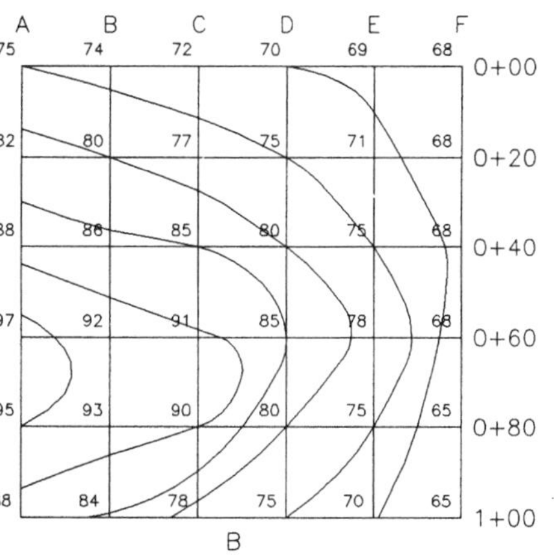

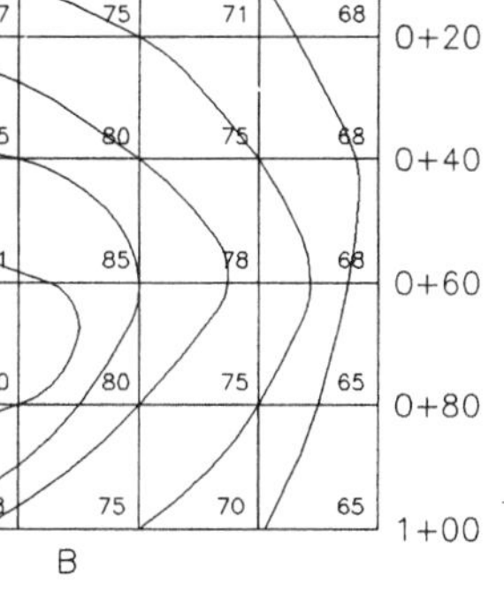

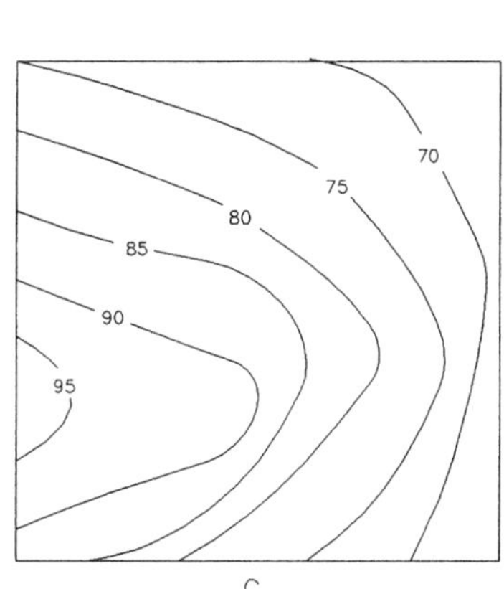

FIGURE 24–6
Contour Map

Prompt	Response
Specify next point or [Undo]:	*Type:* **@100<90** ↵
Specify next point or [Undo]:	*Type:* **@100<0** ↵
Specify next point or [Close/Undo]:	↵
Command:	*Type:* **AR** ↵ (or select Array and use the dialog box)
Select objects:	*Click:* **on the vertical line**
Select objects:	↵
Specify the type of array [Rectangular/Polar]<R>:	*Type:* **R** ↵
Enter the number of rows (- - -)<1>:	↵
Enter the number of columns (111)<1>:	*Type:* **6** ↵
Specify distance between columns (111):	*Type:* **20** ↵
Command:	↵ (Repeat ARRAY)
Select objects:	*Click:* **on the horizontal line**
Select objects:	↵

Note: SNAP ON will allow you to place all elevation labels the same distance from the intersections.

Note: Selecting DTEXT OPTIONS allows you to select the top, middle, or bottom of TEXT in addition to the left, centered, and right justification.

Step 4. Continue, through the Array command, forming an array of 6 rows and 1 column, with −20 units between rows.

Step 5. Label each intersection using Single Line Text, right-justified, height 2.5 in the locations shown. Set SNAP ON, set ORTHO OFF, and set TEXT as the current layer.

Step 6. Place the letters above the grid in the location shown using Single Line Text, centered, height 3.5, with SNAP ON and TEXT as the current layer.

Step 7. Place the station numbers to the right of the grid using Single Line Text, middle/left, height 3.5, simplex font, SNAP ON. Set TEXT as the current layer.

Step 8. With contour as the current layer, use Polyline or Spline to draw a Polyline through each point with an elevation of 70′. You will have to estimate the location of these points on several of the grid lines. For example, the 70′ elevation on the vertical line between E 0+00 and E 0+20 is halfway between the two points. (E 0+00 is 69; E 0+20 is 71.)

Step 9. Use Pedit (Edit Polyline) to change the Polylines to a smooth curve using the *fit-curve* modifier.

Step 10. Draw contours for the 75′, 80′, 85′, 90′, and 95′ elevations using the procedure described for the 70 elevation.

Step 11. Copy the contours and the outer grid lines to the location shown using the Copy command.

Step 12. Place text on the contour lines as shown in Figure 24–6C using the Single Line Text command, height 2.5, TEXT as the current layer.

Step 13. Break the contour lines on each side of the text using the Break command.

Step 14. Place your name in the lower right corner using Single Line Text, right-justified, height 3.5.

Step 15. *Click:* **Layout1, then** *Click:* **OK and set a plot scale of 1 = 40 (after you are in Layout1,** *Click:* **on the viewport boundary and use Properties from the Modify menu to set the standard scale of 1=40.) Place your name in the lower right corner and print the drawing on an 11″ × 8½″ sheet.**

Step 16. Save the drawing in two places with the name EX24-4(your initials) and exit AutoCAD.

PROFILE

Exercise 24–5: Drawing a Profile

A profile (Figure 24–7) is a cross section of the earth taken across a set of contours. Because the area covered is very large and the change in elevation is small compared with the area, the vertical scale is often different from the horizontal scale. This difference in scale makes it much easier to see the change in elevation. A profile can be drawn across any set of contours. The contours are drawn from field notes, as described in Figure 24–6. Then a line is drawn across the contours where the profile is desired. Vertical lines are projected from the intersections of the line with the contours. A grid at a representative scale is then drawn beneath the contour, and the profile is plotted through the intersection of the grid with the vertical lines.

To draw Figure 24–7:

Step 1. Load AutoCAD. *Click:* **Create Drawings-Wizards-Quick Setup.**

Step 2. Make the following settings:

Units: Decimal—1 digit to the right of the decimal point. Accept the defaults for all other unit prompts.

Area: Width: 350
Length: 250

GRID: 10

SNAP: 2

LAYERS: NAME	Color	Linetype	Lineweight
CONTOUR	Magenta	Continuous	Default
GRID	Cyan	Continuous	Default
PROFILE	Green	Continuous	Default

Set CONTOUR as the current layer. Set SNAP ON. Set ORTHO OFF.

Step 3. Draw the contours.
Since there are two scales involved, the contours may be drawn first and then reduced to be compatible with the vertical scale. In this example, reduction will not be necessary. Assume the contours were drawn five times as large as the areas and reduced to 20%. Draw the contours approximately as shown using Polylines and the fit-curve modifiers from Pedit or use Spline. The extreme limits of the outside contour should be approximately 170 wide by 100 high.

Step 4. Set GRID as the current layer and draw a horizontal line across the center of the set of contours using the Line command and the Nearest Osnap mode at each end of the line.

Step 5. Set ORTHO ON and use Copy to copy the horizontal line to be the top line of the grid, the 310 line.

Step 6. Use Array to draw the remaining horizontal lines: 7 rows, 1 column, −10 distance between rows.

Step 7. Use Line to draw a vertical line from the left end of the line across the contours to the left end of the bottom line of the grid.

Step 8. Set a running Osnap mode of Intersection and Copy the vertical line through each contour intersection with the horizontal line.

Step 9. Use Single Line Text, simplex font, to place all text on the drawing. The numbers on the left of the grid can be drawn most easily using Single Line

FIGURE 24–7
Profile

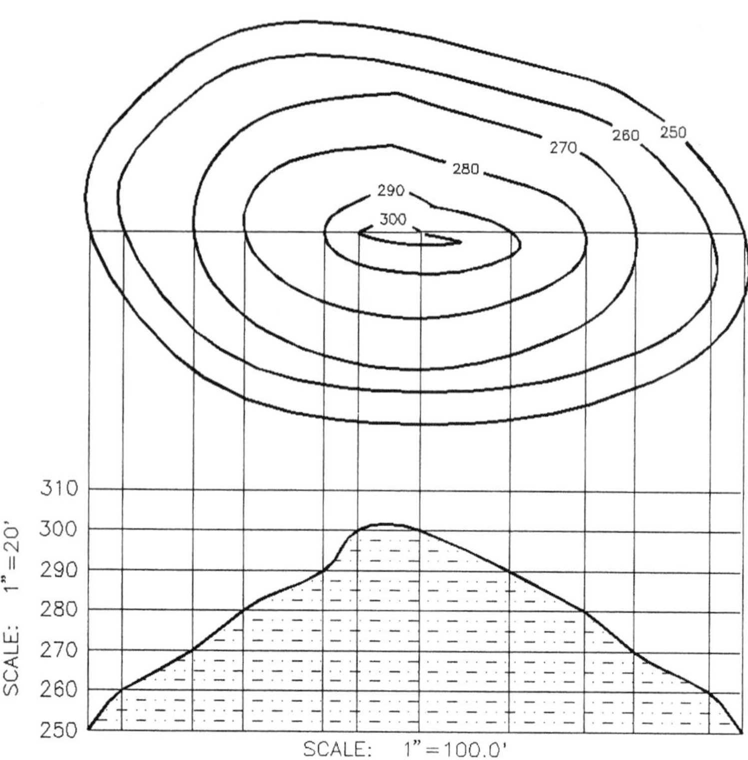

Text, middle, right. Make larger text 3.5 and smaller text, 2.5. Break contours on each side of the text.

Step 10. Use Polyline to draw lines through the intersections of the vertical lines with the corresponding grid lines. Use Pedit-Fit curve to make a curve out of the Polyline.

Step 11. Use Hatch to create the shaded area. The hatch pattern is MUDST with a scale of 20.

Step 12. *Click:* **Layout1, then** *Click:* **OK, and set a scale of 1 = 40 (after you are in Layout1,** *Click:* **on the viewport boundary and use Properties from the Modify menu to set the scale.) Place your name in the lower right corner and print the drawing on an 11″ × 8½″ sheet.**

Step 13. Save the drawing in two places with the name EX24-5(your initials) and exit AutoCAD.

HIGHWAY MAP

Exercise 24–6: Drawing a Highway Map

Refer to Figures 24–8 and 24–9. The highway map of Figure 24–9 is drawn using a centerline down the middle of the highway. This centerline is created with bearings using the Line command, as shown in Figure 24–8. The center for the radius in Figure 24–8 is located by using Offset at a distance of 320′ and clicking on two bearings. Then the radius is drawn using Circle with a radius of 320′. Trim is used to remove the part of the circle that is not needed. The bearings and curves are joined together using Edit Polyline-Join to form a single Polyline so that the road may be created with the use of Offset.

To draw Figure 24–9:

Step 1. Load AutoCAD. *Click:* **Create Drawings-Wizards-Quick Setup.**

Step 2. Make the following settings:

Units:	Select decimal units and surveyor's units.			
Area:	Width: 410 Length: 410			
GRID: 10				
SNAP: 2				
LAYERS:	NAME	Color	Linetype	Lineweight
	CONTOUR	Magenta	Continuous	Default
	HIGHWAY	Yellow	Continuous	Default
	CUT	Cyan	Continuous	Default
	FILL	Green	Continuous	Default
Set HIGHWAY as the current layer.				

Step 3. Use Line to draw two bearings.

Prompt	Response
Command:	**Line** (or *Type:* **L** ↵)
Specify first point:	*Type:* **350, 350** ↵
Specify next point or [Undo]:	*Type:* **@184.1<S56D33′36″W** ↵
Specify next point or [Undo]:	*Type:* **@138.3<S25D20′52″W** ↵
Specify next point or [Close/Undo]:	↵
Command:	**Offset** (or *Type:* **O** ↵)
Specify offset distance or [Through] <Through>:	*Type:* **135** ↵

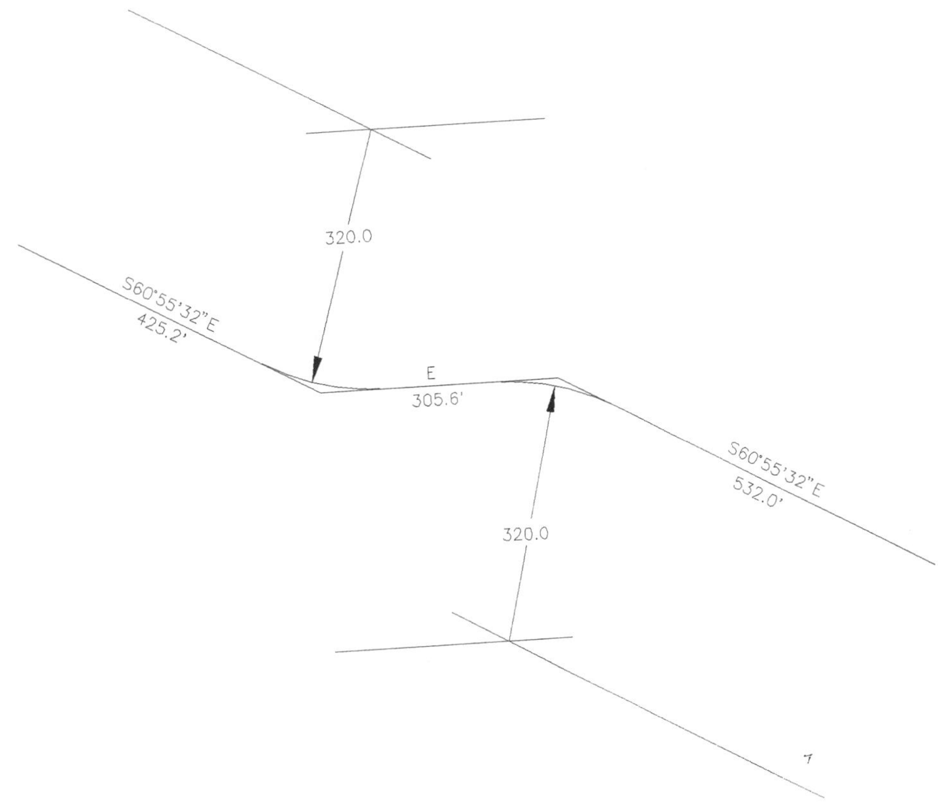

FIGURE 24–8
Highway Map Construction Lines

FIGURE 24–9
Highway Map

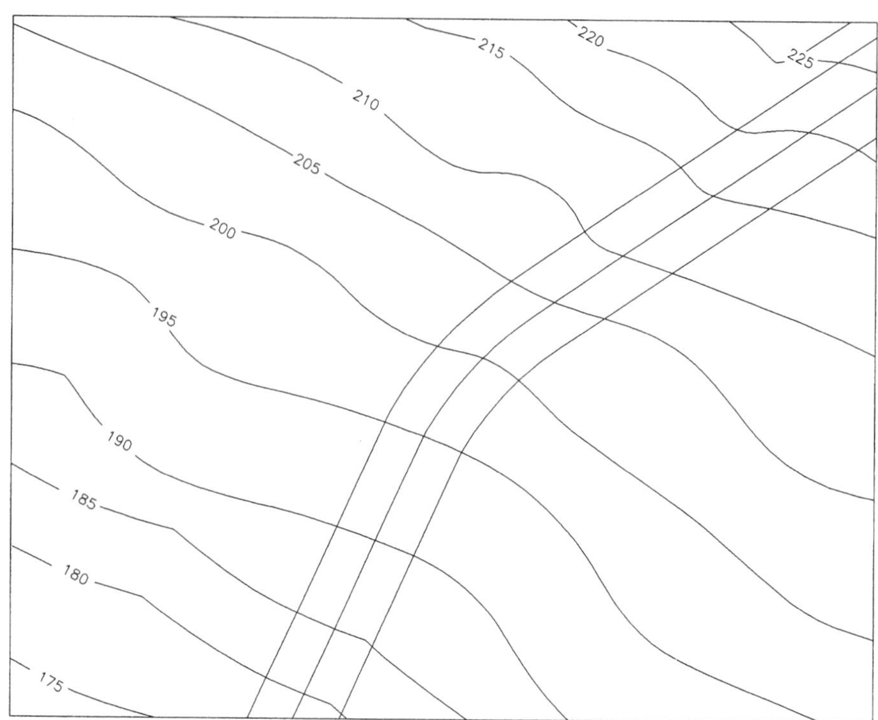

Prompt	Response
Select object to offset:	*Click:* **on one of the bearings**
Specify point on side to offset:	*Click:* **on any point to the right of the bearing**
Select object to offset or <exit>:	*Click:* **on the other bearing**
Specify point on side to offset:	*Click:* **on any point to the right of the bearing**
Select object to offset or <exit>:	↵

Step 4. **Using the intersection of the two offset lines as the center, draw a Circle using Circle-Center, Radius with a radius of 135. Use Trim to remove the unwanted parts of the circle and the bearing. Erase the two offset lines.**

Step 5. **Connect the bearings and the curves to form a single polyline using Edit Polyline-Join.**

Step 6. **Offset the polyline 15′ on each side of the polyline to form the highway.**

Step 7. **Draw a 320 × 250 rectangle around the highway using Line, and Move it to the approximate location shown in Figure 24–9.**

Step 8. **With CONTOUR as the current layer, draw contours to approximate the ones shown. Label contours with Single Line Text, simplex font, 3.5 high. Break contours around labels, as shown.**

Step 9. *Click:* **Layout1, set a plot scale of 1 = 50, place your name in the lower right corner and print the drawing on an 11″ × 8½″ sheet.**

Step 10. **Save the drawing in two places with the name EX24-6(your initials) and exit AutoCAD.**

CUT and FILL

As a highway proceeds through contours, it is often necessary to cut out part of the earth or add to the existing contours. This process is called CUT and FILL (Figure 24–10). In this case contour 200 is the elevation of the highway, and the angle that the contours

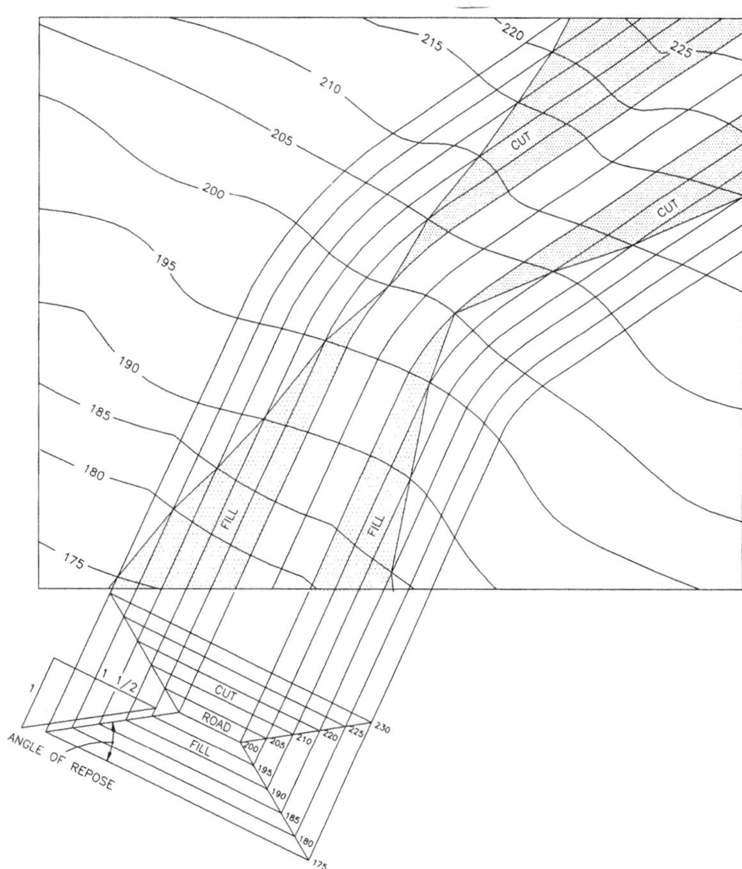

FIGURE 24–10
CUT and FILL

make with the highway is at a ratio of 1:1½ (the angle of respose). With this information, a profile can be established off the end of the road. A vertical scale that is the same as the scale used to draw the highway is used to make the contours.

Exercise 24–7: Making a Cut-and-Fill Drawing

To make the cut-and-fill drawing:

Step 1. Load AutoCAD, open drawing EX24-6(your initials), and save it as EX24-7(your initials).

All layers and settings have been made from Figure 24–9.

Step 2. Set CONTOUR as the current layer.

At a convenient distance from the end of the road, draw a line (the short one with ROAD on it) perpendicular to both sides of the road. You will probably want to draw the left side longer than the width of the road so you can be sure that the lines can be extended to it. Use the Osnap-Perpendicular mode even though it does not touch the right side of the road.

Step 3. Extend both sides of the road to the perpendicular line.

Step 4. From the intersection formed by the sides of the highway and the perpendicular line, draw lines to form the angle of repose at a ratio of 1½ to 1.

Step 5. Offset the line labeled ROAD five times on both sides at an offset distance of 5.

Step 6. **Extend these lines to the angle of repose.**

Step 7. **Offset the highway lines THROUGH the intersection of the cut-and-fill vertical scale with the angle of repose. You will have five lines on each side of the road.**

Step 8. **Extend the highway OFFSET to the furthermost line forming the angle of repose.**

Step 9. **Draw polylines through the intersection of the contour lines and the offset highway lines. There will be four of these lines.**

Step 10. **Add text for CUT and FILL labels using Single Line Text, simplex font.**

Step 11. **Break lines as needed to prepare the drawing for the HATCH pattern. You may have to draw a small scale box (which will be erased later) around the CUT and FILL labels to keep the hatch pattern out of the labels.**

Step 12. **Hatch areas of CUT and FILL using the DOTS pattern. Use scales for the HATCH pattern as follows: 40 for FILL, 25 for CUT.**

Step 13. **Place your name in the lower right corner.**

Step 14. *Click:* **Layout1, then** *Click:* **OK, and set a scale of 1 = 50 using Properties. Print the drawing full scale on an 8½″ × 11″ sheet.**

Step 15. **Save the drawing in two places with the name EX24-7(your initials) and exit AutoCAD.**

EXERCISES

EXERCISE 24–1. Draw Figure 24–2 as described in this chapter.

EXERCISE 24–2. Draw Figure 24–3 as described in this chapter.

EXERCISE 24–3. Draw Figure 24–5 as described in this chapter.

EXERCISE 24–4. Draw Figures 24–6B and 24–6C as described in this chapter.

EXERCISE 24–5. Draw Figure 24–7 as described in this chapter.

EXERCISE 24–6. Draw Figure 24–9 as described in this chapter.

EXERCISE 24–7. Draw Figure 24–10 as described in this chapter.

EXERCISE 24–8. Open drawing EX24–3(your initials) and save it as EX24-8(your initials). Draw a 50′ × 30′ rectangle using the Polyline command inside the building line of Figure 24–5.
Use Area to find:

Building area
Area of the property inside the PL
Difference between building area and property area

Use Single Line Text, 3.5 units high, simplex font to show this information in the lower left corner of the drawing. Print this drawing on an 11″ × 8.5″ sheet.

EXERCISE 24–9. Draw Figure 24–11 using the settings from Figure 24–4. Name the draw ing EX24–9(your initials). Print the drawing on an 11″ × 8.5″ sheet.

EXERCISE 24–10. Draw a contour map similar to Figure 24–6B and 6C from the field notes in Figure 24–12. Name the drawing EX24–10(your initials). Use Figure 24–6 as a prototype. Print the drawing on an 11″ × 8.5″ sheet.

EXERCISE 24–11. Draw a contour map similar to Figure 24–6B and 6C from the field notes in Figure 24–13. Name the drawing EX24–11(your initials). Print the drawing on an 11″ × 8.5″ sheet.

EXERCISE 24–12. Draw a north arrow similar to the one shown as Figure 24–14. Name it EX24–12 (your initials). Draw it on layer 0 with convenient SNAP and GRID settings. The arrow should measure 10 units from tip to tail. Approx imate all other dimensions and change it a little if you like. Print the draw ing on an 11″ × 8.5″ sheet.

FIGURE 24–11
Exercise 24–9

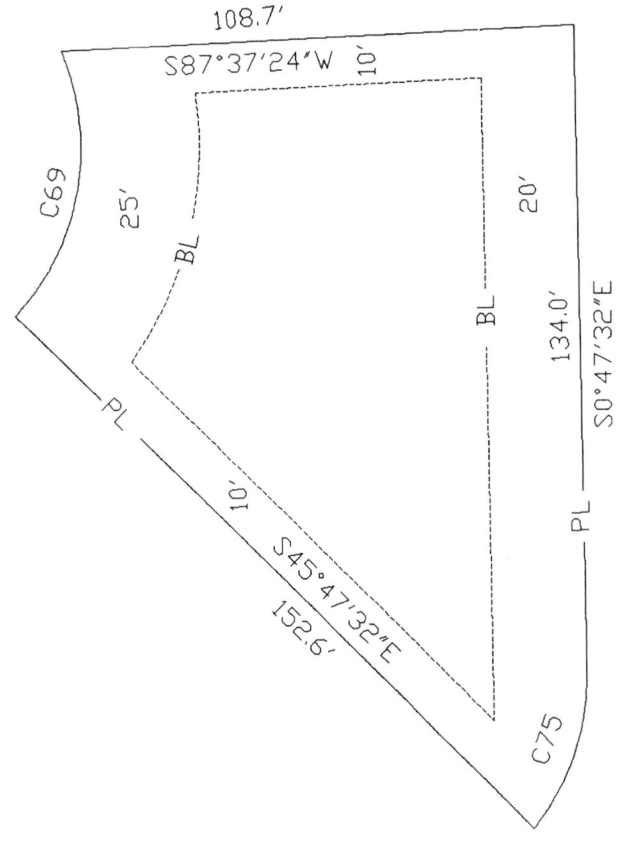

CURVE DATA

CURVE	CHORD BEARING	CHORD LENGTH	CURVE RADIUS
C69	S10°33′59″W	55.4	50′
C75	S19°40′9″W	33.4	50′

	A	B	C	D	E	F
0+00						
0+20						
0+40						
0+60						
0+80						
1+00						

FIELD NOTES

STATION	ELEVATION	STATION	ELEVATION
A–0+00	164.0	D–0+00	160.0
A–0+20	171.0	D–0+20	164.0
A–0+40	177.0	D–0+40	170.0
A–0+60	186.0	D–0+60	170.0
A–0+80	184.0	D–0+80	172.0
A–1+00	177.0	D–1+00	165.0
B–0+00	162.0	E–0+00	158.0
B–0+20	170.0	E–0+20	160.0
B–0+40	173.0	E–0+40	164.0
B–0+60	182.0	E–0+60	167.0
B–0+80	182.0	E–0+80	164.0
B–1+00	172.0	E–1+00	169.0
C–0+00	161.0	F–0+00	157.0
C–0+20	166.0	F–0+20	157.0
C–0+40	174.0	F–0+40	156.0
C–0+60	180.0	F–0+60	156.0
C–0+80	180.0	F–0+80	155.0
C–1+00	167.0	F–1+00	155.0

FIGURE 24–12
Exercise 24–10

A B C D E F

0+00
0+20
0+40
0+60
0+80
1+00

FIELD NOTES

STATION	ELEVATION	STATION	ELEVATION
A-0+00	114.0	D-0+00	110.0
A-0+20	120.0	D-0+20	114.0
A-0+40	127.0	D-0+40	120.0
A-0+60	135.0	D-0+60	120.0
A-0+80	134.0	D-0+80	122.0
A-1+00	127.0	D-1+00	116.0
B-0+00	112.0	E-0+00	107.0
B-0+20	120.0	E-0+20	110.0
B-0+40	123.0	E-0+40	114.0
B-0+60	131.0	E-0+60	117.0
B-0+80	132.0	E-0+80	114.0
B-1+00	122.0	E-1+00	119.0
C-0+00	111.0	F-0+00	107.0
C-0+20	115.0	F-0+20	107.0
C-0+40	124.0	F-0+40	106.0
C-0+60	130.0	F-0+60	106.0
C-0+80	132.0	F-0+80	114.0
C-1+00	118.0	F-1+00	114.0

FIGURE 24–13
Exercise 24–11

FIGURE 24–14
Exercise 24–12

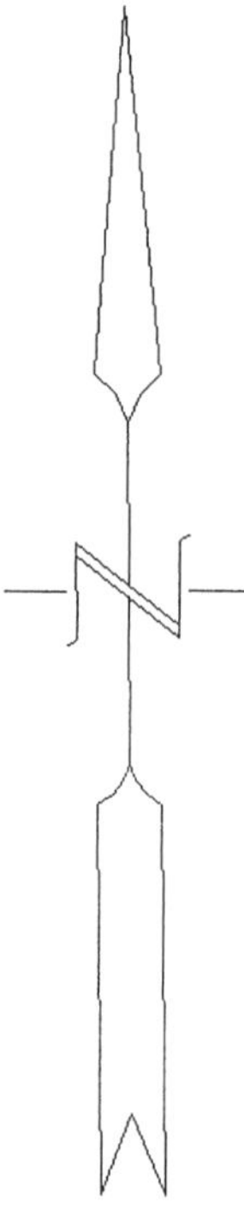

EXERCISE 24–13. Draw Figure 24–15 using the settings from Figure 24–10 (Exercise 24–7). Change:

LIMITS: Lower left corner: 5000,5000
Upper right corner: 6000,6000

Use Single Line Text, simplex font for all lettering except the title block.

Use Single Line Text, COMPLEX for the title-block information. Print the drawing on a 22″ × 17″ sheet.

GRID: 20

SNAP: 5

EXERCISE 24–14. Draw and dimension Figure 24–16. Label with Single Line Text, SIMPLEX, 5 units high. Use the following settings and layers. Print the drawing on an 11″ × 8.5″ sheet.

LIMITS: Lower left corner: 0,0
Upper right corner: 400,200

SNAP: 5

GRID: 10

LTSCALE: 50

DIMSCALE: 50 (or set DIMSCALE = 0; paper space limits = 11,8.5; and use the Mview command with the Fit option to create a paper space viewport.)

DIMASZ: 0

DIMTSZ: .125

DIMTXT: .1

LAYERS:

NAME	Color	Linetype	Lineweight
THICK	Yellow	Continuous	Default
DIM	Green	Continuous	Default
TEXT	Red	Continuous	Default
CL	Cyan	Center	Default
HID	Magenta	Hidden	Default
GL	Blue	Continuous	Default
WL	Blue	Continuous	Default
SL	Blue	Continuous	Default

EXERCISE 24–15. Draw Figure 24–17 using the settings described, with two text styles and fonts. Do not specify a size when you specify a style. Both fonts should be vertical. Center the drawing within the limits. Print to fit on an 11″ × 8.5″ sheet. Make the curb look like the curbs you know about. Notice that some features have been enlarged to make them easier to see. Use the following settings and layers:

LIMITS: Lower left corner: 0,0
Upper right corner: 400,200

SNAP: .5

GRID: 1

LAYERS:

NAME	Color	Linetype	Lineweight
THICK	Yellow	Continuous	Default
HOUSE	Cyan	Continuous	Default
SOD	Green	Continuous	Default
TEXT	Red	Continuous	Default
THIN	Magenta	Continuous	Default

Be sure to Zoom-All before you start.

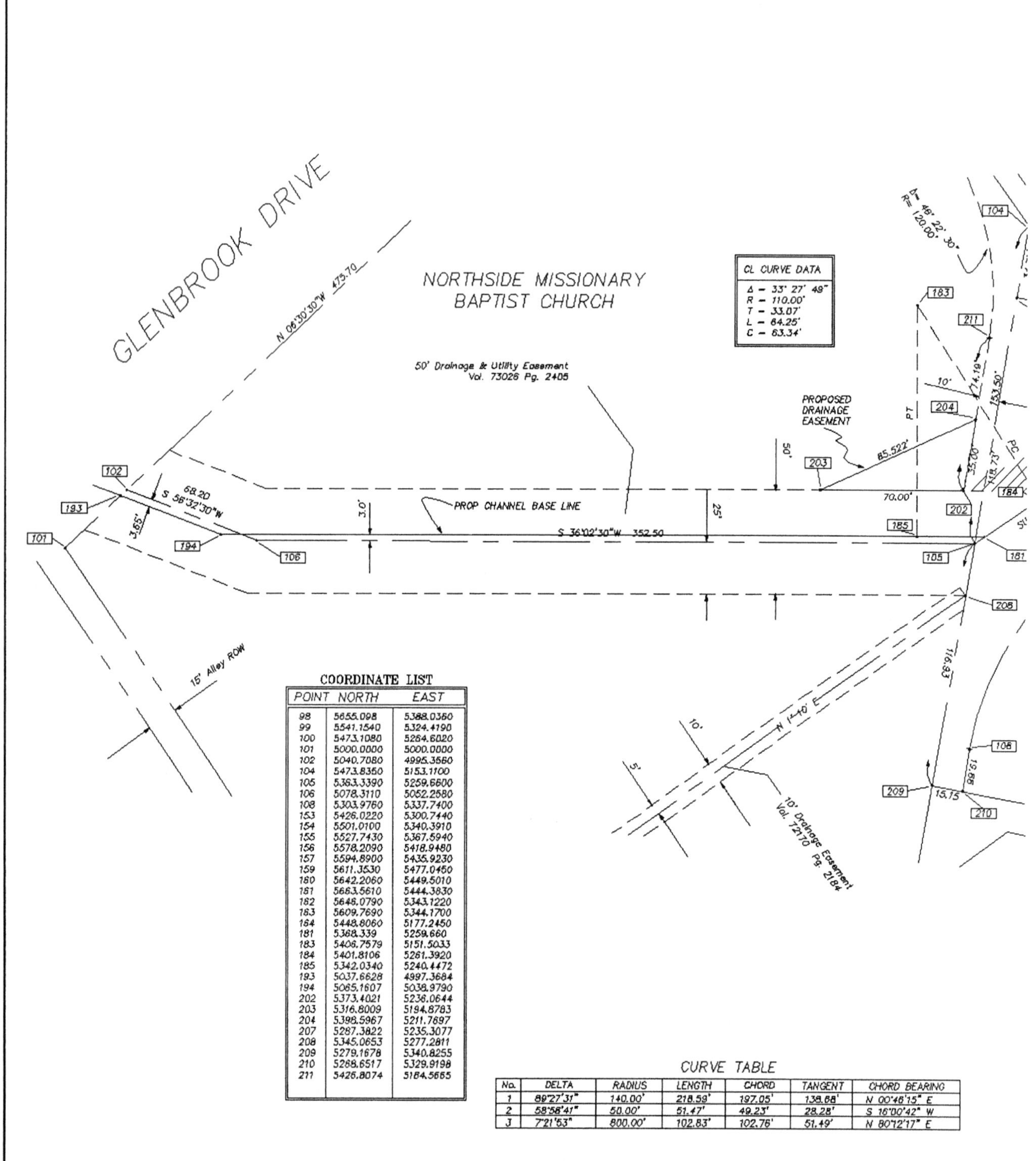

COORDINATE LIST

POINT	NORTH	EAST
98	5655.098	5388.0360
99	5541.1540	5324.4190
100	5473.1080	5264.6020
101	5000.0000	5000.0000
102	5040.7080	4995.3560
104	5473.8350	5153.1100
105	5363.3390	5259.6600
106	5078.3110	5052.2580
108	5303.9760	5337.7400
153	5426.0220	5300.7440
154	5501.0100	5340.3910
155	5527.7430	5367.5940
156	5578.2090	5418.9480
157	5594.8900	5435.9230
159	5611.3530	5477.0450
160	5642.2060	5449.5010
161	5663.5610	5444.3830
162	5646.0790	5343.1220
163	5609.7690	5344.1700
164	5448.8060	5177.2450
181	5368.339	5259.660
183	5406.7579	5151.5033
184	5401.8106	5261.3920
185	5342.0340	5240.4472
193	5037.6628	4997.3684
194	5065.1607	5038.9790
202	5373.4021	5236.0644
203	5316.8009	5194.8783
204	5398.5967	5211.7697
207	5287.3822	5235.3077
208	5345.0653	5277.2811
209	5279.1678	5340.8255
210	5268.6517	5329.9198
211	5426.8074	5184.5665

CURVE TABLE

No.	DELTA	RADIUS	LENGTH	CHORD	TANGENT	CHORD BEARING
1	89°27'31"	140.00'	218.59'	197.05'	138.68'	N 00°46'15" E
2	58°58'41"	50.00'	51.47'	49.23'	28.28'	S 16°00'42" W
3	7°21'53"	800.00'	102.83'	102.76'	51.49'	N 80°12'17" E

FIGURE 24–15
Sheet 1 of 2
Exercise 24–13

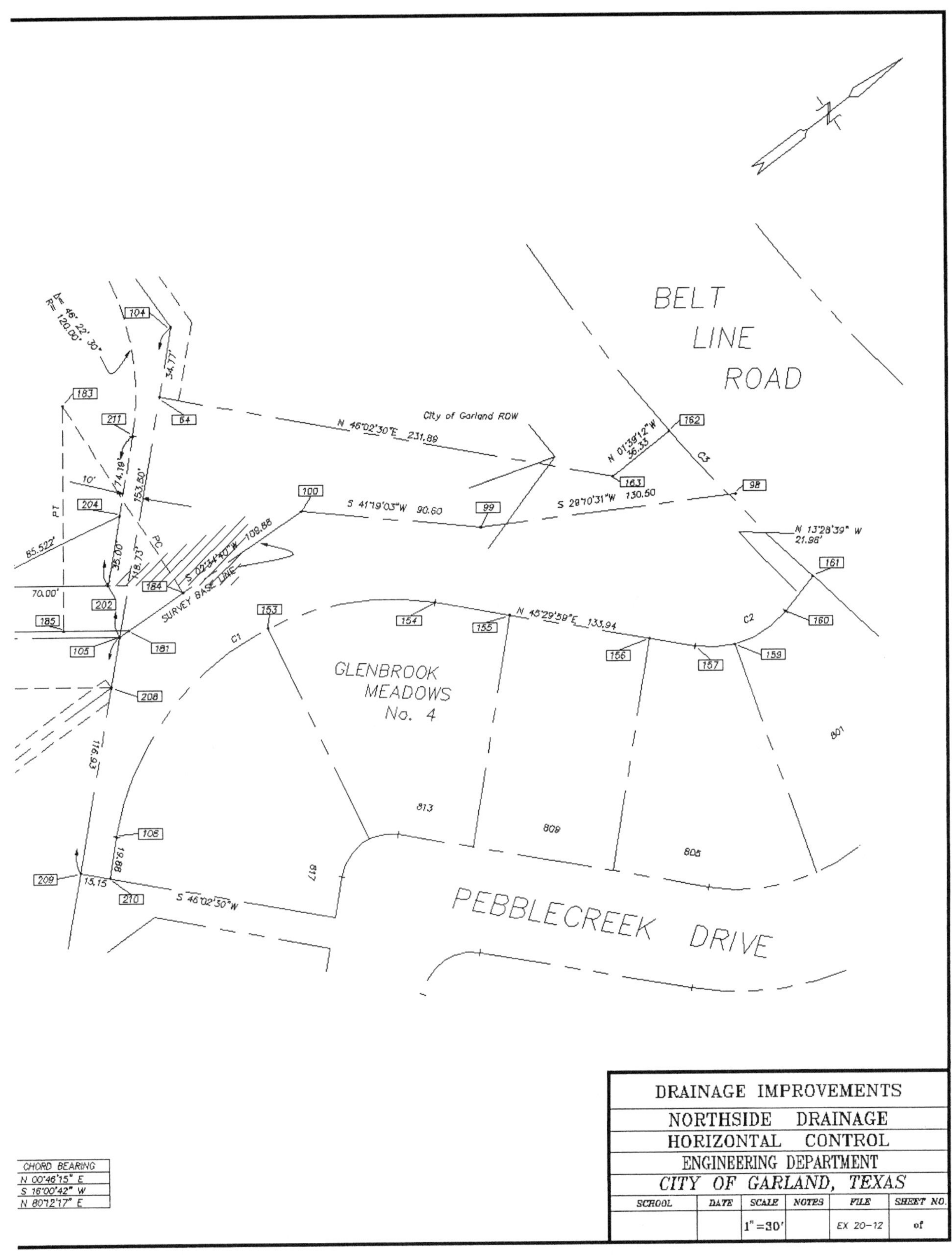

FIGURE 24–15
Sheet 2 of 2

FIGURE 24–16
Exercise 24–14

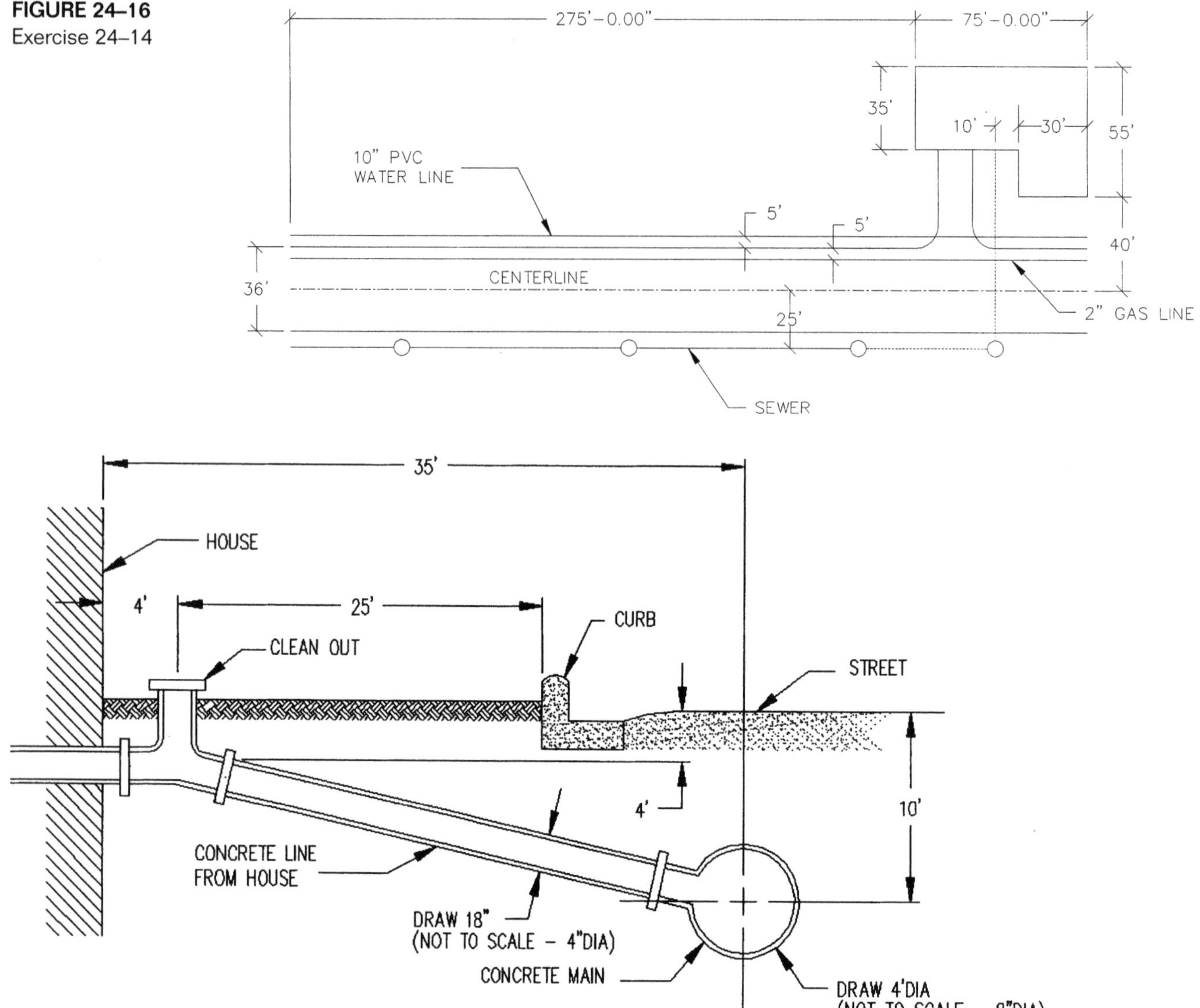

FIGURE 24–17
Exercise 24–15

REVIEW QUESTIONS

Circle the best answer.

1. The selection of decimal units allows drawings to be made
   a. In feet
   b. In inches only
   c. In millimeters only
   d. In any metric measurement
   e. In any unit of measure
2. The selection of surveyors units permits lines to be drawn as bearings.
   a. True
   b. False
3. Which of the following is a correct response to the Line command prompt "To point:" when surveyor's units have been selected?
   a. @100<N30D ↵
   b. @100<N30D0'0" ↵
   c. @100<N30%%D0'0"E ↵
   d. @100<N30D0'E ↵
   e. @100<ND30"0'0E
4. Which of the following surveys does not require elevation measurements?
   a. Topographic
   b. Photo
   c. Plat
   d. Route
   e. Construction

5. Which of the following variables was set to 50 to allow dimensions to be added to the open traverse in Figure 24–2?
   a. Ltscale
   b. Plot Ratio
   c. Dimscale
   d. Dim
   e. Dimvar
6. Which of the following is called a plat?
   a. Land survey
   b. Topographic survey
   c. Geodetic survey
   d. Photo survey
   e. Route survey
7. Which of the following commands is used to discover the length and direction of a bearing?
   a. Dist
   b. Inquiry
   c. List
   d. Type
   e. Status
8. A crossing window may be created (when Erase is selected from the pull-down menu) by
   a. Clicking on a spot that contains no entities and dragging downward to the left
   b. Clicking on a spot that contains no entities and dragging upward to the right
   c. Clicking on a spot that contains no entities and dragging upward to the left
   d. Clicking on a spot that contains no entities and dragging downward to the right
   e. None of the above
9. There is no response to a Single Line Text prompt that will allow text to be placed at the same angle as the bearing.
   a. True
   b. False
10. The linetype of Figure 24–5 that was used to draw the building line is
    a. DASHED
    b. HIDDEN
    c. CONTINUOUS
    d. DASHEDX2
    e. PHANTOM

Complete.

11. List the six survey types:

    ______________________ ______________________

    ______________________ ______________________

    ______________________ ______________________

12. List the setting that allows linetypes such as DASHED to be displayed correctly on a large drawing:

    ____

13. List the command and its option that allowed the contours of Figure 24–6 to be changed from straight polylines to smooth curves:

    ____

14. Why does a profile often have different vertical and horizontal scales?

    ____

15. Why is a HATCH pattern scale of 20 necessary for the profile in Figure 24–7?

    ____

16. A contour is used to show ______________________
17. The curve data described in Figure 24–4 list the bearing under which heading?

    ____

18. Define the term *angle of repose* as it is used in Figure 24–10.

    ____

    ____

19. Describe what is meant by CUT and FILL.

    ____

    ____

20. List the xp zoom scale factor suggested for Figure 24–10.

25 Electronic Applications

OBJECTIVES

After completing this chapter, you will be able to

- □ Make a symbol library for drawing schematic symbols.
- □ Draw schematic diagrams using symbols from the symbol library.
- □ Make a component library for drawing printed circuit boards.
- □ Draw printed circuit board:

  Assembly drawings
  Artwork
  Drill plans

INTRODUCTION

Many types of drawings are used in electronics industries. Some of the most common ones are electronic schematic diagrams and the drawings used to make printed circuit boards. This chapter discusses only schematics and printed circuit board drawings. Many of the other types are mechanical and require no specific knowledge of electronics. Although schematic diagrams may be drawn from an engineer's sketch without knowledge of electronics, schematic diagrams and the drawings for printed circuit boards are unique and must follow certain rules. These rules are presented later in this chapter.

DRAWING TYPES

The four types of drawings to be used in this chapter are

- □ Schematic diagrams
- □ Printed circuit board assembly drawings
- □ Printed circuit board drill plans
- □ Printed circuit board artwork

Figure 25–1 shows these four types and describes how they are used.

- □ The schematic (Figure 25–1A) is the first drawing that is created. This is done when the engineer designs the circuit. It often is drawn as a sketch by the engineer and formalized by the PC designer.
- □ A design layout similar to the component assembly (Figure 25–1B) is then used to determine where components and circuitry will be placed.
- □ The artwork (Figure 25–1C) is created using the design layout.
- □ Copies of parts of the artwork are used to make the drill plan (Figure 25–1D) and the component assembly (Figure 25–1E).

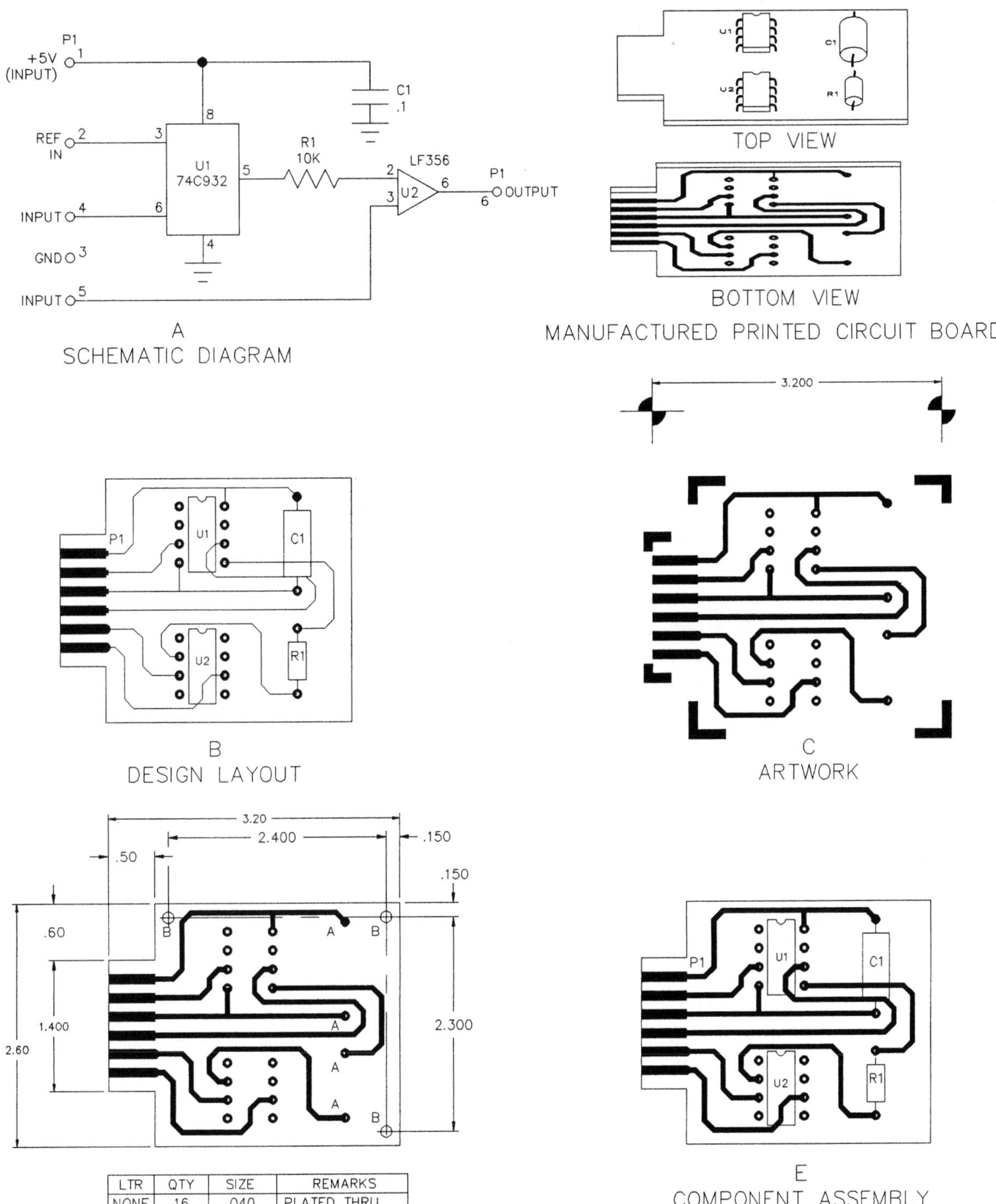

LTR	QTY	SIZE	REMARKS
NONE	16	.040	PLATED THRU
A	4	.063	PLATED THRU
B	3	.125	

FIGURE 25–1
Drawings for Printed Circuit Boards

Let's take this simple circuit from schematic diagram to component assembly using AutoCAD. We begin with a parts library for schematic diagrams.

PARTS LIBRARY

Every printed circuit designer has a library of parts, because he or she must use these parts over and over again. This library is divided into two parts: one part for schematic symbols, the other part for the actual size and shape of components. Let's put both these parts on the same disk. (If you have the time, you might even want to make a pop-down menu for them, as described in the chapter on menu customizing, and copy them into the ACAD directory.) Draw the symbols and save them on disks, one for schematic symbols and one for components.

Be sure to label your disks SYMBOLS and PARTS and make a backup copy of both. Now, let's make schematic symbols and insert them into a schematic diagram.

Exercise 25–1: Drawing Symbols and a Schematic Diagram

Step 1. Load AutoCAD. *Click:* **Create Drawings-Wizards-Quick Setup.**

Step 2. Make the following settings:

Note: If you construct symbol blocks on the 0 layer, they will take on the color of the layer on which they are inserted. Many users prefer to do this instead of constructing symbols on other layers.

Units: Decimal, full size—3 digits to the right of the decimal point

Area: Width: 7
Length: 4

GRID: .2

SNAP: .05

TEXT STYLE AND FONT: SIMPLEX

LAYERS:	NAME	Color	Linetype	Lineweight
	THICK	Yellow	Continuous	Default
	THIN	Cyan	Continuous	Default

Step 3. Draw symbol.

Turn SNAP ON. With THICK as the current layer, draw the outline for the symbol for the 74C932 component shown in Figure 25–2. Put all text on the TEXT layer and all leads on the THIN layer, and make all text .1 high. Do *not* dimension the drawing.

Warning: Be sure SNAP (F9) is ON when you draw and insert symbols so that all symbols can be placed on GRID or SNAP locations.

Step 4. Assign attributes.

After you have drawn the symbol, assign attributes as shown in Figure 25–3. Use TEXT as the current layer.

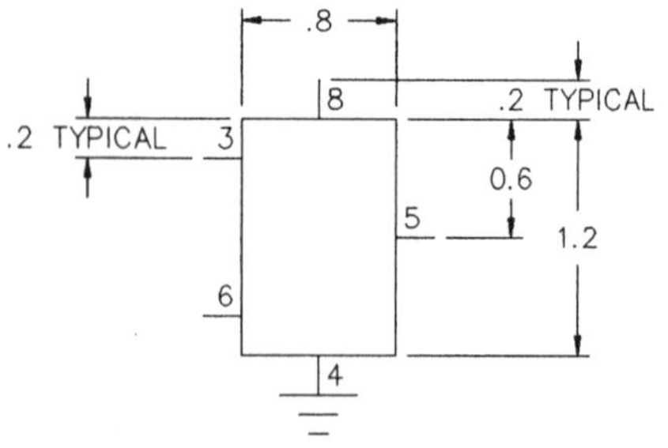

FIGURE 25–2
74C932 Component

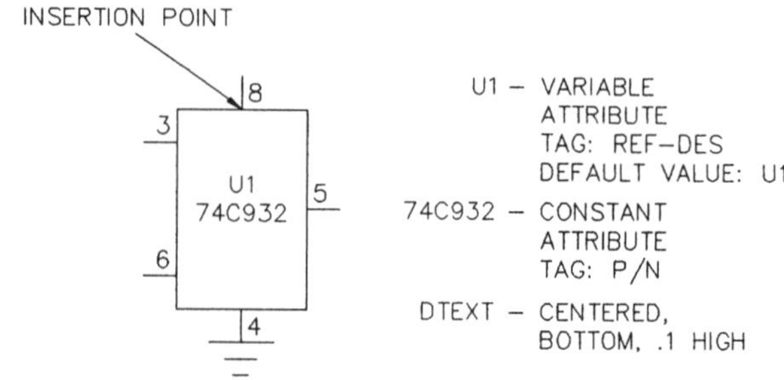

FIGURE 25–3
Wblock for 74C932

- □ Make U1 a variable attribute because it will change (U2, U3, U4, etc.) when you use this symbol several times on the same drawing. The attribute TAG for U1 should be REF-DES for reference designation, the name given to labels that identify the specific part. The default value should be U1.
- □ Make 74C932 a constant attribute. This is the part number that is looked for when a listing of parts is needed. Make this tag P/N. The attribute value will be 74C932.

Step 5. Wblock the symbol.

After attributes are assigned, Wblock the drawing using the name A:\74C932 to place it on the floppy disk, labeled SYMBOL, in drive A.

Step 6. Make Wblocks for the remaining symbols, which are shown in Figures 25–4 through 25–9. Notice that C1 and R1 require both a vertical and a horizontal position because both positions are used a great deal.

Draw the symbol on the THICK layer and all text on the TEXT layer.

Step 7. Draw a schematic diagram.

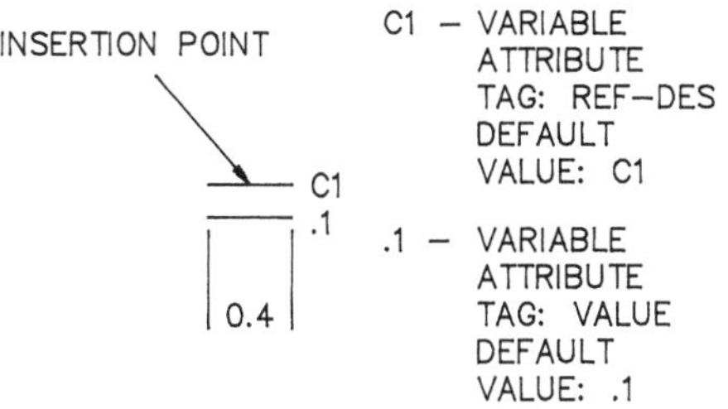

FIGURE 25–4
Vertical Capacitor

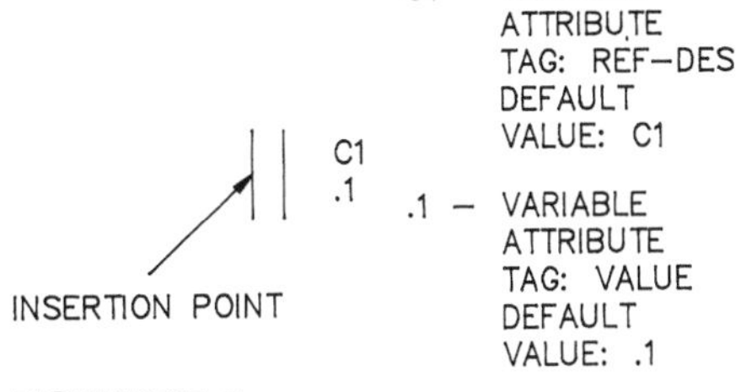

FIGURE 25–5
Horizontal Capacitor

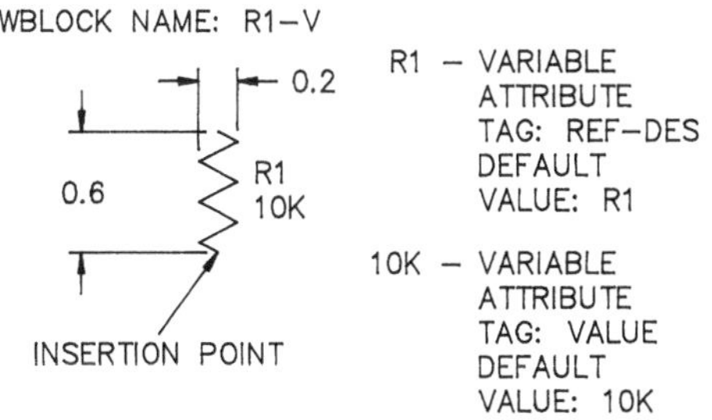

FIGURE 25–6
Vertical Resistor

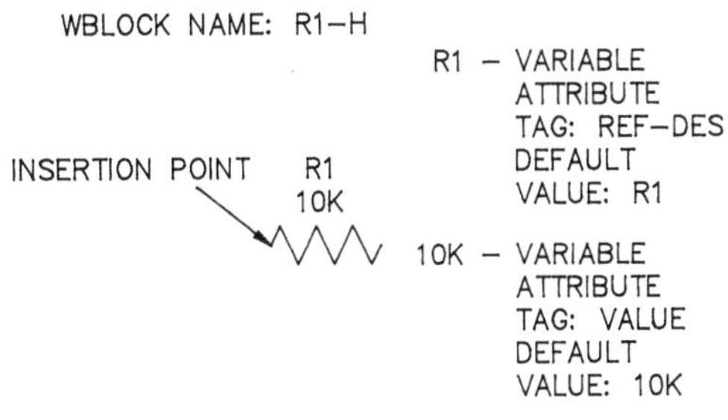

FIGURE 25–7
Horizontal Resistor

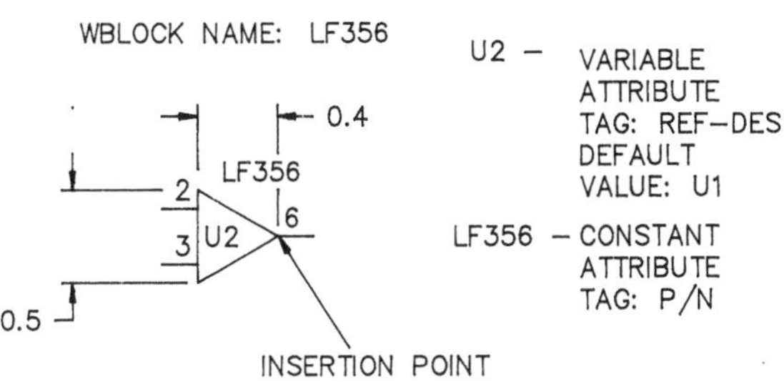

FIGURE 25–8
LF356

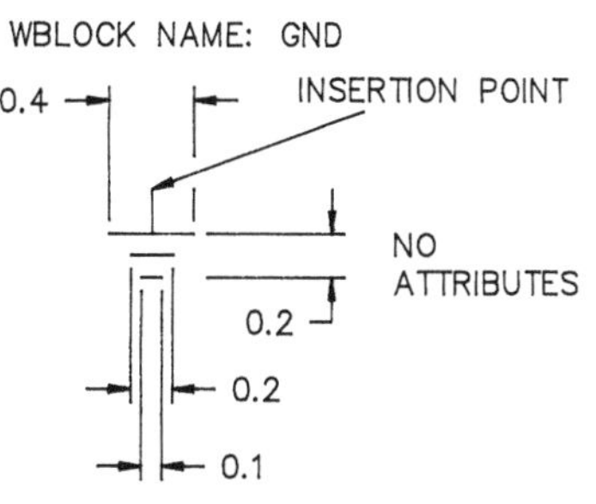

FIGURE 25–9
Ground

FIGURE 25–10
The Schematic Diagram

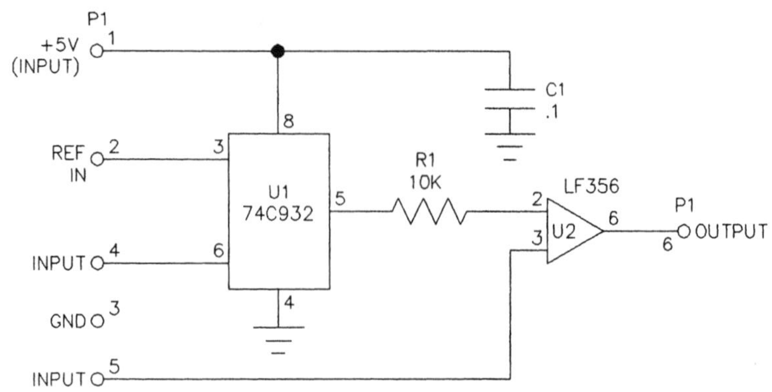

After you have Wblocked all schematic symbols, perform the following procedures, as shown in Figure 25–10.

- □ Insert the appropriate symbols into drawing SCH-1, which is the current drawing. Be sure SNAP (F9) is ON when you insert symbols and draw lines. Connect symbols using lines drawn on the THIN layer.
- □ Draw input and output circles on the THIN layer.
- □ Draw input text using Dtext, right-justified on the TEXT layer.
- □ Draw output text using Dtext, left-justified on the TEXT layer.

Place your name in the lower right corner: Dtext, .1 high, right-justified, bottom, .25 inside, and .25 up from the corner. Save the drawing in two places with the name EX25-1(your initials) and Exit.

The five major rules for good schematic layout are

- □ Place inputs on the left and outputs on the right.
- □ Remove doglegs where possible.
- □ Avoid crossovers.
- □ Don't crowd components and lettering.
- □ Leave the circuit connected exactly as in the sketch.

Figures 25–11 through 25–14 illustrate these rules.

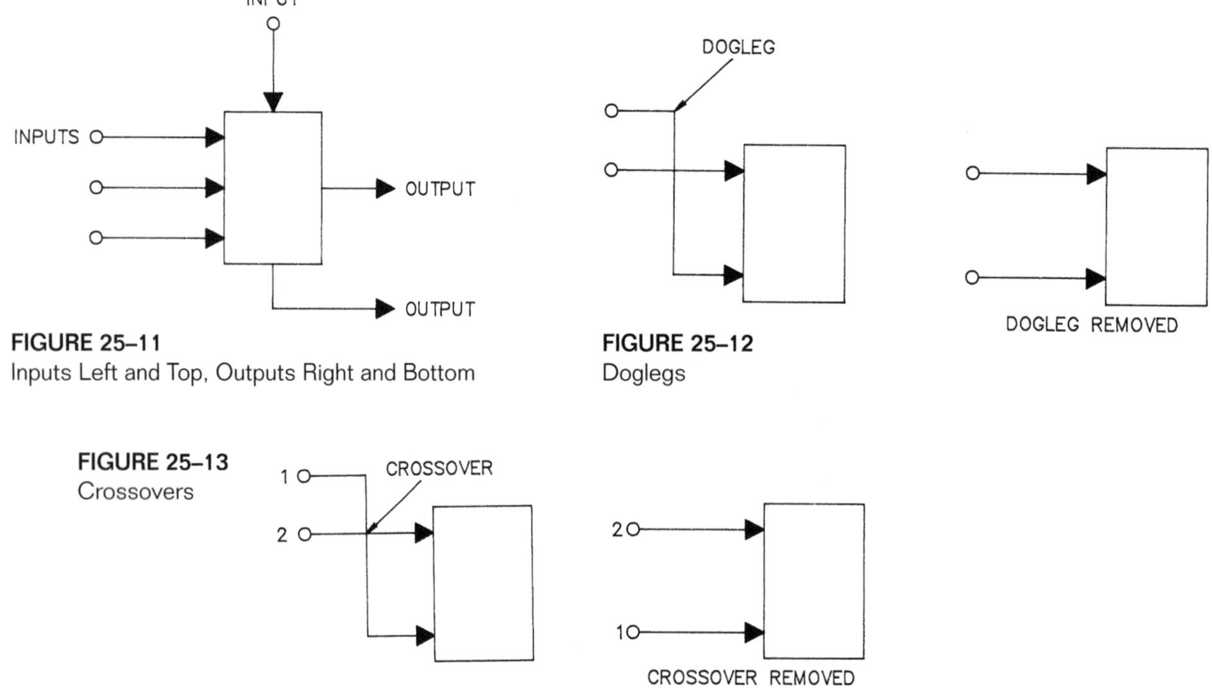

FIGURE 25–11
Inputs Left and Top, Outputs Right and Bottom

FIGURE 25–12
Doglegs

FIGURE 25–13
Crossovers

FIGURE 25–14
Keep Drawings Uncrowded

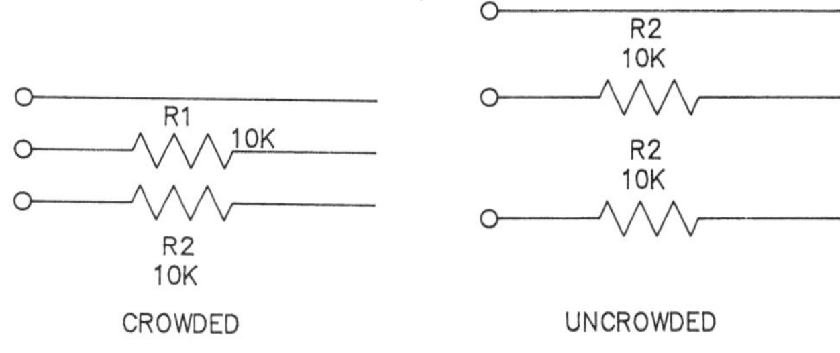

PCB PARTS LIBRARY

Now that the schematic diagram is complete, let's make the printed circuit board drawings. Once again, begin with a parts library, then Insert parts from the library onto the board outline.

Exercise 25–2: Drawing Parts and a Design Layout

Step 1. Load AutoCAD, open drawing EX25-1(your initials) and save it as EX25-2(your initials).

(Most of the same settings from EX25–1 can be used for this drawing.)

Prompt	Response
Command:	*Click:* **Erase** (all the drawing)

Step 2. Add the following layers and reset limits to 11,8.5.

LAYERS:	NAME	Color	Linetype	Lineweight
	TRACE	Cyan	Continuous	Default
	PAD	Cyan	Continuous	Default

Warning: Be sure SNAP (F9) is ON when you draw and insert symbols so that all symbols can be placed on GRID or SNAP locations.

Draw the physical size and shape and assign attributes to the components (parts) needed for this printed circuit and Wblock them to the disk labeled PARTS. Notice that the pin numbers (1 to 8) have been indicated to show you how most ICs are numbered. These should not appear on your drawing. A dot in the upper left corner shows where pin 1 is located. Do *not* put any dimensions on these drawings.

Step 3. With the THICK layer current, draw the component outline for 74C932 (Figure 25–15).

Tip: Be sure to draw all PADS on the PAD layer.

Step 4. Use Donut to draw the pads (connection points) for the 74C932 PCB component with the PAD layer current. Use Donut with .05 ID and .10 OD.

Tip: Be sure SNAP is ON when you draw all parts of the board outline.

Step 5. With the TEXT layer current, assign one attribute to this drawing using Attdef.

FIGURE 25–15
Wblock P74C932

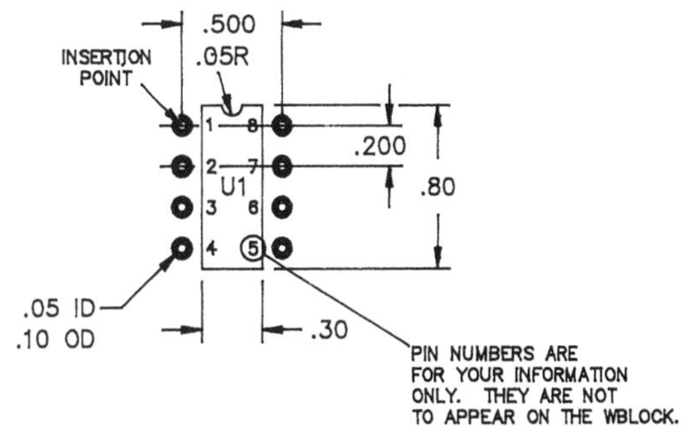

FIGURE 25–16
Wblock PLF356

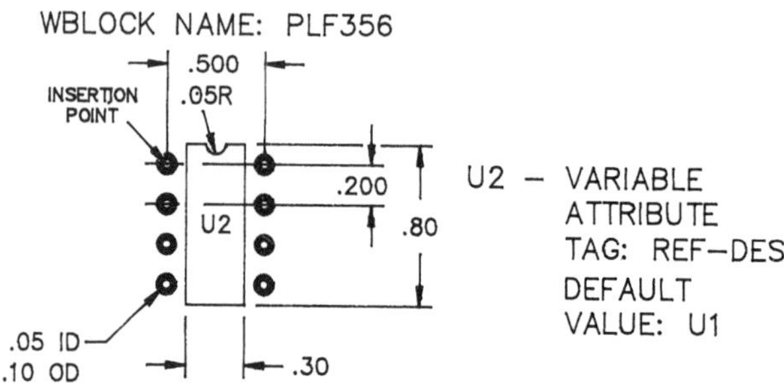

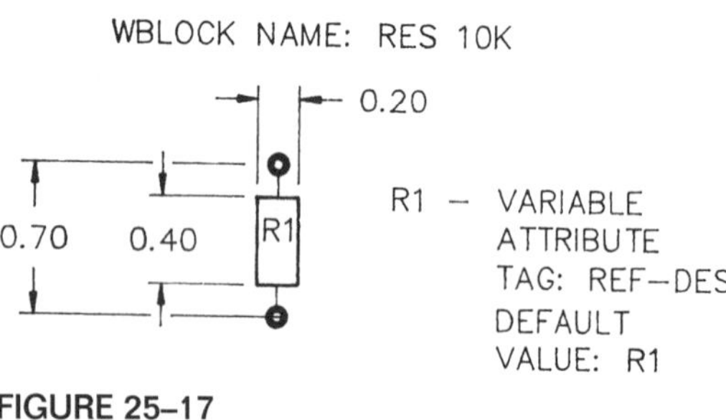

FIGURE 25–17
Wblock RES 10K

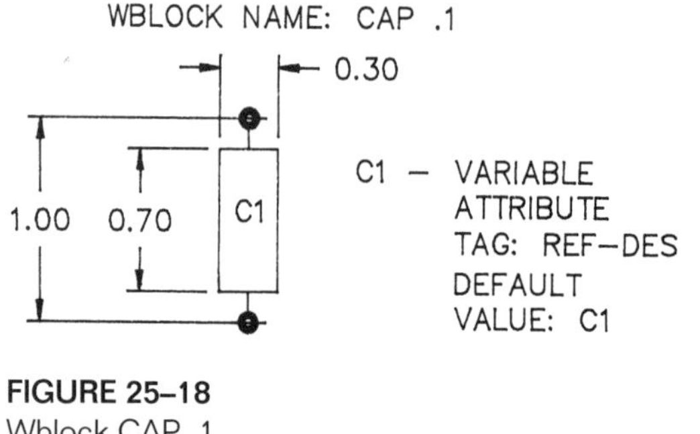

FIGURE 25–18
Wblock CAP .1

Attribute tag: REF-DES
Default attribute value: U1
Center the attribute using Dtext-Middle-Centered.

Step 6. Wblock this component to the disk labeled PARTS, using the name P74C932 (P distinguishes the part from the schematic symbol of the same name). Use the insertion point shown in Figure 25–15.

Use a similar procedure to this one to create the components shown as Figures 25–16 through 25–18. Use the same-size donut for all pads. Make the center of the upper donut the insertion point for R1 and C1 (Figures 25-17 and 25-18). Now draw the board outline, place the components on it, and connect them as described in the schematic diagram to create a design layout.

MAKING A DESIGN LAYOUT

Use the following steps to make a design layout (Figure 25–19).

Step 7. With layer THICK current, draw the board outline using the dimensions shown in Figure 25–20.

FIGURE 25–19
Design Layout

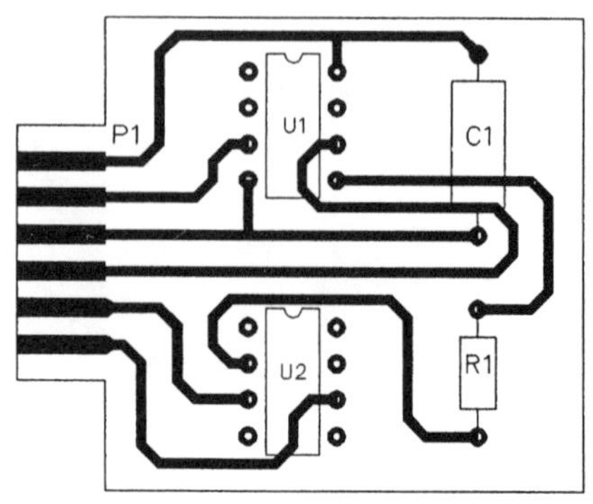

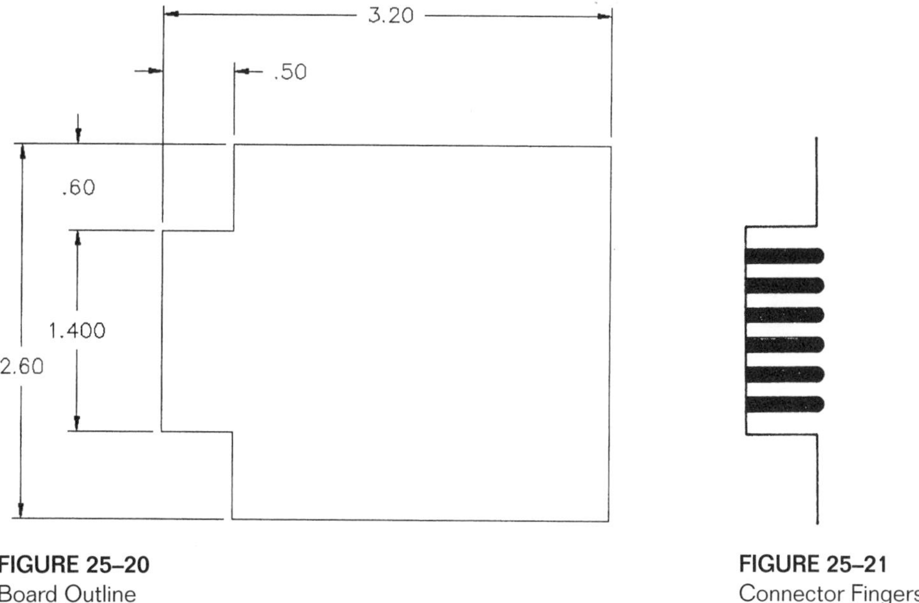

FIGURE 25–20
Board Outline

FIGURE 25–21
Connector Fingers

Step 8. **With TRACE as the current layer, draw one finger on the connector. Use Donut with an inside diameter of 0 and an outside diameter of .1. Draw a construction line through the center of the Donut and then Trim the bottom half. Use Polyline with a beginning and ending width of .1 to draw the first finger (Figure 25–21).**

Warning: Be sure SNAP (F9) is ON when you draw and insert symbols so that all symbols can be placed on GRID or SNAP locations.

Step 9. **Use Array to draw the remaining five fingers. The distance between rows is .200.**

Step 10. **Insert parts from your PARTS disk in the approximate locations shown in Figure 25–22.**

Step 11. **Use Polyline with a width of .05 to draw all connections (called TRACEs) (Figure 25–23). Make sure that no connections cross and that there is a minimum of .05 space between all copper areas (PAD to TRACE, etc.).**

Step 12. **Use a .100, 45° chamfer at all corners to reduce the likelihood that cracks will develop at 90° corners when the board is etched.**

Step 13. **With TEXT as the current layer, add the label P1.**

Step 14. **Print the drawing full scale on an 11″ × 8.5″ sheet.**

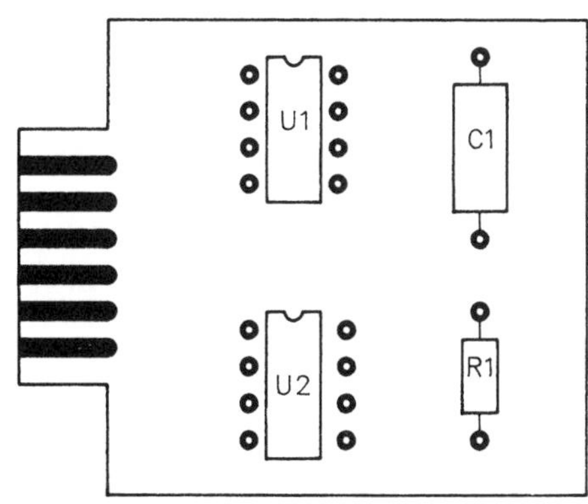

FIGURE 25–22
Insert Parts

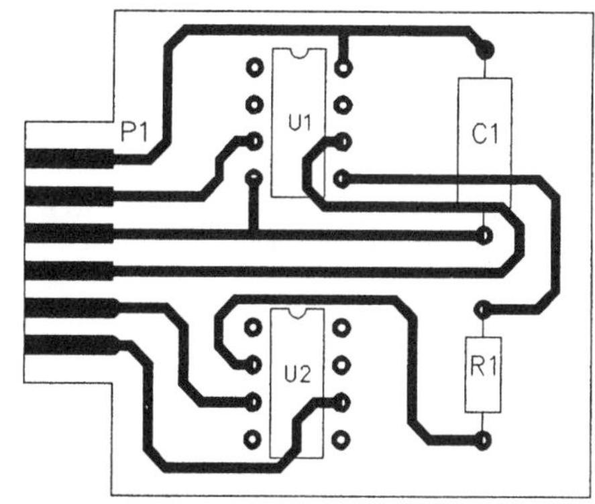

FIGURE 25–23
Completed Design Layout

Step 15. **Save the drawing in two places with the name EX25-2(your initials) and exit AutoCAD.**

The design layout, Figure 25–23, is now complete. Because this is a simple one-sided board, this design layout may be used as the component assembly drawing.

Exercise 25–3: Creating the Artwork

Next, we make a drawing that can be used to etch the copper circuit onto the PC board. This drawing is called an *artwork.*

To create the artwork in Figure 25–24:

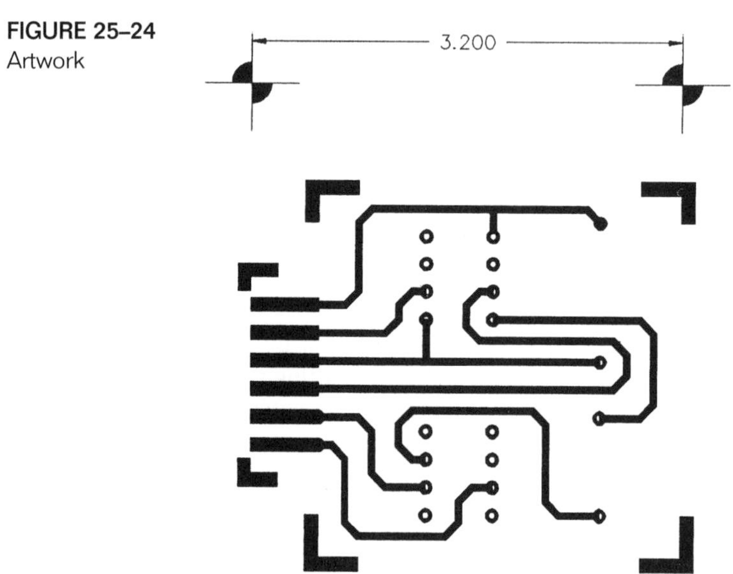

FIGURE 25–24
Artwork

Step 1. **Load AutoCAD, open drawing EX25–2 (your initials), and save it as EX25-3(your initials).**

Step 2. **Explode all blocks.**

Step 3. **Draw marks that locate the corners of the board. Use Polyline width .1 and make sure that the inside of the Polyline marks the corner of the board.**

Step 4. **Draw targets and place them so they are in line with the vertical edges of the board, approximately 1″ above the board. Use a Donut with an ID of 0 and an OD of .3. The lines through the center of the Donut should be .7 long. Use Trim to remove two quarters of the Donut.**

Step 5. **Dimension the distance between targets so the photo shop will know what size to make the film that will be used to etch the circuit.**

Step 6. **Erase all parts of the old PCB-1 drawing that are not needed.**

Step 7. **Print the drawing full scale on an 11″ × 8.5″ sheet.**

Hint: Turn off layers that contain the artwork and any other needed information. Erase all other layers.

Step 8. **Save the drawing in two places with the name EX25-3(your initials) and exit AutoCAD.**

Exercise 25–4: Making a Drill Plan

Now a drawing must be made that tells the fabricator what size to trim the board, what size holes must be drilled, and where the holes are to be located. This is called a *drill plan.*

To create the drill plan (Figure 25–25):

FIGURE 25–25
Drill Plan

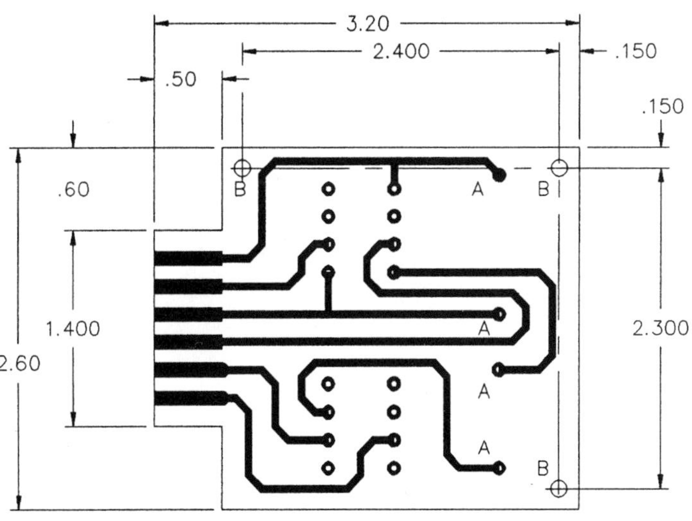

LTR	QTY	SIZE	REMARKS
NONE	16	.040	PLATED THRU
A	4	.063	PLATED THRU
B	3	.125	

Step 1. **Load AutoCAD, open drawing EX25-2(your initials), and save it as EX25-4(your initials).**

Step 2. **Explode all blocks.**

Step 3. **Erase unneeded parts of the old PCB-1.**

Step 4. **Draw the three .125″-diameter tooling holes in the locations shown. These holes are used to hold the board while parts are being soldered in place and other operations are performed.**

Step 5. **Add labels to A and B holes. Notice that the holes for the integrated circuits (U1 and U2) are a different size than the holes for C1 and R1.**

Step 6. **Add dimensions with DIMTXT set at .1, simplex font.**

Tip: Turn off the layers containing the parts of the drawing that you need while erasing.

Step 7. **Add the hole schedule using Line and Dtext, .1, simplex font.**

Step 8. **Print the drawing on an 11″ × 8.5″ sheet.**

Step 9. **Save the drawing in two places with the name EX25-4(your initials) and exit AutoCAD.**

EXERCISES

EXERCISE 25–1. Draw Figure 25–10 as described in this chapter.

EXERCISE 25–2. Draw Figure 25–23 as described in this chapter.

EXERCISE 25–3. Draw Figure 25–24 as described in this chapter.

EXERCISE 25–4. Draw Figure 25–25 as described in this chapter.

EXERCISE 25–5. Draw the schematic diagram in Figure 25–26. Create any new Wblocks needed and place them on your SYMBOLS disk. Use the same layers, SNAP, and GRID as used for Exercise 25–1. Set LIMITS to 11,8.5 and center the drawing within that area. Make sure that SNAP is ON when you draw all parts of the Wblocks and the schematic diagram itself.

EXERCISE 25–6. Prepare an artwork, drill plan, and component assembly drawing for the schematic in Figure 25–26. Use the specifications in Figure 25–27 for the board size and the parts. Make all pads .05 inside diameter and .15 outside diameter. Place E1, E2, and E3 on the same side of the board .250 from the edges and .500 from center to center. Use E3 as the ground pin.

FIGURE 25–26
Exercise 25–5

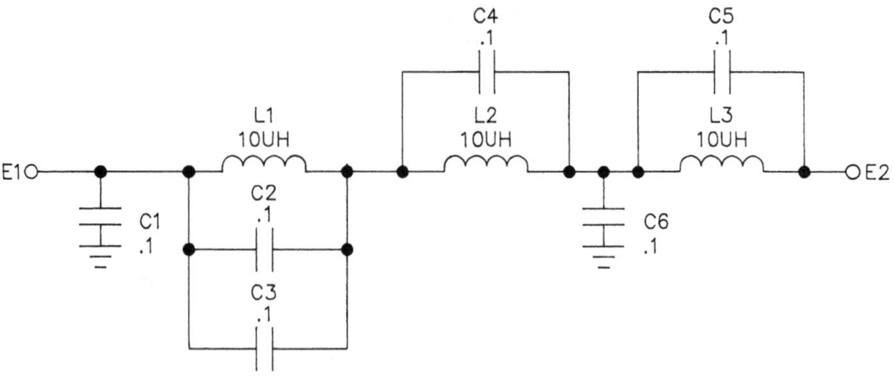

FIGURE 25–27
Specifications for Exercise 25–6

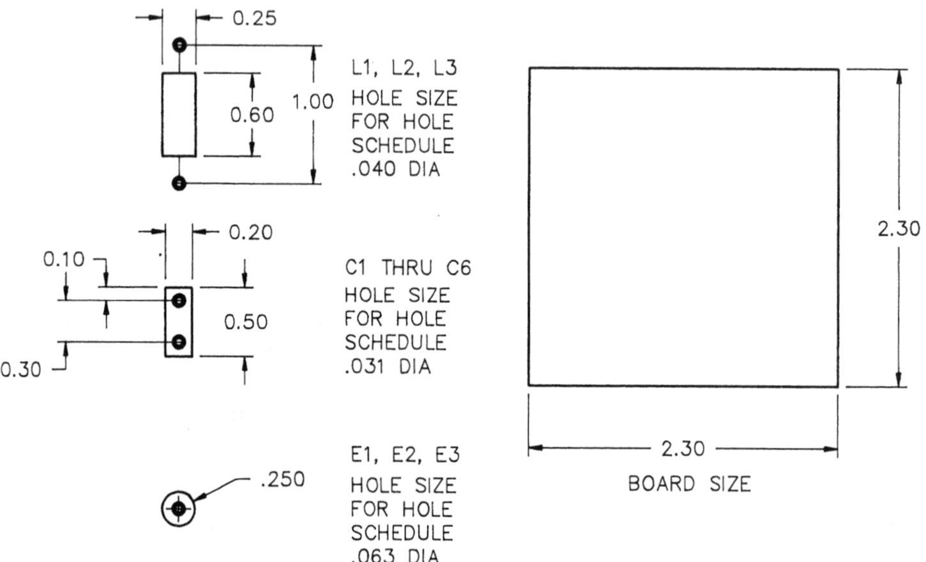

EXERCISE 25–7. Draw the symbols shown as Figure 25–28. Wblock them and place them on your SYMBOLS disk. Assign attributes as indicated. Use settings and layers from SCH-1, Exercise 25-1.

EXERCISE 25–8. Draw the schematic diagram shown as Figure 25–29. Use symbols from Exercise 25-7. Set Limits to 11,8.5 and center the drawing in that area. Be sure SNAP is ON when you draw. The fillets where lines connect should be .25R.

EXERCISE 25–9. Draw the schematic diagram shown as Figure 25–30. Create any new Wblocks needed and place them on your SYMBOLS disk. Use the same layers, SNAP, and GRID as used for Exercise 25–1. Set Limits to 11,8.5 and center the drawing within that area. Make sure that SNAP is ON when you draw all parts of the Wblocks and the schematic diagram itself.

EXERCISE 25–10. Draw the schematic diagram shown as Figure 25–31. Create any new Wblocks needed and place them on your SYMBOLS disk. Use the same layers, SNAP, and GRID as used for Exercise 25–1. Set Limits to 11,8.5 and center the drawing within that area. Make sure that SNAP is ON when you draw all parts of the Wblocks and the schematic diagram itself.

EXERCISE 25–11. Draw the artworks in Figures 25–32 and 25–33 for a two-sided printed circuit board (circuit on both sides of the board, components on only one side). Notice that all the pads for both sides of the board are in the same location (the back side is a mirror image). Draw all pads for the circuit side, Mirror them for the component side, and then draw all connections. Make these separate drawings. Realize that leads are going under some components after they are assembled onto the board. No leads or pads may be closer than .05 to any other copper area.

FIGURE 25–28
Exercise 25–7

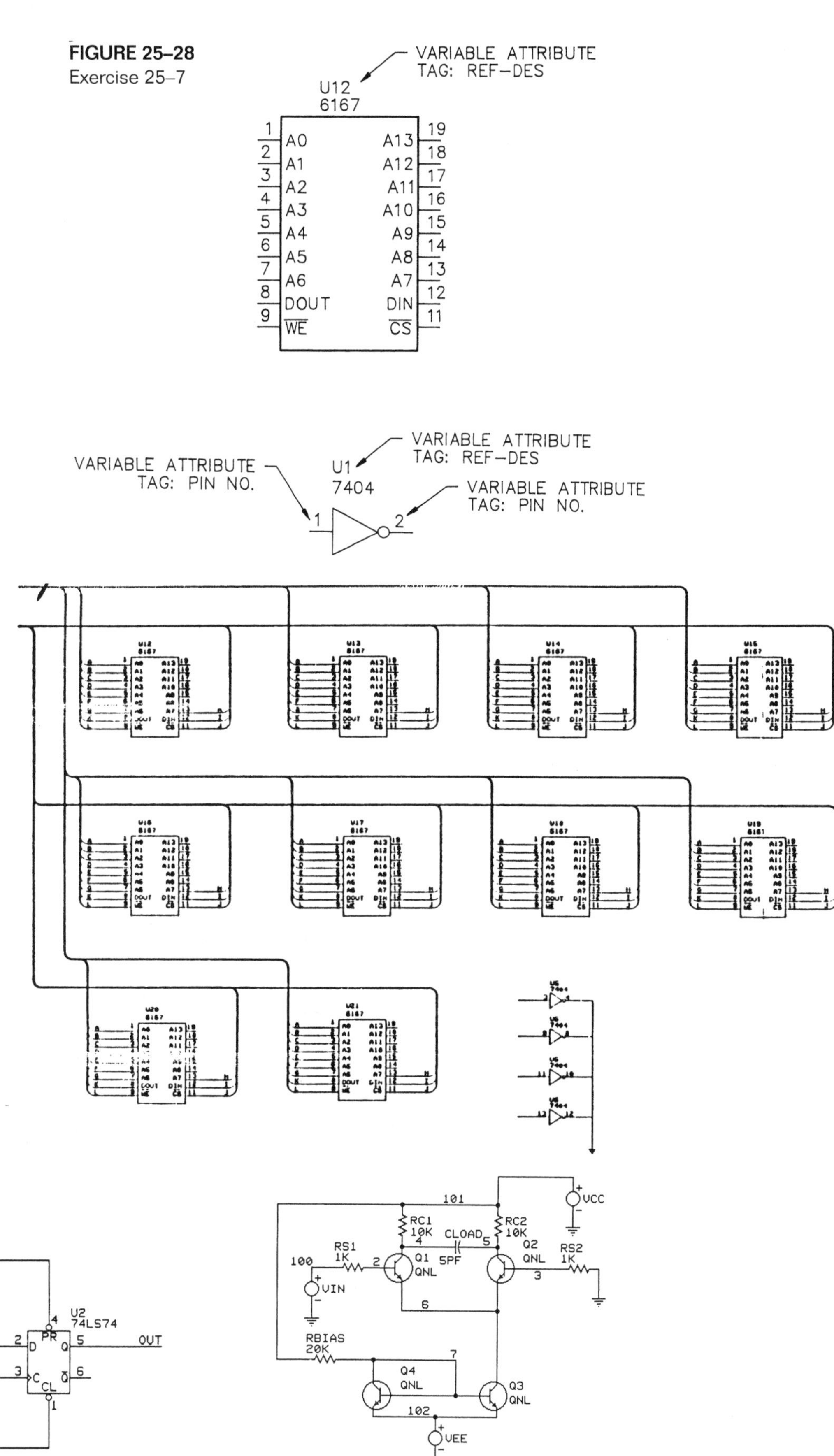

FIGURE 25–29
Exercise 25–8

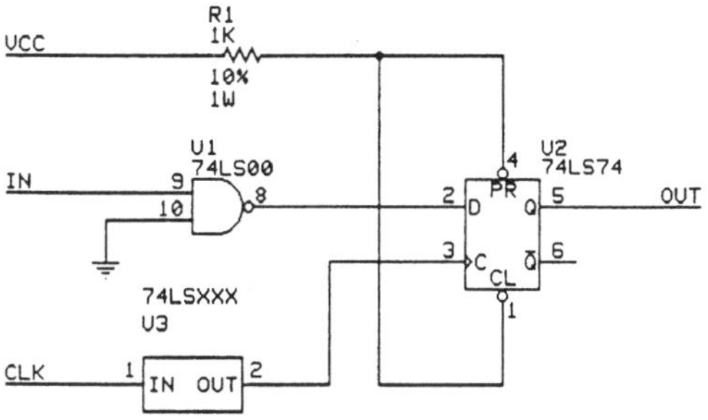

FIGURE 25–30
Exercise 25–9

FIGURE 25–31
Exercise 25–10

FIGURE 25–32
Component Side Artwork
Exercise 25–11

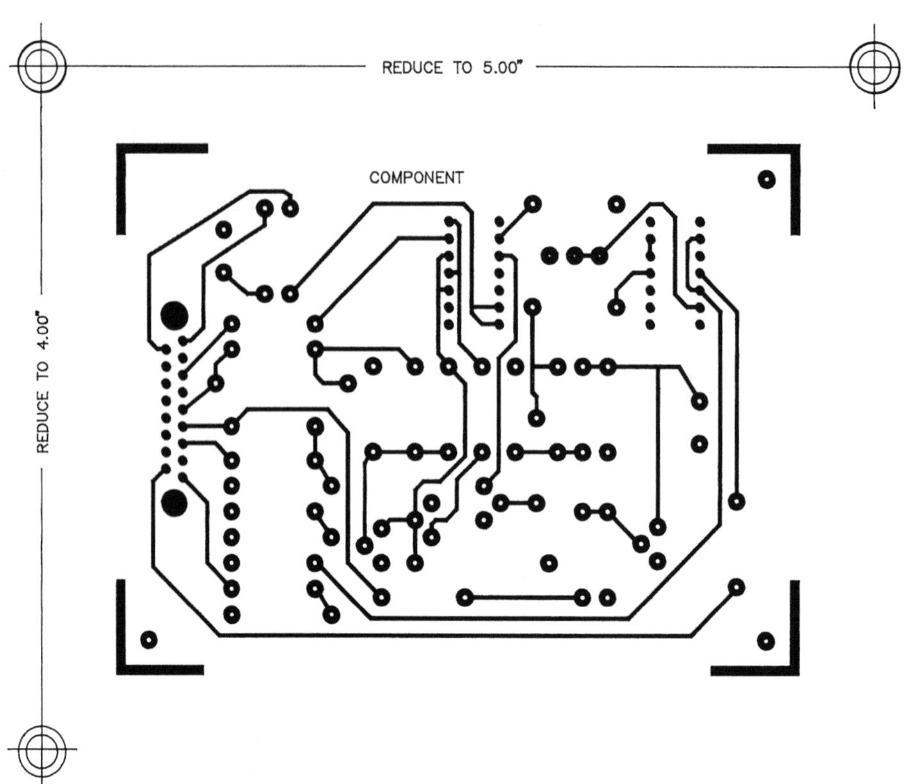

FIGURE 25–33
Circuit Side Artwork
Exercise 25–11

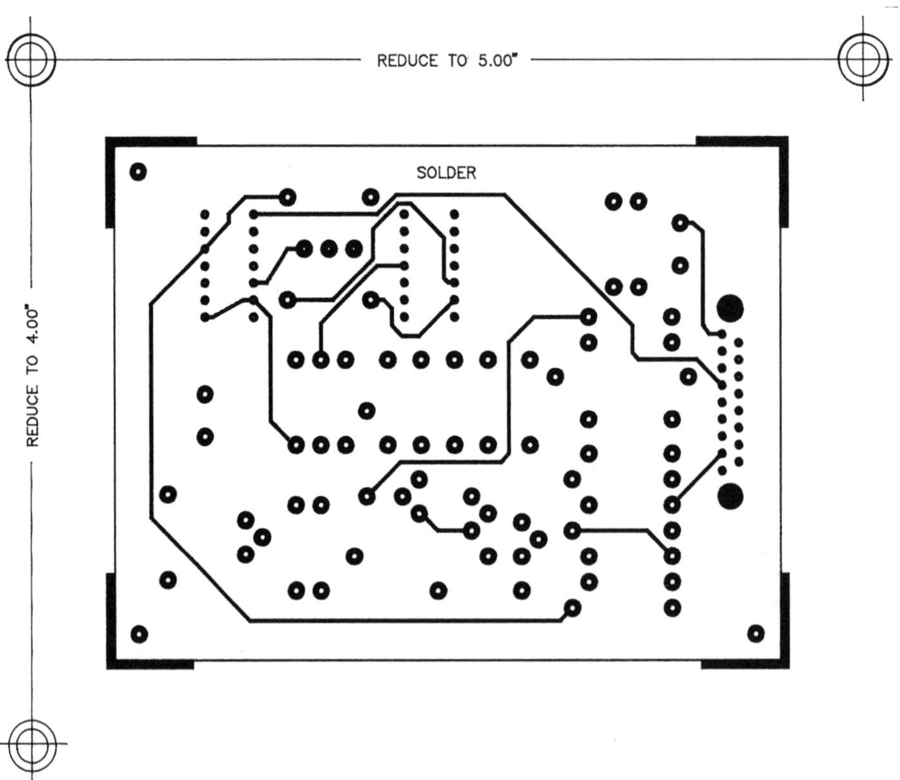

Use the settings from Exercise 25–2. Make four layers, one for PADS, one for circuit side traces, one for component side traces, and one for TEXT. Make sure SNAP is ON when you draw.

EXERCISE 25–12. Draw the components shown in Figure 25–34, Wblock them, and place them on your PARTS disk. Select an appropriate insertion point for each component. Use settings and layers from PCB-1, Exercise 25–1.

EXERCISE 25–13. Draw the component assembly drawing shown in Figure 25–35. Draw the board outline using the dimensions shown. Use the components from Exercise

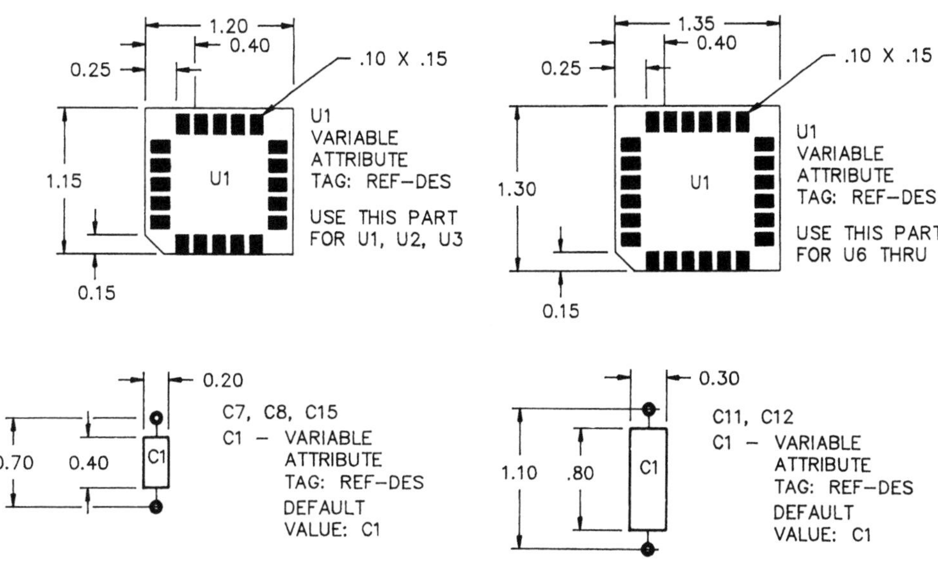

FIGURE 25–34
Exercise 25–12

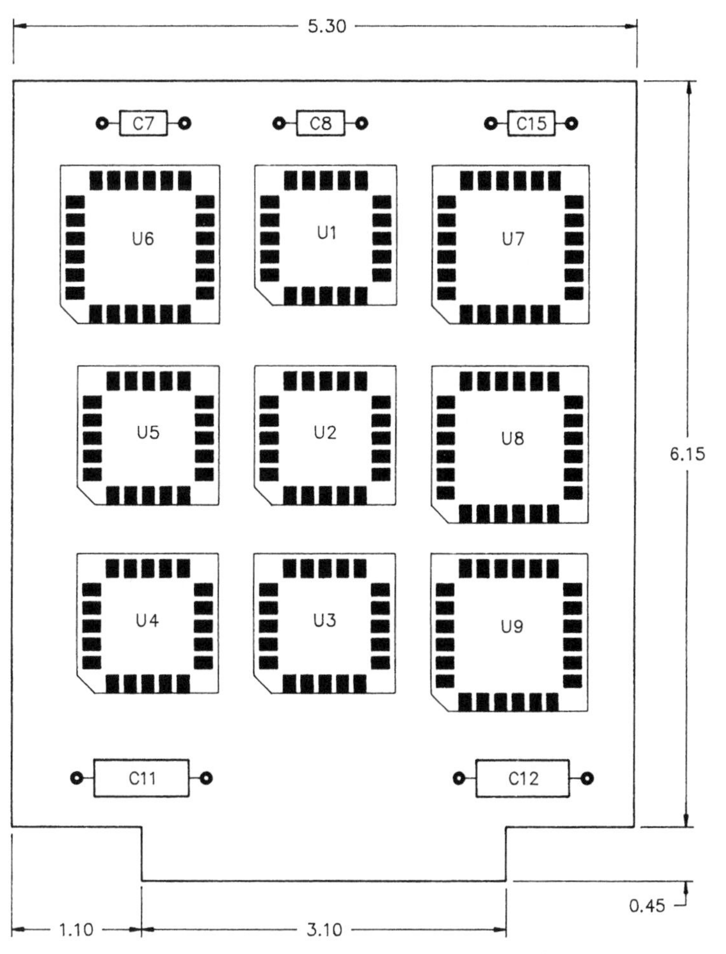

FIGURE 25–35
Exercise 25–13

25–12 and place them in the approximate positions shown. The integrated circuits on this board are surface-mounted components. Surface mounting is a process by which a component is soldered to the surface of a PCB instead of being inserted into holes. Therefore, no holes are required to mount these components onto the board.

REVIEW QUESTIONS

Circle the best answer.

1. An electronic schematic diagram
   a. Provides information about how parts may be purchased
   b. Provides information about how parts are assembled
   c. Provides information about how parts are formed
   d. Provides information about how parts are connected
   e. All the above
2. Printed circuit board designers have two parts libraries. They are:
   a. Schematic symbols and components' physical shapes
   b. Schematic parts and component symbols
   c. Components' shapes and reference designators
   d. Symbols and notes
   e. Component parts and default values
3. Which of the following is similar to a design layout?
   a. Schematic
   b. Artwork
   c. Drill plan
   d. Assembly drawing
   e. None of the above
4. Which of the following would most likely be defined as a variable attribute for a schematic symbol?
   a. U1
   b. 74C932
   c. PIN 3
   d. LF356
   e. GND
5. Which of the following settings *must* be ON when inserting symbols and drawing lines on a schematic diagram?
   a. ORTHO
   b. SNAP
   c. COORDINATES
   d. FILL
   e. LIMITS
6. Which of the following is a connection point on a printed circuit board?
   a. Value
   b. Reference designator
   c. PAD
   d. TARGET
   e. Board outline
7. Which of the following shows the fabricator what the finished size of the board should be?
   a. Design layout
   b. Artwork
   c. Schematic
   d. Drill plan
   e. Assembly drawing
8. Which of the following shows the assembler where to place the components on the board?
   a. Design layout
   b. Artwork
   c. Schematic
   d. Drill plan
   e. Assembly drawing

Complete.

9. Which of the PCB drawing types is used to etch the circuit on the board?

____

10. Which of the PCB drawing types is used to make a design layout?

____

11. How is PIN 1 identified on the Wblock PLF356?

____

12. Why are targets placed on the artwork?

____

26 Electromechanical Packaging Applications

OBJECTIVES

After completing this chapter, you will be able to

- □ Make a parts library for commonly used mechanical parts.
- □ Draw to scale a multilayer design layout for a complex electromechanical assembly.
- □ Draw and dimension a front panel from a design layout.
- □ Draw and dimension a rear panel from a design layout.
- □ Draw and dimension a chassis from the design layout.
- □ Draw and dimension a cover from the design layout.
- □ Draw an assembly drawing and prepare a parts list.
- □ Draw a schematic diagram to connect components.

THE MECHANICAL DESIGN PROCESS

Mechanical designs are used in all metal-fabricating industries. The people who create these designs, mechanical engineers and design drafters, are found in companies as diverse as aerospace, electronics, and air-conditioning manufacturers. Most of these designers follow similar procedures to create the drawings needed to fabricate the parts and assemble them. This procedure follows these steps:

- □ Collect the existing information regarding the size of the final assembly and the individual components to be used. Make outline drawings of the components.
- □ Make a full-scale design layout.
- □ Check the design layout for interference (parts overlapping other parts in the same plane).
- □ Draw and dimension individual parts of the design layout.
- □ Make an assembly drawing and a parts list.
- □ Draw a schematic diagram to connect parts.
- □ Check the final assembly and drawings of individual parts, and make necessary changes.

Although some companies are now using 3-D models for mechanical design, most companies continue to use 2-D drawings for these layouts and final drawings. Perhaps 3-D will become faster to use for design layouts in the near future, but 2-D drawings are presented in this chapter. (You may wish to use solid models for the design layout.)

Let's begin by taking a look at a design layout and the accompanying drawings.

Figure 26–1 shows the preliminary sketches and some of the catalog pages of the parts needed to prepare a design layout. Figure 26–2 shows the design layout. In practice, this drawing is drawn full scale in complete detail, with only the critical center lines shown.

FIGURE 26–1
Preliminary Design Information
Sheet 1 of 5

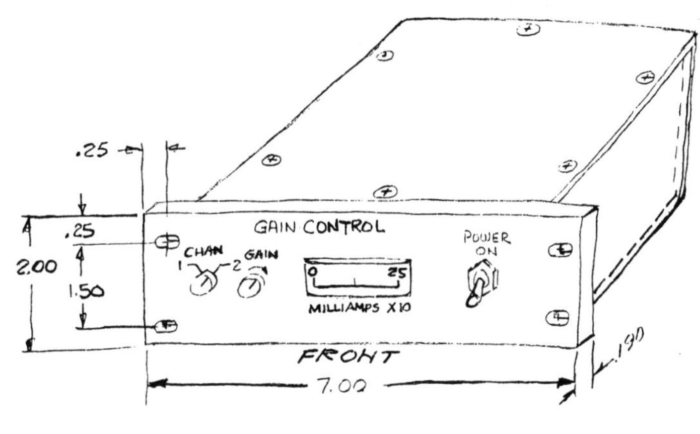

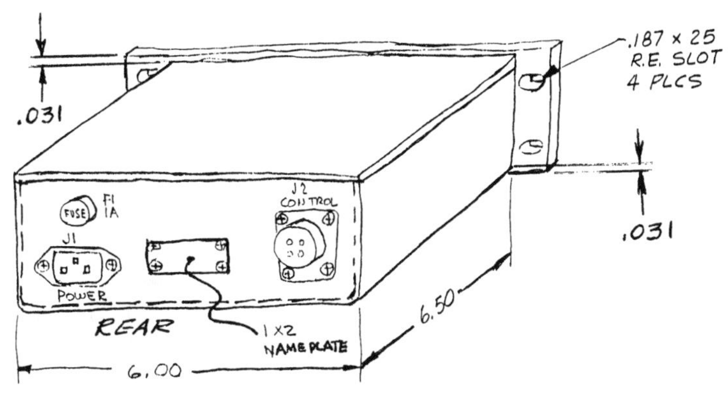

FIGURE 26–1
Sheet 2 of 5

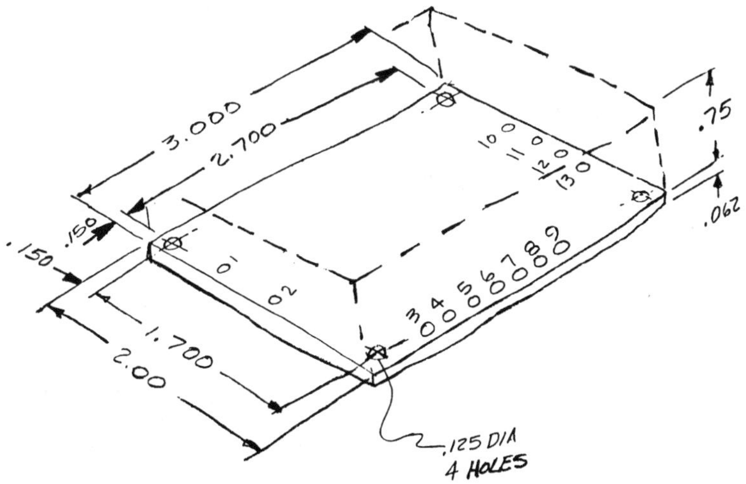

FIGURE 26–1
Sheet 3 of 5

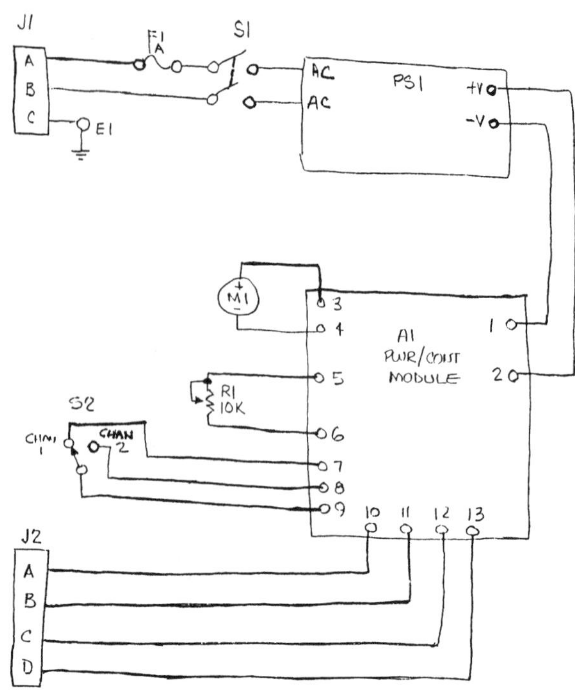

FIGURE 26–1
Sheet 4 of 5

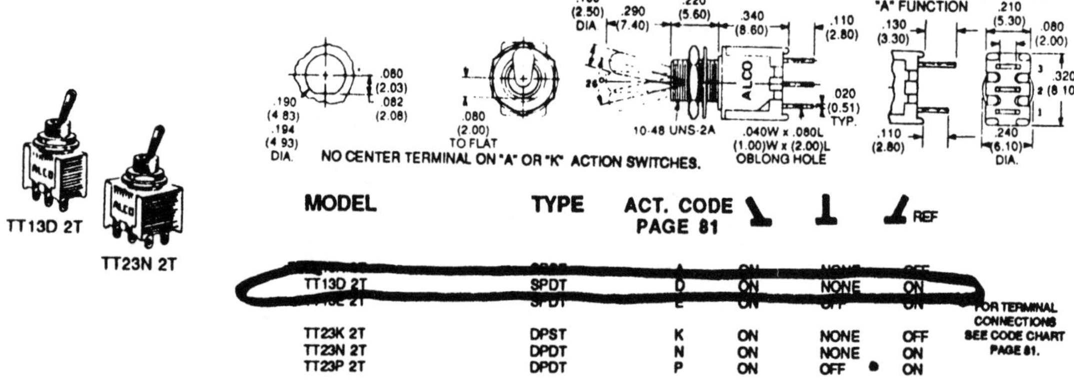

TT SERIES
TOGGLE SWITCHES

MODEL	TYPE	ACT. CODE PAGE 81			REF
TT13D 2T	SPDT	D	ON	NONE	ON
TT23K 2T	DPST	K	ON	NONE	OFF
TT23N 2T	DPDT	N	ON	NONE	ON
TT23P 2T	DPDT	P	ON	OFF	ON

FOR TERMINAL CONNECTIONS SEE CODE CHART PAGE 81.

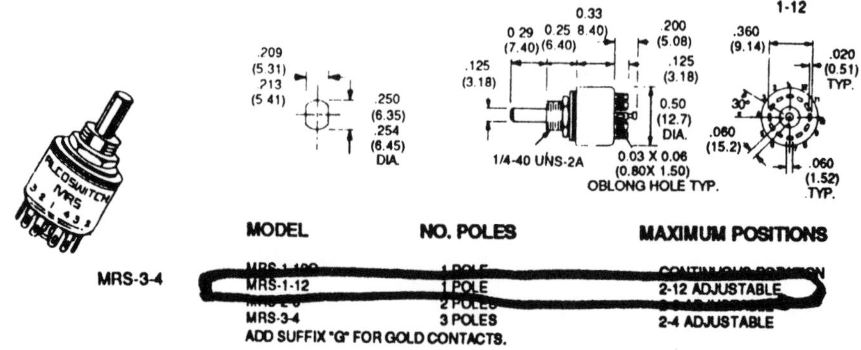

MRS SERIES
MINIATURE ROTARY

MODEL	NO. POLES	MAXIMUM POSITIONS
MRS-1-12	1 POLE	2-12 ADJUSTABLE
MRS-3-4	3 POLES	2-4 ADJUSTABLE

ADD SUFFIX "G" FOR GOLD CONTACTS.

Instrumentation Knobs
RB-67 Series

RB-67-0-M

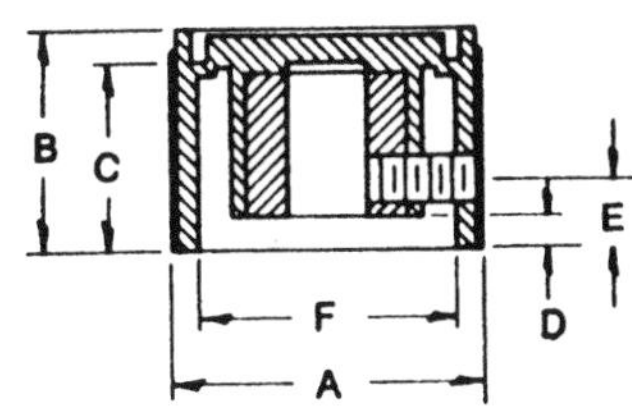

Part Number	A	B	C	D	E	F
RB-67-0-M	.51	.48	.41	.045	.15	.400
RB-67-1-M	.71	[illegible]	[illegible]	[illegible]	[illegible]	[illegible]
RB-67-2A-M	.92	.64	.58	.110	.24	.760
RB-67-2-M	.92	.76	.64	.110	.24	.760
RB-67-3-M	1.25	.66	.55	.115	.24	1.02
RB-67-4A-M	1.50	.66	.56	.110	.24	1.32
RB-67-4-M	1.75	.82	.65	.115	.25	1.53
RB-67-5-M	2.25	.85	.68	.115	.24	2.02

.XX = ±.010
.XXX = ±.005

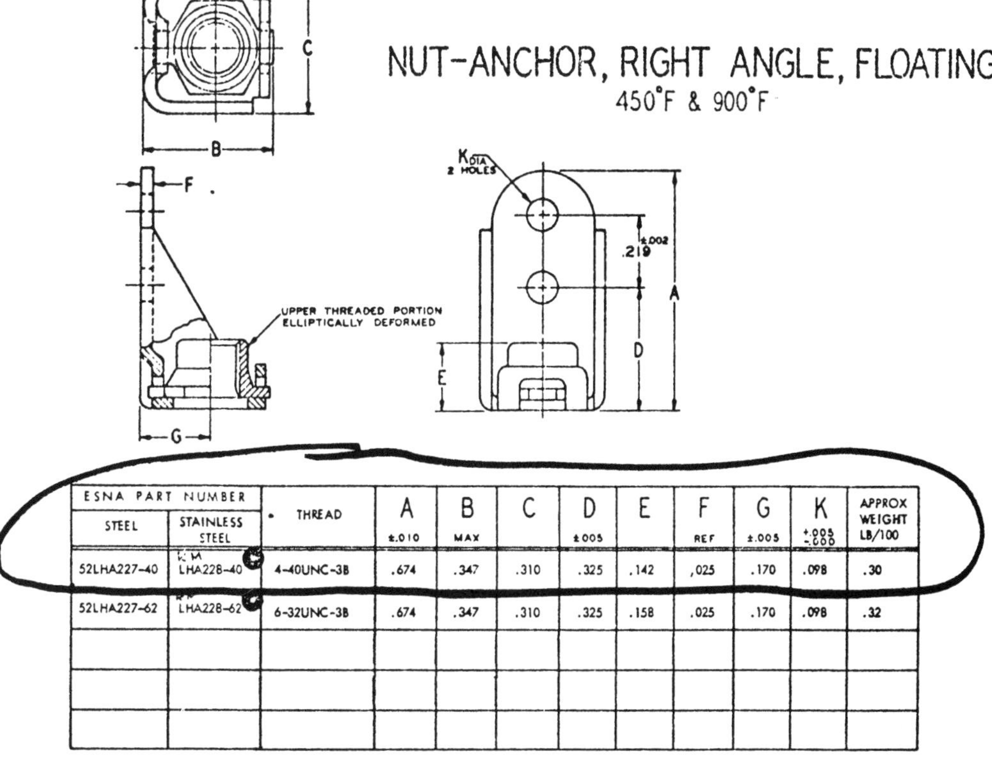

ESNA PART NUMBER		• THREAD	A	B	C	D	E	F	G	K	APPROX WEIGHT LB/100
STEEL	STAINLESS STEEL		±.010	MAX		±.005		REF	±.005	+.005 -.000	
52LHA227-40	LHA228-40	4-40UNC-3B	.674	.347	.310	.325	.142	,025	.170	.098	.30
52LHA227-62	LHA228-62	6-32UNC-3B	.674	.347	.310	.325	.158	.025	.170	.098	.32

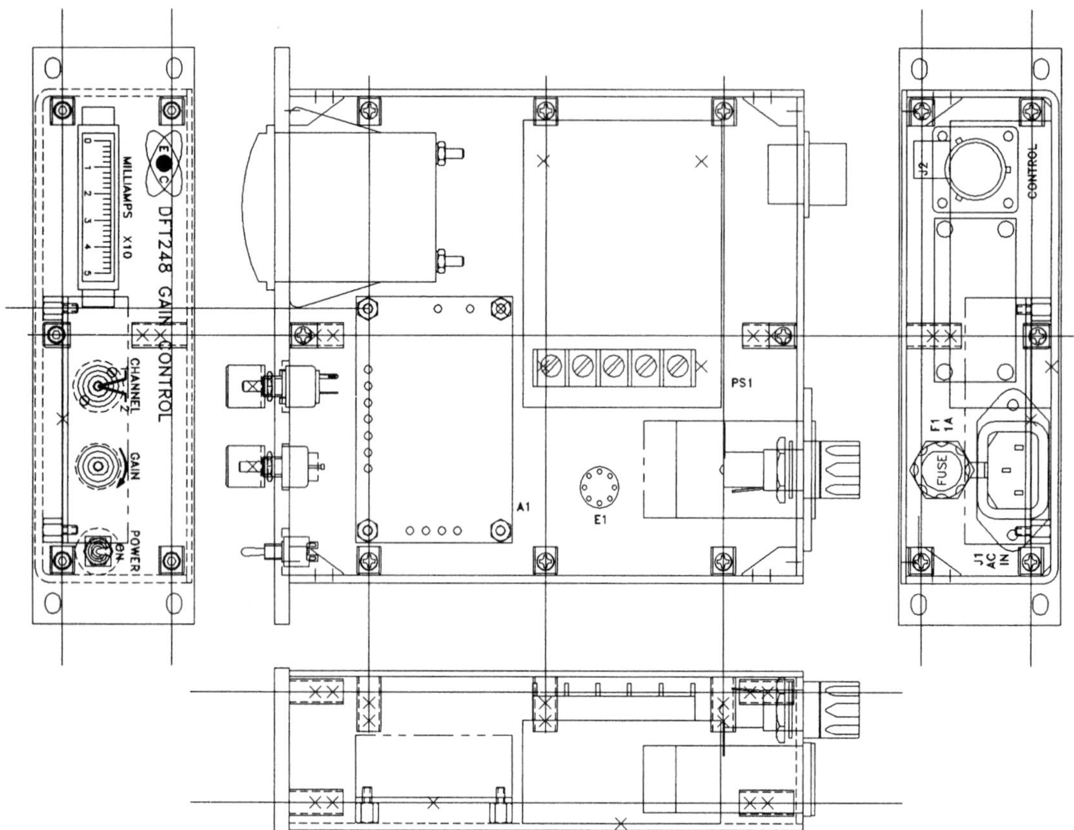

FIGURE 26–2
Design Layout

Figure 26–3 shows one of the detail parts drawings needed for manufacturing. Notice that the drawing shows only one part but has all the information needed to manufacture that part. Most companies follow this procedure because of the need to change, stock, and purchase parts individually and because an individual part may be used in several different assemblies.

Figure 26–4 shows a completed assembly with the accompanying parts list. Sheet 2 of the assembly is a wiring diagram. No dimensions are shown on this drawing. Each different part is called out on the drawing with an item number (the item number is the line number on the parts list). Notice that many of the circles surrounding the item number are split with a horizontal line. The number above the line is the item number. The number below the line is the quantity of that part needed for the assembly. If no quantity is shown, only one of these parts is used.

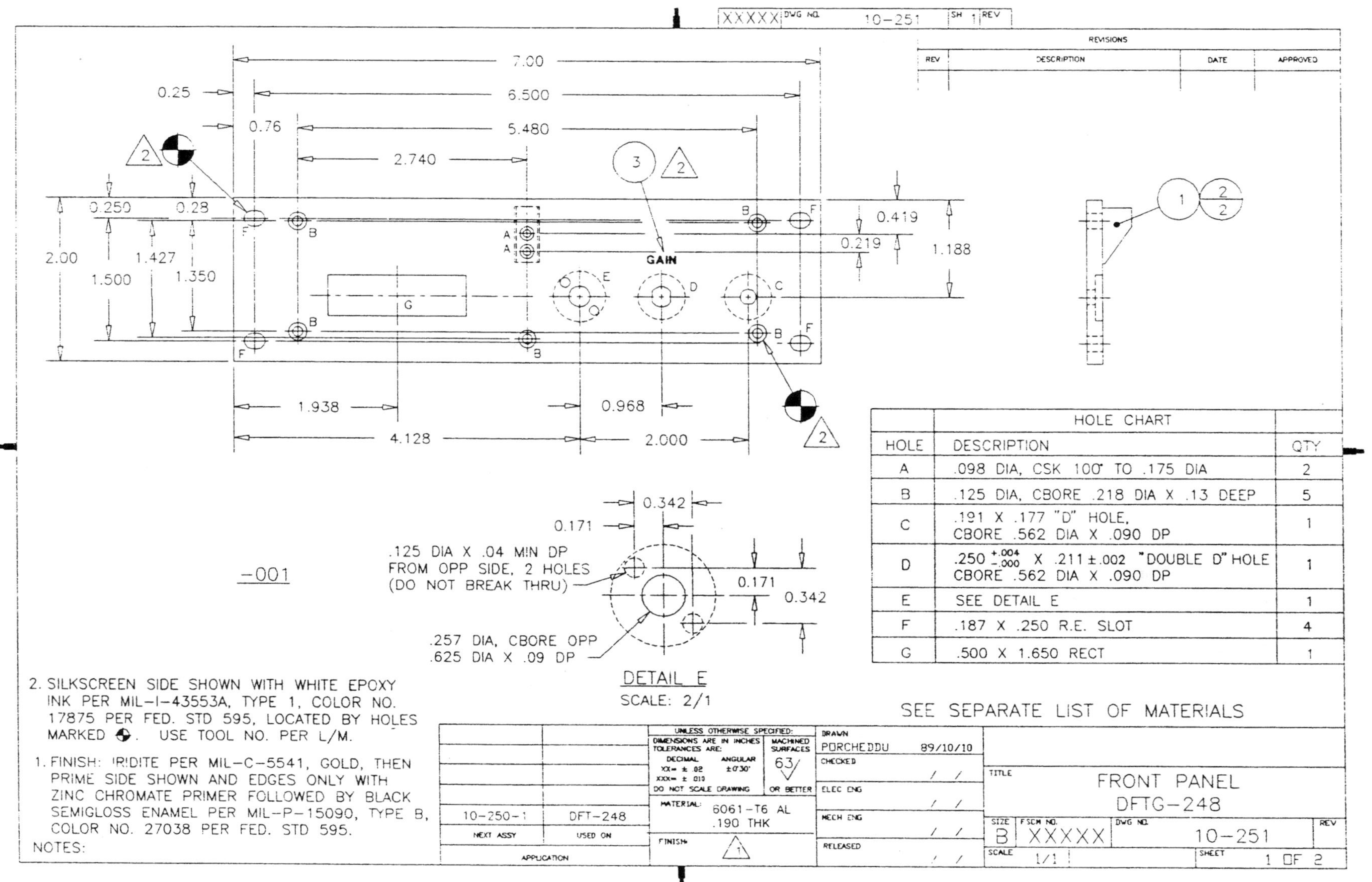

FIGURE 26–3
Detail Part

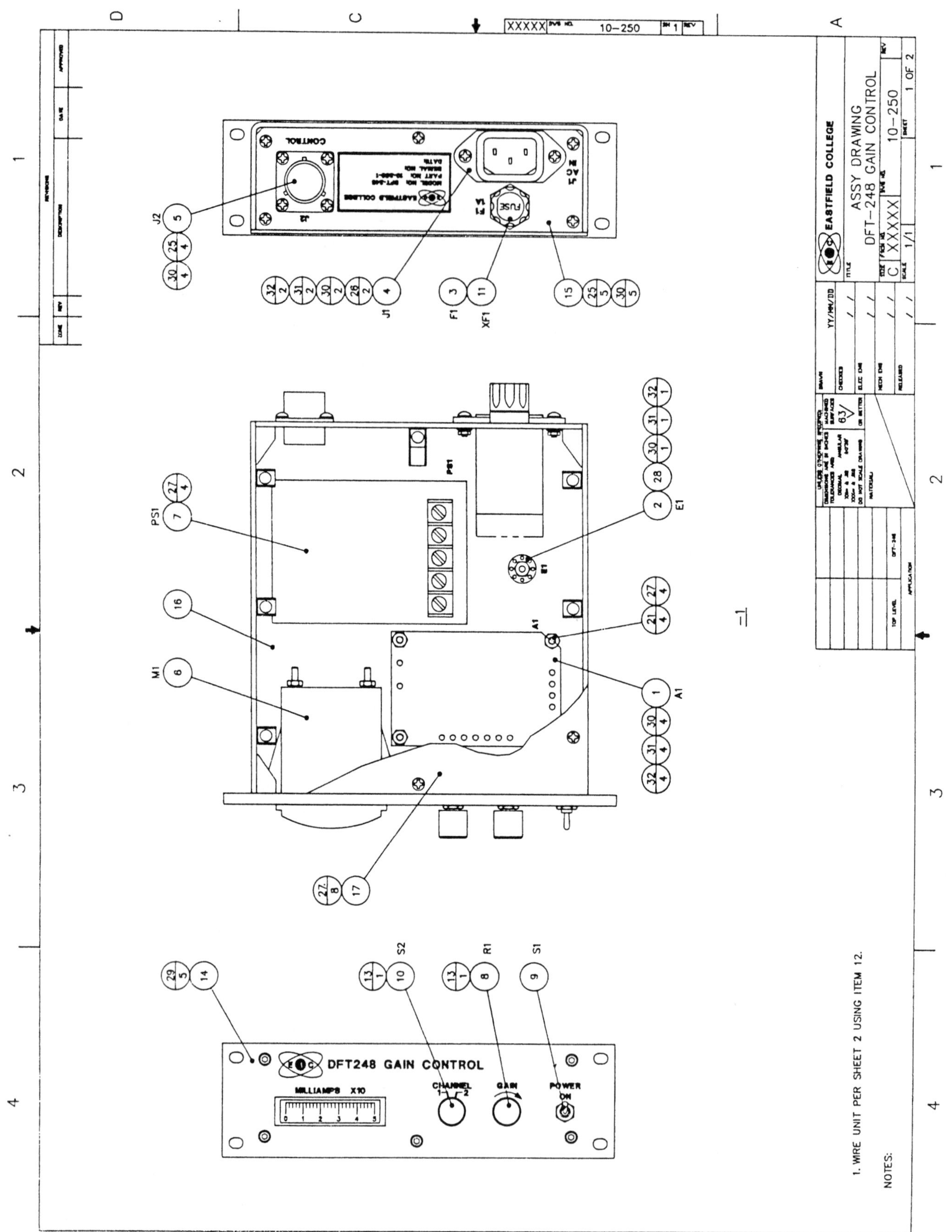

FIGURE 26–4
Assembly Drawing Sheet 1 of 3

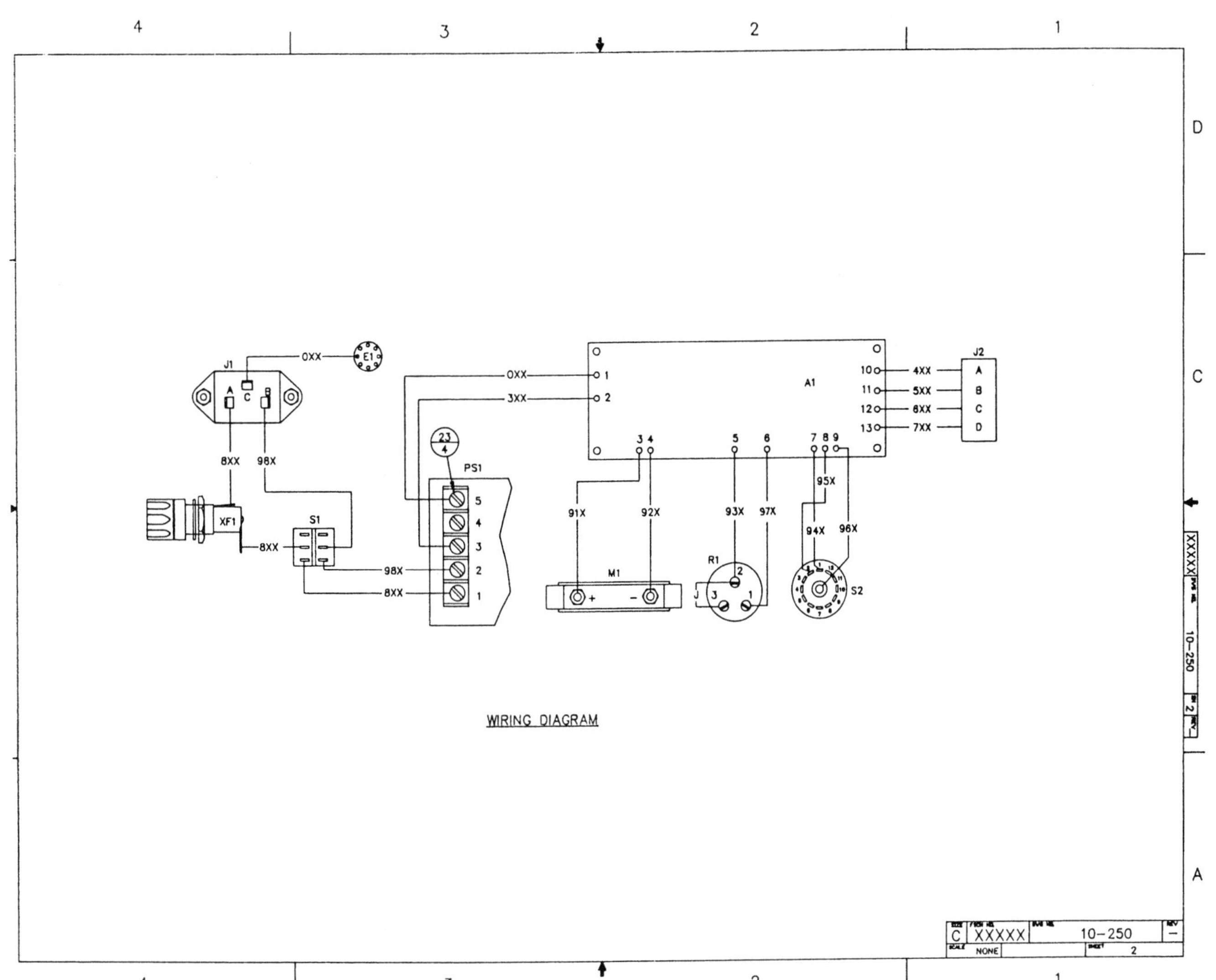

FIGURE 26–4
Wiring Diagram Sheet 2 of 3

LM 10-250 REV DESCRIPTION GAIN CONTROL MODULE SHEET 1 OF 1 DATE 11 NOV 89

FIND NO.	QTY REQ	REV LTR	DESCRIPTION	REFERENCE DESIGNATION	MFGR	MANFACTURER PART NO.	DRAWING NUMBER
1	1		POWER/ CONTROL BOARD	A1		10-231	TBA
2	1		TERMINAL GROUND	E1	CAMBION	190-1037-01-05-00	
3	1		FUSE	F1	LITTLEFUS	3AG-1	
4	1		CONNECTOR AC	J1	CDE	APF300CEE	
5	1		CONNECTOR 4 PIN	J2	CANNON	MS3112E12-4P	
6	1		METER	M1	WESTON	MOD. 111	
7	1		POWER SUPPLY	PS1	TOT POWER	456-CA	
8	1		POTENTIOMETER 10K	R1	ALLEN BRA	WA-10K	
9	1		SWITCH SPDT	S1	ALCOSWIT	TT13D 2T	
10	1		SWITCH ROTARY	S2	ALCOSWIT	MRS-1-12	
11	1		FUSEHOLDER	XF1	LITTLEFUS	342004	
12	AR		WIRE TEFLON NO. 24AWG				
13	2		KNOB		ROGAN	RB-67-0-M	
14	1		FRONT PANEL				10-251-1
15	1		REAR PANEL				10-252-1
16	1		CHASSIS				10-253-1
17	1		COVER				10-254-1
20	AR		THERMAL COMPOUND		THERMAL	250 THERMALCOTE	
21	4		STANDOFF ML-FEM 4-40 X .25L		PROMPTUS	164-01-SS-4-40-7A	
23	4		TERMINAL LUG NO. 4		HOLLINGS	MS23536-148	
25	9		SCREW 4-40 X 5/16L PPH		MIL STD	MS51957-14	
26	2		SCREW 4-40 X 3/8L PPH		MIL STD	MS51957-15	
27	16		SCREW 4-40 X 1/4L PFH		MIL STD	MS24693C2	
28	1		SCREW 4-40 X 5/8L PFH		MIL STD	MS24693C7	
29	5		SCREW 4-40 X 5/16L SOC HD		MIL STD	NAS1352C04-5	
30	12		WASHER FLAT NO. 4 SMALL PAT.		MIL STD	MS15795-004	
31	3		WASHER LOCK NO. 4		MIL STD	MS35338-134	
32	7		NUT HEX 4-40		MIL STD	MS35649-244	
35	REF		SCHEMATIC DFTG-248 GAIN CONTROL MODULE				10-255-1
36	REF		OUTLINE DRAWING DFTG-248 GAIN CONTROL MODULE				10-256-1

FIGURE 26–4
Parts List Sheet 3 of 3

DESIGNING AN ELECTROMECHANICAL ASSEMBLY

Let's work our way through the design of a complex electromechanical assembly, in this case a sheet metal box containing the parts needed to act as a gain control in a larger electronic assembly, such as radar or other sensing equipment. Begin by naming the project and creating directories to contain all the drawings for this project.

Naming the Project and Labeling Two Empty Disks

Step 1. Name the project with your initials, a hyphen, and the letters GC (for gain control) (Example: JMK-GC).

Step 2. Label one disk (your initials)-GC.

The disk labeled (your initials)-GC will contain all final drawings for the project. Label another disk PARTS. This disk will contain all the preliminary drawings and the design layout.

Collecting All Existing Information

For this project the sizes of the box and of its mounting holes have already been determined (Figure 26–5). (It must fit into an existing hole in an electronic rack or chassis.) The components to be located on front and rear panels have also been determined. These locations are approximate, and the components may be moved if necessary, as long as they remain on the front or rear panel, as shown.

In addition, a preliminary parts list (Figure 26–6) has been compiled. This list contains all the parts that must be mounted into the assembly. It also lists the sheet metal parts, the front and rear panels, the cover, and the chassis that must be designed to complete the

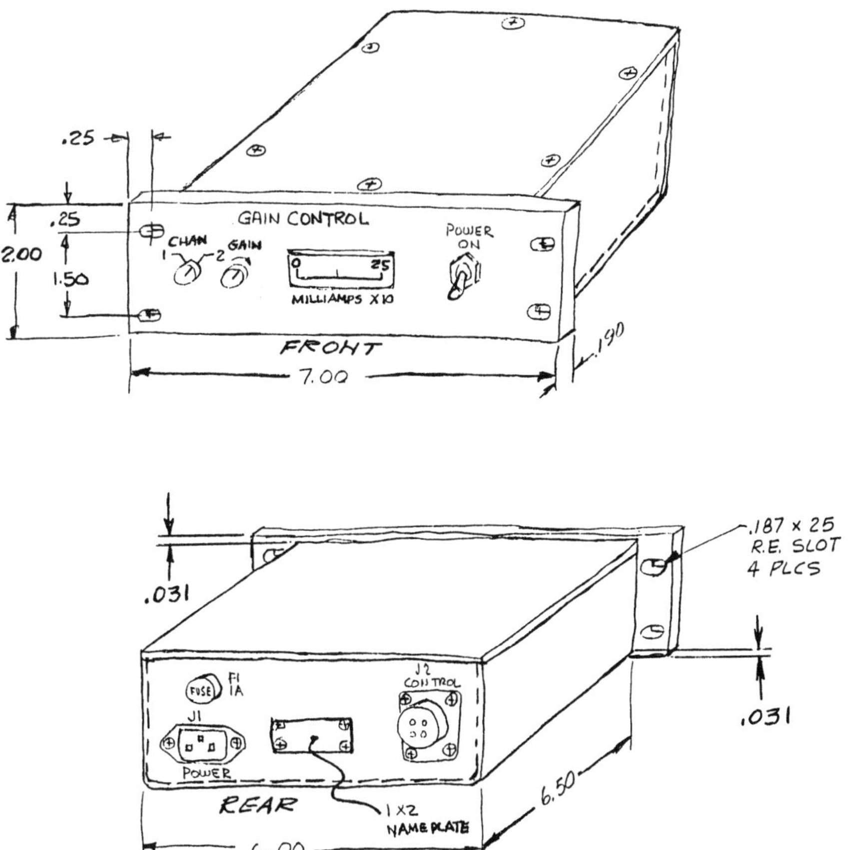

FIGURE 26–5
Preliminary Design Information (External Appearance of Gain Control Module)

Item Number	Quantity Required	Description	Reference Designation	Drawing Number
1	1	Power/control board	A1	
2	1	Terminal ground	E1	
3	1	Connector ac	J1	
4	1	Connector 4 pin	J2	
5	1	Meter	M1	
6	1	Power supply	PS1	
7	1	Potentiometer— 10K	R1	
8	1	Switch—SPDT	S1	
9	1	Switch rotary	S2	
10	1	Fuse	F1	
11	2	Knob		
12	4	Standoff ML-FEM 4-40 × .25L		
13	1	Front panel		
14	1	Rear panel		
15	1	Chassis		
16	1	Cover		
17	*AR	Wire teflon no. 24GA		
18	AR	Thermal compound		
19	4	Thermal lug no. 4		
20	5	Screw 4-40 × 5/16L PPH		
21	17	Screw 4-40 × 1/4L PFH		
22	5	Screw 4-40 × 5/16L SOC HD		
23	10	Washer flat no. 4 small pat.		
24	10	Washer lock no. 4		
25	REF	Schematic DFTG-248 gain control module		

FIGURE 26–6
Preliminary Parts List

assembly. This list may change as the screws, nuts, washers, other fasteners, and wiring are added in order to mount the components onto the assembly and connect the parts with wiring. Notice the heading "Reference Designation." This is a label given to functional parts to help in identifying which part is being discussed or listed.

Exercise 26–1: Drawing Outline Drawings of All Components

Information for outline drawings would normally be obtained from manufacturers' catalogs. It has been simplified for this exercise and is shown as Figures 26–7 through 26–21. At this time draw all these parts and Save them on your disk labeled PARTS. Use the following guidelines:

- □ Draw all parts full scale.
- □ Estimate any dimensions not shown.
- □ Draw parts on layer 0.
- □ Check to make sure all parts are drawn accurately from the given dimensions. Use List and Dist to check all dimensions. An "×" is shown in each view to identify the insertion point (don't draw the ×).
- □ Plan insertion points to place parts in the correct locations in the design layout.
- □ Wblock each view of each part to your disk labeled PARTS. Wblock each view as a separate drawing (Example: Wblock name A:\A1-T ↵).
- □ Print all views of each part. Put each part on a separate 11″ × 8.5″ sheet.

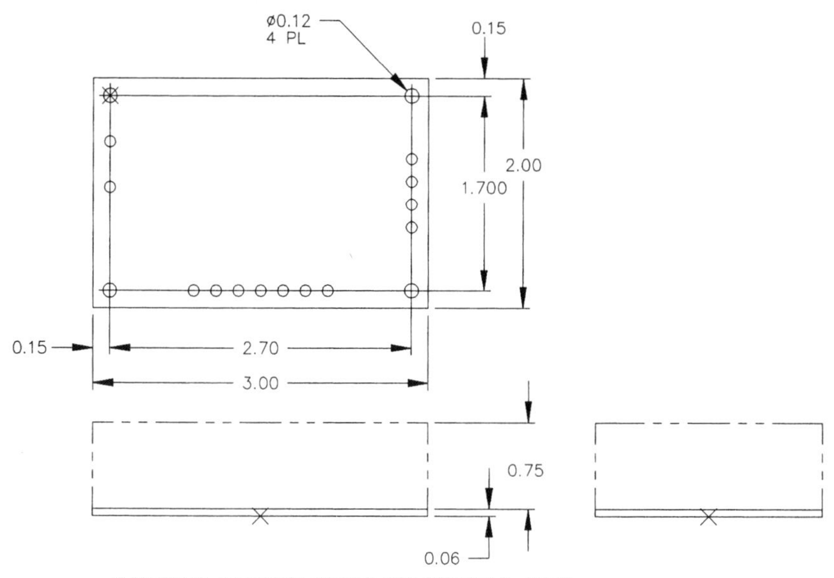

FIGURE 26–7
Top, Front, and Side Views of A1 (Power Control Board)

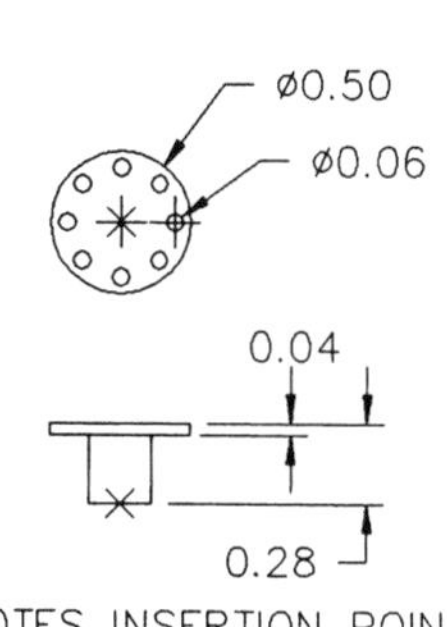

FIGURE 26–8
Top and Side Views of E1 (Terminal Ground)

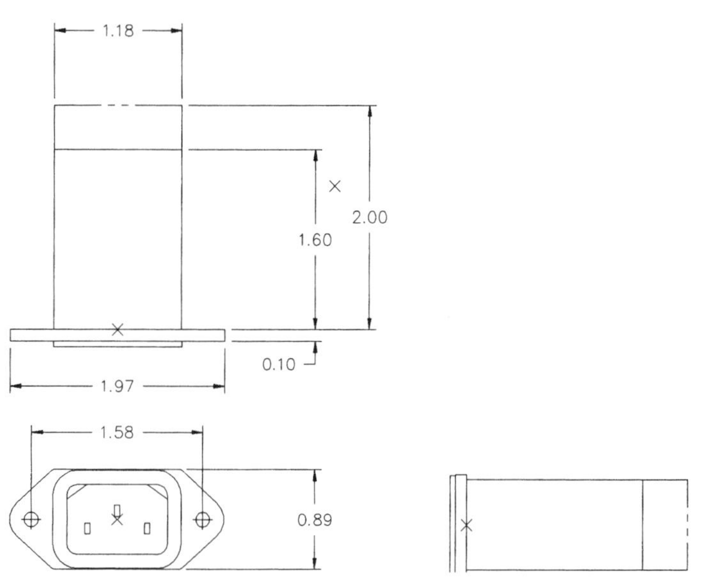

FIGURE 26–9
Top, End, and Side Views of J1 (Connector, ac)

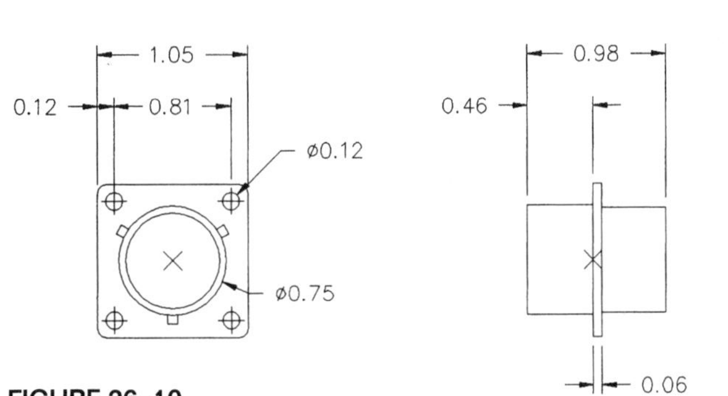

FIGURE 26–10
Front and Side Views of J2 (Connector, 4 Pin)

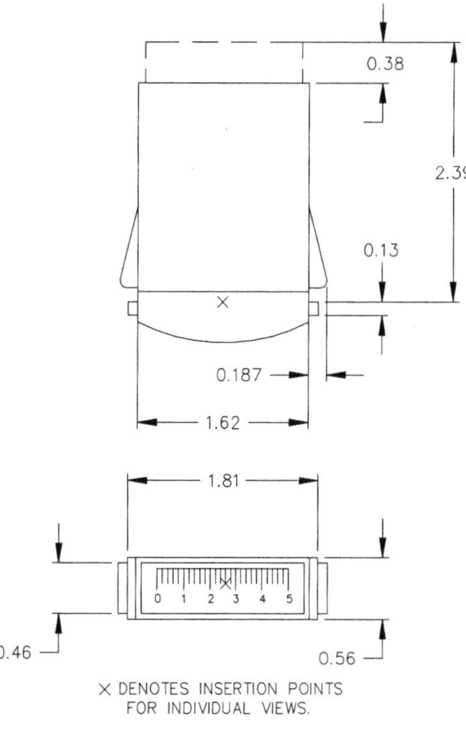

FIGURE 26–11
Top and Front Views of M1 (Meter)

FIGURE 26–12
Top, End, and Side Views of PS1 (Power Supply)

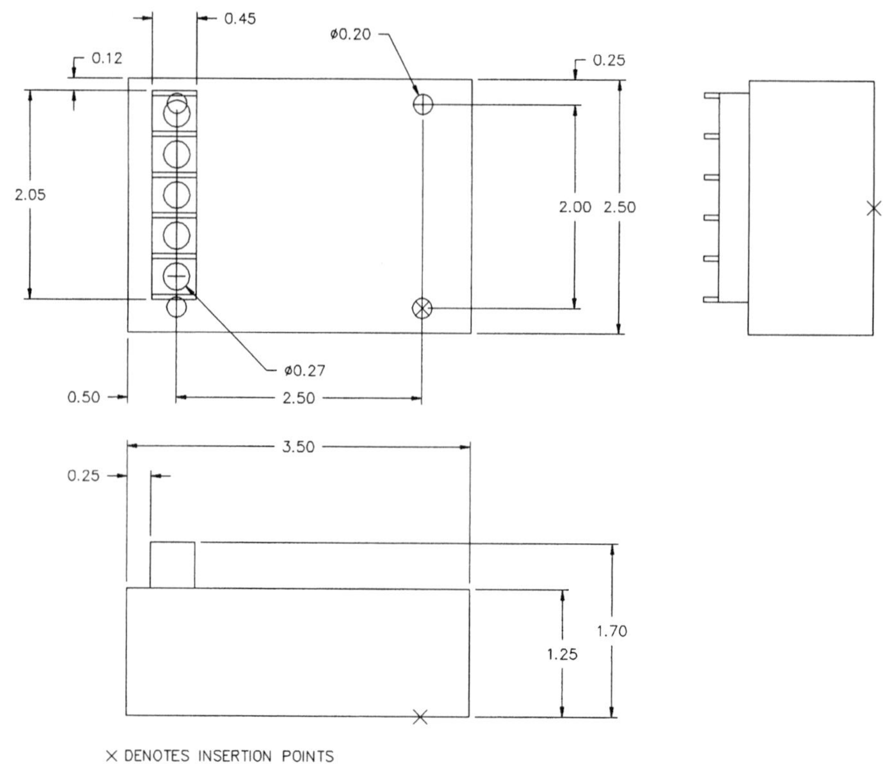

FIGURE 26–13
End, Side, and Rear Views of R1 (Potentiometer)

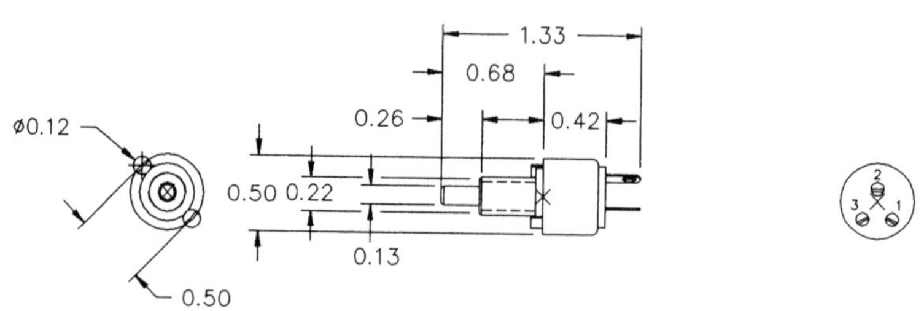

FIGURE 26–14
Top, End, Side, and Rear Views of S1 (Switch SPDT)

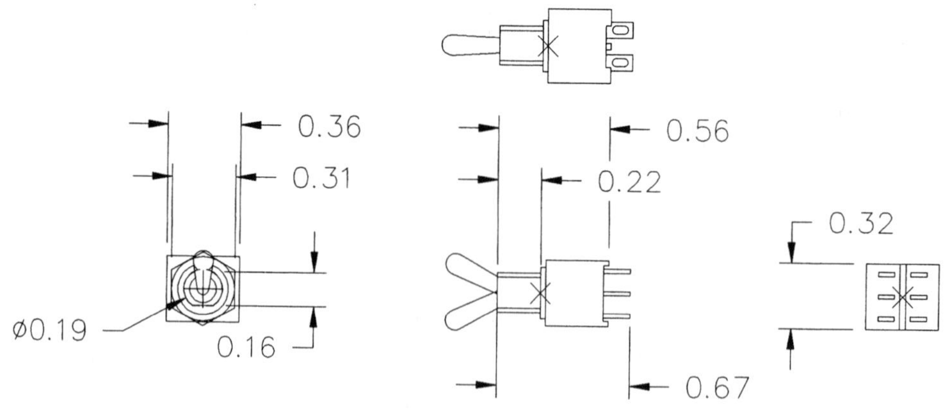

FIGURE 26–15
End, Side, and Rear Views of S2 (Switch, Rotary)

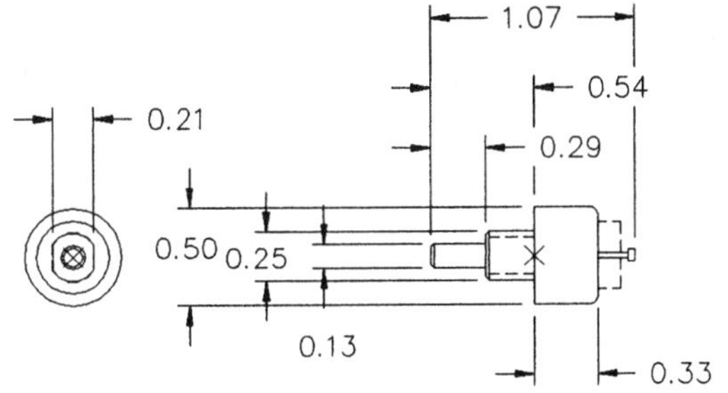

FIGURE 26–16
End, Side, and Rear Views of F1 (Fuse)

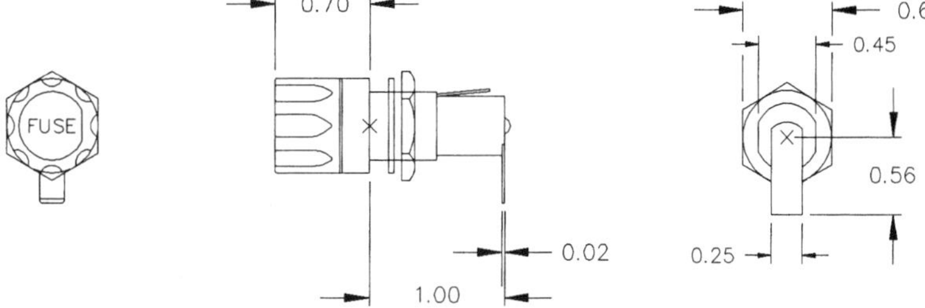

FIGURE 26–17
Front and Side Views of Knob

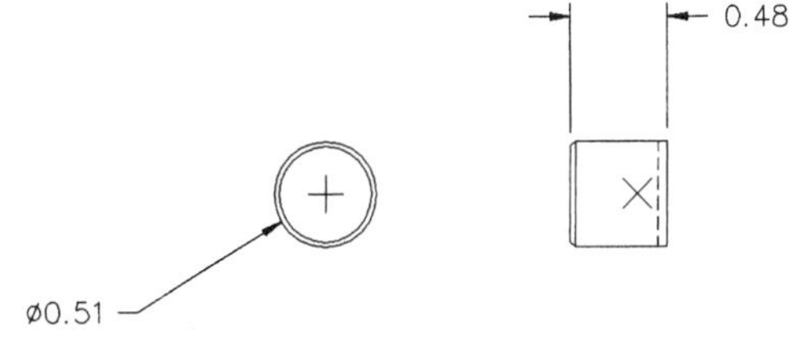

FIGURE 26–18
Top and Side Views of Standoff

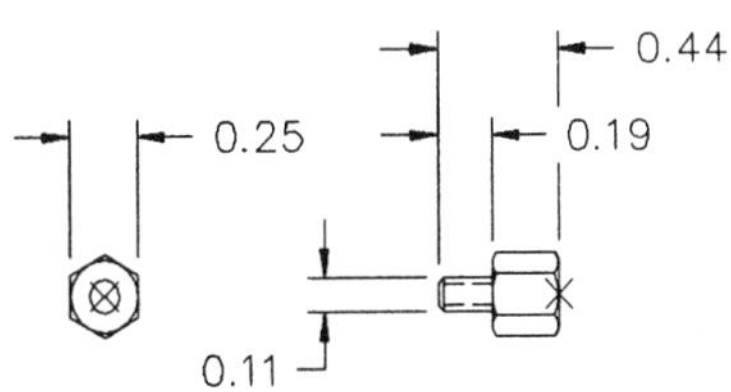

FIGURE 26–19
Top, Side, and End Views of Nutplate

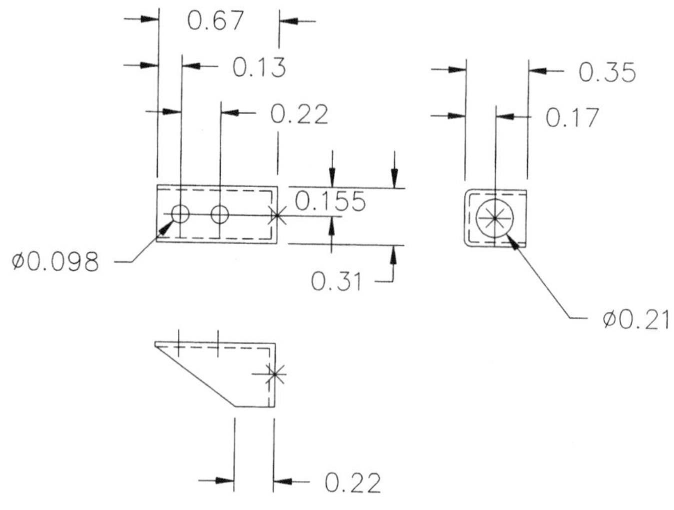

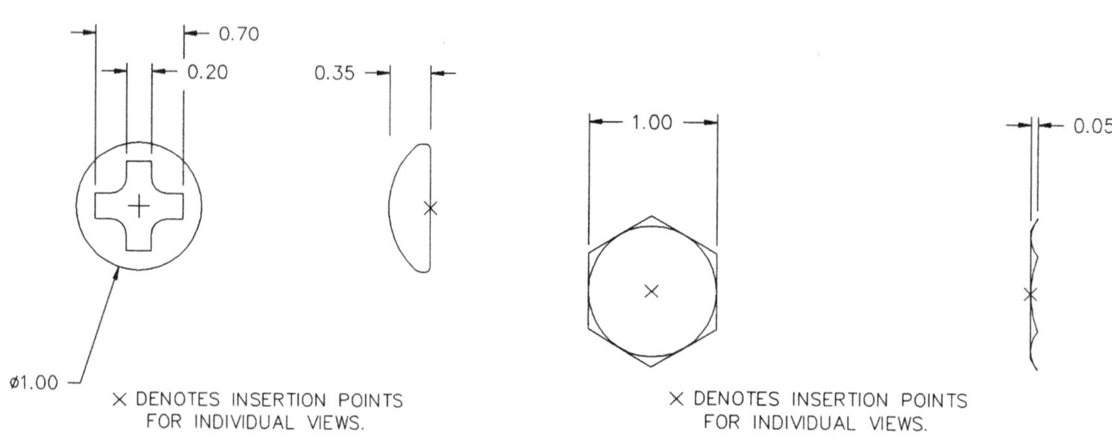

FIGURE 26–20
Screw Head Scaled for Insertion at Any Scale

FIGURE 26–21
Hex Head Scaled for Insertion at Any Scale

Exercise 26–2: Making a Full-Scale Design Layout

Use Figures 26–22 through 26–24.

Step 1. Load AutoCAD. *Click:* **Create Drawings-Wizards-Quick Setup.**

Step 2. Make the following settings:

Units: Decimal—3 digits to the right of the decimal
Area: Width: 22
Length: 17
SNAP: .05
GRID: .2

LAYERS: NAME	Color	Linetype	Lineweight
CHASSIS	Red	Continuous	Default
FRONT	Green	Continuous	Default
REAR	Cyan	Continuous	Default
SHEET METAL	Black	Continuous	Default
SHEET METAL H	Black	Hidden	Default

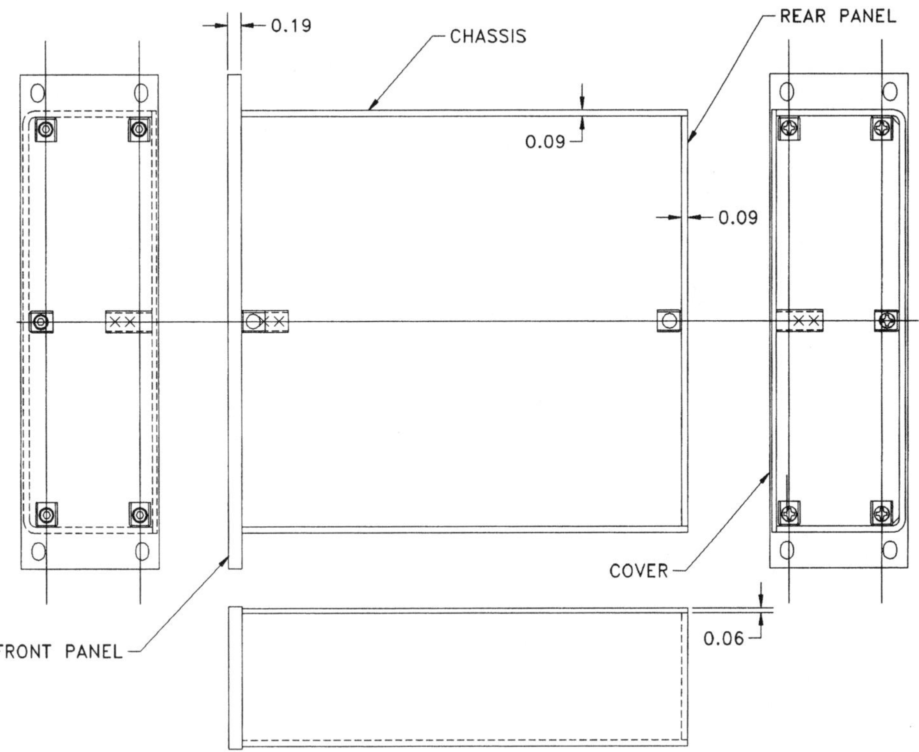

FIGURE 26–22
Sheet Metal Parts

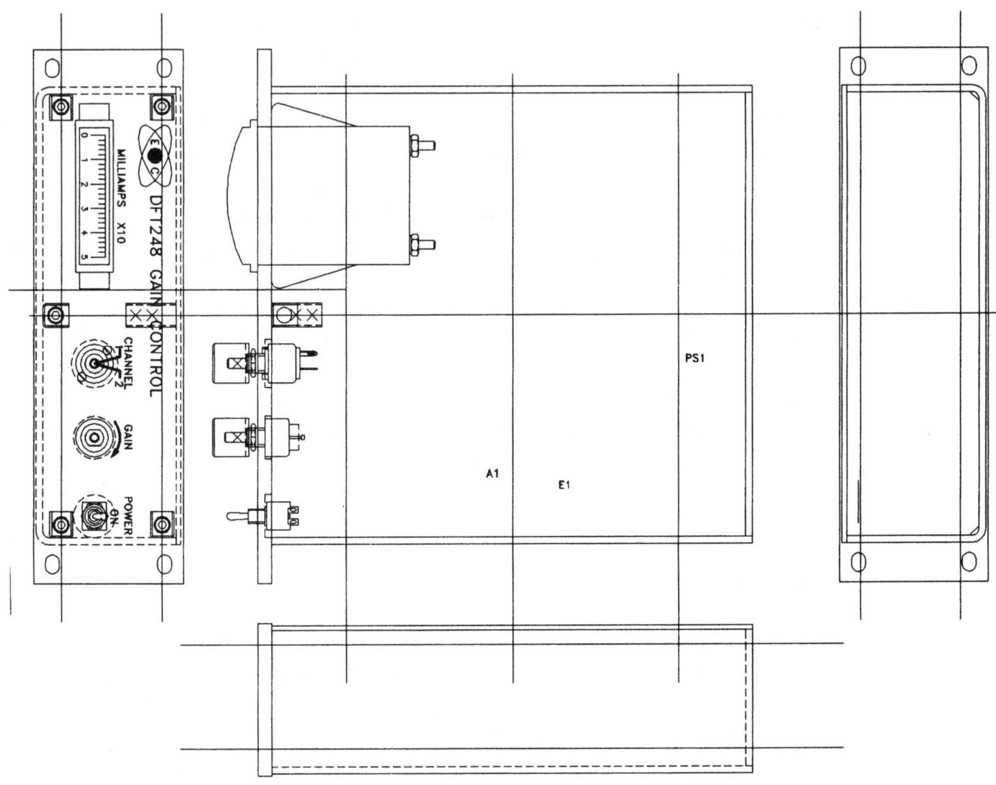

FIGURE 26–23
Front Panel Parts in Place

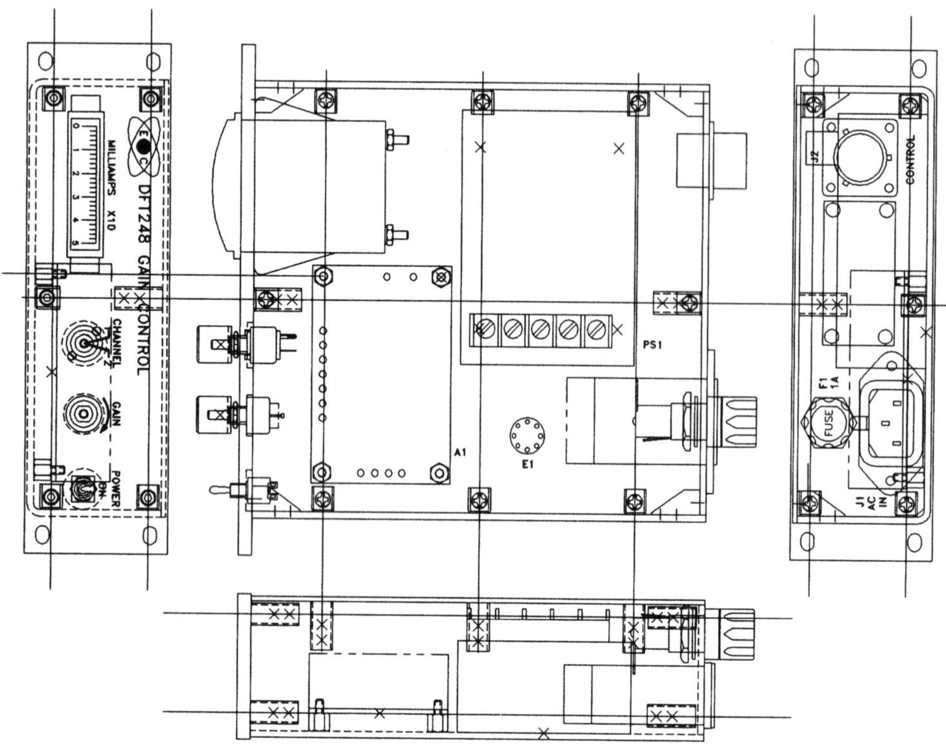

FIGURE 26–24
Complete Design Layout

Step 3. **With layer SHEET METAL current, use the information from Figure 26–5 to draw the outlines for top, side, front, and rear views of the assembly (Figure 26–22). (The view names are what the manufacturing people use, not the standard orthographic view names.) Use layer SHEET METAL H for all hidden lines. All metal thicknesses have been shown on Figure 26–22. Use them to draw thicknesses, but do not show these dimensions on the design layout. Notice that the front panel fits on the outside of the chassis, and the rear panel fits on the inside of the chassis. The cover fits on top of the chassis.**

Step 4. **Show the nutplates that will be riveted to the chassis in appropriate locations so that the cover, front, and rear panels can easily be screwed into these nutplates. Be sure SNAP is ON when you locate these nutplates. Try to locate them on a GRID so that dimensioning of matching holes can be as simple as possible. Nutplates should be located as follows:**

- □ Eight for mounting the top cover (Figure 26–24)
- □ Five for mounting the front panel
- □ Five for mounting the rear panel

Step 5. **Insert components from the disk labeled PARTS onto the design layout (Figure 26–24). Make the appropriate layer current when parts are inserted. For example, FRONT layer should be current when parts are inserted that are mounted on the front panel.**

Place the following parts in holes that are counterbored .090 from the back of the front panel:

Hint: Offset a construction line .090 from the back of the front panel to place S1, S2, and R1.

- □ SWITCH labeled POWER: S1.
- □ SWITCH labeled CHANNEL 1-2: S2; install knob also.
- □ POTENTIOMETER labeled GAIN: R1; install knob also.

Place these three parts on the top and front panel views (Figure 26–23). It is not necessary to draw them in the side view unless there is a possibility that they may interfere with other components. The meter M1 should be placed on the front panel at this time also.

Continue to place parts in the views that are needed to ensure that no parts overlap any others:

- □ Place F1, J1, and J2 on the rear panel.
- □ Place the power supply (PS1) on the chassis as near J1 as possible so that the wires connecting these two components can be short.
- □ Place A1 and E1 on the chassis.
- □ Use Dtext, ROMAND font, .1 height to label components on front and rear panels. Use .2-high letters for the GAIN CONTROL label on the front panel.

Figure 26–24 shows a complete design layout.

Step 6. *Click:* **Layout1, set a Plot scale of 1=2, and print the drawing ½ scale on an 11″ × 8.5″ sheet.**

Step 7. **Save your drawing as 10-250 on your disk labeled PARTS, and exit AutoCAD. Your layout may be quite different, but all the components must be there and must not interfere with each other. After the design layout is complete, parts may be detailed from the layout.**

Exercise 26–3: Drawing and Dimensioning Individual Parts

The individual sheet metal parts (chassis, front panel, rear panel, and cover) may now be accurately drawn and dimensioned as shown in Figures 26–25 through 26–28. (Be sure to fill in the XXXs with your design dimensions.) A good way to ensure that parts will fit after they are manufactured is to do the following:

- □ Copy the design layout for each individual part. Open the design layout, 10-250, and save it as the detail part (Example: 10-253). Erase what you don't need for the individual part.
- □ Dimension using Osnap to ensure that the correct dimension is shown. Use 2-place decimal dimensions where XX is shown and 3-place decimals where XXX is shown.
- □ Insert an appropriately sized drawing format (Chapter 11) around the drawing and change the drawing limits to the format size: 22,17 for the chassis and 17,11 for the other three parts. Complete title block information and add notes. If you do not have a format drawing, you will have to use an Ansi template file and insert your drawing into it. Then change it so it is similar to the ones shown in Figures 26–25 through 26–28. The border of these two formats is .50″ less than the format size all around. (Example: 22″ × 17″ format has a 21″ × 16″ border.) All other sizes for the title block and other format lines may be proportional to the sizes shown.
- □ Use hole sizes shown on Figures 26–25 through 26–28. These sizes are slightly larger than the screws and other fasteners or parts to allow parts to be easily assembled and still function properly.
- □ Save these drawings as 10-251-1, 10-252-1, 10-253-1, and 10-254-1 on your disk labeled (your initials)-GC.

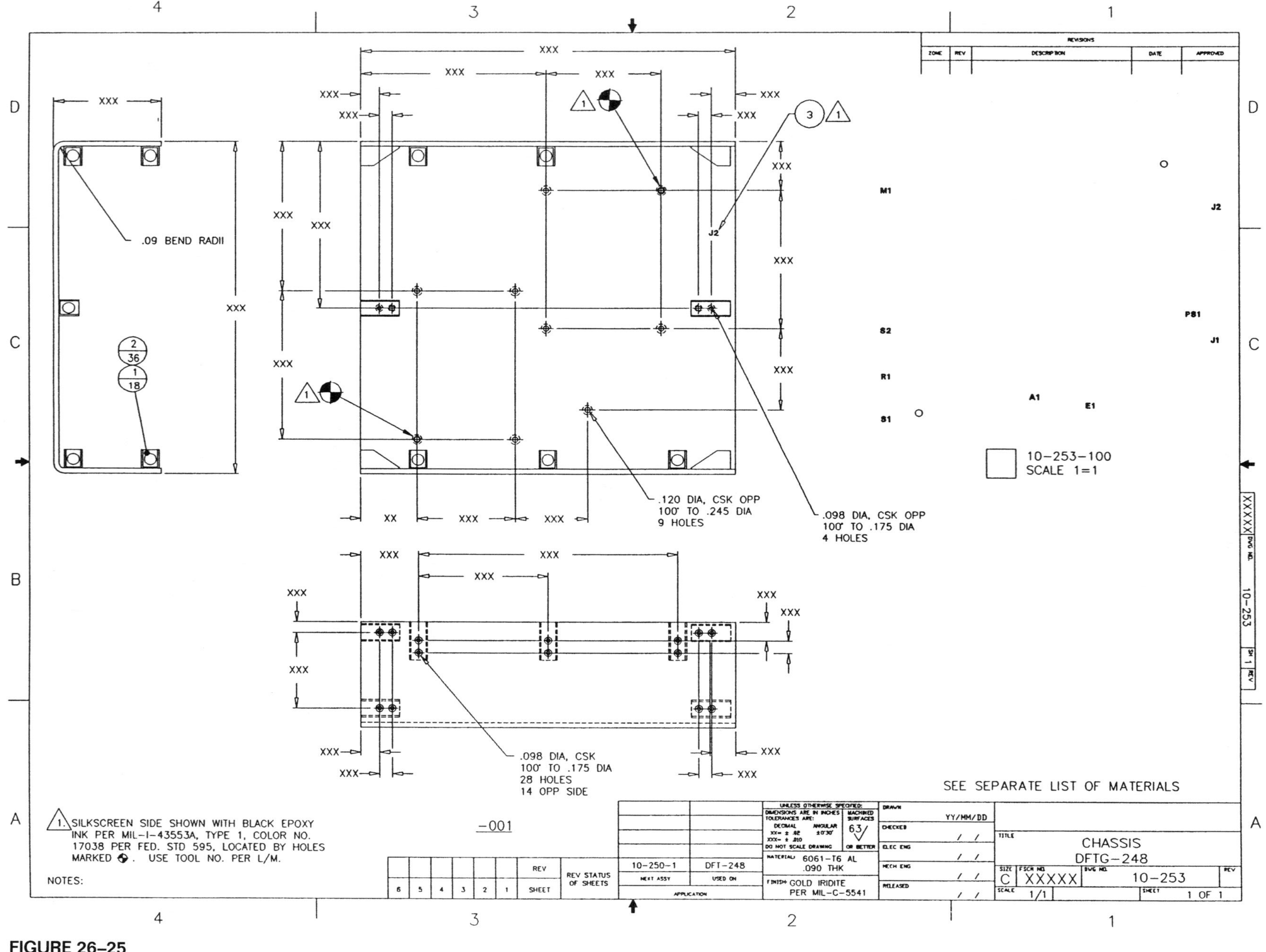

FIGURE 26–25
Detail Drawing of the Chassis

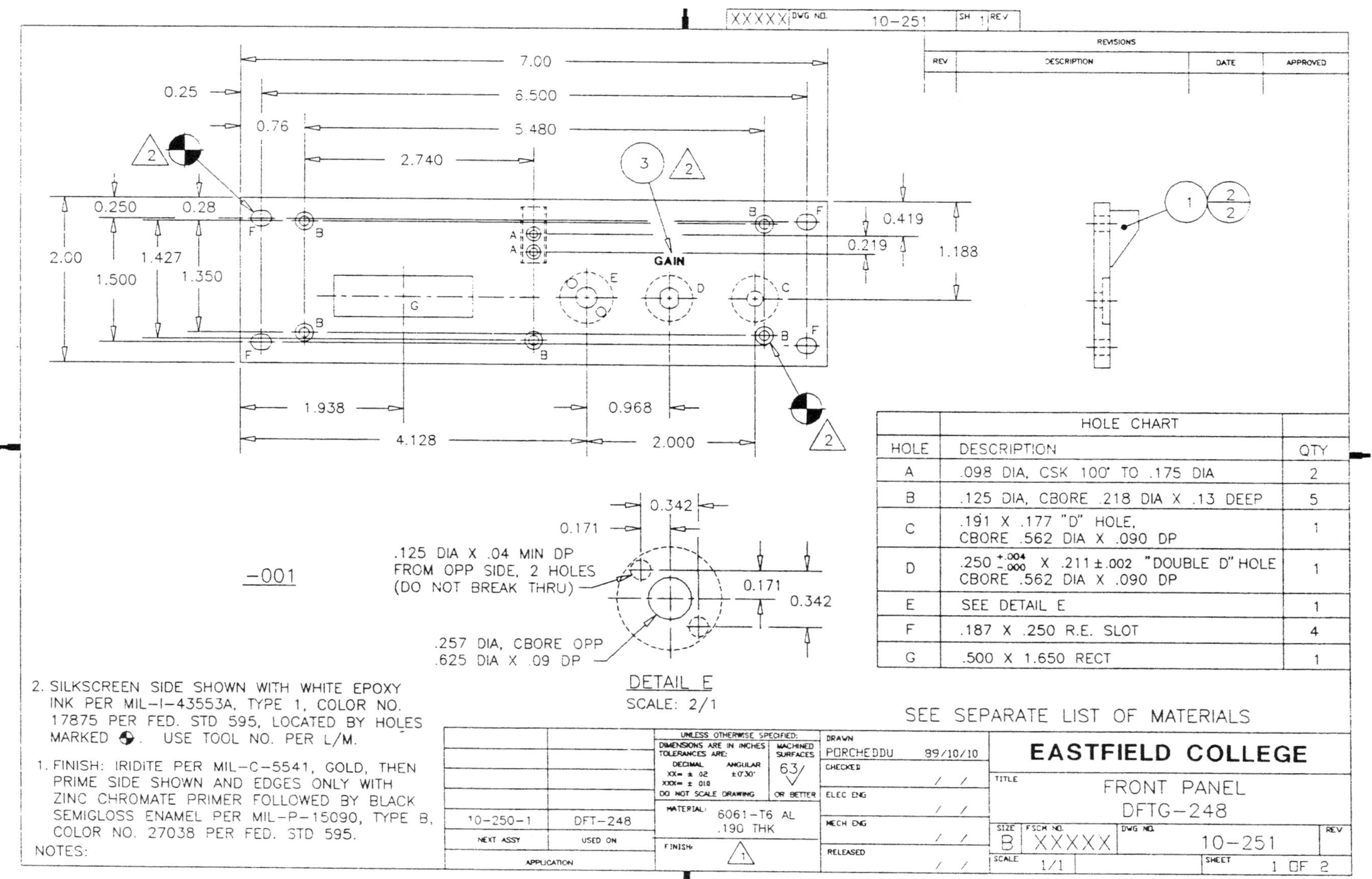

FIGURE 26–26
Detail Drawing of the Front Panel

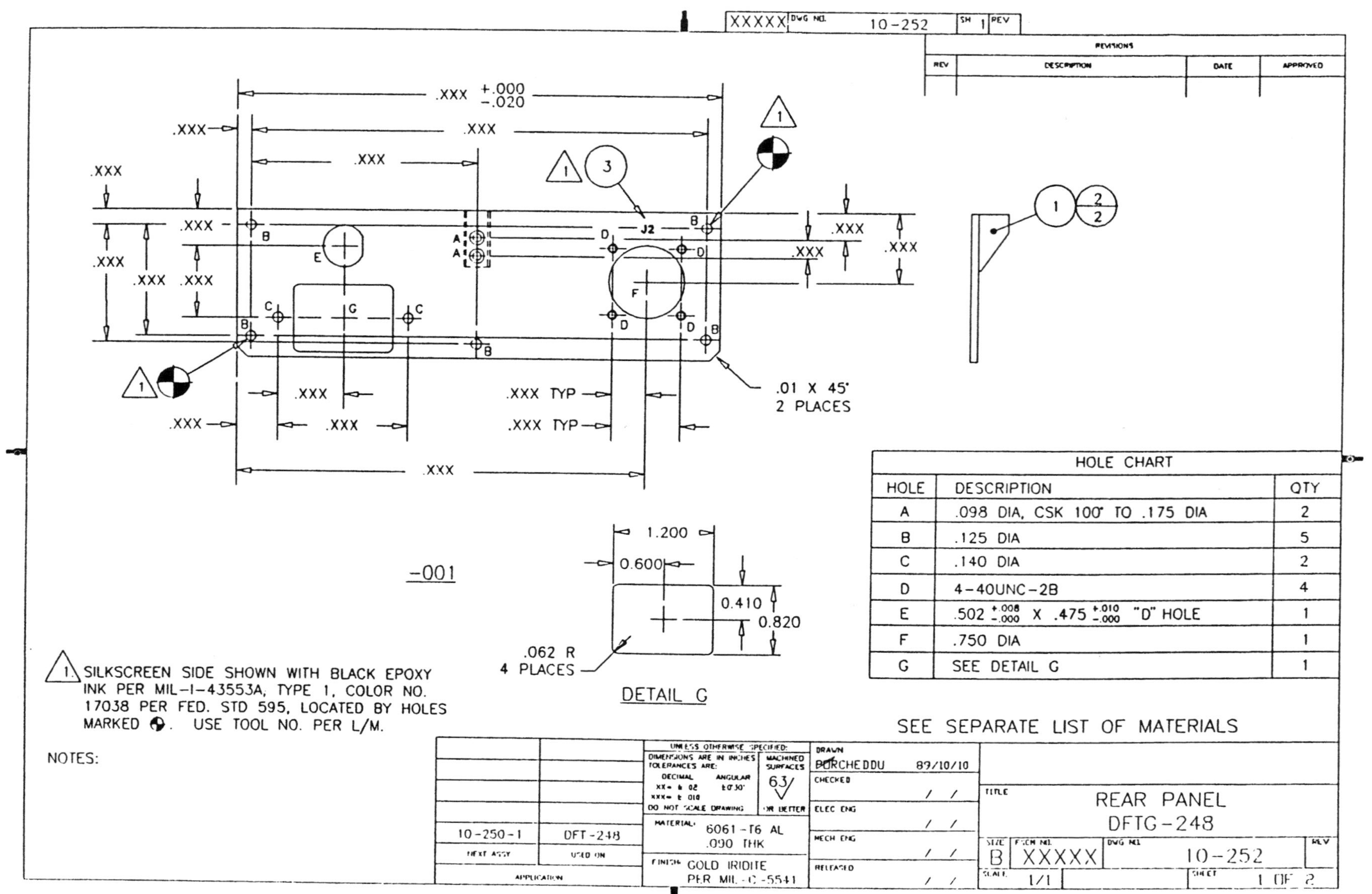

FIGURE 26–27
Detail Drawing of the Rear Panel

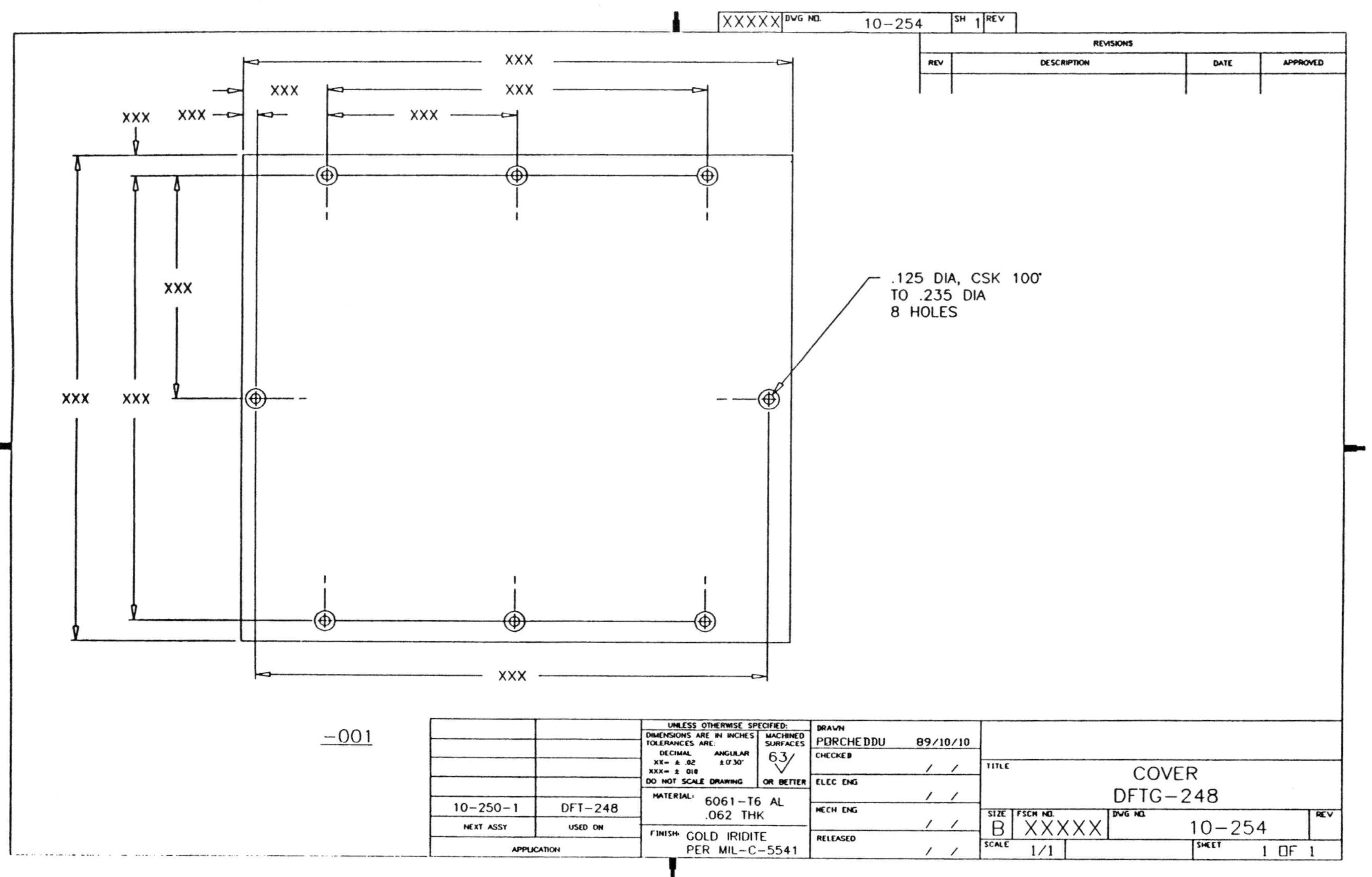

FIGURE 26–28
Detail Drawing of the Cover

Exercise 26–4: Making an Assembly Drawing and a Parts List

A copy of the design layout may be used to make an assembly drawing (Figure 26–29) for this package. *The index numbers on Figure 26–29 will not be the same as the index numbers on your assembly drawing. The index numbers on your assembly drawing must agree with your parts list* (Figure 26–6).

Step 1. Load AutoCAD, open the drawing A:\10-250, and save it as 10-250-1.

Step 2. Erase any unnecessary lines and the side view and Trim lines where appropriate to obtain a drawing similar to Figure 26–29.

Step 3. Insert a 22″ × 17″ format around the drawing on Layout1.

Step 4. Draw callouts and leaders.

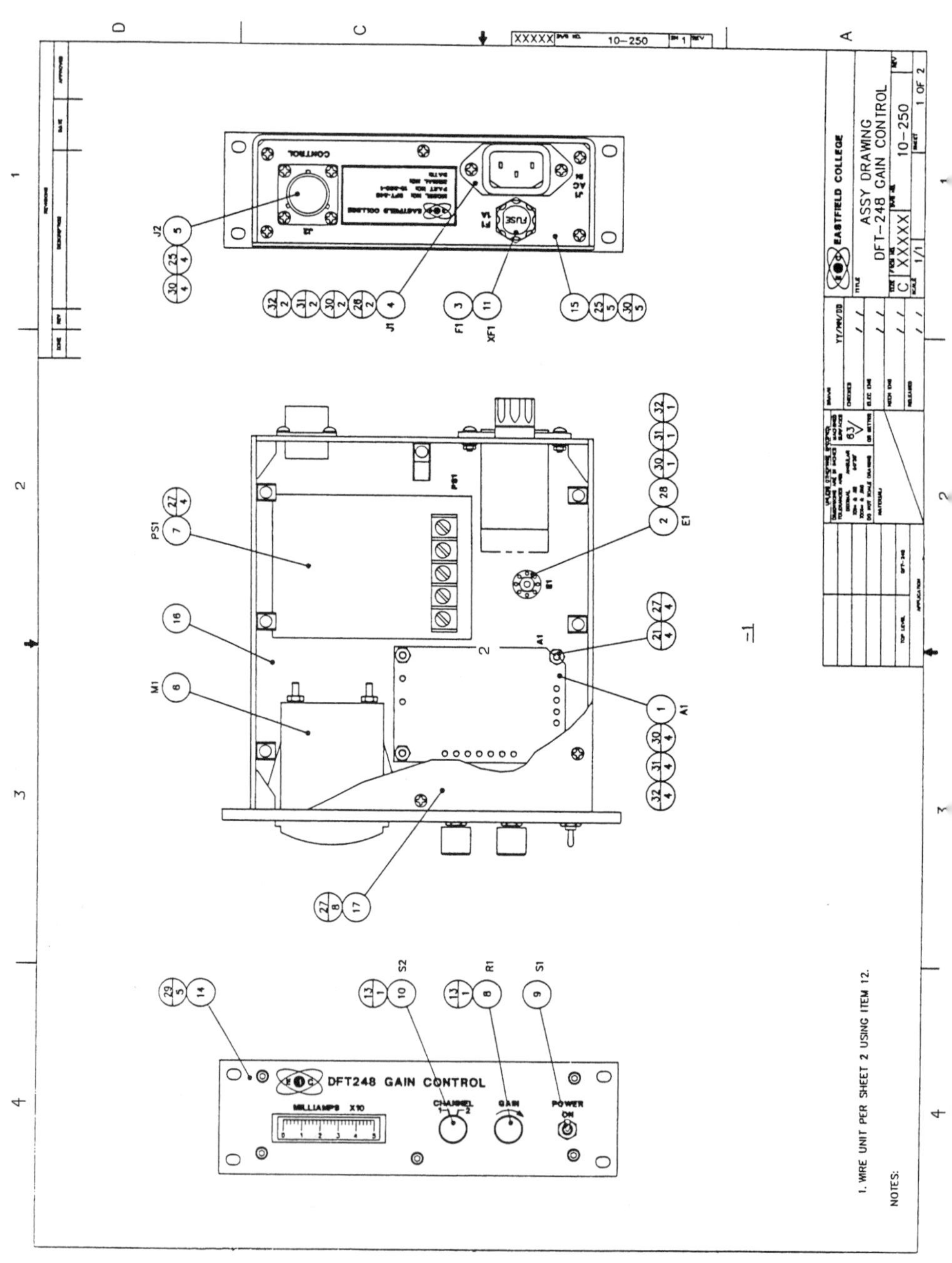

FIGURE 26–29
Assembly Drawing

- □ Use a .625″-diameter circle for the balloons on the end of the callout leader.
- □ Locate all balloons the same distance from the outline of the assembly.
- □ Keep all leaders at an angle to the part they call out. Do not use vertical or horizontal leaders.
- □ Use split balloons where more than one of an item is called out. The number above the line is the index number. The number below is the quantity used for that assembly. Use Dtext, simplex font, .1 high.
- □ Use the following quantities for the balloons showing mounting hardware:

A1: Power control board	4 each, item 12; 4 each, item 21
E1: Terminal ground	1 each, item 21
PS1: Power supply	4 each, item 21
10-251-1: Front panel	5 each, item 22; 5 each, item 23; 5 each, item 24
10-252-1: Rear panel	5 each, item 20; 5 each, item 23; 5 each, item 24
10-253-1: Cover	8 each, item 21

All other components are purchased complete with hardware, so hardware for those parts does not have to be counted.

Step 5. Print the drawing ½ scale on an 11″ × 8.5″ sheet.

Step 6. Save the drawing as 10-250-1 on your disk labeled (your initials)-GC, and exit AutoCAD.

Prepare a parts list similar to Figure 26–6 using an A-size format. You may use AutoCAD or a word processor for the parts list. If you use AutoCAD, make the text with the simplex font, .1 high. Make the space between lines ⅜″. *Make sure the parts list agrees with the index numbers on the assembly drawing.*

Exercise 26–5: Drawing a Schematic Diagram to Connect Wiring

To draw a schematic diagram from Figure 26–30:

Step 1. Load AutoCAD, *Click:* **Create Drawings-Wizards-Quick Setup, and make the appropriate settings.**

Step 2. Draw all symbols approximately twice the size shown on Figure 26–30.

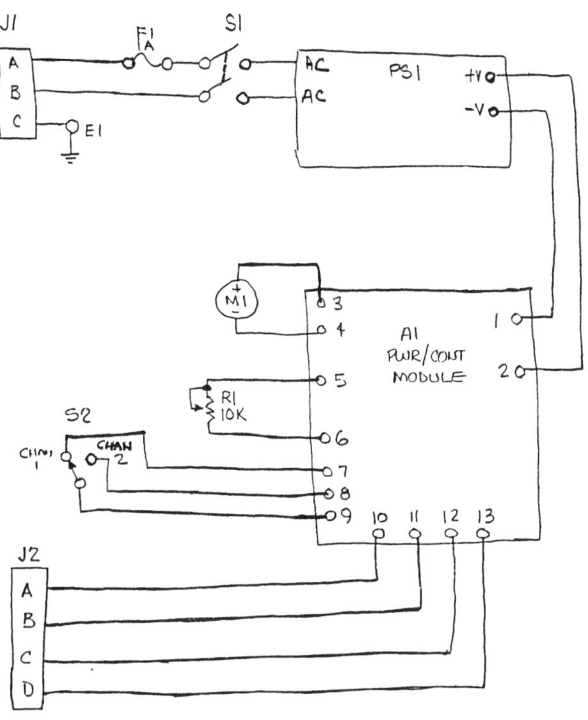

FIGURE 26–30
Preliminary Design Information (Gain Control Module Schematic Diagram)

Step 3. *Click:* **Layout1 and set a Plot scale of 1=2, insert a 17″ × 11″ format around the drawing and give it the drawing number 10-255-1.**

Step 4. **Use Dtext, simplex font, .1 high for all lettering.**

Step 5. **Complete the title block information.**

Step 6. **Print the drawing on an 11″ × 8.5″ sheet.**

Step 7. **Save this drawing as 10-255-1 on your disk labeled (your initials)-GC and exit AutoCAD.**

The project is now complete. Carefully check each line and number on every drawing. Correct all your errors and run another print before submitting the drawing.

EXERCISES

EXERCISES 26–1 through 26–5. Complete the drawing package described in this chapter. Submit prints of all drawings as they are completed, including individual component parts for your library. Design layout, assembly drawings, detail parts, and schematic should be on the sheet size described in the problem.

EXERCISE 26–6. Prepare a complete drawing package from an existing assembly containing no more than 12 parts (excluding hardware). Some calculators are good examples of this type of assembly. Other items, including children's toys, remote controls, and telephones, can also be used. Make a design layout, assembly drawing, schematic, and at least four detail drawings on appropriately sized formats (no smaller than 17″ × 11″). If the item selected is small, make the scale of the drawing 2× (twice the size), 4×, or larger to make the drawings easy to read.

EXERCISE 26–7. Prepare a 3-D model of the drawing package used in Exercises 26–1 through 26–5. Make 3-D models of all parts (do not include screws, washers, and other small hardware) and locate them on the chassis and front and rear panels. Simplify parts as needed, but be sure to maintain all critical dimensions. Position the cover above the Gain Control Module so that all the parts can be seen. Make a four-viewport paper space drawing that includes top, front, right side, and perspective views of the module. Print all four viewports on a single 22″ × 17″ sheet.

REVIEW QUESTIONS

Circle the best answer.

1. The parts to be inserted are created on which layer?
   a. 0
   b. Sheet metal
   c. Front
   d. Rear
   e. All the above
2. The design layout is merely an approximate location of parts.
   a. True
   b. False
3. The front panel contains which of the following?
   a. A1
   b. PS1
   c. J1
   d. J2
   e. S1
4. The rear panel contains which of the following?
   a. R1
   b. S2
   c. J1

d. A1
e. E1

5. The chassis contains which of the following?
   a. A1
   b. R1
   c. S2
   d. J1
   e. J2
6. The assembly drawing is needed to
   a. Tell how parts are assembled
   b. Show how parts are connected electrically
   c. Tell someone how to build the individual parts
   d. All the above
   e. None of the above
7. The schematic diagram is needed to
   a. Tell how parts are assembled
   b. Show how parts are connected electrically
   c. Tell someone how to build the individual parts
   d. All the above
   e. None of the above

Complete.

8. Why are separate layers used for parts located on front panel, rear panel, and chassis?

____

____

____

9. Why is Osnap needed in defining insertion points for parts?

____

____

10. List the detail drawings by DRAWING FILE NAME that were made in this chapter.

____

____

____

11. Describe how the assembly drawing was made in this chapter.

Step 1 _______________

Step 2 _______________

Step 3 _______________

Step 4 _______________

12. List the parts, by reference designation, that are mounted in counterbored holes.

____

____

27 Technical Illustrating Applications

OBJECTIVES

After completing this chapter, you will be able to

- Use 2-D drawings to make the following isometric drawings:

  Exploded views
  Cutaway views

- Learn to reduce drawings to fit standard page sizes.
- Learn to perform common line shading techniques.

Technical illustrating, as it is commonly defined in many manufacturing industries, consists of making the drawings used in proposals, reports, and technical manuals. Probably the most familiar of these manuals are the automobile repair, operation, and maintenance manuals. Similar manuals are used for equipment as complex as military aircraft and as simple as charcoal cookers. Most of these manuals contain similar types of drawings.

DRAWING TYPES

The most common drawing types used in technical illustration are

Schematic diagrams
Block diagrams
Exploded views
Cutaways
Pictorials

Three of these drawing types—schematic diagrams, block diagrams, and pictorials—were covered in earlier chapters. This chapter is concerned only with exploded views and cutaways. Before you start making these drawings, let's talk a little about a shading technique that is used to add interest and clarify complex drawings.

SHADING

One of the most common mistakes beginning illustrators or drafters make is in the area of shading. They almost always try to do too much. The best way to avoid overshading is to find a finished drawing that looks good to you and copy that technique. Never begin to shade a drawing until you have a definite plan.

Single-Line Shading Technique

A good plan that is commonly used is the single-line shading scheme. The details of these techniques are shown in Figures 27–1 through 27–6.

FIGURE 27–1
Highlights and Shadows with Single-Line Shading

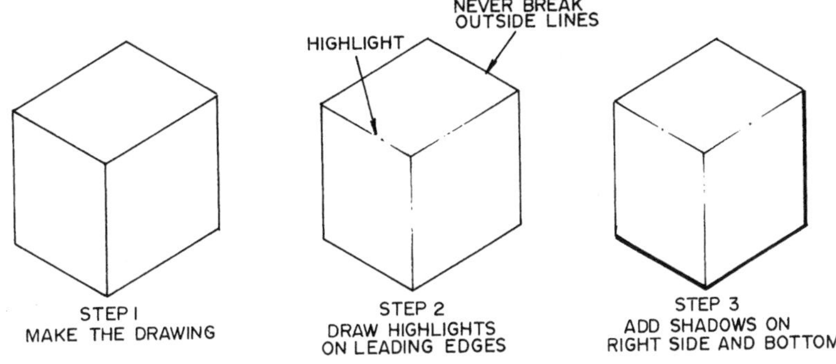

Highlights

Highlights are shown on the leading edges. *Caution: Never break outside lines that form the object* (Figure 27–1).

Shadows

Note: LINEWEIGHTS may also be assigned in the Layer Properties Manager for some shading lines.

Tip: Draw all hole and thread shading patterns using a 1″ ellipse. Wblock them; then Insert them when needed at a scale that supplies the hole size needed. (Example: Scale factor .500 produces a ½″ hole.)

Tip: Use grips to stretch an arc or polyline arc in or out so it fits.

Shadows are shown on the right side and bottom. These are drawn with a thick polyline. To do this, click Polyline and then W after you have picked the first point to specify the width. For the drawings in this chapter, a .02 width for shadows is acceptable. Notice that the shadow on the cylinder shown in Figure 27–2 begins about halfway down on the ellipse and gets thicker; this can be done using a polyline with a different beginning and ending width (0 beginning, .02 ending), or if the Polyline arc is difficult to manage, Offset an ellipse at a distance of .05, Rotate it to form the shadow, Trim the excess, and Hatch the shadow using the solid hatch. The hole-shading technique of Figure 27–3 is good for holes. Notice that the thin shading lines get closer together as they approach the small end of the ellipse. The dark shadow is drawn with one straight line and another ellipse Offset approximately as shown. Trim is then used to eliminate unneeded lines, and a SOLID HATCH pattern may be used for the shaded area.

FIGURE 27–2
Shading Cylinders

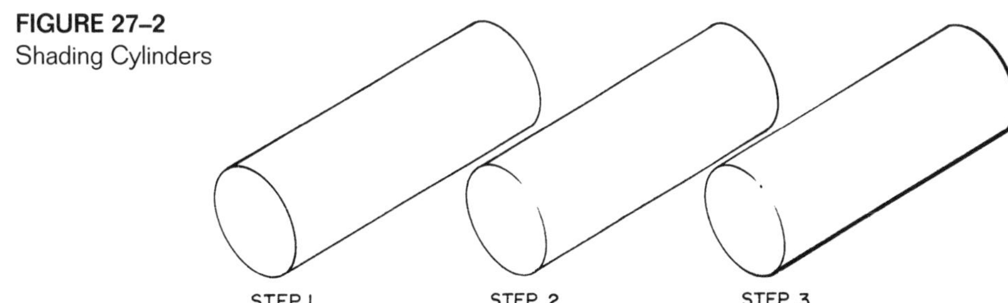

FIGURE 27–3
Shadows for Holes

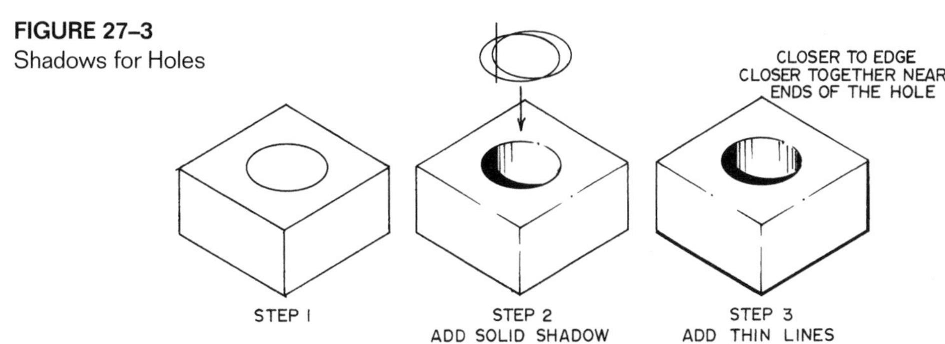

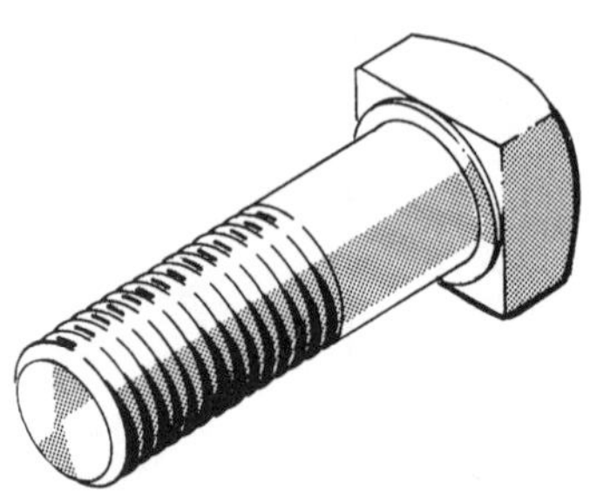

FIGURE 27–4
Shading Threads

Threads

Figure 27–4 shows a good method for drawing threads. The solid black shadows are drawn with a Polyline of different beginning and ending thicknesses and then arrayed with SNAP set at a 30° angle. The small shadow at the top is just a short, uniform thick Polyline (.02 W). It is important to make all the shadows the same length and the same thickness. The highlight is made by drawing two construction lines and Trimming the threads between them to form a uniform highlight, then erasing the construction lines. The dotted shadow is formed by drawing construction lines, hatching the area with the DOTS pattern, and then erasing the construction lines.

Fillets and Rounds

Fillets and rounds are drawn with straight lines that stop short of the corners or with short curved lines (Figure 27–5). The short-curved-line technique does not produce as realistic a result as the straight-line technique and is not used by many illustrators.

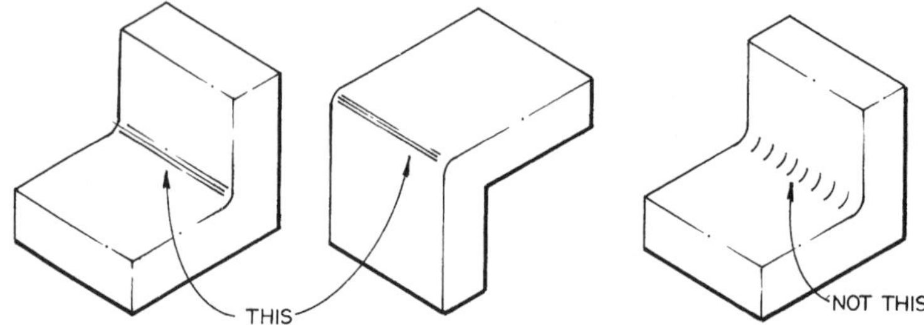

FIGURE 27–5
Shading Fillets and Rounds

Compound Curves

Figure 27–6 shows a method for drawing compound curves. Notice that shading lines are thin and broken and stop short of the edges.

There are many other shading techniques, but these are commonly used for technical manuals. Earlier chapters discuss the use of Shade for 3-D objects. Now let's proceed with exploded views.

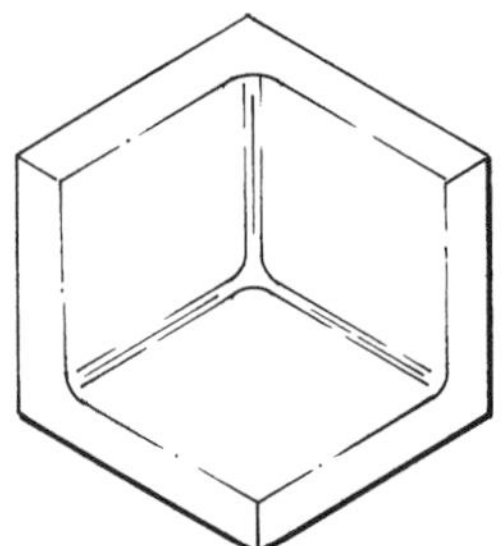

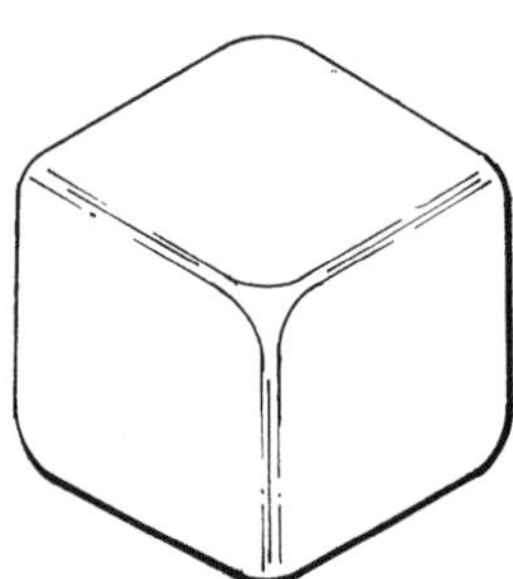

FIGURE 27–6
Shading Compound Curves

EXPLODED VIEWS

Note: The shadow technique of Figure 27–8 that shows a heavy line around all outside edges is also used.

Although a full 3-D model could be used to create an exploded view, creating it would consume more time than most companies are willing to spend, and it does not lend itself to line-shading techniques as described previously. Therefore, only isometric drawings are used for the exploded views in this chapter.

Exploded views are used to tell someone how to assemble, disassemble, repair, install, and identify the parts of an assembly. These parts must be drawn in the correct order and position. Figures 27–7 through 27–10 show four examples of exploded views and describe how they are used.

Now that you have some information about how exploded views are used, let's talk about how to draw them. You may have the actual parts to work from or you may have to start with a 2-D assembly drawing. Since we don't sell equipment with this book for you to take apart, we are going to have to start with the 2-D assembly drawings.

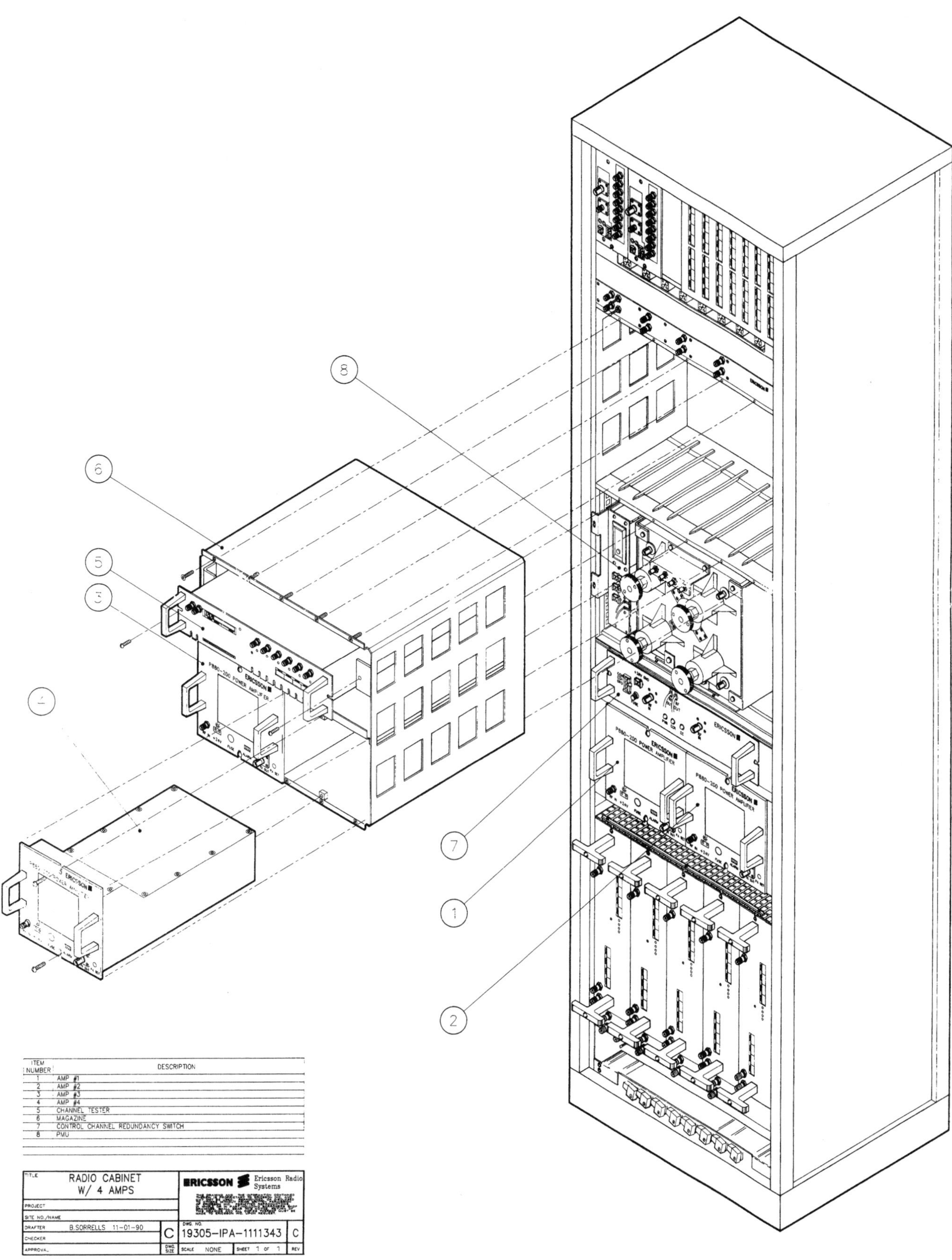

FIGURE 27–7
Exploded View—Assembly Instructions
Courtesy Ericsson Radio Systems Inc.

FIGURE 27–8
Exploded View—Repair Instructions

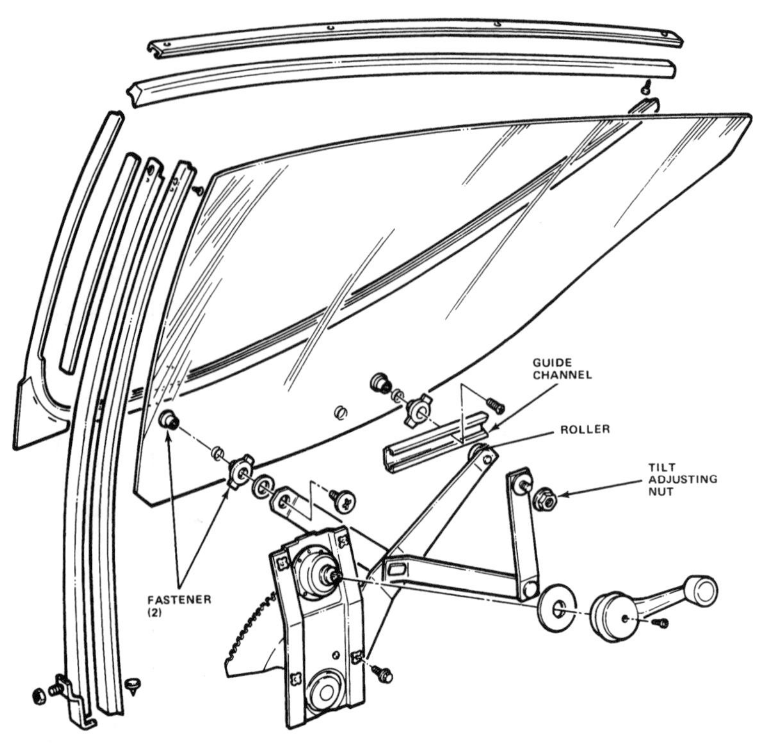

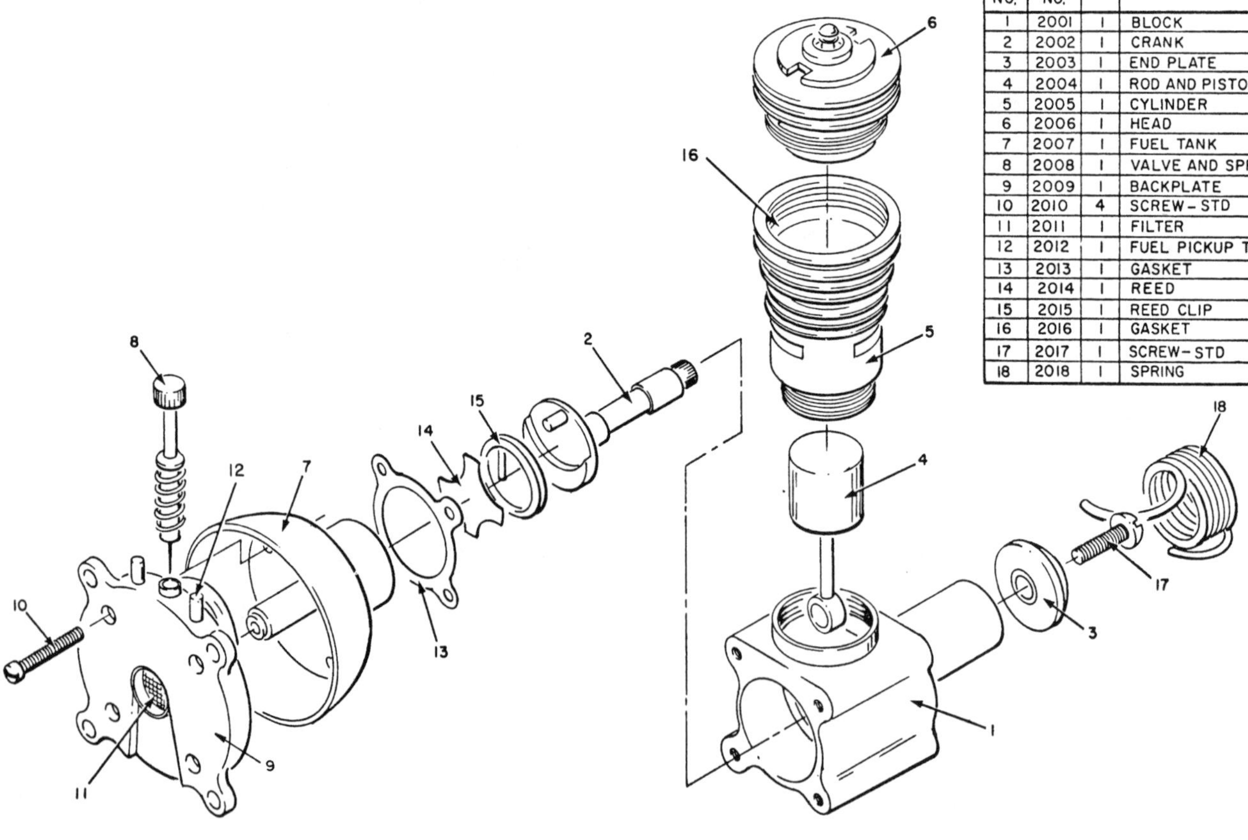

ITEM NO.	PART NO.	QTY	DESCRIPTION
1	2001	1	BLOCK
2	2002	1	CRANK
3	2003	1	END PLATE
4	2004	1	ROD AND PISTON
5	2005	1	CYLINDER
6	2006	1	HEAD
7	2007	1	FUEL TANK
8	2008	1	VALVE AND SPRING
9	2009	1	BACKPLATE
10	2010	4	SCREW - STD
11	2011	1	FILTER
12	2012	1	FUEL PICKUP TUBE
13	2013	1	GASKET
14	2014	1	REED
15	2015	1	REED CLIP
16	2016	1	GASKET
17	2017	1	SCREW - STD
18	2018	1	SPRING

FIGURE 27–9
Exploded View—Installation Manual

FIGURE 27–10
Assembly Instructions

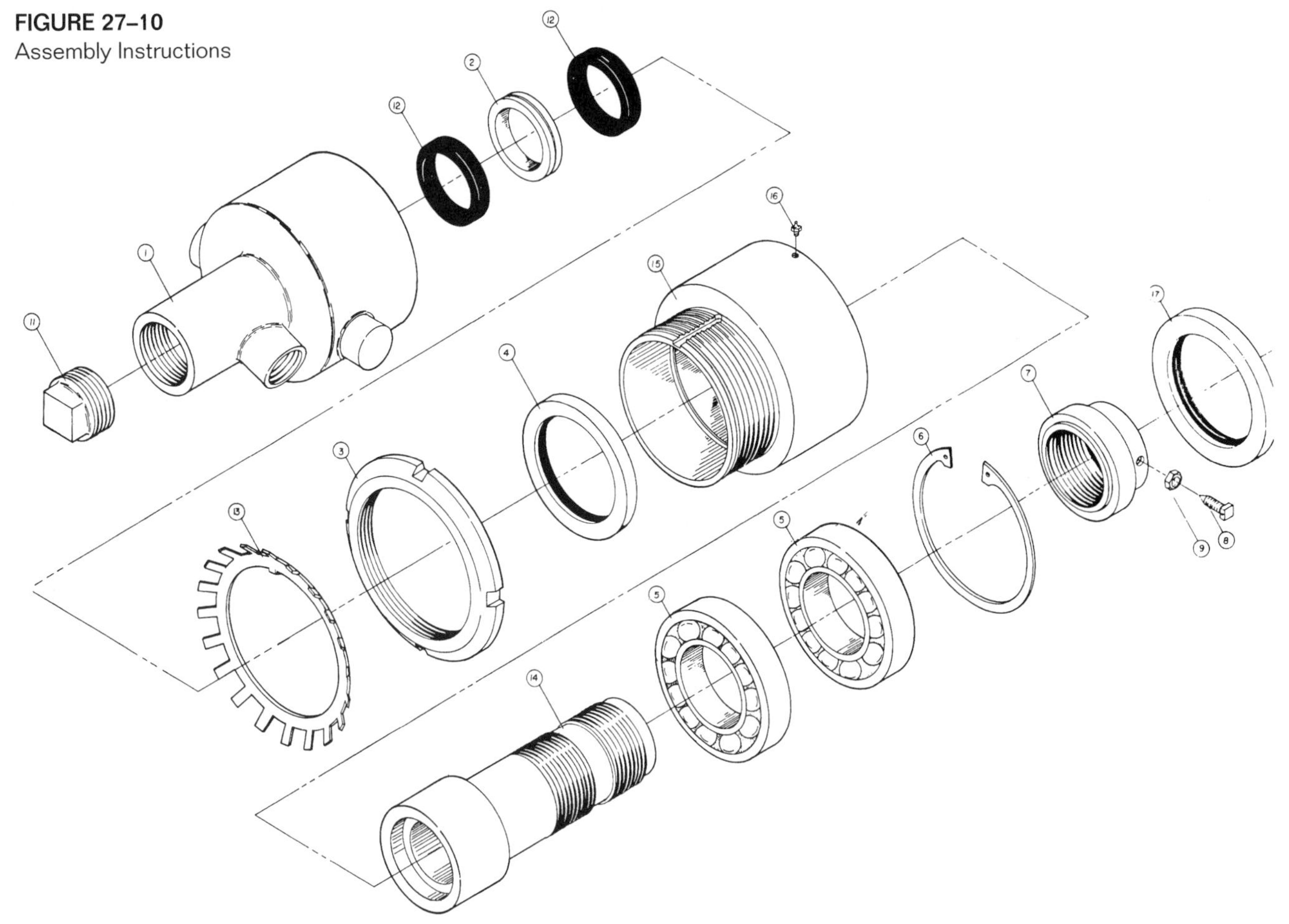

Drawing an Exploded View

Use the following three steps:

1. *Assemble information.* Figure 27–11 is an assembly drawing such as the one that would be furnished to you. Usually this is the starting point. From here, the illustrator orders detail drawings of each one of the parts. He or she gets the drawing numbers from the parts list on the assembly drawing. Often a drawing number is shown, but many times only a part number is listed. Either of these numbers can be used to get detail drawings of the individual parts.

   For the assembly shown in Figure 27–11, eight detail drawings are needed. Often, standard parts such as screws, nuts, bolts, and other fasteners do not have detail drawings. The drawing details for these parts are taken from a standards book or some other reference material such as *Machinery's Handbook* or a good drafting book.

2. *Make a thumbnail sketch.* After you get all the detail drawings (Figures 27–12 through 27–18) and fastener information, the next step is to make a thumbnail sketch of the parts in the order that they will be shown on the final drawing. Figure 27–19 is a good example of a thumbnail sketch. Little detail is shown on this sketch. Its purpose is to give you a plan for your drawing. This plan shows you how many parts you must draw and in what position they must be drawn. For example, the ellipses of item 1 of Figure 27–13 must all be drawn in the top isoplane. Item 2 has ellipses in top and left isoplanes, and item 5 has ellipses in the left isoplane only.

Note: The drawings shown in Figures 27-13 through 27-17 are dual-dimensioned. The top number on all dimensions is in inches. The bottom number is in millimeters.

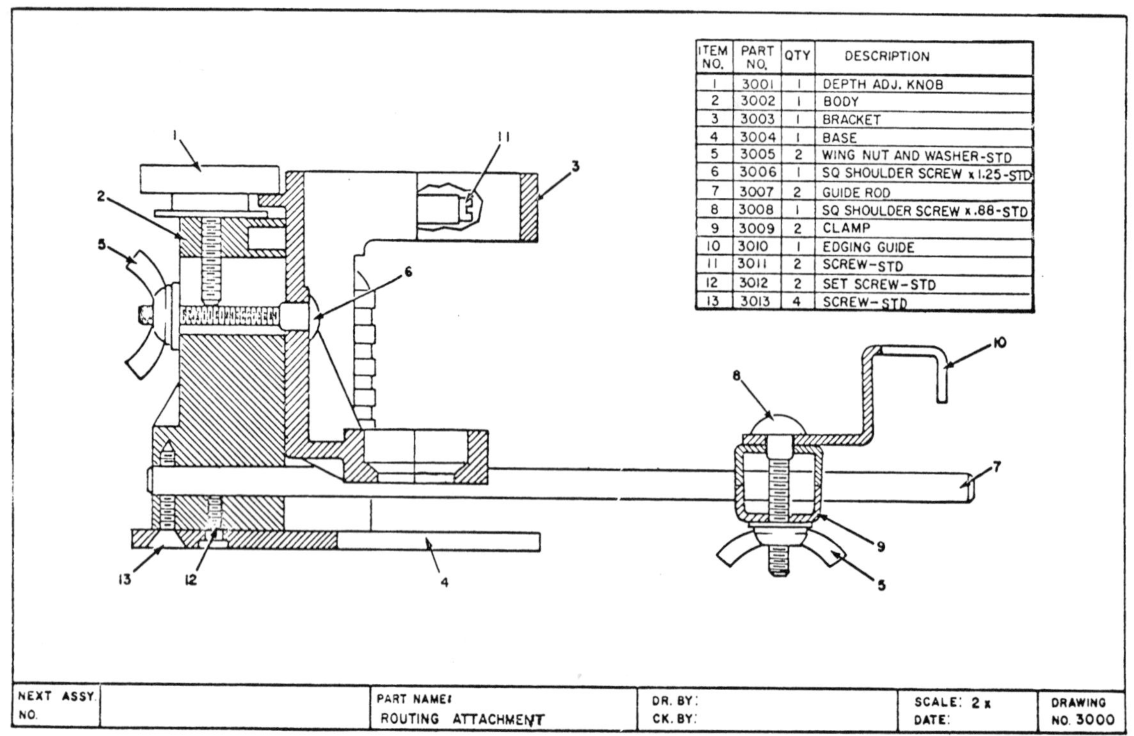

ITEM NO.	PART NO.	QTY	DESCRIPTION
1	3001	1	DEPTH ADJ. KNOB
2	3002	1	BODY
3	3003	1	BRACKET
4	3004	1	BASE
5	3005	2	WING NUT AND WASHER-STD
6	3006	1	SQ SHOULDER SCREW x 1.25-STD
7	3007	2	GUIDE ROD
8	3008	1	SQ SHOULDER SCREW x .88-STD
9	3009	2	CLAMP
10	3010	1	EDGING GUIDE
11	3011	2	SCREW-STD
12	3012	2	SET SCREW-STD
13	3013	4	SCREW-STD

FIGURE 27–11
Assembly Drawing Number 3000

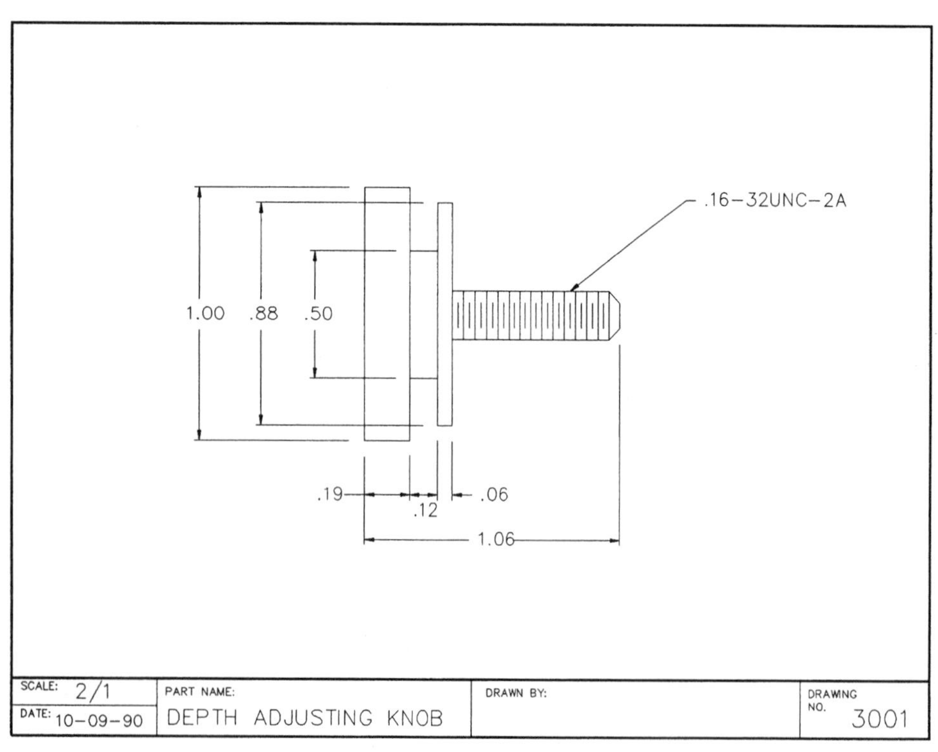

FIGURE 27–12
Detail Drawing Number 3001

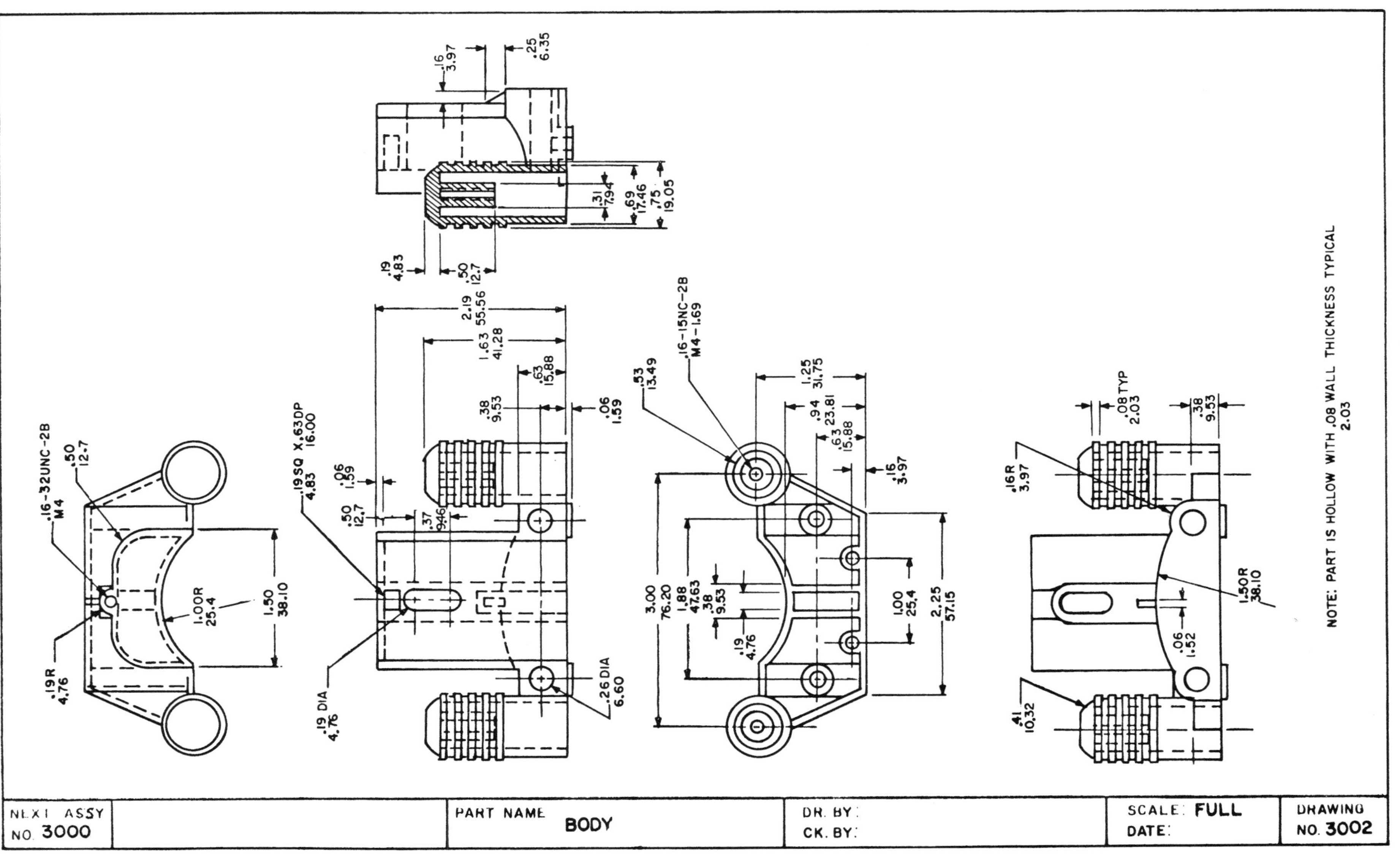

FIGURE 27–13
Detail Drawing Number 3002

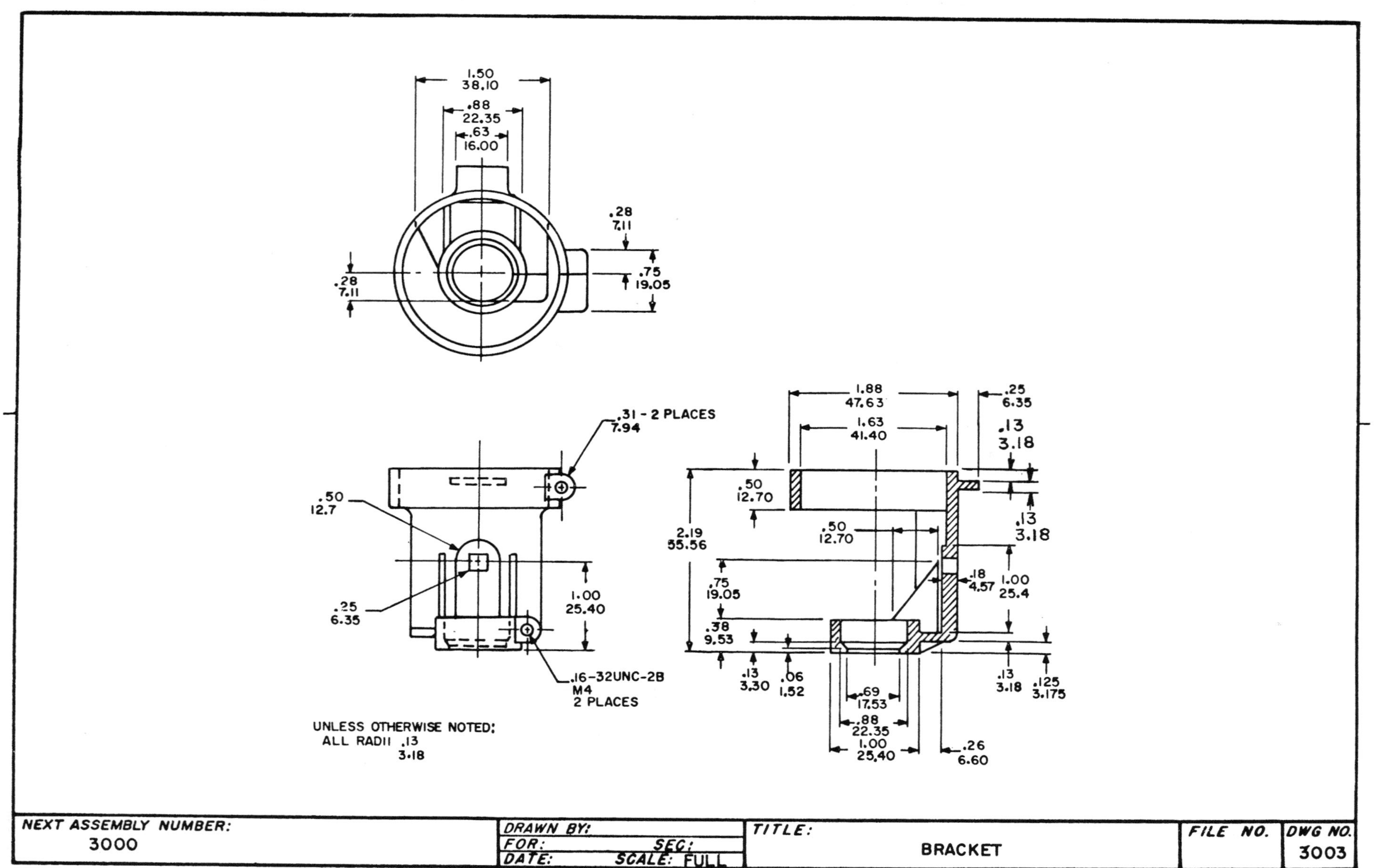

FIGURE 27–14
Detail Drawing Number 3003

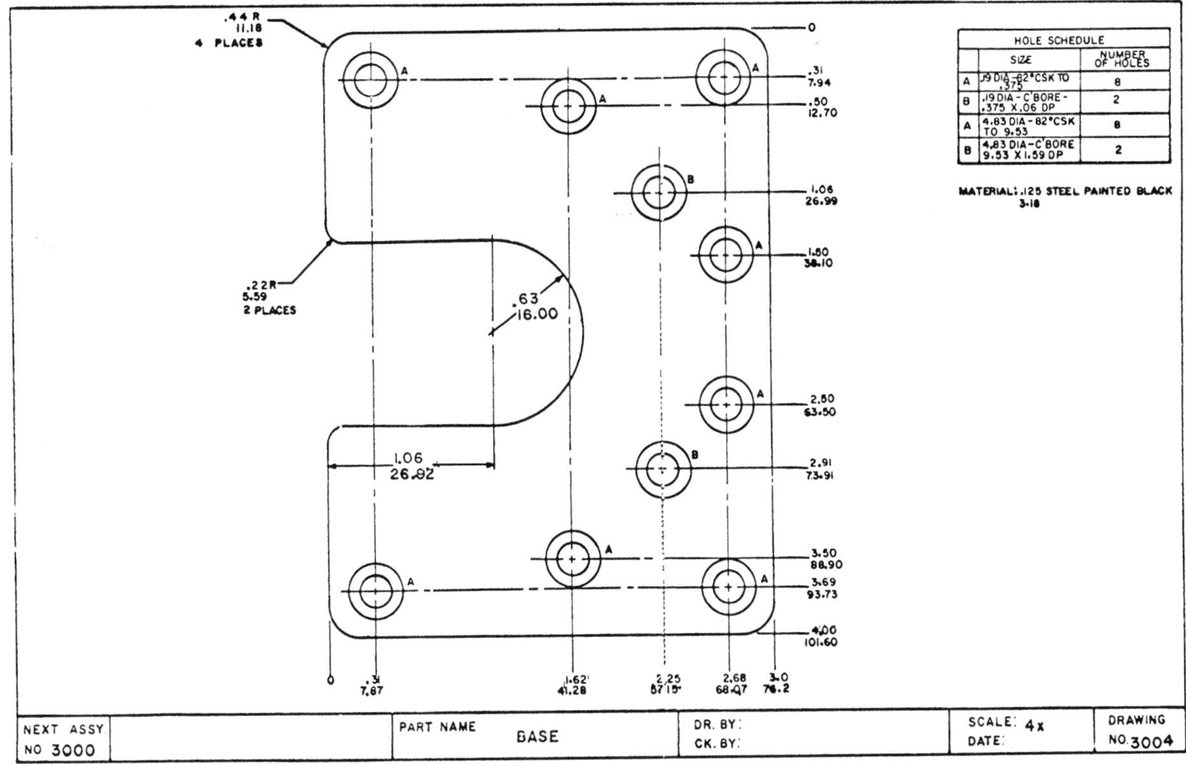

FIGURE 27–15
Detail Drawing Number 3004

FIGURE 27–16
Detail Drawing Number 3007

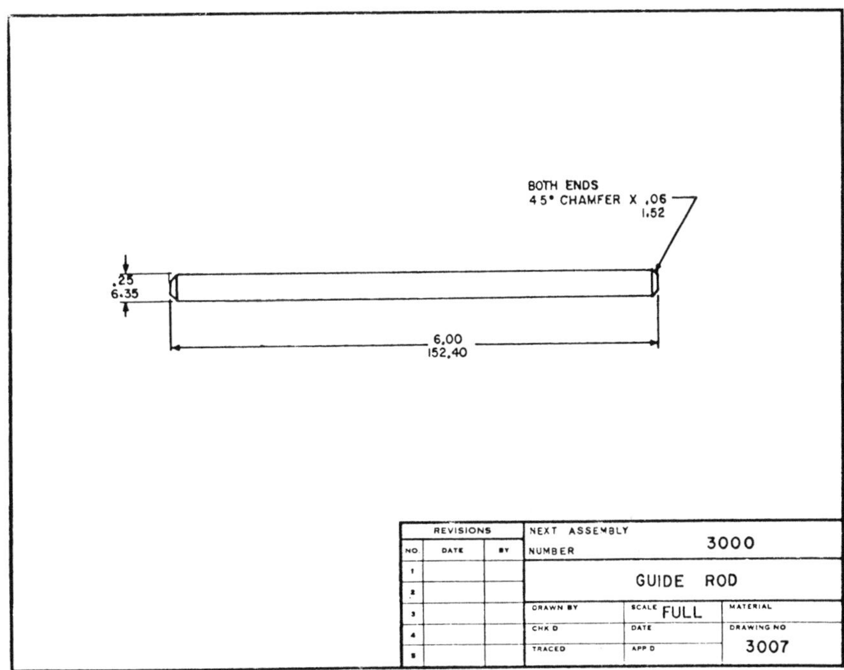

FIGURE 27–17
Detail Drawing Number 3009

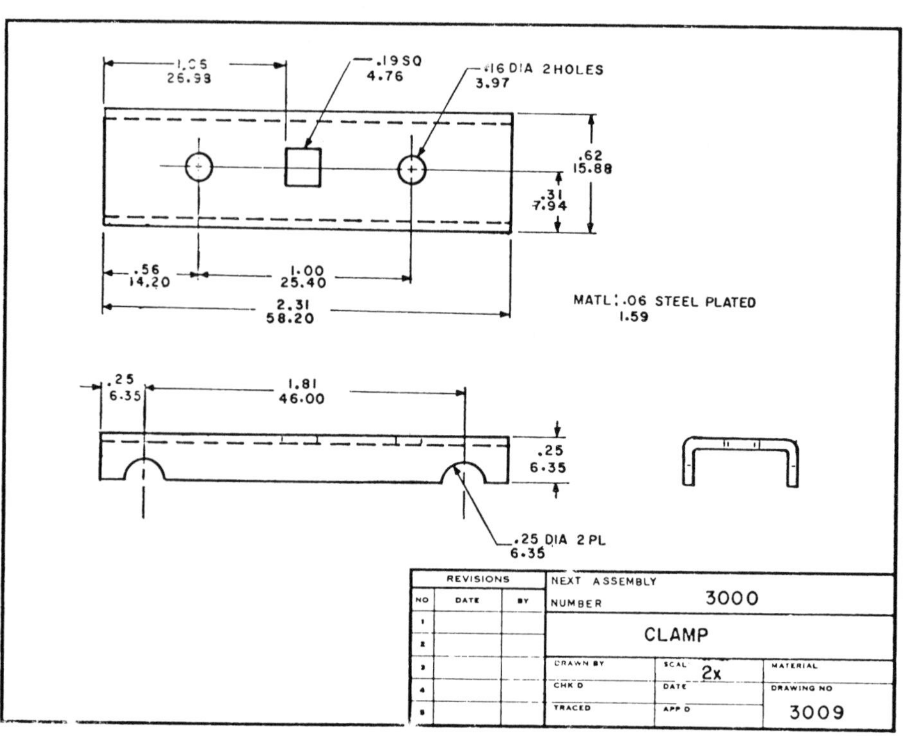

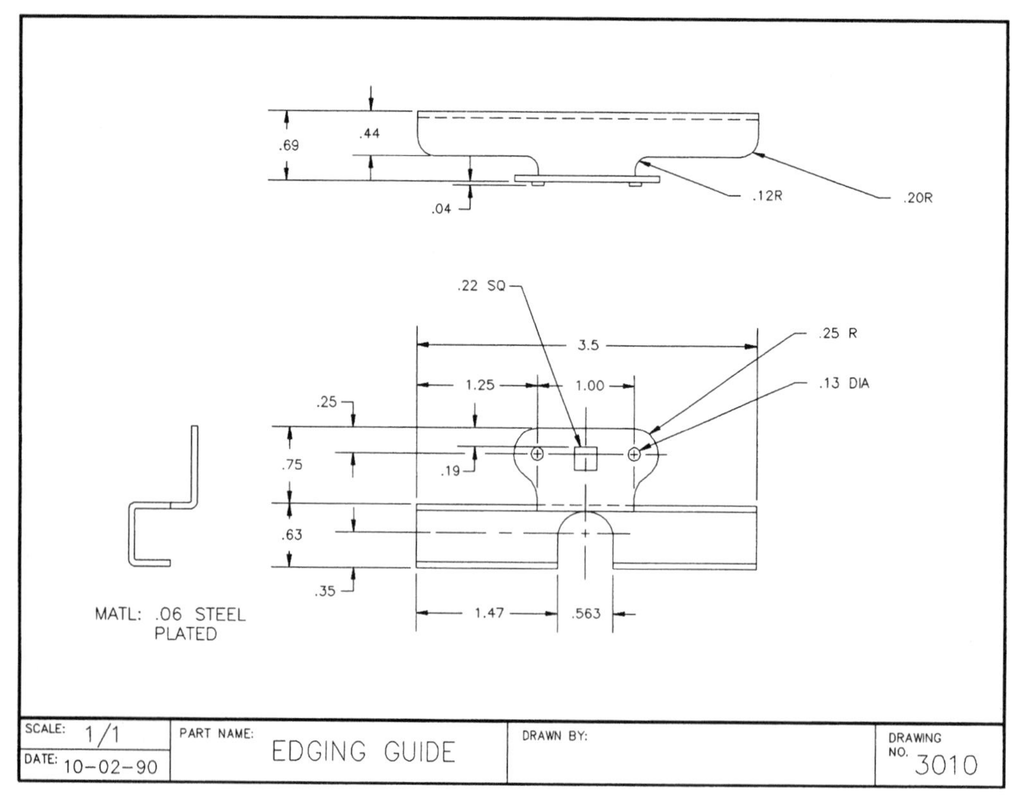

FIGURE 27–18
Detail Drawing Number 3010

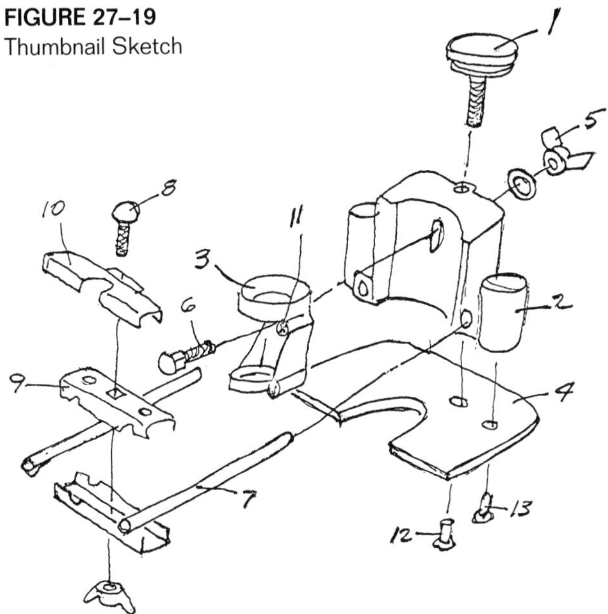

FIGURE 27–19
Thumbnail Sketch

3. *Draw individual parts.* After you reach this point, you are ready to begin drawing. Often, it is best to draw each part full scale in isometric, Save it as a separate drawing, and then Insert it into the exploded assembly. This process lets you draw quickly without having to think too much about the layout. Layouts can become very complicated. Being able to move the pieces around as blocks allows you to make a good layout of the right proportions without a lot of effort.

Sometimes you may need to overlap parts to fit them into an area of a specified size. Move the part to the desired location and then use Trim and Erase to remove any unwanted lines (Figure 27–20). Let's draw two parts and insert them into an exploded view to give you an idea of how this is done.

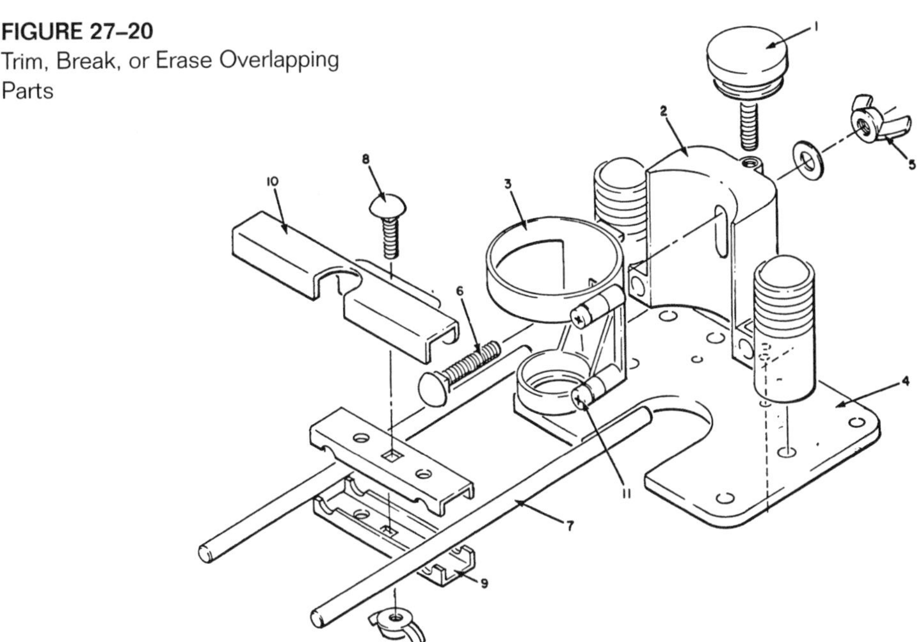

FIGURE 27–20
Trim, Break, or Erase Overlapping Parts

FIGURE 27–21
Drawing Part Number 3001

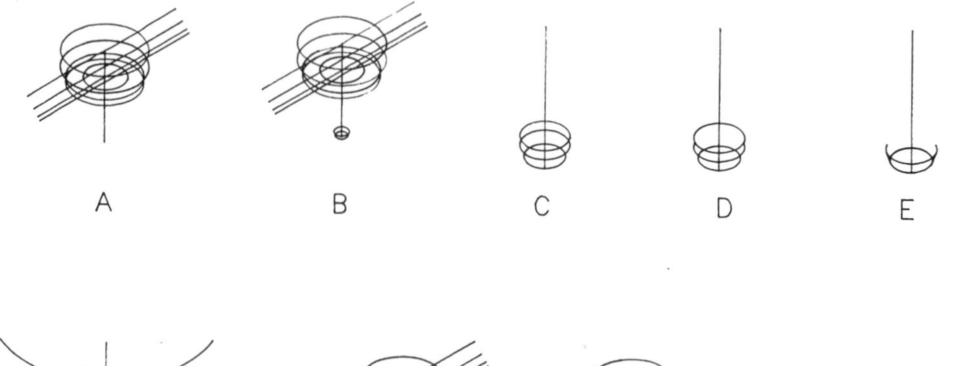

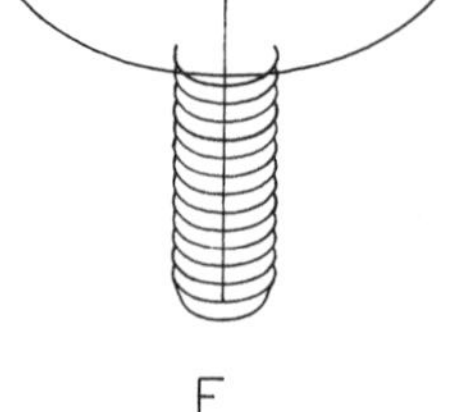

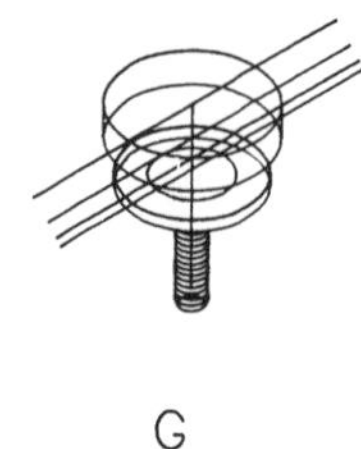

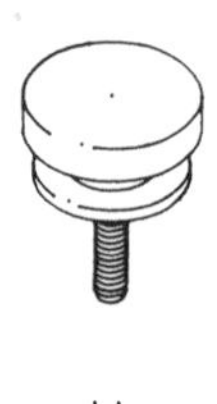

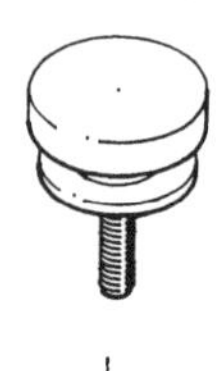

Exercise 27–1: Drawing Part Number 3001 (Figure 27–21)

Refer to Figure 27–12 (the 2-D drawing) and Figure 27–21 (the isometric drawing).

Step 1. Load AutoCAD. *Click:* **Create Drawings-Wizards-Quick Setup.**

Step 2. Make the following settings:

Units: Decimal—3 digits to the right of the decimal point
Area: Width: 7
Length: 4
SNAP: .0625
SNAP STYLE: ISO (use Ctrl-E or the function key F5 to toggle to the top isoplane)
GRID: .125

LAYERS:	NAME	Color	Linetype	Lineweight
	OBJECT	Green	Continuous	Default
	SHADOW	Yellow	Continuous	Default
	EXP	Red	Phantomx2	Default

Step 3. Draw construction lines for the centers of all ellipses with layer 0 current. Begin with one of the 30° lines (Figure 27–21A).

Prompt	Response
Command:	*Select:* **Line** (or *Type:* **L** ↵)
Specify first point:	*Click:* **on a point approximately ½″ above and 1″ to the left of the center of the drawing.**
Specify next point or [Undo]:	*Type:* **@2<30** ↵
Specify next point or [Undo]:	↵
Command:	*Select:* **Copy** (or *Type:* **CP** ↵)
Select objects:	*Click:* **on the line you just drew.**
Select objects:	↵
Specfiy base point or displacement or [Multiple]:	*Type:* **M** ↵ (or *Click:* **MULTIPLE**)

Prompt	Response
Specify base point:	*Click:* on the line
Specify second point of displacement or <use first point as displacement>:	*Type:* **@.19<−90** ↵
Specify second point of displacement or <use first point as displacement>:	*Type:* **@.31<−90** ↵ (.19 + .12 from Figure 27–12)
Specify second point of displacement or <use first point as displacement>:	*Type:* **@.37<−90** ↵ (.31 + .06 from Figure 27–12)
Specify second point of displacement or <use first point as displacement>:	↵
Command:	*Click:* **Line** (or *Type:* **L** ↵)
Specify first point:	*Click:* **Osnap-Midpoint**
Midpoint of:	*Click:* **on the top construction line**
Specify next point or [Undo]:	*Type:* @**1.06<−90** ↵ (Get dimensions from Figure 27–12.)
Specify next point or [Undo]:	↵

Step 4. Now draw all the required ellipses (Figure 27–21A and B) with layer OBJECT current.

Tip: Select running Osnap mode Intersection for ellipses.

Prompt	Response
Command:	*Click:* **Ellipse** (or *Type:* **EL** ↵)
Specify axis endpoint of ellipse or [Arc/Center/Isocircle]:	*Type:* **I** ↵
Specify center of isocircle:	*Click:* **Osnap-Intersection**
INT of	*Click:* **on the intersection of the top 30° construction line with the vertical line** (Figure 27–21A).
Specify radius of isocircle or [Diameter]:	*Type:* **D** ↵ (to select diameter or .5 for radius)
Specify diameter of isocircle:	*Type:* **1** ↵
Command:	↵ **(Repeat ELLIPSE)**
Specify axis endpoint of ellipse or [Arc/Center/Isocircle]:	*Type:* **I** ↵
Specify center of isocircle:	*Click:* **Osnap-Intersection** (*Click:* on the intersection of the second 30° line with the vertical line.)
Specify radius of isocircle or [Diameter]:	*Type:* **.5** ↵
Command:	↵ **(Repeat ELLIPSE)**
Specify axis endpoint of ellipse or [Arc/Center/Isocircle]:	*Type:* **I** ↵
Specify center of isocircle:	*Click:* **Osnap-Intersection** (*Click:* on the intersection of the third 30° construction line with the vertical line.)
Specify radius of isocircle or [Diameter]:	*Type:* **.25** ↵ (the size of the radius of the small circle on the third surface from the top)
Command:	↵ **(Repeat ELLIPSE)**
Specify axis endpoint of ellipse or [Arc/Center/Isocircle]:	*Type:* **I** ↵

Prompt	Response
Specify center of isocircle:	*Click:* **Osnap-Intersection** (*Click:* on the intersection of the third 30° construction line with the vertical line.)
Specify radius of isocircle or [Diameter]:	*Type:* **.44** ↵ (the size of the radius of the large circle on the third surface from the top)
Command:	↵
Specify axis endpoint of ellipse or [Arc/Center/Isocircle]:	*Type:* **I** ↵
Specify center of isocircle:	*Click:* **Osnap-Intersection** (*Click:* on the intersection of the fourth 30° construction line with the vertical line.)
Specify radius of isocircle or [Diameter]:	*Type:* **.44** ↵
Command:	↵
Specify axis endpoint of ellipse or [Arc/Center/Isocircle]:	*Type:* **I** ↵
Specify center of isocircle:	*Click:* **Osnap-Endpoint** (*Click:* on the lower end of the vertical line (Figure 27–21B).)
Specify radius of isocircle or [Diameter]:	*Type:* **.07** ↵ (the size of the radius on the chamfered end of the thread)
Command:	↵
Specify axis endpoint of ellipse or [Arc/Center/Isocircle]:	*Type:* **I** ↵
Specify center of isocircle:	*Click:* **Osnap-Nearest** (*Click:* on a point approximately 1⁄16″ up from the lower end of the vertical line.)
Specify radius of isocircle or [Diameter]:	*Type:* **.08** ↵ (½ of the .16 shown on the thread specification .16-32UNC-2A; .16 is the thread diameter.)

Note: Draw all ellipses in the Top isoplane. Draw as many construction lines as you need and use Osnap-Midpoint and Intersection for ellipse centers. Use Trim to remove the front part of the ellipses.

Tip: Remember to draw a centerline for constructing all cylindrical parts. Draw all ellipses on the same centerlines.

Now all the ellipses are drawn. The remaining tasks are as follows:

- □ Array threads.
- □ Draw lines connecting the ellipses.
- □ Create any necessary distortion for a clearer illustration.
- □ Trim or Erase unneeded lines.
- □ Add highlights and shadows.
- □ Save the drawing with the name 3001.

Step 5. Array threads. Before the threads can be arrayed, the ellipse forming the thread must be trimmed correctly.

Prompt	Response
Command:	*Click:* **Copy** (or *Type:* **CP** ↵)
Select objects:	*Click:* **on the .19-diameter ellipse (Figure 27–21C).** ↵
Specify basepoint or displacement or [Multiple]:	*Click:* **on the center of the ellipse using Osnap-Center.**
Specify second point of displacement or <use first point as displacement>:	*Type:* **@.04<90** ↵
Command:	*Click:* **Trim** (or *Type:* **TR** ↵)
Select cutting edges:	*Click:* **on the upper thread.** ↵

Prompt	Response
Select object to trim or shift-select to extend or [Project/Edge/Undo]:	*Click:* **on the back of the lower thread (Figure 27–21D)** ↵
Command:	*Click:* **Erase** (or *Type:* **E** ↵)
Select objects:	*Click:* **on the upper thread ellipse (Figure 27–21E)** ↵
Command:	*Type:* **-AR** ↵
Select objects:	*Click:* **on the trimmed thread (Figure 27–21F).**
Enter the type of array [Rectangular/Polar]<R>:	*Type:* **R** ↵
Enter the number of rows (- - - -) <1>:	*Type:* **10** ↵
Enter the number of columns (111) <1>:	↵
Enter the distance between rows or specify unit cell (- - - -):	*Type:* **.04** ↵

Note: *Type:* **AR** ↵ (without the minus to use the Array dialog box).

Step 6. Draw lines connecting ellipses (Figure 27–21F and G). You will have to Zoom in on the ellipses. Use Line and Osnap-Endpoint to draw these lines. Ellipses are constructed in several segments, so Osnap-Endpoint allows you to pick the end of the segment that forms the outermost part of the ellipse.

Step 7. Create any distortions you believe are necessary to provide a clearer drawing (Figure 27–21G). In this case the threads and the lower three ellipses of the knob were moved down a little (about .1), so that the smaller ellipse forming the shoulder shows. You may not choose to do this, but this example is used to demonstrate that distortion is acceptable and sometimes is necessary to clarify details.

Step 8. Break two of the uppermost ellipses and draw a POINT to form highlights (Figure 27–21H). You may have trouble using Break on these ellipses. Whether you pick the ends of the BREAK clockwise or counterclockwise, the ellipse often does not appear as you think it should. You may need to break the ellipse at the same point in two places and then use Erase to remove the highlight.

Step 9. Create highlights on the threads (Figure 27–21I). Draw two construction lines approximately .05 apart and use Trim to remove a section of the threads to form a highlight on the threads. Erase the construction lines when you finish trimming.

Step 10. Add shadows with layer SHADOW current (Figure 27–21I). Use the Properties. . . command to change lines on the right side and bottom of the drawing to another layer (SHADOW). Use a thicker black pen for SHADOW LAYER pen location on your plotter to obtain the thick line.

Step 11. Print the drawing full scale on an 8.5″ × 11″ sheet.

Step 12. Save the drawing in two places with the name 3001 and Exit AutoCAD.

Exercise 27–2: Drawing Part Number 3004 (Bottom View)

Refer to Figure 27–15 (the 2-D drawing) and Figure 27–22 (the isometric drawing).

Step 1. Load AutoCAD. Open the drawing 3001 and save it as 3004. (This will allow you to use the settings from 3001.)

Use Ctrl-E or F5 to toggle to the TOP isoplane.

Prompt	Response
Command:	*Click:* **Erase**
Select objects:	*Type:* **ALL** ↵

FIGURE 27–22
Drawing Part Number 3004

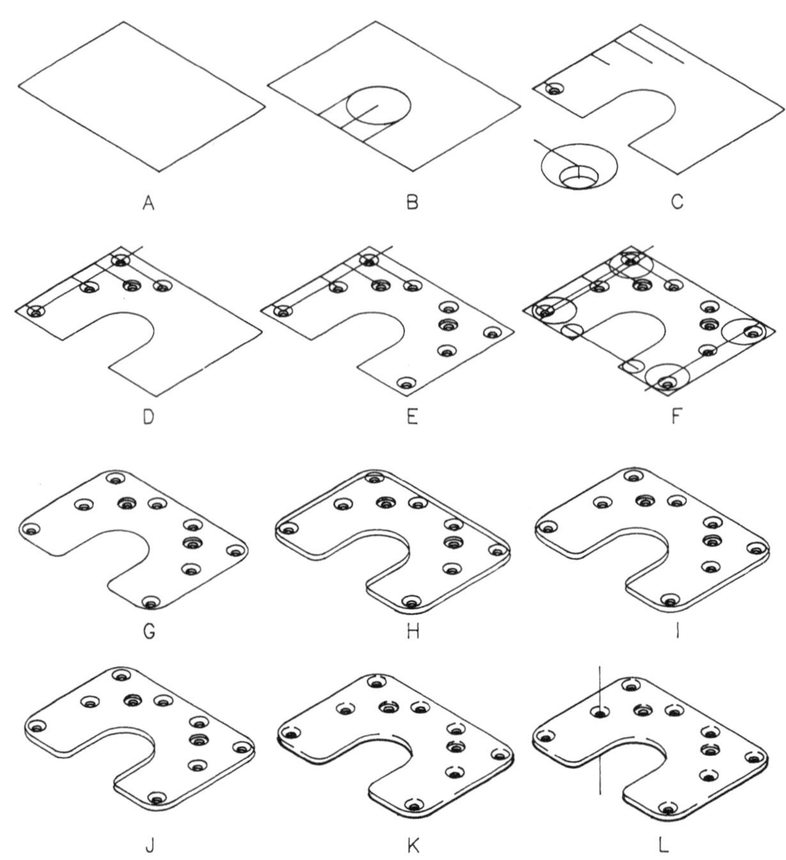

Step 2. Draw the outer lines of the base (Figure 27–22A) with layer OBJECT current.

Prompt	Response
Command:	*Click:* **Line** (or *Type:* **L** ↵)
Specify first point:	*Click:* **on a convenient point for the upper left corner of the base.**
Specify next point or [Undo]:	*Type:* **@3<30** ↵
Specify next point or [Undo]:	*Type:* **@4<150** ↵
Specify next point or [Close/Undo]:	*Type:* **@3<210** ↵
Specify next point or [Close/Undo]:	*Type:* **C** ↵

Step 3. Draw the large ellipse (Figure 27–22B).

Note: Draw all ellipses in the TOP isoplane. Draw as many construction lines as you need and use Osnap-Midpoint and Intersection for ellipse centers. Use Trim to remove the front parts of the ellipses.

Prompt	Response
Command:	*Click:* **Ellipse** (or *Type:* **EL** ↵)
Specify axis endpoint of ellipse or [Arc/Center/Isocircle]:	*Type:* **I** ↵
Specify center of isocircle:	*Click:* **Osnap-From**
Base point:	*Click:* **on the front long line using Osnap-Midpoint**
<Offset>:	*Type:* @**1.06<30** ↵
Specify radius of isocircle or [Diameter]:	*Type:* **.63** (from Figure 27–15) ↵

Step 4. Draw lines to form the edges of the slot (Figure 27–22B). Use Osnap-Endpoint, or quadrant, then draw the edge past the outer line of the base with ORTHO ON. (Perpendicular will give you a 90° angle, which is not what you want.) Use Erase and Trim to remove unnecessary lines.

Step 5. Draw construction lines for the other holes (Figure 27–22C) and draw ELLIPSEs for the first hole. Notice that the construction line for the first countersunk hole has a short vertical line to locate the depth of the countersink. The bottom of the hole may be copied from the ellipse drawn at the endpoint of the vertical line. Use Trim to erase uneeded line segments.

Step 6. Copy the countersunk holes from the endpoint of the first construction line to the endpoints of the other construction lines using Osnap-Endpoint (Figure 27–22D). Notice that one of the holes is a counterbore, not a countersink, and requires a slightly different procedure.

Step 7. Draw or copy construction lines in a similar manner for holes on the right side of the base (Figure 27–22E). (Mirror won't give you what you want.)

Step 8. Draw ellipses and then Trim at all corners to form fillets (Figure 27–22F and G). (Fillet doesn't give you an Isometric fillet.) Erase construction lines.

Step 9. Copy the outside lines of the base to form the metal thickness (@.125< −90) (Figure 27–22H).

Step 10. Erase the back edge of the metal thickness or don't copy it (Figure 27–22I).

Step 11. Draw vertical lines from ellipses to show metal thickness (Figure 27–22J).

Step 12. Break lines to form major highlights (Figure 27–22K). Add shadows using the Properties. . . command to change the shadow lines to the shadow layer (Figure 27–22L).

Step 13. Draw an explosion line through the center of the second countersunk hole to locate the insertion point for part 3002 when you draw and insert that part. (Layer EXP must be current.)

Step 14. Save the drawing in two places with the name 3004 and Exit AutoCAD.

Exercise 27–3: Drawing the Exploded View (Figures 27–23 and 27–20)

Tip: Remember to draw a center line for constructing all cylindrical parts. Draw all ellipses on the same center lines.

The exploded view itself may be constructed after all the individual parts are drawn. You may find it helpful to make this drawing equal to one of the detail parts so that you don't have to make all the settings again. It is probably best to Erase the detail and then Insert the detail drawing again so that it may be moved as a block.

Step 1. Load AutoCAD, open drawing 3001, and save it as 3000.

FIGURE 27–23
Drawing the Exploded View

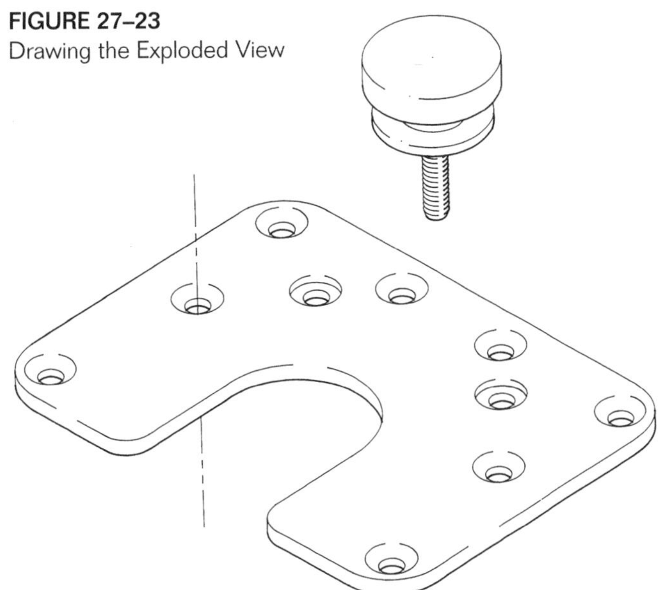

Step 2. Make the following settings:

LIMITS: 17,11			
LAYERS:	NAME	Color	Linetype
	CALLOUTS	Cyan	Continuous
	PARTS-LIST	Blue	Continuous

Step 3. Erase the existing drawing and insert parts.

Prompt	Response
Command:	*Click:* **Erase** (Erase the entire drawing.) ↵
Command:	*Click:* **Insert**

Tip: Zoom in on all areas where Trim or Break is to be used. Use Offset to get a temporary trim line. Erase the offset line after you have trimmed overlapped parts, leaders, or expansion lines.

Insert 3001 and 3004 at a convenient location and move them as needed. Explode and use Erase and Trim after all parts are in position, as shown in Figure 27–20.

Modify drawing 3004 so that the plate shows the counterbores and countersinks from the opposite side as shown in Figure 27–20.

After the drawing is done, you may have to Trim or Break lines where parts overlap and where leaders and explosion lines are drawn (Figure 27–20).

Now let's consider explosion lines, leaders, index numbers, and parts lists one at a time.

Step 4. Add explosion lines with layer EXP current.

Help: If the Phantomx2 Linetype appears continuous, change LTSCALE to .5 or less. *Type:* **LTSCALE** ↵, or pick it from the menu.

Explosion lines are lines that show how the parts fit together. They are thin and have a long dash and two short dashes (the Phantomx2 linetype is fine). You can think of them as a string on which the parts hang. Figure 27–24 shows how they look as they go through several parts. Notice that they go through the entire visible part of any hole. They may sometimes be shown in a hidden form if there are several together and a possibility of confusion exists. These lines are always drawn on isometric axes except in very rare cases. They stay solid when they pass through object lines. The object line is broken where the explosion line passes. Set layer EXP current, then draw all explosion lines. After the explosion lines are completed, the drawing must be reduced to the size at which it will be printed before index numbers and leaders are added. This makes it easy to keep the height of index numbers uniform throughout a book.

Most technical manuals have standard page sizes that make the process of merging text and art a little easier. For most illustrations, these sizes become the LIMITS of a

FIGURE 27–24
Explosion Lines

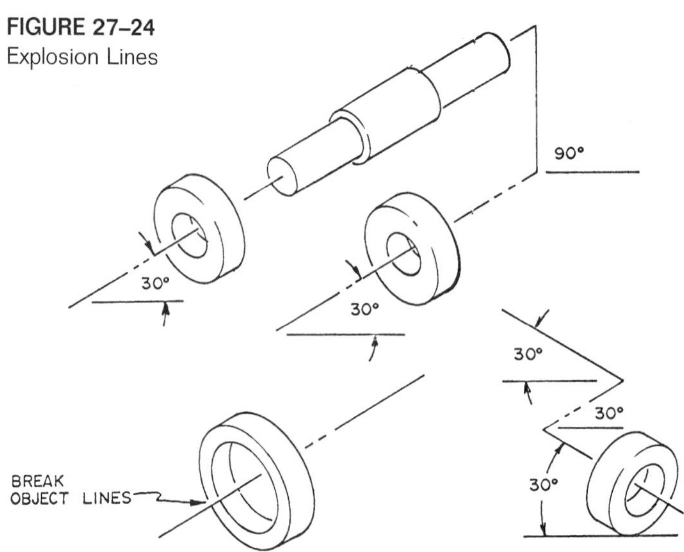

FIGURE 27–25
Standard Illustration Sizes

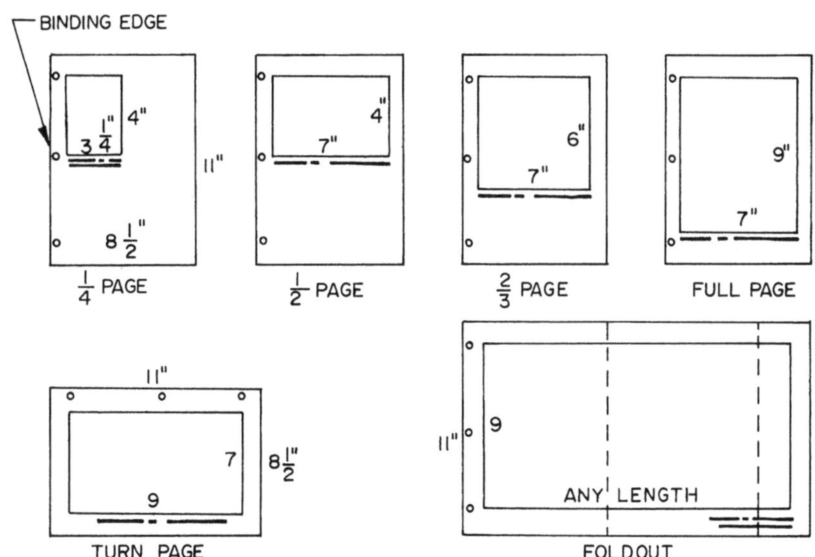

drawing. This drawing is then inserted into a page that has been created with a desktop publishing program.

Step 5. Reduce the drawing to a standard size.

Although different publishers use different sizes, the sizes that follow are common: Standard illustration sizes for 8½″ × 11″ printed pages are 4″ × 7″, 6″ × 7″, and 8¾″ × 7″. Turn pages are 6¾″ × 9″, and foldout pages are 8¾″ high by whatever length is needed. The 3¼″ × 4″ size is called a ¼ page, the 4″ × 7″ size is called a ½ page, etc. Figure 27–25 shows these illustration sizes on printed pages of an 8½″ × 11″ book. Notice that there is a margin at the top, right, and left. Room is left at the bottom of the illustration for a figure title.

Now reduce the drawing shown in Figure 27–20 to a ½-page size (4″ × 7″) before adding leaders and callouts. Change LIMITS to 7,4 and center the drawing within this area. (Make sure the drawing is smaller than 7″ × 4″ so that callouts can be added within that area.)

Step 6. Add leaders with layer CALLOUTS current.

Leaders are the lines that lead from the index number to the part (Figure 27–26). Some have arrows; some do not. Some just touch the part; some break the part. Here again, you have to find out what the customer wants. If he or she doesn't know, use what you think looks good.

The following guidelines for leaders are often used and also meet most military and commercial specifications:

- □ Medium thickness—no arrowhead
- □ As short as practical
- □ Placed at angles between 15° and 75° (None should be horizontal, vertical, or on one of the isometric axes. A fan arrangement is good.)

FIGURE 27–26
Index Numbers and Leaders

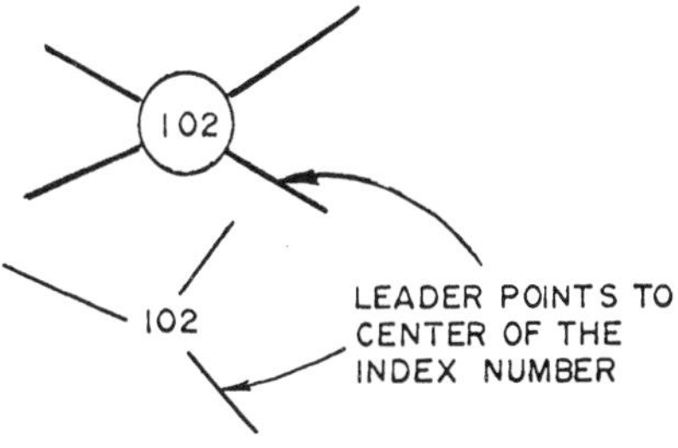

- □ Placed to just break the part about 1⁄16″
- □ Drawn with a break above the leader
- □ Pointed to the center of the index number

Step 7. Add index numbers (callouts) with layer CALLOUTS current.

Index numbers are numbers that label the parts so they can be identified on a parts list. Schemes to number the parts clockwise or counterclockwise, left to right, or top to bottom can work if there are no changes to the drawing. Usually, though, the numbers get out of order on a drawing with many parts. Your best bet is to start with a plan and hope it works.

On small drawings, such as the ones you will work with in this book, the clockwise numbering scheme is fine. Sometimes the index number becomes a complete description, and sometimes phrases are used. Figure 27–27 shows some index numbers and how they are arranged. They can be used either with or without balloons (circles around them). If balloons are used, their diameter is usually three times the height of the index number. *Be sure that all index numbers are straight (horizontal) and in line, and use an acceptable font.*

For the assignments in this chapter use:

- □ Font: SIMPLEX
- □ Height: .1
- □ Leader with arrowhead
- □ No balloon
- □ DIMSCALE: .5

Chapter 17 contains a customized menu that allows you to insert the leader, balloon, and index number with a single click. If you are not using an arrowhead, the Line command with SNAP ON is easier than using Leader from the Dimension menu. If phrases are used, be sure they are flush left or flush right as needed. Dtext makes this very easy to do. The leader should point to the center of the phrase.

Step 8. Print the drawing full scale on an 8.5″ × 11″ sheet.

Step 9. Save the drawing in two places and exit AutoCAD.

FIGURE 27–27
Index Numbers (Callouts)

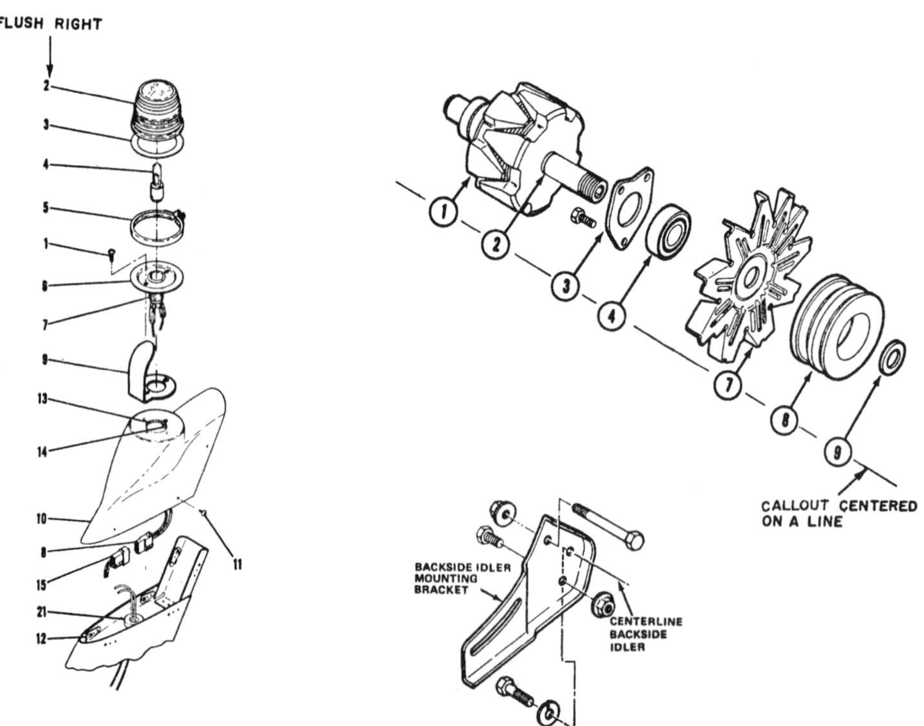

Parts List

The parts list contains the descriptions that identify the parts so they can be ordered or worked with in some way. They have several forms, but most of them look like the following:

Index Number	Part Number	Quantity	Description
1	10050	2 ea.	Wheels ½″ dia.
2	L0326	6 ea.	Springs

Often these lists are on the same page as the illustration. Sometimes they are on another page, but they are usually close together. They are sometimes done by the illustrator. When you make a parts list, be sure that it is not crowded. The space between lines on the parts list is usually three times the height of the lettering between the lines.

Summary

Exploded views usually have these elements:

□ Parts
□ Explosion lines
□ Index numbers
□ Leaders
□ Parts lists

They are drawn in these steps:

□ Get an assembly drawing.
□ Get details of individual parts.
□ Make a thumbnail sketch.
□ Draw parts on separate drawings in isometric using a single-line shading technique.
□ Insert parts in position on an isometric explosion line.
□ Reduce the drawing to the correct page size using Scale.
□ Add explosion lines, leader lines, index numbers, and parts list.
□ Clean up lines on overlapping parts and over leaders and explosion lines using Trim or Break.
□ Check the drawing for accuracy and correct mistakes.

Now, let's move on to cutaways.

CUTAWAYS

Cutaway drawings are among the most impressive of technical illustrations. They are used in many different types of publications, such as advertising pieces, spec sheets, and repair manuals. Examples of cutaway drawings are shown in Figures 27–28 through 27–30.

Although cutaways are impressive drawings and can take a lot of time if the assembly has many parts, they are not difficult. The main thing to remember when drawing cutaways is to complete one part at a time and make sure parts are in the right position. The drawing shown in Figure 27–30 is an excellent example of a complex cutaway. However, study a few individual parts for a moment and you will quickly see that there is nothing here that you have not drawn or could not draw if you knew the shape and size of the part.

There are a few rules and details, however, that will help you with drawing cutaways. The steps listed next cover those rules and details.

Steps for Cutaway Drawing

1. Determine surfaces to be cut.
2. Make a sketch.

FIGURE 27–28
Advertising Cutaway

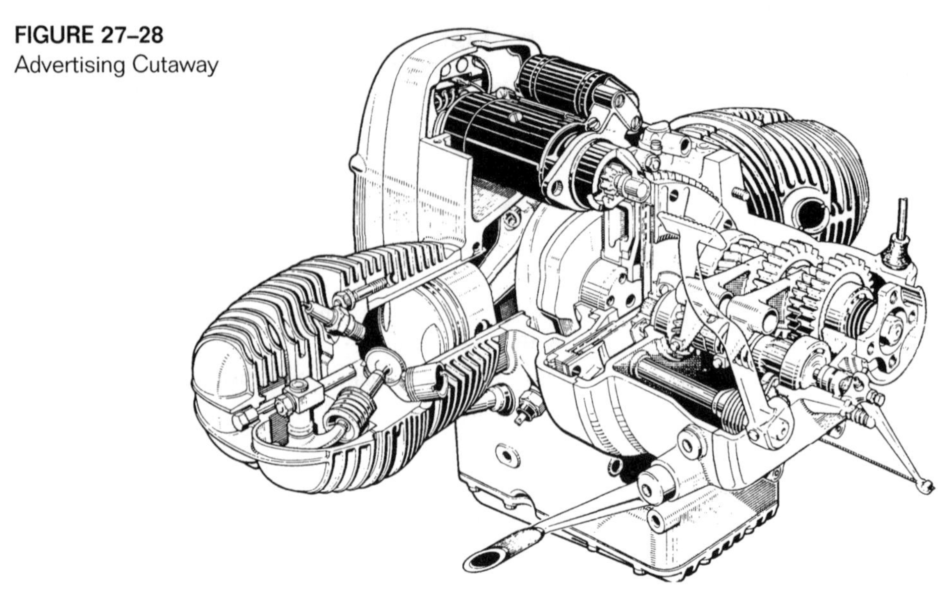

FIGURE 27–29
Architectural Cutaway

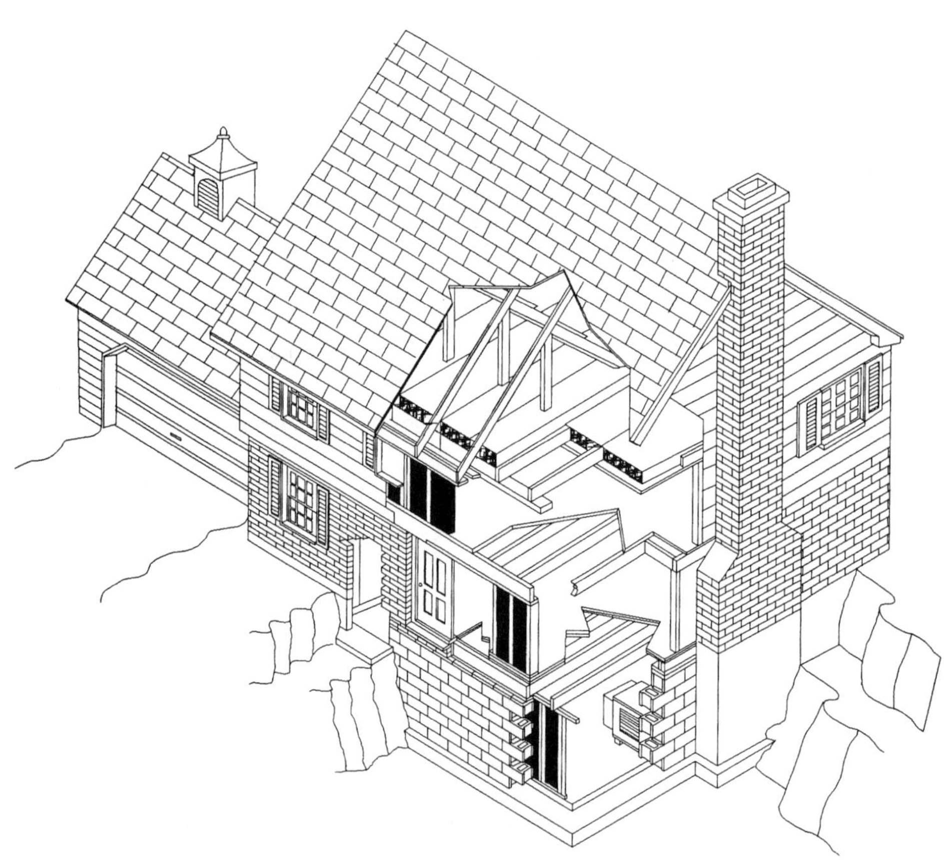

FIGURE 27–30
Mechanical Cutaway

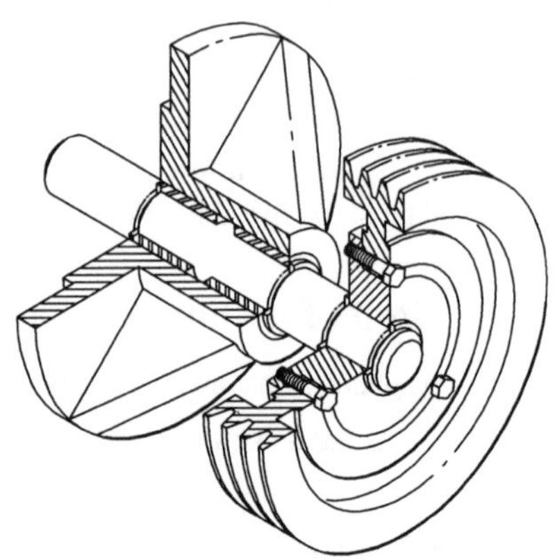

3. Start a new drawing and make settings.
4. Draw cut surfaces.
5. Draw full shapes.
6. Add highlights and shadows.
7. Add shading to cut surfaces.
8. Add callouts.

Now, let's examine each step in detail.

Exercise 27–4: Drawing a Cutaway View

Step 1. Determine surfaces to be cut.

Find out exactly what the drawing is trying to show. When you know the parts to be shown and the correct position, you can determine which surfaces should be cut and how deep the cut should be. If, for example, the drawing in Figure 27–31 were to be shown as a cutaway and your instructions were to show how the vacuum switch works, a cut completely across the upper and lower housing through the magnet and the diaphragm should be used. To show less would hide some of the internal parts that reveal how the switch functions.

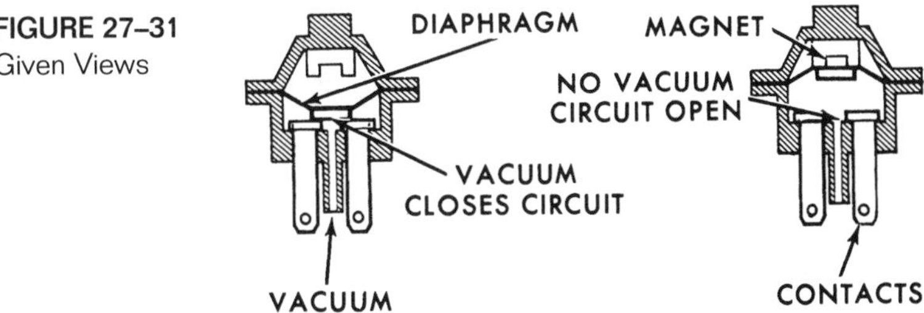

FIGURE 27–31
Given Views

Step 2. Make a freehand sketch.

Making a freehand sketch (Figure 27–32) allows you to decide which isometric position to use and to make the correct decision about which surfaces to cut. This sketch confirms that a full cut across the part is needed to show both contacts. Also, it shows that the top isoplane is a good position for the drawing because it shows how the part functions.

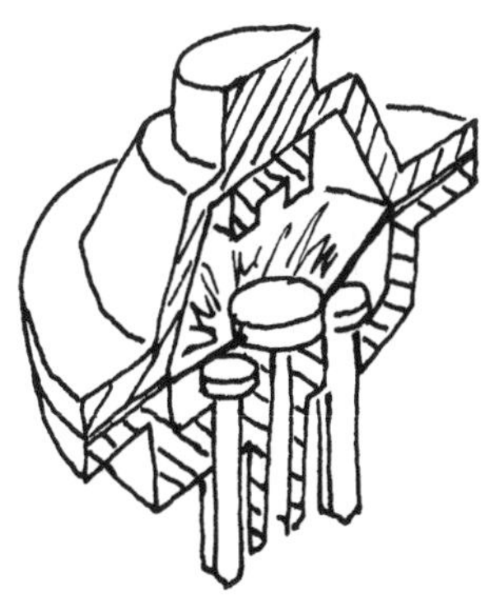

FIGURE 27–32
Freehand Sketch

Step 3. Load AutoCAD, open drawing 3000, and save it to the hard drive with the name CUTAWAY (to use settings from drawing 3000; if you have not drawn 3000, use the settings shown for that drawing).

Step 4. Make the following setting:

LAYERS:	NAME	Color	Linetype	Lineweight
	SHADE	Red	Continuous	Default

Erase all of drawing 3000 that is now CUTAWAY and continue with step 5.

Step 5. Draw cut surfaces.

Tip: If you draw a vertical line through the center of the cut surfaces, you will easily be able to locate the ellipse centers. Then drag their radii to end on the cut surfaces and Trim what you don't need.

Usually, it is best to draw the cut surfaces first (Figure 27–33). However, sometimes some of the parts that are not cut must be drawn first. You will discover that as you proceed through the drawing. Notice that the cut surfaces were drawn just as they appear on the flat views except that isometric angles have now taken the place of horizontal and vertical lines. Measure the drawing as shown in Figure 27–33 and draw it twice size.

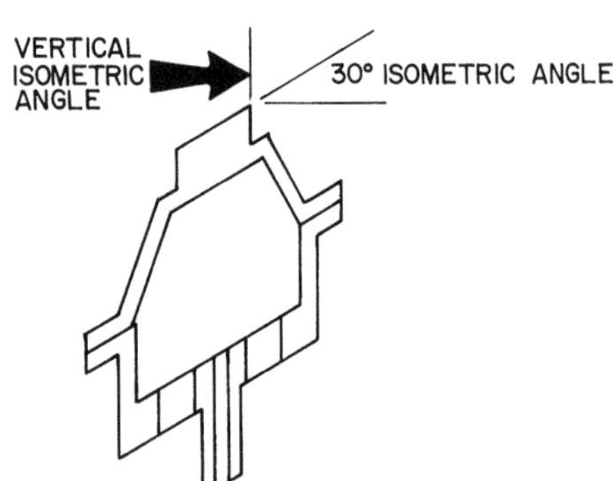

FIGURE 27–33
Draw Cut Surfaces

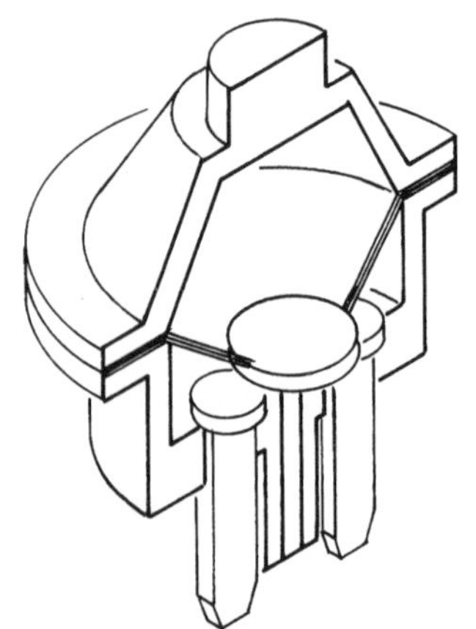

FIGURE 27–34
Draw Full Shapes

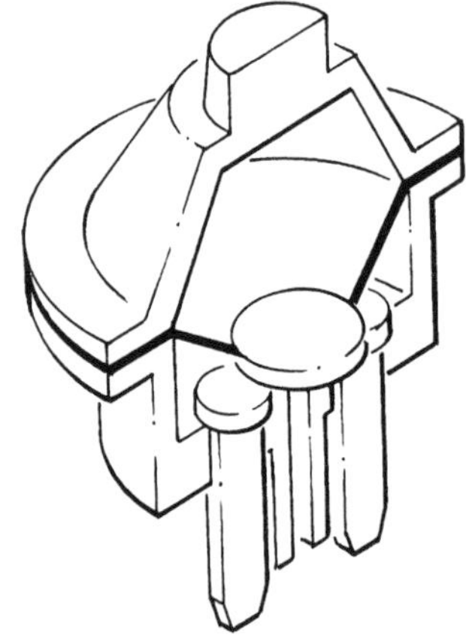

FIGURE 27–35
Add Highlights and Shadows

Step 6. Draw full shapes.

Draw the full ellipses and other shapes, then trim them and complete the uncut parts inside the cut surfaces (Figure 27–34). Here you must be sure that the parts are shown in their correct positions, which you can determine by measuring. If they are in the correct position and still do not show clearly what is intended, do not hesitate to distort dimensions or make additional cuts as long as parts do not get too far out of proportion.

Step 7. Add highlights and shadows.

Use the single-line shading technique to add highlights and shadows (Figure 27–35). The highlights and shadows shown in this figure are about all this drawing requires. If your drawing is a little different, that's probably fine as long as you followed the rules described in this chapter.

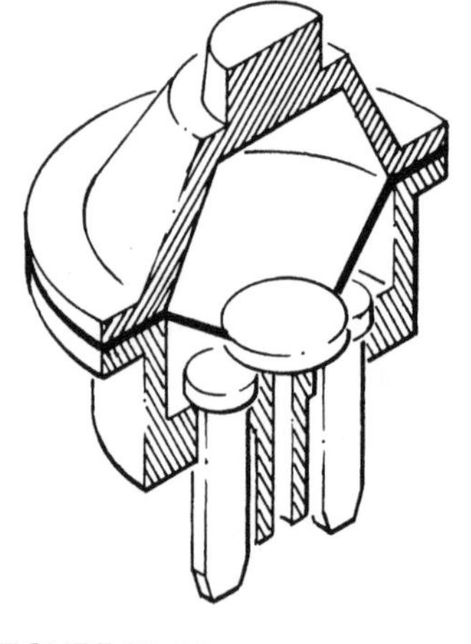

FIGURE 27–36
Add Hatching to Cut Surfaces

Step 8. Add shading to cut surfaces.

In Figure 27–36, a uniform hatch pattern was used on the cut surfaces that looks fine. Notice that the shading lines are at steep angles of 60° in opposite directions (60° and −60°). It is important to make these lines different from isometric angles because they can easily be confused with object lines. A dot pattern works better if there are lots of parts with lines. If the outer surfaces of the object are shaded, no shading is shown on the cut surfaces. The examples shown later in this chapter illustrate these points.

Step 9. Add callouts.

Notice that the lettering in the callout is lined up horizontally (Figure 27–37). The letter end of the leader points to the center of the line of lettering, and the object end just breaks

FIGURE 27–37
Add Callouts

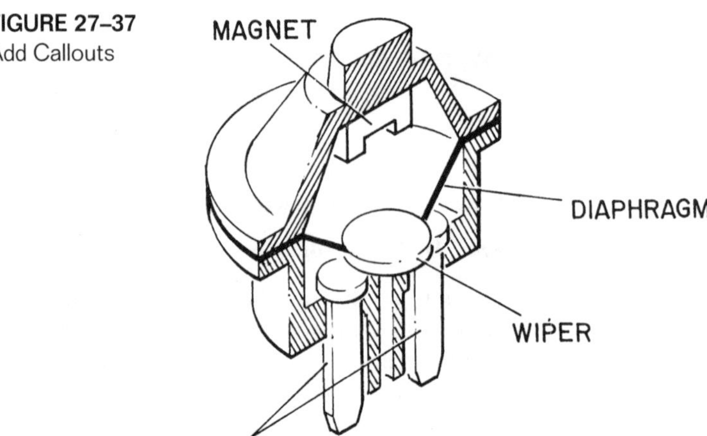

the part about 1⁄16″. Lines of lettering can be centered or arranged flush right if it is convenient. Be sure you follow a consistent pattern and that all callouts are easy to read.

Step 10. Print the drawing on an 8.5″ × 11″ sheet.

Step 11. Save the drawing in two places and exit AutoCAD.

Details for Cutaways

There are a few more details to cover before you begin the following exercises. If you must cut a flat plane, use obtuse angles for the cut, as shown in Figure 27–38. This allows you to show uniform thickness easily by using the opposite isometric angle and does not detract from the drawing as extremely jagged cuts do.

The final detail is that fasteners, shafts, and spheres are shown much more clearly if they are not cut on the drawing. Generally, nothing should be cut in a cutaway that is not necessary to show what is intended. Figure 27–39 is a good example of the selection process.

Now, let's look at another cutaway that has shading on it. Figure 27–40 has a dot pattern in the areas behind the rafters. This is a good technique to use in order to make specific features stand out. Study cutaways as you find them to decide what works and what does not. Not all the drawings you see printed in books and magazines are good ones.

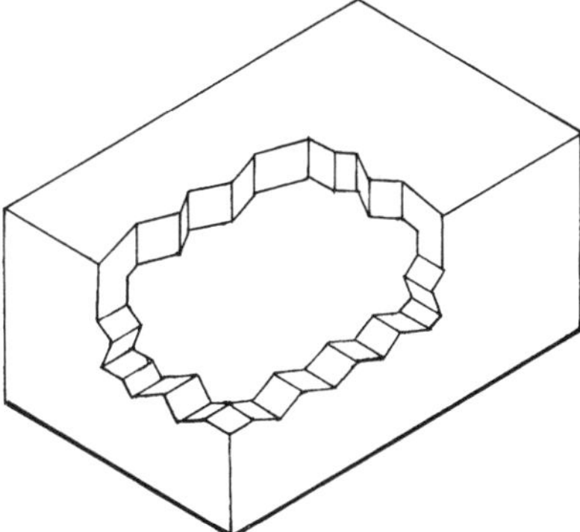

FIGURE 27–38
Obtuse Angles for Cut Surfaces

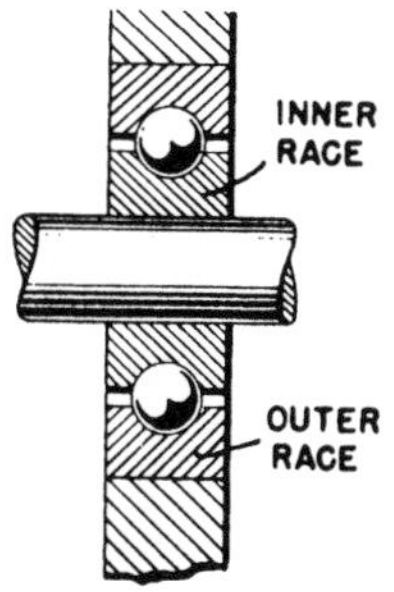

FIGURE 27–39
Shafts and Spheres Are Not Cut in a Section or Cutaway

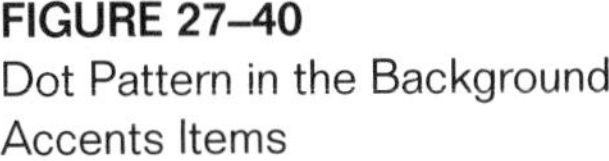

FIGURE 27–40
Dot Pattern in the Background Accents Items

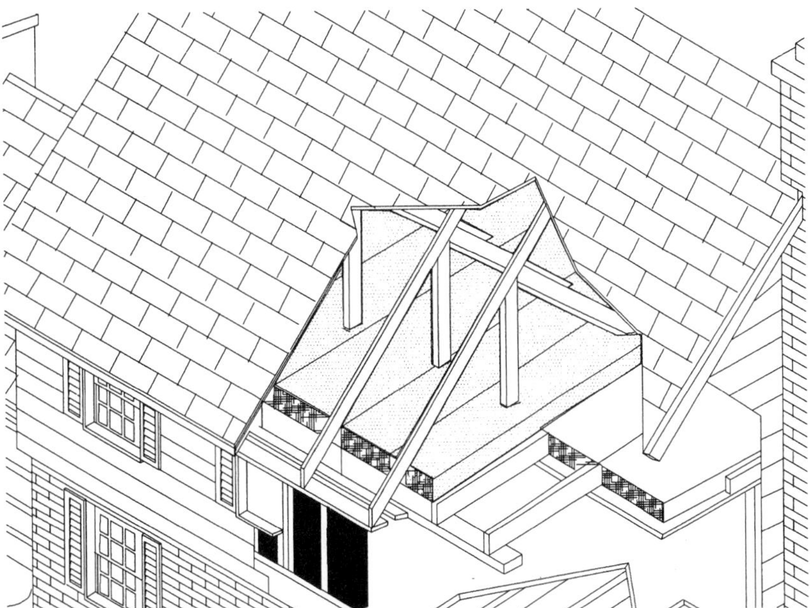

EXERCISES

EXERCISE 27–1. Draw Exercise 27–1 as described in this chapter.

EXERCISE 27–2. Draw Exercise 27–2 as described in this chapter.

EXERCISE 27–3. Draw Exercise 27–3 as described in this chapter. Refer to the assembly drawing, Figure 27–11, and the detail parts, Figures 27–12 through 27–18. Approximate any dimensions not shown. Your drawing will resemble Figure 27–20 but will have some minor differences. Use the following settings and layers:

Area: Width: 7
Length: 4

SNAP: .0625, ISO for the drawing; .0625, STANDARD for callouts and parts list

GRID: .125

LAYERS:

NAME	Color	Linetype	Lineweight
OBJECT	Green	Continuous	Default
SHADOW	Yellow	Continuous	Default
CALLOUTS	Cyan	Continuous	Default
PARTS-LISTS	Blue	Continuous	Default
EXP	Red	Continuous	Default

ALL LETTERING: FONT: simplex.shx HEIGHT: . 1

Leader with arrowhead: DIMSCALE = .5; balloons on index numbers

EXERCISE 27–4. Draw Exercise 27–4 as described in this chapter.

EXERCISE 27–5. Use drawings 10001 through 10009 (Figures 27–43 through 27–48) to make an exploded view of the vise (Figure 27–41). Put on index numbers and a parts list. Make your drawing full scale and then scale it down to a 7″ × 9″ full-page size. Use the single-line shading technique. Put your name in the lower right-hand corner. The top half of Figure 27–42 shows what your final drawing should look like. Use the following settings and layers:

Area: Width: 7
Length: 9

SNAP: .0625, ISO for the drawing; .0625, STANDARD for callouts and parts list

GRID: .125

LAYERS:

NAME	Color	Linetype	Lineweight
OBJECT	Green	Continuous	Default
SHADOW	Yellow	Continuous	Default
CALLOUTS	Cyan	Continuous	Default
PARTS-LISTS	Blue	Continuous	Default
EXP	Red	Continuous	Default

ALL LETTERING: FONT: simplex.shx HEIGHT: .1

Leader with arrowhead: DIMSCALE = .5

FIGURE 27–41
Exploded View of Vise

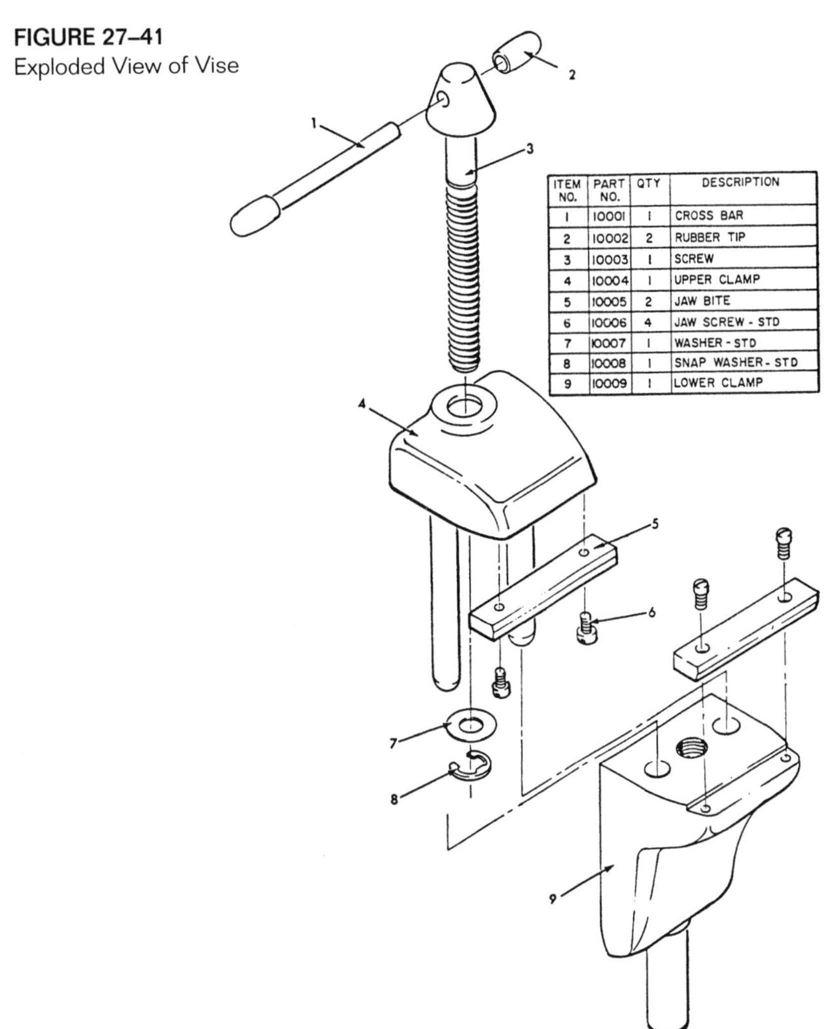

ITEM NO.	PART NO.	QTY	DESCRIPTION
1	10001	1	CROSS BAR
2	10002	2	RUBBER TIP
3	10003	1	SCREW
4	10004	1	UPPER CLAMP
5	10005	2	JAW BITE
6	10006	4	JAW SCREW - STD
7	10007	1	WASHER - STD
8	10008	1	SNAP WASHER - STD
9	10009	1	LOWER CLAMP

FIGURE 27–42
Vise Assembly Drawing

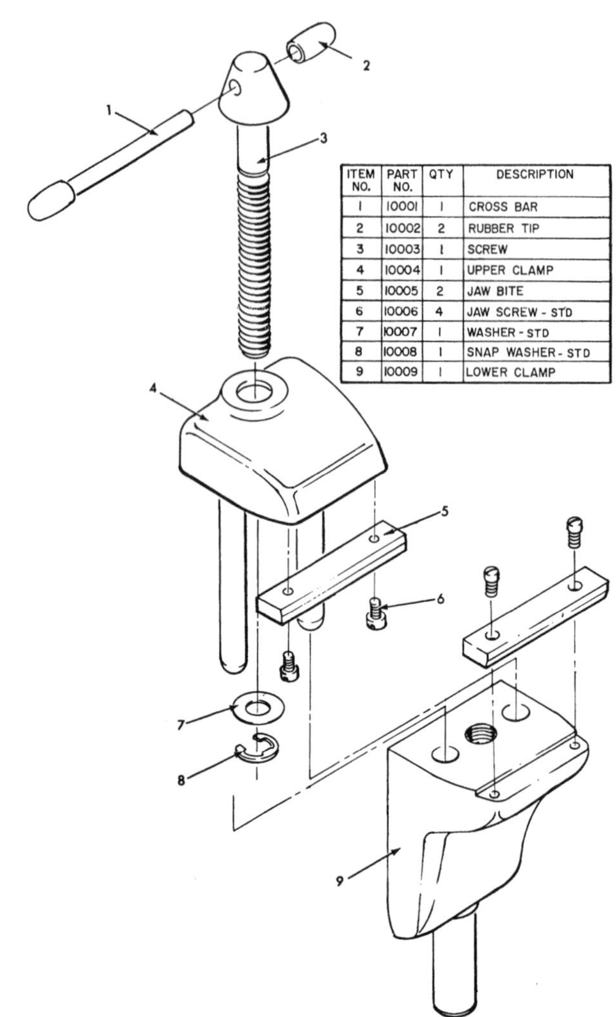

ITEM NO.	PART NO.	QTY	DESCRIPTION
1	10001	1	CROSS BAR
2	10002	2	RUBBER TIP
3	10003	1	SCREW
4	10004	1	UPPER CLAMP
5	10005	2	JAW BITE
6	10006	4	JAW SCREW - STD
7	10007	1	WASHER - STD
8	10008	1	SNAP WASHER - STD
9	10009	1	LOWER CLAMP

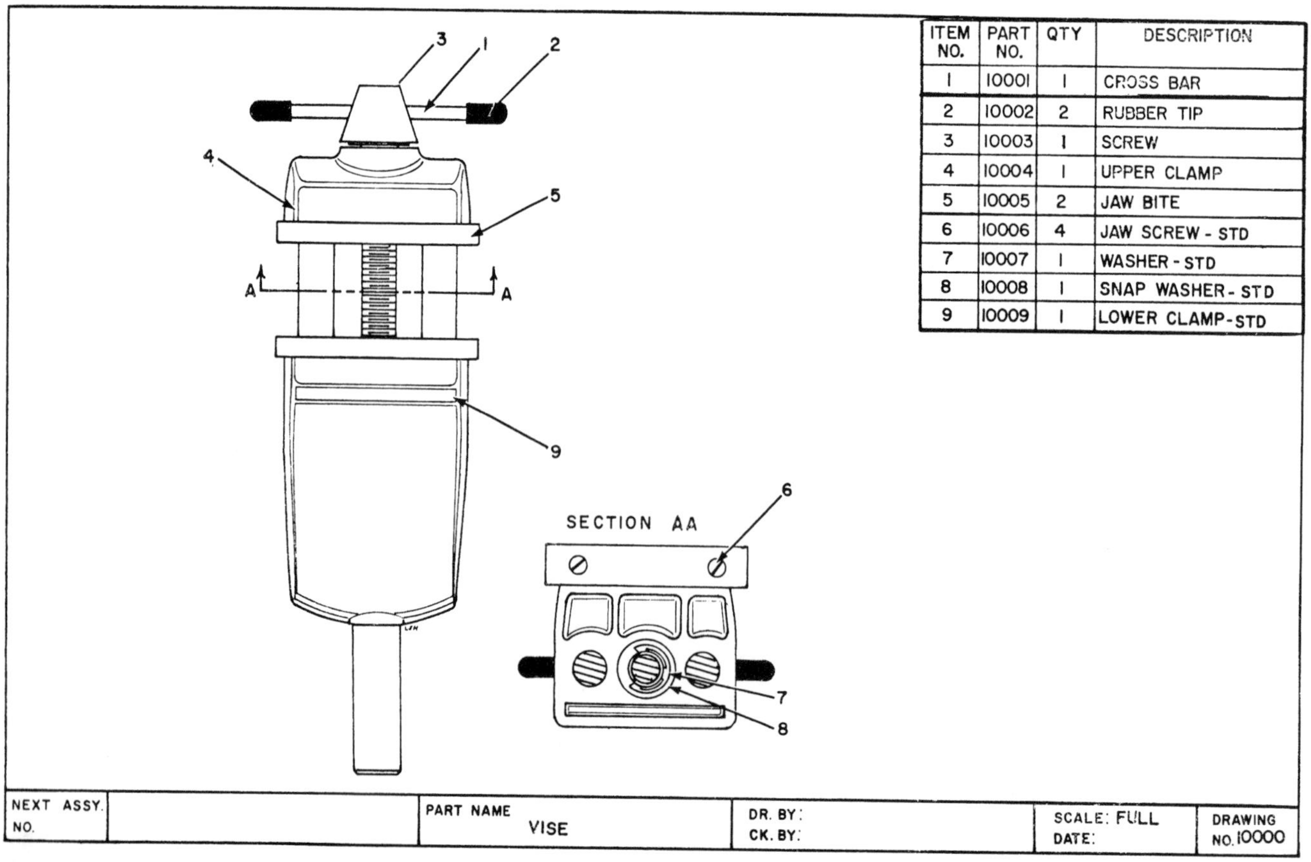

3 1 2
4
5
A A
9
SECTION AA
6
7
8

ITEM NO.	PART NO.	QTY	DESCRIPTION
1	10001	1	CROSS BAR
2	10002	2	RUBBER TIP
3	10003	1	SCREW
4	10004	1	UPPER CLAMP
5	10005	2	JAW BITE
6	10006	4	JAW SCREW - STD
7	10007	1	WASHER - STD
8	10008	1	SNAP WASHER - STD
9	10009	1	LOWER CLAMP-STD

NEXT ASSY. NO.		PART NAME VISE	DR. BY: CK. BY:	SCALE: FULL DATE:	DRAWING NO. 10000

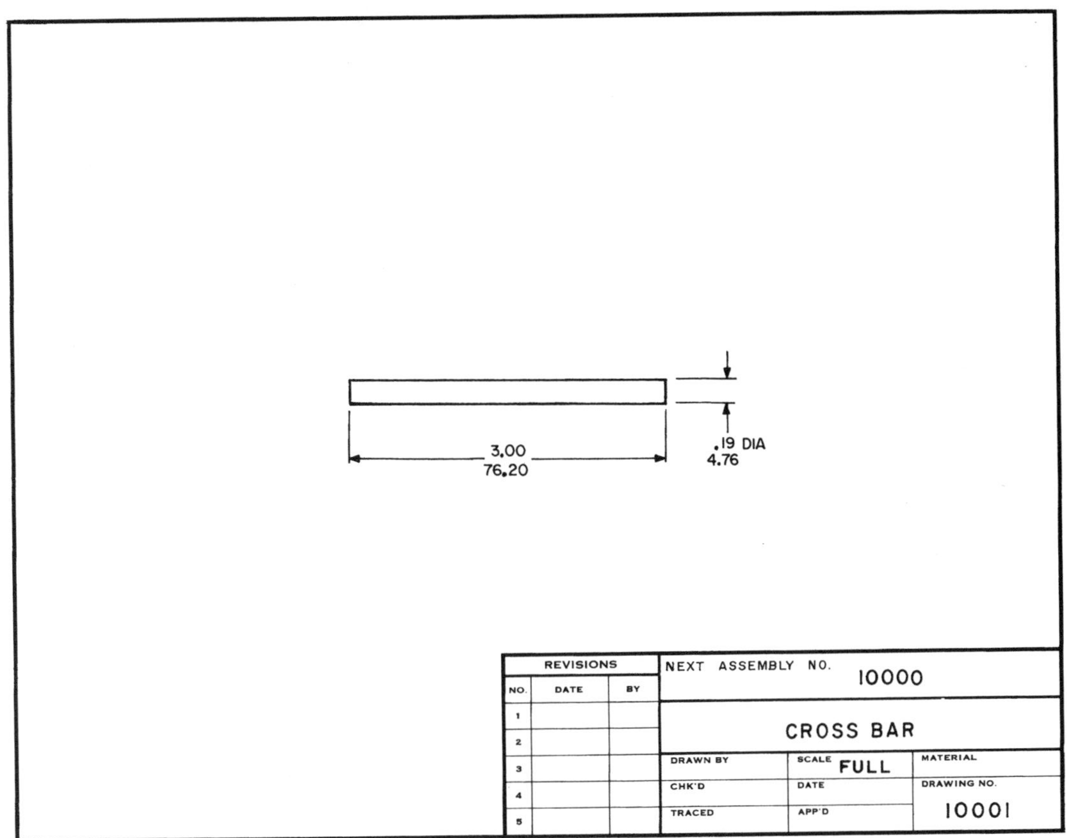

FIGURE 27–43
Cross Bar Detail Drawing

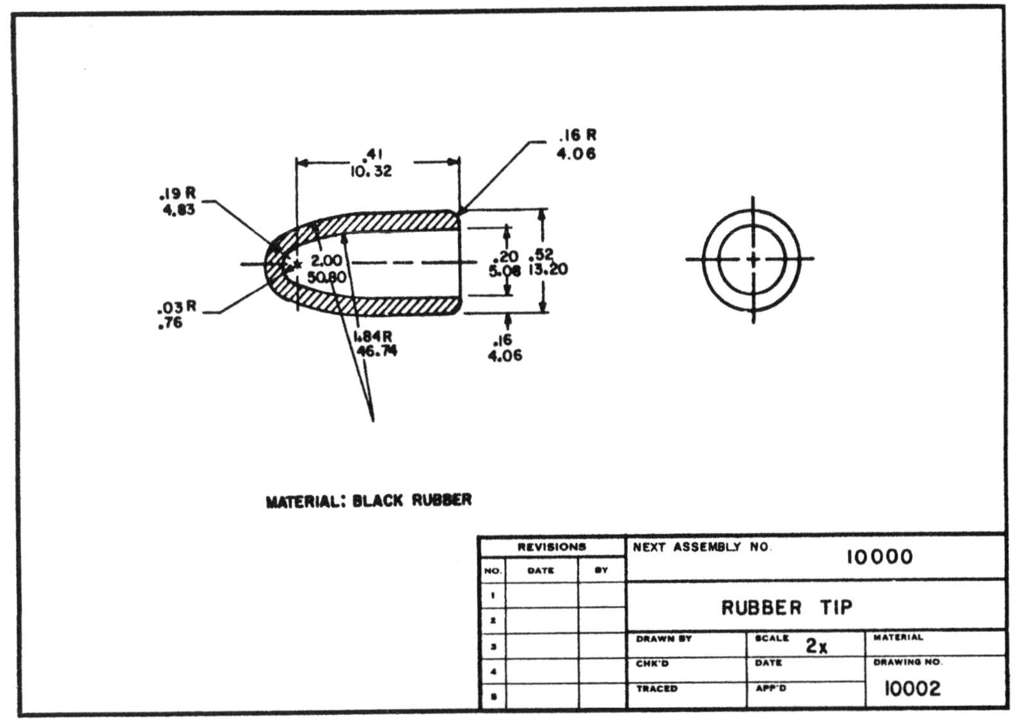

FIGURE 27–44
Rubber Tip Detail Drawing

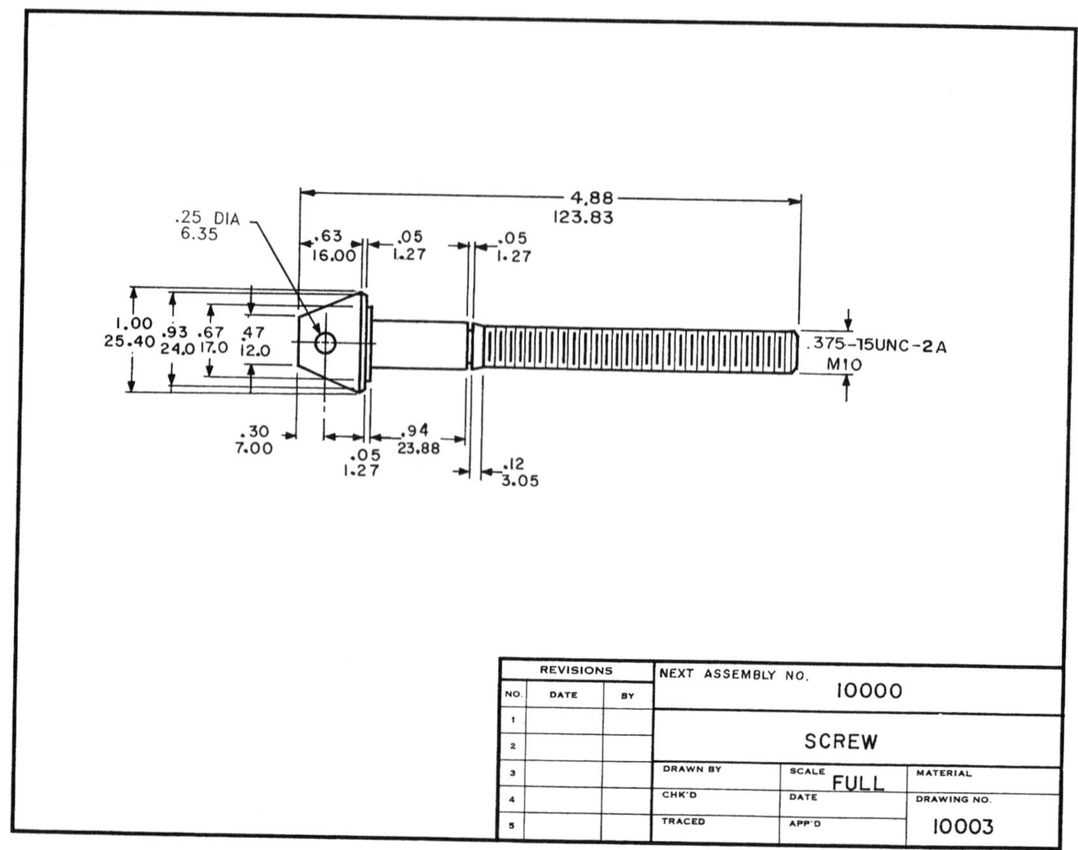

FIGURE 27–45
Screw Detail Drawing

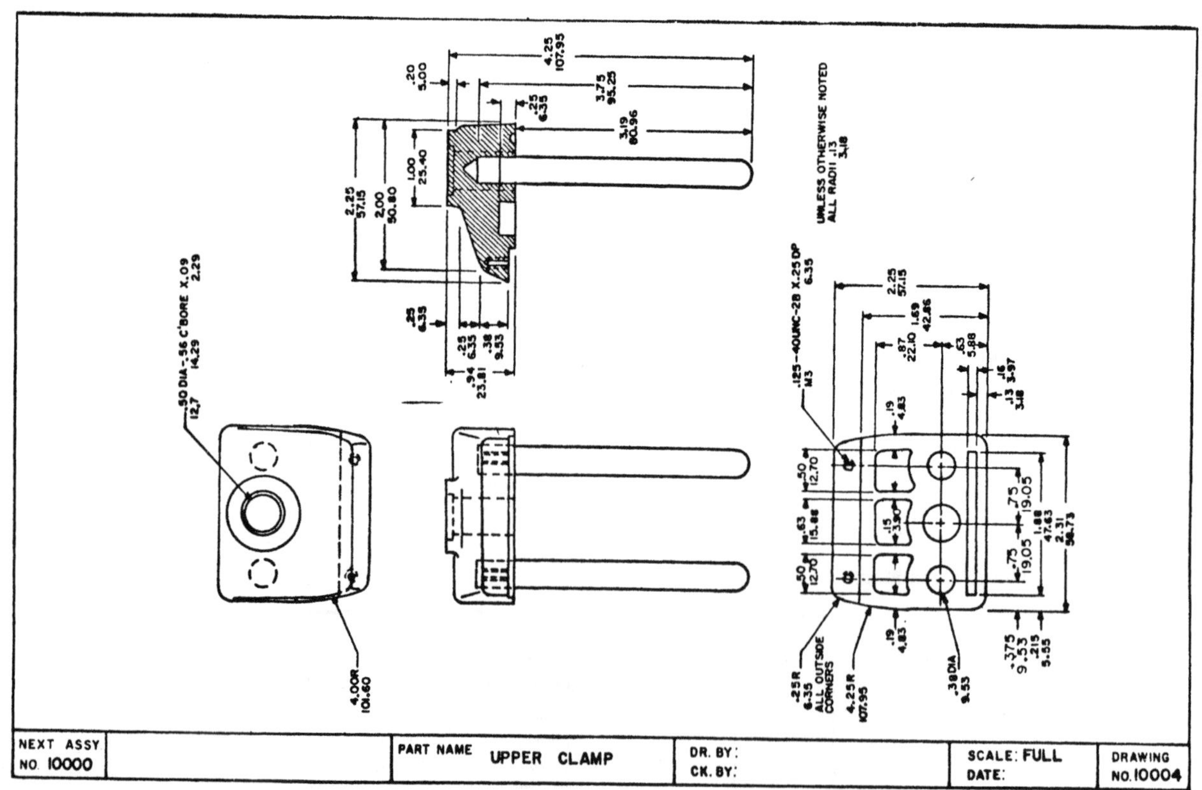

FIGURE 27–46
Upper Clamp Detail Drawing

.20 DIA. THRU .25 C'BORE X .12 DP.
5.08 6.35 3.05
.50
12.7
.30
7.62
.44
11.18
1.72
43.70
2.50
63.50
5°
.25
6.35
.12
3.05
REVISIONS
NO. DATE BY
NEXT ASSEMBLY NO. 10000
JAW BITE
DRAWN BY
SCALE 2x
MATERIAL
CHK'D
DATE
DRAWING NO. 10005
TRACED
APP'D

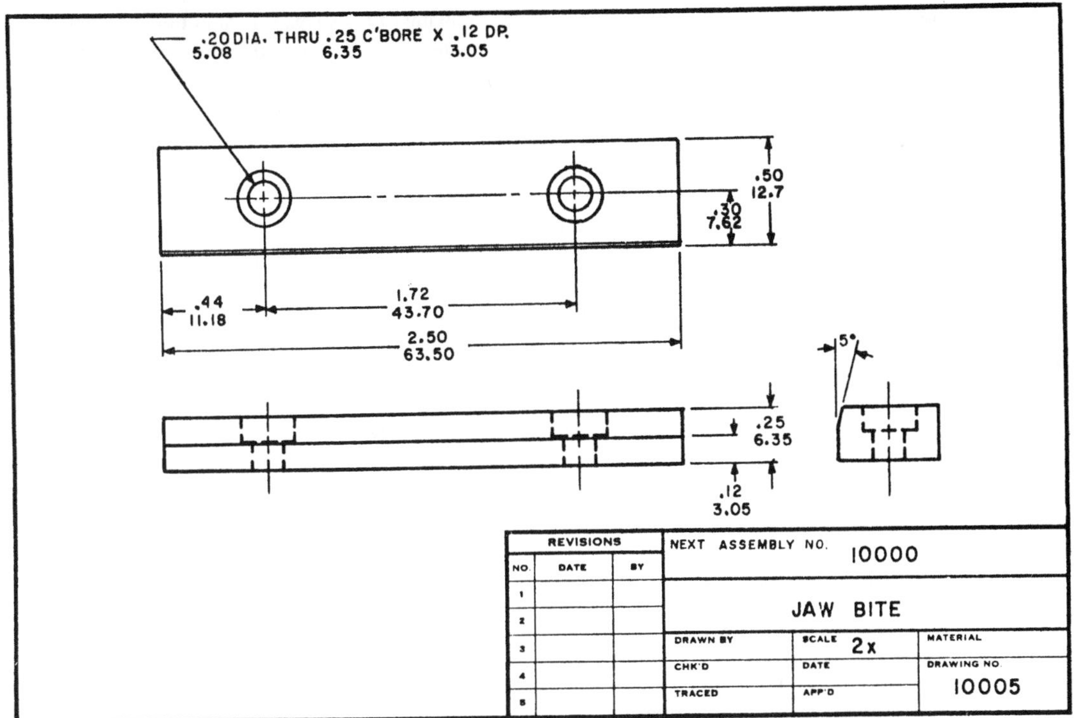

FIGURE 27–47
Jaw Bite Detail Drawing

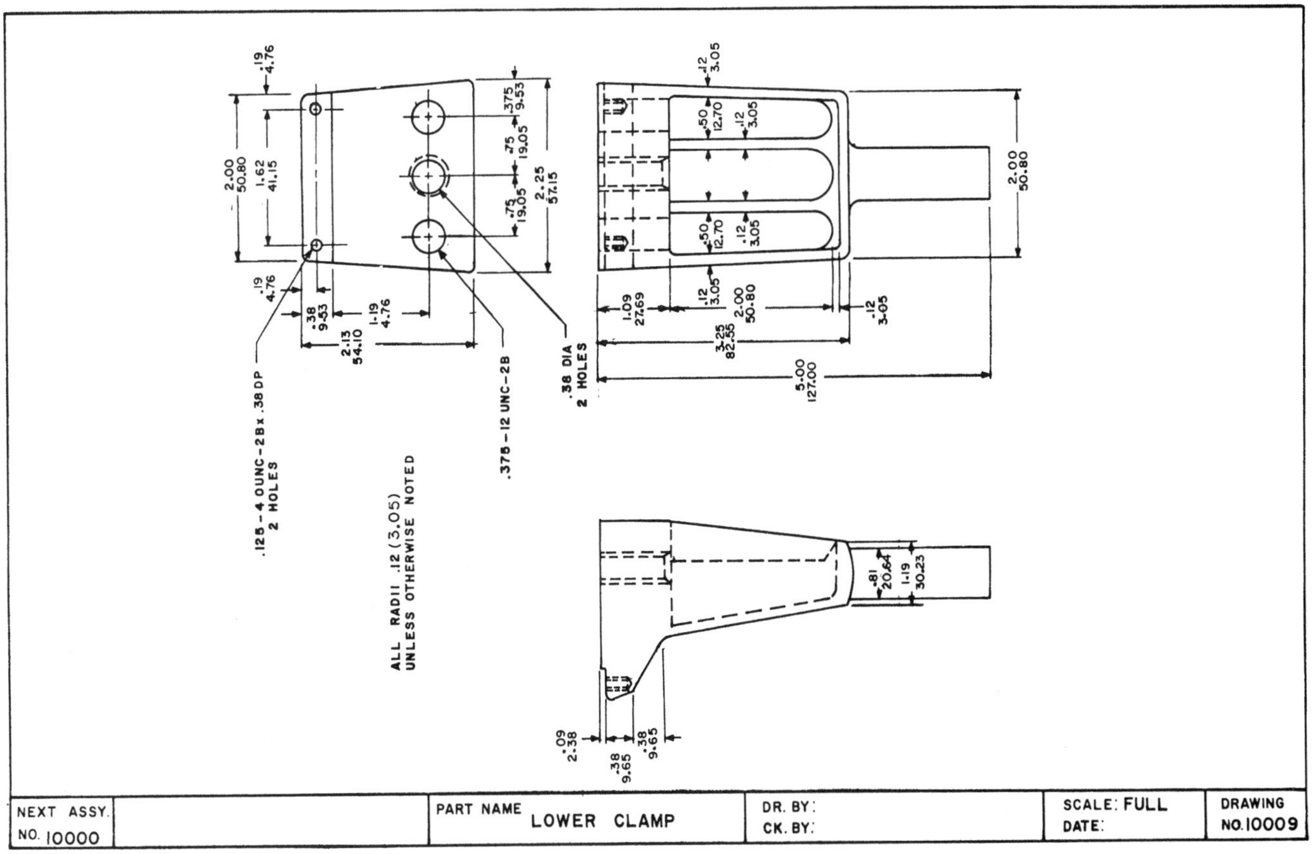

.125-4 OUNC-2B x .38 DP
2 HOLES
ALL RADII .12 (3.05)
UNLESS OTHERWISE NOTED
.375-12 UNC-2B
.38 DIA
2 HOLES
2.00
50.80
1.62
41.15
2.25
57.15
2.13
54.10
3.25
82.55
5.00
127.00
NEXT ASSY.
NO. 10000
PART NAME LOWER CLAMP
DR. BY:
CK. BY:
SCALE: FULL
DATE:
DRAWING
NO. 10009

FIGURE 27–48
Lower Clamp Detail Drawing

EXERCISE 27–6. Make an isometric cutaway drawing of the shape shown in Figure 27–49 using the single-line shading technique. Make the cut with obtuse angle break lines. Center the drawing in an 11,8.5 area (the limits). Place your name so that it ends .5″ over and .5″ up from the lower right corner. Use the same technique as shown in Figure 27–50. Use layers and settings from Exercise 27–1.

EXERCISE 27–7. Make an isometric cutaway drawing of Figure 27–51 using the single-line shading technique. Make the cut with a straight break line. Center the drawing in a 7,4 area. Use Hatch, U, .08 apart for showing crosshatching on cut surfaces. Use the same technique as shown in Figure 27–52. Use layers and settings from Exercise 27–1.

Tip: The fastest way to draw a ¼ cutaway (Figure 27–52) is
- Draw a centerline at a 30° angle.
- Draw one face of the cut surface in its correct position above the center line.
- Mirror the other face of the cut surface.
- Click on the centers of ellipses on the center line and drag their radii to their correct lengths on the cut surface, then Trim what you don't need.

EXERCISE 27–8. Make an isometric cutaway drawing of the three-part assembly shown in Figure 27–53. Draw it using the single-line shading technique. Make the cut with a straight break line. Center the drawing in a 7,6 area (the limits). Cut only the bushing and the pulley. Show the shaft full. Measure this drawing and make your drawing the same size as this drawing. Use layers and settings from Exercise 27–1. Use Hatch, U, .08 apart for crosshatching on cut surfaces. Do not add callouts.

FIGURE 27–49
Cutaway Exercise

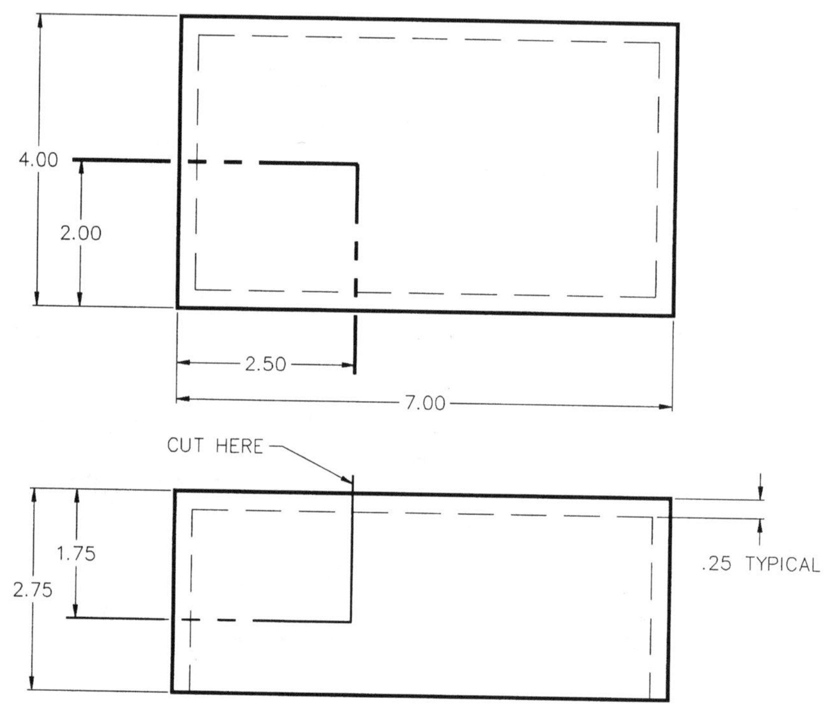

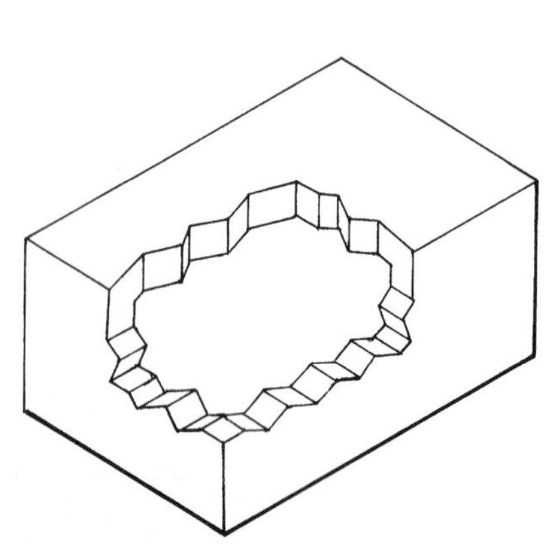

FIGURE 27–50
Cutaway Exercise

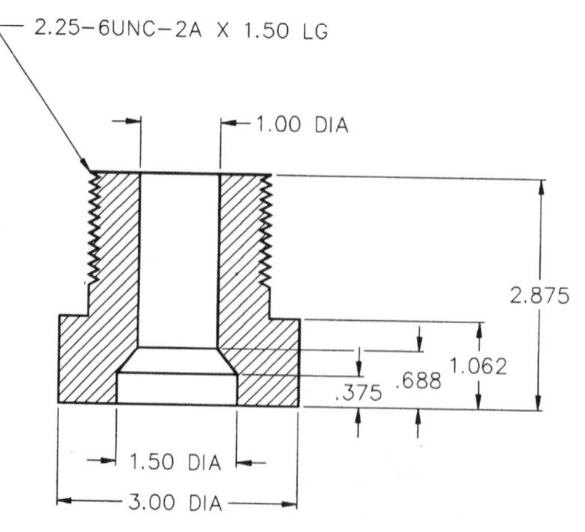

FIGURE 27–51
Cutaway Exercise

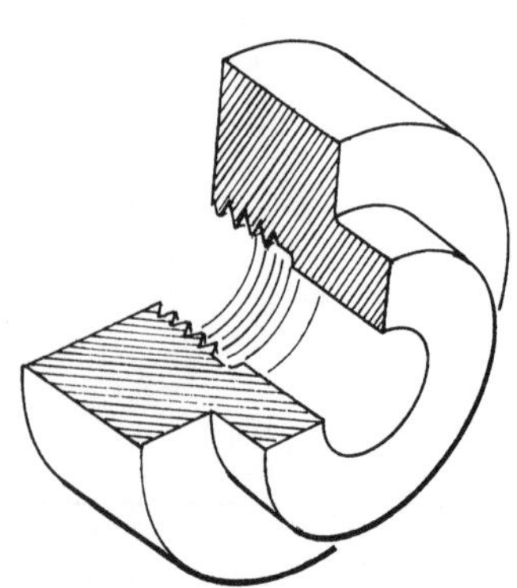

FIGURE 27–52
Cutaway Exercise

FIGURE 27–53
Assembly Cutaway Exercise

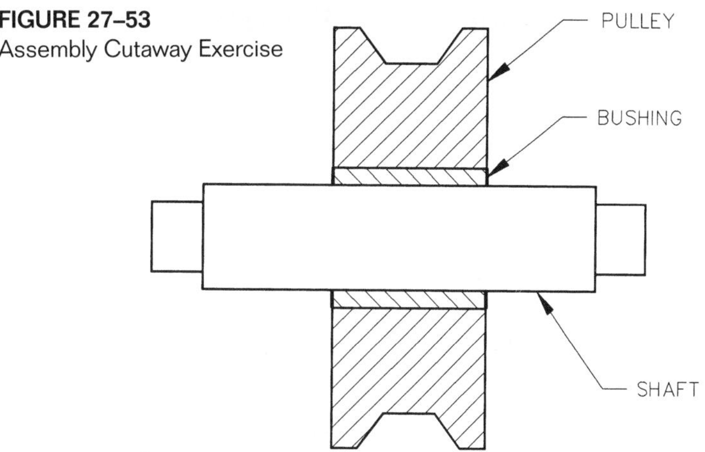

EXERCISE 27–9. Make an isometric cutaway drawing of the assembly shown in Figure 27–54. Cut housing, bushings, pulley, and lock washers one-half. Leave all other parts full. Use layers and settings from Exercise 27–3. Use Hatch, U, .08 apart for crosshatching on cut surfaces. Do not add callouts. Approximate any dimensions not shown.

EXERCISE 27–10. Make an isometric cutaway drawing of one of the objects listed here. (Or draw any other commonly used object that has 5 to 10 separate parts.) Use right-side and bottom-line shading. Make the drawing approximately 9″ and center it on an 8½″ × 11″ sheet. Use LINE or HATCH patterns if needed on cut surfaces.

Objects

Teapot
Flashlight
Door latch assembly
Aerosol can

Do not select an object that is overly complicated. *Make it easy on yourself!*

FIGURE 27–54
Assembly Cutaway Exercise

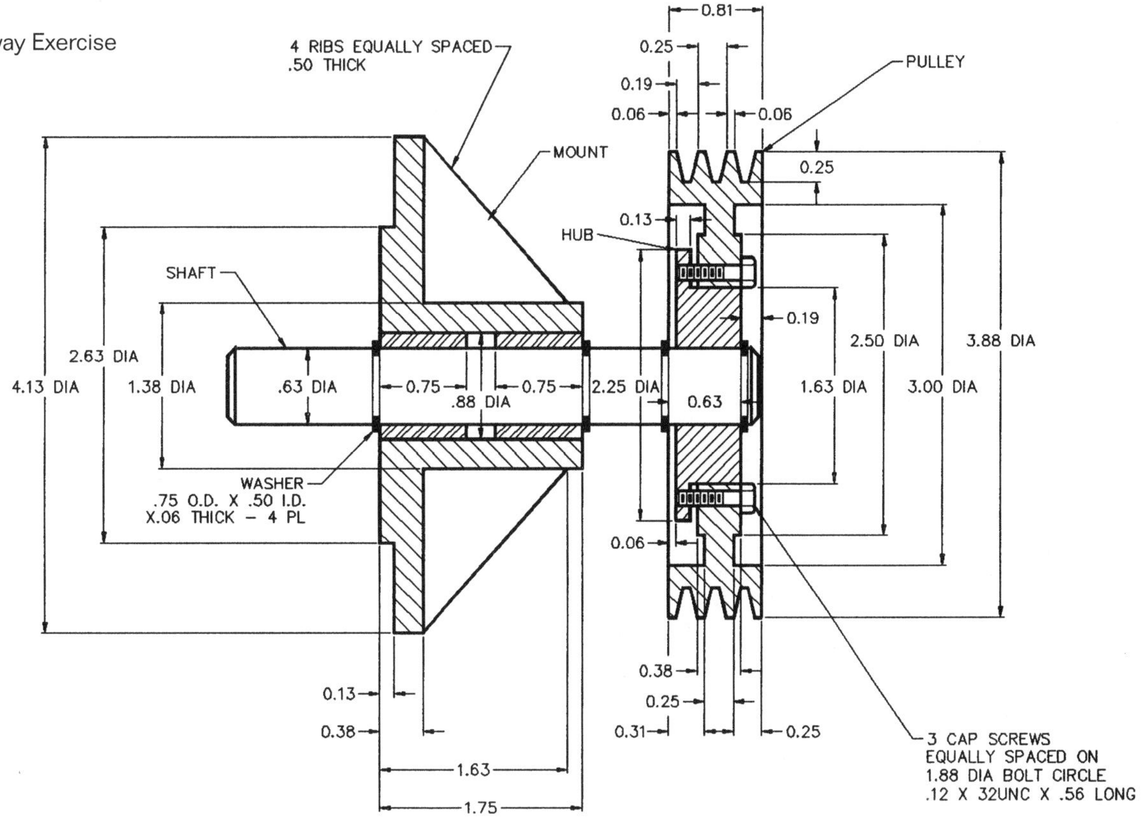

REVIEW QUESTIONS

Circle the best answer.

1. Which of the following commands is used to create a shadow line?
   a. Copy
   b. Change
   c. Line
   d. Polyline
   e. Shadow
2. Highlights are shown on
   a. All interior lines
   b. Selected outside lines
   c. Leading edges
   d. Leading edges and outside lines
   e. Holes only
3. A dotted shadow on threads may be formed with which of the following HATCH patterns?
   a. DOT
   b. DOTS
   c. U
   d. DOTTED
   e. POINT
4. Three-dimensional modeling is described in this chapter.
   a. True
   b. False
5. A 2-D assembly drawing contains which of the following?
   a. Detailed dimensions of each part
   b. A thumbnail sketch
   c. Explosion lines
   d. Right-side and bottom shade lines
   e. Parts list
6. Which two keys must be pressed to toggle from one isoplane to another?
   a. Ctrl-E
   b. Alt-E
   c. Alt-C
   d. Ctrl-F1
   e. Ctrl-C
7. Which of the following must be the starting point for drawing all cylindrical isometric objects?
   a. Ellipses
   b. Outside edges
   c. Center lines
   d. Inside edges
   e. Shade lines
8. Which function key is used to toggle between isoplanes?
   a. F2
   b. F3
   c. F5
   d. F7
   e. F9
9. Distortions are not allowed in technical illustration.
   a. True
   b. False
10. The drawing form used throughout this chapter is
    a. Isometric
    b. Dimetric
    c. Trimetric
    d. Perspective
    e. 3-D modeling

Complete.

11. Describe the purposes of a thumbnail sketch of an exploded view.

____

____

12. List the function key that allows you to toggle to isoplanes.

____

13. Describe why parts are sometimes overlapped on an exploded view.

____

____

14. List the steps for drawing exploded views.

____

____

____

____

____

____

____

____

____

15. List four rules for adding index numbers to an exploded-view drawing.

____

____

____

____

16. Describe the purpose of a freehand sketch for a cutaway drawing.

____

17. Describe how to add highlights and shadows to a cutaway drawing.

____

____

18. Describe how to add shading to cut surfaces of a cutaway drawing.

____

____

19. Describe how fasteners, shafts, and spheres are drawn on a cutaway drawing.

____

20. List the steps for drawing cutaways.

____

____

____

Glossary

Absolute coordinates The location of a point in terms of distances and/or angles from a fixed origin point.

Alias An alternate name for the same command (Example: L is an alias for LINE).

Aliasing The jagged appearance of a curved line or a straight line at an angle.

Aligned dimension A dimension that shows the distance between two points at an angle.

Ambient color A color produced by ambient light.

Ambient light Light that illuminates all surfaces equally.

Angular dimension A dimension that measures angles.

Annotations Notes, text, tolerances, legends, and symbols.

ANSI American National Standards Institute; sets drafting standards.

Anti-aliasing A means of shading the main pixels to reduce the appearance of aliasing.

Array A rectangular or circular pattern of graphical objects.

ASCII American Standard Code for Information Interchange; a standard set of 128 binary numbers representing keyboard information such as letters, numerals, and punctuation.

Aspect ratio The ratio of width to height on the display

Associative dimensions Dimensions that automatically update their values when the associated geometry is modified.

Associative hatching A hatched area that changes as the shape of the area changes.

Attribute Textual information associated with CAD geometry. Attributes can be assigned to drawing objects and extracted from the drawing database. Applications include creating bills of material.

Attribute extraction file A text file to which attribute data is written when it is extracted from a drawing.

Attribute prompt The text that is displayed when a block with an attribute is inserted.

Attribute tag The label that AutoCAD looks for when attributes are extracted.

Attribute template A file used to provide a format for extracted attributes.

Attribute value The text that appears on the block when a block with an attribute is inserted.

AUI Advanced User Interface; a user-interface enhancement that includes on-screen dialog boxes, a menu bar that can be customized, pull-down menus, and icon menus.

Autolisp A programming language contained within the AutoCAD program that is used for writing programs for AutoCAD commands.

Baseline dimensioning A dimension relative to a fixed horizontal or vertical datum or reference.

Base point The first point selected when copying, moving, rotating, inserting, or gripping objects.

Baud rate See *bps*.

Bezier curve A curve defined by a set of control points.

Binary The numerical base, base 2, by which computers operate. The electrical circuitry of a computer is designed to recognize only two states, high and low, which easily translate to logical and arithmetic values of 1 and 0. For example, the binary number 11101 represents the decimal number 29.

Bit (binary digit) The smallest unit of computer data.

Board (printed circuit board) Board onto which components are soldered and connected via etched circuits on the board.

Boot To turn the computer on and start a program.

bps (bits per second) A unit of transmission; also called baud rate.

B-spline curve A curve that passes near a set of control points

Buffer An intermediate storage device (hardware or software) between data handling units.

Busy lamp Indicator on the front of a disk drive that lights when the drive is writing or reading a disk.

Byte A string of 8 bits representing 256 different binary values. A kilobyte (Kbyte) is 1024 bytes.

CAD *C*omputer-*a*ided *d*esign; the use of graphics-oriented computer software for designing and drafting applications.

Chamfer A beveled edge or corner between two otherwise intersecting lines or surfaces.

Chip (integrated circuit) A miniature circuit made by etching electronic components on a silicon wafer.

Clipping The process of setting the display boundaries of graphical items.

Clock Electronic timer used to synchronize computer operations. A clock is an indication of the speed of the computer operations.

Cold boot Starting the computer by turning it off and then on again.

CMYK *C*yan, *M*agenta, *Y*ellow, and *B*lack (key color) A system of creating colors by specifying the percentage of each of the four colors.

Command A word used to initiate a task.

Com port A communications port allowing data to flow into and out of the computer. Most communication ports are serial ports. Digitizers and most plotters are connected to communication ports. Most COM ports have pins rather than holes.

Configuration A particular grouping of computer hardware as a functional unit. It may also include the allocation of hardware resources and sometimes refers to software parameter settings.

Continue dimension A linear dimension that uses the second extension origin of the previous dimension as its first extension origin.

Coons patch A bicubic surface patch interpolated between four adjoining general space curves.

Coordinate filters An AutoCAD feature (also called XYZ point filters) that allows a user to extract individual X, Y, and Z coordinate values from different points in order to create a new, composite point.

Cpolygon A crossing polygon that selects any object crossed by or contained within it.

cpu Central processing unit; it is responsible for arithmetic computations, logic operations, memory addresses, and data and control signal traffic in a computer.

Crosshairs A cursor usually made up of two perpendicular lines on the display screen used to select coordinate locations.

Crossing window A window that selects any object crossed by or contained within the window.

CRT Cathode-ray tube; the video display tube used with computers.

Cursor An indicator on the display screen that shows where the next entered data will appear.

Database Related information organized and stored so that it can be easily retrieved and, typically, used in multiple applications. A noncomputer example of a database is the telephone directory.

Default A parameter or variable that remains in effect until changed. It is what a computer program assumes in the absence of specific user instructions.

Definition points (def points) Points that appear when associative dimensions are created.

DIESEL Direct Interpretively Evaluated String Expression Language. A programming language for customizing menu items.

Diffuse color The predominant color of an object

Digitizing tablet A graphics input device that generates coordinate data. It is used in conjunction with a puck or a stylus.

Dimension style A named group of settings for each dimensioning variable affecting the appearance of a dimension. Also called a dimstyle in AutoCAD.

Dimension text The text that appears in the dimension line.

Dimensioning variables Settings that control the appearance of dimensions.

Direct distance entry A method of defining points that allows the cursor to be moved to indicate the desired direction, then the value is typed.

Directory Groups of files identified by a directory name.

Disk or diskette A thin, flexible platter coated with a magnetic material for storing information.

Disk or diskette drive A magnetic device that writes on and retrieves data from a disk.

Display resolution The number of horizontal and vertical rows of pixels that can be displayed by a particular graphics controller or monitor. For example, 640 columns and 350 rows of pixels can be displayed by a standard EGA graphics controller and color monitor.

Display screen A video-display tube or CRT used to transmit graphical information.

Dithering Combining color dots to display more colors than are really available.

DOS Disk operating system; software that controls the operation of disk drives, memory usage, and I/O in a computer.

Drag To dynamically move the virtual image of a graphical entity across the display screen to a new location using a puck, mouse, or stylus.

Drawing file A collection of graphical data stored as a set (file) in a computer.

Drawing limits The page size specified for a drawing. The grid shows the drawing limits.

Drive A device used to read or write information on a disk or diskette.

DXF Drawing interchange file; a file format used to produce an ASCII description of an AutoCAD drawing file.

Edge A command used to change the visibility of a face.

Edit To modify existing data

Elevation The Z value of an object with reference to the XY-plane.

Embed To copy an object from a source document into a destination document. An embedded object has no link to the program from which the source document was taken.

Endpoint The exact location on a line or curve where it terminates.

Enter key (<hard>) Sometimes called the Return key; it signals the computer to execute a command or terminate a line of text.

Entity An AutoCAD term describing predefined graphical objects that are placed in the drawing using a single command.

Expansion slot Location inside the system unit for the connection of an optional printed circuit board. Expansion slots for optional boards are available in many computers.

Expansion option Add-on hardware that expands power and versatility.

Explode A command that separates blocks and poylines into separate line segments.

Extents The extreme boundary of a drawing without regard to the drawing limits.

External reference A drawing file that is linked (or attached) to another drawing. Also called an xref in AutoCAD.

Extrusion In AutoCAD, the process of assigning a thickness property to a given entity. The direction of the extrusion is always parallel to the Z axis of the UCS in effect when the entity was created.

Face A bounded section of the surface of a modeled object.

Feature control frame The box surrounding a geometric dimension.

File Information stored by a computer.

Fill Solid coloring covering an area bounded by lines and/or curves.

Fillet A curved surface of constant radius blending two otherwise intersecting surfaces; a 2-D representation of the preceding involving two lines or curves and an arc.

Finite Element Analysis (FEA) Numerical technique of approximately determining field variables such as displacements or stresses in a domain. This is done by breaking down the domain into a finite number of "pieces," also called "elements," and solving for the unknowns in those elements.

Finite Element Modeling (FEM) Process of breaking down a geometric model into a mesh, called the finite element mesh model, that is used for finite element analysis.

Fit tolerance The setting that determines how close a B-spline curve passes to the fit points.

Floating viewports Viewports that are not fixed and can be moved, erased,and stretched

Floppy disk A circular plastic disk coated with magnetic material mounted in a square plastic holder. It is used by a computer to store information for use later. It can be inserted or removed from a floppy disk drive at will. It is also called a diskette.

Font A distinctive text typeface, usually named and recognized by the aesthetic appearance of its characters.

Format To prepare a disk to accept data.

Freeze A setting that keeps objects on selected layers from being displayed. A frozen layer is not displayed, regenerated, or plotted. Freezing shortens regeneration time. A frozen layer is not selected when the ALL selection option is used.

Function key A key on the keyboard that can be assigned to perform a task. A function key is typically used as a shortcut to a lengthy string of keystrokes.

Grid An area on the graphics display covered with regularly spaced dots used as a drawing aid.

Grips Small squares that appear on objects selected before a command is activated. After the grips appear the objects can be edited by selecting one of the squares to make it hot and toggling through the available grip modes.

Handle An alphanumeric tag that AutoCAD assigns to every object.

Hard copy A paper printout of information stored in a computer.

Hard disk A rigid magnetic storage device that provides fast access to stored data.

Hardware The electronic and mechanical parts of a computer.

Hatching A regular pattern of line segments covering an area bounded by lines and/or curves.

High density The storage capacity of a disk or disk drive that uses high-capacity disks.

HLS *H*ue, *l*ightness, and *s*aturation. A system of defining color by specifying the amount of these three values.

Hz (hertz) A unit of frequency equal to one cycle per second.

Icon A graphical symbol typically used to convey a message or represent a command on the display screen.

Interface A connection that allows two devices to communicate.

I/O Input/output; a mechanism by which a computer accepts or distributes information to peripheral devices such as plotters, printers, disk drives, and modems.

ISO International Standards Organization, an organization that sets international standards for drawings. *Also,* an abbreviation for isometric, a view or drawing of an object in which the projections of the X, Y, and Z axes are spaced 120° apart, and the projection of the Z axis is vertical.

Isometric snap style A snap style that sets the grid and snap to the isometric angles of 30°, 30°, and 90°.

K (kilobyte) 1024 bytes.

Layer A logical separation of data to be viewed individually or in combination. Similar in concept to transparent acetate overlays.

Layout The tab that allows paper space viewports to be created with scaled insertions of the model space drawing.

Linetype Sometimes called *line font,* it represents the appearance of a line. For example, a continuous line has a different linetype than a dashed line.

Lineweight A setting in the Layer Manager that allows lines on any layer to be assigned a specific width.

Link A copy of a source document that is connected to the source program so that any changes to the source document are reflected in the copy.

Load To enter a program into the computer's memory from a storage device.

M (megabyte) One million bytes.

Macro A single command made up of a string of commands.

Memory An electronic part of a computer that stores information.

Menu A display of programs or tasks.

MHz (megahertz) One thousand hertz.

Microprocessor An integrated circuit "chip" (or set of chips) that acts as the CPU of a computer.

Mirror To create the reverse image of selected graphical items.

Mode A software setting or operational state.

Model A two- or three-dimensional representation of an object.

Model space Model space is where model geometry is created and maintained. Typically, entities in model space are drawn to scale of the design feature. Model space is the complement of paper space. See *paper space*.

Modem (modulator-demodulator) A device that links computers via a telephone line.

Monochrome A video display that features different shades of a single color.

Motherboard The main printed circuit board in a computer to which all other boards are connected.

Mouse A hand-operated, relative-motion device resembling a digitizer puck used to position the cursor on a computer display screen.

Network An electronic linking of computers for communication.

Node An object snap option that allows you to snap to points.

Normal Perpendicular.

Numerical control (NC) Programmable automation of machine tools.

NURBS *N*on*u*niform *r*ational *B*-*s*pline curve. A curve or surface defined by control points.

Object Also called entity; any element such as text, lines, circles, arcs, dimensions, hatching, and polylines used in AutoCAD.

OLE *O*bject *l*inking and *e*mbedding. Objects from a source document are copied into a destination document. When the object is selected in the destination document, the program used to create the source document is activated.

Operating system Also called the disk operating system; software that manages computer resources and allows a user access and control.

Origin The intersection point of the axes in a coordinate system. For example, the origin of a Cartesian coordinate system is the point at which the X, Y, and Z axes meet (0, 0, 0).

Orthographic projection The 2-D representation of a 3-D object without perspective. In drafting, it is typically the front, top, and right-side views of an object.

Ortho mode An AutoCAD setting that permits only horizontal or vertical input from the graphical pointing device (mouse, puck, or stylus).

Osnap Object snap, an AutoCAD setting that allows the user to specify point locations based on existing geometry. This allows for the graphical selection of the precise location of midpoints and endpoints of lines, center points and tangent points of circles and arcs, and the like.

Overwrite To store information at a location where information is already stored, thus destroying the original information.

Pan Redefines the display boundaries without changing magnification; analogous to panning with a camera.

Paper space Space in which documentation graphics such as title blocks, some annotation, or borders can reside. Typically, entities are created in paper space, to the scale at which they will be plotted. Some 3-D features also work in paper space. Working in paper space allows working with nontiled viewports. See *model space*.

Parallel interface Interface that communicates 8, 16, or 32 bits at a time.

Parallel port A connector on the back of the computer that usually has holes rather than pins. This connector always has 25 connections. Most printers are connected to parallel ports.

Parallel printer A printer with a parallel interface.

pc3 file The plotter configuration file. It contains all the specific information needed to operate a particular plotter or printer.

Peripheral An input or output device not under direct computer control.

Perspective projection The simulation of distance by representing parallel lines converging at a vanishing point.

Pick button The button on any pointing device such as a mouse that is used to pick objects or define points—usually the left mouse button.

Pixels (picture elements) Tiny dots that make up a screen image.

Plan view A view perpendicular to a selected face of an object.

Plot style A file containing all the pen assignments, fill style, line endings, and other elements that control how a drawing is plotted.

Plotter A computer-controlled device that produces text and images on paper or acetate by electrostatic, thermal, or mechanical means (with a pen).

PMP file *P*lot *m*odel *p*arameter; a file that contains the custom plotter calibration and paper size data to operate a specific printer or plotter.

Point A location or dot in 3D space specified by X, Y, and Z coordinates.

Point filters A means of individually extracting the X, Y, and Z coordinates of points to specify a new point.

Polar array Objects copied about a center point a specific number of times.

Polar coordinate A coordinate specified by a distance and angle from an origin.

Polygon window A selection window in the shape of a polygon. An item must be contained entirely inside the window to be selected.

Polyline An AutoCAD geometric entity composed of one or more connected segments treated as a single entity. Polylines can be converted into curves.

Port A connection on a computer where a peripheral device can be connected.

Primitive A basic geometric model from which more complex models are constructed. Primitives are points and lines in wireframe models, and simple shapes such as blocks, cones, and cylinders in solid models.

Processor A computer on a chip.

Program A detailed list of instructions that will be quickly, precisely, and blindly followed by a computer.

Prompt A message from the computer software requesting a response from the user.

Puck A hand-operated device with one or more buttons (resembling a mouse) that operates in conjunction with a digitizing tablet; also called a transducer.

RAM (random-access memory) Temporary read/write memory that stores information only when the computer is on.

Read To extract data from a storage device such as a floppy disk or hard disk.

Reflection color The color of a highlight on shiny material.

Regenerate To recompute the screen coordinates from the drawing database so that the screen is refreshed. Redraw does not recompute, as regenerate does.

Relative coordinates Coordinates specified by differences in distances and/or angles measured from a previous set of coordinates rather than from the origin point.

Return button The button on a pointing device used to accept an entry—usually the right mouse button.

RGB *R*ed, green, *b*lue. A system of creating colors using percentages of these three colors.

Right-hand rule Using the fingers of the right hand to remember the relative directions of the positive X, Y, and Z axes of a Cartesian coordinate system. It is particularly useful in AutoCAD in visualizing UCS orientations.

ROM (read-only memory) Permanent computer memory that cannot be written to.

RS-232C Standard interface cable for serial devices.

Running object snap An object snap mode such as endpoint that is automatically active when a point is selected.

Save To store data on a disk.

Script file A file with the extension .scr created in a text editor that executes a set of AutoCAD commands.

Selection window A window used to select objects. Any object must be contained entirely within the window to be selected.

Serial interface An interface that communicates information one bit at a time.

Serial port A connector on the back of the computer that has pins rather than holes. This connector may have either 9 or 25 pins.

Serial printer A printer with a serial interface (receives information one bit at a time).

Snap A means of setting a pointing device to stop at specified intervals on an invisible grid.

Software Computer programs.

Solid model A computer representation of a fully enclosed, three-dimensional shape. Solid models define the space a real object occupies in addition to the surface that bounds the object.

Stylus An input device used like a digitizer puck but that looks like a pen.

Surface model A 3-D representation of an object made of a wire frame on which surfaces are attached. A surface model is hollow; a solid model is solid.

Surface of revolution A surface generated by revolving a profile curve around an axis.

System board The main printed circuit board inside the system unit, into which other boards are connected.

System unit The component that contains the computer parts, disk drives, and option boards.

System variable A setting that determines how the AutoCAD program operates.

Template drawing A drawing file with predefined settings.

Text style A collection of settings that determine the appearance of text.

Thaw A setting that displays frozen layers when that layer is also on.

Thickness A setting that gives height (the Z dimension) to certain objects such as solids, circles, and polylines, making them 3-D objects.

Tilemode An AutoCAD system variable that controls whether viewports are tiled or nontiled when created. When Tilemode is on, you are in model space—viewports are adjacent and cannot be moved, stretched, or erased.

Tracking A means of locating a point relative to other points on the drawing.

Unit A user-defined distance, such as inches, meters, or miles.

User coordinate system A movable, user-defined coordinate system used for convenient placement of geometry; frequently referred to as the UCS.

Vector A mathematical entity with a precise direction and length (but no specific location).

View A graphical representation of a 2-D drawing or 3-D model from a specific location (viewpoint) in space.

Viewpoint A location in 3-D model space from which a model is viewed.

Viewport A bounded area on a display screen that may contain a view. If a viewport is created when TILEMODE is set to 1, then it is tiled. When TILEMODE is set to 0, viewports are created with the Mview command. They are nontiled or model space viewports and reside in paper space. See *model space* and *paper space*.

Virtual screen display The area of the display where AutoCAD can zoom in or out without regenerating the drawing.

Wireframe model A 2-D or 3-D representation of an object consisting of boundary lines or edges of an object.

World coordinate system A fixed coordinate system that defines the location of all graphic items in a drawing or model. It is frequently referred to as the WCS.

Wpolygon See p*olygon window*.

Write To record or store information in a storage device.

Write-enable notch Slot on the side of a floppy disk that, when uncovered, permits the disk to be written on.

Write-protect To cover a floppy disk write-enable notch, thus preventing writing on the disk.

Xref See e*xternal reference*.

XYZ point filters A means of individually extracting the X, Y, and Z coordinates of points to specify a new point.

Zoom The process of reducing or increasing the magnification of graphics on the display screen.

Index

A

B

C

D

E

J

K

L

M

N

O

P

Q

R

S

T

U

V

W

X

Z